SERIALS FOR LIBRARIES:

an Annotated Guide to
Continuations . Annuals . Yearbooks . Almanacs .
Transactions . Proceedings . Directories . Services .

Compiled by

Joan K. Marshall

Neal/Schuman Publishers   ABC-Clio, Inc.

New York   Santa Barbara   Oxford

Published by the American Bibliographical Center—Clio Press
2040 Alameda Padre Serra
Box 4397
Santa Barbara, CA 93103
In association with Neal-Schuman Publishers, Inc.

Copyright © 1979 by Neal-Schuman Publishers, Inc.

All rights reserved. Reproduction of this book, in whole or in part, without written permission of the publisher is prohibited.

Printed and bound in the United States of America.

Library of Congress Cataloging in Publication Data

Marshall, Joan K
 Serials for libraries.

 Includes indexes.
 1. Reference books. 2. Serial publications—
Bibliography. I. Title.
Z1035.1.M27 011'.02 78-31144
ISBN 0-87436-280-6

SERIALS FOR LIBRARIES

CONTENTS

EDITORIAL BOARD   IV
FOREWORD, by Bill Katz   VII
PREFACE   IXIII
INTRODUCTION, by Richard R. Centing   XI
HOW TO USE THIS BOOK   XIII
GENERAL WORKS   3
   Almanacs and Yearbooks   3
   Bibliographies   6
   Biographical Directories and Indexes   15
   Book and Nonprint Media Reviews—Abstracts and Indexes   19
   Directories   21
   Periodical and Essay Abstracts and Indexes   26
   Statistical Works   28
EDUCATION   33
   General Works   33
   Adult and Continuing Education   36
   Elementary and Secondary Education   37
   Higher Education   39
   Instructional Methods and Materials   45
   Special Education   49
   Vocational Education   50
HUMANITIES   53
   General Works   53
   Art and Architecture   55
   Classics   64
   Dance   67
   Language and Literature   68
   Library Science   78
   Motion Pictures   84
   Music   85
   Philosophy   91
   Photography   95
   Religion   97
   Theatre   114
SOCIAL SCIENCES   119
   General Works   119
   Anthropology and Archaeology   120
   Banking and Finance   125
   Business and Economics   129
   Civil Rights and Human Rights   148
   Communications   150
   Consumer Interests   164
   Criminology and Law Enforcement   166
   Ethnic Interests   172
   Folklore   175
   Genealogy and Heraldry   176
   Government and Public Administration   177
   History and Area Studies   183
   Hobbies and Gifts   190
   Home Economics   195
   Housing and Urban Planning   196
   Insurance   199
   Labor and Industrial Relations   200
   Law   207
   Management   216
   Marketing   218
   Occupations and Careers   225
   Patents, Trademarks, and Copyrights   228
   Political Science   230
   Public Finance and Taxation   238
   Real Estate   242
   Social Services   245
   Sociology   250
   Sports and Recreation   253
   Transportation   284
   Travel   296
SCIENCE   323
   General Works   323
   Aeronautics   325
   Astronomy   326
   Biology   326
   Building Technology   330
   Chemistry   331
   Computer Science   333
   Earth Sciences   335
   Electricity and Electronics   337
   Energy and Environmental Studies   339
   Engineering   334
   Geography   347
   Horticulture   348
   Industrial Technology   349
   Marine Science   354
   Mathematics   355
   Medical and Health Science   356
   Metallurgy   371
   Military Science   372
   Mining and Mineralogy   374
   Physics   377
   Psychology and Psychiatry   378
   Veterinary Medicine   381
WHEN TO BUY WHAT   383
AUTHOR/TITLE INDEX   413
SUBJECT INDEX   467

EDITORIAL BOARD

Editor:
Joan K. Marshall
Associate Librarian for Technical Services
Brooklyn College of the City of New York
Brooklyn, New York

Editorial Board:
Sanford Berman
Head Cataloger
Hennepin County Public Library
Edina, Minnesota

Merilyn S. Burke
Serials Librarian
Health Center Library
University of Connecticut
Farmington, Connecticut

Kay Ann Cassell
Director
Bethlehem Public Library
Delmar, New York

Arthur Curley
Deputy Director
Detroit Public Library
Detroit, Michigan

Neal Edgar
Research Librarian
Kent State University Libraries
Kent, Ohio

Elizabeth Futas
Assistant Professor
Division of Librarianship
Emory University
Atlanta, Georgia

Kathleen Heim
Lecturer
Graduate School of Library Science
University of Illinois
Urbana, Illinois

Kenneth Kaplan
Acting Chief Librarian
New York City Community College
City University of New York
New York, New York

Suzanne LeBarron
Reference Librarian, Sociology Department
Minneapolis Public Library and Information Center
Minneapolis, Minnesota

Lydia Lo
Librarian
Shasta College
Redding, California

Barbara S. Marks
Reference Librarian
Bobst Library
New York University
New York, New York

Ellis Mount
Senior Lecturer
School of Library Service
Columbia University
New York, New York

Mimi Penchansky
Head of General Reference and Interlibrary
    Loan Librarian
Paul Klapper Library
Queens College of the City University
    of New York
Queens, New York

Betty-Carol Sellen
Associate Librarian for Reference Services
    and Collection Development
Brooklyn College of the City University
    of New York
Brooklyn, New York

Susan J. Vaughn
Deputy Associate Library for Reference
    Services
Brooklyn College of the City University
    of New York
Brooklyn, New York

Gunta Vittands
Reference Librarian
Wheaton College Library
Norton, Massachusetts

FOREWORD

Serials for Libraries meets a long standing need. Among the thousands of available irregular and annual serials, librarians must make necessary choices. They require all the help they can get in determining what to purchase, what to avoid. And that's what this book is all about. This is a trustworthy guide to the selection of some well known, not so well known, and even a few outcasts in the sea of serials.

The compiler and her editorial board have carefully selected about 2,000 titles which they consider important for libraries. An indication of audience level for each of the titles makes it relatively simple to separate out what is needed for this or that type and size of library. The annotations provide further guidance for the librarian involved in selecting serials or for the reference librarian trying to locate a particular type of serial publication. The annotations are descriptive, offering a feeling for the purpose, scope, and audience of the serial.

Selection was made by subject experts, by librarians, in other words, by people who are drawing from the nitty-gritty daily experience of working with those rewarding, yet challenging irregular serials and annuals. A glance at the qualifications of the compiler and her assistants should be evidence enough of the thought and the skill which have gone into this compilation.

Few are going to agree entirely with the selection. There are some titles I would add, other titles I would delete, but taken on balance the selection is well done. The bibliographical information is full and enough data is given to allow ease of ordering. When this publication goes to another edition, it is hoped that librarians will make further suggestions as to types of materials to be added or excluded. For example, an effort was made to limit most, although not all, of the listings to English language publications from the United States. Should more foreign titles be included? Also, "basics" are interpreted to mean annual and irregular serials found in most academic, school, and public libraries. This is a wide net to cast with the result that there are too many(?) or is it too few(?) technical and specialized serials.

A good reference book is measured by its index, and it is nice to report that the subject index was prepared by Sanford Berman, the expert among experts on how to make an index useful. The bibliographic entries are arranged under broad disciplines or subject categories in the body of this book to provide easy access for the general reader and for librarians involved in the selection of materials, but the user who is seeking materials on a specific topic within a discipline or who needs a cross-disciplinary approach to a topic will find the subject index an invaluable guide. There is also an author-title index for those who want quick reference to a particular title. It provices access by both current and past titles (a great help since serials tend to change names with great frequency), corporate authors, personal authors who have become closely identified with a particular work, and even short, popular titles.

Of equal use, particularly for smaller to medium-size libraries, is the "When to Buy What" list in the appendix. This list provides the month or season when new editions of approximately 880 serial titles should be ordered. Many smaller libraries find it unnecessary or too expensive to purchase every annual or biennial revision of every serial title. Armed with the information provided in this guide, librarians will be better able to control their own orders and ensure that they will get the revised edition they want as soon as it is available. This guide should also help librarians know when they should place a claim for those serial titles which are on standing order.

For all these reasons I recommend *Serials for Libraries* to you — although I quickly add that I am totally biased, as would be anyone who for so long has seen the need for such a work. This first edition is a solid beginning and one which deserves wide support. So with that: thank you Joan Marshall and all who helped make this book possible.

BILL KATZ
Professor, School of Library and Information Science, State University of New York at Albany
Editor, *Magazines for Libraries*

PREFACE

"You are working on WHAT?"
"Serials for Libraries."
"Cereals for—you mean, like corn flakes?!!"

Such is the fame of serials. Periodicals have achieved popular recognition as magazines, but serials are cereals to the general library user.

To librarians in technical services attempting to acquire, claim, process, and assume some measure of bibliographic control over serials, and to librarians in public services attempting to make decisions about serials purchases and reorders, serials are elusive, exasperating, and expensive publications that undergo seemingly continual changes with apparent malicious abandon.

Unannounced title and frequency changes sometimes reflect an unannounced change in the scope of a publication, but often they seem to reflect merely the whims of publishers. Not infrequently a publication, after having gone through a variety of title changes, suddenly reappears under its original title. Titles that had been received regularly suddenly stop coming. The questions that must be asked at this point are myriad. Has the latest issue simply been lost in the mail? Has the work ceased or temporarily suspended publication? Has there been a change in publisher which resulted in the library's order being lost? Has there been a change in title; is it possible that the apparently "new" and unordered publication that was returned to the publisher last week was really the missing title under a new guise? Still other titles die, but unlike you or I, they often rise again like the phoenix, and all of the "ceased publication" notes have to be changed to "suspended publication" notes on the records.

In addition to these problems, serials are proliferating at an alarming rate, are becoming increasingly more expensive, and are rarely reviewed once they have become established. The number of serial titles published increases from year to year. The latest edition of Bowker's *Irregular Serials and Annuals* (1978) lists 32,500 titles; the previous edition listed 30,000 titles. The cost of serials continues to rise, and unlike monographs which are individually selected, serials on standing order are received without prior warning of the increase in price. In larger libraries the proportionate share of library budgets devoted to serial publications is estimated at being from 40 to 60 percent. Many libraries have attempted to stay the take-over of the book budget by serial purchases by establishing a policy of instituting cancellations to offset the cost of new purchases. Selection decisions are hampered, however, by the absence of extensive, current, and regular review media covering serials; reviews are particularly scarce once a title has become established.

Serials for Libraries will not resolve all of the problems connected with the selection, acquisition, and control of serials. But it does provide current information on the contents, frequency, and price of serials which should be of interest to school, junior and senior college, and public libraries. It should be of assistance in selecting new titles, in comparatively reevaluating titles currently received, and in the referral of users to specific serial titles in the library or in another library collection.

Definition of a Serial

The *Anglo-American Cataloging Rules* (American Library Association, 1967) defines a serial as a "publication issued in successive parts bearing numerical or chronological designations and intended to be continued indefinitely. Serials include periodicals, newspapers, annuals (reports, yearbooks, etc.), the journals, memoirs, proceedings, transactions, etc., of societies, and numbered monographic series" (p. 346). A mass of library materials is covered in that definition. *Serials for Libraries* is an attempt to aid librarians in the selection and control of a specific part of that mass.

Criteria for Inclusion

Serial publications included in *Serials for Libraries* are English language titles which are available in the United States, are published on an annual or other regular basis (but not more often than once a year), and are suitable for collection by public, school, and undergraduate college libraries.

Irregular series (but, again, not published more often than once a year) have been included if the title contains information not available elsewhere. U.S. foreign language titles of ethnic interest, important multi-language titles (such as many U.N. and UNESCO publications), and important English language titles not available from a U.S. distributor have also been included on a limited basis.

Serial publications which have been excluded are periodicals (publications issued more often than once a year), newspapers, and monographic series (independent works that are related to one another by a collective series title, for example, *Twayne's World Author Series*. The annual cumulations of periodicals, on the other hand, have been included. Loose-leaf services have generally been excluded because they are periodical in nature; however, a few standard reference services which appear in a loose-leaf format were considered to be so important that they were listed anyway, particularly in the business section. Although U.S. government serial publications are included, they were not covered in depth because of the very large number of titles issued by the government, the often narrow specificity of the publications, and the difficulty encountered in tracking them down for examination.

Serials titles of interest primarily to research and special libraries have generally been excluded. In some subject areas, however, it is difficult to make decisions about the audience for a particular title. Business and science publications, in particular, presented problems. Many of the business titles included would be of interest only in those college libraries supporting programs in business education or in public libraries that have extensive business collections. Science titles often posed even more difficult problems in terms of determining whether a publication is too specialized or technical for an interested college or public library user. Many highly technical works contain information which is needed by and not beyond the understanding of the general special-interest reader. In addition to the difficulty of determining audience level, the sheer number of serial publications in the sciences is overwhelming. A brief glance at *Scientific, Engineering, and Medical Societies Publications in Print* edited by James M. Kyed and James M. Matarazzo (R. R. Bowker, 1976) amply demonstrates the number of conference proceedings, transactions, membership directories, annual reports, and other serial publications that are available in the sciences and that apparently meet our criteria for inclusion. The science titles finally chosen for inclusion are meant to be representative of the types of publications available from both commercial and society or association publishers in the various scientific disciplines; it should not be regarded as a "best" list. The Kyed and Matarazzo book cited above and the invaluable advice of Carole Schildhauer (Barker Engineering Library, Massachusetts Institute of Technology) were of great assistance in making the final selection of titles for inclusion from those submitted by the bibliographers.

As a rule, local publications which are restricted to information about one state or city or which would otherwise be of local interest only have not been included. A few exceptions have been made for state publications which are representative of publications available in other areas, e.g., New York State's *Comprehensive Crime Control Plan* has been included since each state must file a similar plan annually in order to qualify for federal crime control assistance.

Insubstantial publications have not been included unless they provide information not readily available elsewhere. For example, brochures, pamphlets, or catalogs issued by associations, institutions, or private publishers, such as the "Best Books for Young Adults" or "Notable Children's Books" pamphlets issued annually by the American Library Association, have not been covered. Examples of the publications which at first appear to fall into this category but which were included because of the unique information they contain are *WomenSports* magazine's annual list of athletic scholarships available to women and the U.S. Superintendent of Documents' bibliography of subject bibliographies available from the Government Printing Office.

Every effort was made to exclude ceased or suspended publications, but given the nature of serials, some titles which have been included may have ceased, changed title, changed frequency, or risen astronomically in price since they were examined by the bibliographer and the information verified by the editorial staff.

Selection Process

The titles included were selected from titles listed in Bowker's *Irregular Serials and Annuals,* 1976/77 (1976) and its *Supplement* (1976), Sheehy's *Guide to Reference Books* (American Library Association, 1976), *Guide to American Directories* (B. Klein Publications, 1975), various subject bibliographies, and publishers' catalogs. The bibliographers drew upon their subject expertise, personal contact with publishers, and, often, prowling conference exhibits to verify information or locate issues to examine in making the final selection.

A number of extraneous factors entered into the decision to include or exclude a title which, on the basis of the information provided in the sources listed above, presumably met the criteria. In a number of instances, an issue of a title could not be located for examination and there was insufficient information available on the work to justify its inclusion. Corresponding with the publisher was sometimes helpful, but not always. In a few instances, the publisher could not be located, and it was presumed that the publication had ceased, even though cessation could not always be verified. If the only issue of a title available for examination was pre-1976, the title was included only if verification of its current publication could be obtained. Non-current irregular serials were included only if they had a long publishing history, and, whenever possible, the publisher had been contacted to confirm the intent to continue publication.

The potential number of serials which met the criteria stated above is not known. Many titles were excluded for the reasons given above; others may have been overlooked. It is hoped that future editions of *Serials for Libraries* will fill in any gaps that may appear in this initial effort and that users of this volume will submit their suggestions for future improvements.

Acknowledgements

Because serials are so elusive and exasperating, the bibliographers who worked on *Serials for Libraries* found that the work of compiling lists of appropriate titles, locating copies of those titles, and verifying the bibliographic information was far more onerous than anticipated. Without their dogged efforts, this book would not exist. My sincere thanks to all the members of the Editorial Board: Sanford Berman, Merilyn Burke, Kay Cassell, Arthur Curley, Neal Edgar, Elizabeth Futas, Kathleen Heim, Kenneth Kaplan, Suzanne LeBarron, Barbara Marks, Lydia Lo, Ellis Mount, Mimi Penchansky, Betty-Carol Sellen, Susan Vaughn, and Gunta Vittands.

The completion of this project also depended a great deal on the efforts of many others who deserve special mention. Deborah Alterman, Pearl Holford, Myra Rubin, Katherine Rutkowski, Alan Stretton, and Susan Treschan were involved in this project as research assistants and supplied bibliographic information necessary to complete many entries. Carole Schildhauer of the Barker Engineering Library, Massachusetts Institute of Technology, gave much needed assistance in the final selection of titles in the sciences. Eleanore Futas typed all of the entries with speed and incredible accuracy, and helped with the final preparation of the "When to Buy What" section. Sue Rodriguez typed and filed, and refiled, and refiled the author-title index, and assisted in the identification of prices, publishers, and other missing information. Lyda Clifton, Gloria Hassen, and Shirley Rosen of the Brooklyn College Library worked tirelessly and inventively at tracking down elusive bits of missing bibliographic information. Carole Cushmore and the staff of the Baker and Taylor Company provided invaluable assistance with the verification of publication information and supplied much of the information used in preparing the "When to Buy What" listings.

My thanks also to Sanford Berman, subject indexer extraordinaire, for compiling the subject index with his usual insight and consummate skill. And my particular thanks to Patricia Read, my editor at Neal-Schuman Publishers. Without Patsy's skillful editing and sense of organization, and, most importantly, without her calm resolve that impossible deadlines could be met and impossible snags unraveled, this book would still be a mass of 8½ × 11 sheets and 3 × 5 cards cluttering up my apartment.

JOAN K. MARSHALL
October, 1978

INTRODUCTION

Serials for Libraries is going to be a standard reference tool for librarians serving on the frontline of public service at the reference desk; also, it will be essential in technical service areas responsible for verification and ordering of serial titles. This dual purpose should establish *Serials for Libraries* as a primary bibliographic source for librarians assigned the task of selecting new titles for the collection, for reference staffs assigned the duty of locating highly specialized materials, and for all professionals who recognize that current information about serial publications is a major lacuna of librarianship.

Numerous theoretical articles about subscription agents, the claiming process, on-line check-in, title change problems, or cataloging rules can be found in the literature, but few citations discuss the obvious, utilitarian end of compilations like *Serials for Libraries:* to provide summary data on the non-magazine, non-newspaper types of serial (issued either in a bound volume like the *Guinness Book of Records* or cumulating into a volume like the *Congressional Quarterly Almanac*), so that reference staffs can quickly verify the existence of the most effective, precise source capable of answering questions. It is impossible for reference personnel to mnemonically file the titles of all potentially useful serials, and few librarians have heard of, much less seen, all of them. It is to the credit of Neal-Schuman Publishers and Joan Marshall that *Serials for Libraries* was created as a new contribution to the reference literature on serials, one that nicely complements Bill Katz' *Magazines for Libraries*.

It is surprising that few articles or books zero-in on the bond between reference service and reference serials. Murfin and Wynar's *Reference Service: An Annotated Bibliographic Guide* (Libraries Unlimited, 1977) contains only a handful of bibliographic citations which emphasize the interrelationship. One of the clearest general discussions is Andrew D. Osborn's *Serial Publications: Their Place and Treatment in Libraries* (ALA, 1973), which includes a significant chapter on "Reference Work." It confirms that: "The stock-in-trade for standard reference work consists in no small measure of abstracting and indexing services, annuals, directories, government publications, newspaper indexes, statistical works, trade and national bibliographies, who's whos, and a host of other serial publications." My intention has been to establish "reference serials" as a term in the language of library science. When my column of that name was founded in *Reference Serials Review* (April/June 1974), and later transferred to the inaugural number of *Serials Review* (January/June 1975), I made it a point to provide in-depth reviews of already functioning reference serials like *Journalism Abstracts* and *The Atlanta Constitution: A Georgia Index,* both annuals, because I knew that reference departments could squeeze extra mileage out of their budgets (normally divided between books and serials) by submitting one-time purchases of either a run of the serial to date or acquiring only a few recent years. It made good sense to build the collection, even at the expense of the book budget. *The Guinness Book of World Records* could be obtained even if the funds for new subscriptions were frozen. Many of the titles in *Serials for Libraries* fall into this category. Items which are requested constantly like the *Reader's Guide,* and which are issued serially during the year before the bound cumulation comes out, certainly could not be considered for such a buying program—at least in American libraries.

Smaller institutions will also benefit from *Serials for Libraries* because they all too often do not have access to enough information on the spectrum of serials emanating from the presses of commercial publishers, associations, colleges and universities, foundations, and churches. If they have the option to refer library users to larger, nearby institutions which might possess the relevant guide or biographical dictionary, the knowledge of a particular title will certainly help the referred patron when he/she appears at the next reference level.

Whenever I attend the conferences of the American Library Association, I allocate as much time as possible to surveying the exhibits. There is no greater educational tool for neophytes or tenured professionals than the hundreds of exhibits at ALA which allow not only inspection of the myriad new or changing reference serials, but also dialogues with the publishers and vendors of these publications. It is time consuming but instructive to learn who has issued a cumulative index; started an abstracting service; or what back volumes of an annual are in-print for purposes of replacement or fill-in. The final purchase decision can have no better justifier than physical handling and analysis of anticipated subscriptions. You must always beware of promotional hustling, of course, but overall I find that publishers are an honest breed who merely desire some of your time so they can present their case. The Combined Book Exhibit includes some reference serials too and should always be a scheduled stop. *Milton Studies,* an annual evaluated in this first edition of *Serials for Libraries,* was displayed at the 1978 ALA Conference in "A Special Collection of Books and Journals" which was prepared especially for the Conference. Exhibit shopping is a simple method for gathering facts about publications, domestic and international, which should not be neglected by libraries concerned about quality acquisitions.

Book reviews (i.e. book and *serial* reviews) are also a mainstay of the selection process. Library literature has often called for the improvement of our reviewing sources. Those who cannot keep in personal touch with publishers, those who are desk-bound without travel budgets, and those without the recourse of time-consuming trade journal reading are obligated to glean what knowledge they can from reviews, approval plans or traveling salespersons (and their second cousins, the mass-distributed flyer). Approval plans do not tend to display nor traveling salespersons demonstrate the great bulk of reference serials. A cursory examination of such reviewing media as *Booklist, Choice,* and *Library Journal* will reveal that few of the titles in *Serials for Libraries* received current attention. *College & Research Libraries* and *Wilson Library Bulletin* likewise shy away from coverage of the more esoteric or not-new titles in favor of the substantial monographic releases. In the last few years, newer services devoted to reviewing the proliferating flow of titles have arrived: *American Reference Books Annual* (ARBA), *Reference Services Review* (RSR), and *Serials Review* (SR). More comprehensive than their predecessors, these services have vastly improved the climate of professional reviewing.

All serial publications are not going to be reviewed or exhibited at ALA. *Serials for Libraries,* evaluative and descriptive, provides a neat reference package that functions as a selection tool as well as a bibliographic device. Serials in general are gaining attention in our profession; the formation of scholarly journals like *Serials Librarian* (1976) proves the case. I can only hope that *Serials for Libraries* receives wide distribution and informed discussion.

RICHARD R. CENTING
Assistant Professor, Ohio State University Libraries
Formerly Associate Editor, *Serials Review*

HOW TO USE THIS BOOK

ARRANGEMENT

Serials with distinctive titles are entered under title. Serials with generic titles (annual report, membership directory, etc.), those which begin with an acronym or initialism (e.g., *Official AAU Wrestling Handbook*), and reports of government agencies are entered under corporate author.

Titles are arranged under five broad categories (general works, education, humanities, social sciences, and science) and, within categories, by subject (e.g., anthropology, business and economics, etc.). Due to the interdisciplinary nature of so many of the titles included, it was often very difficult to decide where to place a title. Anyone involved in library classification is well aware of the problem; some titles fall neatly into place, others fall neatly into two or even three places, and still others defy rational placement of any sort. In some instances, subject disciplines have been combined, e.g., business and economics, because the titles listed under each were so similar. Because some titles do defy placement, and because so many serials are interdisciplinary, the subject index should be consulted for complete subject access.

There is an ethnic studies section included under the social sciences. Included in this section are general ethnic interest titles which did not fit appropriately into any broad subject category. Titles of ethnic interest that had a subject orientation are included with the subject, e.g., the *Directory for Reaching Minority Groups* is included under "social services" not under "ethnic studies." A women studies section has not been provided since all of the materials dealing with women fell under specific subjects, e.g., the *Directory of Women Writing* is placed in the language and literature section. Subject access to titles dealing with ethnic interests or women studies is provided by the subject index.

There are no internal cross references in the main body of the work. These were not included for two reasons. First, there would have had to be an enormous number of cross references. Second, and more importantly, the decision that a user might reasonably expect to find a title under "language and literature," for example, that has been included in "communications" is a subjective one on the part of the editor. My experience in using books that provide internal cross references is that the reference structure does not meet every user's expectations, and yet it is relied upon by the user since it is there. If a particular title is sought and not found under the "expected" subject in the main body of the text, the author-title index should be consulted. The index provides access by corporate authors, personal authors whose names have become closely associated with a work, all distinctive current and previous titles of a work, and, when appropriate, partial and popular titles.

THE BIBLIOGRAPHIC CITATION

The bibliographic information given for each entry includes author (if appropriate); title; former titles; *ISSN; date begun; frequency;* whether the work includes a bibliography, index, or illustrations; the publisher and address; the distributor (if different from the publisher) and address; the *issue examined* with the date, editor, number of pages, and price; the *audience level*, and *where the volume is indexed*.

The abbreviations used in the citations are:

a.	annual
approx.	approximately
Aud	audience
bi-a.	bi-annual
bibl.	bibliography
cum.	cumulative
Dist	distributor
ed., eds.	editor, editors
freq.	frequency
illus.	illustration(s)
index.	index(es)
irreg.	irregular
m.	monthly
N.S.	new series
q.	quarterly
suppl.	supplement
tri-a.	tri-annual
v.	volume
w.	weekly
w/	with

ISSN

The ISSN (International Standard Serial Number) is an eight digit number that uniquely identifies a serial title. At the time an ISSN is assigned, a corresponding key title is assigned. (In the U.S., this is done by the National Serials Data Program.) Once assigned, the ISSN and the corresponding key title remain attached to the title, whether current or ceased, and is never used again for any other serial publication. If the title of a serial changes, a new ISSN and key title must be assigned; the old ISSN and key title remain attached to the former title.

Although the ISSN was developed primarily as an

aid in the control and identification of serials on an international level, it has a potential for use in the smaller library. It could be a useful, economical, and accurate means of communication between libraries and vendors or publishers, an aid in checking in and claiming serials, and an aid in simplifying interlibrary loan procedures. A problem encountered by the bibliographers, however, was the absence of the ISSN in so many of the serials examined. Many of the ISSN's included in this publication were determined from sources such as Bowker's *Irregular Serials and Annuals,* rather than from the publications themselves. Unfortunately, the *ISSN-Key Title Register* (Library of Congress, 1977) arrived too late to be of assistance to us. That publication lists all ISSN and key title assignments made by the National Serials Data Program through February 1975. I cannot imagine why publishers have been reluctant to include assigned ISSN in their publications, but the post office has come to the rescue. The U.S. Postal Service has been developing an identification number which was to appear on all serial publications if they were to be mailed at second-class rates. The Library of Congress has now convinced the postal service to use the ISSN instead, so we are certain to see the ISSN more prominently displayed on future publications.

DATE BEGUN

Determining the date a publication began is one of those areas where serials are elusive and exasperating. Before learning through experience, it was assumed that between the *Union List of Serials* (Wilson, 1965) and *New Serial Titles* (Library of Congress, 1953–), determining the date of the first issue of a publication would not be difficult. The matter became complicated, as we discovered, by title changes, splits, mergers, suspensions, etc. Whenever possible, the date of the first issue is given. If a serial suspended publication for a time, the date of the first issue and the date of the first issue after publication resumed are both given. If the starting date was uncertain or simply not to be determined, and the volumes examined were numbered, this information is given in parentheses in lieu of the date begun, e.g., (1973 is 15th ed.).

FREQUENCY

The one thing that can be said with absolute certainty about the frequency of serial publications is that it changes frequently. The frequency given is based on the latest information available from the publisher (often the least reliable source), Faxon's *Librarian's Guide to Periodicals, Annuals . . .* (1978), and Baker and Taylor's *Continuation Service Starter List* (1978). In the bibliographic citation, recent changes in frequency are indicated in parentheses following the present frequency. Complex frequency changes are noted in the annotation.

ISSUE EXAMINED

The bibliographic citation is based upon the issue examined by the bibliographer. In some instances, the bibliographer was not able to locate an issue that met our 1976 or later criteria. Bibliographic information about later issues, which were not examined by the bibliographer, is included in parentheses. If bibliographic information about later issues became available, even when the issue examined was 1976 or later, this is also provided in parentheses. Every attempt was made to supply price information as of September 1978. Whenever it was known that a new edition of a title was scheduled for publication in late 1978 or early 1979, this information is noted in the annotation and the price given in the bibliographic citation.

AUDIENCE LEVEL

The abbreviations used are:
- El Elementary School (Grades K through 8)
- Jh Junior High School (Grades 7 through 9)
- Hs High School (Grades 9 through 12)
- Jc Junior College (freshman and sophomore level)
- Cl College (freshman through senior level)
- Pl Public Library (general adult public)
- Pf Professional (librarians and educators)
- Sa Special Audience (special interest audience)

The audience level for any given title was often difficult to determine. Certainly every title indicated as being appropriate for a public library will not be appropriate for every public library. The audience levels indicated can be used at the most as a general guide; the selection of a title must be based upon the needs of the users of a particular library.

The elementary through college and public library audience levels are meant to indicate the appropriateness of a title to the user, not to the professional, in that library. Titles which one might certainly expect to find in an elementary school library for the use of the librarian and classroom teacher are not indicated as *El* (elementary school) but as *Pf* (professional librarian or educator). *Pf* has been used to indicate titles which would be used by librarians and other educators in their work with students and the public. Titles in the Wilson Standard Catalog Series, for example, are designated *Pf* since they are professional selection tools, and *Pl* since they might also be used by the general adult public selecting materials for children and young adults. Titles of professional interest to librarians and other educators (or to other professionals) are designated as *Sa* (special audience). *Sa* has been used also to indicate a level of difficulty and/or specialized interest.

INDEXED IN

This area provides information on where the serial is indexed (the index information included as part of the bibliographic citation indicates whether or not the publication contains its own index). The information was gleaned by the bibliographers and the editorial staff from publishers' blurbs, Faxon's *Librarians' Guide to Periodicals, Annuals* . . . (1978), and various general indexes (e.g., Gale's *Biographical Dictionaries Master Index*). Without going through every possible general index to serial contents, it is very difficult to determine where, if anywhere, a serial title is indexed. Publishers should be encouraged to include this information in their serial publications (along with the ISSN).

ANNOTATIONS

The annotations are meant to be descriptive and comparative. They should provide sufficient, though brief, information to allow the user of this volume to select titles appropriate to a specific library collection. Unfortunately, some of the annotations are too brief. This is an admitted fault and will be corrected in any future editions whenever possible. In this edition, however, it was not possible to reexamine all of the titles that were too scantily annotated, and it was the decision of the editor and the publisher to include them for their bibliographic value.

Titles which are indicated in bold face type in the annotations are included elsewhere in the body of the text.

CONTRIBUTORS AND ADVISORS

AC	Arthur Curley,	*Editorial Board*
AS	Alan Stretton,	*Research Assistant*
BCS	Betty-Carol Sellen,	*Editorial Board*
BSM	Barbara S. Marks,	*Editorial Board*
DA	Deborah Alterman,	*Research Assistant*
EF	Elizabeth Futas,	*Editorial Board*
EM	Ellis Mount,	*Editorial Board*
GV	Gunta Vittands,	*Editorial Board*
JKM	Joan K. Marshall,	*Editor*
KAC	Kay Ann Cassell,	*Editorial Board*
KMH	Kathleen M. Heim,	*Editorial Board*
KR	Katherine Rutkowski,	*Research Assistant*
KSK	Kenneth S. Kaplan,	*Editorial Board*
LL	Lydia Lo,	*Editorial Board*
MBP	Mimi Penchansky,	*Editorial Board*
MR	Myra Rubin,	*Research Assistant*
MSB	Merilyn S. Burke,	*Editorial Board*
NLE	Neal Edgar,	*Editorial Board*
PH	Pearl Holford,	*Research Assistant*
SB	Sanford Berman,	*Editorial Board*
SJV	Susan J. Vaughn,	*Editorial Board*
SLB	Suzanne LeBarron,	*Editorial Board*
ST	Susan Treschan,	*Research Assistant*

SERIALS FOR LIBRARIES

GENERAL WORKS

ALMANACS AND YEARBOOKS

GE 1
Americana Annual. 1923. a. index. Grolier Educational Corp., 575 Lexington Ave, New York, NY 10022. Examined: 1977. Edward Humphrey, ed. approx. 800p. write for price.
Aud: Cl, Pl

Updates the *Americana Encyclopedia*. Divided into two major parts. "Feature Articles of the Year" includes signed articles on topics of current interest, such as the U.S. election, the Bicentennial, and multinational business ethics. The alphabetical section provides access to the year's events in such areas as agriculture, banking, fashion, labor, military affairs, music, polar research, and prizes and awards. Other features include statistical and tabular data, news of societies and organizations, and of major universities and colleges. An alphabetical subject index is provided. KMH

GE 2
The Annual Register. World Events in (year). ISSN 0066-4057. 1758. a. index. illus. Longman Group, 5 Bentinck St, London W1M 5RN, England. Dist: St. Martin's Press, 175 Fifth Ave, New York, NY 10010. Examined: 218th ed., 1976. H. V. Hodson, ed. 541p. $37.50.
Aud: Cl

Reports world events affecting geographic areas, international organizations, religion, science, law, art, sports, and economic and social affairs. A statistical section accompanies the economic chapter. Documents of political and economic importance are included. Obituaries and a Chronicle of Events complete the volume. The emphasis is British, but it is a gauge of world activity. First published in 1758 and edited by Edmund Burke. KSK

GE 3
Britannica Book of the Year. ISSN 0068-1156. 1938. a. index. Encyclopaedica Britannica, 425 N Michigan Ave, Chicago, IL 60611. Examined: 1977. Lawrence K. Lustig, ed. 768p. $12.95; $9.95 to subscribers.
Aud: Cl, Pl

Updates the *Encyclopaedia Britannica*. Divided into four parts including: Feature Articles; People of the Year (biography, Olympic champions, Nobel prize-winners, obituaries); Chronology of Events; and Book of the Year, an alphabetically organized treatment of people, places, and significant developments in areas such as economics, health, literature, science, and sports. Special reports by experts are included throughout the Book of the Year section on subjects such as Australian politics, law of the sea, the 1976 Presidential election, and the Winter Olympics. A statistical supplement updates tables in the basic Encyclopaedia. Provides a subject index which includes article headings from the Book of the Year and which indexes earlier volumes as well as the one at hand. KMH

GE 4
Chases' Calendar of Annual Events. 1958. a. index. illus. Apple Tree Press, Box 1012, Flint, MI 48501. Examined: 1978. William D. Chase, ed. 80p. $7.95.
Aud: El, Jh, Hs, Jc, Cl, Pl

Subtitle: "Special day, weeks, and months in (year)." Arranged by date. Although the calendar is oriented toward the U.S., all well known and some obscure world holidays are also noted. The calendar includes Saint's Days; events such as parades, pageants, and shows; and birthdays of famous men and women. On the whole, a treasury of miscellaneous information. There is an alphabetic name and subject index. JKM

GE 5
Collier's Yearbook. ISSN 0069-5793. 1939. a. index. Crowell-Collier Educational Corp., 866 Third Ave, New York, NY 10022. Examined: 1977. Marion L. Waxman, ed. approx. 625p. $15; $9 to libraries.
Aud: Hs, Jc, Pl

Updates the *Collier's Encyclopedia*. Provides a brief month by month summary of the year's major news events, several feature articles on topics of major interest during the period covered, and an alphabetically arranged update of articles in the basic set. KMH

GE 6
Compton Yearbook. ISSN 0069-8091. 1958. a. Encyclopaedia Britannica, 425 N Michigan Ave, Chicago, IL 60611. Examined: 1977. Richard Pope, ed. 608p. $10.95.
Aud: El, Jh, Hs, Pl

Updates the *Compton's Encyclopedia*. In the 1977 edition, there were four feature articles, 11 special reports on topics of interest during the year covered, and an alphabetically arranged update of articles in the basic set. KMH

GE 7
Facts on File Yearbook. ISSN 0014-6641. 1940. a. w/w. suppls. Facts on File, 119 W 57th St, New York, NY 10019. Examined: 1976, Bob Hollingsworth, ed.; 1977. 1202p. $270.
Aud: Hs, Jc, Cl, Pl

Facts on File summarizes, records, and indexes the news of the world each week. It is issued as a looseleaf digest with a twice-monthly cumulative index (the "blue index") and a quarterly cumulative index (the "yellow index"). The **Yearbook** is a bound compilation of all 52 digests from the previous year with an annual index. All digests are organized into hierarchical sections: world affairs, U.S. affairs, other nations, and miscellaneous. Cumulative indexes are issued at five-year intervals. KMH/JKM

GE 8
The Great Issues Today. (Continues: Great Ideas Today. ISSN 0072-7288.) 1971. a. index. illus. Encyclopaedia Britannica, 425 N Michigan Ave, Chicago, IL 60611. Dist: Hammond Inc., Maplewood, NJ 07040. Examined: 1978. 480p. $11.95.
Aud: Hs, Jc, Cl, Pl

The yearbook supplement to Encyclopaedia Britannica's *Great Books of the Western World*. Consists of lengthy, signed, rather scholarly articles on topics of current interest. The 1978 volume, for instance, contained articles on recent developments and future directions in the arts and sciences, and a lengthy discussion of religion. JKM

GE 9
Guinness Book of World Records. ISSN 0072-9000. (Continues: Guinness Book of Records. ISSN 0300-1676.) 1955. a. index. illus. Guinness Superlatives, 2 Cecil Ct, London Rd, Enfield, England. Dist: Sterling Publishing Co., 2 Park Ave, New York, NY 10016. Examined: 1977. 704p. $8.95; $2.25 pap.
Aud: El, Jh, Hs, Jc, Cl, Pl

Originally intended as a means of peacefully settling arguments about extremes and record performances. Contains records of the biggest, best, most, smallest, worst, and least of just about everything: human beings, animal and plant kingdoms, natural world, universe and space, scientific world, arts and entertainment, business world, world's structures, mechanical world, human world, human achievements, and sports and games. It is profusely illustrated and includes a subject index. Procedures for submitting a record are given at the beginning of the volume. KMH

GE 10
Hammond Almanac of a Million Facts. (Continues: Associated Press Almanac; New York Times Encyclopedic Almanac; CBS News Almanac. ISSN 0090-208X.) 1970. a. index. illus. Hammond Almanac, Maplewood, NJ 07040. Examined: 1977. Sylvia Westerman, ed. 1040p. $5.95.
Aud: Hs, Jc, Cl, Pl

A general information almanac focusing on the U.S. The issue examined was published under the auspices of CBS News and still carried the title *CBS News Almanac*; the title change occurred with the 1978 issue. The 1977 volume opens with a commentary on the previous year by CBS news correspondents, followed by a month by month chronology of events. Topical sections include: U.S. history; U.S. government; taxes/expenditures; finance, industry, labor; travel and transportation; U.S. crime summary; civil rights/race; public health and medicine; earth: facts and figures; stars, planets, and space; U.S. states, cities, and territories; representative American cities; diplomatic affairs; military affairs; education; communications; world biography; popular and classical arts; directory of associations, societies, and foundations; religion; disasters and catastrophes; obituaries; etc. An extensive subject index provides access to the well organized contents. KMH

GE 11
Information Please Almanac, Atlas, and Yearbook. ISSN 0073-7860. 1947. a. index. illus. Simon and Schuster, 630 Fifth Ave, New York, NY 10020. Examined: 1977. Ann Golenpaul, ed. 992p. $6.95; $3.95 pap.
Aud: El, Jh, Hs, Jc, Cl, Pl

A general information almanac focusing on the United States which opens with a summary of the previous year's elections when pertinent, followed by a news summary of the year's events and in depth information on the American economy, celebrated persons, awards, astronomy and calendars, cities, colleges, countries of the world, geography, holidays, religion, presidents, science, states of the U.S., taxes, travel, U.N., vital statistics, and world history. Special features include a crossword puzzle dictionary and zip code directory. A detailed subject index follows the text, and black-and-white maps are included. KMH

GE 12
News Dictionary. (Continues: News Year.) 1964. a. Facts on File, 119 W 57th St, New York, NY 10019. Examined: 13th ed., 1976. Mary E. Clifford, Raymond Hill, and Stephen Orlofsky, eds. 744p. $11.95; $6.95 pap.
Aud: Hs, Jc, Cl

Alphabetical approach to major events, subjects, countries, and individuals making news in a particular year. Based on material published in *Facts on File*. Approach is straightforward and there are ample cross references. JKM

GE 13
Oxbridge Omnibus of Holiday Observances around the World. 1977. a. index. Oxbridge Communications, 1345 Ave of the Americas, New York, NY 10019. Examined: 1977. Christopher Samuels, ed. 144p. $2.95.
Aud: El, Jh, Hs, Jc, Cl, Pl

Provides the dates of government, business, bank, and religious holidays around the world. Banking and business hours are also noted. The volume is cross indexed by name of the holiday, day and date, country and state, and definition of the holiday. JKM

GE 14
Pears Cyclopaedia. ISSN 0079-0362. 1897. a. illus. Pelham Books, 52 Bedford Sq, London WC 1, England. Dist: Transatlantic Arts, N Village Green, Levittown, NY 11786. Examined: 1973; 1976. Mary Barker and Christopher Cook, eds. 976p. £3.75.
Aud: Sa

British one-volume encyclopedia of reference information covering the history of the world, prominent people, English law, religion, medicine, gardening, games, and culture. A substantial color atlas and gazeteer are included. KMH

GE 15
Reader's Digest Almanac and Yearbook. ISSN 0079-9831. 1966. a. index. illus. Reader's Digest Association, Pleasantville, NY 10570. Examined: 1977. 1024p. $5.95.
Aud: Jh, Hs, Cl, Pl

General information almanac oriented toward U.S. interests. A review article on news events is followed by alphabetically arranged topics which include: accidents, animals, arts, awards, books, calendars, climate, Congress, crime, earth, economy, education, elections, history, international relations, newspapers, people, science, sports, travel, women, and deaths. A subject index provides access to specific items, and there are black-and-white illustrations. KMH

GE 16
What They Said. ISSN 0512-5804. 1969. a. index. Monitor Book Co., 195 S Beverly Dr, Beverly Hills, CA 90212. Examined: 8th ed., 1976. Alan F. Pater and Jason R. Pater, eds. 610p. $19.95.
Aud: Hs, Jc, Cl

An annual highlighting the views of prominent people on multiple subjects. It attempts to give the "spoken work the permanence and lasting value of the written word." Prominent people are defined as top-level officials at all levels of government; military officers; academics; corporation officers; diplomats; heads of organizations; celebrities from the entertainment world; and sports figures. The selection of speakers and quotations is of necessity a subjective one. The book is arranged in three parts: national affairs; international affairs; and general, which includes arts, fashion, philosophy, religion, sports, women's rights, etc. Both complete speeches and excerpts of speeches are provided, including the source and date. Under each topic the arrangement is alphabetical by speaker. JKM

GE 17
Whitaker's Almanack. ISSN 0083-9256. 1869. a. index. J. Whitaker and Sons, 13 Bedford Sq, London WC1B 3JE England. Examined: 109th ed., 1977. 1230p. $18.95.
Aud: Cl, Pl

A general information almanac focusing on Great Britain. Astronomical tables are presented in detail for 75 pages. English peerage, parliamentary constituency, parliamentary summary, public officers, judges, municipal officials, ecclesiastical officials, and ecclesiastical authorities make up more than half of the volume. Foreign country information, sport results, and addresses of societies, institutions, and clubs are included. A very extensive subject index (80 pages) precedes the text. KMH

GE 18
World Almanac and Book of Facts. ISSN 0084-1382. 1868. a. index. illus. Newspaper Enterprise Association, World Almanac Div, 230 Park Ave, New

York, NY 10017. Examined: 1977. George E. Delury, ed. 976p. $3.25 pap.
Aud: Jh, Hs, Cl, Pl

A compendium of universal knowledge focusing on the United States, which provides information on nearly all topics. Volumes begin with a news summary of the previous year including, when pertinent, election returns. Governmental offices are listed for municipalities throughout the U.S. Worldwide statistics for agriculture and manufacturing as well as population figures for U.S. cities, counties and states are given. World facts include flags, Rand McNally color maps, athletic and entertainment awards, sports results, and chronological postal information. An extensive index provides access to the information which is almost all tabular. KMH

GE 19
World Book Year Book. ISSN 0084-1439. 1922. a. Field Enterprises Educational Corp., 510 Merchandise Mart Plaza, Chicago, IL 60654. Examined: 1976. Wayne Willie, ed. 608p. $13.50; $8.50 to schools and libraries.
Aud: Jh, Hs, Pl

Begins with a brief month by month chronology of important events in 1975 (the year covered by the volume). Continues with lengthy, signed review articles on broad topics (e.g., James Reston on Focus on the Nation; Sylvia Porter on Focus on the Economy; Alistair Cooke on Focus on the Arts) and lengthy, signed essays on specific topics of current interest. The essays are followed by an alphabetically arranged update of the *World Book Encyclopedia* (including brief obituaries) which is the largest portion of the volume. The full subject index covers the 1974 through 1976 editions. JKM

GE 20
The World in (year): History as We Lived It. a. index. illus. Franklin Watts, 730 Fifth Ave, New York, NY 10019. Examined: 1965, 287p.; 1976. The Associated Press, eds. 300p. $10.95.
Aud: Hs, Jc, Cl, Pl

A *Life*-magazine-style news annual. Chronological arrangement of Associated Press articles and photographs chronicling the year's national and international news events. Indexed by name and subject. A special feature is the 30-page news almanac covering important news events, deaths, awards, U.S. government offices and officials, U.N. representatives, sports, disasters, economics, and various facts about each state. KR/JKM

BIBLIOGRAPHIES

GE 21
Alternatives in Print. 1969. a. New Glide Publications, 330 Ellis St., San Francisco, CA 94102. Examined: 5th ed., 1977/78. Noah Phyllis Levin, ed. 198p. $11.95; $8.95 pap.
Aud: Hs, Jc, Cl, Pl, Pf

Subtitle: "Catalog of social change publications." A "Books in Print" of the small press compiled by the Task Force on Alternatives in Print of the Social Responsibilities Round Table of the American Library Association. Provides access to publications and productions of the counterculture, the Third World, the dissident press, and other small press. Begins with an introduction and a how-to-use section. These are followed by a thesaurus of subject headings used in the volume; subject headings range from abortion to Zionism and include alternative life style, women's liberation, cybernetics, crafts, yoga, and Black liberation. The next section lists publishers by the subject of their publications; for example, under "cybernetics" would be a list of publishers who have titles on that topic. The main part of the work, the list of social change publications, covers approximately 1500 organizations and small presses. It is arranged alphabetically by publisher, and each entry includes the address and a list of publications available with author and price. The address list of social change publishers, arranged geographically, is printed so that it can be photocopied and used for mailing labels. The preface outlines the history of this unique and special tool. The sixth edition, which will be expanded to include over 3000 alternative publishers, will be published by Neal-Schuman Publishers, 64 University Place, New York, NY 10003. KMH/MBP

GE 22
American Book Publishing Record. Annual Cumulation. ISSN 0002-7707. 1965. a. R. R. Bowker, 1180 Ave. of the Americas, New York, NY 10036. Dist: R. R. Bowker, Box 1807, Ann Arbor, MI 48106. Examined: 1965; 1969; 1976. Gertrude Jennings, ed. 1152p. $47.50.
Aud: Cl, Pl, Pf

Cumulates the titles listed in the monthly issues of *American Book Publishing Record;* the monthly issues are a cumulation of Bowker's *Weekly Record.* Arranged by subject according to Dewey classification numbers, with separate sections for juvenile and adult fiction and an author and title index. The entries are compiled from Library of Congress cataloging and from cataloging prepared by the *Weekly Record* staff. Each entry includes: main entry, Dewey and LC classification numbers, title and statement of authorship, edition statement, imprint, collation, series, notes, LC card number, ISBN, binding information, price, subject, and added entry tracings. Excluded are government publications, dissertations, periodicals, pamphlets of less than 49 pages and other ephemeral publications, and most school textbooks. Quinquennial cumulations are available for the years 1960/64, 1965/69, and 1970/74. A 28 year single cumulation, *American Book Publishing Record Cumulative 1950/77* (13v. $1500), is scheduled for Fall 1978 publication. It will include LC and Dewey call numbers and a subject index using LC terms. JKM

GE 23
Best Books for Children. 1960. irreg. index. R. R. Bowker, 1180 Ave of the Americas, New York, NY 10036. Dist: R. R. Bowker, Box 1807, Ann Arbor, MI 48106. Examined: 1970, 272p.; 15th ed., 1978. $12.95.
Aud: Pl, Pf

The 15th edition of this book selection guide, which is to be published in Fall, 1978, lists approximately 5500 books in print for grades kindergarten through six. Titles included are recommended by reliable review sources, committees, and book lists. Arranged by subject, each entry includes a full annotation, bibliographic information, and ordering information. Author, title, and illustrator indexes are included. JKM

GE 24
Bibliographic Guide to Black Studies. ISSN 0360-2710. 1975. a. bibl. G. K. Hall and Co., 70 Lincoln St, Boston, MA 02111. Examined: 1976. 340p. $65.
Aud: Sa

Consists of author, title, and subject entries for all current and retrospective materials cataloged during the year by the New York Public Library's Schomburg Center for Research in Black Culture. Entries, each classified by Dewey Decimal Classification, appear in a dictionary or alphabetical sequence and include full tracings (i.e., subject headings and other added entries). Subject cataloging follows the Library of Congress scheme, augmented by special descriptors developed for the Schomburg Collection. Schomburg acquisitions "cover Black activity wherever peoples of African descent have lived," especially "books by authors of African descent, regardless of subject matter or language." Computer produced in a three column per page format. Supplements the *Dictionary Catalog of the Schomburg Collection of Negro Literature and History* (G.K. Hall, 1962). SB

GE 25
Bibliographic Guide to Conference Publications. 1975. a. G. K. Hall and Co., 70 Lincoln St, Boston, MA 02111. Examined: 1977. 2v. 1055p. $100.
Aud: Cl, Pl, Sa

Provides access to conference publications cataloged by the Library of Congress and the Research Libraries of the New York Public Library. Covers proceedings, reports, and summaries of conferences, meetings, and symposia conducted by both private and governmental organizations throughout the world; includes works published in all languages. Entries are arranged in one alphabet under main entry, added entries, titles, series, and subject headings; each entry provides full LC cataloging information and both LC and NYPL call numbers. JKM

GE 26
Bibliographic Guide to Government Publications—Foreign. ISSN 0360-280X. 1975. a. G. K. Hall and Co., 70 Lincoln St, Boston, MA 02111. Examined: 1977. 2v. 1113p. $115.
Aud: Cl, Pl, Pf

Provides access to foreign documents cataloged by the Library of Congress and the Research Libraries of the New York Public Library. Documents such as parliamentary debates and papers, session laws, correspondence on foreign relations, treaties, departmental reports, censuses, statistical annuals and reports, etc. are included. Covers works in all languages. Entries are arranged in one alphabet under main entry, added entries, title, series, and subject headings; each entry provides full LC cataloging information and both LC and NYPL call numbers. The **Guide** also serves as an annual supplement to NYPL's *Catalog of Government Publications* (G. K. Hall, 1972). SJV

GE 27
Bibliographic Guide to Government Publications—U.S. ISSN 0360-2796. 1975. a. G. K. Hall and Co., 70 Lincoln St, Boston, MA 02111. Examined: 1977. 2v. 1295p. $150.
Aud: Cl, Pl, Pf

Provides access to federal, state, and local documents cataloged by the Library of Congress and the Research Libraries of the New York Public Library. Entries are arranged in one alphabet under main entry, added entries, title, series, and subject headings; each entry provides full LC cataloging information and both LC and NYPL call numbers. The **Guide** also serves as an annual supplement to NYPL's *Catalog of Government Publications* (G. K. Hall, 1972). SJV

GE 28
Bibliographic Index. ISSN 0006-1255. 1937. a. w/2 suppls. H. W. Wilson, 950 University Ave, Bronx, NY 10452. Examined: 1976. Ann Massie Case, ed. 518p. service basis.
Aud: Cl, Pl

Subtitle: "A cumulative bibliography of bibliographies." A list of bibliographies, in English and other languages, which contain at least 50 citations. Entries are arranged by subject. Includes bibliographies published separately or as parts of books or pamphlets. In addition, approximately 2400 periodicals are regularly examined for bibliographic material. Issued in cumulative volumes of varying size from 1937 to 1968 and since then annually. KMH

GE 29
Bibliography: Books for Children. ISSN 0147-250X. 1937. tri-a. index. Association for Childhood Education International, 3615 Wisconsin Ave, Washington, DC 20016. Examined: 1974. 112p. $2.75 pap. (1977.)
Aud: Pl, Pf

An annotated bibliography of approximately 1500 titles recommended for children aged two through twelve. Includes author and title indexes. JKM

GE 30
Books for the Teen Age. ISSN 0068-0192. 1955. a. index. New York Public Library, Fifth Ave and 42nd St, Rm 58, New York, NY 10018. Examined: 1977. Lillian Morrison, ed. 67p. $2.50.
Aud: Jh, Hs, Pl

A list of approximately 1250 titles of special interest to young adults compiled by NYPL librarians who work with teenagers. Arranged alphabetically by author within broad subject categories: "Here/Now"; "The Arts and Fiction"; "Science"; "Action"; "Adventure"; and "Other Things to Do". Includes specific subject and title indexes. EF/JKM

GE 31
Books in Print. ISSN 0068-0214. 1947. a. w/suppl. index. R. R. Bowker, 1180 Ave of the Americas, New York, NY 10036. Dist: R. R. Bowker, Box 1807, Ann Arbor, MI 48106. Examined: 1976/77 suppl., 2500p., $42.50; 1977/78. 4v. $86.50. (1978/79. 4v. $92.50.)
Aud: Cl, Pl, Pf

Author and title index in four volumes to 478,000 titles from 6000 U.S. publishers. Volumes one and two are an alphabetical author index; volumes three and four are an alphabetical title index. Volume four includes a list of active publishers arranged alphabetically by abbreviation, a list of publishers who have been inactive or who have gone out-of-business since the last *Supplement* was issued, and an alphabetical directory of active U.S. publishers. Bibliographic entries include author, title, LC card number, subject and series information, ISBN, publisher, and distributor. **Books in Print** is produced from the BIPS Data Base begun in 1948 primarily as a listing of titles included in **Publishers' Trade List Annual (PTLA).** During the early 1970s, the data base was expanded to include information from publishers whose titles were not included in **PTLA.** Subject access is provided through the companion title **Subject Guide to Books in Print.** Paperbound books are listed in Bowker's semi-annual *Paperbound Books in Print.* KMH

GE 32
Books in Series in the United States. ISSN 0000-0515. 1966/75. bi-a. w/a. suppls. index. R. R. Bowker, 1180 Ave of the Americas, New York, NY 10036. Dist: R. R. Bowker, Box 1807, Ann Arbor, MI 48106. Examined: 1966/75, 2486p., $52.50; 1978 suppl. 1000p. $34.50.
Aud: Cl, Pl, Pf

A bibliography of books published in series in the U.S. between 1966 and 1975 with current information on their availability and price. Sources used in the compilation were Library of Congress MARC files, **Books in Print, Publisher's Trade List Annual, American Book Publishing Record,** and **Irregular Serials and Annuals.** Arranged alphabetically by series main entry. Each series entry includes ISSN and full bibliographic information. Under each series title, books are arranged by number or, if unnumbered, by title. Each book entry includes author or editor, publication date, price, publisher, ISBN, LC card number, and out of print information when applicable. Includes an author and title index to individual works and a subject index to series. A second edition of **Books in Series** is scheduled for publication in December 1978; (approx 3600 pages, tentative price $62.50); this edition will supercede the first edition and its supplement. KMH/JKM

GE 33
British Books in Print. ISSN 0068-1350. (Continues: The Reference Catalogue of Current Literature.) 1874. a. index, J. Whitaker and Sons, 13 Bedford Sq, London WC1B, 3JE England. Dist: R. R. Bowker,

Box 1807, Ann Arbor, MI 48106. Examined: 1976; 1977. 2v. 4701p. $78.
Aud: Cl, Pl

A national inclusive index of books in print and on sale in the United Kingdom with details as to author, title, editor, translator, reviser, year of publication or latest edition, size, number of pages, illustrations, series, binding, price, name of publisher, and ISBN. This is a two volume set. Volume one contains a list of publishers and addresses, a how-to-use section, a section explaining how to order, and a list of series and their publishers. This is followed by the body of the work listing in one alphabet authors, titles, and subjects of British books in print. Volume one covers the letters A-J; volume two completes the alphabet. MBP

GE 34
Children's Books, Awards and Prizes. ISSN 0069-3472. (Continues: Westchester Library System. Children's Books: Awards and Prizes.) 1969. bi-a. index. Children's Book Council, 67 Irving Place, New York, NY 10003. Examined: 1975; 1977. 156p. $4.95.
Aud: Pl, Pf

A listing of the winners of the major children's book awards in the U.S., Canada, Great Britain, and Australia. Arranged alphabetically by name of award, each entry includes a brief history of the award and, with a few exceptions, lists all award winners. For the Newbery, Caldecott, and National Book Awards, finalists are listed in addition to award winners. Includes author/illustrator and title indexes. JKM

GE 35
Children's Books in Print. ISSN 0069-3480. (Continues: Children's Books for Schools and Libraries.) 1962. a. index. R. R. Bowker, 1180 Ave of the Americas, New York, NY 10036. Dist: R. R. Bowker, Box 1804, Ann Arbor, MI 48106. Examined: 8th ed., 1976/77. Gertrude Jennings, ed. approx. 790p. (10th ed., 1978/79. 790p. $29.95.)
Aud: Pl, Pf

The volume begins with a Foreword by Lillian N. Gerhardt, Editor-in-Chief of *School Library Journal,* which defines children's books and describes the liberal approach to selection of the 39,000 titles listed in the current volume. A how-to-use section and a key to abbreviations precede the body of the work which includes an author index, a title index, and an illustrator index. Each entry includes author, title, illustrator, publisher, price, grade level, ISBN, and LC card number when available so that all information is found whether the volume is consulted by author, title, or illustrator. A key to publishers' abbreviations which includes full names and addresses completes the volume. Subject access is through the companion volume **Subject Guide to Children's Books in Print.** MBP

GE 36
Children's Catalog. 1909. quinquennial w/4 a. suppls. index. H. W. Wilson, 950 University Ave, Bronx, NY 10452. Examined: 13th ed., 1976, 1408p., $40 (includes 4 suppls.); 1977 suppl. 166p.
Aud: Pl, Pf

The **Children's Catalog** is part of the Wilson Standard Catalog Series. It is a guide to the best fiction and nonfiction books for children from preschool age to the sixth grade. There is minimal overlap with the **Junior High School Library Catalog**. The 13th edition is an annotated list of 5415 titles with 13,375 analytical entries. The titles included were selected by librarians and specialists in the field of children's literature. The entries, which include full bibliographic descriptions, are arranged by Dewey Decimal Classification; fiction, story collections, and easy books are in separate sections. The use of uniform titles in this edition brings together variant forms of individual folk and fairy tales. Complete author, title, subject, and analytical indexes and a directory of publishers and distributors with complete, current addresses are included. EF/JKM

GE 37
Children's Literature: A Guide to Reference Sources. Supplement. 1972. quinquennial. index. illus. Library of Congress, Children's Book Section, Washington, DC 20540. Dist: Superintendent of Documents, U.S. Government Printing Office, Washington, DC 20402. Examined: 2nd ed., 1977. Virginia Haviland, ed. 413p. $7.75.
Aud: Cl, Pl, Sa

An annotated international list of books, pamphlets, and articles intended for persons concerned with the creation, study, or reading of children's literature. The basic volume was published in 1966 and listed over 1000 items; the first supplement added almost 750 items; the second adds over 900. With the second supplement, bibliographies and critical works on nonprint materials and research in the field of children's literature have been included. Author, title, and subject indexes are provided. JKM

GE 38
Cumulative Book Index. ISSN 0011-300X. 1928. a. w/m. suppls. H. W. Wilson, 950 University Ave, Bronx, NY 10452. Examined: 1976. 2421p. service basis.
Aud: Cl, Pl

Subtitle: "A world list of books in the English language." An international bibliography of books published in the English language arranged by author, subject, and title. Excluded are government documents, most pamphlets, cheap paperbound books, maps, music scores, editions with less than 500 copies printed, and, in general, local, fugitive, or ephemeral materials. The most complete information is provided in the author entry: name, title, series, edition, pagination, price, date, publisher, ISBN, and LC card number. A directory of publishers and distributors appears at the end of the volume. Cumulative volumes were published for the years 1928/32, 1933/37, 1938/42, 1943/48, 1949/52, and 1953/55; biennial cumulations were published between 1957/58 and 1967/68; only the annual volumes have been issued since 1969. KMH

GE 39
Government Reference Books. ISSN 0072-5188. 1968/69. bi-a. index. Libraries Unlimited, Box 263, Littleton, CO 80160. Examined: 4th ed., 1974/75. Alan Edward Schoor, ed. 263p. $11.50.
Aud: Hs, Jc, Cl, Pl

Subtitle: "A biennial guide to U.S. government publications." Includes over 1300 entries arranged by broad subject disciplines: social sciences, science and technology, humanities, and general works. These broad categories are further broken down in such sub-groups as economics and business, energy and energy conservation, etc. Each entry includes author, title, pagination, LC card number, Superintendent of Documents number, and a descriptive annotation. Includes personal author, title, and subject indexes. JKM

GE 40
Guide to Microforms in Print. ISSN 0017-5293. 1961. a. Microform Review, 520 Riverside Ave, Box 405, Saugatuck Sta, Westport, CT 06880. Examined: 1976; 1977. John J. Walsh, ed. 410p. $42.50.
Aud: Cl, Pl

A cumulative, annual listing of microform titles, comprising books, journals, newspapers, government publications, archival material, etc., currently available from micropublishers. Provides bibliographic control for all microform publications (incorporates *International Microforms in Print* beginning with the 1977 edition) except theses and dissertations. Entries are in alphabetic sequence according to author-title following Library of Congress and Anglo-American Cataloging Rules. Bibliographic information includes author, title, volumes, dates, prices, publisher, and type of microform for book, journal, and newspaper entries. Introduction is in English, French, German, and Spanish. A **Subject Guide to Microforms in Print** is also available. KMH

GE 41
Guide to Reference Books. (Continues: Guide to the Study and Use of Reference Books.) 1902. irreg. index. American Library Association, 50 E Huron St, Chicago, IL 60611. Examined: 9th ed., 1976. Eugene P. Sheehy, ed. 1015p. $30.
Aud: Hs, Jc, Cl, Pl, Pf

The standard guide to general reference materials; it is often referred to by the name of the compiler: currently Sheehy, formerly Winchell, and occasionally one still hears references to Mudge, the compiler from 1910 to 1941. The work is divided into five major sections: General Reference Works; The Humanities; Social Sciences; History and Area Studies; and Pure and Applied Sciences. Within each of these sections there are subject subdivisions; within subdivisions, works are classified by form. Entries are given in Library of Congress established form and include bibliographic history, LC call numbers, and descriptive notes. The notes serve as a selection aid. The ninth edition lists approximately 10,000 titles and includes general reference works in all languages. The index includes authors, titles, and subjects in one alphabet. Since the arrangement of the work is designed to facilitate the review of reference works in a field of study, the use of the index is necessary to locate a particular title. Supplements are issued between editions. JKM

GE 42
Guide to Reprints. ISSN 0072-8667. 1967. a. w/June suppl. Guide to Reprints, Box 249, Kent, CT 06757. Examined: 1977. 628p. $39.50.
Aud: Cl, Pl

An annual, cumulative guide in alphabetic order to books, journals, and other material available in reprint form. Includes materials that have gone out-of print-but are now back in print by a photo-offset process—as opposed to recomposing the text. Guidelines for inclusion are: there must be no new composition; the reprint must be bound and full sized; the print edition must be more than 200 copies; and the reprint must be listed in a catalog. A publishers directory is included. Reprint entries are arranged by author and include the original publication date, price, and ISBN number when available. Journals and sets are entered by title; volume numbers and years and ISSN numbers are provided when available. KMH

GE 43
Index Translationum. ISSN 0073-6074. 1932-40; 1948 n.s. a. index. UNESCO, Place de Fontenoy, 75700, Paris, France. Dist: Unipub, Box 433, New York, NY 10016. Examined: no. 26, 1973. 974p. $74.
Aud: Sa

An annual (but late—the 1973 edition was issued in 1976) international bibliography of translations published in UNESCO member nations, though occasionally other nations are included. Arrangement is by country (in French) under the ten major headings of the Universal Decimal Classification. Each entry includes author, title of translation, name of translator, place of publication, publisher, and the language in which the work was written or from which it was translated. An alphabetical list of principal authors follows the main body of the directory. The text is in French and English. The current series of **Index Translationum** began in 1948; from 1932-1940, it was published as a service of the International Institute of Intellectual Cooperation. In 1973, G. K. Hall issued a *Cumulative Index to English Translations* in two volumes which cumulates entries from the 1948-68 annual volumes for translations done in nations where English is the primary language (Australia, Canada, New Zealand, Ireland, South Africa, United Kingdom, and United States). KMH

GE 44
International Publications. 1972. a. International Publications Service, 114 E 32nd St, New York, NY 10016. Examined: 3rd ed., 1975/76. 274p. $7.50.
Aud: Cl, Pl, Pf

Subtitle: "An annual annotated subject bibliography." Lists approximately 7000 publications of publishers and agencies throughout the world which are available through International Publications Service to libraries or individuals trying to build international collections or to fill gaps in existing collections. Sections are arranged by subject. Part one covers serials and series, and publications of international organizations; part two covers monographs. All entries are arranged alphabetically by subject (agriculture, banking, history, philosophy, etc.). Each entry includes author, LC card number, title, date, pages, content notes, price, and a short descriptive annotation. Except in the case of international organizations' publications, the publishers' names are omitted since this is a distributor's catalog. MBP

GE 45
Irregular Serials and Annuals; An International Directory. ISSN 0000-0043. 1967. bi-a. index. R. R. Bowker, 1180 Ave of the Americas, New York, NY 10036. Dist: R. R. Bowker, Box 1807, Ann Arbor, MI 48106. Examined: 1976/77. Emery I. Koltay, ed. 1068p. $55.
Aud: Cl, Pl

Provides bibliographic and purchasing information for 30,000 serials and continuations such as proceedings, transactions, advances, progresses, reports, yearbooks, handbooks, annual reviews, and monographic series published throughout the world. Arranged alphabetically by main entry under 251 subject headings with cross indexes. Entries include title, frequency, country of publication, publisher, Dewey classification number, buying and ordering information, abstract and indexing information, and bibliographic notes. A list of cessations is provided. Index is organized by title. A special feature is the index to publications of international organizations. Supplemented between editions by *Ulrich's Quarterly* and by the *Bowker Serials Bibliography Supplement* which is published intermittently and updates both this title and **Ulrich's International Periodicals Directory.** KMH/JKM

GE 46
Junior High School Library Catalog. 1965. quinquennial w/4 a. suppls. index. H. W. Wilson, 950 University Ave, Bronx, NY 10452. Examined: 3rd ed, 1975, 991p., $42 (includes suppls.); 1977 suppl. 110p.
Aud: Jh, Pl, Pf

The **Junior High School Library Catalog** is part of the Wilson Standard Catalog Series. Designed as a selection aid for librarians and teachers, it covers approximately 6000 fiction and nonfiction titles appropriate for seventh through ninth grade students. In the third edition, coverage of topics of current concern is expanded to include such issues as women's rights, communal living, alcoholism, venereal diseases, etc. The titles included were selected by librarians and experts in the field of young adult literature. The entries, with full bibliographic description, annotations, and recommended *Sears* subject headings, are arranged by Dewey Decimal Classification. Thorough author, title, subject, and analytical indexes, and a directory of publishers and distributors with complete, current addresses are included. EF/JKM

GE 47
Large Type Books in Print. 1970. a. index. R. R. Bowker, 1180 Ave of the Americas, New York, NY 10036. Dist: R. R. Bowker, Box 1807, Ann Arbor, MI 48106. Examined: 1976. 455p. (1978. $17.50.)
Aud: Pl, Sa

A subject arranged list of over 3000 books reproduced in 14 point type or larger for use by the visually impaired. The volume itself is set in 18 point type. Adult trade books, children's books, and school textbooks are included. Entries give author, title, binding, price, type size, book size, discount information, and publisher. Includes a directory of publishers with current addresses, and author and title indexes. The 1978 edition will be available in September 1978. JKM

GE 48
Library of Congress Publications in Print. ISSN 0083-1603. 1935. a. U.S. Library of Congress, Publications Office, Washington, DC 20540. Examined: 1978. Judith Farley and Teena Siggers, eds. 60p. free.
Aud: Cl, Pl, Pf

A list of books, pamphlets, and serials published by the Library of Congress or compiled by members of the Library of Congress staff and published by the Superintendent of Documents or commercial publishers. Out-of-print LC publications which have been reprinted and are available from commercial publishers and music, folk, and literary records available from LC are also included. Full ordering information is provided for each entry including LC card and classification numbers, price, pagination, and contents and cataloging notes where appropriate; entries for recordings note the number of sides and describe accompanying materials. There is an author, title, and subject index, a list of publishers represented in the volume, and a list of Government Printing Office bookstores with full current addresses. JKM

GE 49
Magazines for Libraries. 1969. irreg. bibl. index. R. R. Bowker, 1180 Ave of the Americas, New York, NY 10036. Dist: R. R. Bowker, Box 1807, Ann Arbor, MI 48106. Examined: 2nd ed., 1972. William Katz, ed. 822p. (3rd ed., 1978. $35.)
Aud: Hs, Jc, Cl, Pl, Pf

The third edition of this guide to magazine selection for public, school, and college librarians will be available in October 1978. The now standard work provides descriptive and critical annotations of the editorial content, point of view, and other significant features of approximately 4500 titles. The new edition will annotate approximately 6500 titles. Arranged by subject, each entry includes full bibliographic information, indexing information, and audience level. Includes a title index, a bibliography of periodical bibliographies, and other items of interest to those working with periodicals. JKM

GE 50
Private Press Books. ISSN 0079-5402. 1959. a. bibl. index. Private Libraries Association, Ravelston-South View Rd, Pinner, Middlesex, England. Examined: 1977. David Chambers, ed. $6.
Aud: Sa

This checklist of books issued by private presses "attempts to include the work of all private presses printing in English, and the more important of those printing in other languages." The 1977 edition listed books published in 1974. Arrangement is alphabetical by the issuing press. Entries include basic bibliographical information and a detailed description of the physical book. A bibliography of private printing, divided into general works and literature on individual presses, follows the main section. An index of authors, titles, and presses is provided. KMH

GE 51
Public Library Catalog. 1934. quinquennial w/a. suppls. index. H. W. Wilson, 950 University Ave, Bronx, NY 10452. Examined: 6th ed., 1973. Estelle A. Fidell, ed. 1543p. $65 (includes 4 suppls.).
Aud: Cl, Pl, Pf

The **Public Library Catalog,** a guide to 8765 nonfiction titles selected for inclusion by practicing librarians, is part of the Wilson Standard Catalog Series. Designed for use in public, college, and university libraries as a book selection tool, as an aid in cataloging and classification, and as a readers' advisory aid. Under the author's name, in a classified arrangement, full bibliographic information, suggested subject headings, ISBN's, and annotations are given for each title. There are thorough author, title, and subject indexes, and 15,852 analytical entries for composite works. There is a directory of publishers and distributors with complete, current addresses. Works of fiction are covered by Wilson's **Fiction Catalog.** EF/JKM

GE 52
Publishers' Trade List Annual. ISSN 0079-7855. 1873. a. index. R. R. Bowker, 1180 Ave of the Americas, New York NY 10036. Dist R.R. Bowker, Box 1807, Ann Arbor, MI 48106. Examined: 1977. 6v. $50.
Aud: Cl, Pl

Consists of the catalogs of over 2250 publishers bound together in six volumes. Smaller and specialist publishers whose listings vary in length from one title to only a few pages of publications are listed in a separate section. The major portion of the work contains publishers' catalogs which are more than four pages long. The format of each catalog, and information supplied, varies with the whim of each publisher. There is a single index to publishers listed in both sections. **Books in Print** was originally issued as an index to **PTLA** (as it is usually referred to), but is now generated from its own data base. KMH/MBP

GE 53
Senior High School Library Catalog. 1926. quinquennial w/4 a. suppls. H. W. Wilson, 950 University Ave, Bronx, NY 10452. Examined: 11th ed, 1977. 1416p. $50 (includes suppls.)
Aud: Hs, Pl, Pf

The **Senior High School Library Catalog** is part of the Wilson Standard Catalog Series. A selection aid for librarians and teachers, it covers approximately 5300 fiction and nonfiction titles appropriate for tenth through twelfth grade students. In response to changing curricula, many adult books have been included, and there is greater representation of books about ethnic groups, increased coverage of foreign language dictionaries, and a substantial increase in titles in Dewey 300 and 700 categories. The titles included were selected by librarians and specialists in the field. The entries, with full bibliographic description, annotations, and recommended *Sears* subject headings, are arranged by Dewey Decimal Classification. Thorough author, title, and subject indexes; 17,587 analytical entries; and a directory of publishers and distributors with complete, current addresses are included.
EF/JKM

GE 54
Small Press Record of Books in Print. 1966. a. index. Dustbooks, Box 1056, Paradise, CA 95969. Examined: 5th ed, 1975. Len Fulton, ed. 240p. $6.95. (6th ed. 424p. $8.95 pap.)
Aud: Cl, Pl

The "Cumulative Book Index" of the small press, this bibliography lists books, pamphlets, chapbooks, broadsides, posters, and poem cards published by small, independent presses worldwide. It is a companion volume to **International Directory of Little Magazines and Small Presses** which lists periodicals. The main portion is arranged alphabetically by author; entries include title, publisher, size, pagination, binding, type of printing, price, date, description, and size of press run. Also includes a title index and a publisher/author index with publishers' full addresses. Published irregularly for the first two editions: the first edition covered 1966-68, the second covered 1969-72. It has been published annually since 1973. KMH

GE 55
Standard Periodical Directory. ISSN 0085-6630. 1963. bi-a. index. Oxbridge Communications, 1345 Ave of the Americas, New York, NY 10019. Examined: 5th ed., 1977. John F. Resser, ed. 1715p. $75.
Aud: Cl, Pl

Subtitle: "The largest authoritative guide to United States and Canadian periodicals . . . information on more than 60,000 periodicals." This one volume work provides data on periodicals (any publication having a frequency of at least once every two years) including consumer magazines, trade journals, newsletters, government publications, house organs, directories, transactions, and proceedings. A Table of Contents lists the subject headings under which the listings appear. This is followed by a cross index to subject headings. The body of the work lists in bold face type the title of periodical, address, editor, advertising director, financial officer, year established, frequency, price, circulation, and advertising rates. In addition, a short description of the contents of each periodical is included where available. A title index appears at the end of the volume. KMH/MBP

GE 56
Subject Guide to Books in Print. ISSN 0000-0159. 1956. a. R. R. Bowker, 1180 Ave of the Americas, New York NY 10036. Dist: R. R. Bowker, Box 1807, Ann Arbor, MI 48106. Examined: 1977/78. 2v. $65.
Aud: Cl, Pl, Pf

Subtitle: "Subject guide to (hardbounds, paperbacks, trade books, textbooks, adult books, juvenile) books in print—the available books, new and old, in 62,000 categories with full ordering information." This two volume work begins with a how-to-use section, a key to abbreviations, and a key to publishers' abbreviations which supplies the full name and address of each. The body of the work follows. Works included are listed under LC subject headings arranged alphabetically. There are 62,000 headings with over 51,000 cross references. Information provided in the entries includes author, co-author, editor, co-editor, translator, co-translator, title, number of volumes, edition, LC number, series information, language if other than English, illustrations, grade range, year of publication, type of binding, price, ISBN, publisher's order number, imprint, and publisher. Fiction, poetry, and drama are omitted as are Bibles, but commentaries, histories, and versions of the Bible other than in English are covered extensively. KMH/MBP

GE 57
Subject Guide to Children's Books in Print. ISSN 0000-0167. 1971. a. R. R. Bowker, 1180 Ave of the Americas, New York, NY 10036. Dist: R. R. Bowker, Box 1807, Ann Arbor, MI 48106. Examined: 1976. 453p. $28.50.
Aud: Pl, Pf

Companion volume to **Children's Books in Print.** A listing of approximately 39,000 titles under 8300 subject headings. Includes fiction titles. Information given for each title includes: author, title, publisher, date of publication, price and when it was supplied by the publisher, grade level, binding information, edition statement, number of pages or volumes, ISBN, and illustrator. Includes a directory of the publishers represented in the volume with current addresses. KMH/JKM

GE 58
Subject Guide to Microforms in Print. ISSN 0090-290X. 1962. a. Microform Review, 520 Riverside Ave, Box 405, Saugatuck Sta, Westport, CT 06880. Examined: 1976; 1977. John J. Walsh, ed. 495p. $42.50.
Aud: Cl, Pl

A companion volume to **Guide to Microforms in Print**, this subject guide (incorporating *International Microforms in Print* with the 1977 edition) is a cumulative, annual listing of microform titles comprising books, journals, newspapers, government publications, and archival material currently available from micropublishers. Entry information includes, as appropriate, author, title, volume, date, price, publisher, and type of microform. Subject classification is derived from the Library of Congress' *Outline of the Library of Congress Classifications*. An index to the subject classification is provided, as is a directory of publishers. The introduction is in English, French, German, and Spanish. KMH/MBP

GE 59
Ulrich's International Periodicals Directory. ISSN 0000-0175. (Continues: Ulrich's Periodicals Directory; Periodicals Directory). 1932. bi-a. index. R. R. Bowker, 1180 Ave of the Americas, New York, NY 10036. Dist: R. R. Bowker, Box 1807, Ann Arbor, MI 48106. Examined: 17th ed., 1977/78. 2096p. $57.50.
Aud: Cl, Pl, Pf

Subtitle: "A classified guide to current periodicals, foreign and domestic." Lists in-print periodicals issued more than once a year which are published throughout the world. Annuals and irregular serials are covered in the companion volume, **Irregular Serials and Annuals.** Entries are arranged by subject and include Dewey classification number, Country Code and ISSN, title, subtitle, language(s) of text, year begun, frequency, price, sponsor, publisher, editor, advertising, reviews, abstracting, bibliography, charts, illustrations, patents, statistics, indexes, circulation, format, where indexed, key titles, and former titles. Special features include lists of cessations, new periodicals, publications of international organizations, an ISSN index, and a title index. Supplemented between editions by *Ulrich's Quarterly* and by the *Bowker Serials Bibliography Supplement* which is published intermittently and which updates both this title and Bowker's **Irregular Serials and Annuals.** KMH

GE 60
U.S. Bureau of the Census. Bureau of the Census Catalog. 1946. a. w/m. and q. suppls. index. U.S. Department of Commerce, Bureau of the Census, Washington, DC 20233. Dist: Superintendent of Documents, U.S. Government Printing Office, Washington, DC 20402. Examined: 1977. 255p. $3.25; $19 w/m. and q. suppls.
Aud: Cl, Pl, Pf, Sa

Divided into two sections. The first part lists all publications issued by the Bureau during a specified period with complete ordering information and descriptive annotations. Entries are arranged by subject. There is a list of selected publications of other agencies. Part two lists data files (computer tape and punchcards), special tabulations of data, and other unpublished nonstatistical materials, such as maps and computer programs. It is also arranged by subject and includes sections describing microfiche publications, the personal census records service, and other customer services. The appendix lists government and Census Bureau depositary libraries holding census bureau reports. JKM

GE 61
U.S. Superintendent of Documents. Subject Bibliography Index. 1973. a. Superintendent of Documents, U.S. Government Printing Office, Washington, DC 20402. Examined: 1977. 8p. free.
Aud: Hs, Jc, Cl, Pl, Pf

A subject approach to the 270 subject bibliographies now available free of charge from the Superintendent of Documents. Under Education, for example, 12 bibliographies covering such topics as adult education, drug education, reading, educational statistics, etc. are listed. The bibliographies provide ordering information for each entry, including price and Superintendent of Documents number. The new publication replaces specific subject price lists, such as the *Education Price List*, and is designed to provide up to date information on publications available from the Superintendent of Documents. Libraries can be put on a mailing list to receive future, revised editions. BSM

BIOGRAPHICAL DIRECTORIES AND INDEXES

GE 62
Biographical Dictionaries Master Index. 1975/76. bi-a. Gale Research Co., Book Tower, Detroit, MI 48226. Examined: 1975/76. Dennis La Beau and Gary C. Tarbert, eds. 3v. 2492p. $85.
Aud: Hs, Jc, Cl, Pl

An alphabetical index to more than 50 biographical dictionaries and other reference sources. Provides access to over 800,000 biographical sketches of contemporary men and women in works such as the Marquis Who's Who series (therefore obviating the need to acquire the **Marquis Who's Who Publications: Index to All Books**), **American Men and Women of Science, Directory of American Scholars, Who's Who of American Women, Contemporary Authors**, etc. A very useful reference work; particularly helpful in tracking down individuals who are listed in only a few sources or to find out if they are listed at all. A time saver. JKM

GE 63
Biography Index. ISSN 0006-3053. 1946. tri-a. w/a. and q. suppls. H. W. Wilson, 950 University Ave, Bronx, NY 10452. Examined: 1973/76. 995p. $40.
Aud: Hs, Jc, Cl, Pl

Subtitle: "A cumulative index to biographical material in books and magazines." Guide to biographical materials in over 2200 periodicals, books of individual and collective biography, and incidental biographical material in other books. Material indexed includes obituaries, letters, diaries, and memoirs. Bibliographies, portraits, or other illustrations are noted if they appear with indexed biographies. Juvenile literature is also analyzed. Arranged alphabetically by biographee with a supplementary index by career or occupation. A checklist of composite works analyzed is included. KMH

GE 64
Blue Book: Leaders of the English-Speaking World. ISSN 0067-9240. 1968. a. St. Martin's Press, 175 Fifth Ave, New York, NY 10010. Examined: 1973/74. 1586p. $30. (1977. $45.)
Aud: Cl, Pl

Annual listing of persons in the U.S., Great Britain, and the English-speaking Commonwealth who have "achieved distinction in the arts and sciences, business, or the professions." Each entry provides personal information, home and work addresses, titles and degrees, current and immediate past positions, and publications. JKM

GE 65
Current Biography Yearbook. ISSN 0084-9499. 1940. a. w/m. suppls. H. W. Wilson, 950 University Ave, Bronx, NY 10452. Examined: 1976; 1977. Charles Moritz, ed. 502p. $20.
Aud: Hs, Jc, Cl, Pl
Indexed in: *Biographical Dictionaries Master Index.*

Provides brief, objective biographical articles about living individuals. The 1976 edition includes updated sketches that supersede articles in earlier editions. Emphasis is on individuals prominent in areas such as dance, education, government, journalism, literature, movies, music, photography, politics, publishing, television, and theatre. Obituaries of individuals previously featured are included in each monthly issue and cumulated in the annual volume. Cumulative indexes have been issued at ten year intervals. In 1973, a separate index was issued for 1940-70. Subsequent annual volumes (1972-76) have included cumulative indexes for all volumes since 1970. KMH

GE 66

Dictionary of International Biography. ISSN 0419-1137. 1963. a. Melrose Press, Market Hill, Cambridge CB2 3QP England. Examined: v. 14, 1978. Ernest Kay, ed. 2v. 967p., $65.
Aud: Cl, Pl

Subtitle: "A biographical record of contemporary achievement." Who's who type information, obtained by questionnaire, on over 11,000 persons of international significance. Sketches include references to the person's inclusion in other biographical works. The basis for inclusion is not stated, but this is not a vanity publication. JKM

GE 67

Directory of Significant 20th Century Minority Women in the U.S.A. 1978. freq. not determined. Gaylord Bros., Box 4901, Syracuse, NY 13221. Examined: 1978. Jessie Carney Smith, ed. 500p. $29.95.
Aud: Jc, Hs, Cl, Pl

An alphabetically arranged list of approximately 750 minority women. Each entry indicates the biographee's specific ethnic identity (e.g., tribe is indicated for American Indian women; Chinese, Japanese, or other national origin is indicated for Asian-Americans; etc.), and includes personal who's who type data; a career summary; and generally a statement of the woman's views, beliefs, accomplishments, and ideals written by the biographee herself or by someone who knows her well. Could be used to provide role models for American Indian, Black, Hispanic, and Asian-American (the minority groups covered) girls and young women, in addition to serving as a basic biographical dictionary. JKM

GE 68

International Who's Who. ISSN 0074-9613. 1963. a. Europa Publications, 18 Bedford Sq, London WC1B 3JN England. Dist: Gale Research Co., Book Tower, Detroit MI 48226. Examined: 40th ed., 1976/77; 41st ed., 1977/78. 1908p. $70.
Aud: Cl, Pl
Indexed in: *Biographical Dictionaries Master Index.*

An alphabetical listing of international scope covering persons in all fields. Entries include occupation, birth date, memberships, honors, education, publications, offices, leisure interests, and addresses. Special features include an alphabetical list by nation of reigning royal families (whose biographies are in the main entry sections) and an obituary list of deceased biographees from the previous edition. KMH

GE 69

Marquis Who's Who Publications: Index to All Books. 1974. a. Marquis Who's Who, 200 E Ohio St, Chicago, IL 60611. Examined: 1976; 1977. 565p. $24.95.
Aud: Cl, Pl

An index to the biographical sketches in the Marquis publications **Who's Who in America, Who's Who in the East, Who's Who in the South and Southwest, Who's Who in the Midwest, Who's Who in the West, Who's Who in American Law, Who's Who in Finance and Industry, Who's Who in Government, Who's Who in Religion, Who's Who in the World,** and **Who's Who of American Women.** Also includes, in the same alphabet, an index to sketches in volume six of **Who Was Who in America** and to sketches in the Marquis biographical directories of child development professionals and school district officials. A very useful reference work, but if biographical directories other than Marquis publications are collected, Gale's **Biographical Dictionaries Master Index** is more valuable. JKM

GE 70

Who Was Who in America. ISSN 0083-9345. 1942. tri-a. index. Marquis Who's Who, 200 E Ohio St, Chicago, IL 60611. Examined: 1973/76. 2v. 3614p. $47.50.
Aud: Cl, Pl
Indexed in: *Biographical Dictionaries Master Index; Marquis Who's Who Publications: Index to All Books.*

Sketches removed from **Who's Who in America** because of the death of the biographee have been expanded here to include date of death, and often the cause of death and interment location. The years covered are 1897 to the present. Since volume four, cumulative indexes to other volumes have been included in each issue. These cumulations are very helpful since sketches are occasionally updated. Marquis published *Who Was Who in America: Historical Volume* in 1963 (rev. 1967, 689p.) which covers the years 1607 through 1896 and is "a compilation of sketches of individuals, both of the United States of America and other countries, who have made a contribution to, or whose activity was in some manner related to the history of the United States, from the founding of the Jamestown Colony" to 1897. The *Historical Volume* includes tables of national political figures, first governors and years of admission of the several states, major events in United States history, etc. KHM/JKM

GE 71
Who's Who. ISSN 0083-937X. 1849. a. A. and C. Black, 4-6 Soho Sq, London W1V 6AD England. Dist: St. Martin's Press, 175 Fifth Ave, New York, NY 10010. Examined: v. 129, 1977/78. 2688p. $64.50.
Aud: Cl, Pl
Indexed in: *Biographical Dictionaries Master Index*.

Annual British biographical dictionary on which the formats of all other national who's who publications are based. Alphabetical listing of prominent British personalities including education, positions, honors, publications, recreation, and addresses. Special features include a late supplement, obituaries, and information about the Royal Family. Six volumes containing the biographies removed from **Who's Who** each year on account of death have been published as *Who Was Who*, covering the years 1897-1970. The sketches are, for the most part, unaltered except for the addition of the date of death. KMH

GE 72
Who's Who Among Black Americans. 1975/76. bi-a. index. Who's Who Among Black Americans Publishing Co., Northbrook, IL. Examined: 1975/76. William C. Matney, ed. 772p. $49.95.
Aud: Cl, Pl
Indexed in: *Biographical Dictionaries Master Index*.

Typical who's who type information on approximately 10,000 Black Americans supplied by the biographees. Some Black Americans of significance are not included since they did not wish to be listed in a race-identified biographical dictionary. Alphabetically arranged with a geographic index, and an occupation index by broad categories (e.g., art, behavioral and medical sciences, etc.). JKM

GE 73
Who's Who in America. ISSN 0883-9396. 1899. bi-a. Marquis Who's Who, 200 E Ohio St, Chicago, IL 60611. Examined: 1976. 2v. $79.50.
Aud: Cl, Pl
Indexed in: *Biographical Dictionaries Master Index; Marquis Who's Who Publications: Index to All Books*.

Contains 70,000 entries in two volumes. Alphabetical entries include name, occupation, vital statistics, parents, education, marital information, children, career, career related civic and political activities, nonprofessional directorships, military record, decorations and awards, professional and association memberships, political and religious affiliation, lodges, clubs, publications, home and office addresses. Special features include a necrology of those who appeared in the previous editions; a section listing biographees who appear in regional editions; a section titled "Thoughts on My Life," which includes statements of those principles, ideas, goals, and standards of conduct that have helped biographees to achieve success and high regard; and a list of citations for significant contributions to society. Biographees who have died are entered in **Who Was Who in America.** KMH

GE 74
Who's Who in Canada. ISSN 0083-9450. 1911. bi-a. index. illus. International Press, 643 Yonge St, Toronto, Ontario, Canada. Examined: 64th ed., 1975/76. Ernest Whelpton, ed. 1360p. $85.
Aud: Cl, Pl
Indexed in: *Biographical Dictionaries Master Index*.

An illustrated biographical directory containing standard personal information, education, career, honors, and publications. An alphabetical index precedes the directory and must be used since the directory itself is not arranged alphabetically. KMH

GE 75
Who's Who in the Arab World. ISSN 0083-9752. 1965/66. bi-a. (irreg.) bibl. Publitech Publications, Box 5936, Beirut, Lebanon. Dist: International Publications Service, 114 E 32nd St, New York, NY 10016. Examined: 1974/75. Gabriel M. Bustros, ed. 1734p. $50.
Aud: Cl, Pl
Indexed in: *Biographical Dictionaries Master Index*.

Contains over 4000 biographical notices of individuals from 17 Arab nations: Algeria, Bahrain, Egypt, Iraq, Jordan, Kuwait, Libya, Morocco, Oman, Qatar, Saudi Arabia, Sudan, Syria, Tunisia, United Arab Emirates, Yemen (Arab Republic) and Yemen (People's Democratic Republic). Lebanon is not included since Publitech issues an individual volume for that nation. Sketches include basic biographical data: name, address, education, positions, career, associations, and publications. Biographical sketches are preceded by 1200 pages of introductory material divided in two parts. The first part, Outline of the Arab World, provides a general survey of the history of the Middle East, League of Arab States, the Arab Peninsula, the Maghreb Permanent Consultative Committee, Arab Petroleum, the Suez Canal, the United Nations in the Middle East and the U.N.R.W.A. (United Nations Relief and Worlds Agency). The second part, A Survey of the 17 Arab Countries, covers statistics, geography, religion, history, government, economy, investments, budget, trade, oil industry, educational facilities, banking, media, transport and tourism, embassies, and bibliography. Recommended for general collections primarily for this introductory information rather than for the biographical sketches. KMH

GE 76
Who's Who in the East. ISSN 0083-9760. 1945. bi-a. Marquis Who's Who, 200 E Ohio St, Chicago, IL 60611. Examined: 16th ed., 1977/78. 897p. $52.50.
Aud: Cl, Pl
Indexed in: *Biographical Dictionaries Master Index; Marquis Who's Who Publications: Index to All Books.*

Contains 18,500 names of individuals who have distinguished themselves by continuous achievement in their careers or by election or appointment to public office and who reside in one of the following states or provinces: Connecticut, Delaware, District of Columbia, Maine, Maryland, Massachusetts, New Hampshire, New Jersey, New York, Pennsylvania, Rhode Island, Vermont, New Brunswick, Newfoundland, Nova Scotia, Prince Edward Island, Quebec, and the eastern half of Ontario. Alphabetical entries include name, occupation, vital statistics, parents, education, marital information, children, career, career-related civic and political activities, non-professional directorships, military record, decorations and awards, professional and association memberships, political and religious affiliation, lodges, clubs, publications, home and office addresses. Most biographees furnish their own data but the Marquis staff will compile information when needed. Two classes of persons are included: those of regional reference interest, and those of national interest but of local/regional importance. A special feature is the list of biographees residing in the East who are listed in **Who's Who in America.** KMH

GE 77
Who's Who in the Midwest. ISSN 0083-9787. 1949. bi-a. Marquis Who's Who, 200 E Ohio St, Chicago, IL 60611. Examined: 15th ed., 1976/77. 823p. $49.50.
Aud: Cl, Pl
Indexed in: *Biographical Dictionaries Master Index; Marquis Who's Who Publications: Index to All Books.*

Contains 18,500 names of individuals who have distinguished themselves by continuous achievement in their careers or by election or appointment to office and who reside in one of the following states or provinces: Illinois, Indiana, Iowa, Kansas, Michigan, Minnesota, Missouri, Nebraska, North Dakota, Ohio, South Dakota, Wisconsin, Manitoba, Western Ontario. Entries follow the same format as **Who's Who in the East.** KMH

GE 78
Who's Who in the South and Southwest. ISSN 0083-9809. 1947. bi-a. Marquis Who's Who, 200 E Ohio St, Chicago, IL 60611. Examined: 15th ed., 1976/77. 904p. $49.50.
Aud: Cl, Pl
Indexed in: *Biographical Dictionaries Master Index; Marquis Who's Who Publications: Index to All Books.*

Contains 20,000 names of individuals who have distinguished themselves by continuous achievement in their careers or by election or appointment to office and who reside in one of the following states or territories: Alabama, Arkansas, Washington, DC, Florida, Georgia, Kentucky, Louisiana, Mississippi, North Carolina, Oklahoma, South Carolina, Tennessee, Texas, Virginia, Puerto Rico, Virgin Islands. Entries follow the same format as **Who's Who in the East.** KMH

GE 79
Who's Who in the West. ISSN 0083-9817. 1949. bi-a. Marquis Who's Who, 200 E Ohio St, Chicago, IL 60611. Examined: 15th ed., 1976/77. 823p. $52.50.
Aud: Cl, Pl
Indexed in: *Biographical Dictionaries Master Index; Marquis Who's Who Publications: Index to All Books.*

Contains 18,500 names of distinguished individuals from one of the following states or provinces: Alaska, Arizona, California, Colorado, Hawaii, Idaho, Montana, Nevada, New Mexico, Oregon, Utah, Washington, Wyoming, Alberta, British Columbia, Saskatchewan. Criteria for inclusion and the format of the entries are the same as **Who's Who in the East.** KMH

GE 80
Who's Who in the World. ISSN 0083-9825. 1971/72. bi-a. Marquis Who's Who, 200 E Ohio St, Chicago, IL 60611. Examined: 3rd ed., 1976/77. 767p. $52.50.
Aud: Cl, Pl
Indexed in: *Biographical Dictionaries Master Index; Marquis Who's Who Publications: Index to All Books.*

Typical who's who type information supplied, in most instances, by the biographee. Includes personal data on birthplace, date of birth, parents, spouse, children, and education; a career summary; professional, community, business, or organization affiliations and activities; honors and achievements; and writings. Includes individuals of international significance in all fields of endeavor. JKM

GE 81
Who's Who of American Women. ISSN 0083-9841. 1958. bi-a. Marquis Who's Who, 200 E Ohio St, Chicago, IL 60611. Examined: 1977/78. 971p. $52.50.
Aud: Cl, Pl
Indexed in: *Biographical Dictionaries Master Index; Marquis Who's Who Publications: Index to All Books.*

Contains 21,000 sketches. All women listed in **Who's Who in America** are included. Some Canadians and other nationalities are included if they have an important association with the U.S. Alphabetical entries include name, occupation, vital statistics, parents, education, marital information, children, career, career-related civic and political activities, non-professional directorships, awards, professional and association memberships, political and religious affiliation, clubs, publications, and home and office address. The Marquis staff consults newspapers, magazines, journals, and books by and about women to glean choices for inclusion. Most biographees provide their own data, but Marquis staff has done so when women did not submit data forms. KMH/KAC

GE 82
World Who's Who of Women. 1973. a. illus. World Who's Who of Women, International Biographical Center, Cambridge CB2 3QP England. Examined: 3rd ed., 1976. Ernest Kay, ed. 935p. $50.
Aud: Cl, Pl
Indexed in: *Biographical Dictionaries Master Index.*

Of the 9000 entries, 7000 include a photograph. Each entry gives basic information about the woman's career, achievements, and personal data. KAC

BOOK AND NONPRINT MEDIA REVIEWS—ABSTRACTS AND INDEXES

GE 83
American Reference Books Annual. ISSN 0065-9959. 1970. a. index. Libraries Unlimited, Box 263, Littleton, CO 80160. Examined: v. 7, 1976; v. 8, 1977. Bohdan S. Wynar, ed. 821p. $30.
Aud: Cl, Pl, Pf

Provides reviews of reference books published in the United States during a single year. Categories include: ready reference tools, such as dictionaries, encyclopedias, indexes, directories, bibliographies, guides, concordances, atlases, and gazetteers; serial reference tools (the first review is historical, subsequent reviews at three to five year intervals point out changes in scope and policy); new editions of reference books; foreign titles that have an exclusive distributor in the United States; government publications on a selective basis; and reprints on a selective basis. Each entry includes bibliographic information and a signed review of an average 310 words. Arrangement is by subject with special categories, such as Ethnic Studies or Environmental Sciences and Energy Resources, to reflect topics of current interest. The staff of contributing editors and reviewers are generally specialists in the area in which they evaluate materials. Each edition of **ARBA** has expanded in scope and length of review. KMH

GE 84
Book Review Digest. ISSN 0006-7326. 1905. a. w/m. suppls. index. H. W. Wilson, 950 University Ave, Bronx, NY 10452. Examined: 1976. Josephine Samudio, ed. 1488p. service basis.
Aud: Hs, Jc, Cl, Pl

Subtitle: "An index to reviews of current books." Index to reviews of fiction and non-fiction appearing in 71 selected periodicals. A work of fiction must have four or more reviews to be included; non-fiction must have two or more reviews. Fiction is arranged alphabetically by author; entries include title, pagination, price, publishing information, review excerpts, and citations. Non-fiction is classified according to the *Abridged Dewey Decimal Classification* and subject headings are based on the *Sears List*. A subject and title index are included. In 1976 H. W. Wilson issued *Book Review Digest Author/Title Index* for 1905-1974. From 1921 through 1961, cumulative subject and title indexes appeared every five years in the annual volume; since 1962 the five year cumulative index has appeared as a separate volume. KMH

GE 85
Book Review Index. 1965. a. w/bi-m. suppls. Gale Research Co., Book Tower, Detroit, MI 48226. Examined: 1976. Gary Tarbert, ed. 665p. $68 w/binder.
Aud: Hs, Cl, Pl

Provides citations to reviews in about 325 periodicals of general fiction; of non-fiction works primarily in the humanities, social sciences, librarianship, and bibliography; and of young adult and juvenile works. Inclusion of a citation does not depend upon the number of times the work was reviewed. Symbols indicate children's books. With the 1976 volume, reviews of periodicals are indexed. The arrangement is by author of the work reviewed. Publication of the **Book Review Index** was suspended from 1969 to 1971; a retrospective index covering these years was published in 1974/75. Since 1973 the bi-monthly supplements cumulate in alternate issues. KMH/JKM

GE 86
Children's Book Review Index. ISSN 0147-5681. 1975. a. index. Gale Research Co., Book Tower, Detroit, MI 48226. Examined: 1975, 254p.; 1976. Gary C. Tarbert, ed. $18. (1977. 356p.)
Aud: Pl, Pf

Arranged by author of the title reviewed, each entry includes author, title, and review source with date of issue and page number. Covers literature for children from preschool through age ten. Entries are based upon the indexing of about 325 periodicals and newspapers for Gale's **Book Review Index**; specific children's literature reviewing media covered include *Children Today, Horn Book, School Media Quarterly,* and *Junior Bookshelf*. Since this publication duplicates the entries in **Book Review Index**, most libraries would not need both; however, the children's index would be very useful to school and children's librarians and to parents who do not have ready access to the more inclusive title. JKM

GE 87
Current Book Review Citations. ISSN 0360-1250. 1976. a. w/m. suppls. index. H. W. Wilson, 950 University Ave, Bronx, NY 10452. Examined: 1976, 941p.; 1977 suppls. Paula de Vaux, ed. $75/yr.
Aud: Hs, Jc, Cl, Pl

Indexes book reviews published in more than 1200 book reviewing and subject periodicals. Covers fiction, non-fiction (including science and law books), and children's and young adult titles. Reviews of foreign language books and new editions are included. Cumulates reviews in all other Wilson indexes, as well as covering reviews not listed in any other index. Arranged in two parts: part one cites book reviews under main entry of the work reviewed and provides full citations to reviews; part two is a title index to the first part. The most comprehensive of the book review indexes. KMH

GE 88
Guide to Reviews of Books from and about Hispanic America; Guía a las Reseñas de Libros de y sobre Hispanoamérica. 1972. a. bibl. index. Blaine Ethridge—Books, 13977 Penrod St, Detroit, MI 48223. Examined: 1974. Antonio Matos, ed. 1290p. $45.
Aud: Sa

Cites reviews of nearly 3000 books dealing with Latin America, culled from approximately 400 periodicals. Each citation includes a 25-100 word summary in either English or Spanish. Arrangement is alphabetical by author. Entries for individual works indicate author, title, place of publication, publisher, imprint date, and pagination. A preface and introduction appear in both English and Spanish. Volumes conclude with a title index. Publications indexed are concerned with subjects in the social sciences and humanities. SB

GE 89
Library Journal Book Review. ISSN 0075-9082. 1968. a. index. R. R. Bowker Co., 1180 Ave of the Americas, New York, NY 10036. Dist: R. R. Bowker, Box 1807, Ann Arbor, MI 48106. Examined: 1976; 1977. Janet Fletcher, ed. 828p. $24.95.
Aud: Cl, Pl, Pf

Cumulates, in a classified arrangement, the signed reviews from the preceding year's *Library Journal*. *LJ* reviews provide full bibliographic information and are written by librarians or subject specialists. The cumulation includes an author and title index. Each volume covers approximately 6000 reviews. EF/JKM

GE 90
Media Review Digest. ISSN 0091-5858. (Continues: Multi-Media Reviews Index.) 1970. a. w/semi-a. suppls. index. Pierian Press, Box 1808, Ann Arbor, MI 48106. Examined: v. 7, 1977. C. Edward Wall, ed. 542p. $79.50.
Aud: Cl, Pl, Pf

Subtitle: "The only complete guide to reviews of non-book media." The volume begins with an introduction explaining the scope, arrangement, purpose, and methodology. It contains 40,000 citations and cross references to reviews and descriptions of films and filmstrips, educational and spoken-word records and tapes, slides, transparencies, illustrations, globes, charts, media kits, games, and other miscellaneous media forms. Citations are arranged under the following headings: film and videotape; filmstrip; record and tape; miscellaneous media; film awards and prizes; and mediagraphics. Includes a classified subject index, an alphabetical subject index, and a list of producers and distributors with addresses. Listings are arranged by title within each section. Reviews list name of journal, volume number, date, page, and a plus or minus indicating evaluation by reviewer of film or media. A short annotation is also included where available. Subject sections list films alphabetically and indicate section in which annotation appears. MBP/KMH/BSM

GE 91
Reference and Subscription Books Reviews. ISSN 0080-0430. 1968/70. a. index. American Library Association, 50 E Huron St, Chicago, IL 60611. Examined: 1975/76. ALA Reference and Subscription Books Review Committee, ed. 162p. $10.
Aud: Cl, Pl, Pf

Cumulates the in-depth reviews originally written by librarians for publication in *The Booklist*. The reviewers' aim is to inform potential purchasers of the quality of major reference works which are of general interest and of subscription books. Reviews cover general characteristics of the work, history, scope, purpose, fullness of treatment, style, accuracy, authority of the material, impartial or biased point of view, currency, format, strengths or weaknesses, and usefulness to intended audience. Entries are arranged alphabetically by title. Citations include title, author or editor, pages or number of volumes, place and date of publication, publisher, illustrations, price, and type of bindings available. EF/JKM

GE 92
Reference Sources. 1977. a. index. Pierian Press, 5000 Washtenaw Ave, Ann Arbor, MI 48104. Examined: 1977. Linda Mark, ed. 430p. price varies (see annotation).
Aud: Pf

Arranged by Library of Congress main entry with appropriate cross references. Each entry includes full bibliographic information; price; ISBN and LC card number; an annotation which covers illustration, index, and/or bibliography information; LC subject headings; Dewey Decimal number; the general subject heading under which the title is indexed; full citations to reviews; and, in some instances, quotations from reviews. Includes a broad subject index, an index by LC subject headings, and an index by Dewey Decimal number. The volume is priced on a sliding scale: the cost to libraries with budgets over $25,000 and to libraries in high schools with enrollments over 1000 is $35 a year or $25 if they also subscribe to Pierian's *Reference Services Review*; the cost to all other libraries is $25 or $19.95 if they also subscribe to *Reference Services Review*. JKM

DIRECTORIES

GE 93
Annual International Congress Calendar. 1961. bi-a. index. Union of International Associations, c/o Robert Fenaux, One Rue aux Laines, 1000, Brussels, Belgium. Dist: International Publications Service, 114 E 32 St, New York, NY 10016. Examined: 17th ed., 1977. 332p. $23. (18th ed., 1978. 332p.)
Aud: Sa

A chronological listing of international congresses, conferences, meetings, and symposia sponsored or organized by international or important national bodies in the year covered by the volume and subsequent years. Entries include date, place, address of organizing body, theme, estimated number of participants, number of countries represented, concurrent exhibitions, and reference to the **Yearbook of International Organizations.** Indexes include a geographical index by continent, country, and city; analytical subject index; and international organization index. A last minute listing is included. Updates appear in the journal, *International Associations*, which is also published by the Union of International Associations. KMH

GE 94
Annual Register of Grant Support. ISSN 0066-4049. (Continues: Grant Data Quarterly.) 1967. a. index. Marquis Academic Media, 200 E Ohio St, Chicago, IL 60611. Examined: 11th ed., 1977/78. Deanna Perkis Sclar, ed. approx. 700p. $52.50.
Aud: Jc, Cl, Pl, Pf

A well organized, well indexed survey of current grants available from many sources: business, labor unions, professional organizations, government, and foundations. Arranged by broad subjects such as social sciences, humanities, health and medical sciences, area studies, and environment. For each entry, the purpose of the organization, eligibility requirements, financial data, and duration of grant support are given. Indexes are by subject, organization or program, geographical region, and personnel (trustees, directors, committee members). BSM

GE 95
Awards, Honors, and Prizes. 1969. irreg. index. Gale Research Co., Book Tower, Detroit, MI 48226. Examined: 3rd ed., 1975. Paul Wasserman, ed. v.1, 564p., $38; v.2, 443p., $48.
Aud: Cl, Pl

Subtitle: "An international directory of awards and their donors." Lists 4242 awards and prizes in all fields of activity arranged under the name of the sponsoring body. Entries include name and address, purpose, form and frequency of award, date established, and name and address of the person to contact for application. The subject index provides access to awards by activity. An alphabetical index to awards by name is provided. Volume one covers U.S. and Canadian awards and prizes; volume two lists international and foreign awards and prizes and includes a geographic index. KMH

GE 96
Current British Directories. ISSN 0070-1858. 1953. irreg. index. C. B. D. Research, 154 High St, Beckenham, Kent BR3 1EA England. Examined: 1972/73, 358p.; 1976/77. I. G. Anderson, ed. $27.50.
Aud: Sa

A bibliography of 2750 directories published in Great Britain, the British Commonwealth, and South Africa designed to serve the needs of market researchers, direct mail specialists, librarians, information officers, and book suppliers. The bibliography is divided into three major parts. The first part lists local directories, and is intended to help the user find a place, find a person or organization within a known place, or locate businesses within a particular locality; a place index is included for this section. The second part covers specialized directories of industries, trades, and professions; who's whos; yearbooks; special periodical issues; and general trade directories arranged in alphabetical order by title. The third section includes directories of the British Commonwealth, South Africa, and Pakistan. Entries provide serial numbers; title; publisher's name, address, and telephone; date of first edition; frequency of publication; date; price, pagination; and description of contents. KMH

GE 97
Directory of Associations in Canada; Repertoir des Associations du Canada. 1974. a. University of Toronto Press, Toronto, Ontario, M5S 1A6 Canada. Examined: 1974; 1975. Brian Land, ed. 550p. $45.
Aud: Cl, Pl

Directory of non-governmental, non-profit organizations composed of institutional members which operate with or without a federal or provincial charter, and which were formed for some particular purpose or to advance a common cause, especially of a public nature. Major categories include international associations with branches in Canada; foreign associations with branches in Canada; and, national, interprovincial, provincial, regional, metropolitan, or local associations. Organized in three sections: a guide to the subject index with cross-references; a subject index; and an alphabetical list of associations. Full information is given in the third section including name, address, director, and branches of the association. In English and French. KMH

GE 98
Directory of British Associations and Associations in Ireland. ISSN 0070-5152. 1965. irreg. index. C. B. D. Research, 154 High St, Beckenham, Kent BR3 1EA, England. Dist: Gale Research Co., Book Tower, Detroit, MI 48226. Examined: 5th ed., 1977. G. P. Henderson and S. P. A. Henderson, eds. 457p. $60.
Aud: Cl, Pl, Sa

Lists interests, activities, and publications of trade associations, scientific and technical societies, professional institutes, learned societies, research organizations, chambers of trade and commerce, agricultural societies, trade unions, and cultural, sports, and welfare organizations. Arrangement is alphabetical by name of association. Entries include name, date of formation, address, telephone and telex numbers, officials, branches, subgroups, type of organization, areas of interest, activities, membership data, publications, and previous names. An abbreviation index and subject index are included. British associations and associations in Ireland are not listed in Gale's **Directory of European Associations.** KMH

GE 99
Directory of European Associations. ISSN 0070-5500. 1971. irreg. index. Gale Research Co., Book Tower, Detroit, MI 48226. Examined: 2nd ed., 1976. I. G. Anderson, ed. 2v. v. 1, 557p., $65; v. 2, 315p., $45.
Aud: Cl, Pl, Sa

The first volume, "National Industrial, Trade, and Professional Associations," includes data on over 9000 trade, industrial, and professional associations in all fields of activity in all countries of Europe, except Great Britain and Ireland which are covered in Gale's **Directory of British Associations and Associations in Ireland**. It is arranged by subject, and entries include organization name, address, phone number, membership data, activities, publications, and changes in name. Detailed subject, name, and abbreviation indexes are included. Explanatory information is in English, French, and German. Volume two, "National Learned, Scientific and Technical Societies," was first issued in 1975 and follows the same format.

A third volume, which will cover the arts, sports, and social welfare, is projected. KMH

GE 100
Directory of Organizations and Individuals Professionally Engaged in Government Research and Related Activities. 1935. a. index. Governmental Research Association, Box 387, Ocean Gate, NJ 08740. Examined: 1975/76. 66p. $15.
Aud: Pl, Sa

This slim pamphlet includes "established agencies concerned with the improvement of the organization and administration of government and the promotion of economy and efficiency in the performance of public services." Organizations are listed geographically, and each entry includes date of founding, address, telephone number, name of executive officer, and names of the professional research personnel of member agencies. About half of the individuals listed are members of the Governmental Research Association. There are alphabetical indexes of organizations and individuals. KR/JKM

GE 101
Directory of Research Grants. 1975. a. bibl. index. Oryx Press, 3930 E Camelback Rd, Phoenix, AZ 85018. Examined: 1977/78. Betty L. Wilson, ed. 235p. $34.75.
Aud: Cl, Pl, Sa

Provides up-to-date information on more than 1500 grants, contracts, and fellowships for research, training, and innovative efforts which are available from federal and state governments, private foundations, associations, and corporations. Some foreign entries are included, but the emphasis is on the U.S. Entries are organized by academic discipline and include brief information on the purpose, amount, and the name, address, and telephone number of the sponsor. Each entry's code number corresponds to its number in the Grant Information System. Introductory material includes an article, "The Many Faces of a Grantsperson," and information on preparing proposals. An index of grant names and of sponsoring organizations by type is provided. BSM

GE 102
Encyclopedia of Associations. ISSN 0071-0202. 1956. irreg. index. Gale Research Co., Book Tower, Detroit, MI 48226. Examined: 11th ed., 1977. Margaret Fisk and Mary W. Pair, eds. 3v. v.1, 1456p., $70; v.2, 729p., $50; v.3, $60.
Aud: Cl, Pl

Issued in three parts, the **Encyclopedia of Associations** is the only comprehensive source of detailed information concerning nonprofit American membership organizations of national scope. Also included are for-profit and non-membership groups if their names or activities suggest they are voluntary nonprofit organizations; foreign groups of interest to Americans; international groups if they have a large American membership; local or regional groups if their orientation is outside their immediate vicinity; and citizen action groups and programs. Volume one, "National Organizations of the United States," contains the basic entry for each organization in classified subject order. Each entry includes: name, keyword, arrangement, acronym, address, telephone number, name and title of chief official, founding date, membership, staff, state and local groups, description, mergers and name changes, and conventions. An alphabetical and keyword index provides access by specific subject and by organization name. Volume two, "Geographic-Executive Index," is essentially a reclassification of the information in volume one to provide greater access. It is arranged in two sections, a geographic index and an executive index, with reference back to volume one. Volume three is an inter-edition periodical supplement to volumes one and two which lists new associations and projects. Each supplement contains an index to itself and previous supplements. KMH

GE 103
Foundation Directory. ISSN 0071-8092. (Continues: American Foundations and Their Fields.) 1960. irreg. index. illus. Foundation Center, 888 Seventh Ave, New York, NY 10019. Dist: Columbia University Press, 136 S Broadway, Irvington-on-Hudson, NY 10533. Examined: 6th ed., 1977. Marianna O. Lewis, ed. 661p. $30.
Aud: Cl, Pl
Indexed in: *ERIC*.

After an introductory section covering definitions, legal form, types of foundations, and origin of funding, the descriptive directory lists foundations alphabetically by state and foundation. Entries provide full name, address, date of incorporation, donors' purpose and activities, financial data, officers, IRS employer identification number, and name of the person with whom one should correspond. An index to foundations by city and state; an index to donors, trustees, and administrators; an index to foundations; and an index to fields of interest are included. Appendixes list types of foundations and community foundations. MBP

GE 104
Foundation Grants Index. 1970/71. a. index. The Foundation Center, 888 Seventh Ave, New York, NY 10019. Dist: Columbia University Press, 136 S Broadway, Irvington, NY 10533. Examined: 1976. Lee Noe, ed. 361p. $15. (1977. 443p.)
Aud: Cl, Pl

Subtitle: "A cumulative listing of foundation grants." Arranged alphabetically by state and, within states, by name of the granting agency. Under the name of the foundation, the recipients of grants are listed alphabetically. Grant information provided includes the date the grant was made, the location of the recipient, the amount of the grant, a description of the grant, and a grant identification number. Includes a keyword index, a broad subject index, and an index of recipients; the indexes refer the user to grant numbers. Includes grants of $5000 or more made to nonprofit organizations. The Foundation Center notes in the introduction that although every attempt is made to be inclusive, not all foundations report their grants. Updated between editions by the bi-monthly *Foundation News*. JKM

GE 105
Grants Register. ISSN 0072-5471. 1969. bi-a. bibl. index. St. Martin's Press, 175 Fifth Ave, New York, NY 10010. Examined: 5th ed., 1977/79. Roland Turner, ed. 764p. $25.
Aud: Jc, Cl, Pl

Subtitle: "Post-graduate awards, the English-speaking world." Lists scholarships, fellowships, awards, prizes, and grants offered by government agencies and private organizations in the U.S., the United Kingdom, and Commonwealth countries. Individual colleges and universities are not covered. A detailed subject index leads to entries arranged in eleven subject areas such as professions and occupations, and creative and applied arts. Entries describe grants and provide information on eligibility requirements, application deadlines, amount of grant, and address for correspondence. An index of sponsoring agencies is included. BSM

GE 106
Guide to American Directories. ISSN 0533-5248. 1954. irreg. index. B. Klein Publications, 11 3rd St, Rye, NY 10580. Examined: 9th ed., 1975. Bernard Klein, ed. 496p. $45.
Aud: Cl, Pl

Guide to over 5200 directories of the United States covering industrial, professional, and mercantile categories. Designed to aid business and industry in locating new markets, and to aid organizations, associations, and advertisers in finding current reliable sources of information. Organization is alphabetical by subject (accounting, confectionary, florists, recreation), then by the directory title. Entries include a description of the directory and the address of the distributor or issuing agency. Sections on education and manufacturers are subdivided by state. There is a title index to directories, and rather than providing cross references between subject sections, entries that are appropriate for inclusion in more than one subject category are repeated. KMH

GE 107
International Bibliography of Directories; Internationale Bibliographie der Fachadressbuecher. ISSN 0074-9672. 1962. irreg. index. Verlag Dokumentation, Box 148 Jaiserstr 13, 8023, Pullach bei München, West Germany, Dist: R. R. Bowker, Box 1807, Ann Arbor, MI 48106. Examined: 5th ed., 1973. Michael Zils, ed. 535p. $39.95.
Aud: Sa

Over 6000 directories organized into 15 subject groups and 80 subgroups. Entries include directory name and address. A geographical index provides a regionally organized key to directories listed in the main part. A subject index includes terms which vary from the organization of subject groups. In German and English. KMH

GE 108
Jewish Organizations; A Worldwide Directory. 1971. quadrennial. The American Jewish Committee, Institute of Human Relations, 165 E 56th St, New York, NY 10022. Examined: 2nd ed., 1975. Iva Cohen, ed. 98p. $3.
Aud: Pl

An alphabetical list of Jewish communal service organizations around the world. Organizations are listed by country, with addresses and names of officers when available. A brief description is provided for some organizations. Entries for larger countries, such as France, United States, England, and Canada, are grouped under categories. Telephone numbers are not provided. LL

GE 109
Research Centers Directory. ISSN 0080-1518. 1960. irreg. index. Gale Research Co., Book Tower, Detroit, MI 48226. Examined: 5th ed., 1975. Archie M. Palmer, ed. 1040p. $85.
Aud: Jc, Cl, Pl, Sa

Subtitle: "A guide to university-related and other non-profit research organizations." There are nearly 7000 entries in this publication covering subject area and multidisciplinary research centers. Subject areas covered include agriculture; home economics and nutrition; astronomy; business, economics, and transportation; conservation; education; engineering and technology; government and public affairs; labor and industrial relations; law; life sciences; mathematics; physical and earth sciences; regional and area studies; social sciences; humanities; and religion. Universities and other nonprofit research organizations are listed alphabetically. Information provided includes address, telephone number, director, date of founding, staffing, source of support, principal fields of research, library facilities, and publications. Indexes are by institution, by center, and by subject. The publication is updated by Gale's *New Research Centers* which is issued periodically. BSM/JKM

GE 110

Sources of Serials. ISSN 0000-0523. 1977. freq. not determined. R. R. Bowker, 1180 Ave of the Americas, New York, NY 10036. Dist: R. R. Bowker, Box 1807, Ann Arbor, MI 48106. Examined: 1st ed., 1977. 1547p. $52.50.
Aud: Cl, Pl, Sa

Subtitle: "An international publisher and corporate author directory." An international name and title authority file for all serial publishers included in **Ulrich's International Periodicals Directory, Irregular Serials and Annuals,** and *Ulrich's Quarterly,* all published by R. R. Bowker. Arranged by country, then by publisher and/or corporate author, this guide covers approximately 63,000 publishers and corporate authors in 181 countries. Under each publisher, the titles published or sponsored are listed, and current address information is provided. JKM

GE 111

Women's Organizations and Leaders Directory. ISSN 0092-668X. 1973. bi-a. index. Today Publications and News Service, National Press Bldg, Washington, DC 20045. Examined: 1973; 1975/76. Myra E. Barrer, ed. various paging. $54.
Aud: Jc, Cl, Pl

With the 1975/76 edition, the scope of the **Directory** became international. It is a comprehensive directory and register of living women and organizations concerned about the provision of equal rights and equal opportunities for women. Guide to 17,000 organizations, their goals, leaders, addresses, phone numbers, and publications, arranged in alphabetical order with national, regional, state, local, and committee components. There are five indexes: an alphabetical index of individuals and organizations; a geographical index; indexes of periodical publications issued by each organization in periodical and organization order; and a subject index. A list of subject headings is provided. KAC/KMH

GE 112

Yearbook of International Organizations; Annuaire des Organizations Internationales. ISSN 0884-3814. 1948. bi-a. index. Union of International Associations, One Rue aux Laines, 1000 Brussels, Belgium. Dist: International Publications Service, 114 E 32nd St, New York, NY 10016. Examined: 16th ed., 1977. 806p. $55.
Aud: Cl, Pl, Sa

The Union of International Associations (UIA), founded in 1907, aims to promote the development of international cooperation with special emphasis on international relations of a non-governmental character; to assemble information on international organizations, their meetings, their publications, and activities; to make this information available to interested parties; and to effect research, facilitate mutual relations, and promote study. The UIA's principal mode of activity is to process information and make it widely available through reference books. The **Yearbook** gives information on over 6000 international governmental and non-governmental organizations. Because of the increase in the number of institutions calling themselves "international," the 1977 edition takes a new approach which allows the reader to confront the task of defining internationality. It is divided into two sections. The first lists those organizations genuinely international in character which cover operations in at least three countries, give members the right to elect a governing body and officers, have permanent headquarters and provision for continuity of operation, rotate officers among member countries, derive substantial funds from three or more countries, lead an independent life apart from a parent organization, and give evidence of current activity. Educational, social, and secret organizations are excluded. The second section includes organizations which call themselves international, but which do not qualify under the above criteria. Descriptions of organizations in the first section include organization number, name, main and secondary addresses, date founded, aims, structure, languages, finances, consultative status, NGO relations, activities, conferences, publications, members, classification, and date the information was received. Descriptions in section two include organization number, "other" information, and inactive organizations. Seven indexes provide access to the directory: subject, English name, French name, geographical by headquarters location, initials, subject keywords in English, and subject keywords in French. Special features are supplements on the United Nations, historical notes on the legal position of international associations, and a regional/universal organization name index. Supplemented by the journal *International Associations* which is also published by the Union of International Associations. KMH/SJV

PERIODICAL AND ESSAY ABSTRACTS AND INDEXES

GE 113
Abridged Readers' Guide to Periodical Literature. ISSN 0001-334X. 1935. a. w/9 m. suppls. H. W. Wilson, 950 University Ave, Bronx, NY 10452. Examined: 1976/77. 468p. $25.
Aud: Jh, Hs, Pl

A cumulative author and subject index to periodicals of general interest. The titles are selected by the American Library Association's Committee on Wilson Indexes to reflect the needs of, and provide balanced subject coverage to schools and small to medium size public libraries. With the 1977/78 volume, an index to book reviews will be included as it is in other Wilson indexes. The 1976/77 volume indexed 44 periodicals. Effective with the 1978/79 volume, 56 periodicals will be indexed; 27 of these are new titles selected for indexing, 15 titles will be dropped. Arrangement is the same as that of the **Readers' Guide** from which the indexing is drawn. If a smaller library can afford the difference in price, the unabridged **Guide,** with its coverage of 173 periodicals, is a better investment. JKM

GE 114
Access: The Supplementary Index to Periodicals. ISSN 0095-5698. 1976. a. w/2 suppls. index. Gaylord Bros., Box 4901, Syracuse, NY 13221. Examined: 1976, 720p.; 1977. John Gordon Burke, Kathy Hill, and Ned Kehde, eds. $75.
Aud: Hs, Cl, Pl

Designed to complement existing periodical indexes and to provide access to prominent library-owned periodicals not currently indexed. It will index some of the periodical titles dropped by the **Reader's Guide to Periodical Literature,** and drop any titles which are voted into the **Guide.** The 158 titles covered include: *American Girl, Boy's Life, Camera 35, Country Music, Dance News, Family Circle, Mother Jones, Sepia, Sky and Telescope, Vogue,* and *WomenSports.* Coverage of regional publications (e.g., *Alaska, Atlanta, Miami Magazine,* etc.) is more thorough than in other supplementary periodical indexes. Arrangement is in two parts. The author index provides title of article, periodical, date, page, number of pages required to photocopy the article (a boon for Interlibrary Loan), and illustrations. The second part is a subject index. The two supplements are four-month cumulations appearing in May and December; the annual issue is available in March. KMH

GE 115
Access Index to Little Magazines. ISSN 0363-065X. 1976. a. Gaylord Bros, Box 4901, Syracuse, NY 13221. Examined: 1976. John Gordon Burke, Len Fulton, and Ned Kehde, eds. 302p. $50. (1977. $50.)
Aud: Cl, Pl

An author, title, and subject index to approximately 75 literary magazines not indexed elsewhere. Gaylord also makes available on an annual basis through their *Access Index to Little Magazines Microform Program* a microfilmed edition of all of the magazines indexed ($300/year; $325/year for both the index and the microfilm). The package is a good buy, if affordable, since so many of the magazines included are only elusively acquired. JKM

GE 116
Canadian Essay and Literature Index. ISSN 0316-0696. 1973. a. University of Toronto Press, Toronto, Ontario M5S 1A6, Canada. Examined: 1974, 489p.; 1975. Andrew D. Armitage and Nancy Tudor, eds. $35.
Aud: Cl, Pl

An author, title, and subject index to essays, book reviews, poems, plays, and short stories which have appeared in 80 anthologies and collections and 75 magazines published in Canada. Periodicals indexed in the **Canadian Periodical Index** are not included. The list of periodicals indexed includes holding libraries. The 1974 volume was published in 1976; the 1975 in 1977. KMH

GE 117
Canadian Periodical Index; Index de Periodiques Canadiens. ISSN 0008-4719. (Continues: Canadian Index to Periodicals and Documentary Films; Index de Periodiques et Films Documentaire Canadiens.) 1928.

a. w/m. suppls. Canadian Library Association, 151 Sparks St, Ottawa K1P 5E3 Canada. Examined: 1976; 1977 suppls. Sylvia Morrison, ed. price on request.
Aud: Cl, Pl

An author and subject index to 103 Canadian periodicals (e.g., *Alberta Historical Review, Canadian Historical Review, Newfoundland Quarterly,* and *Tawow*). Entries include author and title of the article indexed, date and name of the periodical in which it appeared, and the number of pages. The listing of films was dropped in 1964 since this duplicated the listing done by the National Library in *Canadiana*. Text in English and French. KMH

GE 118
Essay and General Literature Index. ISSN 0014-083X. 1934. quinquennial w/a. and semi-a. suppls. H. W. Wilson, 950 University Ave, Bronx, NY 10452. Examined: 1970/74, 1781p.; 1977 suppl. Norma Freedman, ed. 385p. $35/yr.
Aud: Hs, Jc, Cl, Pl

An author and subject index to collections of essays and other composite works. Many areas of knowledge are covered, but the humanities and social sciences are stressed. Literary criticism is particularly emphasized. Only twentieth century publications are included. Each volume or supplement contains a complete list of the collections indexed in the volume with full bibliographic information. The first volume covers the period 1930/33; seven year cumulations have appeared between 1934 and 1954. Since 1955, quinquennial cumulations have been issued, the latest being 1970/74. KMH/JKM

GE 119
Index to U.S. Government Periodicals. 1975. a. w/q. suppls. Infordata International, 175 E Delaware Place, Suite 4602, Chicago, IL 60611. Examined: 1975; 1976. 815p. $200.
Aud: Cl, Pl

Subtitle: "A computer-generated guide to 156 selected titles by author and subject." Indexes publications on a wide variety of topics. For example, included in the 1976 edition for the first time are: *Agricultural Finance Review, Agricultural Outlook, Commitment, Education Around the World, Schizophrenia Bulletin,* and *Weekly Weather and Crop Bulletin*. Each article is entered under all logical subject headings rather than using *see also*'s to link topics. The list of titles indexed includes names of editors, addresses, and frequency. Provides much needed access to the wide range of subject matter published in U.S. Government periodicals. JKM

GE 120
New York Times Index; A Book of Record. 1913. a. w/semi-m. suppls. illus. New York Times Co., 229 W 43rd St, New York, NY 10036. Examined: 1976. 1901p. $125; $225 w/semi-m. suppls.; $125 suppls. only.
Aud: Cl, Pl

An author, subject, and title index to the contents of the late city edition of the *New York Times*. Also presents a condensed, classified history of the world consisting of news and editorial matter entered under appropriate subject headings. Corrections to earlier volumes appear at the end of each volume. Continuous publication of the **Index** began in 1913; indexes for 1851-1912, compiled from the *Times'* own files or indexed for the first time, are available from R. R. Bowker. KMH

GE 121
Readers' Guide to Periodical Literature. ISSN 0034-0464. 1900. a. w/semi-m. and q. suppls. H. W. Wilson, 950 University Ave, Bronx, NY 10452. Examined: 1976/77. Zada Limerick, ed. 1290p. $55.
Aud: Jh, Hs, Jc, Cl, Pl

The basic author and subject index to periodicals of general interest covering such titles as *American Home, Business Week, Commentary, Ebony, McCalls, Ms., Oceans, Saturday Review, Time,* and *Writer*. The 1976/77 volume indexed 159 periodicals. Effective with the 1978/79 volume, 173 periodicals will be indexed; 60 of these are new titles selected for indexing, 43 titles will be dropped. Selection of periodicals is by subscriber vote with the advice of the Committee on Wilson Indexes of the American Library Association's Reference and Adult Services Division. Arrangement is by author and subject, and entries include title, author, periodical name, date, and pages. Special features include addresses of the periodicals, whether or not they are available for the blind and physically handicapped, and a book review section. The **Readers' Guide** began in 1900 and was cumulated at intervals from two to five years until 1965 when annual cumulations began. Supplements are issued semi-monthly and cumulated quarterly. In 1944 the H. W. Wilson Co. issued *Nineteenth Century Readers' Guide* using the format of the **Readers' Guide** to cover materials from 1890-1899. In 1935 the **Abridged Readers' Guide** began publication. KMH

STATISTICAL WORKS

GE 122
African Statistical Yearbook; Annuaire Statistique pour l'Afrique. 1970. a. Economic Commission for Africa, Box 3001, Addis Ababa, Ethiopia. Examined: 1974; 1976. 4v.
Aud: Sa

Published in four separate parts (North Africa, West Africa, East Africa, and Central Africa), the **Yearbook** presents statistical data for 44 African countries on population, employment, agriculture, industry, transport, trade, prices, and social statistics. Organization within parts is alphabetical by name of country. Sponsored by the United Nations. KMH

GE 123
American Statistics Index. Supplement. ISSN 0091-1658. a. w/m. suppls. index. Congressional Information Service, 7101 Wisconsin Ave, Suite 900, Washington, DC 20014. Examined: 1976. James B. Allen, ed. 2v. 2036p. $790.
Aud: Sa

Subtitle: "A comprehensive master guide and index to the statistical publications of the U.S. Government." It is published in two volumes. In the first volume, individual publications, periodical publications, and publications in series are abstracted. Abstracts, based on examinations of the original publication, provide full bibliographic data, description of the publication, and tables. The second part is an index to the abstract volume. Indexes are by subject and name; categories; standard classification system; and title and agency report numbers. The comprehensive services provided with a subscription to the **American Statistics Index (ASI)** are fully described in the abstract volume. These include information on acquiring documents from the government and the *ASI* microfiche program wherein *ASI* will provide copies of documents on request. **ASI** began publication with a retrospective edition in 1973 listing federal government statistical publications in part, as of January 1, 1974, as well as significant publications issued since the early 1960s. The annual volume is supplemented monthly. KMH/MBP

GE 124
Annual Abstract of Statistics. 1840. a. index. Her Majesty's Stationery Office, Box 569, London SE1 9NH, England. Examined: 1974; 1976. 487p. £7.50.
Aud: Cl, Pl

Compiled by the Central Statistical Service, this guide provides statistical data for the United Kingdom on area, population, social conditions, education, labor, production, transport and communications, distributive trades, external trade, income, finances, and prices. An index of sources gives the titles of official publications. A subject index provides access to precise topics. KMH

GE 125
Demographic Yearbook; Annuaire Demographique. ISSN 0082-8041. 1948. a. index. United Nations Statistical Office, New York, NY 10017. Dist: International Publications Service, 114 E 32 St, New York, NY 10016. Examined: 27th ed., 1975; 28th ed., 1976. 984p. $45; $34 pap.
Aud: Cl, Pl

A comprehensive collection of international demographic statistics compiled through the cooperation of national statistical services for more than 220 areas throughout the world. Ten-year tables include: world summary, population, infant and maternal mortality, general mortality, marriage, and divorce. Each edition focuses on a particular topic (topics of past editions are listed in the preface), such as natality, mortality, population distribution, ethnic characteristics of the population, or population trends. The 1975 **Yearbook** focused on natality, providing thirty tables. Technical notes explain the criteria for each section in great detail. A subject-matter index covers the content of all published editions. Text is in English and French. KMH/MBP

GE 126
Federal Statistical Directory. (Continues: Directory of Federal Statistical Agencies.) 1935. irreg. index. U.S. Bureau of the Budget, Statistical Policy Division, Washington, DC. Dist: Superintendent of Documents, U.S. Government Printing Office, Washington, DC 20402. Examined: 25th ed., 1976. 270p. $2.50.
Aud: Sa

Prepared by the Statistical Policy Division of the Office of Management and Budget, the directory is designed to facilitate communication among the various U.S. federal offices working on statistical programs. It is a companion volume to **Statistical Services of the United States Government.** Lists, by organizational units within each agency, the names, office addresses, and telephone numbers of key personnel engaged in statistical programs and related activities of the executive branch of the federal government. Includes a building location directory and name index. KMH

GE 127

Guide to Official Statistics. 1976. a. bibl. index. Her Majesty's Stationery Office, Box 569, London SE1 9NH England. Examined: 1976. 391p. £7.50.
Aud: Sa

The 1976 volume is the first post-war edition compiled in response to a recommendation from the Estimates Committee of the House of Commons. Designed to give users a broad indication of whether needed statistics have been compiled and, if so, where they are published. Covers all official and some non-official sources of statistics for the United Kingdom and the Isle of Man. Includes broad content descriptions of all publications containing a significant amount of statistical information. Organization is by broad subjects: general, area, climate, environment, populations, social statistics, agriculture, production, transport, distribution, public services, prices, economy, finance, business, and overseas. Each is subdivided into subtopics. Entries include titles and detailed annotations for each source. An alphabetical key word index provides greater subject access than the classified main list. Details of publisher, price, date, etc. for sources cited in the main section are listed in a separate bibliography with ordering information. KMH

GE 128

Pocket Data Book, U.S.A. ISSN 0079-2403. 1967. bi-a. index. illus. U.S. Bureau of the Census, Washington, DC 20233. Dist: Superintendent of Documents, U.S. Government Printing Office, Washington, DC 20402. Examined: 1973; 1976. 444p. $4.
Aud: Hs, Jc, Cl, Pl

A pocket size compendium of statistics compiled from data collected by various government and private agencies covering a broad spectrum of subjects. The book begins with a short summary of the subjects covered. This is followed by the main section of the book—the tables. Subjects covered are population, vital statistics, immigration, land and environment, government elections, national defense and veterans, law enforcement, labor, health, education, science, welfare, income, prices, parks and recreation, agriculture, forests and fisheries, business enterprise, manufactures, mining, construction and housing, transportation, communications, power, finance and insurance, distribution and services, and foreign commerce. An explanation of terms and an index are included. MBP

GE 129

Statesman's Year Book. ISSN 0081-4601. 1864. a. bibl. index. illus. MacMilliam Press, Little Essex St, London WC2R 3LF, England. Dist: St. Martin's Press, 175 Fifth Ave, New York, NY 10010. Examined: 113th ed., 1976/77; 114th ed., 1977/78. John Paxton, ed. 1572p. $22.50.
Aud: Jc, Cl, Pl

Subtitle: "Statistical and historical annual of the states of the world." Provides concise, up-to-date statistical and general information on the nations of the world. Divided into four parts: international organizations (United Nations, World Council of Churches, SEATO, the Arab League, etc.); the Commonwealth; the United States; and other countries. National entries include information on the constitution and government, area and population, religion, education, communications, judiciary, finance, defense, agriculture, forestry, mining, industry, power, commerce, shipping, roads, railways, aviation, postal service, banking, weights and measures, and diplomatic missions. A bibliography of books providing additional information is included for each country. Special features include comparative statistical tables on wheat, rye, barley, oats, maize, rice, millet, sorghum, sugar, petroleum, territorial sea limits, and top world banks. A place and international organizations index and a products index provide further access. KMH/SJV

GE 130

Statistical Abstract of Latin America. ISSN 0081-4687. 1956. a. index. Latin American Center Publications, University of California, Los Angeles, CA 90024. Examined: 17th ed., 1976; 18th ed., 1977. James W. Wilkie, ed. 449p. $27.
Aud: Cl, Pl

Summarizes socioeconomic and political characteristics of the twenty Latin American countries. Organization is topical (geographic, social, socioeconomic, economic), then alphabetical by nation. Special features in the 1976 volume include an essay, "Measuring the Scholarly Change of Latin American Democracy, 1945-70," and a guide to statistical data for research. A subject index provides access to subtopics within the main section. KMH

GE 131

Statistical Abstract of the United States. ISSN 0081-4741. 1878. a. index. U.S. Bureau of the Census, Washington, DC 20233. Dist: Superintendent of Documents, U.S. Government Printing Office, Washington, DC 20402. Examined: 97th ed., 1976; 98th ed., 1977. William Lerner, ed. 1048p. $11.
Aud: Hs, Jc, Cl, Pl

The standard summary of statistics on the social, political, and economic organization of the United States. Compiled from many statistical publications, both governmental and private. Provides information in about 1400 tables on population, vital statistics, immigration, education, labor, income, prices, elections, communications, energy, transportation, agriculture, forests, mining, construction, manufacturing, foreign commerce, and comparative international statistics. Appendixes include guides to statistics sources, census publications, and state statistical abstracts. Comprehensive subject index. KMH/MBP

GE 132
Statistical Services of the United States Government. 1968. irreg. U.S. Bureau of the Budget, Statistical Policy Division, Washington, DC 20233. Dist: Superintendent of Documents, U.S. Government Printing Office, Washington, DC 20402. Examined: 1975. 234p. $3.40.
Aud: Sa

Prepared by the Statistical Policy Division of the Office of Management and Budget. Provides information on statistical programs of the government in three major parts. Part one describes the federal statistical system and relation of its programs to other organizations. Part two is a description of major economic and social statistical series collected by agencies of the government. The third part lists agency statistical representatives and principal publications. KMH

GE 133
Statistical Yearbook for Asia and the Pacific; Annuaire Statistique pour l'Asie et le Pacifique. ISSN 0085-6711. (Continues: Statistical Yearbook for Asia and the Far East). 1969. a. United Nations Statistical Office, New York, NY 10017. Dist: International Publications Service, 114 E 32nd St, New York, NY 10016. Examined: 8th ed., 1975; 9th ed., 1976. 490p. $25.
Aud: Cl, Pl

Presents statistics on population, human resources, agriculture, fishing, industry, energy, trade, and society for the nations of Asia and the Pacific. Data are published for each nation in alphabetical order by nation. Extensive explanatory notes precede each table. Includes a list of the principal sources used in compiling the statistical data arranged by country, issuing agency, and title of publication used. In English and French. KMH/JKM

GE 134
Statistics Europe. ISSN 0081-5101. 1968. irreg. bibl. index. C. B. D. Research, 154 High St, Bekenham, Kent BR3 1EA, England. Dist: Gale Research Co., Book Tower, Detroit, MI 48226. Examined: 3rd ed., 1976. Joan M. Harvey, ed. 480p. $40.
Aud: Sa

Subtitle: "Sources for social, economic, and market research." Information about statistics sources for each European country arranged in alphabetical order by country. Entries include name and address of national statistical office, libraries, bibliographies of statistics, and major statistical publications on a variety of topics, i.e., production, trade, demography, social, financial. A section on statistics sources for Europe as a whole precedes national listings. Title and subject indexes are included. KMH

GE 135
Statistics Sources. ISSN 0585-198X. 1962. irreg. bibl. Gale Research Co., Book Tower, Detroit, MI 48226. Examined: 4th ed., 1974; 5th ed., 1977. Paul Wasserman and Jaqueline Bernero, eds. 976p. $58.
Aud: Sa

Subtitle: "A subject guide to data on industrial, business, social, educational, financial and other topics for the United States and internationally." Brings together under specific subjects information on sources of data about the U.S. and other countries. Statistical information in sources of international scope is also covered. Exhaustive analysis and indexing of sources such as the **Statistical Abstract of the United States**, trade and professional journals, and key international sources provides a straight alphabetical listing of subjects. A typical entry, "Births and Birth Rates—Age of Mother," refers the user to the U.S. Census data on fertility. Entries include name and address of publisher or issuing body, and title of the publication in which the statistics are included. The selected bibliography of key statistical sources provides an annotated listing of major general statistical compendia available in the English language from governmental and non-governmental sources. Emphasis is on American and international sources. KMH/MBP

GE 136
UNESCO. Statistical Yearbook; Annuaire Statistique. ISSN 0082-7541. (Continues: Statistical Yearbook of the League of Nations.) 1949. a. UNESCO, 7 Place de Fontnoy, 75700, Paris, France. Dist: Unipub, Box 433, New York, NY 10016. Examined: 1975; 1976. 1074p. $66.
Aud: Cl, Pl

A compilation of statistics prepared by the Office of

Statistics with the Statistical Office and the Population Division of the United Nations. Each member state reports periodically on laws, regulations, and statistics relating to its educational, scientific, and cultural life. Includes tables on population, area, exchange rates, literacy, and educational attainment; public and private educational institutions at all levels; science and technology, e.g., human resources and expenditures for research and experimental development; and culture and communications, including libraries, museums, book production, newspapers and other periodicals, paper consumption, film, and television. Each section is preceded by explanatory text. An appendix lists member states and associate members of UNESCO; another lists school and fiscal years. Text in English, French, and Spanish. KMH/MBP

GE 137

United Nations. Statistical Yearbook; Annuaire Statistique. ISSN 0082-8459. (Continues: Statistical Yearbook of the League of Nations.) 1948. a. index. United Nations, Statistical Office, New York, NY 10017. Dist: United Nations Publishing Service, New York, NY 10017. Examined: 28th ed., 1976. 909p. $45; $35 pap.
Aud: Cl, Pl

International statistical data presented in 26 topical chapters: population, human resources, agriculture, forestry, fishing, industrial production, mining and quarrying, manufacturing, construction, energy, internal and external trade, transport, communications, consumption, balance of payments, wages and prices, national accounts, finance, public finance, development assistance, housing, health, education, science and technology, and culture. Data are comparable for the various countries over time to the degree that available statistics permit. Special features include a world summary which summarizes global aggregates, country nomenclature, conversion coefficients and factors from metric to the U.S. system, and a country index. Text is in English and French. KMH/MBP

GE 138

U.S. Bureau of the Census. Census of Population. ISSN 0082-9390. 1790. decennial. illus. U.S. Bureau of the Census, Washington DC 2033. Dist: Superintendent of Documents, U.S. Government Printing Office, Washington, DC 20402. Examined: 1970 Census, Part 34, Sections 1 and 2 (New York). approx. 2400p. price varies; $16.25 for Part 34.
Aud: Cl, Pl

Volume one is published in 58 parts, each covering a different state or territory of the U.S. The volume examined was part 34, section one, covering New York State. Each part contains four chapters: number of inhabitants; general population characteristics; general social and economic characteristics; and detailed characteristics. Each section contains maps, charts, and tables. Breakdowns by country, town, types of persons, education, industry, and metropolitan and non-metropolitan areas. Explanatory text appears in appendixes A, B, and C in section two. There is a table finding guide, i.e., subjects arranged by type of area and table number. MBP

GE 139

U.S. Bureau of the Census. Current Population Reports. a. U.S. Bureau of the Census, Subscriber Services Section (Publications), Washington, DC 20233. Examined: 1977. various pagings. $56.
Aud: Hs, Jc, Cl, Pl

The Bureau of the Census issues serial population reports in seven different series; they are all sold for the single annual subscription price shown above. Subscriptions to single series are not accepted: single copies of individual reports may be ordered from the Superintendent of Documents, U.S. Government Printing Office, Washington, DC 20402. The seven reports are:

P-20 Population Characteristics. Current national, and occasionally regional statistics on geographic residence and mobility, fertility, education, school enrollment, marital status, numbers and characteristics of households and families, and persons of Spanish origin. Approximately 20 reports are issued each year. Some are annual, some are issued less frequently.

P-23 Special Studies. Included in this series is an annual report on the Black population, and reports on the metropolitan/nonmetropolitan population, American youth, and the older population.

P-25 Population Estimates and Projections. Annual estimates of the population of the states by broad age groups, and of the U.S. by age, race, and sex. Annual estimates of the components of population change. Estimates of the population of selected metropolitan areas and their component countries. Projections of the future population of the U.S. and individual states. Approximately 70 reports are issued each year.

P-26 Federal-State Cooperative Program for Population Estimates. Population estimates of counties in selected states in which the figures are prepared by a state agency.

P-27 Farm Population. Data on the size and selected

characteristics of the farm population of the U.S. Issued jointly with the Economic Research Service of the U.S. Department of Agriculture. One or two reports each year.

P-28 Special Censuses. Results of population censuses taken at the request and expense of city or other local governments. Subscription includes only the quarterly and annual summaries which show the total population figures for all the censuses conducted during the period. Individual reports issued for areas of 50,000 or more showing population by age, sex, and race are available from the Bureau of the Census (prices vary).

P-60 Consumer Income. Data on the proportions of families, individuals, and housholds at various income levels. Information is also presented on the relationship of income to age, sex, race, family size, education, occupation, work experience, and other characteristics. A special annual report provides detailed information on low-income families and individuals. Five reports are issued each year. JKM

EDUCATION

GENERAL WORKS

ED 1
America's Educational Press. 1925. irreg. index. Educational Press Association of America, Glassboro State College, Glassboro, NJ 08208. Examined: 32nd ed., 1971. 165p. (33rd ed., 1976. $10.)
Aud: Jc, Cl, Pl, Pf

A classified directory of the periodicals issued by educational organizations in the U.S. and Canada, covering general, national, state, special subjects, and local publications. Each entry includes the frequency of publication, price, publisher or sponsoring organization, editor's name and address, beginning year, circulation, whether or not advertising and book reviews are included, type of publication (journal, newspaper, newsletter, etc.), and method of reproduction (print, mimeograph, etc.). Title and editor indexes are provided. This directory is the only resource for locating many smaller publications; thus it is helpful for librarians, as well as for those wishing to publish. BSM

ED 2
Annual Editions: Readings in Education. ISSN 0095-5787. 1973. a. index. illus. The Dushkin Publishing Group, Sluice Dock, Guilford, CT 06434. Examined: 1978/79. Fred Schultz, ed. 256p. $5.95.
Aud: Hs, Jc, Pl

A collection of articles reprinted from a wide variety of current newspapers and journals in the field of education. Articles are arranged under broad topics. Titles in the series are designed primarily for classroom use, but they also provide a broad overview of the topic for the layperson. Includes a subject index. JKM

ED 3
Catalog of Federal Assistance Programs. ISSN 0097-7802. (Continues: Catalog of Federal Domestic Assistance.) a. index. U.S. Office of Education, Office of Management, Washington, DC 20202. Dist: Superintendent of Documents, U.S. Government Printing Office, Washington, DC 20402. Examined: 1976. 713p. $7.30.
Aud: Jc, Cl, Pl, Pf

Subtitle: "An indexed guide to the federal government's programs offering educational benefits to the American people." Lists all programs available to the general public (institutions and/or individuals) which are administered by the Office of Education and other federal agencies in support of educational services, professional training, or library services. Each program description covers type of assistance provided, purpose, eligibility, and application information. Includes grants, loans, scholarships, insurance, technical assistance, counselling and professional training, and provision of Federal property, facilities, equipment, goods, and services. Extensive indexes cover: administrative agencies; authorization (acts creating programs and index to which programs were created by each); Public Laws and U.S. Codes; key words in titles (KWIC); program name; and beneficiary. Indispensable as much for the indexes as it is for the information on the actual programs. BSM

ED 4
Digest of Educational Statistics. 1962. a. index. National Center for Educational Statistics, Washington, DC. Dist: Superintendent of Documents, U.S. Government Printing Office, Washington, DC 20402. Examined: 15th ed., 1976. W. Vance Grant, ed. 214p. $3.75.
Aud: Hs, Jc, Cl, Pl, Sa

Statistical information on a variety of subjects, including the number of schools and colleges in the U.S., enrollments, faculty, federal funds, libraries, and student performance in standard tests, is presented in 190 tables. Sources of information are noted. The statistics included are of current and national interest, but some provide historical data. Each edition updates earlier volumes, and new charts and tables are often added. Like most statistical publications, it is never entirely up-to-date. BSM

ED 5
Directory of American Scholars. ISSN 0070-5101. 1942. irreg. index. R.R. Bowker, 1180 Ave of the Americas, New York, NY 10036. Dist: R.R. Bowker, Box 1807, Ann Arbor, MI 48106. Examined: 6th ed.,

1974. Jaques Cattell Press, ed. 4v. (7th ed., 1978. 4v. $165; $45 per v.)
Aud: Cl, Pl, Sa
Indexed in: *Biographical Dictionaries Master Index.*

Published in cooperation with the American Council of Learned Societies, the work contains profiles of more than 38,000 scholars. Arranged by broad disciplinary areas in the four volumes: history, English, speech, and drama; foreign languages, linguistics, and philology; and philosophy, religion, and law. Cross references are provided for scholars with major involvement in more than one field. The brief biographies cover personal information, education, position, professional experience, honors, memberships, research interests, and publications. Covers Canadian and U.S. academics. Each volume has a geographic index, and volume four has an index of scholars. The seventh edition is scheduled for publication in December 1978. BSM

ED 6
Directory of Organizations and Personnel in Educational Management. ISSN 0070-6035. (Continues: Directory of Organizations and Personnel in Educational Administration.) 1968. irreg. index. ERIC Clearinghouse on Educational Management, University of Oregon, Eugene, OR 97403. Dist: ERIC Document Reproduction Service, Box 190, Arlington, VA 22210. Examined: 5th ed., 1976. Philip K. Piele and Stuart C. Smith, eds. 81p. $4.67; $.83 microfiche.
Aud: Cl, Pl, Sa

Covers both Canadian and U.S. organizations and individuals active in the field of educational management including those involved in research and those providing services to the educational management profession. Arranged alphabetically. There are subject indexes to organizations and personnel and a geographic index. Availability of publications of both organizations and individuals is indicated. Particularly helpful for those needing consultants. BSM

ED 7
ERIC Educational Documents Index. a. index. Macmillan Information, 866 Third Ave, New York, NY 10022. Examined: 1977. 1585p. $45.
Aud: Cl, Sa

Provides access to abstracts of documents found in the monthly *Resources in Education* and to 700 full collections of ERIC (Educational Resources Information Center) documents on microfiche. There are three indexes: an author index, a subject index, and an institutions or corporate author index. Entries provide titles and accession numbers for the documents or reports. The subject index is divided into two parts, major descriptors and minor descriptors. Descriptors or subject headings are derived from the *Thesaurus of ERIC Descriptors.* JKM

ED 8
Education Directory. 1912. National Center for Educational Statistics, Washington, DC. Dist: Superintendent of Documents, U.S. Government Printing Office, Washington, DC 20402.
Aud: Cl, Pl, Sa
    Part One: State Education Agency Officials. irreg. Examined: 1976/77. 100p.
    Part Two: Public School Systems. a. Examined: 1976/77. $2.65
    Part Three: Colleges and Universities. (Continues: Directory of U.S. Institutions of Higher Education. ISSN 0070-654X.) a. Examined: 1976/77. $6.20.
    Part Four: Educational Associations. irreg. index. Examined: 1976. $1.83.

Beginning in 1894, the directory was published as part of the annual report of the Commission of Education; in 1912, it was incorporated with the U.S. Office of Education *Bulletin*. The present format varies somewhat. Part one lists principal officials in state education and library extension agencies. There was a five-year gap between the last two editions of part one, but the 1976/77 volume was published with the promise that the National Center "plans to publish subsequent directories more frequently." The second part provides tabular information on the 1700 elementary and secondary public school systems in the U.S., as well as on the church organizations which maintain state, regional, or national school systems. The brief entries are arranged by state and include address, grade span, number of schools, enrollment, and the name of the chief administrator. Individual schools are not included. Part three lists only accredited institutions of higher education including two-year, four-year, and occupational postsecondary schools. Entries are arranged by state. The inclusion of names of presidents, deans, and other officers (sometimes including chief librarians) makes this volume particularly useful. More detailed descriptions of the 1662 institutions listed are available in the **College Handbook.** Part four lists international, national, college, and regional associations and foundations with an interest in education. It includes a subject index. Together or separately, these volumes are an invaluable resource, in spite of the irregular publication schedule of the first and last parts. BSM

ED 9
Education Index. ISSN 0013-1385. 1929. a. w/m. and q. suppls. H.W. Wilson Co., 950 University Ave, Bronx, NY 10452. Examined: 24th ed., 1973/74; 27th ed., 1976/77. 901p. service basis.
Aud: Cl, Pl, Sa

A yearly cumulative index to approximately 327 English language educational publications. Yearbooks and monographs are covered selectively; primary coverage is of periodicals. Access is by author and subject in one alphabet; there is a separate author listing of citations to book reviews. Subject areas indexed include administration and supervision; pre-school, elementary, secondary, higher, and adult education; teacher education; vocational education; counseling and personnel service; teaching methods; and curriculum. Fields of study indexed include the arts, comparative and international education, English language arts, health and physical education, multicultural and multiethnic education, religious education, science and mathematics, special education and rehabilitation, and educational research related to areas and fields indexed. Comprehensive, and a standard index in the field. JKM

ED 10
Guide to American Educational Directories. ISSN 0072-8225. 1963. irreg. index. Todd Publications, 11 Third St, Rye, NY 10580. Examined: 4th ed., 1975. Barry T. Klein, ed. 364p. $22.50
Aud: Jc, Cl, Pl, Pf

About 2700 U.S. and some Canadian directories in the field of education are listed. Publishers included are educational organizations, foundations, government agencies, private companies, and research firms. Fully annotated entries are arranged alphabetically by title under 100 subjects, and full bibliographic information is provided. Extremely useful resource, but not for all libraries. BSM

ED 11
Leaders in Education. ISSN 0075-8299. 1932. irreg. index. R.R. Bowker, 1180 Ave of the Americas, New York, NY 10036. Dist: R.R. Bowker, Box 1807, Ann Arbor, MI 48106. Examined: 5th ed., 1974. Jaques Cattell Press, comp. Anne Rhodes, ed. 1309p. $52.50.
Aud: Cl, Pl
Indexed in: *Biographical Dictionaries Master Index.*

Provides biographical information on 17,000 people in American and Canadian education, based on questionnaires. Included are deans and other administrative officers, academic faculty, directors and staff of educational research institutions, state and provincial commissioners of education and some of their staff, leading figures in public and private schools, officers of foundations concerned with education, officials of the U.S. Office of Education and of major educational associations, and authors of important pedagogical books. Entries are arranged alphabetically with specialty and geographic indexes. Expensive, but essential for tracking down otherwise elusive biographies. BSM

ED 12
National Faculty Directory. ISSN 0077-4472. 1971. a. Gale Research Co., Book Tower, Detroit, MI 48266. Examined: 8th ed., 1978. 2v. $115.
Aud: Jc, Cl, Pl

An alphabetical list of about 450,000 members of teaching faculties at 2900 junior colleges, colleges, and universities in the U.S. and at 180 selected Canadian (English-teaching) institutions. Name, institution, and department are given. Non-classroom faculty are not included. There is a list of the institutions. The publication is derived from the data base of the Association of American University Presses, which is maintained for subject oriented mailing lists. Useful for locating people not listed elsewhere and for verifying current addresses. BSM

ED 13
National Union of Christian Schools. Directory and Annual Reports. 1970/71. a. index. The National Union of Christian Schools, 865 28th SE, Grand Rapids, MI 49508. Examined: 1976/77. 285p.
Aud: Pl, Sa

A guide to U.S. and Canadian schools who belong to the National Union of Christian Schools. It lists names of the National Union's Board of Directors, staff, and district board members. The directory section contains tabulated information (history, statistics) and directories of schools, with personnel, addresses, phone numbers, and board officers; affiliate members; societies without schools; teachers, with address, name of school, grades and/or courses taught; and professional organizations. The annual reports section contains the agenda and reports of boards and officers, statistics, and financial records. LL

ED 14
Projections of Educational Statistics to (year). 1966. a. National Center for Educational Statistics, Washington, DC. Dist: Superintendent of Documents, U.S. Government Printing Office, Washington, DC 20402. Examined: 1977. 146p. $3.
Aud: Jc, Cl, Pl, Sa

Each annual issue provides statistical projections for the next ten years for enrollments, graduates, teachers, and expenditures at all levels of education: elementary, secondary, and higher. Sources of statistics are given. Issued by the National Center for Educational Statistics since 1966; in 1964 and 1965 projections were included with the U.S. Office of Education *Circular*. BSM

ED 15
Requirements for Certification of Teachers, Counselors, Librarians, and Administrators. ISSN 0080-1429. (Continues: Requirements for Certification for Elementary Schools, Secondary Schools, and Junior Colleges.) 1935. a. University of Chicago Press, 5801 Ellis Ave, Chicago, IL 60637. Examined: 42nd ed., 1977/78. Elizabeth H. Woellner, ed. 227p. $13.
Aud: Jc, Cl, Pl, Sa

Initial certification requirements for teachers, special education personnel, counselors, librarians, and administrators in the 50 states and in U.S. possessions and territories. Requirements for special fields are generally not included. Arranged by state. BSM

ED 16
Sourcebook of Equal Educational Opportunity. (Continues: Yearbook of Equal Educational Opportunity.) 1975/76. a. index. Marquis Who's Who, 200 E Ohio St, Chicago, IL 60611. Examined: 1975/76, 479p.; 2nd ed., 1976/77. 686p. $34.50.
Aud: Hs, Jc, Cl, Pl, Sa

Presents statistical and factual data on equal educational opportunity in the U.S. Arranged in topical sections with a subject/geographic index. Includes general information on trends in education and the role of the Office for Civil Rights, and sections on education, work opportunities, and attainments of Blacks, Spanish-surnamed Americans, Native Americans, Asian-Americans, and women. Each of the sections on specific population groups provides data on size of the population, social and economic statistics, school enrollment, and educational legislation. A final section provides information on the work of the U.S. Regional Manpower Administration. The title changed in the second edition which was published in late 1977, indicating the book may no longer be an annual. JKM

ED 17
Standard Education Almanac. ISSN 0081-4237. 1968. a. index. Marquis Academic Media, 200 E Ohio St, Chicago, IL 60611. Examined: 1977/78. Jon S. Greene, ed. 675p. $34.50.
Aud: Jc, Cl, Pl, Sa

Provides comprehensive, current coverage of elementary, secondary, higher, and adult education in the U.S., including facts and statistics on funding, legislation, and educational materials. Sources for each selection are noted. Divided into nine sections. Summary essays are presented for each section and for many subsections. Subject areas covered are general education including enrollment, number of teachers, staff, income sources, statistics, and education associations; elementary and secondary education; higher education; adult and continuing education, listing facilities, expenditures, and statistics; equal educational opportunity for Blacks, Spanish-surnamed Americans, Native Americans, and women; bilingual/bicultural instruction and special education for the handicapped; career education; educational resources, covering publishers, public television stations, and AV material producers; education and government; and related statistics such as population characteristics, salaries, funding for research and development, etc. A valuable compendium; the subject, organization, personnel, and geographic indexes make the information easily accessible. BSM

ED 18
World of Learning. ISSN 0084-2117. 1947. a. index. Europa Publications, 18 Bedford Sq, London, WC1B 3JN England. Dist: International Publications Service, 114 E 32nd St, New York, NY 10016. Examined: 28th ed., 1977/78. 2v. $73.50.
Aud: Jc, Cl, Pl

Standard guide to and directory of learned societies, research institutes, libraries, museums, and universities around the world. The latest edition includes open or free universities. Arranged alphabetically by country and institution within each category. Information on each institution varies according to what has been received. For many of the schools, the entries are extensive and include lists of faculty and other officers by department or division, often with degrees; other entries may include only the chief administrator's name. An index to institutions is provided. No other publication is so inclusive. BSM

ADULT AND CONTINUING EDUCATION

ED 19
Continuing Education: A Guide to Career Development Programs. 1977. freq. not determined. bibl. index. Gaylord Professional Publications with Neal-Schuman Publishers, Box 4901, Syracuse, NY 13221.

Examined: 1977. 704p. $39.95.
Aud: Cl, Pl, Sa

A guide to advanced training and adult continuing education programs and courses offered by more than 2000 colleges, universities, organizations, and other institutions. Divided into three sections. The first is an alphabetical listing of institutions by state. Entries provide name and address, a brief description of the type of programs or courses offered, and an indication of credit or degrees given, special programs offered, and subject areas covered. The second section is a directory of organizations which provides general information on the types of seminars, programs, and conferences offered. The third section lists organizations and institutions by career area, e.g., agriculture, management, journalism, library service, building inspection, etc. The appendix includes an annotated list of accredited home study schools, a list of educational television stations active in educational programming, an annotated bibliography of other directories and sources of information about continuing education programs, and a list of continuing education associations. JKM

ED 20
Continuing Education Resource Guide. a. Society for the Advancement of Continuing Education for Ministry, 3401 Brook Rd, Richmond, VA 23227. Examined: 1974/75. 5v. $1; $.25 per v.
Aud: Pl, Sa

A guide to schools, colleges, and universities which offer continuing education programs for clergy and professional church workers. The guides are published for five regions—New England, Mid-Atlantic, South, North Central, and the West; these can either be purchased as a set or individually. Entries are arranged alphabetically by name of institution. Each entry gives: address, contact person if available, type of programs offered, length, tuition or fees, and dates of programs. Principal career centers are also listed. A separate list of contact persons who are not affiliated with specific schools is provided. LL

ED 21
Guide to Independent Study through Correspondence Instruction. (Continues: Guide to Correspondence Studies in Colleges and Universities.) 1964. bi-a. National University Extension Association, Suite 360, One Dupont Circle, Washington, DC 20036. Examined: 1975/77. 43p. $1.
Aud: Hs, Jc, Cl, Pl

Lists courses available from regionally accredited institutions which are members of the Division of Independent Study of the National University Extension Association. Fifty-six subjects are included with numbers referring to the colleges and universities where the courses are offered. The brief entries for each institution include the name of the person to whom correspondence should be sent and general introductory information on admissions, credit, fees, guidance, and special programs. There is a section for handicapped students. BSM

ED 22
Training and Development Organizations Directory. 1978. freq. not determined. index. Gale Research Co., Book Tower, Detroit, MI 48226. Examined: none. (1st ed., 1978. 614p. $45.)
Aud: Pl, Sa

The first edition was scheduled for Spring 1978 publication. Publisher's information states that this new directory will provide "details on the activities and specialties of companies, institutes, and special consulting groups that conduct managerial and supervisory training courses for business firms and government agencies." Entries will indicate the sponsoring organization's address, phone number, founding date, number of professional staff, areas of course emphasis, names of principal staff, target audience, and a description of courses or training offered. JKM

ED 23
Yearbook of Adult and Continuing Education. 1975/76. a. index. Marquis Who's Who, 200 E Ohio St, Chicago, IL 60611. Examined: 3rd ed., 1977/78. 672p. $34.50.
Aud: Cl, Pl

Provides statistical data and research reports on the state of adult education in the U.S., including data on new trends such as lifelong education and education for the senior population. Arranged in topical sections with a subject/geographic index. Topics covered in the 1977/78 edition were: general adult education; lifelong learning; education for senior citizens; continuing professional education; cooperative and career education; alternatives to and innovations in traditional educational programs; and a directory of adult and continuing education organizations. JKM

ELEMENTARY AND SECONDARY EDUCATION

ED 24
Advanced Placement Course Descriptions. 1960. bi-a.

College Entrance Examination Board, 888 Seventh Ave, New York, NY 10036. Dist: College Board Publication Orders, Box 2815, Princeton, NJ 08540. Examined: 1976/77. 13v. $10; $1 per v.
Aud: Jh, Hs, Jc, Pl

Each volume is devoted to a subject, i.e., American history, art, biology, classics, chemistry, English, European history, French language and literature, German language and literature, mathematics, music, physics, and Spanish language and literature. Provides information on college level studies taken in secondary schools for which college credit is granted. Each volume covers a full year course at a designated level. Includes course description and a list of colleges and universities that have reported policies of granting advanced placement and/or credit. Each also gives information on the advanced placement examinations and some sample questions. A guide to the Advanced Placement Program is available upon request. BSM

ED 25
Annual Editions: Readings in Early Childhood Education. 1976. a. index. illus. The Dushkin Publishing Group, Sluice Dock, Guilford, CT 06434. Examined: 1978/79. Judy Spitler McKee, ed. 288p. $6.55.
Aud: Hs, Jc, Pl

A collection of articles arranged under broad topics and reprinted from a wide variety of current newspapers and journals in the field of early childhood education. Titles in the series are designed primarily for classroom use, but they also provide a broad overview of the topic for the layperson. Includes a subject index. JKM

ED 26
Guide to Summer Camps and Summer Schools. ISSN 0072-8705. (Continues: Sargent Guide to Summer Camps and Summer Schools.) 1936. bi-a. index. Porter Sargent Publishers, 11 Beacon St, Boston, MA 02108. Examined: 20th ed., 1977/78. 446p. $10; $7 pap.
Aud: Jh, Hs, Jc, Cl, Pl

Provides brief data on more than 1000 camps and schools in the U.S. and Canada. Those with general programs are arranged by geographical area. Camps offering special interest programs, such as aviation, reading, creative writing, sailing, drama, etc., as well as camps with programs for the handicapped are listed alphabetically by name under the subject classification. There is an index to camps by name. Information provided is brief but sufficient, and includes business as well as camp address, cost, subject, skill orientations, if any, and type of child for whom the program is intended. BSM

ED 27
Handbook of Private Schools. ISSN 0072-9884. a. index. Porter Sargent Publishers, Beacon St, Boston, MA 02108. Examined: 58th ed., 1977. 1460p. $16.
Aud: Pl, Sa

More than 1900 schools, arranged by regions and states, are described in detail. Entries include name of administrative officer, cost, number of students, special programs, and physical facilities. Tutoring programs, summer sessions, religious affiliations, and recreational opportunities are also noted. Classified tables locate schools by type. Camps and a few Canadian and foreign schools are also included. Brief information is provided for an additional 937 boarding and day schools. Useful for parents and for counselors and teachers seeking positions. BSM

ED 28
Lovejoy's Prep School Guide. ISSN 0459-925X. (1968 is 3rd ed.) irreg. index. Simon and Schuster, Rockefeller Center, 630 Fifth Ave, New York, NY 10020. Examined: 4th ed., 1974. Clarence E. Lovejoy, ed. 222p. $9.95; $5.95 pap.
Aud: Jh, Pl

Divided into five sections. The first section lists private, independent schools and includes a brief explanation of schools which are church-controlled or which have Junior ROTC (Reserve Officers Training Corps). The second section covers admission policies of prep schools. The third section focuses on scholarships and lists all schools which belong to the School Scholarship Service. Schools with special programs and curricula are highlighted in the fourth section, and the last section lists each school with a short description and a rating. Includes an index. JKM

ED 29
Patterson's American Education; School Systems and Schools Classified. ISSN 0079-0230. (Continues: Patterson's American Educational Directory.) 1904. a. index. Educational Directories, Box 199, Mt. Prospect, IL 60056. Examined: 1977. Norman F. Elliott, ed. 786p. $29.50.
Aud: Cl, Pl, Sa

The directory is divided into two parts. The first part is a comprehensive listing of more than 7000 schools, arranged by state, then by city and town. Town and county population figures are given, and the names of the superintendent and junior and senior high school principals for each school and school system are given. All private and parochial schools and colleges are included, as are officials of state departments of education, and county superintendents. In part two, schools are listed by academic or vocational offerings. Opportunities for study abroad, correspondence schools, and summer sessions are noted. This section is also available separately for $4. A new feature is a classified list of educational associations and societies. No descriptive information is given about any school, but this directory is still a must for all libraries. BSM

ED 30
Private Independent Schools. ISSN 0078-5399. 1943. a. index. Bunting and Lyon, 238 N Main St, Wallingford, CT 06492. Examined: 1977. 541p. $30.
Aud: Pl, Sa

Subtitle: "A comprehensive guide to American elementary and secondary private schools." Presents data on about 1300 private elementary and high schools based on information provided by the schools themselves. Entries describe the campus, faculty and administration, student body, academic program, student activities, admission requirements, and costs. There are fairly long descriptions of 350 schools; only brief information is provided for the other listings. Day and boarding schools; coeducational and single-sex schools; military, church-related, and international schools; and schools for students with special interests are covered. Most of the schools are college preparatory. A few foreign schools are included. The guide also includes a list of educational associations, an index to schools, and geographical and classified subject indexes. A paperback edition titled *Guide to Private Schools* (1977, $10) includes only the 350 lengthy descriptions and is intended for parents and their children. BSM

ED 31
School Universe Data Book. ISSN 0146-4329. 1976/77. a. index. Curriculum Information Center, Brooks Tower, 1020 15th St, Denver, CO 80202. Examined: 1976/77; 1977/78. 5v. $325; state volumes, $12 to $24.
Aud: Cl, Pl, Sa

Computer-produced information on public, parochial, and other independent schools in the 50 states and the District of Columbia. Provides the name of the 116,000 administrators of state, district, and diocesan schools systems, plus the heads of 4000 independent schools. Street addresses and telephone numbers of school offices, regional and county centers, and public, Catholic, and other independent school buildings are also provided. Includes complete data on enrollments, grade span, type of district or school, and any special education and special training programs. Statistical summaries are provided by county, district, and state, as well as by county and regional centers. The school listings are arranged by state, then by county and district. Preceding each state's listings are indexes to district names and counties. Names, addresses, and telephone numbers of state department of education personnel follow each state listing. Updated and verified by telephone each summer, the information is comprehensive, current, and accurate. This volume pulls together information which is often hard to find and scattered. The entire set is primarily for marketing purposes, but it can be useful in large research libraries. Individual volumes on each state can be purchased separately for $12 to $24, depending on the state, and are a more practical purchase for smaller libraries. BSM

ED 32
Schools Abroad of Interest to Americans. ISSN 0080-6900. 1959. irreg. index. Porter Sargent Publishers, 11 Beacon St, Boston, MA 02108. Examined: 3rd ed., 1975. 448p. $10.
Aud: Sa

Lists over 700 primary and secondary schools in 125 countries. Entries cover curricula, language and other admission requirements, boarding and day facilities, enrollment, and key personnel. Often the language of instruction, composition of student body, and range of college preparation are noted as well. Invaluable for those who need information on schools abroad for American students, such as employees of multinational companies and diplomatic officials. Arranged by continent and then by country. A few postsecondary and specialized schools are included. Indexes to schools, associations, and consultants are provided. BSM

HIGHER EDUCATION

ED 33
Accredited Institutions of Postsecondary Education. ISSN 0065-0862. (Continues: Accredited Institutions of Higher Education.) 1964. a. index. American Council on Education, One Dupont Circle, Washington, DC 20036. Examined: 1977/78. Sherry S. Harris, ed. 356p. $5.50.
Aud: Hs, Jc, Cl, Pl

Subtitle: "A directory of accredited institutions, professionally accredited programs, and candidates for accreditation." Indispensable for the kind of data provided: location, whether private or public, whether liberal arts or special/technical, accrediting agency, date of last accreditation, programs additionally accredited and by whom, type of governance, level of degrees awarded, enrollment, and name of chief executive officer. Junior and community colleges are included, as well as four-year colleges and universities. Arranged by state and alphabetically within each state by name of institution. Appendixes cover major changes in the previous year in two-year and four-year institutions, and the names and addresses of regional and specialized accrediting groups. BSM

ED 34
Barron's Handbook of American College Financial Aid. irreg. Barron's Educational Series, 113 Crossways Park Dr, Woodbury, NY 11797. Examined: 1977. Nicholas C. Proia, ed. 512p. $6.95.
Aud: Hs, Jc, Cl, Pl

Includes information on determining the costs of attending college, how to apply for financial aid, how awards are granted, the types and conditions of grants and loans, the types of financial aid available, and how financial aid packages are administered. Includes the names of financial aid officers at each college and information on when and how to apply for financial aid, plus a glossary of financial aid terms. In 1974 Barron's published a *Handbook of Junior and Community College Financial Aid* in the same format; both are very useful publications, but the junior and community college title is rather out-of-date. JKM

ED 35
Barron's Profiles of American Colleges. (1976 is 10th ed.) irreg. index. Barrons' Educational Series, 113 Crossways Park Dr, Woodbury, NY 11797. Examined: 10th ed., 1976. 2v. 1288p. $33.90; $12.90 pap.
Aud: Jh, Hs, Jc, Cl, Pl

Volume one contains descriptions of over 1450 accredited colleges and universities in the U.S. Descriptions include information on student life, such as drop-out rates, racial composition, religious activities, athletic programs, and regulations on alcohol, automobiles, and curfews; the physical plant; programs and degrees awarded; majors offered; required courses; independent study and experimental programs; costs and financial aid available; and admissions requirements, including requirements and procedures for transfer students. Volume two is an index to major areas of study including schools offering various types of alternatives to traditional study patterns. A special feature is the college selector which groups colleges by degree of selectivity in admissions and average annual cost. Very useful for students and guidance counselors. Regional editions (Midwest, Northeast, South, and West) containing the same information are also available for $3.95 each. JKM

ED 36
Barron's Handbook of College Transfer Information. irreg. Barron's Educational Series, 113 Crossways Park Dr, Woodbury, NY 11797. Examined: 1975. Nicholas C. Proia, ed. 304p. $4.95.
Aud: Hs, Jc, Cl, Pl

Transfer information for over 1400 colleges including admission standards, required examinations, financial aid, and how to apply. A very useful publication, but since it is somewhat out-of-date, the information included would require verification. BSM

ED 37
College Blue Book. 1923. bi-a. index. Macmillan Information, 866 Third Ave, New York, NY 10022. Examined: 1977. David Biesel, ed. 5v. $135; $35 per v.; v. 1-3, $85; v. 1-3 plus v.4 or v.5, $110.
Aud: Jh, Hs, Jc, Cl, Pl

The basic **Blue Book** consists of three volumes. Volume one, "Narrative Descriptions," describes fully, yet concisely, over 3,000 colleges in the U.S. and Canada. Volume two, "Tabular Data," provides brief tabular information on costs, accreditation, enrollment, faculty size, and name of chief administrative officer or registrar. It is arranged by state or province. Volume three, "Degrees Offered by College and Subject," is an indispensable volume which lists the subjects in which degrees are offered under each institution. In the second half of the book, the names of colleges offering degrees in more than 2500 subject areas are listed by subject. A fourth volume, "Scholarships, Fellowships, Grants, and Loans," is edited by M. Lorraine Mathis and Elizabeth I. Dixon. Arranged by broad subject areas, such as environmental studies, area studies, etc., it provides substantial, up-to-date information on the various forms of financial aid. Foundations and institutions are listed alphabetically. Indexes to titles and foundations, level of awards (i.e., community college, college, advanced), and detailed subjects are provided. The fifth volume, "College Blue Book: Occupational Education" (formerly the *Blue Book of Occupational Education),* has 1196 pages and is now in its third edition. It contains five sections: occupational descriptions derived from the

Occupational Outlook Handbook; occupational schools arranged by state and city; curricula and programs of instruction, also arranged by state and city; two-year institutions; and allied medical schools. Unfortunately, it is lacking an index to schools. BSM

ED 38
College Handbook. ISSN 0069-5653. 1941. tri-a. bibl. index. College Entrance Examination Board, 888 Seventh Ave, New York, NY 10036. Dist: College Board Publications, Box 2815, Princeton, NJ 08540. Examined: 1975. Susan F. Watts, ed. 1255p. $6.95.
Aud: Jh, Hs, Jc, Cl, Pl

Describes 2863 colleges and two-year and four-year undergraduate programs, as listed in part three of the **Education Directory**. Detailed descriptions supplied by the colleges are provided for 1662 schools. The other listings include brief descriptions which were taken from other publications. Entries are arranged by state. The information given is ample and includes church affiliation (if any); whether public or private; for men, women, or both; undergraduate and graduate enrollment; accreditation; curriculum and degrees offered; special programs; information for low-income and minority students; freshman requirements; availability of military training; placement tests; counselling; credit; academic regulations; graduate programs; admission requirements; number of admission applications received and accepted; basis for selection of applicants; application procedures; student life and characteristics of freshman class; student activities and athletics; annual expenses; and financial aid available. Altogether a comprehensive volume and a bargain. BSM

ED 39
The College Planning Search Book. 1977/78. a. index. illus. American College Testing Program, Box 168, Iowa City, IA 52240. Examined: 1977/78. John D. Roth, ed. 244p. $5.
Aud: Jh, Hs, Jc, Cl, Pl, Sa

Subtitle: "A guide for students, parents, and counselors." Presents data on costs, admission requirements, institutional and student body characteristics, career programs, majors, and financial aid for over 2700 two-year and four-year colleges. Provides check lists and worksheets for students to use in organizing their ideas while they search for colleges that meet their needs. Describes key steps in planning. A useful and novel approach. BSM

ED 40
Commonwealth Universities Yearbook. ISSN 0069-7745. 1914. a. bibl. index. Association of Commonwealth Universities, 36 Gordon Sq, London WC1 OPF, England. Dist: International Publications Service, 114 E 32nd St, New York, NY 10016. Examined: 53rd ed., 1976. Hugh W. Springer and T. Craig, eds. 4v. $68.50.
Aud: Sa

Subtitle: "A directory to the universities of the Commonwealth and the handbook of their association." The introduction contains 15 authoritative articles, eight of which are substantial descriptions of countries having more than three or four universities. The rest cover secondary education in Commonwealth countries and are written to help students in other countries interpret entrance requirements. The first three volumes, arranged alphabetically by country, cover the universities of the 26 Commonwealth countries plus the Republic of Ireland and the Union of South Africa. Extensive information is provided on each university including the names, titles, and degrees of administrative and teaching staffs arranged by department or school. Entries can run to many pages, depending upon the size of the institution. The fourth volume has a general index and an index to the more than 150,000 names of staff and faculty. Indispensable for institutions with foreign students or for those whose faculty have international interests. Considered a companion volume to *American Universities and Colleges* (published by the American Council on Education; the last edition was published in 1973, and no new edition is planned) and the **International Handbook of Universities**. BSM

ED 41
Comparative Guide to American Colleges for Students, Parents, and Counselors. 1964. irreg. index. Harper and Row, 10 E 53rd St, New York, NY 10022. Examined: 1975. James Cass and Max Birnbaum, eds. 747p. $17.50; $7.95 pap. (8th ed., 1977.)
Aud: Jh, Hs, Pl

The purpose of the guide is "to determine the best possible fit between students' talents, interests, and aspirations, and the environment that individual colleges offer." To this end the publication provides the kind of information students really want to know, such as the degree of freedom students enjoy, the role of students in campus governance, etc. The descriptions of individual colleges vary in length, depth of characterization, and the amount of analytical data provided. The editors have considered the following: "the reputation and academic quality of each institution as measured by objective data; the desire of the college to seek students from other areas of the country; the willingness of a college to reveal comparative and analytical information; and the applicability of the analytical data developed in this volume to specialized institutions such as seminaries, music schools, etc." The volume is arranged by the name of the institution. There are indexes by state, by selectivity of admission, and by religious affiliation. BSM

ED 42
Directory of Predominantly Black Colleges and Universities in the United States of America. 1966. irreg. index. National Alliance of Businessmen, 1730 K St, NW, Washington, DC 20006. Dist: Superintendent of Documents, U.S. Government Printing Office, Washington, DC 20402. Examined: 1969, 85p.; 1977. 107p. free.
Aud: Hs, Jc, Pl

Arranged alphabetically with a geographical index. Entries include the name of the college or university, address, telephone number, names of administrators, current enrollment, degrees offered, number of degrees granted, and the objectives and affiliations of the institution. Includes both private and public institutions. JKM

ED 43
Financial Aids for Higher Education. (Continues: National Catalog of Aids for Students Entering College.) 1963. bi-a. bibl. index. William C. Brown Co., 2460 Kerper Blvd, Dubuque, IA 52001. Examined: 7th ed., 1976/77. Oreon Keeslar, ed. 700p. $14.95.
Aud: Hs, Jc, Cl, Pl

Presents accurate, concise information on more than 3400 programs offering financial assistance to college freshmen. Arranged so that the high school senior can locate appropriate programs by career orientation, by organization or church membership, and by special situation, such as war orphan, child of a member of a particular labor union, or child of an employee of a particular industry or organization. Entries are in alphabetical order and give full information on value, restrictions, eligibility, application procedures, etc. Excellent introductory material on seeking scholarships, planning, national testing programs, the National College Scholarship Service, budgeting, and approved national contests. Indexes provide full access. BSM

ED 44
Graduate and Professional School Opportunities for Minority Students. ISSN 0090-8266. 1969. a. bibl. index. Educational Testing Service, Princeton, NJ 08540. Examined: 6th ed., 1975/76. Louise D. Stone, ed. approx. 120p. $3.
Aud: Cl, Pl

A guide to educational opportunities, mostly in the U.S., for members of minority groups. Information is based on questionnaires sent to graduate and professional schools, not all of whom respond. Discusses resources available to minority students. Schools and departments are listed by subject. Information provided includes: name of person to contact, application fees and procedures, admission application dates, number of students, number of minority students and faculty, and number of minority students receiving financial aid. There is an index of institutions. BSM

ED 45
Graduate Programs and Admissions Manual. 1972. a. bibl. index. Educational Testing Service, Princeton, NJ 08540. Examined: 5th ed., 1976/77. David R. Deener, ed. 4v. $3 per v.
Aud: Cl, Pl

Sponsored by the Council of Graduate Schools and the Graduate Record Examination Board, the four volumes (biological and health sciences; arts and humanities; physical sciences, mathematics and engineering; and social sciences and education) cover 79 majors in 504 institutions. Information on the institution is provided in tabular format. One section covers departments and programs by discipline, and another describes special and interdisciplinary programs. Each section includes general information, admission requirements, and availability of loans, housing, and assistantships. Introductory material covers the admission process, financial aid, and information for foreign students. A sample Graduate Record Examination is provided in each volume. BSM

ED 46
Guide to American Graduate Schools. (1975 is 3rd ed.) irreg. index. Viking Press, 625 Madison Ave, New York, NY 10022. Examined: 3rd ed., 1975. Herbert B. Livesey and Harold Doughty, eds. 437p. $17.50.
Aud: Cl, Pl

The introduction explains the meanings of graduate and professional schools, financial aid, standards, etc. The main portion of the book is comprised of listings of graduate schools in alphabetical order. The school's location is given along with pertinent information on tuition, housing facilities, where to make applications, admission requirements, financial aid, degree requirements, and a list of programs available. The schools are indexed by the state they are located in, field of study, and institutional abbreviations. JKM

ED 47
Handbook on International Study for U.S. Nationals. (Continues: Handbook on International Study.) 1955. irreg. bibl. index. Institute on International Education, 809 United Nations Plaza, New York, NY 10017. Examined: 6th ed., 1976-. Mary Louise Taylor, ed. 5v. $12; $6.95 pap.
Aud: Sa

Formerly a one volume publication, the new edition is being published in five parts. *Study in Europe* was published in 1976; *Study in the American Republics* came next; *Study in Africa South of the Sahara, Study in the Middle East and North Africa,* and *Study in East and South Asia and Oceania* are forthcoming. Judging from what has been published already, these volumes will be a substantial contribution to the literature. The first two volumes run to approximately 300 and 220 pages respectively. Intended for the undergraduate, graduate, or post graduate scholar planning to attend a foreign institution with a definite academic or professional goal in mind. Arranged by country, each entry includes a brief description of higher education, academic year, major university degrees, admission, costs, and housing. Special programs and universities are then listed with addresses, a notation as to whether they are public or private, size of student body, U.S. enrollment (if any), and degrees awarded. Also noted is whether or not a non-degreed candidate may attend. Additional information is provided on fields of study, awards, exchange programs, volunteer and trainee opportunities, organizations providing services, and government regulations. Indexes are by institution, fields of study, organizations, and institutions with their major fields. Appendixes give currency exchange and inflation rates. Extremely comprehensive but the **Handbook** would have to be used in conjunction with something else, such as **World of Learning** or **International Handbook of Universities**, to supplement the information provided. BSM

ED 48
International Handbook of Universities and Other Institutions of Higher Education. ISSN 0074-6215. 1959. tri-a. bibl. index. International Association of Universities, One Rue Miollos, Paris 75732, France. Dist: American Council on Education, One Dupont Circle, Washington, DC 20036. Examined: 6th ed., 1974. H. M. R. Keyes and D. J. Aitken, eds. 1326p. $32.
Aud: Sa

Companion to *American Universities and Colleges* (published by the American Council on Education; the last edition was published in 1973 and no new edition is planned) and **Commonwealth Universities Yearbook**. Covers 110 countries. Institutions are listed alphabetically within the country; in those countries where there are many institutions, the listings are divided into universities and other. This is particularly helpful in the case of countries with many professional and technological institutions. Each entry includes: size of academic staff; student enrollment; lists of faculties, departments, institutes, schools, and colleges; brief descriptions of history and structure (with notes on any cooperative arrangements with institutions in other countries); admission requirements; duration and fields of study; academic year; and fees. Some entries are extensive, others are sparse; on the whole, however, the information appears to be adequate. BSM

ED 49
Lovejoy's College Guide. ISSN 0076-132X. 1940. irreg. index. Simon and Schuster, 630 Fifth Ave, New York, NY 10020. Examined: 1976. Clarence E. Lovejoy, ed. approx. 420p. $4.95 pap.
Aud: Jh, Hs, Jc, Cl, Pl

A reliable long-established publication covering U.S. colleges. It is divided into two parts. In part one, under curricula, are listed 500 careers and special programs, such as advanced placement, early admission decisions, and colleges having facilities for the handicapped, for kosher meals, etc. Descriptions of colleges, arranged by state, are provided in part two. About 3500 schools are covered. A general section discusses college costs, financial aid, admissions, selecting a college, and college religious groups. Sources of information on student loan programs are listed by state. There is an index of colleges. BSM

ED 50
The New Guide to Study Abroad. (Continues: A Guide to Study Abroad.) 1962. irreg. index. Harper and Row, 10 E 53rd St, New York, NY 10022. Examined: 5th ed., 1976/77. John Arthur Garraty, ed. 450p. $11.95; $4.95 pap.
Aud: Hs, Jc, Cl, Pl, Sa

Lists summer and full year programs for high school and college students and for teachers. General introductory chapters cover planning, benefits, preparations, cost considerations, general descriptions of higher education opportunities in several countries, and approaches to foreign study. Divided into sections according to level of student: college and graduate student, pre-college and high school, and teaching positions. There is also a section on summer work and travel abroad programs. Includes programs sponsored by both American and foreign universities, and provides some information on independent study and financial assistance. Appendixes list organizations and agencies promoting foreign study and travel. Subject and institution indexes are provided. Information for each entry is brief but useful. BSM

ED 51
Peterson's Annual Guide to Undergraduate Study. 1966. a. Peterson's Guides, Box 123, Princeton, NJ 08540. Examined: 12th ed., 1978. 1571p.
Aud: Jh, Hs, Cl, Pl

Subtitle: "2800 two-year and four-year colleges and universities in the U.S. and Canada." The guide is compiled from data supplied by the colleges and universities included, therefore it is not complete as some institutions do not submit the information requested. For institutions listed, however, the information is extremely detailed and up to date—more so than in any similar publication. BSM

ED 52
Peterson's Annual Guides to Graduate Study. 1966. a. Peterson's Guides, Box 123, Princeton, NJ 08540. Examined: 1978. Karen C. Hegener, ed. 5v. $75.
Aud: Cl, Pl

A very useful set, but it is not complete as the publisher is dependent upon input from schools and departments, and many do not cooperate. For those institutions that do cooperate the information is extremely detailed and up to date—more so than in any similar publication. A directory of programs precedes the descriptions of individual institutions. The number of volumes and the subject arrangement varies from year to year. Individual volumes may be purchased; prices are listed below. In the 1978 edition, the volumes were: *1350 Graduate Institutions in the U.S. and Canada, An Overview* ($10); *Graduate Programs in the Humanities and the Social Sciences in the U.S. and Canada* ($14); *Graduate Programs in the Biological, Agricultural, and Health Sciences in the U.S. and Canada* ($15); *Graduate Programs in the Physical Sciences in the U.S. and Canada* ($12); and *Graduate Programs in Engineering and Applied Sciences in the U.S. and Canada* ($12). BSM

ED 53
Student Aid Annual. ISSN 0585-4555. 1955. a. index. Chronicle Guidance Publications, Moravia, NY 13118. Examined: 1977/78. 347p. $10.
Aud: Hs, Jc, Cl, Pl

Covers financial aid programs offered nationally and regionally, primarily by private noncollegiate organizations, independent and AFL-CIO affiliated labor unions, and the federal and state governments. Awards, loans, and scholarships are arranged alphabetically by title in two sections, undergraduate and graduate. Covers Puerto Rico and the 50 states. Indexes are by subject for undergraduates and for graduates, and there is a source index to all programs. BSM

ED 54
Study Abroad: International Scholarships, International Courses. ISSN 0081-895X. 1948. bi-a. bibl. index. United Nations Educational, Scientific, and Cultural Organization, 7 Place de Fontenoy, Paris 75700, France. Dist: Unipub, Box 443, Murray Hill Sta, New York, NY 10016. Examined: 21st ed., 1977/78-1978/79. 558p. $7.50.
Aud: Jc, Cl, Pl

Lists several hundred thousand individual scholarships, assistantships, travel grants, courses, and seminars in all academic and professional fields in over 100 countries. Each entry covers: subject and level, location, cost, awards and other benefits, eligibility requirements, and application information. Part one lists scholarships under international organizations and under national institutions by country and by discipline and profession. Part two lists areas of study under broad disciplinary headings and is largely arranged by country. Includes institution and detailed subject indexes. Good information, but complicated to use. The text is in English, French, and Spanish. BSM

ED 55
Summer Study Abroad. ISSN 0081-9379. a. bibl. index. Institute of International Education, 809 United Nations Plaza, New York, NY 10017. Examined: 25th ed., 1977. Gail A. Cohen, ed. 130p. $4.
Aud: Jc, Cl, Pl

Programs sponsored by U.S. and foreign institutions and organizations for those of college age and older, and a few professional opportunities are included. Covers pre-session orientations and study-related work opportunities, as well as some other working positions. Arranged by geographic area, then by country and city. Information on sponsoring institution or organization, dates, eligibility, programs, language of instruction, housing, costs, and application deadline are included for each entry. There is an index of institutions and an appendix listing U.S. consortia. BSM

ED 56
U.S. College Sponsored Programs Abroad: (academic year). ISSN 0082-8602. (Continues: U.S. Academic Programs Abroad and Undergraduate Study Abroad.) 1964. a. (formerly bi-a.) bibl. index. Institute of International Education, 809 United Nations Plaza, New York, NY 10017. Examined: 7th ed., 1977. Gail A. Cohen, ed. 146p. $4.50.
Aud: Jc, Cl, Pl

Arranged by continent, then by country and city, the guide provides full information on academic year programs, including location, dates, enrollment, fields of study, academic level, credits, pre-requisites, program of instruction and instructional language, housing, and travel. There are indexes to fields of study and sponsoring institutions, and the appendix lists consortia. The guide is intended primarily for undergraduates. BSM

ED 57
Whole World Handbook. ISSN 0070-1165. 1972. a. bibl. index. Council on International Educational Exchange, 777 United Nations Plaza, New York, NY 10017. Dist: Simon and Schuster, 630 Fifth Ave, New York, NY 10020. Examined: 4th ed., 1976/77. Margaret E. Sherman, ed. 367p. $2.95.
Aud: Hs, Jc, Cl, Pl

Subtitle: "A student guide to work, study, and travel abroad." Covers summer and academic year programs, providing information and advice on working, studying, and travelling abroad including costs and documents required. Arranged by geographic area and then by country, with introductory information on each area. Information on individual programs is extremely brief. Designed for high school and college level students. BSM

ED 58
WomenSports Magazine: Scholarship Guide Issue. a. Women Sports Publishing Co., Dept. WS1, 230 Park Ave, New York, NY 10017. Examined: 1977. 12p. $.50.
Aud: Hs, Jc, Cl, Pl

A geographically arranged list of about 400 colleges and universities offering approximately 10,000 athletic scholarships to women. The total estimated value of the scholarships is over $7,000,000. Entries include the name of the institution offering the scholarship, the name of the women's athletics director, address, number of scholarships available, and values and kinds of scholarships available. Published as part of the September issue of *WomenSports,* the guide is available separately for 50¢ postage and handling. JKM

ED 59
Yearbook of Higher Education. ISSN 0084-3784. 1969. a. index. Marquis Academic Media, 200 E Ohio St, Chicago, IL 60611. Examined: 9th ed., 1977/78. 727p. $44.50.
Aud: Jc, Cl, Pl

Comprehensive coverage of the world of higher education in the U.S. and considerable information on Canada. Part one is a directory of higher education institutions, two-year and four-year accredited schools, arranged by state. Those in Canada are arranged by province. Names of administrative personnel and department chairpersons are given. Part two includes statistics of U.S. higher education including enrollment, degrees granted, faculty, facilities, income, expenditures, students, and federal funding. Some figures are given for Canada. Part three, "Resource Information in Higher Education," lists associations, ERIC Clearinghouses, U.S. and Canadian consortia, and statewide boards of higher education. Indexes are by names of institutions and associations, and by statistical and resource information. Sources of statistics are listed. A very useful compendium, especially for the statistical information. BSM

INSTRUCTIONAL METHODS AND MATERIALS

ED 60
Audio-Visual Equipment Directory. ISSN 0571-8759. 1953. a. index. illus. National Audio-Visual Association, 3150 Spring St, Fairfax, VA 22030. Examined: 23rd ed., 1977/78. Sally Herickes, ed. 482p. $15; $13.50 to members.
Aud: Pl, Pf, Sa

Based on information supplied by manufacturers, the **Directory** covers more than 2000 models of audiovisual equipment. Seventy-four categories of equipment are listed. The arrangement within each category is alphabetical by company name and then by model. Each entry is accompanied by a picture and includes price, dimensions, weight, and electrical requirements. Foreign equipment available in North America is also listed. Indexes provide a geographical list of dealers and a list of manufacturers with addresses and telephone numbers. Clear and useful, even for the inexperienced. BSM

ED 61
Books for Secondary School Libraries. ISSN 0068-0184. (Continues: Three Thousand Books for Secondary School Libraries.) 1961. irreg. index. R. R. Bowker, 1180 Ave of the Americas, New York, NY 10036. Dist: R. R. Bowker, Box 1807, Ann Arbor, MI 48106. Examined: 5th ed., 1976. 526p. $15.95.
Aud: Pl, Pf, Sa

Compiled by a committee of librarians from member schools of the National Association of Independent Schools, this guide lists titles recommended for use by high school students who intend to go on to college. Arranged by Dewey classification number. Entries include Library of Congress cataloging information. Author, title, and subject indexes and a publisher directory are provided. Approximately 6300 nonfiction titles are listed; topics covered range from basic disciplines, such as literature, art, and social studies, to subjects of current concern, such as ecology, women, race relations, and space travel. JKM

ED 62
Educational Media Yearbook. ISSN 0000-037X. 1973. a. bibl. index. R. R. Bowker, 1180 Ave of the Americas, New York, NY 10036. Dist: R. R. Bowker, Box 1807, Ann Arbor, MI 48106. Examined: 4th ed., 1977. James W. Brown, ed. 559p. $19.95. (1978. $25.)
Aud: Cl, Pf, Sa

A useful compendium with articles by media experts and a huge amount of data of interest to those in educational media. Includes full information on national audiovisual organizations; a conference calendar; lists of foundations and federal granting agencies, doctoral programs, media competitions, prize-winning films, media periodicals, and directories and source lists; a directory of producers, publishers, and distributors; and an extensive bibliography of media about media. The articles review and capsulize significant aspects of the current status of educational media-related activities and developments in a variety of fields; discuss issues and dilemmas; provide guidelines for school and district media programs; and cover research and development, the sales and business outlook, the employment status of recent graduates of media specialist programs, and international media developments. BSM

ED 63-71
Educators Guides. Educators Progress Service, Randolph, WI 53956. Examined: 9v.
Aud: Pf, Sa

ED 63
Educators Guide to Free Audio and Video Materials. 1953. a. index. Examined: 24th ed., 1977. Walter Wittrich and James Berger, eds. 234p. $10.50.

ED 64
Educators Guide to Free Films. ISSN 0070-9395. 1941. a. index. Examined: 37th ed., 1977. John C. Diffor and Mary F. Horkheimer, eds. 731p. $12.75.

ED 65
Educators Guide to Free Filmstrips. ISSN 0070-9409. 1948. a. index. Examined: 29th ed., 1977. John C. Diffor and Mary Horkheimer, eds. 174p. $10.

ED 66
Educators Guide to Free Guidance Materials. ISSN 0070-9417. 1961. a. index. Examined: 16th ed., 1977. Mary Saterstrom, ed. $10.75.

ED 67
Educators Guide to Free Health, Physical Education, and Recreation Materials. ISSN 0424-6241. 1967. a. index. Examined: 10th ed., 1977. $11.

ED 68
Educators Guide to Free Science Materials. ISSN 0070-9425. 1959. a. index. Examined: 18th ed., 1977. 346p. $11.25.

ED 69
Educators Guide to Free Social Studies Materials. ISSN 0070-9433. 1960. a. index. Examined: 17th ed., 1977. 622p. $11.75.

ED 70
Educators Guide to Free Tapes, Scripts, Transcriptions. ISSN 0070-9441. 1953. a. index. Examined: 24th ed., 1977. $11.75.

ED 71
Educators Guide to Free Teaching Aids. ISSN 0070-9387. 1954. a. index. Examined: 23rd ed., 1977. $24.50.

These guides are selected annotated lists of materials that can be borrowed or obtained free of charge for use in elementary and secondary schools. All items have been reviewed by the Educators Progress Service staff. Entries include title, annotation, applicable physical details for type of media (e.g., film entries include running time, size, sound, etc.), source, availability, and restrictions on use. The date of publication of materials listed is included on some, but not all, entries. There are some listings of demonstration curriculum units that incorporate free materials. Includes source and availability lists and clear ordering information for U.S., Canadian, and Australian users. Each subject volume is arranged by type of media; each volume covering a specific medium is arranged by subject. Title and detailed subject indexes are included in all guides. New titles added since the previous edition are marked. The annual revision is sufficiently thorough to warrant replacement purchase. KMH/BSM

ED 72
El-Hi Textbooks in Print. ISSN 0070-9565. (Continues: Textbooks in Print.) 1927. a. index. R. R. Bowker, 1180 Ave of the Americas, New York, NY 10036. Dist: R. R. Bowker, Box 1807, Ann Arbor, MI 48106. Examined: 1976; 1977; 1978. 670p. $29.95.
Aud: Pf, Sa

Arranged by subject, this work indexes more than 30,000 textbooks designed for use in elementary and secondary classrooms. Entries give complete bibliographic and ordering information. Indexes to authors, titles, and textbook series, as well as a list of publishers with addresses are provided. Useful not only for ordering textbooks but also for tracking down elusive titles, especially those in series, which do not appear elsewhere. BSM

ED 73
Elementary Teachers Guide to Free Curriculum Materials. ISSN 0070-9980. 1944. a. bibl. index. Educators Progress Service, Randolph, WI 53956. Examined: 34th ed., 1977. Patricia H. Suttles and Kathleen S. Nehmer, eds. 368p. $10.50.
Aud: Pf, Sa

Like its companion volumes, **Educators Guide to Free Films,** etc., this very useful publication lists materials by subject, and has a subject index (more detailed than the subject arrangement), a title index, and an index of sources with names and addresses for U.S., Canadian, and Australian users. Ample descriptions are provided for materials included. The sections are on different colors of paper for easy access. BSM

ED 74
Guide to Reference Books for School Media Centers. Supplement. 1974/75. bi-a. Libraries Unlimited, Box 263, Littleton, CO 80160. Examined: 1974/75. 131p. $8.
Aud: Pf, Sa

A bibliography of selection tools and reference books for elementary and secondary schools and for junior colleges. The basic volume (1973, 496p., $17.50) listed over 2000 reference works and almost 200 print and nonprint selection tools. The first supplement, published in 1976, adds close to 520 titles. JKM

ED 75
Guides to Educational Media. (Continues: Guides to Newer Educational Media.) 1961. irreg. index. American Library Association, 50 E Huron St, Chicago, IL 60611. Examined: 4th ed., 1977. Margaret I. Rufsvold, ed. 159p.
Aud: Pf, Sa

Identifies and describes catalogs, indexes, lists, and reviewing services which systematically provide information about educational media: films, filmstrips, multimedia kits, programmed instruction materials, discs and tapes, slides, transparencies, and videotapes. The listing is comprehensive, not selective, and covers all levels of education. Provides full descriptions of 245 items, covering scope, arrangement, information in entries, and special features such as indexes and appendixes. The book is arranged alphabetically. The index covers authors, organizations, types of media, and subjects. BSM

ED 76
International Yearbook of Educational and Instructional Technology. (Continues: Association for Programmed Learning and Educational Technology. Yearbook.) 1972/73. a. bibl. Association for Programmed Learning and Educational Technology, Sweet and Maxwell, 11 New Fetter Lane, London, EC4, England. Dist: International Publications Service, 114 E 32nd St, New York, NY 10016. Examined: 1976/77. Anne Howe and A.J. Romiszowski, eds. 555p. $22.50.
Aud: Pf, Sa

Contains useful articles on trends in the field and on the state of educational technology by geographic area. The bulk of the volume is divided into several sections: a directory of associations, organizations, and research centers arranged by geographic area; a subject listing of programmed materials on the market with a list of publishers; and a guide to AV media on the market. The AV media section covers mostly hardware and lists sources of information on software. A rather specialized publication useful for the media person and for marketing purposes. BSM

ED 77-89
NICEM Indexes. National Information Center for

Educational Media, University of Southern California, University Park, Los Angeles, CA 90007. Examined: 1976. 13v. $430; $216.50 microfiche.
Aud: Pf, Sa

ED 77
NICEM Index to Educational Audio Tapes. bi-a. index. Examined: 4th ed., 1976. 28,000 entries. $47; $23.50 microfiche.

ED 78
NICEM Index to Educational Overhead Transparencies. bi-a. index. Examined: 5th ed., 1976. 2v. 60,000 entries. $75.50; $39.50 microfiche.

ED 79
NICEM Index to Educational Records. bi-a. index. Examined: 4th ed., 1976. 25,000 entries. $47; $23.50 microfiche.

ED 80
NICEM Index to Educational Slides. bi-a. index. Examined: 3rd ed., 1976. 28,000 entries. $52.50; $22 microfiche.

ED 81
NICEM Index to Educational Videotapes. bi-a. index. Examined: 4th ed., 1976. 15,000 entries. $29.50; $14.50 microfiche.

ED 82
NICEM Index to 8mm Motion Cartridges. bi-a. index. Examined: 5th ed., 1976. 26,000 entries. $47; $23.50 microfiche.

ED 83
NICEM Index to Environmental Studies—Multimedia. 1976. bi-a. index. Examined: 1st ed., 1976. 26,000 entries. $34.50; $18.50 microfiche.

ED 84
NICEM Index to Health and Safety Education—Multimedia. bi-a. index. Examined: 3rd ed., 1976. 33,000 entries. $47; $23.50 microfiche.

ED 85
NICEM Index to Producers and Distributors. bi-a. index. Examined: 4th ed., 1976. 16,000 entries. $21.50; $11 microfiche.

ED 86
NICEM Index to Psychology—Multimedia. bi-a. index. Examined: 3rd ed., 1976. 28,000 entries. $47; $23.50 microfiche.

ED 87
NICEM Index to 16mm Educational Films. bi-a. index. Examined: 6th ed., 1976. 4v. 100,000 entries. $109.50; $76.50 microfiche.

ED 88
NICEM Index to 35mm Educational Filmstrips. bi-a. index. Examined: 6th ed., 1976. 3v. 70,000 entries. $86.50; $45.50 microfiche.

ED 89
NICEM Index to Vocational and Technical Education—Multimedia. bi-a. index. Examined: 3rd ed., 1976. 32,000 entries. $47; $23.50 microfiche.

This series of indexes achieves what its 1964 predecessor, *Educational Media Index,* attempted to do, that is, to index and describe available nonprint materials. Compiled from the NICEM data bank, these volumes cover all levels of education and all kinds of media. Each entry includes a physical description, contents description, technical information appropriate for the medium, producer and distributor, and audience or grade level. The volumes which are devoted to a particular medium are accessible by subject. The four subject volumes have an index with a more detailed subject breakdown. Altogether, the series provides access to about half a million audiovisual titles. An ambitious project, the series is not perfect. Prices and dates are not included, and reading the complex code is not always a simple matter. BSM

ED 90
National Society for the Study of Education. Yearbook. ISSN 0077-5762. 1902. a. bibl. National Society for the Study of Education, 5835 Kimbard St, Chicago, IL 60637. Dist: University of Chicago Press, 5801 Ellis Ave, Chicago, IL 60637. Examined: 1977. 2v. $12 per v.
Aud: Cl, Pl, Sa
Indexed in: *Education Index.*

Collectively this series represents a current and historical overview of the study of education. It is published in two separate parts each year; occasionally, a third section is issued. Each part is devoted to a particular aspect of education usually of current, and often crucial, interest. Each part is composed of original articles and is edited by someone who is prominent in the particular area examined. From time to time a whole area of education is reviewed and subsequently re-reviewed. The volumes summarize major developments in thought, research efforts, and programs. Includes bibliographies. Individually and collectively indispensable as basic background information. The 1977 volume focused on "The Teaching of English and the Politics of Education"; the 1976 volume featured "Issues in Secondary Education" and the "Psychology of Teaching Methods." BSM

ED 91

A Selective Guide to Materials for Mental Health and Family Life Education. (Continues: Information Research Center for Mental Health and Family Hygiene; IRC Recommends.) 1973. bi-a. bibl. index. Mental Health Materials Center, 419 Park Ave S, New York, NY 10016. Dist: Gale Research Co., Book Tower, Detroit, MI 48226. Examined: 3rd ed., 1976. 947p. $65.
Aud: Pf, Sa

A weighty tome whose price has skyrocketed, but which is still a must if affordable. It presents a comprehensive list of print and nonprint materials, arranged by broad subject category, i.e., child growth and development, adults, and areas of special concern, such as alcoholism, delinquency, drugs, mental illness, disabilities, suicide, etc. Introductory material covers using the guide, ordering materials, using materials effectively, and a "Memorandum to Discussion Leaders." Each item is assigned a full page; the lengthy summary of contents is followed by an evaluation. Audiences and uses are covered in detail. Full ordering information is provided. Prices range from five cents to hundreds of dollars. There is a section on reference materials; a detailed subject index; a subject index for printed materials; an alphabetical listing of printed materials; and an alphabetical list of audiovisual materials. Appendix materials describe the Mental Health Materials Center. BSM

SPECIAL EDUCATION

ED 92

Chicorel Abstracts of Reading and Learning Disabilities Periodicals. 1976. a. Chicorel Library Publishing Corp., 275 Central Park W, New York, NY 10024. Examined: 1977. 906p. $45.
Aud: Cl, Sa

Signed abstracts of periodical articles on reading and learning disabilities. Arranged by broad subject, each abstract provides information on sources used by the author, conclusions reached, and audience level. Includes an author/title index, a subject index, and a list of journals abstracted with ordering information. This publication is volume 19 in the *Chicorel Index* series. JKM

ED 93

Convention of American Instructors of the Deaf. Proceedings. 1850. bi-a. index. illus. Convention of American Instructors of the Deaf, Kansas School for the Deaf, Olathe, KA 66061. Examined: 47th ed., 1975. Robert R. Davila, ed. 671p.
Aud: Sa

The published proceedings "represent not only a complete history of the organization from its founding in 1850, but also document developments and changes in the education of deaf persons during this period." The 1975 volume, subtitled "Our Learning Society—Issues and Themes in the Education of the Deaf," adds to the information accumulated by presenting papers delivered by specialists at the biennial meeting. Sample topics include preparing deaf youths for leadership roles, the deaf learner in a learner's society, current curriculum options as applied to the education of the deaf, etc. Lists of officers, past presidents, previous meetings, and present members, and the constitution of the organization are included. There is an index to the volume. MBP

ED 94

Directory for Exceptional Children. ISSN 0070-5012. 1954. irreg. (formerly bi-a.) index. Porter Sargent Publishers, 11 Beacon St, Boston, MA 02108. Examined: 7th ed., 1972; 8th ed., 1978. approx. 1240p. $25.
Aud: Cl, Pl, Sa

Subtitle: "A listing of educational and training facilities." A comprehensive publication describing more than 4000 schools, clinics, and treatment centers for disturbed, maladjusted, or handicapped children. Both public and private facilities are classified according to the problems with which they primarily deal. Entries, arranged by state within each section, describe facilities, staff, fees, and requirements for acceptance. Federal and state agencies, associations, societies, and foundations are also listed. Canadian resources are now included, as well as a general alphabetical index. The eighth edition was scheduled for publication in January 1978. BSM

ED 95

Educating the Disadvantaged. ISSN 0531-8327. 1968. a. bibl. AMS Press, 56 E 13th St, New York, NY 10003. Examined: 1973. Erwin Flaxman, ed. 498p. (1977. $75.)
Aud: Cl, Sa

An anthology of journal articles chosen from current education journals and documents "representative of significant issues in the education of the disadvantaged." Articles are grouped into the following sections: equal education opportunity, developmental states and ability, teachers and schools, school desegregation, and academic achievement and racial attitudes. KR/JKM

ED 96
Yearbook of Special Education. 1975/76. a. index. Marquis Who's Who, 200 E Ohio St, Chicago, IL 60611. Examined: 3rd ed., 1977/78. 700p. $34.50.
Aud: Cl, Pl

Includes statistical data, research findings and legislative reports on the status of the education and employment of gifted and handicapped persons in the U.S. Arranged in topical sections with a subject/geographic index. In the 1977/78 edition the sections were: general special education; physical education, job placement, and the medical, psychological, and social needs of the mentally retarded; the levels of impairment and employment of speech and hearing impaired persons; current data on the elimination of architectural barriers; employment of blind and visually impaired persons; definitions of and tested teaching techniques for the developmentally disabled; education and employment of gifted and talented persons; the rights of and litigation concerning gifted and handicapped persons; and inpatient facilities for the retarded. JKM

VOCATIONAL EDUCATION

ED 97
American Vocational Association. Yearbook. ISSN 0066-1163. 1967. a. bibl. American Vocational Association, 1510 H St, NW, Washington, DC 20005. Examined: 7th ed., 1974. Melvin L. Barlow, ed. 283p. $10. (11th ed., 1978. $12)
Aud: Cl, Pl, Sa

Each yearbook is individually titled and edited. The 1974 yearbook is entitled "The Philosophy for Quality Vocational Education Programs." It contains nine long essays on various aspects of the yearbook theme. The essays were written by experts in vocational education, general education, economics, home economics, and psychological studies. Many of the articles contain bibliographies, and are addressed primarily to teachers of vocational education. An earlier title in the series is "The Individual and His Education," edited by Alfred H. Krebs. KSK

ED 98
Barron's Guide to the Two-Year Colleges. (1977 is 6th ed.) irreg. index. Barron's Educational Series, 113 Crossways Park Dr, Woodbury, NY 11797. Examined: 6th ed., 1977. 2v. 416p. $17.45; $8.20 pap.
Aud: Jh, Hs, Jc, Cl, Pl

Covers junior and community colleges, technical and vocational institutions, business schools, and four-year colleges and universities offering two-year programs. Volume one provides descriptions of the institutions including admissions requirements, enrollment figures, costs and financial aid, religious affiliation if any, student-teacher ratio, campus size, academic and vocational programs offered, and, for residential colleges, information about student life. Volume two, the occupational program selector, is arranged by programs of study offered by the institutions listed in volume one. JKM

ED 99
Comparative Guide to Two-Year Colleges and Career Programs. 1976. bi-a. index. Harper and Row, 10 E 53rd St, New York, NY 10022. Examined: 1st ed., 1976. James Cass and Max Birnbaum, eds. 545p. $15; $6.95 pap.
Aud: Jh, Hs, Pl

Relatively brief information is given for each institution: size of full-time and part-time student body, admission requirements, degrees offered, programs, academic calendar, facilities, and costs. Entries are arranged by state and then alphabetically by institution. Public and private institutions are included in one list. Useful appendixes cover training programs offering above average job opportunities, an alphabetical list of careers with the institutions offering training in them, and an index of religiously affiliated schools. There is no institution index. BSM

ED 100
Directory of Postsecondary Schools With Occupational Programs. 1970. bi-a. index. National Center for Educational Statistics, Washington, DC. Dist: Superintendent of Documents, U.S. Government Printing Office, Washington, DC 20402. Examined: 3rd ed., 1975/76. Evelyn R. Kay, ed. 405p. $5.50.
Aud: Jh, Hs, Jc, Pl

Nearly 12,000 public and private institutions which offer postsecondary occupational programs below the baccalaureate level are listed. The brief entries, arranged alphabetically by state and city, cover accreditation, telephone number, and programs offered. Some statistical information is provided. Indexes of schools and programs are included. Much less expensive than the **College Blue Book** volume on occupational education, but provides less information. BSM

ED 101
Lovejoy's Career and Vocational School Guide. ISSN

0076-1346. 1955. irreg. index. Simon and Schuster, 1230 Ave of the Americas, New York, NY 10019. Examined: 4th ed., 1973. Clarence E. Lovejoy, ed. approx. 180p. $7.95; $3.95 pap. (1978.)
Aud: Jh, Hs, Jc, Pl

Subtitle: "A source book, clue book, and directory of institutions training for job opportunities." Lists 1550 selected occupations, 679 Army careers, career and trade organizations, and schools offering job training. Schools are arranged by vocation and then by state. Brief information is provided for each school. There is an index to schools. Useful for its inclusion of military career opportunities not found elsewhere. A new edition is scheduled for publication in Fall 1978. BSM

ED 102
Technician Education Yearbook. ISSN 0082-2353. 1963. bi-a. bibl. illus. Prakken Publications, 416 Longshore Dr, Ann Arbor, MI 48107. Examined: 7th ed., 1975/76. Lawrence W. Prakken and Jerome C. Patterson, eds. 350p. $16
Aud: Hs, Jc, Cl, Pl

A nationwide listing of approximately 1850 schools offering technician training. Besides the basic directory, the **Yearbook** also contains brief articles on current problems and innovations in technical education written by professors and other experts in the field. The articles are illustrated with photographs, and frequently include brief bibliographies. Another section contains case studies of vocational programs in specific schools written by professors at those schools. These are also illustrated with photographs. The major section of the book includes the directories of institutions, technologies, and officials. Data are obtained from questionnaires returned by the institutions themselves. The first directory is a listing of institutions offering technician training. It is arranged alphabetically by state, and then by institution within the state. Information includes address, whether the school is public or private, the president and other top administrators, total enrollment, technician enrollment, accreditation, admission requirements, and the types of technologies offered by institutions. Under the name of the technology is a listing of colleges arranged by state. The last listing is a directory of federal and state officials of technician education. Section four gives current occupational information about technicians from the U.S. Bureau of Labor Statistics. Section five gives information on professional organizations that are concerned with technician education, including officers and staffs of those organizations. Finally, there is a bibliography of books, pamphlets, and magazine articles that have been published since the last edition of the **Yearbook** or that were inadvertently omitted from that edition. KSK/BSM

HUMANITIES

GENERAL WORKS

HU 1
Alfred P. Sloan Foundation. Report. ISSN 0065-6216. 1938. a. Alfred P. Sloan Foundation, 630 Fifth Ave, New York, NY 10020. Examined: 1977. 80p. free.
Aud: Cl, Pl

A report on the Sloan Foundation's programs by subject area, plus a financial report and a statement from the president. KAC

HU 2
American Council of Learned Societies. Annual Report. ISSN 0065-7972. 1958. a. American Council of Learned Societies, 345 E 46th St, New York, NY 10017. Examined: 1976/77. 105p. free.
Aud: Cl, Pl

The American Council of Learned Societies is a federation of 42 national scholarly organizations concerned with the humanities or the humanistic aspects of the social sciences. The report includes information on its activities, special projects, awards to individuals, and a financial report. KAC

HU 3
Andrew W. Mellon Foundation. Annual Report. ISSN 0066-1694. 1969. a. Andrew W. Mellon Foundation, 140 E 62nd St, New York, NY 10021. Examined: 1977. 74p. free.
Aud: Cl, Pl

Each issue includes a financial statement, the president's report, and a summary of grants given in major program areas. KAC

HU 4
Annuale Mediaevale. 1960. a. illus. Humanities Press, Atlantic Highlands, NJ 07716. Examined: v. 15, 1975, Herbert H. Petit, ed., 158p.; v. 17, 1976. $10; $13.50 to libraries and institutions.
Aud: Cl, Sa

A journal of scholarly articles concerning aspects of medieval life. Titles of articles in volume 15 include "Some Aspects of Meaning in Anglo-Saxon Art and Literature," "Civic Concern and Iconography in the York Passion Play," etc. There are illustrations accompanying the various articles. JKM

HU 5
British Academy, London. Proceedings. ISSN 0068-1202. 1903. a. Oxford University Press, Ely House, 37 Dover St, London WIX 4AH, England. Dist: Oxford University Press, 200 Madison Ave, New York, NY 10016. Examined: v. 61, 1975; v. 62, 1976. $33.50.
Aud: Cl, Pl

In addition to the annual report of the Academy, the proceedings lists the officers and council members, and sometimes the Academy's fellows. Also included are the presidential address and a collection of lectures given during the year on philosophy, literature, history, economics, and other subjects. KAC

HU 6
British Humanities Index. ISSN 0007-0815. (Continues: Subject Index to Periodicals.) 1962. a. w/q. suppls. index. The Library Association, 7 Ridgmount St, London WC1E 7AE, England. Examined: 1976. B. M. King, ed. 216p. $67.70.
Aud: Cl, Sa

An author and subject index to about 375 current British humanities journals (e.g., *Cambridge Quarterly, Kipling Journal, Poetry Australia, Welsh History Review*). Arranged alphabetically by subject heading. Entries include title, author, magazine title, volume, and pagination. There is an author index in the annual volume. KMH

HU 7
Carnegie Corporation of New York. Annual Report. 1921. a. index. Carnegie Corporation of New York, 473 Madison Ave, New York, NY 10022. Examined: 1974. 106p. free.
Aud: Cl, Pl

Includes the report of the president, a report on programs listing grants and books resulting from grants, a report of the secretary, and a report of the treasurer. There is also a list of grant recipients with their addresses and an index to the lists of grants. JKM

HU 8
Current Research in British Studies by American and Canadian Scholars. ISSN 0590-417X. (Continues: Current Research in British Studies by North American Scholars.) 1953. quadrennial. index. Kansas State University, Military Affairs, Aerospace Historian Publishing, Eisenhower Hall, Manhattan, KS 66506. Examined: 7th ed., 1975. Phyllis W. Butmann and William A. Butmann, eds. 161p. $4.
Aud: Cl, Sa

A catalog of research, including doctoral research, in British and Imperial studies in progress by North American scholars. It is arranged by the time period being studied, with a separate section for British Empire research. The author index includes the addresses of the scholars listed. KAC

HU 9
Ford Foundation. Annual Report. ISSN 0071-7274. 1952. a. bibl. index. illus. Ford Foundation, 320 E 43rd St, New York, NY 10017. Examined: 1977. 75p. free.
Aud: Cl, Pl

A report from the president, a report on the Foundation's programs, and a financial statement are included. There is also a bibliography of books and reports published under Foundation grants. KAC

HU 10
Humanities Index. ISSN 0095-5981. (Continues: Social Science and Humanities Index; International Index to Periodicals.) 1974. a. w/q. suppls. H. W. Wilson, 950 University Ave, Bronx, NY 10452. Examined: 1976/77, 1025p.; Mar. 1978 suppl. 275p. service basis.
Aud: Hs, Jc, Cl, Pl

An author and subject index in one alphabet to over 250 periodicals in the fields of archaeology and classical studies, area studies, folklore, history, language and literature, literary and political criticism, performing arts, philosophy, religion and theology, and related subjects in the humanities. Complete bibliographic information is given under each entry. A separate book review section is arranged alphabetically by author of the work reviewed. A list of the periodicals indexed with address and subscription information is included. Supersedes and expands the humanities portion of the *Social Science and Humanities Index* (1965-74) and the *International Index to Periodicals* (1907-65). KMH

HU 11
Index to Book Reviews in the Humanities. ISSN 0073-5892. 1960. a. Phillip Thomson, 836 Georgia St, Williamston, MI 48895. Examined: v. 17, 1976. Phillip Thompson, ed. 402p. $20.
Aud: Cl, Pl

An index to book reviews in several hundred humanities periodicals. The entries are arranged alphabetically by the name of the author of the work reviewed. Prior to 1970, history and some related social science disciplines were included in the publication's definition of "humanities." Since that date, the disciplines covered are: art and architecture, biography, personal narratives and memoirs, drama and dance, folklore, language and literature, music, philosophy, and travel and adventure. KAC/JKM

HU 12
John Simon Guggenheim Memorial Foundation. Reports of the President and the Treasurer. 1939. a. John Simon Guggenheim Memorial Foundation, 90 Park Ave, New York, NY 10016. Examined: 1976. 145p. free.
Aud: Cl, Pl

Includes a report from the president and the treasurer of the Foundation and biographies of the Foundation's fellows. KAC

HU 13
Journal of the Warburg and Courtauld Institutes. (Continues: Journal of the Warburg Institute.) 1938. a. index. illus. The Warburg Institute, University of London, Woburn Sq, London WC1H 0AB England. Examined: v. 39, 1976. D. S. Chambers and Elizabeth McGrath, eds. 292p. £10.

Contains beautifully illustrated scholarly articles on civilization, religion, art, etc. There is a list of contributors, a general index, an index of manuscripts, and a list of publications available. A section entitled "Notes to Contributors" explains when and how to submit articles for publication. JKM

HU 14
Lilly Endowment, Inc. Report. ISSN 0457-8910. 1950. a. illus. Lilly Endowment, 2801 E Meridian St, Indianapolis, IN 46208. Examined: 1976. free.
Aud: Cl, Pl

An annual report on grants given, investments made, and the financial statement of the Lilly Endowment. KAC

HU 15
Medievalia et Humanistica: Studies in Medieval and Renaissance Culture. ISSN 0076-6127. 1970. a. Cambridge University Press, 32 E 57th St, New York, NY 10022. Examined: v. 8, 1977. Paul Clogan, ed. 224p. $22.50.
Aud: Cl, Pl
Indexed in: *Modern Language Association of America, MLA International Bibliography; Reader's Guide.*

Each issue has a theme, such as medieval poetics, medieval historiography, or medieval and renaissance spirituality. Articles and notes are included. The publication is sponsored by the Comparative Studies in Medieval Literature Section of the Modern Language Association. KAC

HU 16
National Endowment for the Humanities. Annual Report. ISSN 0083-2111. 1966. a. illus. National Endowment for the Humanities, National Foundation on the Arts and the Humanities, Washington, DC 20506. Dist: Superintendent of Documents, U.S. Government Printing Office, Washington, DC 20402. Examined: 10th ed., 1975; 11th ed., 1976. 168p. free.
Aud: Cl, Pl

Includes a report from each division of the National Endowment, a summary of grants and awards made, and a financial report. KAC

HU 17
Renaissance and Modern Studies. ISSN 0486-3720. 1957. a. illus. Sisson and Parker, 25 Wheeler Gate, Nottingham, England. Examined: v. 19, 1975; v. 21, 1977. John Lucas, ed. 141p. £2.75.
Aud: Cl, Sa

A journal of scholarly articles on various aspects of the renaissance or modern times. Poetry is also included in most volumes. Each volume focuses on a specific theme, e.g., the 1977 volume focuses on literature and ideology and includes such articles as "Christopher Caudwell's Illusions," "Orwell in Spain," and "Socialist Fiction in the 1930's." The last section provides notes on contributors and there is a table of contents in the back. Most volumes include illustrations, but there are none in the 1977 issue. JKM

HU 18
Rockefeller Foundation. Annual Report. ISSN 0080-3391. (Continues: Rockefeller Foundation. The President's Review and Annual Report. ISSN 0057-885X.) 1914. a. index. Rockefeller Foundation, 1133 Ave of the Americas, New York, NY 10036. Examined: 1976. John H. Knowles. 122p. free.
Aud: Cl, Pl, Sa

Opens with a list of trustees and trustee committees, a list of headquarters' officers and staff, a list of staff in the foundation's eight divisions (agricultural sciences, arts, health sciences, humanities, international relations, natural and environmental sciences, social sciences, and fellowship and information service), and a list of field staff in various countries. This is followed by a section containing information on organizational meetings and officers and the annual "President's Review." The section on grants and programs, the major portion of the report, provides detailed information on the Foundation's grants and programs in the following areas: conquest of hunger, population and health, education, conflict in international relations, equal opportunity, arts, humanities and contemporary values, quality of environment, special interests and explorations, and study awards. Complete financial statements comprise the final section of the report. There is an index to the volume. JKM

HU 19
Winterthur Portfolio. ISSN 0084-0416. 1964. a. index. illus. University Press of Virginia, Box 3608, University Sta, Charlottesville, VA 22903. Examined: v. 11, 1976. Ian M. G. Quimby, ed. 251p. $10.
Aud: Cl, Pl
Indexed in: *Répertoire d'art et d'archéologie.*

The intent of this publication is "to make available to the serious student an authoritative reference for the investigation and documentation of early American culture." Articles in volume 11 discuss American caricature in the early 19th century, glass productions in the U.S. in the 18th century, Sargent's murals in the Boston Public Library, and architect Stanford White. Contributors include experts from various professions: professors, historians, librarians, and museum curators. Articles are documented and accompanied by illustrations. There is an index of subjects, names, and illustrations in one alphabetical sequence. GV

ART AND ARCHITECTURE

HU 20
American Academy of Arts and Sciences. Records of the Academy. ISSN 0065-6844. (Continues: American Academy of Arts and Sciences. Proceedings.) 1958/59. a. index. American Academy of Arts and Sciences, 165 Allendale St, Jamaica Plain Sta, Boston,

MA 02130. Examined: 1975/76. Stephen Graubard, ed. 153p. $2.50.
Aud: Sa

Contains the charter, statutes, and annual reports of the various committees and officers of the American Academy of Arts and Sciences of Boston. Members of the Academy are listed in a classified section, and an alphabetical index of members is included. GV

HU 21
American Architects Directory. ISSN 0065-695X. 1956. irreg. index. American Institute of Architects, 1735 New York Ave, NW, Washington, DC 20006. Dist: R. R. Bowker Co., 1180 Ave of the Americas, New York, NY 10036. Examined: 2nd ed., 1962; 3rd ed., 1970. 1126p. $38.95. (1978.)
Aud: Cl, Sa
Indexed in: *Biographical Dictionaries Master Index.*

An alphabetical listing of 23,000 living American architects. The directory is sponsored by the American Institute of Architects (AIA) whose members are listed automatically; also lists selected architects who are not members of AIA. Entries provide brief biographical data, present employment, state registrations, lists of up to five principal works, publications, and awards. The preface contains a roster of AIA officers and award winners. Also includes a necrology section and a geographic index. GV

HU 22
American Art Directory. ISSN 0065-6968. (Continues: American Art Annual.) 1898. bi-a. index. illus. R. R. Bowker Co., 1180 Ave of the Americas, New York, NY 10036. Dist: R. R. Bowker Co., Box 1807, Ann Arbor, MI 48106. Examined: 46th ed., 1976. Jaques Cattell Press, ed. 536p. $39.95. (47th ed., 1978. 719p. $42.50.)
Aud: Cl, Pl

Title and frequency vary: v. 1-37, 1898-1945/48 appeared as the *American Art Annual;* 1898-1900 and 1911-1949 irregular; 1901/02 and 1902/03 never issued; 1904-1910 biennial; 1952-1976 triennial. **Who's Who in American Art** was published as part two from 1936-1947, and since then as a separate publication.

Contains geographic listings of art museums, organizations, and art schools in the U.S., Canada, and abroad. The major section lists U.S. museums, libraries, and associations by state. The entries provide specific information, including curators, hours of service, special collections and exhibitions, libraries, publications, and often figures on attendance and income. Canadian art organizations and major museums abroad are listed in separate chapters. The section on U.S., Canadian, and selected foreign art schools provides specific information about faculty, tuition, entrance requirements, and major areas of study. Also includes lists of state arts councils, periodicals and newspapers carrying art notes, scholarships, travelling exhibitions, and booking agencies. Since 1913 this standard reference tool has been published by or for the American Federation of Arts. GV

HU 23
American Research Center in Egypt. Journal. ISSN 0065-9991. 1962. a. illus. American Research Center in Egypt, Princeton, NJ 08540. Dist: J. J. Augustin, Locust Valley, NY 11568. Examined: v. 13, 1976. Gerald E. Kadish, ed. 161p. $20.
Aud: Cl, Sa

A scholarly publication dealing with all periods of Egyptian history and culture: Pharaonic, Hellenistic, Islamic, and modern Egyptian. Issued by the American Research Center in Egypt, it is dedicated to publishing quality research articles. The 1976 issue contains contributions dealing with ancient Egyptian methods of raising weights, the origin of the "cap-crown" of Nefertiti, and observations on 18th dynasty royal sculpture. Articles are amply footnoted and accompanied by plates and diagrams. Also includes a section of signed critical book reviews. GV

HU 24
Annual of Advertising, Editorial, and Television Art and Design with the Annual Copy Awards. (Continues: Annual of Advertising, Editorial, and Television Art and Design. ISSN 0066-4014.) 1921. a. illus. Watson-Guptill Publications, One Astor Plaza, New York, NY 10036. Examined: 55th ed., 1976. Jennifer Place, ed. unpaged (893 items). $25.
Aud: Sa

Title varies: volumes published in 1921-1937, 1940-1941, 1943-1945, and 1947-1950/51 were titled *Annual of Advertising and Editorial Art*; the 1938-1939, 1942, and 1964 volumes were published as *Art Directors Annual of Advertising Art.*

A catalog of works by the finalists in the annual exhibition held as a joint effort by the Art Directors Club and the Copy Club of New York. Works by the 893 finalists in 1976 are arranged by categories: print advertising, radio and television (text), editorials, books, graphic design, and photography and illustration. The numbered entries include information on the art director, writer, photographer, agency, and client and are accompanied by a reproduction of the entry. Recipients of the gold and silver medals are indicated. GV

HU 25
Architectural History. ISSN 0066-622X. 1958. a. illus. Society of Architectural Historians of Great Britain, 8 Belmont Ave, Melton Park, Newcastle-upon-Tyne NE3 5QD, England. Examined: v. 19, 1976. J. Mordaunt Crook, ed. $12.15. (v. 20, 1978.)
Aud: Cl, Sa

A scholarly publication of the Society of Architectural Historians of Great Britain which deals with "significant source material as well as results of original research on the history of architecture in Great Britain." A section of glossy plates appears at the back of each issue. GV

HU 26
Architectural Schools in North America. ISSN 0092-7856. 1947. a. Association of Collegiate Schools of Architecture, 1735 New York Ave, NW, Washington, DC 20006. Examined: 1973/74. David Clarke, ed. 193p. $3. (1977.)
Aud: Cl, Sa

An alphabetical listing of architectural schools in North America which presents tabulated information on the numbers and types of students, degrees offered, fees, faculty, and requirements. The special areas of concentration and activities of schools are mentioned. GV

HU 27
Archives of Asian Art. ISSN 0066-6637. (Continues: Chinese Art Society of America. Archives.) 1945/46. a. index. illus. Asia Society, 112 E 64th St, New York, NY 10021. Examined: v. 30, 1976/77. John Rosenfield, ed. 126p. $15.
Aud: Cl, Sa

A scholarly publication concerned with the history and current state of Asian art. The 1976/77 issue contains extensively illustrated articles dealing with the authenticity of early Chinese handscrolls, the dating of art in Buddhist caves, and a study of a 20th century Japanese graphic designer. Since 1956, acquisitions in the field of Asian art by museums in the U.S. and Canada have been listed; entries include illustrations, dating, and provenance. Prior to 1956, only selected acquisitions of public museums were included. A complete list of acquisitions from 1974 to 1976 appears in the supplement *Museums Acquisitions Register*. There is a cumulated index to the first 20 volumes (1945 to 1965). GV

HU 28
Arts Orientalis. ISSN 0571-1371. 1954. irreg. bibl. illus. Freer Gallery of Art, Smithsonian Institution, Washington, DC 20560. Examined: v. 10, 1975. 105p. $30. (1978.)
Aud: Cl, Sa
Indexed in: *Art Index.*

Subtitle: "The arts of Islam and the East." A joint publication of the Freer Gallery of Art and the University of Michigan Department of Fine Arts. Dedicated to "the beauty and civilization of the East," it seems to fill the gap caused by the cessation of *Ars Islamica* (1934-1951). It contains scholarly articles which are copiously illustrated with plates, line drawings, and maps. Volume two is the "Charles Lang Freer Centennial Volume." Volume ten contains bibliographies of works by M. Loehn and R. J. Geltems as well as articles on Rajput painting, the influence of Li T'ang, and rule line painting in China. Numerous illustrations accompany the text. GV

HU 29
Art and Crafts Market. ISSN 0147-2461. (Continues: Artist's Market; Artist's and Photographer's Market.) 1974. a. index. illus. Writer's Digest, 993 Alliance Rd, Cincinnati, OH 45242. Examined: 1978. Lynne Lapin and Betsy Wones, eds. 655p. $10.95.
Aud: Cl, Sa

Describes 4498 potential purchasers of architectural designs, fine art, cartoons, commercial art, calligraphy, crafts, animation, fashion designs, and other arts and crafts. Entries are classified by type of market and advertising agencies, publishers, galleries, dealers, etc. Entries include the name and address of the person to contact, rate of payment, and type of work solicited. Special needs and tips on breaking into a specific area are offered frequently. Articles provide advice on freelancing techniques and contracts, information on the new copyright law, a section on competitions and exhibitions, and lists of dealers and galleries arranged alphabetically by state. Includes a glossary of art terms and an index of individual buyers. GV

HU 30
Art at Auction: The Year at Sotheby's and Parke-Bernet. ISSN 0084-6783. (Continues: Ivory Hammer; Sotheby's Annual Review.) 1962/63. a. index. illus. Rizzoli International Publications, 712 Fifth Ave, New York, NY 10019. Examined: 1974/75. Anne Jackson,

ed. 464p. (1976/77. $28.50.)
Aud: Cl, Sa

Documents the most important transactions in the art world by listing items sold during that fiscal year at the merged auction houses of Sotheby's of London and Parke-Bernet of New York. Items are arranged by category, i.e., pictures, drawings, and sculptures, with subdivisions for old masters, European, American, and modern artists. Other categories include: prints, manuscripts, books, glass and paperweights, art nouveau and art deco, wine, games, jewelry, etc. Signed commentaries on more general topics are interspersed throughout. Numerous black-and-white and color illustrations accompany the text. GV

HU 31
Art Design Photo. ISSN 0306-817X. (Continues in part: LOMA: Literature on Modern Art.) 1972. a bibl. index. illus. Alexander Davis Publications, 43 South Hill Rd, Hemel Hempstead, Herts, HP1 1JB, England. Dist: Art Book Co., 136 E 65th St, New York, NY 10021. Examined: 1974. Alexander Davis, ed. 220p. $60. (1978.)
Aud: Cl, Pl

An annual bibliography of books, catalogs, and articles on modern art, graphic design, photography, and art libraries. Provides international coverage of late 19th and 20th century art and artists, photography, and graphic design, including ceramics, textiles, jewelry, and fashion as well as art movements, museums, education, and libraries. Arranged first by artists, then alphabetically by subjects. Brief entries provide full bibliographic information. An extensive index provides access to subjects, museums, art terms, photography items. Coverage overlaps that of *Artbibliographies Modern* (Santa Barbara, CA: ABC Clio, 1973-); both publications are successors to *LOMA* which was also edited by Alexander Davis. GV

HU 32
Art Index. 1929. a. w/q. suppls. H. W. Wilson Co., 950 University Ave, Bronx, NY 10452. Examined: 1975/76. 905p. service basis.
Aud: Jc, Cl, Pl

An author and subject index to approximately 152 art periodicals and museum bulletins. The emphasis is on U.S. periodicals, but important foreign titles are covered; the titles indexed are selected by the subscribers. All art fields are included: archaeology, architecture, art history, arts and crafts, fine arts, graphic arts, industrial design, interior design, photography and films, planning and landscape design, and related subjects. Index entries include information about reproductions or other illustrations. There is an index to book reviews, arranged alphabetically by the author of the work reviewed, in a separate section. JKM

HU 33
Art/Kunst. 1972. a. bibl. index. W. Jaeggi, AG, Freie Str 40, CH-4001 Basel, Switzerland. Dist: International Publications Service, 114 E 32nd St, New York, NY 10016. Examined: v. 1, 1972, 88p., $7.50; v. 4, 1975. W. Jaeggi, ed. 116p.
Aud: Cl, Pl

An international bibliography of art books, including exhibition catalogs, published during the previous year. Compiled from information supplied by cooperating publishers. Lists new books in a classified subject arrangement: general aesthetics, art epochs, art forms and techniques, popular arts, arts and crafts, publications about individual artists, and catalogs and guides. Price and ordering information is provided. Contains an index of authors, editors, and artists. GV

HU 34
Art Prices Current. 1907/08; 1921/22. a. index. William Dawson and Sons, Cannon House, Folkestone, Kent CT19 5EE, England. Dist: International Publications Service, 114 E 32nd St, New York, NY 10016. Examined: v. 49, 1971/72. various pagings. $45. (1975, 575p.; 1978.)
Aud: Sa

A British publication that lists sale prices and buyers' names for selected paintings, drawings, miniatures, and prints auctioned during the year at the principal London, continental, and American auction rooms. Issued in two parts starting with volume 29. Part A covers paintings, etc., and part B covers engravings and prints. Entries are arranged numerically with indexes of artists, engravers, and collections. The first series was published from 1907 to 1916; a new series was begun in 1921/22. GV

HU 35
Artists/USA. 1970/71. bi-a. illus. Artists/USA, 1315 Walnut St, Philadelphia, PA 19107. Examined: 1977/78. 176p. $30.
Aud: Cl, Pl

A directory of fewer than 500 selected living American artists and European artists who are currently exhibiting in the U.S. Includes artists who work in the field of painting, sculpture, photography, textile design, and lithography. Arranged alphabetically by artist, entries include: the artist's name and address; awards; galleries, exhibitions, and collections; a short biography; and reproductions of works with title, size, medium, and price. Attempts to bring together the artist and the potential buyer. GV

HU 36
Avery Index to Architectural Periodicals. Supplement. 1963. irreg. G. K. Hall and Co., 70 Lincoln St, Boston, MA 02111. Examined: 1977. 882p.
Aud: Pf, Sa

Reproduces the catalog cards for the periodical holdings of the Avery Architectural Library at Columbia University. A list of the over 500 periodical titles included and a list of periodical titles that were added to the collection between 1973 and 1976 precedes the catalog card reproductions. JKM

HU 37
Bibliographic Guide to Art and Architecture. 1975. a. G. K. Hall, 70 Lincoln St, Boston, MA 02111. Examined: 1977. 861p. $95.
Aud: Cl, Pf, Sa

Supplements *Dictionary Catalog of the Art and Architecture Division*, the Research Libraries of New York Public Library (G. K. Hall, 1975). Contains complete cataloging information for all books and nonprint materials cataloged by the Library of Congress and the New York Public Library Reseach Libraries during the preceding year in the areas of painting, drawing, sculpture, history and design, city planning, printmaking, engraving, costume and metal work. Main entries, added entries, titles, series, and LC subject headings are arranged in one alphabet. JKM

HU 38
Female Artists Past and Present. 1971. irreg. index. Women's History Research Center, 2325 Oak St, Berkeley, CA 94708. Examined: 2nd ed., 1974. 158p. $6; $5 to individual women.
Aud: Cl, Pl, Sa

Contains a listing of individual women artists practicing today. There is also a classified subject index listing women artists under different specialties, i.e., ceramics, drawing, textile arts, etc. Another section lists women working in other areas of the visual arts, including art historians and gallery personnel. Also provides information on contemporary female artists' movements, groups, articles, publications, etc. JKM

HU 39
Fine Arts Marketplace. ISSN 0000-0361. 1973/74. bi-a. index. R. R. Bowker Co., 1180 Ave of the Americas, New York, NY 10036. Dist: R. R. Bowker Co., Box 1807, Ann Arbor, MI 48106. Examined: 1975/76. Paul Cummings, ed. 497p. $16.50.
Aud: Cl, Sa

A directory of organizations, businesses, and individuals concerned with the fine arts field. Provides information on locations, telephone numbers, lists of personnel, products, and areas of special interest. The largest section lists art dealers, photography dealers, auction houses, reproduction publishers, art book stores, and museum stores by geographical area. The services section, which is also arranged by geographical area, lists photographers, packers and movers, insurers, advertising agencies, restorers, and framers. The third major part, the suppliers section, is arranged alphabetically by names of retailers; it does not contain full information about the firms listed but refers the reader back to the first section. In the 1976 edition, photography dealers are listed with retailers. The index of names includes the addresses and telephone numbers of individuals and firms. GV

HU 40
Graphis Annual. ISSN 0072-5528. 1952/53. a. index. illus. Walter Herdeg, Graphis Press, 107 Dufourstrasse, CH8008 Zurich, Switzerland. Dist: Hastings House, 10 E 40th St, New York, NY 10016. Examined: 25th ed., 1976/77. Walter Herdeg, ed. 235p. $37.50.
Aud: Sa

Subtitle: "International annual of advertising and editorial graphics." An international survey of graphics in advertisements, annual reports, booklets, book jackets, magazine covers, trademarks, letterheads, and record covers, and of film and television editorial design. The numbered entries (782 in the 1976/77 edition) are accompanied by black-and-white or color illustrations and a text in English, French, and German that supplies data on title, artist, designer, art director, agency, and publisher. The arrangement of the bilingual text makes browsing difficult since the data are not arranged according to the language; each item is given in all three languages, thus necessitating reference to six different places on a given page. GV

HU 41
Graphis Posters. 1973. a. index. illus. Walter Herdeg, Graphis Press, 107 Dufourstrasse, CH8008 Zurich, Switzerland. Dist: Hastings House, 10 E 40th St, New York, NY 10016. Examined: 1977. Walter Herdeg, ed. 211p. $37.50.
Aud: Sa

Subtitle: "International annual of poster art." An international review of selected poster art covering the previous year. The 1977 edition includes 715 numbered entries arranged by categories: advertising, cultural, social, and consumer posters. Information for each item includes a black-and-white or color reproduction of the poster and a text in English, French, and German which gives title, artist, designer, art director, and agency. The name index lists addresses of poster publishers. GV

HU 42
Illustrators. ISSN 0073-5477. 1959. a. index. illus. Hastings House Publishers, 10 E 40th St, New York, NY 10016. Examined: v. 18, 1977. Don Barron, ed. 496p. $24.50.
Aud: Sa

Subtitle: "The annual of American illustration." The 1977 edition reproduces the entries in the 18th annual national exhibition of the Society of Illustrators which was held in New York City. Included are 497 examples of works by American illustrators in the areas of editorial, institutional, advertising, and book illustration. Category of work, artist, art director, publisher(s), advertising agency, and often the title are given for each entry. Reproductions of illustrations are in black-and-white and in color with a warning that alteration in color may have occurred in the printing process. Book titles are not provided for illustrations which appeared in books, and no biographical data is included about the artists. GV

HU 43
International Auction Records. ISSN 0074-1922. 1967. a. illus. Editions Publisol, 185 E 85th St, New York, NY 10028. Examined: v. 10, 1976. E. Mayer, ed. $52. (v. 12, 1978. $70).
Aud: Sa

Title varies: *International Yearbook of Sales.*

A guide to major sales at auction houses in the U.S. and abroad. The 1976 edition quotes over 25,000 prices collected in the course of the principal sales between January 1975 and January 1976. Entries are classified by general areas (engravings, drawings, watercolors, paintings, and sculptures) and then arranged alphabetically by artist within each area. Name of artist, dates, title of work, a short description, size, price, and place of sale are provided for each item. GV

HU 44
International Who's Who in Art and Antiques. 1972. tri-a. illus. Melrose Press, Market Hill, Cambridge CB2 3QP, England. Dist: Rowman and Littlefield, 81 Adams Dr, Totowa, NJ 07512. Examined: 1st ed., 1972. Ernest Kay, ed. 629p. $37.50. (2nd ed., 1976.)
Aud: Cl, Pl

An international biographical directory that lists selected living artists, art educators, gallery and museum directors, art and antique collectors, dealers and auctioneers, publishers of art and antique books, antiquarian and art booksellers, restorers, etc. Includes over 4,000 entries from 58 countries, arranged alphabetically by biographer. Entries provide a brief curriculum vitae, including exhibitions, awards, and publications. The appendixes include a 64-page section of reproductions and listings of art schools, museums and galleries, art associations, and art scholarships and grants arranged geographically by country within each category. GV

HU 45
Journal of Glass Studies. 1959. a. bibl. index. illus. Corning Museum of Glass, Corning Glass Center, Corning, NY 14830. Examined: v. 18, 1976. John H. Martin, ed. 279p. $15.
Aud: Sa

A specialized publication whose bicentennial issue focuses on John Frederick Amelung, the distinguished 18th century American glassmaker. Articles trace his background, and the issue includes a descriptive catalog of his works (accompanied by numerous plates) and a bibliography on Amelung. There is also a description of archeological excavations conducted at the New Bremen Glass Manufactury and the results of chemical analyses of Amelung glass. A regular feature is the unannotated, classed checklist of articles and books on glass published during the previous year. Volume 15 includes a cumulative index to volumes issued from 1959 to 1973. GV

HU 46
Libraries, Museums, and Art Galleries Year Book. ISSN 0075-899X. (Continues: Greenwood's Library Year Book; British Library Year Book; Librarian's Guide.) 1897. irreg. index. James Clarke and Co., 7 All Saints Passage, Cambridge, England. Dist: R. R. Bowker Co., Box 1807, Ann Arbor, MI 48106. Examined: 1976. Edmund V. Corbett, ed. 254p. $42.50.
Aud: Cl, Sa

A directory of libraries and museums in the United Kingdom and the Republic of Ireland. The section on libraries includes the British Library, public libraries (arranged by name), and special libraries (arranged by town). The second section lists museums, galleries, and stately homes. Entries are arranged geographically under the three categories and contain information on key personnel, hours of opening, admission charges, and selected data on collections. A new edition is scheduled for publication in late 1978. GV

HU 47
Marsyas. ISSN 0076-4701. 1941. bi-a. illus. New York University, 1 E 78th St, New York, NY 10021. Dist: J. J. Augustin, Locust Valley, NY 11560. Examined: v. 17, 1974/75. Paul Yule and Andrew Clark, eds. 127p. $8. (1978/79.)
Aud: Cl, Sa
Indexed in: *Art Index.*

Scholarly publication which includes studies dealing with the history of art and is international in scope. Includes thoroughly documented articles, often accompanied by plates. Articles in the 1974/75 edition discuss Titian's frescoes, aspects of Iranian architecture, and Japanese scroll painting. Each volume contains lengthy summaries of dissertations submitted to the Institute of Fine Arts of New York University, arranged by subject specialization, as well as lists of masters' theses. GV

HU 48
Metropolitan Museum Journal. ISSN 0077-8958. 1968. a. illus. Metropolitan Museum of Art, Fifth Ave and 82nd St, New York, NY 10028. Examined: v. 11, 1976. 143p. $15.
Aud: Sa
Indexed in: *Art Index; Répertoire d'Art et d'Archéologie.*

A scholarly serial which publishes the results of research studies conducted at the Metropolitan Museum of Art. Includes articles and notes, written by staff members and outside scholars, on all the fields of art represented in the Metropolitan Museum. The 1976 issue contains articles, accompanied by numerous plates and illustrations, on the Cesnola Collection's Phoenician inscriptions and the "Story of The Emperor of China" in the Beauvais tapestry series. GV

HU 49
Museum Notes. ISSN 0027-4097. 1943. a. bibl. index. illus. Rhode Island School of Design, Museum of Art, Providence, RI 02903. Examined: v. 63, 1977. Selection 7. Stephen E. Ostrow, ed. 243p. $5.
Aud: Cl, Pl
Indexed in: *Art Index.*

Since 1972 the Providence Museum of Art has been publishing catalogs of specific areas of their collection as special issues of **Museum Notes.** Catalogs in the Selection series include: *American Watercolors and Drawings; British Watercolors and Drawings; Contemporary Graphics; Glass; French Watercolors and Drawings, ca. 1800-1910;* and *Ancient Jewelry.* Selection seven, *American Paintings from the Museum's Collection, ca. 1800-1930,* is an exhibition catalog of 19th and early 20th century American paintings arranged according to subject matter, i.e., landscape, portraits, people and places, and still life. Entries include reproduction of the art work, description, provenance, exhibitions, and an in-depth discussion about the artist and the specific work. Copious footnotes accompany the entries, and a bibliography appears at the end of each catalog item. An alphabetical index of artists refers back to catalog numbers of the paintings. GV

HU 50
Museums of the World; Museen der Welt. 1973. irreg. bibl. index. Verlag Dokumentation, Box 148, Jaiserstr 13, 8023, Pullach bei München, West Germany. Dist: R. R. Bowker Co., Box 1807, Ann Arbor, MI 48106. Examined: 2nd ed., 1975. Eleanor Braun, ed. 808p. $52.50.
Aud: Cl, Pl

Included in this comprehensive directory are art museums and galleries, museums of natural science, museums of science and technology, local and regional museums of natural and cultural history, open-air museums, memorial sites, and special collections. Excluded are zoological and botanical gardens, aquariums, planetariums, buildings and ruins without a museum collection, and small sized museums with less than 20 square meters of exhibit area. The directory lists 17,500 museums in 150 countries. Entries are arranged first by continent and then by country and city. Most of the text is in English, but the alphabetical listings of cities and museums are in the language of the country. The amount of information supplied in each museum entry varies greatly since the directory depends upon responses to a questionnaire. Entries generally list address, name of director or curator, date founded, description of holdings, and number of volumes in the library. There are three indexes which refer to item numbers in the directory: a name index, a geographic index, and a subject index. Compared to the detailed classified indexing of special collections in *The Directory of World Museums* (N.Y.: Columbia Univ. Press, 1975), the subject index in this directory is difficult to use for locating specific collections or archives. The 1975 edition also includes a list of national

HU 51

National Institute for Architectural Education. Yearbook. ISSN 0077-474X. (Continues: National Institute for Architectural Education. Bulletin.) 1964. a. illus. National Institute for Architectural Education, 20 W 40th St, New York, NY 10018. Examined: 1974. 168p. $15.
Aud: Cl, Sa

This is the eleventh yearbook to incorporate reports of the year's activities of the NIAE, design critiques, and award winning projects in one volume. The various awards given out during the preceding year are listed with a description of the winning buildings or sites and several illustrations. An important reference source for those interested in current trends in architecture and architectural education. JKM

HU 52

Official Museum Directory. ISSN 0090-6700. (Continues: Museums Directory of the United States and Canada.) 1971. bi-a. index. American Association of Museums, 2233 Wisconsin Ave, NW, Washington, DC. Dist: National Register Publishing Co., 5201 Old Orchard Rd, Skokie, IL 60076. Examined: 1977. Anita Schneider and Marilyn Hicks Fitzgerald, eds. 891p. $37.50.
Aud: Cl, Pl

Provides directory information for 5474 museums of art, history, and science in the U.S. and Canada. U.S. and Canadian institutions are listed in separate alphabets, arranged by state/province, by city or town, and by institution. Entries include address, principal personnel, type of museum, scope of the collection, description of activities, facilities, fields of research, publications, membership, hours of opening, and admission fees. Alphabetical indexes of institutions, personnel, and institutions by categories are provided. Also includes lists of museum associations in the U.S. and abroad. GV

HU 53

On Site. 1972. a. illus. Site, 60 Greene St, New York, NY 10012. Examined: no. 5 and 6, 1974; no. 7, 1976. Alison Sky, ed. 320p. $14.95.
Aud: Cl, Sa

Each issue deals with a specific theme. The 1974 edition is a double issue which examines energy in the light of new ideas which could shape our environment. Contributors include scientists, sociologists, artists, and architects. Number seven, 1976, titled "Unbuilt America," presents a history of unrealized architectural projects over the past two hundred years, beginning with Thomas Jefferson in 1776 through the Bicentennial proposals in 1976. The publication aims to bridge the gap between the environmental arts and architecture. GV

HU 54

On View. ISSN 0474-1382. 1966/67. a. index. illus. Plaistow Publications, c/o Alan Osborne, 3 New Plaistow Rd, Stratford, London E15 3JA, England. Dist: International Publications Service, 114 E 32nd St, New York, NY 10016. Examined: v. 10, 1976. Alan Osborne, ed. 120p. $10.
Aud: Sa

Subtitle: "A guide to museum and gallery acquisitions in the U.S.A. and U.K." Acquisitions of major British and American museums and galleries are listed in two main sections, the United States and the United Kingdom. Volume ten lists acquisitions from July 1974 through July 1975. Within the country sections, entries are listed alphabetically by cities and towns, then arranged according to subject areas. The U.S. section has a mixed arrangement, e.g. the Boston Museum of Fine Arts is listed under "Boston," but the Cleveland Museum of Art appears under "Ohio." Entries provide a brief description of the item and often include an illustration of the item acquired. An index of institutions precedes the main text. There is also an index of painters and sculptors. GV

HU 55

Penrose Graphic Arts International Annual. ISSN 0079-0710. (Continues: Penrose Annual.) 1895. a. illus. Northwood Publications, Northwood House, 93-99 Goswell Rd, London EC1V 7QA, England. Dist: Hastings House Publishers, 10 E 40th St, New York, NY 10016. Examined: v. 69, 1976. Brian Smith, ed. 256p. $30.
Aud: Cl, Pl

Title varies: *Process Yearbook* (volumes 2-3, 7-8) and *Penrose's Pictorial Annual* (volumes 4-6, 9-19). Publication was suspended between 1917 and 1919 and between 1941 and 1949.

An international review of the graphic arts—its history, present, and future. Issues begin with a survey article covering the developments during the previous year in various geographical areas, e.g., the North American scene or the United Kingdom scene, and in specific subject areas, e.g., page composition by computers. The survey section is followed by articles on diverse topics within the field of graphic arts. The 1976 edition includes articles entitled "Reproducing the Kelmscott Chaucer" and "Newspaper and Magazine Design in Poland," among others. Articles are often accompanied by excellent illustrations and photographs, and the text is printed on multicolored paper. Contributors are well-known, and a short biography (with portrait) of each contributor appears at the end of the work. GV

HU 56
Perspecta; The Yale Architectural Journal. ISSN 0079-0958. 1951. irreg. illus. Perspecta, Yale University, Box 2121, Yale Sta, New Haven, CT 06520. Dist: Wittenborn Art Books, 1018 Madison Ave, New York, NY 10021. Examined: v. 15, 1975. 109p. $10. (1978.)
Aud: Cl, Pl
Indexed in: *Art Index.*

Consists of papers on architecture edited and published by students at the Yale School of Architecture. Issues are devoted to a specific topic and include articles by well-known scholars in the field who are writing for the general public. Number 15 is entitled "Backgrounds for an American Architecture" and focuses on the cultural history of American architecture. Material presented is richly illustrated with maps, plans, and photographs. GV

HU 57
Structurist. ISSN 0081-6027. 1960/61. a. index. illus. Eli Bornstein, Box 378, Sub 6, University of Saskatchewan, Saskatoon, Saskatchewan S7N 0W0, Canada. Dist: Wittenborn Art Books, 1018 Madison Ave, New York, NY 10021. Examined: no. 15/16, 1975/76. Eli Bornstein, ed. 187p. $10.
Aud: Cl, Pl

Devoted to the free exchange and exploration of a wide variety of ideas contributing to man's knowledge of the process of creation in all fields relating to art. Art, defined as a "structure builder," is used as the focus for an interdisciplinary examination of the creative process. Issues deal with a specific topic as it applies to the contemporary art scene. Topics covered include "Art, Language, and Literature" (no. 12), "Space/Time" (no. 15/16), and "Art and Vision: Education of the Sense" (no. 17/18, forthcoming). The 1975/76 edition includes articles dealing with the time/space concept applied to architecture, cinema, photography, and specific art styles. Articles were written by such well-known contributors as Rudolph Arnheim and Wylie Sypher. Articles are fully documented and accompanied by black-and-white and color photographs. Also contains lengthy signed book reviews in the area of modern art. GV

HU 58
U.S. National Gallery of Art. Annual Report. 1969/70. a. illus. National Gallery of Art, Washington, DC 20565. Examined: 1975. 95p. $1.25.
Aud: Cl, Pl

An annual review of the organization and activities of the National Gallery of Art. Includes an outline of the organization; a review of the year's activities written by the director; a list of acquisitions for the previous year; a description of current national arts programs and educational programs; and a listing of staff activities covering lectures, research projects, and publications. An alphabetical roster of major employees appears at the end of the report. GV

HU 59
U.S. National Gallery of Art. Studies in the History of Art. ISSN 0091-7338. (Continues: Report and Studies in the History of Art.) 1971/72. a. illus. National Gallery of Art, Washington, DC 20565. Examined: v. 6, 1974. 214p. $6.50.
Aud: Cl, Sa

Contains scholarly articles on art history written by experts in the field. The majority of contributions concern items owned or exhibited by the National Gallery of Art. The copiously illustrated articles in the 1974 issue deal with painting, medals, sculpture, Russian art collections, and tapestry restoration at the National Gallery. Includes biographical sketches of contributors. The first volume under the new title (1971/72) was a double issue; subsequent volumes have been issued annually. GV

HU 60
Walters Art Gallery. Journal. ISSN 0083-7156. 1938. irreg. illus. Walters Art Gallery, 600 N Charles St, Baltimore, MD 21201. Examined: v. 36, 1977. Ursula McCracken, ed. 136p. $5.
Aud: Sa
Indexed in: *Art Index.*

Includes scholarly, well-documented contributions, accompanied by plates and diagrams, dealing with various aspects of art and archaeology. The 1977 edition is a festschrift to Dorothy Kent Hill, retired Curator of Ancient Art at the National Gallery, and includes a bibliography of her works. Articles discuss ancient art items found at the Walters Art Gallery and Greek and Roman art pieces in other museums. Previous issues have included scholarly examinations of art pieces housed in the Walters Art Gallery and sections of notes on specific areas of the museum. Although the **Journal** is purported to be an annual publication, recent volumes have been issued irregularly; volume 33/34 covered 1970/71, volume 35 was issued without a date, and volume 36 was issued in 1977. GV

HU 61
Whitney Review. ISSN 0511-8824. 1960/61. a. illus. Whitney Museum of American Art, 945 Madison Ave at 75th St, New York, NY 10021. Examined: 1973/74. 48p. free.
Aud: Cl, Sa

Reports on the museum's activities during the preceding fiscal year (July 1-June 30). Includes several articles on the different events that took place at the museum and an annotated list of exhibitions that were held during the year. Lists the entire staff of the museum, committees, friends of the museum, and contributors. There are many illustrations. JKM

HU 62
Who's Who in American Art. ISSN 0000-0191. (Continues in part: American Art Annual.) 1936/37. bi-a. index. R. R. Bowker Co., 1180 Ave of the Americas, New York, NY 10036. Dist: R. R. Bowker, Box 1807, Ann Arbor, MI 48106. Examined: 12th ed., 1976. 576p. $37. (13th ed., 1978. 760p. $42.50)
Aud: Cl, Pl
Indexed in: *Biographical Dictionaries Master Index.*

Volumes one to four (1936/37 to 1940/47) appeared as part two of the *American Art Annual*. The **American Art Directory,** a companion volume which is also published by Bowker, continues the directory of national, regional, and state open exhibitions which was also part of the *American Art Annual*. **Who's Who in American Art** was published every three years in the past, but will now be revised biennially.

Sponsored by the America Federation of Art, this is a biographical directory of approximately 9000 artists, key art administrators, scholars, collectors, critics, dealers, librarians, print makers, silversmiths, etc. Includes people in the world of art who are living in or native to the United States, Mexico, and Canada. Entries are arranged in one alphabet by biographee and often include the following biographical data: art form, birth date, education, works, employment, publications by and about the subject, awards, memberships, style and technique, media, name and address of dealer, and biographee's address. Issues also contain a geographic index of subjects (by state, then city), a professional classification index, and a necrology section. GV

HU 63
Who's Who in Art. 1927. bi-a. Art Trade Press, London, England. Dist: International Publications Service, 114 E 32nd St, New York, NY 10016. Examined: 17th ed., 1974. 554p. $25. (1977.)
Aud: Cl, Pl

A directory of living artists, predominantly British, but also including selected outstanding non-British contemporary artists, designers, craftsmen, critics, writers, teachers, collectors, and curators. The alphabetically arranged entries provide brief biographical notes and list publications, works in permanent collections, awards, and signatures. There is a brief section on the aims and activities of British artists' academies, groups, and societies. Necrologies, and monograms and signatures are listed in separate appendixes. The first four volumes (1927, 1929, 1934, 1948) were issued on an irregular basis, but subsequent volumes have been issued biennially. GV

HU 64
World Collectors Annuary. ISSN 0084-1498. 1946/49. a. bibl. index. illus. World Collectors Publishers, Box 263, Voorburg 2111, Netherlands. Dist: William S. Heinman, 1966 Broadway, New York, NY 10023. Examined: v. 27, 1975. Ame Van Eijk Van Voorthuijsen, ed. $90. (v. 28, 1976. 396p. $95.)
Aud: Sa

Lists alphabetically by artist the paintings, watercolors, pastels, and drawings sold in the major auction houses of the U.S. and Europe. The 1975 edition contains approximately 11,000 entries which consist of a brief description, provenance, place and date of sale, price paid, and bibliographic notes. Reproductions of selected works sold during the year are included. A cumulative index for 1946 to 1972 is available for $60. A supplemental index for 1973/74 has also been issued. GV

CLASSICS

HU 65
American School of Classical Studies at Athens. Annual Report. ISSN 0360-6651. 1881. a. American School of Classical Studies at Athens, Princeton, NJ 08540. Examined: 95th ed., 1976. 61p.
Aud: Sa

Contains the American School's articles of incorporation, names of the Board of Trustees, committees, staff of the school, Council of Alumni Association, and the Auxiliary Fund Association. The reports include those of the director; professor of archaeology; secretary of the school; librarian of the school; directors of excavations, special research fellows, admissions and fellowships, and summer sessions; committee on publications; the Alumni Fund Association; and the treasurer. Many of the reports include financial statements. There is also a list of cooperating institutions. LL

HU 66
Augustinian Studies. ISSN 0094-5323. 1961. a. bibl. Augustinian Institute, Department F-1, Villanova University, Villanova, PA 19085. Examined: v. 6, 1975. Robert P. Russell, ed. 207p. $10. (1977.)
Aud: Cl, Sa

Contains essays and book reviews on the study of St. Augustine and Augustinian influence. As a rule, the articles are published in English, although French and German articles are included occasionally. Most articles provide bibliographical footnotes. There are one or two book reviews of medium length. Sometimes there are reports of various activities and programs at the Augustinian Institute at Villanova University. LL

HU 67
Byzantine and Modern Greek Studies. 1975. a. Basil, Blackwell and Mott, 108 Cowley Rd, Oxford OX4 1JF, England. Examined: v. 3, 1977. Donald M. Nicol, ed. 200p. $15.
Aud: Cl, Sa

"Devoted to all aspects of Byzantine and Modern Greek scholarship." Contains articles representing original research and critical analysis of the society and culture of the Greek-speaking peoples from the Middle Ages to the present. Contributors include both British and American scholars. JKM

HU 68
California Studies in Classical Antiquity. ISSN 0068-5895. 1968. a. illus. University of California Press, 2223 Fulton St, Berkeley, CA 94720. Examined: v.9, 1977. Ronald S. Stroud and Philip Levine, eds. 202p. $8.50.
Aud: Cl, Sa

This edition includes eleven scholarly and technical articles on the philology of classical Greek and Latin. Papers contributed are chiefly by faculty members and graduate students on the various campuses of the University of California. Two examples of articles are "Plato on 'Not'" and "The Secondary Choruses in Aeschylus' *Supplices*." JKM

HU 69
The Classical Association. Proceedings. ISSN 0069-4460. 1903. a. The Classical Association, 31-34 Gordon Sq, London, England. Examined: v. 73, 1976. Christopher Collard, ed. 50p. free to members.
Aud: Sa

The Classical Association aims to promote and sustain interest in classical studies. It organizes annual conferences to give scholars and teachers an opportunity to meet and discuss their problems. The proceedings contain the president's address, report of the general meeting, reports of recent works and publications in the field, accounts of events at the conference, reports of the Association's councils and offices, and a statement of accounts. It also includes a list of officers, reports from other branches, and a list of allied associations. LL

HU 70
Giorgio Levi Della Vida Conference. Publications. 1970. bi-a. index. illus. Gustave E. von Grunebaum Center for Near Eastern Studies, University of California at Los Angeles, Los Angeles, CA 90024. Examined: 5th ed., 1977. Amin Bahni and Speros Vryonis, Jr., eds. 165p.
Aud: Sa

Contains papers presented at the proceedings of the Giorgio Levi Della Vida Conference. These articles are devoted to the study of Islamic civilization. The Giorgio Levi Della Vida Medal is awarded biennially to an outstanding scholarly work in this area. For the issue examined, the medal was awarded to S. D. Goitein whose paper is entitled, "Individualism and Conformity in Classical Islam." All articles include bibliographical references; some articles include illustrations or photographs. Areas of Islamic civilization covered include art, philosophy, classics, culture, religions, and history. It does not include a program or minutes of the conferences. LL

HU 71
Harvard Studies in Classical Philology. ISSN 0073-0688. 1890. a. Harvard University Press, 79 Garden St, Cambridge, MA 02138. Examined: 1975; 1976. Albert Herrichs, ed. $18.50. (v. 81, 1977. 306p.)
Aud: Cl, Sa

An important and long-established collection of scholarly papers, research essays, textual analyses of ancient works, and summaries of dissertations. Published under the auspices of the Department of Classics at Harvard, contributions are primarily by Harvard faculty and graduates. Contributors represent a sufficient number of cognate fields, however, to provide a breadth of scope and diversity of interpretations. AC

HU 72.
Journal of Hellenic Studies. ISSN 0075-4269. 1880. a. bibl. index. illus. Society for the Promotion of Hellenic Studies, 31-34 Gordon Sq, London WC1H 0PP, England. Examined: v. 97, 1977. Ewen Bowie, ed. 248p. $19.
Aud: Cl, Sa

A collection of scholarly articles written largely by European authors. Includes reviews of books published throughout the world on classical Greek studies, including Greek philology, history, archaeology, literature, etc. Includes a list of books received and an author-subject index to reviews. The Society also publishes *Archaeological Reports*, an illustrated annual which includes reports of recent archaeological work in Greece and other parts of the Greek world, the annual report of the Society, a membership list, and a list of pertinent acquisitions by British museums. JKM

HU 73
Journal of Roman Studies. ISSN 0075-4358. 1911. a. index. illus. Society for the Promotion of Roman Studies, 31-34 Gordon Sq, London WC1H 0PP, England. Examined: v. 67, 1977. F. G. B. Millar, ed. 272p. $19.
Aud: Cl, Sa

A collection of articles written primarily by authors from English-speaking countries, though articles written in Latin, French, German, and Greek are also included. Articles are concerned with the cultural, social, economic, and political history of Rome. Contains reviews of books published throughout the world. A report on the Society's proceedings is included in the subscription. JKM

HU 74
The Journal of the Ancient Near Eastern Society of Columbia University. ISSN 0010-2016. 1968. a. bibl. illus. Ancient Near Eastern Society, Columbia University, 602 Kent Hall, New York, NY 10027. Examined: v. 8, 1976. Edward L. Greenstein, ed. 126p. $10.
Aud: Sa

A journal devoted to the study of the Ancient Near East. Many of the articles are on ancient script and writing, such as Akkadian writing and cuneiform. There are also articles on art and culture, with illustrations and photographs. All articles are documented. It does not contain news of the society. The journal was published semi-annually until 1976. LL

HU 75
Teiresias. ISSN 0381-9361. (Continues: Bibliography of Boiotian Studies.) 1971. a. bibl. Teiresias, Department of Classics, McGill University, 855 Sherbrooke St W, Montreal, Quebec H3A 2T7 Canada. Examined: 1976. Albert Schachter, ed. 2v. free to indiv.; $7.50 to institutions.
Aud: Sa

A review and a bibliography of classics. Divided into two sections. Unfortunately, the first part was unavailable for review. The second part is a bibliography arranged in the following sections: archaeological reports, articles, papers read, reviews, bibliographies, and dissertations. The appendix for the issue examined is an epigraphica. The entries are in English, French, German, Greek, and Italian. LL

HU 76
Vergilius. ISSN 0506-7294. 1956. a. bibl. illus. The Vergilian Society, c/o C. P. Twichell, The Choate School, Wallingford, CT 06492. Examined: v. 22, 1976. Janice M. Benario, ed. 64p. $2.
Aud: Sa

The annual report of the Vergilian Society which includes articles, bibliography, book reviews, the report of the director of the Classical Summer School, the annual report of the Secretary, poems, and a list of officers of the Society. The short articles are devoted to Vergilian studies. They include bibliographical references, illustrations, and photographs. Book reviews are of medium length. There is a listing of books received. Intended for those who are interested in Virgil and teachers of classical studies. LL

HU 77
Virgil Society. Proceedings. ISSN 0083-629X. 1961/62. a. bibl. H. W. Walden and Co., 18 Station Approach, Clapham Junction, London SW 11, England. Examined: no. 15, 1975/76. F. Robertson, ed. 29p. $3.64.
Aud: Sa

Contains articles, lectures, poems, and textual criticisms on the works of Virgil. Articles and lectures include bibliographical references. It also contains brief notes on news and events of the society. There is a list of officers but not of members. LL

HU 78
Yale Classical Studies. ISSN 0084-330X. (1975 is v. 24.) irreg. Syndics of the Cambridge University Press, The Pitt Bldg, Trumpington St, Cambridge CB2 IRP, England. Examined: v. 25, 1977. T. F. Gould and C. J. Herrington, eds. 350p.
Aud: Cl, Sa

An international collection of scholarly articles in English directed primarily to the professional Classicist. Each volume in the series deals with a specific area of Classical philology. Volume 24 is devoted to studies on the Greek historians, and volume 25 is devoted to literary studies of Greek tragedy. JKM

DANCE

HU 79
American Dance Therapy Association. Proceedings of the Annual Conference. ISSN 0065-8022. 1966. a. American Dance Therapy Association, 216e-1000 Century Plaza, Columbia, MD 21044. Examined: 1974. 173p. $4.50. (1978.)
Aud: Sa

Contains papers presented at the annual conference of the American Dance Therapy Association by teachers and clinicians working in the field. The 1974 issue includes papers from the ninth annual conference focusing on dance-movement therapy. Previous conferences dealt with defining the dance therapist (1972) and describing the functions of that profession—clinician, researcher, educator (1973). GV

HU 80
Bibliographic Guide to Dance. 1975. a. G. K. Hall, 70 Lincoln St, Boston, MA 02111. Examined: 1977. 768p. $95.
Aud: Cl, Pf, Sa

Provides complete cataloging information for all dance materials, including films, photographs, music scores, videotapes, books, etc., cataloged by the Library of Congress and the New York Public Library Research Libraries during the preceding year. Supplements the *Dictionary Catalog of the Dance Collection*, Performing Arts Research Center, The Research Libraries of the New York Public Library (G. K. Hall, 1974). Access is provided through main entries, added entries, titles, series, and subject headings. JKM

HU 81
Dance Directory. ISSN 0070-2676. 1954/55. irreg. American Alliance for Health, Physical Education, and Recreation, 1201 16th St, NW, Washington, DC 20036. Examined: 9th ed., 1976. 95p. $2.50.
Aud: Hs, Jc, Cl, Pl
Indexed in: *ERIC*.

Subtitle: "Programs of professional preparation in American colleges and universities." A directory of dance programs in the U.S. offering both undergraduate and graduate degrees. Arranged alphabetically by states, then by institutions within a state, entries provide a short description of the institution, pertinent programs offered, personnel involved, and courses and credits offered in the area of dance. A geographical listing of colleges and universities appears at the beginning of the volume. GV

HU 82
Dance Magazine Annual. ISSN 0070-2684. 1967. a. illus. Danad Publishing Co., 10 Columbus Circle, New York, NY 10019. Examined: 1978. Heidi von Obenauer, ed. 282p. $10.
Aud: Sa

Subtitle: "Catalogue of dance artists and attractions, programs, resources, and services." An extensive directory of dance companies, artists, programs, organizations, and sources in the field of dance. Lists U.S. and foreign professional and regional dance companies in a classified arrangement (ballet, ethnic, jazz, etc.); people and companies which provide services for the dance industry (choreographers, designers, photographers); funding agencies in the U.S. and Canada; sponsors; booking organizations; and professional organizations. Entries provide brief directory information, including address, telephone number, and chief personnel. Also includes lists of educational opportunities, books and film publishers, periodicals, and awards in the dance field. GV

HU 83
Dance World. ISSN 0070-2692. 1966. a. index. illus. Crown Publishers, One Park Ave, New York, NY 10016. Examined: v. 12, 1977. John Willis, ed. $16.95.
Aud: Pl, Sa

Provides a pictorial and statistical summary of the past season's dance productions. The emphasis in volume 12 is on New York, covering major and minor dance company offerings from June 1, 1976 through May 31, 1977. It also contains a section on annual summer dance festivals and regional professional dance companies. Arrangement within these sections is by the name of the dance company. Entries include a list of technical and administrative staff, a list of the artists and guest artists, and the company's repertoire for the season. Includes a biographical section on dancers and choreographers, giving birth date, education, debut, selected work experiences, and current affiliation. The volume contains a wealth of black-and-white photographs of dance productions. Performers, choreographers, dance companies, and titles of programs are listed in the index. GV

HU 84
Focus on Dance. ISSN 0071-6294. 1960. irreg. The National Dance Association of the American Alliance for Health, Physical Education, and Recreation, 1201 16th St, NW, Washington, DC 20036. Examined: v. 8, 1976. E. Carmen Imel, ed. 86p. $6.50.
Aud: Sa

Presents papers from the annual conference of the National Dance Association. Volume eight, a bicentennial issue, is devoted to the topic of "Dance Heritage" in America. The "Heritage" section addresses the topics of dance in Mormon Utah, dance in Eskimo society, and a history of the square dance in America. Also includes a "Festival" section which concentrates on 20th century dance and a "Horizon" section which discusses current trends and innovations in the dance field. Previous issues have dealt with the specific themes of dance therapy, and ethnic and recreational dance. GV

LANGUAGE AND LITERATURE

HU 85
African Literature Today. 1968. a. index. Africana Publishing Corp., 101 Fifth Ave, New York, NY 10003. Examined: no. 8, 1976. Eldred D. Jones, ed. 160p. $9.
Aud: Cl, Pl
Indexed in: *Abstracts of English Studies.*

A scholarly source of critical essays and reviews by an international array of contributors. Each issue focuses on a different theme, usually a literary form, e.g., drama, poetry, the novel. Lengthy reviews of important works comprise about half of each issue. Some articles are broad in scope, such as "Roots in African Drama and Theatre"; others are highly specific, e.g., "Language and Meaning in Sarjinka's *The Road*." Arabic as well as sub-Saharan literatures are included. Format is compact and attractive. AC

HU 86
American Literary Scholarship. ISSN 0065-9142. 1965. a. bibl. index. Duke University Press, 6697 College Sta, Durham, NC 27708. Examined: 1971; 1974. James Woodress, ed. $14.75. (1975, 542p.; 1978.)
Aud: Cl, Pl
Indexed in: *Essay Index.*

An important survey of the year's critical writings in the field of American literature. Includes bibliographic essays by a number of distinguished contributors. Part one consists of chapters on major writers (e.g., Poe, Melville, Faulkner); part two focuses on periods and literary forms. Books, dissertations, and articles are cited, with over 250 periodical sources represented in recent volumes. American scholarship is featured almost exclusively, but there is a brief final section on foreign contributors. Modeled on **The Year's Work in English Studies,** and published under the sponsorship of the American Literature Section of the Modern Language Association. AC

HU 87
American Philological Association. Directory. ISSN 0044-779X. 1970. irreg. American Philological Association, 431-432 N Burrowes, Pennsylvania State University, University Park, PA 16802. Examined: 1972; 1975. Robert W. Carrubba, ed. $5.
Aud: Sa

A paperback pamphlet, issued approximately every three years, that lists in two separate sections all personal and institutional members of the American Philological Association. Full address is given for each entry, but institutional affiliations of personal members are not indicated except as part of the address. There is a complete list of officers and committees, including full membership rosters for the latter. AC

HU 88
Author Biographies Master Index. 1978. freq. not determined. bibl. Gale Research Co., Book Tower, Detroit, MI 48226. Examined: none. (1st ed., 1978. Dennis La Beau, ed. 2v. $65.)
Aud: Cl, Pl

Subtitle: "A consolidated guide to bio-bibliographical information concerning authors living and dead as it appears in a selection of the principal biographical dictionaries devoted to authors, poets, journalists, and other literary figures." Similar in format and content to Gale's **Biographical Dictionaries Master Index.** Publisher's information indicates that the material for both titles is drawn from the same computer data base, but since the new publication was not available for examination, it is uncertain how much duplication there is between the two indexes. JKM

HU 89
Best American Short Stories. ISSN 0067-6233. (Con-

tinues: Best Short Stories.) 1915. a. Houghton Mifflin Co., 2 Park St, Boston, MA 02107. Examined: 1975. Martha Foley, ed. $10. (1976. 364p.)
Aud: Hs, Jc, Cl, Pl
Indexed in: *Short Story Index.*

A collection of stories with wide appeal that are drawn each year from popular magazines and literary quarterlies that feature short fiction of quality. *The New Yorker, Sewanee Review, Atlantic,* and *Harpers* are among the journals usually represented. Each volume contains a final section, called "The Yearbook of the American Short Story," which lists notable short stories of the past year and the addresses of American and Canadian magazines which publish short stories. AC

HU 90
Best Poems of (year): Borestone Mountain Poetry Awards. ISSN 0067-6276. (1959 is v. 11.) a. Pacific Books Publishers, Box 558, Palo Alto, CA. Examined: v. 28, 1976. Waddell Austin, ed. 119p. $5.95.
Aud: Jc, Cl, Pl

After examining 300 poems published in popular and scholarly magazines from the English-speaking world in 1975, the editors selected the 75 poems reprinted here. The stated purpose of the annual compilation is "to preserve in book form each year some of the poems of merit that might be lost among countless magazine pages." JKM

HU 91
Bibliographic Annual in Speech Communication. ISSN 0067-6837. 1970. a. bibl. The Speech Communication Association, 5205 Leesburg Pike, Falls Church, VA 22041. Examined: 1975. Patricia C. Kennicott, ed. approx. 375p. $8.
Aud: Cl, Sa

A comprehensive record of graduate work in speech communication, and a basic resource for scholars and teachers in the field. Each volume presents subject bibliographies arranged in six broad categories: mass communication, behavioral studies in communication, rhetorical studies, public address, oral interpretation, and theatrical craftsmanship. In addition, there are abstracts of doctoral dissertations and a list of graduate theses and dissertations. AC

HU 92
Bibliographie Linguistique; Linguistic Bibliography. 1939/47. a. bibl. index. Editions Spectrum, Utrecht, The Netherlands. Dist: International Publications Services, 114 E 32nd St, New York, NY 10016. Examined: 1939/47; 1972; 1973. J. J. Beylsmit, ed. 621p. $39.50.
Aud: Cl, Sa

The most important bibliographic publication of truly international scope in the field of linguistics. It is a comprehensive listing of books, journal articles, and reviews, divided into broad categories (Indo-European, Asiatic, etc.) with highly specific subdivisions. Published under the auspices of the Permanent International Committee of Linguistics, International Council of Philosophy and Humanistic Studies, with support from UNESCO. Annual publication began with a retrospective volume covering the years 1939-47 which was published in 1949. AC

HU 93
Children's Literature Review. ISSN 0362-4145. 1976. a. index. Gale Research Co., Book Tower, Detroit, MI 48226. Examined: 1976. Carolyn Riley, ed. 2v. 440p. $25 per v.
Aud: Pl, Pf

Subtitle: "Excerpts from reviews, criticism, and commentary on books for children and young people." Each author entry provides a brief note on the author, excerpts from general commentaries on the author's work, excerpts from criticism of specific titles, and full citations to additional reviews and commentaries. Each volume contains entries for about 50 authors and an index of authors, critics, and titles that cumulates index entries in all previous volumes. JKM

HU 94
Contemporary Authors. ISSN 0010-7468. 1962. irreg. index. Gale Research Co., Book Tower, Detroit, MI 48226. Examined: v. 65-68, 1977. Jane A. Bowden, ed. 4v. $38 per v. (v. 69-72, 1978. 627p.)
Aud: Hs, Jc, Cl, Pl
Indexed in: *Biographical Dictionaries Master Index.*

Subtitle: "A bio-bibliographic guide to current writers in fiction, general nonfiction, poetry, journalism, drama, motion pictures, television, and other fields." Prior to 1977, this title provided bio-bibliographical information on authors of books only. Beginning with the four 1977 volumes, the focus has been expanded to include significant authors of all types of media. Entries are arranged alphabetically by biographee and include information on personal life, career, writings, and works in progress. References to other biographical/critical sources are provided. Cumulative indexes are included in every other volume; the entire set undergoes continuous revision at five-year intervals. The basic set includes only living authors; in 1975 Gale began publishing *Contemporary Authors—Permanent Series* which covers authors who have been deleted from the basic set. KMH

HU 95
Contemporary Literary Criticism. ISSN 0091-3421. 1973. irreg. index. Gale Research Co., Book Tower, Detroit, MI 48226. Examined: v. 7, 1977. Phyllis Carmel Mendelsohn and Dedria Bryfonski, eds. 563p. $42. (v. 8, 1978. 556p. $42.)
Aud: Hs, Jc, Cl, Pl

Subtitle: "Excerpts from criticism of the works of today's novelists, poets, playwrights, and other creative writers." An ongoing encyclopedia of current literary criticism which brings together criticism of contemporary authors from diverse sources. Presents significant passages from the published criticism of works by well-known creative writers who are living or who have died since January 1, 1960. Twentieth century writers who died prior to 1960 are covered in Gale's **Twentieth Century Literary Criticism.** Each volume presents approximately five excerpts of criticism published during the last 25 years for each of 200 authors, including authors who were not cited in previous volumes as well as new criticism of authors who were previously cited. Entries include references to Gale's **Contemporary Authors** which provides complete bio-bibliographical information on the authors. There is a cumulative index in each volume. KMH

HU 96
Current Trends in Linguistics. 1963. a. bibl. index. Mouton Publishers, Box 482, 173 Frannenslag, The Hague 2076, The Netherlands. Dist: Humanities Press, Atlantic Highlands, NJ 07716. Examined: v. 1, 1963; v. 10, 1973; v. 14, 1976. Thomas A. Sebeok, ed. 952p. $168.
Aud: Cl, Sa

An immense, scholarly compilation devoted to assessing the current state of linguistic research in all fields and all countries. Each volume focuses on a special (usually regional) topic, such as Soviet and East European linguistics or linguistics in North America, and features major scholarly articles and extensive bibliographies. Volume 14 contains an index to all preceding volumes. Published under the auspices of the Center for Applied Linguistics of the Modern Language Association and under the supervision of the International Committee on Linguistic Information. AC

HU 97
Dickens Studies Annual. ISSN 0084-9812. 1970. a. index. Southern Illinois University Press, Box 3697, Carbondale, IL 62901. Examined: v. 1, 1970; v. 5, 1976. Robert B. Partlow, Jr., ed. $15. (v. 6, 1977. 210p.)
Aud: Jc, Cl, Pl

A collection of critical essays, academic in tone, representing virtually all aspects of Dickensiana: structure and character development in the novels, psychological interpretations, Dickens's development as a writer, and his relations with other literary figures. Contributors are primarily faculty members at American universities. There is a thorough index to the ten or so essays in each volume. AC

HU 98
Directory of American Fiction Writers. 1976. bi-a. index. Poets and Writers, 201 W 54th St, New York, NY 10019. Dist: Publishing Center for Cultural Resources, 27 W 53rd St, New York, NY 10019. Examined: 1976. Cherie Fein, ed. 136p. $10; $5 pap.
Aud: Cl, Sa

Lists names, addresses, telephone numbers, work preferences, and recent publications of approximately 800 contemporary fiction writers whose work has been published in the United States. The basic arrangement is geographic, but there is an alphabetical index. Includes a directory of names and addresses of approximately 500 organizations that sponsor workshops and readings; a listing of poetry and fiction anthologies, resources for creative writing teachers, bookstores, and literary organizations; and other information of interest to the creative writer. A joint supplement to this publication and the **Directory of American Poets** is published twice a year and distributed free to all purchasers of the volume. The publishers have also established a telephone information service for latest addresses and phone numbers. AC

HU 99
Directory of American Poets. 1973. bi-a. index. Poets and Writers, 201 W 54th St, New York, NY 10019. Dist: Publishing Center for Cultural Resources, 27 W 53rd St, New York, NY 10019. Examined: 2nd ed., 1975. Cherie Fein, ed. 130p. $12; $6 pap. (1977.)
Aud: Cl, Sa

Lists names, addresses, and telephone numbers of approximately 1500 contemporary poets whose work has been published in the United States. Entries also include publications, but only the most recent. The basic arrangement is geographic, but there is an alphabetical name index and an index of special (such as ethnic) backgrounds. Includes a directory of names and addresses of approximately 500 organizations that sponsor workshops and readings; listings of fiction and poetry anthologies, resources for creative writing teachers, bookstores, and literary organizations; and other information of interest to the creative writer. A joint supplement to this publication and to the **Directory of American Fiction Writers** is published twice a year and distributed free to all purchasers of the volume. The publishers have also established a telephone information service for latest addresses and phone numbers. AC

HU 100
Directory of Women Writing. a. Women Writing Press, RD 3, Newfield, NY 14867. Examined: 1977. Andrea Chesman and Polly Joan, eds. 91p. $3.50.
Aud: Sa

A name and address directory of U.S. women writers. Its purpose is to aid women writers to find one another. KAC

HU 101
Essays and Studies. ISSN 0071-1357. (Continues: English Studies.) 1910-46; 1948. a. John Murray, 50 Albermarle St, London W1X 4BD, England. Examined: v. 24, 1971; v. 29, 1976. E. Talbot Donaldson, ed. 121p. £1.75.
Aud: Cl, Pl
Indexed in: *Essay Index.*

A respected collection of critical and analytical essays on both broad and specific aspects of English literature. Covers all periods and forms, but more often than not the subject is a particular writer, e.g., Chaucer, Shakespeare, Beckett, Behan. Published under the auspices of the English Association with a different editor for each annual volume. The series was formerly published by Oxford at the Clarendon Press; when John Murray began publishing the title in 1948, the designation "new series" was added and the volume number reverted to number one. Volumes published before 1975 are available from Messrs. Dawson and Sons, Cannon House, Park Farm Rd, Folkestone, Kent. AC

HU 102
Essays by Divers Hands. ISSN 0080-4584. (Continues: Transactions of the Royal Society.) 1827. bi-a. Oxford University Press, Ely House, London W1, England. Examined: 1827; 1972. Robert Speaight, ed. (1977. 180p. $11.)
Aud: Cl, Sa
Indexed in: *Essay Index.*

A venerable collection of the lectures delivered during the preceding two seasons before Great Britain's Royal Society of Literature. These volumes constitute the transactions of the Royal Society and were formerly so titled. The essays are far-ranging in scope, featuring luminaries of England's cultural establishment, and are usually on a broad and humanistic plane. Hugh Walpole, St. John Ervine, Harold Nicolson, G. K. Chesterton, and Edmund Gosse have been among its editors. AC

HU 103
Fiction Catalog. 1908. quinquennial w/a. suppls. index. H. W. Wilson, 950 University Ave, Bronx, NY 10452. Examined: 9th ed, 1975. 797p. $45 w/4 suppls. (1976 suppl. 119p.)
Aud: Hs, Jc, Cl, Pl

A guide to 4734 English-language fiction titles, including foreign language titles in English translation. Titles included were selected by librarians working in the field. Classic titles are included even if they are currently out-of-print. Entries are arranged by title-page author, with appropriate cross-references, and include full bibliographic information, a descriptive annotation, and a critical commentary. There are detailed title and subject indexes with appropriate geographical or time subdivisions to aid in selecting fiction from a particular locale or of a particular era. The indexes also provide access to large print books for the visually impaired and include 2069 analytical entries for composite works. There is a directory of publishers and distributors with complete current addresses. Issued as part of the Wilson Standard Catalog Series and designed to be used in conjunction with the **Public Library Catalog** which covers nonfiction titles. EF/JKM

HU 104
Fitzgerald/Hemingway Annual. ISSN 0071-5654. 1969. a. bibl. illus. Gale Research Co., Book Tower, Detroit, MI 48226. Examined: 1960; 1974; 1975. Matthew J. Bruccoli and C. E. Frazer Clark, Jr., eds. (1977. Margaret M. Duggan and Richard Layman, eds. 268p. $24.)
Aud: Cl, Pl

A wide-ranging collection of critical and analytical essays, interviews, reviews, bibliographies, auction information, and even some recently discovered original material by the two major American writers who are usually the subjects of the articles. The volume is generally divided into separate sections on the two authors, but occasionally there are articles which treat them jointly. Of interest to the collector and afficionado as well as to the student or scholar. Gale Research Co. began publishing the **Annual** with the 1977 volume. The 1969-1976 volumes are now available from Bruccoli Clark Publishers, 1700 Lone Pine Rd, Bloomfield Hills, MI 48013. AC

HU 105
French XX Bibliography. ISSN 0085-0888. (Continues: French VII Bibliography.) 1949. a. bibl. index. French Institute, 22 E 60th St, New York, NY 10022. Examined: no. 1, 1949; no. 26, 1974; no. 27, 1975. Douglas W. Alden, Ruth-Elaine Tussing, and Peter C. Hay, eds. $30.
Aud: Cl, Sa

Scholarly, comprehensive bibliography of books and journal articles on all aspects of contemporary French literature. The scope is international, and over 500 periodicals are monitored. Separate sections on authors and subjects are thoroughly cross-referenced. Cumulative indexes are issued every five years. Established under the auspices of the Modern Language Association, the work is now a joint venture of the French Institute-Alliance Française and the Camargo Foundation. AC

HU 106
Index of American Periodical Verse. ISSN 0090-9130. 1971. a. Scarecrow Press, 52 Liberty St, Metuchen, NJ 08840. Examined: 1971; 1975. Sander W. Zulaut and Irwin H. Weiser, eds. 394p. $17.50. (1976. 457p.)
Aud: Hs, Jc, Cl, Pl

A location guide to poems which have appeared during the preceding year in approximately 170 periodicals published in the U.S. and Canada. The basic listing is by author with sub-arrangement by title or first line. Entries include abbreviated periodical title, volume, date, and specific page. A separate section provides editor, address, and latest subscription information for each perioical indexed. An index by title and first line, included in earlier volumes, was discontinued in 1975. AC

HU 107
International Authors and Writers Who's Who. (Continues: Authors and Writers Who's Who. ISSN 0067-2386.) 1934. bi-a. Melrose Press, 3 Market Hill, Cambridge CB2 3QP, England; Gale Research Co., Book Tower, Detroit, MI 48226. Examined: 8th ed., 1977. 900p. $52.50.
Aud: Cl, Pl

Contains brief biographical sketches of noteworthy novelists, poets, playwrights, nonfiction writers, and literary critics. Earlier volumes had a stronger British emphasis since they were first published in England; this edition attempts to cover writers in all nations, as the new title indicates. Entries include name, any pseudonyms or pen names, address, date and place of birth, educational and professional background, dates and titles of published works (including a list of periodical articles published), awards, memberships, and agent. JKM

HU 108
International Who's Who in Poetry. ISSN 0539-1342. 1958. bi-a. index. illus. Melrose Press, 3 Market Hill, Cambridge, England. Dist: Rowman and Littlefield, 81 Adams Dr, Totowa, NJ 07512. Examined: 1974/75. Ernest Kay, ed. 880p. $32.50. (5th ed., 1977. $42.50.)
Aud: Cl, Sa

Provides biographical and bibliographical information on approximately 4500 living poets. Entries include personal data and career information, address, title and date of publications, and periodicals in which poems have appeared (but specific citations are not given). There is an index of pen names, and appendixes list poetry societies, poetry magazines from around the world, awards, and resources. Considerable space is devoted to texts of prize-winning poems and photographs of major poets. Intended scope is international, but English language poets dominate heavily. AC

HU 109
Jewish Book Annual. ISSN 0075-3726. 1942. a. bibl. Jewish Welfare Board, Jewish Book Council, 15 E 26th St, New York, NY 10010. Examined: v. 35, 1977/78. Jacob Kabakoff, ed. 276p. $12.75.
Aud: Pl, Sa

An annual recording of Jewish literary activities and activities of the Jewish Book Council. It contains historical and critical commentaries on Jewish authors, publications, and bibliographies. Bibliographies included in volume 35 are: "American Jewish Nonfiction Books, 1976/77"; "American Jewish Fiction Books"; "Jewish Juvenile Books"; "American Hebrew Books"; "Yiddish Books"; "Anglo-Jewish Books"; "Selected Books on Israel"; and "Jewish Book Council and National Jewish Book Awards." The bibliographies include brief annotations. Hebrew and Yiddish book lists are printed in Hebrew and Yiddish. The list of National Jewish Book Awards is arranged by name of the award, and each entry includes a description of award, names of judges, awardee, and awarded work. There is a list of contributors and editors, but no listing of members. LL

HU 110
Literary and Library Prizes. ISSN 0075-9880. (Continues: Literary Prizes and Their Winners; Famous Literary Prizes and Their Winners.) 1935. irreg. index. R. R. Bowker Co., 1180 Ave of the Americas, New York, NY 10036. Dist: R. R. Bowker Co., Box 1807, Ann Arbor, MI 48106. Examined: 9th ed., 1976. Olga S. Weber, ed. 544p. $19.95.
Aud: Cl, Pl

Lists 367 awards (60 new to the ninth edition) in four major areas: International, American, British, and Canadian. Arranged alphabetically by name of award, entries include sponsor, criteria, and list of recipients. An alphabetical name index provides access to prizes and winners. Library awards have been included since the fourth edition published in 1959. KMH

HU 111
Milton Studies. ISSN 0076-8820. 1969. a. University of Pittsburgh Press, 127 N Bellefield Ave, Pittsburgh, PA 15260. Examined: 1969; 1975; 1976. James D. Simmonds, ed. $17.50. (v. 10, 1977. $14.50.)
Aud: Cl, Sa

A collection of lengthy articles (averaging over 3000 words each) intended as a forum for Milton scholarship and criticism. In addition to critical interpretations of aspects of the poet's work and occasional biographical material, there are also studies of broader historical and literary contexts, the work of Milton's contemporaries, traditions which influenced his art and thought, contemporary religious and political movements, Milton's influence on other writers, and the history of critical response to his work. There are no book reviews. AC

HU 112
Modern Humanities Research Association. Annual Bibliography of English Language and Literature. ISSN 0066-3786. 1920. a. bibl. index. Modern Humanities Research Association, Kings College, Strand, London WC2R 2LS England. Dist: Cambridge University Press, Bentley House, 200 Euston Rd, London NW1, England. Examined: v. 48, 1976. Derek Roper, ed. $17.75. (v.49, 1977. 951p.)
Aud: Cl, Sa

An outstanding basic bibliography of books, journal articles, and pamphlets on English language and literature. Though some U.S. publications are included, there is an understandable emphasis on British materials. Recent volumes include over 15,000 bibliographic citations, representing will over 1000 sources. The language entries are arranged by broad subjects: vocabulary, grammar, and semantics. The literature chapters include: Old English, Middle English, and 16th, 17th, 18th, 19th, and 20th centuries. There are separate indexes to writers and subjects treated; authors, editors, translators, etc.; anonymous works; and works in facsimile. AC

HU 113
Modern Humanities Research Association. MHRA Annual Bulletin. ISSN 0076-9975. 1927. a. Modern Humanities Research Association, Kings College, Strand, London WC2R 2LS England. Dist: University of Colorado, Boulder, CO 80309. Examined: 1973; 1976. D. A. Wells, ed. $6.
Aud: Cl, Sa

A guide to research activities and publications of this important British literary association, now international in membership, which is dedicated to the promotion of advanced study and research in the modern humanities, especially European languages and literatures. The **Bulletin** also includes lists of research in progress and lists of members, officers, and committees. AC

HU 114
Modern Language Association of America. MLA International Bibliography of Books and Articles on the Modern Languages and Literatures. ISSN 0024-8215. (Continues: American Bibliography; Annual Bibliography.) 1921. a. bibl. index. Modern Language Association of America, 62 Fifth Ave, New York, NY 10011. Examined: 1974. 3v. $25. (1976. 3v. v. 1, 312p.; v.2, 386p.; v. 3, 204p.)
Aud: Cl, Sa

The most important bibliographic guide to current scholarship in the modern languages and literatures. In the present format there are three volumes which are available separately or in a single library edition. Volume one covers general, English, American, Medieval, and Celtic literature and folklore. European, Asian, African, and Latin-American literature are covered in volume two. Volume three is devoted to linguistics. The books and articles are selected by a committee of 150 scholars, and approximately 3000 periodicals are monitored. The addition of the word "international" to the title in 1963 signalled an extensive enlargement in scope. MLA published a complimentary three-volume annual, *MLA Abstracts*, 1970 through 1975. AC

HU 115
The Nathaniel Hawthorne Journal. 1971. a. bibl.

index. illus. Gale Research Co., Book Tower, Detroit, MI 48226. Examined: 1977. C. E. Frazer Clark, Jr., ed. 320p. $24.
Aud: Cl, Pl

Includes previously unpublished writings by Hawthorne and his contemporaries and biographical, bibliographical, and critical studies. Featured in the 1977 volume is Hawthorne's "Slender Means," the royalties from which he used to support himself through his literary apprenticeship and to publish his first novel. Also included are articles on a wide variety of Hawthorne scholarship, for example, "Who Wrote Hawthorne's First Diary," "Hawthorne's Presence in *Moby-Dick*," "Hawthorne and the Civil War," and "Hawthorne and the Revision of American Art History." Each volume includes a checklist of recent Hawthorne scholarship and book reviews of significant titles in the field. Prior to the 1977 volume, the *Journal* was published by Bruccoli Clark Publishers, 1700 Lone Pine Rd, Bloomfield Hills, MI 48013; the 1971-76 volumes are available from Bruccoli Clark. JKM

HU 116
Nebula Award Stories. ISSN 0077-6408. 1965. a. Harper and Row, 10 E 53rd St, New York, NY 10022. Examined: v. 10, 1975. James Gunn, ed. 254p. (v. 12, 1977. $8.95.)
Aud: Hs, Jc, Cl, Pl

Published for the Science Fiction Writers of America. Includes several novellas and short stories selected by that organization from popular American science fiction magazines. Also includes listings of Nebula and Hugo award winners from the past ten years. JKM

HU 117
New African Literature and the Arts. ISSN 0077-7994. 1966. irreg. Third Press, Joseph Okpaka Publishing Co., 444 Central Park W, New York, NY 10025. Examined: v. 2, 1970; v. 3, 1973. Joseph Okpaka, ed. 394p. $8.95.
Aud: Jc, Cl, Pl, Sa

A collection of essays, articles, literary criticism, and poetry written primarily by authors of African origin. Subjects treated range from African culture and folklore to science and communication. Many of the essays in volume three were originally presented at the first Pan-African Culture Festival held in Algeria in 1969. Biographical notes on the contributors are included. JKM

HU 118
New Dimensions Science Fiction. ISSN 0099-0906. (Continues: New Dimensions.) 1971. a. Harper and Row, 10 E 53rd St, New York, NY 10022. Examined: no. 1, 1971, 246p.; no. 8, 1978. $9.95.
Aud: Hs, Jc, Cl, Pl

An anthology of approximately 14 original science fiction stories which "attempt to negotiate the difficult middle course between the old and the new" in contemporary science fiction. The tales are prefaced by an introduction and biographical information on each author. KR/JKM

HU 119
Oxford Slavonic Papers. ISSN 0078-7256. 1950. a. Oxford University Press, Ely House, London W1, England. Dist: Oxford University Press, 200 Madison Ave, New York, NY 10016. Examined: 1950; 1975; 1976. Robert Auty, J. L. I. Fennell, and I. P. Foote, eds. 122p. $17. (1977.)
Aud: Cl, Sa
Indexed in: *Essay Index*.

A scholarly collection of original articles and documents, plus occasional bibliographic essays and review articles, relating to the languages, literatures, culture, and history of Russia and other Slavonic nations. The volumes are divided into "Old Series" (1950-1967, edited by S. Korovalov) and "New Series," but the general purpose and scope have remained relatively unchanged. Although articles are always in English, each volume includes contributions by scholars from all over the world. AC

HU 120
Prize Stories. ISSN 0079-5453. 1919. a. Doubleday and Co., 245 Park Ave, New York, NY 10017. Examined: 1974; 1975. William Abrahams, ed. $7.95.
Aud: Hs, Jc, Cl, Pl
Indexed in: *Short Story Index*.

An anthology of short stories by American writers that are winners of the O. Henry Awards, a memorial prize established by the Society of Arts and Sciences. The better literary periodicals (*New Yorker, Atlantic*) are always well represented, but fiction from more popular magazines (*Redbook, Mademoiselle*) is found to a greater extent here than in the similar collection, **Best American Short Stories.** Past editors have included Blanche Colton Williams, Harry Hansen, Herschel Brickell, Paul Engle, and Richard Poirier. AC

HU 121
Proof. ISSN 0079-6980. 1971. a. index. illus. J. Faust

and Co., Box 5616, Columbia, SC 29205. Examined: 1971; 1974. Joseph Katz, ed. $22.50. (1977.)
Aud: Cl, Sa

Subtitle: "The yearbook of American bibliographical and textual studies." A scholarly collection in attractive format featuring essays on first editions, variant drafts and editions, and publication histories of important works in American literature. There are also review articles, facsimile illustrations, and a register of current publications. AC

HU 122
The Romantic Movement. ISSN 0557-2738. 1964. a. bibl. University of Colorado, Boulder, CO 80309. Examined: v. 12, 1974; v. 13, 1975. David V. Erdman, ed. $8.
Aud: Cl, Sa

A selective and critical bibliography, compiled by a committee of the Modern Language Association, designed to cover a "movement" rather than a period. For example, although the English section is confined largely to the years 1789-1837, other sections extend over different time spans. It attempts to include all books and articles of scholarly merit on European Romanticism. There are descriptive, and sometimes critical, annotations. Also available as a supplement to the September issue of the quarterly publication *English Language Notes*. From 1936 to 1963 the bibliography was issued as part of *Philological Quarterly*. In 1973 Pierian Press reprinted the 1936 to 1970 volumes as *The Romantic Movement Bibliography* (7v.). The reprint is not a cumulative edition, but it does include an index by name, reviewer, and subject to the entire work and a cumulative list of periodical title abbreviations that have been used. AC/JKM

HU 123
Science Fiction Book Review Index. ISSN 0085-5979. 1970. a. index. H. W. Hall, 3608 Meadow Oaks Lane, Bryan, TX 77801. Examined: v. 17, 1976. H. W. Hall, ed. $5.
Aud: Hs, Cl, Pl

A slim but comprehensive guide to reviews of science fiction books representing all levels: adult, juvenile, technical. Reviews of historical, critical, and bibliographic works are also included. Citations represent approximately 60 periodicals. Basic arrangement is by author with an index to book titles. AC

HU 124
Shakespeare Studies. ISSN 0582-9399. 1965. a. Burt Franklin Co., 235 E 44th St, New York, NY 10017. Examined: 1965; 1976. J. Leeds Barroll III, ed. $8. (v. 7, 1974. 518p.)
Aud: Cl, Sa
Indexed in: *Modern Language Abstracts*.

A handsomely-printed collection of research essays, criticism, and extensive book reviews by English and American scholars on literary, philosophical, aesthetic, and theatrical aspects of Shakespeare's plays and their production. Editorial offices are at the University of Tennessee, but there is an international advisory board. AC

HU 125
Shakespeare Survey. ISSN 0080-9152. 1948. a. bibl. illus. Cambridge University Press, Bentley House, 200 Euston Rd, London NW1, England. Examined: 1948; 1974; 1975. Kenneth Muir, ed. $19.95. (v. 29, 1976, 191p., $19; v. 30, 1977. 214p. $21.95.)
Aud: Cl, Sa
Indexed in: *Essay Index*.

A collection of essays, reviews, and information on performances, intended as a critical survey of the year's contributions to Shakespearean study and production. Each volume reviews new books, journal articles, and productions around the world. Essays focus on some special topic, such as the comedies or Shakespeare's use of language. There are full-page photographs of scenes from major productions. The first 18 volumes were edited by Allardyce Nicoll. AC

HU 126
Short Story Index. ISSN 0098-3756. (Continues: Index to Short Stories.) 1900. a. w/quinquennial cum. bibl. index. H. W. Wilson Co., 950 University Ave, Bronx, NY 10452. Examined: 1969/73 cum. Gary L. Bogart and Estelle A. Fidell, eds. 639p. $30. (1976, 199p.; 1977. $20.)
Aud: Jh, Hs, Jc, Cl, Pl

A guide to short story fiction appearing in anthologies and, since 1974, in approximately 45 periodicals. Entries are indexed under author, title, and subject. Each volume includes an alphabetical list of the collections indexed with full bibliographic information, a directory of publishers and distributors, and a directory of periodicals indexed. The first volume in the set, published in 1953, covers the years 1900-49 and supersedes the *Index to Short Stories* (1923-36). With the publication of the 1974/78 cumulation, approximately 112,500 short stories published in collections or periodicals will have been indexed. Basic to readers' advisory as well as reference services. AC/JKM

HU 127
Something about the Author. 1971. irreg. bibl. index. illus. Gale Research Co., Book Tower, Detroit, MI 48226. Examined: v. 13, 1978. Anne Commire, ed. 257p. $25.
Aud: El, Jh, Pl
Indexed in: *Biographical Dictionaries Master Index.*

Subtitle: "Facts and pictures about contemporary authors and illustrators of books for young people." A children's version of Gale's **Contemporary Authors.** Provides information on the lives, careers, and works of popular contemporary authors and illustrators of children's books. Authors who died prior to 1961 are covered in Gale's **Yesterday's Authors of Books for Children.** Entries include personal and career information, complete bibliographies, critical commentary, examples of book illustrations and jacket designs, and often, photographs of the author and personal comments. Well illustrated and set in large size type. Each volume contains about 200 entries and a cumulative index of authors and illustrators. JKM

HU 128
Speech Communication Association. Directory. ISSN 0081-3648. (Continues: Speech Association of America. Directory.) 1941. irreg. index. Speech Communication Association, 5205 Leesburg Pike, Falls Church, VA 22041. Examined: 1941; 1964; 1973/74. Robert N. Hall, ed. $7.
Aud: Cl, Sa

A list of names, addresses, degrees, and major professional interests of members of the national Speech Communication Association and four regional affiliate groups. Also includes lists of officers and committees, selected journals, institutions and administrative officers of speech in higher education; graduate degree programs; a checklist of books, equipment, and supplies; and an extensive geographic index of members by state and locality. Issued from 1941 to 1969 by the Association under its earlier name; the new title took effect with the 1970/71 volume. AC

HU 129
Speech Index. ISSN 0081-3656. 1935. irreg. Scarecrow Press, 52 Liberty St, Box 656, Metuchen, NJ 08840. Examined: 4th ed., 1966, Roberta Briggs Sutton, ed., 947p., $22.50; 1971/75 suppl. Charity Mitchell, ed. 126p. $8.50.

Subtitle: "An index to collections of world famous orations and speeches for various occasions." The basic volume indexes speeches published in 259 anthologies by author, subject, and type of speech in a single alphabet. Each edition cumulates the contents of previous editions and supplements, as well as indexing new anthologies. The latest supplement (1971/75) covers an additional 33 anthologies. JKM

HU 130
Tennessee Studies in Literature. ISSN 0497-2384. 1956. a. University of Tennessee Press, 293 Communications Bldg, Knoxville, TN 37916. Examined: 1958; 1959; 1976. Richard M. Kelly, ed. 126p. $7.50. (v. 22, 1977. $7.50.)
Aud: Cl, Sa
Indexed in: *Essay Index; Modern Language Abstracts.*

A collection of essays on a wide range of literary themes. Frequently individual issues focus on a special general topic, such as American literature, 18th century literature, and others of similar breadth. An introductory section provides an abstract of each essay in the volume. Although there is no formal geographic restriction on source of essays, contributions from Southern scholars are particularly encouraged. AC

HU 131
Thomas Hardy Year Book. ISSN 0082-416X. 1970. a. illus. Toucan Press, Mound Durand, St. Peter Port, Guernsey, C.I., England. Examined: 1970; 1973/74; v. 5, 1975. J. Stevens Cox and G. Stevens Cox, eds. 108p. (v. 7, 1977. $.96.)
Aud: Cl, Sa
Indexed in: *British Humanities Index.*

A small but charming and useful collection of critical and biographical essays, research articles, and memorabilia about the life and times of Thomas Hardy, his physical and cultural environment, and other Dorset writers of the 19th century. A particularly attractive feature is the frequent inclusion of previously unpublished photographs of Hardy's Wessex from an extensive private collection in the editors' possession. AC

HU 132
Tulane Studies in English. ISSN 0082-6758. 1949. irreg. Tulane University, Department of English, New Orleans, LA 70118. Examined: v. 21, 1974. Huling E. Ussery, ed. 131p. $8.
Aud: Cl, Sa
Indexed by: *Abstracts of English Studies; Modern Language Abstracts.*

This scholarly journal is a collection of articles dealing with history and criticism of English and American literature. The 1974 volume includes seven articles. Only those who hold a doctoral degree in English from Tulane University may publish in this journal. JKM

HU 133
Twentieth Century Literary Criticism. 1978. irreg. index. Gale Research Co., Book Tower, Detroit, MI 48226. Examined: v. 1, 1978. Dedria Bryfonski and Phyllis Carmel Mendelson, eds. 604p. $38.
Aud: Hs, Jc, Cl, Pl

Subtitle: "Excerpts from criticism of the works of novelists, poets, playwrights, and other creative writers of the era 1900-1960." International in scope, this reference tool presents significant passages from published criticism of the works of creative writers who died between 1900 and 1960. For each of the 28 authors included in the first volume, there is also a brief biographical summary and a list of principal works. Intended to be a companion volume to Gale's **Contemporary Literary Criticism** which covers authors now living and those who have died since 1960. A cumulative index to authors and critics will be included in subsequent volumes. AS/JKM

HU 134
Women and Literature. 1971. irreg. bibl. index. illus. Women and Literature Collective, Box 441, Cambridge, MA 02138. Examined: 3rd ed., 1976. 212p. $3.50.
Aud: Cl, Pl

Subtitle: "An annotated bibliography of women writers." Arranged by country and by century with a section of anthologies and one of works about literature. The American and British sections are the most extensive, but works by women in Africa, Asia, Australia, Canada, Europe, and Latin America are also included. There is an author and subject index. KAC.

HU 135
Write on, Woman! 1977. a. index. Lynne D. Shapiro, 92 Horatio St, 4S, New York, NY 10014. Examined: 1977. Lynne D. Shapiro, ed. 32p. $3.50.
Aud: Sa

Subtitle: "A writer's guide to U.S. women's/feminist/lesbian alternate press periodicals." Lists pertinent information about each periodical such as the type of material published, deadlines, the degree of interest in unsolicited manuscripts, and whether the periodical pays for its articles. There is an index by type of material published. KAC

HU 136
Yearbook of Comparative and General Literature. ISSN 0084-3695. 1952. a. bibl. Comparative Literature Office, Ballantine Hall 402, Indiana University Press, Bloomington, IN 47401. Examined: 1952; 1975; v. 25, 1976. Horst Frenz, ed. 132p. $5.
Aud: Cl, Sa

A collection of articles, symposia, reviews of professional works, news and notes, and a bibliography of literary works in English translation. Earlier volumes contain an annual bibliography of comparative literature, but this was discontinued after 1970. Published in collaboration with the Comparative Literature Committee of the National Council of Teachers of English, the American Comparative Literature Association, and the Comparative Literature Section of the Modern Language Association. AC

HU 137
Yearbook of Comparative Criticism. ISSN 0084-3709. 1968. a. Pennsylvania State University Press, University Park, PA 16802. Examined: 1968; v. 7, 1976. Joseph P. Strelka, ed. 306p. $12. (v. 8, 1977. 281p. $13.75.)
Aud: Cl, Sa

A collection of essays by noted literary scholars that is devoted to the methodology of literary study with an international perspective. Contributions address fundamental questions and principles of literary theory, comparison of methods of literary criticism, and application of different methods to practical examples in literary history. Each volume has a special focus, e.g., literary criticism and psychology, literary criticism and sociology, and perspectives in literary symbolism. AC

HU 138
Yearbook of English Studies. 1971. a. Modern Humanities Research Association, Kings College, Strand, London WC2R 2LS, England. Examined: v. 3, 1973; v. 7, 1977. G. K. Hunter and C. J. Rawson, eds. 340p. £10.
Aud: Cl, Sa

A scholarly collection of essays and reviews on the literature and language of English-speaking countries. Beginning in 1978, there will also be specially commissioned articles on a broad topic or theme. Articles tend toward specific rather than general subjects, and contributors are primarily from the universities of the United Kingdom. More than half of each volume consists of lengthy, frequently comparative reviews of scholarly works on English literature from all over the world, including publications in other languages. AC

HU 139
Year's Work in English Studies. ISSN 0084-4144.

1919/20. a. bibl. index. John Murray, 50 Albemarle St, London W1X 4BD, England. Dist: Humanities Press, Atlantic Highlands, NJ 07716. Examined: 1919/20; v. 55, 1974. James Redmond, ed. 610p. $15.75.
Aud: Cl, Sa

A selective survey, with descriptive and critical commentary, of recent books and journal articles published in Europe or America on English literature. Present format consists of chapters on major chronological and subject divisions (history and criticism, English language, Middle English, Shakespeare, 20th century, etc.). In recent years it has included a separate chapter on American literature. A useful companion to the Modern Humanities Research Association's **Annual Bibliography of English Language and Literature**, which is much more comprehensive but lacks annotations. Published under the auspices of the English Association. Publication is rather late; the 1974 volume was published in 1977. AC

HU 140

Year's Work in Modern Language Studies. ISSN 0084-4152. 1929/30. a. bibl. index. Modern Humanities Research Association, King's College, Strand, London WC2R 2LS, England. Dist: International Publications Service, 114 E 32nd St, New York, NY 10016. Examined: v. 33, 1971; v. 37, 1975. Glanville Price and David A. Wells, eds. $40. (v. 38, 1976. 1094p.)
Aud: Cl, Sa

A critical survey of books and periodicals published during the previous year in the fields of literary and linguistic studies. The scholarly bibliographic essays are divided into major sections: general linguistics, Medieval Latin, Romance languages (extensively subdivided by specific language and period), and Celtic, Germanic, and Slavonic languages. Approximately 1000 sources are cited in the most recent volume. There are very detailed name and subject indexes. AC

HU 141

Yesterday's Authors of Books for Children. 1977. irreg. bibl. index. illus. Gale Research Co., Book Tower, Detroit, MI 48226. Examined: 1977. Anne Commire, ed. 2v. 609p. $25 per v.
Aud: El, Jh, Pl

Subtitle: "Facts and pictures about authors and illustrators of books for young people from early times to 1960." Provides bio-bibliographical information on children's authors and illustrators who died prior to 1961. Living authors and authors who have died since 1961 are covered in Gale's **Something about the Author.** Each volume will cover about 60 authors and illustrators. The author and illustrator index in each volume will cumulate index entries from all previous volumes. Well illustrated with portraits, drawings, and photographs. In addition to personal and professional information on each author or illustrator, entries include listings of secondary sources, such as books, journal articles, films, filmstrips, and recordings, about the author's life and work. JKM

LIBRARY SCIENCE

HU 142

Advances in Librarianship. 1970. a. bibl. index. Academic Press, 111 Fifth Ave, New York, NY 10003. Examined: 1977. Melvin J. Voight and Michael H. Harris, eds. 344p. $22.50.
Aud: Sa
Indexed in: *Library Literature; Library and Information Science Abstracts; Information Science Abstracts.*

A literature review of topics in the field of librarianship which are deemed important for the year by the editors. Such topics as the machine and cataloging, bibliotherapy, trends in library education, relevance, public librarianship, sound recordings, and women in librarianship have appeared in recent volumes. Each article includes excellent bibliographies of works on the topic under discussion. There is a subject and author index to each volume. EF

HU 143

American Library Association. ALA Membership Directory. 1949. a. American Library Association, 50 E Huron St, Chicago, IL 60611. Examined: 1977. 256p. $10; free to institutional members.
Aud: Sa

A directory of both personal and institutional members of the American Library Association, including foreign members. The directory gives title, address (usually business), and place of employment. The listing is arranged alphabetically. The volume also provides information on the ALA organization covering headquarters staff, charter, membership by state, officers, etc. EF

HU 144

American Library Association. The ALA Yearbook. 1976. a. bibl. index. illus. American Library Association, 50 E Huron St, Chicago, IL 60611. Examined: 1977. Robert Wedgeworth, ed. 432p. $25.

Aud: Sa
Indexed in: *Library Literature*.

Subtitle: "A review of library events." Provides information about activities, events, and organizations that reflect the diverse interests of the American Library Association for the year preceding the publication of the volume, i.e., the 1977 edition reviews activities in 1976. Individual contributors, notable in the profession, write articles about topics of interest to the association and its membership. The topics have included library education, public librarianship, the British Library, the ALA Centennial celebration, etc. EF

HU 145
American Library Association. Audiocassette Programs from the Annual Conference. 1972. a. American Library Association, 50 E Huron St, Chicago, IL 60611. Examined: 1977. 45 cassettes. $11.95 per cassette.
Aud: Sa

Audiocassettes made from tapes of selected programs at ALA's annual conference. Topics covered in the 1977 publication include: "How to Avoid the Practice of Law When Giving Legal Reference Service in Public and University Libraries," "Economics of Providing Information and Services," "Upstairs, Downstairs: Approaches to Selecting, Acquiring, and Processing Microforms," "Indexes and Periodical Use," "Subject Heading Control in Catalog Management," "Public Service and the On-Line Catalog," "Ethnic Pluralism: The Emerging American Identity—from Fragmentation to the New Pluralism," and "The Prostitution of Information: Fees for Service." Discounts from 10-30 percent are given on orders of 10-51 cassettes. JKM

HU 146
American Library Association. Directory of Library Science Libraries. 1976. a. American Library Association, Library Education Division, 50 E Huron St, Chicago, IL 60611. Examined: 1976. Carol S. Nielson and Kathryn Hall, eds. 50p. $1.
Aud: Cl, Pl

Describes the library science library facilities in 24 accredited library schools. The alphabetically arranged descriptions include hours of opening, number of seats, periodical holdings, classification system used, etc. A useful referral resource. JKM

HU 147
American Library Association. Handbook of Organization. 1970/71. a. index. American Library Association, 50 E Huron St, Chicago, IL 60611. Examined: 1977/78. 130p. $4; free to members.
Aud: Sa

A guide to the structure of the American Library Association, its officers, council members, committee members, staff, representatives, etc. The directory also contains background information on the association including the functions of all the units and awards, citations, and scholarships given by the ALA. All the publications of the association and its divisions are enumerated, and copies of the constitution and the bylaws are included. There is a general index and a name index. EF

HU 148
American Library Directory. ISSN 0065-910X. 1923. bi-a. index. R. R. Bowker, 1180 Ave of the Americas, New York, NY 10036. Dist: R. R. Bowker, Box 1807, Ann Arbor, MI 48106. Examined: 29th ed., 1974/75, 1242p; 30th ed., 1976/77. Jaques Cattell Press, ed. $45. (31st ed., 1978. 1390p. $47.50.)
Aud: Jc, Cl, Pl, Sa

Directory of public, university, college and junior college libraries. Also listed are special libraries, including armed forces, medical, law, religious, institutional, and recreational libraries. Entries give name, address, telephone number, personnel (sometimes an abbreviated listing), income and expenditures, number of volumes, microform holdings, etc. For libraries with special collections, the number of vertical file drawers is indicated; college and university entries note the enrollment. Arranged by state or province, then by city or town; population statistics are given for each. EF

HU 149
American Society for Information Science. Proceedings. ISSN 0040-7870. 1964. a. bibl. index. American Society for Information Science, 1155 16th St, NW, Washington, DC 20036. Dist: Knowledge Industry Publications, Two Corporate Park Dr, White Plains, NY 10604. Examined: v. 13, 1976, 176p. w/10 microfiche; v. 14, 1977. 127p. w/10 microfiche. $17.50; $14 to members.
Aud: Sa
Indexed in: *Library Literature; Information Science Abstracts; Library and Information Science Abstracts*.

The printed proceedings of the annual American Society for Information Science conference are published before the conference begins. Contains abstracts written by the authors of papers they will deliver at the conference. Where the papers are available in full, they have been put on microfiche and included in a packet in the back of the volume. Each volume reflects the special theme of that year's conference. In 1977 the theme was "Information Management in the 1980's." EF

HU 150

Annual Review of Information Science and Technology. ISSN 066-4200. 1966. a. index. American Society for Information Science, 1155 16th St, NW, Washington, DC 20036. Dist: Knowledge Industry Publications, 2 Corporate Park Dr, White Plains, NY 10604. Examined: v. 10, 1975, Carlos Cuadra, ed., $27.50; v. 11, 1976. Martha Williams, ed. $28. (v. 12, 1977. 389p.)
Aud: Sa
Indexed in: *Information Science Abstracts; Library Literature.*

Includes a comprehensive literature review and state-of-the-art reports on selected topics in the field of information science and technology, such as design and evaluation of information systems, bibliotherapy, information needs and uses, document retrieval, etc. Each volume includes a thorough author/subject/name index. A cumulative index covering the 1966 through 1975 volumes is available. EF

HU 151

Association of American Library Schools. Directory. 1943. a. index. Association of American Library Schools, 471 Park Lane, State College, PA 16801. Examined: 1976. Lucille Wert, ed. 84p. $3.
Aud: Sa

Lists all accredited and non-accredited programs in library schools in the U.S. and Canada. Provides the names of the deans and directors of each program with their addresses and telephone numbers, as well as names of faculty members with their areas of specialization. EF

HU 152

Association of Research Libraries. ARL Statistics. 1968/69. a. Association of Research Libraries, 1527 New Hampshire Ave, NW, Washington, DC 20036. Examined: 1975/76. Suzanne Frankie, comp. 46p. free.
Aud: Sa

Statistics are provided by the 105 members of the Association of Research Libraries. Includes statistics on materials budget, size of collection, number of staff, and general expenditures. EF

HU 153

Biographical Directory of Librarians in the United States and Canada. (Continues: Who's Who in Library Service.) (1955 is 3rd ed.) irreg. American Library Association, 50 E Huron St, Chicago, IL 60611. Examined: 5th ed., 1970. Lee Ash, ed. 1250p. $45.
Aud: Sa
Indexed in: *Biographical Dictionaries Master Index.*

Provides biographical information on approximately 20,000 librarians, archivists, and information scientists. Entries indicate date and place of birth, name of spouse, education, foreign language facility, positions held, other important career or special assignments, organizations, major honors, publications, principal areas of professional interest, and mailing address. Information is compiled from questionnaires mailed to librarians in North America. JKM

HU 154

British Librarianship and Information Science. ISSN 0071-5662. (Continues: Fives Years' Work in Librarianship; Year's Work in Librarianship.) 1972. quinquennial. bibl. index. Library Association, 7 Ridgmount St, Store St, London SC1, England. Examined: 1971/75. 379p.
Aud: Sa

Aims to present a general picture of what happened in British librarianship during the five years examined, as opposed to an anthology or critical review of the literature. The editors solicit scholarly articles (the subjects and emphases of which are changed quinquennially) from professionals in the field in order to obtain this current overview. Articles are arranged by section category. Includes a complete subject and title index, abbreviations lists, lists of reference, and corrections to earlier editions. KR/JKM

HU 155

Council on Library Resources. Report. ISSN 0070-1181. 1956/57. a. index. Council on Library Resources, One Dupont Circle, Suite 620, Washington, DC 20036. Examined: 1975. 56p. free.
Aud: Sa.
Indexed in: *ERIC.*

Annual report of the expenditures, grants, and programs that the Council has sponsored during the previous year. The document gives names of recipients of grants and the exact nature of their research. There is an index to grants. This publication is of particular interest to librarians who wish to seek grants to assist in research efforts. *Library Literature* provides access to summaries of or excerpts from the report which are published in the periodicals it indexes. EF

HU 156
Directory of Government Document Collections and Librarians. 1974. irreg. index. Congressional Information Service, 7101 Wisconsin Ave, Suite 900, Washington, DC 20014. Examined: 1978. 544p. $22.50.
Aud: Hs, Jc, Cl, Pl

Compiled and edited by the American Library Association's Government Documents Round Table. The main portion of the work presents detailed descriptions of approximately 2300 U.S. libraries' holdings of federal, state, local, foreign, and international government documents. Each description includes the names of staff responsible for the collection and the library's access policy. There are indexes by category of documents collected, staff, and other persons and organizations involved in government documents activities. JKM

HU 157
Directory of Special Libraries and Information Centers. 1963. irreg. index. Gale Research Co., Book Tower, Detroit, MI 48226. Examined: 4th ed., 1977. Margaret L. Young, Harold C. Young, and Anthony Kruzas, eds. 3v. v. 1, 1187p., $74; v. 2, 657p., $45; v. 3, $60.
Aud: Hs, Jc, Cl, Pl

Covers special libraries, research libraries, information centers, archives, and data centers managed by government agencies, business, industry, newspapers, educational institutions, nonprofit organizations, and societies in the fields of science, technology, medicine, law, art, religion, history, social science, and humanistic studies. Volume one, "Special Libraries and Information Centers in the U.S. and Canada," provides an alphabetical list of libraries by sponsoring organization or institution with a subject index. Entries include the name of the library, the address and telephone number, the head librarian or manager, founding date, size of the staff, subject areas covered by the collection, any special collections, book holdings, microforms, periodicals, services offered, publications, any automated operations, and any networks or consortia of which the library is a part. Volume two is a geographic-personnel index. The two volumes are updated between editions by volume three, "New Special Libraries," which is published periodically (subscription includes four inter-edition issues). A valuable reference tool for high schools, colleges, and public libraries. Libraries with limited budgets or with a defined clientele may wish to consider purchasing individual volumes in Gale's companion publication, the **Subject Directory of Special Libraries and Information Centers.** EF/JKM

HU 158
Financial Assistance for Library Education. (Continues: Fellowships, Scholarships, Grants-in-Aid, Loan Funds, and Other Financial Assistance for Library Education.) 1961. a. index. American Library Association, Library Education Division, 50 E Huron St, Chicago, IL 60611. Examined: 1976/77. Margaret Myers, ed. 79p. $.50.
Aud: Jc, Cl, Pl

Describes scholarships, fellowships, etc., worth over $500 for assistance in library education. Descriptions include the amount of the award, the number of awards available, and the eligibility requirements. Awards granted by state and provincial library agencies, associations, and similar organizations in the U.S. and Canada are arranged by state or province. National and regional awards are arranged alphabetically. There is a list of accredited library schools and an index to financial awards for special groups and for degrees at other than the master's level. JKM

HU 159
LIST: Library and Information Services Today. 1971. a. index. Gale Research Co., Book Tower, Detroit, MI 48226. Examined: 1976. Paul Wasserman, ed. 633p. $46.85.
Aud: Sa

Subtitle: "An international registry of research and innovation." Contains descriptions of on-going library-related research in traditional fields of study, e.g., agriculture, literature, and medicine, as well as in such emerging fields as women's studies, environmental studies, American Indian studies, etc. Citations are arranged by subject, then by principal investigator. Entries usually include a statement of the purpose of the study. Indexes to investigators, titles, organizations, geographic areas, funding agencies, types of libraries, subjects, and acronyms and initialisms are provided. The first three volumes were produced by Science Associates, then the publication was taken over by Gale Research Company. EF

HU 160
Library Lit: The Best of (year). ISSN 0085-2767. 1971. a. Scarecrow Press, 52 Liberty St, Metuchen, NJ 08840. Examined: 1977. Bill Katz, ed. 349p. $12.
Aud: Sa

A panel of judges and the editor cull 30 of the best articles from library periodicals published during the previous year. The selection aims at being a "crystallization of all that is exciting and progressive" in librarianship. General categories are: libraries and librarians, technical services/technical processes, communication and education, and the social prerogative. A list of contributors is included. Bibliographies often accompany the articles. KR/JKM

HU 161
Library Networks. ISSN 0145-9627. 1974/75. bi-a. bibl. index. Knowledge Industry Publications, 2 Corporate Dr, White Plains, NY 10604. Examined: 3rd ed., 1978/79. Susan K. Martin. approx. 130p. $29.50; $24.50 soft cover.
Aud: Pf, Sa

Surveys the history of and current developments in library networks. Chapter titles include: "The Scope of Networking"; "Implications of Machine-Readable Data"; "Network Organization"; "Suppliers to the Market"; "Network Management"; "National Efforts"; and "Networks and the Future." The appendix lists 26 library networks in North America and their members. Includes an extensive bibliography and index. JKM

HU 162
Library Statistics of Colleges and Universities. 1939/40. bi-a. U.S. Department of Health, Education, and Welfare, Education Division, Washington, DC 20202. Dist: Superintendent of Documents, U.S. Government Printing Office, Washington, DC 20402. Examined: 1973/74, 2v., v. 1, 300p., $1.70; v. 2, 98p., $3.25; 1975/76. Stanley Smith and Nicholas Osso, eds. v. 1, 397p., $5.25.
Aud: Cl, Sa

Provides statistics on college and university libraries as part of HEGIS (Higher Education General Information Survey) which began in 1967 and LIBGIS (Library Information Survey) which started in 1975. This statistical survey includes data on library collections, staffing, expenditures, and developmental areas for 2980 colleges and universities representing 98.1 percent of the college population in the U.S. The statistics are issued in two volumes which are not necessarily published simultaneously. Volume one includes institutional data, and volume two includes summary data. EF

HU 163
Microforms: The Librarians' View. 1976. irreg. bibl. index. illus. Knowledge Industry Publications, 2 Corporate Dr, White Plains, NY 10604. Examined: 1978/79. Alice Harrison Bahr, ed. approx. 130p. $24.50.
Aud: Pf, Sa

Reports on recent trends and developments in the use, care, handling, and storage of microforms. Covers such topics as computer-output-microform (COM), economics of microforms, the proposed American National Standards Institute (ANSI) microforms standards, acquisition tools, microform viewing equipment, and both traditional and innovative uses of microforms in libraries. The appendixes list MARC-FICHE users and selected microform cabinet manufacturers, and provide sample microform policy statements. There is a detailed bibliography and an index to the volume. JKM

HU 164
National Commission on Libraries and Information Science. Annual Report to the President and Congress. ISSN 0091-2972. 1971/72. a. National Commission on Libraries and Information Science, 1717 K St, NW, Washington, DC 20036. Dist: Superintendent of Documents, U.S. Government Printing Office, Washington, DC 20402. Examined: 1975/76. 89p. $2.
Aud: Sa

Describes the activities of the National Commission on Libraries and Information Science (NCLIS), including studies it has conducted in the past year, goals and objectives of the group, administration and organization, members of the Commission, etc. EF

HU 165
OCLC Annual Report. (Continues: Ohio College Library Center. Annual Report.) 1967/68. a. OCLC, 1125 Kinnear Rd, Columbus, OH 43212. Examined: 1975/76. Frederick G. Kilgour, ed. 21p. free.
Aud: Sa

In early 1978 the governmental structure of the Ohio College Library Center was changed to provide national, rather than state-wide, control. At the same time, its name was changed to OCLC which, in the words of the news release announcing the change, does not stand for anything. The report provides yearly statistics, describes new projects which OCLC has engaged in for the past year, and updates ongoing projects. Includes a list of members of the Board of Trustees and members of the system. Also includes grants that OCLC has been awarded and its budget. The publication is of particular interest to those libraries using or contemplating the use of the OCLC system of card production and/or serials control. EF/JKM

HU 166
SHARE: A Directory of Feminist Library Workers. (Continues: Sisters Have Resources Everywhere: A

Directory of Feminist Library Workers.) 1975. a. index. Women Library Workers, Box 9052, Berkeley, CA 94709. Examined: 3rd ed., 1978. Carole Leita, ed. 58p. $3.
Aud: Sa
Indexed in: *Directory Information Service*.

Arranged geographically by state and, within state, by name. The entries are prepared by the persons included; each includes home and usually work address and phone number, and a statement of the resources the person has to share. Resources to share range from offers of temporary living space to offers of assistance and sharing of experience on subjects such as credit unions, co-oping, publishing, and single-parenting. Name, subject, organizational affiliation, and publications indexes are included. Formerly biennial; annual publication was announced in the third edition. JKM

HU 167
Special Library Association. Annual Directory Issue. ISSN 0038-6723. 1948. a. index. Special Library Association, 235 Park Ave S, New York, NY 10003. Examined: v. 68, no. 10, 1977. Nancy M. Viggiano, ed. $12; free to subscribers.
Aud: Sa

A directory of the Special Library Association. Includes information on the history; honors and awards; chapter, affiliate, and division membership statistics; officers; staff; committee members; divisions and sections; representatives to other associations; structure; etc. A new directory entitled "Institutions Where SLA Members Are Employed: An SLA Directory" will be available in Fall 1978 for $15. EF

HU 168
Subject Directory of Special Libraries and Information Centers. 1963. irreg. index. Gale Research Co., Book Tower, Detroit, MI 48226. Examined: 4th ed., 1977. Margaret L. Young, Harold C. Young, and Anthony Kruzas, eds. 5v. 1437p. $125; $30 per v.
Aud: Hs, Jc, Cl, Pl

A rearrangement by subject of the entries in Gale's **Directory of Special Libraries and Information Centers.** Volume one covers business and law libraries, including military and transportation libraries; volume two lists education and information science libraries, including picture, audiovisual, publishing, rare book, and recreational libraries; volume three lists health sciences libraries, including all aspects of basic and applied medical sciences; volume four covers social sciences and humanities libraries, including area/ethnic, art, geography/map, history, music, religion/theology, theater, and urban/regional libraries; and volume five covers science and technology libraries, including agricultural, environmental/conservation, and food science libraries. Entries indicate the name of the library, the address and telephone number, the name of the head librarian or manager, size of the staff, subject specialization, size of holdings, services provided, publications, etc. Arranged by subject within each subject volume. The individual volumes are much less expensive than the complete **Directory** and would be useful to the subject specialist and in smaller general libraries that have a defined clientele. JKM

HU 169
U.S. Library of Congress. Annual Report of the Librarian of Congress. ISSN 0083-1565. 1866. a. index. Library of Congress, Washington, DC 20540. Dist: Superintendent of Documents, U.S. Government Printing Office, Washington, DC 20402. Examined: 1975. approx. 90p. $6.40.
Aud: Sa

Details the activities of the Library of Congress during the preceding year. Includes the *Annual Report* of the Register of Copyrights. The report is supplemented by the *Quarterly Journal of the Library of Congress. Library Literature* provides access to summaries of or excerpts from the **Report** which are published in periodicals it indexes. EF

HU 170
University of Illinois at Urbana-Champaign. Clinic on Library Applications of Data Processing. Proceedings. ISSN 0069-4789. 1963. a. bibl. index. University of Illinois, Graduate School of Library Science, Champaign, IL 61820. Dist: University of Illinois Publications Office, 249 Armory Bldg, Champaign, IL 61820. Examined: 1976. J. L. Divilbiss, ed. 164p. $8.
Aud: Sa
Indexed in: *Library Literature*.

The proceedings of the annual clinic given at the University of Illinois Graduate School of Library Science on data processing applications in libraries. Although each volume has a different theme (the 1976 volume focuses on the economics of library automation), the series as a whole gives librarians an overview of what has happened and is happening in the field of library automation. EF

MOTION PICTURES

HU 171
Film Literature Index. ISSN 0093-6758. 1973. a. w/q. suppls. Filmdex, Albany, NY. Dist: R. R. Bowker, Box 1807, Ann Arbor, MI 48106. Examined: 1975. Vincent J. Aceto, Jane Graves, and Fred Silva, eds. 609p. $67.50.
Aud: Cl, Pl

An author and subject index to approximately 140 film journals and to writings on film in about 150 general scholarly periodicals. Access to the articles indexed is also provided under name of performer, director, cinematographer, film title, festivals and awards, and professional societies. The quarterly supplements are available only from Filmdex. The annual cumulations are somewhat late in publication; the 1973 and 1974 volumes were published in 1975, and the 1975 volume was published in 1977. KMH

HU 172
Film Review Digest Annual. 1976. a. index. KTO Press, Kraus-Thomson Organization, Millwood, NY 10546. Examined: 1977. David M. Brownstone and Irene M. Franck, eds. 394p. $35.
Aud: Cl, Pl

Cumulates the quarterly issues of *Film Review Digest*. Contains about 1500 abstracts of film reviews that appeared in 26 U.S., British, and Canadian publications. Reviews are arranged alphabetically by film title; about 300 feature films that opened in the U.S. during the preceding year are covered. Includes a separate index of reviewers, a list of awards, and a "people and film titles" index. KR/JKM

HU 173
International Film Guide. ISSN 0074-6053. 1964. a. index. Tantivy Press, 108 New Bond St, London W1Y 0QX England. Dist: A. S. Barnes and Co., Cranbury, NJ 08512. Examined: 1976. Peter Cowie, ed. 608p. $4.95. (1978. $6.95.)
Aud: Pl

Provides information on the year's events in the motion picture industry throughout the world. Brief articles present information on the state of feature film production, recent "important" films, leading film groups, film shorts, film distributors, and film festivals in 50 countries. A section entitled "Directors of the Year" includes a biographical sketch and a filmography of leading film directors. There is a list of film festivals with approximate dates, a brief history of the festival, where to write for information, and, occasionally, recent festival award winners. A separate section on television includes information on public television in America, the British Broadcasting Corporation (BBC), winners of the Emmy Awards and other major television awards, major television production companies, and television events in Finland, France, Greece, Italy, and the Netherlands. Also includes listings of preview theaters, film insurance companies, film transporters, film archives, film schools, film magazines, industry or government sponsored films, film studios and labs, etc. There is a brief section of reviews of recent books on the film industry. Includes many advertisements, often making it difficult to follow the text. There is an index to advertisers. JKM

HU 174
International Motion Picture Almanac. ISSN 0074-7084. (Continues: Motion Picture and Television Almanac.) 1929. a. index. illus. Quigley Publishing Co., 1270 Sixth Ave, New York, NY 10020. Examined: 49th ed., 1978. Richard Gertner, ed. 680p. $15.
Aud: Pl, Sa

Subtitle: "Reference tool of the film industry." A complete compendium of information on the motion picture industry. The 19 sections in the 49th edition include: statistics on theater grosses, expenses, attendance, etc.; the Great Hundred, a list of outstanding motion pictures; an extensive who's who listing; feature films released during the preceding year; services, covering all film-related services from animal trainers to film distributors; talent and literary agencies; publicity representatives; corporations; theater circuits, i.e., companies owning three or more individual theaters; drive-in theaters; equipment; non-theatrical motion pictures; film related organizations; the press, covering trade publications, newspapers, fan magazines, and magazine film editors; the industry self-regulation code; the film industry in Great Britain and Ireland; world market; and international film festivals. There is a subject index and an index to advertisers. JKM

HU 175
New York Times Film Reviews. 1969/70. bi-a. index. Arno Press, 3 Park Ave, New York, NY 10016. Examined: 1975/76. 365p. $60.
Aud: Cl, Pl, Sa

Includes photo reprints of film reviews arranged chronologically as they appeared in the *New York Times*. Reviews are indexed by film title; individuals mentioned, i.e., performers, producer, director, screenwriter, etc.; and producing or distributing corporation. Supplements the original six-volume set, *New York Times Film Reviews: 1896-1970* (Arno Press, 1970). KR/JKM

HU 176
Screen World. ISSN 0080-8288. 1949. a. index. illus. Crown Publishers, 419 Park Ave S, New York, NY 10016. Examined: v. 27, 1976. John Willis. 256p. $12.95. (1978. $9.95.)
Aud: Pl

(Title varies: *John Willis' Screen World.*)

A pictorial review of the year in motion pictures. Sections include: top box office stars; domestic films released in the U.S. (with cast and credits); promising new actors; Academy Award winners for all previous years in the categories of best picture, best actor, best actress, best supporting actor and actress, best director, best foreign film, and special awards; foreign films released in the U.S.; biographical data on film actors; and obituaries for the preceding year. There is a name and film title index. JKM

MUSIC

HU 177
African Music. ISSN 0065-4019. (Continues: African Music Society. Newsletter.) 1954/57. irreg. index. African Music Society, Box 138, Roodeport, Transvaal 1725, South Africa. Examined: v. 5, 1975/76. Andrew Tracey, ed. 162p. $15.
Aud: Sa

Indexed in: *Music Index; RILM Abstracts of Music Literature.*

Contains scholarly articles in the field of African music. The 1975/76 issue includes the following articles: "Structural Levels of Rhythm and Form in African Music," "Talking Drums of Nigeria," "Zulu Soul Songs," and "Swahili Epic Poetry: A Musical Study." Also contains numerous critical book reviews and a list of films dealing with African music. Volume five cumulates contents of all previous volumes. GV

HU 178
American Society of University Composers. Proceedings of the Annual Conference. ISSN 0066-0701. 1966. a. American Society of University Composers, c/o American Music Center, 2109 Broadway, Suite 15-79, New York, NY 10023. Examined: 1972/73. Warner Hutchinson, ed. 111p. (v. 11, 1978. $8.)
Aud: Sa

Indexed in: *Music Index; RILM Abstracts of Music Literature.*

Contains the text of the speeches and panel discussions presented at the annual national conference of the American Society of University Composers, as well as papers delivered at two regional meetings. Includes a list of members arranged geographically. GV

HU 179
Annual Index to Popular Music Record Reviews. ISSN 0092-3486. 1972. a. bibl. index. Scarecrow Press, Box 656, 52 Liberty St, Metuchen, NJ 08840. Examined: 1975. Andrew D. Armitage and Dean Tudor, eds. 552p. $20. (1978.)
Aud: Hs, Jc, Cl, Pl

An index to reviews of popular music recordings in the U.S., England, and Canada. In each of 13 categories (rock, mood-pop, country, old-time and bluegrass, folk, ethnic, jazz, blues, soul, popular religious, show band, and humor), the year's recordings are listed with full discographic information and complete citations for reviews. Entries are numbered and assigned an evaluative number (0-5). Each section begins with a discographic essay and a list of the best recordings for the year. The 1975 edition indexes 5084 reviews appearing in 64 publications during the year; the 1972 annual covered 35 sources and included 3679 reviews. The number of citations has remained relatively stable in subsequent editions—5906 in 1973, 5158 in 1974. An annotated list of periodicals indexed, a directory of record labels, a listing of specialty record stores, an artist index, and an anthology index (arranged by title of album) are also provided. GV

HU 180
Bibliographia Musicologica; Bibliography of Music Literature. ISSN 0084-7844. (Continues: Joachimsthal Documentation.) 1968. a. index. Joachimsthal Publishers, Box 2238, Utrecht, The Netherlands. Examined: v. 6, 1973. A. M. Joachimsthal, ed. 157p. (v. 8, 1975. $48.50.)
Aud: Sa

An international bibliography of non-periodical publications in music literature, including monographs, dissertations, and selected pamphlets. Numbered entries are arranged alphabetically by author and appear in the language of the publication; items are not annotated. A detailed subject/name index is included. Volumes are sometimes late in appearing; the 1975 volume was not published until 1977. GV

HU 181
Bibliographic Guide to Music. (Continues: Book Guide to Music.) 1975. a. G. K. Hall, 70 Lincoln St, Boston, MA 02111. Examined: 1977. 477p. $70.
Aud: Cl, Pf, Sa

Supplements the *Dictionary Catalog of the Music Collection,* the Research Libraries of the New York Public Library (G. K. Hall, 1964). Contains complete catalog entries, arranged in one alphabetical sequence, for all music materials cataloged by the Library of Congress and the Research Libraries of the New York Public Library during the preceding year. Covers all forms of materials, including scores, record catalogs, manuscripts, periodicals, librettos, etc. Access is provided through main entries, added entries, titles, series, and subject headings. Prior to 1975, G. K. Hall issued *Book Guide to Music* which contained publications cataloged only by the Library of Congress. JKM

HU 182
Billboard International Buyer's Guide of the Music-Record Industry. ISSN 0067-8600. 1960/61. a. Billboard Publications, 9000 Sunset Blvd, Los Angeles, CA 90069. Examined: 1977/78. Lee Zhito, ed. 410p. $10.
Aud: Sa

An international guide to music suppliers and services. Listings for the U.S. encompass record companies, sheet music jobbers, wholesalers, professional organizations, and services and supplies allied with the record/tape industry. Entries are usually arranged by state within the specific topics. The international section offers similar coverage, but the main arrangement is by country, then by topical areas. Entries include address and telephone number, list of key personnel, major products or services, and often, international representatives and firms represented. GV

HU 183
Billboard International Directory of Recording Equipment and Studio Directory. ISSN 0067-8627. 1970. a. Billboard Publications, 1515 Broadway, New York, NY 10036. Examined: 1977/78. Lee Zhito, ed. 110p. $10.
Aud: Sa

Provides listings of manufacturers and companies involved in the recording industry. Includes a listing of recording studio equipment manufacturers and importers in the U.S., with address and telephone number, key personnel, and a list of products; a geographically arranged listing of U.S. and international recording studios describing the services available; and a list of independent record producers. GV

HU 184
British Music Yearbook. (Continues: Music Yearbook.) 1972/73. a. index. Bowker Publishing Co., Box 5, Epping, Essex CM16 4BV, Great Britain. Dist: R. R. Bowker Co., Box 1807, Ann Arbor, MI 48106. Examined: 4th ed., 1976. Arthur Jacobs, ed. $22.50. (5th ed., 1977/78. 780p. $27.50.)
Aud: Cl, Sa

A survey and directory, focusing primarily on the British music scene, with statistics and reference articles for the year. Divided into eleven sections: a section called "Musicians of the Year" (Benjamin Britton in 1976, Tito Gobbi in 1975) which contains discographies; a survey of statistics of the British musical scene; reference articles on laws, insurance, income tax, and copyright; offices and societies; professional performances; festivals and competitions; records; publishing and press; education, libraries, and museums; music in places of worship; and a miscellaneous section covering military and folk music, etc. Includes a brief alphabetical subject index. GV

HU 185
Buyer's Guide to the World of Tape. ISSN 0090-9033. 1972. a. illus. ABC Leisure Magazines, Great Barrington, MA 02130. Examined: 1977. Wayne Armentrout, ed. 116p. $1.50.
Aud: Pl

The major part of this publication is a list of tape equipment by categories, including open reel, cassette, 8-track cartridge, compacts, portables, automobile, microphones, headphones, and accessories. Entries within sections are alphabetically arranged by the name of the manufacturer and include model number, listing of major features, weight, price, and, often, illustrations. Also includes informative articles on how to make good tape recordings, how to choose tapes, and how to edit tapes. A glossary of tape terminology appears in the front section. GV

HU 186
Composium Directory of New Music. 1971. a. Crystal Record Co., Box 65661, Los Angeles, CA 90065. Examined: 1977. 66p. $6.95; $4.95 pap.
Aud: Sa

An annual index of both published and unpublished contemporary classical compositions by living composers. All items listed are available for purchase or rental. The major section lists composers alphabetically and provides a brief biography and a description of each work covering length of performance, difficulty, price, and publisher (with address). The second section lists the compositions by ensemble and instrument or voice. GV

HU 187
Consort; Journal of the Dolmetsch Foundation. 1929. a. index. illus. Dolmetsch Foundation, 14 Chestnut Way, Godalming, Surrey, GU7 1TS, England, Examined: no. 32, 1976. Shelagh M. Godwin, ed. 44p. $7.
Aud: Sa
Indexed in: *Music Index; RILM Abstracts of Music Literature.*

Publication suspended from 1936 to 1948.

Includes scholarly articles in the field of classical musicology. The 1976 edition contains materials about Italian opera, early 17th century English keyboard music, the music of the pharaohs, and performance of 18th century Italian orchestral music. Signed book and record reviews appear in each edition. GV

HU 188
Contributions to Music Education. 1972. a. index. Ohio Music Education Association, c/o Melvin C. Platt, School of Music, Kent State University, Kent, OH 44242. Examined: no. 5, 1977. Melvin C. Platt, ed. 91p. free.
Aud: Cl, Sa

Published and funded by the Ohio Music Education Association. Contains scholarly articles about music education, concentrating on the state of music education in Ohio. Also contains signed critical reviews of books in the field of music education. Volume five contains an author and title index for the first five volumes. GV

HU 189
Directory of Music Faculties in Colleges and Universities U.S. and Canada. (Continues: Directory of Music Faculties in American Colleges and Universities. ISSN 0419-3040) 1967/68. bi-a. College Music Society, Music Department, State University of New York, Binghamton, NY 13901. Examined: 6th ed., 1976/77. various pagings. $12.
Aud: Hs, Jc, Cl, Pl
Indexed in: *Music Index; RILM Abstracts of Music Literature.*

A computer generated directory of music faculties in 1373 U.S. and Canadian institutions of higher education. Divided in four sections. The first section is a directory of departments of music arranged alphabetically by state or province, then by name of institution. Entries provide address and telephone number, degrees offered, and a list of faculty members indicating special fields of interest. Sections two and three provide the same data arranged by faculty names and areas of specialization, respectively. The last section lists graduate degrees in music and institutions which grant the specific degrees; this section was published separately before 1972. GV

HU 190
Galpin Society Journal. ISSN 0072-0127. 1948. a. illus. Galpin Society, Rose Cottage, Boislane, Chesham Bois, Bucks HP6 6BP, England. Examined: v. 30, 1977. 188p. $7.75.
Aud: Sa
Indexed in: *Music Index; RILM Abstracts of Music Literature.*

A specialized publication dedicated to the dissemination of research in the history, construction, and use of musical instruments. International in scope, it contains scholarly articles accompanied by numerous illustrations. The 1977 edition covers such topics as "Oboes, Bassoons, and Bass Clarinets Made by Hartford, Connecticut Makers Before 1815," "Tongan Musical Instruments," and "The Maltese Zagg." Also contains signed critical book reviews. GV

HU 191
High Fidelity; Records in Review. ISSN 0073-2095. 1955. a. index. The Wyeth Press. Great Barrington, MA 02130. Examined: 22nd ed., 1977. Edith Carter, ed. 465p. $9.95.
Aud: Pl, Sa

An annual anthology of long, critical, signed reviews of serious musical recordings on disc and tape compiled from *High Fidelity* magazine for the previous year. Reviews are arranged alphabetically by composer and subdivided further for frequently recorded artists. Reviews of collections are listed separately in a Recitals and Miscellany section and encompass vocal collections, choral collections, chamber music, string, orchestral, woodwind, and medieval and renaissance music. Includes a complete index of performers. GV

HU 192
High Fidelity's Test Reports. ISSN 0090-3981. 1973. a. illus. ABC Leisure Magazines, Great Barrington, MA 02130. Examined: 1978. John W. P. Mooney, ed. 330p. $3.95.
Aud: Sa

A compilation of laboratory and listening tests originally published in *High Fidelity* magazine and conducted by the editors of that publication and the technical staff of the CBS Technology Center (a division of Columbia Broadcasting System). Covers products currently available in the audio marketplace. Products are grouped by category: amplifiers, tuners, receivers, speakers, turntables, cartridges, headphones, tape equipment, and system accessories. Within each area, entries are arranged alphabetically by brand name and accompanied by a short description covering model number, price and warranty, and manufacturer's address. The comment section presents a technical evaluation of the item, usually accompanied by graphs and tables. A fifteen-page glossary briefly defines technical terms. GV

HU 193
Index to Record and Tape Reviews. ISSN 0097-8256. 1971. a. index. Chulainn Press, Box 770, San Anselmo, CA 94960. Examined: 1974, 571p.; 1975. Antoinette O. Maleady, ed. 635p. $20. (7th ed., 1977. $42.50.)
Aud: Cl, Pl

Subtitle: "A classical music buying guide." Provides citations to reviews of classical recordings on discs or tape which appeared in British, Canadian, and U.S. journals. The 1974 edition covered 18 periodicals; the 1977 volume covers 37 periodicals. It is arranged in three sections: an alphabetical index by composer; an index to music in collections arranged by manufacturer; and a performer index to recordings listed in the other two sections. Previous editions included spoken records, but this feature has been dropped. Each citation gives disc/tape label and number, variant numbers, and citations to reviews with a system of plus and minus signs to indicate the critical viewpoint of the reviewer. Contains many cross references to numbered items in the various sections. GV

HU 194
International Folk Music Council. Yearbook. ISSN 0074-6096. (Continues: Journal of the International Folk Music Council.) 1969. a. International Folk Music Council, Department of Music, Queen's University, Kingston, Ontario, Canada. Examined: v. 7, 1975. 191p. $15. (v. 10, 1978. $12.)
Aud: Sa
Indexed in: *Music Index; RILM Abstracts of Music Literature.*

Contains scholarly articles in the international folk music field and surveys publications and recordings in the field. Volume seven contains contributions by scholars dealing with ethnomusicology in Serbia, Tokyo festival music, songs of Bengal, etc. Most articles are written in English, but articles in French and German are also included. GV

HU 195
International Music Guide. 1976. a. index. illus. Tantivy Press, London, England. Dist: A. S. Barnes and Co., Box 421, Cranbury, NJ 08512. Examined: 1977. Derek Elley, ed. 282p. $5.95.
Aud: Cl, Pl

Provides a factual survey of the world's music scene from autumn through summer of the preceding year, with emphasis on the U.S. and Great Britain. A world survey section contains informative general articles and lists of premieres, with an evaluation of performances, in Western Europe, the Middle East, and the U.S. The reviews section covers live and selected recorded music, as well as "affiliated genres of popular music." Also contains a report on audio equipment and lists of music shops, schools, and periodicals in Great Britain and the U.S. GV

HU 196
International Percussion Reference Library. Catalogue. ISSN 0085-219X. 1963. bi-a. Arizona State University, Music Department, Tempe, AZ 85281. Examined: v. 6, 1974. Sue E. Stancu, ed. 42p. $2.50. (1978.)
Aud: Sa

Intended to be a central reference source for all compositions, featuring percussion instructional materials and recordings of percussion performance. The catalog includes only items found in the Arizona State University library; it is essentially a classed bibliography providing full citations and indicating degree of difficulty. GV

HU 197
International Society for Music Education. ISME Yearbook. (Continues: International Music Educator.) 1973. a. B. Schott's Sohne Musikverlag, Weihergarten 7, Postfach 3640, D-65 Mainz, Germany. Examined: v. 4, 1977. Egon Kraus, ed. 130p.
Aud: Cl, Sa

Includes the main papers delivered at UNESCO-sponsored International Society for Music Education (ISME) conferences and seminars. The stated purpose is "to publish articles from different countries and continents dealing with actual problems in the various fields of music education and related disciplines." Each conference has a unifying theme, e.g., "Music as a Dimension of Lifelong Education" in 1976 and "The Education of the Professional Musician" in 1977. Articles are short, and all have been translated into English. The 1975 volume, "Challenges in Music Education," was issued as a separate publication and contains papers from the 11th international conference of ISME. GV

HU 198
International Who's Who in Music and Musicians Directory. (Continues: Who's Who in Music and Musicians' International Directory.) 1935. bi-a. Melrose Press, 3 Market Hill, Cambridge CB2 3QP, England. Dist: Gale Research Co., Book Tower, Detroit, MI 48226. Examined: 7th ed., 1975. 1848p. $37.50. (8th ed., 1978. 1178p. $59.50.)
Aud: Cl, Pl
Indexed in: *Biographical Dictionaries Master Index.*

An alphabetically arranged biographical directory of approximately 12,000 living musicians, international in scope, which provides who's who style information: vital statistics, education, career, compositions, honors, recordings, and publications. Seven geographically arranged appendixes list orchestras, music organizations, major awards and competitions, major festivals, major concert halls and opera houses, major conservatories, colleges and universities of music, and Masters of King's/Queen's Music. GV

HU 199
Music and the Artists Directory. ISSN 0077-2380. (Continues: Music Journal Artists' Directory.) 1966/67. a. index. Sar-Les Music, 370 Lexington Ave, New York, NY 10022. Examined: 1977. Robert Cumming, ed. 170p. $5.
Aud: Pl, Sa

Lists U.S. and Canadian orchestras, opera companies, music festivals, and concert series, arranged by state and province within the country divisions. Entries include address, telephone, and succinct information on main executives, number of productions, and seating capacity. The two indexes, one an alphabetical listing of artists and attractions, the other a subject classed arrangement of the same, are keyed to the section on artists' managers and representatives. GV

HU 200
Music in Higher Education. ISSN 0077-2410. 1967. a. National Association of Schools of Music, 11250 Roger Bacon Dr, No. 5, Reston, VA 22090. Examined: no. 9, 1974/75. 52p. $5. (1976/77.)
Aud: Cl, Sa

A summary of statistical data about music education in U.S. colleges and universities compiled from annual reports of 428 member institutions. Tables present data regarding enrollment and degrees offered, faculty and their salaries and tenure, budgets and expenditures, etc. A list of new music facilities is included. GV

HU 201
Musica Disciplina. ISSN 0077-2461. (Continues: Journal of Renaissance and Baroque Music.) 1946. a. index. illus. American Institute of Musicology, E. P. San Silvestro, Rome, Italy. Dist: Hanssler-Verlag, Bismarckstrasse 4, 7303 Newhausen, Stuttgart, West Germany. Examined: v. 30, 1976. Armen Carapetyan, ed. 146p. $15.
Aud: Sa
Indexed in: *Music Index; RILM Abstracts of Music Literature.*

Subtitle: "Yearbook of the history of music, medieval and Renaissance." A scholarly yearbook dedicated to publishing research articles and inventories of manuscript scores in the specific area of medieval and Renaissance music. Volume 30 contains documented articles about medieval polyphony at Canterbury, accompanied by numerous plates, and a description and inventory of an anonymous medieval chanson. Previous editions contain bibliographies of books and doctoral dissertations in this area, but this feature was eliminated in volume 30. A cumulative author/subject index to the first 20 volumes is available. GV

HU 202.
Musical America International Directory of the Performing Arts. (Continues: Musical America; High Fidelity-Musical America Directory Issue.) 1968/69. a. ABC Leisure Magazines, Great Barrington, MA 01230. Examined: 1977. Shirley Fleming, ed. 500p. $12.
Aud: Sa

A directory of performing artists, primarily U.S. and Canadian. Its purpose is to advertise the artists and services. The major listing is arranged by subject categories (orchestras, dance companies, festivals, music schools, music magazines, etc.), with geographical divisions under each category. There is also an international directory, arranged by country, covering the same subject categories. Also includes reports of activities and new artists, submitted by leading concert managers of the U.S. and Canada, arranged alphabetically by company. GV

HU 203
National Association of Schools of Music. Directory. ISSN 0547-4175. 1950. a. National Association of Schools of Music, 11250 Roger Bacon Dr, No. 5, Reston, VA 22090. Examined: 1976. 102p. $2.
Aud: Hs, Jc, Cl, Pl

Provides an alphabetical listing of accredited schools of music in the U.S. Entries give address, telephone number, department and principal personnel, and degrees granted. Also includes an alphabetical list of executives of member institutions and a list of members arranged by state. GV

HU 204
National Association of Schools of Music. Proceedings of the Annual Meeting. ISSN 0077-3409. 1934. a. National Association of Schools of Music, 11250 Roger Bacon Dr, No. 5, Reston, VA 22090. Examined: no. 65, 1977. 216p. $3.
Aud: Cl, Sa

Presents the minutes of the annual meeting of the National Association of Schools of Music (52nd Annual Meeting, Atlanta, GA, 1976) and reports of committees and officers. Also lists officers, commissions, and member institutions, and publishes papers presented at the general session, regional meetings, workshops, and interest group sessions of the Association. Papers in the 1977 edition address the topics of: music in higher education in Canada, methods for evaluating music libraries, and management techniques for music executives. GV

HU 205
Organ Yearbook. ISSN 0078-6098. 1970. a. illus. Uitgeverij Frits Kauf B.V., Postbox 20, 2707, Netherlands. Examined: v. 7, 1976. Peter Williams, ed. 192p.
Aud: Sa
Indexed in: *RILM Abstracts of Music Literature*.

Subtitle: "A journal for players and historians of keyboard instruments." Devoted to technical studies of keyboard instruments, especially the organ, written primarily in English. The 1976 edition presents scholarly articles on the history of organ building in Portugal and England and on industrialized organ building. It also includes an inventory of new and restored organs in France, Germany, and Italy. A major section is devoted to reviews of music, books, and recordings in this area. GV

HU 206
Pennsylvania Music Educators Association. Bulletin of Research in Music Education. 1969. a. Pennsylvania Music Educators Association, Graduate Division, West Chester, PA 19380. Examined: v. 7, 1976. Ira Singleton, ed. 47p. free to qualified personnel.
Aud: Cl, Sa
Indexed in: *Music Article Guide*.

A publication of the Pennsylvania Music Educators Association dedicated to promoting research and the utilization of research findings to introduce innovative teaching techniques in music. Articles in volume seven address the topics of mini-courses in middle schools, guitar use in schools, and discipline problems in the music class, among others. Authors stress the successful application of methods described in actual teaching experiences. GV

HU 207
Popular Music Periodicals Index. ISSN 0095-4101. 1973. a. bibl. index. Scarecrow Press, 52 Liberty St, Metuchen, NJ 08840. Examined: v. 4, 1975. Dean Tudor and Andrew D. Armitage, eds. 349p. $15. (1978.)
Aud: Jc, Cl, Pl

Provides full indexing for 55 English language periodicals and selective indexing for 12 additional titles in the popular music field. An annotated list of journals indexed is included in the preface. The main section of the work consists of a subject index of 20 main categories with numerous sub-topics and extensive cross references. Within subdivisions, listings are by artists or groups, agents, concerts or festivals, instruments, songs and music, contests and awards, and record companies. The author index provides cross references for pseudonyms. Includes a bibliography of books in the field of popular music which received favorable reviews. GV

HU 208
Royal Musical Association, London. Proceedings. ISSN 0080-4452. 1874/75. a. index. Royal Musical Association, c/o Malcolm Turner, British Museum, Great Russell St, London WC1B 3DG, England. Examined: v. 100, 1973/74. Edward Olleson, ed. 247p. (v. 104, 1978. $8.95.)
Aud: Cl, Sa
Indexed in: *Music Index; RILM Abstracts of Music Literature*.

Includes papers presented at various conferences of the British Royal Musical Association during the previous year. The 1973/74 volume contains scholarly articles about classical music, comments on recent Mozart research, a discussion of Donizetti's various operas, and an examination of the influence of Viennese popular comedy on the music of Haydn and Mozart. There is also a list of members and past presidents of the association. GV

HU 209
Schwann Artists Catalog. ISSN 0582-1487. (Con-

tinues: Schwann Artist Listing Long Playing Record Catalog; Schwann Artist Issue Catalog.) 1953. irreg. W. Schwann, 137 Newberry St, Boston, MA 02116. Examined: 1976. 280p. $3.95 pap.
Aud: Pl, Sa

A listing of currently available, long-playing, classical records and tapes by name of performer. The same records and tapes are listed by composer and title in the monthly *Schwann-1* and the semi-annual *Schwann-2*, respectively. Listings are arranged in sections by type of performance. The first section lists orchestras, trios, quartets, etc., with sub-sections for composers. The second section lists conductors and their groups. Section three lists instrumental soloists arranged by instrument. The fourth section covers choral groups, operatic groups, and vocalists. Entries include information on composer, title, performance, label, and item number. Prices are not included since they are subject to frequent changes. Popular and jazz music are covered in the two other Schwann publications noted above. GV

HU 210
Schwann Children's Record and Tape Guide. 1964. a. W. Schwann, 137 Newberry St, Boston, MA 02116. Examined: 1977. Richard Blackham, ed. 18p. $1.
Aud: Pl, Sa

Lists more than 1700 currently available records, as well as cartridge and cassette tapes, for children. Entries are arranged by title and include label and an identifying number. A price list is appended. GV

HU 211
Soundings: A Music Journal. ISSN 0081-2080. 1970. a. University College, Cardiff Press, Box 78, Cardiff, CF1 1XL, Wales. Examined: v. 6, 1977. Stephen Walsh, ed. 120p. $4.
Aud: Sa
Indexed in: *Music Index; RILM Abstracts of Music Literature*.

This scholarly journal in the general field of music research is a Welsh publication with an international editorial policy. The 1977 issue features well-documented articles about Baroque music, the history of Welsh music, and editions of Borodin's symphonies. GV

HU 212
Studies in Music. ISSN 0081-8267. 1967. a. University of Western Australia, Nedlands, 6009 WA, Australia. Dist: Theodore Front Musical Literature, Alfred A. Kalmus, 131 N Robertson Blvd, Beverly Hills, CA 90211. Examined: no. 10, 1976. Frank Callaway, ed. 107p. $6.
Aud: Sa

The stated purpose is to report the results of musicological studies in Australia and New Zealand. Includes scholarly essays by university faculty dealing with international musical topics, e.g., Stockhausen, Neapolitan comic opera, and the Vihuela, an ancient Spanish instrument. Also includes a section of "Notes on Pacific Music" and a subject-arranged list of theses on musical subjects that have been accepted or that are in progress at Australian universities. Contents of the 1967-1975 volumes are cumulated at the end of the 1976 issue. GV

HU 213
Yearbook for Inter-American Musical Research; Anuario Interamericano de Investigacion Musical. ISSN 0066-5274. (Continues: Interamerican Institute for Musical Research. Yearbook; Anuario.) 1965. a. index. illus. University of Texas Press, Austin, TX 78712. Examined: v. 10, 1974. Gilbert Chase, ed. 234p. $5. (v. 13, 1977. $5.)
Aud: Sa
Indexed in: *Music Index; RILM Abstracts of Music Literature*.

Features lengthy articles on music research in the U.S. and Latin America. The scholarly contributions are written in English and Spanish. Signed, critical book reviews and a section of shorter, unsigned reviews are included. GV

PHILOSOPHY

HU 214
American Catholic Philosophical Association. Proceedings. ISSN 0065-7638. 1926. a. bibl. index. American Catholic Philosophical Association, The Catholic University of America, Washington, DC 20064. Examined: v. 49, 1975. George F. McLean, ed. 259p. $5. (1977.)
Aud: Cl, Sa
Indexed in: *Catholic Periodical and Literature Index*.

Primarily the papers presented at the annual meeting of the Association. Each annual meeting has a different theme. In 1975, the theme was "Philosophy and Civil Law." The papers are of medium length and include bibliographical references. The last section of the volume contains reports of committees and officers, and minutes of the meeting. There is a list of officers and committees but not of members. LL

HU 215

American Philosophical Association. Proceedings and Addresses. ISSN 0065-972X. 1927. a. bibl. index. illus. American Philosophical Association, University of Delaware, Newark, DE 19711. Examined: v. 50, 1977. Norman E. Bowie, ed. $10.
Aud: Cl, Sa
Indexed in: *Philosopher's Index.*

The official publication of the American Philosophical Association. The yearly volume contains the proceedings of their meetings and the meetings of the eastern, pacific, and western divisions. It includes presidential addresses, news of the divisions, committee reports, information on grants and fellowships, news on the teaching of philosophy, awards and prizes, and general news of membership activity. The presidential addresses include bibliographical references and illustrations. Also includes the Association's constitution and a list of officers. Members are not listed. LL

HU 216

Aristotelian Society for the Systematic Study of Philosophy. Proceedings. ISSN 0066-7374. 1887/96; 1900. a. Methuen and Co., 11 New Fetter Lane, London, EC4, England. Examined: v. 75, 1975. 247p. (1977.)
Aud: Sa
Indexed in: *Philosopher's Index.*

Contains the papers read before the Society during the previous year. Papers cover all aspects of Aristotelian philosophy. Includes the president's address and a list of officers and members. The membership list indicates name, year the person was elected as a member, and address or institutional affiliation. The program of the annual conference is also included. LL

HU 217

Bibliography of Society, Ethics, and the Life Sciences. ISSN 0094-4831. 1973. a. index. Hastings Center, Institute of Society, Ethics, and the Life Sciences, 360 Broadway, Hastings-on-Hudson, NY 10706. Examined: 1976/77. Sharmon Sollitto, ed. 82p. $3.50.
Aud: Cl, Pl, Sa

A bibliography of materials on ethics in relation to the bio-medical sciences. Includes introductory readings in ethics and the life sciences, ethical theory, history of medical ethics, codes of professional ethics, medical ethics education, values, ethics and technology, behavior control, death and dying, experimentation and consent, genetics, fertilization and birth, health care delivery, population and birth control, scarce medical resources, transportation, and hemodialysis. Entries under each section are arranged alphabetically by author. Each entry includes title, place and name of publisher, date or volume number, and inclusive pages. Monographs are briefly annotated. LL

HU 218

Boston College. Studies in Philosophy. ISSN 0068-0354. 1966. irreg. bibl. Boston College, Chestnut Hill, Boston, MA 02167. Examined: v. 4, 1975. Frederick J. Adelmann, ed. 128p. $15. (1977.)
Aud: Cl, Sa
Indexed in: *Philosopher's Index.*

Presents articles on less common themes that affect contemporary problems in philosophy. The theme changes with each issue. In volume four, the articles, which were written by Russian authors and translated into English, centered on "Philosophical Investigations in the U.S.S.R." There are some bibliographical footnotes, but no extensive bibliography. LL

HU 219

Comitatus; A Journal of Medieval and Renaissance Studies. ISSN 0069-6412. 1969. a. bibl. illus. Center for Medieval and Renaissance Studies, University of California, 405 Hilgard Ave, Los Angeles, CA 90024. Examined: v. 8, 1977. Tanis Thorne, ed. 75p. $2.50; $4 to institutions.
Aud: Cl, Pl

An interdisciplinary journal on medieval and Renaissance studies. It includes studies and papers on culture, philosophy, literature, arts, and other related subjects. Articles include bibliographical references and some illustrations. There is a book review section. The journal is edited by graduate students at the Center for Medieval and Renaissance Studies. LL

HU 220

Danish Yearbook of Philosophy. ISSN 0070-0614. 1964. a. bibl. illus. International Booksellers and Publishers, Munksgaard, 35 Noerre Soegade, DK 1370, Copenhagen K, Denmark. Dist: Humanities Press, 300 Park Ave S, New York, NY 10010. Examined: v. 12, 1975. Mogens Bleguad, ed. 128p. (v. 14, 1977. $13.11.)
Aud: Cl, Sa
Indexed in: *Philosopher's Index.*

Contains essays on philosophy and psychology. The essays are all in English and are 20 to 50 pages long. Includes bibliographical references and some illustrations. There is no index. LL

HU 221
Directory of American Philosophers. ISSN 0070-508X. 1962. bi-a. index. Philosophy Documentation Center, Bowling Green University, Bowling Green, OH 43403. Examined: 8th ed., 1976/77. Archie J. Bahm, ed. 329p. $27.
Aud: Hs, Jc, Cl, Pl

Covers philosophical activities in the U.S. and Canada. Organized in three parts. Parts one and two are organized geographically by states or provinces, then alphabetically by colleges and universities which offer courses in philosophy. Each entry includes information on department and address, data on accreditation, type of control, type of student body, type of academic calendar, levels and kinds of offerings, enrollment, highest level of instruction in philosophy, phone number of the division, and a list of professors with title, position, and major/special. The first two parts also contain information on assistantships, societies, centers and institutes, and journal publishers. Part three contains statistics on size of philosophical departments, highest level of specialization offered by each department, and the number of philosophers in each state or province with national totals. Part four contains indexes of universities and colleges, societies, centers, councils and institutes, journals, and publishers, and a list of names and addresses of philosophers. LL

HU 222
Franciscan Studies. 1941. a. bibl. The Franciscan Institute, St. Bonaventure University, St. Bonaventure, NY 14778. Examined: v. 35, 1975. Conrad L. Harkins, ed. 275p. $10. (1977.)
Aud: Sa
Indexed in: *Catholic Periodical and Literature Index; Philosopher's Index.*

Contains essays, studies, and a bibliography in philosophy, Franciscan scholarly subjects, and related fields. Primarily in English but includes a few articles in Latin. The papers include bibliographical references. Books that have been received by the publication are listed but not reviewed. LL

HU 223
International Studies in Philosophy. 1968. a. bibl. "Filosoffia," 26, Piazza Statuto, 10144, Torino, Italy. Examined: v. 7, 1975. Augusto Guzzo, ed. 279p. $15. (1977.)
Aud: Sa

Subtitle: "A yearbook of general philosophical inquiry." Contains papers and articles of general philosophical inquiry. Articles are mostly written in English, though some are in other European languages. Articles include bibliographical references. Includes book reviews of medium length; about 10 to 20 titles are reviewed in an issue. LL

HU 224
The Locke Newsletter. 1969. a. Roland Hall, Department of Philosophy, University of York, Heslington, York, England. Examined: no. 7, 1976. 152p. $5.50; free to Locke scholars.
Aud: Sa
Indexed in: *Philosopher's Index.*

A journal devoted to the works of Locke and Lockian thought. It contains articles, papers, and criticisms on the subject. There is a section for queries and answers to readers' questions. Special features include a list of recent Locke publications and book reviews. LL

HU 225
Manchester Literary and Philosophical Society. Memoirs and Proceedings. ISSN 0076-3721. a. bibl. illus. The Society, 36 George St, Manchester, England. Examined: v. 117, 1974/75. 159p. $8.55. (v. 120 due October 1978.)
Aud: Sa

The Society's interests include literature and philosophy in all fields of knowledge, such as the philosophy of science. The memoir section contains articles of medium length on literature and philosophy. Bibliographical references are included, and occasionally illustrations are featured. The proceedings include obituaries, annual reports, meetings, and lists of past presidents of the Society, council members, and members of the Society. The members' list does not include addresses. LL

HU 226
Nomos. ISSN 0078-0979. 1958. a. bibl. index. Lieber-Atherton Press, 1841 Broadway, New York, NY 10023. Dist: New York University Press, 21 W Fourth St, New York, NY 10012. Examined: no. 1, 1958; no. 17, 1977. J. Roland Pennock and John W. Chapman, eds. 348p. $17.50.
Aud: Sa

The yearbook of the American Society for Political and Legal Philosophy. Comprised of revised scholarly papers (with further comments) presented at the annual meetings, supplemented by other papers written by members of the Society. Each year's articles discuss a specific theme, i.e., volume one deals with authority, volume 17 focuses on human nature in politics. Each volume is separately indexed. KR/JKM

HU 227
The Philosopher's Index. 1967. a. w/q. suppls. index. Philosophy Documentation Center, Bowling Green State University, Bowling Green, OH 43403. Examined: 1976, Richard H. Lineback, ed., 403p.; v. 11, 1977. 399p. $22.50; $45 to institutions. (q. suppls., $18; $35 to institutions.)
Aud: Cl, Pl

Subtitle: "An international index to philosophy periodicals." Arranged by author of the article indexed. Each entry includes the full title of the article, a citation to the journal in which it appeared, and, if available, an abstract. In most cases the abstracts are supplied by the author. In a few instances the abstracts are written by the Philosophical Institute of the University of Dusseldorf or by the staff of the **Philosopher's Index**; these abstracts are identified as not having been supplied by the author. Includes a personal name and topical subject index; a list of periodicals indexed with current address, frequency, and price; and a book review index. LL/JKM

HU 228
Philosophic Exchange. 1969. a. bibl. illus. Center for Philosophic Exchange, State University of New York, Brockport, NY 14420. Examined: v. 2, no. 1, 1975; no. 2, 1976. D. A. Wells, ed. 86p. $5.50.
Aud: Sa
Indexed in: *Philosopher's Index*.

Subtitle: "The annual proceedings of the Center for Philosophic Exchange." The Center was established "to conduct a continuing program of philosophic inquiry relating to both academic and public issues." The proceedings contain articles presented by philosophers of varying nationalities who have been invited by the Center to present papers. The papers include bibliographical references and photographs of the authors. LL

HU 229
Question. ISSN 0079-919X. (Continues: Rationalist Annual.) 1968. a. bibl. Rationalist Press Association, 88 Islington High St, London N1, England. Dist: Prometheus Books, 923 Kensington Ave, Buffalo, NY 14215. Examined: v. 9, 1976. Hector Hawton, ed. 96p. $1.80.
Aud: Sa

Contains essays on rationalist philosophy and thought. Includes bibliographical references. LL

HU 230
Royal Society of Canada. Transactions; Société Royale du Canada. Memoires. ISSN 0035-9122. 1882. a. bibl. University of Toronto Press, Toronto, Ontario M5S 1A6, Canada. Examined: 4th series, v. 14, 1976. 322p. $7.50.
Aud: Sa
Indexed in: *Biological Abstracts; Engineering Index.*

Contains papers presented at the annual symposium of the Royal Society of Canada. The papers are devoted to topics in the humanities, social sciences, and sciences. Organized in sections according to subject: joint symposium, l'academie des lettres et des sciences humaines/academy of humanities and social sciences, and academy of sciences. Articles are in either English or French and include bibliographical references. The presidential address given at the annual meeting is included. LL

HU 231
Traditio. ISSN 0362-1529. 1943. a. bibl. index. illus. Fordham University Press, Bronx, NY 10458. Examined: v. 32, 1976. Edwin A. Quain, ed. 474p. $17.50.
Aud: Cl, Sa
Indexed in: *Catholic Periodical and Literature Index; Philosopher's Index*.

Subtitle: "Studies in ancient and medieval history, thought, and religion." Includes studies, essays, bibliographical works, and articles on ancient and medieval history, primarily in the areas of religion and thought. Organized in three sections: articles, miscellany, and bibliographical studies. The articles are of considerable length (30-40 pages). Most are in English, with a few in French, German, or Latin. The miscellany section contains shorter articles on various aspects of life and culture during these periods. The bibliographical articles are substantive and scholarly. There are no book reviews. All articles include bibliographical references. LL

HU 232
Tulane Studies in Philosophy. ISSN 0082-6766. 1950. a. Tulane University, Department of Philosophy, 304 Tilton Hall, New Orleans, LA 70118. Examined: v. 25, 1976. Robert C. Whittemore, ed. 118p. $5.
Aud: Cl, Sa
Indexed in: *Philosopher's Index*.

Contains short and medium length articles on philosophy and contemporary thought. Includes bibliographical references. There are no book reviews. LL

PHOTOGRAPHY

HU 233
Black Photographer's Annual. ISSN 0090-7197. 1973. a. index. illus. Black Photographer's Annual, 55 Hicks St, Brooklyn, NY 11201. Dist: Light Impressions Corp., Box 3012, Rochester, NY 14614. Examined: 1976. Joe Crawford, ed. 118p. $12.95; $5.95 pap. (6th ed., 1978.)
Aud: Hs, Jc, Cl, Pl

The aim of this catalog of work by Black photographers is stated by James Baldwin in the preface to the 1976 edition as ". . . a study of means, and styles, of confrontation." The first section is a collection of photographs by various Black photographers dealing with Black experiences. Artists are identified by name only; no further information is given. The second part, called "Portfolios," features selected portfolios of famous Black photographers and includes a short biographical sketch of artists represented. GV

HU 234
British Journal of Photography Annual. ISSN 0068-2217. (Continues: British Journal of Photographic Almanac.) 1861. a. bibl. index. illus. Henry Greenwood and Co., 24 Wellington St, London WC2, England. Dist: American Photographic Book Publishing Co., East Gate and Zeckendorf Blvds, Garden City, NY 11530. Examined: 1977. G. W. Crawley, ed. 216p. $17.95.
Aud: Cl, Pl

The purpose of this publication is to present some of the year's best photographs with feature articles, formulary, and descriptions of the technical process. It is arranged in three major sections. Part one consists of 110 pages of photographs with short resumés by the artists. The second section includes general articles on photography; a survey of the year's activities in color photography, education, audiovisual aids, graphic reproductions, and photographic galleries; and an international directory and bibliography (often annotated) of organizations, galleries, and publishers. The third section consists of technical information about black-and-white and color processing, including tables and formulas. From 1861 to 1961 the work was published as the *British Journal of Photographic Almanac*, incorporating *The Year Book of Photography and Amateur's Guide* and *The Photographic Annual*. GV

HU 235
Creative Camera International Year Book. ISSN 0306-3909. 1975. a. illus. Coo Press, 19 Doughty St, London WC1N 2PT, England. Dist: Light Impressions Corp., Box 3012, Rochester, NY 14614. Examined: 1976. Colin Osman and Peter Turner, eds. 236p. $20.
Aud: Hs, Jc, Cl, Pl

Presents collections of photographs arranged according to specific themes. The 1976 edition has major sections entitled "Young Contemporaries" and "Landscape in a Modern Age," plus shorter sections on specific photographers. Each collection of photographs includes prefatory remarks. Emphasizes the art of photography, not the techniques. Includes a brief biographical sketch of photographers represented as well as excellent black-and-white photographs. GV

HU 236
Directory of Professional Photography. ISSN 0070-6140. 1940. a. Professional Photographer's Association of America, PPA Publications, 1100 Executive Way, Oak Leaf Commons, Des Plaines, IL 60018. Examined: 1976. Frederick Quellmalz, ed. 243p. $25.
Aud: Pl, Sa

An international directory of professional photographers and suppliers of products and services. Includes a geographically arranged listing of photographers giving the address and area of specialization and a list of photographic suppliers listed alphabetically by company, by categories of products and services, and by geographical areas. GV

HU 237
Photographer's Market. ISSN 0147-247X. 1978. a. bibl. index. illus. Gaylord Bros., Box 4901, Syracuse, NY 13221. Examined: 1978. Melissa Milar and William Brohaugh, eds. 408p. $9.95.
Aud: Pl, Sa

A guide to "1616 places where freelance photographers can sell their work." Potential markets are arranged by specific areas: advertising agencies, audiovisual firms, book publishers, public relations firms, and stock photo agencies. Includes a section about periodicals which is further subdivided by the type of publication, i.e., consumer magazines, trade journals, newspapers. Entries include a short description of the photographic policies of each buyer, rates of payment, whom to contact, and helpful tips to the freelancer. General articles advise the photographer about preparing a portfolio, mailing works, copyright, and model releases. Listings of competitions and exhibitions, foundations and grants, galleries, professional organizations and clubs, workshops, and firms (state by state) which offer technical services for photographers are included. GV

HU 238
Photographis. ISSN 0079-1830. 1966. a. index. illus. Walter Herdeg Graphis Press, 107 Dufourstrasse, CH-8008 Zurich, Switzerland. Dist: Hastings House Publishers, 10 E 40th St, New York, NY 10016. Examined: 1977. Walter Herdeg, ed. 227p. $37.50.
Aud: Sa

Subtitle: "International annul of advertising photography." An international catalog of advertising photography of the previous year arranged according to the type of publication in which it appeared: magazines and newspapers, booklets, folders, catalogs and programs, calendars, editorial photography and magazine covers, house organs. The trilingual text (English, French, German) which accompanies the numbered photograph entries includes a short description, title, designer, agency, photographer, publisher, and art director. Photographs appear in black-and-white as well as color. GV

HU 239
Photography Annual. ISSN 0075-1849. 1951. a. illus. Ziff-Davis Publishing Co., One Park Ave, New York, NY 10016. Examined: 1978. H. M. Kinzer, ed. 184p. $1.95.
Aud: Cl, Pl

A compilation of photographic works, most from the previous year, presenting selected representative folios by various photographers. Each artist is described briefly, followed by black-and-white and color reproductions of the artist's work. GV

HU 240
Photography Market Place. ISSN 0095-439X. 1975/76. a. bibl. index. R. R. Bowker Co., 1180 Ave of the Americas, New York, NY 10036. Dist: R. R. Bowker Co., Box 1807, Ann Arbor, MI 48106. Examined: 1975/76, Fred W. McDarrah, ed., 436p., $14.95; 1977. 502p. $15.50.
Aud: Pl, Sa

This "complete sourcebook for still photography" includes approximately 5500 services and products of interest to U.S. photographers. Includes sections about picture buyers and sellers, sources of equipment and technical services, model agencies and supportive services, photographic agencies and organizations, schools and career opportunities, and a major section on photography books and periodicals. Each entry provides complete address, telephone numbers, and names of key personnel. Most listings are arranged geographically by state or alphabetically by organizations. Includes an extensive annotated bibliography of picture books and reference books. GV/JKM

HU 241
Photography Year. ISSN 0090-4406. 1973. a. index. illus. Time-Life Books, Time and Life Bldg, Rockefeller Center, New York, NY 10020. Examined: 1975. 242p. (1978. $19.95.)
Aud: Cl, Pl

This international yearbook on photography provides information on major shows, newly discovered photographers, status of the current market place, annual awards and prizes, recent books, and a major section on new equipment and technology. Also includes a news roundup covering obituaries, new collections, and news of people in the field. Each section begins with a brief commentary, followed by illustrations, most in color but there are some black-and-white illustrations. All illustrations are credited. GV

HU 242
Photography Year Book. ISSN 0079-1865. 1936. a. illus. Argus Books, Station Rd, Kings Langley, Hertfordshire, England. Dist: International Publications Service, 114 E 32nd St, New York, NY 10016. Examined: 1977. John Sanders, ed. unpaged. $19.95.
Aud: Cl, Sa

An international catalog of color and black-and-white photography for the previous year. Photographic entries are arranged in a numbered sequence which corresponds to the trilingual commentary (English, German, and Spanish or French) at the back of the volume. The commentary lists the name of photographer, type of camera, lens and film used, shutter speed, aperture, developer, and type of paper. Photographs are beautifully reproduced, and, due to the process of "screenless lithography," exact color reproduction is assured by the editors. The **Year Book** was not published between 1939 and 1946. In 1947, it was published under the title *Photography To-Day*. GV

HU 243
Photo-Lab Index. 1939. a. w/q. suppls. index. illus. Morgan and Lester, 145 Palisade St, Dobbs Ferry, NY 10522. Examined: 32nd ed., 1974. Ernest M. Pittaro, ed. 1000p. (1977. $39.95; q. suppls., $12.50.)
Aud: Pl, Sa

Subtitle: "Cumulative formulary of standard recommended photographic procedures." A basic manual of "recommended photographic procedures in a standardized form" which provides information on exposure, film speeds, filter factors and illumination, and depth of field. It discusses the developing and printing of various types and brands of film (times, formulas, toners, etc.) and contains sections on slides, copying, and photomechanical data. Sections one through eight pertain to specific manufacturers; sections nine through fifteen contain general information by subject area, e.g., optics and filter data, lighting and exposure, enlarging, photographic chemicals, motion pictures and audiovisuals, etc. All sections have an index in the beginning, and the introduction contains a condensed over-all index which can be consulted when a specific manufacturer is not known. Material is accompanied by formulas, tables, graphs, and charts. GV

RELIGION

HU 244
American Baptist Churches in the U.S.A. Directory. ISSN 0091-9381. (Continues in part: American Baptist Convention. Yearbook.) 1971. a. index. American Baptist Churches in the U.S.A. Valley Forge, PA 19481. Examined: 1976. Robert C. Campbell, ed. $4. (1977. 310p.)
Aud: Pl, Sa

A complete directory of the American Baptist Churches (ABC) in the U.S.A. Includes information on the organization of the ABC with names and designations of members of the General Board and those on the international and national levels. The material is organized from the general to specific. An index of names is found after each section. Other affiliated or related organizations are listed, including missions and missionaries. The last third of the directory is an alphabetical registry of professional leaders of the ABC, giving names, addresses, and categorical occupations. For ordained ministers, the year of ordination is also given. Two tables provide data on the historical and biennial meetings of the ABC and give a summary of denominational statistics. Individual churches are listed in the "Directory of Churches and Professional Staff," which is arranged alphabetically by state. LL

HU 245
American Baptist Churches in the U.S.A. Yearbook. ISSN 0092-3478. (Continues in part: American Baptist Convention. Yearbook.) 1907. a. index. American Baptist Churches in the U.S.A., Valley Forge, PA 19481. Examined: 1976. Robert C. Campbell, ed. $4. (1977. 284p.)
Aud: Sa

Summarizes the activities of the executive offices of the American Baptist Churches. Covers the offices of the general secretary, Board of Educational Ministries, and the Ministers and Missionaries Benefit Board. Financial reports for each office are appended at the end of each section. Under the heading for each office is a roster of officers. Programs and projects are listed along with the most significant event of the year for each office or subordinate organization. Regional reports concentrate on general problems and summarize work done in specific areas, such as medicine, education, missions, etc. LL

HU 246
American Bible Society. Annual Report. 1916. a. index. American Bible Society, 1865 Broadway, New York, NY 10023. Examined: 1975, 125p.; 1976. 126p. free.
Aud: Sa

The yearbook and directory of the American Bible Society. Contains information on the Society's officers and managers and its history; a report of the annual meeting; information on personnel changes; reports on library activities, volunteer activities, and world services provided; and a treasurer's report. The directory includes names of officers, department heads, and headquarters personnel; a list of members by regional societies; and the Society's constitution, charter, and bylaws. LL

HU 247
American Jewish Organizations. Directory. ISSN 0065-8979. (Continues: American Synagogue Directory.) 1957. bi-a. H. Frenkel, 24 Rutgers St, New York, NY 10002. Examined: 8th ed., 1973. 189p. $12. (9th ed., 1975.)
Aud: Pl, Sa

A directory of Jewish organizations in the U.S. and Canada. Lists over 5800 synagogues, organizations, schools, and Israeli institutions. Synagogues are coded by affiliation, i.e., Orthodox, Conservative, Reform, or Traditional. LL

HU 248
American Jewish Year Book. ISSN 0065-8987. 1899. a. bibl. index. American Jewish Committee, Jewish Publication Society of America, 165 E 56th St, New York, NY 10022. Examined: v. 77, 1977. Morris Fine

and Milton Himmelfarb, eds. $15. (v. 78, 1978. 714p.)
Aud: Hs, Jc, Cl, Pl

Presents a record of the year's events and trends in American and world Jewish life. Contains special articles on various aspects of Jewish life, statistical and demographic data, summaries of events and trends affecting Jewish life in specific countries of the world, and lists of Jewish organizations, federations, and periodicals. Also includes monthly calendars, a brief necrology, and a subject index. Volume 77 contains a list of special articles which appeared in volumes 51 through 76. SB/KMH/LL

HU 249
American Lutheran Church. Yearbook. ISSN 0569-6348. 1960. a. index. illus. Augsburg Publishing House, 426 S Fifth St, Minneapolis, MN 55415. Examined: 1977. Arnold R. Mickelson, ed. 432p. $2.75.
Aud: Pl, Sa

The American Lutheran Church is comprised of the American Lutheran Church, the Evangelical Lutheran Church, and the United Evangelical Lutheran Church. The directory is arranged topically beginning with a church calendar and lectionary calendar, followed by information on the organization of the Church, names of the officers of the national and subordinate units of the Church, and related associations both here and abroad, such as the Lutheran World Relief, World Council of Churches, U.S. Conference of World Council of Churches, and other cooperating churches. Includes indexes to personnel and institutions; a geographical listing of congregations; clergy members; statistics; a necrology; a separate list for the clergy of the Evangelical Lutheran Church of Canada; and a list of recent graduates of the theological seminaries with pictures and brief vita. LL

HU 250
Anglican Yearbook. ISSN 0517-774X. 1890. a. index. Anglican Church of Canada, Anglican Book Centre, 600 Jarvis St, Toronto, Ontario M4Y 2J6, Canada. Examined: 1977. 181p. $5.
Aud: Pl, Sa

Lists the bishops of the Anglican Church of Canada and also the primates and prolocutors. Includes information on the organization of the General Synod, finances, diocesan and parish statistics, Anglican Foundation of Canada, archives, church house library, overseas personnel of the Anglican Church of Canada, societies of the church, dioceses (bishops, offices, parishes, and clergy), Anglican chaplains to the Canadian forces, officers of the provincial synods, universities and schools (residential schools, religious communities, social service resources), and general information. The latter category lists some church headquarters, Anglican book store outlets, diocesan conference centers, church papers, Canadian Episcopate, and alphabetical lists of communities served in Canada, bishops, clergy, deaconesses, and church Army personnel. LL

HU 251
Annual Directory: Houses of Prayer. 1976. a. Clarity Publishing, 75 Champlain St, Albany, NY 12204. Examined: 1976; 1977/78. 108p. $4.95.
Aud: Pl, Sa

An alphabetical list of over 70 Catholic houses of prayer in the U.S., with a few in Canada and abroad. The publication is intended for use by those who seek a special place to come together to renew their faith through prayer. It lists the name, address, phone number, the sponsoring community or church with founding date of the house, and names of contact persons. Includes a short statement on the spirituality thrust and guest policy. The appendixes group the houses of prayer by geographical location and by purpose (such as serving only their own religious community, primarily to men or women) and those that offer hermitage opportunities. LL

HU 252
Association of Theological Schools in the United States and Canada. Bulletin. ISSN 0362-1472. (Continues: American Association of Theological Schools. Bulletin; Association of Theological Schools. Directory.) 1937. freq. varies. Association of Theological Schools, Box 396, Vandalia, OH 45377. Examined: 1977. Jesse H. Zigler, ed. 7v.
Aud: Cl, Pl, Sa

Consists of seven parts which have various frequencies. Parts one through three, five, and six are published biennially. Part one gives information on the organization, constitution, and bylaws of the Association of Theological Schools (ATS); part two lists officers, committees, and commissions; part three gives procedures, standards, and criteria for membership; part five includes policy statements; part six is the minutes and proceedings of the biennial meeting. Part four, the directory, is published annually and includes information on schools. Each entry indicates address, phone number, chief executive officer, denomination, affiliation, size of faculty, library size, enrollment, and degrees offered. Part seven, the membership list, is published semi-annually and includes names of member schools with accredited degrees offered and date of previous and next accreditation periods. A binder is provided to hold the parts. The **Bulletin** absorbed the *Directory* after 1972; it had been published separately as a biennial. LL

HU 253

Baptist Federation of Canada. Proceedings; Minutes Report. ISSN 0522-3547. 1955. tri-a. bibl. index. illus. Baptist Federation of Canada, 91 Queen St, Box 1298, Brantfort, Ontario M3T 5T6, Canada. Examined: 1970/73. R. Fred Bullen, ed.
Aud: Sa

Contains the minutes and proceedings of the previous triennium of the Baptist Federation of Canada, reports of the committees and organizations, and a summary of church statistics arranged geographically. Information provided includes number of churches, baptisms, membership, and finances; many photographs of the meetings are included. Also included is a list of Canadian Baptist publications. LL

HU 254

Baptist Missionary Association of America. BMAA Directory and Handbook. ISSN 0525-4655. (Continues: Baptist News Service. Directory and Handbook. ISSN 0091-2743.) 1970. a. index. Baptist News Service, Box 97, Jacksonville, TX 75766. Examined: 1976/77. Leon Gaylor, ed.
Aud: Pl, Sa

A comprehensive guide to the work of the Baptist Missionary Association of America (formerly North American Baptist Association). Provides complete information on the organization, doctrine, statistics, church membership, baptismal records, expenditures, and value of church property. General contents include a basic description and history of the BMAA, general directories and tables, related district and state associations, BMAA statistics, directory of missionaries, directory of church location, music and youth directors, and ordained and licensed ministers. The directory for ordained and licensed ministers is an alphabetical list, organized by state, giving address and phone number. LL

HU 255

The Baptist Union Directory. ISSN 0302-3184. (Continues: Baptist Handbook.) 1861. a. index. The Baptist Church House, 4 Southampton Row, London, WC1B 4AB, England. Examined: 116th ed., 1977/78. 298p. $3.35.
Aud: Sa

The directory of the Council of the Baptist Union of Great Britain and Ireland. It contains proceedings and reports of the annual assembly and lists of associations, churches, statistics, ministers and lay preachers, and educational and social institutions associated with the Council. Entries in the directory of ministers include information on degrees, granting institution, dates of attendance, positions held and dates, and address. Church statistics are arranged by location, giving name of the church, date of organization, number of members, name of minister(s), and name of church secretary. LL

HU 256

A Biographical Directory of Clergymen of the American Lutheran Church. 1962. decennial. illus. Augsburg Publishing House, 426 S Fifth St, Minneapolis, MN 55415. Examined: 2nd ed., 1972. Arnold R. Michelson, ed. 1054p. $15.
Aud: Pl, Sa

An alphabetical listing of the clergy of the American Lutheran Church. Entries include information on date and place of ordination, date and place of birth, parents, marital status, education, honors, publications, offices held, service or other employment, and retirement status. Portraits are included when available. The volume is prefaced by a brief list of the general officers of the American Lutheran Church. A list of removals from the clergy roster is appended at the end. LL

HU 257

Biographical Directory of Negro Ministers. 1965. irreg. G. K. Hall, 70 Lincoln St, Boston, MA 02111. Examined: 1975. Ethel L. Williams, ed. 580p. $28.
Aud: Pl, Sa

An interdenominational directory published every three to four years of 1442 Black ministers and clergymen in the U.S. It is an alphabetical listing giving information on birth date, names of parents, education, marital status, children, positions held, awards and honors, publications, and address. Includes geographic and denominational access. LL

HU 258

Broadman Comments: On the International Bible Lessons for Christian Teaching, Convention Uniform Series. ISSN 0068-2721. 1945. a. index. Broadman Press, 124 Ninth Ave N, Nashville, TN 37234. Examined: 1977/78. Donald F. Ackland, ed. 384p. $3.95.
Aud: Sa

A guide to the study of the Bible based on the International Sunday School Lessons, Uniform Series. Organized by six-year cycles of study. The publication seeks to achieve a good balance in the study of history and doctrine, Old and New Testament, spiritual enrichment, and community concern. Arranged according to the academic calendar from September to August. An area of study is assigned to each quarter. Each lesson contains two scriptural passages, studying the Bible, analyses of the passages, techniques for applying the lesson, and suggestions for teaching the class which includes an outline. A list of titles from Broadman on studying and teaching the Bible precedes each quarter of study. There is an index to scriptural passages. LL

HU 259

Canadian Society for the Study of Religion. Proceedings. Société Canadienne pour l'Etude de la Religion. Actes. ISSN 0317-4972. 1968. a. CSSR/SCER, Queen's Theological College, Kingston, Ontario, Canada. Examined: 1976. D. Franklin, ed. 35p.
Aud: Sa

Contains summaries of proceedings, primarily the papers presented at the annual convention. Includes a conference program, minutes, treasurer's report, and a list of members with addresses. In English and French. LL

HU 260

Catholic Almanac. ISSN 0069-1208. (Continues: National Catholic Almanac.) 1971. a. index. Our Sunday Visitor, Huntington, IN 46750. Examined: 1978. Felician A. Foy, ed. 703p. $11.95; $7.95 pap.
Aud: Cl, Pl

Originated remotely from *St. Anthony's Almanac* published by the Franciscans of Holy Name Province from 1904 to 1929. Issued by the *Franciscan Magazine* from 1931-1933 and by St. Anthony's Guild from 1936-1971. Called *The National Catholic Almanac* from 1940-1969. Acquired by *Our Sunday Visitor* in 1971.

Provides an overview of events in the prior year focusing on the Catholic church. A special reports section covers various topics each year. Special reports in the 1978 volume covered the canonization of St. John Newman and in-hand reception of Holy Communion; reports in the 1977 volume covered the Assembly of the Synod of Bishops, Indochina refugee resettlement, marriage encounter, Catholic charismatic renewal, and the proposed ordination of women. Covers dates and events in church history, ecumenical councils, popes, canonizations, encyclicals, the Synod of Bishops, cardinals, and the Vatican. Church doctrine is outlined. Catholic biographies and worldwide statistics are provided. Men's and women's religious orders and Catholic educational institutions are listed with addresses. There is an extensive subject index. KMH

HU 261

Catholic Periodical and Literature Index. ISSN 0008-8285. (Continues: Catholic Periodical Index; The Guide to Catholic Literature.) 1967/68. bi-a. w/bi-m. suppls. bibl. Catholic Library Association, 461 W Lancaster Ave, Haverford, PA 19041. Examined: v. 18, 1975/76. Catherine M. Pilley, ed. 565p. $60.
Aud: Cl, Pl

An author and subject index to 124 Catholic periodicals (e.g., *Augustinian Studies, Catholic Theological Society of America Proceedings, Journal of Ecumenical Studies, New Scholasticism, The Teilhard Review*), and an annotated author-title-subject bibliography of adult books by Catholics, with a selection of Catholic interest books by other authors. Author, title, and subject entries are arranged in one alphabet. **The Catholic Periodical and Literature Index** began in 1967 with the merger of *The Catholic Periodical Index* (1930-1966) and *The Guide to Catholic Literature* (1888-1967). The new title continued the volume numbering of the *Index* and began with volume 14. KMH

HU 262

Catholic Telephone Guide. ISSN 0147-5959. 1934. a. index. illus. The Catholic News, 86 W Broad St, Fleetwood/Mt. Vernon, NY 10552. Examined: 43rd ed., 1977. Victor L. Ridder, ed. 274p. $15.
Aud: Pl, Sa

A directory and buyer's guide serving the Catholic Church in the New York metropolitan area. It includes the archdioceses and dioceses of New York, Brooklyn, and Rockville Centre (Long Island), and, in New Jersey, Newark, Trenton, Paterson, and Camden. Categories of information are arranged under the name of the diocese. Categories include diocesan or archdiocesan officials, churches, seminaries, novitiates, Catholic charities, institutions, universities, colleges, and schools. Entries in these categories give: name, address, phone number, name(s) of director, pastor, or list of officers (depending on nature and size of organization). Additional directory information is listed for the following: Eastern rite churches, religious communities, organizations, and activities. Includes alphabetical lists of priests (religious order, institution, address), chaplains of hospitals and institutions, military chaplains, summer camps, and Catholic publications; an advertisers' index; and a buyer's guide. Advertisements for religious items and services are found throughout the guide. LL

HU 263
Catholic Theological Society of America. Proceedings. ISSN 0069-1267. 1946. a. bibl. index. Catholic Theological Society of America, Mahwah, NJ 07430. Examined: v. 31, 1976. Luke Salm, ed. 262p. $7.50.
Aud: Sa

The proceedings of the sessions and business reports of the Society. The general sessions include the major address of the conference, with categorical responses from the members of the Society; reports of seminar workshops, including presentations and summaries; balance sheets on current issues; and the presidential address. The topics covered in the 1976 issue are contemporary Christian theologies, infallibility, civil religion, ecumenism, and religious education. Includes the secretary's and the treasurer's reports and a list of officers of the Society. There is no list of members. LL

HU 264
Central Conference of American Rabbis. Yearbook. ISSN 0069-1607. 1890. a. index. Central Conference of American Rabbis, 790 Madison Ave, New York, NY 10021. Examined: 86th ed., 1977. Elliot L. Stevens, ed. 342p. $10.
Aud: Sa

The purpose of the Central Conference of American Rabbis is to preserve and promote Judaism. Its yearbook contains reports and papers of the Conference officers and committees; lists of officers, standing committees, commissions, and conference representatives; and programs of the convention. All committee and commission reports are included, with action taken printed in bold face type. Papers on religious and current social issues are presented. There is a list of memorial tributes to distinguished members who died in the previous year. The appendix includes listings of charter members, CCAR conventions, and past presidents; a necrology; a catalog of CCAR publications; suggestions for procedures in rabbinical-congregational relationships; constitution and bylaws; code of ethics for rabbis; executive board activities; and a list of members arranged alphabetically, then geographically. The alphabetical list includes name, degrees, position, congregation or institution, and address. The geographical listing, arranged by location and name of congregation, gives only the rabbi's name and year of his ordination. LL

HU 265
Christian Church. Yearbook and Directory. (Continues: Disciples of Christ. Yearbook and Directory. ISSN 0420-0713.) 1969. a. index. Christian Church, 222 S Downey Ave, Indianapolis, IN 46219. Dist: Christian Board of Publication, Box 179, St Louis, MO 63166. Examined: 1976. Betty H. Sanders, ed. 554p. $9.95 pap.
Aud: Pl, Sa

Contains a description of the organization, directory of the church, reports, ecumenical and fraternal relationships, statistical reports of congregations, summary and comparative reports, and a ministers' directory with related lists of chaplains and seminary students and a necrology. Directory of the church includes: general officers, board and cabinet members, administrative staff, and lists of committees, divisions, and departments. Reports of the church are taken from the minutes and proceedings of the previous year. Statistics on local congregations are arranged geographically. Entries include name, address, phone number, size of membership, church income, mission finance, and outreach finance. Ministers' directory is an alphabetical listing; entries cover name, address, whether ordained or licensed, and position or type of ministry. LL

HU 266
Christian Periodical Index. ISSN 0069-3871. 1956. a. (formerly quinquennial w/a. and q. suppls.) bibl. index. Christian Librarian's Fellowship, 910 Union Rd, West Seneca, NY 14224. Examined: 1971/75, 544p.; 1976. Ruth G. Butler, ed. 137p. $13.
Aud: Cl, Pl, Sa

Subtitle: "An index to subjects, authors, and book reviews." A selected index to 43 Christian periodicals that are chosen by the members of the Christian Librarian's Fellowship. One or two of the periodicals are published in Australia or England. All are in English. Subjects and authors are included in one alphabet, with subject headings printed in caps. There is a separate book review section indexed by author, with name of reviewer indicated. LL

HU 267
Church Overseas. ISSN 0578-2341. 1963. bi-a. index. illus. Canadian Baptist Overseas Mission Board, 217 St. George St, Toronto, Ontario, Canada. Examined: 1972. E. J. Bell, ed. 152p. $1.
Aud: Sa

A review of the overseas church work of the Canadian Baptist Overseas Missions (CBOM). The work of four overseas missions—Kenya, Zaire, India, and Bolivia—were reported in the issue examined. The reports consist of articles written by the missionaries involved. The data given is not consistent; each mission focuses on different events, tasks, people, and mission work. Photographs of missionaries and overseas mission work are featured liberally. Maps and some statistics can be found—in this case for Kenya. A directory of officers of the CBOM and a missionary directory are also included. LL

HU 268
The Church Pulpit Year Book. ISSN 0069-4002. a. index. Chansitor Publications, 46 Bedford Row, London, WC1R 4L4, England. Examined: 1976, 299p.; 1977. 307p. £3.
Aud: Sa

Contains the scriptural texts and two suggested sermons for the Anglican church service. One sermon is linked to the scriptural text for Holy Communion, and the other deals with the lessons for Evensong. The sermons can be used without alteration, or ministers can add their own materials. The sermons and scriptural readings are arranged according to the church calendar. There is a special section for secular holidays such as Mothering Sunday and Remembrance Sunday. LL

HU 269
Clerical Directory of the Protestant Episcopal Church. ISSN 0578-4980. 1968. bi-a. w/suppls. Church Hymnal Corp., 800 Second Ave, New York, NY 10017. Examined: 1977. 700p. $10.
Aud: Pl, Sa

Lists all ordained clergy of the Episcopal Church. Each entry includes: address, position (or retired), place and date of birth, names of parents, education, ordinations date and name(s) of ordaining bishop(s), marital status, employment record, associations, honor and awards, and publications. There is a separate list of depositions and removals, giving the name of the deposed clergy member, reference to his/her previous biographical listing, diocese, and the date and presiding bishop when the action was taken. The 1977 edition reflects changes made from October 1, 1974 to October 31, 1976. LL

HU 270
College Theology Society. Proceedings. ISSN 0069-5750. (Continues: Society of Catholic College Teachers of Sacred Doctrine. Proceedings.) 1955. a. bibl. Seabury Press, 815 Second Ave, New York, NY 10017. Examined: 1975. Thomas McFadden, ed. 214p. $5.
Aud: Sa

Selected essays from the annual convention of the College Theology Society. The 1975 edition is entitled "Liberation, Revolution, and Freedom: Theological Perspectives." The essays are by noted theologians and teachers of theology or religious studies. The approach is well-rounded, covering liberation of the Third World, women, and minority movements. The underlying theme is connected with classical Christian values. Articles include bibliographical references. There is no index. A list of contributors is found at the end. The introduction sheds some light on the 1974 convention, otherwise no convention program is found. The editor is chairman of the College of Theology at St. Joseph's College in Philadelphia. LL

HU 271
Confessions in Dialogue. 1972. irreg. index. World Council of Churches, 150 Route de Ferney, 1211 Geneva 20, Switzerland. Examined: 3rd ed., 1975. Nils Ehrenstrom. 266p.
Aud: Sa

Subtitle: "A survey of bilateral conversations among world confessional families." Contains conversations between confessional churches on church union negotiations. The purpose of the publication is to furnish documentation and summaries of these conversations. It is organized as a survey of ecumenical dialogue, particularly in the area of theological and ecclesiastical problems. The table of contents lists the following sections: descriptive accounts of the conversations; aims of the conversations; methods and procedures; subject matters (i.e., scripture, worship, and bilateral dialogue); bilateral conversations—problems and possibilities; concluding reflections; and recommendations. Includes a list of editions of documents and a directory of agencies on church union. Although this is an irregular publication, it has been revised consistently to update hard-to-find information on ecumenical dialogue. LL

HU 272
Conservative Congregational Christian Conference. Annual Report. a. Conservative Congregational Christian Conference, Box 171, Hinsdale, IL 60521. Examined: 26th ed., 1975. Willis E. Joiner, ed. 62p.
Aud: Pl, Sa

Lists annual meeting locations, officers, committees, budget, treasurer's report, gift income from churches, auditor's report, constitutions and bylaws, area representatives, regional fellowships, member churches, ordained ministers, licensed ministers, conference care, individual lay members, and conference benefactors. Entries for member churches include: address, name of pastor and clerk, year organized, year joined CCC, membership, expenses, and missionary giving. The lists of ordained and licensed ministers gives name, address, and place of service. Does not include written reports or minutes of annual meetings. LL

HU 273
Consultation on Church Union. Digest. ISSN 0589-4867. 1962. irreg. Consultation on Church Union, 227 Alexander St, Princeton, NJ 08540. Examined: 12th ed., 1974. Paul A. Crow, Jr., ed. 97p. $2.50.
Aud: Pl, Sa

Title varies: *Digest of the Proceedings of the Meeting*.

Includes articles and addresses of the plenary session of the Consultation on Church Union (COCU), an ecumenical organization of nine Protestant churches with observers from the Catholic, Anglican, and Friends churches. The goal of COCU is to work toward a united church. The meetings focus on dogmatic, worship, or liturgical issues; church structure; and spirited fellowship. Members, participants, observers, and guests are listed by denomination with title, office, and address. The issue examined had a supplementary section for official records, including the minutes and appendixes, financial reports, and personnel. LL

HU 274
Deseret News Church Almanac. ISSN 0093-786X. 1974. a. index. illus. Deseret News, Box 838, Salt Lake City, UT 84110. Examined: 1977. William B. Smart, ed. 306p. $1.95.
Aud: Pl, Sa

An annual compilation of events as reported in the *Church of the Latter Day Saint Church News*. Features include: major events of the past year, the year in review, historical chronology of the church, general authorities—current, general authorities—historical data, stakes of the church, missions and regions, membership statistics, departments and auxiliaries, interesting facts, and an index. The section on general authorities includes biographical data and pictures of past and current presidents of the church. The section on the stakes of the church is arranged chronologically. Each entry includes information on: name, locality, date of organization, name of president, names changed (or disorganized), and number of stakes. The section on missions and regions includes addresses of missions, missionaries called and serving annually, full-time missions—historical data, regional representatives of the twelve regions of the church, areas of the church, and area conferences. The almanac was prepared by the staff of *Deseret News* in cooperation with the staff of the history department of the Church of the Latter Day Saints. LL

HU 275
Directory of Campus Ministry. ISSN 0070-5209. 1970. a. U.S. Catholic Conference, The Center for Applied Research in the Apostolate, 1312 Massachusetts Ave, NW, Washington, DC 20005. Examined: 1970/72. 217p.
Aud: Cl, Pl, Sa.

A guide to Catholic Campus ministry in the U.S. Lists over 2000 public, private, and church-related institutions, arranged alphabetically by state and diocese. Each entry includes: address; affiliation or control; accessibility to cultural centers, such as libraries, museums, theaters; enrollment; and breakdown of enrollment when available. Chaplaincies and names of chaplains are listed when available with names, addresses, phone numbers, and a brief description of religious services and programs. There is a separate index of chaplains, which gives name, diocese, and state. The directory is restricted to the U.S. Catholic Conference. LL

HU 276
Directory of Lutheran Churches in Canada. ISSN 0316-800X. 1954. a. Lutheran Council in Canada, 365 Hargrave St, Suite 500, Winnipeg, Manitoba R3B 2K3, Canada. Examined: 21st ed., 1976. W. Schultz, ed. 72p. $1.50.
Aud: Pl, Sa

A combined listing of the Lutheran churches in Canada including the Evangelical Lutheran Church of Canada, the Lutheran Church in America—Canada Section, and the Lutheran Church—Canada. It lists the executive administrations and their offices and associated or related agencies and institutions, including campus ministries, with the names of officers or contact persons. Included are two directories, one for congregations and the other for clergy. The congregation directory is arranged alphabetically by place names with information on name of congregation, church body, membership count, location, and name of pastor. The clergy roster is a straight alphabetical listing of clergy members with address, phone number, and church body affiliate. LL

HU 277
Directory of the Armenian Church in North America and Church Calendar. ISSN 0419-3709. 1961. a. Diocese of the Armenian Church of America, 630 Second

Ave, New York, NY 10016. Examined: 1978. 21p. free.
Aud: Pl, Sa

Title varies: *Directory of the Armenian Church*.

A directory and calendar for the Armenian Church in America. Arranged in two parts. The first part includes a monthly calendar, with Saint's days and holy days noted, and a list of daily Bible readings. The second part is the directory. It provides historical and descriptive information about the church and lists primates and clergy, parishes of the eastern and western dioceses, notes on the Armenian community in America, principal Armenian organizations, the Armenian press in the U.S., and Armenian day schools. LL

HU 278
Ecumenical Directory of Retreat and Conference Centers. 1974. irreg. index. Jarrow Press, 90 Madison St, Denver, CO 80206. Examined: 2nd ed., 1975. Philip Deemer, ed. 270p. $15.
Aud: Pl

A directory and guide to retreats or spiritual conferences, primarily for members of the Christian faith. The centers listed are ecumenical, unless otherwise noted, and are located in the U.S. and Canada. They are listed alphabetically first by state or province, then by city or town. Information is given on events, accommodations, rates, chapels, use for non-religious groups, schedule, conductors, reservations, and camping. Under events, it also lists what types of conferences or retreats are offered. Address and phone number are provided, including the name of the contact person. LL

HU 279
Episcopal Church Annual. ISSN 0071-1012. 1830. a. index. illus. Morehouse-Barlow Co., 78 Danbury Rd, Wilton, CT 06897. Examined: 1977. Ronald T. Lau, ed. 506p. $10.
Aud: Pl, Sa

Provides a comprehensive guide to the Protestant Episcopal Church. Contains information on general organization, statistics, official agencies, institutions and organizations, special services for the military and the handicapped, religious orders, diocesan and parochial lists, clergy, and presiding bishops. Includes a section on the larger Anglican communion. There is an index to advertisers for church supplies and services. LL

HU 280
Episcopal Church Calendar. ISSN 0421-3122. (Continues: Episcopal Church Lesson Calendar.) a. Morehouse-Barlow Co., 98 Danbury Rd, Wilton, CT 06897. Examined: 1975. $5.50 pap.
Aud: Pl, Sa

The official calendar of the Episcopal Church. It lists according to the church year from the first Sunday of Advent to the day before Advent: collects, scriptural lessons, Psalm readings, hymns, propers and prefaces, altar colors, and holy days/feast days. In the issue examined, the calendar is arranged according to the *Trial Use Prayer Book* (Services for Trial Use) and the *Prayer Book* (Book of Common Prayer). Additional hymns are listed separately. LL

HU 281
Fact Book on Theological Education. 1971. a. index. Association of the Theological Schools, Box 396, Vandalia, OH 45377. Examined: 1976/77. Marvin H. Taylor, ed. 109p. $10.
Aud: Cl, Pl

A statistical guide to the institutional members of the Association of Theological Schools (ATS). Statistical tables are organized under the following categories: enrollment, number and distribution of personnel, finances—revenues and expenditures, and compensation. Brief descriptive analyses are given in each category. Statistics on distributions and trends in enrollment are provided by degree program, sex, and race. The second half of the book is classified by schools and includes more detailed statistical tables in each category. The statistical tables on schools cover denominational affiliation, administrative officers' distribution, faculty distribution, library staff distribution, and analyses of revenues, expenditures, and compensations. Names and addresses of institutions are not provided. LL

HU 282
Friends World Conference Committee. American Section. Friends Directory. bi-a. Friends World Committee for Consultation, Section of the Americas, 1506 Race St, Philadelphia, PA 19102. Examined: 1977/78. 100p. $1.75.
Aud: Pl, Sa

Subtitle: "Meetings for worship in the Western Hemisphere." A list of Friends Meetings in Canada, the Caribbean, Mexico, Central and South America, and the U.S. The Meetings are arranged alphabetically under state or province. Entries include the name of the Meeting (with the Yearly Meeting affiliation), address, time of the meeting for worship on Sunday, and name and address of the clerk or pastor. There are additional listings for Friends information centers around the world. Friends elementary and secondary schools, colleges and adult study centers, homes in the U.S., and headquarters of various Friends organizations. LL

HU 283
Garuda. ISSN 0046-5445. 1971. irreg. illus. Vajradhatu, 1111 Pearl St, Boulder, CO 80302. Examined: 1971; 1972; 1974; 1976. Chogyäm Trungpa Rinpoche and Michael Kohn, eds. 88p. $3.95.
Aud: Pl, Sa

Includes writings on the thoughts and teaching of Chogyäm Trungpa Rinpoche, with other works by distinguished and lay teachers, scholars, and artists in the Buddhist tradition. Includes many illustrations and photographs. Some issues contain news and the schedule of Chogyäm Trungpa's appearances. Also featured are poetry and artistic photographs. Each issue has a different theme. LL

HU 284
General Association of Regular Baptist Churches. Yearbook. ISSN 0431-1396. 1952. a. illus. Regular Baptist Press, 1300 N Meacham Rd, Schaumberg, IL 60172. Examined: 1977. Merle R. Hull, ed. 154p. $3.50; $2 pap.
Aud: Pl, Sa

The General Association of Regular Baptist Churches was founded in 1932 by a group of churches which had withdrawn from the Northern Baptist Convention. Its directory lists fellowshipping churches, Christian day schools, mission churches, pastors, missionaries and Christian workers, chaplains, and annual meetings. Church listings are arranged alphabetically by city and state. Entries include: name of church, address, name and address of pastor, and phone number. Provides additional information on how to enter the fellowship, recommendations on books and periodicals, auditors' report, and projects approved by state associations. Also includes the most recently amended constitution, statistics, and a list of current church officers with their pictures. LL

HU 285
Guide to Social Science and Religion in Periodical Literature. ISSN 0017-5307. (Continues: Guide to Religious and Semi-religious Periodicals; Guide to Religious Periodicals.) 1964. a. index. National Periodical Library, Box 47, Flint, MI 48501. Examined: v. 12, 1976. Albert M. Wells, ed. 157p. $47.50.
Aud: Cl, Pl, Sa

A guide to 93 periodicals in the social sciences and religion, with primary emphasis on religious periodicals. It is arranged alphabetically by subject. Entries include title of article, title of periodical, date, page, author, and number of words in article. There are no book reviews. LL

HU 286
Handbook of Denominations in the United States. 1951. quinquennial. bibl. index. Abingdon Press, 201 Eighth Ave S, Nashville, TN 37202. Examined: 6th ed., 1975. Frank S. Mead, ed. 320p. $5.95.
Aud: Cl, Pl, Sa

A concise handbook giving descriptive history, statistics, and basic doctrines of 250 religious bodies in the U.S. Covers the major religions: Christianity, Judaism, Bahai, and Spiritualism. Organized by the major groups; sub- or splinter groups are named and briefly described under the major denomination. Denominations are arranged alphabetically by names. Entries include the origin, organization, history, doctrine and beliefs, missionary efforts, and some basic statistics on membership and related institutions. A special feature is a list of "Headquarters of Denominations" which includes addresses and names of chief officials. Compiler, Frank S. Mead, is an authority on the historical and contemporary church. LL

HU 287
Hebrew Studies. ISSN 0146-4094. (Continues: Hebrew Abstracts. ISSN 0438-895X.) 1955. a. bibl. The National Association of Professors of Hebrew in American Institutions of Higher Education, Strickler Hall, University of Louisville, Louisville, KY 40208. Examined: 17th ed., 1976. Israel T. Naamani, ed. 193p. $2.
Aud: Cl, Sa

Subtitle: "A journal devoted to the Hebrew language, the Bible, and related areas of scholarship." Includes articles on the Bible, Hebrew language, and the teaching of Hebrew studies. Also includes lectures and essays presented at conferences of the National Association of Professors of Hebrew. All articles are written in English and include bibliographical references. There is a section of brief reviews of monographs, new periodicals, and journal articles. LL

HU 288
Index to Mormonism in Periodical Literature. ISSN 0073-5981. 1966. a. Church of Jesus Christ of Latter-day Saints, Historical Department, Public Services, 50 E North Temple St, Salt Lake City, UT 84150. Examined: 1976. Kevin L. Bashore, ed. 292p. $5.
Aud: Pl, Sa

An index to 20 periodical titles, most of which are published by the Mormon church or affiliated organizations. Other periodicals are indexed only when they contain articles which pertain to Mormons or Mormonism. It is arranged alphabetically by subject or person. The index is designed for a comprehensive audience, from children to research scholars. LL

HU 289
Index to Religious Periodical Literature. ISSN 0019-4107. 1949/52. bi-a. w/semi-a. suppls. American Theological Library Association, 5600 S Woodlawn, Chicago, IL 60637. Examined: v. 12, 1975/76. Fay Dickerson, ed. 880p. $80 w/semi-a. suppls.
Aud: Cl, Pl, Sa

An index to 203 English, French, and German religious periodicals. Covers scholarly articles in the fields of church history, biblical literature, theology, history of religions, sociology and psychology of religion and related areas of the humanities, and current events. There are three sections: an author index, a subject index, and a book review index. The author index includes abstracts of some articles. Book reviews are indexed by author. Entries include information on title, periodical, publisher, date, author of review article, and volume and page number. Subscription includes three semi-annual supplements and the biennial cumulation. LL

HU 290
Institute of Jewish Studies. Bulletin. 1972. a. bibl. Institute of Jewish Studies, University College, London, Gower St, London WC1E 6BT, England. Dist: Bulletin of the Institute of Jewish Studies, Subscription Department, London WIA AW2, England. Examined: v. 3, 1975. R. Loewe and C. Abramsky, eds. 107p. $3.22. (1978.)
Aud: Sa

Devoted to Jewish learning, including biblical, Talmudic, and Midrashic literature, philosophy, mysticism, Hasidism, and modern Jewish thought. Six or seven articles of approximately 20 pages each are published in each volume; all include bibliographical references. Includes book reviews of three to five titles in each yearly volume and a seminar record, giving dates, names of lecturers, and titles of papers presented at the Mocatta Library at the University College. Most of the articles are in English, some are in Hebrew. LL

HU 291
Jednota Annual; Furdek. ISSN 0419-4873. 1962. a. bibl. illus. First Catholic Slovak Union, 3289 E 55th St, Cleveland, OH 44127. Examined: 1977. Joseph C. Krajsa, ed. 303p.
Aud: Pl, Sa

Contains articles, biographies, history, and news about the Slovak Catholic church, clergy, and church people. There is no definite format. Articles are of varying lengths; many are written by members of the clergy. Longer articles include bibliographical references. Poems are also included. There is one book review in the 1977 issue. Also includes articles from the Jednota's 39th Convention souvenir book. A special feature is the list of Jednota College Scholarship grant winners which includes a brief vita and picture of each winner. Photographs and drawings are included. LL

HU 292
Jednota; Katolicky Kalendar. 1897. a. bibl. illus. Jednota Printery, Box 150, Middletown, PA 17057. Examined: 1977. Jozef C. Krajsa, ed. 260p. $3.
Aud: Pl, Sa

A directory and yearbook of the First Catholic Slovak Union. The text is in Slovak. The first part contains articles about the church and proceedings from the church convention. The second part contains a church directory which lists church leaders, clergy, religious orders, and church periodicals and publications. A calendar which notes Saint's days and holy days is found at the end. It is illustrated with photographs. Poems are included often. LL

HU 293
Journal of Mormon History. ISSN 0094-7342. 1974. a. bibl. Mormon History Association, Box 7010, University Sta, Provo, UT 84601. Examined: v. 2, 1975. Richard W. Sadler, ed. 88p. $4.
Aud: Pl, Sa

Contains articles of medium length on Mormons and Mormonism. It includes bibliographical references. There are no book reviews. A list of officers of the association is found on the back cover. LL

HU 294
Journal of the General Convention of the Protestant Episcopal Church. 1789. tri-a. index. illus. Seabury Press, 821 Second Ave, New York, NY 10017. Examined: 1973; 1976. 1379p. $15.
Aud: Pl, Sa

Summarizes the proceedings of the triennial General Convention of the Protestant Episcopal Church. Divided into five sections: the directory; the General Convention journal, covering actions taken in both houses; concurrent actions; reports of committees, boards, etc; and a supplement containing reports of special meetings, the rules of order, and amendments. The Constitution and canons are listed separately with an index. The work is compiled by the Executive Council from the minutes of the Convention. LL

HU 295
Lutheran Church in America. Minutes of Biennial Convention. ISSN 0460-010X. 1960. bi-a. index. Lutheran Church in America, Board of Publication, 2900 Queen Lane, Philadelphia, PA 19129. Examined: 8th, 1976. James R. Crumley, Jr., ed. 909p.
Aud: Pl, Sa

The proceedings of the biennial convention, including the reports from all church committees, offices, and institutions. It has a complete list of church officers and of delegates to the convention. Divided into two sections, reports and exhibits. Detailed minutes are reported for each department, committee, or division. Many of these include activities and planned programs for the next two years. Statistics are given wherever applicable. The exhibits include the constitution and bylaws, approved constitutions for congregations, standards of acceptance into and continuance in the ministry of the Lutheran Church in America, and proper sources of calls. LL

HU 296
Lutheran Church in America. Yearbook. ISSN 0460-0118. (Continues: United Lutheran Church in America Yearbook; Augustana Annual Yearbook.) 1963. a. index. Lutheran Church in America, Board of Publications, 2900 Queen Lane, Philadelphia, PA 19129. Examined: 1977. 493p.
Aud: Pl, Sa

The directory of the Lutheran Church in America (LCA) which is comprised of the American Evangelical Lutheran Church, the Augustan Evangelical Lutheran Church, the Finnish Evangelical Lutheran Church, and the United Lutheran Church. It includes several directories: the organization of the church, national and international agencies and institutions, clerical roll, missionaries and lay associates, faculty of institutions, campus ministries, a list of statistical tables, and the LCA program and budget. Personal entries indicate only the address, synod, and whether or not the individual is retired. Faculty members are listed by name under their affiliated institution. The 1977 issue includes short articles on the 1976 church convention and the 1976/78 church calendar. There is an index to advertisers. LL

HU 297
Lutheran Church—Missouri Synod. Lutheran Annual. 1910. a. index. Concordia Publishing House, 3558 S Jefferson Ave, St Louis, MO 63118. Examined: 1977. Ralph R. Reinke, ed. 516p. $2.
Aud: Pl, Sa

A directory to the Lutheran Church—Missouri Synod. It is arranged by organization of the church boards, officers, and auxiliary organizations and related associations, including educational and social institutions. Clerical and lay workers are listed under the following categories: pastors, teachers, directors of Christian education, lay ministers and parish workers, and deaconesses. Entries include address, phone numbers, and name of synod. There is also a directory of congregations in the U.S. and Canada. Information provided for each congregation includes name of church, address, time of services, name of pastor, and phone number. A list of principal stations in world areas is appended. LL

HU 298
Measuring Mormonism. ISSN 0094-5633. 1974. a. bibl. Association for the Study of Religion, 3646 East 3580 South, Salt Lake City, UT 84109. Examined: 1976. Glenn M. Vernon, ed. 58p. $2.
Aud: Sa

A collection of articles on various sociological aspects of Mormonism. Articles in the 1976 issue examine church attendance, variations in church membership, and stress in Mormonism. The articles are scholarly and include bibliographical references and case studies; some also have statistical tables. There are generally four or five articles in each issue. LL

HU 299
Mennonite Yearbook and Directory. 1905. a. index. illus. Mennonite Publishing House, 616 Walnut Ave, Scottdale, PA 15683. Examined: v. 67, 1976. James E. Horsch, ed. 167p. $2.95.
Aud: Pl, Sa

Reflects the life and the structure of the Mennonite Church in North America. Lists the work of the conferences and related organizations and projects. Contains a regional directory, conference and district directory, overseas Mennonite churches, Beadry Amish directory, general board, board of congregational ministries, board of education, mission board, mutual aid board, publication board, inter-Mennonite projects, world Mennonite directory, statistics, and a ministerial directory. The regional directory of congregations includes names of district conferences, coordinating committee offices, appointees to church board, and individual churches arranged by state. The conference and district directory of congregations lists committees and officers, members of the women's missionary and service commission, and names and addresses of congregations. It also includes general information and statistics. Entries in the ministerial directory include name, address, telephone number, status and function, date of birth, date of ordination and/or license as deacon, congregational name and number, conference affiliation, and region in which the person lives. Schools and colleges are listed in the directory of church organizations. LL

HU 300

Mission Handbook: North American Protestant Ministries Overseas. ISSN 0093-8130. (Continues: North American Protestant Ministries Overseas.) 1951. tri-a. bibl. index. Missions Advanced Research and Communication Center, 919 W Huntington Dr, Monrovia, CA 91016. Examined: 11th ed., 1976. 589p. $10.
Aud: Pl, Sa

Provides descriptive and statistical data on all North American Protestant overseas ministries and related agencies. It gives an account of mission activities during the last three years. Personnel and financial information are listed with statistics and analyses of the surveys. Mission agencies, mission associations, countries of service, schools, and professors of mission are also listed. LL

HU 301

Mission Yearbook of Prayer. ISSN 0544-4330. 1892. a. index. United Presbyterian Church, 475 Riverside Dr, New York, NY 10027. Examined: 1973. 345p. $1.25.
Aud: Pl, Sa

Provides concise and timely information on mission work and missionaries in the U.S. and overseas, arranged in a calendar format for those who wish to support and pray for mission work. Includes information on missionaries, fraternal workers and national church works, missions and Christian education, workers, campus chaplains in colleges and universities, and military chaplains. Indexes provide a more organized format for access to specific information. LL

HU 302

Moravian Church in America. Daily Texts and Directory and Statistics. 1730. a. Board of Educational Ministries, 5 W Market St, Bethlehem, PA 18018. Examined: 1976, 2v.; 1978. 440p. $3; $2.50 pap.
Aud: Pl, Sa

Arranged in two sections. In 1976, the two sections were published as separate volumes; in 1978, both parts are included in one volume. The first is a devotional work which is arranged according to the calendar year. Each day's entry includes Bible texts with hymn verses and prayers. A list of historical notes of organizations in the U.S. and Canada and of the world-wide Moravian Church is appended. The second part is the Moravian Church in America directory. This includes information on: bishops, ministers in active service, directors of Christian education, missionaries, retired or released ministers, widows of Moravian ministers, retired missionaries, addresses of missionary apartments, Northern Province boards and agencies, Southern Province boards and agencies, interprovincial boards, educational institutions, Moravian book shops, church journal, church causes, prayer days and special emphases, location of churches, statistics, and a directory of officials. LL

HU 303

National Association of Catholic Chaplains. Annual Convention Proceedings. 1965. a. illus. The National Association of Catholic Chaplains, Division of Chaplain Services, U.S. Catholic Conference, 1312 Massachusetts Ave, NW, Washington, DC 20005. Examined: 10th ed., 1975. David Baeten, ed.
Aud: Pl, Sa

Contains the minutes and reports of the association's annual convention. The report of the executive director includes data on membership, association chapters, committees, and associated activities. The minutes of the business meetings are summarily listed. Keynote addresses are reprinted along with photographs of speakers and activities at the meeting. Does not include lists of members or future meeting locations. Election results are given. LL

HU 304

National Council of Churches. Division of Overseas Ministries. Report. ISSN 0077-412X. 1965. a. illus. National Council of Churches in the USA, Division of Overseas Ministries, 475 Riverside Dr, New York, NY 10027. Examined: 1972, 72p.; 1975. 87p. free.
Aud: Pl, Sa

Area reports of the overseas ministries are arranged geographically and provide a brief description of current activities and the involvement of the Division of Overseas Ministries in local affairs. Lists participating organizations, officers, and executive staff. Includes a financial statement with denominational receipts, and reports on the strategy and technical area program, activities of the Church World Services, division-wide services, and the World Council of Churches. Presents the budget and program for the following year. There are many photographs illustrating missionary work overseas. LL

HU 305
Official Catholic Directory. ISSN 0078-3854. 1817. a. index. P. J. Kenedy and Sons, Box 729, New York, NY 10022. Examined: 1977. A. J. Corbo, ed. $41. (1978. 1455p. $39.50.)
Aud: Cl, Pl, Sa

A comprehensive directory of the Roman Catholic Church in the U.S., the Canal Zone, Puerto Rico, the Virgin Islands, Agana, Carolina and Marshall Islands. Foreign missionary activities, Canada, and Mexico are also covered, but less thoroughly. It is divided into three parts. Part one covers the church hierarchy, e.g., Vatican officials, cardinals, patriarchs, and Roman Curia. Part two is a directory of the U.S. Catholic Church with listings of archdioceses, dioceses, extraterritorial sees, and overseas missions; statistics; religious orders; and officials and clergy of the Catholic Church in the U.S. Part three provides the same information for Canada and Mexico. Information for each archdiocese and diocese includes names of clergy, parishes, missions, and parochial schools. Also included are the institutions, such as colleges and universities, hospitals, nursing homes, religious communities, layman organizations, and diocesan cemeteries. A special feature in the 1977 edition is a recapitulation of statistics at the end of each diocese listing. The alphabetical list of clergy gives the name, address, religious order, and diocese. An index and a special "Hints and Helps" section are particularly helpful in the use of the directory. LL

HU 306
The Organization of the United Methodist Church. 1970. irreg. index. Abingdon Press, 55 E 55th St, New York, NY 10022. Examined: 1977. Jack M. Tull. 174p. $4.95 pap.
Aud: Sa

A general information source on the United Methodist Church based on its *Book of Discipline*. It explains historical origins, church structure and membership, theology and beliefs, ministry and episcopacy, and the judicial administration. LL

HU 307
Orthodox Church in America. Yearbook and Church Directory and Calendar. a. illus. Orthodox Church in America, Department of Religious Education, Box 675, Syosset, NY 11701. Examined: 1977. 88p. $5.
Aud: Pl, Sa

The directory of the Orthodox Church in the U.S., Canada, Mexico, and South America. It lists church officers and organization, parishes, clergy, choir directors, church school coordinators, Eastern Orthodox military chaplains, vital statistics, Orthodox Youth Rally, sponsors and patrons, seminaries and foundations, and the Historical Society of the Orthodox Church in America. The directory is organized hierarchically from the Primate to the clergy. Section on dioceses lists churches by location; entries include name of church, date of foundation, language of services, clergy, readers and/or teachers, and choir directors. Clergy entries include name and address, but no personal information is given. There is a separate directory of parishes, arranged by state, giving location, name, and address. The 1977 edition features news and photographs of St. Vladimir's Theological Seminary. A church calendar, which lists feast and fast days, and includes scriptural readings for the departed and for special occasions, is available separately. LL

HU 308
Philadelphia Yearly Meeting of the Religious Society of Friends. Proceedings and Yearbook. (Continues: Messenger of the Philadelphia Yearly Meeting of Friends.) a. index. Philadelphia Yearly Meeting, Friends Center, 1515 Cherry St, Philadelphia, PA 19102. Examined: 26th ed., 1976. 199p.
Aud: Pl

Includes the minutes of the Yearly Meeting sessions, annual accounts and budget, and reports of committees, sections, and Friends organizations. Individual committee reports give an account of activities, programs and goals; most reports also include financial summaries. The yearbook section includes an alphabetical listing of monthly meetings, Quarterly Meeting reports, membership statistics, a calendar of local meetings, and general information on Friends homes and retirement communities, schools and colleges, and organizations. There is a directory of Friends under appointment arranged by the Quarterly Meetings, sections, or committees; there is also a separate alphabetical list of Friends with addresses. LL

HU 309
Religious Books and Serials in Print. 1978. freq. not determined. index. R. R. Bowker, 1180 Ave of the Americas, New York, NY 10036. Dist: R. R. Bowker, Box 1807, Ann Arbor, MI 48106. Examined: none. (1978/79. approx. 1650p. $39.50.)
Aud: Cl, Pl, Sa

The first edition is to be published in Fall 1978, and therefore was not available for examination. The publisher's catalog states: "Covering all religions as well as metaphysics, the occult, theology, ethics and related philosophical subjects—this new guide lists some 35,000 available titles of all kinds under 5000 subject areas. Full ordering and bibliographical data is provided in each entry. Includes a separate Bible section, author and title indexes, separate indexes for children's and religious fiction, and a directory of all publishers represented with current addresses." JKM

HU 310
The Religious Public Relations Council. Directory. 1950. bi-a. index. Religious Public Relations Council, Rm 1031, 475 Riverside Dr, New York, NY 10027. Examined: 1974/75; 1976/77. 64p. $2.
Aud: Pl

The membership directory of the Religious Public Relations Council. Members are listed alphabetically by chapters. Officers and fellows are listed separately. Each entry includes name, position held, name of firm or organization, address, and phone number. Council members are public relations officers in religious settings or are involved in publishing as religious editors or staff. LL

HU 311
The Religious Society of Friends. Handbook. 1955. quinquennial. index. Friends World Committee for Consultation, Drayton House, 30 Gordon St, London WC1H 0AX, England. Dist: Friends World Committee, American Section and Fellowship Council, 152-A N 15th St, Philadelphia, PA 19102. Examined: 6th ed., 1972. 84p. $1.20.
Aud: Pl

A list of Societies of Friends around the world. Arranged in broad geographical areas by continent. Entries include information on the location of Yearly Meetings, Friends missions, Meetings connected with the Friends Service Council, and names of other Meetings. More detailed information is provided for individual Meetings including date of establishment, number of members and Meetings, address, and publications. Also lists schools, colleges, centers for study, Friends publications, Friends centers and offices, Friends reference libraries, and membership statistics. The **Handbook** has been published quinquennially since 1962. LL

HU 312
A Sociological Yearbook of Religion in Britain. 1966. a. bibl. SCM Press, 56 Bloomsbury St, London WC1, England. Examined: 8th ed., 1975. Michael Hill, ed. 184p. £2.80.
Aud: Cl, Pl

Contains articles on the sociology of religion, embracing both contemporary and historical, theoretical and empirical studies. Articles are written primarily from a British point-of-view. Most include bibliographical references. LL

HU 313
Solomon Goldman Lectures; Perspectives in Jewish Learning. ISSN 0079-1016. 1965. a. bibl. The College of Jewish Studies Press, Spertus College of Judaica, 618 S Michigan Ave, Chicago, IL 60605. Examined: v. 1, 1965. Monford Harris, ed. 85p. $7; $5 pap.
Aud: Cl, Pl

An annual volume dedicated to Jewish learning. It is not restricted in any particular field. It contains lectures by Jewish scholars that were delivered at Spertus College. Each issue contains four or five articles ranging from ten to twenty pages in length and including bibliographical references. LL

HU 314
Southern Baptist Periodical Index. ISSN 0081-3028. 1965. a. Southern Baptist Convention, Historical Commission, 127 Ninth Ave, Nashville, TN 37234. Examined: 1975. Davis C. Woolley, ed. 240p. $6.75.
Aud: Cl, Pl

An index to 46 Southern Baptist periodicals. Entries are arranged alphabetically by subject and include title, author(s), periodical, volume, page, date of issue, and an indication of whether there are illustrations. LL

HU 315
Spiritual Community Guide for North America. ISSN 0160-0354. 1972. irreg. bibl. index. illus. Howard S. Weiss, Spiritual Community Guide, Box 1080, San Rafael, CA 94902. Examined: 1972. Amir Latif, ed. 208p. $2.95. (1975/76, $3.50; 4th ed., 1979. 256p. $5.95.)
Aud: Pl, Sa

A spiritual guide and handbook oriented primarily to Eastern religion and philosophy, but also to Native American spiritual beliefs. Divided into three major sections: a directory of spiritual growth centers; a handbook of holy men and teachers; and a guide to community centers and organizations that promote spiritual growth. Entries in the directory include a description of the sect or type of devotion, meditation, and/or teaching; address; and phone number. The handbook section includes articles on spiritual growth and communication that are written by teachers, holy men, and gurus. The third section lists community centers, schools, bookstores and libraries, food stores, restaurants, bakeries, etc., in the U.S. and Canada. Entries are arranged alphabetically by state and indicate the type of service or products available. A glossary, photographs of spiritual leaders, and a list of publications are included. LL

HU 316
Tarbell's Teacher's Guide to the International Bible Lessons for Christian Teaching of the Uniform Course. ISSN 0082-1713. 1905. a. bibl. Fleming H. Revell Co., Old Tappan, NJ 07675. Examined: 73rd ed., 1977. Frank S. Mead, ed. 412p. $5.95.
Aud: Pl, Sa

A guide for teachers in church school programs of all denominations. Lesson plans are based on the International Sunday School lessons and are arranged according to the academic calendar. Each weekly lesson focuses on a different theme and includes two versions of the scriptural passage (taken from the King James Bible and the Living Bible unless otherwise indicated), home daily Bible readings, a background description of the passages, notes on the printed text, suggestions for teachers, and separate topics for adults and for young people. There is a list of recommended audiovisual aids with the producers' addresses. LL

HU 317
Trinity Journal. (Continues: Trinity Studies.) 1971. a. bibl. Trinity Evangelical Divinity School, 2045 Half Day Rd, Deerfield, IL 60015. Examined: v. 5, 1976. Timothy Erdel, ed. 170p. $2.
Aud: Pl
Indexed in: *New Testament Abstracts*.

Subtitle: "A journal of student scholarship." Contains articles and reviews on religion, biblical studies, church history, mission, theology, religion, and philosophy. Most of the contributors are students at the Trinity Evangelical Divinity School. Articles are of short to medium length and include bibliographical references. LL

HU 318
Unitarian Historical Society, London. Transactions. ISSN 0082-7800. 1917. a. Lindsey Press, 1-6 Essex St, Strand, London WC2 England. Examined: v. 16, no. 3, 1977. $4.50.
Aud: Cl, Pl

Contains articles and notes dealing with Unitarian history or of interest to Unitarians in Great Britain. Each issue includes six to ten book reviews, most with brief annotations, and a separate review section on new periodicals and journal articles. There is also a list of officers. LL

HU 319
Unitarian Universalist Directory. ISSN 0082-7827. 1961. a. index. illus. Unitarian Universalist Association, 25 Beacon St, Boston, MA 02108. Examined: 1977. Joan A. Fitzgerald, ed. 223p. $5; $6 to libraries; free to members.
Aud: Pl

Provides basic information about the association. The two major listings are churches and fellowships, and ministers in fellowships. The churches are arranged alphabetically by state and city. Entries include: address and phone number, district, date of organization, names of ministers, religious education program, president/chairperson, number of members, church school enrollment, total expenditure, annual fund contribution, and sustaining friends contribution. The ministers in fellowships listing is arranged alphabetically by name. Entries include: address, present settlement, date of ordination, education, and recent settlements. Other lists provide names and addresses of associate officers and trustees, committees, widows of Unitarian Universalist ministers, religious educators, affiliated organizations, finances and general assembly, and bylaws and rules. The issue examined includes photographs of recently built churches. LL

HU 320
United Church Board for World Ministries. Annual Report and Calendar of Prayer. ISSN 0145-0824. 1961. a. index. illus. United Church Board for World Ministries. 475 Riverside Dr, New York, NY 10027. Examined: 1977. David M. Stowe, ed. 68p. $1.
Aud: Pl, Sa

The first section, the annual report, contains brief accounts of and reports on world ministries, world issues, service priorities, overseas seminars, and evangelism. Also contains a personnel report, financial report, an "in memoriam" list, and lists of officers, members of the Board of Directors, corporate members, honorary members, and the missionaries' roll of honor. The calendar is arranged by geographical areas. A description of the work of the church, missionaries, and the type of missionary work taking place in a particular country accompanies each month's calendar, with specific days set aside for prayer and meditation. The number of days set aside varies according to the size and involvement of the church in the particular area. Photographs are included. A separate list of overseas missionaries with names and addresses is provided. An organizational chart is found on the back cover. LL

HU 321

United Church of Christ. General Synod. Minutes. ISSN 0501-221X. 1957. bi-a. index. United Church of Christ, 297 Park Ave S, New York, NY 10010. Examined: 10th ed., 1975. 161p. $2.
Aud: Cl, Pl, Sa

Contains all the minutes of action taken at the General Synod. The index provides access to reports, statements, financial and budget statements, issues and priorities, resolutions, and other Synod activities. The appendix includes lists of elected officers, members of the councils, commissions, and boards; standing rules of the current Synod; reports of the treasurer; addresses presented at the Synod; worship program; and a list of conference delegates with addresses. The organization of the church is described, and a list of church officers is provided at the beginning of the report. LL

HU 322

United Church of Christ. Yearbook. (Continues: Yearbook of the Congregational Christian Churches; Congregational Yearbook; Christian Annual.) a. index. United Church of Christ, 297 Park Ave S, New York, NY 10010. Examined: 1972. 512p. $7.
Aud: Cl, Pl, Sa

Provides statistics, financial summaries, and a directory of the officers, lay workers, educational institutions, and churches of the United Church of Christ. Arranged in five sections: United Church of Christ directory, annual church statistics, directory of ministers, necrology, and directory of continuing organizations. Entries in the church statistics section are listed alphabetically by location and include name of church, year organized, name of pastor, the year pastor was called, total membership, church school enrollment, mission support, and local church expenses. Entries for ministers include name, ministerial designation, year ordained, and address. LL

HU 323

United Methodist Church (United States). General Minutes of the Annual Conference of the United Methodist Church. ISSN 0503-3551. (Continues: Methodist Church (United States). General Minutes of the Annual Conference of the Methodist Church in the U.S. and Canada.) 1968. a. index. Methodist Church, The Council on Finance and Administration, 1200 Davis St, Evanston, IL 60201. Examined: 1975. Norman L. Conrad, ed. 1288p.
Aud: Pl, Sa

A record of the United Methodist Church's annual meeting with statistics. Contains procedural notes; a map of conferences and areas of the United Methodist Church; lists of bishops and officers of both general and jurisdictional conferences and annual conferences; statistical summaries; a general membership roll of military service personnel; a statistical review; the business proceedings of the annual conference; lists of missionaries, deaconesses, and military and civilian chaplains; decisions of the judicial council; and an index of annual conference ministerial members. Statistical information on individual conferences includes: membership, church school attendance, salaries, property values, operating expenses, ministerial support, and benevolences. The index of annual conference ministerial members includes probationers and associate members. It lists names and year of "full connection" or probationary status with United Methodist Church for each minister and a page reference to the conference and the location of the church the minister is connected with. No biographical information is provided. LL

HU 324

United Presbyterian Church in the U.S.A. Minutes of the General Assembly. ISSN 0082-8548. 1879. a. index. United Presbyterian Church in the U.S.A., Publications Division, 475 Riverside Dr, Rm 1201, New York, NY 10027. Examined: 1973, 2v.; 1975, 3v.; 1977. 2v. v.1, 990p.; v.2, 874p. $4.
Aud: Pl, Sa

Issued in seven series since 1879: series 1, v.1-23, 1879-1900; series 2, v.1-21, 1901-1921; series 3, v.1-17, 1922-1938; series 4, v.1-13, 1939-1951; series 5, v.1-16, 1952-1957; series 6, v. 1-9, 1958-1966; and series 7, v.1- , 1967/68-.

Recent issues have been divided into two volumes, the Journal of Proceedings, and Statistics. The Journal of Proceedings contains the minutes of Assembly committees and the permanent judicial commission; reports of agencies, councils, committees, and commissions; reports from corresponding bodies and theological seminaries; regulations, standing rules, and general rules for judicatories; and lists of moderators, stated clerks, and officers. Reports are occasionally issued in a third volume. The Statistics volume provides information on additions and removals from the list of ministers, changes in the list of churches, United Presbyterian chaplains on active duty, church contributions to the Fifty Million Fund, commissioned church workers, subordinate units, and various statistical summaries. It also includes listings for each affiliated church with name, location, names and addresses of clergy, congregational report, and reports to the General Assembly. LL

HU 325
United States Catholic Mission Council. Mission Handbook. (Continues: United States Catholic Missionary Personnel Overseas. ISSN 0082-9560.) 1950. bi-a. U.S. Catholic Mission Council, Rm 500, 1325 Massachusetts Ave, NW, Washington, DC 20005. Examined: 1974. 33p. $1.
Aud: Cl, Pl, Sa

Following actions taken in Vatican Council II, the National Conference of Catholic Bishops established the United States Catholic Mission. The handbook lists U.S. missionaries only, meaning those who are U.S. citizens by birth or by naturalization. It is organized in three parts: U.S. Catholic Mission Council (gives origin and purpose, organization, activities), U.S. Catholic Mission inventory, and useful information. Part two is in two sections. Section A lists U.S. Catholic personnel serving abroad, including religious priests and brothers, religious sisters, lay personnel, U.S. diocesan priests, and U.S. foreign missionaries; section B covers U.S. Catholic Mission fields abroad which includes countries served by U.S. Catholic personnel, field distribution of U.S. Catholic missionaries, and field distribution by areas. Religious orders are listed by name, locations served, and number of religious serving. Mission institutes and seminars and missions sending groups of lay personnel abroad are also listed. LL

HU 326
Who's Who in Religion. ISSN 0160-3728. 1975. a. Marquis Who's Who, 200 E Ohio St, Chicago, IL 60611. Examined: 2nd ed., 1977. 736p. $55.
Aud: Cl, Pl
Indexed in: *Marquis Who's Who Publications: Index to All Books*.

A biographical directory of individuals involved with religion or religious work in the U.S. and Canada. Lists over 16,000 church officials, clergy, religious educators, and lay leaders. Each entry includes name, position, vital statistics, parents, education, marital status, children, career, additional religious activities or secular employment, civic and political activities, institutional directorships, decorations or awards, professional and other political or club affiliations, writings, and home and office address. LL

HU 327
World Buddhism; Vesak Annual. ISSN 0084-1447. 1960. a. bibl. illus. Buddhist Publications, 153-3 Dutugemunu St, Nugegoda, Sri Lanka. Examined: 1976. 63p. $4.50.
Aud: Pl, Sa

Contains articles, essays, and some poetry dealing with Buddha and Buddhism. Many articles center on the teaching of Buddhism and the interpretation of Buddhist thoughts, and include bibliographical references. Published in English. LL

HU 328
World Conference of Friends. Report. ISSN 0429-7326. 1920. irreg. illus. Friends World Committee for Consultation, Woodbrooke, Selly Oak, Birmingham, 29, England. Dist: Friends World Committee for Consultation, American Section and Fellowship Council, 1506 Race St, Philadelphia, PA 19102. Examined: 4th ed., 1968. 190p. $.92.
Aud: Pl, Sa

Contains the programs, reports, statements, and messages of the World Conference of Friends. It also lists conference officers, committees, observers, planning committee, representatives, and the gathering participants. The plenary sessions are briefly noted. Keynote addresses, reports, statements, and messages are printed in full. Includes local press reviews. The 1968 issue was the report of the fourth world conference which was held in Greensboro, N.C. This conference is held about once every ten years. LL

HU 329
World Council of Churches. Minutes and Reports of the Central Committee Meetings. ISSN 0083-1684. 1948. a. World Council of Churches, 150 Route de Ferney, CH-1211 Geneva 20, Switzerland. Dist:World Council of Churches, 475 Riverside Dr, Rm 439, New York, NY 10027. Examined: 29th ed., 1976. 114p. (30th ed., 1977. 123p. $4.80.)
Aud: Pl, Sa

Contains the reports and proceedings of the annual meeting of the World Council of Churches. Reports are organized according to the structure of the WCC. Committee reports from all world-wide units are included. The appendixes include lists of participants and members of unit committees, the committee on the General Secretariat, the staffing and nominations committee, and the finance committee; the report of the review committee; abstracts of current world issues; and the budget. A list of documents available on request is attached. LL

HU 330
Yearbook of American and Canadian Churches. ISSN 0084-3644. (Continues: Federal Council Year Book; Year Book of the Churches; Handbook of the Churches; Yearbook of American Churches.) 1916. a. index. illus. Abingdon Press, 201 8th Ave S, Nashville, TN 37202. Examined: 45th ed., 1977. Constant H. Jacquet, Jr., ed. 287p. $8.95.
Aud: Cl, Pl

Provides comprehensive information on churches in the U.S. and Canada. It lists established religious bodies and their related organizations, excluding religious cults and sects. The entry for each religious body includes a list of churches, officers, and subordinate units with addresses; a brief description of the history; publications; and substantial church statistics. Special features include lists of international religious cooperating bodies, regional and local ecumenical agencies, church related colleges and theological seminaries, and service agencies, and a calendar of Christian and Jewish religious observances. The information is prepared and edited by the Office of Research and Evaluation of the National Council of Churches in the U.S.A. LL

HU 331
Zionist Year Book. ISSN 0084-5531. 1951. a. index. illus. The Zionist Federation of Great Britain and Ireland, Rex House, 4-12 Regent St, London SW1Y 4PG England. Examined: 1977. Jane Moonman, ed. 343p. £3.
Aud: Sa

Contains feature articles on Zionist life and concerns, a directory of Zionist organizations, a directory of Jewish organizations, a section on Israel, obituaries of well-known Zionists, and a Zionist who's who section. The directory of Zionist organizations covers the World Zionist Organization, Jewish agencies, the Zionist Federation of Great Britain and Ireland, national Zionist organizations, Greater London Zionist societies, Zionist organizations abroad, Israeli trade and banking associations, and other Zionist organizations in the United Kingdom. The general Jewish directory includes world Jewish population, Board of Deputies of British Jews, World Jewish Congress, communal organizations in Great Britain, communal organizations abroad, and a list of chief rabbis and rabbinates. The section on Israel provides a description of the development of the Yishur; useful addresses for the Oleh; a directory of organizations, clubs, educational institutions, political parties, etc; and lists of the diplomatic and consular corps, and government tourist offices. LL

THEATRE

HU 332
American Theatre Association. Directory of Members. ISSN 0569-4396. (Continues: American Educational Theatre Association. Directory of Members.) 1965/66. a. American Theatre Association, 1317 F St, NW, Washington, DC 20004. Examined: 1974. Anthony Reid, ed. 185p. $6. (1976. Sharon Davis, ed. 135p.)
Aud: Cl, Sa

Lists organizations, bylaws, officers, and members of the American Theatre Association. Members are listed alphabetically with their divisional affiliation and address, and geographically by state and city. Schools of drama are also listed geographically with addresses and the name of the main administrator of the program. GV

HU 333
Best Plays of (year). (Continues: Burns Mantle Best Plays.) 1899. a. bibl. index. illus. Dodd, Mead and Co., 79 Madison Ave, New York, NY 10016. Examined: 1976/77. Otis L. Guernsey, Jr., ed. 483p. $15.
Aud: Hs, Jc, Cl, Pl

A comprehensive survey of theatrical activity in the U.S. and Canada with numerous charts and surveys. The season's Broadway, Off-Broadway, and Off-Off-Broadway productions are described. Credits, casts, performances, attendance, illustrations, a history of the production, and synopsis of scenes are provided for New York productions. A directory of professional regional theatre lists productions outside New York and selected international ones. As in previous editions, condensations of ten outstanding plays are printed, but biographical information about theatrical personalities has been eliminated. Each edition cumulates lists of long-runs on and off Broadway and of recipients of New York Drama Critics Circle Awards, Pulitzer Prizes, and other awards. Contains bibliographies of recently published plays and drama recordings. GV

HU 334
The Best Short Plays. 1968. a. Chilton Book Co., Radnor, PA 19089. Examined: 1975, 340p.; 1978. Stanley Richards, ed. 392p. $10.50.
Aud: Hs, Jc, Cl, Pl

An annual collection of one-act plays by new and well known playwrights. Most of the plays included in each yearly volume are not available elsewhere. The 1975 volume includes plays by two "Obie" winners, Terrence McNally and Israel Horovitz. The 1978 edition contains twelve plays, some of which are currently running in New York. JKM

HU 335
Bibliographic Guide to Theatre Arts. 1975. a. G. K. Hall, 70 Lincoln St, Boston, MA 02111. Examined: 1977. 255p. $55.
Aud: Cl, Pf, Sa

Contains complete catalog records for theatre arts materials cataloged by the Library of Congress and the Research Libraries of the New York Public Library during the preceding year. Covers materials in the areas of the stage, radio, television, film, vaudeville, nightclub performances, puppetry, the circus, etc. Main entries, added entries, subject headings, titles, and series are arranged in one alphabet. Supplements the *Catalog of the Theatre and Drama Collections*, the Research Libraries of the New York Public Library (G. K. Hall, 1967). JKM

HU 336
Cavalcade and Directory of Acts and Attractions. ISSN 0090-2993. 1973. a. illus. ABC Leisure Magazines, Amusement Business Division, 2160 Patterson St, Cincinnati, OH 45214. Examined: 1977. 198p. $10.
Aud: Sa

A comprehensive directory for talent buyers and promoters. Shows, radio programs, and touring attractions are listed in three major categories: musical and theatrical; outdoor attractions; and circus, variety, and specialty acts. Entries include data on type of attraction, facilities at which it has appeared, and name of booking agent. A directory of agents and their addresses appears at the end of the volume. GV

HU 337
Directors Guild of America. Directory of Members. 1966. a. index. Directors Guild of America, 7950 Sunset Blvd, Hollywood, CA 90046. Examined: 11th ed., 1977/78. 437p. $5.
Aud: Pl, Sa

Lists the officers, administrative staff, members of the national board of directors, important bylaw provisions, and the 4875 members of the Directors Guild of America (DGA). Membership listings include name, guild category (e.g., director, stage manager, production manager, etc.), and, at the member's discretion, home, business, and/or agent's addresses; credits; and current assignments. Fortunately, most members choose to include the additional information in their entries, making this a more valuable reference tool for the industry and for the general public. The volume also includes a geographic and category index of members; a list of agents and one of attorneys and business managers with addresses and phone numbers; lists of recipients of the DGA Award for Television Direction, the DGA Award for Theatrical Direction, the D. W. Griffith Award, and the DGA Critics Award; and an index of advertisers. JKM

HU 338
Empirical Research in Theatre. 1971. a. Bowling Green State University, Center for Communications Research, 322 South Hall, Bowling Green, OH 43403. Examined: v. 5, 1975. David Addington and Allen N. Kepke, eds. 60p. $2. (v. 8, 1978.)
Aud: Sa
Indexed in: *Sociological Abstracts*.

A scholarly publication which focuses on methodological studies of the theater that utilize the research methods of the social sciences. Volume five includes a research report on developing a self-teaching program in dialect training for actors and on the use of interaction analysis as a tool for understanding actor/director interaction during dramatic rehearsals. GV

HU 339
Encore. ISSN 0071-0164. 1948. a. illus. National Association of Dramatic and Speech Arts, Shaw University, Box 124, Raleigh, NC 27602. Dist: Joseph Adkins, NADSA, Fort Valley State College, Fort Valley, GA 31030. Examined: 1977. H. B. Caple, ed. 37p. $2.
Aud: Cl, Sa
Indexed in: *Theatre/Drama Abstracts*.

Contains scholarly and creative writing about black theatre and rhetoric, especially as it is reflected on the U.S. college scene. The 1977 issue contains two original short plays, reports on college productions, an article on Ed Bullins, and news about playwriting contents. The "bookshelf" section contains brief critical notes about recent books dealing with the theatre. GV

HU 340
International Mimes and Pantomimists. IMP Directory. ISSN 0095-2087. 1974/75. a. bibl. International Mimes and Pantomimists, c/o E. Gilbert, Route 3, Spring Green, WI 53588. Examined: 1974/75. 97p. $12.
Aud: Sa

In spite of the title, the major section of this *Directory* consists of a briefly annotated bibliography of mime and pantomime which is divided into sections (books, articles, scripts, and films), each arranged by author. Location symbols are often provided for these items. The directory section lists individuals involved in this field, arranged by country, and describes special services offered and special areas of concern. A third section provides international coverage of courses, teachers, and institutions in the field. GV

HU 341
National Directory for the Performing Arts and Civic Centers. ISSN 0092-0738. 1973. irreg. index. Handel and Co., Box 503, Dallas, TX 75221. Dist: Wiley-Interscience, 605 Third Ave, New York, NY 10016. Examined: 2nd ed., 1975. Beatrice Handel, ed. 182p. $50. (3rd ed., 1978.)
Aud: Cl, Sa

Presents a compilation of information on performing arts organizations and performance facilities in the United States. The directory is arranged by state, city, and then category (i.e., facility, dance, instrumental music, vocal music, performing arts series, and theater). Entries for facilities describe type, seating capacity, stage type, address, telephone number, management and staff, and availability for rental. For organization entries, information on status, purpose, management, budget, officers, income season, etc., is given. Includes an alphabetical index by the name of facility or organization and a subject index. A companion volume is the *National Directory of the Performing Arts/Educational* (2nd ed., 1975) which lists institutions of higher education in the U.S. with programs in dance, music, and theater. It is arranged by state, then alphabetically by institution. Each entry provides a brief overview of areas of specialization, degrees, faculty, facilities, etc. Both of these directories have just been published in a third edition; combined price for the set is $87.50. GV

HU 342
National Playwrights Directory. 1977. freq. not determined. index. illus. Gale Research Co., Book Tower, Detroit, MI 48226. Examined: 1st ed., 1977. Phyllis Johnson Kaye, ed. 374p. $15.
Aud: Cl, Pl

A project of the O'Neill Theater Center. Provides brief biographical information on more than 500 living American playwrights. Each entry includes brief data on personal life and professional achievements; home address; agent's name, address, and phone number; a list of plays indicating availability and where they have been produced; and, often brief synopses of plays and a photograph of the playwright. There is an index to plays mentioned with asterisks indicating those plays for which a synopsis has been included. JKM

HU 343
New York Theater Annual. 1976/77. a. illus. Gale Research Co., Book Tower, Detroit, MI 48226. Examined: 1976/77. Catherine R. Hughes, ed. 212p. $20. (1977/78. $20.)
Aud: Pl, Sa

Covers all Broadway and Off-Broadway productions, as well as selected Off-Off-Broadway shows, opening or continuing runs during the preceding season (June 1—May 31). The entry for each play includes full production and cast listings, opening and closing dates, a brief plot summary, excerpts from major reviews, and one or more photographs. JKM

HU 344
Performing Arts Resources. ISSN 0360-3814. 1974. a. bibl. Drama Book Specialists Publishers, 150 W 52nd St, New York, NY 10019. Examined: v. 2, 1975. Ted Perry, ed. 129p. $12.50. (1978.)
Aud: Cl, Pl

Sponsored by the Theatre Library Association to provide "documentation for theatre, film, television and popular entertainments." Excludes material on music and dance. Articles in volume two cover a wide range of subjects: the preservation of film archives, an annotated bibliography of prompt scripts and signed copies of Sheridan's *The Rivals*, and a descriptive catalog of the filmic materials (books, equipment, films) relevant to the history of the cinema which can be found in the Gershwin Collection at the University of Texas, Austin. An overview of performing arts research collections in New York, a survey of U.S. resources in teaching radio and television history, and an annotated reference bibliography of theater in American fiction, 1774-1850, were some of the topics included in volume one (1974). GV

HU 345
Play Index. 1949. quinquennial. index. H. W. Wilson

Co., 950 University Ave, Bronx, NY 10452. Examined: 1968/72. Ester A. Fidell, ed. 403p. $20.
Aud: Hs, Pl

Indexes by author, title, and subject plays which appear in collections as well as plays published individually during the five-year period. The listings under author or main entry include a brief synopsis, the number of acts or scenes, size of the cast, number of sets, and bibliographical information. Plays are also listed by type of cast (e.g., all female, puppets, etc.) and number of players. There is a list of the collections indexed in the volume and a directory of publishers and distributors with addresses. The 1973/77 volume is scheduled for publication in Fall 1978. KMH/JKM

HU 346
Research Opportunities in Renaissance Drama. ISSN 0098-647X. (Continues: Opportunities for Research in Renaissance Drama; Renaissance Drama. ISSN 0486-3739.) 1956. a. bibl. illus. Modern Language Association Conference on Research Opportunities in Renaissance Drama, c/o David M. Bergeron, Department of English, University of Kansas, Lawrence, KS 66045. Examined: v. 19, 1976. David M. Bergeron, ed. 137p. free.
Aud: Cl, Sa

Scholarly publication in the field of Renaissance drama with an international scope. Contributors are members of the teaching profession in Canada, England, and the United States. The 1976 issue contains an annotated bibliography on folk-drama scholarship, a chronological chart of Elizabethan and Jacobean dramas and their Spanish origin, an annotated bibliography on Renaissance children's companies, and a list of contemporary Renaissance drama productions. A medieval supplement, edited by Sheila Lindenbaum, contains a review of scholarship on liturgical drama 1965-1975; the first part of this critical bibliographical essay appeared in volume 18 (1975). GV

HU 347
The Scene. ISSN 0090-5259. 1972. a. illus. New Egypt Publications, 5 Beekman St, New York, NY 10038. Dist: Horizon Press, 156 Fifth Ave, New York, NY 10010. Examined: v. 4, 1977. Stanley Nelson, ed. 271p. $5.
Aud: Cl, Pl, Sa

Subtitle: "Plays from Off-Off-Broadway." An annual survey of Off-Off-Broadway theater which includes a guide to Off-Off-Broadway theaters in New York City, texts of numerous plays which have appeared in these theaters in recent years, and introductory material about the role of the little theater movement in the broader area of experimental theater. Photographs of stage scenes and illustrations of set designs are sometimes provided. Volume four contains a special section on the London counterpart of Off-Off-Broadway, the Fringe, including a survey article, a bibliography, and scripts of selected plays produced on the London stage. GV

HU 348
Theatre Annual. ISSN 0082-3821. 1942. a. illus. Hiram College, Hiram, OH 44234. Examined: v. 33, 1977. John V. Falconiere, ed. 112p. $2.
Aud: Cl, Sa

A publication devoted to information and research in the arts and history of the theater which offers scholarly contributions on international aspects of theater. The 1977 issue contains articles about aspects of works by Tennessee Williams, Edward Albee, and David Storey. The 1976 issue contains a monograph by Glenn Litton (Case Western Reserve University) on "The American Musical Theater in the 1950's," a bicentennial celebration of an art form unique to the United States. GV

HU 349
Theatre, Film and Television Biographical Master Index. 1978. freq. not determined. Gale Research Co., Book Tower, Detroit, MI 48226. Examined: none. (1978. $30.)
Aud: Cl, Pl

A new publication in Gale's "Biographical Index Library." Format is similar to the **Biographical Dictionaries Master Index.** Since the new title was not available for examination, it is uncertain how much overlap in coverage there will be between the two publications. Publisher's information states: "This new volume is a key to sources covering the stage, screen, opera, popular music, radio and television . . ." Among the reference titles indexed are the *ASCAP Biographical Dictionary,* **International Motion Picture Almanac**, the *Oxford Companion to Film, Who Was Who on Screen, Who's Who on the Stage,* **Who's Who in the Theatre**, etc. JKM

HU 350
Theatre Studies. (Continues: Ohio State University, Columbus. OSU Theatre Collection. Bulletin.) 1954. a. bibl. index. illus. Ohio State University, Theatre Research Institute, Department of Theatre, 1089 Drake Union, Columbus, OH 43210. Examined: no. 22, 1975/76. 76p. $2.

Aud: Cl, Sa
Indexed in: *Guide to the Performing Arts; Theatre/Drama Abstracts*.

The official journal of the Ohio State University Theatre Research Institute. Reports on scholarly research in the history of the theater. The 1975/76 issue contains scholarly articles dealing with scenery in Renaissance drama, the Innsbruck Easter Plays, and the American frontier play. It also includes critical reviews of selected dissertations and theses and reviews of bibliographical works in the field of theater history. A cumulative index to the first 20 volumes was included in volume 20 (1973/74). GV

HU 351
Theatre World. ISSN 0082-3856. (Continues: Daniel Blum's Theatre World.) 1944/45. a. index. illus. Crown Publishers, One Park Ave, New York, NY 10016. Dist: Crown Publishers, Distribution Center, 34 Engelhard Ave, Avenel, NJ 07001. Examined: v. 33, 1976/77. John Wills, ed. 288p. $15.95.
Aud: Hs, Jc, Cl, Pl

An annual survey of the American theater, focusing on Broadway and Off-Broadway productions. Lists complete casts, dates of opening and closing, and statistics about performances. Contains brief biographical sketches of outstanding performers, producers, directors, and designers and numerous illustrations from productions and portraits of performers. Professional regional companies outside New York City, national touring companies, and annual Shakespeare festivals are also included. GV

HU 352
Who's Who in the Theatre. ISSN 0083-9833. 1912. irreg. Sir Isaac Pitman and Sons, 39 Parker St, Kingsway, London WC2B 5PB, England. Dist: Gale Research Co., Book Tower, Detroit, MI 48226. Examined: 15th ed., 1972. Ian Herbert, ed. (16th ed., 1977. 1416p. $50.)
Aud: Cl, Pl
Indexed in: *Biographical Dictionaries Master Index; Theatre, Film, and Television Biographical Master Index*.

A major reference work on the English-language theater. The main feature is the biography section which includes approximately 2500 entries on actors, actresses, directors, playwrights, producers and designers, historians, etc. Entries are arranged alphabetically by stage name and provide a short personal history, theatrical credits, publications, memberships and awards, and address and telephone number. Broadway and Off-Broadway play bills and London play bills cover New York and London performances, giving theater, title, opening date, and credits. There are also listings of long-runs in London and New York plus a tabulation of London and New York theaters covering premieres, seating capacities, and box office information. Also includes an obituary section which lists people who have died since the previous edition and a roster of people in previous editions who are no longer included. The 15th edition includes an index to London play bills from 1921 to 1965. GV

SOCIAL SCIENCES

GENERAL WORKS

SS 1
Brookings Institution. Annual Report. ISSN 0068-2802. 1962. a. illus. Brookings Institution, 1775 Massachusetts Ave, NW, Washington, DC 20036. Examined: 1970. James D. Farrell, ed. free.
Aud: Cl, Pl

Details the annual activities of the Brookings Institution, a nonprofit organization devoted to research, education, and publication in economics, government, foreign policy, and the social sciences in general. It opens with a brief overview of the Institution's purpose, financing, administration, and research activities, and a list of the Board of Trustees and officers. This is followed by the president's review which gives an overview of Brookings' activities for that year. Next are reports from the directors of the economic studies, governmental studies, and foreign policy studies programs, giving reviews of research completed and research in progress. There are also reports from the directors of the advanced study program, the social science computation center, and the publications program. Appendixes list: staff of the Institution; fellows, guest scholars, and frequent contributors to activities of the advanced study program; publications for the year (books, reports, articles, etc.); and selected public and professional service activities of the senior staff. The financial report of the Institution is also included in the appendixes. Illustrated with photos, including portraits of various Brookings' officials and authors. KSK

SS 2
National Council for the Social Studies. Yearbook. ISSN 0085-3720. 1931. a. bibl. illus. National Council for the Social Studies, 1201 16th St, NW, Washington, DC 20036. Examined: 1975. Raymond H. Muessig, ed. 308p. (1978.)
Aud: Cl, Sa
Indexed in: *Social Science Citation Index.*

The National Council for the Social Studies is the professional organization of educators at all levels who are interested in the teaching of social studies. The **Yearbook** reflects the interests of this group. Each issue is devoted to a specific theme or problem in the social sciences. The 1975 volume is entitled "Controversial Issues in the Social Sciences: A Contemporary Perspective." It contains eight lengthy essays by professors of education and sociology in colleges, high school social science instructors, and members and directors of associations and groups concerned with vital issues. Some topics that are discussed are: traditional sex modes and values, the study of death, majority rule, integration, perils to our planet, and nation-states vs. world organization. All of the articles contain bibliographies or bibliographical footnotes; one essay ends with a list of teaching materials. Black-and-white photographs are scattered throughout the volume. Emphasis in each article is placed on how the teacher can present these controversial issues in the classroom. KSK

SS 3
Social Sciences Citation Index. ISSN 0091-3707. 1972. a. w/2 suppls. Institute for Scientific Information, 325 Chestnut St, Philadelphia, PA 19106. Examined: 1976. Stephen R. Aaronson, ed. $1500. (1977. 7587p.)
Aud: Cl, Sa

A massive, complex index to the literature of the social sciences. Patterned after its companion volume **Science Citation Index** which also covers selected materials in the social sciences. Covers more than 3000 journals, 2000 of which are covered selectively. Issued in three parts. Part one is the citation index which lists specific articles or works by cited author; entries indicate sources in which the work was cited. The second part, the source index, is arranged by author and provides full bibliographic data on the sources indicated in the first part. Whenever possible the author's address is included. The third part is the "Permuterm Subject Index." Subject headings are derived from combining significant terms in the title and subtitle of a particular work "to form all possible pairs of terms." References in the subject index are to names appearing in the second part. There is also a "corporate address index." The format is difficult, and the type is quite small and bothersome. The annual cumulations contain a long guide for users of the volume which should be studied carefully; the user's guide is available separately. Designed primarily for academic use, the **Index** is most valuable for wide-ranging searches. The data file is available for computer searching. NLE

SS 4
Social Sciences Index. ISSN 0094-4920. (Continues: Social Science and Humanities Index; International Index to Periodicals.) 1974. a. w/q. cumulations. H. W. Wilson, 950 University Ave, Bronx, NY 10452. Examined: 1975/76. Joseph Bloomfield, ed. 1077p. service basis.
Aud: Hs, Jc, Cl, Pl

An author and subject index to over 250 periodicals in the fields of anthropology, area studies, economics, environmental science, geography, law and criminology, medical sciences, political science, psychology, public administration, sociology, and related subjects in the social sciences. Complete bibliographic information is given under each entry. Book reviews are arranged alphabetically by author of the work reviewed in a separate section. A list of the periodicals indexed with address and subscription information is included. Supersedes and expands the social science portion of the *Social Science and Humanities Index* (1965-74) and the *International Index to Periodicals* (1907-65). KMH

SS 5
Stanford Journal of International Studies. ISSN 0081-4326. (Continues: Stanford University School of Law. International Society. Proceedings.) 1968. a. bibl. Stanford University School of Law, Stanford, CA 94305. Examined: v. 10, 1975; v. 11, 1976. Edward A. Schneider, ed. $5.25.
Aud: Cl, Sa
Indexed in: *ABC Pol Sci; Index to Foreign Legal Periodicals; Index to Periodical Articles Related to Law; International Political Science Abstracts; Legal Periodicals Index; PAIS; Social Science Citation Index.*

Each annual volume focuses on a particular subject or theme. Recent volumes have covered the multinational corporation (1976), China's changing role in the world economy (1975), and evolving approaches to development (1974). The **Journal** is interdisciplinary and offers a broad approach to international problems. Articles are contributed by both professionals and students. Includes book reviews. SJV

SS 6
Yivo Annual of Jewish Social Science. ISSN 0084-4209. 1946. bi-a. bibl. index. Yivo Institute for Jewish Research, 1048 Fifth Ave, New York, NY 10028. Examined: v. 16, 1976. David Roskies, ed. 423p. $8.
Aud: Sa
Indexed in. *Historical Abstracts; America: History and Life.*

Contains lengthy articles on Jewish social issues. Each volume has a different theme. The theme of the 1976 issue was the Jewish labor movement in America. Articles include bibliographical references. Although the title is the **Yivo Annual,** the publication is issued biennially. LL

ANTHROPOLOGY AND ARCHAEOLOGY

SS 7
American Anthropological Association. Annual Report and Directory. ISSN 0065-6933. 1969. a. American Anthropological Association, 1703 New Hampshire Ave, NW, Washington, D.C. 20009. Examined: 1977. 62p. $3.
Aud: Cl, Sa

Report by the president of the Association on its activities and major concerns of the previous year. Provides information on the issues confronting anthropologists in academic and international political situations; information and statistics on the internal operations of the organization; and information on employment patterns and training programs for anthropologists. Reports of the editors of the major Association publications and reports from committees and representatives to other scholarly groups are included. Also includes information on submitting manuscripts for publication by the Association. The directory section lists officers, titles of publications, addresses, membership dues, dates and places of the annual meeting of the Association, and 40 other groups with related interests, including regional and special interest associations. BCS

SS 8
Annual Editions: Readings in Anthropology. ISSN 0095-5582. 1975/76. a. bibl. index. illus. Dushkin Publishing Group, Sluice Dock, Guilford, CT 06437. Examined: 1977/78. David M. Rosen, ed. 276p. $4.95. (1978/79. 320p. $6.55.)
Aud: Cl, Pl

A selection of articles on cultural and social anthropology concentrating on contemporary peoples. Articles are grouped under a number of broad topics. They are reprinted from both professional and general publications. Topics covered in the 1977/78 volume included such current issues as sex roles, the culture of poverty, the impact of the West on other cultures, and drug addiction. Emphasis is on the relevance of anthropological methods for the study of the present human condition, including that of the people in the U.S. BCS

SS 9
Annual Review of Anthropology. ISSN 0084-6570. (Continues: Biennial Review of Anthropology.) 1972. a. bibl. index. illus. Annual Reviews, 4139 El Camino Way, Palo Alto, CA 94306. Examined: v. 5, 1976. Bernard J. Siegel, ed. 406p. $17.
Aud: Cl, Sa
Indexed in: *Biological Abstracts; Chemical Abstracts; Language and Language Behavior Abstracts; Multi-Media Reviews Index.*

A critical review and appraisal of the year's work in anthropology. Each chapter focuses on a specific topic and is written by a recognized expert in that area. Chapters provide analytical, rather than critical, reviews of specific publications and/or an overview of the subject area. Physical, social, and cultural anthropology are covered. The 1976 issue includes a long chapter on problems in anthropological bibliography that is of potential interest to librarians. Each chapter includes a bibliography with full citations for all publications discussed. There is a cumulative author and chapter title index to the first five volumes included in volume five. BCS

SS 10
Archaeological Institute of America. Annual Meeting Paper Abstracts. 1974. a. Archaeological Institute of America, 53 Park Place, Rm 802, New York, NY 10007. Examined: 1974, 81p.; 1977. 44p. $3.50.
Aud: Cl, Sa

This publication, without covers and stapled at the corner, gives summaries of the papers presented at the general meetings of the Archaeological Institute held in December of each year. Many are reports of field work, others are studies of previously unpublished material. The information is brief. The author and his/her affiliation is given followed by a brief summary of what was presented. The arrangement is not explained; it appears to be by the geographic region where the work is being done. Provides a brief survey of what is being studied and where. BCS

SS 11
Archaeological Institute of America. Bulletin. 1909. a. Archaeological Institute of America, 53 Park Place, Rm 802, New York, NY 10007. Examined: v. 67, 1975/76. 48p. (v. 68, 1976/77. 55p. $3.)
Aud: Cl, Sa

The Archaeological Institute of America was founded in 1879 to bring together the professional and the nonprofessional interested in the "search for an understanding of the human past." The Bulletin reports on the activities of the Institute in the furtherance of this aim. In addition to reports on the annual operations of the Institute, there is information on current archaeological projects, fellowship awards, and publications. Brief summaries of field work projects with names and addresses of staff directors are included. A list of the 80 regional societies affiliated with the Institute is provided with full addresses. There is also a list of the Institute's lectures and programs for the year and the name of the local societies at which they were given. Programs include lectures, symposia, films, and field trips. BCS

SS 12
Archaeological Society of New Jersey. Bulletin. 1948. a. bibl. illus. Archaeological Society of New Jersey, Humanities Bldg, Rm 104, Seton Hall University, South Orange, NJ 07079. Examined: no. 31, 1974, 33p.; no. 33, 1976. Bruce Dahlgren, ed. 44p. $2.50.
Aud: Cl, Sa

Contains articles on archaeological digs in the New Jersey area, with special emphasis on the Indians of the Upper Delaware; the excavation of historical sites; and the examination of colonial artifacts. Also includes reprints of early accounts of contacts between Native Americans and European settlers. The 1976 issue was a special edition, focusing on the ceremonial dress of the Delaware Indian. There are numerous illustrations and photographs. BCS

SS 13
Archaeological Survey Annual Report. ISSN 0068-6182. 1958. a. bibl. illus. University of California, Los Angeles, Department of Anthropology, Los Angeles, CA 90024. Examined: v. 14, 1972. Nancy L. Farrell, ed. 255p. $5.
Aud: Cl, Sa

The UCLA Archaeological Survey attempts to find and identify archaeological sites in Southern California and to sponsor excavations of these sites before they are destroyed by residential and other types of development. This publication presents a report on the year's work of the sponsoring body as well as research papers on results of excavation work in the area.

Papers on research methods and on findings in specific site excavations are also included. BCS

SS 14

Archaeology of Eastern North America. ISSN 0360-1021. 1973. a. illus. Eastern States Archaeological Federation, Island Field Museum, RD 2, Box 126, Milford, DE 19963. Examined: v. 4, 1976, 128p.; v. 5, 1977. Louis A. Brennan, ed. $7.
Aud: Pl, Sa
Indexed in: *Abstracts in Anthropology*.

Articles concentrate on archaeological study and research in areas of the eastern U.S. There are articles of interest to both the scholar and the general reader. Urban areas as well as more remote areas are covered. The 1976 issue contains numerous maps and photographs of artifacts. The 1977 volume includes articles on recent discoveries and discussions of the nature and relevance of contemporary archaeology. BCS

SS 15

Eastern States Archaeological Federation. Bulletin. 1941. a. Eastern States Archaeological Federation, Island Field Museum, RD 2, Box 126, Milford, DE 19963. Examined: no. 34, 1975. Martha Potter Otto, ed. 17p. $1.
Aud: Cl, Sa
Indexed in: *Abstracts in Anthropology*.

Contains minutes and proceedings of the annual meeting of the Federation and reports of the numerous state societies which make up the Federation. The reports include information on membership, contents of publications, and state archaeological projects and digs. Any event of relevance to archaeologists in a given state, for instance lawsuits instituted by Indian Americans, is noted in the reports. The state reports give extensive details on specific site activity. Abstracts of papers on archaeological activity and research presented at the annual meeting are also included; the 1975 issue contains 23 abstracts. BCS

SS 16

Fieldwork Opportunities Bulletin. a. Archaeological Institute of America, 53 Park Place, Rm 802, New York, NY 10007. Examined: 1977; 1978. 25p. $3.
Aud: Cl, Pl

Lists job opportunities in archaeological excavations and programs. Each job description indicates whether or not volunteers are accepted and whether there is a staff position open. Advice is given on what excavation work is like, who is most likely to find it suitable, and how to apply for jobs. The job listings are arranged by country and then by site. Listings indicate purpose of the project, requirements, person to whom to apply, expenses and/or salary, and whether college credit is available. Both U.S. and foreign locations are covered. There is also a list of other sources of information on opportunities for this type of activity. Projects listed include offerings for both the professional and the amateur. BCS

SS 17

Films: The Visualization of Anthropology. 1972. tri-a. index. Audio-Visual Services, 17 Willard Bldg, Pennsylvania State University, University Park, PA 16802. Examined: 1976/77. Lori A. Baldwin, ed. 159p. free.
Aud: Cl, Sa

A catalog listing 16mm films from the collection of Audio-Visual Services at Pennsylvania State University. Each entry includes an annotation of the film with a brief description and, in some cases, a critical commentary. Each entry also includes title, a distributor code, release date, running time, catalog number, and rental and purchase prices. Complete information on how to obtain the films is provided in the introduction. Arranged by the sub-disciplines of anthropology and then by cultural areas. There is a detailed table of contents and a title index. BCS

SS 18

Historical Archaeology. ISSN 0440-9213. 1967. a. bibl. illus. The Society for Historical Archaeology, Department of Sociology and Anthropology, Wayne State University, Detroit, MI 48202. Dist: Michael J. Rodeffer, Ninety Six Historic Site, Box 325, Ninety Six, SC 29666. Examined: v. 9, 1975. John D. Combes, ed. 105p. (v. 12, 1978. $20.)
Aud: Sa
Indexed in: *Abstracts in Anthropology*.

A collection of articles on various aspects of historical archaeology, varying from the highly technical to the descriptive. The 1975 volume includes several articles on methodology as well as articles and book reviews related to underwater archaeology, a relatively new field with a scanty literature. The book review section is lengthy and the reviews are analytical and critical. BCS

SS 19

International Bibliography of Social and Cultural Anthropology. ISSN 0085-2074. 1955. a. bibl. index. Tavistock Publications, 11 New Fetter Lane, London EC4P 4EE England. Dist: Aldine Publishing Co., 529 S Wabash Ave, Chicago, IL 60605. Examined: v. 19,

1973, 443p.; v. 20, 1974, 477p.; v. 24, 1976. Britta Rupp, ed. $45.
Aud: Cl, Sa

One of four bibliographies in the *International Bibliography of the Social Sciences* series which is prepared by the International Committee for Social Sciences Documentation. The first five volumes were published by UNESCO, Paris, as part of *Documentation in the Social Sciences*.

Contents include a list of periodicals covered, a detailed plan of the classification scheme for the bibliography, an author index, and a subject index. The detailed bibliographic entries are listed by author under appropriate subject. Books, journals, and conference proceedings are included. The coverage is world wide. Titles are in the language of publication, and titles of articles published in languages other than French or English are translated into English. The volume for 1973 contained 4760 bibliographic entries. The classification scheme for the bibliography has very detailed subdivisions. BCS

SS 20

International Committee on Urgent Anthropological and Ethnological Research. Bulletin. ISSN 0538-5865. 1958. a. bibl. International Committee on Urgent Anthropological and Ethnological Research, c/o Institut fuer Voelkerkunde, Universitatsstraase 7 A-1010 Vienna, Austria. Examined: no. 15, 1973; no. 16, 1974; no. 17, 1975. Anna Hohenwart-Gerlachstein, ed. 127p. $6.50.
Aud: Cl, Sa

Published under the auspices of UNESCO upon recommendation of the International Council for Philosophy and Humanistic Studies and with the financial help of the Austrian Academy of Sciences. Includes articles on ethnological groups whose identity and traditional lifestyle are in danger of disappearing because of the impact of other cultures. The articles report on the existence of these groups, studies to date on the culture of these groups, and the need for recording their traditions, systems, and values before the impact of encroaching influences results in cultural disintegration. Articles are written in English, French, and German. BCS

SS 21

Levant: Journal of the British School of Archaeology in Jerusalem. ISSN 0075-8914. 1969. a. bibl. illus. The British School of Archaeology in Jerusalem, 2 Hinde News, Marylebone Lane, London, W1M 5RH England. Examined: v. 9, 1977. P. R. S. Moorey, ed. 178p. $13.20.
Aud: Sa

A journal devoted to the archaeology of Palestine and its neighboring countries from ancient times to the 19th century. It includes articles on excavations, explorations, and archaeological analyses, accompanied by illustrations and photographs. Many of the articles deal with classical and religious interests. Most include bibliographical references. Features some news of members of the British School of Archaeology in Jerusalem. LL

SS 22

Muse. ISSN 0077-2194. 1967. a. illus. University of Missouri-Columbia, Museum of Art and Archaeology, Columbia, MO 65201. Examined: 10th ed., 1976. Gladys D. Weinberg, ed. 48p. $3.
Aud: Cl, Pl, Sa

Contains articles on objects in the museum's collection and on the museum's activities and acquisitions. The reports on acquisitions provide descriptive information on each new item including place, date, and culture of origin and are accompanied by numerous photographic illustrations. Cultures represented include African, Central and South American, Far Eastern, Greek, and Roman. The 1976 issue includes a fully-illustrated article on the silver of Paul Revere in the museum's collection. This annual is free to libraries and other institutions with publications to exchange. BCS

SS 23

The New Hampshire Archaeologist. ISSN 0077-8346. 1950. a. bibl. illus. New Hampshire Archaeological Society, Averill Rd, Brookline, NH 03033. Examined: 18th ed., 1975. Paul Holmes, ed. 23p. $4.
Aud: Sa

Includes reports on current archaeological projects in the state of New Hampshire. Provides information on location of the site, discoveries made, and implication of the research for understanding the prehistory of the area. Also includes a list of the Society's officers and information on applications for membership. BCS

SS 24

Oklahoma Anthropological Society. Bulletin. 1953. a. bibl. illus. Oklahoma Anthropological Society. Dist: Mel Phillips, Secretary/Treasurer, Oklahoma Anthropological Society, 2217 Arlington Dr, Oklahoma City, OK 73108. Examined: v. 25, 1976. Don Wyckoff, ed. 158p. $5.
Aud: Cl, Sa

Indexed in: *Abstracts in Anthropology.*

The Society is dedicated to the scientific collection, preservation, classification, and study of American Indian ethnological and archaeological remains and materials. The bulletin reports on the year's activities on behalf of the fulfillment of these goals. There are detailed reports on archaeological site excavations with numerous photographs and illustrations. Some reports survey large projects, others analyze specific artifacts uncovered and their possible cultural significance. BCS

SS 25

Ontario Archaeology. ISSN 0078-4672. 1954. bi-a. bibl. illus. Ontario Archaeological Society, Box 241 Postal Sta P, Toronto, Ontario M5S 258, Canada. Examined: no. 28, 1976. $3.
Aud: Cl, Sa
Indexed in: *Abstracts in Anthropology.*

Collection of articles on prehistory describing excavation prospects, techniques used in specific projects, and analysis and interpretation of archaeological sites and discoveries. The emphasis is on sites and materials relating to the Ontario area. The issue examined contained a long bibliography on Ontario archaeology. BCS

SS 26

Pacific Anthropologists. ISSN 0078-7418. 1962. irreg. index. Pacific Scientific Information Center, Box 6037, Honolulu, HI 96818. Examined: 1974. Edwin H. Bryan, Jr., ed. 68p. $2.
Aud: Sa

A directory of persons who are studying human cultures in the Pacific. Entries are arranged alphabetically by name and note address and specialization, including both the geographic area and the particular research interest, e.g., Fiji-social change. The publisher indicates a desire to publish the directory annually, depending upon funds available. Five issues have been published to date. BCS

SS 27

Southern Indian Studies. ISSN 0085-6525. 1949. a. bibl. illus. Archaeological Society of North Carolina, University of North Carolina, Box 561, Chapel Hill, NC 27514. Examined: v. 24, 1972. Joffre W. Coe, ed. 53p. $2. (1978.)
Aud: Sa

Features scholarly reports on archaeological research and study of prehistoric Indian cultures in the southern area of the U.S. Includes information on the location of the site under investigation, the materials examined, and assumptions made about the cultures from the study of the physical evidence found. Illustrations include charts, drawings, and photographs. Back issues are available in microfilm from Microfilming Corporation of America (21 Harrison Rd, Glen Rock, NJ 07452). BCS

SS 28

Syesis. ISSN 0082-0601. 1968. a. bibl. illus. British Columbia Provincial Museum, 601 Belleville St, Victoria, British Columbia, Canada V8V 1X4. Examined: v. 7, 1974; v. 8, 1975. Robert F. Scagel, ed. 264p. $5. (v. 11, 1978.)
Aud: Sa
Indexed in: *Biological Abstracts.*

Publication of studies of the natural and human history of the Pacific Northwest, covering Alaska, British Columbia, Washington, Idaho, and Montana. The primary emphasis is on British Columbia. The publication is intended for the professional. There are long articles, brief notes on research, announcements of professional interest, and book reviews. Occasional supplements usually focus on a specific topic and are issued and priced separately. BCS

SS 29

Texas Archaeological Society. Bulletin. ISSN 0082-2930. 1929. a. bibl. illus. Texas Archaeological Society, Southern Methodist University, Box 165, Dallas, TX 75275. Examined: v. 47, 1976. Thomas R. Hester, ed. 286p. $12.
Aud: Cl, Sa
Indexed in: *Abstracts in Anthropology.*

The Texas Archaeological Society has as its purpose the study of the human past in Texas and contiguous areas. Articles in the **Bulletin** reflect this goal. The 1976 issue contains articles on research on prehistorical and historical sites in Texas and Mexico. Articles describe methodology and provide an analysis of findings. There are numerous photographs, drawings, and charts. The literary quality of the writing makes the information accessible to both the specialist and the interested layperson. Back issues of the **Bulletin** are available from the Society and from University Microfilms (300 N Zeeb Rd, Ann Arbor, MI 48106). BCS

SS 30

Wenner-Gren Foundation for Anthropological Research. Report. ISSN 0083-7997. 1942. a. bibl. Wenner-Gren Foundation, 14 E 71st St, New York, NY

10021. Examined: 1974. 96p. free. (1975. 88p.)
Aud: Sa

Report of the Wenner-Gren Foundation's activities during the preceding year. Includes descriptions of conferences and symposia, details on the subject and work-to-date of research projects sponsored by the Foundation, and numerous references to recent publishing activity indicating authors, titles, and sources for materials. Provides a survey of what is being studied in the field of anthropology, where research is taking place, and where findings are being reported. All areas of the world are included, as are both prehistorical and historical cultures. BCS

SS 31
Yearbook of Physical Anthropology. ISSN 0096-848X. 1945. a. bibl. illus. American Association of Physical Anthropology, 1703 New Hampshire Ave, NW, Washington, D.C. 20009. Examined: v. 19, 1975. John Buettner-Janusch, ed. 196p. $6. (1978.)
Aud: Cl, Sa

Contains lengthy articles on physical anthropology, and papers presented at the annual meetings of the American Association of Physical Anthropologists. Most of the articles are in English. There is a selective guide to graduate training in physical anthropology that provides information about graduate training "of substance" in the United States and other countries. The entry for each school lists the faculty and their specialties, degrees offered, number of graduate students enrolled, requirements for the Ph.D., and department addresses. BCS

BANKING AND FINANCE

SS 32
Accountants' Index. 1920. a. (bi-a. to 1970.) American Institute of Certified Public Accountants, 1211 Ave of the Americas, New York, NY 10036. Examined: 25th ed., 1976. Jane Kubat, ed. 1170p. $42.50.
Aud: Cl, Sa

An author/subject index to materials published by the American Institute of Certified Public Accountants. Includes books, periodicals, pamphlets, and some government documents. Subject areas covered include accounting, financial management, investments, and special businesses and industries. Provides a convenient list of journal and book publishers specializing in the subject fields covered. Dictionary arrangement with *see* and *see also* references. NLE

SS 33
American Institute of Certified Public Accountants. Accounting Trends and Techniques. 1946. a. index. illus. American Institute of Certified Public Accountants, 1211 Ave of the Americas, New York, NY 10036. Examined: 1976. George Dick and Richard Rikert, eds. 397p. $30.
Aud: Cl, Sa

Analyzes accounting practices revealed in 600 annual reports to stockholders of selected industrial and merchandising companies for the preceding fiscal year. The text is arranged in six topical sections, and there are many tables showing trends over the past three years in different accounting matters, such as terminology, financial statement format, and other events reflected in the financial statements. Includes a subject index and an appendix of company names. KR/JKM

SS 34
Analysts Handbook. 1964. a. w/m. suppls. Standard and Poor's Corp., 345 Hudson St, New York, NY 10014. Examined: 1977. 102p. $230.
Aud: Sa

Subtitle: "Composite corporate per share data—by industries." Selected income data are kept up-to-date quarterly and compare group price actions such as sales, profit margins, earnings, dividends, book value, and capital expenditures. The basic value of this publication is that it enables users to compare companies to the industry action as a whole. Over 50 industrial groupings such as aerospace, chemicals, food, leisure time, pollution control, and tobacco are compared to 400 industrials both in statistical summaries and in stock price index graphs. Sections also compare utilities, transportation, and financial groupings. Designed only for the expert, but essential for the specific information presented. NLE

SS 35
Credit Manual of Commercial Laws. ISSN 0070-1467. (Continues: The Credit Man's Diary; The Credit Diary and Manual of Commercial Laws; The Credit Manual of Commercial Laws with Diary.) 1958. a. index. National Association of Credit Management, 475 Park Ave S, New York, NY 10016. Examined: 1977. George Kohlik, ed. 994p. $24.
Aud: Sa

Offers an abstract of federal and state legislation and rulings of interest to credit executives. Begins with feature articles on such topics as recent cases of interest to creditors and recent federal and state legislation. The bulk of the manual is made up of over 30 chapters on such topics as: uniform commercial code, contracts, terms of payment, retail installment sales laws, federal and state consumer protection legislation, credit cards, antitrust and trade regulation laws, community property laws, liens, bad check laws, assumed or fictitious names, sales and use taxes, fraudulent conveyances, bankruptcy procedures, the bankruptcy act as amended, international trade, and state bond laws. The final chapter is a glossary of legal terms. There is an index by subject and state. Some chapters summarize the laws in each state regarding the subject areas covered. NLE/KSK

SS 36

Credit Union Yearbook. ISSN 0074-4468. (Continues: International Credit Union. Yearbook.) 1954. a. Credit Union National Association, 1617 Sherman Ave, Madison, WI 53703. Examined: 1977. approx. 30p. free.
Aud: Pl

The Credit Union National Association existed from 1934 until 1964, changing in that year to CUNA International, and then becoming the World Credit Union. The present association was established in 1970. Its yearbook contains considerable data on the credit union form of cooperative banking arrangement. Information is presented clearly in graphs with a brief explanatory text. Includes a concise explanation of the credit union system, how it operates, and its values and advantages, and a convenient list of credit union associations with addresses and at least one officer's name and title for each. NLE

SS 37

Directory and Guide to the Mutual Savings Banks of the United States. 1958/59. a. National Association of Mutual Savings Banks, 200 Park Ave, New York, NY 10017. Examined: 52nd ed., 1975/76; 1977. 221p. $25.
Aud: Pl

Provides usual directory information, arranged geographically. Includes general information on the organization and structure of the banking industry as well as some abbreviated sections on banking regulations. NLE

SS 38

Directory of American Savings and Loan Associations. ISSN 0070-5098. 1955. a. T. K. Sanderson Organization, 200 E 25th St, Baltimore, MD 21218. Examined: 22nd ed., 1976/77; 23rd ed., 1978. T. K. Sanderson, ed. 443p. $35.
Aud: Pl, Sa

Presents information on savings and/or building and loan associations and co-operative banks. Banks are listed alphabetically by state and city. Entries give complete association name, whether stock or mutual, area codes, telephone numbers, zip codes, executives, branch offices, whether state or federally chartered, and whether insured or uninsured. Intended for use by such organizations as insurance companies, funds, banks, credit unions, and others needing access to banking information. This is a first source of information and should be used with a bank directory since the basic structure of these associations is different. NLE

SS 39

The Dow Jones Investor's Handbook. 1978. a. Dow-Jones Books, Box 300, Princeton, NJ 08540. Examined: 1978. Maurice L. Farrell, ed. 153p. $4.95.
Aud: Cl, Pl

Subtitle: "A convenient reference to stock and bond market indicators." A four-page essay for the layman, "Can the Economy Still Expand?," summarizes the current U.S. economic situation and prefaces the records, tables, charts, etc. that make up the bulk of the handbook. The table of contents lists the following chapters: "Dow-Jones Average," "Barron's Indices," "New York Stock Exchange Data," and "Stock and Bond Trading for 1977." Includes over 2000 over-the-counter securities quotations. KR/JKM

SS 40

Finance Facts Yearbook. ISSN 0430-4705. 1961. a. National Consumer Finance Association, 1000 16th St, NW, Washington, D.C. 20036. Examined: 1975. 79p. free.
Aud: Cl, Pl

Consumer finance companies specialize in small loans. This yearbook details the operations of these institutions, and of sales finance companies, industrial banks, and industrial loan companies. It provides an analysis of the consumer sector, covering population, labor force, education, consumer income, expenditures, savings, and the use of credit. Also includes data about finance companies and industrial banks. The brief list of references is useful for further study. Basic, at times almost telegraphic, information. NLE

SS 41

Investment Companies. ISSN 0075-0271. (Continues: Investment Companies and Their Securities.) 1941. a. Weisenberger Financial Services, 870 Seventh Ave, New York, NY 10017. Examined: 37th ed., 1977. Paul A. Johnston, ed. 601p. $96.
Aud: Sa

A text book on modern American investment companies, how they are constituted, how they operate, how they are funded, and what to avoid when considering the use of one of them. It is intended to be a source of factual information on mutual funds and other types of investment companies. Information is compiled from company reports to stockholders and statistical services. None of the data was subjected to independent verification, but the massive compilation has its own merits, one being the extent of the information. Covers more than 750 investment companies of all types. General information about investment companies includes techniques of investment, regulations, definitions of investment terms, services offered, and how to select an investment company. Also describes the various categories of investment companies currently practicing. The major share of the volume covers the important area of mutual funds and closed end investment companies. NLE

SS 42

Moody's Bank and Finance Manual. ISSN 0027-0814. 1928. a. Moody's Investors Service, 99 Church St, New York, NY 10007. Examined: 1977. Robert P. Hanson, ed. 3288p. $240.
Aud: Sa

The purpose of Moody's ratings is to provide investors with a simple system of gradation by which the relative investment qualities of bonds may be determined. Companies are rated on a scale of nine, from Aaa to C. Terms used and techniques applied are carefully delineated, as are disclaimers concerning Moody's omniscience. What is true of **Moody's Bank and Finance Manual** in this general sense is true of all Moody publications. It provides a detailed introduction explaining the techniques used plus a number of special lists, e.g., 100 largest banks in the free world; largest banks by amount of deposits; and a number of investment tabulations. Covers American bank and trust companies, savings and loan associations, international banks, federal credit agencies, investment companies, real estate companies, finance companies, and insurance companies. Information is received from the companies themselves, the Securities and Exchange Commission, and federal and state regulatory agencies. Coverage is massive; provides information on 3100 American banks alone. A loose-leaf volume accompanies the basic two-volume set and keeps the information current. NLE

SS 43

Moody's Dividend Record. 1930. a. w/w. suppls. Moody's Investors Service, 99 Church St, New York, NY 10007. Examined: v. 47, 1976. 190p. $110. (v. 48, 1977. 192p.)
Aud: Sa

Lists American and selected foreign stock exchange ex-dividend procedures, previous record sales, dividends declared, income bond interest payments, preferred stocks called, stock dividends and splits, and other detailed information relating directly to dividends. The annual volume cumulates and supersedes all previously issued weekly supplements. The annual is valuable for historical information, but without the weekly supplements, its value is limited. NLE

SS 44

Moody's Handbook of Common Stocks. ISSN 0027-0830. (Continues: Moody's Handbook of Widely Held Common Stocks.) 1965. a. w/q. suppls. index. Moody's Investors Service, 99 Church St, New York, NY 10007. Examined: 1977. Stanley Birkson, ed. $30; $90 w/suppls. (Spring 1978 suppl. 488p.)
Aud: Sa

Provides quick and easy access to basic financial and business information on over 900 stocks with investor interest. Displays information mainly in price charts, statistics, and analyses which are revised quarterly. Each quarterly supplement has an addenda for late-reporting companies. Includes a how-to-use section, an index of companies by major line of business, a discussion of the economic outlook, an analysis of stock price movements by industry, and long-term charts on popular stock market averages. Charts are based on the Dow-Jones Industrial Average, Moody's Utility Index, the New York Stock Exchange Index, and the American Stock Exchange Index. Each company report usually includes information on capitalization, earnings, some background, recent developments, prospects, and basic statistical information. Decisions and evaluations are not included. NLE

SS 45

Moody's Industrial Manual. ISSN 0027-0849. 1909. a. index. Moody's Investors Service, 99 Church St, New York, NY 10007. Examined: 1977. Robert P. Hanson, ed. 3808p. $300.
Aud: Sa

Covers companies listed on the New York Stock Exchange, the American Stock Exchange, and regional American exchanges. A section of international industrial companies also is included. The listings are based on information provided by the companies and selected federal and state agencies. The financial statements are provided in a uniform manner and are intended to be neutral and without bias. Special features include a geographical index and a classified list of companies by industry and product. Each company's description covers capital structure, a brief history, subsidiaries, principal plants, officers, and finances. The financial structure is analyzed in a variety of descriptions and tabular presentations. This basic source for information on bonds is kept up to date by *Moody's Industrial News Reports,* a loose-leaf service published semi-weekly. NLE

SS 46
Moody's Over-the-Counter (OTC) Industrial Manual. ISSN 0027-0865. 1970. a. index. Moody's Investors Service, 99 Church St., New York, NY 10007. Examined: 1977. 1344p. $280.
Aud: Sa

Includes a key to Moody's bond ratings, Moody's preferred stock ratings, definitions, an alphabetical index, and several special features such as a geographical index, a classification of companies by industries and products, and Over-the-Counter industrial stock splits. Information for each company includes: history, background, mergers, acquisitions, subsidiaries, business and products, and principal plants and properties. Kept up to date by *Moody's Industrial News Reports;* each annual volume replaces semi-weekly issues and provides a reservoir of historical information. NLE

SS 47
Moody's Public Utilities Manual. ISSN 0027-0873. 1928. a. Moody's Investors Service, 99 Church St, New York, NY 10007. Examined: 1977. 2562p. $240.
Aud: Sa

Among the companies covered in this manual are electric and gas utilities, gas transmission companies, and telephone and water companies. The listing for each company includes a capital structure table which gives the highlights of outstanding bond and stock issues and information on the history, background, mergers, acquisitions, subsidiaries, business details, construction programs, and principal plants and properties. Data relating to rates, franchises, and contracts are also presented. Includes names and titles of officers and directors, general counsel, auditors, date of the annual meeting, number of stock holders and employees, and the full address of the corporation. Each company's bond structure is detailed. The numerous combinations are complex but are carefully described and detailed. NLE

SS 48
Mutual Fund Fact Book. ISSN 0077-2550. 1965. a. illus. Investment Company Institute, 1775 K St, NW, Washington, DC 20006. Examined: 1977, 89p.; 1978. 92p. $2.95.
Aud: Cl, Pl

An introduction to mutual funds intended for the general public. About half the volume is devoted to discussions of such topics as an analysis of holders of mutual funds, an explanation of how shares are sold and of the regulations governing sale, an explanation of what mutual funds are, etc. The remainder of the volume consists of statistical tables analyzing mutual funds from various points of view, e.g., a table illustrating mutual funds dividends and distributions to shareholders for 1961-74. Most of the tables cover a 10 to 15 year time span. Also included is a glossary of mutual funds terminology. JKM

SS 49
National Fact Book of Mutual Savings Banks. 1961. a. illus. National Association of Mutual Savings Banks, 200 Park Ave, New York, NY 10017. Examined: 1974; 1977. 63p. free.
Aud: Sa

Provides detailed information on the savings bank industry and its role in savings and mortgage markets. Financial structure, deposits, capital market investments, income, and insurance are among the major topics covered in statistical tables and narrative descriptions. Much of the information is primarily of use to those who work with and interact with mutual savings banks. While the scope is narrow, the information is detailed and "official." This annual compilation is kept up-to-date by the *Savings Bank Journal* and the Association's annual report. NLE

SS 50
Rand McNally International Bankers Directory. ISSN 0360-7445. 1876. a. illus. Rand McNally and Co, Box 7600, Chicago, IL 60680. Examined: 1977. $115.50.
Aud: Cl, Pl

Subtitle: "The banker's blue book." Presents a tremendous amount of information on the banking industry. Special features include: a numerical list of banks in the United States, arranged by routing number, with a detailed and informative section on how routing numbers are built; a diagram showing features of printed U.S. currency and how to detect counterfeit bills; a section on the Federal Reserve System that is possibly a better source of information than some publications issued by the federal government; a useful section on discontinued bank titles; and a digest of banking laws. There is also a section on accessible banking points for non-bank towns in the U.S. that should be of interest to smaller communities. A first choice title. NLE

SS 51
Savings and Loan Fact Book. ISSN 0581-8761. 1954. irreg. illus. United States Savings and Loan League, 111 E Wacker Dr, Chicago, IL 60601. Examined: 21st ed., 1974; 24th ed., 1977. 128p.
Aud: Jc, Cl, Pl

Intended as a reference source on savings, home ownership, residential construction, and financing. Statistical information is displayed in tables and charts, and there are many clear and readable narrative passages which are authoritative and packed with details. Provides background information on many aspects of the savings and loan business, and some well-selected and organized information on appropriate government agencies. Includes a good glossary. This publication is a good beginning source for economics and banking information. NLE

SS 52
Securities Law Review. ISSN 0080-8474. 1969. a. index. Clark Boardman Co., 435 Hudson St, New York, NY 10014. Examined: 1976. Harold S. Bloomenthal, ed. 855p. $35.
Aud: Sa

A compilation of recent legal periodical writing in the securities regulation field. The articles and additional materials span the 12-month period following publication of the previous annual. There is an introductory survey by the editor which places the selected articles in context and refers to other research articles. The articles are then divided into a number of sections, with such titles as Securities Act Amendments, Disclosure, Shareholder Fraud, and International Securities Regulation. They are reprinted from such journals as the *Columbia Law Review, Journal of Corporation Law, NYU Law Review,* and the *Cornell Law Review.* A cross-reference table of the original periodical citations and the corresponding page numbers in this volume is appended. Contributors to the annual are listed alphabetically in the author and subject index at the end of the volume. All articles contain extensive footnotes. KSK

BUSINESS AND ECONOMICS

SS 53
American Cooperation. ISSN 0065-793X. 1925. a. index. illus. American Institute of Cooperation, 1129 20th St, NW, Washington, DC 20036. Examined: 1976/77. Beryle Stanton, ed. 522p. $8.20.
Aud: Sa

Contains articles, statistics, and other information of use to those who are interested in farm cooperatives. Geared for employers, managers, directors, and members of cooperatives, as well as educators, communicators, and policy-makers. Includes the proceedings of the National Institute on Cooperative Education, plus articles on research in the field and marketing strategies. The book is divided into sections and chapters on the future of cooperatives, current issues in the field, specific instances of cooperatives at work, legal foundation, the importance of marketing, and educational opportunities. It also includes a section on the activities of the American Institute of Cooperation. The final section contains statistical reports on types of cooperatives (rural electric, rural telephone, etc.) and annual reports from the national organization highlighting the past year's activities. There is a list of the officers, trustees, and committees of the AIC, and a subject—title—name index to the entire book. Illustrated throughout with photographs, portraits of the authors of the articles, and tables. Each annual volume bears the title of that year's institute. KSK

SS 54
The American Register of Exporters and Importers. ISSN 0065-9967. 1945. a. index. American Register of Exporters and Importers, 38 Park Row, New York, NY 10038. Examined: 1975, $30; 33rd ed., 1978. 850p.
Aud: Pl, Sa

The title describes the scope of this publication, but a list of the contents reveals its many values. It covers U.S. foreign service posts; American chambers of commerce abroad; foreign chambers of commerce in the U.S.; banks in world trade; custom house brokers and freight forwarders; and branches of the U.S. Bureau of International Commerce. Contains product indexes in English, Spanish, French, and German. One of the other valuable features is the advertisements which are also indexed. This listing of export and import concerns does not claim to be complete, but the edition examined seems to have covered the field fairly well. NLE

SS 55
American Statistical Association. Business and Economic Statistics Section. Proceedings. ISSN 0066-0736. 1954. a. index. illus. American Statistical Association, 806 15th St, Suite 640, Washington, DC

20005. Examined: 1972. 496p. (1977. $15.)
Aud: Sa

Includes papers presented under the sponsorship of the Business and Economics Statistics Section at the annual meeting of the American Statistical Association. An index of participants, a table of contents, and a listing of contributed papers precede the texts of the papers. Topics include such items as national data banks, multinational corporations, statistical systems in Canada, economic forecasting, stock markets, and census reports. Some articles contain bibliographical references; others are illustrated with charts, tables, and figures. KSK

SS 56

Anglo American Trade Directory. ISSN 0066-1813. 1916. bi-a. American Chamber of Commerce (United Kingdom), 75 Brook St, London W1Y 2EB, England. Examined: 59th ed., 1975/76. S. G. Harman, ed. 462p. $50.
Aud: Sa

Includes a list of members of the American Chamber of Commerce, American chambers of commerce in foreign countries, a section on America in Britain with information on services and regulations, and a section on Britain in America with travel and commercial information helpful for the British businessperson in America. The major part of the book is the trade register which attempts to list all British and American businesses having trade and/or investment relations with each other. The edition examined contains 13,000 entries and seems to be fairly complete in its information. Most names the average user would want are included. A good starting point, but other sources often have other, more complete information. Useful as a complement to the Dun and Bradstreet group and other publications. Updated by monthly supplements published in conjunction with *Anglo-American Trade News.* NLE

SS 57

Annual Editions: Readings in Business. ISSN 0090-4309. 1972. a. index. illus. Dushkin Publishing Group, Sluice Dock, Guilford, CT 06437. Examined: 1978/79. Joseph G. Mattingly, Jr., ed. 224p. $5.95.
Aud: Hs, Jc, Cl, Pl

A collection of articles reprinted from newspapers, news magazines, and trade journals. Designed to support introductory business courses at the high school or college level, the collection also provides an overview of current business trends and techniques for the general reader. Articles are frequently illustrated with charts, graphs, tables, and photographs, and occasionally include references for further reading. JKM

SS 58

Annual Editions: Readings in Economics. ISSN 0090-4430. 1973/74. a. Dushkin Publishing Group, Sluice Dock, Guilford, CT 06437. Examined: 1973/74. 400p. (1978/79. 305p. $6.25.)
Aud: Jc, Cl, Pl

An anthology of articles from various magazines (*Time, Duns Review, Forbes, Harvard Business Review,* etc.) printed in facsimile reproduction format. The essays are either by the staffs of periodicals like *Business Week* or by well-known economists, politicians, and social scientists. The readings are divided into a number of sections, with titles such as: "What Power Do Labor Unions Have To Influence the U.S. Economy?" Within these sections are grouped a number of relevant essays. At the beginning of the collection is a guide that helps the reader find any topic wherever it forms an important part of the discussion in the articles. Designed for use in introductory courses in economics. KSK

SS 59

Annual Editions: Readings in Microeconomics. 1976. a. index. illus. Dushkin Publishing Group, Sluice Dock, Guilford, CT 06437. Examined: 1978/79. 224p. $5.95.
Aud: Hs, Jc, Cl, Pl

A collection of articles originally published in newspapers, magazines, and business and economics journals during the preceding year. Articles frequently include statistical charts, tables, and graphs. Arranged under topical sections. Designed to provide supplementary readings for microeconomics courses in high schools or colleges, the collections can also serve as a broad introduction to the field for the general reader. JKM

SS 60

AudArena Stadium Guide and International Directory. ISSN 0067-0537. (Continues: Arena, Auditorium, Stadium Guide. ISSN 0518-3979.) 1958. a. Billboard Publications, Amusement Business Division, 1515 Broadway, New York, NY 10036. Examined: 1977. Irwin Kirby, ed. 288p. $25 pap.
Aud: Pl, Sa

Most listings in this directory are for the United States, although Canada, Europe, the Middle East, Africa, and Asia are also covered. The listings are geographically arranged, for the U.S. by state, then city; for

Canada by Province; and for the other regions by country. Included are arenas, auditoriums, stadiums, exhibit halls, sports facilities, concert halls, and convention sites. Each listing includes phone number, manager, seating, size, fee, nearby hotels, and parking. There are quick reference guides to seating size: up to 5,000; 5,001-10,000; 10,001-15,000. There is also a list of booking agencies. SLB

SS 61
Basebook. ISSN 0093-8025. (Continues: Predicasts Basebook.) 1973. a. Predicasts, 200 University Circle Research Center, 1100 Cedar Ave, Cleveland, OH 44106. Examined: 1976. Robert Baumgartner, ed. 586p. $150.
Aud: Cl, Sa

The preface to the 1976 edition states: "The data in the **Basebook** are measures of market size. The time series reflect the cyclical sensitivity of the various products and industries. The series are arranged by modified Standard Industrial Classifications, a hierarchical system in which the more general items are listed first, followed by subdivisions which have more detailed coding. To find a series in the **Basebook,** the user can 1) use the alphabetical guide (yellow pages) to find the SIC codes for products and services, 2) use the table of contents to pick out broad subject headings and then scan the entries for the item needed. . .While the **Basebook** will be available in printed form only once a year, the data are updated quarterly and are available to customers through our on-line PTS system." The statistical abstracts are divided into seven sections: general economics; agriculture; extraction and construction; manufacturing; transportation, communications, and utilities; trade and financial services; and government. These larger sections are then subdivided into smaller units, e.g., trade and financial services is broken up into lodging, business, repair, recreation, medical, household, professional, science, and education. There is a listing of source materials for the statistics which indicates the full name of the publication from which the data were taken, publisher, address, frequency of publication, annual subscription, and the price of a single issue. KSK

SS 62
Benefit-Cost and Policy Analysis. ISSN 0091-3227. 1972. a. index. illus. Aldine Publishing Co., 529 Wabash Ave, Chicago, IL 60605. Examined: 1974. R. E. Zeckhauser, ed. 514p. $24.95.
Aud: Cl, Sa

Subtitle: "An Aldine annual on forecasting, decision-making and evaluation." An anthology of essays on the various aspects of policy analysis. The papers are reprinted from other books and serials. In the 1974 volume, the book is divided into three sections. Part one, "The Use of Knowledge in Policy Formulation," addresses practical policy issues on such subjects as nuclear reactor safety and how to save gasoline. Part two, "Distributional Considerations," analyzes the consequences of various policies. Part three, "The Application of Policy Analysis," presents an overview of policy analysis as an operating practical discipline. Many of the scholarly articles contain footnotes, bibliographical references, charts and graphs, and tables. There is an index at the end of the volume. The final yearly selection of articles to be included and organization is made by a member of the editorial board, an expert on public policy, who presents an introductory overview of work and trends in the field. KSK

SS 63
Bibliographic Guide to Business and Economics. 1974. a. G. K. Hall and Co., 70 Lincoln St, Boston, MA 02111. Examined: 1977. 3v. 1851p. $190.
Aud: Cl, Sa

Provides complete cataloging information for titles acquired and cataloged by the Library of Congress and/or the Research Libraries of the New York Public Library in the fields of economics, transportation and communications, business administration, finance, insurance, public finance and taxation, demographics, labor relations, etc. Main entries, added entries, titles, series, and subject headings are interfiled in one alphabetic sequence. JKM

SS 64
Bibliography of Appraisal Literature. 1974. bi-a. index. American Society of Appraisers, Dulles International Airport, Box 17265, Washington, DC 20041. Examined: 1st ed., 1974. Dexter D. MacBride, ed. 769p. $30.
Aud: Cl, Sa

Provides references to all types of literature in all areas of appraising: real property, personal property, intangibles, utilities, machinery and equipment, technical evaluation, and appraisal administration. Geared for practitioners, students, researchers, and the public. The data has been separated into 15 major subject classifications, i.e., appraisal theory and rural property; recreational property; public utilities; natural resources; fine arts, objects of value, and collectors' items; intangible property; machinery and equipment;

costs; land industry; transportation; and government property and concerns. Each subject classification is further divided into sub-categories. Entries are arranged alphabetically by author and include title, publication source, date, and page reference. Each of the 15 sections opens with an introductory commentary on the reference sources and the subject field by an expert in the area. There is an index of authors at the end of the volume. The data has been input and corrected by computer technology. KSK

SS 65

Bibliography of Corporate Social Responsibility: Programs and Politics. 1971. a. bibl. index. Bank of America Corp., Box 37000, San Francisco, CA 94137. Examined: v. 6, 1977. Nadene Mathews, ed. 78p. $2.
Aud: Cl, Sa

Designed to serve as a resource for information dealing with the impact of contemporary social problems on business and society, and with the response to those problems by corporations, government bodies, and other groups. Covers books, periodical articles, reports, and speeches available from corporations, government offices, libraries, foundations, etc. The items are listed under 20 major subject categories such as aging and the aged, the arts, consumers and consumerism, education, employment, energy, pollution, etc. These categories are further divided into more specific subject headings. Each entry includes the name of the company or organization supplying the item, address, title, article, date, and a brief annotation. Most materials listed are available at no charge from the companies that produce them. MBP

SS 66

Bibliography of Publications of University Bureaus of Business and Economic Research. ISSN 0066-8761. 1957. a. index. West Virginia University, Bureau of Business Research, College of Business and Economics, Morgantown, WV 26506. Examined: v. 20, 1975. Dennis R. Leyden and Stanley J. Kloc, eds. 209p. $7.50.
Aud: Cl, Sa

Provides "a convenient reference document to publications of the Association for University Business and Economic Research (AUBER) and the members of the American Assembly of Collegiate Schools of Business (AACSB) which do not appear in the traditional indexes." Many of the publications deal with topics beyond the narrowly construed confines of business and economics. The first section lists items by subject category in alphabetical order. The second section lists publications by their institutions of origin. The third section is the author index, where an individual author's works are referenced by index numbers which correspond to those listed in the preceding section. Information is gathered from computer-oriented questionnaires. Subjects in section one include: general economics, economic growth, domestic monetary and fiscal theory, international economics, administration, agriculture, and manpower and welfare programs. KSK

SS 67

Business Books and Serials in Print. ISSN 0146-5953. (Continues: Business Books in Print. ISSN 0000-0369.) 1973. a. index. R. R. Bowker, 1180 Ave of the Americas, New York, NY 10036. Dist: R. R. Bowker, Box 1807, Ann Arbor, MI 48106. Examined: 1977. 1232p. $37.50.
Aud: Sa

Provides full ordering information and bibliographic data on more than 31,500 titles in the areas of economics, industry, finance, management, industrial psychology, and other business related topics. Indexed by author, title, and subject. Includes a directory of publishers represented in the volume with current addresses. Serials have been included for the first time in the 1977 edition and are indexed by title and subject. KMH

SS 68

Business Periodicals Index. ISSN 0007-6961. 1958. a. w/m. and q. suppls. H. W. Wilson Co., 950 University Ave, Bronx, NY 10452. Examined: v. 19, 1977. 1200p. service basis.
Aud: Hs, Jc, Cl, Pl

A cumulative subject and author index to over 270 English language periodicals covering a wide variety of fields related to business and industry, including banking, advertising and public relations, communications, occupational health and safety, and specific businesses and trades, among others. The publisher indicates that the 1977/78 volume will provide more complete coverage of biographical sketches of business leaders. Book reviews are arranged alphabetically by author in a separate section. This is a basic source for periodical materials on business. Since the cost is determined on a service basis, most libraries should be able to afford this index as a guide to their own collections and a key to outside materials. NLE

SS 69

Business Statistics. ISSN 0090-7669. 1932. bi-a. index.

U.S. Bureau of Economic Analysis, Washington, DC 20230. Dist: Superintendent of Documents, U.S. Government Printing Office, Washington, DC 20402. Examined: 1975. 280p. $15.15.
Aud: Sa

Issue examined is the 20th in a series presenting historical data for approximately 2500 series that appear in the monthly *Survey of Current Business* (ISSN 0039-6222). Data are shown annually for the years 1947 to 1974, quarterly for 1964 to 1974, and monthly for 1971 to 1974. These spans rotate every two years as new issues appear so that the most current information is the most complete. The bulk of material is statistical and covers general business, commodity prices, construction and real estate, domestic trade, labor force information, foreign trade, and information in 13 broad categories of business and industry. Provides explanatory notes, sources of data, and historical data. A useful general index and another summary source that makes individual business publications less necessary. NLE

SS 70
Carnival and Circus Booking Guide. ISSN 0090-2985. 1972. a. illus. Billboard Publications, Amusement Business Division, 1717 West End Ave, Nashville, TN 37203. Examined: 1976/77. Irwin Kirby, ed. 28p. $1.50.
Aud: Sa

Compiled by the staff of *Amusement Business,* another Billboard publication. The first part contains articles of general interest to those in the carnival and circus business. The main body is the survey of carnivals and circuses. Surveys are mailed to carnival firms, with follow-up phone calls for further information. Each entry includes: name of company, address and phone number, the various areas and festivities for which it plays, the number of units it has, how many miles it travels annually, items it carries (rides, shows, games), whether it has generators and transformers, whether it operates year-round or not, the number of transportation facilities (tractors, trailers, autos, etc.) it has, the name of the president, and, if necessary, the names of other officers such as general manager, secretaries, concession managers, etc. Circus listings include name of circus, address and phone number, names of top executives, the various regions in the U.S. it plays in (geared to a map), the number of performances it played the previous year, whether it carries programs of food and drink, the number of miles it travels annually, the transportation facilities it uses, and whether it has telephone crews. Advertisements and photos are included in the articles section. KSK

SS 71
Commodity Year Book. ISSN 0069-6862. 1939. a. Commodity Research Bureau, One Liberty Plaza, New York, NY 10006. Examined: 1977. Henry Jiler, ed. 385p. $21.
Aud: Sa

Designed to be accompanied by three other publications: *Futures Market Service, Commodity Chart Service,* and *Statistical Abstract Service.* Each of the three updates contains current information, and each provides different arrangements of commodity information. Includes a variety of statistical tables on nearly 100 basic raw commodities and unfinished products. Provides information on imports, exports, stock, production, yields, prices, etc. Convenient tables of U.S. wholesale commodity prices, U.S. Retail Price Index, U.S. Industrial Production Index, U.S. Gross National Product, national income, and personal income — all boiled down to one page at the end of each commodity. Good information, briefly stated, with clear and easy-to-apprehend tables. NLE

SS 72
The Conference Board. Cumulative Index. ISSN 0069-8350. 1963. a. The Conference Board, 845 Third Ave, New York, NY 10022. Examined: 1977. free.
Aud: Cl, Pl

The Conference Board was formerly the National Industrial Conference Board, and its publications continue to cover many of the same areas, e.g., business economics, public affairs administration, financial administration, and international operations management. The 1977 cumulation focuses on research published in the last ten years. Coverage is not comprehensive since obsolete and out-of-date titles are deleted. A dozen or more Conference Board serials are indexed, so the volume is useful for any library from the small to the large research. The range of subject matter is very broad — from accountability to zip codes. Indexes the Conference Board's publications only, but much of this material is very valuable. Individual titles can be selected, and many of them are inexpensive. A good general tool, and the price is right. NLE

SS 73
Custom House Guide. ISSN 0070-2250. 1862. a. index. Custom House Guide, 401 N Broad St, Philadelphia, PA 19108. Examined: 113th ed., 1976. Edward H. Kiernan, ed. 2000p. $72.
Aud: Sa

Covers tariff schedules, duty rates, ports, the international revenue code, customs information, shipping and commercial regulations, reciprocal trade agreements. Over 2000 pages are devoted to the details of import regulations, how to solve problems and answer questions, and what the problems and questions actually are. Several indexes and a logical arrangement help to approach the information. Essential for the business which does any buying abroad and for information in related areas. NLE

SS 74
Direction of Trade. ISSN 0012-3226. 1958. a. w/12 m. supps. The Secretary, International Monetary Fund, Washington, DC 20431. Examined: 1970/74. 334p. $10.
Aud: Sa

Issued by the International Monetary Fund's Statistics Bureau as a supplement to *International Financial Statistics*. Issues examined provide trade-by-country data over a seven-year period for 151 countries. Data are given in U.S. dollars. Covers 80 to 85 percent of the world's exports and imports. Introductory information is in French and Spanish. Provides data for the world as a whole, industrial countries, and "other Europe," and then information country-by-country. Information between countries is coded by a list in each volume; the coding saves space. The work deals with both detailed and summary data for international information, and is the basic source for much of this information. The subscription is a good buy. NLE

SS 75
Directory of American Firms Operating in Foreign Countries. ISSN 0070-5071. 1955/56. irreg. Simon and Schuster, One W 39th St, New York, NY 10018. Examined: 8th ed., 1975. Juvenal L. Angel, ed. 1622p. $75.
Aud: Sa

Lists "over 4500 American corporations that control 17,000 foreign business enterprises." Includes "only those firms that are in good standing" and companies "in which American firms or individuals have a substantial direct capital investment." The listings are arranged in two sections. The first lists firms alphabetically by name and includes U.S. address, president's name, foreign officer in charge of the overseas operation, principal products or services, and the country or countries of operation. The second section lists firms by country and includes home office address (U.S.), names and address of each subsidiary or branch, products manufactured or distributed and/or services rendered. A table of contents lists countries and page numbers. KR/JKM

SS 76
Directory of Franchising Organizations. ISSN 0070-556X. 1959. a. Pilot Books, 347 Fifth Ave, New York, NY 10016. Examined: 16th ed., 1975. 63p. $2.95.
Aud: Pl, Sa

Lists the leading U.S. franchise opportunities by type of service. Each listing includes name, address, a brief description of the service or type of business, and an indication of the approximate investment required by potential purchasers. Clear warning is given to potential franchise purchasers; the editors strongly advise individuals to investigate each company thoroughly before investing. KR/JKM

SS 77
Directory of Hotel and Motel Systems. a. American Hotel and Motel Association, 888 Seventh Ave, New York, NY 10019. Examined: 1977. Rose Vinckus, ed. 292p. $10 pap.
Aud: Sa

A directory of hotel and motel systems operating three or more hotels, motels, or resorts. It is arranged alphabetically by name of the system, and includes major officers, executive office address, phone number, name of each hotel or motel, city, and number of rooms. One is referred to the **Hotel and Motel Red Book,** published by the same association, for more detailed information about individual establishments. SLB

SS 78
Directory of New England Manufacturers. 1936. a. index. George D. Hall Co., 20 Kilby St, Boston, MA 02109. Examined: 1977. 920p. $79.
Aud: Sa

Issued with the editorial cooperation of the New England Council. Arranged in four tabbed sections. The first section lists manufacturers in New England alphabetically with company name and address. The second section is a geographical listing of manufacturing concerns with the firm's name, address, telephone number, names of executives, description of products, and Standard Industrial Classification number. The third section lists New England banks by city or town; entries indicate name, address, phone number, chief executive's name, and banking facilities available. Section four lists manufacturers in a classified product heading index. A table of contents and a few pages of almanac-type information on New England manufacturing preface the main body of the volume. KR/JKM

SS 79
Directory of North American Fairs and Expositions. (Continues: Cavalcade and Directory of Fairs. ISSN 0069-1291.) Amusement Business, 1717 West End Ave, Nashville, TN 37203. Examined: 1976. Irwin Kirby, ed. 96p. $25.
Aud: Sa

A guide to fairs and expositions in the U.S. and Canada. Includes all known fairs or agricultural expositions running three or more days, as well as stock shows and other appropriate events. Augmented lists of fairs will be in the spring and summer special issues of *Amusement Business*. The beginning of the **Directory** contains a brief industry market study on revenues, spending, expenses, and attendance. There follows a one-page listing of fair association meetings. The directory section lists fairs by state, then by city. Information on each fair includes: name, address, phone number, manager and any other officials, facilities, attendance data, area from which it attracts an audience, attractions, and dates that it played during the year. At the end of the volume is a chronological listing of fairs by date and location. Information is obtained by mailings and telephone calls. Contains advertisements of fairs. NLE

SS 80
Directory of Texas Manufacturers. ISSN 0070-6450. 1933. a. index. University of Texas at Austin, Bureau of Business Research, Austin, TX 78712. Examined: 26th ed., 1975. 2v. $25 pap.
Aud: Sa

The first volume lists manufacturers alphabetically by name, by geographical location, then by home office and parent company. The geographical listings are arranged by city or town and include the most complete information: name and address of firm, name and address of the parent company (if different), form of organization of the company, year of establishment, area of product distribution, number of employees, ownership and administration, product description, and Standard Industrial Classification code number. Volume two lists manufacturers by product code number and includes an alphabetical index to products. KR/JKM

SS 81
Dow Jones-Irwin Business Almanac. 1977. a. index. illus. Dow Jones-Irwin, 1818 Ridge Rd, Homewood, IL 60430. Examined: 1977, 661p.; 1978. Sumner N. Levine, ed. 783p. $15; $9.95 pap.
Aud: Cl, Pl, Sa

Contains brief, survey articles, several tables, and many statistical charts covering current trends and developments in all areas affecting business, finance, and economics. Some data on international trade are also included. The 1977 volume included several special articles on legislation, regulatory matters, taxation, investments, accounting practices, labor relations, and international business trends; a calendar of international trade shows and fairs; and a glossary of commercial definitions and abbreviations. The 1978 volume adds a listing of executive recruiting agencies, a list of "useful telephone numbers for obtaining quick access to business and economic information," a listing of labor contract expiration dates for major labor unions, and many other special features. A concise, extremely useful business reference tool. JKM

SS 82
Eastern Manufacturers and Industrial Classified Directory and Buyers Guide. 1936. a. illus. Bill Directory Publishers, 2112 Broadway, New York, NY 10023. Examined: 1976. 189p. $15 pap.
Aud: Pl, Sa

Popularly known as the "yellow book." Provides information for the potential purchaser of all types of materials, supplies, equipment, and services. Format is similar to the telephone company's yellow pages, alphabetically arranged, "descriptive business classification headings," i.e., adhesives, grinding, machine shops, etc. Entries include firm name, address, and phone number. There are no cross references and no index. Paid advertisements are mixed with free classified listings. Covers: New York, New Jersey, Connecticut, Pennsylvania, West Virginia, Massachusetts, Maine, Rhode Island, Delaware, Maryland, the District of Columbia, New Hampshire, and Vermont. KR/JKM

SS 83
Economic and Social Progress in Latin America. Annual Report. ISSN 0095-2850 (Continues: Socio-Economic Progress in Latin America. Annual Report. ISSN 0074-0888.) 1972. a. illus. Inter-American Development Bank, Washington, DC 20577. Examined: 1974. 485p. free to libraries. (1976. 446p.)
Aud: Cl, Pl

"Purpose of the report is to present a detailed review of developments in Latin America in their two principal aspects, economic and social. To that end, it is divided in two parts; the first one comprises a regional description of general and sectoral trends; the second one consists of such an analysis on a country-by-country basis. Each chapter in the second part is accompanied by a statistical summary. At the end of the report is a statistical appendix with 48 tables of regional indicators." The report is based on official information and statistical data available to the Inter-American Development Bank by the end of a certain year. The 1974 volume covers trends since 1970, with particular emphasis on 1973 and 1974. The regional analysis section is divided into five chapters: general economic trends, the external sector, the financing of development, regional economic integration, and social development trends. The country summaries cover Caribbean as well as Latin American nations. The statistical appendix includes tables on population data, national accounts, public finance balance of payments, primary commodity exports, and oil and related energy data. KSK

SS 84
Economic Survey of Europe. ISSN 0070-8712. 1948. a. illus. United Nations Publications, LX 2300, New York, NY 10017. Dist: International Publications Service, 114 E 32nd St, New York, NY 10016. Examined: v. 15, 1973. 172p. $7. (v. 16, pt. 1, 1974.)
Aud: Cl, Pl

Prepared by the Secretariat of the Economic Commission for Europe, this serial serves the needs of the Commission and helps in reporting on world economic conditions. The survey is divided into two large chapters on recent economic developments in Western Europe and recent economic developments in Eastern Europe and the Soviet Union. Each chapter is further divided into four to six parts: chapter one covers oil, economic prospects, and Southern European developments; chapter two covers production trends, investment, and foreign trade. Tables and charts are used throughout the survey. KSK

SS 85
Economic Survey of Latin America. ISSN 0070-8720. 1949. a. illus. United Nations Publications, LX 2300, New York, NY 10017. Examined: 1972. 241p. (1974. 339p. $12.)
Aud: Cl, Pl

"Part one of the survey reviews the economic developments observed in a particular year both in Latin America as a whole and in each individual country. Part two presents a brief account of economic trends in the individual Latin American countries. Production results, the fiscal sector, and the balance of payments are analyzed for each country, and the main developments in connection with economic policy are discussed. Part three comprises three special studies on planning processes and on the development of the mining and energy sectors." Statistical tables and figures are utilized extensively throughout the survey. The survey is prepared by the U.N.'s Economic Commission for Latin America. KSK

SS 86
Economics: Encyclopedia. ISSN 0090-4422. 1973/74. irreg. bibl. illus. Dushkin Publishing Group, Sluice Dock, Guilford, CT 06437. Examined: 1973/74. 279p. $5.95.
Aud: Jc, Cl, Pl

Over 10,000 short articles are arranged alphabetically and tied together by a system of cross references and item guides. Both *see* and *see also* references are used. Subject maps show the interrelationships among the 1000 articles on each of 21 areas of economic study. Item guides point out relationships between individual articles in the book. Consult references, at the end of an article, are numerically keyed to a classified bibliography at the back of the volume. All articles are prepared by experts working in their own fields. Articles of 200 words or more are signed, shorter pieces are unsigned. Photographs, tables, charts, and graphs are liberally used. This encyclopedia is geared for the nonprofessional reader. The bibliography at the end is divided into over two dozen sections representing the major study areas of economics. KSK

SS 87
Encyclopedia of Business Information Sources. ISSN 0071-0210. (Continues: Executives' Guide to Information Sources.) 1970. irreg. Gale Research Co., Book Tower, Detroit, MI 48226. Examined: 3rd ed., 1976. Paul Wasserman, ed. 667p. $42.
Aud: Jc, Cl, Pl, Sa

Subtitle: "A detailed listing of primary subjects of interest to managerial personnel, with a record of sourcebooks, periodicals, organizations, directories, handbooks, bibliographies, and other sources of information on each topic." An invaluable guide to information on 1280 subjects including public utilities, minority business, retail trade, environment, fund raising, copyright, etc. Lists under each subject dictionaries, almanacs, bibliographies, professional societies and associations, statistical sources, etc., with name and address of publishers and price where appropriate.

The listings range from basic, introductory materials to very specialized periodicals or statistical sources. Valuable as a selection guide for librarians and as a basic guide for students, business people, and the general public. JKM

SS 88

Exporters Encyclopedia World Market Guide. ISSN 0149-8118. 1904. a. Dun and Bradstreet, 99 Church St, New York, NY 10007. Examined: 72nd ed., 1977. Peter F. Greene. $120. (73rd ed., 1978. 1600p. $210.)
Aud: Sa

This Dun and Bradstreet publication even includes a few maps showing time zones, world population, world languages, and a plain, but adequate Mercator projection world map by the American Map Company, one of the better publishers. Other features are an exporters' service directory; information on export orders, markets, and export know-how; and other data needed by those who trade abroad. The 17-page section on France contains demographic information and data on banks, cable rates, exchange control, legal information, consulates, marketing regulations, trade laws, and pollution. Also provides information on consumer protection, mail regulations, ports, and more. Accompanied by a "fact file" in a separate binder containing updated and supplementary information. A valuable manual which can be used in place of a number of other tools as the first place to look for basic business information. NLE

SS 89

Food and Agriculture Organization of the United Nations. Production Yearbook. ISSN 0071-7118. (Continues: Yearbook of Food and Agricultural Statistics, Part One.) Food and Agriculture Organization of the United Nations, 00100 Rome, Italy. Dist: Unipub, Box 433, Murray Hill Sta, New York, NY 10016. Examined: v. 30, 1977. 116p. $15.
Aud: Cl, Sa

Provides statistical information on all aspects of food and agriculture production throughout the world in the form of tables and graphs. Covers index numbers of agricultural production, food supplies, wages, freight rates, etc. Text is printed in English, French, and Spanish. JKM

SS 90

Food and Agriculture Organization of the United Nations. Trade Yearbook. ISSN 0071-7126. (Continues: Yearbook of Food and Agricultural Statistics, Part Two.) Food and Agriculture Organization of the United Nations, 00100 Rome, Italy. Dist: Unipub, Box 433, Murray Hill Sta, New York, NY 10016. Examined: v. 30, 1977. 354p. $13.50.
Aud: Cl, Sa

Presents statistics on international trade in major world agricultural products. Text is printed in English, French, and Spanish. Statistical information is provided by the individual governments through questionnaires or through published documents which are then examined by the editorial staff. JKM

SS 91

Foreign Trade Marketplace. 1977. freq. not determined. index. Gale Research Co., Book Tower, Detroit, MI 48226. Examined: 1st ed., 1977. George J. Schultz, ed. 662p. $48.
Aud: Cl, Sa

A handbook and directory of foreign trade covering approximately 5000 consultants, companies, and organizations active in international trade. The first section provides a narrative overview entitled "Developing a Foreign Trade Strategy." The second section is a subject-classified directory drawn from government data banks. Listings are arranged under specific subheadings within five general categories: commercial activities: export-import; government and organizational activities; media, promotion, and information activities; procedures; and transportation, trade zones, and communications. Includes a subject and geographic index. JKM

SS 92

Fortune Double 500 Directory. 1970. a. index. Fortune Double Directory, Time Inc., 541 N Fairbanks Ct, Chicago, IL 60611. Examined: 1972. 39p. $3.75.
Aud: Sa

Subtitle: "Who did the best and the worst. . . of the largest United States industrial corporations and the 50 largest banks, life insurance, diversified financial, retailing, transportation, and utility companies." Originally published in the May and June issues of *Fortune Magazine*. Comprised of comparative lists of data on profits, assets, sales, etc. of the first 500 largest industrial corporations, and then the second 500 largest corporations. Includes a brief essay on corporate activities during the preceding year and an alphabetical index of the "fifty-largest" lists. KR/JKM

SS 93

Handbook of International Trade and Development Statistics. 1964. irreg. illus. United Nations Publica-

tions, Sales Section, Rm A-3315, New York, NY 10017. Examined: 1976. 657p. $24.
Aud: Cl, Pl

"Intended to provide a complete basic collection of statistical data relevant to the analysis of the problems of world trade and development." It may be an overstatement to say it provides a complete basic collection. However, the data presentation is quite different from other sources; it is analytically presented in the hope that interpretation will be easier. The presentation is much simpler, and the beginner may find this a good place to start a data search. U.N. data is as neutral as possible, and as many sources as can be tapped easily are used. Contains over 100 types of tables giving various comparisons and rankings. Excellent source for overall economic data. The text is in English and French. NLE

SS 94

Hotel and Motel Redbook. ISSN 0073-3490. (Continues: Hotel Redbook; The Official Hotel Redbook and Directory; U.S. Official Hotel Directory.) 1886. a. index. American Hotel Association Directory Corp., 888 Seventh Ave, New York, NY 10019. Examined: 1977. G. M. Barbara Rugowski, ed. 675p. $16.50.
Aud: Cl, Pl

Official directory of American Hotel and Motel Association members including hotels, motels, and resorts in the United States and other countries. The directory is divided into five major sections. U.S. hotels and motels are listed in alphabetical order by state and town; entries include name, address, number of rooms, telephone number, rates, and location. International hotels and motels are arranged in alphabetical order by nation and town; entries parallel those in the U.S. section. Resorts and condominiums are also arranged in alphabetical order by state and town, and by nation and town; entries include minimum daily and weekly rates for rooms and suites, recreational facilities, kitchen facilities, and mail service. Business meeting facilities in domestic and foreign properties are also listed in alphabetical order by state and town; entries note capacity of largest function room, number of meeting rooms of various seating capacities, availability of audio-visual equipment, and recreational facilities. There is a list of suppliers of products and services who are Allied Members of the American Hotel and Motel Association. A foreign language index listing hotels with key employees able to communicate in French, Spanish, German, or Japanese, and an index to advertisers are provided. Special features include a U.S. road map and information about the American Hotel and Motel Association. SLB

SS 95

Ice Rink Directory and Hockey Buyers Guide. (Continues: World Ice Rink Directory.) a. Billboard Publications, Amusement Business Division, 1515 Broadway, New York, NY 10036. Examined: 1977. 43p. $3 pap.
Aud: Pl, Sa

Contains a market report, equipment buyer's guide to producers, and a product listing for those companies that provide ice rink and hockey related products. The major portion of the book is an alphabetical arrangement of ice rinks by state, giving the address, size, when open, services offered, and instructions given. Canadian ice rinks are listed by province at the end. SLB

SS 96

International Bibliography of Economics. ISSN 0085-204X. 1952. a. bibl. index. Tavistock Publications, 11 New Fetter Lane, London EC4P 4EE, England. Dist: Aldine Publishing Co., 529 S Wabash Ave, Chicago, IL 60605. Examined: v. 24, 1975. 513p. $55.
Aud: Cl, Sa

One of four bibliographies in the *International Bibliography of the Social Sciences* series which is prepared by the International Committee for Social Sciences Documentation. The first nine volumes were published by UNESCO.

Contents include a list of periodicals covered, a detailed plan of the classification scheme for the bibliography, an author index, and a subject index in both English and French. The detailed bibliographic entries are listed by author under appropriate subject. Books, journals, conference proceedings, and government publications are indexed. The coverage is world wide. Titles are in the language of the publication, and titles of articles published in languages other than French or English are translated into English. The classification scheme for the bibliography has very detailed subdivisions. JKM

SS 97

Jane's Major Companies of Europe. ISSN 0075-3041. 1970. a. index. B. P. C. Publishing, Paulton House, 8 Shepherdess Walk, London NI 7LW, England. Dist: Franklin Watts, 730 Fifth Ave, New York, NY 10019. Examined: 1977. Jonathan Love, ed. 1250p. $74.50.
Aud: Sa

A directory of European companies, arranged into six

(A-F) sections: Finance (banking, financial, insurance, property); Services (utilities, transport, shops, publishing and printing, hotels, beers, wines and mineral waters, etc.); Light Industry and Industrial Chemicals (timber and wood products, textiles, footwear, tobacco, foods, china and glass, chemicals and pharmaceuticals); Engineering (electrical, electronics and telecommunications, aircraft and motors, docks and ship repairs); Building (building materials, builders, and roads); and Metals and Minerals (coal, iron and steel, metals, gas and oil, and mining). Information for each company includes address, phone and telex numbers, end of its financial year, directors, management, constitution, subsidiaries, activities, recent developments, stock information, and number of employees, among other items. In the front of the book are classified indexes arranged by field of business, an alphabetical index of companies, and an index of countries. There is also a summaries section which gives salient points of company activity, ownership, and performance at a glance. KSK

SS 98

Japan Economic Yearbook. ISSN 0075-3246. 1954. a. index. The Oriental Economist, Nihonbashi, Tokyo, Japan. Dist: International Publications Service, 114 E 32nd St, New York, NY 10016. Examined: 1976/77. 339p. $30.
Aud: Cl, Sa

"A comprehensive economic yearbook in the English language devoted exclusively to the study and analysis of Japan's economic, financial, and industrial developments." Divided into sections. The first section includes a chronology (general economy) and reports and tables on various economic trends. The second section examines specific industries and is arranged by type of industry. The third section is a list of major companies with date established, address, phone, president, capital, type of company (manufacturer, production, or business). There is also an index to companies. KR/JKM

SS 99

Journal of Behavioral Economics. ISSN 0090-5720. 1972. a. bibl. Western Illinois University, Center for Business and Economic Research, Macomb, IL 61455. Examined: v. 3, 1974. Fred L. Fry, ed. 371p. $6. (v. 7, 1978.)
Aud: Cl, Sa

"An interdisciplinary journal aimed toward academicians, both inside and outside the economics discipline, and to practitioners in business and non-profit organizations. The two goals of the journal are to 1) further knowledge of real world economic phenomena by integrating psychological and sociological variables into economic analysis, and 2) promote inter-disciplinary research by academicians and practitioners dealing in economics, the behavioral sciences, and social policy. The editors are particularly interested in substantial articles which are co-authored by scholars representing different social science disciplines. The journal may also include, from time to time, symposium articles emphasizing an inter-disciplinary approach to a current economic problem. Potential articles should draw heavily upon current literature surrounding the subject area, including findings and analysis and be written in terms understandable by readers from other disciplines. Unpublished dissertations treating inter-disciplinary topics are invited." The issue examined contains seven articles on such topics as housing preferences of the elderly, wages, bargaining, time preference, and unemployment insurance. There is a symposium on health care, also containing seven articles. It also includes a book review section. All reviews are signed. Bibliographical references, tables, and charts accompany most of the articles. KSK

SS 100

Kelly's Manufacturers' and Merchants' Directory. ISSN 0075-5370. 1880. a. index. Kelly's Directories, Neville House, Eden St, Kingston-upon-Thames, Surrey KT1, 1BY, England. Examined: 1972/73. 2v. v. 1, 2076p.; v. 2, 3461p. (1977. $60.)
Aud: Sa

Subtitle: "List of manufacturers and merchants, alphabetical and classified." Presents information on international supply and sales outlets for buyers and sellers. The lists are arranged in two volumes. Volume one covers Great Britain, Northern Ireland, and the Republic of Ireland, and volume two covers Europe, Africa, the Americas, Asia, and Oceania. Both volumes are indexed by trade. Importers and exporters are listed by their products. Entries include trade descriptions, addresses, telephone numbers, telegraphic addresses, and telex numbers. The information is verified and updated each year. KR/JKM

SS 101

Mail Order Business Directory. ISSN 0085-2953. 1955. bi-a. B. Klein Publications, 11 Third St, Rye, NY 10580. Examined: 1972. Barry T. Klein, ed. 377p. (1976. $30.)
Aud: Pl, Sa

Subtitle: "A complete guide to the mail order market." Presents advice and information for people interested in selling products to U.S. mail order houses. Lists 4800 of the "most active mail order firms" alphabetically by state and city. Information is compiled from questionnaires sent to the firms and supplemented by information from "trade sources and direct contact with the companies themselves." Listings include name, address, and type of product carried. KR/JKM

SS 102

National Bureau of Economic Research Annual Report. ISSN 0077-3611. 1920. a. National Bureau of Economic Research, 261 Madison Ave, New York, NY 10016. Examined: 56th ed., 1976. 114p. free.
Aud: Cl, Sa

"The National Bureau was organized in 1920 in response to a growing demand for objective determination of the facts bearing upon economic problems, and for their interpretation in an impartial manner. The National Bureau concentrates on topics of national importance that are susceptible to scientific treatment." Each annual report has a distinctive title; the 1976 report is entitled "Research Priorities Amidst Changing Economic and Social Values." The first part is a report by the president of the Bureau in which he discusses future research possibilities. The main body consists of brief staff reports on research that is under way. It is divided into seven areas: economic and social performance; urban, regional, and environmental studies; human behavior and social institutions; financial and industrial institutions and processes; international studies; measurement methods and operations; and conference workshops and other programs. There are reports on the officers and finances of the Bureau and on new publications that have appeared or will be forthcoming during the year. Occasionally tables, charts, and bibliographies of NBER papers appear in the staff reports. KSK

SS 103

National Minority Business Directory. ISSN 0077-5231. (Continues: National Black Business Directory.) 1969. a. index. National Buy-Black Campaign, 1115 Plymouth Ave N, Minneapolis, MN 55411. Examined: 1971. 60p. $12.50.
Aud: Sa

A directory of "black-owned firms engaged in profit-making ventures of a national scope." Criterion for inclusion being that at least 50 percent of the firm be black-owned. Firms supplied the information listed in the brief abstracts which include firm name, address, phone number, president/owner, product or service, and last year's gross. The arrangement is by goods or service and then alphabetical by state and firm. The publishers, National Buy-Black Campaign, supply information on these and other minority-owned firms in the U.S. for a "nominal fee." Includes sketches of the achievements of black industrial and scientific pioneers of the past, a thorough table of contents, and a cross reference index. KR/JKM

SS 104

New Jersey State Industrial Directory. 1901. a. index. State Industrial Directories, 2 Penn Plaza, New York, NY 10001. Examined: 1976. unpaged. $80.
Aud: Cl, Sa

Similar in format to the **New York State Industrial Directory**. Information on firms may be obtained by knowing firm name, geographical location (by county), or product category. Includes three tabbed sections: alphabetical, geographical, and classified buyers guide. A research staff has updated data on each firm through questionnaires and research in business reference sources. Firms were included only if they were manufacturers "with six or more employees." KR/JKM

SS 105

New York State Industrial Directory. ISSN 0548-9067. 1963. a. index. State Industrial Directories, 2 Penn Plaza, New York, NY 10001. Examined: 1975. unpaged. $80.
Aud: Sa

A regional directory of manufacturers arranged for ready access by manufacturer's name or product. Information was obtained by a research staff and by questionnaires sent to the firms. All companies are listed free of charge. The book is tabbed like a dictionary into the following sections: alphabetical; metropolitan, Manhattan and upstate; and classified. Maps precede each county in the geographical section (the largest section in the book) locating the county in the state and giving population and area code. The firms can be located by name through the alphabetical index which gives the town and county in which they are located; by county, through the geographical listing which includes name, corporate affiliation, address, telephone number, Standard Industrial Classification Code number, product description, plant size, property size, number of employees, company offices, and location of branch plants in New York City; and by product category, through the classified section which lists address, telephone number, and county location. KR/JKM

SS 106
Official Hotel-Motel Directory and Facilities Guide. ISSN 0072-9167. a. index. Hotel Sales Management Association, 362 Fifth Ave, New York, NY 10001. Examined: 1975/76. Frank W. Berkman, ed. 188p. $5 pap.
Aud: Sa

A directory of hotels, motels, and resorts that belong to the Hotel Sales Management Association. Listings are arranged by country and, in the United States, by state. The countries are not listed alphabetically, but the Table of Contents doubles as an alphabetical index. There is also a very complete index to individual facilities. After some introductory information on the Association, the main body of the book provides the country-by-country listing. Entry for each establishment includes number of rooms, address, phone, TWX, director of sales or other officer(s), and often a description of facilities. There are many advertisements. SLB

SS 107
Pan American Development Foundation. Annual Report. ISSN 0552-9913. 1964. a. illus. Pan-American Development Foundation, 1625 I St, NW, Rm 622, Washington, DC 20006. Examined: 1976. unpaged.
Aud: Jc, Cl, Sa

The Foundation's fundamental philosophy is "to put tools in the hands of those who will use them." It determines where private efforts are needed, and then brings these needs to the attention of private citizens, business, and civic groups throughout the Americas. The annual report briefly lists the Foundation's activities during the year. After listing the officers and members of the Board of Trustees, it includes a message from the president. The report then lists each country and outlines the aid each has received. The Foundation's financial report is also presented along with a table of the health, education, and economic development programs of the organization. Illustrated throughout with photographs. KSK

SS 108
Per Jacobsson Foundation. Proceedings of the Lecture Meeting. ISSN 0079-0761. (Continues: Per Jacobsson Memorial Lecture. ISSN 0079-077X.) 1964. a. Per Jacobsson Foundation, International Monetary Fund Bldg, Washington, DC 20431. Examined: 1976. Gordon Williams, ed. 29p. free.
Aud: Cl, Sa

Proceedings of the lecture meetings of the Foundation which take place in various countries. After welcoming and opening remarks, the principal paper is given by the main speaker. Principal papers have covered such topics as monetary policy, the role of bankers, monetary gold, international banking, international payments, and why banks are unpopular. After the paper is presented, it is commented on by other speakers. Questions asked by the audience and brief biographies of the speakers are included. The proceedings are published in English, French, and Spanish. The last pages list the Founding sponsors, Board of Directors, Foundation officers, and previous publications. KSK

SS 109
Plant Location. ISSN 0554-2731. 1959. a. bibl. illus. Simmons-Boardman Publishing Corp., 350 Broadway, New York, NY 10013. Examined: 1976. Fredric Good, ed. 240p. $12.
Aud: Sa

Subtitle: "The industrial and economic development workbook." "Designed for use at the inception of the site-selection process." Material in the U.S. section is arranged geographically by census region. A regional map is presented, followed by detailed information on each state in that region. In the Canadian section there is a map of Canada, followed by material on each province. Information on each state and province includes: financial assistance to industry, tax rates, advanced education facilities, listing of cities with population over 25,000, employment, hours and earnings, industrial mix, wage survey, unemployment, environmental controls, railroads and airlines serving cities of 25,000 or more, electric and gas utilities serving cities over 25,000, climate, mineral production, and a listing of industrial development counselors. A Plant Location Brochure Service provides free brochures and literature from advertisers to interested readers who want more detailed information on a certain area. Contains many illustrated advertisements. KSK

SS 110
President Directory. 1967. a. index. illus. Diamond-Time, 1-2-3 Kita Aoyama, Minatu-Ku, Tokyo 107. Dist: Time Inc., Time/Life Bldg, Rockefeller Center, New York, NY 10020. Examined: 1976. 122p. $12.
Aud: Sa

Subtitle: "Japan's 500 leading industrial corporations." Compiled and edited by the editorial department of Diamond-Time, a joint venture of Time Inc. and Diamond Publishing Co., a Japanese publisher of economic periodicals and books. Covers the fiscal year prior to the year in the title (i.e., fiscal year April 1974 to March 1975 for the 1976 edition). Geared to those interested in Japan's economy, market, and business enterprises. After some articles on events during the fiscal year, the annual continues with statistical maps (in color) illustrating various aspects of the Japanese economy. It includes a list of the 1121 leading Japanese mining/manufacturing corporations ranked by sales; lists of the 200 leading Japanese exporting corporations ranked by value of exports; a list by industry of the leading exporting corporations ranked by value of exports; and a list of the 200 leading foreign capital-affiliated corporations in Japan. There are alphabetical indexes of the mining/manufacturing corporations and the non-manufacturing corporations. Advertisements are scattered throughout. Formerly the annual only listed the top 500 mining/manufacturing corporations; now it lists all those listed on the Tokyo, Osaka, and Nagoya stock exchanges. KSK

SS 111

Puerto Rico. Department of the Treasury. Office of Economic Research. Economy and Finances. ISSN 0079-7871. 1955. a. illus. Department of the Treasury, Office of Economic Research, San Juan, PR 00905. Examined: 1975. 35p. free.
Aud: Jc, Cl

An annual review of business and finance in Puerto Rico. "Business is described in terms of aggregate economic indicators. Finance is viewed in terms of operations of the principal financial institutions, both private and public, and the fiscal operations of the Commonwealth Government." The first third of the report looks at economic activity (consumption, employment and unemployment, net income, agriculture, world trade, etc.). The second part covers private financial activity (banking, savings and loan associations, mortgages, personal loan companies, and insurance companies). The final section focuses on public finances (taxes, government expenditures, public debt, tax legislation, etc.). The report contains tables throughout on such items as employed persons by industry group, assets of banks, deposits and types of loans of banks, and government receipts by sources. Charts and figures are also included in the survey. KSK

SS 112

Research in Corporate Social Performance and Policy. 1978. a. bibl. JAI Press, Box 1285, Greenwich, CT 06830. Examined: v. 1, 1978. Lee Preston, ed. 350p. $12.50; $25 to institutions.
Aud: Cl, Sa

An annual compilation of scholarly articles reflecting current research on "the impact of the large corporation on its social environment and the development and implementation of corporate social policy." The initial volume contained 16 articles written primarily by professors at leading U.S. colleges and universities and arranged in two sections, theoretical foundations and empirical evidence, and research approaches and analytical issues. The appendix examines instruments for social performance and policy research. JKM

SS 113

Research in Economic History. 1976. a. bibl. illus. JAI Press, Box 1285, 321 Greenwich Ave, Greenwich, CT 06830. Examined: v. 1, 1976. Paul J. Uselding, ed. 371p. $12.50; $25 to institutions. (v. 2, 1977. 385p. $12.50; $25 to institutions.)
Aud: Cl, Sa

Subtitle: "An annual compilation of research." Publishes "research papers that are longer than a conventional, journal-length article yet shorter than a monograph." Essays contain "historical scholarship, presentation of new evidence, conceptual freshness and creativity, and analytical rigor." There are nine papers in the first volume including: "Manufacturing in the Antebellum South"; "Transference and Development of Institutional Constraints upon Economic Activity"; "The Centuries of American Inequality"; "English Open Fields as Behavior Towards Risk"; "The Business Advisory Council of the Department of Commerce, 1933-1961: A Study in Corporate/Government Relations"; "Stagflation in Historical Perspective: The Napoleonic Wars Revisited"; "Cross-Spectral Analysis of Long Swings in Atlantic Migration"; "Socio-Economic Patterns of Migration from the Netherlands in the 19th Century"; and "In Dispraise of the Muckrakers: U.S. Occupational Mortality, 1890-1910." All of the articles contain tables and/or figures. Each article also includes a bibliography at the end of the paper. KSK

SS 114

Research in Experimental Economics. 1978. a. bibl. JAI Press, Box 1285, Greenwich, CT 06830. Examined: v. 1, 1978. Vernon L. Smith, ed. 365p. $12.50; $25 to institutions.
Aud: Cl, Sa

A scholarly journal containing original papers based on laboratory and field experiments in the fields of economics and econometrics. The first volume includes nine articles covering such topics as "Volunteer Bias in Experiments in Economics"; "An Experimental Analysis of Decision Making Procedures for Discrete Public Goods"; and "Labor Supply Behavior of

Animal Workers." An extremely specialized collection suitable only for university or research collections in economics. JKM

SS 115
Research in Finance. 1978. a. JAI Press, Box 1285, Greenwich, CT 06830. Examined: v. 1, 1978. Haim Levy, ed. 350p. $12.50; $25 to institutions.
Aud: Cl, Sa

Like other series published by JAI Press, this title is an annual cumulation of original, scholarly papers written primarily by university faculty in the U.S. The six articles in the first volume included such titles as "Consumption and Saving in Economic Development"; "An Inter-Industry Approach to Econometric Cost of Capital Estimation"; "Test of Capital Asset Pricing Hypotheses"; etc. Articles would be of interest to college students in the fields of business, economics, and finance, and to corporate financial officers. JKM

SS 116
Research in International Business and Finance. 1978. a. JAI Press, Box 1285, Greenwich, CT 06830. Examined: v. 1, 1978. Robert G. Hawkins, ed. 475p. $12.50; $25 to institutions.
Aud: Cl, Sa

It appears that each volume will focus on a particular theme or subject. The first volume focuses on "The Economic Effects of Multinational Corporations." It includes ten lengthy, scholarly articles, many of which include responses/commentaries by various corporate executives, academics, and/or government officials. Articles cover such diverse topics as taxation, collective bargaining and labor relations, local control of natural resources, and other aspects of the relations between multinational corporations and their host countries. JKM

SS 117
Standard and Poor's Register of Corporations, Directors and Executives. ISSN 0079-3825. (Continues: Poor's Register of Directors of the U.S. and Canada; Poor's Register of Corporations, Directors, and Executives: U.S. and Canada.) 1928/29. a. w/3 suppls. index. Standard and Poor's Corp., 345 Hudson St, New York, NY 10014. Examined: 1977. E. Murphy, ed. 3v. v. 1, 2397p.; v. 2, 1590p.; v. 3, 807p. $140.
Aud: Cl, Sa
Indexed in: *Biographical Dictionaries Master Index.*

In three volumes with cumulative supplements. Volume one lists corporations alphabetically by business name. Information for each corporation includes: address; phone number; officers and directors; primary accounting firm, bank, and law firm; Standard Industrial Classification code; annual sales; number of employees; division names and functions; products; and whether the company is a subsidiary or division of another corporation. Volume two is a register of directors and executives, arranged alphabetically by name. Information includes: principal business affiliation with official title; business address; residence; and, where obtainable, place and year of birth, college and year of graduation, and fraternal memberships. Volume three contains the indexes and is divided into six color-coded sections: Standard Industrial Classification index (green); Standard Industrial Classification codes (pink); geographic index (buff); new individual additions (blue); obituary section (green); and new company additions (blue). Kept up to date by a series of cumulating and superseding supplements; only the latest is necessary. A major source of corporate information and an addition to the information in Who's Who publications. NLE/KSK

SS 118
Surveys of Consumers. ISSN 0085-3410. (Continues: Survey of Consumer Finances. ISSN 0081-9727.) 1972. a. University of Michigan, Institute for Social Research, Ann Arbor, MI 48106. Examined: 1972/73. Burkhard Strumpel et al., eds. 235p. $10.50. (1974/75. R. T. Curtin, ed. 325p. $14.)
Aud: Cl, Sa

Subtitle: "Contributions to behavioral economics." The second volume (1972/73) of a new serial published by the Economic Behavior Program of the Survey Research Center. Its predecessor, the annual *Survey of Consumer Finances,* was published continuously from 1960-1970, and the data from prior annual surveys were published in the *Federal Reserve Bulletin* from 1945-1959. The current volume is in three parts. "Part one contains substantive theoretical and methodological articles, based on the diverse research projects of the Economic Behavior Program. Part two contains a summary of the findings of six quarterly surveys of consumer sentiment. Part three outlines the survey methodology and procedures which are used by the Survey Research Center." The articles are based on scholarly research and usually include extensive tables and some references. The outlook charts and tables in part two are preceded by six chapters which analyze the outlook for consumer demand within a certain period of time, usually one or two months. Part three contains a sample questionnaire used to gather the data. KSK

SS 119
Swimming Pool Weekly and Swimming Pool Age Data and Reference Annual. ISSN 0082-0466. 1932. a. index. illus. Hoffman Publications, 3000 NE 30th Place, Box 11299, Fort Lauderdale, FL 33306. Examined: 1977. Dave Kaiser, ed. 362p. $6 pap.
Aud: Pl, Sa

Divided into seven sections. The first section is a buyer's guide which is a directory of equipment, supplies, and services. It is arranged by subject and includes suppliers' addresses. There is a directory of pool industry associations, arranged by state, which includes the president's name and address. The wholesale distributors directory is arranged by state and gives the name and address of each distributor. The pool award winner section includes good photographs, specifications, and price. The basic technical features section is a series of articles on such subjects as solar energy and pool renovation. The public pool design and financing section includes photographs, statistics, and articles. The pool design feature is a series of articles on specialized pool designing. There is an index to advertisers. SLB

SS 120
Thomas Grocery Register. ISSN 0082-4151. 1898. a. Thomas Publishing Co., One Penn Plaza, New York, NY 10001. Examined: 1974. John Kovac, ed. 2v. 952p. $60.
Aud: Sa

Subtitle: "The official buyers and sellers guide of the grocery and allied trades." Volume one gives data on supermarket chains, wholesalers, brokers, exporters, and warehouses. It also includes an alphabetical listing of companies and organizations. Volume two lists manufacturers, importers, and other sources for food and non-food products, equipment and machinery, and industry related services. It is arranged in three sections: products and services, brand names, and an alphabetical listing of companies and organizations. Each section is tabbed (like a large dictionary) and includes an introduction which explains the arrangement, data therein, and where to look for further information on the companies. Advertisers (yellow pages style) are included in the "brokers" and "warehouses" sections. KR/JKM

SS 121
United Nations. Department of Economic and Social Affairs. World Economic Survey. ISSN 0084-1714. 1948. a. illus. United Nations Publications, LX 2300, New York, NY 10017. Dist: International Publications Service, 114 E 32nd St, New York, NY 10016. Examined: 1972. 109p. (1974, $9.50; 1976. 200p.)
Aud: Cl

Reviews current trends in the world economy. After giving an over-all view spotlighting world production and trade, the book examines recent trends in the developed market economies, centrally planned economies (Eastern Europe, Soviet Union, China), and in developing nations. Each chapter looks at production and use of resources for each area, plus the states of internal and external balance. Illustrated throughout with tables which cover such subjects as world agricultural production, U.S. balance of payments, industrial growth in Eastern Europe, and the growth of total production for developing countries. Sources for the tables are given. U.N. documents are referred to by their symbolic letters and numbers. Text is in English, French, and Spanish. KSK

SS 122
U.S. Agency for International Development. Proposed Foreign Aid Program; Summary Presentation to the Congress. ISSN 0082-8637. (Continues: Proposed Economic Assistance Programs.) 1963. a. illus. U.S. Agency for International Development, Department of State, Washington, DC 20523. Dist: Superintendent of Documents, U.S. Government Printing Office, Washington, DC 20402. Examined: 1968. 297p.
Aud: Cl, Pl

Provides members of Congress with a summary of the foreign aid program proposed for a fiscal year. Figures for the fiscal year before the date of the volume are estimates, while figures for prior years represent actual obligations. The present fiscal year figures represent proposed programs. Various chapters list priorities, private resources for development, impact on the American economy of foreign aid, and specific requests for countries in Latin America, Asia, and Africa. There is an analysis of the fiscal year request by funding categories including contributions to international organizations, and an appendix of selected tables including statistics on basic economic data for the less developed non-communist areas. Charts are also included in the volume. KSK

SS 123
U.S. Bureau of the Census. Census of Manufacturers. ISSN 0082-9374. 1810. quinquennial. illus. U.S. Bureau of the Census, Washington, DC 20233. Dist: Superintendent of Documents, U.S. Government Printing Office, Washington, DC 20402. Examined: 1967. 3v.
Aud: Sa

Divided into three parts: summary and subject statistics; industry statistics; and area statistics. The set examined was based on the 1967 census of manufacturers, which was part of the economic census covering 1967. Input is received from trade and professional associations, individual companies, federal and state agencies, labor unions, and research and educational organizations. Summary tables include sizes of establishments, inventories, expenditures for plant and equipment, materials and water consumed, and numerous analytical tables. Industrial chapters are divided into about 20 major groups, each subdivided by specific industries. The result is hundreds of industrial categories, each with an array of statistical tables. Details are myriad, and the comparison of years serves for a growth analysis. Volumes are issued extremely late; the 1967 volume was not published until 1971, and the 1972 volume was issued in 1975. NLE

SS 124

U.S. Bureau of the Census. County Business Patterns. ISSN 0082-9463. 1946. a. illus. U.S. Bureau of the Census, Washington, DC 20233. Dist: Superintendent of Documents, U.S. Government Printing Office, Washington, DC 20402. Examined: 1975. 129p.
Aud: Sa

The 1975 issues are the 22nd in the series presenting the first quarter employment and payroll statistics by county and industry. Provides data covering most of the economic divisions of the country, such as agricultural services, mining, construction, manufacturing, transportation, public utilities, wholesale trade, retail trade, finance, insurance, real estate, and services. Each separate piece for each state includes a useful "General Explanation" which details the information included and how it is organized. The organization for each state is the same. Maps and pie charts display some data. Also includes much information on employers, payrolls, and other data. Convenient breakdown, but data is not interpreted and the user must be sophisticated. Primary source for the information covered. NLE

SS 125

U.S. Bureau of the Census. Foreign Commerce and Navigation of the United States. 1820/21. irreg. U.S. Bureau of the Census, Washington, DC 20233. Dist: Superintendent of Documents, U.S. Government Printing Office, Washington, DC 20402. Examined: 1965. 3v. v. 1, 594p.; v. 2, 809p.; v. 3, 926p. $24.25.
Aud: Sa

The frequency of this publication has varied over the years. Data included is published in numerous other federal documents in intervening years, but the summaries provided here are valuable for historical and demographic data. The 1965 issue is in three volumes: Standard International Trade Classification (STIC) commodity by country; area and country by STIC; and Schedule A and Schedule B commodity by country. This publication is the "top of the line" for the information included, even if the data is dated. Only a few libraries may need this since the STIC is available in other sources, but librarians need to know about this source. NLE

SS 126

U.S. Council on International Economic Policy. International Economic Report of the President Transmitted to the Congress. ISSN 0091-2492. 1973. a. illus. Council on International Economic Policy, Executive Office Bldg, Washington, DC 20500. Dist: Superintendent of Documents, U.S. Government Printing Office, Washington, DC 20402. Examined: 1977. 194p. $4.85.
Aud: Cl

The President of the United States traces the progress made in the past year by the U.S. in dealing with the major economic issues facing the world. Part one shows the U.S. position in the world economy. This part discusses world economic conditions, the U.S. international economic position (balance of trade), and developments in the U.S. International economic policies regarding developing nations, energy, agriculture, East-West trade, law of the sea, and questionable payment abroad. Part two deals with selected current international economic issues. Among the subjects dealt with (one to a chapter) are: food and agriculture, East-West trade and finance, multinational corporations, international anti-trust developments, export promotion and market developments, trade regulation and restraint, international investment patterns, energy resources, international labor comparisons, air transportation and tourism, ocean shipping, technology, and U.S. trade and industrial pollution. Both sections are illustrated with brightly colored charts, maps, figures, and illustrations. Appendix A is a report to the President of the U.S. on the activities of the Council on International Economic Policy during the year. Appendix B is comprised of statistical tables on international economic comparisons, U.S. foreign trade, U.S. international transactions, the international investment position of the U.S., economic assistance, energy, minerals, agriculture, and manufactured goods. Finally, there is a brief chronology of selected events during the year which affected U.S. international economic policy. KSK

SS 127
U.S. Federal Supply Service. Index of Federal Specifications and Standards. ISSN 0364-1414. (Continues: U.S. Federal Supply Bureau. Federal Standard Stock Catalogue, Section 4, Federal Specifications, Part I; Index to Federal Specifications, Standards, and Handbooks.) 1952. a. index. U.S. Federal Supply Service, General Services Administration, Washington, DC. Dist: Superintendent of Documents, U.S. Government Printing Office, Washington, DC 20402. Examined: 1974. 335p. (1977. $13.50.)
Aud: Cl, Sa

Provides alphabetical, numerical, and federal supply classification listings of federal specifications, federal standards, federal handbooks, and qualified products lists in general use throughout the federal government. "The index lists federal standardization documents which have been printed and distributed, including those which are mandatory for use, and identifies the sources from which these documents may be obtained. Supplements to the index indicate the dates on which the use of new *Federal Specifications and Standards* become mandatory. Each index, issued in January, is a consolidation of the previous index and its December cumulative supplement." The alphabetical and numerical listings are divided into federal specification, federal standards, and federal handbooks. Information for each title includes: title of the document, document number, QPL (Qualified Products Lists) letter, FSC (Federal Supply Classification) code, PREP letter (for Government agency use only), date of the latest specification or standard, and the price of coordinated documents. The numerical listing of federal and interim federal specifications lists titles by document number. Another listing gives federal standardization documents by FSC number. Some volumes include a complete list of cancelled and superseded documents. KSK

SS 128
U.S. Industrial Outlook; With Projections to (year). 1973. a. illus. U.S. Department of Commerce, Washington, DC 20233. Dist: Superintendent of Documents, U.S. Government Printing Office, Washington, DC 20402. Examined: 1978. 479p. $5.45.
Aud: Sa

Filled with charts, diagrams, and statistical tables. Concentrates the knowledge, experience, and judgment of 100 experts qualified to describe 200 industries. Designed to assemble statistics, monitor and interpret trends, and delineate key elements for each industry described. Figures and projections (for the next ten years) are based on the previous year's dollar, and inflationary factors are included. Also based on the Standard Industrial Classification. Each issue includes brief and readable articles by government specialists on the economy and statistics. A goldmine of data on the economy. Organized in such a way as to relate to some of the other statistical materials and sources available. NLE

SS 129
U.S. Internal Revenue Service. Statistics of Income: Business Income Tax Returns. (Continues: Statistics of Income: U.S. Business Tax Returns.) 1954. a. index. illus. U.S. Internal Revenue Service, 1111 Constitution Ave, NW, Washington, DC 20224. Dist: Superintendent of Documents, U.S. Government Printing Office, Washington, DC 20402. Examined: 1974. E. J. DiPaolo, ed. 232p. $3.25.
Aud: Cl, Sa

Includes financial estimates based on sample returns of sole proprietorships and partnerships. Changes in business income tax law and industrial classification are explained. Basic subjects covered include: adjusted gross income, depreciation, farm proprietorships, income statements, industry classification, partnerships, size classifications, and state income taxes. The 1974 edition was published in 1977. SJV

SS 130
U.S. Internal Revenue Service. Statistics of Income: Corporation Income Tax Returns. 1954. a. index. illus. U.S. Internal Revenue Service, 1111 Constitution Ave, NW, Washington, DC 20224. Dist: Superintendent of Documents, U.S. Government Printing Office, Washington, DC 20402. Examined: 1972. Joel R. Stubbs, ed. 248p. $4.
Aud: Cl, Sa

Provides corporate income tax data based on a sample of unaudited corporation income tax returns. Statistics are presented on receipts, deductions, net income, income tax liability, tax credits, and distributions to stockholders. Major classifications of the data are industry and size groupings based on total assets and business receipts. An historical summary of corporate income tax statistics from 1963 to 1972 is presented. The 1972 edition was published in 1977. SJV

SS 131
U.S. National Bureau of Standards. Annual Report.

(Continues: Technical Highlights of the National Bureau of Standards. ISSN 0083-1905.) 1902. a. illus. National Bureau of Standards, Washington, DC 20234. Dist: Superintendent of Documents, U.S. Government Printing Office, Washington, DC 20402. Examined: 1975. 32p.
Aud: Cl, Pl

Gives a brief history of the National Bureau of Standards' founding and some highlights of its past activities. It describes some of its present activities and research in various fields (energy, computers, measurement, the environment, promoting better materials use, product safety, etc.), and the information services provided by the NBS. Finally, it gives information on the Bureau's organization, funds and facilities, and staff. NBS committee and panel members are listed. Illustrated throughout with photographs. KSK

SS 132
Who's Who in Finance and Industry. ISSN 0083-9523. (Continues: Who's Who in Commerce and Industry.) 1936. bi-a. Marquis Who's Who, 200 E Ohio St, Chicago, IL 60611. Examined: 19th ed., 1975/76. 812p. $47.50.
Aud: Cl, Pl, Sa
Indexed in: *Biographical Dictionaries Master Index.*

A biographical directory of business executives; information is gathered from current media and surveys. Attempts to include individuals who have accomplished some outstanding achievement, who are known in a field but not outside of it, who are leaders of certain firms, or who are known to have expertise in any sub-field of finance and industry. There is a helpful list of abbreviations which should be consulted. Provides standard Marquis format and information. Contains names not found in other directories or general guides to business directories. There is no approach by firm name. NLE

SS 133
World Trade Annual. ISSN 0512-3739. 1963. a. United Nations, Statistical Office, New York, NY 10017. Dist: Walker and Co., 720 Fifth Ave, New York, NY 10019. Examined: 1973; 1975. 5v. $165.
Aud: Sa

Issued in five separate volumes. Volume one covers food, beverages, tobacco, and inedible crude materials, except fish, animal, and vegetable oils and fats. Volume two covers mineral fuels and chemicals. Volume three is entitled "Manufactured Goods Classed Chiefly by Material Other Than Food, Fuels, Chemicals, Machinery, and Transport Equipment." Volume four covers miscellaneous manufactured materials, and volume five covers machinery and transport equipment. Provides summarized and detailed trade statistics by commodity and by trading partner. Tables are arranged by commodity. Data is supplied by the 24 principal trading countries of the world. Published rather tardily; the 1975 edition was issued in late 1977. KMH

SS 134
World Trade Annual. Supplement. ISSN 0512-3747. 1964. a. United Nations Statistical Office, New York, NY 10017. Dist: Walker and Co., 720 Fifth Ave, New York, NY 10019. Examined: 1973. 5v. $75.90 per v.
Aud: Sa

Subtitle: "Trade of the industrialized nations with Eastern Europe and the developing nations." Data is presented in a format comparable to the **World Trade Annual.** The five volumes cover Eastern Europe and the U.S.S.R., South and Central America, Africa, the Near East, and the Far East, respectively. Provides information on the total trade of each county or region according to the Standard International Trade Classification (SITC) and the trade of each section, division, group, subgroup, and item of the SITC. KMH

SS 135
World Wide Chamber of Commerce Directory. 1965. a. Johnson Publishing Co., Box 455, Loveland, CO 80537. Examined: 1976/77. 225p. $7.
Aud: Pl

A complete list of chambers of commerce in the U.S. Each entry notes the manager or president of the chamber, address, and telephone number. Canadian and foreign chambers, foreign embassies and consulates in the U.S., and U.S. consulates and embassies throughout the world are also listed. KMH

SS 136
Yearbook of Industrial Statistics. (Continues: The Growth of World Industry.) 1963. a. index. United Nations, Department of Economic Affairs, New York, NY 10017. Dist: United Nations Publishing Service, New York, NY 10017. Examined: 1975. 2v. v. 1, 691p.; v. 2, 706p. $62.
Aud: Cl, Pl

Presents statistics of world industry in two volumes. Volume one includes tables showing major industries in each country and international tables showing the index numbers of industrial production and employment for the world. The national tables are arranged alphabetically by country, and the introduction for each country explains how the data were compiled. The second volume deals specifically with annual production statistics for 527 industrial commodities. It is arranged by commodity, then by nation, and figures indicate the total industrial production of each item. Retrospective data are included in both volumes. There are four indexes: 1) commodities according to International Standard Industrial Classification (ISIC) codes; 2) commodities in alphabetical order by name; 3) countries by name; and 4) countries by ISIC code. The 1975 volume was published in 1977. NLE/KMH

SS 137

Yearbook of International Trade Statistics. ISSN 0084-3822. (Continues: International Trade Statistics.) 1951. a. United Nations, Statistical Office, New York, NY 10017. Dist: United Nations, U.N. Publications, LX 2300, New York, NY 10017. Examined: 1975; 24th ed., 1976. 2v. v. 1, 968p.; v. 2, 731p. $50.
Aud: Cl, Pl, Sa

Published in two volumes. Volume one, "Trade by Country," provides detailed data on the imports and exports of 149 countries. Summary tables showing trade flow between countries and the contribution of each nation to the trade of its region and of the world are provided. Some tables provide historical data. Volume two, "Trade by Commodity," analyzes the imports and exports of each nation by commodity and includes commodity matrix tables. The introduction details the structure of the tables in both volumes and provides general information on international trade. NLE/KMH

CIVIL RIGHTS AND HUMAN RIGHTS

SS 138

American Civil Liberties Union. Annual Report. a. illus. American Civil Liberties Union, 22 E 40th St, New York, NY 10016. Examined: 1977. 35p. free.
Aud: Pl

Presents highlights of the year's work of the American Civil Liberties Union (ACLU) and of important legislation and judicial decisions implemented during the preceding year. Arranged in brief topical sections, e.g., access to the courts, political surveillance, abortion, voter law, school desegregation, capital punishment, sexual privacy, women's rights, etc. Also lists ACLU officers, members of the Board of Directors, and members and officers of the National Advisory Council. JKM

SS 139

Freedom in the World: Political Rights and Civil Liberties. 1978. a. illus. Freedom House, 20 W 40th St, New York, NY 10018. Examined: 1978. Raymond D. Gastil, ed. 320p. $20.
Aud: Cl, Pl

An expansion of Freedom House's *Comparative Survey of Freedom*. Part one deals with purposes and assumptions. Tables indicate comparative levels of freedom in various countries. Part two gives definitions and distinctions. Part three summarizes conditions of freedom in every independent nation, with descriptions of political-economic systems, policy ratings of freedom, and the nature of the ethnic or nationality situation. SJV

SS 140

Human Rights Organizations and Periodicals Directory. ISSN 0098-0579. 1973. bi-a. index. Meiklejohn Civil Liberties Institute, 1715 Francisco St, Berkeley, CA 94701. Examined: 1977. David Christiano, ed. 147p. $6.75.
Aud: Jc, Cl, Pl

Contains approximately 500 entries of organizations and publications dedicated to social change and the expansion and protection of human rights. Listings are arranged alphabetically by group and include address, publications, and an annotation describing the group's activities. There is a subject index. SJV

SS 141

National Association for the Advancement of Colored People. NAACP Annual Report. ISSN 0077-3212. 1910. a. illus. National Association for the Advancement of Colored People, 1790 Broadway, New York, NY 10019. Examined: 1961; 1962; 1963; 1964; 1965; 1966. $1.
Aud: Sa

Reports discuss activities in the area of civil rights engaged in by various divisions of the NAACP. Reports have focused on such diverse activities as the plight of the Black worker, getting out the vote, the march to freedom, the civil rights front, and the legal, religious, educational, and labor struggles of NAACP members. Each volume includes a chronological abstract of news highlights relating to civil rights' struggles, financial statements, and membership and convention activities, with photographs of outstanding members. SJV

SS 142

The Sexual Barrier. 1970. irreg. Marija Matich

Hughes, 2422 Fox Plaza, San Francisco, CA 94102. Examined: 1972 suppl., 35p.; 1977. Marija Matich Hughes, ed. 843p. $35.
Aud: Cl, Pl

Subtitle: "Legal, medical, economic, and social aspects of sex discrimination." A bibliography of materials on women in employment. Covers legal aspects of employment, pay differentials, professional opportunities, general employment information, and discrimination. Books, pamphlets, and government documents in English are listed. Supplements are issued between editions. KAC

SS 143
U.S. Commission on Civil Rights. The State of Civil Rights: A Report of the United States Commission on Civil Rights. ISSN 0161-9233. 1976. a. U.S. Commission on Civil Rights, Washington, DC 20425. Dist: Superintendent of Documents, U.S. Government Printing Office, Washington, DC 20402. Examined: 1977. 36p. $1.
Aud: Hs, Cl, Pl, Sa

The annual report presented to Congress by the U.S. Commission of Civil Rights detailing executive, legislative, and judicial actions taken that relate to civil rights, plus other developments in the area of equal opportunity. Provides an overview of progress — or the lack of progress — in employment, education, housing, women's rights, the administration of justice, and political participation. SJV

SS 144
Women in (year). ISSN 0095-1536. 1965. a. illus. U.S. Citizens' Advisory Council on the Status of Women, 53306 Constitution Ave, Washington, DC 20008. Dist: Superintendent of Documents, U.S. Government Printing Office, Washington, DC 20402. Examined: 1971. Fran Henry, ed. $1.25. (1975. 142p.)
Aud: Jc, Cl, Pl

The annual report of the U.S. Citizens' Advisory Council on the Status of Women. The first section includes a summary of the accomplishments and activities of women during the year and provides information about the Equal Rights Amendments, the appointment of women to high posts in the government, recent Supreme Court decisions affecting women, equal employment opportunities, and child care, among other topics. The next section summarizes the recommendations and activities of the Council. There are assorted appendixes which list the number of women promoted to high level positions in governments, national organizations that support the ERA, and excerpts from speeches. SJV

SS 145
Women's Rights Almanac. 1974. a. bibl. illus. Elizabeth Cady Stanton Publishing Co., 5857 Marbury Rd, Bethesda, MD 20034. Dist: Harper Colophon Books, 10 E 53rd St, New York, NY 10022. Examined: 1974. Nancy Gager, ed. 620p. $5.95.
Aud: Hs, Jc, Cl, Pl

A handbook on women's "social, political, and legal status." Special features include: a state-by-state statistical and factual directory; essays on major issues of importance to women (e.g., ERA, abortion, divorce and marriage, etc.); and an overview of the International Women's Movement. Provides a variety of useful information, bibliographies, and lists of national and local organizations and other resources. Covers the areas of: "politics, government, legal rights, employment, education, abortion, rape, consumer protection, marriage and divorce, birth and health, women's organizations, child care, and a chronology of events, issues, and people." KR/JKM

SS 146
Yearbook of the European Convention on Human Rights. 1959. a. bibl. index. Martinus Nijholl, Lange Voorhout 9-11, Box 269, The Hague, Netherlands. Examined: v. 16, 1973, 516p., $65; v. 17, 1974. 704p. $82.70. (v. 18, 1975. $59.10.)
Aud: Cl, Sa

Part one of this volume contains basic texts relating to the European Commission and the European Court of Human Rights plus developments in the Council of Europe concerning human rights. Part two includes decisions of the European Commission and the European Court. Part three includes debates and decisions in various countries relating to the European Convention on Human Rights. Text is in French and English. SJV

SS 147
Yearbook on Human Rights. ISSN 0084-4098. 1946. bi-a. United Nations Publications, United Nations, LX 2300, New York, NY 10017. Examined: 1973/74. 327p. $15.
Aud: Cl, Sa

Deals with human rights as defined in the Universal Declaration of Human Rights. Part one is devoted to national developments. Forty-two states relate progress in various aspects of human rights, i.e., right to work, right of petition, right of asylum, freedom of religion, freedom of assembly, etc. Material is arranged under the subject categories presented in the Declaration. Part two covers independence and self-government movements in trust and non-self-governing territories. Part three contains information on international activities and United Nations' participation in the field of human rights. SJV

COMMUNICATIONS

SS148
AB Bookman's Yearbook. ISSN 0065-0005. 1949. a. bibl. index. illus. Antiquarian Bookman, Box 1100, Newark, NJ 07201. Examined: 1976. Jacob L. Chernovsky, ed. part 1, 183p.; part 2, 335p. $7.50.
Aud: Sa

Subtitle: "Specialist book trade annual for all bookmen, dealers, publishers, librarians and collectors." This work contains articles, annotated bibliographies, and a column, "Antiquarian Book Notes," of interest to the collector and other specialists concerned with out-of-print, antiquarian, and specialized books. The body of the work reproduces catalogs and advertisements of book dealers. Part one, "The New and the Old," contains catalogs of specialist and antiquarian reprinters, specialist book publishers, and specialist trade services. Part two, "The Old and the New," contains similar catalogs and advertisements of specialist book sellers ("Reference Directory of Specialist and Antiquarian Book Sellers"), a book trade services directory, and a dealer's list of desiderata and offerings. The services directory is arranged by subject. Additional information included are lists of definitions of interest to specialists in the field, poetry, an index of advertisers, rate lists, and ordering information. MBP

SS 149
American Book-Prices Current. ISSN 0091-9357. 1894/95. a. American Book-Prices Current, Bancroft-Parkman, 121 E 78th St, New York, NY 10021. Examined: 1976. Katherine Kyes Leab and Daniel J. Leab, eds. $65.
Aud: Pf, Sa

Essential tool for buying, selling, and evaluating books, serials, autographs, manuscripts, broadsides, and maps based on actual figures realized at auction. Arranged in two parts. Part one covers books, including broadsides, single-sheet printings, maps and charts, and uncorrected proof copy. Part two covers autographs and manuscripts, including original illustrations for printed books, documents, letters, typescripts, corrected proofs, single photographs, and signatures. Entries are alphabetical by author and include full title, publishing information, a physical description of the item, and a key to the season's sales. Indexes have been issued at five year intervals since 1916; the latest is 1970-75. KMH

SS 150
American Book Trade Directory. ISSN 0065-759X. (Continues: American Book Trade Manual; American Booktrade Directory.) 1915. a. index. R. R. Bowker, 1180 Ave of the Americas, New York, NY 10036. Dist: R. R. Bowker, Box 1807, Ann Arbor, MI 48106. Examined: 22nd ed., 1975/76, 669p.; 24th ed., 1978/79. Jaques Cattell Press, eds. 925p. $47.50.
Aud: Pf, Sa

Lists booksellers and publishers in the U.S., Great Britain, Ireland, and Canada; wholesalers in the U.S. and Canada; and foreign book dealers. Divided into six sections. Section one covers retail outlets in the U.S. arranged alphabetically by state and city. Entries include name of store, address, telephone number, manager, buyer, branch stores, type of books, and subject specialties. Another section provides information on volume of sales, percent of specialties handled, and size of operation. The second section lists wholesalers of paperbacks, hardbounds, and magazines. The third section includes lists of exporters and importers, auctioneers, export representatives, private book clubs, greeting card publishers, imprints and publishing houses that are no longer active, and foreign language book dealers. The fifth section covers the book trade in Canada, Great Britain, and Ireland. An alphabetical index to retailers and wholesalers listed in the first sections completes the volume. KMH/MBP

SS 151
American Newspaper Markets Circulation. 1961. a. index. illus. American Newspaper Markets, Box 182, Northfield, IL 60093. Examined: 16th ed., 1977/78. 932p. $35; $25 pap.
Aud: Sa

Subtitle: "Comprehensive print analysis showing circulation and penetration in every U.S. county, in every U.S. metropolitan area, in television viewing areas for every U.S. daily newspaper, every U.S. Sunday newspaper, all regional sales groups, five national supplements, 24 leading magazines." The volume is divided into five sections: 1) metropolitan area print analysis; 2) state section; 3) television viewing areas; 4) tables and rankings; 5) geographical listing of advertisers. Section one is comprised of tabulations by metropolitan area; name of publication; population; households; retail sales; morning, evening, and Sunday circulation; and sales group memberships. The state section, arranged alphabetically, lists newspapers by city, with the same information as in a county area print analysis. This section also includes a state map indicating circulation and a newspaper circulation summary. The TV viewing area section, ranking cities by number of viewers with breakdown of areas within city, contains tables ranking population, households, retail sales, and effective buying income, and a TV viewing area print analysis with similar information as that contained in sections one and two. Section four, tables and rankings, contains comparisons and tables that amplify and add to the overall picture presented in earlier sections of the book. Finally, there is a complete ranking of U.S. newspapers by total daily circulation. MBP

SS 152

Assembling. 1970. a. illus. Assembling Press, Box 1967, Brooklyn, NY 11202. Examined: 1977. Richard Kostelanetz and Henry James Korn, eds. approx. 400p. $6.95. ($4.95 ea. for earlier editions.)
Aud: Sa

Subtitle: "A collection of otherwise unpublishable manuscripts." Manuscripts are selected and printed by the invited contributors. All contributors submit 1000 copies of no more than three 8½" × 11" sheets containing whatever they wish printed at their own initiative and expense. **Assembling** agrees in return to collate and bind everything received. The initial issue had roughly 150 pages; the most recent, the Seventh Assembling (1977), had over 400 pages. In the next three years, with the National Endowment for the Arts' support, the publishers hope to issue three volumes with 600, 1000, and 1800 pages, respectively. Contributions include experimental and innovative art, poetry, fiction, etc., in many colors, textures, and formats. MBP

SS 153

Audiovisual Market Place (AVMP). ISSN 0067-0553. 1969. a. (bi-a. until 1976.) index. R. R. Bowker, 1180 Ave of the Americas, New York, NY 10036. Dist: R. R. Bowker, Box 1807, Ann Arbor, MI 48106. Examined: 1977. James S. Barnes and Olga S. Weber, eds. 438p. $23.50.
Aud: Cl, Pl, Sa

Subtitle: "A multi-media guide." A comprehensive register of organizations, firms, and personnel in the AV industry that also serves as a buyer's guide to equipment and instructional materials for the classroom and for media production. There are 25 sections arranged under three broad categories: AV Software, which covers producers and distributors, production companies, production services, public radio and television program libraries, and AV cataloging services; AV Hardware, which lists manufacturers and dealers; and Reference. Entries in the first two sections include name of the firm, address, phone, executives, materials produced or distributed, and audience served. Producers and distributors are listed alphabetically by name and by subject or type of media. Equipment manufacturers are listed alphabetically by state. The reference section includes an annotated list of reference books and directories, a classified index of reference books, a calendar of events, an annotated list of media-oriented periodicals and trade journals with ordering information, an advertising rate schedule for periodicals and journals, an annotated list of media-related associations, a list of festivals and awards with addresses, a glossary of terms, and a general index. KMH/BSM

SS154

Ayer Directory of Publications. (Continues: Ayer Directory of Newspapers, Magazines, and Trade Publications. ISSN 0067-2696; N. W. Ayer and Son's Directory of Newspapers and Periodicals.) 1880. a. index. illus. Ayer Press, W Washington Sq, Philadelphia, PA 19106. Examined: 108th ed., 1976; 110th ed., 1978. 1277p. $54.89.
Aud: Cl, Pl

Comprehensive list of newspapers and periodicals which originate in the U.S., Puerto Rico, Virgin Islands, Bermuda, the Republic of Panama, and the Philippines. Canadian publications were included in earlier volumes. Titles included are published four or more times a year. School and smaller college publications, local church publications, and most house organs are excluded. Basic organization is alphabetical by state, then by town. Entries for publications include name, printing technique, date begun, day(s) published, political orientation, rate, columns, width, depth, subscription price, and circulation. At the head of each state basic information is given about industry, agriculture, and manufacturing, as well as newspaper and periodical statistics. Information about industry and population is also provided for towns. Maps precede the geographical listings. Indexes include: publications by special interests (e.g., building materials, water supply); editors of newspapers with more than 100,000 circulation; agricultural publications by class;

foreign language publications issued in the U.S.; Jewish, fraternal, Black, college, and religious publications; magazines organized by subject (men's, sports, etc.); trade, technical, and class publications; and publications by frequency of issuance. KMH/MBP

SS 155

Best Editorial Cartoons of the Year. 1973. a. index. illus. Pelican Publishing Co., 630 Burmaster St, Gretna, LA 70053. Examined: 6th ed., 1977. Charles Brooks, ed. 160p. $9.95. $4.95 pap. (7th ed., 1978. $10.57.)
Aud: Hs, Jc, Cl, Pl

The history of the year as depicted in the work of more than 130 noted editorial cartoonists working for U.S. and Canadian newspapers and periodicals. In the 1977 edition, 25 major topics are covered including the presidential campaign, the Montreal Olympics, and the Wayne Hays scandal. JKM

SS 156

Best in Covers. ISSN 0361-2066. 1975. a. index. illus. RC Publications, 6400 Goldsboro Rd, NW, Washington, DC 20034. Dist: Watson-Guptill Publications, 1515 Broadway, New York, NY 10036. Examined: 1975. Nicholas Polites, ed. approx. 100p. $13.95.
Aud: Pl, Sa

The volume examined presents color and black-and-white photographs of magazine, book, and record covers selected by a panel of experts in various fields of communication, book publishing, magazine publishing, writing, illustration, advertising, etc. Descriptive text accompanies each reproduction. Indexes to clients, publishers, and record companies; magazines, book titles, and album titles; art directors, designers, and design firms; and illustrators and photographers precede the body of the work. MBP

SS 157

Book Auction Records. ISSN 0068-0095. 1902. a. index. Dawsons of Pall Mall, Cannon House, Folkestone, Kent, England. Dist: International Publications Service, 114 E 32nd St, New York, NY 10016. Examined: 1974/75; 1975/76. Wendy Y. Heath, ed. 421p. $55.
Aud: Pf, Sa

Subtitle: "A priced and annotated annual record of international book-auctions." Provides listings of books sold at auction during the previous year. Arrangement is by author and entries include title, description of book, when and where sold, and price. A key to sales lists all sales indexed as well as auctioneers represented. Functions not merely as a record of current sale prices, but as a guide to the features which determine the value of a book. Issued quarterly from 1902 through 1940/41, it has been published annually since. KMH

SS 158

Bookman's Price Index. ISSN 0068-0141. 1964. a. Gale Research Co., Book Tower, Detroit, MI 48226. Examined: v. 12, 1977. Daniel F. McGrath, ed. 739p. $52.
Aud: Pf, Sa

Subtitle: "Guide to the values of rare and other out-of-print books." An annual guide to the values of rare and other out-of-print books and sets of periodicals. The volume begins with a How to Use This Book section, followed by a list of dealers represented in this volume with their addresses. The arrangement is alphabetical by author within each entry. The following information is given: author's name, title, place and date of publication, description of the book, including its condition when offered by the dealer, name of dealer publishing catalog, number of catalog in which offered and item number within the catalog, date (or year of receipt) of the catalog in which the book is offered, and price at which offered. MBP

SS 160

Bowker Annual of Library and Book Trade Information. ISSN 0068-0540. (Continues: American Library Annual; American Library Annual and Book Trade Almanac; American Library and Book Trade Annual.) 1955. a. index. R. R. Bowker, 1180 Ave of the Americas, New York, NY 10036. Dist: R. R. Bowker, Box 1807, Ann Arbor, MI 48106. Examined: 21st ed., 1976, 653p.; 22nd ed., 1977. Nada Beth Glick and Sarah L. Prakken, eds. 703p. $25.70.
Aud: Pf, Sa

Annual update of the library and book trade. Includes overviews of general library developments, federal agencies, national libraries, and national associations written by the appropriate authorities (e.g., Alphonse F. Trezza on the National Commission on Libraries and Information Science; Russell Shank on the Smithsonian; Clara Jones on the American Library Association). Summaries of legislation, funding, grants, copyright, library education, and placements provide concise encapsulation of the year's developments. The chapter on library and book trade statistics includes data on library expenditures and building, Association of American Publishers, statistics, and book prices. A chapter on international library and book trade news highlights developments in various nations (Iran, Mexico, Australia in 1977; United Kingdom, Norway, Korea, People's Republic of China in 1976). The section entitled Reference and Directory Information covers literary prizes, best sellers, library associations, and book trade directories. Appendixes include a calendar of library and book trade meetings and the text of PL 94-533, the Copyright Act. Serves as an organizing tool of important information for librarians and book trade professionals. KMH/MBP

SS 161
Broadcasting Cable Sourcebook. 1972/1973. a. index. Broadcasting Publications, 1735 DeSales St, NW, Washington, DC 20036. Examined: 1978. Sol Taishoff, ed. 368p. $20.
Aud: Sa

Lists cable television systems in the U.S. and Canada alphabetically by state and then by city. The description of each system includes the address, area served, number of subscribers, charges, and affiliated TV stations. There are chapters which list program suppliers, equipment, multiple system operators, etc. There is an index and a list of abbreviations used in the beginning of the book. GV

SS 162
Broadcasting Yearbook. ISSN 0068-2713. (Continues: Broadcast Yearbook-Marketbook Issue.) 1933. a. index. illus. Broadcasting Publications, 1735 De Sales St, NW, Washington, DC 20036. Examined: 1976; 1977. Sol Taishoff, ed. various paging. $30.
Aud: Cl, Pl, Sa

"The most comprehensive directory to the business of broadcasting." Divided into six sections. The first section contains articles on the history of broadcasting media, a capsule summary of the industry, a major section on the Federal Communications Commission, directories of group ownership and newspaper/magazine cross-ownership, a tabular record of station trading, and a list of broadcast facilities by state. Section B, Television, includes an ADI (Areas of Dominant Influence) market atlas with coverage maps and market ratings, directories of TV stations with call letters and channels, and a history of TV station transfers. Section C, Radio, contains a directory of AM and FM radio stations in the U.S. and Canada and statistical tables of broadcasting interest. Section D covers broadcast advertising and includes directories of advertising agencies, station representatives, media planning services, and TV and radio codes, and a section on networks and programming with complete data on personnel and programs arranged by subject. The last two sections provide information on equipment and engineering. Section E has a list of manufacturers, a directory of consulting engineers, and a buyer's guide to equipment and services. Section F lists professional services, associations, government agencies, congressional committees, unions, and educational institutions connected with the broadcast industry. There are tables of contents for each section and a general index. MBP

SS 163
CATV Systems Directory, Map Service, and Handbook. ISSN 0091-1984. (Continues: CATV Systems Directory and Map Service. ISSN 0068-4767.) 1966. a. illus. Communications Publishing Corp., 1900 W Yale, Englewood, CO 80110. Examined: 1975/76. Robert A. Searle, ed. 150p. $8.95; $23.90 w/*CATV Buyer's Guide*.
Aud: Sa

The contents of this directory, divided into four sections, are compiled from material furnished by federal agencies and cable systems operators and from research by the editors. Section A contains CATV industry statistics, a list of the largest U.S. and Canadian systems, summary of CATV rules, official top-100 TV market list, glossary of terms, and lists of government agencies and committees, CATV associations, public interest and information and technical groups, etc. In each case where pertinent, names, addresses, phone numbers, and personnel are indicated. Section B (U.S. CATV Systems), alphabetically arranged by state, provides detailed information on individual cable television systems. Information provided includes city, name, address, and phone number of system, date began, number of subscribers, channels, rates, and plant. Canadian CATV system listings (section C) contains similar information. Section D, CATV map section, contains maps arranged alphabetically by state and shows the location of systems within each of CATV-served communities and the 35-mile radius of each TV station. MBP

SS 164
Cassell's Directory of Publishing in Great Britain, the Commonwealth, Ireland, South Africa, and Pakistan. ISSN 0069-097X. 1960/61. bi-a. index. Cassell and Co., 35 Red Lion Sq, London, C1R 4SG England. Dist: International Publications Service, 114 E 32nd

St, New York, NY 10016. Examined: 1973/74; 1976/77. Claire Sotnick, ed. 581p. $17.50.
Aud: Cl, Pl, Sa

Directory of the book trade divided into two major parts. "The Publishing and Promotion of Books" includes entries on publishers in the geographic area delineated by the title. Entries include address, subjects published, and names of staff. Bookclubs, literary prizes, and a calendar of literary and trade events are also included. Part two, "Representatives and Services," lists authors' agents, pictures and photo agencies, translators, indexers, etc. Indexes of subjects, publishers, and agents are provided. KMH

SS 165

Catholic Press Directory. ISSN 0008-8307. 1923. a. index. illus. Catholic Press Association of the U.S. and Canada, 119 N Park Ave, Rockville Centre, NY 11570. Examined: 1977. John S. Randall, ed. 120p. $8 pap.
Aud: Sa

Subtitle: "Official media reference guide to Catholic newspapers and magazines in the U.S. and Canada." This pamphlet-style publication lists information about the Catholic organizations, as well as information about the Catholic Press Association. The first section provides information about national newspapers, newspaper representatives, diocesan newspapers arranged by state, Canadian newspapers, and other diocesan newspapers. Entries list name, address, and phone number, personnel, advertising rates, mechanical requirements, subscription price, circulation figures, and some descriptive text. The magazine section is divided into three sections; the first lists Catholic magazines alphabetically, the second covers other language publications, and the third covers diocesan directories. The same information is provided here as in the newspaper section. The Catholic Press Association section lists general publisher members, service members, staff members, associate members, officers and directors, etc., with mailing information about each. An index to publications and to advertisers is included. MBP

SS 166

Children's Media Market Place. 1978. a. bibl. Gaylord Professional Publications in association with Neal-Schuman Publishers, Box 4901, Syracuse, NY 13221. Examined: 1978. Deirdre Boyle, ed. 400p. $15.95 pap.
Aud: Pl, Pf

Covers every area of children's media, delineates the market, and provides directory information for users, buyers, reviewers, producers, and distributors of children's media. Books, audiovisual materials, realia, games, television, learning programs, wholesalers, bookstores, agents, reviewing services and reviewers, events, federal agencies and programs, organizations, and selection tools are among the topics covered. Each entry includes name, address, telephone number, key personnel, etc. JKM

SS 167

Communication Yearbook. 1977. a. bibl. index. Transaction Books, New Brunswick, NJ 08903. Examined: 1977. Brent D. Ruben, ed. 656p.
Aud: Cl, Sa

Published under the auspices of the International Communication Association. Attempts to synthesize and present an overview of current publications and trends in communications. Includes solicited papers on general topics chosen by the editors; general overviews of current trends in theory and research in various fields within communications; and "competitively selected studies of outstanding current research/conference proceedings." Papers are indexed by author, topic, concept, and methodology. KR/JKM

SS 168

Directory of the College Student Press in America. ISSN 0085-0020. 1967. tri-a. index. National Council of College Publications Advisors, Indiana State University, Terre Haute, IN 47809. Dist: Oxbridge Publishing Corp., 150 E 52 St, New York, NY 10021. Examined: 3rd ed., 1976. 237p. $20.
Aud: Hs, Jc, Cl

Lists periodicals published by college students alphabetically by state and school. Information includes name of publication, name of faculty advisor, annual budget, date began, frequency, press run, number of columns, and size. College enrollment is also listed. Included in the volume are statistics on the college student press; guidelines for a free and responsible student press; a bibliography covering aspects of the press, photography, cartoons, law, magazines, etc.; lists of scholastic, high school, and journalistic press associations and societies; a list of suppliers and vendors; and indexes of college newspapers, college yearbooks, and college magazines. MBP

SS 169

Editor and Publisher International Yearbook. ISSN 0424-4923. (Continues: Editor and Publisher Year-

book.) 1920/21. a. index. Editor and Publisher, 850 Third Ave, New York, NY 10022. Examined: 1977. Robert U. Brown, ed. 515p. $25.
Aud: Sa

Indexed in: *Business Periodicals Index; Industrial Arts Index.*

Divided into six sections covering newspapers published in the U.S.; those published in Canada; those published in foreign countries; news and syndicate services, mechanical equipment; and organizations, industry services, and supplies. Newspaper listings include name, address, phone, personnel, circulation, advertising rates, and mechanical specifications. Sections one, two, and three are arranged alphabetically by geographical location. Section four is broken down to news, picture and press services, feature news and picture syndicate services, comic section groups and networks, etc. Short listings provide name, address, and personnel. The supplies and service section lists services alphabetically with names of suppliers of each. The final section lists diverse data about newspapers, TV correspondents in the U.S., newsprint statistics, films about newspapers, schools and departments of journalism, current award winners, advertising clubs in the U.S., etc. An index to the contents and one to advertisements completes the volume. MBP

SS 170

Editor and Publisher Market Guide. 1924. a. Editor and Publisher, 850 Third Ave, New York, NY 10022. Examined: 1977. Robert U. Brown, ed. 502p. $50.
Aud: Sa

Provides current data for the 1500 U.S. and Canadian markets served by daily newspapers. Includes 14 point comparable market surveys. After market rankings, the guide presents surveys of cities served by daily newspapers arranged alphabetically by state and town. Entries include estimates of population, retail sales, income, and householders for every county and city served by a daily newspaper. KMH

SS 180

Feature Films on 8mm and 16mm. ISSN 0071-4100. (1977 is 5th ed.) irreg. index. R. R. Bowker, 1180 Ave of the Americas, New York, NY 10036. Dist: R. R. Bowker, Box 1807, Ann Arbor, MI 48106. Examined: 5th ed., 1977. 422p. $21.95.
Aud: Pl, Pf

Subtitle: "A directory of feature films available for rental, sale, and lease in the United States." A guide to about 16,000 commercially produced films, documentaries, experimental films, and animations. Films included range from early silent classics through films produced in 1975. Titles listed are based upon availability, not upon place of production. Entries provide running time, director, actors, producing studio, and distributor. Includes indexes to directors and to film serials. JKM

SS 181

Gebbie Press All-in-One Directory. ISSN 0097-8175. 1972. a. index. Gebbie Press, Box 1000, New Paltz, NY 12561. Examined: 7th ed., 1978. Amalia Gebbie, ed. unpaged. $45.
Aud: Pl, Sa

Communications libraries would do well to consider purchasing this compact media directory aimed at professional public relations practitioners. The "all-in-one" in the title refers to the ten fields covered: daily newspapers, weekly newspapers, radio AM-FM stations, television stations, general (consumer) magazines, business papers, trade press, Black press, farm publications, and news syndicates. Intended as an aid to setting up public relations mailing lists in the print and broadcast fields, information listed includes current address, circulation, frequency, and intended audience. Arrangement is by category (if a publication) or by state and city (if TV or news). Individual pages are unnumbered, but publication categories (table included) and a publications name index are included, and sections are segmented by colored pages to distinguish type of media readily, i.e., green pages contain TV and radio stations. KR/JKM

SS 182

Guide to College Courses in Film and Television. 1969. bi-a. index. American Film Institute, John F. Kennedy Center for the Performing Arts, Washington, DC 20566. Dist: Acropolis Books, 2400 17th St, NW, Washington, DC 20009. Examined: 1975. Sam L. Grogg, Jr., ed. 286p. $8.95.
Aud: Jh, Hs, Jc, Cl, Pl

Covers film and television courses in 791 U.S. and foreign schools. Entries for U.S. colleges and universities are arranged by state and include detailed information on degrees offered, size of program, names of faculty, scholarships available, and a brief summary describing the intent of the program, major areas of study, course titles, teacher training courses, and facilities available. Foreign schools are listed by country. Additional sections include lists of schools by degrees offered and by majors, and a list of schools with media study courses for teachers. There is an index to schools. BSM

SS 183
Index to the Contemporary Scene. ISSN 0092-7392. 1971. a. bibl. index. Gale Research Co., Book Tower, Detroit, MI 48226. Examined: v. 1, 1971, 122p.; v. 2, 1972. David W. Brunton, ed. 120p. $14.
Aud: Cl, Pl

Subtitle: "An analytical guide to the contents of recent monographs, collections, symposia, anthologies, handbooks, guides, surveys, and other works of nonfiction dealing with topics of current interest." Includes works on currently important topics in the social sciences and popular culture, i.e., environmental crisis, women's movement, educational reform, the occult and new religions, etc. The volume begins with a list of books indexed arranged by author and including complete bibliographical data including price. Each book is assigned a code letter and number. The index section of the volume consists of an alphabetical subject list. Each subject is assigned one or more code numbers referring to the volumes on the list. Volume one covers books published in 1971, but it was not published until 1973. Volume two, published in 1975, indexes books published in 1972. MBP

SS 184
International Book Trade Directory. 1978. freq. not determined. R. R. Bowker, 1180 Ave of the Americas, New York, NY 10036. Dist: R. R. Bowker, Box 1807, Ann Arbor, MI 48106. Examined: none. (1978. approx. 512p. $35.)
Aud: Cl, Pl, Sa

This publication will be available in July 1978. The publisher's catalog entry says: "This landmark first edition concentrates on those booksellers who handle foreign publications. It provides information on some 30,000 booksellers and wholesalers in 170 countries outside North America. Organized alphabetically by country and city, each entry includes: name, address, telephone number, subject specialization, type of trade (hardback, paperback, wholesale, export, import, library supplier, second-hand, antiquarian)." JKM

SS 185
The International Directory of Little Magazines and Small Presses. ISSN 0084-9979. (Continues: Directory of Little Magazines; Directory of Little Magazines and Small Presses.) 1965/66. a. index. Dustbooks, Box 1056, Paradise, CA 95969. Examined: 12th ed., 1976/77, 349p.; 13th ed., 1977/78. Len Fulton and Ellen Ferber, eds. 440p. $11.95; $8.95 pap.
Aud: Cl, Pl, Pf

Comprehensive guide to the constantly changing world of independent publishing. Arrangement is alphabetical by press/magazine with cross references from imprints to full entries. Magazine entries include: name, name of press, editor(s), address, phone number, type of material used, additional comments by editors including recent contributors, frequency of publication, one year subscription price, single copy price, sample copy price, founding year, average number of pages, page size, production method, circulation, reporting time on manuscripts, payment rates, rights purchased and/or copyright arrangements, ad rates, discount schedules, back issue prices, number of issues published in previous year, number expected for current year, areas of interest for review materials, and membership in small magazine/press organizations. Press listings provide the same type of detailed information. Additional access is provided through three indexes: subject, regional, and distributors, jobbers, and agents. A list of organization acronyms is also included. KMH/MBP

SS 186
International Index to Film Periodicals. ISSN 0000-0388. 1972. irreg. index. International Federation of Film Archives, 38 Ave des Ternes, Paris, France. Dist: St. Martin's Press, 175 Fifth Ave, New York, NY 10010. Examined: 1973, Michael Moulds, ed.; 1976. 395p. $17.95.
Aud: Cl, Pl, Sa

The index is a project undertaken by the Documentation Commission of the International Federation of Film Archives to coordinate documentation efforts in film archives throughout the world. It begins with a section on how to use the index, a list of abbreviations, and a list of periodicals indexed, with addresses. Entries are arranged by subject, i.e., general reference material; institutions; festivals and conferences; distribution; exhibition; society and cinema; film education; aesthetics, theory, and criticism; history of the cinema; individual films; biography; and miscellaneous. Entries include name of author, title of article, periodical, volume issue, date, page numbers, a brief description of content, and type of item (i.e., article, film review, interview, etc.). All Western languages are covered. An author index and an index of subject headings complete the volume. MBP

SS 187

International Literary Market Place. ISSN 0074-6827. (Continues: European Literary Market Place 1975/76.) 1966. a. index. R. R. Bowker, 1180 Ave of the Americas, New York, NY 10036. Dist: R. R. Bowker, Box 1807, Ann Arbor, MI 48106. Examined: 11th ed., 1977/78. Peter Found, ed. 469p. $24.50.
Aud: Cl, Pl

Companion volume to **Literary Market Place**. Arranged alphabetically by country, the directory lists European publishers, major libraries, major booksellers, library associations, literary associations and societies, literary periodicals, book trade organizations, book trade reference books and journals, library reference books and journals, literary agents, and book clubs. Information provided includes name, address, telephone number, subject(s), and ISBN publisher's prefix. There is a short discussion of the copyright conventions, followed by an annotated list of international book trade, literary, and library organizations as well as an annotated list of United Nations agencies, an international bibliography, a list of international literary prizes, a book trade calendar, and a discussion of ISBN. An alphabetical index to the entire volume provides access by subject, publishers, prizes, and personal names. MBP

SS 188

International Television Almanac. ISSN 0539-0761. 1956. a. index. Quigley Publishing Co., 159 W 53rd St, New York, NY 10019. Examined: 22nd ed., 1977. Richard Gertner, ed. $16. (1978. 625p.)
Aud: Cl, Pl, Sa

The volume contains statistics and other valuable data concerning the world of television. A list of poll and award winners, an index to advertisers, and an index to subjects begin the volume. An extensive who's who section provides brief biographical data on those connected with the motion picture and television industry, including credits where applicable. The "Pictures" section lists information about feature film releases from 1955 to 1975, distributors of 16mm feature films, and credits for feature films released in 1975/76. Names, addresses, staff, and other pertinent data is provided in sections on companies in the field, producers/distributors, stations, advertising agencies/station representatives, organizations, services, talent and literary agencies, publicity representatives, programs, the press, the industry in Great Britain and Ireland, the world market, and the television code. MBP

SS 189

Jaeger and Waldmann World Telex Directory. 1952. a. Telex-Verlag Haeger and Waldmann, OHG, Postfach 160, Holzhofallee 38, 6100 Darmstadt, West Germany. Dist: International Publications Service, 114 E 32nd St, New York, NY 10016. Examined: 26th ed., 1978. 4v. $100.
Aud: Sa

This international directory of telex and teletype (TWX) numbers appears in four volumes. Volume one (Europe) and volume two (America, Asia, and Australia) comprise section A. This is an alphabetical section arranged by country and, within each country, by company name. It contains complete telex data and postal addresses of subscribers. Part B, volume three, comprises the classified trades section or yellow pages. This is an alphabetical index classified by trades (specified in English, French, and German) and arranged alphabetically by country within each classification. This section also contains a company information list (white pages) with detailed company information including names of directors and managers; products; services; products exported, imported, and traded; and languages of correspondence. Volume four, part C, is an alphabetical and numerical listing of answerback codes. MBP

SS 190

Literary Market Place. ISSN 0075-9899. 1940. a. index. R. R. Bowker, 1180 Ave of the Americas, New York, NY 10036. Dist: R. R. Bowker, Box 1807, Ann Arbor, MI 48106. Examined: 38th ed., 1978. Janice Blaufox, ed. 841p. $22.50
Aud: Cl, Pl, Sa

Subtitle: "The directory of American book publishing." The volume is arranged by the following categories: publishers; book trade, literary, advertising, and media associations; book trade events; courses, conferences, and contests; agents and agencies; services and suppliers; direct mail promotion; review, selection, and reference; radio, television, and motion pictures; wholesale export and import; book manufacturers; magazine and newspaper publishing; and names and numbers. Each broad division is subdivided. Entries in the major sections provide name, address, telephone, telex, and cable numbers, officers and personnel, foreign representatives, and description. Many entries are annotated. The names and numbers section is color-coded in yellow and lists, with address and phone number, each person or firm included elsewhere in the directory. The **International Literary Market Place** is a companion volume. MBP

SS 191

Marconi's International Register. (Continues: International Cable Address Directory.) 1898. a. index. Telegraphic Cable and Radio Registrations, 1600 Harrison Ave, Mamaroneck, NY 10543. Examined: 1977. L. G. Smith, Jr., ed. $45.
Aud: Sa

The primary objectives of this volume are to facilitate international communication and to promote trade at home and overseas. The register is divided into six sections. The first section is a comprehensive list of the principal firms of the world that have international contacts, arranged alphabetically by name, giving postal addresses, cable addresses, telex and telephone numbers, and the particulars of the business. Section two, the "International Trade Index and Buyer's Guide," lists trade headings in alphabetical order subdivided by country. Section three lists trade names, brands, and trade marks as a guide for buyers who know the brand name but not the manufacturer. Remaining sections include an English index of product headings, a legal section, and a cable address index which provides access by cable addresses to the firms listed in the first section. MBP

SS 192

Media Report to Women. Index/Directory. 1973. a. index. Media Report to Women, 3306 Ross Place, NW, Washington, DC 20008. Examined: 1976, Donna Allen, ed.; 1977. 59p. $6.
Aud: Cl, Pl

An annual cumulative index to *Media Report to Women* and a directory of women's media groups and individual women active in the media. Areas included are news services, radio-TV, video and cable groups, film, art, music, periodicals, presses, and other related media. An index to volumes one through four (1972-76) is included in the 1977 edition. KAC

SS 193

Microform Market Place. 1974. bi-a. index. Microform Review, Box 1297, Weston, CT 06880. Dist: R. R. Bowker, Box 1807, Ann Arbor, MI 48106. Examined: 1976/77. Alan M. Meckler, ed. 194p. $15.95.
Aud: Sa

Subtitle: "An international directory of micropublishing." A comprehensive directory to every micropublisher in the United States and abroad. Divided into ten sections: directory of micropublishers; reprographic centers; subject index; geographic index; mergers and acquisitions; microform jobbers; organizations involved with micrographics education; bibliography of primary sources; calendar of meetings; and a names and numbers directory. The directory of micropublishers, which is the heart of the work, lists micropublishers' names alphabetically with addresses, telephone numbers, key personnel, and major microform programs. The subject index lists publishers under headings in which they offer microforms. The names and numbers index lists individuals and firms mentioned elsewhere in the directory. The geographic index provides access to publishers by state and country. The bibliography is annotated. MBP

SS 194

The Micropublishers' Trade List Annual. ISSN 0361-2635. 1977. a. index. Microform Review, Box 1297, Weston, CT 06880. Examined: 1977. Jeanne Short, ed. approx. 12000p. on microfiche. $80.
Aud: Sa

Presents in loose-leaf format the catalogs and brochures of micropublishers throughout the world. Catalogs and brochures are printed on microfiche (4" × 6") and placed in pockets in an alphabetical arrangement by name of publisher. About 12,000 pages from hundreds of publishers are included in this edition. A printed index lists micropublishers alphabetically with number of fiche. The volume is similar to **Publishers Trade List Annual** in that it exactly reproduces catalogs and brochures of publishers indicating authors, titles, prices, and bibliographic data of all micropublications available. MBP

SS 195

Midwest Media. a. index. Midwest Newsclip, 360 N Michigan Ave, Chicago, IL 60601. Examined: 1977. Deborah Homsher, ed. 164p. $40.
Aud: Sa

The spiral-bound volume is divided into three sections, each designated by a change in paper color. The first section covers special interest, trade, religious, ethnic, and Black publications within the six-county Chicago area. Publications are listed alphabetically. Entries include name, address and phone number of the publisher; editors and columnists; circulation; deadline for submission of copy; classified and display advertising rates; and other pertinent information. Information about wire services, correspondents, national periodicals, and Chicago area magazines and newspapers is also provided. Section two provides the same type of information for downstate weekly publications and Missouri daily papers. The third section, Electronic Media, is subdivided into four parts: Radio/Chicago; TV/Chicago; Radio/Suburban, Illinois, Indiana; and TV/Illinois. In the first two parts, stations are listed alphabetically by call letters; the other two parts are arranged alphabetically by location. Each entry provides name, address, phone number, format, newscasts, area of transmission, time on air, network affiliation, wire services, managerial personnel, and special programs such as talk shows or discussion programs. The publisher also offers, for an additional fee, a newsclip service and a pressure-sensitive mailing label service covering the areas and/or publications included in the volume. MBP

SS 196

Motion Picture Market Place. 1976/77. a. Little, Brown and Co., 34 Beacon St, Boston, MA 02106. Examined: 1976/77. Tom Costner, ed. 510p. $12.95.
Aud: Cl, Sa

Surveys in directory format all aspects of the theatrical and television business in the U.S. Provides access to individuals and companies involved in production, distribution, and exhibition. Entries are arranged by subject, e.g., agents, casting agencies, dubbing, major studios, props, stunts, wardrobe, etc. KMH

SS 197

National Newspaper Association. NNA National Directory of Weekly Newspapers. 1921. a. index. illus. National Newspaper Association, 1627 K St, NW, Suite 400, Washington, DC 20006. Examined: 57th ed., 1977. approx. 330p. (1978. $25.)
Aud: Sa

The volume begins with a description of the American Newspaper Representatives Service and a directory of American newspaper representatives. This is followed by a table of weekly newspaper statistics. The body of the work is arranged alphabetically by state. Each section contains a map showing counties and population, a list of counties, and a key to contents. The listings for each state, arranged in tabular format, include city, zip code, area designation (i.e., Agriculture, Industrial, Mining, Oil, Resort, Suburban, County Seat), population, newspaper, line rate, days published, circulation, number of columns, column width, production information, policy and alcoholic beverage advertising (i.e., acceptance or non-acceptance of liquor, beer, or wine advertising), phone number, publisher's name, and county in which newspaper is published. A list of newspaper trade associations with addresses, phone numbers, and managers; a list of national advertisers and advertising agencies; and an index to states in the directory are also included. MBP

SS 198

National Radio Publicity Directory. 1972. a. index. illus. Peter Glenn Publications, 17 E 48th St, New York, NY 10017. Examined: 1974/75, 295p.; 5th ed., 1977/78. Brian J. Smith, ed. $70.
Aud: Sa

Subtitle: "Cross referenced information on network, syndicated and local talk shows from all fifty states, plus Montreal and Toronto." The volume appears in loose-leaf format. Local stations and talk shows are listed alphabetically by state. Entries include station call letters, AM or FM, watts, network affiliation, subjects covered, time slots, person to contact, and type of material sought. Separate sections cover network shows, syndicated shows, and college and education stations. There is an index by station format and by topics discussed. Listings under each topic are arranged alphabetically by state, then by call letters. A map of telephone area codes and time zones is also provided. MBP

SS 199

National Telecommunications Conference. Record. ISSN 0077-5878. (Continues: National Telemetering Conference. Proceedings.) 1972. a. Institute of Electrical and Electronics Engineers, 345 E 47th St, New York, NY 10017. Examined: 1977. 3v.
Aud: Cl, Sa
Indexed in: *Engineering Index.*

Contains papers presented at the National Telecommunications Conference on such topics as fiber optics, computer communications, microwave devices, etc. EM

SS 200

North American Film and Video Directory. ISSN 0362-7802. index. R. R. Bowker, 1180 Ave of the Americas, New York, NY 10036. Dist: R. R. Bowker, Box 1807, Ann Arbor, MI 48106. Examined: 1976. 284p. $25.
Aud: Cl, Pl, Pf

Subtitle: "A guide to media collections and services." A geographically arranged list of more than 2000 college, public, special, museum, or archival libraries with media centers that have collections of 25 or more 16mm films. Each entry provides information on staff, size and subject emphasis of collection, loan or rental policies, budget, publications, and facilities. Also provides statistics on other types of media collected. There is an index to institutions with special collections and an appendix which lists film cooperatives and circuits. JKM

SS 201
Publishers' International Directory. 1970. a. index. R. R. Bowker, 1180 Ave of the Americas, New York, NY 10036. Dist: R. R. Bowker, Box 1807, Ann Arbor, MI 48106. Examined: 7th ed., 1977. 890p. $80.
Aud: Cl, Pl, Sa, Pf

A geographically arranged list of approximately 37,000 active publishers in 145 countries in Europe, the Americas, Africa, and Oceania. Each entry includes the company name, address, telephone number, specialization, and, if available, ISBN prefix. Subject index identifies publishers geographically according to specialization. Includes a directory of book trade and library associations. Also includes the *ISBN Publishers' Index*; this index is published by Verlag Dokumentation and is distributed in the Western Hemisphere by Bowker. It is available separately for $22. JKM

SS 202
Radio Amateur's Handbook. ISSN 0079-9440. 1925. a. index. illus. American Radio Relay League, 225 Main St, Newington, CT 06111. Examined: 55th ed., 1978. Tony Dorbuck, ed. 664p. $13.50; $8.50 pap.
Aud: Sa

Consists of 25 chapters containing all the information the radio amateur needs to construct and operate all kinds of ham radios and stations, i.e., how to build sets, how to operate them, how to order equipment, etc. Some of the chapters included in the volume are "Amateur Radio," "Radio Design Technique and Methods," "Solid State Fundamentals," "VHF and UHF Receiving Techniques," "Test Equipment, Construction Practices and Data Tables," "Assembling a Station," and "Operating a Station." Many diagrams and photographs are included with the explanatory text. Also includes information on federal regulations and types of equipment; a list of abbreviations used in text and drawings; a list of abbreviations for CW work; international prefixes; and vacuum tube data tables and lists. An index completes the volume. MBP

SS 203
Series, Serials and Packages. ISSN 0082-1373. 1949. a. w/suppl. index. Broadcast Information Bureau, 30 E 42nd St, Suite 1211, New York, NY 10017. Examined: v. 18, 1977, Avra Leah Fliegelman, ed.; v. 19, 1978. approx. 234p. $144 w/suppl.
Aud: Sa

A television tape source book. Detailed information is provided for all television series including stars, storyline, number of episodes, running time, year of production, etc. Includes information previously listed in the Broadcast Information Bureau's *TV Free Film Source Book,* which is no longer published. MBP

SS 204
TV Feature Film Source Book. ISSN 0082-1357. 1949. a. Broadcast Information Bureau, 30 E 42nd St, Suite 1211, New York, NY 10017. Examined: v. 18, 1977. Avra Leah Fliegelman, ed. $159.
Aud: Sa

Lists over 21,000 feature film titles available for TV on film or tape. Gives all pertinent information about the film, i.e., actors, directors, title, time, subject, and format. The name, address, and phone number of the distributor are also provided. MBP

SS 205
TV Season (year). 1976. a. index. Oryx Press, 3930 E Camelback Rd, Phoenix, AZ 85018. Examined: 1974/75. Nina David, ed. 201p. $13.95. (1973/74; 1975/76.)
Aud: Pl

This is a list of the regularly scheduled television shows presented by ABC, CBS, NBC, and PBS. The programs are listed alphabetically; each entry includes the name, network, type of show, limited descriptive material, characters, and credits (producer, director, writer, announcer, etc.). In addition, the book includes a list of the shows cancelled during the season, summer shows, the Emmy awards, and a fifteen-page "Who's Who in TV" for the 1974-75 season. The who's who section doubles as an index to individuals listed in the main text. MBP

SS 206
Television Contacts. (1976 is 5th ed.) a. index. Larimi Communications, 151 E 50th St, New York, NY 10022. Examined: 8th ed., 1978. Michael Smith, ed. 595p. $90.

Aud: Sa

A directory of information enabling publicists or other users to contact local television stations and programs throughout the country. Arranged alphabetically by state and city, each entry includes call letters, channel number, address, and telephone number of TV station; names of station personnel, e.g., program, news, sports, women's, and film directors; complete information about news shows and whether they accept features and business news; general format of current local interview programs, and the name of the host and contact at each show; whether a program will use scripts, color slides, product samples, black and white photos, or color film; all special programs which deal with consumerism, ecology, health, energy, the aging, games, food, and travel; and audience figures. A complete listing of all television stations and one of all syndicated and network television programs are included, as is a cross-index permitting the user to locate programs and stations by call letters and cities and states. A monthly change bulletin ($10 annually) and a daily update titled *Hotline* ($20 annually) are also available. MBP

SS 207

Television Factbook. ISSN 0085-268X. (Continues: TV Directory: Television Rates and Fact Book.) 1946. a. index. illus. Television Digest, 1836 Jefferson Place, NW, Washington, DC 20036. Examined: v. 46, 1977. Dawson B. Nail, ed. 2v. (v. 47, 1978. 2v. v. 1, 1056p.; v. 2, 1072p. $85.50.)
Aud: Sa

Subtitle: "The authoritative reference for the advertising, television, and electronics industry." The first volume, "Stations," provides information on U.S. and Canadian television stations, educational television, American forces television, and group ownership of stations. An international TV directory is included. Entries are arranged alphabetically by state, city, and call letters, and include name and address of licensee, telephone and teletype numbers, ownership information, personnel, circulation statistics, and advertising rates. There are statistical tables and a map indicating the area served for each station listed. The second volume, "Services," contains a wide array of miscellaneous information covering such aspects of the television industry as equipment manufacturers, related congressional committees, consulting engineers, market rankings and research, publications in TV and related fields, CATV ownership, attorneys and public relations personnel in the industry, and television satellites. The second volume includes an index to the contents of both volumes. MBP

SS 208

United States Postal Service. Directory of Post Offices with ZIP Codes. 1955. a. Superintendent of Documents, U.S. Government Printing Office, Washington, DC 20402.
Aud: Hs, Jc, Cl, Pl

Originally loose-leaf form with quarterly updates. Now annual and updated by the weekly *Postal Bulletin*. Zip codes have been included since the 1963 edition. JKM

SS 209

United States Postal Service. ZIP Code Directory. 1965. a. Superintendent of Documents, U.S. Government Printing Office, Washington, DC 20402. Examined: 1977. 1857p.
Aud: Hs, Jc, Cl, Pl

A list of zip codes arranged by state, and by city or county, as appropriate. Includes zip code maps, postal regulations, and package wrapping and mailing instructions. JKM

SS 210

Used Book Price Guide. ISSN 0083-4807. 1972. quinquennial. Price Guide Publishers, 525 Kenmore Sta, Kenmore, WA 98028. Examined: 1972, Mildred S. Mandeville, ed., 2v., $45; 1977 suppl. $39.
Aud: Pf, Sa

Subtitle: "An aid in ascertaining prices." Contains retail prices asked by used book dealers for 74,000 titles in the basic set and 40,000 titles in the supplement. Comprises a basic reference work for the buying and selling of American and British used books from all periods and all fields. Entries are arranged alphabetically by author and include title, place of publication, date of publication, size, binding, price in dealer's catalog, and any other identifying points such as dealer's code number or condition. Includes a list of abbreviations, a list of dealer codes, a list of bibliographies and reference books found useful in the used book trade, and a few points of general information relating to the field. MBP

SS 211

Willing's Press Guide. ISSN 0000-0213. 1874. a. index. Thomas Skinner Directories, RAC House, Lansdowne Rd, Croydon CR9 2HE England. Dist: IPC Magazines, 205 E 42nd St, New York, NY 10017. Examined: 103rd ed., 1978. approx. 800p. $22.50.
Aud: Sa

Guide to the newspaper and magazine press of the

United Kingdom, and to the principal publications of Europe and the United States. Provides an alphabetical list of newspapers and periodicals published in Great Britain and Ireland, including year of establishment, when published, price, and publishers' name and address. Other publications are listed by country. A classified index provides subject access. Special features include a list of daily newspapers, Sunday newspapers, and Greater London newspapers. London addresses of provincial papers are included. There is a county and town index to newspapers. Leading publishers and their periodicals are also listed. MBP

SS 212

Working Press of the Nation. ISSN 0084-1323. 1949. a. index. National Research Bureau, 424 N Third St, Burlington, IA 52601. Examined: 28th ed., 1977. Milton A. Paule and Lillian Gaines, eds. 5v. $109.50; $40 per v.
Aud: Cl, Pl

A comprehensive roster of press, news services, feature syndicates, and house organs. Issued in five volumes. Volume one, "The Newspaper and Allied Services Directory," is devoted to the exclusive listings of newspapers, news services, newsreels, and photo services. One section lists the personnel of all editorial departments of daily newspapers and all personnel of allied services in the U.S. and Canada. Daily newspapers are listed alphabetically by title and by location in two sections; entries include address, phone, circulation, politics, and key personnel. A listing of editors and writers arranged alphabetically by subject specialty follows. Other sections cover weekly newspapers, Black newspapers, religious weeklies, foreign language newspapers, Sunday magazine newspaper supplements, daily papers which publish a weekend television supplement, news services, news picture services, and newsreel companies. Volume two, the "Magazine and Editorial Directory," is divided into seven sections. The first three sections list service, trade, professional, and industrial publications under broad subject classifications. There are separate sections of farm and agricultural publications and of consumer publications, an alphabetical list of all publications by title which includes the address and editor, and three sections which group publications by areas of interest. In the last three sections, entries indicate name, address, executives, editors, deadlines, subscription rates, editorial analyses, circulation, etc. The third volume, the "Radio and Television Directory," contains eleven sections covering radio stations in the U.S. and Canada arranged by state; principal radio stations arranged by call letters; radio directors and personnel arranged by subject (i.e., disc jockeys, sports directors, etc.); local radio programs listed by type such as children's, civic, farm, entertainment, etc.; radio stations listed by power and by location; radio and television networks and their personnel; television stations in the U.S. and Canada listed by state or province; principal television stations and their personnel arranged by call letters; TV directors and personnel by categories; local television programs in the U.S. and Canada; and public/educational television stations in the U.S. arranged geographically. The fourth volume, the "Feature Writer and Syndicate Directory," lists free-lance feature writers alphabetically by name and by subject specialties, free lance photographers, feature syndicates and their personnel, publications served by free lance writers indicating circulation and type of articles each magazine accepts and sources of photographs. The directory is designed to aid public relations personnel who need to contact free lance writers, photographers, or firms directly. Volume five, "Gebbie House Magazine Directory," provides detailed information about internal and external house organs of more than 3500 companies, clubs, government agencies, and other groups in the U.S. and Canada. Publications are listed alphabetically by sponsor with address, title, editor, year began, frequency, length, size, printing method, printer, circulation, and editorial policy. There are indexes by title of publications, by location of sponsor, by industry classification of sponsor, and by circulation. There is also an alphabetical listing of printers by city and state and a section of questions and answers about the house magazine field. Until 1976, this volume was published separately under the title *House Magazine Directory/Gebbie House Magazine Directory*. KMH/MBP

SS 213

World Radio TV Handbook. 1947. a. Billboard Publications, One Astor Place, New York, NY 10036. Examined: 31st ed., 1977. Jens Frost, ed. $10.95.
Aud: Hs, Jc, Cl, Pl

A complete directory of international radio and television designed to aid the international radio listener. The text is in English; the introductions are in French, Spanish, and German. Opens with articles relating to broadcasting. Main section contains detailed information on radio stations and broadcasting operations in every country in the world. Entries are arranged by country and include names and addresses of broadcasting companies, names and titles of leading officials, and lists of broadcasting stations in each country including frequencies, wavelengths, transmitter power, call signs (if used), and station names. Program information is also provided including times, frequencies, and beaming areas of the broadcasts in each language. A listing of the shortwave stations of the world by frequency and long and medium wave stations by continents is presented. Special features include: World Time in All Countries; Time Zone Chart of the World; maps; Sets Country by Country; and a special editorial section called "Listen to the World." KMH

SS 214
Writers and Artists Yearbook. ISSN 0084-2664. 1906. a. index. Adam and Charles Black, 4,5, and 6 Soho Sq, London W1U 6AD England. Dist: Writer Inc., 8 Arlington St, Boston, MA 02116. Examined: 70th ed., 1977. 462p. $8.95.
Aud: Pl, Sa

Subtitle: "A directory for writers, artists, playwrights, writers for film, radio and television, photographers, and composers." The British counterpart of **Writer's Market**. Provides information on markets for writers in newspapers and magazines, books, theatre, film, radio, and television. Opportunities for artists, designers, and photographers are also listed. Includes general information on copyright, libel, literary agents, indexing, societies, and clubs. KMH

SS 215
Writer's Directory. ISSN 0084-2699. 1970. bi-a. St. James Press, La Montagu News N, London W1, England. Dist: St. Martin's Press, 175 Fifth Ave, New York, NY 10010. Examined: 1976/78. A. S. Burack, ed. 1236p. $25.
Aud: Sa.

Contains a list of abbreviations, an index to authors by writing categories, and a list of writers with biographical data about each. Listings include date and place of birth, description of writing specialty, positions held, publishers, and all publications, as well as complete mailing address. An obituary section lists deceased writers alphabetically with date of death. The volume concludes with a directory of American, Australian, British, Irish, Canadian, New Zealand, South African, and Rhodesian publishers with addresses. Writers listed have produced and had published at least one full length book in English of fiction, non-fiction, poetry, or drama. MBP

SS 216
Writer's Handbook. ISSN 0084-2710. 1936. a. Writer Inc., 8 Arlington St, Boston, MA 02116. Examined: 1977. A. S. Burack, ed. 840p. $14.95. (1978. 809p.)
Aud: Cl, Pl, Sa

A practical guide for the aspiring professional writer arranged in four parts. The first three parts consist of articles of the "how to" variety on numerous aspects of writing for publication. Part four, the "Writer's Market," is a guide to some 2500 sources of publication for fiction, non-fiction, poetry, and fillers, including juvenile and other special categories. Book, magazine, radio, television, and stage possibilities are listed, but most entries are periodicals. Address, editors, editorial requirements, and amount of payment are given. There is also a list of literary agents. AC

SS 217
Writer's Market. ISSN 0084-2729. 1929. a. index. Writer's Digest, F and N Publishing Corp., 9933 Alliance Rd, Cincinnati, OH 45242. Examined: 48th ed., 1977; 49th ed., 1978. Jane Koester and Bruce Joel Hillman, eds. 894p. $13.50.
Aud: Pl, Sa

Subtitle (1978): "4,454 places to sell your books, articles, fiction, fillers, plays, gags, verse—and more!" The beginning section, "Freelance at Work," contains essays with advice to the writer on every aspect involved in preparing, mailing, and selling manuscripts, copyright, dealing with rejections, and fees. The market section of the book is arranged by broad subjects: book publishers; trade, technical and professional journals; company publications; consumer publications; farm publications; and opportunities and services. These sections are subdivided by specific subject areas, such as accounting, real estate, sports, travel, insurance, jewelry, journalism, and humor. Entries are arranged alphabetically under the specific subjects and provide name, address, editor, type of manuscripts sought, royalties and contracts offered, and a short description of the publishing firm listed. This description is supplied by the firm itself. The section on opportunities and services covers audiovisual markets, literary services, contests, awards, greeting card publishers, picture sources, play producers, syndicates, writers' clubs and conferences, etc. A subject index provides access to all sections. MBP

SS 218
Writer's Yearbook. ISSN 0084-2737. 1930. a. illus. Writer's Digest, F and W Publishing Corp., 9933 Alliance Rd, Cincinnati, OH 45242. Examined: 1976. John Brady, ed. (1977. $2 from publisher; $1.50 on newsstand.)
Aud: Pl, Sa

In magazine format, the yearbook consists of about twenty articles written by specialists in the field covering how to write, research, and sell. Some articles in the 1976 edition are: "How to Research for Specialized Markets," by Elizabeth McGough; "The Joy of Sexy Writing," by D. R. Butler; "There's Gold in Them Thar Treasure Stories," by Ben Townsend; "How to Write How-To's," by Charles Self, Jr.; "No Horsing Around: This Market Needs Writers," by Doreen Bush; "Breaking into Songwriting," by Jim Fragali; "Writing and Editing a Newsletter," by Regina Hackett; "Rod Serling's Last Interview," by Linda Brevelle; "One Man Bank: Syndicating Your Own Cartoon Strip," by James Childress; and "New Market: Community Directories," by James L. Moore. There are sections listing markets for articles, fiction, poetry, books, and cartoons. Entries include addresses, descriptions, and prices paid for items submitted. MBP

CONSUMER INTERESTS

SS 219

Consumer Complaint Guide. 1971. irreg. Macmillan Information, 866 Third Ave, New York, NY 10022. Examined: 1977. 497p. $10.95; $4.95 pap. (1979. 510p.)
Aud: Pl

A single source of information to help the consumer locate the right person or agency to help with his particular problem. Divided into three parts. The first part, "Consumer in the Marketplace," offers advice to buyers before they purchase products. Part two, "How and to Whom to Complain," provides information on locating the right agency to help with various consumer problems. The third section, "Who's Who in the Marketplace," lists companies engaged in providing consumer products and services. Listings include industry and trade organizations, state and local consumer agencies, national and international consumer organizations, and federal agencies. KMH

SS 220

Consumer Guide. a. bibl. index. illus. Consumer Guide, 3323 W Main St, Skokie, IL 60076. Examined: v. 53, 1974, Lawrence Teeman, ed., $20; 1977. 130p.
Aud: Pl, Sa

Each volume focuses on a different product or service area. The 1974 volume is subtitled "Rating the Diets"; it includes a brief overview and a separate chapter on various fad diets. Each chapter includes references to articles in medical journals to support its critique of the diet. There is an index to the volume. The 1977 volume is subtitled "Canning, Preserving, and Freezing." MBP

SS 221

Consumer Protection Guide. 1978. a. The Free Press, 200D Brown St, Riverside, NJ 08075. Examined: 1978. Joseph Rosenbloom, ed. 410p. $10.95; $4.95 pap.
Aud: Pl

Subtitle: "How to get your money's worth from the experts." A guide for the consumer to various service professions, e.g., doctors, lawyers, real estate agents, etc. Provides an overview of each profession covering type of services offered, qualifications needed to practice, complaint procedures, and relevant state licensing boards and professional associations. Some sections include information on how to select a qualified professional. Also includes a directory of private and governmental agencies that handle consumer problems. JKM

SS 222

Consumer Reports Buying Guide. (Continues: Consumers Union Reports.) 1936. a. index. Consumers Union of the U.S., 256 Washington St, Mount Vernon, NY 10550. Examined: 41st ed., 1976; 42nd ed., 1977. 416p. $3. (1978. 431p.)
Aud: Pl

A compilation of major test reports, brand and model ratings, and general consumer guidance which have appeared in the monthly issues of *Consumer Reports*. Product evaluations are presented under broad subject categories, e.g., kitchen and laundry, foods, outdoor recreation, home workshop, photography, home and personal care, automobiles, etc. Each product report indicates model number tested, name and address of manufacturer, price, size, and the Consumer Reports' rating. An alphabetical index to products concludes the volume. Originally published as the December issue of *Consumer Reports* magazine, it is also available as a separate publication. KMH/MBP

SS 223

Consumers Index to Product Evaluations and Information Sources. ISSN 0094-0534. 1973. a. w/q. suppls. bibl. index. Pierian Press, Box 1808, Ann Arbor, MI 48106. Examined: v. 2, 1974; v. 4, 1976, 263p.; v. 5, 1977. Linda Mark, ed. $39.50.
Aud: Hs, Jc, Cl, Pl, Sa

Aimed at the general consumer, the business office, and the educational-library community. Provides access to reviews and evaluations of products in 109 periodicals. The index is classified into 14 categories of consumer interest: consumerism and general information; the family, investments, finances, and employment; health and personal care; food; beverage and tobacco; clothing; the home; sports, recreation and hobbies; sight and sound; transportation; travel and vacations; office and business management; education and the library; and miscellaneous. Special features include a lengthy, annotated bibliography of books, pamphlets, and consumer aids for each of the 14 categories in the index and an annotated directory of the periodicals indexed. A product index is included. KMH

SS 224
Consumers' Research Magazine Handbook of Buying. ISSN 0069-9241. (Continues: Consumer Bulletin Annual.) 1930. a. index. illus. Consumers' Research, Washington, NJ 07882. Examined: v. 52, 1977. J. Schlink, ed. 224p. $2.95.
Aud: Pl

This buying guide is originally published as the October issue of the oldest monthly consumer product test magazine in the U.S., *Consumers Research* (m. $10/yr.). Following impartial research, CR's staff assigns descriptive annotations and ratings (recommended, intermediate, and not recommended) to hundreds of brands of products. Automobiles, stereos, household appliances, and clothing were some of the categories reviewed in the issue examined. Short articles counseling the potential consumer preface each product category, and references to earlier *Consumers' Research* articles are included after many of the reviews. The index is thorough, and the text is adequately illustrated. Overlap between this publication and the **Consumer Reports Buying Guide** is not as great as one would expect; both are useful in large and public libraries. KR/JKM

SS 225
Directory of Government Agencies Safeguarding Consumer and Environment. ISSN 0070-5586. 1968. a. Serina Press, 70 Kennedy St, Alexandria, VA 22305. Examined: 1976. Daniel Sprecher, ed. 135p. $9.95.
Aud: Pl

Intended to help consumers contact federal and state agencies for complaints, advice, or information. Name, address, and phone number of the agencies are given. Arranged in 19 categories, including air pollution, automobile safety, consumer protection, food and drugs, insurance, noise abatement, pesticides, radiation, water pollution, weights and measures, etc. SJV

SS 226
Encyclopedia Buying Guide. ISSN 0361-1094. 1963. bi-a. bibl. index. R. R. Bowker Co., 1180 Ave of the Americas, New York, NY 10036. Dist: R. R. Bowker Co., Box 1807, Ann Arbor, MI 48106. Examined: 1975/76. Kenneth L. Kister, ed. 282p. $16.50.
Aud: Hs, Jc, Cl, Pl, Pf

Subtitle: "A consumer guide to general encyclopedias in print." A buying guide which evaluates 36 nonspecialized encyclopedias on the American market. Categories include adults, children, very young readers, and handy reference. The guide is divided into three parts: the general information section gives the purpose, history and limitations of encyclopedias, industry sales practices, consumer protection information, advice on comparison shopping, and how to evaluate individual sets. The second section, "Encyclopedias at a Glance," is a chart providing statistical data. The final section includes encyclopedia profiles of individual sets which detail strong and weak points, exceptional features, and best potential audience. Appendixes include information on discontinued encyclopedias, almanacs, and yearbooks, a bibliography of articles about encyclopedias, a directory of consumer protection agencies, and a directory of publishers and distributors. A title and subject index is included. This biennial publication is a successor to *General Encyclopedias in Print* (1962); the second edition is scheduled for publication in June 1978. KMH

SS 227
Food Co-op Directory. 1973. irreg. Food Co-op Directory, 106 Girard SE, Albuquerque, NM 87106. Examined: 6th ed, 1977. Wild R. Turkey, ed. 58p. $3; $1.50 to individuals and non-profit groups.
Aud: Pl

Provides key information about more than 2300 food co-ops in the U.S. and Canada, including buying clubs, cooperative stores, warehouses, bakeries, restaurants, etc. Divided into four basic sections: federations, warehouses, and regional contacts; newsletters; listings of co-ops; and unclassifieds. Listings in section one provide name, address, phone number, and a code indicating whether listee is a federation, warehouse, or a regional contact. Section two lists names and mailing addresses of newsletters printed by food co-ops. Section three is arranged alphabetically by state or province. Listings appear in zip code order. Codes indicating what kind of co-op the listing covers are included. Section four includes advertisements of publications and products of interest to those interested in food co-ops. MBP

CRIMINOLOGY AND LAW ENFORCEMENT

SS 228

American Correctional Association. Annual Congress of Corrections. Proceedings. (Continues: American Prison Association. Proceedings.) 1870. a. American Correctional Association, 4321 Hartwick Rd, Suite L208, College Park, MD 20740. Examined: 1975. 303p. $14. (1976.)
Aud: Sa

The Annual Congress of Corrections provides a forum for examining correctional problems and issues. Besides normal convention business, the proceedings include the general session addresses and the sectional meeting papers. The latter are taken from panel discussions on all aspects of correctional practice including chaplaincy, citizen participation, volunteers, classification, jails, legal issues, juvenile offenders, probation, parole, research, and treatment. SJV

SS 229

Annual Editions: Readings in Criminal Justice. 1976. a. bibl. index. illus. Dushkin Publishing Group, Sluice Dock, Guilford, CT 06437. Examined: 1978/79. Donal E. J. MacNamara, ed. 256p. $5.95.
Aud: Hs, Jc, Cl, Pl

Contains reprints of newspaper, magazine, and journal articles in the field of criminal justice published during the preceding year. Articles are selected by an editorial board and arranged under broad topical categories. Many include photographs, charts, and suggestions for further reading. The collection is designed for use in high school and college classrooms, but it is also useful as an overview of current events, trends, and techniques in the area of criminology and justice for the general reader. JKM

SS 230

Collected Studies in Criminological Reseaarch. ISSN 0079-5300. 1967. a. Council of Europe, Publications Section, Strasbourg, France. Dist: Manhattan Publishing Co., 225 Lafayette St, New York, NY 10012. Examined: v. 14, 1976. 72p. (v. 15, 1977. $10.)
Aud: Sa

Each volume is devoted to a particular subject in the field of European crime problems (crime statistics, evaluation and planning, narcotics, etc.). The issue contains a number of essays by experts in the field that analyze aspects of the particular subject. Some papers have notes and references appended at the end. Some volumes contain reports presented to the Criminological Colloquium, others include papers read before the Conference of Directors of Criminological Research Institutes. SJV

SS 231

Crime and Justice. 1972. a. bibl. AMS Press, 56 E 13th St, New York, NY 10003. Examined: 1971/72. Jackwell Susman, ed. 491p. $15. (1977.)
Aud: Cl

An anthology of current essays dealing with controversial aspects in the field of crime and justice. Highly technical articles have been omitted, as were readings that were mainly methodological. Articles are reprinted from such magazines as *Criminology, Washington Law Review, NYU Law Review, American Sociologist, Journal of Marriage and the Family, Fortune,* and *Issues in Criminology.* Articles are divided into sections, e.g., social values affecting crime, community influences and effects on crime, etc. Most articles have either bibliographies or extensive footnotes. SJV

SS 232

Criminal Justice Periodical Index. 1975. a. w/2 suppls. index. University Microfilms International, 300 N Zeeb Rd, Ann Arbor, MI 48106. Examined: 1976. Carolyn A. Dyer, ed. approx. 350p. $65.
Aud: Jc, Cl, Sa

An author and subject index to over 80 periodicals in the field of criminal justice. Coverage is broad: criminology, criminal justice, law enforcement, and social issues, such as drug abuse and other social problems, are included. Book reviews, film reviews, and court cases are indexed. The index is easy to use and up to date, but very specialized. University Microfilms offers an article copy service to complement the index. SJV

SS 233

Directory: Juvenile and Adult Correctional Departments, Institutions, and Agencies and Paroling Authorities of the United States and Canada. ISSN 0070-5373. (Continues: Directory of Correctional Institutions and Agencies of the United States of America.) 1955. a. American Correctional Association, 4321 Hartwick Rd, Suite L208, College Park, MD 20740. Examined: 1978. 284p. $11.
Aud: Sa

A comprehensive directory listing juvenile and adult correctional institutions in the U.S. and Canada. A statement concerning the organization and administration of corrections is provided for each state. Members of state boards of corrections, parole boards, and youth service departments are listed. Information for each institution includes address, telephone number, administrator, year opened, normal capacity, average population, type of inmate, and age limits. Following the main directory are lists of federal penitentiaries, state planning agencies, military facilities, and correctional service agencies. Next is a section on Canadian federal institutions, national parole board organizations, and provincial institutions. There is a map of parole board organization in the U.S. and its territories and a list of parent agencies responsible for administering U.S. correctional services. A statistical summary gives fiscal resources, personnel, and juvenile and adult prison population by state. Title varies slightly for various editions. Great Britain was included in earlier editions. KSK/SJV

SS 234
International Association of Chiefs of Police. The Police Yearbook. (Continues: International Association of Chiefs of Police. Proceedings.) 1894. a. International Association of Chiefs of Police, 11 Firstfield Rd, Gaithersburg, MD 20760. Examined: 1974, 228p.; 1977. R. B. Argrisani and B. L. Rathbun, eds. 411p. $5.
Aud: Sa

Contains the papers and proceedings of the annual conference including workshop papers, international seminars, annual awards, committee reports, etc. A section on education and training covers current trends in police training, physical fitness training programs, a criminal justice education accreditation update, and other relevant material. Workshops and international seminars focus on such topics as female police, police/labor relations, citizen groups to combat crime, narcotics traffic, and terrorism. The appendix lists current officers of the International Association of Chiefs of Police (IACP), headquarters staff, conference cities, past presidents, and constitutions and rules. SJV

SS 235
International Review of Criminal Policy. ISSN 0074-7688. 1952. a. bibl. United Nations, Department of Economic and Social Affairs, New York, NY. Dist: United Nations Publications, LX 2300, New York, NY 10017. Examined: no. 31, 1974; no. 32, 1976; no. 33, 1977. 97p. $7.
aud: Cl, Sa

Frequency varies: issued semi-annually from 1952-1957 and in 1959, 1961, and 1962; published annually in 1958, 1960, 1963-72; issued biennially from 1972-1976.

Each volume contains substantial articles on a particular aspect of criminal policy, prevention of crime, and treatment of offenders. The scope is international, and the authors are experts in their areas. The second section contains reports of the activities of international organizations concerned with criminal policy. The volume concludes with summary reports of United Nations meetings and committees in the area of crime and social policy. Earlier editions had greater bibliographic emphasis. The text is in English, French, and Spanish. SJV

SS 236
International Yearbooks of Drug Addiction and Society. 1973. a. bibl. index. Sage Publications, 275 S Beverly Dr, Beverly Hills, CA 90212. Examined: v. 3, 1975. Luiz R. Simmons, ed. 325p. $17.50.
Aud: Cl, Sa

Each annual volume focuses on a particular aspect of drug addiction and the many ways in which it affects society. Volume one is entitled "Discrimination and the Addict"; volume two is "Drugs, Politics, and Diplomacy: The International Connection"; and volume three is entitled "Communication Research and Drug Education." The target audience for each volume varies. Volume three is directed toward professional educators and media producers with articles written by educators and practitioners. Each article includes a bibliography, and there is a selected bibliography at the end of the volume. SJV

SS 237
Law Enforcement and Criminal Justice Education Directory. (Continues: Law Enforcement Education Directory.) 1972/73. irreg. illus. International Association of Chiefs of Police, Professional Standards Division, 11 Firstfield Rd, Gaithersburg, MD 20760. Examined: 1975/76. Richard W. Kobetz, ed. 759p. $9.75. (1977.)
Aud: Hs, Jc, Cl, Pl

Unique directory for the student preparing for a career in criminal justice. Information is collected by questionnaire and arranged in four sections. Section one gives tabular data on degrees and enrollment. Section two lists schools by state with addresses and degrees offered. Section three lists colleges with coordinator, courses offered (undergraduate and graduate), degrees offered, number of students, faculty, and graduates. Section four gives information on financial assistance. SJV

SS 238

Law Enforcement Desk Reference and Police Official's Diary. 1976. a. Law Enforcement Desk Reference, Box 7333, Trenton, NJ 08628. Examined: 1978. I. B. Zeichner, ed. 320p. $16.50.
Aud: Sa

A combination quick-reference encyclopedia and daily and monthly planner and diary. Includes pertinent federal and state laws with addresses of federal and state agencies. There is an emergency section with procedures for handling firearms, chemical spills, poisoning, first aid, emergency care, etc. Glossaries of drug slang, CB slang, and law, motor vehicle, policy wagering, and pornographic terms are included. There is also a statistics section and other special sections. SJV

SS 239

National Directory of Law Enforcement Administrators: Prosecution, Correctional, and Judicial Agencies. ISSN 0547-6224. 1962. a. National Police Chiefs and Sheriffs Information Bureau, 828 N Broadway, Milwaukee, WI 53202. Examined: v. 11, 1975. M. E. Wyrick, ed. 187p. (1977. $19.85.)
Aud: Sa

All listings are verified or validated by direct contact through first-class mail, personal visits, or long distance telephone calls. The first listing, county law enforcement, is arranged by state, and provides the name of the county, the county seat, and the names of county sheriffs and prosecutors. The next section lists, by state and municipality, the names of municipal chiefs of police. Briefer sections on state criminal investigation units and motor vehicle division authorities follow. Next is a state-by-state listing of state police and highway patrols, followed by a listing of federal agencies (FBI, U.S. Customs Service, Drug Enforcement Administration, U.S. Marshals' Offices, U.S. Secret Service field offices, U.S. attorneys of the Department of Justice, and the Treasury Department's Bureau of Alcohol, Tobacco and Firearms). There are lists of state and federal correctional institutions and a directory of U.S. courts. The back cover shows the color and expiration dates of automobile license plates for that year. KSK

SS 240

National Institute of Law Enforcement and Criminal Justice. Annual Report. 1974. a. bibl. Law Enforcement Assistance Administration, U.S. Department of Justice, Washington, DC 20531. Dist: Superintendent of Documents, U.S. Government Printing Office, Washington, DC 20402. Examined: 1975. 79p. $1.90.
Aud: Cl, Sa

The National Institute of Law Enforcement and Criminal Justice is the research arm of the Law Enforcement Assistance Administration. Its report provides a description of various research programs in the areas of citizen participation in criminal justice, police, courts, legal services, punishment, and corrections. There is a list of awards with a summary of the winning projects. A bibliography of the Institute's publications is appended. SJV

SS 241

National Institute of Municipal Law Officers. NIMLO Municipal Law Review. (Continues: Municipalities and the Law in Action.) 1936. a. National Institute of Municipal Law Officers, 839 17th St, NW, Washington, DC 20006. Examined: v. 37A, 1974. Charles S. Rhyne, ed. $11. (1977.)
Aud: Sa

A record of municipal legal experiences within a certain year. It reviews the activities of the National Institute of Municipal Law Officers and its various committees. The committees reporting cover airports, annexation, municipal bonds, building codes and fire prevention ordinance, city-state relations, civil liberties, computers and municipal law, condemnation, contracts, sewage disposal, federal-city relations, public housing, labor relations, local government personnel, public utility problems, taxes, traffic and parking, urban renewal, water problems, and zoning and planning. Most of these committee reports were given at the annual conference of NIMLO. A number of the reports contain footnote references. Following these committee reports, which take up the bulk of the volume, are staff papers on selected subjects in the field of municipal law. KSK

SS 242

New York State Division of Criminal Justice Services. Comprehensive Crime Control Plan. 1969. a. illus. State of New York, Division of Criminal Justice Services, Office of Planning and Program Assistance, 80 Centre St, New York, NY 10007. Examined: 1977. 372p. free.
Aud: Sa

Each state which seeks funding under the Crime Control Act of 1973 and the Juvenile Justice and Delinquency Prevention Act of 1974 must submit an annual plan to the Law Enforcement Assistance Administration. They have various titles, i.e., *Crime Control Plan* (New York) and *Criminal Justice Plan* (New Jersey). The guidelines from LEAA emphasize a multi-year plan which includes crime analysis, system description, problem identification, and multi-year forecasting of expenditures and accomplishments. The New York plan is in eight sections: Planning Process; Policies and Principles; Crimes and Arrests in New York State; Criminal Justice System in New York State; Juvenile Justice System in New York State; Problems and Needs Statewide; Standards and Objectives for Programs; and The Annual Action Program with Fund Allocation Information. A good source of local and statewide crime statistics and a summary of ongoing research in criminal justice. SJV

SS 243
Police and Law Enforcement. 1972. a. index. AMS Press, 56 E 13th St, New York, NY 10003. Examined: v. 2, 1973/74. James T. Curran, Austin Fowler, and Richard H. Ward, eds. 392p. $15. (1977.)
Aud: Cl, Sa

"A collection of contemporary materials which focus on the crucial issues and controversies in American law enforcement. . .published for students of criminal justice, for law enforcement administrators and practitioners, and for concerned citizens as a catalyst for inquiry and analysis." The essays included have appeared either in professional police magazines or in general periodicals such as *New York* and *The American Scholar*. The anthology is arranged into five sections: the police — socio-political perspectives; crime and the community: offenders, victims, and the law enforcement role; police work—studies in practitioner behavior, attitude, role, and role perception; police management and professional ethics; and law enforcement and the future—trends and predictions. Within each section are a number of essays which explore aspects of the particular topic. Some papers have footnotes or illustrative tables. There is a subject index appended. KSK

SS 244
Police Yearbook. ISSN 0079-2950. 1961. a. Davis Publishing Co., 250 Potrero St, Santa Cruz, CA 95060. Examined: 1972. J. Robert Lansberry, ed. 245p. $6. (1977.)
Aud: Sa

Contains 1000 questions taken from police promotional examinations given in major U.S. cities during a particular year. The book is divided into ten sections with 100 multiple-choice type questions presented in each section. The areas covered are: supervision/administration/management (in two sections); public and community relations; training; budgets; reading comprehension; reports, charts, graphs, and ratings; electronic data processing and reports; riots, revolts, patrol, traffic, and juveniles; investigation/criminalistics/fingerprints; vice; law/evidence and corrections; and drugs and general knowledge. Answer keys, in yellow paper, are at the end of each section. KSK

SS 245
Probation and Parole. ISSN 0079-5615. 1969. a. Probation and Parole Officers Association, Box 408, Madison Square Sta, New York, NY 10010. Examined: v. 6, 1974. Philip Snowden Dobbs, ed. 56p. (v. 9, 1978. $4.50.)
Aud: Cl, Sa
Indexed in: *Abstracts on Criminology and Penology.*

The professional journal of the New York State Probation and Parole Officers Association. Its goal is "to increase and improve communication between probation and parole staff on all levels in the state. . .All disciplines related to correction and rehabilitation are encompassed, with particular attention given to articles relating to conditions in New York State." Articles are on such topics as prison sentencing, the Black probation officer, and youth counseling. The articles often contain tables, statistics, and footnotes. KSK

SS 246
U.S. Department of Justice. Annual Report of the Attorney General of the United States. ISSN 0082-9943. 1870. a. illus. U.S. Department of Justice, Constitution and 10th St, NW, Washington, DC 20530. Dist: Superintendent of Documents, U.S. Government Printing Office, Washington, DC 20402. Examined: 1976. 240p. $1.75.
Aud: Cl, Pl, Sa

Summarizes activities of the previous year for each office within the Department of Justice. Chapter summaries provide a description of the Office and its major programs. Includes the Offices of U.S. Attorneys, Solicitor General, Legal Counsel, Professional Responsibility, Legislative Affairs, Policy and Planning, Special Prosecutor, Management and Finance, Antitrust, Criminal, Civil, Civil Rights, Land and Natural Resources, Tax, F.B.I., LEAA, Bureau of Prisons, Immigration and Naturalization, Drug Enforcement, Community Relations, U.S. Marshals, U.S. Parole Commission, and the Pardon Attorney. SJV

SS 247
U.S. Federal Bureau of Investigation. Annual Report. 1918/19. a. illus. U.S. Federal Bureau of Investigation, 9th St and Pennsylvania Ave, NW, Washington, DC 20535. Examined: 1976. 27p.

Aud: Hs, Jc, Cl, Pl

A review of the FBI's activities covering investigative operations (organized crime, bank robberies, fugitives, kidnaping, extortion, police killings, skyjacking, etc.), national security matters (domestic terrorism, bombings), and other Bureau activities. Information is presented in a summary narrative. KSK

SS 248

U.S. Federal Bureau of Investigation. Uniform Crime Reports for the United States. (Cover title: Crime in the U.S.) ISSN 0082-7592. 1930. a. w/q. suppls. illus. Federal Bureau of Investigation, Washington, DC 20535. Dist: Superintendent of Documents, U.S. Government Printing Office, Washington, DC 20402. Examined: 1975. 297p. $1.50.
Aud: Jc, Cl, Pl

Provides a nationwide view of crime based on police statistics contributed by local law enforcement agencies. The first section is a narrative summary of the crime totals for the particular year. The rest of the volume consists of tabular information on crime and criminals, persons arrested, and law enforcement employees. Crime statistics are presented by state and city in the following categories: homicide, rape, robbery, aggravated assault, burglary, larceny, and motor vehicle theft. The figures on law enforcement employees include the number of assaults on officers and employment statistics. This section also includes a narrative summary on law enforcement officers. KSK

SS 249

U.S. Federal Bureau of Prisons. Annual Report. 1930. a. illus. U.S. Federal Bureau of Prisons, 101 Indiana Ave, NW, Washington, DC 20357. Examined: 1973. 25p. free.
Aud: Jc, Cl, Pl

The early history of the Federal Bureau of Prisons is outlined briefly, then the events of the year are reported. All aspects of federal prisons (staff training, vocational education, treatment programs, offenders, rights, new facilities construction, and future plans) are covered. A map of the federal correction system and a list of locations of institutions and community treatment centers are provided at the end of the volume. Illustrated throughout with photographs. KSK

SS 250

U.S. Federal Bureau of Prisons. Statistical Report. ISSN 0565-0380. (Continues: National Prisoner Statistics Bulletin.) 1949. a. illus. U.S. Federal Bureau of Prisons, Data Base Management, 320 First St, NW, Washington, DC 20534. Examined: 1974/75. Donald L. Miller, ed. 121p. free.
Aud: Jc, Cl, Pl

A record of the number and characteristics of those individuals who have been committed by federal courts to the custody of the U.S. Attorney General. Trend tables, volume summaries, and distributions of offender characteristics comprise this report. Trend tables provide comparative statistics for the last ten years on size, movement, average time served, and average sentence length of federal offenders. Summaries of the year's admissions and discharges, and comparisons of prison statistics over a four-year fiscal period are included. There are tables showing prison population, admissions, and discharges at the end of the fiscal year, plus figures on escapes and apprehensions. The volume includes a glossary of sentence procedures; a list of Bureau of Prisons, institutions, and community centers; and a map of the federal correctional system. Issued 1926-1946 by the Bureau of the Census under the title: *Prisoners in State and Federal Prisons and Reformatories.* KSK

SS 251

U.S. Law Enforcement Assistance Administration. Annual Report. ISSN 0565-6567. 1968/69. a. illus. Law Enforcement Assistance Administration, U.S. Department of Justice, Washington, DC 20531. Dist: Superintendent of Documents, U.S. Government Printing Office, Washington, DC 20402. Examined: 8th ed., 1976. 107p. $2.50.
Aud: Cl, Pl

As a major funding agency for state and local criminal justice systems, the Law Enforcement Assistance Administration assists in strengthening and improving their programs. Projects funded cover every aspect of criminal justice including police, courts, corrections, victim assistance, white collar crime, organized crime, and elimination of corruption. The Annual Report covers the organization and budget of LEAA. An overview of the components of the agency emphasizing their major activities is also provided. A statistical appendix shows comparative funding patterns. There is a list of regional offices. SJV

SS 252

U.S. Law Enforcement Assistance Administration. Expenditure and Employment Data for the Criminal Justice System. 1965. a. illus. U.S. Department of Justice, Law Enforcement Assistance Administration, Washington, DC 20402. Dist: Superintendent of Documents, U.S. Government Printing Office, Wash-

ington, DC 20402. Examined: 1976. 387p. $4.40.
Aud: Cl, Sa

Includes expenditure and employment data for federal, state, and local government criminal justice activities. Tables show the summary amounts for the criminal justice system. There are six sections covering police protection, judicial, legal services and prosecution, public defense, corrections, and other criminal justice activities. SJV

SS 253
U.S. National Criminal Justice Information and Statistics Service. Capital Punishment. (Continues: U.S. Bureau of Prisons. National Prisoner Statistics: Executions.) 1971/72. a. illus. U.S. National Criminal Justice Information and Statistics Service, 633 Indiana Ave, NW, Washington, DC 20530. Dist: Superintendent of Documents, U.S. Government Printing Office, Washington, DC 20402. Examined: 1976. 61p. $1.20.
Aud: Cl, Sa

Provides information on the number of persons on death row at the beginning and end of the year and differentiates the population by age, sex, race, marital status, level of education, legal status at the time of arrest, offense for which sentenced, and length of time on death row. Information is collected by a mail canvas of correctional authorities. The report is part of the National Prisoner Statistics Program. Information has been collected since 1962 and published in various series. Includes a narrative summary, charts, and tables. SJV

SS 254
U.S. National Criminal Justice Information and Statistics Service. Criminal Victimization in the United States: A Comparison of (year) and (year) Findings. 1973. a. illus. U.S. National Criminal Justice Information and Statistics Service, 633 Indiana Ave, NW, Washington, DC 20530. Dist: Superintendent of Documents, U.S. Government Printing Office, Washington, DC 20402. Examined: 1975/1976. 133p. $1.25.
Aud: Cl, Sa

Supplements the basic report *Criminal Victimization in the United States, 1973.* Presents crime statistics and findings of the victimization surveys of the National Crime Survey Program. The 1975/76 **Findings** were not published until 1978. The report is based on a national survey of households and businesses assigned to assess the extent and type of criminal victimization. It focuses on certain types of offenses: for individuals, rape, robbery, assault, and personal larceny; for households, burglary, household larceny, and motor vehicle theft; and for commercial establishments, burglary and robbery. It attempts to measure changes in victimization rates and to assess the impact of crime on society. SJV

SS 255
U.S. National Criminal Justice Information and Statistics Service. Prisoners in State and Federal Institutions. ISSN 0082-917X. 1971/73. a. U.S. National Criminal Justice Information and Statistics Service, 633 Indiana Ave, NW, Washington, DC 20530. Dist: Superintendent of Documents, U.S. Government Printing Office, Washington, DC 20402. Examined: 1975. 46p. $1.20; single copy free.
Aud: Cl, Sa

Provides information on the number and movement of state and federal prisoners, and measures the year-end prison population. The narrative summary concentrates on distribution of population, female prisoners, new court commitments, recidivists, and releases. The information has been collected in various formats since 1926. The present series dates back to 1971 and is part of the National Prisoner Statistics program. SJV

SS 256
U.S. National Criminal Justice Information and Statistics Service. Sourcebook of Criminal Justice Statistics. 1973. a. index. U.S. National Criminal Justice Information and Statistics Service, 633 Indiana Ave, NW, Washington, DC 20530. Dist: Superintendent of Documents, U.S. Government Printing Office, Washington, DC 20402. Examined: 1976. Michael J. Hindelang, ed. 865p. $11.
Aud: Hs, Jc, Cl, Pl

A compilation of statistics from a variety of government and private agencies focusing on state and local data with a nationwide scope. The material is divided into six major sections: "Characteristics of the Criminal Justice System" provides data on criminal justice agencies, expenditures, workload, and personnel; "Public Attitudes Toward Crime and Criminal Justice Related Topics" gives results of opinion polls on death penalties, victimization, gun control, drug use, etc.; "Nature and Distribution of Known Offenses" provides data on the extent of illegal activity; "Characteristics and Distribution of Persons Arrested" counts arrestees by age, sex, race, and area; "Judicial Processing of Defendants" gives information on the number of juveniles and adults processed through the system; and "Persons Under Correctional Supervision" provides information on persons on probation and parole, and population of federal, state, and local institutions. Each section includes a brief narrative introduction and full bibliographic information. This publication could serve to replace many specialized sources in smaller libraries. SJV

SS 257

U.S. National Criminal Justice Information and Statistics Service. Trends in Expenditure and Employment Data for the Criminal Justice System. 1971/73. a. illus. National Criminal Justice Information and Statistics Service, U.S. Law Enforcement and Assistance Administration, Washington, DC 20531. Dist: Superintendent of Documents, U.S. Government Printing Office, Washington, DC 20402. Examined: 1971/75. 132p. $2.30.
Aud: Cl, Sa

Summarizes data on public expenditure and employment for criminal justice activities at the federal, state, and local level. Statistics are abstracted from the Law Enforcement and Assistance Administration's annual report **Expenditure and Employment Data for the Criminal Justice System.** Police, judicial activities, legal services, public defense, corrections, and other activities are covered. The introduction provides a summary of findings and trends. SJV

ETHNIC INTERESTS

SS 258

Akademiska Dzive. ISSN 0516-3145. 1958. a. bibl. illus. Akademiska Dzive, One Vincent Ave S, Minneapolis, MN 55405. Examined: v. 19, 1977. Magdalene Rozentale, Gunta Rosentale, and Elizens Skurupijs, eds. $4.
Aud: Cl, Sa

A vehicle for relatively short papers on all aspects of Latviana (e.g., philosophy, literature, history), together with book reviews and reports on Latvian intellectual life and education in America, Australia, and elsewhere. Illustrated with historic photographs and portraits, as well as contemporary graphics. Published entirely in Latvian, with English language abstracts. SB

SS 259

American Irish Historical Society. The Recorder. ISSN 0034-1665. 1901. a. illus. American Irish Historical Society, 991 Fifth Ave, New York, NY 10028. Examined: v. 36, 1975, 165p.; v. 37, 1976. Gavin Murphy, ed. free to members.
Aud: Hs, Jc, Cl, Pl

Contains short essays, memoirs, biographical profiles, and poetry on topics both Irish and Irish-American. Contributors range from journalists and historians to politicians and business executives. SB

SS 260

American-Italian Historical Association. Proceedings of the Annual Conference. 1968. a. bibl. American Italian Historical Association, 209 Flagg Place, Staten Island, NY 10304. Examined: 8th ed., 1975. 177p. $5.
Aud: Cl, Sa

Papers, together with subsequent comment and discussion, on specific conference themes: "Ethnicity in American Political Life: The Italian American Experience" (1968, O.P.); "The Italian American Novel" (1969, $1.50); "An Inquiry into Organized Crime" (1970, $2.50); "Power and Class: The Italian-American Experience Today" (1971, $2.50); "Italian American 'Radicalism': Old World Origins and New World Developments" (1972, $2.50); "The Religious Experience of Italian Americans" (1973, $4.00); "The Interaction of Italians and Jews in America" (1974, $4.00); and "The Urban Experience of Italian Americans" (1975). Proceedings are published somewhat late; the 1975 proceedings were published in 1977. SB

SS 261

The American Sephardi. 1966. a. bibl. illus. Sephardic Program, Yeshiva University, 186th St and Amsterdam Ave, New York, NY 10033. Examined: v. 7 and 8, 1975. Herman P. Salomon, ed. 176p. $5.
Aud: Sa

Subtitle: "Journal of the Sephardic Studies Program of Yeshiva University." Contains articles, poetry, news items, and book reviews on Sephardic heritage. Articles are in English and Spanish; most of them are illustrated and include biographical references. Book reviews cover both books and journal articles. Includes a special section for Sephardic activities. LL

SS 262

Black Review. ISSN 0067-9119. 1971. a. illus. William Morrow and Co., 105 Madison Ave, New York, NY 10016. Examined: no. 2, 1972. Mel Watkins, ed. (1976. 158p.)
Aud: Hs, Cl, Pl

A collection of essays, short stories, and poems covering all areas of the Black experience—politics, arts, literature, history. Most are written by Black artists. The issue examined contains 13 essays and poetry selections varying from three to 30 pages in length. Black-and-white drawings by Ellsworth Attoby are interspersed throughout. JKM

SS 263
Ethnic Studies Bibliography. 1976. a. index. University of Pittsburgh, University Center for International Studies, G-6 Mervis Hall, Pittsburgh, PA 15260. Examined: 1978. $30.
Aud: Cl, Sa

An index to periodical literature on ethnic studies. Approximately 120 periodicals are indexed for ethnic studies material. The author, subject, geographic area, proper name (e.g., names of laws or organizations), and journal name indexes precede the citations. Each citation includes author, title, periodical citation, an abstract, an indication of the inclusion of statistical tables, etc., names of persons cited, and name and topical subject descriptors. JKM

SS 264
Finnish Americana. 1978. a. bibl. illus. Finnish Americana, 2208 Third St, NW, New Brighton, MN 55112. Examined: v. 1, 1978. Michael G. Karni, ed. 120p. $4.
Aud: Hs, Jc, Cl, Pl

Subtitle: "A journal of Finnish American history and culture." Contains essays, fiction, poetry, edited letters and documents, criticism, and book reviews dealing with "all aspects of the history and culture of the Finns in North America." The first issue includes two short stories, nine reviews, and six articles (e.g., "The Feminist Dilemma in the Finnish Immigrant Community"; "Finnish Place Names as a Form of Ethnic Expression in the Middle West"; and "The America Letters: Immigrant Accounts of Life Overseas."). Illustrations range from maps and photographs to manuscript facsimiles. SB

SS 265
Gratz College Annual of Jewish Studies. 1972. a. bibl. index. illus. Gratz College, Tenth St and Tabor Rd, Philadelphia, PA 19141. Examined: v. 5, 1976. Isidore Davis Passow and Samuel Tobias Lachs, eds. $5.
Aud: Cl, Sa

Academic and bibliographic studies on Judaism and Jewish education, culture, and history, emphasizing the Jewish-American experience. Among the most recent contributions are: "Beginnings of Jewish Education in America"; "Synagogue Music in the Early American Republic"; "The Influence of the Bund on the Jewish Socialist Movement in America"; "A Contribution to American-Jewish Bibliography"; "The Development of Jewish Camping in the United States"; and "Attitudes Toward Women's Role: Does a 'Jewish Subculture' Exist in America?" SB

SS 266
Harvard University Seminar in Ukrainian Studies. Minutes. ISSN 0362-8078. 1970/71. a. bibl. Committee on Ukrainian Studies, Harvard Ukrainian Research Institute, 1581-1583 Massachusetts Ave, Cambridge, MA 02138. Examined: no. 6, 1975/76. Uliana Pasicznyk, ed. $3; $5 to libraries and institutions.
Aud: Cl, Sa

Contains one- to six-page summaries of the 30 or more papers presented during the academic year, together with ensuing discussions. A selected bibliography concludes each report. Themes for recent sessions ranged from Czarist censorship and "the Ukrainian obsession in Gogol's life and work" to the legal basis for recognizing Ukrainian statehood from 1917 to 1920 and "the strength of Ukrainian as compared with other Slavic languages." SB

SS 267
Hebrew Union College Annual. ISSN 0360-9049. 1924. a. bibl. illus. Hebrew Union College Annual, 3101 Clifton Ave, Cincinnati, OH 45220. Examined: v. 46, 1975. Sheldon H. Blank, ed. 532p. $15.
Aud: Cl, Sa

Contains scholarly essays—variously written in English, Hebrew, German, and French—covering "the total range of Hebraica and Judaica." An alphabetical index of authors for volumes 1-45 appears as an appendix to volume 46. In 1976, HUCA inaugurated a series of *Hebrew Union College Annual Supplements* with publication of Yosef Hayim Yerushalmi's *Lisbon Massacre of 1506 and the Royal Image in the Shebet Yehucah,* a 91-page monograph ($7.50 from Ktav, 75 Varick St, New York, NY 10015). SB

SS 268
Herzl Year Book. 1959. a. bibl. illus. Herzl Press, Theodor Herzl Institute, 515 Park Ave, New York, NY 10022. Examined: v. 4, 1961/62. Raphael Patai, ed. 396p.
Aud: Pl

Subtitle: "Essays on Zionist history and thought." Sponsored by the Theodor Herzl Institute which conducts research and educational activities on Zionist history and thought. Features lengthy scholarly articles, 20-50 pages, which include biographical references. A list of contributors is provided. There are no news articles and no index. LL

SS 269
Index to Literature on the American Indian. 1970. irreg. bibl. Indian Historical Press, 1451 Masonic Ave, San Francisco, CA 94117. Examined: 1973. J. Henry, ed. $12.
Aud: Jh, Hs, Jc, Cl, Pl

An index to more than 700 popular and scholarly journals and books. It is compiled by Native American scholars and published by the American Indian Historical Society. Arranged by subject and within subject by author. Full bibliographic information is given for each entry. Includes an extensive bibliography of periodicals published by Native American organizations and peoples. JKM

SS 270
Jewish National Fund. Yearbook. a. Jewish National Fund, Youth and Education Department, 42 E 69th St, New York, NY 10021. Examined: 1977. Leon L. Wolfe, ed. approx. 40p. $1; free to schools.
Aud: Pl

Includes articles, essays, and reports dealing with many aspects of Israel, Zionism, and American Jewish life. Articles are arranged under broad subject categories. The 1977 volume celebrates "The Tenth Anniversary of Jerusalem Reunited" and includes articles under such subject headings as: America and Israel; Israel and the Bicentennial; My Friend Jimmy Carter; Zionism: Looking Ahead; Israeli Women: Golda Meir; Women in the Air Force; Women in the Police; Builders of Eretz Israel in JNF Stamps; and Personalities. An obituaries section is also included. MBP

SS 271
Journal of Croatian Studies. ISSN 0075-4218. 1960. a. bibl. Croatian Academy of America, Box 1767, Grand Central Sta, New York, NY 10017. Examined: v. 14/15, 1973/74; v. 16, 1975. Jerome Jareb and Karlo Mirth, eds. $12.
Aud: Cl, Sa

Subtitle: "Annual review of the Croatian Academy of America." Primarily contains essays and research on Croatian and Croatian-American history, economics, politics, sociology, and literature. Also includes extensive book reviews, reports on Croatian Academy meetings, obituaries, and occasional literary works, usually in both Croatian and English. SB

SS 272
Journal of Mexican American History. ISSN 0047-2581. 1970. a. bibl. index. Journal of Mexican American History, Box 13861, University of California at Santa Barbara, Santa Barbara, CA 93107. Examined: v. 4, 1974. Joseph P. Navarro, ed. $15. (v. 7, 1977.)
Aud: Cl, Sa
Indexed in: *America: History and Life; Humanities Index.*

The purpose of the **Journal** is "to do something about the scholarly neglect of the history of Mexicans in the United States." Features substantive essays, often based on primary sources; reprinted historical documents, and critical reviews. Articles in volume four include: "Mexican Americans on St. Paul's Lower West Side"; "Health and the Mexican Americans in Los Angeles, 1850-1861"; "Mexican American Labor before World War II"; "Latin Images in American Films, 1929-1939"; and "Anglo-American Attitudes towards the Hispanos, 1846-1861." Volumes one to three consisted of two issues each. SB

SS 273
Norwegian-American Studies. ISSN 0078-1983. 1926. irreg. bibl. illus. Norwegian-American Historical Association, St. Olaf College, Northfield, MN 55057. Examined: v. 27, 1977. Kenneth O. Bjork, ed. 323p. $7.50.
Aud: Cl, Sa

An amalgam of Norwegian-Americana, including scholarly essays, annotated bibliographies, memoirs, short plays, historical documents (e.g., letters, official reports, diaries), and occasional graphics. Recent volumes have featured "Notes of a Civil War Soldier," "Factors in Assimilation: A Comparative Study," "From Norwegian State Church to American Free Church," "Berdahl Family History and Rolvaag's Immigrant Trilogy," "Polygamy among the Norwegian Mormons," Rodney Nelson's one-act "Popcorn Man," and data on recently cataloged archival material. Volumes 2, 3, 7, 12, and 13 are out of print; other volumes are available for $5. SB

SS 274
The State of Black America. 1976. a. National Urban League, The Equal Opportunity Bldg, 500 E 62nd St, New York, NY 10021. Examined: 1978. 204p. $5.
Aud: Hs, Jc, Cl, Pl

The first issue of this publication outlined the status of Black Americans in our Bicentennial year. The 1978 edition is a review of the changes, or of the absence of change, in the status of Black Americans from 1966 to 1976. It consists of essays, with bibliographic footnotes, by scholars on the economy, the economic status of Black families and children, education, housing, social welfare, and politics. Included are conclusions drawn from the essays and recommendations for policy changes by the National Urban League. Also includes statistical tables. JKM

SS 275
Ukrainian Academy of Arts and Sciences in the United States. Annals. 1951. irreg. bibl. illus. The Academy, 206 W 100 St, New York, NY 10025. Examined: v. 13, no. 35/36, 1973/77. I. S. Koropeckyj, ed. 372p. $15.
Aud: Sa

Scholarly essays and extensive bibliographies covering many aspects of both the historical and the contemporary Ukraine. Some issues center on a specific theme, e.g., economics, history, linguistics. All issues typically conclude with a "chronicle" of Academy-sponsored activities and signed obituaries. SB

SS 276
U.S. Bureau of Indian Affairs. American Indian Calendar. a. U.S. Bureau of Indian Affairs, Washington, DC 20233. Dist: Superintendent of Documents, U.S. Government Printing Office, Washington, DC 20402. Examined: 1974; 1976. 40p. $.80.
Aud: Jh, Hs, Jc, Cl, Pl

A guide to established ceremonial occasions, dances, feasts, and other celebrations held on or near American Indian reservations. Arranged by state and, within state, chronologically by the date of the event. JKM

SS 277
YIVO Bleter. ISSN 0084-4217. 1931. bi-a. bibl. YIVO Institute for Jewish Research, 1048 Fifth Ave, New York, NY 10028. Examined: v. 45, 1975. Joshua A. Fishman, ed. 162p. $6.
Aud: Cl, Sa

Printed wholly in Yiddish, with English language abstracts. Volumes are composed of academic essays, archival documents, and reviews, now mainly devoted to single themes or topics, e.g., volume 43 on "Jews in England" and volume 45 on "Jews in Central and Eastern Europe in the 18th and 19th Centuries." Volumes 31-43 are available at $5 each; volume 44 is $6. SB

SS 278
Zapisy. New Series. (Continues: Zapisy. Old Series.) 1962. a. bibl. illus. Byelorussian Institute of Arts and Sciences, 3441 Tibbet Ave, Bronx, NY 10463. Examined: v. 16, 1975. Vitaut Tumash, ed. $8.
Aud: Cl, Sa

Consists of articles, memoirs, notes, documents, book reviews, and conference reports concerning Byelorussian history, culture, and "emigre" life, all printed in Cyrillic with English language summaries of major essays. Recommended for public libraries that serve a Russian-speaking population. SB

FOLKLORE

SS 279
Calendar of Festivals. (Continues: Calendar of Folk Festivals and Related Events.) 1971. a. bibl. illlus. The National Council for the Traditional Arts, 1346 Connecticut Ave, NW, Suite 1118, Washington DC 20036. Examined: 1977. Nancy Dolliver, ed. $3.25.
Aud: Hs, Jc, Cl, Pl

A directory of folk celebrations in the U.S., with some entries for Canada. Emphasis is on non-commercial events, although others are included if the editors consider them important. The entries are arranged by state and then chronologically within each state. Information for each event includes the name of the festival, the exact location, the name and address of the contact person, sponsors, and a brief description of the main features of the festival. If there is an admission charge, it is given. Most entries also indicate whether the festival takes place indoors or outdoors, if there are camping facilities, and if food is available. There are many entries for community-based traditional folk gatherings and for celebrations of Native American peoples. Festivals of music, dance, crafts, and folk celebrations are included. BCS

SS 280
Folklore Annual. ISSN 0071-6782. 1969. a. bibl. Center for Intercultural Studies in Folklore and Oral History, University of Texas at Austin, S. W. B. 306, Austin, TX 78712. Examined: no. 6, 1974. John H. McDowell, ed. 81p. free.
Aud: Sa

A collection of graduate student publications in folklore. The articles in the issue examined covered a variety of topics, from material on the Black community in Austin to the Quechua-speaking community in Bolivia. The journal reflects the interests of the University of Texas program. It is not limited to peasant, minority, or so-called primitive groups, but includes any setting where people communicate face-to-face. The approach to folklore here emphasizes a close examination of text. BCS

SS 281
Good Old Days Christmas Annual. 1966. a. illus.

Tower Press, Box 426, Seabrook, NH 03874. Examined: 1976. Edward J. Kutlowski, ed. 85p. $1.25.
Aud: Pl

Contains stories, cartoons, drawings, photographs, and poems providing a nostalgic view of what Christmas was like in the "good old days." There are comic strips relating to Christmas in the 1930's and 1940's, and advertising for holiday wares and supplies from the 1920's. The stories are predominantly anecdotes about a memorable Christmas in the life of the writer. There are sketches of Christmas customs in other countries. Many of the photographs are of the family-album type. BCS

SS 282
Northeast Folklore. ISSN 0078-1681. 1958. a. bibl. illus. The Northeast Folklore Society, South Stevens Hall, University of Maine, Orono, ME 04473. Examined: v. 17, 1976. Edward D. Ives, ed. 134p. $4.
Aud: Cl, Pl
Indexed in: *Abstracts of Folklore Studies.*

Contains the songs, legends, tales, and traditions of New England and the Atlantic provinces of Canada. Text is in English and occasionally in French. Each issue is devoted to a specific aspect of regional folklore or to a comparative study. There is an emphasis on oral history with recorded interviews of people involved with the topic under consideration. Issues have included: "Suthin': An Oral History of a Woods Operation at Little Musquash Lake, Maine, 1946"; "Cree Tales and Beliefs"; "Me and Fannie: The Oral Autobiography of Ralph Thornton"; "Jones Tracy: Tall Tale Teller from Mount Desert Island"; and "Twenty One Folksongs from Prince Edward Island." There are many photographs and illustrations. Out-of-print back issues are available from the Johnson Reprint Co. Membership in the Society is $3 and provides the subscriber with **Northeast Folklore** and the Society's *Newsletter.*

GENEALOGY AND HERALDRY

SS 283
Daughters of the American Colonists Lineage Book. 1929. a. index. National Society Daughters of the American Colonists, 2205 Massachusetts Ave, NW, Washington, DC 20008. Examined: v. 18, 1974; v. 19, 1975. Josephine W. Vincent, ed. 460p.
Aud: Pl

A simple listing giving the woman's name, the names of colonists from whom she is descended, and the order of descent. There is a brief informational note about the colonist in order to identify him/her. Contains an index to the Society's members and an ancestors index. Out-of-print volumes are available on microfilm from Bell and Howell (1700 Shaw Ave, Cleveland, OH 44112). BCS

SS 284
Genealogical Periodical Annual Index. 1962. a. index. The Yankee Bookman, 3602 Maureen Lane, Bowie, MD 20715. Examined: v. 14, 1975. Laird C. Towle, ed. 62p. $9.50. (1978.)
Aud: Pl

A surname, locality, topical, and book review index to genealogical periodical literature. Heraldry is also included. The list of periodicals cited contains 117 genealogical periodicals, with an additional 39 family association publications entries. The introduction gives detailed instructions on how to use the index, outlines the scope of coverage, and describes how to obtain material indexed. BCS

SS 285
Hereditary Register of the United States of America. 1972. a. index. illus. Hereditary Register Publications, 444 Camelback Rd, Phoenix, AZ 85012. Examined: 1973; 1976. John Griffin Richardson Rountree, ed. 876p. $32.50.
Aud: Pl

Contains information on American hereditary societies, including their membership requirements, objectives, programs, history, and publications. Also lists present and past officers. Part two lists family associations, with names, addresses, and publications. Part three, the "Hereditary List," is a listing of officers and prominent members of the societies with biographical data. There is an alphabetical listing of society names in the index. BCS

SS 286
Roll of Arms. 1928. irreg. illus. New England Historic Genealogical Society, 101 Newbury St, Boston, MA 02116. Examined: 1972, part 8. 31p. $12.50.
Aud: Pl

Parts one and two were reprinted from the *New England Historical Genealogical Register.* Provides names of American families having registered arms, with descriptions and line drawings. Arranged by registration number. There is also an alphabetical list of the surnames included in each part. The introduction to part eight give information on the propriety and impropriety of the use of heraldic ornaments, and states that the Committee registers only arms which have been "rightfully borne in this country." BCS

GOVERNMENT AND PUBLIC ADMINISTRATION

SS 287

American Public Works Association. APWA Directory. (Continues: APWA Yearbook.) 1969/70. a. index. American Public Works Association, 1313 E 60th St, Chicago, IL 60637. Examined: 1976/77. 575p. $20.
Aud: Sa

Contains lists of members with addresses, arranged alphabetically and geographically (by state or province, and city). Members include government officials concerned with public works, sewage disposal, sanitation, highways, and health services; equipment manufacturers; officials of public utility companies; and engineering and public administration. The **Directory** also includes lists of association officers, chapter officers, committee members, and APWA staff members. EM/JKM

SS 288

Annual Editions: Readings in American Government. ISSN 0090-547X. 1971. a. index. illus. Dushkin Publishing Group, Sluice Dock, Guilford, CT 06437. Examined: 1978/79. Bruce Stinebrickner, ed. 320p. $6.55.
Aud: Hs, Jc, Cl, Pl

Contains facsimile reproductions of articles published in newspapers, magazines, and journals designed for use in high school and college courses in American government. Articles are arranged in broad topical sections, each of which is prefaced by a summary/overview. The table of contents directs the reader to specific topics within each section, and the index provides further reader assistance. Also useful as an introduction to American government and current issues in government for the general reader. JKM

SS 289

The Book of the States. 1935. bi-a. index. illus. The Council of State Governments, Iron Works Pike, Lexington, KY 40511. Examined: v. 21, 1976/77 Paul Albright, ed. 673p. $21. (v: 22, 1978/79. 654p. $21.)
Aud: Cl, Pl

Attempts to provide authoritative information on the structure, working methods, financing, and functioning of state governments. Covers the legislative, executive, and judicial branches. Major state services (education, transportation, human services, public protection, housing and development, natural resources, and labor relations) are also surveyed. Intergovernmental relations (interstate, federal-state, and state-local) are outlined. Emphasis is on activities during the two years between editions. Individual state entries give nickname, motto, flower, bird, tree, song, stone, date entered the Union, the state capital, selected officials, supreme court, legislature, and selected statistics. Two supplements appear in the years between publication of the biennial volumes: *State Elective Officials and the Legislatures* and *State Administrative Officials Classified by Function*. SJV

SS 290

Braddock's Federal-State-Local Government Directory. 1976. a. index. Braddock Publications, 1028 Connecticut Ave, NW, Washington, DC 20036. Examined: 1976. 249p. $3.95. (1977/78.)
Aud: Hs, Jc, Cl, Pl

A privately published, easy-to-use directory of information on government at all levels, with emphasis on the federal government. It gives the address and phone number for officials in the White House, executive departments, independent agencies/commissions, regulatory agencies, U.S. Senate, U.S. House of Representatives, congressional caucuses, selected congressional commissions, courts, specialized sources for statistical information, and the communications media. For each state, the governor, lieutenant governor, secretary of state, attorney general, and officers of the legislature are listed. There is a list of state and local government publications. Includes such handy information as area codes, time zones, and forms of address. Good one-volume reference source. SJV

SS 291

Clements' Encyclopedia of World Governments. 1974. bi-a. illus Political Research, 5th fl, Continental Bldg, Dallas, TX 75201. Examined: 1976. John Clements, ed. 362p. $85.
Aud: Hs, Jc, Cl, Pl

Basically a survey of the governments of independent nations. Articles are arranged alphabetically and follow a standard format. For each country there is a reproduction of the flag; photograph of the government head; description of the government (with charts); historical highlights; basic statistics; and officials. Information is primarily provided by the governments of the respective countries. Includes a brief section on international organizations; a glossary; time dials; addresses of foreign embassies in the U.S.; and geographical charts for the continents. SJV

SS 292
Congressional Directory. 1857. a. index. illus. U.S. Congress, Joint Committee on Printing, Rm S151, U.S. Capitol, Washington, DC 20510. Dist: Superintendent of Documents, U.S. Government Printing Office, Washington, DC 20402. Examined: 95th Congress, 1st Session, 1977. Lawrence F. Kennedy, ed. 1126p. $8.50.
Aud: Jc, Cl, Sa

The most complete directory of federal government officials and others related to the function of government. A biographical section covering senators and representatives is followed by listings of state delegations, terms of services, committees and committee staffs (names and addresses), and committee assignments of senators and representatives. There is a directory of administrative or legislative assistants and secretaries and a statistical section on the Congress. The section on the Capitol includes floor plans and a history of the building and grounds. Executive departments are outlined, including each agency and its personnel. Lists each international organization in which the U.S. has representation, foreign diplomatic representatives and consular offices in the U.S., and U.S. diplomatic and consular offices abroad. The last section deals with the press (print, radio, and television) on Capitol Hill. Beginning in 1978, there will be a paperback supplement instead of a new **Directory,** omitting most non-congressional information and material that does not change significantly in a year. SJV

SS 293
Congressional Information Service. CIS/Annual. 1970. a. bibl. index. Congressional Information Service, Montgomery Bldg, Washington, DC 20014. Examined: 1978. 2v. $260.
Aud: Jc, Cl, Pl, Sa

Cumulates the monthly issues of *CIS/Index*; can be purchased separately as a two-volume set or included with an annual subscription to the *Index* ($270-$690 depending on library budget). The first volume contains abstracts of congressional documents, including committee hearings and prints; House and Senate reports, documents, and special publications; and Executive reports and documents. Each abstract includes full bibliographic information, SuDocs number for ordering the document from the Government Printing Office, the entry number in the *Monthly Catalog,* and the CIS number for retrieval of the document from the *CIS Microfiche Library.* The second volume is a cumulative index of subjects and names. It also includes five supplementary indexes to bill, report, and document numbers, and to names of Committee and Subcommittee Chairmen. A five-year cumulative index for 1970-1974 is available ($385; $265 w/subscription to other CIS publications). JKM

SS 294
Congressional Staff Directory. 1959. a. index. Congressional Staff Directory, Box 62, Mt. Vernon, VA 22121. Examined: 1977. Charles B. Brownson, ed. 840p. $19.50.
Aud: Cl, Pl

Concentrates on the staffs of the members of Congress. Listings cover state delegations, staffs of each senator and of senate committees, staffs of joint committees, staffs of each representative and each house committee, key personnel of executive departments and agencies plus biographies of congressional staff. Includes difficult-to-locate information, such as room locations, telephone numbers, and job titles of key staff members. Cities and towns over 1500 population are listed with congressional district and current representative.

SS 295
Council of State Governments. Suggested State Legislation. 1941. a. index. The Council of State Governments, Iron Works Pike, Lexington, KY 40511. Examined: v. 35, 1976, 185p., $6.50; v. 37, 1978. 224p. $7.50.
Aud: Sa

Contains proposals approved by the Committee on Suggested State Legislation of the Council of State Governments. These suggested measures are cast in the form of bill drafts which, along with the accompanying explanatory statements, are for the use of state officials, members of legislative bodies, and legislative staff agencies. The volume is distributed to governors, legislators, and other state officials. "The suggested draft legislation constitutes no more than suggestions with respect to the problems posed. It should, therefore, be introduced only after careful consideration of local conditions." Sources of the proposed acts are states, the federal government, and legislative service agencies. A cumulative index of measures published in previous volumes of **Suggested State Legislation,** covering the period 1941-1973, is available from the Council. Supplements covering the 1974-76 volumes appear at the back of the 1976 volume. The 1978 edition includes drafts of the following legislation: Business Takeover Act, Hearing Aid Dealers Regulation, Life Care and Payments Contracts Act, Private Security Licensing and Regulatory Act, and Sexual Assault Act. KSK/SJV

SS 296
Countries of the World and Their Leaders. (Continues Countries of the World.) 1974. irreg. bibl. index. illus. Gale Research Co., Book Tower, Detroit, MI 48226. Examined: 4th ed., 1978. 1154p. $24.
Aud: Hs, Jc, Cl, Pl

Subtitle: "The U.S. Department of State's report on the status of the world's nations..." Contains profiles of 168 nations and territories based on the Department of State's "Background Notes on Countries of the World." Each profile covers population and demographic statistics, history, government, political conditions, economy, foreign relations, relations with the U.S., principal government officials, and members of the U.S. Diplomatic Mission; and includes a brief, current bibliography. Profiles often include maps and other illustrations. The volume also contains: the State Department's "Status of the World's Nations" which provides a brief statistical survey of each nation and a checklist of nations which have gained independence since 1943; the CIA's "Chiefs of State and Cabinet Members of Foreign Governments"; and the State Department's "International Alliances" which covers the United Nations, NATO, the European Communities, Organization of African Unity, etc. KR/JKM

SS 297
County and City Data Book. 1949. quinquennial. index. illus. U.S. Bureau of the Census, Washington, DC 20233. Dist: Superintendent of Documents, U.S. Government Printing Office, Washington, DC 20402. Examined: 1977. 1011p. $19.50.
Aud: Jc, Cl, Pl

A convenient one-volume compilation of government statistics selected from recent censuses and surveys of government and private agencies. All sources used are indicated. Includes statistics on land area, population, vital statistics, labor force, school enrollment, social security, bank deposits, housing, local government finances and employment, elections, crime, wholesale and retail trade, selected services, mineral industries, agriculture, etc. Data are provided for census regions, divisions, states, Standard Consolidated Statistical Areas, Standard Metropolitical Statistical Areas, and cities of 25,000 population. SJV

SS 298
The County Year Book. ISSN 0099-1015. 1975. a. bibl. index. illus. National Association of Counties, 1735 New York Ave, NW, Washington, DC 20036. Examined: 1977. 300p. $21.
Aud: Cl, Pl

Compiled by the National Association of Counties and the International City Management Association. Data is derived from questionnaires sent to county officials. The majority of the information is presented in tabular form. Part A covers administrative and legislative trends. Part B covers finances and employment. Part C treats services provided by counties. Part D describes the various administrative arrangements including increased use of computers and collective bargaining arrangements. The directory section contains names of county officials, and professional associations and organizations serving county governments. An excellent section on references lists basic sources of information on all phases of county administration. Companion volume to **The Municipal Year Book**. SJV

SS 300
Dod's Parliamentary Companion. ISSN 0070-7007. 1832. a. index. Sell's Publications, Sell's House, 39 East St, Epsom, Surrey, England. Examined: 1978. 893p. £7.
Aud: Sa

A compact biographical directory to the Royal Family, peers, and members of the House of Commons. Precedence, forms of address, parliamentary terms, and various ministries and public offices are also given. Election results are provided for each constituency for the last general election. SJV

SS 301
Federal Election Commission. Annual Report. 1975. a. index. illus. Federal Election Commission, 1325 K St, NW, Washington, DC 20463. Examined: 1976. Ann Lang Irvine, ed. 142p.
Aud: Cl, Sa

The Federal Election Commission (FEC) has the enforcement jurisdiction for the Federal Election Campaign Act covering disclosure campaign limitations and public financing. Its **Annual Report** highlights events of the year affecting this jurisdiction and discusses compliance and enforcement. Recommendations for changes in the act are also presented. Appendixes give a chronology of events, amendments to the Act, proposed regulations and amendments, selected FEC opinions, an index to opinions, and FEC Federal Register notices. SJV

SS 302
Federal Employees Almanac. ISSN 0071-4127. 1954. a. illus. Federal Employees News Digest, Box 457, Merrifield, VA 22116. Examined: 1976; 1977. Joseph Young, ed. $1.85.
Aud: Sa

An indispensable volume for Federal employees that would also be of interest to those considering entering federal employment. Provides information pertaining to federal benefits, working conditions, take-home pay tables, retirement, health insurance, injury compensation benefits, social security, grievance procedures, promotion, etc. Volume is updated every year to provide the most current information. SJV

SS 303
Index to Current Urban Documents. 1972/73. a. w/q. suppls. index. Greenwood Press, Westport, CT 06880. Examined: v. 5, 1976/77. Mary Kalb, ed. 379p. $145 w/3 q. suppls.
Aud: Cl, Sa

Indexes local government documents, state documents that deal with a city or county, and federal documents pertaining to Washington, D.C. Arrangement is alphabetical by place name then by city department or agency, country department, regional organization, state department, and quasi-public organization. A subject index follows. Bibliographic data include author (agency), title, year, and whether the document contains an appendix, bibliography, or charts. Most documents listed are available on microfiche through the *Urban Documents Microfiche Collection*. SJV

SS 304
Moody's Municipal and Government Manual. ISSN 0545-0233. (Continues: Moody's Manual of Investments: American and Foreign Government Securities.) 1955. a. index. illus. Moody's Investors Service, 99 Church St, New York, NY 10007. Examined: 1977. Robert Hanson, ed. 2v. 4560p. $365.
Aud: Sa

A reference service listing issuers of municipal or government bonds including federal agencies, states, counties, cities, school districts, and foreign governments. The annual volume summarizes activities of issuing agency, with a description of bonded debt, financial statistics, valuations, taxes, and Moody's bond rating. The "Special Features Section" includes tables and charts on municipals and general economic statistics. A loose-leaf service, *Moody's Municipals and Governments,* published twice weekly, keeps the publication current. SJV

SS 305
The Municipal Year Book. 1934. a. bibl. index. illus. International City Management Association, 1140 Connecticut Ave, NW, Washington, DC 20036. Examined: v. 44, 1977. 388p. $27.50. (v. 45, 1978. 428p.)
Aud: Cl, Pl

Subtitle: "The authoritative source book of urban data and developments." An indispensible source of information on all facets of urban management. Data are collected from questionnaires sent to all cities with populations over 2,500. Content and emphasis vary from year to year. Regular features include profiles of individual cities; employment, salaries, and expenditures of police, fire, and refuse collection and disposal departments; city payrolls; and information sources for major areas of local government administration. Special features in the 1977 edition include analyses of municipal elections; personnel practices in police service; productivity improvements; and annexation and corporate changes. A section on Canada gives information on economic policy and salaries of officials, police, and fire fighters. The directory section is a guide to organizations and people involved in local government management. Names, addresses, and services offered by national organizations to municipalities are listed. Companion volume to **The County Year Book**. SJV

SS 306
National Association of Regional Councils. Directory. 1969. a. National Association of Regional Councils, 1700 K St, NW, Washington, DC 20006. Examined: 9th ed., 1977. 44p.
Aud: Sa

A directory of regional councils or agencies which have multijurisdictional local government representation on their governing bodies, multipurpose or multifunctional programs, legal status which allows them to receive funds, and full-time staffing. There are 669 such councils listed in the 1977 directory. Entries are arranged by state and include name, address, telephone number, and key personnel. SJV

SS 307
The National Directory of State Agencies. 1974. bi-a. Information Resources Press, 2100 M St, NW, Washington, DC 20037. Examined: 2nd ed., 1976/77. Nancy D. Wright and Gene P. Allen, eds. 646p. $51.60.
Aud: Cl, Pl

Divided into two major parts: an alphabetical list of state agencies by state and then by agency, with the name of official in charge and address; and a list of state agencies by function and by state. The appendix lists associations of state government officials and state government information numbers and addresses. KMH

SS 308
Profiles of State Planning Associations in the United States. 1964. quadrennial. American Society of Planning Officials, 1313 E 60th St, Chicago, IL 60637. Examined: 2nd ed., 1966. 56 leaves (loose-leaf format). $2. (5th ed., 1974. 55 leaves.)
Aud: Sa

Issued bienially from 1968-1970.

A list of state planning associations arranged alphabetically by state. Entries are based on survey responses from the organizations themselves, and include the following information: when founded; purpose; membership; any local divisions; governing body (officers, board of directors); committees; paid staff; headquarters; financial support; number of meetings it holds (regular, special, board of directors); publications; special activities (e.g., legislation, assistance to new planning agencies, public education, inquiry answering, library of basic planning materials, cooperation with other groups, etc.); and current address. KSK

SS 309
Public Papers of the Presidents of the United States. ISSN 0079-7626. 1957. a. index. illus. Office of the Federal Register, National Archives and Records Service, General Services Administration, Washington, DC 20408. Dist: Superintendent of Documents, U.S. Government Printing Office, Washington, DC 20402. Examined: 1974. 2v. v 1, 713p., $12.50; v. 2, 841p., $16. (1975. v. 1, 1004p.)
Aud: Cl, Pl

In 1957 the Office of the Federal Register decided to publish annual volumes containing the public messages and statements of the U.S. presidents. The series covers presidents since Harry S. Truman; three volumes for Herbert Hoover (1929-1931) have been published. Text includes White House press releases, materials issued by the White House press office, and news conferences. Arrangement is chronological. A list of White House releases not included in the volume; a complete list of all proclamations, executive orders, and similar documents; and a list of reports of the President to Congress are included in the appendixes. SJV

SS 310
State Information and Federal Region Book. 1973. bi-a. illus. Potomac Books, Box 40604, Washington, DC 20016. Examined: 1977. Susan Lukowski and Cary T. Grayson, Jr., eds. 306p. $14.50.

A directory of basic facts about each state covering state officers, major state services, state legislative officials, officials of the state supreme court, and the U.S. senators and representatives from each state. The offices of Federal agencies located in each state are included. Also includes maps. This publication would be very useful in a small or medium-sized collection. SJV

SS 311
The State of Black Politics. 1977. a. Joint Center for Political Studies, 1426 H St, NW, Washington, DC 20005. Examined: 1977. $10.
Aud: Jc, Cl, Pl

Includes a listing of Black federal appointees, members of the Congressional Black Caucus and their staffs, minority staff aides to state governors, and biographical sketches of Black mayors elected since August 1976. Analyzes the growth in the number of Black officials and concentrates on the results of the 1975 and 1977 elections. This publication grew out of the Center's **National Roster of Black Elected Officials.** SJV

SS 312
Taylor's Encyclopedia of Government Officials: Federal and State. ISSN 0082-2183. 1967/68. bi-a. w/q. suppls. index. illus. Political Research, 510 Continental Bldg, Dallas, TX 75201. Examined: 1977/78. John Clements, ed. 285p. $150 w/q. suppls.
Aud: Hs, Jc, Cl, Pl

Contains the text of important historical documents; emblems; and lists of presidents, U.S. departments and bureaus, members of Congress and congressional committees, members of the judiciary, ambassadors and, for each state, federal and state elected officials and delegates to national conventions. The volume concludes with 150 basic questions and answers on government. SJV

SS 313
U.S. Bureau of the Census. Census of Governments. ISSN 0082-9358. 1850. quinquennial. illus. U.S. Bureau of the Census, Washington, DC 20233. Dist: Superintendent of Documents, U.S. Government Printing Office, Washington, DC 20402. Examined: 1972. 7v. (1977.)
Aud: Cl, Sa

Furnishes information on number and characteristics of state and local governments in the U.S. Value of taxable property, public employees and payrolls, government revenue expenditure, debts, and financial assets are covered. Volume one, "Government Organization," lists number, size, and special function of state and all local governments. Volume two covers taxable property values and assessment-sales price ratios. Volume three focuses on public employment indicating number of employees, payrolls, labor-management relations for each local government. Volume four, "Government Finances," covers school districts, special districts, counties, municipalities, and townships. Volume five discusses local government in metropolitan areas. Volume six covers topical studies such as employee retirement systems, state payments to local governments, and historical statistics. Includes a graphic summary with charts and maps. Volume seven contains state reports. This *Census* is updated by various publications of the Bureau of the Census. SJV

SS 314
U.S. Bureau of the Census. Chart Book of Governmental Data; Organization, Finances, and Employment. ISSN 0360-2508. (Continues: Chart Book on Government Finances and Employment. ISSN 0082-9420.) 1966. a. illus. U.S. Department of Commerce, Washington, DC 20233. Dist: Superintendent of Documents, U.S. Government Printing Office, Washington, DC 20402. Examined: 1973. 20p. $.85.
Aud: Jc, Cl

Provides a summary of key facts on governmental organization, finance, and employment which have been drawn from recent Bureau of the Census reports. With each chart is listed the publication from which the data were drawn. A description of each of the publications appears at the end of the graphic material. Charts are divided into eight chapters: government organization, government finances, state and local government finances, state government finances, local government finances, property tax data, state and local government retirement systems, and public employment and payrolls. The charts are in color. KSK

SS 315
U.S. Bureau of the Census. City Employment in (year). ISSN 0091-9209. 1946. a. illus. U.S. Bureau of the Census, Washington, DC 20233. Dist: Superintendent of Documents, U.S. Government Printing Office, Washington, DC 20402. Examined: 1975. 20p. $.65.
Aud: Cl

Presents city government employment and payroll statistics. For cities with over 50,000 population, data are reported by function and population size-group. SJV

SS 316
U.S. Bureau of the Census. County Government Employment in (year). 1974. a. illus. U.S. Bureau of the Census, Washington, DC 20233. Dist: Superintendent of Documents, U.S. Government Printing Office, Washington, DC 20402. Examined: 1976. 17p. $.70.
Aud: Cl

Employment and payroll statistics are presented by function and population-size group for all county governments. Presents individual figures for counties over 100,000 population. SJV

SS 317
U.S. Bureau of the Census. Local Government Employment in Selected Metropolitan Areas and Large Counties. 1971. irreg. illus. U.S. Bureau of the Census, Washington, DC 20233. Dist: Superintendent of Documents, U.S. Government Printing Office, Washington, DC 20402. Examined: 1974. 119p. $2.15.
Aud: Cl

Examines local government employment and payrolls in the 72 largest standard metropolitan statistical areas. SJV

SS 318
U.S. Bureau of the Census. Public Employment in (year). 1940. irreg. illus. U.S. Bureau of the Census, Washington, DC 20233. Dist: Superintendent of Documents, U.S. Government Printing Office, Washington, DC 20402. Examined: 1976. 32p. $.90.
Aud: Cl

Tables give employment and payroll data for state and local governments by function and type of government. Statistics on number of public employees, average earnings, and full-time equivalent employment by function are presented. Some historical summary information is also included. SJV

SS 319
United States Government Manual. (Continues: United States Government Organization Manual; United States Government Manual.) 1935. a. index. illus. Office of the Federal Register, National Archives and Records Service, Washington, DC 20408. Dist: Superintendent of Documents, U.S. Government Printing Office, Washington, DC 20402. Examined: 1977/78. Richard L. Claypool, ed. 882p. $6.50. (1977/78 suppl. 156p. $2.75.)
Aud: Cl, Sa

The official handbook of the federal government. It covers the legislative, judicial and executive branches of government, but focuses on the Executive and its departments and agencies. It describes the purposes and programs of each agency and lists top personnel, address, and phone number. The latest **Manual** provides references to the *Federal Register* or the *Code of Federal Regulations* for the most recent statement of organization. Quasi-official agencies and multilateral and bilateral international organizations are treated briefly. Sources for further information are provided for each entry. In 1977/78, a *Supplement* was issued indicating changes in personnel. SJV

SS 320
Washington Information Directory. 1975/76. a. bibl. index. Congressional Quarterly, 1414 22nd St, NW, Washington, DC 20037. Examined: 3rd ed., 1977/78. Robert E. Healy, ed. 865p. $18.
Aud: Pl

A guide to governmental and non-governmental sources of information in Washington, D.C. It is organized by 16 broad subject areas, such as communications, economics and business, energy, law and justice, etc. Entries under these categories are listed by executive branch, Congress, and private organizations. There are summaries for each of the 16 chapters. Entries include address, phone, personnel, and a summary of the organization's activities. A reference bibliography is included for each subject area. There is a detailed subject index and an agency and organization index. This directory differs from others in that its basic approach is by subject, not agency. Appendixes list members of Congress, executive departments, foreign embassies, state and local officials, labor unions, and regional and religious organizations. The texts of the Freedom of Information Act and the Privacy Act are also appended. SJV

SS 321
Who's Who in Government. 1972/73. bi-a. index. Marquis Who's Who, 200 E Ohio St, Chicago, IL 60611. Examined: 3rd ed., 1977/78. 753p. $55.50.
Aud: Cl, Pl
Indexed in: *Biographical Dictionaries Master Index; Marquis Who's Who Publications: Index to All Books.*

Contains biographical information on key men and women in all departments of the federal government and on selected officials in local, state, and international governments. Entries include name, position, vital statistics, parents, education, marital status, children, career, career-related activities, civic activities, political activities, non-professional directorships, military record, decorations and awards, professional and other memberships, political affiliation, religion, lodges, clubs, writings, home address, and office address. Two useful indexes are included, an index by general topic and one by government departments. SJV

SS 322
Women of the (no.) Congress. 1957. bi-a. illus. U.S. Women's Bureau, 200 Constitution Ave, NW, Washington, DC 20210. Dist: Superintendent of Documents, U.S. Government Printing Office, Washington, DC 20402. Examined: 1976, 94th Congress, 2nd Session. 112p. free.
Aud: Hs, Jc, Cl, Pl

A biographical directory which includes brief sketches and photographs of women elected to the Senate or House of Representatives during the years covered by the volume. Includes a statistical chart illustrating the number of women who have served in Congress from 1917 to the present. Useful for ready access to information on women in national public office, but duplicates material in the **Congressional Directory.** JKM

HISTORY AND AREA STUDIES

SS 323
Africa (year). 1966. a. illus. Stryker-Post Publications, 888 17th St, NW, Washington, DC 20006. Examined: 1977. Pierre Etienne Dostert, ed. 105p. $2.25.
Aud: Hs, Jc, Cl, Pl

A volume in the publisher's *World Today Series*. The introductory chapters deal with the pre-colonial period and the colonial period in African history. Following these chapters, sections on individual countries are presented by region. Basic facts on each country (area, population, ethnic background, language, religions, currency, etc.) are presented. The history, culture, economy, and a paragraph speculating on the future are also provided for each country. Black-and-white maps and photographs illustrate the text. SJV

SS 324
Africa Contemporary Record: Annual Survey and Documents. 1968/69. a. bibl. index. illus. Africana Publishing Co., 101 Fifth Ave, New York, NY 10003. Examined: v. 8, 1975/76. Colin Legum, ed. $50. (v. 9, 1976/77.)
Aud: Cl, Sa

Examines the affairs of Africa within an African context. After an analysis of the year's events, essays on current issues are presented. They are basically political in tone and examine outside participation in African affairs. A country-by-country survey stresses political, foreign, social, and economic affairs. Presentation of data is basically in narrative form. Part three of the volume presents the texts of documents important in the political, social, and economic development of Africa. They cover activities of the Organization of African Unity, the United Nations, Afro-Asian Peoples' Solidarity Organization, and dealings with Commonwealth and non-aligned countries. Political, social, and economic agreements are also included. SJV

SS 325
Africa South of the Sahara. ISSN 0065-3896. 1971. a. bibl. illus. Europa Publications, 18 Bedford Sq, London WC1B 3JN, England. Dist: Gale Research Co., Book Tower, Detroit, MI 48226. Examined: 1976/77, 1149p.; 7th ed., 1977/78. 1183p. $63.
Aud: Cl, Pl

Surveys all the nations of Africa south of the Sahara (other African nations are covered in Europa's companion volume, **The Middle East and North Africa**). Part one, "Background to the Continent," includes articles written by scholars on such topics as "Industry in Africa" and "The African Languages." The second part covers regional organizations such as the East African Community and the Organization of African Unity. Part three presents surveys of each country covering physical and social geography, history, an economic survey, and a statistical survey. A directory of government, diplomatic representation, judicial system, publishers, radio and television, finance, trade and industry, transport, tourism, and education, and a bibliography are provided for each country. The final part, "Other Reference Material," includes a who's who of the area, calendars, a list of primary commodities, a section on weights and measures, a list of research institutes, and a select bibliography. KMH/SJV

SS 326
Africa Year Book and Who's Who. 1977. a. illus. Africa Journal, Kirkman House, 54A Tottenham Court Rd, London W1P 0BT, England. Dist: R. R. Bowker Co., 1180 Ave of the Americas, New York, NY 10036. Examined: 1977. Raph Uwechue, ed. 1364p. $40.
Aud: Cl, Pl

Produced by indigenous African editors and specialists. It treats the entire continent as an interdependent whole and proposes to correct the prevailing impression of Africa as a hodge-podge of countries. A record of important political, cultural, economic, and social events during the preceding year begins the volume. Part one covers geography, people, economy, communication of the continent. Part two describes official African organizations and includes their charters and other important political documents. Part three examines each country and provides a visitor's guide. Part four covers African participation in various international organizations. Part five is a record of African participation in sports. Part six is a who's who listing with standard biographical information. SJV

SS 327
America: History and Life. Part C, American History Bibliography. (Continues: Writings on American History.) 1974. a. American Bibliographic Center, Clio Press, Riviera Campus, 2040 Alameda Padre Serra, Santa Barbara, CA 93103. Examined: v. 14, 1977. 294p. service basis.
Aud: Cl

America: History and Life "abstracts or cites articles, books, and dissertations in U.S. and Canadian studies, from prehistory to the present." Beginning with volume eleven, 1974, it is published in four parts. Part A provides abstracts and citations of articles in over 1900 domestic and foreign journals and is issued three times a year. Part B, a semi-annual publication, cites book reviews appearing in 130 history journals. Part C cumulates the listings of the first two parts on an annual basis and also includes citations to dissertations. It is arranged in sections entitled North America, Canada, the U.S. (subdivided into three sections: National History to 1945; 1945 to Present; and Regional History), History, Humanities, and Social Sciences. Each citation includes a reference to the abstract in Part A, Part B, or *Dissertation Abstracts International*. Part D is an annual index to the first three parts. SJV

SS 328
Anglo-Saxon England. 1972. a. bibl. illus. Cambridge University Press, Bentley House, 200 Euston Rd, London NW1 2DB, England. Dist: Cambridge University Press, 32 E 57th St, New York, NY 10022. Examined: v. 4, 1975. (v. 6, 1977. 300p. $31.)
Aud: Cl, Pl

Articles on all aspects of Anglo-Saxon studies. There is a bibliography for the previous year which is arranged by subject and includes books, articles, and significant reviews. KAC

SS 329

Annual Bibliography of British and Irish History. 1975. a. index. Humanities Press, Atlantic Highlands, NJ 07716. Examined: 1975. G. R. Elton, ed. 155p. $20. (1976. 193p.)
Aud: Cl

A scholarly reference work covering the history of England, Scotland, Wales, and Ireland. Books, articles, and official publications are included. It is divided into 13 sections with subject subdivisions. They are: bibliography, archives, reference, and historiography; general works; Roman Britain; England 450-1066; England 1066-1500; England and Wales 1500-1714; Britain 1715-1812; Britain 1815-1914; Britain since 1914; Medieval Wales; Scotland before the union; Ireland to 1640; and Ireland since 1640. The first volume covers publications in 1975. It is important for its currency as well as its comprehensiveness. STV

SS 330

Annual Editions: Readings in American History, Post-Civil War. (Continues in part: Readings in American History. ISSN 0090-4511.) 1972. a. index. illus. Dushkin Publishing Group, Sluice Dock, Guilford, CT 06437. Examined: 1978/79. Robert J. Maddox, ed. 256p. $5.95.
Aud: Hs, Jc, Cl, Pl

Like other titles in the Annual Editions series, this collection contains reproductions of articles originally published in newspapers, magazines, and scholarly journals. It is designed for use as supplementary reading for high school and college courses in American history from the Civil War to the present. Articles are selected by an editorial board and are arranged in broad topical sections. Many include charts and illustrations; some include suggestions for further reading. JKM

SS 331

Annual Editions: Readings in American History, Pre-Civil War. (Continues in part: Annual Editions: Readings in American History. ISSN 0090-4511.) 1972. a. index. illus. Dushkin Publishing Group, Sluice Dock, Guilford, CT 06437. Examined: 1978/79. Robert J. Maddox, ed. 256p. $5.95.
Aud: Hs, Jc, Cl, Pl

A companion to **Readings in American History, Post-Civil War.** Contains reproductions of newspaper, magazine, and journal articles dealing with early American history. Designed for use in high school and college classrooms, but also useful as an introductory reader for the general public. Articles often include illustrations, and there is a subject index. JKM

SS 332

Bibliographic Guide to North American History. 1977. a. G. K. Hall, 70 Lincoln St, Boston, MA 02111. Examined: 1977. 554p. $65.
Aud: Pf, Sa

Covers U.S. colonial history, state and local history, constitutional history, plus Canadian political and constitutional history. It represents publications cataloged by the New York Public Library with additional titles from Library of Congress MARC tapes. Full bibliographic information is provided as are New York Public Library classification codes and Library of Congress call numbers. All the entries are arranged in one alphabetical sequence. All types of materials are included. The volume serves as an annual supplement to the *United States Local History Catalog* of the Research Libraries of the New York Public Library. SJV

SS 333

Bibliography of Asian Studies. 1969. a. index. Association for Asian Studies, Lane Hall, University of Michigan, Ann Arbor, MI 48109. Examined: 1972; 1974. 510p. $8.50.
Aud: Cl

Presents comprehensive coverage of western language scholarly monographs and articles dealing with East, South, and Southeast Asia. The basic arrangement is geographic—by region then by country. Entries are provided for the following categories: anthropology and sociology, arts, biography, economics, education, geography, history, language, library and information sciences, literature, philosophy and religion, politics and government, psychology and psychiatry, and science and technology. The bibliography was part of the *Journal of Asian Studies* from 1941 to 1968. The 1974 volume was published in 1977. SJV

SS 334

Bibliography of Old Norse-Icelandic Studies. ISSN 0067-7213. 1963. a. index. The Royal Library, Nhistians Brygge 8, DK 1219, Copenhagen K, Denmark. Examined: 1963; 1964; 1973; 1974. Hans Bekker-Nielsen, ed. $5.25. (15th ed., 1978.)
Aud: Cl, Sa

An annotated record of noteworthy books, journal articles, and reviews on a broad range of Old Norse-Icelandic subjects. Listings represent the works of historians, archaeologists, literary critics, bibliographers, runeologists, and philologists. Each volume contains an introductory essay on some aspect of Old Norse studies. There is also a helpful subject index. AC

SS 335

Canada Yearbook; Annuaire du Canada. ISSN 0068-8142. 1867. a. bibl. index. Statistics Canada, Publications Distribution, Ottawa, Ontario K1A 0T6, Canada. Examined: 1972, 1404p.; 1975. $18.50.
Aud: Hs, Jc, Cl, Pl

Annual review of economic, social, and political developments in Canada. Preliminary chapters on physiography, constitution, and government are followed by extensive tabular data on demography, health, education, labor, scientific research, natural resources, agriculture, mining, energy, housing, transportation, manufacturing, communications, trade and finance. Appendixes include functions of government organizations, Canadian honors, books about Canada, and government information services. Subject index provides access to data. The 1975 volume was not published until 1977. KMH

SS 336

Canadian Almanac and Directory. ISSN 0068-8193. 1847. a. index. Copp Clark Publishing Co., 517 Wellington St W, Toronto, Ontario M5V 1G1, Canada. Dist: Fearon Publishers/Pitman Publishing Corp., 6 Davis Dr, Belmont, CA 94002. Examined: 130th ed., 1977. Susan Walters, ed. $28.95.
Aud: Jc, Cl, Pl

Functions as a Canadian yearbook with a detailed directory of municipal, provincial, and federal governments. Data on courts, judges, hospitals, ministries, government departments, and municipalities are provided for each province. An alphabetical table of contents precedes the body of the work and a detailed index follows. Special features include a directory of law firms and a post office and shipping guide. A complete up-to-date guide to Canadian governmental, business, cultural, ecclesiastical, financial, and educational institutions. KMH

SS 337

Corpus Almanac of Canada. ISSN 0315-7083. (Continues: Corpus Canadian Almanac.) 1974. a. index. illus. Corpus Publishers Services, 151 Blon St W, Toronto, Ontario M5S 1S4, Canada. Dist: International Scholarly Book Service, Box 555, Forest Grove, OR 97116. Examined: 12th ed., 1977. Margot J. Fawcett, ed. $29.50.
Aud: Cl, Pl

Compendium of facts about Canada. An extensive directory of libraries, publishers, museums, associations, and societies precedes the main portion of the work. Sections cover such topics as the year's events, government (national, provincial, territorial, municipal), communications, education, religion, law, real estate, business, finance, taxation, transportation, and demography. There is an extensive subject index. Black-and-white maps are included. KMH

SS 338

Directory of Historical Societies and Agencies in the United States and Canada. 1956. bi-a. index. American Association for State and Local History, 1400 Eighth Ave S, Nashville, TN 37203. Examined: 10th ed., 1975/76. Donna McDonald, ed. 434p. $10.
Aud: Sa

Contains information on state, county, municipal, regional, and special interest historical societies. It is the basic reference work for organizations on the North American continent dealing with local history. Information is compiled by questionnaire. Each entry includes name, mailing address, telephone number, year founded, paid director or elected officer to whom mail should be addressed, number of members, employees, and volunteers. Any magazine published is listed and major programs engaged in at the time of compilation are included in the entry. Contains a general index and a special interest index that lists over 100 entries under "genealogical societies." Beginning with the 11th edition (1978), volumes will be published every three years instead of biennially. SJV

SS 339

Face the Nation. 1971. a. index. Scarecrow Press, 52 Liberty St, Box 656, Metuchen, NJ 08840. Examined: v. 19, 1976. CBS News, eds. $27.50.
Aud: Hs, Jc, Cl, Pl, Sa

Subtitle: "The collected transcripts from the CBS radio and television broadcasts." Volumes 1-13, covering 1954-1970, were published in 1971 ($229.50). Each subsequent volume includes transcripts of the weekly CBS radio and television interview program broadcast during the previous year with a complete name, subject, and issue index. The in-depth interviews with leading politicians, diplomats, and other public personalities provide important supplementary information for any historical or sociological study of the times. Students will especially find this reference source valuable as a supplement to textbook and periodical literature. JKM

SS 340
The Far East and Australasia. 1969. a. bibl. illus. Europa Publications, 18 Bedford Sq, London WC1B 3JN, England. Dist: Gale Research Co., Book Tower, Detroit, MI 48226. Examined: 1976/77. 1331p. $66. (9th ed., 1977/78. 1251p.)
Aud: Cl, Pl

Subtitle: "A survey and directory of Asia and the Pacific." Covers states and territories east of Afghanistan, the Soviet Union, Australia, New Zealand, and the Pacific Isles. The introduction includes articles on population, trade, and religion. The second section provides information on regional cooperative organizations. The main section includes descriptions of each country, arranged under four broad regions: South Asia, South East Asia, East Asia, and Australasia and the Pacific Isles. Each description covers the geography, history, economy, religion, judicial system, press, education, defense, etc. A directory of major institutions and government representatives and a bibliography are also provided for each country. The final section consists of reference materials such as calendars, a who's who listing, a table of weights and measures, a list of research institutes, and a selected bibliography on the region. Maps are included. KMH/SJV

SS 341
The Far East and Southwest Pacific. 1968. a. illus. Stryker-Post Publications, 888 17th St, NW, Washington, DC 20006. Examined: 1977. Harold C. Hinton, ed. 90p. $2.25.
Aud: Hs, Jc, Cl, Pl

A volume in the publisher's *World Today Series*. After a brief historical introduction to the peoples of Asia, their religious beliefs, economic background, and political status, each country is treated individually. Basic facts on the area, population, capital, climate, language, religion, flag, etc. are provided. A more detailed discussion of the history, culture, economy, and future prospects is also included for each country. There are black-and-white photographs, maps, and drawings. SJV

SS 342
Great Britain. Central Office of Information. Britain: An Official Handbook. 1948/49. a. bibl. index. illus. Her Majesty's Stationery Office, 49 High Holborn, London WC1V 6HB, England. Dist: Pendragon House, 220 University Ave, Palo Alto, CA 94301. Examined: 1977. 509p. £6. (1978. 488p.)
Aud: Cl

A quick reference guide to economic and administrative aspects of life in Great Britain exclusive of the Commonwealth. Covers broad areas such as government, social welfare, education, defense, law, economy, arts, sports, and recreation. Includes maps, photographs, and charts. SJV

SS 343
Handbook of Latin American Studies. ISSN 0072-9833. 1935. a. bibl. index. University of Florida Press, 15 NW 15th St, Gainesville, FL 32601. Examined: no. 36, 1974; no. 37, 1975. Dolores Moyano Martin, ed. $25. (no. 38, 1976. 695p.)
Aud: Cl

A classified annotated bibliography of books and periodical articles concentrating on Latin American studies. Beginning with volume 26, the publication was divided into two volumes, humanities and social sciences, each appearing every other year. The social science volume covers anthropology, economics, education, geography, government and politics, international relations, and sociology. Humanities covers art, folklore, history, language, literature, music, and philosophy. Each section is compiled by contributing editors who prepare an introductory statement on the bibliographic highlights since the last volume. Sources are international in scope. Each volume has an author and subject index. SJV

SS 344
Historic Documents. 1972. a. index. Congressional Quarterly, 1414 22nd St, NW, Washington, DC 20037. Examined: 1975; 1976; 1977. Robert A. Diamond, ed. 969p. $37.
Aud: Jc, Cl

Attempts to provide easy access to historic documents of more than transitory interest. A broad subject range is covered. The publication includes presidential statements, court decisions, press conferences, commission reports, special studies, and speeches of national or international importance. Each document is preceded by introductory material and sometimes a short summary of subsequent developments. The arrangement is basically chronological. There is a cumulative index covering 1972-1976. SJV

SS 345
Index to Book Reviews in Historical Periodicals. 1972. a. bibl. Scarecrow Press, 52 Liberty St, Box 656, Metuchen, NJ 08840. Examined: 1975. John W. Brewster and Joseph A. McLeod, eds. 685p. $22.50.
Aud: Cl, Pf, Sa

Indexes the book reviews published in approximately 100 English language scholarly journals and historical society periodicals. Review citations are arranged alphabetically by author of the work reviewed and indexed by title. Publication of the **Index** actually began in 1975, when retrospective volumes for 1972, 1973 and 1974 were issued. The 1975 volume, published in 1977, provides the most complete coverage yet. Could serve as a useful acquisitions tool, particularly once the publication schedule becomes more firmly established. JKM

SS 346
International Bibliography of Historical Sciences. 1926. a. Librairie Armand Colin, Paris, France. Examined: v. 42, 1973. Michel Francois and Nicolas Tolu, eds. 361p.
Aud: Cl

A selective and descriptive bibliography of books and articles published for the International Committee of Historical Sciences. Entries are in all languages. The headings change language each year. Arrangement is classified and chronological. The 1973 volume was not published until 1976. SJV

SS 347
Japan Almanac. 1972. a. illus. Mainichi Newspare, 1-1-1 Hitotsubashi, Chiyoda-ku, Tokyo 100. Japan. Examined: 1976. $12.
Aud: Cl, Pl

Subtitle: "A comprehensive handbook on Japan." An annual English language almanac on all aspects of Japanese life. Provides a chronology of major events of the previous year, history, political parties, current government officials, economic statistics, trade, industrial and cultural information. Similar data is given for each prefecture. An extensive directory with addresses of museums, organizations, institutions of higher education, and major companies, as well as a who's who listing provide up-to-date data. Extensive statistical tables on all aspects of Japanese society (population, price indexes, Gross National Profit, traffic, criminality) make up the last portion. KMH

SS 348
Latin America. 1967. a. illus. Stryker-Post Publications, 888 17th St, NW, Washington, DC 20006. Examined: 1977. Jon D. Cozean, ed. 107p. $2.25.
Aud: Hs, Jc, Cl, Pl

A volume in the publisher's *World Today Series*. The introductory chapters include an historical overview of Latin America, Puerto Rico and its political status, drugs in Latin America, and the Organization of American States. Following these general chapters are specific sections on each country covering area, population, climate, political status, religion, ethnic background, history, culture, economy, and future prospects. Arranged in brief, convenient format. Illustrated with black-and-white photographs and maps. SJV

SS 349
Latin America. ISSN 0094-7458. 1972. a. index. Facts on File, 119 W 57th St, New York, NY 10019. Examined: 1977. Lester A. Sobel, ed. 213p. $11.95.
Aud: Hs, Jc, Cl, Pl

This annual records major economic and political events in Latin America and the Caribbean. Information is compiled from the weekly **Facts on File** reports of world events. Articles are brief—about as long as an almanac article. Arrangement is by country, and there is a subject/name/country index. Facts listed include: important occurrences, economic development, guerrilla operations, labor action, diplomatic relations, government corruption, political maneuverings, student activism, military affairs, etc. "A conscientious effort was made to record all events without bias and to produce a reliable and useful reference tool...for researchers, students, educators, and librarians." KR/JKM

SS 350
The Middle East and North Africa. ISSN 0076-8502. (Continues: Middle East.) 1948. a. bibl. illus. Europa Publications, 18 Bedford Sq, London WC1B 3JN, England. Dist: Gale Research Co., Book Tower, Detroit, MI 48226. Examined: 24th ed., 1977/78. 936p. $54.50.
Aud: Cl, Pl

A major reference source covering the Middle East and Northern Africa. Part one is a general survey including articles on the politics, economy, foreign relations, and religions of the region. Part two covers regional organizations involved in the area. Part three includes signed articles on each country covering the geography, history, economy, and statistics, with a directory of major institutions and a selected bibliography. Part four contains reference materials such as a who's who listing, weights and measures, research institutes, and a bibliography. SJV

SS 351
The Middle East and South Asia. 1967. a. illus.

Stryker-Post Publications, 888 17th St, NW, Washington, DC 20006. Examined: 1977. Ray L. Cleveland, ed. 98p. $2.25.
Aud: Hs, Jc, Cl, Pl

A volume in the publisher's *World Today Series*. The historical introduction covers the emergence of civilization through British expansion. Following this, each country is treated individually. The basic facts given include area, population, language, ethnic background, religion, currency, etc. There are also sections devoted to history, culture, the economy, and the future prospects of the country. A few bibliographic references are given. Black-and-white photographs and maps are included. SJV

SS 352
Middle East Annual Review. 1975. a. illus. Rand McNally, Box 7600, Chicago, IL 60680. Examined: 1978. Michael Field, ed. 400p. $14.95.
Aud: Cl, Pl, Sa

A business oriented review focusing on economic affairs. Organized in two parts. The introductory section consists of nine signed articles on such topics as political developments, the OPEC, oil, civil engineering, banking, the Arab boycott, and minerals. These chapters are followed by signed analyses of 28 Middle Eastern countries. The information provided includes banking hours, public holidays, major hotels, health advice to the traveler, the press of the country, main commodities imported and exported, balance of payments, etc. Sources of the information are not cited. Useful for students of the area, persons doing business in the area, and for travellers. Illustrated with good maps and medium-quality photographs. SJV

SS 353
Middle East Contemporary Survey. 1978. a. Africana Publishing Co., 101 Fifth Ave, New York, NY 10003. Examined: 1978. Colin Legum, ed. 900p. $60.
Aud: Cl, Pl

The volume covers the national affairs and international relations of the Middle Eastern countries during the year prior to the date of the volume. Political, economic, military, and international events are discussed. SJV

SS 354
Middle East Yearbook. ISSN 0308-1699. 1977. a. illus. K Magazines, 63 Long Acre, London WC2E 9JH England. Dist: Franklin Watts, 730 Fifth Ave, New York, NY 10019. Examined: 1978. John Wallace, ed. 320p. $25.
Aud: Cl, Pl

Prepared by the Centre for Middle Eastern and Islamic Studies of the University of Durham in England. The first section is an atlas which covers the physical features, temperature, precipitation, vegetation, population, agriculture, minerals, oil, and communications of Middle Eastern countries. Text accompanies the maps. Following the atlas, there are signed essays on topics of current concern; the essays include many statistical charts and maps. The volume includes a section on "Information for Businessmen" which gives for each country the language, holidays, business hours, travel tips, commerce, etc. A country-by-country presentation provides facts and figures and basic background information for 22 countries. SJV

SS 355
New African Yearbook. 1964. a. Franklin Watts, 730 Fifth Ave, New York, NY 10019. Examined: 1978. 288p. $25.
Aud: Cl, Pl

Contains up-to-date facts, figures, statistics, and trends on 52 African countries. SJV

SS 356
Oral History Review. (Continues: Proceedings of the Oral History Association Annual Colloquia.) 1973. a. Oral History Association, University of Vermont, Burlington, VT 05401. Examined: 1973;1977. Samuel B. Hand, ed. 86p. $4.
Aud: Cl, Sa
Indexed in: *Historical Abstracts; America: History and Life.*

A combination of state-of-the-art articles on oral history and the business proceedings of the Oral History Association. Articles deal with legal factors, psychological factors, ethics, uses in teaching, international aspects, and trends in the use of oral history. Each issue also reviews the annual colloquium of the Association and gives various reports of committees. A book review section includes books on technique and examples of published uses of oral history. SJV

SS 357
Scottish Studies. ISSN 0036-9411. 1957. a. index. illus. University of Edinburgh, School of Scottish Studies, 27 Geroge Sq, Edinburgh EH8 9LD, Scotland. Examined: v. 20, 1976. John MacQueen, ed. $12. (v. 21, 1977.)
Aud: Cl, Pl

Subtitle: "The journal of the School of Scottish Studies, University of Edinburgh." Each volume presents a wide range of research into Scottish traditional life. Articles, notes, and book reviews are included. An index to the first ten volumes is available. The text is occasionally in Scots or Gaelic. KAC

SS 358
The Soviet Union and Eastern Europe. 1970. a. illus. Stryker-Post Publications, 888 17th St, NW, Washington, DC 20006. Examined: 1977. Samuel L. Sharp, ed. 101p. $2.24.
Aud: Hs, Jc, Cl, Pl

A volume in the publisher's *World Today Series*. About half of the volume is alloted to coverage of the Soviet Union, and the remainder to other countries of Eastern Europe. Basic facts such as area, population, climate, language, religion, commercial products, former political status, chief of state, etc., are presented in a handy format. The history of the Soviet Union, particularly its political history, is covered quite extensively with many photographs, maps, and genealogical charts. A discussion of each country's culture, economy, and future prospects is also included. This volume would be a good companion to the conventional travel guide. SJV

SS 360
West Africa Annual. ISSN 0083-8144. 1963. a. illus. John West Publications, 212 Broad St, Lagos, Nigeria. Dist: International Publications Service, 114 E 32nd St, New York, NY 10016. Examined: 9th ed., 1975. L. K. Lakande, ed. 429p. $15.
Aud: Jc, Cl, Sa

General geographical, economic, political, cultural, historical surveys of each of the 16 countries in West Africa. An eight-page general survey introduces this English language annual, followed by surveys of the 16 countries. The survey lengths vary from a paragraph to two pages; statistics are plentiful in the text as well as in tables. Maps of each section preface the serendipitous chapters. A table of contents guides the reader. The printing is less than perfect (some tables need to be read in a mirror), and the language in the text is rather formal and labored. KR/JKM

SS 361
The West Indies and Caribbean Yearbook. ISSN 0083-8233. 1929. a. index. illus. Caribook, 1255 Yonge St, Toronto, Ontario, Canada M4W 123. Examined: 47th ed., 1976/77. Colin Rickards, ed. $27.50.
Aud: Cl, Pl

Directory of nations in the West Indies and Caribbean detailing climate, government, public and social services, utilities, communications, resources, industries, finance, trade, tourism, and business. Provides travel information, a gazetteer, maps, and an advertising index. KMH

SS 362
Writings on American History. 1975. a. bibl. index. KTO Press, Millwood, NY 10546. Examined: 1976. James J. Dougherty and Marcia G. Castaneda, eds. 269p. $15.
Aud: Cl, Sa

Subtitle: "A subject bibliography of articles." Published under the auspices of the American Historical Association. Originally published as supplements to the *Annual Report* of the American Historical Association (1906-1939/40). In 1948, the National Historical Publications Commission assumed responsibility for the compilation of the bibliography and published until 1961. In 1976, Kraus-Thomson (KTO Press) published a four-volume set covering 1962-1973 publications. Volumes are now published on an annual basis. Derived from the "Recently Published Articles" section of the *American Historical Review* which reviews over 1500 historical journals published throughout the world. Citations to journal articles and dissertations are cited in "broad chronological and, in the U.S. list, geographical categories." A title-keyword (subject) index and an author index are provided. Some foreign journals are indexed, but most of the writings are in English. KR/JKM

HOBBIES AND GIFTS

SS 363
American Numismatic Society. Annual Report. ISSN 0569-6720. (Continues: American Numismatic Society. Proceedings.) 1962. a. illus. American Numismatic Society, Broadway and 156th St, New York, NY 10038. Examined: 1975. Leslie A. Elan, ed. 118p. free.
Aud: Sa

The main section of the report, entitled "The Coin Cabinet," presents an illustrated description of new accessions, arranged by country. Reports on the library, publications, the photography department, awards, educational activities, staff activities, finances, and officers follow. There is a final section entitled "Lists and Tables" that lists various categories of members and donors. SLB

SS 364
The Antique Trader Weekly. Annual of Articles on Antiques. 1972. a. index. illus. The Antique Trader Weekly, Box 1050, Dubuque, IA 52001. Examined: 1976. 450p. $7.95 pap.
Aud: Pl

An annual compilation of articles which appeared in *The Antique Trader Weekly* during the previous year. Articles are indexed by subject and objects mentioned. There are many good quality photographs and illustrations. An oversized, paperbound annual printed on newsprint pages. SLB

SS 365
Antiques and Their Prices. (Continues: Antiques and Their Current Prices.) 1950. bi-a. index. illus. E. G. Warman Publishing, 540 Morgantown Rd, Uniontown, PA 15401. Examined: 13th ed., 1976. Edwin G. Warman. 634p. $9.95 pap.
Aud: Pl

The first section lists glass patterns in two parts, clear glass patterns and colored glass patterns. Listings are arranged by name and include a brief description of the general brand, a hand drawn illustration, price for various types of objects, such as bowls, tumblers, etc. It includes an index to patterns with two or more names. The larger general section is arranged alphabetically by category, for example, ABC plates, almanacs, etc. There is a brief description and history for each category, then specific items are listed with their prices. The book includes many black-and-white photographs. SLB

SS 366
The British Antiques Yearbook. (Continues in part: The International Antiques Yearbook.) 1968/69. a. bibl. index. illus. Art and Antique Yearbooks, Hestergate House, Vauxhall Bridge Rd, London SW1V 1HF, England; and Larry Ross c/o Connoisseur Magazine, 224 W 57th St, New York, NY 10019. Dist: International Publications Service, 114 E 32nd St, New York, NY 10016. Examined: 1974/75; 1976/77. Marcell d'Arge Smith, ed. 952p. $25.
Aud: Pl, Sa

After an art sales review for the previous year, the main portion of the book presents a directory and guide to both London and provincial antiques dealers, arranged by area. Dealer entries include address, hours, if an appointment is necessary, and specialty. Maps of areas are included. There are also lists of packers and shippers, trade services and suppliers, auctioneers and salesrooms, fairs and fair calendars, associations, appropriate periodicals, and book publishers. There is a specialists index and an index to dealers. Many advertisements throughout. SLB

SS 367
British Numismatic Journal and Proceedings of the British Numismatic Society. 1903. a. index. illus. British Numismatic Society, Warburg Institute, Woburn Sq, London WC1H 0AB, England, Examined: v. 44, 1974. Michael Dolley, H. E. Paga, and M. Melaré-Radiffe, eds. 108p. $17.
Aud: Sa
Indexed in: *British Humanities Index.*

Presents scholarly research in the field of British numismatics. The 1974 volume includes a lengthy documented article on the Mint of Watchet in Somerset. Issues include proceedings of the previous year's meeting of the British Numismatic Society and long critical reviews of books in the field. GV

SS 368
Buying and Selling United States Coins. ISSN 0068-4562. 1970. a. bibl. index. illus. Western Publishing Co., 1220 Mound Ave, Racine, WI 53404. Examined: 1974. Kenneth E. Bressett and R. S. Yeoman, eds. 128p. $1.25 pap. (8th ed., 1977.)
Aud: Pl

The introduction says this book "contains all essential information needed to collect, buy, and sell U.S. coins." It is written for the layperson who wishes to become a serious collector or a casual accumulator. There is a short bibliography at the beginning, and hints on buying and selling. The major portion is arranged chronologically by coin type, from oldest to newest. Entries include photographs, dates, quantity minted, and average dealer and retail prices for fair, good, and very good condition. SLB

SS 369
Coin Collectors' Handbook. 1954. a. index. illus. Doubleday and Co., 501 Franklin Ave, Garden City, NY 11530. Examined: 1970/71. Fred Reinfeld, ed. 153p. $5.95. (1976. 154p.)
Aud: Pl

There are a few introductory articles of interest, but the main portion of this book consists of the directories, including a catalog of U.S. coins, a catalog of U.S. tokens, and a catalog of Canadian coins. Catalogs are arranged by type of coin and year minted. Entries include illustrations, quantity minted, and approximate value. There is also a checklist of American coin clubs arranged geographically, a glossary of terms, and an index. SLB

SS 370
Coin World Almanac. 1976. a. bibl. index. illus. Amos Press, Box 150, Sidney, OH 45365. Dist: Wehman Brothers, Ridgedair Ave, Morris County Mall, Cedar Knolls, NJ 07927. Examined: 1976. 833p. $10.
Aud: Pl

Subtitle: "A handbook for coin collectors." Presents encyclopedic information for coin collectors. Contains articles and tables covering U.S. coin designs, assay commissioners, and mint medals, with information on artists, models, and dates. Includes a coin catalog; lists of museums, auctions, and famous collections; and an unannotated international bibliography of numismatic publications. GV

SS 371
Comic Book Price Guide. 1970. a. illus. Bob Overstreet, 2905 Vista Dr, NW, Cleveland, TN 36311. Dist: Crown Publishers, 419 Park Ave S, New York, NY 10016. Examined: 1977. Robert M. Overstreet, ed. 443p. $7.95 pap.
Aud: Pl

A price guide to American comic books. The lengthy introduction includes much information of use to the collector, such as storing books, market report, investors data, starting a collection, selling, and much more. There is an extensive table of contents. The main portion of the book is arranged alphabetically by the name of the comic, from *Abbie an' Slats* to *Zorro*. Many of the entries include an illustration of one copy. The entries indicate dates published, notable illustrators, publisher, and average prices for each issue number sold in the last year in good, fine, or mint condition. There are two large sections of advertisements. SLB

SS 372
Contemporary Crafts Market Place. ISSN 0095-2710. 1975/76. a. bibl. index. R. R. Bowker Co., 1180 Ave of the Americas, New York, NY 10036. Examined: 1975/76. American Crafts Council, comp. 502p. $13.95 pap.
Aud: Cl, Pl

An extensive directory that lists craft shops and galleries by state; national, regional, and state craft organizations; courses or craft schools by state, indicating degrees, offered subjects, and address; suppliers, arranged by subject area; and packing, shipping, and insurance agents. There is a calendar of regularly scheduled craft events, arranged by state, and a listing of publications, arranged by type (e.g., periodical or reference) and subject. The list of publications does not include annotations. There is a very complete index. SLB

SS 373
Craft, Model, and Hobby Industry Annual Trade Directory. ISSN 0011-0752. (Continues: Annual Basic Hobby Industry Trade Directory.) 1946. a. index. illus. Hobby Publications, 229 W 28th St, New York, NY 10001. Examined: 1977. Geoffrey Wheeler, ed. 208p. $8 pap.
Aud: Pl, bsa

A magazine-format annual produced by the monthly magazine *Craft, Model and Hobby Industry*. After a trade commentary, it lists manufacturers, book and magazine publishers, wholesalers, manufacturers' representatives, department and chain store buyers, industry suppliers, and associations. All entries provide address, phone number, and contact person. There is a classified index of products which refers back to the full listings. SLB

SS 374
Crafts Annual. 1973. a. New York State Craftsmen, 27 W 53rd St, New York, NY 10019. Dist: Publishing Center for Cultural Resources, 27 W 53rd St, New York, NY 10019. Examined: 25th ed., 1978. 36p. $1.
Aud: Pl

Contains articles of interest to craftspersons. The 1978 issue includes articles on how to start a crafts business; how to make money, market products, and manage a home based business; and suggestions for appropriate legal agreements between craftspersons and buyers. Approximately one-third of the 36 pages are devoted to advertisements. JKM

SS 375
Current Coins of the World. ISSN 0070-1882. (Continues: Catalog of Modern World Coins.) 1966. a. index. Western Publishing Co., 1220 Mound Ave, Racine, WI 53404. Examined: 5th ed., 1972. R. S. Yeoman, ed. 256p. (1978. $5.50.)
Aud: Pl

Identifies coins of all countries in all metals issued during the past 25 years. Listings are arranged under country, metallic content, design, and denomination. Coins are then listed chronologically. Each entry indicates the catalog number, the denomination, the date of issue, and the estimated value. SLB

SS 376
Franklin Mint. Limited Editions. (Continues: Franklin Mint. Numismatic Issues.) 1965/69. quinquennial w/a. suppls. index. illus. Franklin Mint, Franklin Center, PA 19063. Examined: 1972. Herman Baron, ed. 303p. $6.
Aud: Pl

An annual reference catalog that lists coins, medals, tokens, and other collector's items produced by the Franklin Mint during the preceding year. Each entry includes a fairly large illustration of the product, name, sculptor, catalog number, type of metal, and number minted. Sections include "Coins of the Realm," "Commemorative Series," "Art Series," "Promotional Series," "Individual Issues," "Additional Products," and "Updated Mintage Figures." A cumulative index from 1965-1973 is available. SLB

SS 377
Guide Book of United States Coins. ISSN 0072-8829. 1946. a. index. illus. Western Publishing Co., 1220 Mound Ave, Racine, WI 53404. Examined: 28th ed., 1975; 30th ed., 1977. R. S. Yeoman, ed. 256p. $3.95.
Aud: Pl

Subtitle: "The red book of United States coins (year)." An illustrated catalog of coins which covers U.S. coins from 1616 to the present. The first section deals with coins and tokens of Colonial days and the second part lists regular U.S. coins arranged according to denominations, from half-cents through double eagles. Entries provide brief description, mint report, and retail price for coins in various conditions. The introduction offers various tips on coin collecting and selling and a brief history of American coinage. SLB

SS 378
Handbook of United States Coins, with Premium List. (Cover title: Blue Book of U.S. Coins.) ISSN 0072-9949. 1942. a. index. illus. Western Publishing Co., 1220 Mound Ave, Racine, WI 53404. Examined: 34th ed., 1977. R. S. Yeoman, ed. 128p. $2.95.
Aud: Sa

A handbook for collectors of U.S. coins. Includes prefatory advice on collecting, selling, and cleaning coins and information on mints and mint markets. The major part of the work lists coins issued (half-cents through double eagles). Each section focuses on a specific denomination and includes a general introduction, then an illustrated listing of coins in the category, with printing dates, quantities minted, and dealer prices for various conditions of the coin. SLB

SS 379
International Art and Antiques Yearbook. ISSN 0538-4311. (Continues: The Antiques Yearbook; The International Antiques Yearbook.) 1949/50. a. index. illus. Antiques Yearbooks, London, England. Dist: Hearst Books, Division of Hearst Magazines, 250 W 55th St, New York, NY 10019. Examined: 1976. 1918p. $24.95.
Aud: Sa

An international directory of antiques dealers, auctioneers, salesrooms, packers, and shippers, arranged alphabetically by country and then city. Includes dealers in Europe, English-speaking countries, Israel, and Japan. Entries give address, telephone number, hours of business, and area of specialization. Also provides a list of antiques dealers' associations, a list of selected antiques and art periodicals arranged by country of publication, and a calendar of the year's international antiques fairs. There is an index of specialists arranged by country. SLB

SS 380
The Kovels' Complete Antiques Price List. 1969. a. illus. Crown Publications, 419 Park Ave S, New York, NY 10016. Examined: 9th ed., 1976. Ralph Kovel and Terry Kovel, eds. 724p. $7.95 pap.
Aud: Pl

Subtitle: "A guide to the market for professionals, dealers and collectors." Arranged alphabetically by item, this annual lists the current prices for each antique or collectible from antique shows, sales, flea markets, and auctions held during the preceding fiscal year. Many entries specify size, age, color, and pattern, and current price, and are illustrated with color and black-and-white photographs. SLB

SS 381
The Lyle Official Antiques Review. 1971/72. a. index. illus. Lyle Publications, Glenmayne, Galashiels, Silkirkshire, TD1 3PT, England. Dist: Charles Scribner's Sons, 597 Fifth Ave, New York, NY 10017. Examined: 1971/72; 1974/75. Tony Curtis, ed. 523p. $12.40. (1977. 606p. $11.04.)
Aud: Pl, Sa
Indexed in: *Catholic Periodical and Literature Index.*

Includes guides to silvermarks, British monarchs, and British periodicals, and articles on "The Art Market," "British Antiques Exporters," "Erotic Antiques," etc. The major portion of the book is an alphabetical listing of antiques by type of object, from beds to water colors. Each listing includes black-and-white drawing, brief description, and current price in British pounds. Also presents exchange rates and a money conversion table. There is a limited amount of advertising. SLB

SS 382
Minkus New American Stamp Catalog. ISSN 0076-9061. 1953. a. illus. Minkus Publications, 116 W 32nd St, New York, NY 10001. Examined:1978. Ben Blumenthal, ed. 366p. $7.50.
Aud: Pl

The introduction explains that this catalog is "divided into sections consisting of stamps issued for particular purposes or recognized by collectors as separate groups," e.g., regular postal issue, commemorative issues, airmail, special delivery, postage due, etc. There are about 50 of these divisions. Within the divisions the stamps are listed by date of issue. Entries include illustration, purpose, verbal description of design, watermark, perforation, catalog number, colors, quantity distributed, first date of usage, prices for used and unused stamps, number of stamps on block, plate block and sheets, and minor varieties of the same stamps in a different color or any other significant difference. There are also listings of stamps of U.S. possessions, chronologically arranged. Includes excellent instructions for using the book and reading the entries. SLB

SS 383
Minkus New World Wide Stamp Catalog. ISSN 0076-907X. 1955. a. index. illus. Minkus Publications, 116 W 32nd St, New York, NY 10001. Examined: 1977/78. George Tlamsa, ed. 3v. $16.50 pap.
Aud: Pl, Sa

Arranged in three parts covering the British Commonwealth and Ireland, Free Asia and Africa, and Latin America, respectively. Within each part, countries are arranged alphabetically, and there is an index to each part to clarify where specific territories and possessions can be found. Brief demographic and historical data are provided for each country, followed by a chronological listing of stamps including illustrations and an indication of paper variety, color, perforation, watermark, printing method, size, and price for used and unused stamps. The explanation of how to use the volume is excellent. JKM

SS 384
Pick's Currency Yearbook. ISSN 0079-2063. 1955. a. index. illus. Pick Publishing Corp., 21 West St, New York, NY 10006. Examined: 21st ed., 1976/77. 800p. $150.
Aud: Sa

Provides descriptions and appraisals of 112 major currencies and accessory units throughout the world as well as several minor currencies. Surveys the year's developments in international monetary exchange through text, tables, and charts. Includes tables showing monthly gold bar and coin prices over the last ten years, monetary depreciation over the last ten years, and similar statistics. Discusses exchange rate structures throughout the world, resident and nonresident restrictions on currency exchange and transfer, and domestic currency restrictions. A comprehensive source of information on world currencies for the business professional or the amateur. The first 19 volumes, 1955-74, are available on microfilm for $350. JKM

SS 385
Scott's Specialized Catalogue of U.S. Stamps. 1900. a. index. illus. Scott Publishing Co., 530 Fifth Ave, New York, NY 10036. Examined: 1974. James B. Hatcher, ed. 735p. (1977. $20; $14 pap.)
Aud: Pl

Lists various groups of U.S. stamps in very specialized divisions, including envelopes, revenues, private die proprietary, hunting permit, locals, Christmas seals, etc. Each entry includes illustration, catalog number, design, denomination, color, and price for uncanceled and canceled stamps. There is a subject index. SLB

SS 386
Scott's Standard Postage Stamp Catalogue. 1867. a. index. illus. Wehman Brothers, Ridgedale Ave, Morris County Mall, Cedar Knolls, NJ 07927. Examined: 133rd ed., 1977. James G. Hatcher, ed. 4v. v. 1, $13; v. 2, $15; v. 3, $15; v. 4, $15.
Aud: Pl

Volume one of this international stamp directory covers U.S., U.N., and British Commonwealth; volumes two, three, and four cover Europe, Africa, Asia, Latin America, arranged alphabetically by country. After a short description of each country, its stamp issues are listed chronologically with illustrations, description, denominations, and value of the principal stamps, both used and unused. The U.S. section includes information about Confederate stamps, newspaper stamps, and stamped envelopes, and an index of commemorative issues. Offers concise information for the collector. SLB

SS 387
Standard Catalog of World Coins. 1971. bi-a. index. illus. Krause Publications, Iola, WI 54945. Examined: 1975; 1977. Chester L. Krause and Clifford Mishler, eds. 1600p. $19.50 pap.
Aud: Pl

Lists world coins by country, then chronologically. Each entry includes an illustration, date, mintage, and average market value by condition. There is an index by country and by coin denomination. A table of exchange rates and a silver and gold coin value chart are also included. SLB

SS 388
Standard Catalogue of Canadian Coins, Tokens, and Paper Money. 1952. a. index. illus. Charlton International Publishing, 299 Queen St W, Toronto, Ontario M5V 129, Canada. Examined: 1977. J. E. Charlton, ed. 289p. $4.50 pap.
Aud: Pl

Lists Canadian coins by type, date, quantity, and retail value based on condition. Paper money is arranged by bank, amount, year, and condition. Also includes a list of merchants and miscellaneous notes, scrip, and bonds. Some historical background is given throughout. There are price range charts of selected paper money, tokens, and coins. SLB

HOME ECONOMICS

SS 389
Better Homes and Gardens Christmas Ideas. (Title page: Creative Christmas Ideas from Better Homes and Gardens.) ISSN 0405-6590. 1952. a. index. illus. Special Interest Publications, Meredith Corp., 1716 Locust St, Des Moines, IA 50336. Examined: 1976. Richard Boyer, ed. 176p. $1.50 pap.
Aud: Pl

Includes decorating and gift ideas, with instructions on how to make them, and some recipes. The well organized table of contents and an index to instructions make this magazine-format annual work better than most. There is advertising throughout. SLB

SS 390
Celebrate! ISSN 0361-0896. (Continues: Celebrate! The Magazine for Cake and Food Decorators. bi-m.) 1974. a. index. illus. Wilton Enterprises, 833 W 115th St, Chicago, IL 60643. Examined: v. 2, 1975; v. 3, 1976; v. 4, 1977. Eugene T. Sullivan and Marilynn C. Sullivan, eds. 160p. $9.95.
Aud: Pl

Each annual is arranged chronologically to present cake decorating ideas for the appropriate season of the year. The decorating ideas are presented with magnificent color photographs and detailed instructions. Most of the instructions are geared to those with previous cake decorating experience. There are also feature articles on specialized skills and on awards. A subject index is included. SLB

SS 391
Decorative Art and Modern Interiors. ISSN 0070-3206. (Continues: Decorative Art in Modern Interiors.) 1906. a. illus. Studio Visa, 35 Red Lion Sq, London, WC1R 4SG, England. Dist: Viking Press, 625 Madison Ave, New York, NY 10022. Examined: 1973/74; 1974/75; 1975/76. Maria Schofield, ed. 192p. $29.50.
Aud: Cl, Pl

Each issue concentrates on a specific theme, e.g., light and color as elements of interior architecture, city development and private dwellings, and apartments and houses. Includes photographs of approximately 20 design plans related to the theme. The introduction is in English, German, Spanish, and French. The text accompanying the photographs is in English. Two other specialized trends and reviews also appear. A list with addresses of all manufacturers and designers represented in that volume is provided. SLB

SS 392
Family Circle Great Ideas Christmas Helps. 1966. a. illus. The Family Circle, 488 Madison Ave, New York, NY 10022. Examined: 1976. Arthur Hettich, ed. 144p. $1.35 pap.
Aud: Pl

Contains instructions on how to sew, knit, bake, build, and glue over 250 gifts. Also provides instructions for making decorations for doors, walls, trees, mantles, and tables. Recipes are included. A section of color photographs of the projects provides page references to the detailed instructions that follow. There is no table of contents or index. Advertising is included throughout. SLB

SS 393
House and Garden Color Guide. 1976. a. bibl. illus. Conde Nast Publications, 350 Madison Ave, New York, NY 10017. Examined: 1976. Louis Oliver Gropp, ed. 124p. $1.75 pap.
Aud: Pl

A guide to the use of color in the home. Includes articles on home decorating, remodeling, and building; general techniques; how to add color with crafts; and information on new products. There is an extensive annotated bibliography of booklets arranged by subject, with publisher's or distributor's address and price. There are many color and black-and-white photographs. SLB

SS 394

McCall's Needlework and Crafts Christmas Make-It Ideas. 1950. a. illus. McCall's Needlework and Crafts Publications, The McCall Pattern Co., 230 Park Ave, New York, NY 10017. Examined: 1976. Charlotte Brem, ed. 162p. $1.65 pap.
Aud: Pl

Provides detailed instructions on how to make various Christmas decorations and gifts. There is no table of contents or index; a section of color photographs of the projects indicates the pages where the instructions can be found. Includes advertising throughout. SLB

SS 395

Spare-Time Furniture Projects. 1963. a. bibl. illus. Davis Publications, 229 Park Ave S, New York, NY 10003. Examined: 1977. Joe Daffron, ed. 96p. $1.50 pap.
Aud: Pl

This magazine-format annual contains some special features, such as an annotated list of valuable homeowner booklets and an introduction to Citizens Band radio. There are several articles on tools, materials, and techniques for making furniture. Provides illustrated instructions for making Early American, modern, and traditional furniture. SLB

SS 396

Woman's Day Best Ideas for Christmas. 1950. a. illus. Fawcett Publications, Fawcett Bldg, Greenwich, CT 06830. Dist: Fawcett Publications, 1515 Broadway, New York, NY 10036. Examined: 1976. Frank Bowers, ed. 128p. $1.10 pap.
Aud: Pl

Includes some food ideas, many gift and decorations ideas, and some party ideas. Table of contents for this magazine-format annual works fairly well as an index. There are advertisements throughout. SLB

SS 397

Woman's Day Granny Squares. 1974. a. illus. Fawcett Publications, One Fawcett Place, Greenwich, CT 06830. Examined: no. 5, 1977. Marion Lyons, ed. 96p. $1.29 pap.

Aud: Pl

This magazine-format needlework annual contains instructions for making a variety of items from crocheted "granny squares." There is also a basic crochet lesson and a guide to abbreviations and terms. SLB

HOUSING AND URBAN PLANNING

SS 398

Building Officials and Code Administrators International. BOCA Basic Housing-Property Maintenance Code. (1975 is 5th ed.) tri-a. index. Building Officials and Code Administrators International, 1313 E 60th St, Chicago, IL 60637. Examined: 1975. 27p. $3.75.
Aud: Cl, Pl, Sa

"This code prescribes the minimum requirements for buildings used for human occupancy and habitation. . .The concept of this code is that all repairs, alterations, extensions or other construction required by this code are to be made in accordance with the applicable requirements of the building code or such other building regulations legally in force in the jurisdiction. Similarly, the installation of all plumbing, electrical, heating, air conditioning, ventilating or similar systems installed as required by this code. . ." This code supplements the *BOCA Basic Building Code.* Articles one and two give details on administration and enforcement of the code, as well as definitions of terms. The next three articles give environmental requirements (exterior and interior structure), space and occupancy requirements, and the responsibilities of persons for maintenance, cleanliness, disposal of rubbish, etc. There is a subject index. It is advised that the code be administered by a division of the local building department. The code is revised every three years. KSK

SS 399

Building Officials and Code Administrators International. BOCA Basic Mechanical Code. ISSN 0360-4152. 1971. irreg. index. illus. Building Officials and Code Administrators International, 1313 E 60th St, Chicago, IL 60637. Examined: 2nd ed., 1975. 270p. $9.50.
Aud: Cl, Pl, Sa

"Sets forth comprehensive regulations for the safe installation and maintenance of mechanical facilities where great reliance was previously placed on accepted practice and engineering standards." Changes in the codes are published in supplements; completely new editions are prepared every three years with all approved changes since the previous edition. After introductory articles on administration and enforcement, and definitions, the code gives requirements on: heating, cooling and ventilating; steam and hot water heating systems and process piping; boilers and pressure vessels; gas, liquid, and solid fuel piping and equipment; chimneys and vents; mechanical refrigeration; incinerators; fire suppression systems; and air pollution control. Appendixes list accredited authoritative agencies, accepted engineering practice standards, material standards, and water sprinkler systems with basic components. There is a subject index, with references to section numbers. Illustrated throughout with tables and figures. KSK

SS 400
Building Officials and Code Administrators International. BOCA Basic Plumbing Code. ISSN 0098-1702. (1970 is 2nd ed.) tri-a. illus. Building Officials and Code Administration International, 1313 E. 60th St, Chicago, IL 60637. Examined: 3rd ed., 1975. 187p. $9.50.
Aud: Cl, Pl, Sa

Establishes minimum plumbing standards, in terms of performance objectives, with specific requirements for implementation. Changes in the code are published periodically in supplements to the code in a form convenient for adoption by local governments. A new edition is published every three years and contains all approved changes in the design and installation of plumbing systems since the previous editions. Includes chapters on basic principles, administration and enforcement, definitions and general regulations, and articles on more specific aspects of plumbing, such as materials, drainage systems, storm drains, vents and venting, plumbing fixtures, hospital plumbing, sewage-disposal, water supply and distribution, inspection tests, and maintenance. The appendixes cover building water supply distribution systems; typical symbols and drawings; tables, rules, and conversion calculations; and maximum rates of rainfall for various cities. Tables are used throughuot the code to illustrate various regulations. The codes are designed for adoption by state or local governments. KSK

SS 401
Downtown Mall Annual and Urban Design Report. ISSN 0364-586X. (Continues: Downtown Malls. ISSN 0098-7557.) 1975. a. bibl. illus. Alexander Research and Communications, Downtown Research and Development Center, 270 Madison Ave, Suite 1505, New York, NY 10016. Examined: v. 3, 1977. Lawrence A. Alexander, ed. 84p. $14. (v. 4, 1978. $16.)
Aud: Cl, Pl, Sa

A collection of essays on various aspects of urban revitalization. The authors are experts in architecture, urban planning, construction technology, and design. Some of the articles are downtown case studies on such cities as Rome, N.Y.; Williamsport, Pa.; Augusta, Ga.; and Kingston, N.Y. These case studies are followed by the Urban Idea File, a collection of photographs of mall areas in the cities described in the case studies and of malls in other locations. This is followed by a series of articles on such subjects as historic preservation, graphic design, construction techniques, and what benefits can be produced from a mall. There is a directory of downtown malls arranged alphabetically by state, then by city. Each entry includes the name of the mall, the executive director of the project, the company responsible for the mall, and the company's address and phone number. Following the directory is a bibliography on downtown urban design and malls compiled by the Downtown Research and Development Center. The bibliography includes books, articles, and special studies. Biographical notes on the contributors complete the volume. KSK

SS 402
Tri-State Regional Planning Commission. Annual Regional Report. ISSN 0092-2358. (Continues: Tri-State Transportation Commission. Annual Report.) 1971/72. a. illus. Tri-State Regional Planning Commission, One World Trade Center, New York, NY 10048. Examined: 1975/76, 16p.; 1976/77. 19p. free.
Aud: Cl, Pl, Sa

Annual report of the Commission which was formed by the legislators of Connecticut, New Jersey, and New York to carry out regional planning in the tri-state region. The report outlines outstanding events of the particular year; tells what and who the commissioners are and how the Commission works; details its efforts in such areas as interstate and intrastate rail service, appointment of federal housing assistance, reviews of community development projects, inventory of air pollution emissions, etc.; and outlines its expenditures. Includes photographs of the Commission's regional conference and lists members of the Commission's technical advisory group and citizen advisory panel. KSK

SS 403
Urban Affairs Annual Reviews. ISSN 0083-4688. 1967. a. bibl. Sage Publications, 275 S. Beverly Dr, Beverly Hills, CA 90212. Examined: v. 12, 1977. 304p. $20.
Aud: Cl

Each volume in the series has a separate title and different editors. Volume 12, for example, is entitled "Comparing Urban Service Delivery Systems" and is edited by Vincent Ostrom and Frances Pennell Bish. Scholarly papers by American and foreign social scientists address themselves to the theme of that particular volume. All the papers contain bibliographies; some utilize tables and figures. The Editorial Advisory Board for the series is international in scope. KSK

SS 404
Urban Institute. Annual Report. ISSN 0092-7481. 1969/70. a. illus. Urban Institute, 2100 M St, NW, Washington, DC 20037. Examined: 1974. B. J. Stiles, ed. 45p. free. (1976.)
Aud: Cl, Pl, Sa

The Urban Institute conducts research on public policy issues such as the economy, energy, housing conditions, mass transit, the control of urban growth, and social programs (welfare, national health insurance). The purpose of the research efforts is "to bring insight to the effects of prospective public actions." The **Annual Report** analyzes the Institute's research in various fields. It is divided into subject sections including distribution of income and wealth, transportation, housing, social services, etc. At the end of each section is a listing of current books and articles on the topic. The report also covers the activities of the Institute's special divisions, such as the land use center and the cable television information center. The last section gives financial and corporate information, e.g., sources of support, balance sheets, expenditures, and lists of officers, trustees, and research staff. Scattered illustrations, mostly drawings, are included. KSK

SS 405-410
U.S. Bureau of the Census. Annual Housing Survey. a. illus. U.S. Bureau of the Census, Washington, DC 20233. Dist: Superintendent of Documents, U.S. Government Printing Office, Washington, DC 20402.
Aud: Cl, Pl, Sa

SS 405
Part A: General Housing Characteristics. ISSN 0360-0513. Examined: 1976. 281p. $3.20.

SS 406
Part B: Indicators of Housing and Neighborhood Quality. ISSN 0360-5329. Examined: 1976. 178p. $2.75.

SS 407
Part C: Financial Characteristics for the Housing Inventory. Examined: 1976. 259p.

SS 408
Part D: Housing Characteristics of Recent Movers. Examined: 1976. 141p.

SS 409
Part E: Urban and Rural Housing Characteristics. Examined: 1976. 204p.

SS 410
Part F: Financial Characteristics by Indicators of Housing and Neighborhood Quality. Examined: 1976. 455p.

These annual reports on current housing are sponsored by the U.S. Department of Housing and Urban Development and conducted by the U.S. Bureau of the Census. Each part presents tabular information for the U.S. as a whole, and then for the regions: Northeast, North Central, South, and West. Appendixes at the end of each volume explain geographic area classifications, definitions of subject characteristics, and source and reliability of the estimates. A map of the regions and geographic divisions of the U.S. and a textual introduction and overview of the tabular information begins each volume. KSK

SS 411
U.S. Department of Housing and Urban Development. Annual Report. ISSN 0565-2820. 1965. a. illus. U.S. Department of Housing and Urban Development, Washington, DC 20410. Dist: Superintendent of Documents, U.S. Government Printing Office, Washington, DC 20402. Examined: 1976. 68p. $1.35.
Aud: Cl, Pl, Sa

A narrative record of major activities of all programs administered by the Department of Housing and Urban Development (HUD) during the calendar year. The **Report** first gives the highlights and a summary of HUD's activities during the year. The rest of the volume is devoted to a description of each department or office in HUD, starting with the Office of the Secretary, narrating what that particular division did during the year. Among the assistant secretaries there are, for example, offices for community planning and development, consumer affairs and regulatory functions, legislative affairs, and fair housing and equal opportunity. At the end of the report is a list of advisory bodies to the department. Illustrated throughout with black-and-white photographs of urban scenes. KSK

SS 412
Woodall's Directory of Mobile Home Communities. ISSN 0094-1891. (Continues: Woodall's Trailer Park Directory; Woodall's Mobile Home Park Directory.)

1946. a. index. illus. Woodall Publishing Co., 3500 Western Ave, Highland Park, IL 60035. Dist: Simon and Schuster, 1230 Ave of the Americas, New York, NY 10020. Examined: 1975. 400p. $5.95.
Aud: Pl

Lists and rates mobile home parks. Every year Woodall's inspectors visit every mobile home park in the country. Star ratings (from one to five) are given to the area visited. The **Directory** is arranged alphabetically by state, then by city. Provides directions on how to get to each park from the town under which it is listed. Contains a few articles on mobile home maintenance and buying, and a list of associations that are active in the mobile home industry. Some brief listings of Canadian mobile communities and a list of transport companies are also included. Advertisements for mobile home communities take up more than half of each page. KSK

INSURANCE

SS 413
Hine's Insurance Counsel. 1908. a. Hine's Legal Directory, 443 Duane St, Box 71, Glen Ellyn, IL 60131. Examined: 47th ed., 1955/56. James R. Collins and Edward E. Collins, Jr., eds. 550p. $8; $5.50 to libraries. (69th ed., 1978.)
Aud: Sa

"A directory of qualified and experienced attorneys with special interest in insurance and transportation practice. Reference section includes insurance companies with legal-claim officials, insurance and transportation organizations, state insurance officials, transportation lines, and handwriting experts." There are lists of, among other things, insurance companies, insurance company groups, transportation lines, etc. Listings are arranged by state, then by city. Included in each listing is the name of the law firm, its partners and associates, its interests (claims, etc.), the companies it represents, and transportation clients (if any). There are some very brief listings of attorneys in Puerto Rico, Canada, West Indies, Mexico, etc. KSK

SS 414
Insurance Almanac. ISSN 0074-0675. 1913. a. index. Underwriter Printing and Publishing Co., 291 S Van Brunt St, Englewood, NJ 07631. Examined: 1977. Donald E. Wolff, ed. 684p. $30.
Aud: Cl, Pl, Sa

Subtitle: "Who, what, when and where in insurance." Lists U.S. insurance companies, agents, adjusters, groups, etc. by type (management group, life, reciprocals, health, etc.). Listings note business address, officers, territories covered, date of establishment and types of insurance offered. There is an index of companies, and the table of contents gives further directory assistance. A handful of advertisements are sprinkled through the text. Most of the data is compiled from an insurance journal, *The Weekly Underwriter*. KR/JKM

SS 415
Life Insurance Fact Book. ISSN 0075-9392. (Continues: Life Insurance Fact Book. ISSN 0075-9406.) 1946. a. index. illus. American Council of Life Insurance, 1850 K St, NW, Washington, DC 20006. Examined: 32nd ed., 1977. 128p. $.50.
Aud: Pl, Sa

Formerly issued by the Institute for Life Insurance. Provides current and historical statistical information on the "U.S. business of all legal reserve life insurance companies operating in this country and the total domestic and foreign business of U.S. life companies." The clear, well-documented text is supplemented by a variety of tables, graphs, and charts showing life insurance ownership, payments, assets and premium receipts, how life insurance dollars are used, life expectancy, causes of death, etc. Includes a list of state insurance officials; mortality tables; a list of historic dates; an annotated list of life insurance organizations with addresses, phone numbers, and chief officers; and a combined glossary and subject index. JKM

SS 416
New Group Health Insurance. a. Health Insurance Institute, Statistical Services, 1850 K St, NW, Washington, DC 20006. Examined: 1977. 16p. free.
Aud: Pl

A brief summary of the Health Insurance Institute's annual survey of new group health insurance policies. Includes a section comparing trends in group insurance plans over the last five years. Employees may find the information valuable as a standard to which their own company's benefit program can be compared. JKM

SS 417
Pension Facts. a. bibl. American Council of Life Insurance, 1850 K St, NW, Washington, DC 20006. Examined: 1977. 63p. free.
Aud: Pl, Sa

Provides brief, up-to-date information on a wide variety of pension programs and on federal legislation affecting pensions and retirement plans. Chapters include: "Pension and Retirement Plans—A Review"; "The 1974 Federal Pension Legislation"; "Major Pension and Retirement Programs in the U.S."; "Private Pension Plans with Life Insurance Companies"; and "Government-Administered Pension Plans." Includes a glossary, a list of "Historic Dates of U.S. Pension and Retirement Plans," an annotated bibliography of books and pamphlets, and a list of periodicals which often include articles or information on pensions. There are a number of clear, useful tables for quick reference. An excellent introductory source for anyone interested in finding out more about retirement and pensions, and a handy information tool for those working in the field. JKM

SS 418
Source Book of Health Insurance Data. ISSN 0073-148X. 1959. a. index. illus. Health Insurance Institute, 1850 K St, NW, Washington, DC 20006. Examined: 19th ed., 1977/78. 80p. free.
Aud: Pl, Sa

Provides current information on all aspects of the health insurance business in the U.S. Statistical data is presented in clear, easy-to-read tables and charts covering such facts as premium rates, benefits payments, number of persons insured, etc. for the major forms of health insurance, e.g., hospital, surgical, regular medical, major medical, disability, and dental. Includes a glossary and a subject index. Statistics were compiled from the annual reports of insurance companies, government agencies, and hospital and medical associations. A valuable reference source for anyone interested in health care and health insurance. JKM

LABOR AND INDUSTRIAL RELATIONS

SS 419
Chamber of Commerce of the United States of America. Employee Benefits. ISSN 0069-2433. (Continues: Fringe Benefits.) 1947. bi-a. illus. Chamber of Commerce of the U.S., 1615 H St, NW, Washington, DC 20062. Examined: 1973. Fred D. Lindsey, ed. 32p. $3.
Aud: Jc, Cl, Pl

Provides statistical information on the scope and nature of employee benefits. Contains both textual matter and statistical tables. The text includes a summary of findings, facts on the distribution of benefit payments, average benefit payments, industry and regional variations, pension and insurance costs, percent of companies paying employee benefits, wage and payroll data, and a comparison of employee benefits over a 20-year period. The tables include data on: distribution of employee benefits for the year, employee benefits by type of payment, benefits as percent of payroll by region and industry groups, pension and insurance payments by industry groups, employee payroll deductions for pensions and insurance, wage data by industry groups, and a comparison of employee benefits over a 20-year period for over 150 companies. Some of this information is presented in chart form as well as in tables. KSK

SS 420
Dictionary of Labour Biography. 1972. bi-a. index. Augustus M. Kelley, 300 Fairfield Rd, Fairfield, NJ 07006. Examined: v. 1, 1972, 388p.; v. 2, 1974, 454p.; v. 3, 1976. Joyce M. Bellamy and John Saville, eds. 236p. $25.
Aud: Cl, Sa

A biographical directory of individuals who were active in the organizations and institutions of the British Labour Movement and/or who influenced the development of radical and socialist ideas in Great Britain. Coverage extends from the beginning of modern industrialism in the late 18th century to the present. Living persons are excluded. Format is similar to the British *Dictionary of National Biography*. Well edited and thorough. Includes a consolidated name index and a subject index. KR/JKM

SS 421
Directory of National Unions and Employee Associations. (Continues: Directory of National and International Labor Unions in the United States. ISSN 0070-5896.) 1971. bi-a. index. illus. U.S. Bureau of Labor Statistics, Washington, DC 20210. Dist: Superintendent of Documents, U.S. Government Printing Office, Washington, DC 20402. Examined: 1974. 156p.
Aud: Sa

A factbook on union structure and membership. The main portion of the **Directory** is a list of unions affiliated with the AFL-CIO and those unaffiliated unions which have collective bargaining agreements with different employers in more than one state. Information was gathered from questionnaires sent to each union or association listed. Other sections cover the structure of the labor movement, developments in labor during the preceding two years, union membership statistics, and functions of unions. Includes many statistical tables, a name index, and a union and employee association index. Presented in a loose-leaf format and updated between editions by periodic supplements. KR/JKM

SS 422
Employment and Earnings: United States. (Continues: Employment and Earnings Statistics for the United States. ISSN 0071-013X.) 1909. a. illus. U.S. Bureau of Labor Statistics, Department of Labor, Washington, DC 20210. Dist: Superintendent of Documents, U.S. Government Printing Office, Washington, DC 20402. Examined: 1972, 720p.; 1975. 784p.
Aud: Jc, Cl, Pl

Each volume is cumulative from 1909. Current volumes are based on the 1967 Standard Industrial Classification (SIC). Presents detailed industry statistics on U.S. non-agricultural work force. Only national data is presented. Each industry title is identified by an appropriate SIC code. Summary tables at the beginning of the volume give information on employees on manufacturing payrolls, average weekly earnings, labor turnover rates, etc. The tables are followed by charts and graphs that illustrate the statistical data. Another section gives detailed employment, hours and earnings, and labor turnover statistics by industry. The major part of the book gives detailed statistics, by industry, on employment, hours and earnings, and labor turnover. Included are monthly and annual averages on employment covering all employees, women, production workers in manufacturing, etc. Also shown are average weekly and hourly earnings, average weekly and overtime hours, job vacancies, and labor turnover rates. Following these detailed statistics, there is a section on seasonally adjusted data, indexes of aggregate weekly man-hours and payrolls, and statistics on job vacancies in manufacturing, by selected industry. Footnotes and a technical note on how the data have been collected complete the volume. KSK

SS 423
Labor Relations Yearbook. ISSN 0075-7489. 1966. a. index. Bureau of National Affairs, 1231 25th St, NW, Washington, DC 20037. Examined: 1976. 618p. $12.
Aud: Cl

A record of the year's activities in labor-management relations. Part one begins with a chronology of major events for the current year, followed by a list of major contract settlements in both manufacturing and non-manufacturing industries. Multistate settlements are listed first, followed by settlements for particular states. Increases and other provisions are given for each agreement. The rest of part one includes reports and articles on: general bargaining information, employee benefits and fringes, bargaining problems and techniques, strikes, labor relations conferences and studies, labor organizations, and the role of the federal government in labor relations. Part two is devoted to special analyses of court decisions involving specific labor-relations cases selected from the BNA's *Labor Relations Reporter*. The facts of the case and its background are presented, and the significance of the court's decision is analyzed. Part three presents tables of basic economic data. Included are major contract expirations for the upcoming year, wages and fringes, report on work stoppages, employment and unemployment for a four-year period, an urban retired couple's budget, and the GNP. A narrative summary of the data precedes each table. A topical index and a table of cases cited are also provided. KSK

SS 424
Minorities and Women in State and Local Government. 1973. a. U.S. Equal Employment Opportunity Commission, Washington, DC 20506. Dist: Superintendent of Documents, U.S. Government Printing Office, Washington, DC 20402. Examined: 1974. 6v. v. 1, 247p., $3.75; v. 2, 225p., $3.75; v. 3, 224p., $3.75; v. 4, 216p., $3.75; v. 5, 220p., $2.75; v. 6, 198p., $3.25. (1975. 7v.)
Aud: Jc, Cl, Pl

A statistical compilation based on reports filed by state and local governments in accordance with the Equal Employment Opportunity Act of 1972. The six volumes included in the 1974 annual are: U.S. Summary; State Governments; County Governments; Municipal Governments; Township Governments; and Special Districts. KSK

SS 425
Minority Group Employment in the Federal Government. 1969. a. U.S. Civil Service Commission, Washington, DC. Dist: Superintendent of Documents, U.S. Government Printing Office, Washington, DC 20402. Examined: 6th ed., 1974. 137p. $1.75. (1977. $6.05.)
Aud: Jc, Cl, Pl

A statistical compilation arranged by federal employing agency. Provides data on minority group full-time civilian employment by the federal government. The minority groups covered are Native Americans, Asian-Americans, Blacks, and Spanish-surnamed Americans. Data included are numbers of employees, pay system of the agency, and grade or salary level of minority employees. JKM

SS 426
Public Employment. 1940. a. U.S. Bureau of the Census, Department of Commerce, Washington, DC. Dist: Superintendent of Documents, U.S. Government

Printing Office, Washington, DC 20402. Examined: 1976. Alan V. Stevens, ed. 32p. $.70.
Aud: Cl

Includes statistical tables on civilian public employment in the U.S. during the past year. A narrative introduction tells how the data were gathered as well as its reliability, and analyzes the trends in public employment represented by the data. The introduction also includes some small tables, such as state and local government employment by function and by type of government. The rest of the volume gives tables that illustrate statistics such as public employment and payrolls by level of government and by function; number of public employees by level of government and by state; and full-time equivalent employment per 10,000 population of state and local governments by function and by state. KSK

SS 427

Report on National Survey of Compensation Paid Scientists and Engineers Engaged in Research and Development Activities to the U.S. Atomic Energy Commission. ISSN 0093-4267. 1968. a. Battelle Memorial Institute, Columbus Laboratories, 505 King Ave, Columbus, OH 43201. Dist: Superintendent of Documents, U.S. Government Printing Office, Washington, DC 20402. Examined: 1970. $2.50.
Aud: Sa

Presents the results of an annual survey conducted by the Columbus Laboratories of Battelle Memorial Institute under a contract with the U.S. Atomic Energy Commission. After explaining the sampling plan used to gather the statistics, the report analyzes the data and trends turned up by the survey. This explanatory material is followed by the salary tables themselves. The tables are arranged into lettered sections. The titles of the various sections include: total survey tables; bachelor's degree; master's degree; doctorate degree; middle management; median curves (supervisory level by degree level); non-degreed employees; working-as-occupation; sex; medical doctors; trend analysis; standard industrial classification, etc. An appendix gives examples of survey questionnaires. KSK

SS 428

Salary and Benefit Information for Middle Management Personnel for U.S. and Canada. 1973. a. Administrative Management Society, Maryland Rd, Willow Grove, PA 19090. Examined: 1976. 40p. $75; $50 to members.
Aud: Cl, Pl

Provides salary data and fringe benefit information for exempt middle management personnel. Top management positions are excluded. The survey presents data for middle management employees in certain firms and from selected cities in the U.S. and Canada. Twenty job titles were selected as representative positions that would be found in all types of business. Survey data on salaries by type of business is presented for the U.S. as a whole, as well as Canada and five geographic regions (Eastern, West Central, East Central, Southern, and Western). This is followed by a summary of annual salary levels for middle management positions in the U.S. and Canada. There is information on the latest trends in company policies on work hours, paid vacations and holidays, and sick leave pay, plus an outline of insurance plans and pension plans provided by the company. All annual base compensation is reported in thousands of dollars. KSK

SS 429

U.S. Bureau of Labor Statistics. Analysis of Work Stoppages. ISSN 0082-9013. 1941. a. U.S. Bureau of Labor Statistics, Department of Labor, Washington, DC 20210. Dist: Superintendent of Documents, U.S. Government Printing Office, Washington, DC 20402. Examined: 1974. Frances E. Kanterman, ed. 76p. $1.80. (1975. 80p. $2.20.)
Aud: Sa

Provides a detailed statistical presentation of work stoppages during the year. Beginning the volume is a one-page summary of highlights of the strike picture for the year. This is followed by the statistical tables which analyze work stoppages in the U.S. by month, by size and duration, by industry group and size, by union affiliations, by contract status and size, by major issue, in government by major issue and union participation, by region and state, by state and metropolitan area, by contract status and mediation, and by major issue and type of settlement — to name only a few of the tables. Following this data is an appendix containing an historical record of work stoppages by state for a 40-year period. Information on the scope of the publication, definitions, and the methods used to gather the data is included at the back of the volume. KSK

SS 430

U.S. Bureau of Labor Statistics. Handbook of Labor Statistics. ISSN 0082-9056. 1924/26. a. U.S. Bureau of Labor Statistics, Department of Labor, Washington, DC 20210. Dist: Superintendent of Documents, U.S. Government Printing Office, Washington, DC 20402.

Examined: 1971. 369p. (1977. 361p. $5.50.)
Aud: Jc, Cl

A compilation of statistics derived from the various series produced by the Bureau of Labor Statistics. Each table is historically complete, beginning with the earliest reliable and consistent data and running through the current calendar year. Related series from other governmental agencies and foreign countries are included. The data are grouped under economic subject matter headings without regard to the surveys or other sources from which the information was derived. Technical notes describing major statistical programs and identifying the tables derived from each program precede the tables. Subject headings used for each group of tables include: labor force, employment (characteristics, industry, state and region, area and city, job vacancies and labor turnover, training), unemployment (characteristics, industry, insured unemployed), hours, productivity and unit labor costs, compensation (wages, earnings by industry, earnings by region and state, supplementary compensation, social insurance), prices and living conditions (consumer price index, wholesale price index, consumer expenditures, family budget), unions and industrial relations (union membership, work stoppages, labor relations), industrial injuries, foreign labor statistics, and general economic data (GNP, national income, distribution of families by income). KSK

SS 431

U.S. Bureau of Labor Statistics. Union Wages and Hours Surveys; Local Transit Operating Employees. ISSN 0082-9099. 1936. a. illus. U.S. Bureau of Labor Statistics, Department of Labor, Washington, DC 20210. Dist: Superintendent of Documents, U.S. Government Printing Office, Washington, DC 20402. Examined: no. 1903, 1975, 16p.; no. 1974, 1977. 18p. $.45.
Aud: Jc, Cl, Pl

The Bureau of Labor Statistics also conducts annual surveys of wage rates and scheduled hours of work for specified crafts or jobs as provided in labor-management agreements which are published as *Trades; Printing Trades; Motortruck Drivers;* and *Grocery Store Employees*. All of the survey publications follow the same format. These studies present the wage rates in effect on the first workday in July, as reported to the Bureau by appropriate local labor organizations in each of the cities included in the survey. A narrative at the beginning of the survey gives a summary plus survey findings of wage trends, industry averages, cost-of-living additives, regional and city averages, hours of work, and supplementary benefits. This is followed by tables that give data on wage rate indexes in the U.S. since 1929, average wage rates for the year ending July 1, wage-rate distribution, cents-per-hour changes in wage rates, weekly hours in the U.S., average wage rates and changes, average wage rates by population, etc. Also given are two charts that show annual percent increases in wage rates of local-transit operating employees by classification for a ten-year period, and annual increases in current and constant-dollar wage rates of local-transit operating employees and in the Consumer Price Index over a ten-year period. The appendix outlines the scope and methods of the survey. KSK

SS 432

U.S. Civil Service Commission. Manpower Statistics Division. Occupations of Federal White-Collar Workers. 1960. a. illus. U.S. Civil Service Commission, Manpower Statistics Division, Washington, DC 20415. Dist: Superintendent of Documents, U.S. Government Printing Office, Washington, DC 20402. Examined: 1975. 215p. $3.05.
Aud: Jc, Cl, Pl
Indexed in: *Congressional Information Service Index*.

Released as part of the SM-56 series of personnel statistics reports. Presents statistical information on full-time federal civilian white-collar employment by occupation, grade, salary, sex, geographic location, and major employing agency. Includes comparisons with previous years. The report begins with highlights of the federal white-collar work force for the year, followed by a narrative profile of such workers accompanied by charts. The statistical tables are divided into two appendixes, one for the current year, the other for the past year. Both sections contain the following information on full-time federal civilian white-collar employment: major geographic area by sex; pay system categories by sex, worldwide; employment and average salary by major geographic area and sex; occupational distribution by grade, worldwide; occupational distribution by selected agency, worldwide; and grade distribution of employment and average salary by major geographic area and sex. KSK

SS 433

U.S. Civil Service Commission. Manpower Statistics Division. Pay Structure of the Federal Civil Service. 1946. a. U.S. Civil Service Commission, Manpower Statistics Division, Washington, DC 20415. Dist: Superintendent of Documents, U.S. Government

Printing Office, Washington, DC 20402. Examined: 1976. 42p. $.55.

Aud: Jc, Cl, Pl

Indexed in: *Congressional Information Service Index.*

Presents salary and wage information on full-time federal civilian employees. The report begins with a narrative that gives the background of the federal pay structure, statutory and other pay systems information, how the annual salary and wage survey is conducted, and highlights of the survey. This is followed by a brief series of statistical charts that give information on such items as distribution of full-time employment by pay category and the distribution of full-time employment by geographic area. Finally, there are the statistical tables which contain information on such items as: employment in foreign service pay systems; distribution of employees by salary interval and pay system; employees by federal agency and pay system; and a chronology of general pay schedule legislation. There is an appendix of salary schedules (general schedule, foreign service, VA, etc.) showing salaries for all civil service grades. KSK

SS 434

U.S. Civil Service Commission. Manpower Statistics Division. Study of Employment of Women in the Federal Government. ISSN 0097-7764. (Continues: Federal Civilian Employment of Women.) 1966. a. U.S. Civil Service Commission, Manpower Statistics Division, Washington, DC 20415. Dist: Superintendent of Documents, U.S. Government Printing Office, Washington, DC 20402. Examined: 10th ed., 1975. 356p. $2.55.

Aud: Cl, Pl

Presents statistical information on full-time federal civilian white-collar employment by agency, grade or salary equivalency, sex, and occupation. It starts with a page of highlights from the study, then tells how the data was gathered and how to read the figures. This is followed by some narrative and charts that give general findings. The rest of the volume is devoted to the statistical tables. Information in the tables covers all federal agencies. The first set of tables indicates full-time white-collar employment by agency and geographic area and by general schedule equivalent grades and other pay systems. The same information is also broken down by occupational group. Next are tables of full-time white-collar employment worldwide for all agencies by special categories within occupational group. Finally, there are statistics for full-time white-collar employment worldwide by occupational group. At the end of the volume is a general schedule of annual salary rates. KSK

SS 435

U.S. Department of Labor. Manpower and Automation Research. ISSN 0076-4132. 1963. a. U.S. Department of Labor, Office of Manpower, Automation, and Training, 14th St and Constitution Ave, NW, Washington, DC 20210. Dist: Superintendent of Documents, U.S. Government Printing Office, Washington, DC 20402. Examined: 1965, 116p.; no. 41, 1975. 41p. $1.05.

Aud: Cl, Sa

Lists contract and grant research sponsored by the Office of Manpower, Automation, and Training, under the Department of Labor's Manpower Administration. Subject areas of research include counseling and guidance, education, labor force, job finding and placement, mobility, occupations, projections, technological change, general training, women, and youth. Part one lists projects initiated during the fiscal year covered by the publication, alphabetically arranged by name of contractor. Part two lists ongoing projects initiated before the fiscal year. Information in both parts includes name of contractor, address, contract number, the project title, principal staff, objectives and procedures of the contract, status of the project, and, where possible, highlights of findings. Part three provides a selected list of completed projects, giving contractor, principal investigator, and title of the project. An appendix lists alphabetically by state depository libraries where copies of research reports can be located. Another appendix gives guidelines for submission of contract research proposals. KSK

SS 436

U.S. Department of Labor. Employment and Training Administration. Research and Development Projects. (Continues: Manpower Research and Development Projects; Manpower Research Projects. ISSN 0082-9994.) 1963. a. index. U.S. Department of Labor, Employment and Training Administration, 14th and Constitution Ave, NW, Washington, DC 20210. Examined: 1977. 294p. free.

Aud: Cl, Sa

Summarizes the projects funded by the Office of Research and Development of the Employment and Training Administration. Includes all projects completed within a three year span. The first four chapters describe projects in the following areas: program planning and administration, programs and techniques, the labor market, and economic and social policies. Chapter five is devoted to institutional, dissertation, and small-grant research projects. Within each major area there are divisions into smaller subject fields, e.g., programs and techniques covers projects in education, public employment programs, welfare recipient programs, worker assessment and orientation, etc. Each project listing includes the following information: name of project, institution that is handling it, name of person in charge, contract or grant number, whether it is still in progress or completed, subject descriptors, and, where provided, a brief description of the project's purpose. Chapter six lists projects relating to foreign trade and U.S. investment abroad. Appendixes give guidelines of submission of R & D proposals, conditions for doctoral dissertation grants and small grant research projects under CETA, and an excerpt from the 1973 CETA Act. There are indexes of contract and grant numbers, contractor and grantee organizations, individuals associated with contracts and grants, and research subjects. KSK

SS 437

U.S. Equal Employment Opportunity Commission. Equal Employment Opportunity Report. ISSN 0083-0526. 1966. a. U.S. Equal Employment Opportunity Commission, G St NW, Washington, DC 20506. Dist: Superintendent of Documents, U.S. Government Printing Office, Washington, DC 20402. Examined: 1970, 2v., 1474p.; 1975. Frank A. Haughton, ed. 2v. $11.50.
Aud: Jc, Cl, Pl

A collection of employment data compiled by the Equal Employment Opportunity Commission based on reports submitted by all employers of 100 or more employees. Omitted from the figures are temporary employees and those who work for government employers. Listings cover nine occupational categories (officials and managers, professionals, technicians, sales workers, office and clerical, craftsmen-skilled, operatives-semiskilled, laborers-unskilled, service workers) and four minority groups (Black, Asian-American, Native American, and Spanish-surnamed American) which are divided into male and female. Volume one contains tables for minority group employment by occupation, sex, and state, followed by data on minority group employment for selected states by industry, occupation, and sex. The second volume contains totals for Standard Metropolitan Statistical Areas and for selected industries in these areas. The list of SMSA and a list of industries are provided at the beginning of the first volume. KSK

SS 438

U.S. Federal Mediation and Conciliation Service. Annual Report. ISSN 0083-0771. 1948. a. illus. U.S. Federal Mediation and Conciliation Service, Department of Labor Bldg, 14th St and Constitution Ave, NW, Washington, DC 20210. Dist: Superintendent of Documents, U.S. Government Printing Office, Washington, DC 20402. Examined: no. 29, 1976. 80p. $1.30.
Aud: Cl, Pl

Annual report for the fiscal year reflecting the activities of the Federal Mediation and Conciliation Service (FMCS). The report begins with a brief introduction to the functions of the Service, then continues with a description of its activities in the private sector and in public employee bargaining; its role as a mediator in disputes; the activities of the office of technical services, the office of arbitration services, the office of the general counsel, office of administration, and the FMCS's public information service. The report is illustrated throughout with photographs of the FMCS in action and its leading officials. There are also statistical tables on such subjects as the size of bargaining units in negotiations, federal agency cases, length of renewed contracts, and the number and percentage of closed FMCS dispute mediation cases. Appendixes give the text of the Labor-Management Relations Act of 1947 (Titles one and two) and the Health Care Act. There is a listing of the regional offices of the FMCS and a map showing the location of each. KSK

SS 439

U.S. National Labor Relations Board. Annual Report. ISSN 0083-2200. 1936. a. index. U.S. National Labor Relations Board, 1230 16th St, NW, Washington, DC 20572. Dist: Superintendent of Documents, U.S. Government Printing Office, Washington, DC 20402. Examined: 41st ed., 1976, 257p.; 42nd ed., 1977. 257p. $2.55.
Aud: Cl

Describes the activities of the National Labor Relations Board during the year. The first chapter summarizes the NLRB's activities showing highlights in case activity, operations, and decisions. The jurisdiction of the Board is examined in the next chapter. Succeeding sections discuss the following aspects of the NLRB: effect of concurrent arbitration proceedings, board procedure, representation proceedings, unfair labor practices, supreme court litigation, contempt litigation, enforcement litigation, injunction litigation, and special and miscellaneous litigation. These narrative discussions are followed by an index of cases mentioned, a glossary of terms used in statistical tables, and a subject index to annual report tables. The rest of the report is devoted to statistical tables covering the fiscal year. Among other items, there are tables for: total cases received, closed, and pending; types of unfair labor practices alleged; industrial and geographic distribution of cases received; analysis of elections conducted in representation cases closed; and distribution of unfair labor practice situations received. The introductory chapter contains charts illustrating the number of contested board decisions issued and the amount of back pay received by discriminatees. KSK

SS 440
U.S. National Labor Relations Board. Digest and Index of Decisions of the National Labor Relations Board. Annual Supplements. ISSN 0076-4132. 1951. a. index. U.S. National Labor Relations Board, 1230 16th St, NW, Washington, DC 20572. Dist: Superintendent of Documents, U.S. Government Printing Office, Washington, DC 20402. Examined: 1970. 919p.
Aud: Sa

A selective guide to decisions issued by the Board. Arranged into a number of sections: definitions, evidence, investigation and certification of representatives, jurisdiction, jurisdictional dispute proceedings, practice and procedure, remedial orders (employers), remedial orders (unions), unfair labor practices (employers), unfair labor practices (unions), and unit appropriate collective bargaining. Each entry has a number and a title, followed by a brief (one paragraph to one page) description of the Board's decision, and the NLRB volume and decision number where the full decision may be read. The index in the front of the book outlines the various topics and sub-topics that are covered by the volume. There is also an alphabetical subject index to employees that the NLRB either decided upon (included) or refused to decide (exclusions), accompanied by citation number to the full decision. KSK

SS 441
U.S. National Mediation Board. Annual Report. ISSN 0083-2286. (Continues: Annual Report of the Mediation Board.) 1935. a. U.S. National Mediation Board, 1230 16th St, NW, Washington, DC 20572. Dist: Superintendent of Documents, U.S. Government Printing Office, Washington, DC 20402. Examined: 1975, 85p., $1.15; 1977. 115p.
Aud: Cl, Pl

Summarizes the activity of the National Mediation Board for the previous fiscal year; the new fiscal year ends September 30. After a brief summary and observations on the Board's projects during the current year, there is a discussion of the cases handled by the Board and their disposition. Chapters on mediation disputes, representation disputes, arbitration and emergency boards, wage and rule agreements, interpretation and application of agreements, and organization and finances of the NMB follow. Appendix A gives the report of the National Railroad Adjustment Board. Appendix B gives lists of neutral arbitrators and referees that were appointed. Finally, appendix C gives a list of tables, e.g., number of cases received and disposed of within the past forty years; disposition of mediation cases by method, class of carrier, and issue involved; number of cases disposed of by major groups of employees; strikes in the railroad and airline industries, etc. KSK

SS 442
U.S. Women's Bureau. Handbook on Women Workers. ISSN 0083-3622. (Continues: Handbook of Facts on Women Workers.) 1948. bi-a. bibl. index. illus. U.S. Women's Bureau, Department of Labor, Washington, DC 20210. Dist: Superintendent of Documents, U.S. Government Printing Office, Washington, DC 20402. Examined: 1975. 435p. $7.50.
Aud: Cl, Pl

Presents facts relating to the present economic, civil, and political status of women. Divided into three parts: women in the labor force, laws governing women's employment and status, and institutions and mechanisms to advance the status of women. Part one gives information and statistics in both text and tables on women as workers; women's employment by occupations and industries; income and earnings; education, training, and employment; and the outlook for women workers. Part two describes federal and state labor laws of special interest to women, maternity standards, and the civil and political stetus of women. Part three describes federal machinery for advancing women's status, as well as various commissions on the status of women and international activities. There is an appendix of reference sources that list women's organizations and another that offers a bibliography of selected publications from the U.S. Department of Labor. There is a subject index for the entire handbook. Parts one and two include an introduction that highlights the information that follows. Illustrated with charts. KSK

SS 443
Yearbook of Labour Statistics. ISSN 0084-3857. 1935/36. a. International Laborer Organization, Publications, CH 1211 Geneva 22, Switzerland. Dist: International Laborer Organization, 1750 New York

Ave, NW, Washington, DC 20006. Examined: 36th ed., 1976. $37.95.
Aud: Cl, Pl

Summarizes principal labor statistics in 180 countries and territories arranged by topic (employment, unemployment, hours of work, productivity, wages, prices, accidents, disputes), then by continent and nation. Arrangement is explained in a separate table. Introductions to each topic outline their scope. In English, French, and Spanish. Supplemented by the quarterly *Bulletin of Labour Statistics*. KMH

LAW

SS 444
American Bar Association. Law Student Division. Federal Government Legal Career Opportunities. ISSN 0065-7476. (Continues: Federal Government Job Opportunities for Young Lawyers.) 1952. a. index. American Bar Association, Law Student Division, 1155 E 60th St, Chicago, IL 60637. Examined: 1975. David Martin, ed. 158p. $4. (1978. Susan Gilmore, ed. $4.)
Aud: Cl, Sa

Lists the various branches of the federal government (legislative, judicial, and executive departments, and independent agencies) and details the job opportunities for attorneys in the various areas or departments within each branch. Each departmental listing includes: anticipated openings, number of attorneys employed, location of positions, entrance grades and qualifications, opportunities for experienced attorneys, special selection factors, nature of legal work, training and opportunities for promotion, quasi-legal positions for law graduates, how to apply, opportunities for specialization, summer employment (if any), and additional information. Some of these headings are omitted from department listings if they are not applicable. The preface to the book includes a chart of the U.S. government and a brief chapter on the government lawyer (benefits, eligibility, etc.). There is an index of the various government agencies and of type of occupations. KSK

SS 445
The American Bench. 1977. a. Reginald Bishop Forster and Associates, 121 W Franklin Ave, Minneapolis, MN 55404. Examined: 1977. Mary Reincke and Jeannen C. Wilhelmi, eds. 1906p. $80.
Aud: Sa

Attempts to provide comprehensive coverage of the American judiciary. Over 14,500 judges on federal and state courts are included. Jurisdictional and geographic information is provided for federal and state courts. There are maps of judicial divisions and a list of judges in alphabetical order giving title, court level served, and office address. The biographies were contributed by the judges and include personal data, education, important decisions, authorship, honors, awards, interests, and civic activities. SJV

SS 446
American Journal of Jurisprudence. ISSN 0065-8995. (Continues: National Law Forum.) 1956. a. bibl. index. University of Notre Dame, Notre Dame Law School, Notre Dame, IN 46556. Examined: v. 21, 1976. Charles E. Rice and Robert E. Rodes, eds. 215p. $7.50. (1977. 240p.)
Aud: Cl, Pl, Sa
Indexed in: *Catholic Periodical and Literature Index; Index to Legal Periodicals.*

A publication of the Natural Law Institute which is "dedicated to a critical examination of the significance of natural law for our times. To this end it seeks to provide a meeting ground for discussion and a clearinghouse for information. Scholarly contributions from the point of view of any intellectual discipline, whether scientific, historical, political, legal, philosophical, or theological, and whether favorable or unfavorable to the natural law approach, will be welcome." Each issue contains approximately nine scholarly articles, plus a limited number of lengthy book reviews. A bibliography compiled by Joachim Bohnert includes books and articles on natural law, jurisprudence, and related areas published in Germany, Switzerland, Austria, France, and Italy during that particular year. The publishing date of each issue is in the fall, but teachers may obtain a list of the articles which will appear in the next issue of the **Journal**, plus a short summary of each article, in the spring. Back stock and reprint rights of the **Journal** are held by and are available from William S. Hein and Co., 1285 Main St, Buffalo, NY 14209. KSK

SS 447
American Society of International Law. Proceedings. ISSN 0066-0647. 1907. a. index. American Society of International Law, 2223 Massachusetts Ave, NW, Washington, DC 20008. Examined: 69th ed., 1975; 70th ed., 1976; 71st ed., 1977. James A. R. Nafziger, ed. 301p. $9.
Aud: Cl, Sa
Indexed in: *Index to Legal Periodicals; Social Science Citation Index.*

Covers the annual meeting of the American Society of International Law (ASIL). It includes the papers of the various panel discussions, luncheon addresses, and the speech given at the annual dinner, plus papers presented during the semifinal and final rounds of the Philip C. Jessup International Law Moot Court Competition. Appendixes include the report of the Executive Secretary of the Association of Student International Law Societies, a list of current officers and committees of the ASIL, and its incorporation act, constitutions, and regulations. Many of the papers in the proceedings contain bibliographical footnotes. Topics of the panels cover various current subjects of interest in international law, such as payments abroad, control of terrorism, environmental protection, human rights, the law of the sea, access to supplies and resources, boycotts, etc. Cumulative indexes have been published for 1907-1920, 1921-1940, and 1941-1960. KSK/SJV

SS 448

Annual Legal Bibliography. ISSN 0073-0793. 1961. a. index. Harvard Law School Library, Publications L347, Langdell Hall, Cambridge, MA 02138. Examined: v. 17, 1977. Margaret M. Moody and Margaret L. Aycock, eds. 667p. $60.
Aud: Cl, Sa

A cumulation of *Current Legal Bibliography* which is a selected list of books and articles received by the Harvard Law School Library. Four basic areas are covered: common law jurisdictions, civil law and other jurisdictions, private international law, and public international law. Includes an analytical table of contents and a subject and geographic index. Entries are not annotated. SJV

SS 449

Annual Review of Population Law. 1974. a. Law and Population Programme, The Fletcher School of Law and Diplomacy, Tufts University, Medford, MA 02155. Examined: 1974; 1975; 1976. 184p.
Aud: Cl, Sa

Produced under the auspices of the International Advisory Committee on Population and Law. Later editions will be published by the United Nations Fund for Population Activities.

Laws are listed by subject under broad categories, i.e., general population policy, fertility regulation, family status and welfare, children and child welfare, public welfare, public health, education, property and economic factors, migration, and census and vital statistics. A second table of contents provides access by country and international organizations. The body of the publication provides texts and references to constitutions, legislation, regulations, legal opinions, and judicial decisions relating to population law. SJV

SS 450

Annual Survey of African Law. ISSN 0066-4405. 1967. a. bibl. index. Rex Collings, 69 Marylebone High St, London W1, England. Dist: Rowman and Littlefield, 81 Adams Dr, Totowa, NJ 07512. Examined: 1972; 1973. Neville Rubin and Eugene Cotran, eds. 384p. $47.50. (1978.)
Aud: Cl, Sa

Covers law and legal developments in the countries of Africa during one year. Most of the articles are written by legal scholars from the particular country. Africa is divided into Commonwealth African countries, Francophonic African countries, and others. Areas covered include constitutional law, administrative law, judicial system, criminal law and procedure, family law and succession, property law, commercial law, tax law, civil practice and procedure, and labor law. Each volume includes a bibliographic chapter of books and articles on African legal problems. It covers the continent, regions, and individual countries. Format is narrative. A table of cases and a table of statutes are included. South Africa is covered in the bibliographic chapter but not in the legal surveys. SJV

SS 451

Annual Survey of American Law. ISSN 0066-4413. 1942. a. bibl. index. Oceana Publications, Dobbs Ferry, NY 10522. Examined: 1976. Terry C. Pelster, ed. 797p. $20.
Aud: Cl, Sa
Indexed in: *Index to Legal Periodicals.*

A publication of the New York University School of Law. Staff members of the **Annual Survey,** as well as outside authorities (professors, lawyers), describe the latest legal developments taking place during the year in various fields. Each chapter focuses on a particular area and covers the rulings and decisions that affect that field. Subjects include banking, federal Indian law, sex discrimination, criminal procedure and law, labor law, torts, consumer protection, family law, communications law, legal and constitutional history, securities regulation, bankruptcy, First Amendment rights, environment, health, copyright, election law, military law, and property. At the end of the book there is a table of cases discussed throughout the annual and a topical index. Each chapter contains numerous bibliographical footnotes and references.

Some volumes are issued for a single year (1976), others contain two dates on the volume (1973/74, 1974/75). KSK

SS 452
Bibliographic Guide to Law. 1974. a. G. K. Hall and Co., 70 Lincoln St, Boston, MA 02111. Examined: 1977. 2v. 1307p. $75.
Aud: Cl, Pf, Sa

Provides complete Library of Congress cataloging information for titles in the fields of U.S. law, international law and arbitration, treaties, and foreign law that were acquired and cataloged by the Library of Congress and the Research Libraries of the New York Public Library during the preceding year. Titles, main entries, added entries, series, and subject headings are interfiled in one alphabetical sequence for easy access. Useful as a selection and cataloging tool for librarians, volumes also have value for students and professionals in the field as a guide to current literature. JKM

SS 453
British Yearbook of International Law. 1920/21. a. index. Oxford University Press, 200 Madison Ave, New York, NY 10016. Examined: v. 46, 1972/73. Sir Humphrey Waldock and R. Y. Jennings, eds. 567p. £11.50. (1977.)
Aud: Cl, Sa
Indexed in: *Legal Periodicals Index.*

A scholarly annual which treats and comments on leading issues in international law, such as territorial and boundary disputes, conflicts of laws, jurisdiction, contested jurisdiction, and abuse of rights. The leading articles are written by international experts. The next section gives briefer summaries of opinions and decisions. Decisions of British courts involving international law, the Court of Justice of the European Communities, and the European Convention on Human Rights are discussed in narrative format. A lengthy section is devoted to signed book reviews of considerable length. A cumulative index covering 1920/21 to 1960 is available. Publication was suspended between 1940 and 1943. SJV

SS 454
Canadian Yearbook of International Law; Annuaire Canadien de Droit International. ISSN 0069-0058. 1963. a. index. University of British Columbia Press, 2075 Westbrook Place, Vancouver, BC, V6T 1W5, Canada. Examined: v. 14, 1976. C. B. Bourne, ed. 430p. $10.
Aud: Cl, Sa

Indexed in: *Index to Legal Periodicals; Canadian Periodical Index.*

Published under the auspices of the Canadian Branch, International Law Association. Articles and reviews are in either French or English, primarily the latter. The articles, comprising over half of the yearbook, present scholarly views on various subjects in the field of international law, such as the new power balance of third world nations in the U.N., the doctrine of denial of justice, humanitarian law, and the teaching of international law in Canada. The longer articles are followed by short notes and comments. Next is a compilation of Canadian practice in international law during the year as reflected in public correspondence and statements of the Department of External Affairs. There is also a compilation of important Canadian cases reported during the preceding year in the fields of public international law and conflict of laws. Finally, there is a book review section including short to medium length, signed reviews. KSK

SS 455
Cases Decided in United States Court of Customs and Patent Appeals; Customs Cases Adjudged in the Court of Customs and Patent Appeals. (1975/76 is v. 73.) a. index. Superintendent of Documents, U.S. Government Printing Office, Washington, DC 20402. Examined: v. 73, 1975/76. Helen G. Nassif, ed. 140p. $5.25.
Aud: Sa

Summaries of cases tried before the Court of Customs and Patent Appeals. Each case involves litigation by the U.S. against various companies and institutions in matters revolving around tariff laws and dutiable importations, exemptions, and the classification of articles for duty free entry. Besides the opinions of the Court, the serial includes a table of cases reported and a table of cases cited, the action of the U.S. Supreme Court in the cases that are appealed, indexes of subject matters, statutes construed and referred to, and an analysis of the cases by section. KSK

SS 456
Catalogue: An Index to Indian Legal Materials and Resources in the National Indian Law Library. ISSN 0092-3419. 1973/74. bi-a. index. Native American Rights Fund, 1506 Broadway, Boulder, CO 80302. Examined: 1976. various paging. $20.
Aud: Cl, Pl, Sa

Indexes the National Indian Law Library's holdings on Native American litigation and related issues. In three parts. Part one lists materials by subject. If an item concerns litigation, a brief description is provided. Each item is assigned an acquisitions number. Part two lists materials by acquisitions number with detailed information on holdings. Part three is a plaintiff/defendant and an author/title index to part two. Most materials are available on request from the Library for a per-page reproduction charge. JKM

SS 457
Comparative Juridical Review. ISSN 0069-7893. (Continues: Comparative Judical Review.) 1964. a. bibl. Rainforth Foundation, Pan American Institute of Comparative Law, 3001 Ponce de Leon Rd, Coral Gables, FL 33134. Examined: v. 13, 1976. Mario Diaz-Cruz, ed. 249p. free.
Aud: Pf

A publication of the Pan American Institute of Comparative Law, a facility of the Rainforth Foundation. A bilingual publication, each article is presented first in Spanish, then in an English translation. The papers deal with various aspects of Spanish and Cuban law, such as unjust enrichment, factoring, and simulation. Each article contains bibliographic footnotes. At the end of the volume are unsigned book reviews of medium length, also in English and Spanish. KSK

SS 458
Corporate Counsel's Annual. (1977 is 12th ed.) a. bibl. index. Matthew Bender and Co., 235 E 45th St, New York, NY 10017. Examined: 12th ed., 1977. Harold Friedman, John P. O'Brien, and Herbert S. Schlagman, eds. 2v. 1718p. $37.50.
Aud: Cl, Sa

Offers the past year's articles in the main areas of interest to the corporate attorney and house counsel. Volume one is divided into four parts: corporate law and developments, securities regulations, antitrust and trade regulation, and labor relations. Volume two is in three parts: commercial law—the uniform commercial code, international law, and federal taxation. Each part includes articles on specific aspects of the topic written by experts in the field who analyze the subject and any developments that have occurred in it during the preceding year. The articles are reprints from law journals. At the end of each of the seven sections is an annotated bibliography. The index to both volumes is at the end of volume two. Formerly in one volume, the annual has been issued in two volumes since 1976. KSK

SS 459
Customs and Practices of Notaries Public and Digest of Notary Laws in the U.S. ISSN 0070-2269. 1966. bi-a. index. illus. National Notary Association, 23012 Ventura Blvd, Woodland Hill, CA 91364. Examined: 4th ed., 1974. 168p. $5.80.
Aud: Sa

"Written in lay language, this book is addressed to the notary public in the U.S. who is not an attorney." The first part of the book is divided into nine chapters which contain information on the history of the notary public; what a notary public is; what a notarization is and why it is necessary; the powers, functions, and practice of notaries public; and the notary public's limitations, obligations, and civil and criminal liability. The second part of the volume is a digest of notary laws in the 50 states and the District of Columbia. Each state digest includes the state seal; the qualifications, powers, and duties of a notary in that state; and reasons for his/her removal or resignation. The appendix of the book contains the text of the uniform acknowledgement act (as amended). An index and some sample forms are included at the end of the volume. KSK

SS 460
Digest of Legal Activities of International Organizations and Other Institutions. ISSN 0070-4857. 1967. a. irreg. index. Oceana Publications, Dobbs Ferry, NY 10522. Examined: 3rd ed., 1976. unpaged. $50.
Aud: Cl

Compiled by UNIDROIT (International Institute for the Unification of Private Law). The first edition was published in 1967, the second in 1974, and the third appeared in 1975. The international organizations are arranged by subject in encyclopedia fashion. The volume begins with three lists: an index to international and interfederal organizations, a list of addresses of the organizations, and a list of initials and acronyms. A subject index follows. Under each broad subject is listed the particular aspect of that subject that the organization is concerned with, the name of the organization and the branch concerned with that aspect, terms of reference, a brief summary of the subject, preparatory work, state of work, and other information. A supplement to the 1976 edition is in process. KSK

SS 461
Directory of Law Libraries. (Continues: Law Libraries in the United States and Canada.) (1976 is 18th ed.) bi-a. American Association of Law Libraries, 53 W Jackson Blvd, Rm 1201, Chicago, IL 60604. Dist: Commerce Clearing House, 4025 W Peterson Ave, Chica-

go, IL 60646. Examined: 18th ed., 1976, 132p.; 19th ed., 1978. 146p. $10; $5 to AALL members.
Aud: Cl, Sa

A compilation of information about law libraries throughout the world. Data is obtained from computer printouts mailed to each library listed in the last edition, from new membership records at American Association of Law Libraries headquarters, and from AALL chapter officials. U.S. listings are confined to information about responding law libraries in three categories: institutional members of the AALL; law libraries employing one or more members who are AALL members; and unaffiliated law libraries with collections of 10,000 or more volumes. Information about responding libraries outside the U.S. is included without regard to AALL affiliation or size of collection. Following the section on the bylaws and constitution of the AALL, there is a geographical breakdown of law libraries. An asterisk preceding the name of a library or an individual indicates AALL membership. Information in each entry includes name of library, number of volumes, address, librarian's name, and the names of any AALL members who work there. Canadian and foreign law libraries are also listed geographically. Information on the certification of law librarians and a list of current AALL officers and chapters are appended. KSK/SJV

SS 462

Directory of Law Teachers. ISSN 0070-573X. (Continues: Directory of Teachers in Member Schools.) 1922. a. West Publishing Co., 50 Kellogg Blvd, St. Paul, MN 55102. Examined: 1976; 1977. 1089p. $15.
Aud: Sa

Listing in this directory is open to anyone who is on the faculty of a law school that belongs to the American Association of Law Schools, is on the American Bar Association's list of approved schools, is part of a university accredited by an appropriate regional accrediting agency, or is a Canadian Associate. Teachers are listed alphabetically by school and by subject. A list of law schools in the U.S. and Canada is included. SJV

SS 463

Directory of Lawyer Referral Services and Committees. ISSN 0070-5748. (Continues: Directory of Lawyer Referral Services, Legal Aid and Defender Services, and Legal Assistance Offices of the Armed Forces.) 1962. a. American Bar Association, 1155 E 60th St, Chicago, IL 60637. Examined: 1977. unpaged. free.
Aud: Cl, Pl

Compiled by the standing committee on lawyer referral service of the American Bar Association. The first part is a listing of lawyer referral services arranged by state, then city. Each entry includes the name of the referral service, name of the bar association, the services director or executive director, address, and phone number. There is also a selected listing of Canadian services. The second part is a listing of legal aid and defender offices, which includes the name of the program or society, address, and phone number. The name and address of the public defender, if there is one, are also supplied. Finally, there is a listing of legal assistance offices of the armed forces, first arranged by state, then by branch of service (Army, Navy, Air Force, and Coast Guard). The name, address, and phone number of the office are provided. KSK

SS 464

Directory of Women Law Graduates and Attorneys in the U.S.A. ISSN 0092-1416 (Continues: Directory of Women Attorneys in the United States. ISSN 0092-1416) 1972. bi-a. Ford Associates, 701 S Federal Ave, Butler, IN 46721. Examined: 1974; 1977. Lee Ellen Ford, ed. 5v. $46.50.
Aud: Sa

A mimeographed directory of women law graduates and attorneys in all states, arranged alphabetically by state. There is an introductory statistical summary article on women attorneys. The information is presented differently for each state. There is more information for some states than others. In some states, e.g., Connecticut, those who passed the bar examination and have feminine sounding names are listed. Often there are year-by-year listings of female members of a law school graduating class. Basic information given is name and address. The **Directory** is difficult to use and must contain many errors. However, it is one of a kind and does show the increasing numbers of women in the legal profession. SJV

SS 465

Environment Law Review. 1970. a. index. Clark Boardman Co., 435 Hudson St, New York, NY 10014. Examined: 1976, H. Floyd Sherrod, ed., 699p., $32.50; 1977. 725p. $39.50. (v. 9, 1978. $39.50.)
Aud: Cl

A collection of articles reprinted from various American law journals. The editor has written an introductory survey of the current literature and an overview of the developments in the law of environmental control which precedes the articles in the collection. Each edition includes materials which appear during the preceding year. In the 1976 volume, articles are grouped under broad subject categories: perspectives; energy and the environment; pollution control; land use planning; and environment and litigation. This arrangement varies from year to year. Each section contains from two to four articles. A cross-reference table of original law review citations and corresponding page numbers to the particular volume is appended at the end of the text. Finally, there is a subject and author index. There is no bibliography, but there are many references in the footnotes to each article. This title would be useful in a library which has an interest in environmental law but lacks the budget to subscribe to the major law periodicals. KSK/SJV

SS 466

Index to Legal Periodicals. ISSN 0019-4077. 1926. a. w/m. and q. suppls.; tri-a. cum. index. H. W. Wilson Co., 950 University Ave, Bronx, NY 10452. Examined: 1926/28; 1973/76. Tatana Sahanek and Madeleine Michael, eds. 1333p. service basis.
Aud: Cl, Sa

Published for the American Association of Law Libraries. Indexes more than 374 periodicals published in the U.S., Canada, Great Britain, Ireland, Australia, and New Zealand. Yearbooks, annual institutes, and annual reviews are also covered. Divided into three parts: a combined subject and author index, a table of cases, and a book review index. Each annual and three-year cumulative volume includes a list of subject headings and cross references. SJV

SS 467

Index to Periodicals Related to Law. 1958. a. w/q. suppls. index. Glanville Publications, Dobbs Ferry, NY 10522. Examined: v. 19, no. 4, 1977. Roy M. Mersky and J. Myron Jacobstein, eds. 64p. $25.
Aud: Cl, Pl

A selective index to periodicals in the social and behavioral sciences of interest to the legal community. These periodicals are not indexed in the **Index to Legal Periodicals** or the *Index to Foreign Legal Periodicals*. The annual volume consists of four parts: an index to subject headings, an index to articles by subject, an author index, and a list of periodicals indexed. There is a ten-year cumulation covering 1958-1968 and a five-year cumulation covering 1969-1973. SJV

SS 468

International Court of Justice. Yearbook. 1946/47. a. International Court of Justice, Peace Palace, The Hague 2012, Netherlands. Dist: United Nations Publications, Rm LX 2300, New York, NY 10017. Examined: 31st ed., 1976/77. 144p. $5.
Aud: Sa

Provides general information concerning the International Court of Justice, its organization, jurisdiction, activities, and administration. The texts of the documents by which the Court was created are given. The composition of the court and biographies of the judges are included. Jurisdiction is examined, and texts governing jurisdiction are given. A review chapter on the work of the Court examines cases reviewed that year and the decisions of the Court. Publications and finances are also covered. SJV

SS 469

Juvenile Law Litigation Directory. 1972. a. index. Institute of Judicial Administration, Juvenile Justice Standards Project, 80 Fifth Ave, Rm 1501, New York, NY 10011. Examined: 1972. J. Lawrence Schultz and Patricia Pickrel, eds. unpaged. free.
Aud: Sa

Contains names and addresses of lawyers who have had experience in or developed useful materials on juvenile law litigation. It is compiled on the basis of form letters sent to hundreds of offices nationwide which are engaged in juvenile litigation. After an initial listing of national organizations, there is a list of law offices arranged alphabetically by state and city. Names of individual lawyers in each office are listed in the order that they appeared on the reply forms. Under each office there is a list of issues currently or recently litigated by that office, as reported by the office. At the back is an index of issues. Each issue has been assigned a numbered category. The categories are based on the organization of the volumes of the planned Juvenile Justice Standards. Each law office has also been assigned a category number. Following each category number appears the office number of each office engaged in that kind of litigation. KSK

SS 470

Lawyer's Desk Reference (LDR). (Continues: Sources of Information for the Trial Lawyer and the Legal Investigator.) (1975 is 5th ed.) bi-a. bibl. index. illus. Lawyers Cooperative Publishing Co., Aqueduct Bldg, Rochester, NY 14603; Bancroft-Whitney Co., San Francisco, CA 94107. Examined: 5th ed., 1975, 1404p.; 1977. Harry M. Philo, Dean A. Robb, and Richard M. Goodman, eds. 218p. $40.
Aud: Sa

The fifth edition is subtitled: "Technical sources for conducting a personal injury action." **LDR** is geared for the lawyer handling his/her first negligence case, the tort specialist, and the law firm whose practice is from 10 to 50 percent in the field of negligence law. Written primarily for the plaintiff trial lawyer, it is equally useful to the defense counsel. It includes a list of expert witnesses in various fields; resource guides to medical sources, drug products, and environmental sources; manuals on automobile accident investigation; consumer and household products; investigations of farm injuries, railroad accidents, public utility injuries, and construction accidents; lists of admiralty sources, safety equipment manufacturers, and safety organizations; discussions of various safety standards and codes; a list of government information centers; sources in international safety; a bibliography of technical safety publications and safety films; a chapter on discriminatory torts; a section on swimming pools; and a final chapter on worker's compensation sources. Contains a series of appendixes, including a checklist of legal theories of liability. There is a subject index. The 1977 issue supplements the basic volume. KSK

SS 471
The Lawyer's Directory. 1882. a. Lawyers Directory Publishers, Box 768, Charlottesville, VA 22902. Examined: 77th ed., 1959. 974p. (1977. $25 w/2 suppls.)
Aud: Cl, Sa

Contains a section on federal and state taxes which shows when specific taxes are due and explains relevant governmental procedures; a section on federal and state inheritance taxes; a digest of laws for all states and U.S. possessions, Canada and its provinces, and principal foreign countries; a digest of patent, trademark, and copyright laws; a list of foreign embassies and legations in Washington, D.C.; a list of U.S. embassies, legations, and consular offices throughout the world; a list of members of legal departments of leading U.S. corporations; and a selected list of leading lawyers throughout the world with biographical data. KSK

SS 472
Legal Aid Review. 1902. a. illus. The Legal Aid Society of New York, 11 Park Place, New York, NY 10007. Examined: v. 65, 1967. Allison M. Coudert and Paula C. Rand, eds. 43p. free to contributors to the Society. (v. 68, 1972. 40p.)
Aud: Jc, Cl, Pl

Each issue is devoted to a single theme or issue, i.e., youth and the courts, theory and practice of legal aid, prisons, narcotics laws. Essays of general interest on the subject discuss aspects of this issue. There is a biography and portrait of each contributor. Also includes excerpts of speeches given at the annual meetings of the Legal Aid Society as well as before other groups. At the end of each issue are "legal aid notes," brief items on activities and services of the Legal Aid Society, plus a listing of the Society's officers, directors, and committees for that particular year. KSK

SS 473
Legal Medicine Almanac. ISSN 0075-8590. 1969. a. bibl. index. illus. Appleton-Century Crofts, 292 Madison Ave, New York, NY 10017. Examined: 1973; 1974; 1976. Cyril H. Wecht, ed. 436p. $26.50.
Aud: Sa

Attempts to aid pathologists, clinical physicians, forensic scientists, and attorneys in keeping abreast of the areas of legal medicine and forensic science. These areas have grown in importance in the criminal justice system and there is a growing awareness of the need for increased education and practical information. Each chapter is written by a practicing expert. Titles include "Firearm Fatalities," "Battered Child Syndrome," "Exhumation," "Suicide Notes," "Drug Manufacturers Liability," and "Forensic Dentistry." SJV

SS 474
Martindale-Hubbell Law Directory. (Continues: Martindale's American Law Directory; Hubbell's Legal Directory.) 1931. a. Martindale-Hubbell, One Prospect St, Summit, NJ 07901. Examined: 110th ed., 1978. 7v.
Aud: Sa

Divided into five sections. The main listing, the geographic section, is the roster of the Bar of the United States, Canada, and the Pacific Territories with ratings. The foreign section lists lawyers of standing in other parts of the world. The biographical section lists lawyers by state, city, then law firm. The fourth section is a digest of laws for each state, the District of Columbia, Puerto Rico, and the Virgin Islands. Uniform and Model Acts, and U.S. copyright, patent, and trademark laws are included. The American Bar Association section presents directories of officers, lawyer referral services, legal aid and defender offices, legal assistance offices, and public interest practice firms. Codes of professional responsibility and judicial contact are included. SJV

SS 475

Pre-Law Handbook. ISSN 0075-8264. 1967. a. Association of American Law Schools, Law School Admission Council, Suite 370, One Dupont Circle, NW, Washington, DC 20036. Dist: Educational Testing Service, Law School Admission Council, Box 944, Princeton, NJ 08540. Examined: 1977/78. Rennard Strickland, ed. 375p. $4.
Aud: Cl

Subtitle: "Annual official guide to ABA approved law schools." An alphabetical listing of law schools approved by the American Bar Association. Information provided includes introductory comments about the school, library and physical facilities, basic program of study and degree requirements, activities, admission criteria and procedures, expenses and financial aid, housing, placement, and information on the grade point averages and Law Scholastic Aptitude Test (LSAT) scores of students admitted the previous year. Introductory articles give information on the legal profession, preparing for law school, application process, and the law school experience. BSM/SJV

SS 476

Supreme Court Historical Society. Yearbook. ISSN 0362-5249. 1976. a. bibl. illus. Supreme Court Historical Society, 1511 K St, NW, Washington, DN 20005. Examined: 1977. William F. Swindler, ed. 119p. $12.50. (4th ed., 1978.)
Aud: Cl, Pl

Intended for general readers, the **Yearbook** features articles and illustrations on persons and events in the history of the Court. Examples of some article titles are: "My Father the Chief Justice," by Charles P. Taft; "The Court in the Age of Marshall"; "Presidents vs. the Courts"; and "Women and Other Strangers at the Bar." Three regular departments follow the articles: de minimis, or judicial potpourri, a series of shorter historical sketches; the court in recent literature, a bibliography of recent major books on the subject; and the Society: res gestae, which is an annual report on the Supreme Court Historical Society. The volume is well illustrated with portraits and historical scenes. The articles are written by historians, judges, professors, and law librarians, and some contain footnotes. KSK

SS 477

The Supreme Court Review. ISSN 0081-9557. 1960. a. University of Chicago Press, 5801 Ellis Ave, Chicago, IL 60637. Examined: 1976. Philip B. Kurland, ed. 343p. $25. (1977. 339p.)

Aud: Cl, Sa
Indexed in: *Social Science Citation Index; Index to Legal Periodicals.*

Dedicated to criticism and critical opinion of the Supreme Court. Articles are of substantial length, well documented, and written by scholars in the field. Includes articles dealing with individual court decisions and those surveying trends in the court's actions. The 1976 volume includes such articles as "Buckley v. Valeo: The Special Nature of Political Speech," "Michelin Tire Co. v. Wages: Enhanced State Power to Tax Imports," "The Supreme Court and Federal Jurisdiction: 1975 Term," "Washington v. Davis: Quantity, Quality, and Equality in Employment Testing," and "The Deterrent Effect of the Death Penalty Facts and Faiths." All articles contain extensive footnotes. SJV

SS 478

U.S. Code Congressional and Administrative News. 1939. a. index. West Publishing Co., Box 3526, St Paul, MN 55165. Examined: 1976. 5v. $90 w/m. suppls.
Aud: Cl, Pl

Provides the text of current federal legislation and the legislative history or background and purpose of the legislation. Messages of the President, presidential proclamations, executive orders, administrative regulations, and finding tables are also included. Material can be coordinated with the *United States Code Annotated; Federal Tax Regulations; Internal Revenue Code* (all West publications); and the *Code of Federal Regulations.* SJV

SS 479

U.S. Department of Justice. Office of the Attorney General. Report of the Attorney General to the Congress of the U.S., on the Foreign Agents Registration Act of 1938, as Amended, for the Calendar Year (date). 1945. a. U.S. Department of Justice, Attorney General, Washington, DC 20530. Dist: Superintendent of Documents, U.S. Government Printing Office, Washington, DC 20402. Examined: 1975. 314p. $1.
Aud: Cl, Sa

The first report covered the period June 18, 1942 to December 31, 1944. Since 1950, the report has been issued annually. The publication analyzes the principal trends in the propaganda material disseminated within the U.S. in the English language on behalf of foreign principles and geographical areas. Principal publications are set forth, along with approximate circulation figures per issue. There is an alphabetical list of all registrants whose registrations were in active status during the year and the countries they represent. There is also a listing by geographical area and nationality of registrants whose statements were in active status at any time during the calendar year. Three five-year cumulations (1945/49, 1950/54, and 1955/59) are available. SKS

SS 480

U.S. Department of State. Digest of United State Practice in International Law. ISSN 0095-3369. (Continues: Digest of International Law.) 1973. a. index. U.S. Department of State, Washington, DC 20520. Dist: Superintendent of Documents, U.S. Government Printing Office, Washington, DC 20402. Examined: 1973/74, $7.50; 1975/76. Eleanor McDowell, ed. 947p. $11.
Aud: Cl, Sa

A record of significant developments in U.S. practice in international law. Includes chapters on such subjects as the individual in international law, state representation, the law of treaties, jurisdiction, law of the sea, aviation and space law, state responsibility for injuries to aliens, international economic law, environmental and health affairs, scientific educational and cultural affairs, peaceful settlement of disputes, legal regulation of use of force, and private international law. Each chapter includes a description of events, quotes from speeches and statements, legal decisions, and texts of treaties and agreements affecting the particular area under review. There is a summary table of contents, followed by a more detailed table. A complete index to the entire volume is provided. There is no bibliography, but there are references to other readings throughout the book. SKS/SJV

SS 481

U.S. Environmental Protection Agency. A Collection of Legal Opinions. ISSN 0361-0673. 1973. a. U.S. Environmental Protection Agency, Office of General Counsel, 401 M St, SW, Washington, DC 20460. Dist: U.S. Department of Commerce, National Technical Information Service, Springfield, VA 22161. Examined: v. 1, Dec. 1970/Dec. 1973. 620p.
Aud: Cl, Sa

The first volume, which was not released until 1975, is "a collection of the more significant Environmental Protection Agency legal opinions which were written by the attorneys in the Office of General Counsel from EPA's formation in 1970 through December 31, 1973. Statutes which are interpreted include the Clean Air Act of 1970, the Federal Water Pollution Act, the Norse Control Act, the Solid Waste Disposal Act, the National Environmental Policy Act, and the Federal Pesticide Control Act of 1972." Subsequent opinions will be released in annual updates. KSK

SS 482

United States Statutes at Large. 1789. a. index. Office of the Federal Register, Washington, DC 20408. Dist: Superintendent of Documents, U.S. Government Printing Office, Washington, DC 20402. Examined: v. 88, 1974. 2v. 2545p. (v. 89, 1975. 1512p. $24.)
Aud: Cl, Sa

A two-volume set that contains the laws and concurrent resolutions enacted during each session of the Congress, as well as proclamations. Each volume includes lists of bills enacted into public law, public laws, bills enacted into private laws, and proclamations. The full text of the public laws are then presented. Volume two also carries the complete texts of private laws, concurrent resolutions, and proclamations; a guide to legislative history of public laws; and a table of laws. Both volumes contain subject indexes and an index of individuals mentioned in joint resolutions. The laws are arranged numerically by P.L. (Public Law) number. Volume 89 was not published until 1977. KSK

SS 483

Who's Who in American Law. 1977. a. Marquis Who's Who, 200 E Ohio St, Chicago, IL 60611. Examined: 1977. 607p. $52.50.
Aud: Sa

A biographical directory listing over 20,000 lawyers, judges, law school deans and professors, leading state and federal prosecutors, and justice department officials. Personal and professional data are provided for each biographee. SJV

SS 484

World Legal Directory. ISSN 0075-8213. (Continues: World Law Directory.) 1969. irreg. index. World Peace Through Law Center, 400 Hill Bldg, Washington, DC 20006. Examined: 1st ed., 1969. Cristine R. Forbes, ed. 448p. $35. (1973. $35.)
Aud: Cl, Sa

A computerized directory of the international legal profession. Contains the names and addresses of practicing lawyers; judicial officials; members of the high courts and bar associations; law schools; and law libraries throughout the world. All countries are listed in alphabetical sequence; the name of each country is followed by the population, official language, and capital city. Practicing lawyers are listed according to city for most countries. Often the name and address of each lawyer is followed by date admitted to practice, law school attended, and languages spoken. An index to lawyers by country and state is included at the back. The directory will be updated and revised by computer. KSK

SS 485

Yearbook of School Law. 1933. a. bibl. index. National Organization on Legal Problems in Education, 835 Western, Topeka, KS 66606. Examined: 1976. Philip K. Piele, ed. 335p. $7.95.
Aud: Cl, Pl, Pf

Reviews the previous year's major cases of school law and includes digests of case law. Provides an annotated bibliography of selected research studies in the field. Each chapter, written by an authority in the field, covers a particular topic such as liability, school property, school finance, teachers and other employees, pupils, and higher education. Since 1976 collective bargaining has been a chapter; governance, once a separate chapter, is now subsumed in others. A recommended resource for institutional libraries at all levels. BSM

SS 486

Yearbook of the International Law Commission. ISSN 0082-8289. 1949. a. bibl. Publication Service, United Nations, New York, NY. Dist: International Publications Service, 114 E 32nd St, New York, NY 10016. Examined: 1974. 2v. v. 1, $12.
Aud: Sa

Details the activities of the Commission. In two volumes, with volume two having two parts. Volume one gives the summary records of the meetings of the U.N.'s International Law Commission for that particular year. Part one of volume two contains documents of that session, such as reports of special rapporteurs, documents submitted by members of the Commission, and the report of the Commission to the U.N. General Assembly. Part two of volume two contains a special report by the Attorney General and documents of that particular session of the Commission prepared by the Secretariat. The 1974 **Yearbook** contains a long report in part two on the legal problems relating to the utilization and use of international rivers, with a bibliography and documentation on that subject appended. Also discusses the succession of states in respect of treaties and most-favored-nation clauses. KSK

MANAGEMENT

SS 487

Bank Administration Institute. Biennial Survey of Bank Office Salaries. ISSN 0525-4620. 1965. bi-a. illus. Bank Administration Institute, Personnel Administration Commission, Box 500, 303 S Northwest Hwy, Park Ridge, IL 60068. Examined: 1975. 180p. $10; $5 to members.
Aud: Cl, Sa

Information is derived from survey forms received from Bank Administration Institute member banks. Banks are grouped into nine geographic regions: New England, Mid-Atlantic, South Atlantic, East-South Central, East-North Central, West-North Central, West-South Central, Mountain, and Pacific. Information on officers' salaries is presented for banks with under fifty million dollars, and banks with fifty million dollars and over. In the former, thirteen officer positions are surveyed, while in the latter, forty positions are surveyed. Salary ranges for each officer classification are presented in tabular form according to bank resource size. The data presented in the first set of tables show salaries for all nine regions combined, followed by a separate treatment of each region. The data are presented in the same way for banks both under and over fifty million dollars. Maps precede each region section, outlining the area covered in that part. KSK

SS 488

Bank Administration Institute. Biennial Survey of Bank Personnel Policies and Practices. ISSN 0067-3536. 1962. bi-a. illus. Bank Administration Institute, Personnel Administration Commission, 303 S Northwest Hwy, Park Ridge, IL 60068. Examined: 1972. 26p. $4.
Aud: Cl, Sa

Presents the results of a survey of bank personnel policies and practices. For each subject covered there is an analysis of the survey, plus tabular data. Among the topics surveyed are: ratios of personnel to deposits, percentage of women to total staff, percentage of part-time to full-time personnel, annual turnover, personnel policies and practices, wage and salary policies, time off with pay policies, training and development, holidays, vacations, rest and lunch periods, medical insurance, pension plan, profit sharing plan, pregnancy, personnel publications and records, and present or future bank personnel problems. KSK

SS 489

Best's Safety Directory; Safety—Industrial Hygiene—

Security. (Continues: Best's Safety Maintenance Directory; Best's Environmental Control and Safety Directory. ISSN 0067-6322.) 1946. a. index. illus. A.M. Best Co., Park Ave, Morristown, NJ 07960. Examined: 15th ed., 1975. Kathleen M. Guindon, ed. 1038p. $2. (1977.)
Aud: Cl, Sa

Subtitle: "Featuring OSHA guidelines and the manual of modern safety techniques." Serves two functions: it summarizes important standards of OSHA (Occupation Safety and Health Act) giving ways to implement the new rules, and secondly, it offers a buying guide on safety products and services. Each subject section (eye and face protection, respiratory protection, etc.) begins with OSHA's requirements on that particular aspect of industrial safety. After the safety measures are discussed and illustrated, there is a product guide for the section. The product is described, and then a list of manufacturers is provided. The basic sections are: OSHA and basic safety techniques; personal protection; noise control and hearing protection; warning and communication; machine, tool, and welding safety; materials handling; lighting and electrical safety; fire safety; first aid; industrial hygiene and hazardous materials; and industrial security. Numerous advertisements are scattered throughout. Also includes indexes to the advertisers and their catalogs, a product index, an index of OSHA standards by paragraph numbers, and a source index of manufacturers' addresses. There is a detailed table of contents and an index of OSHA standards and requirements. KSK

SS 490
Bricker's International Directory of University-Sponsored Executive Development Programs. ISSN 0361-1108. 1970. a. Bricker Publications, Box 265, South Chatham, MA 02659. Examined: 1973. George W. Bricker, ed. 304p. $55. (v. 10, 1978. $59.50.)
Aud: Sa

A listing of all United States, Canadian, United Kingdom, and Australian in-residence, university-sponsored executive development programs, as well as English-speaking programs of similar nature on the European continent. The programs described treat management in the broad sense, are not confined to a single industry or single management function, and are at least two weeks in duration. Each program description includes: name of institute, name of program and when it was inaugurated, sponsor, program location and duration, dates of particular year's sessions, tuition, descriptions of participants and faculty, official contact, subject matter, methods of instruction, special features, facilities (accommodations, sports, etc.), and a recommendation regarding the suitability of U.S. and Canadian programs for certain types or levels of executives. An appendix gives summary data for U.S. and Canadian programs (guide for preliminary selection of programs by level of management, starting dates, duration, and size of class). KSK

SS 491
Directory of Exenutive Recruiters. ISSN 0090-6484. 1971. a. Consultants News, Templeton Rd, Fitzwilliam, NH 03447. Examined: 1976. James H. Kennedy, ed. 144p. $5.
Aud: Sa

Compiled and published by *Consultants News*, the confidential newsletter of the consulting profession. Utilized by executive job-seekers, corporate officers in charge of managerial recruiting, and the executive search/management consulting business. It lists over 1000 firms and offices that are retained by management to locate executives. The main section is an alphabetical listing of recruiting firms, giving name of firm and full address for U.S., Canadian, and Mexican locations (city only for overseas locations). Most listings also have information on salary ranges of jobs for which they recruit and the areas or businesses in which they specialize. Appendixes list employment agencies and other firms in executive recruiting on fee-paid basis and women in executive recruiting. There is a geographical locator arranged alphabetically by state, then by cities; within each city the firms are listed alphabetically. KSK

SS 492
Directory of Municipal Management Assistants. ISSN 0363-0552. 1954. a. International City Management Association, 1140 Connecticut Ave, NW, Washington, DC 20036. Examined: 1975. 20p.
Aud: Sa

A directory of assistants to city and county managers and to administrators and councils of government directors. Information for the directory was obtained through a questionnaire sent by the International City Management Association to cities, counties, and councils of governments. Tables give information on municipal assistants by position title, sex and position, race or ethnic background, mean age and position title, and ICMA membership of municipal assistants by position title and membership category. The second part is a directory of assistants to municipal officials arranged alphabetically by state, and then by municipality within the state. Information includes the name of the assistant, and the assistant's job title, age, education, annual salary, and the date of appointment. Information on the municipality includes population and form of government. KSK

SS 493
Dun and Bradstreet Reference Book of Corporate Managements. ISSN 0070-7627. (Continues: Dun's Reference Book of Corporate Management; Moody's Handbook of Corporate Managements. ISSN 0545-0209.) 1967. a. Dun and Bradstreet, 99 Church St, New York, NY 10007. Examined: 11th ed., 1977/78. 1687p. $95.
Aud: Cl, Sa

Contains data on directors and selected officers of approximately 2400 companies which have annual sales of $20 million or more and/or 1000 employees. Data were compiled from Dun and Bradstreet records. Arranged by company, the listing gives the address and phone number as well as the Dun and Bradstreet number. Next are listed the names of the principal officers, including the chief executive officer, chairman of the board, president, executive and senior vice presidents, vice presidents, secretary, and treasurer. Provides the following data on each individual listed: business and professional occupations; additional principal business affiliations outside the corporation, date of birth, marital status, and education. After the corporation listings is a yellow page section which lists the officers in straight alphabetical sequence with title and principal corporate affiliation for each. Subscribers to the directory must agree to return it to Dun and Bradstreet upon receipt of a new edition or on the termination of the subscription. Furthermore, the title page notes the restriction that the use of the volume is limited to the confidential use of subscribers. KSK

SS 494
Fairchild's Financial Manual of Retail Stores. ISSN 0071-3716. 1923. a. index. Fairchild Publications, Book Division, 7 E 12th St, New York, NY 10003. Examined: 49th ed., 1976. Robin Feldman, ed. 376p. $40.
Aud: Cl, Sa

A directory of retail stores arranged in alphabetical order by the name of the store. Before the listing there are some statistics for the leading general merchandise chains, leading drug chains, and leading food chains. Each listing contains the following information: name of company, address and phone number, names and titles of officers, names of directors, a brief description of its business activities and where its main stores are located, its divisions and subsidiaries, transfer agents, stock exchanges, the number of stores at the end of the special year, sales and earnings over a seven-year period, common stock and common stock equity, income account, assets and liabilities, and a statistical summary of the store's working capital, current ratio, shareholders equity, etc. At the end of the directory is an index of store names, with many cross-references (e.g., Abraham and Straus, see Federated Department Stores, Inc.). KSK

SS 495
Ideas for Management. Proceedings of the Annual Conference. ISSN 0073-4624. 1948. a. illus. Association for Systems Management, 24587 Bagley Rd, Cleveland, OH 44138. Examined: 1972. R. B. MacCaffrey, ed. 153p. $12
Aud: Cl, Sa

Presents the papers delivered at the annual meeting of International Systems. The speakers are either administrators or college professors. Topics deal with aspects of the system field that would be of interest to managers. Subjects covered include, for example, basic systems analysis, how to improve profits, protecting corporate computer information, management of time, computer simulation, management by objectives, and training systems personnel. A picture of each speaker is included. Articles often use figures and illustrations, and some have bibliographies or footnotes attached. KSK

MARKETING

SS 496
American Drop-Shippers Directory. ISSN 0065-8103. 1964. a. illus. World Wide Trade Service, Box 283, Medina, WA 98039. Examined: 1977. George Lucas, ed. 22p. $3.
Aud: Sa

A guide to wholesale supply sources for the drop-shipping industry. Geared for dealers who want to locate a supplier for a specific item or items which he/she then sells or distributes to his/her own customers. Suppliers are listed in alphabetical order by the items they furnish. The name and address of the supplier are given. Some of the listings briefly describe the item that the supplier provides or any special service that the drop-shipper gives his customers. Contains advertisements from some of the wholesale sources of supply. KSK

SS 497

American Marketing Association. Proceedings. ISSN 0065-9231. (Continues: Abstracts of Papers of the Conference. ISSN 0065-9215.) 1921. a. bibl. index. illus. American Marketing Association, 222 S Riverside Plaza, Chicago, IL 60602. Examined: 1975. Edward M. Mazze, ed. 712p. $23.95; $17.95 to members.
Aud: Sa

The present series incorporates the Association's *Combined Proceedings* and its *Papers of the Conferences*. Each volume has a specific title. The 1975 edition is entitled "Marketing in Turbulent Times" and "Marketing, the Challenges and the Opportunities." These were the titles of the two conferences held by the American Marketing Association in Chicago and Rochester. The papers have been separated into 13 sections, which have each been further divided into three or more divisions. Divisions include: "The Management of Marketing Activities"; "Research in Marketing"; "Buying Behavior"; "Industrial Markets"; "Physical Distribution"; "Advertising"; "New Challenges to Marketing Editors"; etc. Many of the papers have charts, graphs, tables, and bibliographies. There are author and subject indexes. KSK

SS 498

Annual Editions: Readings in Marketing. 1973. a. index. illus. Dushkin Publishing Group, Sluice Dock, Guilford, CT 06437. Examined: 1978/79. Richard Wendel, ed. $6.55 pap.
Aud: Hs, Jc, Cl, Pl

A collection of articles reprinted from newspapers, magazines, and journals published during the preceding years. Designed to supplement high school and college courses in marketing, the readings cover current developments and issues in all aspects of marketing. Many articles include tables, charts, photographs, and other illustrations. Useful as an introduction to the field of marketing for the general reader. Includes a subject index. JKM

SS 499

Bradford's Directory of Marketing Research Agencies and Management Consultants in the United States and the World. ISSN 0068-063X. (Continues: Survey and Directory, Marketing Research Agencies in the United States; Bradford's Survey and Directory of Marketing Research Agencies in the U.S. and the World.) 1943. bi-a. index. Bradford's Directory of Marketing Research Agencies, Box 276, Department E, Fairfax, VA 22030. Examined: 13th ed., 1971/72. Ernest S. Bradford, ed. 288p. $23.50. (1977/78.)
Aud: Sa

Provides "manufacturers, advertising agencies, and others with a list and description of reliable marketing research agencies in the U.S. and abroad." Includes indexes of marketing research agencies and management consultants, both in the U.S. and abroad; functions of various trade associations; a directory of agencies and consultants arranged alphabetically by state, then city, then by name of the firm (also includes the agency's address, phone number, the services it provides, its directors, when it was established, and its association memberships); a section on Canadian, Puerto Rican, and Mexican agencies; and a directory of other foreign agencies and consultants arranged alphabetically by country. This is followed by a classified list of agencies that offer specific services, arranged by the service offered, e.g., agricultural research, data analysis and processing, marketing consultants, etc. There is an alphabetical index of personnel which includes an abbreviated list of associated agencies. Finally, there are statistical tables of population estimates for the U.S. and population estimates/projections for other countries. KSK

SS 500

Directory of Corporate Affiliations. (Continues: Directory of Corporate Affiliation of Major National Advertisers. ISSN 0070-5365.) 1967. a. index. National Register Publishing Co., 5201 Old Orchard Rd, Skokie, IL 60076. Examined: 1976. Anita Schneider, ed. 554p. + 97p. index. $40. (1978. $79.)
Aud: Sa

Subtitle: "Who owns whom." Gives "the corporate structure of major corporations, their divisions, subsidiaries, and affiliates." Section one lists parent companies arranged alphabetically. Information for each company includes address and phone number, its officers (president, chairman of the board, treasurer, etc.), the names of its subsidiaries, if any, divisions, if any, and foreign subsidiaries, if any. There are also letter symbols which indicate if the company is listed on the New York Stock Exchange, American Stock Exchange, and eight other stock exchanges, as well as if it is being traded over the counter. This major section is followed by a smaller section, separately paged and arranged alphabetically, which is the index of divisions, subsidiaries, and affiliates. Next to the name of the division or affiliate is the name of the parent company. Updated by supplements. The 1978 edition includes a geographic index, arranged by state and city, which is—very oddly—issued as a separate booklet but included in the price. KSK

SS 501
Dollars and Cents of Shopping Centers. ISSN 0070-704X. 1961. tri-a. index. illus. Urban Land Institute, 1200 18th St, NW, Washington, DC 20036. Examined: 1969. J. Ross McKeever, ed. 228p. $30; $22.50 to members.
Aud: Sa

Subtitle: "A study of receipts and expenses." Prepared under the auspices of the Shopping Center Study Committee of the Community Builders Council of the Urban Land Institute. Includes various supplements. Operating statistics are furnished for hundreds of shopping centers in the U.S. and Canada. Data have been combined into several different chapters devoted to regional, community, and neighborhood shopping centers. Within each chapter the topic has been divided into various subtopics, e.g., operating results as a group, operating results by geographic area and by age group, summary of tenant information tables, and tenant information tables—summary of tenant characteristics. There is a separate chapter on Canadian shopping centers. Another chapter gives supplementary information, such as changes in operating results, capital costs, enclosed mall regional shopping centers, tenants by operational type, merchants associations, and a parking index. Appendixes provide definitions, procedures, and an outline of a standard manual of expense accounts for shopping centers. Finally, there is a subject index and an index of statistical tables. KSK

SS 502
Dun and Bradstreet International Market Guide; Continental Europe. ISSN 0419-8204. 1961. a. Dun and Bradstreet, International Office, 99 Church St, New York, NY 10007. Examined: 1978. $535.
Aud: Sa

Designed for sales development, market analysis, and revision of customer and prospect lists. Provides market data and other general information on geographic areas as well as specific businesses. General information on each country is presented, and the entire volume is revised annually. The Trade Classification Code helps identify potential trade outlets. Addresses are complete enough for direct mail purposes and can be used as duty and area directories for non-business purposes as well. Kept up to date with supplements provided as a part of the subscription service. Provides intensive coverage of approximately 20 market areas, each concentrated in one continental European country. Essential for international business contacts. KSK

SS 503
Dun and Bradstreet Middle Market Directory. ISSN 0070-7600. 1964. a. Dun and Bradstreet, 99 Church St, New York, NY 10007. Examined: 1977. $125. (1978. 4067p.)
Aud: Sa

Lists business enterprises in the U.S. with an indicated worth of $500,000 to $999,999. Includes the usual clear Dun and Bradstreet explanation of the symbols used and the arrangement of each entry; the usual abbreviation list; a how-to-use-the-directory section; a helpful section on the Standard Industrial Classification Codes; and four sections which list businesses in four ways: alphabetically, geographically, by product classification, and by D-U-N-S numbers. The title describes the work's contents and limitations; it provides the information expected of all Dun and Bradstreet publications. Useful as a companion to the **Million Dollar Directory**. NLE

SS 504
Dun and Bradstreet Million Dollar Directory. ISSN 0070-7619. 1959. a. w/semi-a. suppls. Dun and Bradstreet, 99 Church St, New York, NY 10007. Examined: 1977. $150. (1978. 5082p.)
Aud: Sa

Covers one percent of the 4.2 million U.S. businesses that have a net worth of one million dollars or more. Lists businesses, utilities, transportation companies, banks, stock brokers, wholesalers, and retailers. Also includes domestic subsidiaries of foreign companies which qualify. Much of the information provided is duplicated in other publications. Lists businesses alphabetically (with cross references from divisions), by D-U-N-S number, geographically, and by product classification. Gives basic information on top management. The information provided here is also available in a number of machine formats from Dun and Bradstreet. Listings are clearly explained, and the instructions at the front of the volume are excellent. Useful as a companion to **Middle Market Directory**. NLE

SS 505
Guide to Consumer Markets. (Continues: Graphic Guide to Consumer Markets. ISSN 0072-551X.) 1963. a. index. illus. Conference Board, 845 Third Ave, New York, NY 10022. Examined: 1976/77. Helen Axel, ed. 295p. $25; $5 to members.
Aud: Sa

Geared for marketing representatives and planners. Information has been gathered by the Conference Board from government and trade sources. The statistics are divided into six main sections, all focusing on various aspects of consumers: population, employment, income, expenditures, production and distribution, and prices. The employment chapter provides detailed statistics on the labor force by age and sex, employment and unemployment, occupations, working wives, average hours and earnings, employment by industry, and employment and earnings by states and metropolitan area. Following the main chapters are sections on definitions, census and survey sources, a list of graphs, and a subject index. The statistics are presented with no narrative summary of their meaning and significance. KSK

SS 506

Handbook of Independent Advertising and Marketing Services. 1971. a. Executive Communications, 400 E 54th St, New York, NY 10022. Examined: 1973. Sue Fulton, ed. $20 to libraries. (1978. 111p.)
Aud: Sa

Begins with a preface on independent services in advertising and marketing functions, explaining why they are being used more and more and what is behind the growth of independent services. The preface also outlines some cautions in the use of independent services. The services are then listed under ten specialized areas: independent creative teams, ad agencies offering modular services, new product workshops, media services, broadcast production consultants, graphic and package design firms, marketing implementation services, sales promotion firms, marketing/management consultants, and direct marketing firms. There is a preface to each of these ten sections which briefly describes the type of service offered and offers suggestions on how to use them. Within each section, the services are listed in no particular order, neither alphabetically nor geographically. The volume is unpaged and there is no index, making it slightly difficult to use. Information on each service includes address, phone number, chief executive, whether it is a division or subsidiary of another agency, and a paragraph explaining its particular services, specialties, awards it has won, important clients, and other general information. For additional information on any firm in the **Handbook** (or those not listed), the subscriber may phone or write the publisher. Bound in a loose-leaf binder. KSK

SS 507

International Directory of Marketing Research Houses and Services. ISSN 0074-459X. (Continues: Directory of Marketing Research Houses and Services.) 1962. a. index. American Marketing Association, New York Chapter, 420 Lexington Ave, New York, NY 10017. Examined: 1977. Pat Ryan, ed. 158p. $18.
Aud: Sa

Also known as the *Green Book*. An alphabetical listing, by company name, of the marketing research industry. Information for each firm includes address, phone number, officers (president, executive vice president, chairman of the board, etc.), a brief description of its specialty, and any special services that it provides for its clients. If the firm has branches in the U.S. or in some other country, the address and director of that office is given. Some of the companies also include advertisements in the *Green Book*. After the main directory there are additional pages of "late listings" for companies not in the main list. There is a geographic index, arranged alphabetically by state for U.S. listings, and by country for foreign entries. Entries in the geographic index include the name of the company, the city in which it is located, and its telephone number. There is also an index of the principal personnel of all companies, arranged alphabetically by the last name of the officer. Finally, there is a listing of computer programs used by some of the companies, with page number(s) indicating which firm makes use of it. KSK

SS 508

Madison Avenue Handbook. ISSN 0076-2148. 1956. a. illus. Peter Glenn Publications, 17 E 48th St, New York, NY 10017. Examined: 20th ed., 1976/77. Brian J. Smith, ed. 188p. $11.95.
Aud: Cl, Sa

Most of the book lists, in tabbed sections, New York City services and agencies, but there are also brief sections with maps on Boston, California, Chicago, Detroit, the South, and Canada, and a section of general trade-related information. Listings include stores; beauty firms; props and rental services; media; agencies (advertising, public relations, talent, etc.); TV, film, and sound production houses; photographers; illustrators; designers and copywriters; and printing services. Includes a useful map of New York City showing the locations of studios, agencies, and media offices. Designed primarily for those working in advertising and public relations, the **Handbook** would also be useful for students and others interested in breaking into related areas of business. KR/JKM

SS 509

Marketing Economics Key Plants. ISSN 0076-4531. (Continues: Market Statistics Key Plants. ISSN 0098-1397.) 1960. bi-a. Marketing Economics Institute, 441

Lexington Ave, New York, NY 10017. Examined: 1975, 2 sections, 311p and 304p., $60; 1977. section 1, 301p.; section 2, 291p. $80.
Aud: Pf

Subtitle: "Guide to industrial purchasing power." Information is arranged to "help the industrial marketer make a quick and easy determination of the size of the market for his/her products and services and to give him/her a ready panoramic view of how prospective customers are distributed geographically across the length and breadth of the U.S." The table of contents is divided into two sections, A and B. The first part lists regions and states; the second part gives the Standard Industrial Classification (SIC) code for various industries. The first half of the guide lists the key plants arranged by state and county. Information includes county, plant name, address, SIC code, and number of employees. The second half gives the key plants arranged by SIC industries. In this way, all meat packing plants, for example, are together. State and county locations, addresses, and employee figures are also provided for each plant. KSK

SS510
Marketing Guide. ISSN 0093-125X. 1973. a. Medical Economics Co., 550 Kinderkamack Rd, Oradell, NJ 07649. Examined: 1975. Joel H. Goldberg. 16p. $5.
Aud: Sa

Subtitle: "Consumer spending patterns for over 300 product lines sold in drugstores from *Drug Topics*." An annual survey conducted by *Drug Topics* that summarizes the previous year's sales of drugstore products. A one-page narrative summary of significant trends for that year is followed by three-year figures that compare the major product categories to the market as a whole and in drugstores alone. The figures also include the drugstore's percentage share of market. Categories include packaged medication; sickroom and convalescent aids; first aid and foot products; baby and feminine needs; pet products; dieting aids; hair and shaving products; oral hygiene and hand products; cosmetics and other toiletries; household goods, hosiery, and sundries; magazines and stationery; and photographic supplies, tobacco, fountain items, and liquor. The last page contains footnotes. KSK

SS 511
Merchandise and Operating Results of Department and Specialty Stores. (1976 is 51st ed.) a. National Retail Merchants Association, Financial Executive Division, 100 W 31st St, New York, NY 10001. Examined: 51st ed., 1976. Jay Scher, ed. 227p. $40; $25 to members.
Aud: Sa

The introduction states: "All the information presented in this report is based upon actual departmental and classification merchandising information reported to the National Retail Merchants Association (NRMA) for incorporation in this survey. Cooperating companies first matched their department and classification to the corresponding MOR merchandising groups. They then provided actual dollar information which was converted into MOR ratio format in accordance with the computer programs written expressly for this purpose . . . this computer program also provides for the automatic determination and print-out of the results published herein . . . The tables presented are photo reproductions of the output reports generated by the computer." After explaining the procedures and terms used in the survey, the report then gives a listing of MOR merchandise groupings (adult female apparel; hobby, recreation, and transportation; etc.). Next are the department store inventory price indexes. Most of the remainder of the book consists of departmental merchandising and operating results for the previous year. The results are divided into sections based on monetary profits from sales. The print-outs give merchandising and inventory data, sales data, and expenses for each item sold. All of the data in the survey are given in the form of a computer print-out. KSK

SS 512
National Association of Chain Drug Stores. NACDS Lilly Digest. ISSN 0092-8410. 1950. a. illus. Eli Lilly and Co., Pharmaceutical Division, Box 618, Indianapolis, IN 46206. Examined: 1977. David J. Carter, ed. 71p. free.
Aud: Sa

Subtitle: "A survey of community pharmacy operations for (year)." "Contains detailed information on financial data voluntarily submitted by independent community pharmacists in the U.S." The statistical charts and tables are arranged into specific information sections. After a summary of community pharmacy operations during the previous year, there are chapters on sales and expenses, prescription department analysis, prescription-oriented pharmacies, net profit, regional variations, pharmacy location, rent, balance sheets, and financial ratios. The "heart" of the **Lilly Digest** gives financial operations during the year according to sales and number of prescriptions dispensed daily. These tables start with sales under

$140,000 and end with sales $600,000 and over. A pharmacist may use this data and compare it with figures from his or her own business. KSK

SS513
Nationwide Directory of Apparel and Accessories Buyers Exclusive of New York Metropolitan Area. 1964. a. index. Salesmen's Guide, 1140 Broadway, New York, NY 10001. Examined: 1967. Edward R. Blank, ed. 352p. $40. (1978. 972p. $50.)
Aud: Sa

Geared to manufacturers, salesmen, and distributors who sell to the mass merchandising retail field. The volume lists discount stores, variety store chains, supermarket store chains, and drug store chains that deal in men's and boys' wear, ladies' wear, infants' to teens' wear, and accessories (jewelry, handbags, belts, etc.). It is arranged alphabetically by state, then city, then by name of store. Information includes address, phone number, type of store (supermarket, drug, etc.), and the name of the persons in the firm who are responsible for specific lines of merchandise. There are some listings for firms in the Metropolitan New York and New Jersey areas, but they are not complete. At the end of the volume, there is an alphabetical index of all firms with the name of the city and state in which they are located. KSK

SS 514
New York Publicity Outlets. ISSN 0077-9024. 1954. a. index. Public Relations Plus, New York Publicity Outlets, Box 327, Washington Depot, CT 06794. Examined: 1975. Harold D. Hansen. 203p. $29.50. (1978. 227p. $39.50.)
Aud: Sa

Subtitle: "Guide for public relations people, covering key personnel on media located within a 50-mile radius of Columbus Circle." Begins with a contents guide to Connecticut, New Jersey, and New York. For each city in these states there are page references to where information can be found in daily newspapers, weekly newspapers, and radio and TV stations. This is followed by a subject guide to magazines and an alphabetical list of magazines. Next are the directories for Manhattan daily newspapers, daily newspapers in other boroughs, metropolitan area daily newspapers, foreign language newspapers, Black press, news services, special interest news services, foreign news services, news photo services, special interest daily newspapers, feature syndicates, syndicated Sunday magazines, New York correspondents for out-of-town newspapers, and metropolitan area weekly newspapers. Information for each title includes address, phone number, frequency, and the names of the publisher, editors, and departmental editors. This is followed by a directory of radio stations (network and independent) in New York City and surrounding areas, radio guest interview programs, TV stations, and TV guest interview programs. For the interview shows, there is information on whom to contact, among other items. Finally, there is the magazine editorial guide. Magazines are arranged by subject (business and finance, home interest, men's interest, etc.), then alphabetically by name of magazine. Information for each title includes number of subscribers, address, editors and publisher, when it is mailed to subscribers, and the editorial interest of the magazine. At the end of the book is an alphabetical index. KSK

SS 515
Principal International Businesses. 1974. a. Dun and Bradstreet, 99 Church St, New York, NY 10007. Examined: 1978. 4334p. $500.
Aud: Sa

Subtitle: "The world marketing directory." Introductory material is in English, French, German, and Spanish. Lists international businesses geographically, alphabetically, and by product classification. Presents information on thousands of businesses in countries around the world. The businesses are selected by Dun and Bradstreet on the basis of their size, national prominence, and international interest. Section one (white pages) lists businesses geographically. Countries are listed alphabetically, and businesses are listed alphabetically within the country. Information on each business includes: D-U-N-S number, import/export indicator, business name, parent company, business address, cable address or telex number, sales volume, employees, SIC number, lines of business, and chief executive. Section two (yellow pages) lists companies by line of business as indicated by Standard Industrial Classification number. Within each SIC category, countries are listed alphabetically by province or state, city and business name. Information for each listing includes business name, street address, city, state, or province, and SIC number. Section three (blue pages) is a complete alphabetical listing of all companies appearing in the **Directory.** Information for each listing includes business name, street address, city, province or state, postal codes (where applicable), and country. KSK

SS 516
Standard Directory of Advertisers. ISSN 0081-4229.

(Continues in part: Standard Advertising Register; McKittrick Directory of Advertisers.) 1907. a. index. National Register Publishing Co., 5201 Old Orchard Rd, Skokie, IL 60076. Examined: 1976/77. Anith Schneider, ed. $68.50. (1978. 1122p.)
Aud: Sa

Issued in two parts. The geographical edition was examined; a classified edition, which includes nine monthly supplements, is also available. A guide to 17,000 corporations. The publisher is a subsidiary of Standard Rate and Data Service, and probably rearranges data available in the SRDS services. Primarily a guide to the agency which serves a particular company. Includes special indexes to trademarks and other approaches useful for corporation searches. A list of advertising associations provides addresses and a contact person. Names, addresses, phone numbers, products, and various classifications are provided for each company listed. Rather specialized, but a good source, if it is current, for contact names. Useful as a way to approach many corporations for additional information, services, product complaints, etc. KSK

SS 517
Surplus Dealers Directory. ISSN 0081-9662. 1950. a. illus. Institute of Surplus Dealers, 520 Broadway, New York, NY 10012. Examined: 1966. Fred D. Reder, ed. 82p. $10. (1977. 168p.)
Aud: Sa

A directory of firms that are in the business of handling government and industrial surplus. It is divided into two types of listings: classified (lists firms by the type of merchandise they deal in, i.e., auto parts, clothing and camping supplies, general surplus, etc.) and alphabetical (lists firms alphabetically with their addresses and a letter that indicates whether they deal wholesale, retail, wholesale and retail, or general surplus). The **Directory** also gives the current officers, board of governors, and past presidents of the Institute of Surplus Dealers. Advertisements are scattered throughout. KSK

SS 518
Thomas Register of American Manufacturers and Thomas Register Catalog File. ISSN 0082-4216. 1905. a. index. illus. Thomas Publishing Co., One Penn Plaza, New York, NY 10001. Examined: 67th ed., 1977. Walter E. Willets, ed. 12v. $69. (68th ed., 1978. 12v. $75.)
Aud: Sa

The first seven volumes list products and services by type according to the modified noun system, i.e., "antennas, radar" instead of "radar antennas." At the end of volume seven is a product index in which products are not listed by the modified noun system. Under the name of the product or service is a list of manufacturers or sources listed alphabetically by state, then city, then by company. In the middle of volume seven, on colored paper, is a list of trade and brand names, arranged alphabetically. Following the listing is the company name and address. Volume eight contains a listing of U.S. companies in alphabetical order. Information for each firm includes company name, address, names of company officials, whether the company advertises in the **Register,** asset ratings, telephone numbers, cable addresses, a symbol that indicates whether a company solicits export business, names of subsidiary companies and affiliated companies, and a symbol indicating that a company catalog is available in the "Thom Cat" Section (volumes nine through twelve). The last four volumes contain company catalogs bound alphabetically by company name. Advertisements giving more detailed information about a product or service can be found in the first eight volumes. Separately paged supplements called "Important Addenda" accompany some volumes. KSK

SS 519
United States and Canadian Mailing Lists. ISSN 0075-2893. 1950. bi-a. Fritz S. Hofheimer, 88 Third Ave, Mineola, NY 11501. Examined: 1971/72. Irene Hofheimer, ed. 146p.
Aud: Sa

Catalog of lists that are available to the direct mail advertiser. Arranged alphabetically by subject category. Key words will lead to any desired category. To avoid repetition of full titles for a series of entries whose key word (or words) are identical, capitals are used for the first entry in the series, and those following are indented. The figure to the left of a title is the current approximate number of addresses available for that list. To the right of the title is the price. Most of the lists are for the U.S., although there are eight pages of Canadian listings. Counts given are nationwide unless otherwise indicated. Hofheimer will supply the direct mail advertiser with mailing addresses on gummed labels or in list form. Some subject categories are broken down by state; however, states not shown are also available. KSK

SS 520
Who Owns Whom. North American Edition. ISSN 0083-9310. (Continues: Who Owns Whom: International Subsidiaries of U.S. Companies.) 1973. a. Who

Owns Whom, 24 Tufton St, London SW1P 3RA, England. Examined: v. 8, 1976/77. G. W. Mann, ed. 906p. $25.
Aud: Cl, Pl, Sa

Lists some 50,000 parent, subsidiary, and associate companies. Gives full coverage of Canadian and Mexican groups, and lists several thousand companies registered in many different countries in which U.S. companies have holdings. Abbreviations of company designations are a necessary key to understanding contents. The guide to alphabetical order unlocks the special arrangement which is not by library filing rules. Sections for Canada and Mexico are divided into parent and senior associate companies, and subsidiary and associate companies. Includes sections on U.S. international and U.S. companies with foreign subdivisions and associates. A useful starting place to trace corporate management and ownership. KSK

SS 521
Who's Who in Training and Development. ISSN 0092-4598. (Continues: American Society for Training and Development. Membership Directory. ISSN 0569-776X.) 1970. a. index. illus. American Society for Training and Development, Box 5307, 6414 Odana Rd, Madison, WI 53705. Examined: 1977. Michael H. Cook, ed. 216p. $25; $5 to members.
Aud: Sa

Describes the American Society for Training and Development (ASTD), gives the names and a photograph of its current officers and past presidents, plus a listing of its committees, staff, chapters, and division officers. The ASTD annual report and its code of ethics are presented. The directory section is divided into two parts: members listed alphabetically (includes titles, organization in which the member works, address, and telephone number), and members listed by organization (arranged alphabetically by company). There are also listings of division members, organization memberships, articles of incorporation and bylaws of the ASTD, ASTD policy, and an index to advertisers. The publication is intended primarily for ASTD members. The copyright prohibits "use of this directory in offering merchandise or services for sales." KSK

OCCUPATIONS AND CAREERS

SS 522
Airline Guide to Stewardess and Stewards Careers. ISSN 0065-4914. 1968. a. illus. Passenger and Inflight Service Magazine, 665 LaVilla Dr, Miami Spring, FL 33166. Dist: Arco Publishing Co., 219 Park Ave S, New York, NY 10003. Examined: 1976/77. Alexander Clark Morton, ed. 127p. $5.95.
Aud: Hs, Jc, Pl

Published by *Passenger and Inflight Service,* the trade magazine of the flight service field. Arranged alphabetically by airline, the **Guide** provides the future flight attendant with information he or she will need to decide on what airline to join. After general information on how to apply to an airline for a position, on the job interview, and on training schools, the **Guide** presents three statistical tables (age requirement, height requirement, and a flight attendant report). Information on each airline is then presented. Data shown include: eligibility, salaries, union, training, uniforms, base assignments, fringe benefits, pass and travel benefits, where and how to apply, and general information. Information about U.S. airlines is presented first, followed by a listing of Canadian and Caribbean airlines. Finally, there is a brief history of flight attendants, and information on what to do after retirement. Lavishly illustrated with photographs. KSK

SS 523
College Placement Annual. ISSN 0069-5734. 1957. a. index. illus. College Placement Council, Box 2263, Bethlehem, PA 18001. Examined: 1977. Warren E. Kauffman, ed. 404p. $5; $3 to members.
Aud: Jc, Cl, Pl

Provides information on the positions customarily offered to college graduates by principal employers. The opening pages contain brief articles of general interest to job-hunters, such as strategies on how to locate information, prepare resumes, and take interviews, and whether to go to graduate school. Also gives the principles and practices of college career planning, placement, and recruitment for those who wish to enter the field. The major section of the volume is the listing of employers, arranged alphabetically by company name. Data presented for each organization include: name and address, parent firm if the organization is a subsidiary, name and title of the designated recruitment representative, a brief description of the organization's business, date established, approximate number of employees, area of recruitment, indication of summer and/or foreign employment, and occupational openings for which the organization will recruit. Some employers have taken full-page ads to provide fuller information. The alphabetical listing of employers is by occupation, by geographic area, and by special employment categories, i.e., employers who have opportunities of special interest for experienced personnel and doctoral-degree holders, as well as those with summer and foreign employment available. There is an index of occupational categories and an index of advertisers. KSK

SS 524
Collegiate Summer Employment Guide. 1972. a. American Collegiate Employment Institute, 1081 Western Blvd, Los Angeles, CA 90024. Examined: 1977. Christopher C. Hall, ed. (1978. 265p.)
Aud: Jc, Cl, Pl

A verified list of employers who plan to hire students for recreational, camp, park, and resort jobs. Organized by type of job, i.e., national park, summer camp, resort, career training, summer theater, overseas, service, federal agencies, and miscellaneous. Entries include contacts, dates available, addresses, and salaries. KMH

SS 525
Directory of College Placement Offices. ISSN 0070-5284. 1960. a. index. College Placement Council, Box 2263, Bethlehem, PA 18001. Examined: 1973/74. Warren E. Kauffmann, ed. 140-. (1975/76. $8; $5 to members).
Aud: Jc, Cl

A listing of college placement offices arranged alphabetically by name of state, then by name of college or university. Entries include the location of the college; the name, title, and telephone number of the placement director; the date on which interviews begin; special requirements for the scheduling of interviews; months in which the institution has graduating classes; and an indication of whether the placement office serves alumni. There is a list of all four-year colleges, followed by a listing of two-year colleges who are members of the Council. Includes an index of institutions and an index of personnel. KSK

SS 526
The Directory of Overseas Summer Jobs. ISSN 0020-6051. a. bibl. Vacation-Work, 9 Park End St, Oxford, England. Dist: National Directory Service, 252 Ludlow Ave, Cincinnati, OH 45220. Examined: 1977, Charles J. James, ed., 155p., $6.95; 1978. 208p. $7.95.
Aud: Hs, Cl, Pl

Lists a wide variety of job openings throughout the world, although most are in Western Europe. Full-time summer work, both paid and volunteer, is the primary emphasis, and details of jobs available with specific employers are provided. Organizations and agencies which arrange jobs are also listed. Arranged alphabetically by country with a supplement for England, Scotland, and Wales. Each national entry includes a brief overview of employment opportunities and visa or work permit requirements. Job entries include salary, description of available positions, length of work, and qualifications. Special features include tips on applying for a job, useful publications on overseas work, and late entries. A useful publication even though the majority of the jobs appear to be in hotels (as waiters, waitresses, chambermaids, etc.) and in summer camps. KSK/BSM

SS 527
Looking for Employment in Foreign Countries Reference Handbook. 1968. bi-a. bibl. index. World Trade Academy Press, 50 E 42nd St, New York, NY 10017. Dist: Simon and Schuster, Reference and Technical Book Division, One W 39th St, New York, NY 10018. Examined: 6th ed., 1972. Juvenal Londono Angel, ed. 727p. $25.
Aud: Cl, Pl

A reference guide to employment overseas. Contains chapters with general information on employment abroad; why people seek foreign work, who should go overseas, qualifications for overseas work, the interaction between Americans and the foreign environment, visas and passports, and avenues to overseas employment (how people can find out about and obtain jobs). There are also chapters that address specific aspects of the topic including: compensation, benefits, and contracts; occupations with the most possibilities of employment in foreign countries; preparing a job resume; different types of consultants that undertake overseas projects; working for the U.S. government in foreign countries; employment guide to U.N. agencies; a list of nonprofit American organizations operating abroad; overseas opportunities for teachers; and positions with multinational corporations. The rest of the handbook gives employment and marketing profiles for most foreign countries. The countries are arranged into five main groups: Western Hemisphere; the Near East and South Asia; East Asia and Australasia; some African nations; and Western Europe. The entry for each country within a group includes: the employment of foreign personnel in that country, residence and working permit requirements, requirement for foreign professionals, working contract and termination, convertibility and repatriation of profits or salaries, payment of taxes by foreigners working in a foreign country, business etiquette and customs, productivity and skills, labor legislation and organizations, employer organizations, factors affecting labor-management relations, human resources, education and health services, agencies offering possibilities of information about employment in the country, and planning and development patterns and programs. Includes a bibliography of material on employment abroad and an index of subjects and countries. KSK

SS 528

Occupational Outlook Handbook. a. index. illus. U.S. Department. of Labor, Bureau of Labor Statistics, Washington, DC 20213. Dist: Superintendent of Documents, U.S. Government Printing Office, Washington, DC 20402. Examined: 1976/77. 781p. $7. (1978/79. 840p. $11; $8 pap.)
Aud: Jc, Pl

Describes hundreds of occupations in the U.S. Information is arranged in 13 clusters of related jobs: industrial production and related occupations; office; service; education and related occupations; sales; construction; transportation; scientific and technical; mechanics and repairers; health; social scientists; social service; and art, design, and communications-related occupations. The listing for each occupation includes: D.O.T. (Dictionary of Occupational Titles) code numbers; the nature of the work; places of employment; training, other qualifications, and advancement; employment outlook; earnings and working conditions; and sources of additional information. Following the occupational outlooks, there is a section on industrial outlooks. Within each major industry can be found: the nature and location of the industry; occupations in that industry; training, other qualifications and advancement; employment outlook; earnings and working conditions; and sources of additional information. Includes a D.O.T. index and an index to occupations and industries. The **Handbook** is illustrated with photographs of the various occupations. At the beginning of the book are articles on where to go for more information, tomorrow's jobs, and how employment projections are made. Updated between editions by the *Occupational Outlook Quarterly* ($4/yr. from the Superintendent of Documents). KSK

SS 529

The Performance Dynamics' Worldwide Directory of Job Changing Contacts. 1972. a. Performance Dynamics, Publishing Division, 17 Grove Ave, Verona, NJ 07044. Examined: 1974/75. Robert J. Jameson, ed. 98p. $10.
Aud: Sa

Subtitle: "A directory of the U.S. and foreign firms that recruit for employment positions at $10,000 and above." Listings are grouped according to ten geographical regions: New England, New York City, Mid-Atlantic and Mid-South, Southeast, Chicago, Midwestern and Plains, Rocky Mountain, Southwest, Los Angeles, and Pacific. There is also an international section listing firms in foreign countries. Entries for each firm are arranged alphabetically within each region and include letter code which designates a firm's primary activity, e.g., executive search firms, management consultant firms, or employment agencies; firm's name, address, and telephone number; area of specialization; and, for certain firms, the name of key executives. An asterisk indicates a company which the publisher considers to be most active in the U.S. in recruiting for the higher salaried positions. The listings for foreign companies omit the letter code. The 1974/75 edition is an expansion of the material in *The Professional Job Hunting System* (2nd ed.). KSK

SS 530

Summer Employment Directory of the United States. ISSN 0081-9352. 1952. a. w/suppl. National Directory Service, 252 Ludlow Ave, Cincinnati, OH 45220. Examined: 27th ed., 1978. Mynena A. Leith, ed. 208p. $7.95; $2.50 suppl.
Aud: Hs, Jc, Cl, Pl

Provides full information on 90,000 summer jobs, primarily in U.S. and Canadian recreational areas, which are open to high school seniors, college students, teachers, nurses, foreign students, and retirees. Information on the jobs comes from the employers. The jobs are arranged alphabetically by state, and within each state, by categories of employers (summer camps, resorts and hotels, national parks, amusement parks, business and industry, ranches, summer theaters, summer schools, conference and training centers, and restaurants). Each listing includes: name of the organization, location, type of employees needed (i.e. college students and teachers, etc.), employment dates, specific openings, salaries, and the name and address of the person receiving applications. Includes a few positions in Canada and the West Indies. Provides some general information about summer employers, information for students outside the U.S., procedures for making job applications, a sample letter of application, and a resume form. A new directory is issued each November; a supplement covering job listings which were received after the directory went to press is issued in February. KSK/BSM/KMH

SS 531

Teaching Abroad. 1973. irreg. bibl. index. Institute of International Education, 809 United Nations Plaza, New York, NY 10017. Examined: 2nd ed., 1976. Gail A. Cohen, ed. 87p. $4.

Aud: Jc, Cl, Sa

Provides basic information on teaching opportunities. Describes organizations and sponsors conducting teaching abroad programs for U.S. elementary and secondary school teachers, adult education and college-level program teachers, as well as opportunities for guidance counselors and administrative personnel. Introductory information covers qualifications, requirements, and application procedures. Arranged by geographic area, each entry gives brief description of the sponsoring organization or agency, academic levels, subject areas, location, requirements, benefits, duration, and application procedures. There is an index of sponsors and institutions. The appendix lists embassies and their addresses in the U.S. BSM

SS 532

World-wide Summer Placement Directory. ISSN 0512-3879. 1952. a. Advancement and Placement Institute, 169 N 9th St, Brooklyn, NY 11211. Examined: 1977. Beth Verssen, ed. 110p. $10.
Aud: Hs, Jc, Cl, Pl

Lists over 100,000 U.S. and foreign summer jobs, including permanent career and part-time opportunities in industry, government, recreation, travel agencies, summer camps, theaters, work camps, service projects, and gift shops. Also lists trainee positions for teachers and college students. Arranged in two section: foreign countries in alphabetical order, and and the U.S. arranged by section, then by state. Information provided for each entry is brief but adequate. Permanent career opportunities are included in a separate section. BSM

PATENTS, TRADEMARKS, AND COPYRIGHTS

SS 533

Annual Institute on Patent Law. Lectures. ISSN 0553-3864. 1963. a. bibl. index. Matthew Bender and Co., 235 E 45th St, New York, NY 10017. Examined: 1977. Virginia Shook Cameron, ed. 483p. $28.50.
Aud: Sa

Subtitle: "Proceedings of the Annual Institute on Patent Law, sponsored by the Continuing Legal Education Center of the Southwestern Legal Foundation on the Campus of the University of Texas at Dallas." Each volume also has a distinctive title, e.g., "Protecting Intellectual Rights," 1964; "Enforceability of Rights," 1965; "Patent Law Annual," 1966/77. The volume consists of lectures delivered at the Institute. Speakers include lawyers, business executives, and representatives from the U.S. government. Subjects of some of the talks include: government ownership of patents, taxation of sales and exchanges of patents, consent decrees in patent cases, how to obtain the antitrust division's assistance in preventing or remedying violations of federal law, protecting inventions in a changing Europe, the new copyright act, and recent developments in patent law. All of these articles contain bibliographical references. There is a table of cases cited in the articles (including footnote references) and a subject index. KSK

SS 534

Copyright Laws and Treaties of the World. Supplements. ISSN 0069-9969. 1956. a. UNESCO, 7 Place de Fontenoy, 75700 Paris, France. Dist: Unipub, Box 433, New York, NY 10016. Examined: 1977. 3v. $315.
Aud: Sa

Compiled by UNESCO and the World Intellectual Property Organization (WIPO) with the cooperation of the Copyright Office of the U.S.A. and the Industrial Property and Copyright Department of the Department of Trade and Industry of the United Kingdom. The basic volume was published in 1956 and is supplemented annually with new and revised material. The unbound supplements can be inserted in a looseleaf binder(s). The volumes are arranged in alphabetical order by name of country. Within each country are the texts of its copyright statutes, including international agreements. Each country has a separate table of contents page (in blue) which gives each law or treaty an item number and indicates which items have expired. At the end of the alphabetical listings are supplementary sections covering laws and treaties that deal with territories of various countries, multilateral conventions (such as the Universal Copyright Convention), and a miscellany that includes, among other items, Rome convention rights, Caracas copyright agreement, and the Washington copyright convention. Instructions for adding the supplements to the binders are provided. KSK

SS 535

Decisions of the United States Courts Involving Copyrights. ISSN 0070-3176. 1910. bi-a. index. U.S. Copyright Office, the Library of Congress, Washington, DC 20540. Dist: Superintendent of Documents, U.S. Government Printing Office, Washington, DC 20402. Examined: 1971/72. Benjamin W. Rudd, ed. 971p. (1975/76. 1530p. $13.75.)
Aud: Cl, Sa

Compilation of federal and state copyright cases, as well as cases involving related subjects in the field of intellectual property, reported during a two-year period. The table of cases in the front of the volumes gives both the plaintiff's and the defendant's name. Cases are arranged in alphabetical order by the name of the plaintiff. Details of the case and the decision of the judge are given, as well as *See Also* citations which refer to earlier or subsequent phases of the same or connected litigation. An appendix gives a supplemental list of cases which do not directly involve copyright, but which may be of possible interest. They are summarized rather than printed in full. Following this appendix is a list of works (books, musical compositions, scripts, trademarks, art works, etc.) involved in the cases. There is a subject index and summaries of cases. The publication is a biennial, but it appears two years after the last year covered, i.e., the 1971/72 volume was published in 1974, the 1975/76 volume in 1978. A cumulative index for the years 1909-70 is available from the Superintendent of Documents (540p., $6.90). KSK

SS 536

Patent Law Review. ISSN 0079-0168. 1969. a. bibl. index. Clark Boardman Co., 345 Hudson St, New York, NY 10014. Examined: 1976. Thomas E. Costner, ed. 510p. $32.50.
Aud: Cl, Sa

A selection of articles on intellectual property that have appeared during the past year. Most of the essays have appeared in law journals, but there are also several unpublished articles grouped in a separate section. The articles are arranged into six broad subject fields: general considerations, licensing, taxation, patent misuse, trademarks, and copyrights. All of the articles include bibliographical footnotes. The first essay in the volume is a survey and overview of recent developments in patent law. The original page numbers of law review material reprinted in the collection are indicated in brackets on each text page. There is a subject and author index at the end of the volume. KSK

SS 537

Trademark Register of the United States. ISSN 0082-5786. (Continues: The Trademark Renewal Register.) 1967. a. index. Patent Searching Service, 422 Washington Bldg, Washington, DC 20005. Examined: 1975, 1110p.; 1976, 1144p.; 1977. Cyril W. Sernak, ed. $54.
Aud: Cl, Pl

The 1975 edition marks the beginning of the use of the newly adopted International Classification Schedule by the U.S. Patent and Trademark Office. Trademark applications filed before August 31, 1973, are classified in accordance with the existing U.S. Classification Schedule. The **Register** is a publication of current trademarks registered and renewed since 1881 in the U.S. Patent and Trademark Office for all classes of products, goods, and services. Only registrations currently in force are listed. Each entry is alphabetically listed by class with date of registration and registration number. The contents page lists all of the classes in three groups (international classification, services—international, and prior U.S. classification). Examples of classes are chemicals, jewelry, communication, tobacco products, wines, and glassware. An appendix gives the complete international and U.S. classifications. KSK

SS 538

U.S. Copyright Office. Annual Report of the Register of Copyrights. ISSN 0090-2845. 1898. a. U.S. Library of Congress, Copyright Office, Washington, DC 20559. Examined: 76th ed., 1973. 18p. free.
Aud: Cl, Pl

The reports are reprinted from the *Annual Report of the Librarian of Congress* for the fiscal year ending June 30. Gives the major developments in the copyright field during the fiscal year. Among the items covered are copyright law revision, administrative developments within the copyright office, copyright business during the year, official publications of the Office, legislative developments, judicial developments (including court decisions related to copyright), and international copyright developments. Following the narrative summary there are a series of tables: international copyright relations of the U.S., number of registrations by subject matter in the past five years, number of articles deposited during the past five years, number of articles transferred to other departments of the Library of Congress, gross cash receipts, fees and registrations for the last six years, and a summary of copyright business. KSK

SS 539

U.S. Patent and Trademark Office. Commissioner of Patents and Trademarks. Annual Report. ISSN 0083-3002. (Continues: U.S. Patent Office. Annual Report of the Commissioner of Patents.) 1837. a. U.S. Department of Commerce, Patent and Trademark Office, Washington, DC 20231. Dist: Superintendent of Documents, U.S. Government Printing Office, Washington, DC 20402. Examined: 1976. 31p. $.15.
Aud: Cl, Pl

Describes events in the field of patents and trademarks and activities of the U.S. Patent and Trademark Office over the last fiscal year. After a brief narrative summary of highlights of the year, the report provides statistical tables. The data on patents includes: summary of patent examining activities, patent applications filed, patents issued, patent applications pending, patents issued to U.S. residents, patents issued by the U.S. to residents of foreign countries, and U.S. patent applications filed by residents of foreign countries. The statistical data on trademarks includes tables on pending trademark applications; summary of trademark examining activities; applications for trademark registrations; renewals and affidavits; trademarks issued, renewed, and published; and U.S. trademark applications and registrations to foreign residents. Finally, there are general statistical data, including actions on petitions to the commissioner, summary of contested cases in patent and trademark office during the year, cases in litigation, litigation report (other jurisdictions, cases reported), a summary of patent and trademark office services furnished for fees or without charge to the public and government agencies, income from fees, operating cost, and end of year employment. KSK

SS 540

U.S. Patent and Trademark Office. Index of Patents Issued from the U.S. Patent and Trademark Office. ISSN 0083-3037. 1920. a. index. U.S. Patent Office, Washington, DC 20231. Dist: Superintendent of Documents, U.S. Government Printing Office, Washington, DC 20402. Examined: 1975. 2v. v. 1, 2242p., $26; v.2, 461p., $8.80. (1976. v. 1, $18.50; v. 2, $8.75.)
Aud: Sa

Prior to 1970 published as part of the *Annual Report of the Commissioner of Patents*. It is now issued in two volumes. Volume one is a list of patentees; volume two is an index to inventions by subject. Volume one begins with a brief index of applicant and assignees of patent applicants. Most of the volume is taken up with the list of patentees, arranged by the first significant character or word of the name. There are many "see" references from a company name or the name of a co-inventor to the name of the patentee. Each entry includes a brief sentence describing the patent, followed by the patent numbers. The first volume also includes briefer lists of reissue patentees, design patentees, plant patentees, defensive publications, and disclaimers and dedications. In volume two, the subject of invention of each invention issued during the year is identified by the class and subclass numbers of the official U.S. Patent and Trademark Office classification at the time the patent was issued. The index is arranged in numerical order by class numbers, and then by subclasses. Design patents, plant patents, and defensive publications are listed separately from regular patents. To find further information on a particular subject, it may be necessary to use other publications of the Patent and Trademark Office. KSK

SS 541

U.S. Patent and Trademark Office. Index of Trademarks Issued from the U.S. Patent and Trademark Office. ISSN 0083-3045. (Continues: Index of Trademarks Issued by the U.S. Patent Office.) 1928. a. U.S. Patent Office, Washington, DC 20231. Dist: Superintendent of Documents, U.S. Government Printing Office, Washington, DC 20402. Examined: 1975. 389p. $7.90. (1976. 393p. $8.)
Aud: Cl, Pl

An alphabetical listing of trademark registrants. Includes the registrants of all trademarks issued during the current year, as well as registrants of trademarks published in the *Official Gazette*. It also includes registrants of trademark registrations renewed, cancelled, surrendered, amended, disclaimed, corrected, etc., during the current year. It provides the name of the trademark, the city and state (if U.S.) or city and country (if foreign) of the company, and the trademark number. KSK

POLITICAL SCIENCE

SS 542

The Almanac of American Politics. 1972. a. index. illus. E. P. Dutton and Co., 201 Park Ave S, New York, NY 10003. Examined: 1978. Michael Barone, Grant Ujifusa, and Douglas Matthews, eds. 1029p. $16.95.
Aud: Hs, Jc, Cl, Pl

Attempts to provide a political portrait of the nation by state and by district. Primarily devoted to national politics, but includes information about state governors. Gains, losses, and significant trends are noted from election to election, as are key votes in the House and Senate. A frank, nitty-gritty political analysis is provided for each state, accompanied by census data indicating share of federal tax burden and federal tax outlay, economic base, and voter characteristics. Each congressional district is profiled in the same manner. Listings for each senator and representative give vital statistics, committees, group ratings, key votes, and results of various elections. SJV

SS 543
America Votes: A Handbook of Contemporary American Election Statistics. ISSN 0065-678X. 1956. bi-a. illus. Congressional Quarterly, 1414 22nd St, NW, Washington, DC 20037. Examined: v. 12, 1976. Richard M. Scammon, ed. 360p. $35.
Aud: Cl, Pl

Examines American electoral behavior through election statistics. Covers results of presidential elections from 1948-76, and results of presidential primary races in 1976. Each state is profiled and vote counts are given for all major elected offices. SJV

SS 544
American Enterprise Institute for Public Policy Research Review: (year) Session of the Congress. 1973. a. illus. American Enterprise Institute for Public Policy Research, 1150 17th St, NW, Washington, DC 20036. Examined: 1976. 44p. $2.
Aud: Jc, Cl, Pl

Provides a brief summary of one session of Congress, covering legislation enacted and legislation not enacted. Major actions are grouped into subject categories and discussed. Congressional action on the President's budget is reviewed. The appendix gives the history of bills enacted into laws. SJV

SS 545
American Foreign Relations: A Documentary Record. (Continues: Documents on American Foreign Relations. ISSN 0070-6973.) 1971. a. index. New York University Press, 21 W 4th St, New York, NY 10011. Examined: 1974. Richard P. Stebbins and Elaine P. Adam, eds. 613p. $26.50. (1977.)
Aud: Cl

Primarily a collection of official American documents, but other documents are included when relevant. The major areas of emphasis are arms control, the Atlantic Alliance, and detente; American policy in Asia, Middle East, Far East, Africa, and South Asia; war in Indochina; international cooperation; and international economic and financial affairs. Each area is broken down into sub-categories. Includes much of the background information and critical commentary formerly provided in the series *The United States in World Affairs*. An important source for foreign affairs collections. SJV

SS 546
Amnesty International Report. (Continues: Amnesty International. Annual Report. ISSN 0569-9495.) 1977. a. Amnesty International Publications, 10 Southampton St, London WC2E 7HF, England. Dist: Amnesty International, USA, 2112 Broadway, Rm 405, New York, NY 10023. Examined: 1977. 352p. $3.95.
Aud: Cl, Sa

Amnesty International is an independent human rights movement working for the release of "prisoners of conscience." It opposes all types of torture and the death penalty. Its task is to monitor governments' adherence to the Universal Declaration of Human Rights. The **Report** covers Amnesty International's relations with other international organizations and its campaign against torture and the death penalty. The major part of the work is devoted to a country by country survey of human rights. The 1977 **Report** covers 116 countries. SJV

SS 547
Annual of Power and Conflict. 1971. a. Institute for the Study of Conflict, 17 Northumberland Ave, London WC2N 5BJ, England. Examined: 1st ed., 1971; 3rd ed., 1973/74; 5th ed., 1975/76. Brian Crozier, ed. 167p. $11.25.
Aud: Cl, Sa

Focuses on the actions of extremist groups throughout the world and weighs changes in the balance of political influence. A regional article provides a framework for the country by country analysis. Then the political status, population, and armed forces personnel are given for each country. Major emphasis is on revolutionary challenges to internal security. For example, the 1975/76 volume entry for the United States covers the Weather Underground, Black Liberation Army, Symbionese Liberation Army, New World Liberation Front, and Fuerzas Armadasde Liberacion Nacional (FALN). An appendix lists extremist organizations with their orientation and status. SJV

SS 548
Annual Review of United Nations Affairs. ISSN 0066-4340. 1949. a. Oceana Publications, Dobbs Ferry, NY 10522. Examined: 1975. Joseph T. Vambery, ed. 216p. $17.50. (1976. 464p.)
Aud: Cl, Sa

Attempts to be "a source of basic information, a ready reference book, and a starting point for further research." Includes as much information as possible about activities at the United Nations during the preceding year. Part one reports on activities under broad topics, such as political and security questions, decolonization, apartheid, economic questions, social questions, human rights, international law, outer space, environment, science and technology, and population. The analytical table of contents lists any United Nations agency involved in a particular activity. Part two, a recent addition, consists of appendixes covering the four main bodies of the United Nations (the General Assembly, the Security Council, the Economic and Social Council, and the Trusteeship Council) and lists the agendas of their meetings, all documents issued by them, and their resolutions and decisions. This publication is important because it is more current than the official United Nations publications and provides more complete bibliographic control. SJV

SS 549

Basic Facts About the United Nations. 1947. a. illus. United Nations, Office of Public Information, New York, NY 10017. Examined: 1977. 115p. $1.50.
Aud: Hs, Jc, Cl, Pl

A simple, well organized guide to the structure and workings of the United Nations. It covers the origins, purposes, principles, main organs, and activities of the United Nations. Descriptions of the major agencies are included. Membership and date of admission are given for all countries. SJV

SS 550

Canadian Annual Review of Politics and Public Affairs. ISSN 0315-1433. 1960. a. index. University of Toronto Press, Toronto, Ontario, M5S 1A6 Canada. Examined: 1975. 363p. $35. (1976. 442p.)
Aud: Cl, Sa

A narrative review of Canadian politics. The text is divided into broad subject categories. One section covers the session of Parliament and Ottawa's relations with the provinces, particularly with Quebec. Another section deals with each province separately, concentrating on economic and political activity. The section titled "External Affairs and Defense" deals with Canadian-American relations and Canada's interactions with the rest of the world. A section titled "The National Economy" presents overview chapters on prominent economic issues. A Canadian calendar and obituaries are included. SJV

SS 551

Congress and the Nation: A Review of Government and Politics. 1945/64. quadrennial. index. illus. Congressional Quarterly, 1414 22nd St, NW, Washington, DC 20037. Examined: 1973/76. Patricia Ann O'Connor, ed. 1271p. $49.50.
Aud: Cl, Pl

Each volume presents a legislative and political summary of one presidential term, based primarily on the **Congressional Quarterly Almanac.** The arrangement follows broad legislative areas. Chronologies and important votes are recorded. The first volume in the series covered 1945-64; subsequent volumes are quadrennial. SJV

SS 552

Congressional Quarterly Almanac. 1945. a. index. illus. Congressional Quarterly, 1414 22nd St, NW, Washington, DC 20037. Examined: v. 32, 1976; v. 33, 1977. Carolyn Mathiasen, ed. 1448p. $70.
Aud: Cl, Pl

A major source of information on the activities of Congress. Volume 32 highlights the events of the 94th Congress, Second Session, 1976. Organization is by area of legislation, i.e., economic policy, energy and environment, foreign policy, national security, housing and urban affairs, labor and manpower, agriculture, law enforcement and judiciary, consumer policy, Congress and government, health policy, education and science, welfare policy, transportation and communications, budget and appropriation. The Session is summarized, and roll call votes are recorded. A glossary of terms and a chapter on how a bill becomes law are included. SJV

SS 553

Congressional Roll Call. 1970. a. index. illus. Congressional Quarterly, 1414 22nd St, NW, Washington, DC 20037. Examined: 1977. $9.
Aud: Cl, Pl

A member by member survey of votes in the House and Senate of the preceding year's congressional session. Analyzes key votes on major issues. Special voting studies cover bipartisan voting, the conservative coelition, North-South split, party unity, presidential support-opposition, voting participation, and freshman voting. The remainder of the volume includes roll call votes of the Senate and House as reported in the *Congressional Record.* SJV

SS 554

Election Index. 1966. bi-a. index. Congressional Staff Directory, Mount Vernon, VA 22121. Examined: 1976. Charles B. Brownson, ed. 274p. $7.
Aud: Cl, Pl

Includes biographical sketches of the incumbent and all candidates for each voting district in each state. Brief statistics for past elections are given. Also lists campaign managers and their addresses. SJV

SS 555
Europa Year Book. ISSN 0071-2302. (Continues: Orbis Encyclopedia of Extra-European Countries; The Encyclopedia of Europe; Europa Year Book.) 1959. a. Europa Publications, 18 Bedford Sq, London WC1B 3JN, England. Dist: Gale Research Co., Book Tower, Detroit, MI 48226. Examined: 18th ed., 1977. 2v. 3350p. $94.50; v.1, $42.50; v. 2, $56. (19th ed., 1978.)
Aud: Cl, Pl

Published in two volumes. Volume one covers international organizations, Europe, Cyprus, and Turkey. Volume two covers the countries of Africa, the Americas, Asia, and Australasia. Provides information on the political, economic, commercial, and social institutions of the world. The listings of international organizations include detailed information on background, membership, addresses of staff, branch offices, budget, organizational structure, subsections, publications, activities, etc. Entries for specific nations are arranged alphabetically and include geographic, historical, government, defense, economic, transportation, social welfare, education, and census data. Tables provide up-to-date statistics. Information is updated annually, and a "Late Information" feature at the beginning of each volume provides last minute changes. Since 1963, information on educational and learned societies and institutions has been omitted from this publication and included in **World of Learning.** SJV

SS 556
Guide to Graduate Study in Political Science. ISSN 0091-9632. 1972. a. index. illus. American Political Science Association, 1527 New Hampshire Ave, NW, Washington, DC 20036. Examined: 1977. 376p. $4. (7th ed., 1978. 408p. $5.)
Aud: Cl, Pl

An alphabetical listing of political science programs at the graduate level. Information given for each program includes admission requirements, financial aid, degree requirements, program descriptions, and a list of faculty. PhD programs and Masters programs are presented in tabular format. There is a faculty index. SJV

SS 557
International Bibliography of Political Science. ISSN 0085-2058. 1953. a. index. Tavistock Publications, 11 New Fetter Lane, London EC4 England. Dist: Aldine Publishing Co., 525 S Wabash Ave, Chicago, IL 60605. Examined: v. 24, 1975. 328p. $36.
Aud: Cl, Sa

This volume is part of the *International Bibliography of the Social Sciences* series. It is a classified listing of books, pamphlets, periodical articles, and government publications in the field of political science. The bibliography is international in scope, covering publications issued in a variety of languages. The entries and the author and subject indexes are in English and French. An outline of the detailed classification system is included. SJV

SS 558
International Yearbook and Statesmen's Who's Who. ISSN 0074-9621. 1953. a. index. Kelly's Directories, Neville House, Eden St, Kingston-upon-Thames, Surrey, KTI IBY, England. Examined: 25th ed., 1977. Robert M. Bradford, comp. 821p. $40. (26th ed., 1978. 803p.)
Aud: Jc, Cl, Pl

Divided into three parts. Part one, the smallest section, gives information on international and national organizations such as the United Nations, specialized agencies of the U.N., affiliated agencies of the U.N., inter-governmental organizations, and other international and national organizations. Part two comprises the international yearbook; after giving charts on the organization of the foreign ministries of the five great powers (Britain, U.S.A., France, China, and U.S.S.R.), the states of the world are presented in alphabetical sequence. It includes, for each country: name of capital, head of state, national flag, constitution and government, local government, legal system, area and population, currency, finance, banks, production, industry and commerce, communications (railways, shipping, air), newspapers, education, atomic energy, and religion. Part three is the "Statesmen's Who's Who" section. Names of the leaders and important figures of all countries are presented alphabetically. Information includes name, nationality, date of birth, profession, education, career, memberships, publications, clubs, and home and office addresses. There is a general index with names of countries, international organizations, etc. KSK

SS 559
International Yearbook of Foreign Policy Analysis. ISSN 0095-1471. 1974. a. bibl. index. Crane, Russak and Co., 52 Vanderbilt Ave, New York, NY 10017. Examined: v. 1, 1974; v. 2, 1975. Peter Jones, ed. 266p. $15.
Aud: Cl, Sa

Contains original papers by foreign policy experts covering the principal events in the field of foreign policy during the previous year. The activities of the U.S., the Soviet Union, China, and the European community are covered each year. Remaining articles concentrate on major actions or trends in foreign policy. SJV

SS 560
International Yearbook of Foreign Policy Studies. 1973. a. bibl. Sage Publications, 275 S Beverly Dr, Beverly Hills, Ca 90212. Examined: v. 1, 1973; v. 3, 1975. Patrick J. McGowan, ed. 213p. $17.50.
Aud: Cl, Sa

This publication was launched to pursue the study of foreign policy grounded within the empirical research traditions of the social sciences. It hopes to contribute to the further conceptualization and measurement of foreign policy behavior. It is international in scope and the editorial board and the contributors are internationally representative. Articles cover the development of the field, description, explanation, prediction, and evaluation. About nine to ten articles are published each year. A bibliography of foreign policy studies is also included in each volume. SJV

SS 561
National Roster of Black Elected Officials. ISSN 0092-2935. 1970. a. index. Joint Center for Political Studies, 1426 H St, NW, Washington, DC 20005. Examined: v. 7, 1977. 262p. $15.
Aud: Jc, Cl, Sa

The 1977 volume lists the names, titles, and addresses of 4311 Black American men and women holding elective office in the U.S. Arrangement is by state with entries grouped by level of office, i.e., federal, state, county, municipality, law enforcement, school districts, and special districts. A description of each level of office is given for each state. The introductory material provides summary statistics on Black participation in American politics. Earlier editions provided more detailed analyses. This feature will now be included in a new publication entitled **The State of Black Politics** which will also be published annually. SJV

SS 562
Political Handbook of the World. ISSN 0079-3035. (Continues: Political Handbook and Atlas of the World.) 1927. a. index. illus. McGraw-Hill Book Co., 1221 Ave of the Americas, New York, NY 10036. Examined: 1977. Arthur S. Banks, ed. 604p. $24.95. (1978. 627p.)
Aud: Cl, Pl

Subtitle: "Governments, regional issues and intergovernmental organizations as of (date)." Each country is listed alphabetically by the customary English name. Besides basic facts, the information focuses on political status, political leaders, politics and political parties, legislatures, cabinets, the news media, and diplomatic representation. A section on regional issues covers Western Europe, Eastern Europe, Latin America, the Middle East, South Asia, Southeast Asia, and Sub-Saharan Africa. The emphasis is on regional political activity. Entries for each intergovernmental organization cover the date of establishment, purpose, headquarters, principal organs, membership, origin and development, structure, and activities. Appendixes list U.N. members and present selected statistical indexes. SJV

SS 563
Presidency (year). 1974. a. index. illus. Congressional Quarterly, 1414 22nd St, NW, Washington, DC 20037. Examined: 1974; 1975; 1976. 192p. $5.25.
Aud: Jc, Cl, Pl

Continues an annual survey begun during the Nixon presidency. The year's activities are reviewed in summary essays on broad topics, including economic policy, foreign policy, housing, welfare policy, health policy, etc. Presidential nominations and confirmations are listed. One chapter is devoted to voting studies. Presidential messages to Congress, veto messages, news conferences, and major statements are included. Much of the information is available elsewhere, but ease of access makes this a useful publication. SJV

SS 564
Public Affairs Information Service. Bulletin. ISSN 0033-3409. 1915. a. w/w. & q. suppls. Public Affairs Information Service, 11 W 40th St, New York, NY 10018. Examined: 1976 (and suppls.) Robert S. Wilson, ed. $85; $180 w/w & q. suppls.
Aud: Jc, Cl, Pl

A subject index to books, pamphlets, government documents, reports of public and private agencies, and articles in over 1,000 periodicals. Covers materials published in the English language throughout the world. Commonly referred to as *PAIS*, it is issued in three forms: the annual permanent volume, weekly bulletins, and quarterly cumulations. A five-year cumulated author index, *Public Affairs Information Service Bulletin Author Index 1965-1969*, was published by Pierian Press in 1973. In 1977, Carrollton Press published a *Cumulative Subject Index to the Public Affairs Information Service Annual Bulletins*

1915-1974. Foreign publications are covered in the *PAIS Foreign Language Index*. JKM

SS 565
Sage Yearbooks in Politics and Public Policy. 1975. a. bibl. Sage Publlications, 275 Beverly Dr, Beverly Hills, CA 90212. Examined: v. 1, 1975, 320p., $17.50; v. 2, 1976, 286p., $17.50; v. 3, 1977. Stuart S. Nagel, ed. 288p. $17.50.
Aud: Cl, Sa

This series is intended to promote the application of political science to policy problems. Each volume is a collection of articles by political scientists and others involved in shaping public policy. Articles are selected on the basis of application of scientific methods to issues of broad significance. Articles usually include bibliographies. Each volume deals with a specific theme, i.e., "What Government Does" is the focus of volume one, volume two deals with "Public Policy Evaluation," and volume three covers "Public Policy Making in a Federal System." SJV

SS 566
Scandinavian Political Studies. Examined: 0080-6757. 1966. a. Universitetsforlaget, Blindern, Oslo 3, Norway. Dist: Sage Publications, 275 S Beverly Dr, Beverly Hills, CA 90212. Examined: v. 1, 1966; v. 9, 1974; v. 10, 1975. Erik Allardt, ed. 222p. $17.50. (1977.)
Aud: Cl

Sponsored by the Political Science Associations in Denmark, Finland, Norway, and Sweden. Includes articles on various areas of political research. The authors are Scandinavian scholars and the emphasis is local. The field of political studies in interpreted broadly; such topics as local planning, labor radicalism, communications, and public expenditures are covered. Some earlier volumes concentrated upon a single theme. SJV

SS 567
United Nations. Delegations to the General Assembly. ISSN 0070-3303. (Continues: United Nations. List of Delegations.) 1946. a. United Nations Publications, LX 2300, New York, NY 10017. Examined: 1976. 399p. $4. (32nd ed., 1977. 420p.)
Aud: Sa

Lists the committees of the United Nations General Assembly with names of members and room location at U.N. headquarters. Also lists each member country, with its representatives and advisers, and all specialized agencies. Addresses of the delegations in New York City are given. SJV

SS 568
United Nations. Yearbook. ISSN 0082-8521. 1947. a. index. United Nations Publications, New York, NY 10017. Examined: v. 28, 1974. 1170p. $35. (1977.)
Aud: Cl, Sa

Divided into two parts. Part one covers activities of the United Nations during the preceding year in five areas: political and security issues (disarmament, space, atomic energy, the Middle East, etc.); economic and social issues (trade, development, environment, refugees, human rights, etc.); issues relating to trust and non-self-governing territories and the Declaration on Granting Independence; legal issues (terrorism, aggression, International Court of Justice, etc.); and administrative and budgetary activities. References to relevant U.N. documents are given at the end of each chapter. Part two provides a short annual summary of the activities of the International Atomic Energy Agencies, International Labour Organisation, Food and Agricultural Organization, UNESCO, World Health Organization, International Bank, International Finance Corporation, International Development Association, International Monetary Association, International Civil Aviation Organization, Universal Postal Union, International Telecommunications Union, and the World Meterological Organization. The Charter and structure of the United Nations are included, and there is a list of U.N. information centers and offices. Usefulness is diminished by the lack of currentness. SJV

SS 569
U.S. and the Developing World: Agenda for Action. 1973. a. Praeger Publishers, 111 Fourth Ave, New York, NY 10003. Examined: 1974. James W. Howe, ed. 208p. $15.
Aud: Cl, Pl

The 1974 edition analyzes the crisis in the world resulting from energy shortages and hunger, how it affects developing nations, and how the U.S. can help solve these new problems. A series of articles analyzes particular aspects of the energy and hunger crisis. They are written by members of the Council and address such issues as "energy shock," the politics of scarcity, food, the need for an international oceans regime, assistance to developing nations, and public opinion and government policy. The first essay, "U.S. Foreign Policy and Development," provides a general survey of the major issues. Following the papers is a statistical section which gives figures on the development gap; trade between developed and developing countries; energy, raw materials, and food; the poorest developing countries; infant mortality rates; world exports; oil exports; world fish catch; and trends in private investment in developing countries. Sources for the statistics are given at the bottom of each page. KSK

SS 570
U.S. Bureau of the Census. Congressional District Atlas. 1960. bi-a. illus. U.S. Bureau of the Census, Washington, DC 20233. Dist: Superintendent of Documents, U.S. Government Printing Office, Washington, DC 20402. Examined: 95th Congress, 1977. unpaged. $4.25.
Aud: Cl, Pl

Presents maps showing the boundaries of congressional districts and includes listings identifying the district in which counties and incorporated municipalities within each state are located. There are state maps and inset maps for more detail. No names of members of Congress are given. SJV

SS 571
U.S. Bureau of the Census. Congressional District Data Book. Examined: 0082-9447. 1961. irreg. U.S. Bureau of the Census, Washington, DC 20233. Dist: Superintendent of Documents, U.S. Government Printing Office, Washington, DC 20402. Examined: 93rd Congress, 1973/74. 550p. $8.30. (1976/77. $12.70.)
Aud: Cl, Pl

Reference volume providing a statistical picture of each Congressional district. Incorporates information from censuses of population, housing, agriculture, business, manufactures, and mineral industries and from governmental and private sources. SJV

SS 572
U.S. Department of State. United States Treaties and Other International Agreements. ISSN 0083-3487. 1950. a. index. U.S. Department of State, Bureau of Public Affairs, 2201 C St, NW, Washington, DC 20250. Dist: Superintendent of Documents, U.S. Government Printing Office, Washington, DC 20402. Examined: v. 26, 1976, 3v., 3910p.; v. 27, 1977/78. 4v. 2278p. $20 per v.
Aud: Cl, Sa

Prior to publication of this compilation, treaties and other international agreements were printed in the *U.S. Statutes at Large*. Each annual volume is issued in three parts. The full texts of each treaty or agreement are arranged numerically as originally published in *Treaties and Other International Acts* (TIAS). At the end of each part is a subject index to the contents of that volume. A cumulative index, 1950-1970, has been published separately. The text of the treaty is often in both English and in the language of the other country. SJV

SS 573
U.S. Department of State. Treaties in Force. ISSN 0083-0194. 1958. a. U.S. Department of State, Washington, DC 20250. Dist: Superintendent of Documents, U.S. Government Printing Office, Washington, DC 20402. Examined: 1977. 391p. $1.50.
Aud: Cl, Sa

Subtitle: "A list of treaties and other international agreements of the United States in force." This list was published in 1932, 1941, 1955, and 1956. It has been an annual since 1958. It includes all treaties and international agreements that have not expired or been denounced by the parties, and have not been replaced or superseded. Part one lists bilateral treaties and agreements by country or political entity with subject subheadings. Citations are given to the full text. Part two includes multilateral treaties arranged by subject. States which are parties to the agreement are given. Citations are to the full text. The list is updated weekly in the *Department of State Bulletin*. SJV

SS 574
U.S. Political Science Documents. 1975. index. University Center for International Studies, University of Pittsburgh, G-6 Mervis Hall, Pittsburgh, PA 15260. Examined: 1975, 2v.; 1976. 2v. v. 1, 1251p.; v. 2, 861p. $91.50.
Aud: Cl, Sa

A bibliographic approach to the literature of political science which offers "specificity of subject analysis and control." It is a retrospective, rather than a current awareness, tool. Volume one includes five indexes to the literature: author/contributor, subject, geographic area, proper name, and journal. Volume two includes the document descriptions. There can be as many as 11 items of information for each document including assession number, author, title, contributors, source, abstract, special features (tables, charts, figures, maps, etc.), individuals cited (those whose work is cited in text, footnotes, references), key subject descriptor, key geographic areas, and proper names (events, organizations, geographic areas, legislation, etc.). SJV

SS 575

The Universal Reference System: Political Science, Government and Public Policy Series. Annual Supplement. ISSN 0364-5908. 1967. a. bibl. IFI/ Plenum Data Co., Plenum Publishing Corp., 227 W 17th St, New York, NY 10011. Examined: 1976. George W. Johnson, ed. 3v. 2600p. $295.
Aud: Sa

The Universal Reference System is a computerized information retrieval system for the social and behavioral sciences. The ten-volume *Political Science, Government and Public Policy Series* was completed in 1965. Annual supplements have been published since 1967. Each supplement includes an index of descriptors, abstracts of the books and journals indexed, and a bibliographic index to the abstracts. Entries in the bibliographic section indicate author, title, format, year of publication, key terms, and additional terms. The abstract section gives full bibliographic citations. This source would be most valuable in a research collection. SJV

SS 576

Who's Who in American Politics. ISSN 0000-0205. 1967/68. bi-a. index. R. R. Bowker Co., 1180 Ave of the Americas, New York, NY 10036. Dist: R. R. Bowker Co., Box 1807, Ann Arbor, MI 48106. Examined: 6th ed., 1977/78. Anne Rhodes, ed. 1170p. $52.50.
Aud: Cl, Pl
Indexed in: *Biographical Dictionaries Master Index.*

A biographical directory of approximately 20,000 men and women active in politics and government in the U.S. at the national, state, or local level, Each entry indicates party affiliation; date and place of birth; names of parents, children, and spouse; education; past and present political, government, and business positions; military service; publications; memberships; religion; voting residence; and mailing address. Lists of the President and his cabinet, state delegations to Congress, governors, and state party chairpersons are included. SJV

SS 577

World Military and Social Expenditures. 1974. a. WMSE Publications, Box 1003, Leesburg, VA 22075. Examined: 1976. Ruth Leger Sivard, ed. 31p. $2.50. (1977. 31p. $2.50.)
Aud: Jc, Cl, Sa

The publishers state that "the purpose of this report is to provide an annual accounting of the use of world resources for social and for military purposes, and an objective basis for assessing relative priorities." Military and social statistical data from basic sources are brought together for comparative purposes. Alternative types of spending are proposed. The Statistical Annex provides three very useful tables. The first outlines military and social trends from 1960-1974 for developed and developing countries. Table two gives comparative resources for 132 countries in general economic areas (population, area, GNP); public expenditures (military, international, peacekeeping, education, health, and foreign economic aid); and human resources (armed forces, teachers, and physicians). Table three gives a per capita ranking of 132 countries in military and social indicators. SJV

SS 579

The Year Book of World Affairs. ISSN 0084-408X. 1947. a. bibl. index. Stevens and Sons, 11 New Fetter Lane, London EC4P 4EE England. Dist: Westview Press, 1989 Flatiron Ct, Boulder, CO 80301. Examined: v. 31, 1977. George W. Keeton and Georg Schwarzenberger, eds. 364p. $27.50.
Aud: Cl, Sa

Published under the auspices of the London Institute of World Affairs. Presents research articles of lasting importance. World affairs in interpreted very broadly. Topics in the 1977 issue include aspects of foreign policy, economics, arms control, government, and education. The topics are examined in depth by recognized scholars. SJV

SS 580

Yearbook on International Communist Affairs. ISSN 0084-4101. 1966. a. bibl. index. Hoover Institution Press, Stanford University, Stanford, CA 94305. Examined: 11th ed., 1977. Richard F. Staar, ed. 612p. $25. (1978. 497p.)
Aud: Cl, Pl

Provides basic data and preliminary evaluations concerning organizational and personnel changes, attitudes toward domestic and foreign policies, and activities of Communist parties and international front organizations throughout the world. Organization is by region (Eastern Europe, Western Europe, Asia and the Pacific, The Americas, Middle East and Africa), then alphabetically by nation. Each nation's Communist organizations are profiled in a detailed essay which includes membership, auxiliary organizations, domestic activities, and views on international issues. An extensive bibliography and index of names is included. SJV

PUBLIC FINANCE AND TAXATION

SS 581
Facts and Figures on Government Finance. ISSN 0071-3678. 1941. bi-a. index. Tax Foundation, 50 Rockefeller Plaza, New York, NY 10020. Examined: 16th ed., 1971. Elsie Watters, ed. 279p. $5. (1977.)
Aud: Cl, Pl

Contains information on tax rates, expenditures, and government debt. Federal finance is derived from publications of the U.S. Bureau of the Budget and U.S. Treasury Department. Data on the operations of state and local governments and all governments combined is derived from the Bureau of the Census. The statistical tables that follow are arranged in sections, e.g., federal government, state governments, local governments, etc. There is a glossary of terms used by different governmental agencies and a topical index. This publication is issued by the Tax Foundation, a private, nonprofit organization whose aim is to be "a national information agency for those who are concerned with problems of government expenditure, taxation, and debt." KSK

SS 582
Federal Tax Handbook. 1947. a. index. illus. Prentice-Hall, Englewood Cliffs, NJ 07632. Examined: 1978. 632p. $7.50.
Aud: Cl, Pl

Presents U.S. federal tax information in a clear and concise manner for organizations and individual taxpayers. A summary of tax legislation approved in the previous year is followed by a calendar and tax tables. New regulations, court decisions, rulings, and procedures are incorporated. A very detailed index provides access to the main section. Useful for answering ordinary tax questions. References are given to Prentice-Hall's *Federal Taxes* volume for further information. SJV

SS 583
Federal Tax Regulations. 1954. a. index. West Publishing Co., Box 3526, St Paul, MN 55165. Examined: 1978. 2v. 4572p. $57.
Aud: Cl, Sa

Contains the rules and regulations of the Treasury Department which deal with income, estate, and gift taxes. The regulations included interpret the statutory provisions and illustrate methods of compliance. All pertain to the Internal Revenue Code of 1954 or Title 26 of the U.S. Code of Federal Regulations. Any changes made after the bound volumes appear are noted in the *U.S. Code Congressional and Administrative News* pamphlets. SJV

SS 584
J. K. Lasser's Your Income Tax. ISSN 0084-4314. 1937. a. index. illus. Simon and Schuster, Rockefeller Center, 630 Fifth Ave, New York, NY 10020. Examined: 1978. J. K. Lasser, ed. 314p. $3.95.
Aud: Pl

A simplified manual for preparing tax returns. Major sections include: exemptions; compensation, wages, and salary; travel, entertainment, and other job expenses; sick pay, disability pensions, and accident and health benefits; moving expense deductions; how dividends are taxed; how interest is taxed; business or professional income; sales of property, stocks, and capital assets; when pensions and annuities are taxed; reporting of farm income or loss; income from rents and royalties; income from partnerships; trust estates; prizes, scholarships, damages, life insurance; what you should know about the "Zero Bracket Amount"; deductions for contributions, medical expenses, casualty, theft, etc.; figuring tax liability; taxes withheld; declaring and paying estimated tax; filing the return; tax-saving ideas and planning; a guide to estate taxes; and checklists to reduce taxes. A comprehensive subject index follows the guide. Special features include: "Basic Tax Facts," "Guide to Preparing Your Income Tax Return," and, in the 1977 issue, "Guide to 1977 Tax Reduction and Simplification Act." SJV

SS 585
Municipal Index. ISSN 0077-2151. 1924. a. index. illus. Morgan-Grampian Publishing Co., Berkshire Common, Pittsfield, MA 01201. Examined: 51st ed., 1977. W. L. Forestell, ed. 856p. $30. (52nd ed., 1978. 840p. $30.)
Aud: Sa

Subtitle: "The purchasing guide for city, township, county officials and consulting engineers." Published under the auspices of *American City* magazine. Presents useful information for government officials such as city and county expenditures, federal funding guide, and lists of conferences, conventions, and meetings. Includes a three-year index to articles appearing in *The American City and County* magazine. The bulk of the directory is devoted to product and service information and advertising. Maps of all states are included, and lists of selected city and county officials and purchasing agents are given. The source is very specialized but includes much useful information. SJV

SS 586

Setting National Priorities: The (year) Budget. ISSN 0085-6045. 1971. a. index. illus. Brookings Institution, 1775 Massachusetts Ave, NW, Washington, DC 20036. Examined: 1976; 1978. Joseph A. Pechman, ed. 443p. $11.95; $4.95 pap.
Aud: Cl, Sa

The stated purpose of this series is "to explain the President's budget, examine alternative policies, and evaluate the budgetary implications of the various options for the short and long run." In light of the complexity of the annual budget document, it hopes to be a step toward increasing public awareness and understanding. Besides analyzing the budget as a whole it treats various issues having major impact on the budgetary process. The 1978 volume covers defense, employment, medical care costs, social security, welfare reform, the cities, and energy within the context of their effect on the national budget. The tables and statistics include some retrospective material so comparisons with past years can be made. SJV

SS 587

State Tax Handbook. ISSN 0081-4598. 1964. a. illus. Commerce Clearing House, 4025 W Peterson Ave, Chicago, IL 60645. Examined: 1976. 671p. $8.50 pap.
Aud: Cl, Pl

Outlines the tax system of each state and the District of Columbia and lists the appropriate tax administration for each state. The major portion of the volume is a tax chart of each state. The constitutional basis of the tax is given and the tax system is described, giving title of tax (yield and percent), basis of rates, and due rates. Consumer Clearing House also publishes guidebooks to individual state taxes on an annual basis. SJV

SS 588

U.S. Bureau of the Census. City Government Finances in (year). (Continues: Summary of City Finances in (year).) 1966. a. illus. U.S. Bureau of the Census, Washington, DC 20233. Dist: Superintendent of Documents, U.S. Government Printing Office, Washington, DC 20402. Examined: 1975/76. 116p. $2.30.
Aud: Cl, Pl

Summarizes city government finances, including data on city-operated utilities; selected city finance items; finances of individual cities and selected urban towns and townships with populations over 50,000; and finances of the 48 largest cities. A list of definitions is also included. SJV

SS 589

U.S. Bureau of the Census. County Government Finances in (year). 1972/73. a. illus. U.S. Bureau of the Census, Washington, DC 20233. Dist: Superintendent of Documents, U.S. Government Printing Office, Washington, DC 20402. Examined: 1975/76. 74p. $1.75.
Aud: Cl, Pl

Presents statistics for county governments and their independent agencies. Lists revenues and expenditures of county-operated utilities by state, finances of county government by population groups, finances of individual governments of counties of over 100,000 population, and per capita amounts of selected financial items. Appendix table shows finances of individual city-counties, classed as municipalities, with over 100,000 population. SJV

SS 590

U.S. Bureau of the Census. Finances of Employee-Retirement Systems of State and Local Governments in (year). 1965. a. illus. U.S. Bureau of the Census, Washington, DC 20233. Dist: Superintendent of Documents, U.S. Government Printing Office, Washington, DC 20402. Examined: 1975/76. 33p. $.85.
Aud: Cl

Presents yearly statistics on receipts, benefits and withdrawal payments, and cash and security holdings of employee-retirement systems administered by state and local governments. SJV

SS 591

U.S. Bureau of the Census. Governmental Finances in (year). 1940. a. illus. U.S. Bureau of the Census, Washington, DC 20233. Dist: Superintendent of Documents, U.S. Government Printing Office, Washington, DC 20402. Examined: 1975/76. 73p. $1.35.
Aud: Cl, Pl

Includes nationwide statistics on federal, state, and local government finances. Local governments covered include counties, municipalities, townships, school districts, and special districts. Current fiscal data are given on revenue, expenditures, utility revenue, and government insurance trust revenue. SJV

SS 592

U.S. Bureau of the Census. Local Government Finances in Selected Metropolitan Areas and Large Counties: (year). 1966. a. illus. U.S. Bureau of the Census, Washington, DC 20233. Dist: Superintendent of Documents, U.S. Government Printing Office,

Washington, DC 20402. . Examined: 1974/75. 147p. $2.55.
Aud: Cl, Pl

Presents summary data on local government in selected standard metropolitan statistical areas. Shows general revenue by source; direct general expenditure by type and by function; revenues and expenditures of utilities; total expenditures for personal services; and cash and security holdings. SJV

SS 593

U.S. Bureau of the Census. State Government Finances in (year). 1965. a. illus. U.S. Bureau of the Census, Washington, DC 20233. Dist: Superintendent of Documents, U.S. Government Printing Office, Washington, DC 20402. Examined: 1975. 65p. $1.40.
Aud: Cl, Pl

Presents detailed statistics on state government finances. Provides data on financial aggregates; expenditure by character and object and by type and function; expenditure by function for capital outlay; indebtedness; cash and security holdings; and population and personal income. SJV

SS 594

U.S. Bureau of the Census. State Tax Collections in (year). 1966. a. illus. U.S. Bureau of the Census, Washington, DC 20233. Dist: Superintendent of Documents, U.S. Government Printing Office, Washington, DC 20402. Examined: 1977. 38p. $1.05.
Aud: Cl, Pl

Itemizes state tax revenues by type of tax including sales and gross receipts tax; license taxes; excise taxes on gasoline, sales, and cigarettes; and individual income taxes. SJV

SS 595

U.S. Excise Tax Guide. ISSN 0083-0534. a. index. Commerce Clearing House, 4025 W Peterson Ave, Chicago, IL 60646. Examined: 1973. 456p. $6. (1977. 456p.)
Aud: Sa

Explains excise law provisions enacted prior to the date of publication. Also shown are new regulations as well as important rulings and court decisions. Includes rate tables and checklists of taxable and nontaxable items. The checklists are not detailed; instead paragraph numbers next to the item refer the reader to more complete information in the text. Chapters in the explanatory text, which follows the excise tax forms, rates, and lists, include sections on retailers and manufacturers excise taxes; stamp taxes; taxes on wagering, playing cards, and games; truck and bus highway use tax; regulatory taxes; alcohol and tobacco taxes; machine guns and other firearms; and returns, payment refunds, and penalties. Throughout the book, page numbers are on the top of the page, paragraph numbers on the bottom. A topical index at the end refers the reader to paragraph numbers. SJV

SS 596

U.S. Internal Revenue Service. Annual Report of the Commissioner. ISSN 0083-1476. 1863. a. index. illus. U.S. Internal Revenue Service, 1111 Constitution Ave, NW, Washington, DC 20224. Dist: Superintendent of Documents, U.S. Government Printing Office, Washington, DC 20402. Examined: 1974. 115p. $1.50.
Aud: Cl, Pl

Describes the activities of the IRS in collecting taxes during the year. Chapters are arranged by topics such as: service to the taxpayer, collecting revenue, ensuring compliance by audits and investigations, technical activities, international programs, legal activities, planning and research, energy activities, and the internal management of IRS. Appendixes include an IRS functional chart, a map of regions and districts, a list of IRS officials, commissioners of the IRS from 1862 to the present, and statistical tables (Internal Revenue collections by principal sources, number of returns filled, costs incurred by IRS, etc.). A subject index is included. Illustrated with photos and charts. KSK

SS 597

U.S. Internal Revenue Service. Annual Report of the Secretary of the Treasury on the State of the Finances. ISSN 0083-1476. 1863. a. index. illus. U.S. Internal Revenue Service, 1111 Constitution Ave, NW, Washington, DC 20224. Dist: Superintendent of Documents, U.S. Government Printing Office, Washington, DC 20402. Examined: 1975, 591p., $5.15; 1976. 627p.
Aud: Cl, Sa

Provides a summary of the major domestic and international developments which affected activities of the U.S. Treasury. Treasury operations for the year are reviewed and reports from various departments of the Treasury are included. Presents various statistics, and statements and remarks of the Secretary of the Treasury on public debt operations, capital markets and debt management, domestic economic policy, tax policy, trade and raw materials policy, investment and energy policy, international monetary affairs, and developing nations. A *Statistical Appendix* is published in a separate volume (1976, 367p., $3.70). SJV

SS 598

U.S. Internal Revenue Service. Statistics of Income: Individual Income Tax Returns. 1954. a. index. illus. U.S. Internal Revenue Service, 1111 Constitution Ave, NW, Washington, DC 20224. Dist: Superintendent of Documents, U.S. Government Printing Office, Washington, DC 20402. Examined: 1973. Jack Blacksen, ed. 247p. $3.60.
Aud: Cl, Sa

Data presented are derived from a stratified sample of individual income tax returns for a given year. It gives estimates of taxpayer's income, exemptions, deductions, and tax. Includes state and regional income data, explanations of terms, and an historical summary covering 1964-1973. A detailed chapter is devoted to the sampling method used. The 1973 edition was published in 1976. SJV

SS 599

U.S. Master Tax Guide. ISSN 0083-1700. (Continues: U.S. Tax Guide.) 1933. a. index. Commerce Clearing House, 4025 W Peterson Ave, Chicago, IL 60646. Examined: 1975. 543p. $7. (61st ed., 1978. 560p. $12; $8 pap.)
Aud: Cl, Pl

Explains in everyday language the tax rules affecting personal and business transactions. In each annual edition emphasis is on the preparation of the previous year's federal income tax returns, but there is also information on the tax consequences of the current year's transactions. It utilizes the Internal Revenue code, plus the official rulings and regulations of the Treasury Department and the decisions of the court. The first part of the book features tax tables. Among the rate tables are those for individual withholding rates, corporate rates, estate and gift tax rates, and miscellaneous tax rates. The tables are followed by check lists which show income items, deductions, etc., which make up most federal tax returns. The main part of the **Guide** is the explanatory text which includes chapters on individuals, corporations, partners and partnerships, trusts-estates-decedents, exempt organizations and retirements plans, tax accounting, gross income, sale or exchange of property, deductions, depreciation and depletion, stocks and bonds, foreign income, returns, payment of tax, and administration and procedure. An index with reference to paragraph numbers in the main text completes the volume. A tax calendar for the particular year is also included. KSK

SS 600

U.S. Office of Management and Budget. The Budget of the United States Government. 1923/24. a. index. illus. Executive Office of the President, Office of Management and Budget, Washington, DC 20503. Dist: Superintendent of Documents, U.S. Government Printing Office, Washington, DC 20402. Examined: 1978/79. 506p. $4.
Aud: Cl, Sa

The basic budget document of the U.S. government. It includes the message of the President to Congress, a summary of the budget, long range projections and economic assumptions, and federal programs by function. The budgetary process is explained in detail, and summary tables are provided for each agency of the government. SJV

SS 601

U.S. Office of Management and Budget. The Budget of the United States Government. Appendix. 1951/52. a. index. illus. Executive Office of the President, Office of Management and Budget, Washington, DC 20402. Dist: Superintendent of Documents, U.S. Government Printing Office, Washington, DC 20402. Examined: 1978. 1123p. $12.
Aud: Cl, Sa

The most detailed of all the budget documents. Detailed budget estimates are given for each government agency. There are schedules of permanent positions for all agencies giving number of positions and salary. Supplemental appropriation requests are listed. Off-budget federal entities and government sponsored enterprises are also included. SJV

SS 602

U.S. Office of Management and Budget. Catalog of Federal Domestic Assistance. 1965. a. index. Executive Office of the President, Office of Management and Budget, Washington, DC 20503. Dist: Superintendent of Documents, U.S. Government Printing Office, Washington, DC 20402. Examined: 1977. 860p. $18.
Aud: Cl, Sa

Lists and describes all federal programs and activities which provide assistance to the public. The 1977 volume described 1046 programs administered by 55 different federal agencies. The assistance is available from governmental or political subdivisions, domestic profit or nonprofit corporations, institutions, and individuals. Covers grants, loans, loan guarantees, scholarships, mortgage loans, and insurance; assistance in the form of federal property, facilities, equipment, goods, or services; technical assistance, counseling, and training; statistical and other information;

and service activities of regulatory agencies. The program descriptions give eligibility requirements, application procedures, deadlines, and persons to contact, among much other information. There are numerous indexes to facilitate use including agency program, function, popular name, applicant eligibility, and subject indexes. SJV

SS 603
U.S. Office of Management and Budget. Issues 78. (Continues: Seventy Issues.) 1977. a. illus. Executive Office of the President, Office of Management and Budget, Washington, DC 20503. Dist: Superintendent of Documents, U.S. Government Printing Office, Washington, DC 20402. Examined: 1977. 289p. $8.90.
Aud: Jc, Cl, Pl

A new budget document intended to provide more general information about various aspects of the U.S. budget. It is geared toward the general reader. The information is presented by broad category, i.e., defense, agriculture, health, commerce and transportation, and law enforcement. The text indicates the effect the current budget will have on the particular program or agency and how money will be allocated. Background information and fact sheets are given for certain areas. SJV

SS 604
U.S. Office of Management and Business. Special Analysis Budget of the United States Government. 1978. a. Executive Office of the President, Office of Management and Budget, Washington, DC 20503. Dist: Superintendent of Documents, U.S. Government Printing Office, Washington, DC 20402. Examined: 1978/79. 329p. $3.25.
Aud: Cl, Sa

Contains 17 special analyses relevant to the budgetary process. Part one includes economic and financial analyses which reflect the way the government finances the economy. Part two furnishes information on social program areas such as education, training, employment, health, income security, civil rights, and crime reduction. Part three presents trends and development in selected areas of government activity. Other sections provide more in-depth analyses of budget data. SJV

SS 605
U.S. Office of Management and Budget. The United States Budget in Brief. 1951. a. illus. Executive Office of the President, Office of Management and Budget, Washington, DC 20503. Dist: Superintendent of Documents, U.S. Government Printing Office, Washington, DC 20402. Examined: 1978/79. 92p. $1.75.
Aud: Hs, Jc, Pl

A more concise, less technical summary of the Federal budget. It corresponds roughly to the basic document **The Budget of the United States Government.** Explanatory tables and a glossary have been added. Includes data for earlier years as well as for the current fiscal year. SJV

SS 606
Your Federal Income Tax Annual. 1943. a. index. illus. U.S. Internal Revenue Service, 1111 Constitution Ave, NW, Washington, DC 20224. Dist: Arco Publishing Co., 219 Park Ave S, New York, NY 10003. Examined: 1978. 192p. $1.50 pap.
Aud: Pl

Designed to aid the general public in the preparation of federal income tax returns. Examines each part of the tax return form and explains the laws which apply. New provisions and various reminders to ease preparation of the return are outlined in the introduction. The main body of the work is divided into seven parts: part one covers the return itself; part two focuses on various types of incomes; part three discusses adjustments to income; part four covers deductions; part five explains capital gains and losses; part six deals with other gains and losses, such as sales of business or property, casualties, and thefts; and part seven covers credits and special tax computations. Provides examples of tax returns and various tables. There is a comprehensive index, and toll-free telephone numbers are given for help in answering tax questions. SJV

REAL ESTATE

SS 607
American Industrial Real Estate Association Journal. ISSN 0065-8642. 1961. a. index. illus. American Industrial Real Estate Association, 5670 Wilshire Blvd, Los Angeles, CA 90036. Examined: v. 15, 1976/77. Lee Segal, ed. 32p. $2.
Aud: Sa

The American Industrial Real Estate Association (AIR) was founded to organize industrial real estate specialists and promote cooperation among its members. Its annual journal contains articles relating to the field of industrial real estate, giving perspectives by experts on new developments in the profession. Subjects of the two- to three-page articles include land titles, adversary bidding in construction contracting, an architectural viewpoint on planning successful facilities, industrial applications of solar energy, prestressed concrete, property assessments, and energy consumption. Also included is the AIR roster of members which gives the name of the member, address, and phone number. Also listed are candidates for membership and affiliate members (companies, corporations, etc.). Illustrated with portraits of the officers and authors, drawings, and advertisements. There is an index to advertisers. KSK

SS 608

E-R-C Directory: Employee Relocation Real Estate Services. ISSN 0071-0113. (Continues: Directory of Appraisers and Brokers.) 1964. a. illus. Employee Relocation Council, 333 N Michigan Ave, Chicago, IL 60601. Examined: 1977. 1139p. $5.
Aud: Sa

Geared for industries which need a single source of information on real estate brokers and appraisers who are specialists in selling and/or acquiring homes for employees who are transferred from one location to another. Listings are organized and presented from the standpoint of the industry user rather than the lister. There is a section of Metro area maps that can be used in locating brokers and appraisers in bedroom communities surrounding the major metropolitan areas. Another section has postal zone maps for fifty major cities which can be utilized to help determine those brokers and appraisers who are closest to a given property. The next major section is the directory of appraisers (pink pages). Appraisers are listed by last name, in alphabetical order, within each city or community that they serve. Information includes: firm affiliation (if any), area code and local phone number, the year he or she started making residential appraisals, professional designations awarded to the appraiser, address, corporations served by the appraiser, and the appraiser's other activities. Following this section is a directory of brokers (yellow pages). Firm names are arranged alphabetically within the individual communities served. Information includes firm name, address, person in charge of the office, real estate and employee housing services offered, corporations served, number of offices, median price of homes available through firm, person in charge of employee relocation work, and means of working with other brokers. Finally, there is a brief listing of miscellaneous services (blue pages), including referral services, housebuying companies, van lines, area counselling, publishing companies, and special services. KSK

SS 609

National Association of Real Estate Investment Trusts. REIT Handbook of Member Trusts. ISSN 0092-4865. (Continues: National Association of Real Estate Investment Funds. NAREIF Handbook of Member Trusts. ISSN 0550-4333.) 1966. a. index. National Association of Real Estate Investment Trusts, 1101 17th St, NW, Washington, DC 20036. Examined: 1975/76. G. N. Buffington, ed. 833p. $40.
Aud: Sa

Contains background and biographical information on each trust for use by financial analysts, mortgage brokers, bankers, and others interested in basic background information about NAREIT members. The trusts are listed alphabetically. Information for each trust includes: name, location of its principal office, background of the trust, officers, current investment policy, fee policies, trustees, public offerings and private placements of debt and equity, per share history, independent auditor and counsel, a detailed balance sheet giving the assets and liabilities of the trust, statement of income, notes to the financial statements, and, finally, the opinion of the CPA about the trust. The logo of the trust is shown. At the end of the **Handbook** is an index of trust officers, trustees of trusts, and officers of independent contractors and/or investment advisors. KSK

SS 610

National Real Estate Directory. (Continues: National Real Estate Investor Handbook and Directory.) 1961. a. index. illus. Communication Channels, 6285 Barfield Rd, Atlanta, GA 30328. Examined: 9th ed., 1970. Sy Nicholson, ed. 255p. $6.
Aud: Sa

Presents data and information on realtors and others in real estate. Includes a survey of the apartment market in selected cities, information on apartment tenants, articles on the U.S. office market and the hospitality industry, a profile of mobile homes, a shopping center operating survey, checklists on buying a building, mortgage applications, condominiums, and an article on what to look for in modernizing a building. The main section includes directories for various professions and services in the U.S. and Canada. Among the categories listed are: appraisers, banks, builders-contractors-developers, building maintenance and office cleaning, consultants and counsellors, franchising systems, hotels and motels, insurance, land companies, port authorities, real estate management, public utility companies, realtors-brokers, and shopping centers. Each category is listed in alphabetical order by state. Information for each listing includes company name, address and, where applicable, the person in charge of the company. Finally, there are highlights from the annual National Real Estate Conference (sponsored by the *National Real Estate Investor*). This section includes the edited speeches, seminars, and question-and-answer periods at the Conference. Illustrated throughout with advertisements. Contains an index to advertisers. The $6 cost of the **Directory** is included in the $28 subscription to the *National Real Estate Investor* (ISSN 0027-9994. 1959. m.). KSK

SS 611
National Roster of Realtors. ISSN 0090-1741. (1973 is 54th ed.) a. index. illus. Hamats Publishing Co., 427 Sixth Ave SE, Cedar Rapids, IA 52406. Examined: 54th ed., 1973. Shirley Boyce, ed. 564p. $35; $12 to realtors.
Aud: Sa

The opening pages give information on the institutes, councils, and societies of the National Association of Realtors (NAR). Includes a photograph of the president of each organization and a brief summary of its activities, purposes, etc. The actual roster includes the names and addresses of all realtors in the U.S. and Canada (members of the NAR) by boards. Arranged alphabetically by state, each listing begins with the state board of realtors, followed by the board of realtors for each city in the state. Included for each board are the names and addresses of the president, executive vice president, secretary, and the members of the board. A number of realtors have advertisements in the roster and there is an index to these advertisers. There is also a brief listing of foreign members of the NAR, plus a comprehensive listing of the officers and past presidents of the NAR and its affiliate councils and divisions. KSK

SS 612
Site Selection Handbook. ISSN 0080-9810. 1956. a. index. illus. Conway Research, Peachtree Air Terminal, 1954 Airport Rd, Atlanta, GA 30341. Examined: 1977. Linda L. Liston, ed. 4v. $35; $10 per v.
Aud: Sa

Composed of four quarterly editions, each separately titled. Pages are numbered consecutively. *Corporate Real Estate Management,* published in February, features an index of corporate real estate for major firms, a survey of corporate real estate managers' professional training, responsibilities, compensation and staff organization, a checklist of site selection factors, and other reference data on corporate real estate acquisition and management. *Industry's Guide to Geo-economic Planning,* published in May, features geographical listings of several thousand development organizations in the U.S. and Canada; a state-by-state presenting of tax incentives, financing programs, and special services offered to industry by state governments; statistical summaries of U.S. and Canadian industrial growth factors and quality of life indicators in the fifty states. *Environment, Energy and Industry,* published in September, includes an index of state and federal environmental control agencies, state and federal energy-related agencies, a survey of state pollution control incentives and financing programs, the annual awards for distinguished service in environmental planning, and other reference data on environmental and energy trends. The *Office and Industrial Parks Index,* published in November, contains a geographical guide to industrial parks, office parks, research parks, airport, rail and port sites, and other reference data to assist industrial facility planners in selecting prepared industrial sites. The four-volume **Site Selection Handbook** is included in the subscription price to *Industrial Development* magazine. KSK

SS 613
U.S. Bureau of Land Management. Public Land Statistics. ISSN 0082-9110. 1962. a. index. illus. U.S. Bureau of Land Management, Division of Records System, Department of the Interior, Washington, DC 20240. Dist: Superintendent of Documents, U.S. Government Printing Office, Washington, DC 20402. Examined: 1976. 186p. $2.75.
Aud: Cl

Surveys the activities of the Bureau of Land Management which is part of the Department of the Interior. Part one gives statistical information on lands of the U.S. and possessions, including data on areas of states, grants to states, and land owned by the U.S. Part two has statistics on the program operations of the Bureau of Land Management. It covers land management, land disposition and use, forest management, outdoor recreation and wildlife, range management, resource conservation and development, minerals leased or sold, locatable minerals, classification and investigation, protection — fire and trespass, and public land surveys. Part three is devoted to adjudication, appeals, and hearings in cases involving the Bureau. Part three also includes tables on administration and finance (receipts from leases, sale of lands, etc.). There is a subject index. KSK

SS 614
Where to Retire on a Small Income. ISSN 0511-8719.

1950. bi-a. illus. Harlan Publications, 1000 Prince St, Greenlawn, NY 11740. Grosset and Dunlap, 51 Madison Ave, New York, NY 10010. Examined: 1975. Norman D. Ford, ed. 208p. $2.95. (20th ed., 1977. $3.95.)
Aud: Pl

Subtitle: "Where to enjoy the good life on little." A guide to the cities and towns where a person can retire cheaply. Contains articles on various aspects of retirement, such as "Eight Major Points in Choosing a Place to Retire"; "Retiring in a Mobile Home"; "Free College Education When You Retire"; "Housing and Rentals"; and "America's Most Livable, Worry-Free Towns." The major part of the volume is a guide to individual places. This section is divided into regions: the East, the Gulf States, the Southwest, California, the Pacific Northwest, and America's Island Paradises. Some of these regions are further divided into smaller sections (e.g., the East is divided into the Ozarks-Ouachitas, the Atlantic Seaboard, and New England). Finally, within each of these parts are a number of states or regions. Description of each city or town within a state covers population, location, major attractions, housing, outdoor activities, culture, and approximately how much it may cost to live there. At the end of the guide is a brief directory of America's leading retirement hotels. Includes a section of black-and-white photographs of some of the locations described and a series of weather maps that give information on rainfall, frost free days, average temperatures, etc. KSK

SS 615

Woodall's Retirement and Resort Communities. ISSN 0145-577X. (Continues: Woodall's Directory of Mobile Home Communities; Woodall's Mobile Home Parks and Retirement Communities.) 1976. a. illus. Woodall Publishing Co., 500 Hyacinth Place, Highland Park, IL 60035. Dist: Grosset and Dunlap, 51 Madison Ave, New York, NY 10010. Examined: 3rd ed., 1978. $5.95.
Aud: Pl

"An illustrated directory and price guide to leisure living opportunities coast-to-coast." The body of the volume is an alphabetical listing by state, retirement region, and facility of all types of housing geared to various types of retirement living. Each section begins with a state map and a short essay about the climate, living conditions, and services. Each entry provides name of facility, special services, location area, onsite recreation, security, community services, eligibility, fees, and business history. Each region entry includes a map indicating location of region within state. The third edition begins with a series of essays of interest to retirees covering such topics as how and why to use the volume, how to choose a suitable retirement home, today's mobile home, budgeting for retirement, and excerpts from Rosefsky's *Guide to Financial Security in the Mature Family*. KSK

SOCIAL SERVICES

SS 616

ACTION (Service Corps). Annual Report. ISSN 0092-086X. 1971/72. a. ACTION, Washington, DC 20525. Dist: Superintendent of Documents, U.S. Government Printing Office, Washington, DC 20402. Examined: 1975. 47p.
Aud: Hs, Jc, Cl, Pl

ACTION is the federal agency charged with designing opportunities for volunteer service. Its annual report details the work of its major programs: the Peace Corps, VISTA, Retired Senior Volunteer Program, Youth Challenge Program, etc. Includes a report on recruitment, international and domestic operations statistics, and a financial statement. JKM

SS 617

American Association of Marriage and Family Counselors. Register. a. American Association of Marriage and Family Counselors, 225 Yale Ave, Claremont, CA 91711. Examined: 1978. 354p. $5.
Aud: Cl, Pl, Sa

The Association's organizational handbook and membership directory. Clinical members of the Association are listed alphabetically and geographically. The geographic section is arranged by state, and within states by zip code. Canadian members and members living outside of North America are included. An authoritative list since "the minimum standard for clinical membership is an earned Master's degree from an accredited institution in marriage and family counseling or an appropriate behavioral science or mental health profession, plus two years of experience in marriage and family counseling under supervision acceptable to the Membership Committee" of the Association. Also lists officers and committee members; U.S., Canadian, and International affiliates; the Association's code of professional ethics; and standards to be followed by members in advertising their services. JKM

SS 618

American National Red Cross. Annual Report. ISSN

0080-0384. 1901. a. illus. American National Red Cross, 17th and D Sts, NW, Washington, DC 20006. Examined: 1976. free.
Aud: Pl

Includes a seven-page report to the American people describing the activities of the Red Cross during the past year. Photographs of activities are included. A list of present and incoming officers, indicating city and state of residence and offices held, follows. Statistical highlights covering the activities discussed in section one and a financial statement are also provided. The financial report is extremely detailed; it contains an explanatory text and balance sheets covering all public support and revenues and all functional expenses. Published in the *Congressional Series of U.S. Public Documents* since 1901. MBP

SS 619

Annual Handbook for Group Facilitators. ISSN 0094-601X. (1973 is 2nd ed.) a. bibl. illus. University Associates Publishers, 7596 Eads Ave, La Jolla, CA 92037. Examined: 2nd ed., 1973. J. William Pfeiffer and John E. Jones, eds. 292p. $12.50.
Aud: Sa

A compendium of articles, forms, papers, etc. compiled in an effort to share theory, information, and practical application ideas in an organized way. The volume is divided into segments covering structured experiences, instrumentation, lecturettes, theory, and resources. There are thumb guides to these sections. Each segment is preceded by an introduction. Articles, if not signed, are credited to the specific specialist who contributed or was responsible for the material. The resource section contains book reviews, a glossary of terms, an annotated bibliography, and an overview of this aspect of the field. Other sections also contain pertinent bibliographic references. This is an annual handbook written by practitioners for practitioners. Most forms, charts, exercises, and instruments, although copyrighted, may be copied or modified for use in education/training designs. Subjects included are sex-role stereotyping, traditional American values, self-disclosure, involvement, risk taking, transactional analysis, human relations, and many others in the practice of group leadership. MBP

SS 620

Child Welfare League of America. Directory of Member Agencies and Associates. (Continues: Child Welfare League of America. Directory of Member Agencies.) a. Child Welfare League of America, 67 Irving Place, New York, NY 10003. Examined: v. 40, 1973. 111p. $3.50. (1977. $7.)
Aud: Cl, Pl

A list of agencies in the U.S. and Canada which provide services for children. Agency services covered include adoption services, day care centers, institutional care for children, maternity homes, social services for children under different situations, etc. Each agency entry notes the service it offers. The directory is divided into two sections, member agencies and associates. In each section U.S. listings are followed by Canadian listings. States and provinces are listed alphabetically with city and town listings following. Also contains a list of officers and members of the Board of Directors; a list of administrative, professional, and technical staff; a description of the League's services; requiements for accredited membership; and definitions of child welfare services. MBP

SS 621

Directory for Reaching Minority Groups. 1970. irreg. U.S. Department of Labor Apprenticeship and Training Bureau, Washington, DC 20402. Dist: Superintendent of Documents, U.S. Government Printing Office, Washington, DC 20402. Examined: 1973. 214p. $2.85.
Aud: Jh, Hs, Jc, Cl, Pl

A list of organizations and individuals prepared to provide information on job training and opportunities to minority groups. Arranged geographically by state and city. Some of the organizations included are the NAACP, the National Urban League, and the Bureau of Indian Affairs. Each entry includes name, address, and telephone number. Provides a list of Black higher educational institutions, fraternities, and sororities. JKM

SS 622

Directory of Agencies Serving the Visually Handicapped in the U.S. 1928. bi-a. index. American Foundation for the Blind, 15 W 16th St, New York, NY 10011. Examined: 18th ed., 1973; 19th ed., 1975. 398p. $10.
Aud: Cl, Pl

This directory has two sections. The first part lists agencies alphabetically by state or U.S. possession. It covers educational services, residential schools, library services, rehabilitation services, and local services arranged by town. Entries include name, address, and phone number of the agency; name of the director; a short description of the services offered, including financial assistance; date established; and organizations to which the agency belongs. The second section lists specialized agencies and organizations such as service for deaf-blind persons, medical research organizations, dog guide schools, and other organizations interested in services to the blind. There is an alphabetical index to agencies. Volume 20, which was supposed to have been published in 1977, is still being compiled; it will probably be released in 1979 without a date. MBP

SS 623

Directory of Counseling Services. ISSN 0094-7512. (Continues: Directory of Approved Counseling Agencies.) a. index. International Association of Counseling Services, 1607 New Hampshire Ave, NW, Washington, DC 20009. Examined: 7th ed., 1973, 273p.; 8th ed., 1974. $4. (1975, $5.25 pap.; 1977. 125p.)
Aud: Jc, Cl, Pl, Sa

An extensive introduction explaining the history and purpose of the association, a section on guidelines for college and university counseling services, and a section on criteria for approval of community, junior, and technical college counseling services begin the volume. Accredited counseling services are then listed alphabetically by state. Each agency listing includes name, address, phone number, sponsor, hours, types of counseling, other services offered, clientele, fees, method of applying, director, and staff. Provisional members are listed alphabetically with the same type of information in a separate section. Provisional members are agencies that have taken the first step toward full accreditation. Canadian agencies are listed in both sections. There is an index to directors of counseling services. MBP

SS 624

Encyclopedia of Social Work. ISSN 0071-0237. (Continues: Social Work Year Book.) 1929. irreg. bibl. index. National Association of Social Workers, Publication Sales, 1425 H St, NW, Washington, DC 20005. Examined: 16th ed., 1971. Robert Morris, ed. 2v. 1645p. $22.50. (17th ed., 1977. 2v. 1702p. $40.)
Aud: Sa
Indexed in: *Abstracts for Social Workers.*

This two-volume work contains articles and biographies written by specialists in the field and a section on statistics. An index completes the set. Articles vary in length from a short paragraph to many pages, and cover subjects such as addiction, crime and delinquency, family services, housing, health care, self-help groups, social action, and youth service agencies. Many articles contain bibliographic references. A list of contributors with their present titles and addresses is included. The statistical section contains tables covering U.S. population, marriage and divorce rates, birth rates, immigrants by region of origin, national health expenditures, etc. MBP

SS 625

Help: The Useful Almanac. 1976/77. a. illus. Consumer News Service, 813 National Press Bldg, Washington, DC 20045. Examined: 1976/77; 1977/78. Arthur E. Rouse, ed. $4.95 pap.
Aud: Pl

Presents consumer information under five topical sections: dealing with the system; household products and services; money and taxes; transportation and communication; and energy and environment. Information is presented in the form of tables, charts, and text. There are some inaccuracies in the textual materials and tables, but this work is still a valuable compilation of facts important to all consumers. MBP

SS 626

Humanidad. ISSN 0441-4144. 1967. a. bibl. Universidad de Puerto Rico, Escuela Graduada de Trabajo Social, Recinto de Rio Piedras, Puerto Rico. Examined: no. 1, 1967; no. 3, 1969; no. 4, 1970; no. 5, 1971; no. 6, 1972; no. 7, 1973. Rosa Celeste Marin, ed. 40-50p. free.
Aud: Cl, Sa

Published by the Graduate School of Social Work of the University of Puerto Rico, these annual volumes in magazine format (8½" × 11") contain short signed articles in Spanish or English covering issues pertinent to the field of social work. Articles are written by faculty members and graduate students of the University's Department of Social Work, and cover such topics as poverty and its implications in the teaching of health and illness; biographies of social reformers; student participation in school administration; the Puerto Rican family and its function in social control; social work as a profession; origins of the profession of social work in Puerto Rico; and family planning in Puerto Rico. All articles include bibliographies pertinent to the subject discussed. MBP

SS 627

International Rescue Committee. Annual Report. ISSN 0538-9461. 1946. a. illus. International Rescue Committee, 386 Park Ave S, New York, NY 10016. Examined: 1976. 20p. free. (1977.)
Aud: Cl, Pl

Provides a brief history of the International Rescue

Committee tracing its work in helping refugees from tyranny and oppression throughout its years of existence. The 1976 report includes discussions of activities during the preceding year on the Indochina Refugee Program, the Thailand Medical Program, Hong Kong, Kurdish refugees from Iran, the European Refugee Program, refugees from Latin American Countries, and refugees from Angola. Also includes a brief financial report itemizing income, expenditures, and costs of program service during the year; and lists of officers, members of the Board of Directors, IRC offices throughout the world, and government agencies, private groups, and individuals who contributed to the Committee. MBP

SS 628
Invest Yourself: Volunteer Service Opportunities. (Continues: Involvement and Action: A Catalogue of Opportunities; Invest Your Summer.) 1944. a. index. Commission on Voluntary Service and Action, 475 Riverside Dr, Rm 700A, New York, NY 10027. Examined: 1976, 63p.; 1977. Charles Hull Jacobs, ed. $2.
Aud: Hs, Jc, Cl, Pl

A pamphlet publication listing voluntary service opportunities each year. Includes a section on how to use the guide; a short description of the Commission on Voluntary Service and Action; a list of part-time and local service opportunities; a discussion of what it means to be a full time volunteer; and listings of opportunities for volunteers under 18 years of age and for adult voluntary service. The latter two listings are arranged by categories of skills needed, e.g., health care, education, social work, business, trade skills, etc. Listings include dates volunteers should apply, location, season needed (if applicable), costs (if any), and a description of the service required. Sections on work camps/group services, intercultural exchange, additional agency resources, and reference to host families are also included. An index to agencies completes the volume. MBP

SS 629
Jewish Social Service Year Book. ISSN 0075-3742. a. illus. Council of Jewish Federations and Welfare Funds, 575 Lexington Ave, New York, NY 10022. Examined: 1976. Alvin Chenkin, ed. (1978/79. $7.)
Aud: Sa

Subtitle: "An analysis of service and financial statistics." Presents a summary of the service and financial experience of Jewish family and children's services, child care agencies, and homes for the aged in the U.S. and Canada during the previous year. The body of the work consists of statistical tables covering these services and their financing. The tabular information is based directly on reports from the agencies and institutions listed at the end of the volume. Tables cover: movement of cases during the year, volume of direct service cases, financial assistance, group treatment, counseling fees, Jewish family life education, volunteer services, sources of operating receipts, etc. Although the volumes are supposed to be annuals, no edition was published in 1977. MBP

SS 630
Public Welfare Directory. 1940. a. illus. American Public Welfare Association, 1155 16th St, NW, Suite 201, Washington, DC 20036. Examined: v. 34, 1973. Perry Frank, ed. $25. (v. 38, 1977/78. Michele Moore, ed. 389p.)
Aud: Cl, Pl, Sa

Contains an outline of the administrative structure of public welfare and related programs at the federal, state, and local levels. Listings include public agencies or agencies expending public funds; federal agencies and regional personnel who have contacts with state welfare departments; state public welfare departments; territorial and commonwealth welfare agencies; local public welfare agencies; and county welfare departments. Covers agencies in the U.S. and Canada. Key personnel, addresses, telephone numbers, fees for services, and description of services are included in each entry. Entries are arranged alphabetically by state. Program responsibilities are indicated by symbols in the left margin of each entry, when applicable; a key to symbols is included. Appendix section contains reproduced documents relating to services, disability and health insurance, how to get information from the U.S. Veterans Administration, how to get help for handicapped dependents of military personnel, etc. MBP

SS 631
Schools of Social Work with Accredited Master's Programs. (Continues: Graduate Professional Schools of Social Work in Canada and the U.S.A.) 1974. a. Council on Social Work Education, 345 E 46th St, New York, NY 10017. Examined: 1977. 19p. free.
Aud: Cl, Pl

Schools offering accredited master's degree programs followed by those which offer a post-master's program are listed by state. In addition, schools that are working toward accreditation are mentioned. School name, address, telephone number, and the name of the dean or director are provided. BSM

SS 632
Seeing Eye Annual Report. 1939. a. illus. Seeing Eye, Morristown, NJ 07960. Examined: 1975/76. Elliott Averett, President. free.
Aud: Pl, Sa

Provides a comprehensive explanation of the services and a brief history of the organization. Includes descriptions of the training of seeing eye dogs and their future owners, student services, field services, information services, and the organization's grants program. A complete financial statement with a list of grants by type and by institution, and a list of officers and members of the Board of Trustees are appended. MBP

SS 633
Social Work Practice. ISSN 0081-0568. 1962. a. index. Columbia University Press, 136 S Broadway, Irvington-on-Hudson, NY 10533. Examined: 1971; 1975. 252p.
Aud: Sa

Subtitle: "Selected papers delivered at the annual forum of the National Conference on Social Welfare." The purpose of the annual forum is to "provide a national forum for the critical examination of basic problems and issues in the social welfare field." The papers selected for inclusion reflect developmental changes in social work practice and the expansion of the field into new areas. The volume includes a list of contributors with their titles and addresses, a table of contents, abstracts of each paper included arranged alphabetically by author, and the full texts of the papers. An index and list of papers from the forum which are not included conclude the volume. MBP

SS 634
Sourcebook on Aging. 1977. freq. not determined. index. Marquis Who's Who, 20 E Ohio St, Chicago, IL 60611. Examined: 1977. 663p. $34.50.
Aud: Cl, Pl

Presents statistical and narrative information collected from a variety of government and private sources. Divided into ten parts covering population statistics; innovative health services; economic concerns, such as the adequacy of social security, housing problems, and federal housing legislation; age discrimination and the older worker; lifelong education programs; special concerns of older persons, such as crime, transportation, and credit; and listings of federal legislation, regulations, and agencies concerned with aging and the older population. Includes subject and geographic indexes. JKM

SS 635
Techniques of Marriage and Family Counseling. ISSN 0091-8385. 1972. a. bibl. American Institute of Family Relations, 5287 Sunset Blvd, Los Angeles, CA 90027. Examined: v. 5, 1976, 132p.; v. 6, 1977. Paul Popenoe, ed. $15.
Aud: Sa

A compilation of short papers presented at the American Institute of Family Relations' annual workshop on Techniques of Marriage and Family Counseling. A foreword by the editor traces the history of the Institute and describes its purpose. This is followed by papers written by psychologists, counselors, and doctors who are specialists in the field of family counseling. Papers cover subjects such as love in modern society, the sexual aversion syndrome, psychodrama, nutrition and counseling, etc. An annotated bibliography for marriage counselors containing complete bibliographic information concludes the work. A short biography of each contributor is also included. MBP

SS 636
What Every Veteran Should Know. ISSN 0083-9108. 1934. a. index. Veterans Information Service, Box 111, East Moline, IL 61233. Examined: 41st ed., 1978. George D. Spilman, ed. 400p. $4.
Aud: Sa

This service officers' guide familiarizes the user with the scope of federal benefits, services, and entitlements, and the best approaches eligible veterans and their dependents can use to obtain those benefits. Arranged alphabetically by subject. There is also a detailed index (chapter and page numbers given), and a quick reference "edge index." Charts on the inside front and back covers of this paperback give the latest benefit rates. The preface clearly states that this is a reference guide and does not have the effect of law, and advises all veterans to contact their Veterans Administration for help in completing claims. Many veterans seeking to file their own claims would find this book a boon. Monthly supplements are available ($8/yr.) to keep the annual guide up-to-date. KR/JKM

SS 637
Wise Giving Bulletin. 1944. a. National Information Bureau, 419 Park Ave S, New York, NY 10016. Examined: 1977. M. C. Van de Workeen, ed. 6p. free.
Aud: Pl

Subtitle: "A reporting and advisory service for contributors." Lists the National Information Bureau's (NIB) eight basic standards with examples illustrating how the NIB applies these standards to its evaluations of agencies. The standards require an agency to have an active and responsible governing board, a legitimate purpose, specific fund-raising practices, cooperation with established agencies, ethical promotion methods, etc. Tabulations of funds received and expended by selected charities are also included. NIB also published a free monthly *Wise Giving Guide* containing ratings of national non-profit organizations based on the NIB basic standards in philanthropy. MBP

SOCIOLOGY

SS 638

American Sociological Association. Proceedings of the Annual Meeting. 1905. a. index. American Sociological Association, 1722 N St, NW, Washington DC 20036. Examined: 72nd ed., 1977.
Aud: Sa

Contains all of the abstracts of papers submitted by authors to the executive office prior to the date of publication. Abstracts appear in session order. The topic index classifies papers by general subject area, and references indicate session numbers rather than page numbers. Subject areas covered include age, altruism, American Indians, anomie, Asian Americans, behavioral sociology, belief systems, blocks, children and youth, China, communes, corporate crime, divorce, disaster, ecology, fertility, homosexuality, housing, sociology of leisure, knowledge, labor market, Marxian sociology, phenomenology, police, sociolinguistics, suicide, women, etc. An author index appears at the end of the volume. MBP

SS 639

Annual Editions: Readings in Marriage and the Family. ISSN 0095-6155. 1974. a. index. illus. Dushkin Publishing Group, Sluice Dock, Guilford, CT 06437. Examined: 1978/79. 224p. $5.95.
Aud: Hs, Jc, Cl, Pl

A collection of newspaper, magazine, and journal articles reflecting current sociological, psychological, historical, political, and other perspectives on marriage and the family. Coverage includes both popular and scholarly publications. Articles are arranged under broad topical categories and include charts, tables, and other illustrations describing the current (and past) state of the family in society. Designed as a supplement to high school and college classroom studies, the collection also will interest the general reader. JKM

SS 640

Annual Editions: Readings in Social Problems. ISSN 0094-9183. 1973. a. index. illus. Dushkin Publishing Group, Sluice Dock, Guilford, CT 06437. Examined: 1978/79. 256p. $5.95 pap.
Aud: Hs, Jc, Cl, Pl

Designed for use in high school and college courses which treat various social problems. Reproduces articles published in newspapers, magazines, and journals reflecting current issues, legislation, and sociological, political, and psychological perspectives on social problems. Articles include charts, tables, and other illustrations, and there is a subject index to the volume. Similar in format to other titles in the *Annual Editions* series. JKM

SS 641

Annual Editions: Readings in Social Psychology. 1976. a. index. illus. Dushkin Publishing Group, Sluice Dock, Guilford, CT 06437. Examined: 1978/79. L. Patrick McGovern. 320p. $6.55.
Aud: Hs, Jc, Cl, Pl

A collection of articles published in newspapers and professional magazines and journals selected by an editorial board for use in social psychology courses at the high school and college levels. Articles are frequently illustrated and sometimes include bibliographies or suggestions for further reading. Although some scholarly material is included, the collection reflects a broader perspective (and has broader appeal) than most academic journals in the field. Useful for the general reader who wants a basic introduction to current issues in the field as well as for the student. JKM

SS 642

Annual Editions: Readings in Sociology. ISSN 0090-4236. 1972. a. index. illus. Dushkin Publishing Group, Sluice Dock, Guilford, CT 06437. Examined: 1978/79. 320p. Jacqueline Scherer, ed. $6.55.
Aud: Hs, Jc, Cl, Pl

A collection of articles reproduced from newspapers, magazines, and trade professional journals reflecting various concerns and issues in the field of sociology. Arranged in broad topical sections with a more detailed subject index provided at the end. Designed as a supplementary reader for high school and college introductory sociology courses, this collection can also serve as a current, broad introduction to the field for the general reader. JKM

SS 643

Annual Editions: Readings in Unexplored Deviance. 1977. a. index. illus. Dushkin Publishing Group, Sluice Dock, Guilford, CT 06437. Examined: 1978/79. Charles Swanson, ed. 224p. $5.95.
Aud: Jc, Cl, Pl

Like other titles in the *Annual Editions* series, this volume contains reproductions of newspaper, magazine, and journal articles published during the preceding year and arranged under broad topical sections. Articles reflect current theories and issues involved in the study of deviancy. The collection is designed as a supplementary reader for sociology courses focusing on various aspects of deviancy, but it could also serve as an overview of the field for the general reader. Articles occasionally include suggestions for further reading and frequently include illustrations. JKM

SS 644

Annual Editions: Readings in Urban Society. 1977. a. index. illus. Dushkin Publishing Group, Sluice Dock, Guilford, CT 06437. Examined: 1978/79. Jacqueline Scherer, ed. 224p. $5.95.
Aud: Hs, Jc, Cl, Pl

A new title in the *Annual Editions* series. Follows the same basic format as other works in the series in that it gathers together articles from newspapers, magazines, and professional journals published during the preceding year. Articles reflect many different approaches to current issues and trends in the study of urban society. They are grouped into topical sections, each of which is prefaced by a general overview. This series will appeal to students as well as to the general public. Smaller libraries who are not able to afford a large number of periodical subscriptions will find the annual volumes useful as a comprehensive collection of current thought in the field as reflected in both popular and scholarly journal articles. JKM

SS 645

Annual Editions: Readings on Aging. 1977. a. index. illus. Dushkin Publishing Group, Sluice Dock, Guilford, CT 06437. Examined: 1978/79. Harold Cox, ed. 256p. $5.95 pap.
Aud: Hs, Jc, Cl, Pl

A collection of newspaper, magazine, and journal articles on various aspects of aging and service to the aging. Articles are arranged under broad topics and are selected to provide a cross-section of current issues, trends, and theories in the field. The *Annual Editions* series is designed as a supplementary source for high school and college courses, but the volumes also provide an interesting, up-to-date survey of the field for general readers. JKM

SS 646

Annual Review of Sociology. ISSN 0360-0572. 1975. a. bibl. index. illus. Annual Reviews, 4139 El Camino Way, Palo Alto, CA 94306. Examined: 1977. Alex Inkeles, ed. v. 1, 479p.; v. 2, 436p.; v. 3, 453p. $17.
Aud: Cl, Sa

Contains scholarly articles identifying the critical issues in the field of sociology and current research bearing on these issues, and explicating and evaluating individual and collective efforts to resolve these issues. The purpose of this review is to raise the standards of research in specific areas of sociological study and in the discipline at large. Articles are arranged under ten major subject headings: differentiation and stratification, political sociology, social processes, institutions, individual and society, formal organization, urban sociology, demography, policy, theory, and methods. A table of contents precedes the articles. Each article is followed by a substantial bibliography. The second volume contains a cumulative index of contributing authors for volumes one and two. MBP

SS 647

Berkeley Journal of Sociology: Critical Review. ISSN 0067-5830. 1955. a. University of California at Berkeley, Graduate Sociology Union, 410 Barrows, Berkeley, CA 94720. Examined: v. 15, 1970; v. 16, 1971; v. 17, 1972; v. 18, 1973/74. Oscar Werdmuller, ed. approx. 200p. $5.50.
Aud: Cl, Sa
Indexed in: *Sociological Abstracts*.

Offers critical review essays on the recent literature in sociology and related disciplines. Its aim is to challenge the social sciences to confront the crisis of the world with intellectual curiosity, historical awareness, and theoretical competence. Articles are scholarly, and many are written by members of the "New Left." They are approximately ten to 40 pages long. Subjects covered include the women's movement, the Black graduate student, Marxism and modern economics, participatory democracy, power, sex, and non-verbal communication, etc. Each volume contains short biographical essays about the authors. A photo-offset publication. MBP

SS 648

Guide to Graduate Departments of Sociology. 1969. a. index. American Sociological Association, 1722 N St,

NW, Washington, DC 20036. Examined: 4th ed., 1972/73. $10. (1976. 212p.)
Aud: Cl, Sa

Lists alphabetically by name of college or university pertinent information about graduate departments of sociology. Each entry includes name, address, and phone number of the university; name of department; chairperson; graduate degree offered; number of degrees granted in year; financial aid available; graduate student enrollment; number of new admissions; special programs; and names, titles, and degrees held by full and part-time departmental faculty. A table of course offerings and special programs and indexes of faculty and of departments by school are included. MBP

SS 649
Harris Survey Yearbook of Public Opinion. ISSN 0085-1442. 1970. irreg. index. Louis Harris and Associates, 1270 Ave of the Americas, New York, NY 10020. Examined: 1970. Graham M. Bright, ed. 574p. $47.50. (1977.)
Aud: Hs, Jc, Cl, Pl

Subtitle: "A compendium of current American attitudes." Summarizes public opinion on issues of interest to the American public in the course of the preceding year. Special attention is accorded government and politics, but public attitudes on the energy crisis, foreign affairs, the economy, crime and corrections, health and medicine, personal and family concerns, sports, and the arts are also surveyed. MBP

SS 650
International Bibliography of Sociology. ISSN 0085-2066. 1957. a. index. Tavistock Publications, 11 New Fetter Lane, London EC4P 4EE, England. Dist: Aldine-Atherton, 529 S Wabash Ave, Chicago, IL 60605. Examined: v. 25, 1975. Adrian Mayer, ed. (1976, 390p.; 1977. $48.)
Aud: Cl, Sa

A volume in the *International Bibliography of the Social Sciences* series. After an explanatory preface in English and French, the volume contains a list of periodicals consulted and the classification scheme. The bibliography section is arranged by subject, and articles are listed alphabetically by author under each subject. Listings are numbered (5761 in this volume) and include author, title, name of journal, volume number, issue number, date, and page numbers. Book listings provide full bibliographic data including number of pages. An author index and a subject index in English and French complete the volume. Subjects covered include social sciences research, methodology, and theory; culture; socialization; social life; social structure; population; family; ethnic group; environment; community; economics; labor; politics; social problems; social services; and social work, among others. MBP

SS 651
Inventory of Marriage and Family Literature. ISSN 0094-7814. (Continues: International Bibliography of Research in Marriage and the Family.) 1967. a. index. University of Minnesota Press, 2037 University Ave SE, Minneapolis, MN 55455. Examined: 1973/74, 376p.; 1975/76. David H. L. Olsen and Nancy S. Dahl, eds. 638p. $35.
Aud: Cl, Pl, Sa

Attempts to index all significant research on marriage and the family which has appeared in books, periodicals, government documents, and pamphlets. The bibliography is arranged by broad subjects and includes indexes by specific subject, author, and key word. Of particular interest to women studies personnel for the access it provides to research on the role of women in the family. KAC

SS 652
Population and Family Planning Programs. 1969. a. The Population Council, One Dag Hammarskjold Plaza, New York, NY 10017. Examined: 9th ed., 1978. Dorothy L. Nortman and Ellen Hofstatter, comps. 104p. $3.95.
Aud: Cl, Pl, Sa

Subtitle: "A Population Council fact book." A survey of the current state of family planning programs and population growth in developing countries. The major part of the work consists of 23 tables grouped under four headings: demographic, social, and economic characteristics; government positions on population growth and matters related to family planning; indicators of family planning program input; and indicators of family planning output. Explanatory text accompanies the tables including notes on sources and limitations of the data presented. Wherever possible, the tables cover through 1976 and span a five-year period. Data were obtained primarily from replies to questionnaires sent in early 1977 to population and family planning program administrators, supplemented by statistics compiled by United Nations and U.S. agencies. JKM

SS 653

Population and the Population Explosion: A Bibliography. ISSN 0091-2263. 1970. a. index. Whitson Publishing Co., Box 322, Troy, NY 12181. Examined: 1975, 173p.; 1977. Charles W. Triche and Diane S. Triche, eds. 407p. $17.
Aud: Cl, Pl, Sa

The bibliography is arranged alphabetically by author in four sections: books and government publications, demographic periodical literature, medical periodical literature, and sociological periodical literature. The items listed are not annotated. The medical section lists periodical articles on birth control, abortion, contraceptives, sterilization, etc. Includes an author index. KAC

SS 654

Recent Sociology. ISSN 0080-0023. 1969. a. Macmillan, 866 Third Ave, New York, NY 10022. Examined: no. 1, 1969, Hans Peter Dritzel, ed.; no. 2, 1970, 234p.; no. 3, 1971, 301p.; no. 4, 1972. 350p. $2.95.
Aud: Cl, Sa

An annual collection of reprints of articles by sociologists that appeared in earlier issues of sociology journals or books. It "attempts to tell the reader about new developments and recent issues in the field of sociology." Each volume is dedicated to a specific topic reflecting current issues in society and sociology. The first volume, entitled *Recent Sociology on the Basis of Politics,* contains articles relating to the political implications of sociological perspectives; an analysis of social power; the sociology of grass-roots movements; social classes and political participation; and social research and political rationality. Subsequent volumes have been entitled: "Patterns of Communicative Behaviour" (volume two); "The Social Organization of Health" (volume three); and "Family, Marriage, and the Struggle of the Sexes" (volume four). MBP

SS 655

Sociological Methodology. ISSN 0081-1750. 1969. a. bibl. index. illus. American Sociological Association, 1722 N St, NW, Washington, DC 20036. Dist: Jossey Bass Publishers, 615 Montgomery St, San Francisco, CA 94111. Microfilm Dist: University Microfilms, 300 N Zeeb Rd, Ann Arbor, MI. Examined: 1976. David R. Heise, ed. 284p. $13.50.
Aud: Sa

A collection of essays, selected by a board of editorial consultants, which makes "a vigorous attack on the problems of defining theoretical and naturalistic structures even when interval-scale measurements are unavailable or intrinsically impossible." Emerging from the various approaches are generalizations that may become the base for the development of more valid methodologies in the future. Chapters five to nine are based on the proceedings of a seminar devoted to causal analysis of nominal and ordinal variables. A name index and a subject index are included at the end of the volume. Contributors to this volume include: Paul W. Holland, Samuel Leinhardt, Leo A. Goodman, James A. Davis, David K. Hildebrand, James D. Laing, Howard Rosenthal, H. M. Blalock, Jr., and Robert K. Leik. MBP

SS 656

U.S. Office of Management and Budget. Social Indicators. 1973. illus. U.S. Office of Management and Budget, Statistical Policy Division, Washington, DC. Dist: Superintendent of Documents, U.S. Government Printing Office, Washington, DC 20402. Examined: 1973. Paul F. Krueger, ed. $7.80. (1976. 258p.)
Aud: Pl, Sa

Subtitle: "Selected statistics on social conditions and trends in the United States." A collection of statistics selected and organized to describe social conditions and trends in the U.S. Eight major social areas are examined: health, public safety, education, employment, income, housing, leisure and recreation, and population. Each chapter contains a brief text, charts (in four colors), technical notes, and tables. Sources for data shown in the charts are given in the tables. Within each category examined, broad areas of social interest or concerns are identified, i.e., under the heading health, the identified social concerns are long life, life free from disability, and access to medical care. These concerns are then defined and analyzed to reveal the general status of the population and how the concern relates to other national issues. MBP

SPORTS AND RECREATION

SS 657

Accidents in North American Mountaineering. ISSN 0065-082X. 1948. a. The American Alpine Club, 113 E 90th St, New York, NY 10028; The Alpine Club of Canada, Box 1026, Banff, Alberta T0L 0C0 Canada. Examined: 1977. John E. Williamson and E. Whalley, eds. 57p. $1.50 pap.
Aud: Sa

Includes the reports of the safety committees of the American Alpine Club and the Alpine Club of

Canada. There are descriptions of each accident, including place, date, and an analysis of the event. The accident descriptions are given first for Canada and then for the U.S. Provides a list of the officers, with addresses, of the Mountain Rescue Association, and retrospective, as well as current, statistics on mountaineering accidents. Mountain rescue groups are listed by state and province. SLB

SS 658
Alaska Fishing Guide. ISSN 0361-3984. 1974/75. a. index. illus. Alaska Northwest Publishing Co., Box 4-EEE, Anchorage, AK 99509. Examined: 1976. 172p. $3.95 pap.
Aud: Sa

Designed for one planning to fish in Alaska, the guide begins with general information about the state, covering geography, transportation with current prices, and all types of information on equipment, clothing, and boats for the fishing trip. Seasons, limits, and fees are also listed. The major section of the book concerns game fish. The varieties are described and sometimes illustrated; an illustration of the gear needed for each variety is provided. There is some discussion of where each game fish might be found. This information is further amplified in a section on fishing spots in Alaska, which is arranged by area and which notes the mileage between spots and the type of fish to expect. There is also a chapter on trophy fish contest rules and a description of major fishing regions. Includes many photographs and a complete index. SLB

SS 659
Alaska Hunting Guide. ISSN 0095-5760. 1973. a. index. illus. Alaska Northwest Publishing Co., Box 4-EEE, Anchorage, AK 99509. Examined: 1973. Editors of Alaska Magazine, eds. 170p. $3.95 pap.
Aud: Sa

Designed for one planning to hunt any type of animal in Alaska, the guide begins with an introduction to the state, including climate, demographics, and transportation, with current prices. There is a large section on wildlife which discusses the various species and gives illustrations of tracks, maps of distribution in the state, general descriptions, and directions for hunting. There are also sections on outfitting for an Alaskan hunt, trophies, ways to hunt in Alaska, and current game laws, and a field guide for trophy hunters. There are brief chapters on sport fishing and other activities possible in Alaska. Many photographs and a complete index are also provided. SLB

SS 660
Amateur Athletic Union of the United States. Directory. a. illus. Amateur Athletic Union of the United States, 3400 W 86th St, Indianapolis, IN 46268. Examined: 1977; 1978. 132p. $4 pap.
Aud: Cl, Pl

Lists names and addresses of officers and committee members of the Amateur Athletic Union. The categories included are national officers, officials, and staff; national committee chairmen (sic); international federation representatives; AAU regional representatives; U.S. sports governing bodies; voting allied bodies; association officers; and national administrative and sports committees. An alphabetical listing of all names included in the directory, with addresses, follows. There is also a map with a key to regions and associations. This directory is the only source for some of this information, such as the names and addresses of AAU officers in any given state. SLB

SS 661
Amateur Athletic Union of the United States. Official Handbook of the AAU Code. ISSN 0091-3405. 1973. a. index. illus. Amateur Athletic Union of the United States, 3400 W 86th St, Indianapolis, IN 46268. Examined: 1973; 1977; 1978. 164p. $4 pap.
Aud: Sa

A compilation of all the provisions and regulations relating to the AAU. Constitutional provisions relating to the Union and its members, including details of governance, are listed first, followed by provisions recommended for inclusion in association constitutions and by-laws. Detailed provisions relating to athletes and athletic events are noted. The appendix includes a description of each district association territory, agreements with other sports associations, and samples of application, registration, and sanction forms. The entire handbook is well indexed. SLB

SS 662
Amateur Athletic Union of the United States. Athletic Library. Official AAU Diving Rules. 1974. a. bibl. index. illus. Amateur Athletic Union of the United States, 3400 W 86th St, Indianapolis, IN 46268. Examined: 1977. John Walker, ed. 93p. $3 pap.
Aud: Cl, Pl

Primarily a list of current AAU diving rules, with changes noted at the beginning. Includes rules for Senior, Age Group, Junior Olympic, and Masters Diving. There is also a complete directory with names and addresses of members or chairpersons of all committees. Previous season results are given. Retrospective information is limited to a few diving awards. The index is only for the rules. SLB

SS 663-673
Amateur Athletic Union of the United States. Athletic Library. Official AAU Handbook Series. Amateur Athletic Union of the United States, 3400 W 86th St, Indianapolis, IN 46268.

SS 663
Official AAU Basketball Handbook. ISSN 0090-4414. 1918. bi-a. index. illus. Examined: 1951/52; 1972/74; 1975/76. 76p. $3 pap.
Aud: Hs, Jc, Cl, Pl

SS 664
Official AAU Baton Twirling Handbook. ISSN 0361-221X. bi-a. illus. Examined: none. (1978/80. 44p. $3.50 pap.)
Aud: Hs, Jc, Cl, Pl

SS 665
Official AAU Boxing Handbook. quadrennial. illus. Examined: 1977/80. 111p. $3 pap.
Aud: Hs, Jc, Cl, Pl

SS 666
Official AAU Gymnastics Handbook. ISSN 0091-3391. (Continues: AAU Gymnastics Yearbook; AAU Gymnastics Guide.) 1973/74. bi-a. illus. Examined: 1957; 1962/63; 1973/74. Jerry F. Hardy, et al., eds. 123p. $3 pap.
Aud: Hs, Jc, Cl, Pl

SS 667
Official AAU Junior Olympics Handbook. bi-a. Examined: none. (1978. 156p. $.75 pap.)
Aud: Jh, Hs, Pl

SS 668
Official AAU Physique Handbook. bi-a. Examined: none. (1977/78. 112p. $5 pap.)
Aud: Hs, Jc, Cl, Pl

SS 669
Official AAU Powerlifting Handbook. bi-a. Examined: none. (1977/78. 44p. $3 pap.)
Aud: Hs, Jc, Cl, Pl

SS 670
Official AAU Synchronized Swimming Handbook. a. bibl. illus. Examined: 1966; 1977. Jeff Lichter, ed. 149p. (1978. 160p. $3.50 pap.)
Aud: Hs, Jc, Cl, Pl

SS 671
Official AAU Trampoline and Tumbling Handbook. bi-a. Examined: none. (1977. 88p. $5 pap.)
Aud: Jh, Hs, Jc, Cl, Pl

SS 672
Official AAU Weightlifting Handbook. (Continues: Official AAU Weightlifting Rule Book.) bi-a. illus. Examined: 1974/75. George L. Nagy, ed. 72p. (1977/78. 96p. $3.50 pap.)
Aud: Hs, Jc, Cl, Pl

SS 673
Official AAU Wrestling Handbook. a. illus. Examined: 1975/76. Dick Torio, ed. 88p. (1977. 96p. $3 pap.)
Aud: Hs, Jc, Cl, Pl

Each handbook contains a section of current official rules of the Amateur Athletic Association for the sport and a section of historical and past-season records. Some of the handbooks include special features as well. The **Boxing Handbook** includes International Rules and Junior Olympic Rules, and a boxing history section which lists all past winners of the Olympics, Pan American championships, U.S.A. Amateur Boxing Hall of Fame, National and New York Golden Gloves, CISM (International Military Sports Council) championships, and interservice championships. It also has several articles of interest to officials and to those organizing local amateur boxing programs. The **Gymnastics Handbook** provides information on apparatus, compulsory exercises, and junior gymnastics rules. The **Synchronized Swimming Handbook** includes names and addresses of AAU committee members, illustrations of figures used and score sheets, a selected bibliography, and lists of previous award winners in all divisions and members of the Hall of Fame. The **Wrestling Handbook** also includes illustrations and a sample score sheet, as well as information for officials, requirements for participation in international amateur wrestling cultural exchanges, and both the International Rules of Greco-Roman and Freestyle Wrestling and the International Rules of Sambo Wrestling. An addendum to the **Wrestling Handbook** was issued in 1978 under the title *AAU Official Wrestling Rules Addendum* (1978, 44p. $3.50); it notes changes in the rules of competition for the three wrestling forms. SLB

SS 674
Amateur Athletic Union of the United States. Athletic Library. Official AAU Judo Rules. 1975. bi-a. illus. Amateur Athletic Union of the United States, 3400 W 86th St, Indianapolis, IN 46268. Examined: 1975. James Lee Nicholes, ed. 51p. $3 pap. (1978/80. 56p. $3.50 pap.)

Aud: Hs, Jc, Cl, Pl

This rules guide is scheduled for biennial publication, although the second edition, 1977, was delayed due to changes in international rules. It will be published in 1978. The guide includes both men's and women's rules for shiai and katu, as well as scoring rules for Junior shiai. There are diagrams for scoring and for organizing tournaments. SLB

SS 675
Amateur Athletic Union of the United States. Athletic Library. Official AAU Karate Rules. 1977. bi-a. illus. Amateur Athletic Union of the United States, 3400 W 86th St, Indianapolis, IN 46268. Examined: 1977/78. Caylor Adkins, Ed Hamile, and Ed Parker, eds. 84p. $3.50 pap.
Aud: Hs, Jc, Cl, Pl

Primarily a list of rules with no index, but a fairly complete table of contents. Both the rules and the appendixes stress safety and medical precautions. The rules include men's and women's kata rules, international kata rules, and international sparring rules. The appendixes include definitions of terms used by judges, illustrations of referees signals, illustrations of positions for match area, scoring charts, and elimination systems. There are also samples of all required forms and checklists. SLB

SS 676
Amateur Athletic Union of the United States. Athletic Library. Official AAU Tae Kwon Do Rules. 1977. quadrennial. illus. 1977. Amateur Athletic Union of the United States, 3400 W 86th St, Indianapolis, IN 46268. Examined: 1977/80. Dong Ja Yang, ed. 40p. $3 pap.
Aud: Hs, Jc, Cl, Pl

Primarily a list of rules, without an index but with a complete table of contents. The rules include contest rules of Tae Kwon Do and world Tae Kwan Do federation match rules. There are illustrations of certain attacks and safety apparatus. At the beginning is a complete directory, with names and addresses, of the National AAU Tae Kwon Do Committee. SLB

SS 677
Amateur Athletic Union of the United States. Athletic Library. Official AAU Track and Field Rules. bi-a. index. Amateur Athletic Union of the United States, 3400 W 86th St, Indianapolis, IN 46268. Examined: 1977. 164p. $3 pap.
Aud: Cl, Pl, Sa

Includes rules of competition for track, field, race walking, and cross country competitions. Also includes 1976 world and American records for indoor and outdoor track and field events. An addendum is issued between editions to note changes in the rules of competition and new world and American records. JKM

SS 678
Amateur Athletic Union of the United States. Athletic Library. Official Rules for Competitive Swimming. (Cover title: AAU Official Rules: Swimming.) ISSN 0091-3413. (Continues: Rules for Competitive Swimming, Diving, Water Polo.) 1955. a. index. Amateur Athletic Union of the United States, 3400 W 86th St, Indianapolis, IN 46268. Examined: 1976, William A. Lippman, Jr. and Ann Aiple Colwell, eds., 112 p., $3 pap.; 1978. 128p. $3.50 pap.
Aud: Hs, Jc, Cl, Pl

Primarily a list of rules, with major rule changes noted at the beginning. A directory with names and addresses of all committee members, a glossary of swimming words and terms, official records, and previous season results are included. There is a combined index to rules, records, and results. SLB

SS 679
Amateur Athletic Union of the United States. Athletic Library. Official Rules for Water Polo. (Cover title: AAU Official Water Polo Rules.) ISSN 0093-5786. a. illus. Amateur Athletic Union of the United States, 3400 W 86th St, Indianapolis, IN 46268. Examined: 1977, Andrew J. Burke, ed., 79p., $3 pap.; 1978. 80p. $3.50 pap.
Aud: Hs, Jc, Cl, Pl

This list of rules is not indexed, but there is a fairly complete table of contents. Rules for specific age groups, rules for women's water polo, and Junior Olympic rules are included. A directory of committees includes names only. A retrospective list of award winners is provided. There is a directory, by region, of referees including name, address, and rating (as rated by an AAU sub-committee), and an alphabetical directory of officials giving only name and address. SLB

SS 680
Amateur Hockey Association of the United States. Official Guide. ISSN 0516-8635. a. illus. Amateur Hockey Association of the United States, 10 Lake Circle, Colorado Springs, CO 80906. Examined: 1977. Don Clark, ed. 63p. $2 pap.
Aud: Hs, Jc, Cl, Pl

A guide to association officers and officials, rules and regulations, and past season activities. Names and addresses are included for all national officers, members of the board of directors, district registrars, district referees-in-chief, and officers of state associations. Rules and regulations for registration, membership, and championships, as well as other organizational rules, are included. These are not the playing rules, which are included in a separate publication. All-time and past season winners are listed for all divisions. Includes discussions of the Canada Cup, World Championship, and World Championship for Juniors; universally drafted players; American players in the major league; citation awards; and team pictures. There is a brief history of ice hockey in the United States. There is no index, but the fairly complete table of contents can serve as an index. SLB

SS 681

Amateur Hockey Association of the United States. Rule Book. bi-a. index. illus. Amateur Hockey Association of the United States, 10 Lake Circle, Colorado Springs, CO 80906. Examined: 1977/78. 84p. $2 pap.
Aud: Hs, Jc, Cl, Pl

Includes names and addresses of the district registrars and names of the rules committee. The rules are completely indexed. Major rule changes and housekeeping changes are noted. There are illustrations of equipment and rinks, as well as illustrations and descriptions of official signals. SLB

SS 682

Amateur Skating Union of the United States. Official Handbook: Speed Skating. ISSN 0516-866X. 1930. bi-a. illus. Amateur Skating Union of the United States, 4423 W Deming Place, Chicago, IL 60639. Examined: 1975. Milan Novak, ed. 83p. $2.50; free to libraries.
Aud: Hs, Jc, Cl, Pl

This biennial handbook is currently the only source for speed skating rules and records. The Amateur Skating Union provides a free copy to libraries when requested on a letterhead. Contains the names and addresses of officers and members, the rules, the constitutions and bylaws of the Union; speed skating history; members of the Hall of Fame; and historical records. There are diagrams for all types of tracks used. SLB

SS 683

Amateur Softball Association of America. Official Rule Book and Guide. ISSN 0065-6739. (Continues: Softball Rules; Official Guide and Rule Book.) 1934. a. illus. Amateur Softball Association of America, Box 11437, Oklahoma City, OK 73111. Examined: 1948; 1954; 1976. 192p. $1.50.
Aud: Hs, Jc, Cl, Pl

Includes names of the commissioners. Complete rules are listed, but they are poorly indexed. The emphasis is on previous season statistics and winners. Retrospective information includes members of the Hall of Honor and some past individual champions, both women and men. SLB

SS 684

Amateur Trapshooting Association. Official Trapshooting Rules. ISSN 0065-6747. a. index. illus. Amateur Trapshooting Association, Box 458, Vandalia, OH 45377. Examined: 1977. 38p. free.
Aud: Jc, Cl, Pl

This small rulebook contains the official rules for the association, and information about the organization for those who wish to join or compete officially. There is a subject index to the rules. SLB

SS 685

American Alpine Journal. ISSN 0065-6925. 1929. a. index. illus. The American Alpine Club, 113 E 90th St, New York, NY 10028. Examined: 1977. H. Adams Carter, ed. 336p. $8.50 pap.
Aud: Pl

Primarily a series of separately authored articles on expeditions, areas, and equipment. Also includes the names of current officers and directors, and members of all committees. After the articles, there are many signed, brief discussions of recent expeditions, arranged by geographical area. A description of club activities, several book reviews, obituaries of climbers killed in the last year, proceedings from the annual meeting, and a list of club publications are also included. There is a complete index and many high quality black-and-white photographs, as well as some hand drawn illustrations. SLB

SS 686

Archery-Golf Guide. 1972/74. bi-a. bibl. American Alliance for Health, Physical Education and Recreation, National Association for Girls and Women in Sport, 1201 16th St, NW, Washington, DC 20036. Examined: 1976/78. Judith A. Jenkins and G. Jean Cerra, eds. 158p. $2.50 pap.
Aud: Hs, Jc, Cl, Pl
Indexed in: *ERIC*.

The next edition of the biennial guide, scheduled for May 15, 1978 publication, will combine archery and fencing and will be entitled *Archery-Fencing Guide*. In the **Archery-Golf Guide** there are separate sections for each sport; the archery section is far more extensive than the golf section. The names and addresses of the guide committees for each section are included. There are individually authored articles on history, technique and tips, bibliographies, and visual aids. The archery section includes the rules of the International Archery Federation and the National Field Archery Association. SLB

SS 687
Argosy Boating Annual. 1976. a. illus. Popular Publications, 420 Lexington Ave, New York, NY 10017. Examined: 1977. Nick Karas, ed. 98p. $1.50 pap.
Aud: Pl

This magazine-format annual consists of two major sections. First there are a few feature articles by separate authors on boat repair, boating areas, and specific kinds of boats, such as pontoons. There is also a large new product section arranged by type of boat and accessories. The new product section entries include a photograph, description, specifications, price, and manufacturer's address. SLB

SS 688
Argosy Fishing Annual. 1975. a. bibl. illus. Popular Publications, 420 Lexington Avenue, New York, NY 10017. Examined: 1977. Nick Karas, ed. 98p. $1.50 pap.
Aud: Pl

Following magazine format, this annual includes longer feature articles than other titles in the Argosy series. The articles are on various types of fishing, although the 1977 annual concentrates on bass fishing. Each entry in the section on new fishing gear includes a photograph, a description, and the manufacturer's address, but not the price. There is a bibliography of fishing literature which is well annotated. There are photographs throughout. SLB

SS 689
Argosy Hockey Yearbook. a. illus. Popular Publications, 420 Lexington Ave, New York, NY 10017. Examined: 1977. Lou Sahadi, ed. 98p. $1.50 pap.
Aud: Pl

This magazine-format annual has more general interest articles than many of the other Argosy publications. It includes a one-page description of each team, with photographs, which gives the previous win-loss record and top scorers. There is some prediction involved in the description. The annual lacks a complete roster for each team. The photographs are of good quality. SLB

SS 690
Argosy Hunting Annual. 1974. a. illus. Popular Publications, 420 Lexington Ave, New York, NY 10017. Examined: 1976. Clare Conley, ed. 98p. $1.50 pap.
Aud: Pl

Like other Argosy annuals, this guide follows magazine format. It contains feature articles by different authors on how to hunt certain game, cooking wild game, and hunting techniques. It includes new product listings for guns, arranged by manufacturer, which describe the new guns and their prices. There are other articles on equipment, though the guide is not designed as a purchaser's catalog. Photographs and illustrations are scattered throughout. SLB

SS 691
Association for Intercollegiate Athletics for Women. AIAW Directory. (Continues in part: AIAW Handbook-Directory.) 1971/72. a. Association for Intercollegiate Athletics for Women, American Alliance for Health, Physical Education and Recreation, 1201 16th St NW, Washington, DC 20036. Examined: 1975/76, 176p., $3.50 pap.; 1977/78. 100p. $4 pap.
Aud: Jc, Cl, Pl

The 1975/76 edition was the last edition to combine the Handbook and the Directory of the Association for Intercollegiate Athletics for Women (AIAW). The current directory lists officers, representatives, regions, and member institutions of the AIAW. It also includes scholarship information and data on 26 sports in which intercollegiate programs for women are offered, showing which of these are offered at each member school. The appendix gives schedules of AIAW national championships in 15 sports and AIAW JC/CC championships in four sports, with a listing of sports advisory committees for both and selected references. SLB

SS 692
Association for Intercollegiate Athletics for Women. AIAW Handbook of Policies and Operating Procedures. ISSN 0090-9106. (Continues in part: AIAW Handbook-Directory.) 1971/72. a. Association for Intercollegiate Athletics for Women, American Alliance for Health, Physical Education and Recreation, National Association for Girls and Women in Sport, 1201 16th St NW, Washington, DC 20036. Examined: 1975/76, 176p., $3.50 pap.; 1977/78. 96p. $5 pap.

Aud: Jc, Cl, Pl

The 1975/76 edition was the last to combine the Handbook and the Directory of the Association for Intercollegiate Athletics for Women (AIAW). The current handbook is briefer, 96 pages, and contains policies and operating procedures; statements on the structure, purposes, and membership of AIAW; lists of officers, representatives, and committee members; recruitment regulations for awarding of financial aid to student athletes; procedures for national championships; AIAW eligibility rules; and procedures and penalties for rule infractions. SLB

SS 693

Baseball Blue Book. 1909. a. index. illus. Baseball Blue Book, 7225 30th Ave N, Box 40847, St. Petersburg, FL 33743. Examined: 1956; 1976. 806p. $15 pap.
Aud: Pl

The emphasis is on professional baseball, although some information on the Babe Ruth League and Little League is included. Team directories for the American and National Leagues are very complete; they include coaches, game coverage, hotels in the area, managers, park statistics, schedules, scouts, trainers, and umpires. Other features include the government of organized professional baseball and a list of statisticians. One of the largest and most unusual features is the curnt Agment of National Association of Professional Baseball Leagues with a detailed index. This is probably the only easily obtainable source for the Agreement which includes information on franchises, how often teams may play, and so on. SLB

SS 694

Baseball Guidebook. ISSN 0403-6104. 1957. a. illus. Maco Publishing Co., 380 Madison Ave, New York, NY 10017. Examined: 1977. Vito Stellino, ed. 88p. $1.50 pap.
Aud: Hs, Pl

This brief, magazine-format guide includes a few feature articles on the baseball draft, nostalgia, and baseball cards. The major portion of the guide is a discussion of each professional team. Each team entry covers strengths, weaknesses, new faces, outlook, prediction for final standing, officers, stadium address, playing field distances, team and player statistics for previous season, and team finishes for all seasons. The guide could be used as a reference tool, but it is probably better as a popular reading item. SLB

SS 695

Baseball Illustrated. 1964. a. illus. Complete Sports Publications, 333 Johnson Ave, Brooklyn, NY 11206. Examined: 1977. Jim McNally, ed. 86p. $1 pap.
Aud: Hs, Pl

This magazine-format annual has much the same mateial as several other baseball annuals. The title would imply that its illustrations are its notable feature. The black-and-white photographs are of medium to good quality, and there are several very good quality color "pin-ups." There is a brief statistical review of the previous season and a few feature articles on players and teams. For each league there are previews and predictions, including a page on each team that contains a discussion of the current team's strengths and weaknesses. The team roster simply includes name and position. SLB

SS 696

Baseball Record Book. ISSN 0078-4605. 1949. a. index. illus. Sporting News, 1212 N Lindbergh Blvd, Box 56, St. Louis, MO 63166. Examined: 1963; 1969; 1972; 1977. Joe Marcin, ed.; Leonard Gettelson, comp. 560p. $3 pap.
Aud: Pl

This very complete record book is devoted exclusively to professional baseball. It lists, with updates from the previous season, all individual and club records. In recent years the book has become easier to use since it now includes a table of contents and a single, all inclusive index in the back. SLB

SS 697

Baseball Rules. (Cover title: Baseball Rule Book.) a. index. illus. National Federation of State High School Associations, 400 Leslie St, Box 98, Elgin, IL 60120. Examined: 1976; 1977. Clifford B. Fagan, ed. 63p. $.85 pap.
Aud: Hs, Jc, Cl, Pl

Includes the complete National Federation baseball rules, with changes emphasized by screening; names and addresses of the National Federation Baseball Rules Committee; field diagrams; table of contents; and index. The National Federation also issues the *Baseball Case Book* (1978, $1.20 pap.), an annual publication which illustrates how the rules should be applied in game situations, and *Baseball Umpires' Manual* (1977/78, $.85 pap.), an annual publication intended for those officiating interscholastic games for schools that are members of the Federation. SLB

SS 698

Basketball Case Book. ISSN 0525-4663. a. index. Na-

tional Federation of State High School Associations, Federation Place, Box 98, Elgin, IL 60120. Examined: 1977/78. Brice B. Durbin and Edward S. Steitz, eds. 94p. $1.20 pap.
Aud: Hs, Jc, Cl, Pl

The case book is designated as an official supplement to **Basketball Rules** by the National Basketball Committee of the United States and Canada. The situations used for the cases are from accounts, reports, and summaries of situations of games received from "basketball leaders in all sections of the country." There is a glossary of technical terms used. The case book is arranged by subject, with a complete index, and gives play, ruling, and reference to official rule section where appropriate. The National Federation also issues the *Basketball Officials' Manual* (1977/78, 57p., $1.10 pap.), a biennial publication intended for those officiating interscholastic games for schools that are members of the Federation. SLB

SS 699

Basketball Guide. (Continues in part: Basketball Guide. ISSN 0065-7018. bi-a.) 1949/50. a. illus. American Alliance for Health, Physical Education, and Recreation, National Association for Girls and Women in Sport, 1201 16th St, NW, Washington, DC 20036. Examined: 1976/77. Helen Knierim, ed. 128p.; 1978/79, $2 pap.
Aud: Hs, Jc, Cl, Pl
Indexed in: *ERIC*.

When this guide became an annual in 1976, it retained its old title but part of the contents was taken up by two other publications, *Basketball Rules* (1977/78, $.75 pap.), an annual beginning in July, 1977 and **Basketball-Volleyball Tips and Techniques,** a biennial beginning July, 1977. The new annual guide includes a summary of rule changes, conversions for basketball, and regulations for championships in various sized schools as determined by the Association for Intercollegiate Athletics for Women. AIAW championships are listed. There is a detailed officiating section which tells how to become a rated official. The rules are reprinted in the Alliance's *Basketball Rules*. SLB

SS 700

Basketball Handbook. bi-a. illus. National Federation of State High School Associations, Federation Place, Box 98, Elgin, IL 60120. Examined: 1976/77; 1977/78. M. F. Sprunger. Clifford B. Fagan, ed. 79p. $.85 pap.
Aud: Hs, Jc, Cl, Pl

The foreword states that the handbook "was written for the purpose of providing both the necessary background and rules knowledge for the groups principally concerned with the game." The book is in three parts. The first part, "The Game," provides a historical survey of the growth of basketball and changes that have taken place in the rules and equipment requirements. Part two is on playing the game. It is intended to provide the player with a basic knowledge of the rules and includes examinations for self testing. Part three focuses on officiating and includes discussion of the rules to assist the official and self examination tests. Appendixes contain information for scorers and timers. There is no index or table of contents. Illustrations of official basketball signals are included. SLB

SS 701

Basketball Rules. (Continues: National Basketball Committee. Official Basketball Guide.) 1941. a. index. illus. National Federation of State High School Associations, Federation Place, Box 98, Elgin, IL 60120. Examined: 1941/42; 1976/77. 60p. $.85 pap.
Aud: Hs, Pl

Provides the complete rules for boys and girls interscholastic basketball competition. Rule changes since the last volume are noted. Includes an index and a diagram of the basketball court. SLB

SS 702

Basketball Rules—Simplified and Illustrated. a. illus. National Federation of State High School Associations, Federation Place, Box 98, Elgin, IL 60120. Examined: 1977/78. Brice B. Durbin and S. Clifford Harper, eds. 111p. $1.50 pap.
Aud: Hs, Pl

Intended by the editors to be appropriate for officials, coaches, players, and spectators. There is no index, but a table of contents lists the general subject areas. Over 240 situations and plays are demonstrated with a brief description and hand drawn illustrations. Technicalities should be verified in the more detailed **Basketball Rules** or the **Basketball Guide**. SLB

SS 703

Basketball-Volleyball Tips and Techniques. (Continues: Basketball Guide. ISSN 0065-7018; Volleyball Guide. ISSN 0065-7050.) 1977. bi-a. bibl. illus. American Alliance for Health, Physical Education, and Recreation, National Association for Girls and Women in Sport, 1201 16th St, NW, Washington, DC 20036. Examined: 1977/79. Ruth Gunden, ed. 93p. $2.25 pap.
Aud: Hs, Jc, Cl, Pl
Indexed in: *ERIC*.

The edition examined was the first biennial edition of this guide. There will still be annual editions of the **Basketball Guide** and *Basketball Rules*, and the annual editions of **Volleyball Guide** and *Volleyball Rules*. These annual editions are designed to reflect changes in rules or other current information. The biennial edition focuses on instructions which to not need such rapid updating. It includes a separate section for each sport. For each section, the names and addresses of the committee responsible for the content are listed. There are several individually authored articles directed to teachers and coaches, a list of audio-visual aids, and selected references. The bibliography on volleyball is much more extensive than that for basketball. SLB

SS 704
Bass Master Fishing Annual. a. illus. Bass Anglers Sportsman Society of America, One Bell Rd, Montgomery, AL 36109. Examined: 1977. Bob Cobb, ed. 95p. $1.50 pap.
Aud: Pl

This specialized magazine-format annual contains a few feature articles, but the major portion of the guide is a forecast of the coming season's bass fishing in various regions of the country. For each region (e.g., Mississippi River, Ohio River, swamp, etc.), there is a map of the area, a discussion of the type of fishing, seasonal expectations, and a directory including when to go, where to stay, where to write for maps, suggested lures, suggested fishing patterns suggested gear, license fees, and where to write for additional information. There is also a discussion of new tackle, including some photographs and a description, and a directory of manufacturers by specialty. SLB

SS 705
Best Sports Stories. ISSN 0067-6292. 1944. a. illus. E. P. Dutton and Co., Two Park Ave, New York, NY 10016. Examined: 1975. Irving T. Marsh and Edward Ehre, eds. 350p. $9.95.
Aud: Pl

After the prize-winning stories in the categories of Best News-Coverage Story, Best News-Feature Story, and Best Magazine Story, there are stories arranged by sport. The author and the original publication are noted. There is also a section for photograph, with prizes for best action and best feature photograph. All stories and photographs are chosen by a committee named in the introduction. All of the stories are non-fiction. SLB

SS 706
Big Ten Records Book. 1948. a. index. illus. Big Ten Service Bureau, Office of the Commissioner, 1111 Plaza Dr, Schaumburg, IL 60195. Examined: 1976/77. 273p. $3 pap.
Aud: Cl, Pl

Subtitle: "The encyclopedia of Big Ten athletics." Includes a directory for each of the Big Ten schools with many useful details, such as colors and nicknames, officers, coaches, athletic plant units, and photographs of stadiums. The updated retrospective records are divided into sections for fall, winter, and spring sports. The special directories include individual and team NCAA titles, conference personnel, history, conference trainers, Big Ten chronology, Robert C. Woodworth Award winners, Conference Medal of Honor winners, and Big Ten Skywriters Hall of Fame. SLB

SS 707
Blue Book of College Athletics. 1931. a. index. illus. Rohrich Corp., 1940 E Sixth St, Cleveland, OH 44114. Examined: 1976/77. 433p. $7 pap.
Aud: Cl, Pl

Entries are alphabetically arranged by the name of the school. Each entry includes the address, phone number, enrollment, colors, team nickname, band, stadium, athletic director, and all coaches for various sports, with individual phone numbers in some cases. It also includes the win-loss record for the previous season in football and basketball, which is not included in the **Blue Book of Junior College Athletics.** There is a listing of associations of coaches, commissioners, and officials. The index classifies the schools by state. SLB

SS 708
Blue Book of Junior College Athletics. ISSN 0520-2973. 1958. a. index. Rohrich Corp., 1940 E Sixth St, Cleveland, OH 44114. Examined: 1977. 164p. $5 pap.
Aud: Jc, Pl

Entries are alphabetically arranged by the name of the school. Each entry includes the address, phone number, enrollment, colors, team nickname, band, stadium, athletic director, and all coaches for various sports, with individual phone numbers in some cases. There is a conference appendix. Colleges are classified by state in a separate index. SLB

SS 709
Bob Wallack's Hunter's Guns. (Continues: Steve

Ferber's Hunter's Guns; Ross Carpenter's Hunter's Guns.) 1953. a. illus. Maco Publishing Co., 380 Madison Ave, New York, NY 10017. Examined: 1976. Bob Wallack, ed. 62p. $1.25 pap.
Aud: Pl

Arranged in magazine format, this guide includes several feature articles of interest to hunters, such as one on high country mule deer and another on hunter safety. The major portion of the guide is a listing of guns, arranged by type, e.g., rifles, shotguns, and handguns. Each entry includes photograph, model name and number, and general specifications. Price is not included. There is a list of manufacturers' addresses at the end. SLB

SS 710
Bob Zwirz' Fishing Annual. ISSN 0363-5538. 1972. a. index. illus. Charger Productions, 34249 Camino Capistrano, Capistrano Beach, CA 92624. Examined: 1977. Bob Zwirz, ed. 130p. $1.50 pap.
Aud: Pl

This annual is very similar to **Bob Zwirz' Fishing Guide** which is published annually by the same company. The format, a combination of articles on types of fishing, equipment, and accessories, is almost exactly the same, although the content of all articles and lists of accessories are different. There are equipment listings which include description, price, and manufacturer address. There are articles on fly-typing and competitions, and comparative articles on boats. An index to advertisers is included. SLB

SS 711
Bob Zwirz' Fishing Guide. a. index. illus. Charger Productions, 34249 Camino Capistrano, Capistrano Beach, CA 92624. Examined: 1977. Bob Zwirz, ed. 130p. $1.50 pap.
Aud: Pl

Includes more articles on fishing equipment than other magazine-format fishing annuals. There are special feature articles on how to fish for certain species, but the majority of articles focus on fishing rods, boats, and accessories. The articles on equipment generally include photographs, descriptions or lengthy discussions about specific items, comparisons of various models, and in some cases, prices. There is an index to advertisers. Similar in format, but not in content, to **Bob Zwirz' Fishing Annual,** which is issued by the same publisher. SLB

SS 712
The Book of Baseball Records. (Continues: Little Red Book of Baseball.) 1925. a. index. Seymour Siwoff, 500 Fifth Ave, New York, NY 10036. Examined: 1952; 1971; 1977. Seymour Siwoff, ed. 360p. $5.
Aud: Pl

A statement on the cover says: "Endorsed by the American and National Leagues. The authentic publication of all official major league baseball records, including world series and all-star games." The most unique feature is the list of all previous club presidents, and the dates of their terms in office. The book includes the standard individual and team records, updated by previous season. Also unique is the listing of world series managers and umpires. There are rosters for each world series and individual world series records. SLB

SS 713
Bow and Arrow Magazine's Bowhunter's Annual. 1976. a. index. illus. Gallant Publishing Co., 34249 Camino Capistrano, Capistrano Beach, CA 92624. Examined: 1976. Box Springer, ed. 114p. $1.50 pap.
Aud: Pl

This magazine-format annual is unique in the material that it covers. It contains several feature articles on hunting animals with bow and arrow. There are several guides to appropriate equipment; entries include photograph, description, price, and manufacturer's address. There is a directory, by state, of bowhunting seasons, listing name and address of regulating agency, hunting season for different types of animals, and license fees. There is an index to advertisers. Photographs are included throughout the book. SLB

SS 714
Bowling-Fencing Guide. 1954/56. bi-a. bibl. illus. American Alliance for Health, Physical Education, and Recreation, National Association for Girls and Women in Sport, 1201 16th St, NW, Washington, DC 20036. Examined: 1975/77. Joyce H. Curtis and Mary Heinecke, eds. 167p. $2 pap.
Aud: Hs, Jc, Cl, Pl
Indexed in: *ERIC.*

The bowling section contains specialized articles on various aspects of bowling, a list of research on bowling, a bibliography of bowling articles and books, and a list of visual aids available. Duckpin rules and scoring, and tenpin rules and regulations are included. The fencing section has feature articles on such topics as teaching beginners, evaluation, and starting a high school program. There are sections on scoring, fencing research, a bibliography, and a list of visual aids available. Officiating services and standards for officials' ratings are listed. Includes complete fencing rules. In January, 1979, the new biennial will be *Bowling-Golf Guide.* Fencing will be combined with archery in May, 1978, as the *Archery-Fencing Guide.* SLB

SS 715
Boys' Gymnastic Rules. a. illus. National Federation of State High School Associations, Federation Place, Box 98, Elgin, IL 60120. Examined: 1977/78. Brice B. Durbin, ed. 165p. $2 pap.
Aud: Jh, Hs, Pl

Includes photographs, names, and addresses of members of the Gymnastics Rules Committee. The inside cover lists major rule changes. The rules have no index, but a table of contents lists general subject areas. Rules changed are identified by a screened background. There are many illustrations of equipment and correct forms for competitors. A high school dual meet competition score sheet is included. SLB

SS 716
Canadian Football League. Official Record and Information Manual. a. Canadian Football League, Suite 908, 11 King St W, Toronto M5H 2A3, Canada. Examined: 1976. Gord Walker, ed. 112p.
Aud: Pl

Contains information not included in other professional football guides. It has the address, officers, head coaches, stadium, and colors for all the Canadian teams; records and highlights from the previous season; lists of all-star teams, major awards, and members of the Hall of Fame; and a list of all-time records for the league. There is also a history section, a listing of all previous Grey Cup games, coaching records, and year-by-year standings. There is a current roster for the teams, which includes for each player position, height, weight, date of birth, pre-professional team, and years with current team. The upcoming season schedule is given. SLB

SS 717
Complete Handbook of Pro Hockey. 1974. a. illus. Signet Books, New American Library, Box 999, Bergenfield, NJ 07621. Examined: 1976. Zander Hollander, ed. 354p. $1.95 pap.
Aud: Hs, Pl

Contains information on both National Hockey League and World Hockey League teams, with a breakdown under each team by players. Player information includes pictures and individual records. There are both previous season statistics and all-time records. The coming season schedule and information about radio stations that will broadcast the games are also included. SLB

SS 718
Cord Sportfacts Fisherman Annual. ISSN 0590-8817. 1970. a. illus. Cord Communications Corp., 25 W 43rd St, New York, NY 10036. Examined: 1977. David T. Pratt, ed. 82p. $1.25 pap.
Aud: Pl

Following magazine format, this annual includes several feature articles by various authors arranged into sections titled "Magic Methods," "Freshwater Fights," "Saltwater Sluggers," and "Sassy Smallfry." There is an accessories listing including photograph, description, price, and manufacturer's address. There is a brief list of free booklets, brochures, and catalogs of possible interest. Photographs are included throughout. SLB

SS 719
Cord Sportfacts Fishing Report. a. illus. Cord Communications Corp., 25 W 43rd St, New York, NY 10036. Examined: 1977. David T. Pratt, ed. 82p. $1.25 pap.
Aud: Pl

Includes several feature articles by various authors arranged into sections titled "Rivers, Lakes, and Streams"; "Offshore and Inshore"; and "Ways and Means." There is also a listing of new fishing boats, including photograph, description, and address of manufacturer. There is a brief list of free booklets, brochures, and catalogs of possible interest. Photographs are included throughout. SLB

SS 720
Cord Sportfacts Guns Guide. ISSN 0590-6776. a. illus. Cord Communications Corp., 25 W 43rd St, New York, NY 10036. Examined: 1976. David T. Pratt, ed. 98p. $1.25 pap.
Aud: Pl

A magazine-format annual which includes several feature articles on equipment. The largest portion of the magazine is a buyer's directory, divided into scope sights, rifles, handguns, and shotguns. Each entry in the buyer's directory includes an illustration, description, and price. There is a list of free literature of interest to shooters and hunters. SLB

SS 721
Cord Sportfacts Hockey Guide. ISSN 0591-0374. a.

illus. Cord Communications Corp., 25 W 43rd St, New York, NY 10036. Examined: 1974. Martin Lader, ed. 96p. $.75 pap.
Aud: Hs, Pl

In magazine format, this guide has several articles and "exclusives" on professional hockey. For the National Hockey League, there is a team-by-team roundup; this is not a directory, but a discussion of past performances, current expectations, and individual player records for the previous season. There are also articles on the World Hockey Association, but no team roundup. SLB

SS 722

Cord Sportfacts Hunting. 1971. a. illus. Cord Communications Corp. 25 W 43rd St, New York, NY 10036. Examined: 1976. David T. Pratt, ed. 96p. $1.25 pap.
Aud: Pl

This magazine-format annual contains fewer and shorter articles than other titles in the Cord Sportfacts series. Most of the articles are on how to hunt various animals, but there are a few on equipment, including descriptions and prices for "Guns of the Year." A lot of space is given to medium-quality pictures. SLB

SS 723

Daiwa Fishing Annual. 1976. a. illus. Aqua-Field Publications, 342 Madison Ave, New York, NY 10017. Examined: 1977. Steve Ferber, ed. 96p. $1.75 pap.
Aud: Pl

Like the other Aqua-Field publications, this magazine-format annual carries a major manufacturer's name in the title. This does not seem to affect the content, although there is not a new products listing for accessories, as is true of most fishing annuals of this type. There are many feature articles by separate authors, arranged into sections for black bass fishing, freshwater fishing tactics, trout and salmon fishing, and saltwater fishing tactics. There are good quality photographs throughout. SLB

SS 724

Dixie Gun Works Mussleloaders' Annual. a. illus. Aqua-Field Publications, 342 Madison Ave, New York, NY 10017. Examined: 1977. Steve Ferber, ed. 96p. $1.75 pap.
Aud: Sa

Like all Aqua-Field annuals, the title incorporates a company name. This does not seem to have a great deal of influence on the material in the magazine-format guide, however. The guide includes a series of feature articles on mussleloaders by separate authors. The articles include competitions, hunting, and technique. There is one article on knives. There are good quality photographs throughout. SLB

SS 725

The Encyclopedia of Football. (Continues: The Official Encyclopedia of Football.) 1952. a. illus. A. S. Barnes and Co., Cranbury, NJ 08512. Examined: 1952; 1971; 1976. Roger Treat, ed. 719p. $14.95.
Aud: Pl

The most complete year-by-year history of professional football available. Arranged chronologically from 1919 to the present. Includes descriptions and scores of championship games for each year and a roster for every team. Retrospective individual champions and all-time leaders are listed. Also very useful is the all-time roster, arranged alphabetically by player, listing college, professional position, and years played with what teams. Other features include a history and information on extinct leagues, an historical list of coaches for each team, a sample standard player contract, and the National Football League's Digest of Rules. At the end are diagrams of each professional stadium. SLB

SS 726

Fawcett's Hunting Journal. 1975. a. illus. Fawcett Publications, Fawcett Bldg, Greenwich, CT 06830. Examined: 1977. Frank Bowers, ed. 96p. $1.25 pap.
Aud: Pl

This magazine-format annual includes a series of separately authored articles on the latest products, deer hunting, hunting skills, and other general interest information. There are some high quality photographs. More space is given to the articles than to the photographs; therefore, this hunting annual contains more information than others of the same format. SLB

SS 727

Field and Stream Bass Fishing Annual. a. illus. CBS Publications, Popular Magazine Group, 383 Madison Ave, New York, NY 10017. Examined: 1977. Glenn L. Sapir and Ken Schultz, eds. 95p. $1.25 pap.
Aud: Pl

This fairly specialized magazine-format annual has a good selection of articles by separate authors. It includes results of major tournaments from the past season; discussions of best bass fishing divided by region, including the West, Midwest, South, East, Canada, and South of the Border; tips on tackle and techniques; and other features, such as recipes for bass. There are good quality photographs throughout. SLB

SS 728
Field and Stream Fishing Annual. ISSN 0362-6385. 1976. a. illus. CBS Publications, Popular Magazine Group, 383 Madison Ave, New York, NY 10017. Examined: 1977. Glenn L. Sapir and Ken Schultz, eds. 97p. $1.25 pap.
Aud: Pl

Features a wide variety of articles on several types of fish and how to cook them. Includes good quality photographs and more articles than most of the fishing annuals of this type. SLB

SS 729
Field and Stream Hunting Annual. ISSN 0361-3011. 1975. a. illus. CBS Publications, Consumer Publishing Division, One Fawcett Place, Greenwich, CT 06830. Examined: 1975; 1977. Glenn L. Sapir and Ken Schultz, eds. 96p. $1.50 pap.
Aud: Pl

Includes many feature articles by different authors, primarily on how to hunt various types of animals and birds. Every year there is a special section on deer and some articles on cooking wild game. There are also a few articles on equipment and technique. The 1977 edition includes a listing of each state's steel shot laws. There are good quality photographs throughout. SLB

SS 730
Field Hockey-LaCrosse Guide. ISSN 0065-7026. 1950/52. bi-a. bibl. illus. American Alliance for Health, Physical Education and Recreation, National Association for Girls and Women in Sport, 1201 16th St, NW, Washington, DC 20036. Examined: 1976/78. Linda K. Nixon and Eleanor Kay Hess, eds. 252p. $1.50 pap.
Aud: Hs, Jc, Cl, Pl
Indexed in: *ERIC*.

While there are many changes being planned for other guides issued by the National Association for Girls and Women in Sport, this guide is scheduled to continue publication in the same format, biennially on even years. A separate section is devoted to each sport. The names and addresses of the guide committee in each field are included. There is information on appropriate sport associations; individually authored articles on history, techniques, conditions, and other tips; bibliographies and lists of visual aids; information on officiating; and rules. The rules are also available separately in the biennial publication, *Field Hockey-LaCrosse Rules* (1977, $1.50 pap.). SLB

SS 731
Field Hockey Rules: Boys and Girls. a. National Federation of State High School Associations, Federation Place, Box 98, Elgin, IL 60120. Examined: none. ($.85 pap.)
Aud: Jh, Hs, Pl

Although no copy was available for examination, this work is recommended based on the quality of other publications issued by the National Federation. Similar publications such as **Baseball Rules** and **Official Football Rules** provide a complete list of the rules with an index and the names and addresses of the committee members responsible for preparing the rules. New rules are indicated by screening. SLB

SS 732
Fishing Guidebook. ISSN 0428-5190. 1958. a. illus. Maco Publishing Co., 380 Madison Ave, New York, NY 10017. Examined: 1976. John Brett, Jr., ed. 74p. $1.25 pap.
Aud: Pl

Contains a few articles by separate authors on technique, types of fish, equipment, and cooking fish. Several articles have far more photographs—of doubtful value—than words. The comparative guide to selecting a fishing rod and the accessories section which includes photographs, descriptions, and manufacturers' addresses are useful. If one cannot select all the magazine-format fishing guides listed, this would probably be the first to eliminate. SLB

SS 733
Fishing World Annual. a. illus. Allsport Publishing Corp., 51 Atlantic Ave, Floral Park, NY 11001. Examined: 1977. Keith Gardner, ed. 87p. $1.50 pap.
Aud: Pl

In magazine format, this annual has a variety of feature articles by various authors on types of fish and fishing, a couple of articles specifically on fishing technique, and a large illustrated section on how to make oversize fly-rod lures and bugs. There are a few book reviews and a very brief listing of new products. High quality color photographs which assist in fish identification are also included. SLB

SS 734
Football Action. a. illus. Sports Eye, Great Neck, NY

11021. Examined: 1977. David Scott, ed. 162p. $1.75 pap.
Aud: Pl

The major focus of this magazine-format annual is predicting winners and assisting those interested in betting on professional and college football. There is a discussion of "power action points" which are listed for each team and used in predicting winners. Most of the articles concern betting and predictions. There is an entry for each professional team which gives the schedule, past season scores, veteran roster, and a discussion and rating for offensive backfield, receivers, and line; and defensive line, linebackers, secondary, and specialists. The college entries for the seven conferences, Ivy League, and major independents include a brief discussion and prediction. There is a schedule of all professional games and of those colleges discussed. National Football League statistics are provided for the entire league, though not by team or player. Includes medium-quality, black-and-white photographs. SLB

SS 735

Football Case Book. a. index. National Federation of State High School Associations, Federation Place, Box 98, Elgin, IL 60120. Examined: 1977. Brice B. Durbin, ed. 103p. $1.20 pap.
Aud: Jh, Hs, Pl

Arranged in the order of the Federation's football rules. There is a presentation of situations, "most of which have actually occurred and some of which have been devised simply to stimulate thinking." The play and ruling are both given, with reference to the appropriate rule section. At the end is a code of ethics for athletics officials. A subject index is included. The National Federation also issues two related annual publications which were not examined: *Football Rules— Simplified and Illustrated* (1978, $2.25 pap.) and *Football Officials' Manual* (1978/79, $1.10 pap.). SLB

SS 736

Football Handbook (Includes Flag Football). a. illus. National Federation of State High School Associations, Federation Place, Box 98, Elgin, IL 60120. Examined: 1977/78. Brice B. Durbin, ed. 96p. $1.10 pap.
Aud: Jh, Hs, Pl

Presents the primary and basic phases of football play. It is divided into six parts which include the historical evolution of the rules; material directed to coaches' responsibilities to the students who participate; material for the players, covering basic rules and a section on duties of the captain; an extensive discussion of the rules for officials; spectator sportsmanship and purposes of interscholastic athletics for spectators; and playing rules for flag football and touch football. Appendixes include a listing of football fundamentals, illustrations of officials' signals, and a summary of penalties. There is no index or table of contents. SLB

SS 737

Football Register. ISSN 0071-7258. 1966. a. Sporting News, 1212 N Lindbergh Blvd, Box 56, St. Louis, MO 63166. Examined: 1969; 1976. Mike Douchant and Moe Marcin, eds. 427p. $5.50 pap.
Aud: Pl

Alphabetical listing of all currently active National Football League players. Entries include nicknames, birth dates, and playing records. SLB

SS 738

Game Plan College Basketball. 1977. a. illus. Game Plan Magazines, 201 S Main St, North Syracuse, NY 13212. Examined: 1977. David Leonard, ed. 106p. $2.25 pap.
Aud: Pl

Includes much the same material as other magazine annuals on college basketball. Its special feature is that it rates the difficulty of a team's schedule for the coming season and predicts team placement at the end of the season. The entries for colleges are arranged by region and give name, previous season win-loss record, a brief discussion of the team, and scoring/rebounding averages of the players. There is a fairly elaborate "Stat-Key" national preview, based on a team's power. The current season playing schedule is included. SLB

SS 739

Game Plan Pro Basketball. 1977. a. illus. Game Plan Magazines, 201 S Main St, North Syracuse, NY 13212. Examined: 1977. David Leonard, ed. 106p. $2.25 pap.
Aud: Pl

A magazine-format annual with information similar to other pro basketball annuals of the same format. Its specialty is predicting the season's outcome for each team and the "Stat-Key" system of measuring the potential of basketball teams in terms of rated power. The annual includes previews for each team, with a two-page discussion and some photographs. There are also a few special articles and complete National Basketball Association schedules. The photographs are of very good quality. SLB

SS 740
Girls Gymnastics Judging Manual. (Continues: Girls Gymnastics Manual.) bi-a. illus. National Federation of State High School Associations, Federation Place, Box 98, Elgin, IL 60120. Examined: 1976/77 and 1977/78. Dolores J. Paulsen and Clifford B. Fagan. 125p. $2.25 pap. (1978/79 and 1979/80.)
Aud: Jh, Hs, Pl

The manual is "written specifically for individuals who serve as judges of girls gymnastics competition at secondary school level." It includes information on scoring, many illustrations of compulsory and optional exercises, and comparisons of the correct and incorrect form. Duties and responsibilities of superior and acting judges are listed. There is no index or table of contents. SLB

SS 741
Girls Gymnastics Rules. a. illus. National Federation of State High School Associations, Federation Place, Box 98, Elgin, IL 60120. Examined: 1977/78. Brice B. Durbin, ed. 129p. $2.25 pap. (1978/79.)
Aud: Jh, Hs, Pl

Includes photographs, names, and addresses for members of the Girls Gymnastics Rules Committee. The rules have no index, but there is a table of contents to subject areas. Many illustrations of correct forms, the code of ethics for judges, coaches, and competitors; conduct of coaches and competitors; and points of emphasis are also included. SLB

SS 742
Goal Post College Football. 1975. e. index. illus. Goal Post Publications, Box 185, Liverpool, NY 13088. Examined: 1976. Mark Valenti, ed. 114p. $1.75 pap.
Aud: Pl

Arranged in an easy-to-read, magazine-like format. It begins with an index to teams and covers previous season conference standings and the top 20 college teams. The Goal Post "accur-rate" system for predicting winners is discussed and demonstrated. The guide lists All-American and all-sectional players. The team entries, arranged by division, include current schedule, offense, defense, and a summary of team quality. There are some medium quality photographs of players. SLB

SS 743
Goal Post Pro Football. 1975. a. illus. Goal Post Publications, Box 185, Liverpool, NY 13088. Examined: 1976. Mark Valenti, ed. 114p. $1.95 pap.
Aud: Pl

Like **Goal Post College Football,** this guide is arranged in an easy-to-read, magazine-like format. It gives previous season statistics and television game schedules, and discusses and describes the Goal Post "accur-rate" system for predicting winners. The team directory, arranged by conference, includes current schedule, description, discussion of offense and defense, and veteran and rookie rosters. SLB

SS 744
Golf Digest Annual. ISSN 0071-176X. 1949. a. illus. Golf Digest, 495 Westport Ave, Norwalk, CT 06856. Examined: 1977. Nick Seitz, ed. 228p. $1.50 pap.
Aud: Pl

This guide is issued as the February issue of *Golf Digest,* but it is also available separately. It features articles on pro tours and instruction, as well as articles on amateurs. The 32-page record book includes all-time and past season records. There is a directory of more than 1,000 places to play and other features. Includes coming season schedule for men's and women's professional, amateur, Juniors, and some international tournaments. SLB

SS 745
Golf Magazine Yearbook. 1958. a. illus. Times Mirror Magazines, 380 Madison Ave, New York, NY 10017. Dist: Subscription Service Office, Box 2786, Boulder, CO 80302. Examined: 1977. John M. Ross, ed. 218p. $1.25.
Aud: Pl

This guide is published as the February issue of *Golf Magazine,* but it can be purchased separately. It includes instructional articles and features. The "Year-Round Reference" section contains a complete history of winners and current season tournament schedules. "Who's Who in Tournament Golf" lists men, then women, alphabetically arranged. Each entry includes age, height, weight, home city, and review of history in golf. It does not include a course directory. There are also several special departments. SLB

SS 746
Golf Tips Annual. 1978. a. illus. Werner Book Corp., 606 Wilshire Blvd, Santa Monica, CA 90401. Examined: 1978. Donald H. Werner, ed. 81p. $1.95 pap.
Aud: Pl

Contains several articles on how to improve one's golf game and style. It is liberally illustrated with good quality photographs. The articles are geared toward the general audience that plays golf for fun or amateur competition. SLB

SS 747

Gridiron News Pro Yearbook. a. illus. National Sports Publishing Corp., 150 E 58th St, New York, NY 10022. Examined: 1977. Donald R. Wall, ed. 162p. $1.50 pap.
Aud: Pl

Another popular football annual in magazine format. The detailed previous season statistics make this guide more useful for reference than some others of this type. The statistics are spread throughout the magazine between articles about each professional team. The format, which is not well indexed, can cause confusion. Team entries are arranged by American and National Conference, but in no particular order; there is no index, so it can be difficult to find a particular entry. Each team entry includes the coming schedule; last year's scores; and a veterans roster which lists name, number, position, size, birth date, college, and games played in previous season. There is also an illustrated depth chart showing the players' positions and a general discussion of the team. Feature articles, a preview and schedule for the Canadian Football League, and Hall of Fame enshrinees are also included. SLB

SS 748

A Guide for the College-Bound Student Athlete. a. National Collegiate Athletic Association, Box 1906, Shawnee Mission, KS 66222. Examined: 1977. 15p. $5 per 50 copies.
Aud: Jh, Hs, Pl

This brief pamphlet is a summary of the NCAA rules and regulations governing recruiting, eligibility, and financial aid. It is in an easy-to-read format, listing what a student may and may not do to be in accord with regulations followed by NCAA colleges. SLB

SS 749

Guide to Cross Country Skiing. 1975. a. illus. Times Mirror Magazines, 380 Madison Ave, New York, NY 10017. Examined: 1977. Editors of *SKI* Magazine, eds. 136p. $1.95.
Aud: Pl

The major emphasis of this guide is on where to go cross country skiing. Entries are arranged by region, state, and area. Each entry includes a description of services offered, contact name, and the address and phone number. There are articles on technique and equipment, and many other features and departments. Written in an easy reading style and well illustrated. SLB

SS 750

Guinness Book of Olympic Records. 1964. quadrennial. illus. Sterling Publishing Co., 419 Park Ave S, New York, NY 10016; Bantam, 414 E Golf Rd, Des Plaines, IL 60016. Examined: 1964; 1975. Norris D. McWhirter and A. Ross McWXhirter, eds. 256p. $1.95 pap. (Bantam.)
Aud: Jh, Hs, Jc, Cl, Pl

Includes a brief history of the Olympics. Lists Olympic medal winners since 1896 in the 21 sports currently in the summer events, and medal winners since 1908 in the seven sports currently in the Winter Olympics. A viewer's guide to rules and scoring methods is also included. The 1975 edition contained an unpaged insert of the events scheduled for the 1976 Montreal Olympics. SLB

SS 751

Guinness Sports Record Book. 1972. bi-a. index. illus. Sterling Publishing Co., 419 Park Ave S, New York, NY 10016. Examined: 1972. Norris D. McWhirter and A. Ross McWhirter, eds. 160p. $4.95; $4.89 plb.
Aud: Pl

Taken from the **Guinness Book of World Records,** this book follows the same format and uses the same pictures. It covers all sports and many games. Before the listing of various records, there is usually a short but useful history. It is well indexed. SLB

SS 752

Gun Digest. ISSN 0072-9043. 1946. a. index. illus. Digest Books, 540 Frontage Rd, Northfield, IL 60093. Examined: 1976. John T. Amber, ed. 448p. $8.95 pap.
Aud: Pl

Includes a wide variety of articles by separate authors on many types of guns, information of interest to collectors, and some information on knives. There is a large section for reviewing new products. The new products listings are arranged by type of gun, with a section on sights and scopes. Each entry includes photograph, model name, specifications, features, and price. There is a briefly annotated Arms Library, arranged by subject interest, which is very complete. There is also a listing of periodical publications, arms associations in the U.S. and abroad, and a directory of the arms trade, arranged by subject, which includes manufacturers' addresses. Includes a fairly complete index. SLB

SS 753

Gun World Hunting Guide. 1972. a. index. illus.

Gallant Publishing Co., 34249 Camino Capistrano, Capistrano Beach, CA 92624. Examined: 1976. Bob Zwirz, ed. 122p. $1.50 pap.
Aud: Pl

Contains several feature articles by different authors on hunting various types of game, with a few articles on selecting and using different types of equipment. There are discussions of products in two sections: handmade folder knives and optical equipment. Each entry in the optical equipment directory includes a photograph, description and specifications, and manufacturer's address. Medium-quality photographs are included throughout. SLB

SS 754
Guns and Ammo Annual. ISSN 0072-906X. 1965. a. illus. Petersen Publishing Co., 8490 Sunset Blvd, Los Angeles, CA 90069. Examined: 1973. E. G. Bell, Jr., ed. 368p. $4.95 pap.
Aud: Pl

The magazine-format annual combines special interest features for those interested in the history of guns, for collectors, and for those who seek to purchase. Besides the wide variety of articles on types of guns, techniques for hunting, and new equipment, there are several catalogs of specific gun models. Catalog entries include photograph, model name, price, size and weight, and description. There is a directory of manufacturers and suppliers which includes addresses. SLB

SS 755
Guns Annual Book of Handguns. 1974. a. illus. Publisher's Development Corp., 8150 N Central Park Ave, Skokie, IL 60076. Examined: 1974; 1977. Jerome Rakusan, ed. 98p. $2.95 pap.
Aud: Pl

Although the major focus of this annual is a catalog of currently available handguns, there are also several feature articles on types of guns and competitions. Some of the articles are new for the annual, others are reprinted from *American Handgunner and Guns*. The catalog sections are for double action revolvers, single action revolvers, double action semi-autos, single action semi-autos, miscellaneous handguns, air pistols, black power handguns, and handguns kits. The catalog entries include photograph, model, specifications, and price. There is a directory of manufacturers, with addresses. SLB

SS 756
Guns Illustrated. ISSN 0072-9078. 1969. a. illus. Digest Books, 540 Frontage Rd, Northfield, IL 60093. Examined: 1971. Editors of Gun Digest, eds. 224p. (1977. $6.95 pap.).
Aud: Pl

This is a catalog intended for the potential buyer. It is arranged by manufacturer and covers handguns, shotguns, rifles, sights, scopes, mounts, and surplus firearms. For each item produced by the manufacturer, there is a photograph, name, detailed description, and price. There is no subject index, so one must know the manufacturer's name to find the particular gun or type of equipment one is seeking. SLB

SS 757
Gymnastics Guide. ISSN 0533-9054. 1963/65. bi-a. American Alliance for Health, Physical Education and Recreation, National Association for Girls and Women in Sport, 1201 16th St, NW, Washington, DC 20036. Examined: none. (1975/77. $4 pap.)
Aud: Jh, Hs, Jc, Cl, Pl
Indexed in: *ERIC*.

No edition of this biennial guide has been examined. However, based on the high quality of other guides published by the National Association for Girls and Women in Sport, it is undoubtedly an important tool. It is assumed that the guide includes articles on technique, officiating, and rules, and a bibliography. SLB

SS 758
Hockey Register. ISSN 0090-2292. (Continues in part: Pro and Senior Hockey Guide.) 1972. a. Sporting News, 1212 N Lindbergh Blvd, Box 56, St. Louis, MO 63166. Examined: 1972/73; 1976/77. Herb Elk, ed. 576p. $5.50 pap.
Aud: Pl

Alphabetical listing of all players currently active in all professional hockey leagues. Entries include birth date and place, physical measurements, and records for entire playing career in junior leagues or above. Includes player's sold, selected, traded record. Was included in the *Pro and Senior Hockey Guide* until 1972; that guide is now entitled **Pro and Amateur Hockey Guide**. SLB

SS 759
Horse and Rider All-Western Yearbook. 1973. a. illus. Rich Publishing, Box 555, Temecula, CA 92390. Examined: 1977. Ray Rich, ed. 137p. $2.25 pap.
Aud: Pl

A magazine-format yearbook which contains many separately authored articles in the areas of training aids, breeding, and veterinary advice, and special features on a variety of subjects of interest to horse riders and trainers. There are many good quality photographs and illustrations, but the narrative is not neglected, making this a useful annual. Advertisements are kept to a minimum. SLB

SS 760
Hunting Guide. ISSN 0073-4101. (Continues in part: Gun Handbook Hunting Guide.) 1965. a. illus. Davis Publications, 229 Park Ave S, New York, NY 10003. Examined: 1975. Bob Steindler, ed. 87p. $1.35 pap.
Aud: Pl

Contains a wide variety of articles by separate authors on equipment, game cooking, and technique. The unique feature of this hunting annual is a hunting forecast, arranged by state, which describes results from previous year and gives some state regulations. The government department responsible for hunting regulations in each state is given, with address. There are poor- to medium-quality photographs throughout. SLB

SS 761
The Indianapolis 500 Yearbook. 1946. a. index. illus. Carl Hungness and Associates, 4914 W 16th St, Speedway, IN 46224. Examined: 1974; 1976. Carl Hungness, ed. 224p. $10.95 plb.; $4.95 pap.
Aud: Pl

A very high quality, magazine-format annual with excellent photographs. There are many articles of both historical and current interest. Provides a title and subject index to the previous three annuals. The driver biographies for the current year include a photograph and the driver's experience in the year's race, with a few additional notes of interest. There is also a performance record for each driver which includes every Indianapolis 500 that the driver has entered. SLB

SS 762
Ithacagun Hunting and Shooting Annual. ISSN 0361-4999. 1976. a. illus. Aqua-Field Publications, 342 Madison Ave, New York, NY 10017. Examined: 1977. Steve Ferber, ed. 95p. $1.75 pap.
Aud: Pl

Like the other Aqua-Field Publications, this magazine-format annual carries the name of a major manufacturer in the title. This does not seem to affect the content of the articles, although there is not a new products listing as in most of the hunting annuals. There are feature articles on hunting many types of game, with a special section on bear hunting. There are also articles on shooting and gunsmithing. Good-quality photographs throughout. SLB

SS 763
Journal of the Philosophy of Sport. ISSN 0094-8705. 1974. a. bibl. index. Philosophic Society for the Study of Sport, c/o Susan Cook, Leisure Education Office, Centennial College, Warden Woods Campus, 651 Warden Ave, Scarborough, Ontario MI1 326, Canada. Examined: 4th ed., 1977. Harold J. Vander Zwagg, ed. 131p. (5th ed., 1978. $5.50.)
Aud: Cl, Pl
Indexed in: *Philosopher's Index.*

The primary purpose of the Philosophic Society for the Study of Sport is "to foster interchange and scholarship among those interested in the scholarly study of sport." The **Journal** does not have a central theme; rather, it is a collection of articles which represent the growing body of knowledge in the relatively new discipline, sport philosophy. The 1977 edition included articles on "Zen, Yoga and Sport"; "Eastern Philosophy for Western Athletes"; "Alienated Youth and Creative Sports Experience"; and "Some Aristotelian Notes on the Attempt to Define Sport." Since the 1976 edition, the annual address of the president of the Society has been included in an appendix. Each of the articles includes bibliographic notes. JKM

SS 764
Little League Baseball Inc. Handbook With Rules and Regulations. ISSN 0458-9575. (Continues: Little League Baseball Inc. Official Rules.) 1952. a. index. illus. Little League Baseball Inc., Box 1127, Williamsport, PA 17701. Examined: 1965; 1970; 1975. 65p. $.35.
Aud: Sa, El, Jh, Pl

Lists members of the Board of Directors, officers, and regional headquarters addresses. Defines purpose, structure, qualifications, tryouts, and regulations. Official playing rules are indexed. SLB

SS 765
Major League Year and Notebook. a. Baseball Blue Book, 7225 30th Ave N, Box 40847, St. Petersburg, FL 33743. Examined: none. (1978. $30.)
Aud: Pl

Although no sample was examined, this annual is mentioned because of the quality of the **Baseball Blue Book** published by the same company. The publisher states that the book "is a mini-library on the Major

League players. Personal information such as physical size and age, even home addresses, can be easily located. Offensive and pitching records are from the previous year and career totals in each category are indexed. Also, years and days of service and first pro years are listed. In the back is a section on all players who were on a list (suspended, disabled, etc.) the previous year." The publisher is correct in stating that "some of this information cannot be found anywhere else," particularly the home addresses of players and the names of players who were on one of the suspended or disabled lists. SLB

SS 766
Marathon Handbook. ISSN 0360-9928. 1974. a. illus. World Publications, Box 366, Mountain View, CA 94040. Examined: 1975. Editors of *Runner's World,* eds. 111p. $1.95 pap. (1977.)
Aud: Pl

Chapters include descriptions of some runners, how to judge your time, current season calendar of marathon races, and all-time marathon time records. There are schedules, all-time lists, and previous season times for other races, including shorter and longer races, race walking, and 24-hour relay. SLB

SS 767
Minor League Digest. a. Baseball Blue Book, 7225 30th Ave N, Box 40847, St. Petersburg, FL 33743. Examined: none. (1978. $30.)
Aud: Pl

No copy of this work was examined, but it is recommended because of the quality of the **Baseball Blue Book** issued by the same publishers. The publishers state that the book is "the most comprehensive statistical book ever published about minor league players. Every player who appeared in one game or more for any minor league club is listed with his complete offensive statistics. In addition, his reserving club, his qualification, his first pro year and all his vital statistics are recorded. The same information for all pitchers, with the pitching record, is also found inside." No other baseball publication was located that provided this information. SLB

SS 768
National Baseball Congress. Official Baseball Annual. ISSN 0077-3549. 1935. a. index. illus. National Baseball Congress, 338 S Sycamore, Wichita, KS 67213. Examined: 1943; 1974/75; 1977. K. F. Harris, ed. various paging. $4.25 pap.
Aud: Pl

Provides a history of the National Baseball Congress which began in 1931 for non-professional players. Several individually paged sections include lists of regulations for team managers and sponsors, rules and results for the national tournament, results of regional tournaments, summaries of state tournaments and district tournaments, and affiliated leagues. Discusses and lists affiliated umpires associations and lists NBA certified umpires for each state. Lists scorers by state, NBA all-time records, and the official rules, which are indexed. SLB

SS 769
National Basketball Association Official Guide. ISSN 0078-3862. 1958. a. index. illus. Sporting News, 1212 N Lindbergh Blvd, Box 56, St Louis, MO 63166. Examined: 1971/72; 1976/77. Matt Winick, ed. 512p. $3.50 pap.
Aud: Pl

Emphasis is on previous season results and records. There is a team directory, with address, officers, coaches, and schedule. Gives current official rules, which are indexed. There is some historical information on all-time record holders. SLB

SS 770
National Collegiate Athletic Association. Annual Reports. ISSN 0077-8794. (Continues: National Collegiate Athletic Association Yearbook.) 1906. a. National Collegiate Athletic Association Publishing Service, Box 1906, Shawnee Mission, KS 66222. Examined: 1975/76. 221p. $2 members; $3 nonmembers.
Aud: Sa

The opening section covers administrative organization and provides names and addresses of all officers. The reports include a statistical review of the past year, financial and other informational reports of all sports committees, and informational reports of all other NCAA committees. The minutes of all executive board and council meetings, detailed financial reports for all sports, and a report of the treasurer are also included. There is no index, but the table of contents is very complete. Another annual NCAA publication, the *National Collegiate Athletic Association Manual* (1978, $3 pap.; $2 to members), contains current NCAA legislation including its constitution, by-laws, interpretations, executive regulations, enforcement procedure, and recommended policies. The *National Collegiate Athletic Association Directory* (1978, $2 pap.; $1 to members) is an annual publication which provides a roster of members by district and division and a listing of NCAA committees. SLB

SS 771

National Collegiate Athletic Association. Official Gymnastics Rules. 1968. a. index. illus. National Collegiate Athletic Association Publishing Service, Box 1906, Shawnee Mission, KS 66222. Examined: 1973; 1976. 48p. $1 pap.
Aud: Cl, Pl

New rules changes are noted at the beginning. There are also equipment specifications and exercise illustrations. SLB

SS 772

National Collegiate Championships. a. National Collegiate Athletic Association Publishing Service, Box 1906, Shawnee Mission, KS 66222. Examined: none. ($3 pap.)
Aud: Cl, Pl

The publisher states that this book includes "history and records of National Collegiate Championship events conducted since 1883 and detailed summaries of the championships of the previous year. Covers 18 sports." Recommendation is based on the quality of other NCAA publications; no copy was available for examination. SLB

SS 773

National Cutting Horse Association. Rule Book. 1963. a. National Cutting Horse Association, Box 12155, Fort Worth, TX 76116. Examined: 1977. 29p.
Aud: Pl

The small rule book is intended for use in the contest arena. For the sake of standardization the rules also include those for judging. A section for the Youth Division, points on judging and showing, and suggestions for show management are also included. SLB

SS 774

The National Directory of College Athletics. Men's Edition. 1967. a. index. illus. Ray Franks Publishing Ranch, Box 7068, Amarillo, TX 79109. Examined: 1977/78. Ray Franks, ed. 424p. $9 pap.
Aud: Hs, Jc, Cl, Pl

The cover states that this directory is an official publication of the National Association of Collegiate Directors of Athletics. Its primary audience focus is athletic officials of senior and junior colleges in the U.S. and Canada. The men's edition is more extensive than the women's edition of the same directory. The major sections of the book are a listing of senior, junior, and Canadian colleges, arranged by name of the school. Entries provide address, telephone number, conference, enrollment, colors, nickname, stadium, fieldhouse, athletic director, and coaches for all sports. Sometimes there is a photograph of the athletic director. Unlike the women's edition, this directory includes a geographical index to the schools listed. There are several articles and records for many of the athletic associations, some game schedules, and a listing of all conferences which includes officers, addresses, and member schools. There is also a college travel guide which lists hotels and motels that cater to college athletic squads and that have been recommended by athletic officials. SLB

SS 775

National Directory of College Athletics. Women's Edition. (Continues: National Directory of Women's Athletics. ISSN 0092-5489.) 1973. a. illus. Ray Franks Publishing Ranch, Box 7086, Amarillo, TX 79109. Examined: 1977. Ray Franks, ed. 200p. $6 pap.
Aud: Hs, Jc, Cl, Pl

The major portion of the book is the listing of senior, junior, and Canadian colleges and their athletic programs for women. Colleges are listed by name under each category. Entries include address, conference, enrollment, colors, nickname, stadium, fieldhouse, president, athletic director, phone number, and coaches for each sport. Indicates scholarships offered for any given sport. Some entries include a photograph of the athletic director. There are a few articles of interest and some tournament records. Lacks a geographic index to the colleges listed. SLB

SS 776

National Directory of High School Coaches. ISSN 0417-5956. 1963. a. Athletic Publishing Co., Box 931, Montgomery, AL 36102. Examined: 1964; 1976/77. John Allen Dees, ed. 508p. $15.95.
Aud: Sa

The title varies; sometimes it is simply *Directory of High School Coaches*. The directory is arranged geographically by state, then city. Entries include the name of the school, sports coaches, address, and phone number. Also included are the records of the national interscholastic track and field, and swimming. The directory states that it is "recognized by National Federation of State High School Athletic Associations." SLB

SS 777

National Federation of State High School Associations. Official Handbook. a. National Federation of State High School Associations, Federation Place,

Box 98, Elgin, IL 60120. Examined: 1977/78. 112p. $.90 pap.
Aud: Sa

This handbook serves as a general guide to the association and to rules of the association. Includes governing information, purposes, election, articles of incorporation, an overview of all programs offered by the Federation, and the standards for athletic and non-athletic events. Non-athletic events include music, forensics, and drama competition. There is also discussion of non-school-sponsored activities and criteria for evaluating them. Includes a listing of all awards and their past recipients. It lists optional limitations that exist, state sponsored competitions, and state championships for each state. There is also a detailed survey of high school sports participation in each state. The administrative section includes past officers, administrative organization with name and length of term for all officers, and committee members. The directory of member state associations and staff members, which is arranged by state, includes address, telephone number, executive director, publication, annual meeting, number of employees, when joined the Federation, and number of high schools and students. SLB

SS 778
National Football Guide. ISSN 0081-3788. 1970. a. illus. Sporting News, 1212 N Lindbergh Blvd, Box 56, St Louis, MO 63166. Examined: 1970; 1976. Joe Marcin and Larry Wigge, eds. 400p. $3.50 pap.
Aud: Pl

Strongest emphasis is on the previous season and current team information, which makes this a very important football annual. The directories for the teams include officers, coaches, address, stadium, colors, training sights, upcoming schedule, and previous season scores. Emphasis is on summaries of all previous season's games, arranged chronologically, including description and box score. There are recaps of all super bowl games, all-time pro football records, and retrospective individual leaders. College information is limited to previous season all-America team and television schedules for the current season. SLB

SS 779
National Football League. Official Record Manual. ISSN 0077-4588. (Continues: National Football League. Record Manual.) 1941. a. illus. National Football League, 410 Park Ave, New York, NY 10022. Examined: 1971; 1976. NFL Public Relations Department and Seymour Siwoff, comps. 406p. $1.95 pap.
Aud: Pl

Concentrates on previous season records for the National Football League exclusively. Includes some all-time team and individual records, as well as team directories and current schedule. Official signals and helmet insignia are illustrated. SLB

SS 780
National Hockey League Guide. 1970/71. a. index. National Hockey League, 920 Sun Life Bldg, Montreal, Quebec H3B 2W2, Canada. Dist: National Hockey League Services, Suite 2480, Two Pennsylvania Plaza, New York, NY 10001. Examined: 1970/71; 1976/77. Ron Andrews, ed. 668p.
Aud: Pl

Provides team directories for all National Hockey League teams, with address, telephone and TWX number, officers and other personnel, club and uniform colors, and TV and radio stations that cover the games. There is an additional list of all player personnel for the team that season. Player entries include height, weight, birth place and date, last season's team, and status. There are previous season records and selected all-time records and award winners. SLB

SS 781
National Motorsports Annual. (Continues: National Automotive Annual.) 1966. a. index. illus. National Automotive Publications, Box S, Farmingville, NY 11738. Examined: 1976. George Houraney, ed. 72p. $2.50 pap.
Aud: Pl

Includes information on American Hot Rod Association, American Motorcycle Association, International Hot Rod Association, NASCAR, National Hot Rod Association, and USAC. There is mention of all-time winners, but the emphasis is on the previous season and the upcoming season, with a calendar of events from March to February in the back. Also includes a drag strip listing, including location, address, telephone, and nearby motels. There are high-quality photographs throughout. SLB

SS 782
New Fishing. ISSN 0092-1734. 1953. a. illus. Maco Publishing Co., 380 Madison Ave, New York, NY 10017. Examined: 1977. John Brett, ed. 72p. $1.25 pap.
Aud: Pl

This brief, magazine-format annual is comprised of a series of articles on types of fish, fishing equipment, and recipes. The articles are provided courtesy of various individuals and organizations. There are fewer articles than in other annuals of this type, but it does include a limited guide to new equipment and tackle with photographs, descriptions, and manufacturers' addresses. Several illustrations and medium-quality photographs are included. SLB

SS 783
Official Baseball Dope Book. ISSN 0067-4265. (Continues: Baseball Dope Book.) 1942. a. index. illus. Sporting News, 1212 N Lindbergh Blvd, Box 56, St Louis, MO 63166. Examined: 1976. Joe Marcin, Chris Roewe, and Larry Wigge, eds. 240p. $1.50 pap.
Aud: Pl

One of the most important features of this annual is that it includes a complete roster for the current season for each professional team. The player rosters list uniform number, right- or left-handed pitching and hitting, height, weight, birth date, previous season club, and some lifetime statistics. These rosters are included in a very extensive team-by-team directory which also contains officers, yearly standings, and a diagram and description of the team's stadium. The guide also includes the officers and offices of the Baseball Commission; American and National League complete current schedule; statistics, arranged by league, for leading pitchers and hitters; no-hit games; Hall of Fame members; and lifetime batting and pitching averages for players active the previous season. There are statistics on the All-Star games since 1933, wins and losses for all World Series, and World Series attendance and money, and a very useful directory which gives an illustration of each team's insignia, a detailed description of the uniform, and an explanation of team colors. SLB

SS 784
Official Baseball Guide. ISSN 0078-3838. 1942. a. index. illus. Sporting News, 1212 N Lindbergh Blvd, Box 56, St Louis, MO 63166. Examined: 1973; 1977. Joe Marcin, et al., eds. 560p. $3 pap.
Aud: Pl

Perhaps the single most important baseball annual because of the amount of detailed information it provides about each team and the previous season results. The team directories include officers, address, scouts, park location, and field dimensions. There is a descriptive essay on the previous season for each team and a complete schedule and scores. Does not include current team rosters, although there are previous season team photographs with the last names of the players. (Final rosters are available so late that the best sources for them are some of the magazine-format annuals.) There are updated retrospective records, and records, player statistics, and averages for all AAA, AA, and A minor league teams, as well as rookie leagues. SLB

SS 785
Official Baseball Rules. ISSN 0078-3846. 1950. a. index. illus. Sporting News, 1212 N Lindbergh Blvd, Box 56, St Louis, MO 63166. Examined: 1963; 1967; 1976. 111p. $1 pap.
Aud: Hs, Jc, Cl, Pl

This is the baseball code used by all professional teams. It is useful for amateur teams as well, which is why so many audience levels are recommended. The rules are indexed and there are diagrams for the field, pitcher's mound, and the glove. SLB

SS 786
Official Football Rules. 1932. a. index. illus. National Federation of State High School Associations, Federation Place, Box 98, Elgin, IL 60120. Examined: 1935; 1974; 1975; 1978. 91p. $1.10.
Aud: Jh, Hs, Pl

Current rules with index. Gives screened background to rules changes from year before. The 1978 edition includes six-man and eight-man rules changes. SLB

SS 787
Official National Collegiate Athletic Association Baseball Guide. ISSN 0473-8950. 1958. a. index. illus. National Collegiate Athletic Association Publishing Service, Box 1906, Shawnee Mission, KS 66222. Examined: 1975; 1977. 136p. $2 pap.
Aud: Jc, Cl, Pl

Begins with a national preview/review, then includes a preview/review for each of seven regions. Regional reviews provide descriptive discussion, win-loss records, and percentages for each team. Also includes a review of last season's championships and statistical leaders, and some all-time statistics. Official rules are paged and indexed separately at end. SLB

SS 788
Official National Collegiate Athletic Association Basketball Guide. 1897. a. illus. National Collegiate Athletic Association Publishing Service, Box 1906, Shawnee Mission, KS 66222. Examined: 1977. 180p. $2 pap.
Aud: Jc, Cl, Pl

Begins with a national preview/review, then provides a preview/review for seven regions. The last season's championships and statistical leaders are given, as well as members of the All-American Team. A large portion of the book is devoted to current season schedules and past season results. Does not include rules, which are published separately. The NCAA also issues two related annual publications, the *Official National Collegiate Athletic Association Basketball Scorebook* ($2 pap.) which is designed for use in scoring games at all levels of play, but especially at the college level, and the *Official National Collegiate Athletic Association Basketball Scores* ($1 pap.) which contains game-by-game scores of the past season for all schools that are members of the NCAA. SLB

SS 789
Official National Collegiate Athletic Association Basketball Rules and Casebook. ISSN 0094-5234. (Continues: NCAA Basketball Guide.) 1970. a. index. illus. National Collegiate Athletic Association Publishing Service, Box 1906, Shawnee Mission, KS 66222. Examined: 1942/42; 1977. Dr. Edward S. Steitz, ed. 68p. $1 pap.
Aud: Jc, Cl, Pl

This publication was previously a part of the **Official National Collegiate Athletic Association Basketball Guide**; now it is only published under separate cover. Includes the rules as adopted by the National Basketball Committee of the U.S. and Canada. In addition to current rules, it notes changes in the rules since the past season. A court diagram, illustrations of officials' signals, and Points of Emphasis are also included. The NCAA also publishes *Official Read-Easy Basketball Rules* ($1 pap.), an annual publication which the association calls " a popularized people's version of the Official Basketball Rules for new or long-time basketball fans." SLB

SS 790
Official National Collegiate Athletic Association Football Guide. 1891. a. illus. National Collegiate Athletic Association Publishing Service, Box 1906, Shawnee Mission, KS 66222. Examined: 1976; 1978. 176p. $2 pap.
Aud: Jc, Cl, Pl

Begins with previews/reviews by region which include descriptions and team records for previous season. There are general reviews of the previous season's bowl games and divisional championship games. Lists current schedules with each team's previous season record. All-American team members and statistical leaders are also listed. Rules are not included as they are published separately. The NCAA also issues *National Collegiate Athletic Association Football Records* ($2 pap.), an annual publication that includes modern college football records (both individual and team), all-time statistical leaders, coaching records, win streaks, longest plays, and all-American teams since 1889. SLB

SS 791
Official National Collegiate Athletic Association Football Rules Interpretations. (Cover title: NCAA Official Football Rules.) a. index. illus. National Collegiate Athletic Association Publishing Service, Box 1906, Shawnee Mission, KS 66222. Examined: 1976. David M. Nelson, ed. 176p. $2 pap. (1978.)
Aud: Jc, Cl, Pl

Includes rules changes from previous season, football code, diagram of field, and the official rules with index. The official rules interpretations are also indexed. Rules and interpretations are paged separately. SLB

SS 792
Official National Collegiate Athletic Association Ice Hockey Guide. (Continues: Official Ice Hockey Rules of the NCAA; Official Ice Hockey Guide.) 1928. a. index. illus. National Collegiate Athletic Association Publishing Service, Box 1906, Shawnee Mission, KS 66222. Examined: 1952; 1974; 1977. 112p. $2 pap.
Aud: Jc, Cl, Pl

Begins with a national preview/review section arranged by region. Emphasis is on the previous season. Including All-American team members. Also covers Collegiate Hockey's Hall of Fame and high school results. There is a directory of ice hockey officials. The rules are listed at the end, separately paged and indexed. SLB

SS 793
Official National Collegiate Athletic Association Skiing Rules. ISSN 0473-8977. (Continues: Official NCAA Boxing, Gymnastics, Skiing Rules.) 1963/64. a. index. National Collegiate Athletic Association Publishing Service, Box 1906, Shawnee Mission, KS 66222. Examined: 1977. 56p. $1
Aud: Jc, Cl, Pl

Changes from previous season rules are noted. Includes charts and tables for scoring. SLB

SS 794
Official National Collegiate Athletic Association Soccer Guide. a. index. illus. National Collegiate Athletic

Association Publishing Service, Box 1906, Shawnee Mission, KS 66222. Examined: 1977. Donald Y. Yonker, ed. 128p. $2.
Aud: Jc, Cl, Pl

Begins with a national preview/review section which covers the national collegiate championship, the previous season's All-American team, divisional championships, and previous season records of member colleges. There is a junior college section, a high school roundup, and a list of records and honor awards. ISAA and NSCAA officers and officials are also listed. Emphasis is on previous season, rather than retrospective, records. The official rules section is separately paged and indexed. SLB

SS 795
Official National Collegiate Athletic Association Swimming Guide. 1945. a. illus. National Collegiate Athletic Association Publishing Service, Box 1906, Shawnee Mission, KS 66222. Examined: 1945; 1955; 1975; 1977. 128p. $2 pap.
Aud: Jc, Cl, Pl

Begins with a national preview/review section. The guide covers NCAA championships, with heavy emphasis on the previous season. Includes dates for upcoming season meets. There is a junior college and high school section which includes records and administrative procedures. The official rules are paged separately at the end, with changes noted before the main body of the rules. SLB

SS 796
Official National Collegiate Athletic Association Water Polo Rules. a. National Collegiate Athletic Association Publishing Service, Box 1906, Shawnee Mission, KS 66222. Examined: none. (1978. $1 pap.)
Aud: Jc, Cl, Pl

According to the publisher, this work includes "official rules of play for college water polo. Also rules changes for coming season, field diagram, and officials' signals." No copy was available for examination. SLB

SS 797
Official Read-Easy Football Rules. 1974. a. index. illus. National Collegiate Athletic Association Publishing Service, Box 1906, Shawnee Mission, KS 66222. Examined: 1976. Arnie Burdick, ed. 32p. $1 pap.
Aud: Pl

Provides a discussion of rules changes and then lists the rules, with humorous illustrations. The format makes the rules easy to read. Rules are indexed. Officials' signals are illustrated on the book's covers. SLB

SS 798
Official Rules of Sports and Games. 1949. bi-a. illus. Kaye and Ward, 21 New St, London, EC3M 4NT, England. Dist: Sports Shelf, Box 634, New Rochelle, NY 10802. Examined: 1976/77. 862p. $22.50.
Aud: Pl

Gives the British rules for 26 sports, with diagrams of playing areas for each sport. The acknowledgments include addresses for official British sports associations. SLB

SS 799
Official United States Tennis Tournament Directory. ISSN 0145-7977. 1977. a. United States Tennis Survey, 1013 Cornwell Place, Ann Arbor, MI 48104. Examined: 1977. 253p. $5 pap.
Aud: Pl

Covers all types of tournaments, with the listing for a year, from February through March of the next year. The major portion of the book is a listing of tournaments arranged by state. Within each state, listings are arranged chronologically and include tournament name; place; name, address, and telephone number of contact person; age division; prize money; type of court; divisions within the tournament; and circuit in which the tournament is included. There are sections for major circuits, giving date, place, and divisions; a chronological schedule for world team tennis; and addresses of major tennis organizations. SLB

SS 800
Official World Series Records. ISSN 0078-3900. 1953. a. index. Sporting News, 1212 N Lindbergh Blvd, Box 56, St Louis, MO 63166. Examined: 1963; 1971; 1976. Leonard Gettelson, comp. 487p. $3.50 pap.
Aud: Pl

The subtitle explains that this annual contains the complete box scores of all games from 1903 to the current year. It is arranged chronologically. For each year there are a few paragraphs discussing the Series and the complete box scores, with added notes for each game within the Series. In recent issues, the annual listings include attendance and financial figures. The descriptions from year-to-year are identical; the difference is that new games are added and the all-time records are updated. SLB

SS 801

Parents Guide to Accredited Camps; Midwestern Edition. (Continues in part: National Directory of Accredited Camps for Boys and Girls.) 1952. a. index. illus. Camping Magazine, American Camping Association, Bradford Woods, Martinsville, IN 46151. Examined: 1977. 66p. $2.40.

Aud: Pl

One of four titles in a series of magazine-format regional editions which replace the *National Directory of Accredited Camps for Boys and Girls.* Also replaces the November/December edition of *Camping Magazine,* although these guides are not editions of *Camping Magazine.* All editions are arranged by state and list for each camp the address, director(s), telephone number, clientele, and program. There are indexes to specialized camps and specialized clientele. There is also an owners/directors index. The primary focus is on the U.S., but the guides include some international camps which are repeated in each regional edition. The states covered in the Midwestern Edition are Illinois, Indiana, Iowa, Kansas, Kentucky, Michigan, Minnesota, Missouri, Nebraska, North Dakota, Ohio, South Dakota, and Wisconsin. SLB

SS 802

Parents Guide to Accredited Camps; Northeastern Edition. (Continues in part: National Directory of Accredited Camps for Boys and Girls.) 1952. a. index. illus. Camping Magazine, American Camping Association, Bradford Woods, Martinsville, IN 46151. Examined: 1977. 82p. $2.40.

Aud: Pl

Follows the same format as other regional editions in the Parents Guide' series. The states covered in the Northeastern Edition are Connecticut, Delaware, Maine, Maryland, Massachusetts, New Hampshire, New Jersey, New York, Pennsylvania, Rhode Island, Vermont, Virginia, Washington, D.C., and West Virginia. SLB

SS 803

Parents Guide to Accredited Camps; Southern Edition. (Continues in part: National Directory of Accredited Camps for Boys and Girls.) 1952. a. index. illus. Camping Magazine, American Camping Association, Bradford Woods, Martinsville, IN 46151. Examined: 1977. 38p. $2.40.

Aud: Pl

The states covered in the Southern Edition, the third in the Parents Guide' series, are Alabama, Arkansas, Florida, Georgia, Louisiana, Mississippi, North Carolina, Oklahoma, South Carolina, Tennessee, and Texas. The type of information provided and the format are the same for all the regional editions in the Parents Guide' series. SLB

SS 804

Parents Guide to Accredited Camps; Western Edition. (Continues in part: National Directory of Accredited Camps for Boys and Girls.) 1952. a. index. illus. Camping Magazine, American Camping Association, Bradford Woods, Martinsville, IN 46151. Examined: 1977. 63p. $2.40.

Aud: Pl

The type of information provided and the format are similar to other regional editions in the Parents Guide' series. The states covered in the Western Edition include Alaska, Arizona, California, Colorado, Hawaii, Idaho, Montana, Nevada, New Mexico, Oregon, Utah, Washington, and Wyoming. SLB

SS 805

Petersen's Pro Football Annual. ISSN 0079-5526. 1960. a. index. illus. Petersen Publishing Co., 8490 Sunset Blvd, Los Angeles, CA 90069. Examined: 1976. Chuck Benedict, ed. 46p. $1.95 pap.

Aud: Pl

Magazine format with medium to high quality photographs. Includes special articles; team directories with helmet insignia; previous season results; a one-page discussion on offense and defense; and special teams. Does not include addresses. There is a section on predictions, NFL rule changes, roster of NFL game officials, past season statistics, and a complete list of winners and losers of the Super Bowl. SLB

SS 806

Pro and Amateur Hockey Guide. ISSN 0079-550X. (Continues: Pro and Senior Hockey Guide.) 1968. a. illus. Sporting News, 1212 N Lindbergh Blvd, Box 56, St Louis, MO 63166. Examined: 1968/69; 1972/73; 1976/77. Larry Wigge and Joe Marcin, eds. 304p. $3.50 pap.

Aud: Pl

When the publisher changed the name to "Pro and Amateur" in 1972, the professional players' lifetime records were dropped. These were then picked up in a separate publication, **Hockey Register.** The guide now includes current directories with addresses and team symbols for the National Hockey League and the World Hockey Association, and team records for both the professional and the amateur leagues for the previous year. The directory for the amateur leagues does not give individual team addresses. There is some historical data on awards and records, although strong emphasis is on the previous season. There are also career records of recently retired players who are not included in the **Hockey Register,** since it is limited to current players. SLB

SS 807
Pro Basketball Illustrated. 1966. a. illus. Complete Sports Publications, 333 Johnson Ave, Brooklyn, NY 11206. Examined: 1977/78. Raymond O'Neill, ed. 70p. $1.25 pap.
Aud: Pl

This magazine-format annual clearly stresses its illustrations. The black-and-white photographs are of medium to good quality. There are very good quality color pin-ups. Some feature articles on players and a brief page of reviews and predictions for each National Basketball Association team are provided. The team rosters are not included. SLB

SS 808
Pro Football Illustrated. 1964. a. illus. Complete Sports Publications, 333 Johnson Ave, Brooklyn, NY 11206. Examined: 1976. Jim McNally, ed. 106p. $1.25 pap.
Aud: Pl

Easy-to-read, magazine format. Contains medium quality photographs, and some special articles. Lists previous season statistics comparatively by passers, rushers, receivers, and punters. Provides information about teams in the National Football Conference and American Football Conference. The team entries are arranged by conference and division, with two pages for each team. These team discussions include offense, defense, PFI forecast, and schedule. There are no team rosters. SLB

SS 809
Pro Hockey. ISSN 0079-5569. 1969. a. illus. Pocket Books, Simon and Schuster, 1230 Ave of the Americas, New York, NY 10021. Examined: 1974/75. Jim Proudfoot, ed. 224p. $2.50 pap.
Aud: Pl

Emphasis is on the National Hockey League, although the issue examined also contained brief information on the World Hockey Association. The team directory for the NHL contains addresses, officers, colors, and farm teams. There is a summary of the previous season and brief biographies of team members. All-time records are included. There is an explanatory section entitled "How Hockey Works." SLB

SS 810
Pro Quarterback. 1969. a. illus. Popular Publications, 420 Lexington Ave, New York, NY 10017. Examined: 1977. Lou Sahadi, ed. 114p. $1.95 pap.
Aud: Pl

A popular, magazine-format annual. There are a few high quality color photographs, which is somewhat unique for this type of publication. The name is misleading because the focus is not on quarterbacks, although there is a Pro Quarterback of the Year. It is primarily a discussion of each team. The team discussions, easily found from the table of contents, cover offense, defense, and a general analysis. There is a veteran roster with number, position, size, professional experience, birth date, college, and games played in previous season. General statistics from the previous season, a completed schedule of games, and a television schedule are also included. SLB

SS 811
Ring Boxing Encyclopedia and Record Book. 1942. a. index. illus. Ring Book Shop, 120 W 31st St, New York, NY 10001. Examined: 1959; 1974; 1977. Nat Loubet and John Ort, eds. 848p. $13.50.
Aud: Pl

Gives records of all champions of all divisions, arranged and indexed by weight division. Also lists active fighters from other countries. The entries for each fighter sometimes include a photograph, and always include the date of fight, opponent, and results in each round. The arrangement is somewhat confusing, but the information is very inclusive. SLB

SS 812
Runner's Almanac. 1972. a. illus. World Publications, Box 366, Mountain View, CA 94040. Examined: 1974. 93p. $1.95 pap.
Aud: Pl

Divided into four major sections. The first section is a review of the previous season, giving record breakers and major meet winners. The second section, Framework, discusses the organization of running as it currently exists, gives categories and definitions for events, and lists all athletic associations that sponsor any running events and all college conferences with their addresses. The third section concerns running records and gives the time, name, and date for each record in all divisions. The final section is an extensive one entitled "Where to Go." Arranged by state, followed by entries for Canada, it covers population, weather, AAU District, race contacts, major races, colleges, top athletes, and doctors. Addresses are provided for every entry within the states. SLB

SS 813
Ski Info: The Equipment Book. 1976. a. index. illus. Forrest Publications, 20 Hill St, Morristown, NJ 07960. Examined: 1978. Jim Avalanch Smith, ed. 352p. $5.95 pap.
Aud: Pl

Intended as a current guide to available ski equipment. It is divided into the broad areas of Alpine Equipment, Cross Country Equipment, and Accessories. Each of these areas is further divided for easy access to information. Each equipment entry includes photograph, brief description, and approximate price. There are also some equipment and feature articles. A brand names index and a manufacturers index are provided. SLB

SS 814
Ski Magazine's Guide to Cross Country Skiing. 1974. a. bibl. illus. Times Mirror Magazines, 380 Madison Ave, New York, NY 10017. Examined: 1977. Michael Brady, ed. 136p. $1.95 pap.
Aud: Pl

This magazine-format guide is divided into sections with several articles on technique, equipment, and general features. There is a directory of more than 250 ski areas in the U.S. and Canada, arranged by region, i.e., East, Midwest, West, and Canada. The entry for each ski area includes name, description, fees, equipment available, how to get there, and the name, address, and phone number of a contact person. At the end of the area directory is a lengthy list of local area trail guides with bibliographic information and price. SLB

SS 815
Skiing Rules. a. American Alliance for Health, Physical Education, and Recreation, National Association for Girls and Women in Sport, 1201 16th St, NW, Washington, DC 20036. Examined: none. (1977/78. $1.50 pap.)
Aud: Jh, Hs, Jc, Cl, Pl

No edition of this annual guide has been examined. However, based on the high quality of the other guides and rulebooks published by the National Association for Girls and Women in Sport, it is important to bring this rulebook to your attention. SLB

SS 816
Soccer Rules. a. illus. National Federation of State High School Associations, Federation Place, Box 98, Elgin, IL 60120. Examined: 1977. Brice B. Durbin, ed. 71p. $.85 pap.
Aud: Jh, Hs, Pl

Includes photographs and names and addresses of the soccer rules committee. The inside cover lists major rules revisions. There is no index, but the table of contents provides access to subject areas. In addition to the list of rules, there are comments on the rules; suggestions for tournament progression; dual officiating system; and a lengthy play rulings section, arranged in the order of the official rules, which gives situations and the correct ruling for that situation. SLB

SS 817
Softball Guide. 1939. a. bibl. index. illus. American Alliance for Health, Physical Education, and Recreation, National Association for Girls and Women in Sport, 1201 16th St NW, Washington, DC 20036. Examined: 1977/79. Donna A. Lopiano, ed. 185p. $2.25 pap.
Aud: Jh, Hs, Jc, Cl, Pl

Softball has been linked with volleyball as well as with track and field in various previous editions. This guide includes the official softball rules for girls and women, with an index. Explanations of officiating are also included. There are articles on tips and techniques and an annotated bibliography, as well as a listing of audiovisual aids and recent softball research. SLB

SS 818
Softball Rules. 1939. bi-a. index. American Alliance for Health, Physical Education, and Recreation, National Association for Girls and Women in Sport, 1201 16th St, NW, Washington, DC 20036. Examined: 1976/78. 153p. $.75 pap. (1977/79.)
Aud: Jh, Hs, Jc, Cl, Pl

These rules are reprinted as a separate publication from the National Association for Girls and Women in Sport's current **Softball Guide**. An index is included. SLB

SS 819
Sports Afield Fishing Annual. 1938. a. bibl. illus. The Hearst Corp., 57th St at Eighth Ave, New York, NY 10019. Examined: 1975. Lamar Underwood, ed. 136p. $1.25 pap.
Aud: Pl

This magazine-format guide is comprised of a series of

feature articles on all types of fishing by different authors. There are articles on various types of fish, equipment, and strategy. An annotated list of fishing books and a list of catalogs that might be of interest are also included. There are many photographs. SLB

SS 820

Sports Afield Gun Annual. ISSN 0490-5326. 1953. a. illus. Hearst Corporation, 57th St at Eighth Ave, New York, NY 10019. Examined: 1975. Lamar Underwood, ed. 144p. $1.25 pap.
Aud: Pl

Lists new guns in catalog form, divided by shotguns, high-power rifles, rimfire rifles, and handguns. Catalog entries include a photograph, description, and price. There are far more feature articles than usually found in this type of annual. The articles are longer and provide far more statistical and comparative information than most gun annuals. There are, for example, gun specification charts and performance tables, an annotated list of books for gun buffs, and a directory of firearms and distributors. SLB

SS 821

Sports Afield Hunting Annual. a. bibl. illus. The Hearst Corp., 57th St at Eighth Ave, New York, NY 10019. Examined: 1976. Lamar Underwood, ed. 120p. $1.25 pap.
Aud: Pl

This magazine-format annual includes a series of feature articles on all types of hunting, each by a different author. Covers both bird and animal hunting with some discussion of equipment. An annotated list of books for hunters and a list of catalogs that might be of interest are included. There are many photographs. SLB

SS 822

Sports All Stars Baseball. 1953. a. illus. Maco Publishing Co., 380 Madison Ave, New York, NY 10017. Examined: 1976. Vito Stellino, ed. 74p. $1.25 pap.
Aud: Pl

This magazine-format baseball annual is primarily devoted to a few feature articles on professional players. There are photographs and previous season statistics of American League and National League All-Star players. There is also a forecast for each league by the editor. If one cannot select all of the magazine-format baseball annuals, this would be the first to pass over. SLB

SS 823

The Story of the Olympic Games; 776 B.C. to (year.) 1936. quadrennial. index. J. B. Lippincott, E Washington Sq, Philadelphia, PA 19105. Examined: 1965; 1977. John Kieran, Arthur Daley, and Pat Jordan, eds. 575p. $12.50.
Aud: Hs, Jc, Cl, Pl

Prior to the 1977 edition which covers winter games, only summer games were included. There is a descriptive chapter on each Summer Olympics held, arranged by year. The description gives many highlights from the games, including any unusual events that occurred and the political environment at the time. A full record of past winners is provided. SLB

SS 824

Street and Smith's Baseball Yearbook. ISSN 0491-1520. 1941. a. illus. Conde Nast Publications, 350 Madison Ave, New York, NY 10017. Examined: 1976. Sam E. Andre, ed. 136p. $1.25 pap.
Aud: Pl

Contains special articles and an American and National League roundup which discusses each team's previous season. There is a composite box score of the previous World Series. The lack of statistics, records, and directories makes this yearbook more suited for popular reading than reference. SLB

SS 825

Street and Smith's College and Pro Official Basketball Yearbook. ISSN 0092-511X. 1970/71. a. illus. Conde Nast Publications, 350 Madison Ave, New York, NY 10017. Examined: 1974/75. Jim O'Brien, ed. 167p. $1 pap.
Aud: Pl

Begins with previous season ratings, college statistics, all-time high school records, the college tournament schedule for current season, and women's outlook. The college preview is arranged by region, not by individual teams. The professional preview is also arranged by region and includes a short paragraph on each team and regional schedules. There is a complete college schedule at the end. SLB

SS 826

Street and Smith's Official Yearbook; College Football. ISSN 0092-3214. 1940. a. index. illus. Conde Nast Publications, 350 Madison Ave, New York, NY 10017. Examined: 1976. Sam E. Andre, ed. 176p. $1.50 pap.
Aud: Pl

Easy-to-read, magazine-like format. Begins with an index of teams. There is a descriptive national preview, and a short discussion of each team, arranged by division. Includes schedules and a selectors' chart which indicates the comparative strength of the teams scheduled to play. SLB

SS 827
Street and Smith's Official Yearbook; Pro Football. ISSN 0092-3214. 1972. a. illus. Conde Nast Publications, 350 Madison Ave, New York, NY 10017. Examined: 1976. Sam D. Andre, ed. 160p. $1.50 pap.
Aud: Pl

This yearbook is also in an easy-to-read, magazine-like format. It includes information about the draft and a description of previous season Super Bowl and division championships. There is a three-page article on each team, arranged by American and National Conference, then by division. The articles cover team leaders, current schedules, previous season scores, roster of veterans, rookies, and free agents. Also lists members of the professional Hall of Fame. Provides brief information on each team in the Canadian Football League. NFC and AFC previous season records and the current NFL schedule are also provided. SLB

SS 828
Swimming and Diving Case Book. a. illus. National Federation of State High School Associations, Federation Place, Box 98, Elgin, IL 60120. Examined: 1977/78. Brice B. Durbin, ed. 47p. $1.10 pap.
Aud: Jh, Hs, Pl

Arranged in the order of the official rules of the Federation. There is no index, but the table of contents lists general subject areas. Situations that have been developed from questions raised in administering interscholastic meets are included. The situation, the ruling on the decision that was made, and comments referring to the appropriate official swimming and diving rules are included. Appendixes give guidelines for judging diving, illustrations of diving silhouettes, and a diving scoring table. SLB

SS 829
Swimming and Diving Rules and Records. (Continues: Swimming Rules.) a. index. National Federation of State High School Associations, Federation Place, Box 98, Elgin, IL 60120. Examined: 1977/78. Brice B. Durbin, ed. 111p. $1.05 pap.
Aud: Jh, Hs, Pl

Includes photographs, names and addresses of the Swimming and Diving Rules Committee. Major rule revisions are listed inside the cover. The rules have a complete index. There is also information on how to apply for the honor roll, and a list of honor roll members, boys and girls, for the past season. There are state meet results for the previous season and winners, by state, for boys and girls. The state meet listings give overall scores for the school, results, and time for each event. Information on how to apply for record listing with the Federation is included. Also includes the National Interscholastic Swimming Records, and all-time winners for boys high school, girls high school, and prep school. SLB

SS 830
Tennis Annual. 1966. a. illus. Tennis Features, 495 Westport Ave, Norwalk, CT 06856. Examined: 1976. Shepherd Campbell, ed. 128p. $3.
Aud: Pl

First published as the February issue of *Tennis Magazine,* the **Annual** can also be purchased separately. There are features on tennis instruction, and the previous season record coverage is extensive, including player statistics, tournament results, pro, amateur, junior champions, and all-time records. Other features follow in the form of special reports and perspectives on players for the current season. There is a preview/review for other racquet sports, i.e., badminton, paddleball, paddle tennis, platform tennis, racquetball, squash, and table tennis. None of the other racquet sports has a separate annual reporting service at this time. SLB

SS 831
Tennis—Badminton—Squash Guide. ISSN 0065-7042. (Continues: Tennis-Badminton Guide.) 1972/74. bi-a. bibl. illus. American Alliance for Health, Physical Education, and Recreation, National Association for Girls and Women in Sport, 1201 16th St, NW, Washington, DC 20036. Examined: 1976/1978. Sharon L. Van Oteghen, Georganna S. Cottman, and Caryl M. Newhoff, eds. 230p. $2.50 pap.
Aud: Jh, Hs, Jc, Cl, Pl

Includes a separate section for each sport; the tennis section is the most extensive. Each section includes articles on technique and strategy, the rules, bibliographies, and a list of visual aids. For tennis and badminton, there is also information on techniques of officiating. The names and addresses for each committee involved with this guide are provided. SLB

SS 832

Track and Field Guide. (Continues: Softball-Track and Field Guide.) 1962/64. a. bibl. illus. American Alliance for Health, Physical Education, and Recreation, National Association for Girls and Women in Sport, 1201 16th St, NW, Washington, DC 20036. Examined: 1976/78. Elizabeth Sadler, ed. 174p. $1.75 pap.
Aud: Jh, Hs, Jc, Cl, Pl

Track and Field Guide, formerly a biennial, is scheduled to be published annually as of 1978. It will maintain the current title, but it will only contain rules. Biennial editions, under the title *Track and Field Tips and Techniques*, will continue, with the next one scheduled for 1979 publication. The last biennial guide contains the rules, NAGWS officiating services, discussions of pentathlon and cross country, articles on technique, a bibliography, and records from elementary through collegiate, American World, and Olympic competitions. There is an appendix with illustrations of required forms and a glossary. Other than the rules and required forms, it is expected that the rest of the material will be in the biennial *Track and Field Tips and Techniques*. SLB

SS 833

Track and Field Rules and Records; Boys and Girls. a. index. illus. National Federation of State High School Associations, Federation Place, Elgin, IL 60120. Examined: 1972; 1977. Clifford B. Fagan, ed. 135p. $1.50 pap. (1978.)
Aud: Jh, Hs, Pl

Rules that have been changed are screened for quick reference. Lists previous season results for both boys and girls, as well as boys' and girls' all-time national interscholastic records. SLB

SS 834

United States Figure Skating Association. Official USFSA Rulebook. (Continues: USFSA Rulebook.) 1941. a. index. illus. United States Figure Skating Association, Sears Crescent, Suite 500, City Hall Plaza, Boston, MA 02108. Examined: 1976/77. 267p. $3.50.
Aud: Pl

The regulations and rules are listed by type, e.g., trophy and medal, amateur states, etc. Figures and jumps are illustrated. Past history of United States Figure Skating Association, all-time champions, and the latest competitions schedules are included. SLB

SS 835

United States Polo Association. Yearbook. ISSN 0083-3118. 1890. a. index. illus. United States Polo Association, 1301 W 22nd St, Executive Plaza, Suite 706, Oak Brook, IL 60521. Examined: 1977. 224p. $10.
Aud: Pl

Serves as a guide to association rules, events, and past records. Names of current and past officers and committee members are listed. The rules include an index and appropriate illustrations. Also listed are all member clubs, schools, and colleges. All events sponsored by the association are listed, with entry qualifications. Past winners and team members are given, often with a photograph of winners from season immediately preceding. For each circuit there is a summary and list of results from the past year. Finally, there is a list of recommended handicaps for members which includes the member's name, club, and address. SLB

SS 836

United States Ski Association. Directory. ISSN 0083-3258. a. index. United States Ski Association, 1726 Champa St, Suite 300, Denver, CO 80202. Examined: 1976/77. 77p.
Aud: Sa

First lists the names, addresses, and officers of all committees of the association and of all affiliated associations. Then the by-laws of the association and the names, addresses, and phone numbers of all association members are listed. This membership list includes organizations as well as individuals. SLB

SS 837

United States Squash Racquets Association. Official Year Book. ISSN 0083-3398. 1925. a. index. illus. United States Squash Racquets Association, 211 Ford Rd, Bala-Cynwyd, PA 19004. Examined: 1977/78. 143p. $6 pap.
Aud: Pl, Sa

A guide to national and regional squash racquet activity and tournaments. Lists national championships, limited international contests, and results of national association activities for Canada, Mexico, intercollegiate, and professional. There are full reports of the United States Women's Squash Racquets Association and regional reports from around the country. Photographs are often included in the reports. Names and addresses of the officers for both the U.S. Squash Racquets Association and the Women's Squash Racquets Association, national tournament rules, playing rules, and historical data such as past champions are included. There is an index to advertisers. Included with the yearbook is a separate 12-page pamphlet with the current season tournament schedules, including date, location, events, and ball and geographic restrictions. SLB

SS 838
United States Tennis Association. The Official USTA Yearbook and Tennis Guide with the Official Rules. (Continues: United States Lawn Tennis Association Yearbook. ISSN 0083-1557.) 1937. a. bibl. index. illus. Harold O. Zimman, 156 Broad St, Lynn, MA 01901. Examined: 1977. 528p. $6.
Aud: Pl, Sa

Extensive directory of USTA officers and committees, with addresses. Other sections are concerned with Association business, such as changes in the by-laws. A retrospective listing of USTA officers since 1881 is provided. Describes the previous season in detail, including results and player portraits. Lists many awards with all previous winners. For each tennis association, or section of the USTA, provides a list of officers with addresses and a photograph, description of the previous year's activities, former winners of major championships, and rankings within the section. There are also past records for all age groups; international results and records; Davis Cup history; and results and history for several major competitions. Includes the official rules of lawn tennis and the constitution of the USTA. While the table of contents is very complete, the yearbook is somewhat difficult to use without a good subject index. SLB

SS 839
United States Volleyball Association. Annual Official Volleyball Rules and Reference Guide. ISSN 0083-3592. (Continues: U.S. Volleyball Association. Official Volleyball Guide and Rules Book.) 1920. a. bibl. illus. United States Volleyball Association, Guynes Printing Co., 615 N Stanton St, El Paso, TX 79001. Dist: H. E. Wilson Co., Box 77065, San Francisco, CA 94107. Examined: 1977. Marvin D. Veronee, ed. 240p. $2.50 pap.
Aud: Pl, Sa

Contains information on the United States Volleyball Association and volleyball in regions, with addresses of regional offices, names of officials, and schedules for tournaments. There are also feature articles. Previous season championships are listed. Missing is a listing of retrospective championships. There is a bibliography of books, films, and magazines on volleyball. Sections on becoming an official, scoring, conducting tournaments, and the official rules of the association for playing the game are also included. SLB

SS 840
Volleyball Guide. (Continues in part: Volleyball Guide. ISSN 0065-7050. bi-a.) 1957/59. a. illus. American Alliance for Health, Physical Education, and Recreation, National Association for Girls and Women in Sport, 1201 16th St, NW, Washington, DC 20036. Examined: 1976/77. Helen Knierim, ed. 93p. $1.75 pap. (1977/78.)
Aud: Jh, Hs, Jc, Cl, Pl

A volleyball guide has been published by this association for several decades, often in combination with another sport, such as softball. In the 1957/59 edition it became a separate, extensive biennial guide with articles, a bibliography, and rules. In 1977 another change was made in order to keep pace with changes in the sport. It is now a shorter, annual publication which just contains official rules and interpretations, and regulations for competition officiating. Some of the information in the older guide is now contained in **Basketball-Volleyball Tips and Techniques,** a biennial publication first issued in July 1977. The rules are also available in a separate publication, *Volleyball Rules* (1977/78, $.75 pap.), which is also published by the association. SLB

SS 841
Volleyball Rules. a. index. illus. National Federation of State High School Associations, Federation Place, Box 98, Elgin, IL 60120. Examined: 1977/78. Clifford B. Fagan, ed. 67p. $.85 pap.
Aud: Jh, Hs, Pl

Includes photographs, names, and addresses of Volleyball Rules Committee. The major rule revisions are noted inside the cover. The rules are for both boys and girls and are indexed, with rule changes indicated by screened background. Includes illustrations of playing area and signals. There are also comments on the rules, state meet results for previous season, boys and girls state champions, tournament procedures, officiating mechanics, scoresheet, and line-up sheet. SLB

SS 842
Who's Who in Baseball. 1915. a. illus. Who's Who in Baseball Magazine Co., 250 Hudson St, New York, NY 10013. Examined: 1968; 1976; 1977. Seymour Siwoff, ed. 160p. $1.50 pap.
Aud: Pl

Alphabetically arranged by player with a separate section for pitchers. Entries for each player include picture, birth place and date, and lifetime playing record. Those included seem to be only players that are still active. The 1977 edition has added box scores for league championship series and World Series, as well as team statistics and standing for previous season. SLB

SS 843
World of Tennis. 1969. a. index. illus. Simon and Schuster, 1230 Ave of the Americas, New York, NY 10020. Examined: 1973. John Barrett, ed. 352p. $3.95 pap.
Aud: Pl, Sa

Subtitle: "A BP and Commercial Union yearbook." The emphasis is on British tennis. Begins with a description and history of BP International Tennis Fellowship. There are articles on "Putting Your Game Together"; discussion and complete round results of four major world open championships; previous Commercial Union Grand Prix season winners in all geographic areas; previous season results of world match play; description, round results, and all-time records and winners of international team competitions; and international rankings. Biographies of all-time greats are alphabetically arranged and include birthplace and date, name of spouse, and playing records. Includes a section on tennis in the U.S.; previous season results of national tournaments, listed by country; and historical data for six major tournaments. SLB

SS 844
Wrestling Officials Manual. 1964. bi-a. National Federation of State High School Associations, Federation Place, Box 98, Elgin, IL 60120. Examined: 1976/77; 1977/78. Clifford B. Fagan, ed. 48p. $.85 pap.
Aud: Sa

Intended for use at meets and tournaments sponsored by member schools of the Federation to provide uniform procedures in wrestling matches at the interscholastic level. There is no index, but the table of contents guides one to broad subject areas. The subjects covered include pre-meet duties; during the match; awarding points; out-of-bounds, stalling, illegal and potentially dangerous holds; technical violations; near falls and falls; injuries and defaults; stalemates; coaching and correction of errors; and interpretations of the official rules. SLB

SS 845
Wrestling Rules. a. illus. National Federation of State High School Associations, Federation Place, Box 98, Elgin, IL 60120. Examined: 1977/78. Brice B. Durbin, ed. 95p. $1.05 pap.
Aud: Jh, Hs, Pl

Names, addresses, and photographs of the Wrestling Rules Committee are included. The rules do not have an index, but a table of contents lists the general subject areas. Illustrations of equipment are provided. There are photographs to illustrate holds and an illustrated officials signal chart. Previous season state meet results are arranged by state, and indicate each school's total scores, and winners in each weight division. There is an article on controlling weight reduction. SLB

TRANSPORTATION

SS 846
Aircraft Owners and Pilots Association. AOPA's Airports U.S.A. (Continues: AOPA Airport Directory. ISSN 0065-4906.) 1962. a. index. illus. Aircraft Owners and Pilots Association, Air Rights Bldg, 7315 Wisconsin Ave, Washington, DC 20014. Examined: 1977. Maria L. St. Peter, ed. 608p. $7.50; $4.75 to AOPA members.
Aud: Pl, Sa

Subtitle: "A special listing of over 13,500 aircraft landing sites, plus supplemental material prepared especially for general aviation pilots and aircraft owners." Preliminary information in the book includes weather and flight information numbers, airport customs facilities, aeronautical charts, terminal control area graphics, and airport diagrams (arranged alphabetically by state). The major portion of the directory is an alphabetical listing of U.S. landing facilities, including airports in U.S. territories, arranged alphabetically by state. Each listing gives name of city or town, name of airport, airport identifier, sectional chart, geographical coordinates, field elevation, distance and direction airport is from city, area code and telephone number, runway headings, flight hazards, brand of aircraft fuel available, type of transportation available from the airport to the community, type of food service at airport, lights on runway, type of plane storage, landing fee information, overnight lodgings and tourist attractions, etc. After the airport section, there are listings for seaplane bases and for heliports. Privately owned and operated airport facilities are included in the listings. Government facilities closed to the general public are not listed. There is a cross-reference index arranged by airport name. KSK

SS 847
American Association of State Highway Officials.

AASHO Reference Book of Member Department Personnel and Committees. ISSN 0516-9445. a. illus. American Association of State Highway Officials, 341 National Press Bldg, Washington, DC 20004. Examined: 1973. 144p. $2.50. (1978.)
Aud: Sa
Indexed in: *Engineering Index.*

Presents data about the Association and its members. Includes general office information, a list of officers for the year, a statement of the purpose of the organization, a map of the U.S. showing the regions of the organization, a chart showing AASHO committee structure, a list of annual meetings and past presidents, information on the regional associations of highway officials, and the awards given by the AASHO. The main section is a directory of member department personnel, arranged alphabetically by state, listing name of department, address and phone number, and department personnel (central office staff and division engineers). The directory is followed by a listing of AASHO committees, including standing committees, subcommittees, and special committees. Finally, there is a directory of college/university engineering departments. NLE

SS 848

American Public Transit Association. Transit Fact Book. (Continues: American Transit Association. Transit Fact Book. ISSN 0149-3132.) 1974/75. a. index. American Public Transit Association, 1100 17th St, NW, Suite 1200, Washington, DC 20036. Examined: 1976/77. 47p.
Aud: Cl, Sa

Contains a summary of transit policy for the year, a glossary of transit industry terms, and a glossary of financial terms. Also presents statistical data related to revenue, fares, seating capacity of buses, energy consumption, etc., in both tabular and graphic form. EM

SS 849

American Trucking Trends. Statistical Report. (Continues: American Trucking Associations Report. ISSN 0066-0892.) 1947. a. index. illus. American Trucking Associations, Department of Economics, 1616 P St, NW, Washington, DC 20036. Examined: 1974, 40p.; 1976 statistical suppl. 24p.
Aud: Sa

Contains charts and graphs on the American trucking industry. After a page devoted to the structure of the industry and another page that briefly surveys industry activities for the year, the rest of the report gives brief narrative summaries and statistical charts on such items as: industry growth, ton-miles, mileage and safety, carrier size and location, motor freight tonnage, products, revenue, taxes, costs, manpower, equipment, and innovations. A subject index is provided. A statistical supplement to the 1975 edition had to be issued because of delays caused by the Interstate Commerce Commission's (ICC) redefinition of terms and the adoption of a new uniform system of accounts. Much of the information on historical trends and patterns has been modified, and other published data from the ICC has also been delayed, sometimes for as long as two years. Therefore, the American Trucking Associations has published an abbreviated version of *Trends*, which includes discontinuations of some data and tables and indicates some inconsistencies in data already included. KSK

SS 850

Analysis of the World Tank Ship Fleet. 1942. a. illus. Bulk Cargo Ship Product Group, Sun Shipbuilding and Dry Dock Co., Chester, PA 19013. Examined: 1976. Larry Liddle, ed. $10.
Aud: Sa

Contains information on the world tank ship fleet, including statistical tables, charts, and written summaries. After a brief summary and a conclusions section, the first major section focuses on the world tank ship fleet. Data here include world inventory, flag of registry, carrying capacity, average speed by flag, deadweight tonnage and speed, distribution of capacity, new construction, and specialty vessels. The next section discusses tank ship charter markets. The last section gives statistical tabulations on such items as carrying capacity changes during the year by flag of registry, average vessel characteristics by deadweight tonnage, ownership by group according to flag of registry (world fleet and U.S. owned tank ships), and tank ships on order or under construction by deadweight tonnage composition and country of construction. KSK

SS 851

Boat Owner's Buying Guide. ISSN 0067-9321. 1959. a. index. illus. Yachting Publishing Corp., 50 W 44th St, New York, NY 10036. Examined: 1974. Kimball Aamodt, ed. 296p. (1977. $2.50 pap.)
Aud: Pl

As the title suggests, the focus is on boats and equipment that can be purchased. There are many advertisements in the magazine-format guide, but the general listings seem to have been prepared independently of the manufacturers. A large portion of the book is arranged by type of boat, such as inboard, specialized, outboard, etc. Under each of these headings, there is a list of manufacturers which includes available models, size, draft, horsepower, and basic price. There are also equipment listings which cover all important details, and a listing of marine services, such as architects, mail order firms, testing services, etc., arranged by state, which provides the address of each company and a few details. An index of boats, engines, and equipment, and a separate advertisers index are also included. SLB

SS 852
Boating Industry Associations. BIA Certification Handbook. ISSN 0067-9402. 1956. a. illus. Boating Industry Associations, 401 N Michigan Ave, Chicago, IL 60611. Examined: 1978. 61p. $5 pap.
Aud: Sa

The Boating Industry Associations is a federation of manufacturers of all types of boating equipment. The certification program outlined in this handbook is intended "to help manufacturers comply with established standards and safety regulations, and to help inform the public of such compliance when purchasing equipment." The handbook, then, is a listing of the specifications for safety certification of boats, trailers, outboard motor oil, and outboard motor horsepower. Illustrations are included when appropriate. KSK

SS 853
Chilton's Auto Repair Manual. ISSN 0069-3634. 1968. a. index. illus. Chilton Book Co., Automotive Editorial Department, Chilton Way, Radnor, PA 19089. Examined: 1978. John H. Weise, ed. $13.95.
Aud: Jc, Cl, Pl, Sa

Divided into two basic sections. The car section lists individual makes and models by name under the manufacturer. Entries include engine identification codes, diagrams depicting engine firing order and distributor wiring, specification tables, and a description with illustrations of various systems and component parts. The second section, the unit repair section, describes trouble-shooting and overhaul procedures for the major components and systems of the cars listed in the first section. It covers charging and starting systems, ignition, carburetors, emission control, engine rebuilding, brakes, steering, and mechanical data. Metric conversion tables are provided at the end of the volume. Separate indexes are provided for each manufacturer listing in the car section. There are also indexes to each unit repair section. The table of contents serves as an index to the volume as a whole. KSK

SS 854
Containerization: A Bibliography. ISSN 0069-9314. (Continues: Bibliography of Economics of Containerization.) 1967. a. bibl. Northwestern University, Transportation Center Library, Levercone Hall, 2001 Sheridan Rd, Evanston, IL 60201. Examined: 1968/69. Dorothy V. Ramm, comp. 47p. $3. (1975/76. 26p. $2.)
Aud: Sa

A listing of materials in the collection of the Transportation Center Library. The 1970 edition supplements and updates the *Bibliography on Economics of Containerization* (1968), which covers the period January 1965 to June 1968. The material relates to both the technical and economic aspects of containerization. The bibliography is divided into seven parts: general and intermodal, air, motor, rail, inland water, marine, and bibliographies. Most of the citations are for periodical articles. Information for each entry includes author, title, name of magazine, date, page number, whether the item is illustrated, and the languages of the article (if it is bilingual). For books, information includes author, title, edition statement (if any), place of publication, publisher, date, and the number of pages. Finally at the end of the bibliography, there is a list of periodicals indexed with addresses and a list of book publishers, also with addresses. KSK

SS 855
Cycle Buyers Guide. 1968. a. illus. Ziff-Davis Publishing Co., One Park Ave, New York, NY 10016. Examined: 1977. Bill Ochel Tree, ed. 144p. $1.95 pap.
Aud: Pl

Primarily a catalog of current motorcycles, arranged by manufacturer. Under the manufacturer, each model is described in detail, with a photograph. There are similar listings for minicycles, minibikes, and motorized bicycles. The accessories list includes photographs and descriptions. There are a few articles, a competition calendar, ten best buys, and fifteen cycle tests. A chart with the laws and regulations concerning motorcycles in all states and a listing of catalogs and brochures available are also included. SLB

SS 856
Cycle Tests. (Cover title: Popular Cycling's Cycle Tests.) a. illus. Coronado Book Corp., 12301 Wilshire Blvd, Los Angeles, CA 90025. Examined: 1974; 1977. Tom Beesley, ed. 99p. $1.50 pap.
Aud: Pl

This magazine-format annual would be of interest to those in the market for a motorcycle and to those who want to keep up with new models. The tests on each model discussed are apparently made just for this publication. There are about 20 models tested. The three- or four-page entry for each bike includes good-quality photographs, a discussion of performance and special features, a recommendation, a numerical evaluation which assigns a potential of 100 points to each model, and specifications for the model. SLB

SS 857

Cycle World Road Test Annual and Buyer's Guide. (Continues: Cycle World Road Test Annual.) 1971. a. illus. Cycle World Magazine, 1499 Monrovia Ave, Newport Beach, CA 92663. Examined: 1976. Bob Atkinson, ed. 202p. $2 pap.
Aud: Pl

Includes about 20 tests (e.g., road tests, enduro tests, motocross tests, etc.) for a variety of specific motorcycle models. There is a two- or three-page description of the test results for each model, photographs, and model specifications. The other major portion of the annual is the buyer's guide, arranged by manufacturer and model. For each model there is a photograph, description, specifications, and suggested retail price. There are good-quality photographs throughout. SLB

SS 858

Directory of Shipowners, Shipbuilders and Marine Engineers. ISSN 0070-6310. 1902. a. index. IPC Industrial Press, Dorset House, Stamford St, London SE1 9LU, England. Dist: IPC America, 205 E 42nd St, New York, NY 10017. Examined: 1977. Douglas Woodyard, ed. 1386p. $20.40.
Aud: Sa

Arranged in 14 sections including a section on shipowners with names and addresses of shipping companies, directors or partners, marine and engineer superintendents, ships in the fleets, and the builders of the respective hulls and engines; a list of container shipping services giving names and addresses of shipping companies with ships running regular services for transporting containers, and names and characteristics of ships in fleets and of ships on order; a list of ferry operating companies that indicates names, addresses, characteristics of ships, and the services in which the companies operate; a tugs and service craft section; a listing of shipbuilders, ship repairers, and drydock owners with names and addresses, directors and principal officers, capacities of berths and docks; a geographical index to shipbuilders and repairers; a section on marine engine builders; a list of consultants including naval architects, marine engineers, ship surveyors, and specialists; and lists of experiment tanks, international organizations, British associations, other national associations, classification societies, and government and official agencies. Finally, there are four indexes: ship index (names of ships and owning companies), personnel index to directors and personnel listed in shipowners and other sections, a general index, and an index to the advertisers. KSK

SS 859

Greenwood's Guide to Great Lakes Shipping. ISSN 0072-7490. 1958. a. illus. Freshwater Press, 463 The Arcade, Cleveland, OH 44114. Examined: 1968, 678p.; 16th ed., 1975. John O. Greenwood, ed. $18. (v. 19, 1978. 562p. $22.)
Aud: Sa

Provides technical and non-technical information regarding all phases of Great Lakes commercial traffic and shipping. Each section is tab indexed, and there is also a table of contents. There are 26 sections covering bulk freight vessels, package freighters and carferries, crane vessels and cargo barges, self-unloaders and tank vessels, tug vessels, ocean-saltwater vessels and fleets, fuels used by vessels, compartment-carrying capacities of freighters, an alphabetical listing of Great Lakes fleets, grain elevators, ore loading and unloading docks, coal docks, general cargo docks and stevedoring, a longevity table, port profiles, salvage, etc. Includes mileage tables, a glossary of shipping terms, and fold-out maps. Scattered throughout the directory are colored plates of ships. Each section begins with an explanation of the terms used in that particular part. Advertisements are scattered throughout, and there is an advertising index at the end of the volume arranged both by category and by city. KSK

SS 860

Inland River Guide. 1972. a. index. illus. Waterways Journal, 701 Chemical Bldg, 721 Olive St, St. Louis, MO 63101. Examined: 1976. Dan Owen, ed. 542p. $20.
Aud: Sa

Divided into ten major sections. The first section lists barge and towing companies alphabetically by name of company. Information on each company includes address, area served, whether it has towboats and barges for hire, personnel of company, and affiliated firms. Section two lists public terminals by river locations. For readers who know the name of a company but not its specific location on a waterway, an alphabetical index has been compiled. Also lists private terminals. Fleeting and harbor services are listed in section three by river location. Section four, shipyards, and repair yards, is arranged by river location and includes an alphabetical listing of yards. Section five presents listings of marine contractors and dredging firms. Section six lists midstreamers by river location. Remaining sections are listings of brokers/professionals, including marine surveyors, marine divers, salvage firms, marine insurance, and marine schools; distributors/suppliers of such items as anchors, barge cleaning equipment, deck equipment, diesel engines, etc.; and government agencies/associations, including U.S. Coast Guard, U.S. engineers, and Public Health Service facilities. The final section, Miscellaneous, covers marine leasing/financing, marine radio stations, bridge clearances, and local statistics. Each of these ten sections is tab indexed. Illustrated advertisements are scattered throughout. KSK

SS 861
Institute of Transportation Engineers. Membership Directory. ISSN 0148-1070. (Continues: Institute of Traffic Engineers. Membership Directory.) 1977. a. Institute of Transportation Engineers, 1815 N Fort Meyer St, Suite 905, Arlington, VA 22209. Examined: 1977. Bess Balchen, ed. 224p. $20.
Aud: Sa

Along with an alphabetical and geographical directory of members, the volume includes lists of past officers, honorary members, and staff members. Member listings include name, home and office addresses, and office phone numbers. EM

SS 862
International Road Federation. World Survey of Current Research and Development on Roads and Road Transport. (1977 is 12th ed.) a. index. International Road Federation, 1023 Washington Bldg, Washington, DC. Examined: 1977. 744p.
Aud: Cl, Sa

Contains surveys of roads and describes the state of all projects in 27 countries. Also updates information for 24 areas previously surveyed. There is a subject index to project reports. KSK

SS 863
International Symposium on Transport and Handling of Minerals. Minerals Transportation: Proceedings. ISSN 0094-7466. 1971. bi-a. bibl. index. illus. Miller Freeman Publications, 500 Howard St, San Francisco, CA 94105. Examined: 1st ed., 1971. 421p. $24.50. (2nd ed., 1973. 448p. $27.50.)
Aud: Sa

Geared for the mineral and transport industries. Examines trends and innovations in the shipping and handling of minerals. The opening pages give brief biographies of the authors (accompanied in most cases by a photograph) and abstracts of their papers. This is followed by the papers themselves. Most of the papers are technically oriented, covering such topics as dusting and spillage of ore cargoes, deterioration of coal during storage and transportation, briquetting and compacting methods, ports, pneumatic handling, ocean transportation, marine insurance, and impediments to transport innovation. Many of the articles contain illustrations and tables. Some include bibliographical references. Following a number of the papers are transcriptions of discussion or question and answer periods. There is a subject index. KSK

SS 864
Jane's All the World's Aircraft. ISSN 0075-3017. (Continues: Jane's All the World's Air-Ships.) 1909. a. index. illus. Macdondald and Jane's Publishers, Paulton House, 8 Shepherdess Walk, London N1 7LW, England. Dist: Franklin Watts, 730 Fifth Ave, New York, NY 10019. Examined: 67th ed., 1976/77. John W. R. Taylor, ed. 860p. $72.50.
Aud: Jc, Cl, Pl, Sa

"Intended to provide its professional readers with a completely reliable and up-to-date reference work on the products of the world's aircraft industry." Prefatory matter includes alphabetical and classified lists of advertisers, a foreword outlining important events in the aerospace and aircraft field during the preceding year, and a list of official records. The main body of the book is divided into the following subject areas: aircraft, homebuilt aircraft (including man-powered and racing aircraft), sailplanes and hang gliders, lighter-than-air airships, lighter-than-air balloons, RPVs and targets, air-launched missiles, spaceflight and research rockets, satellites and spacecraft launched during the year, and aero-engines. Each section is arranged by country, and within each country, aircraft industries are listed in alphabetical order. Each company's entry lists head office, telephone numbers, and directors, and provides a brief summary of its activities and a description of the various types of aircraft that it manufactures. Most of the aircraft descriptions are accompanied by a photograph and sketches of the aircraft. Includes indexes to the aircraft, sailplanes, missiles, rockets, and aero-engines described in the text. Advertisements, some in color, are in the front of the volume. Photos, diagrams, and detailed specifications provide reliable, up-to-date information of surprising depth and complexity. KSK

SS 865

Jane's Freight Containers. ISSN 0075-3033. 1968. a. illus. Macdonald and Jane's Publishers, Paulton House, 8 Shepherdess Walk, London N1 7LW, London. Dist: Franklin Watts, 730 Fifth Ave, New York, NY 10019. Examined: 7th ed., 1974/75. Patrick Finlay, ed. £15.95. (8th ed., 1976/77, 1300p., $72.50; 9th ed., 1977/78. $72.50.)
Aud: Cl, Pl, Sa

Covers port facilities and inland transport in Europe, Africa, Asia, Australia, and the Americas. Contains information on ship operators, non-vessel operating carriers, equipment leasing, containers of various sorts, international road and rail transport, and airports and air freight. Nearly any type of information on containerized shipping can be located here. The photographs, diagrams, and maps make the volume almost essential. In this directory, the photographs and brief essays on operations are virtually a text on this relatively new method of shipping and transportation. The title is so wide-ranging that it fulfills many needs as a general directory of business and industrial information. KSK

SS 866

Jane's Surface Skimmers; Hovercraft and Hydrofoils. ISSN 0075-305X. (Continues: Jane's Surface Skimmer Systems.) 1967/68. a. bibl. index. illus. B.P.C. Publishing, Paulton House, 8 Shepherdess Walk, London N1 7LW, England. Dist: Franklin Watts, 730 Fifth Ave, New York, NY 10019. Examined: 10th ed., 1976/77. Roy McLeavy, ed. 424p. $60.
Aud: Cl, Pl, Sa

A directory of manufacturers of air cushion vehicles (ACV), skimmers, and hydrofoils. Part one lists ACV manufacturers and design groups alphabetically by country, then by name of company. Information for each company includes address, executives, previous designs, and detailed analyses of the various models it manufactures. Photos and diagrams of the models are included in the listing. The following sections include ACV operators, ACV trailers and heavy lift systems, air cushion landing systems, tracked skimmers, and air cushion applicators, conveyors and pallot. Following these smaller sections is a longer directory of hydrofoil manufacturers. Next are additional smaller chapters on sailing skimmers, hydrofoil operators, powerplants, and propulsion systems. The final section includes a selected bibliography of books and articles on ACVs, hydrofoils, etc.; listings of licensing authorities, selected amateur-built hovercraft, ACV clubs and associations, ACV consultants, and hydrofoil consultants; and a glossary of ACV and hydrofoil terms. There is an index of company names and model names. Advertisements are in the beginning and end of the book. KSK

SS 867

Jane's World Railways. ISSN 0075-3084. 1951. a. illus. Macdonald and Jane's Publishers, Paulton House, 8 Shepherdess Walk, London N1 7LW, England. Dist: Franklin Watts, 730 Fifth Ave, New York, NY 10019. Examined: 1976. Paul J Goldsack, ed. £15.95. (1977. 580p. $72.50.)
Aud: Cl, Pl, Sa

Provides an alphabetical list of advertisers, then a classified list of manufacturers of locomotives, rolling stock, signalling and train control equipment, and diesel engines. Includes tabular information on railroads and information by country on rail systems and on rapid transit. The foreword paints a picture of railway economics, especially for the major countries. Includes details about legislation and important developments in national control. Filled with pictures and diagrams of rolling stock, this book is handy also for the make-from-scratch hobbyist. Information is clear, concise, and compact. The article on the National Railroad Passenger Corporation (Amtrak) is detailed enough for most beginning purposes. KSK

SS 868

Lloyd's Register of American Yachts. ISSN 0076-0226. 1903. a. index. illus. Lloyd's Register of Shipping, 17 Battery Place, New York, NY 10004. Examined: 1976. 1192p. $35.
Aud: Sa

Includes names, dimensions and full particulars of known U.S. and Canadian yachts. Yachts whose sail areas are less than 350 square feet or less than 35 feet in length on water line are excluded unless such crafts are owned by a subscriber to the book. The major section is an alphabetical arrangement by name of yacht. Entries include call letters, official number, name, former names, sail number, type, owner, port of registry, home port, size, builder, designer, year and place built, and engine particulars. There is also an index to private flags by owners' names; a color section illustrating flags; a listing of yachts by signal letters; former names of yachts with reference to present names; club abbreviations; and names and addresses of yacht owners. KSK

SS 869

Log of the Star Class: Official Rule Book. ISSN 0076-

9455. 1922. a. index. illus. The International Star Class Yacht Racing Association, 1301 Waukegan Rd, Glenview, IL 60025. Examined: 1976. C. Stanley Ogilvy, ed. 285p. $2 pap.
Aud: Pl, Sa

A directory of officers and fleets, as well as a rule book and a source of current and historic results and winners. Names and addresses for officers are included, as are addresses of the secretary of each district fleet. There is a summary of the world championship races, and a summary with complete results of all other races. Also includes the constitution of the association, a sample entry form, specifications, rules, names and addresses of active certified star measurers, and a lengthy directory of star class yachts. Entries in the directory indicate yacht name, fleet, owner, club, builder, and year built. There is an index of fleet symbols, an index of builders, and an index to the rules and regulations. KSK

SS 870
MVMA Motor Vehicle Facts and Figures. ISSN 0067-253X. (Continues: Automobile Facts and Figures; Motor Truck Facts.) 1927. a. index. illus. Motor Vehicle Manufacturers Association of the U.S., Statistics Department, 320 New Center Bldg, Detroit, MI 48202. Examined: 1976, 104p.; 1977. 96p. free.
Aud: Jc, Cl, Pl, Sa

The tabular data is divided into three major sections: production/registration; use and owners; and economic impact. The introduction provides an overview of events during the past year, presented in narrative form and illustrated with charts. The production section reviews factory sales, factory installations of selected equipment, world production and assemblies, U.S. motor vehicle retail sales, national and state registrations, average age of cars and trucks, and figures on motor buses. Part two shows the number of households that own cars, size and use of truck fleets, driver licenses by state, U.S. drivers by age and sex, number of Americans who drive to work, travel between cities, use of trucks, school buses, highway safety figures, traffic fatalities, fuel consumption, and pollution control devices. Part three gives tables on the motor vehicle industry and related employment, wholesalers, retail auto dealers, automotive parts, hardware stores, U.S. automotive exports and imports, and taxes on motor vehicles and highways. Each of the three sections is preceded by a one-page summary of trends in the industry during the past year. There is a subject index at the end of the book. NLE

SS 871
Merchant Vessels of the United States (Including Yachts). ISSN 0076-650X. 1866. a. index. U.S. Coast Guard, Department of Transportation, 400 7th St, SW, Washington, DC 20590. Dist: Superintendent of Documents, U.S. Government Printing Office, Washington, DC 20402. Examined: 1975. 2286p. $26.
Aud: Sa

Published in compliance with the provisions of the Act of Congress approved July 5, 1884. Contains the names of American merchant vessels and yachts having uncancelled marine documents, i.e., registers, enrollments and licenses, or licenses. An explanation of terms and abbreviations precedes the main list of vessels. Information for each vessel includes: its official number; signal and radio call letters (if any); rig designation; name of vessel; tonnage (gross and net); dimension in feet; hull; when built; where built; service; horsepower; name of owner; and home port. There is a brief list of mortgaged vessels and vessels that are lost, abandoned, or otherwise subject to removal from documentation. A list of ships arranged by signal and radio call letters follows. Another section provides a list of current names of ships indicating former names held by the ships, and a list of former ship names that indicates the name currently in use. Three briefer sections show vessels lost, vessels abandoned or removed for other causes, and vessels sold or transferred to aliens; all have been removed from official records. There is an index of managing owners which indicates the owner's address and the name and official number of his/her ship(s). A monthly supplement is available from the Coast Guard. KSK

SS 872
Moody's Transportation Manual. ISSN 0027-089X. 1928. a. illus. Moody's Investors Service, 99 Church St, New York, NY 10007. Examined: 1977. 1232p. $240.
Aud: Cl, Pl, Sa

Subtitle: "Railroads, airlines, shipping, traction, bus, and truck lines." Covers approximately 1000 enterprises, including oil pipe lines, bridge companies, and automobile and truck leasing and rental companies, in addition to those companies listed in the subtitle. Maps of many of the larger railroad companies are a useful feature. There are also maps for some airlines and bus companies. These are general maps only and do not provide full information on smaller, local routes. Based on stockholders' reports, reports to the Interstate Commerce Commission, and reports to the Securities and Exchange Commission. Numerous features analyze the structure of the industry and the various companies covered. Of special value is the analysis of the railroads. Similar in format, type of information, and value to other Moody publications. NLE

SS 873
Motor Auto Repair Manual. ISSN 0077-1708. 1938. a. index. illus. Hearst Books, Motor Book Department, 250 W 55th St, New York, NY 10019. Examined: 1976. Louis C. Forier, ed. $12.95. (1979. approx. 1300p. $14.95.)
Aud: Jc, Cl, Pl, Sa

Combines car maintenance and repair facts from over 300 factory manuals. Arranged in two sections, car information and general service information. Section one is arranged alphabetically by manufacturer and contains specific technical data and repair procedures. It includes specification data as well as the repair and service operations for each individual make, model, and year. The chapter on manufacturers' makes and models is preceded by an index of component systems and specific related service operations. Section two has information on component systems that are shared by several car makers. It lists technical data and hundreds of general service procedures for carburetors, alternators, transmissions, and other systems that are identical or substantially the same for any make or model. The manual is illustrated throughout with photographs and diagrams. KSK

SS 874
Motor Parts and Time Guide. ISSN 0077-1716. (Continues: Motor's Flat Rate and Parts Manual.) 1910. a. illus. Hearst Books, Motor Publications, 250 W 55th St, New York, NY 10019. Examined: 49th ed., 1977. David Lewis, ed. 1296p. $22.
Aud: Jc, Cl, Pl, Sa

Arranged in chapters devoted to particular car makes or models. The first page of each chapter contains a detailed operation and parts index. This is followed by car model identifications, front grille illustrations, and engine identification code. An operation time section and a parts section for each repair function follow. Specific functions include maintenance and lubrication, emission controls, tune-up and ignition, fuel system and intake manifold, exhaust system, starting motor, alternator, etc. Each of these functions is divided into time and parts. The times are compiled from available manufacturer and shop data and are provided only as an estimating guide. The parts entries indicate part name, car manufacturer's part number, interchangeability, and suggested retail price. Includes illustrations of auto parts as well as photos of front grilles. KSK

SS 875
Motor Truck Repair Manual. ISSN 0098-3624. (Continues: Motor's Truck and Diesel Repair Manual. ISSN 0077-1724.) 1947. a. index. illus. Hearst Books, 250 W 55th St, New York, NY 10019. Examined: 30th ed., 1977. 1472p. $21.95.
Aud: Sa

Provides step-by-step maintenance and repair instructions for a wide variety of truck and utility vehicle makes and models built between 1966 and 1977. Covers all major U.S. manufacturers and most, if not all, popular truck models. Also includes repair and maintenance specifications for gasoline and diesel engines, including those used in tractors and other farm and off-road vehicles. Illustrated throughout with charts, photographs, and diagrams. Similar in format to the **Motor Auto Repair Manual.** With the increasing popularity of pick-up trucks and various recreational vehicles, there should be a need for this useful guide in many libraries. JKM

SS 876
Ports of the World. ISSN 0079-4066. 1896. a. index. Benn Brothers, 125 High St, Colliers Wood, London SW19 2JN, England. Examined: 1976. 883p. (1978. $43.95.)
Aud: Cl

Describes features of the ports, including latitude and longitude, depth, services offered, officials, railroad facilities, statistics on vessels and tonnage handled, etc. Arranged geographically with ports of the United Kingdom listed first, followed by the continents. EM

SS 877
Power Boat Annual; Accessory Directory. ISSN 0085-5057. 1968. a. bibl. index. illus. Marine Publications, c/o Ralph Wilbur, 130 Shepard St, Lawrence, MA 01843. Examined: 1973. Harland Wilbur, ed. 176p. $3.50 pap.
Aud: Sa

The major section of the book is a display of boats by class, i.e., size. Within each class, there is no particular arrangement and no index to any given model. A photograph, model name, manufacturer, size, weight, capacity, hull configuration, type of power, and price are indicated for each model. Many of the entries refer to another, more complete display, which includes a larger photograph and more detailed description, and which is obviously paid for by the manufacturer. The accessory showcase section is fully indexed. For each accessory, a photograph, description, manufacturer, and price is provided. There is also a manufacturer's address directory, a lengthy nautical bookshelf with annotations, and tear-out reader reply cards. SLB/KSK

SS 878

Railway Passenger Car Annual. 1973/74. a. illus. RPC Publications, Box 296, Godfrey, IL 62035. Examined: v. 3, 1976. W. David Randall, ed. 187p.
Aud: Sa

"The purpose of this book is to present in a concise form a car by car description of all railway passenger equipment in service on the U.S. and Canadian roads." Part one lists all passenger cars in revenue service on U.S. and Canadian railroads during the year, as well as passenger cars retained for special excursions, business cars, and railway service. Railroads are listed in alphabetical order. Part two lists revenue passenger equipment in transit service during the year. The systems are listed geographically east to west in the U.S. and Canada. Part three lists passenger cars owned by private organizations and individuals. The organizations are listed first, and then individuals are listed in alphabetical order. Illustrated throughout with photographs of a variety of passenger cars. The place and time when each photo was taken are noted in the captions. Each listing also notes the company that built the car and the year it was built. Succeeding issues will update previous volumes by listing cars that have been retired, scrapped, or wrecked; any new cars placed in service; and any changes in passenger car ownership or numberings. KSK

SS 879

Reed's Nautical Almanac; American-East Coast Edition. 1931. a. illus. Hearst Books, 250 W 55th St, New York, NY 10019. Examined: 1977. 854p. $12.95. (1979. 854p. $12.95.)
Aud: Pl, Sa

Subtitle: "Navigator's and pilot's factbook." Presents current nautical information for the east coast of North America from Nova Scotia to the Caribbean Islands and the Gulf of Mexico. Includes weather information, tides and tidal stream charts, first aid information, safety rules and regulations, astronomical tables, a glossary of nautical terminology, laws of the sea, etc. A separate European edition is available from Thomas Reed Publications, 36/37 Cock Lane, London EC1A 9BY, England. Useful for both the amateur and the professional sailor. JKM

SS 880

Sailboat and Sailboat Equipment Directory. 1967. a. bibl. index. illus. Sail Magazine, Bernard A. Goldhirsh, 38 Commercial Wharf, Boston, MA 02110. Examined: 1973. Murray L. Davis, ed. 344p. $2 pap.
Aud: Pl

Magazine format with several major sections, each well indexed. First is the gear and equipment section, arranged by category, which lists names and addresses of manufacturers. The second section is a geographical listing by region of U.S. and Canadian sailmakers, with addresses and services offered. The major section covers sailboats and is arranged by daysailers, multihulls, iceboats, handsailers, and cruisers. Each entry, paid for by the manufacturer of the boat, includes boat name, manufacturer, address, description, statistics, price, plan, and photograph. There is also a listing of sailing schools, a sailor's library, and a brokerage section which consists of ads by firms. An index to all known U.S. and Canadian sailboats with manufacturer, address, and size, and an index to class associations with the secretaries' addresses are also provided. SLB

SS 882

Steam Passenger Service Directory. ISSN 0081-542X. 1966. a. index. illus. Empire State Railway Museum, Box 666, Middletown, NY 10940. Examined: 1975. Marvin H. Cohen, ed. 152p. $2.50. (12th ed., 1977. 160p.)
Aud: Pl

Subtitle: "An illustrated directory listing tourist railroad, trolley, and museum operations with regularly scheduled or intermittent passenger service." Attempts to include every tourist railroad operation in the U.S. and Canada about which reliable information can be obtained. Arranged by state, then by city, entries include the name of the railroad or museum; whether it is standard gauge; location; details on the railroad's route or the museum's exhibits and displays; schedule; fare or admission; types of trains the railroad has or the types of locomotives in the museum; availability of refreshments on the train, restaurants in depots, or refreshments, gift shops, and picnic areas in museums; and the mailing address and phone number. A photograph of the railroad's chief locomotive or the museum's main exhibit is included in each listing. Guest coupons for various museums or railroads are included. There is an index of listings. There are advertisements in the front and back of the book. KSK

SS 883

**Transportation Research Forum. Proceedings: An-

nual Meeting. ISSN 0091-2468. 1962. a. illus. Richard B. Cross Co., Box 405, Oxford, IN 47971. Examined: v. 18, 1977. 669p. $25.
Aud: Cl, Sa

Includes papers read at the annual meeting of the Transportation Research Forum (TRF), as well as some of the proceedings of the Canadian Transportation Research Forum. TRF's purpose "is to provide a common meeting ground or forum for the discussion of ideas and research techniques applicable to economic, management, and public policy problems involving transportation." Each annual meeting has a theme; "Transportation in Transition" is the theme of the 1977 volume. The annual meeting papers are divided into sections, with each section containing two to four papers on a particular aspect of the theme. Section titles include: aviation issues, freight car utilization, goods movements in the U.S., inland waterway and port issues, intercity trucking, maritime trade, railroad freight rates, urban bus operations, and urban transportation by auto/van pools and taxicabs. Most of the individual papers are of a technical nature and include charts, statistics, references, and tables, plus an occasional illustration. Many of the research papers address the various aspects of energy conservation and the environment within the broader context of transportation. KSK

SS 884

Transportation Telephone Tickler. ISSN 0447-9181. 1950. a. index. illus. Journal of Commerce, 99 Wall St, New York, NY 10005. Examined: 1970. Donald J. Green, ed. 2v. v. 1, 608p.; v. 2, 1200p. $15.
Aud: Sa

Volume one includes a classified index to advertisers; a directory of transportation companies (shipping, air, trucking) in the New York area; lists of associations, banks, consulates, professional services, and departments of the U.S. government; and international mail and conversion tables. Volume two lists port authorities, shipping, consulates, airlines, mail services, trucking, freight handlers, railroads, and other transportation information, arranged alphabetically by city. Many advertisements are included in both volumes. KSK

SS 885

Trinc's Blue Book of the Truck Industry. ISSN 0082-6494. 1944. a. index. Trinc Transportation Consultants, 475 L'enfant Plaza SW, Suite 4200, Washington, DC 20024. Examined: 1976. Harry E. Hawkins, ed. 295p. $125

Aud: Sa

Presents selected information from the annual reports filed with the Interstate Commerce Commission by class one and class two motor carriers of property for the preceding year. The book is arranged in three color-coded sections: summaries by commodities carried and territory served; management and control; and basic accounts and statistics. The first section is very brief and includes statistics for general freight and household goods summarized in 20 territorial groups. In part two, companies are listed alphabetically, with mailing address, ownership and type of organization, names and titles of principal officers and directors, and names of companies controlled. Following this are tabular figures for general freight carriers, arranged by the 20 territorial groups (New England, Midwest, South-Central, etc.). Information in this section includes total assets, operating revenues, salaries, insurance, personnel, mileage, average load and haul, etc. The third section gives statistics by type of commodity that the carrier hauls, i.e., household goods, petroleum products, refrigerated products, agricultural products, motor vehicles, building materials, and other special carriers. There is an index of carriers; each listing in the index includes name of carrier, city and state, page reference, and a letter code referring to principal commodities carried. KSK

SS 886

U.S. Civil Aeronautics Board. Aircraft Operating Cost and Performance Report. ISSN 0082-9609. 1965/1966. a. index. U.S. Civil Aeronautics Board, Washington, DC 20428. Dist: Superintendent of Documents, U.S. Government Printing Office, Washington, DC 20402. Examined: v. 9, 1974/75. 122p. $1.95.
Aud: Sa

Presents unit cost and performance data for transport aircraft operated by U.S. certified route air carriers during a two-year period. Unit operating cost and performance data for turbine aircraft operated by U.S. supplemental air carriers during a one-year period are also presented. The data are grouped into three parts: equipment group by carrier group; equipment type by carrier group; and equipment type by individual carrier. The data are arranged in tables with columns indicating: operation and carrier; cabin configuration; equipment group; equipment type; carrier; and time period covered. Appendixes include indexes of carriers and equipment, the method of computing derived data, aircraft operating cost and performance data for supplemental carriers, and a glossary of terms. Each table is divided into two parts, the aircraft operating expenses and the performance and characteristics. The former covers flying operations, maintenance of flight equipment, and depreciation and rentals on flight equipment, while the latter contains utilization, aircraft capacity, speed, productivity, fuel, and traffic. KSK

SS 887
U.S. Coast Guard. Boating Statistics. ISSN 0565-1530. 1959. a. U.S. Coast Guard, Department of Transportation, c/o Commandant (G-BP), Washington, DC 20590. Examined: 1976. 35p. free.
Aud: Sa

Includes statistics on boat numbering registration, boating accidents, and other boating-related activities collected from the 47 states having federally approved boat numbering systems, the Virgin Islands, Puerto Rico, District of Columbia, and Guam. Also provides information on the other states and American Samoa from Coast Guard numbering records. The table of contents acts as an index to the detailed accident tables. There is also a discussion of boat safety efforts and research by the Coast Guard, a glossary of definitions of terms used in recording boating accident statistics, and a copy of the form used for boating accident reports. SLB

SS 888
U.S. Department of Transportation. Annual Report. ISSN 0563-4157. 1967. a. U.S. Department of Transportation, Washington, DC 20590. Examined: 1975. 7)p. $1.70.
Aud: Cl

Covers agency activities and important developments in such areas as accident prevention, environmental aspects, energy conservation, system development, emergency transportation, etc. EM

SS 889
U.S. Federal Aviation Administration. Census of U.S. Civil Aircraft. ISSN 0069-1437. (Continues: Statistical Study of U.S. Civil Aircraft; U.S. Active Civil Aircraft by State and County.) 1964. a. Department of Transportation, Federal Aviation Administration, Office of Management Systems, Washington, DC 20591. Dist: National Technical Information Service, Springfield, VA 22161. Examined: 1975. Betty V. Cayce, ed. 389p. $1.50.
Aud: Sa

Contains an annual count of all registered civil aircraft in the U.S. Registered aircraft include aircraft of the U.S. air carriers and those in general aviation. Data in the report are compiled from official aircraft registration and airman certification records maintained by the Data Service Division, FAA Aeronautical Center, and from official airport records maintained by the System Planning Division, Airports Service. The report is made up of tables divided into three parts: U.S. registered civil aircraft, air carrier aircraft, and general aviation aircraft. Information covered in the various tables includes: registered U.S. civil aircraft by type and year of manufacture, total civil aircraft production by aviation category and type, active pilots and flight instructors, composition of U.S. air carrier fleet by type of aircraft, general aviation air traffic activities, and estimated hours flown in active general aviation by types of flying, rotorcraft, glider, balloons and dirigibles, and amateur-built aircraft. Some of the tables analyze trends over a ten-year period. There is a glossary of terms used in the publication. KSK

SS 890
U.S. Urban Mass Transit Administration. Urban Mass Transportation Abstracts. ISSN 0090-8223. 1972. a. index. U.S. Department of Transport, 2100 Second Ave SW, Washington, DC 20540. Dist: Urban Mass Transportation Administration (National Technical Information Service, U.S. Department of Commerce), 5285 Port Royal Rd, Springfield, VA 22151. Examined: 1977. 369p. $6.
Aud: Cl

Contains abstracts of research and development project reports, university technical reports, and other technical publications. Includes title, personal author, corporate author, and geographic indexes. EM

SS 891
Ward's Automotive Yearbook. ISSN 0083-7229. a. index. illus. Ward's Communication, 28 W Adams, Detroit, MI 48226. Examined: 1977. Harry A. Stark, ed. 382p. $35.
Aud: Cl, Sa

Contains articles, descriptions, tables, statistics, and summaries of the automobile industry. It is divided into sections, including industry trends, imported vehicles, recreational vehicles, materials and processes, tires, production, retail sales, registrations, Canadian report, car manufacturers, truck manufacturers, and construction/farm equipment manufacturers. Each section begins with a contents page. Following these sections is a directory of automotive suppliers arranged alphabetically by company, giving address and phone number, officers, the products, and trademark. A product guide to automotive suppliers follows. An index of advertisers and a subject index are provided. Includes illustrations of automobile models. KSK

SS 892
Waterway Guide; The Yachtsman's Bible: Mid-Atlantic. 1947. a. bibl. index. illus. Marine Annuals, 238 West St, Box 1486, Annapolis, MD 21404. Examined: 1977. Hugh Whall, ed. 392p. $5.95 pap.
Aud: Pl

One of a series of three guides arranged by geographical regions. Each regional section includes distance map, description of various ports and areas, important navigating information, some sightseeing, contact phone numbers, and nautical maps of areas discussed. There is an extensive cruising glossary with addresses and phone numbers of coast guard stations for the region, distance tables, daily current predictions and current tables, mail drops, coast guard radio beam for the region, weather station information, golf, liquor laws, fishing, and charts and publications available from Waterway Guide Service. Some practical information is included in the "Tips for Traveling" section. Includes indexes to subjects, advertisers, and cities and harbors. The Mid-Atlantic edition covers the New York Bay, New Jersey Waters, Delaware Bay, Delmarva Coast, Chesapeake Bay, Intracoastal Waterway, Sounds and Outer Bank, Morehead City to Charleston, and Charleston to Florida. SLB

SS 893
Waterway Guide; The Yachtsman's Bible: Northern. 1947. a. bibl. index. illus. Marine Annuals, 238 West St, Box 1486, Annapolis, MD 21404. Examined: 1977. Hugh Whall, ed. 428p. $5.95 pap.
Aud: Pl

This is the second of the three *Waterway Guides*. Follows the same format and provides the same type of information as the Mid-Atlantic edition. Covers New York Bay, Long Island and the Sound, Rhode Island/Massachusetts Waters, Cape Cod and the Islands to Boston, Massachusetts/New Hampshire Waters, Down East/The Gulf of Maine, Hudson River, Champlain Waterways, Erie Canal, Lake Ontario/U.S. and Canadian Waters, and Island Waterways of the Northeast. SLB

SS 894
Waterway Guide; The Yachtsman's Bible: Southern. 1947. a. bibl. index. illus. Marine Annuals, 238 West St, Box 1486, Annapolis, MD 21404. Examined: 1977. Hugh Whall, ed. 400p. $5.95 pap.
Aud: Sa

The third *Waterway Guide* covers Florida East Coast/Northern Waters, Okeechobee Waterway, Florida East Coast/Southern Waters, Fort Lauderdale, Greater Miami, Florida Keys, Bahamas, Florida West Coast/Southern Waters, Florida West Coast/Northern Waters, Gulf Coast/Alabama to Mexico. It follows the same basic format as the other two *Waterway Guides*, but it does not include current tables or a "Tips for Traveling" section. SLB

SS 895
World Automotive Market. (Continues: Global Automotive Market Survey and World Motor Census; World Automotive Market Survey and Motor Census.) 1931. a. illus. Automobile International, 386 Park Ave S, New York, NY 10016. Examined: 1976. Bernard Zinober, ed. 42p. $8.
Aud: Cl, Pl, Sa

Includes motor vehicle assembly and production statistics for approximately two dozen countries for the preceding two years; a world motor census, showing the number of cars, trucks, and buses in operation during the year; a table of cars and trucks in the world's leading countries and a world map indicating vehicles on the road; a table of vehicle exports to most countries of the world; statistics on gasoline and diesel fuel usage in selected countries over a five-year period; and statistical information on U.S. exports of vehicles, spare parts and accessories, service equipment, and related automotive supplies to various countries. KSK

SS 896
World Cars. ISSN 0084-1463. 1962. a. index. illus. Hearst Books, 250 W 55th St, New York, NY 10019. Examined: 16th ed., 1977. Automobile Club of Italy, comp. 440p. $24.95. (17th ed., 1979. 440p. $26.95.)
Aud: Pl

Presents specifications for new car models produced in 35 countries. Entries for each car include a photograph and information on engine capacity and operation, transmission system, chassis, steering, brakes, electrical equipment, maintenance, performance, factory price and U.S. price, and variations and optional accessories. Also includes a directory of car manufacturers throughout the world; sections on major racing competitions throughout the world, electric cars, the "coachbuilder's art," and the state-of-the industry in leading car-producing nations; and three indexes. JKM

SS 897

World Motor Vehicle Data. ISSN 0085-8307. 1971. a. Motor Vehicle Manufacturers Association of the U.S., Statistics Department, 320 New Center Bldg, Detroit, MI 48202. Examined: 1975. 160p. $20. (1976. 184p. $20.)
Aud: Cl, Pl, Sa

A statistical compilation of international motor vehicle data for the previous year. The data in the report, which includes production totals by manufacturer and by country, are supplied by foreign government agencies, trade associations, private services, and the press. The first part of the report gives selected world vehicle data, such as world motor vehicle production during the year, the world's ten leading manufacturers, world vehicle registrations, and historical world vehicle data (e.g., production since 1900, exports from 1926 to the present, new and total registrations from the late twenties to the present). The rest of the report gives data on motor vehicles by continent (Africa, Asia, Europe, Eastern Europe, Oceania, and the Western Hemisphere), then by individual country. Information provided for each country includes motor vehicle production, production by manufacturers, vehicle production by models, and total vehicle registrations. KSK

SS 898

Worldwide Yacht Charter and Boat Rental Guide. 1970. a. index. illus. Detroit Publication Consultants, 18226 Mack Ave, Grosse Pointe, MI 48236. Examined: 1977. 51p. $3 pap.
Aud: Sa

Primarily a listing by geographical area of yachts available for charter. These listings include yacht name, length, sail, power or motor-sailer, yacht description by designer or builder, rig, number of berths, whether operated bareboat or with captain, and rates. There is an index to the geographical areas, which can be states, regions, countries, or continents. There are also some practical articles about how to charter and where to go. Includes worldwide listing of sailing schools which gives name, address, rates, type of courses, minimum age allowed, and phone number. SLB

SS 899

Yearbook of Railroad Facts. ISSN 0084-2997. (Continues: Yearbook of Railroad Information; Railroad Facts; Railroad Information.) 1965. a. index. illus. Association of American Railroads, Economics and Finance Department, 1920 L St, NW, Washington, DC 20036. Examined: 1976. 65p. free.
Aud: Cl, Pl, Sa

Summarizes railroad operations during the preceding year and provides some historical statistics on railroad operations in the U.S. as a whole and in the three principal districts to which railroads are assigned for statistical purposes (eastern, southern, and western districts). The figures deal primarily with class one line-haul railroads, those having annual operating revenues of $3,000,000 or more. A narrative outlook reviewing the previous year's activities and giving an industry outlook for the upcoming year precedes the statistics section. The statistics section covers: income, revenues from freight and passengers, expenses, taxes, state railroad taxes, passenger service deficit, loadings, tonnage, passenger miles by classes, freight train miles. cars per average train, mileage by states, miles of track, locomotives in service, types of freight equipment, new and rebuilt miles of track, locomotives in service, types of freight equipment, new and rebuilt equipment, employment and annual wages, and statistics of Amtrak and Auto Train Corporation. At the end of the yearbook is a subject index to the entire volume. Illustrated with photographs and occasional charts. KSK

TRAVEL

SS 900

Air Travel Bargains. ISSN 0065-4868. 1965. a. index. illus. Air Travel Bargains Worldwide Guidebook, Box 897, Coconut Grove, Miami, FL 33133. Dist: Simon and Schuster, 1230 Ave of the Americas, New York, NY 10020. Examined: 1975. Jim Woodman, ed. 384p. $2.95 pap.
Aud: Pl

After some basic information on air travel bargains, a guide to aircraft, and a vocabulary of airline terms, the major focus of the book is to describe, by large geographic region, those airlines that travel from the U.S. and those that travel exclusively within a region. The regions are Europe, Middle East and Asia, Africa, the Caribbean, Bahamas and Bermuda, Mexico and Central America, South America, the Pacific and Orient, U.S. and Canada, and around the world. Within these areas the airlines are listed, with schedules, by best bargain fares and best bargain tours. There is a travel information section which consists of advertisements from several airlines. There are several indexes. Many sample air fares and schedules are provided. SLB

SS 901

American Executive Travel Companion. (Cover title: Guide to Traveling on Business in 50 States.) ISSN 0363-535X. 1976. a. index. Guides to Multinational Business, Box 92, Boston, MA 02138. Examined: 1976. 384p.
Aud: Pl, Sa

Although some basic information one would need while traveling is included in the section on major business cities, the primary purpose of the guide is to provide instant facts and figures on the states and cities included. These facts focus on economics, business, and communications. There are many individual chapters on such topics as atomic energy, the press, military installations, income tax deductions, and so on, all providing current addresses or statistics. Several sections of the book are intended to be written in, such as the appointment calendar, expense record, and business address and telephone directory. There is a very complete index. SLB

SS 902

Automobile Association. AA Budget Guide to Europe. 1976. a. illus. Automobile Association, Publication Division, Fanum House, Basingstoke, Hampshire, RG21 2EA, England. Dist: Standing Orders, 156 Fifth Ave, New York, NY 10010. Examined: 1977. Liz Hyde, ed. 236p. $6.95 pap.
Aud: Pl

This budget guide is concerned exclusively with accommodations. After an article on the vineyards of Bordeaux, there is a lengthy introduction containing practical information on when to travel, climate, budgeting, distances, preparation, buying petrol, the law abroad, health, and money conversion. The address of each national tourist office for the countries covered is also listed. The major portion of the guide is a gazetteer for each country. For each city or town, the guide lists recommended accommodations; each listing indicates whether it is a hotel, inexpensive guest house, farmhouse, etc. There is a separate listing of self-catering accommodations where no housekeeping is provided. A 42-page atlas is also included. SLB

SS 903

Automobile Association. AA Guide to Camping and Caravanning. (Continues: Camping and Caravanning Handbook.) 1973. a. illus. Automobile Association, Publication Division, Fanum House, Basingstoke, Hampshire, RG21 2EA, England. Dist: Standing Orders, 156 Fifth Ave, New York, NY 10010. Examined: 1977. Gillian McWilliam and Roger McWilliam, eds. 287p. $6.95 pap.
Aud: Pl

Lists campsites for England, Wales, Scotland, and Ireland that have been inspected by the Automobile Association. There is a clear introduction on how to use the guide and several articles on winter storage and spring overhaul, law, towing, and sites open all year. The major section is a gazetteer for each country, with campsites arranged by region. The entries include a quality rating, map reference, season, restrictions and facilities, and a description of the area. The map references refer to a 52-page atlas which follows. For each country there is also information on the countryside, picnic sites and rest areas, tourist information offices, and ferries and tolls. SLB

SS 904

Automobile Association. AA Guide to Camping and Caravanning on the Continent. 1976. a. illus. Automobile Association, Publication Division, Fanum House, Basingstoke, Hampshire, RG21 2EA, England. Dist: Standing Orders, 156 Fifth Ave, New York, NY 10010. Examined: 1977. Patricia Kelly, ed. 361p. $8.95 pap.
Aud: Pl

Includes camp sites that have been inspected by the British and West German automobile clubs or recommended by members, affiliated motoring organizations, national tourist offices, and other reliable sources. After brief introductory practical tips and a clear description of how to read a gazetteer entry, there follows the gazetteer arranged alphabetically by country and city or town. For each site there is a telephone number, map reference, description, and codes as to facilities and price. The map references refer to a 72-page atlas. SLB

SS 905

Automobile Association. AA Guide to Continental Motoring. 1974/75. a. index. illus. Automobile Association, Publication Division, Fanum House, Basingstoke, Hampshire, RG21 2EA, England. Dist: Standing Orders, 156 Fifth Ave, New York, NY 10010. Examined: 1977. 554p. $6.95 pap.
Aud: Pl

This motoring guide is oriented to accommodations, but includes a great deal of information useful to a person driving in Europe. The introduction provides practical information, such as emergency help. For each country, additional detailed information on laws and regulations, holidays, automobile club offices, etc., is provided. For each country there is also a gazetteer arrangement of hotels and garages. These entries include the map reference for the town, recommended hotels with facilities, and garages with indications as to when petrol is available and towing services. There is a 56-page atlas and a subject index. City maps are provided in the gazetteer section. SLB

SS 906
Automobile Association. AA Guide to Guesthouses, Farmhouses and Inns. 1976. a. illus. Automobile Association, Publication Division, Fanum House, Basingstoke, Hampshire, RG21 2EA, England. Dist: Standing Orders, 156 Fifth Ave, New York, NY 10010. Examined: 1977. Barry Francis, ed. 287p. $6.95 pap.
Aud: Pl

A budget guide to accommodations and restaurants in England, Channel Islands, Isle of Man, Wales, Scotland, and Ireland. After a brief introduction, the major portion of the book is a gazetteer arranged by the areas mentioned. The gazetteer section has separate listings for guesthouses, hotels and inns, farmhouses, and picnic sites and rest areas. The accommodations entries include address, telephone, map reference, facilities, season, and price. There are separate listings after the gazetteer for establishments offering meals for about £1.50 and for budget price chain restaurants. Both accommodations and restaurants are rated. A 52-page atlas is included. SLB

SS 907
Automobile Association. AA Guide to Holiday Houses, Cottages and Chalets. (Continues: AA Guide to Self-Catering Holiday Accommodation.) 1976. a. illus. Automobile Association, Publication Division, Fanum House, Basingstoke, Hampshire, RG21 2EA, England. Dist: Standing Orders, 156 Fifth Ave, New York, NY 10010. Examined: 1977. Jean Heselden, ed. 139p. $6.95 pap.
Aud: Pl

This guide to accommodations where one does one's own cooking and housekeeping includes England, Isle of Man, Wales, and Scotland. There are some introductory remarks on the advantages of self-catering and clear instructions on using the guide. The major portion is a gazetteer arranged by the regions mentioned. Each town or area mentioned includes a map reference. The accommodations entries include address, booking contact, telephone, description, season, length of stay required, facilities and price. Separate listings of unusual holiday homes that have been converted from a wide variety of buildings, and tourist information offices are also provided. There is a 50-page atlas. The accommodations have been inspected by the Automobile Association. SLB

SS 908
Automobile Association. AA Guide to Hotels and Restaurants in Great Britain and Ireland. (Continues: AA Guide: Hotels and Restaurants in Great Britain.) index. illus. Automobile Association, Publication Division, Fanum House, Basingstoke, Hampshire, RG21 2EA, England. Dist: Standing Orders, 156 Fifth Ave, New York, NY 10010. Examined: 1977. Jean Heselden, ed. 669p. $8.95 pap.
Aud: Pl

Lists hotels and restaurants in England, Channel Islands, Isle of Man, Wales, Scotland, and Ireland that have been inspected by the Automobile Association. Inclusion assumes recommendation, but ratings give further guidelines as to facilities and quality. There are feature articles on the consumer, hospitality, Eastern cuisine, the art of drinking, and the wine label story. The major portion of the book is a gazetteer beginning with London and continuing with the areas as mentioned above. The London section includes a separate index and many quick reference lists. Entries throughout include rating, address, facilities, price, and credit cards accepted. The restaurant entries also mention specialities, and sometimes include a brief description. There are a wide variety of quick reference lists at the end and a 52-page atlas. SLB

SS 909
Automobile Association. AA Guide to Stately Homes, Museums, Castles and Gardens. (Continues: Britain's Heritage Guide to Stately Homes, Castles and Gardens.) 1976. a. index. illus. Automobile Association, Publication Division, Fanum House, Basingstoke, Hampshire, RG21 2EA, England. Dist: Standing Orders, 156 Fifth Ave, New York, NY 10010. Examined: 1977. Gail Harada, ed. 334p. $6.95 pap.
Aud: Pl

Includes not only the types of places listed in the title, but also art galleries, zoos, monuments, and wildlife parks found in England, Scotland, Wales, and North Ireland. There are several feature articles on tracing ancestors, windmills and watermills, and haunted houses. The major portion of the book is a gazetteer arranged by region and indicated by a map grid. Each city, town, or area has a map reference and a listing of places to visit. The place entries include a brief description, season, hours, admission price, and parking.

There is a detailed index to towns and places of interest, as well as a 52-page atlas. SLB

SS 910
Baxter's Eurailpass Travel Guide. 1971. a. illus. Rail-Europe, Box 3255, Alexandria, VA 22302. Examined: 1976/77. Robert Baxter, ed. 335p. $6.95 pap.
Aud: Pl

Begins with a basic introduction about Eurailpass and goes on to explain cost, station symbols, how the book is organized, trip planning, suggestions and air fares, and stopover programs. After the main body of the book, there are special interest articles on places of interest and tours not offered with Eurailpass. Includes useful addresses, aid offices, USO offices, and many other useful lists. There is a chapter for each of the 13 countries included in Eurailpass; each includes general information, illustrations of the rail station, a list of nearby hotels, rental information that might be relevant (such as for bicycles and skis), points of interest, inter-city services, international connections, and a useful information section on prices of lockers, currency exchange, and miscellaneous tidbits. The line-drawn maps of countries, cities, and stations are very basic, missing some details, and, in some cases, too small to see. SLB

SS 911
Baxter's USA Bus Travel Guide. 1973. a. illus. Rail-Europe, Box 3255, Alexandria, VA 22302. Examined: 1976. Robert Baxter, ed. 247p. $6.95 pap.
Aud: Pl

A guide to "how to travel by bus and see the U.S.A. and Canada." It is oriented to Greyhound, since that bus line offers the Ameripass. After an explanation of the Ameripass and some basic travel by bus information, there are several suggested itineraries. The major portion of the book is arranged by geographical region and the major cities within each region. The city entries include some history, sights, information about the bus depot's facilities, and, in some cases, about YMCA/YWCA accommodations. There is a directory of YMCA/YWCA accommodations in the back, which gives address, phone number, price, and distance from the bus depot. There are several other useful lists and directories, such as Greyhound tours and telephone numbers. The selected bus schedules listed are almost impossible to read, due to the size of the print. There are some hand-drawn street and area maps of limited value. The issue examined was the Bicentennial issue and included a section on the American Revolution and Bicentennial calendar. SLB

SS 912
Baxter's USA Rail Pass Guide. (Continues: Baxter's U.S.A. Train Travel Guide.) 1973. a. index. illus. Rail-Europe, Box 3255, Alexandria, VA 22302. Examined: 1976. Robert Baxter, ed. 319p. $6.95 pap.
Aud: Pl

This guide is on "how to travel by train and see the USA and Canada." The name of the guide has been changed because it is now oriented to Amtrak's USARail Pass. Provides explanatory material on the pass and some basic information on traveling by train. The major portion of the book is arranged by geographical region and major cities within those regions. City entries include some history, sights, explanation and illustration of train depots, and YMCA/YWCA accommodations. This section is followed by many special chapters, including U.S. National Parks, itineraries, tours, a station index, and schedules for specific trains. There is a listing of hotels by state and city, with no particular explanation as to why those hotels were chosen. There is also a separate directory of YMCA/YWCA accommodations. Includes some hand-drawn area and street maps. SLB

SS 913
Bazak Guide to Israel. 1966. irreg. index. illus. Bazak Israel Guidebook Publishers, 2 Shvil Hatenufa, Kiryat Hamelacha, Tel Aviv, Israel. Dist: Harper and Row, 10 E 53rd St, New York, NY 10022. Examined: 7th ed., 1976/77. Anthony S. Pitch, Miriam Dorfzaun, and Hannah Carmeli, eds. 456pp. $5.95 pap. (8th ed., 1977/78.)
Aud: Pl

Begins with a section about the country that covers the land, history, state, people, communities of Israel, religion, current holiday calendar, the Kibbutz, and archaeology. The well-indexed practical information section includes government tourist information bureaus abroad, divided by country, with addresses and phone numbers. This section also includes entry regulations, accommodations, and a Hebrew phrase guide. The restaurant guide is separate, rather than with the regional entries, and is more extensive than other Bazak Guides. The restaurants are rated and if they are kosher that is noted. Six regions are included with tourist routes, maps, sights, places of worship, useful addresses, and accommodations for each region. There is a brief place name index. Some advertisements and low quality photographs. SLB

SS 914
Bazak Guide to Italy. 1975. a. index. illus. Bazak Is-

rael Guidebook Publishers, 2 Shvil Hatenufa, Kiryat Hamelacha, Tel Aviv, Israel. Dist: Harper and Row, 10 E 53rd St, New York, NY 10022. Examined: 1975/76. Anthony S. Pitch and Miriam Dorfzaun, eds. 600p. $5.95 pap.
Aud: Pl

The opening section covers the land, history, state, economy, people, entertainment, religion, festa calendar, art, literature, and music. The food and wine section does not list restaurants, but tells, by region, what one might expect to be best. The restaurants are listed and rated within the regional sections. There is no notation to indicate whether or not they are kosher. There is a detailed practical information section, including "Italy on a Shoestring," as well as the other information provided in a Bazak guide. There are separate sections of 14 regional areas, each of which begins with a description of the base city and tours from that city. The regional sections include maps, sights, walks, accommodations, and useful addresses. Places of worship are not listed. There are some medium-quality photographs and some advertisements. SLB

SS 915

Bazak Guide to Portugal. 1973. irreg. index. illus. Bazak Israel Guidebook Publishers, 2 Shvil Hatenufa, Kiryat Hamelacha, Tel Aviv, Israel. Dist: Harper and Row, 10 E 53rd St, New York, NY 10022. Examined: 3rd ed., 1976/77. H. Carmeli and M. Dorfzaun, eds. 431p. $5.95 pap.
Aud: Pl

The introductory material on Portugal covers the land, history, government, economy, people, art and culture, religion and folklore, festa calendar, the bullfight, and entertainment. The detailed practical information section is similar to other Bazak guides, but includes additional information on hunting and fishing, and budgeting your time. The food and wines section is a discussion of what one might expect to be best in the various regions of Portugal. The restaurants themselves are listed and rated in the regional entries, with no notation as to whether they are kosher. There are five regional entries, with a base city in each. The city is described, and sights, accommodations, entertainment, and tours are suggested. The tours also list sights, accommodations, and restaurants. There are maps throughout, and some advertisements and medium-quality photographs. There is a place name index. SLB

SS 916

Bazak Guide to Spain. 1972. a. index. Bazak Israel Guidebook Publishers, 2 Shvil Hatenufa, Kiryat Hamelacha, Tel Aviv, Israel. Dist: Harper and Row, 10 E 53rd St, New York, NY 10022. Examined: 1976/77. H. Carmeli and M. Dorfzaun, eds. 576p. $5.95 pap.
Aud: Pl

The guide opens with a general discussion of Spain, including the land, people, economy, history, art, the bullfight, religion, and folklore, and a fiesta calendar. The practical information section includes a list of Spanish tourist offices, by country, with addresses and phone numbers. It also discusses language, entry regulations, accommodations, and other useful information. The food and wines section is not a list of restaurants, but rather a discussion of the types of food and wines available in the various regions of the country. The restaurants are listed in the regional entries. There is no discussion or notation of kosher restaurants. There are 13 regions, with several tours in each, given. Sights, accommodations, and entertainment are described for each region. Places of worship are not listed. There is a brief place name index, maps throughout, some advertisements, and a few medium-quality photographs. SLB

SS 917

Better Homes and Gardens Travel Ideas. 1969. a. illus. Meredith Corp., 1716 Locust St, Des Moines, IA 50336. Examined: 1973. Neil Kuehnl, ed. 224p. $1.50 pap.
Aud: Pl

This magazine-format guide contains one-page entries on various areas, divided into such subject categories as Historic America, Scenic Seacoasts, Parks and Gardens, City Sights, Rivers and Lakes, Vacation Surprises, Canada, and Family Camping. Each of the area entries includes suggestions for where to stay and eat and some possible activities. There is also a list of places to contact for further information. There are several special feature articles as well. The "Library of Travel Ideas" includes an extensive list of free materials available. SLB

SS 918

Camping and Caravaning France. ISSN 0076-7735. a. illus. Michelin, 47 Ave de Breteuill, 76451, Paris, France. Dist: Michelin Guides and Maps, Box 188, Roslyn Heights, NY 11577. Examined: 1976. 248p. $4.95 pap.
Aud: Pl

The text of this guide to camp sites in France is in

English, French, German, and Dutch. There are explanatory notes, a 22-page atlas and quick reference lists to sites with modern facilities, pleasant sites, main sites for winter holidays, and principal residential caravan sites in the Paris area. There is a gazetteer arranged by city or town that gives all the particulars for each site. Entries include a rating, access, amenities and general characteristics, facilities, season, conditions of admission, and charges. SLB

SS 919
Charter Flight Directory. a. Travel Information Bureau, Box 105, Kings Park, NY 11754. Examined: 1976. Jens Jurgen, ed. 36p. $2.25 pap.
Aud: Cl, Pl

The directory covers over 25,000 charter flights. There is a listing for both OTC (One-Stop Inclusive Tour Charters) and ITC (Inclusive Tour Charters). The entries include airlines, number of flights, length, itinerary, schedules for current year, and minimum package price. There is also a directory of charter flight operators, a list of current Eurailpass rates, and Eurailpass order blanks. SLB

SS 920
Country Vacations U.S.A. (Continues: Farm, Ranch and Countryside Guide. ISSN 0085-0438; Farm and Ranch Vacation Guide.) 1949. bi-a. illus. Farm and Ranch Vacations, 36 E 57th St, New York, NY 10022. Examined: 1976. Pat Dickerman, ed. 223p. $3.50 pap.
Aud: Pl

The guide begins with very clear instructions on its use. After some short introductory essays, the major portion of the book is arranged by geographical region and then by state. Extensive information is provided for each farm, ranch, or other type of country place to stay, including contact person(s), address and description of location, number of units, weekly rates, adults and/or children, other specific information about facilities, a narrative description, and a recommendation. Only recommended places are included in the guide. There is an appendix of foreign languages spoken at the places listed. SLB

SS 921
Dollar Wise Guide to California and Las Vegas. bi-a. illus. The Frommer/Pasmantier Publishing Corp., 380 Madison Ave, New York, NY 10017. Dist: Simon and Schuster, 1230 Ave of the Americas, New York, NY 10020. Examined: 1977/78. Rena Bulkin. 297p. $4.50 pap.
Aud: Pl

Although this guide does have a budget focus, it includes expensive and moderate priced as well as inexpensive accommodations and restaurants. After a brief introduction, the book is arranged by cities and regions. The regional sections include maps, with the concentration of restaurants and accommodations. There is some discussion of sights. The Las Vegas chapter is extremely brief and is not very helpful for those traveling on a budget. SLB

SS 922
Dollar Wise Guide to England. 1969. bi-a. illus. Frommer/Pasmantier Publishing Corp., 380 Madison Ave, New York, NY 10017. Dist: Simon and Schuster, 1230 Ave of the Americas, New York, NY 10020. Examined: 1975/76. Stanley Haggart and Darwin Porter. 311p. $4.50 pap.
Aud: Pl

As the title implies, the focus is on a budget trip to England with the emphasis on medium-priced travel. After an introduction, there is a discussion about inexpensive ways to travel to and within England. Rather than just listing inexpensive hotels and restaurants, the guide arranges them by area and indicates which price range they fall into. There are several chapters on London, including staying and eating, sights and entertainment, and shopping. The chapters on other trips within the country and to Scotland and Wales list sights and provide budget information. There are area and city maps throughout. SLB

SS 923
Dollar Wise Guide to France. 1971. bi-a. illus. Frommer/Pasmantier Publishing Corp., 380 Madison Ave, New York, NY 10017. Dist: Simon and Schuster, 1230 Ave of the Americas, New York, NY 10020. Examined: 1977/78. Stanley Haggart and Darwin Porter. 359p. $4.50 pap.
Aud: Pl

Like other *Dollar Wise* guides, the focus of this work is on budget travel to France. There is a beginning chapter on inexpensive ways to fly to France and to travel within the country. The several chapters on Paris include hotels and restaurants in all price ranges, a guide for students and senior citizens, sights, and entertainment. The chapters on other areas within the country include both sights and price guides to hotels and restaurants. City and area maps are provided throughout. SLB

SS 924
Dollar Wise Guide to Japan and Hong Kong. (Contin-

ues: Japan on $10 A Day; Japan and Hong Kong on $10 A Day.) 1970. bi-a. illus. Arthur Frommer, 380 Madison Ave, New York, NY 10017. Dist: Simon and Schuster, 1230 Ave of the Americas, New York, NY 10020. Examined: 1974/75. John Wilcock. 311p. $3.50 pap.
Aud: Pl

Follows the typical *Dollar Wise Guide* format. The opening section discusses inexpensive ways to travel to and within Japan. There are several chapters on Tokyo, including budget hotels and restaurants, daytime and nighttime amusements, and important names and addresses for emergencies. The chapters on trips to other parts of Japan list both sights and budget hotels and restaurants. There is one section on Hong Kong, which includes the budget guide as well as activities and tours. There are several city and area maps throughout. SLB

SS 925

Egon Ronay's Dunlop Guide: Hotels, Restaurants and Inns in Great Britain and Ireland. (Continues: Egon Ronay's Dunlop Guide to Hotels and Restaurants In Great Britain and Ireland. ISSN 0070-9468.) 1957. a. illus. Egon Ronay Organization, Queen's House, Leicester Sq, London, WC2H 7DE, England. Dist: British Book Center and Association of Pergamon Press, Fairview Park, Elmsford, NY 1?523. Examined: 1975. 796p. $8.95 pap.
Aud: Pl

The title has changed often; earlier titles were *Egon Ronay's Dunlop Guide to Hotels and Restaurants in the British Isles,* and, before that, *Egon Ronay's Guide to Hotels, Restaurants, Pubs, and Inns.* The guide is recommended for a young audience since it includes economy evening meals in London. There are separate listings, including only the name of the establishment, of starred restaurants, rated hotels, graded wine lists, and bargains. The main body of the text is arranged by area, with restaurants, hotels, and inns listed alphabetically. Establishment entries include a description, address, rating, approximate cost, hours, and days closed. The hotel descriptions also include information about late arrivals, last dinner, and parking. There is a 32-page section of maps. SLB

SS 926

Eurail Guide; How to Travel Europe by Train. ISSN 0085-0330. 1971. a. illus. Saltzman Companies, 27540 Pacific Coast Hwy, Malibu, CA 90265. Examined: 1975. Marvin L. Saltzman and Kathryn M. Saltzman, eds. 384p. $5.95 pap. (1978. $8.95 pap.)
Aud: Pl

This guide is arranged into a number of subject chapters. It includes planning an itinerary; several four-day and one-day itineraries, including train number and time and sights; outstanding scenic journeys; British Rail trips; special articles on featured trips; guides to timetables and stations; eating on the train; baggage; train travel translations; rail station facilities, arranged by city; and a Eurail Guide Route Chart, which includes travel time and price. Since the guide is without indexes, it is difficult to locate all the schedules and charts included. SLB

SS 927

Europe on $10 a Day. (Continues: Europe on $5 a Day; Europe on $5 and $10 a Day.) 1957. a. illus. Arthur Frommer, 380 Madison Ave, New York, NY 10017. Dist: Simon and Schuster, 1230 Ave of the Americas, New York, NY 10020. Examined: 1976/77. Arthur Frommer, ed. 675p. $4.95 pap.
Aud: Pl

The opening section is titled "Getting There"; subsequent sections on the major cities cover sights, transportation, inexpensive places to stay (including dorms, starvation and sub-starvation budgets), capsule vocabularies for the essentials of life, menu translations in seven languages, European trains, money rates, packing to save money, inexpensive auto rentals, and bargain shopping tips. There are several maps for all cities, trolley or subway maps, and a wide variety of specialized maps. Because it is a budget guide, the book should be of interest to college audiences. Title changes over the years reflect inflation. SLB

SS 928

Fielding's Guide to the Caribbean Plus the Bahamas. ISSN 0071-4755. 1968. a. index. illus. Fielding Publications, 105 Madison Ave, New York, NY 10016. Examined: 1976. Jeanne Harman and Harry E. Harman III. 780p. $9.95. (1978. $10.95.)
Aud: Pl

The beginning section discusses trip preparation and provides detailed information on how to go by plane or ship. After a general description called "Let's Be Islanders," there are chapters of about 20 pages on each island. These sections include practical information about places to stay, tipping, laundry, things to see and buy, and where to get travel information. SLB

SS 929

Fielding's Low-Cost Europe. ISSN 0071-4798. (Con-

tinues: Fielding's Super Economy Europe.) 1967. a. illus. Fielding Publications, 105 Madison Ave, New York, NY 10016. Examined: 1974. Nancyk Temple Fielding, eds. 978p. $3.95 pap. (1977. $4.95 pap.)
Aud: Pl

The emphasis of this guide is on budget travel. After some practical introductions on cutting costs, preparation, student travel, and European living, the book is arranged by country and then by areas within the country. Entries for major cities include maps, budget suggestions on accommodations, dining, students, night life, activities, transportation, and shopping. There are also detailed travel tips for each country, including things not to buy and local rackets, as well as more traditional advice. Although there is no index, the table of contents is extensive and can serve as an index. SLB

SS 930

Fielding's Selected Favorites: Hotels and Inns, Europe. ISSN 0092-9506. 1972. a. Fielding Publications (with William Morrow and Co.), 105 Madison Ave, New York, NY 10016. Examined: 1974. Dodge Temple Fielding, ed. 460p. $4.95 pap.
Aud: Pl

After an introduction which gives basic advice about staying in hotels, the rest of the book consists of a country-by-country listing of favorites and alternatives. The favorite hotels, usually from 12 to 20 for each country, are listed in a table, giving address, phone number, telex, number of accommodations, prices, and remarks. There is then a paragraph discussing each of these favorites. A brief discussion of the alternative establishments follows, generally with a hint as to why they are not favorites. The amount of information provided about the alternatives varies. SLB

SS 931

Fielding's Selective Shopping Guide to Europe. ISSN 0071-478X. 1957. a. index. Fielding Publications (with William Morrow and Co.), 105 Madison Ave, New York, NY 10016. Examined: 1972. Nancy Fielding and Temple Fielding, eds. 224p. $3.95.
Aud: Pl

Begins with a guide to comparative clothing sizes and sample U.S. Customs duties. The rest of the book is arranged by country and major city or cities. Shopping hours in each country are given. The best shops in each city are listed, arranged by type of item one might buy. There is also a "Things to Buy" guide for each country and a cautionary paragraph on what to watch out for. A complete index by products is provided. SLB

SS 932

Fielding's Travel Guide to Europe. ISSN 0071-'801. 1948. a. index. illus. Fielding Publications, 105 Madison Ave, New York, NY 10016. Examined: 1975. Temple Fielding, ed. 1392p. $9.95. (1978. $10.95.)
Aud: Pl

The emphasis of this guide is on travel tips, restaurants, and accommodations. After a detailed practical introduction on preparation, the guide is arranged by country. For each country there is a brief discussion of the major cities; information on language, people, and attitudes towards tourists; lengthy descriptions of hotels and restaurants; and discussion of transportation, sights, sports, things to buy and not to buy, and local rackets. There are discussions of other items such as cigarettes, drinks, and festivals for some of the countries. There is only one general map of Europe, and a detailed index. SLB

SS 933

Fodor's Austria. ISSN 0071-6340. 1951. a. index. illus. David McKay Co., 750 Third Ave, New York, NY 10017. Examined: 1977. Eugene Fodor, ed. 419p. $11.95.
Aud: Pl

Begins with the Fodor's usual "Facts at Your Fingertips" section which provides planning information as well as addresses and information one might need during a visit. The "Austrian Scene," another standard feature in the Fodor guides, is a collection of essays on the way of life, history, arts, traditional events, food and drink, and shopping. The section also includes a satirical essay, as do most Fodor guides. The "Face of Austria" is arranged by area and discusses where to stay and what to do, as well as giving practical information for that area. There is a German-English vocabulary and 16 pages of maps. Primarily a read-before-you-go guide. SLB

SS 934

Fodor's Belgium and Luxembourg. ISSN 0071-6359. 1951. a. index. illus. David McKay Co., 750 Third Ave, New York, NY 10017. Examined: 1977. Eugene Fodor, ed. 312p. $10.95.
Aud: Pl

The usual Fodor "Facts At Your Fingertips" section has a complete table of contents, which is not true of all Fodor guides. There are two sections for each country. The "Belgian Scene" covers way of life, history, arts, traditional events, a satire, food and drink, and shopping. The "Face of Belgium" is the regional guide to the country, concentrating on sightseeing, although there is some practical information, and hotel and restaurant listings. There is a brief section on the "Luxembourg Scene" describing the country and its people, and a two-part section titled the "Face of Luxembourg" which covers sights and entertainment. There is a glossary of English, French, and Dutch-Flemish terms and a 16-page atlas. There are city plans and photographs throughout. SLB

SS 935
Fodor's Caribbean, Bahamas, and Bermuda. ISSN 0071-6561. 1962. a. index. illus. David McKay Co., 750 Third Ave, New York, NY 10017. Examined: 1970; 1977. Eugene Fodor, ed. 607p. $9.95.
Aud: Pl

After an introduction, there is the usual "Facts at Your Fingertips" section which is indexed in the back of the book. General background chapters on the entire area cover the people, history, arts, food, rum, flowers, and sports. There is also a brief section on each island or island group. The regional chapters include information on sightseeing, practical information, and some hotel and restaurant listings. There are photographs and maps throughout, including a large foldout map and a complete index. SLB

SS 936
Fodor's Cruises Everywhere. 1977. bi-a. index. illus. David McKay Co., 750 Third Ave, New York, NY 10017. Examined: 1977. Eugene Fodor and Robert C. Fisher, eds. 366p. $12.95; $9.95 pap.
Aud: Pl

Publisher's information indicates that this will be published biennially, but the first two editions, 1977 and 1978, have been annual. There are several articles in a section entitled "Planning Your Cruise," which present a wide variety of information on such items as off-season cruises, clothing, gratuities, etc. There is a list of ports of call which does not cover many African points "because of unsettled political conditions and lack of definite information concerning proposed cruises in that part of the world." The ports of call are arranged by region, then country. There is brief information on weather, sightseeing, restaurants, entertainment, shopping, and holidays. Perhaps most unique is the section on shipping lines and their ships, which is arranged alphabetically and gives the name of the line, an illustration of one of their vessels, and prices, facilities, and cruise areas for all their vessels. There is also a schedule of cruises, organized by shipping line name, which does not provide specific dates in the schedule, but the routine they regularly follow. A supplement gives the home addresses for the shipping lines, as well as the United Kingdom and United States addresses. There is an index to places and an index to ships and shipping lines. SLB

SS 937
Fodor's Czechoslovakia. ISSN 0071-6367. 1951. bi-a. index. illus. David McKay Co., 750 Third Ave, New York, NY 10017. Examined: 1973; 1977. Eugene Fodor, ed. 432p. $12.95.
Aud: Pl

In fairly standard Fodor format, this guide begins with "Facts at your Fingertips," followed by a section on Czech history, arts, folklore, and food and drink. The "Face of Czechoslovakia" section has sights and practical information for the area being covered. There is a tourist vocabulary and a foldout map. This is primarily a read-before-you-go guide. SLB

SS 938
Fodor's Europe. ISSN 0071-6375. 1936. a. index. illus. David McKay Co., 750 Third Ave, New York, NY 10017. Examined: 1976. Eugene Fodor and Robert C. Fisher, eds. 1047p. $12.95; $9.95 pap.
Aud: Pl

The standard Fodor "Facts at Your Fingertips" section includes information on planning, special interest travel, getting to Europe, staying in Europe, getting around, and leaving. The largest section is an up-to-date overview of Europe which includes a chapter on each country, covering the history, food and drink, sports, shopping, and other practical information. Includes 33 city plans. The traveler's atlas at the end is merely adequate. Both a read-before and take-with-you guide. SLB

SS 939
Fodor's France. ISSN 0071-6383. 1951. a. index. illus. David McKay Co., 750 Third Ave, New York, NY 10017. Examined: 1975; 1977. Eugene Fodor, ed. 540p. $12.95; $9.95 pap.
Aud: Pl

Includes the standard "Facts at Your Fingertips" section with a complete table of contents. There is an additional introduction called "The French Way of Life." The "French Scene" section includes creative France, history, some popular fallacies, and dining.

There is a separate "Face of Paris" section which covers where to stay, sightseeing, dining, entertainment, and shopping. The "Face of France" is a regional guide to the country, which concentrates on sightseeing, although there is also practical information and some hotel and restaurant listings. There is an English-French tourist vocabulary, a complete index, and a 15-page atlas. There are photographs and city plans throughout. SLB

SS 940
Fodor's Germany; East and West. ISSN 0071-6391. 1951. a. index. illus. David McKay Co., 750 Third Ave, New York, NY 10017. Examined: 1974. Eugene Fodor, ed. 501p. $12.95; $9.95 pap.
Aud: Pl

There are 16 pages of maps, and black-and-white, as well as color photographs. "Facts at Your Fingertips" has a separate table of contents, which is not true of all Fodor guides. There are some special sections on West Germany. The "Face of Germany" is divided into sections on Western, Southwestern, Southeastern, and Northern Germany, West Berlin, and East Germany. Each section includes sights to see, and practical information listings. Only a small portion of the book is devoted to East Germany. There is an English-German vocabulary. This is primarily a read-before-you-go guide. SLB

SS 941
Fodor's Great Britain. ISSN 0071-6405. 1951. a. index. illus. David McKay Co., 750 Third Ave, New York, NY 10017. Examined: 1975, 1977. Eugene Fodor and Robert C. Fisher, eds. 560p. $12.95; $9.95 pap.
Aud: Pl

The guide follows the usual Fodor format, with the addition of an introduction entitled "Why Come to Britain." The "Facts at Your Fingertips" section has a complete table of contents. "The British Scene" includes a current description, history, creative Britain, what's on in Britain, food and drink, and a satirical chapter. The other section, the "Face of Britain," is the regional guide to England, the Isle of Man, Wales, Scotland, the Channel Islands, and Northern Ireland. These chapters on the regions concentrate on sightseeing, although there is also practical information and some hotel and restaurant listings. There is an English-American vocabulary "explaining the common language that divides us." There is also an index, and a 16-page atlas. There are photographs and maps throughout. SLB

SS 942
Fodor's Greece. ISSN 0071-6413. 1951. a. index. illus. David McKay Co., 750 Third Ave, New York, NY 10017. Examined: 1977. Eugene Fodor and William Curtis, eds. 368p. $9.95.
Aud: Pl

The usual Fodor "Facts at Your Fingertips" has a complete table of contents. The other two major sections of the book also follow Fodor format. There is the "Greek Scene," which includes background and histoty, Greek mythology, folklore, sailing in Greek waters, and food and drink. The "Face of Greece" section is the regional guide to the country, with three chapters on Athens. The islands are also included. Chapters on the regions concentrate on sightseeing, although there is also practical information and some hotel and restaurant listings. There is an English-Greek tourist vocabulary, a complete index, and an eight-page atlas. There are city plans and photographs throughout. SLB

SS 943
Fodor's Hawaii. ISSN 0071-6421. 1961. a. index. illus. David McKay Co., 750 Third Ave, New York, NY 10017. Examined: 1977. William W. Davenport, et al., eds. 352p. $9.95.
Aud: Pl

Following the typical Fodor format, the guide includes "Facts at Your Fingertips," a section on each island, and a large section on "The Hawaiian Scene." Each island section includes a map, an essay, and exploring and other practical information. The foreword was written by James A. Michener. SLB

SS 944
Fodor's Holland. ISSN 0071-643X. 1951. a. index. illus. David McKay Co., 750 Third Ave, New York, NY 10017. Examined: 1975; 1977. Eugene Fodor, ed. 340p. $10.95.
Aud: Pl

"Facts at Your Fingertips" has a complete table of contents. The other two major sections of the book also follow Fodor format. There is the "Dutch Scene," which includes a general discussion of the country, art, folklore, history, food, shopping, and water sports particular to Holland. The other section, the "Face of Holland," is the regional guide to the country, and includes two chapters on Amsterdam. Chapters on the regions concentrate on sightseeing, although there is also practical information and some hotel and restaurant listings. There is an English-

Dutch vocabulary, a complete index, and a 16-page map appendix. There are high-quality photographs throughout. SLB

SS 945
Fodor's Hungary. ISSN 0071-6448. 1951. bi-a. index. illus. David McKay Co., 750 Third Ave, New York, NY 10017. Examined: 1971; 1977. Eugene Fodor, ed. 421p. $9.95
Aud: Pl

Begins with the usual "Facts at Your Fingertips," which has a complete table of contents. The "Hungarian Scene" includes a discussion of the people, history, arts, food and drink, and folklore. The "Face of Hungary" is the regional guide to the country; it includes three chapters on Budapest. The chapters on the regions concentrate on sightseeing, although there is also practical information and some hotel and restaurant listings. There is a tourist vocabulary, a foldout map, photographs throughout, and a complete index to places. SLB

SS 946
Fodor's India. ISSN 0071-6456. 1963. a. index. illus. David McKay Co., 750 Third Ave, New York, NY 10017. Examined: 1974. Eugene Fodor and William Curtis, eds. 600p. $12.95.
Aud: Pl

Although this guide has been an annual, the publisher is no longer advertising that it will be revised yearly; therefore it may become an irregular or biennial publication. The Fodor format varies slightly in this guide, which begins with an introduction concerned with geography, demography, and way of life. The usual "Facts at Your Fingertips" section does not have a separate table of contents, but is still useful for planning as well as for information one might need while in the country. The other two major sections of the book follow Fodor format. The "Indian Scene" includes history, women, architecture, painting and sculpture, music, dance, literature, and cuisine, and the "Face of India" is the regional guide to the country. There is a Hindi-English vocabulary, a complete index, and some city plans. There is no atlas. SLB

SS 947
Fodor's Ireland. ISSN 0071-6464. 1968. a. index. illus. David McKay Co., 750 Third Ave, New York, NY 10017. Examined: 1977. Eugene Fodor and Robert C. Fisher, eds. 316p. $11.95.
Aud: Pl

The format is basically like the other Fodor guides, but the "Facts at Your Fingertips," with its table of contents, is toward the end of the book. Added to this edition is a section entitled "Ireland—Town By Town," which is a guide to hotels and restaurants. The entries vary in completeness in this listing. The other two sections of the book follow Fodor format. The "Irish Scene" includes history, language, eating, sports, and shopping. The "Face of Ireland," the regional guide to the country, concentrates exclusively on sightseeing. There is an English-Irish vocabulary, an index, and maps throughout. The 1977 guide excludes Northern Ireland because of the political situation which makes travel there dangerous. SLB

SS 948
Fodor's Israel. ISSN 0071-6588. 1967. a. index. illus. David McKay Co., 750 Third Ave, New York, NY 10017. Examined: 1976. Eugene Fodor, ed. 448p. $10.85.
Aud: Pl

This guide begins with a discussion of postwar Israel and an introduction to the country. There is the usual "Facts at Your Fingertips," with a complete table of contents. There is also a geographic and demographic section. The "Israeli Scene" covers history, the Seventh Day, women, creative Israel, and food and drink. The "Face of Israel" is the regional guide to the country, and includes chapters on Tel Aviv, Jerusalem, and Haifa, as well as regions. These chapters concentrate on sightseeing, although there is also practical information and some hotel and restaurant listings. There is an English-Hebrew vocabulary, which includes some Arabic terms. There is a complete index, and city plans and photographs throughout. SLB

SS 949
Fodor's Italy. ISSN 0071-6472. 1951. a. index. illus. David McKay Co., 750 Third Ave, New York, NY 10017. Examined: 1977. Eugene Fodor, ed. 519p. $12.95.
Aud: Pl

The usual Fodor "Facts at Your Fingertips" has a complete table of contents. The "Italian Scene" covers history, creative Italy, and food and drink. The "Face of Italy" includes separate chapters on major cities such as Rome and Florence. The regional chapters concentrate on sightseeing, although there is some practical information and some hotel and restaurant listings. There is an English-Italian vocabulary, a who's who on Olympus, and a 16-page atlas. There is a complete index and city plans and photographs throughout. SLB

SS 950
Fodor's Japan and Korea. ISSN 0071-6480. (Continues: Fodor's Guide to Japan and East Asia.) 1962. a. index. illus. David McKay Co., 750 Third Ave, New York, NY 10017. Examined: 1976. Eugene Fodor and Robert C. Fisher, eds. 512p. $13.95; $9.95 pap.
Aud: Pl

After an introduction, there is the usual "Facts at Your Fingertips" which has a complete index in the back of the book. There are two major sections for Japan. The first discusses the people, the Japanese spirit, arts, region, food and drink, shopping, and practical information; it is also indexed in the back of the book. The "Face of Japan" is the regional guide to Japan; it includes separate chapters on major cities. The chapters on the regions concentrate on sightseeing, although there is also practical information and some hotel and restaurant listings. The brief section on Korea deals exclusively with South Korea and includes practical information, sightseeing, and some hotels and restaurants. For both countries, there is a very brief guide to the language. There are maps and photographs throughout and a complete index. SLB

SS 951
Fodor's London: A Companion Guide. ISSN 0071-6596. 1971. a. or bi-a. index. illus. David McKay Co., 750 Third Ave, New York, NY 10017. Examined: 1977. Richard Moore, ed. 305p. $8.95; $5.95 pap.
Aud: Pl

In recent years this guide has come out annually; it is still advertised as an annual by the publisher, but the 1977 edition says it is revised each year or each second year. This guide does not follow the Fodor country guide format. Instead it begins with a section entitled "Planning Your Trip," which covers the cost, getting there, arrival, where to stay (which is a list of hotel groups and consortia, not a guide to specific hotels and restaurants), traveling in Britain, and departure. A section with practical information for London follows. There is a section of hotels arranged by quality and cost, including addresses, and brief descriptions. Restaurants are listed by cost and ethnic specialty; listings include the address and a brief description. Information on entertainment, shopping, London for young people, and literary London is provided, and there are sections on exploring Central London and environs. Sightseeing sections include descriptions, directions, area maps, and floor plans for some buildings. There is a complete index. SLB

SS 952
Fodor's Mexico. ISSN 0071-6499. 1972. a. index. illus. David McKay Co., 750 Third Ave, New York, NY 10017. Examined: 1977. Eugene Fodor and Robert C. Fisher, eds. 562p. $12.95; $9.95 pap.
Aud: Pl

The "Facts at Your Fingertips" section includes information on planning, a section on student travel and study, and information for Mexican representatives. There are articles on cost guides, methods of traveling to Mexico, travel within Mexico, retirement and investing in Mexico, and leaving. The "Mexican Scene" covers history, art, folklore, and bullfighting for beginners. The "Face of Mexico" discusses various regions of the country, Mexico City, and Acapulco. Appendixes include a tourist vocabulary and street maps. Throughout are high-quality color and black-and-white photographs. SLB

SS 953
Fodor's Morocco. ISSN 0071-6502. 1965. a. index. illus. David McKay Co., 750 Third Ave, New York, NY 10017. Examined: 1976. Eugene Fodor and William Curtis, eds. 366p. $10.95.
Aud: Pl

After an introduction, there is the usual "Facts at Your Fingertips" section with a complete table of contents. The "Moroccan Scene" includes history, way of life, civilization, folklore and dance, food and drink, and arts and crafts, while the "Face of Morocco" concentrates on sightseeing. The latter section also provides practical information, and some hotel and restaurant listings. There is an Arab and Berber glossary and a complete index. There are some city plans and photographs throughout. SLB

SS 954
Fodor's Portugal. ISSN 0071-6510. 1951. a. index. illus. David McKay Co., 750 Third Ave, New York, NY 10017. Examined: 1977. Eugene Fodor and William Curtis, eds. 310p. $11.95.
Aud: Pl

Follows the standard format of the Fodor country guides. "Facts at Your Fingertips" has a complete table of contents. The "Portuguese Scene" covers history, arts and letters, traditions and folklore, and food and drink. The "Face of Portugal" includes three chapters on Lisbon. There is an English-Portuguese vocabulary, a complete index, one map of the country, and city plans and photographs throughout. SLB

SS 955
Fodor's Scandinavia. ISSN 0071-6529. 1951. a. index.

illus. David McKay Co., 750 Third Ave, New York, NY 10017. Examined: 1973. Eugene Fodor, ed. 542p. (1977. $13.95.)
Aud: Pl

The usual Fodor "Facts at Your Fingertips" includes information on planning, travel to Scandinavia, arriving, staying at hotels, food, how to travel in Scandinavia, and leaving. The "Scandinavian Scene" covers history, art, food and drink, sports, and shopping. There are sections on Denmark, Sweden, Finland, and Iceland. Each country's section includes history and what to see. Supplements include a vocabulary and a 16-page tourist atlas. SLB

SS 956
Fodor's South America. ISSN 0071-6537. 1966. a. index. illus. David McKay Co., 750 Third Ave, New York, NY 10017. Examined: 1977. Eugene Fodor and Robert C. Fisher, eds. 621p. $12.95; $9.95 pap.
Aud: Pl

In addition to Fodor's usual "Facts at Your Fingertips," there is a lengthy background section on South America, then separate sections on each country, including maps and special areas of high interest. Practical information is provided for each country. There is a very brief tourist vocabulary in Spanish and Portuguese. SLB

SS 957
Fodor's South-East Asia. (Continues: Fodor's Guide to Japan and East Asia.) 1975. irreg. index. illus. David McKay Co., 750 Third Ave, New York, NY 10017. Examined: 1976/77. Eugene Fodor and Robert C. Fisher, eds. 511p. $12.95.
Aud: Pl

After two introductory chapters, there is the usual "Facts at Your Fingertips" which is indexed in detail in the back index. The other two major sections of the book basically follow Fodor format. The "Southeast Asian Scene" includes way of life, history, creative Southeast Asia, and religion. The "Face of Southeast Asia" is arranged by country. Each country entry includes a map and is evenly divided between sightseeing and practical information, including some hotel and restaurant listings. There is no attempt to include a tourist vocabulary. The detailed index is arranged by country, with a separate index for practical information and places. There are a few photographs. SLB

SS 958
Fodor's Soviet Union. ISSN 0095-1358. 1975. a. index. illus. David McKay Co., 750 Third Ave, New York, NY 10017. Examined: 1976/77. Eugene Fodor and Robert C. Fisher, eds. 543p. $13.95.
Aud: Pl

The format for this guide varies slightly from the other Fodor guides. There is an introduction that covers geography, demographics, and the way of life. The "Facts at Your Fingertips" section does not include the usual table of contents, but is still useful for planning as well as for information one might need while in the country. The "Soviet Scene" includes history, peoples, art and architecture, literature, lively arts, and food and drink. The "Face of the Soviet Union" is a regional guide, and includes lengthy sections on Moscow and Leningrad, with city plans. The regional section concentrates on sightseeing, although there is also practical information and some hotel and restaurant listings. The English-Russian tourist vocabulary includes the Russian alphabet. There is a complete index, but no atlas. There are photographs throughout. SLB

SS 959
Fodor's Spain. ISSN 0071-6545. 1955. a. index. illus. David McKay Co., 750 Third Ave, New York, NY 10017. Examined: 1977. Eugene Fodor and William Curtis, eds. 390p. $12.95; $9.95 pap.
Aud: Pl

The format is basically like the other Fodor guides, but the "Facts at Your Fingertips," with its table of contents, is toward the end of the book. This edition also includes a section entitled "Spain—Town by Town," which includes a guide to hotels and restaurants, and other practical information. The entries vary in completeness in this listing, but they serve as a guide to quality and price of the establishments included. The "Spanish Scene" covers the land and people, way of life, history, creative Spain, bullfighting for beginners, sports, and food and drink. The "Face of Spain" is the regional guide to the country, with separate chapters on Madrid and Barcelona. This section concentrates exclusively on sightseeing. There is an English-Spanish vocabulary, a complete index, and a 16-page atlas. There are city plans and photographs throughout. SLB

SS 960
Fodor's Switzerland. ISSN 0071-6553. 1951. a. index. illus. David McKay Co., 750 Third Ave, New York, NY 10017. Examined: 1977. Eugene Fodor, ed. 371p. $10.95.
Aud: Pl

This guide includes Liechtenstein. After an introduction to Switzerland, there is the usual "Facts at Your Fingertips" with a complete table of contents. The "Swiss Scene" covers the landscape, way of life, history, creative Switzerland, food and drink, and sports. The "Face of Switzerland" is the regional guide to the country, with chapters on Geneva and Lausanne. The regional sections concentrate on sightseeing, although there is practical information and some hotel and restaurant listings. There is a separate section on the Principality of Liechtenstein, which includes practical information and sights. There is an English-French-German-Italian vocabulary, a complete index, and a single map of Switzerland. There are city plans and photographs throughout. SLB

SS 961
Fodor's Tunisia. 1973. irreg. index. illus. David McKay Co., 750 Third Ave, New York, NY 10017. Examined: 1975. Eugene Fodor, William Curtis, and Robert C. Fisher, eds. 288p. $10.95. (1977.)
Aud: Pl

For the first three years, this guide came out annually; publisher's information indicates it will probably be issued biennially now. The usual "Facts at Your Fingertips" has a complete table of contents. As in a few other Fodor guides, there is also a facts and figures section which is more geographic and demographic in approach. The other two major sections of the book follow Fodor format. The "Tunisian Scene" includes history, food and drink, and arts and crafts. The "Face of Tunisia" is the regional guide to the country, and concentrates on sightseeing, although there is practical information and some hotel and restaurant listings. There is an English-French-Arabic vocabulary, a brief index, and a foldout map. There are city plans and photographs throughout. SLB

SS 962
Fodor's Turkey. ISSN 0071-6618. 1969. a. index. illus. David McKay Co., 750 Third Ave, New York, NY 10017. Examined: 1973; 1977. Eugene Fodor and William Curtis, eds. 414p. $9.95.
Aud: Pl

After an introduction, there is the usual "Facts at Your Fingertips" with a complete table of contents. The "Turkish Scene" includes history, art and architecture, and food and drink. The "Face of Turkey" is the regional guide to the country. The chapters on the regions and major cities concentrate on sightseeing, although there are some hotel and restaurant listings and practical information. There is a Turkish-English vocabulary and brief information on Greco-Roman mythology and archaeology. There are photographs and area maps throughout, a foldout map, and a complete index. SLB

SS 963
Fodor's USA. 1977. a. index. illus. David McKay Co., 750 Third Ave, New York, NY 10017. Examined: 1977. Eugene Fodor and Robert C. Fisher, eds. 931p. $14.95; $9.95 pap.
Aud: Pl

The guide includes an index to the standard "Facts at Your Fingertips" section, a feature which most Fodor guides don't have. There are sections on the "American Scene" and distinctively American vacations. Some states and major cities are in more than one section, since the book is divided first by "America's Travel Wonders" and "America's Vacationlands," and then regionally within those sections. There is a good geographical index to compensate for the arrangement of material. For each state the necessary practical information is included. SLB

SS 964
Fodor's Yugoslavia. ISSN 0071-657X. 1951. a. index. illus. David McKay Co., 750 Third Ave, New York, NY 10017. Examined: 1976/77. Eugene Fodor, ed. 328p. $10.95.
Aud: Pl

This guide has been issued annually through the 1978/79 edition, but publisher's information does not promise that this practice will continue. After an introduction to the country and its people, there is the standard "Facts at Your Fingertips" with a complete table of contents. The other two major sections of the book follow Fodor format. The "Yugoslav Scene" includes history, creative Yugoslavia, folklore, food and drink, and sports. The "Face of Yugoslavia" concentrates on sightseeing, although there is some practical information and some hotel and restaurant listings. There is a tourist vocabulary which includes a Cyrillic and Latin alphabet, a complete index, and an eight-page atlas. There are city plans and photographs throughout. SLB

SS 965
Funspot Directory. ISSN 0071-9951. 1968. a. index. Billboard Publications, Amusement Business Division, 1515 Broadway, New York, NY 10036. Examined: 1975. Irwin Kirby, ed. 93p. $15 pap.
Aud: Pl, Sa

Includes a few articles of interest to those in the

amusement park business, but the major focus is the directory of amusement parks, tourist attractions, and zoos in North America arranged by state and city. Entries include location, phone number, facilities, attendance for year, dates opereting, hours, cost, and manager. There is also a directory, again arranged by state and city, of state amusement, travel, and trade organizations, giving addresses and phone numbers. Advertising is included throughout; there is an index of advertisers. SLB

SS 966
Good Food Guide. ISSN 0072-5005. 1951. a. illus. Consumer's Association, 14 Buckingham St, London WC2, England. Dist: British Book Center, 153 E 78th St, New York, NY 10021. Examined: 1973. Christopher Driver, ed. 752p. $12.50.
Aud: Pl

The main body of the book lists recommended restaurants, in alphabetical order, under England, Wales, Channel Islands, Scotland, Northern Ireland, Republic of Ireland, and London. Each entry includes a description, address, reservations, hours, price range, parking, credit cards accepted, and access for handicapped. There are some specialized lists, with just the restaurant names, by interest, for example, Outstanding Value, 85p. Lunches, and Open after Midnight. There is also a glossary of menu terms, a 36-page touring section, and 16 pages of maps. Recommended especially for a young audience since the price information can be helpful to those traveling on a tight budget. SLB

SS 967
Greece on $10 a Day. (Continues: Greece and Yugoslavia on $5 and $10 a Day.) 1965. bi-a. illus. Arthur Frommer, 380 Madison Ave, New York, NY 10017. Dist: Simon and Schuster, 1230 Ave of the Americas, New York, NY 10020. Examined: 1976/77. John Wilcock, ed. $3.95 pap.
Aud: Pl

As the title implies, the focus of this guide is on budget travel to Greece. After an introduction, there is a discussion of inexpensive ways to get to Greece by air, and by train, ship, or bus from Europe. There are several chapters on Athens, including a general description, a list of budget hotels and low cost meals, sightseeing, nighttime entertainment, and useful names and addresses for emergencies. The chapters on trips from Athens to other islands include both sights to see, and budget hotels and restaurants. Several city and area maps throughout. The guide was published annually from 1967 to 1970. SLB

SS 968
Hawaii on $15 and $20 a Day. 1964. a. illus. Arthur Frommer, 380 Madison Ave, New York, NY 10017. Dist: Simon and Schuster, 1230 Ave of the Americas, New York, NY 10020. Examined: 1977/78. Faye Hammel and Sylvan Levey, eds. 295p. $4.50 pap.
Aud: Pl

The emphasis throughout this guide is on saving money. It begins with tips on saving money while getting to Hawaii. There are several chapters on Honolulu, covering hotels, restaurants, transportation, shopping, and sightseeing. There are also chapters on each island, listing places to stay and eat and where to go sightseeing. A Hawaiian vocabulary is at the end. Primarily a read-before-you-go type of guide, although it could be useful during a trip as well. SLB

SS 969
Hosteling Holidays. 1956. a. American Youth Hostels, Metropolitan New York Council, 132 Spring St, New York, NY 10012. Examined: 1977. 16p. free.
Aud: Pl

Lists trips available to members of the Metropolitan New York Council of American Youth Hostels. People from anywhere in the country may become members. The Council offers trips in North America and Europe, lasting one to four weeks. The listings include a description of the itinerary, dates, price, and age limits, which are usually 16-18 years. Occasionally 14- and 15-year-olds are included, but the maximum age for travelers is 18. SLB

SS 970
Ireland on $10 a Day. 1967. bi-a. illus. Arthur Frommer, 380 Madison Ave, New York, NY 10017. Dist: Simon and Schuster, 1230 Ave of the Americas, New York, NY 10020. Examined: 1975/76. Beth Bryant, ed. 287p. 1977. $4.50 pap.
Aud: Pl

This guide focuses on budget travel to and in Ireland. After an introduction, there is an extensive budget survey of Ireland which covers planning, accommodations, meals, student discounts, shopping bargains, and entertainment. There is also information on inexpensive ways to get to Ireland. All the chapters on specific cities and areas of the country include budget information, as well as sights and entertainments. There are names and addresses useful for emergencies. A reader's selections chapter describes what others have done and where they have stayed successfully. There are area and city maps throughout. The guide was issued annually from 1967 to 1969; it is now a biennial publication. SLB

SS 971

Jewish Travel Guide. ISSN 0075-3750. (Continues: World Guide for Jewish Travellers.) 1950. a. index. illus. Jewish Chronicle Publications, 25 Furnival St, London EC4, England. Dist: Hartmore House/Associated Booksellers, 147 McKinley Ave, Hartford, CT 06606. Examined: 1970/71. Green Flag, ed. 304p. $3.45 pap.
Aud: Pl

The purpose of this guide is to direct travelers to synagogues, Jewish organizations and, in the case of Great Britain and Israel, to kosher hotels and restaurants. The Great Britain and Israel hotel and restaurant listings are rated as to strictness of kosher observance; establishments that are not kosher are not included. The United States section is arranged by state and includes only organizations and synagogues. Most other countries are included and are arranged by city, with synagogues and organizations. There is also information on airlines and how to assure kosher observance while in transit. There is a place index and an index to advertisers. Some photographs, but no maps, are included. SLB

SS 972

Leahy's Hotel-Motel Guide and Travel Atlas. ISSN 0075-8329. 1903. a. index. illus. American Hotel Register Co., 226 W Ontario St, Leahy Bldg, Chicago, IL 60610. Examined: 1976. James F. Leahy, ed. 128p. $15. (1977. $16.)
Aud: Pl

Oversize format in two parts. The first part is a listing of hotels and motels by state and town for the United States; by town for Puerto Rico; by province, then town for Canada; and by town for Mexico. The population of each town is noted, followed by a listing of hotels and motels which includes address, number of rooms, eating plan, lowest rate, and season, if any. The second section is a reprint of the **Rand McNally Road Atlas of the U.S., Canada, and Mexico.** There is also a complete index. SLB

SS 973

Let's Go: The Student Guide to Europe. ISSN 0075-8868. 1960. a. illus. E. P. Dutton and Co., 201 Park Ave S, New York, NY 10003. Examined: 1975/76; 1977/78. Ralph E. Hallo, ed. 704p. $4.95.
Aud: Jc, Cl, Pl

Although aimed at students, the guide would be of interest to anyone attempting to travel on a budget. The planning section includes information on work and study opportunities and such matters as drug laws and where to get help if arrested. Arranged alphabetically by country (Israel, Turkey, and North Africa are included) and area. The entries vary in extensiveness, but all include information on orientation, accommodations, and food. The longer entries also include touring information, useful addresses and telephone numbers, sights, museums, etc. There are simply-drawn maps of limited use. The guide is written by the Harvard Student Agencies (4 Holyoke St, Cambridge, MA 02138). SLB

SS 974

Let's Go: The Student Guide to the United States and Canada. ISSN 0090-788X. 1972. illus. E. P. Dutton and Co., 2 Park Ave S, New York, NY 10016. Examined: 1972/1973. Mopsy Strange Kennedy and Steven D. Stark, eds. 704p. $3.95 pap.
Aud: Pl

The introduction includes information for foreign visitors, as well as information on packing, accommodations, food and various types of transportation. In the introduction, as well as throughout the rest of the guide, the focus is on low cost travel. The United States is arranged by region, then state and city. Canada is arranged by province. For each state there is a brief amount of general information. The city entries contain introductory information, attractions (with hours), inexpensive accommodations and restaurants, nightlife, and, in some cases, a map. Missing is an index, and this reviewer could not locate any of the "dope on dope" that is supposed to be included. SLB

SS 975

Let's Halt Awhile in Great Britain and Ireland. 1933. a. index. illus. Ashley Courtenay, 16 Little London, Chichester, Sussex, England. Dist: Hastings House, 103 E 40th St, New York, NY 10016. Examined: 1976. Ashley Courtenay. 616p. $9.95.
Aud: Pl

A guide to those hotels and inns in England, Wales, Scotland, Isles of Scilly, the Channel Islands, and Ireland which the author and his colleagues recommend. Arranged by geographic regions, with a separate section on London, the guide covers various areas of England, Wales, Scotland, and Ireland. A brief international chapter lists hotels from several countries. Each section includes an area map and a map referring to the recommended hotels. There are discussions of hotel groups as well as individual hotels. For each hotel there is generally a photograph, list of facilities, phone number, and a descriptive paragraph on the view, atmosphere, and restaurants. There is an alphabetical place index. SLB

SS 976
Mexico and Guatemala on $10 a Day. (Continues: Mexico and Guatemala on $5 and $10 a Day.) 1962. bi-a. illus. Arthur Frommer, 380 Madison Ave, New York, NY 10017. Dist: Simon and Schuster, 1230 Ave of the Americas, New York, NY 10020. Examined: 1977. Tom Brosnahan and Jane Kretchman, eds. 421p. $4.95 pap.
Aud: Pl

This guide begins with a discussion of the forms of transportation available. Three sections show various routes to Mexico City. The six chapters on Mexico City cover rooms on a budget, meals on a budget, day and night activities, and listings for various types of information and assistance. There are six chapters on other areas of Mexico and six chapters on Guatemala. The appendixes include a shopping guide, basic vocabulary, and menu terms. Several maps are provided. SLB

SS 977
Michelin Red Guide Series: Benelux. ISSN 0076-7743. a. index. illus. Michelin Services de Tourisme, 46 Ave de Breteuil, 75341 Paris 7, France. Dist: Michelin Guides and Maps, Box 188, Rosyln Heights, NY 11577. Examined: 1976. 354p. $4.95 pap. (1978. $5 pap.)
Aud: Pl

The annual *Red Guide Series* focuses on listing and rating hotels and restaurants in a particular country. This guide includes more history and sights for each town than other books in the series. The explanations and the lexicon are written in Dutch, English, French, and German; the beginning articles on the history and the entries on history and sights within each town are only in French. Belgium, Luxembourg and Holland are covered separately; each section is arranged alphabetically by town. The hotel and restaurant entries list season open, facilities, price, restrictions, and rating as to class and standard of comfort. There are good area and town maps throughout and a place index at the end. SLB

SS 978
Michelin Red Guide Series: France. ISSN 0076-7778. a. index. illus. Michelin Services de Tourism, 46 Ave de Breteuil, 75341 Paris 7, France. Dist: Michelin Guides and Maps, Box 188, Roslyn Heights, NY 11577. Examined: 1976. 1179p. $8.95. (1978. $10.)
Aud: Pl

Like the other books in the Michelin *Red Guide Series*, this book is primarily a listing of hotels and restaurants. The text is in English, French, German, and Italian; the index to the section on Paris is only in French. Towns and cities within France are arranged alphabetically, and there is a lengthy section on Paris and its environs. Hotels and motels are listed for each town, and some sights are mentioned. The format and type of information provided is the same for all works in the series. Good area and town maps are provided. SLB

SS 979
Michelin Red Guide Series: Germany. ISSN 0076-7751. a. illus. Michelin Services de Tourisme, 46 Ave de Breteuil, 75341 Paris 7, France. Dist: Michelin Guides and Maps, Box 188, Roslyn Heights, NY 11577. Examined: 1976. 783p. $8.95. (1978. $9.)
Aud: Pl

This guide is similar in format to other titles in Michelin's annual *Red Guide Series*. The text for the Germany annual is in English, French, German, and Italian. There are brief sections on distances, recommendations to tourists, town plans, and outstanding cuisine. There is a complete explanation on how to use the guide, which is important because entries are primarily in code. The main body is an alphabetical list of towns with hotel and restaurant entries for each. There are good area and town maps throughout. SLB

SS 980
Michelin Red Guide Series: Great Britain and Ireland. a. index. illus. Michelin Tyre Co., 81 Fulham Rd, London SW3 6RD, England. Dist: Michelin Guides and Maps, Box 188, Roslyn Heights, NY 11577. Examined: 1976. 532p. $7.95.
Aud: Pl

Another title in Michelin's *Red Guide Series* which lists and rates hotels and restaurants for the countries included. The explanations and brief articles in this annual are in English, French, Italian, and German; the index to London and any other entries included are in English. The guide includes a full explanation to the coding system used in the entries. It is arranged by country and covers England and Wales, Scotland, Northern Ireland, Channel Islands, Isle of Man, and Republic of Ireland. There are important details and maps given at the beginning of each country. The towns and cities are alphabetically arranged, with a brief mention of sights and a listing of hotels and restaurants. There is a lengthy section on London, with an indexed, foldout map and more discussion of sights. SLB

SS 981

Michelin Red Guide Series: Italy. ISSN 0076-7786. a. index. illus. Michelin Services de Tourisme, 46 Ave de Breteuil, 75341 Paris 7, France. Dist: Michelin Guide and Maps, Box 188, Roslyn Heights, NY 11577. Examined: 1976. 670p. $7.95. (1978. $8.95.)
Aud: Pl

Follows the same format as other titles in the *Red Guide Series*. The explanations and brief articles in this annual are in English, French, German, and Italian; the index for the section on Rome, and any statements in the entries are in Italian. Towns and cities within Italy are arranged alphabetically, with a longer section on Rome that provides more information about sights than is usual. There are good area and town maps throughout. SLB

SS 982

Michelin Red Guide Series: Paris and Environs. ISSN 0076-7794. a. index. illus. Michelin Services de Tourisme, 46 Ave de Breteuil, 75341 Paris 7, France. Dist: Michelin Guides and Maps, Box 188, Roslyn Heights, NY 11577. Examined: 1976. 64p. $1.75 pap.
Aud: Pl

This guide to hotels and restaurants is available in an English only edition. There is a subway and city map, a guide to the code used in the entries, some practical hints, and an index to hotels and restaurants. Restaurants are first listed by name only in an interest arrangement. These include outstanding cuisine, open-air, food specialties, and those under 50 francs. The complete hotel and restaurant entries for Paris are listed by district and include address, phone number, facilities, and price. Restaurants are also rated by class and standard of comfort. Paris environs are arranged alphabetically, with the same style of entry. There is also a glossary of menu terms. SLB

SS 983

Michelin Red Guide Series: Spain and Portugal. ISSN 0076-776X. a. illus. Michelin Services de Tourisme, 46 Ave de Breteuil, 75341 Paris 7, France. Dist: Michelin Guides and Maps, Box 188, Roslyn Heights, NY 11577. Examined: 1976. 405p. $5.95. (1978. $7.95.)
Aud: Pl

The format and type of information provided in this guide is similar to other works in Michelin's *Red Guide Series*. In addition to the standard English, French, German, and Italian, this text includes Spanish and Portuguese. There is a fairly lengthy lexicon included for each country, and a discussion of the foods and wines unique to each. Towns are arranged alphabetically, with brief mention of the important sights and a list of hotels and restaurants. There are good area and town maps throughout. SLB

SS 984

Milepost: All-the-North Travel Guide. ISSN 0361-1361. 1948. a. index. illus. Alaska Northwest Publishing Co., Box 4-EEE, Anchorage, AK 99509. Examined: 1976. Bob Henning, ed. 498p. $5.95.
Aud: Pl

This travel guide is arranged by the possible routes one might take to reach Alaska, and therefore includes information on the Yukon, British Columbia, Northwest Territories, and Alberta, as well as Alaska. Many highway routes are given. These include maps, detailed information on towns, fishing sites, and camping sites along the way. There is also current information on railroads and marine access routes. Each major attraction in Alaska has a section that includes photographs, practical information, history and economy, names of hotels and campgrounds, transportation, and attractions. There is a general information section and a place name index. SLB

SS 985

Mobil Travel Guide: California and the West. ISSN 0076-9827. 1960. a. index. illus. Rand McNally and Co., Box 7600, Chicago, IL 60680. Examined: 1976. 240p. $3.95 pap. (1978. $4.95 pap.)
Aud: Pl

The *Mobil Travel Guides* are designed primarily for those traveling by car through the United States. Each guide is arranged by state, then city. General information is provided for each state. For each city there is a listing of what to see and do, annual and seasonal events, and places to stay and to eat, including quality ratings, addresses, prices, and facilities. Each guide also includes tear-out money saving coupons. This guide covers Arizona, California, Nevada, and Utah. It provides an excellent road atlas to the region and the individual states. SLB

SS 986

Mobil Travel Guide: Great Lakes Area. ISSN 0076-9789. 1960. a. index. illus. Rand McNally and Co., Box 7600, Chicago, IL 60680. Examined: 1976. 237p. $3.95 pap. (1978. $4.95 pap.)
Aud: Pl

The format and type of information provided in this guide are similar to the other Mobil regional travel guides. States covered are Illinois, Indiana, Michigan, Ohio, and Wisconsin. An excellent road atlas is included. SLB

SS 987
Mobil Travel Guide: Middle Atlantic States. ISSN 0076-9797. 1960. a. index. illus. Rand McNally and Co., Box 7600, Chicago, IL 60680. Examined: 1976. 265p. $3.95 pap. (1978. $4.95 pap.)
Aud: Pl

The guide provides a road atlas and other information common to the Mobil regional travel guides for Delaware, the District of Columbia, Maryland, New Jersey, North Carolina, Pennsylvania, South Carolina, Virginia, and West Virginia. SLB

SS 988
Mobil Travel Guide: Northeastern States. ISSN 0076-9800. 1960. a. index. illus. Rand McNally and Co., Box 7600, Chicago, IL 60680. Examined: 1976. 296p. $3.95 pap. (1978. $4.95 pap.)
Aud: Pl

One of the Mobil regional travel guides, this book covers Connecticut, Maine, Massachusetts, New Hampshire, New York, Rhode Island, and Vermont. It provides an excellent road atlas to the region, in addition to the other travel information common to the series. Montreal, Quebec, and Toronto are also covered briefly, though there is no atlas for these areas. SLB

SS 989
Mobil Travel Guide: Northwest and Great Plains States. ISSN 0076-9819. 1960. a. index. illus. Rand McNally and Co., Box 7600, Chicago, IL 60680. Examined: 1977. 261p. $3.95 pap. (1978. $4.95 pap.)
Aud: Pl

This Mobil regional travel guide covers Idaho, Iowa, Minnesota, Montana, Nebraska, North Dakota, Oregon, South Dakota, Washington, and Wyoming. The format, information provided, and special features are similar to those of other titles in the Mobil series. SLB

SS 990
Mobil Travel Guide: Southeastern States. ISSN 0076-9835. 1960. a. index. illus. Rand McNally and Co., Box 7600, Chicago, IL 60680. Examined: 1977. 263p. $3.95 pap. (1978. $4.95 pap.)
Aud: Pl

Another Mobil regional travel guide which follows the same format and provides the same type of information as other guides in the Mobil series. The region covered in this work includes Alabama, Florida, Georgia, Kentucky, Mississippi, and Tennessee. SLB

SS 991
Mobil Travel Guide: Southwest and South Central Area. ISSN 0076-9843. 1960. a. index. illus. Rand McNally and Co., Box 7600, Chicago, IL 60680. Examined: 1976. 275p. $3.95 pap. (1978. $4.95 pap.)
Aud: Pl

This guide provides a road atlas and other features and information common to the Mobil regional travel guides for Arkansas, Colorado, Kansas, Louisiana, Missouri, New Mexico, Oklahoma, and Texas. SLB

SS 992
Mobil Vacation and Business Guide. 1976. a. illus. Rand McNally and Co., Box 7600, Chicago, IL 60680. Examined: 1976. 351p. $4.95 pap.
Aud: Pl, Sa

This guide was designed as a supplement to the Mobil regional travel guide series. It includes some national maps, maps of each of the 53 cities covered, and maps of major airports. The city maps are too small to be very useful. Entries are arranged alphabetically by city and cover history, business, convention facilities, recreation and entertainment, historical areas, sightseeing, general references, and lodgings and restaurants with addresses, descriptions of facilities, and ratings noted for each. SLB

SS 993
Myra Waldo's Travel and Motoring Guide to Europe. 1964. a. index. illus. Macmillan Publishing Co., 866 Third Ave, New York, NY 10022. Examined: 1973, 863p.; 1977. $14.95; $9.95 pap.
Aud: Pl

The guide begins with informational sections on ship and air travel; what to take; travel arrangements; passports and visas; timing; weather; customs; Europe by car; and information points, which lists the various countries' national travel offices and their New York addresses. The main portion of the book is an alphabetical arrangement by country which includes such information as specific weather data, passport and visa, currency, tipping, transportation, basic words and phrases, sports, electricity, sightseeing areas, hotels, restaurants, and driving tours. A limited number of specific hotels and places of interest are listed, perhaps because of the number of countries included. SLB

SS 994
Myra Waldo's Travel Guide to South America. 1968.

quadrennial. index. illus. Macmillan Publishing Co., 866 Third Ave, New York, NY 10022. Examined: 1976. Myra Waldo, ed. 422p. $12.95.
Aud: Pl

Begins with three suggested itineraries and tips on what to take and what to expect. About 40 pages are devoted to each country, including a weather strip, map, and practical information on transportation, tipping, etc. The capital and major cities in each country are given detailed coverage. SLB

SS 995
New England Guide. ISSN 0077-8222. 1957. a. illus. Stephen W. Winship and Co., Box 1108, Concord, NH 03301. Examined: 1977/78. Earl J. Smith, ed. 158p. $1 pap.
Aud: Pl

Subtitle: "The big book of New England." A quality magazine-format guide to New England which has sightseeing as its primary focus. There are some feature articles on accommodations, restaurants, old houses, yankee boats, etc. The major portion of the guide is arranged by state and region, then alphabetically by town. For each town or area listed, there is a description of its characteristics and of what might be interesting to observe. If there are specific places in a town that one can visit, the season and price are noted. Maps can be found throughout and a separate map of New England is included. There are some high-quality color photographs. The price is not an indication of low quality, but rather of the numerous advertisements. SLB

SS 996
New Settler's Guide for Washington, D.C. and Communities in Nearby Maryland and Virginia. ISSN 0097-8213. 1974. a. index. illus. Robert B. Minogue, 8824 Tuckerman Lane, Potomac, MD 20854. Examined: 1977/78. Robert B. Minogue, ed. 184p. $2.95 pap.
Aud: Sa

A quality magazine-format guide oriented toward persons moving to the Washington, D.C. area. Emphasis is on taxes, real estate, and schools. There are some feature stories, but the major portion of the book is arranged by county and town, with maps for each county and living information for each town, such as type of community, taxes, transportation, public services, schools, churches, recreation, medical facilities, and shopping. The feature articles could be of interest to the traveler. SLB

SS 997
New York on $15 a Day. 1960. bi-a. illus. Arthur Frommer, 380 Madison Ave, New York, NY 10017. Dist: Simon and Schuster, 1230 Ave of the Americas, New York, NY 10020. Examined: 1976/77. Joan Hamburg and Norma Ketay, eds. 201p. $3.95 pap.
Aud: Pl

Includes sections on finding a budget hotel, eating cheaply and well, sights and cultural attractions, walks, one-day excursions, bargain nightspots, shopping, and budget tips for children. There is a very interesting section called "Helpful New York City Listings" which includes alcoholism assistance centers, babysitters, dentists, etc. SLB

SS 998
New Zealand on $10 a Day. 1976/77. bi-a. illus. Arthur Frommer, 380 Madison Ave, New York, NY 10017. Dist: Simon and Schuster, 1230 Ave of the Americas, New York, NY 10020. Examined: 1976/77. Beth Bryant. 219p. $3.95 pap.
Aud: Pl

The primary focus of this guide is on budget. After an introduction, there is a budget survey of New Zealand which includes inexpensive travel plans; accommodations such as hostels, camping, Y's, and farmhouse holidays; eating; shopping; and activities. After a chapter on getting to and traveling in New Zealand, there are several chapters on specific cities and areas. These area chapters include maps, specific practical information, and names and descriptions of budget accommodations, restaurants, and shopping areas. There is some information on sights and how to reach them. SLB

SS 999
Rand McNally Campground and Trailer Park Guide. ISSN 0079-9610. (Continues: Rand McNally Guidebook to Campgrounds and Rand McNally Travel Trailer Guide. ISSN 0079-9645.) 1971. a. illus. Rand McNally and Co., Box 7600, Chicago, IL 60680. Examined: 1971/73; 1977. 620p. $6.95 pap. (1978. $7.95 pap.)
Aud: Pl

The national directory covers Canada and all of the United States except Hawaii. There are mileage charts and maps for each state. Arranged by state and town, detailed listings of sites note size, prices, types of facilities, activities, addresses, and telephone numbers. CB radio listings and sanitary disposal stations are also listed. Regions are paged separately so that they can be purchased individually. SLB

SS 1000
Rand McNally Historic America Guide. ISSN 0079-9737. (Continues: Rand McNally Vacation Guide.) 1971. a. Rand McNally and Co., Box 7600, Chicago, IL 60680. Examined: none. (1977. $6.95 pap.)
Aud: Pl

While no copy was inspected, this guide is included based on the high quality of the other Rand McNally guides. Publisher's information states that the guide "tells of events and covers more than 2,800 places of interest that are important to the founding of our nation." It lists historic shrines, monuments, battlefields, museums and residences in all 50 states, covering 400 years of history. Entries include prices, hours, and how to get there. There are 50 full-color maps and 175 illustrations in color and black-and-white. SLB

SS 1001
Rand McNally National Park Guide. ISSN 0079-9629. 1967. a. bibl. index. illus. Rand McNally and Co., Box 7600, Chicago, IL 60680. Examined: 1977. Michael Frome, ed. 212p. $5.95 pap.
Aud: Pl

The guide includes some excellent maps. The major portion of the book is alphabetically arranged by park name; this section includes high-quality color photographs, history, and a practical guide. There are additional sections on how to enjoy the parks without a car; enjoying the other parklands; Washington, D.C.; archaeological, historical, natural, and recreational areas; environment; and new park programs, services, and areas. This is one of the better Rand McNally guides, perhaps because it is not co-sponsored by a commercial company. There is one recommended book with each park entry. SLB

SS 1002
Rand McNally Road Atlas of the United States, Canada, and Mexico. a. index. illus. Rand McNally and Co., Box 7600, Chicago, IL 60680. Examined: 1975. 128p. (1977. $3.95 pap.)
Aud: Pl

A large, colorful encyclopedia of the road. Maps are arranged by individual state or province, and many city and metropolitan area map inserts (or if very large, city maps) are included. The index to countries, cities, and towns is arranged by state or province (the three countries have separate indexes). Helpful features include: map legend, motor law information (by state), toll roads list, U.S. interstate highway map, mileage charts (city to city), driving time maps, list of selected AM/FM radio stations, miles-per-gallon computer, sign language (international hieroglyphs) of the road, and a telephone area and zip code map of the U.S. The 1975 issue has a centerfold map of the Revolutionary War and an index to Bicentennial points of interest. KR/JKM

SS 1003
Sav*on*Hotels. (Cover title: Sav-On-Hotels Across Europe.) ISSN 0098-4507. 1969. a. illus. Traveltips, Box 11061, Oakland, CA 94611. Examined: 1976. 56p. $2.25 pap.
Aud: Pl

This brief guide is oriented strictly to finding budget accommodations in Europe. There are a few travel hints and an explanation of the choices and entry style. There is a section of budget hotels arranged by country which includes name, address, telephone, and price in dollars. The motel section is also arranged by country and contains the same information. An unusual section is on Paradores, Albergues, and Pousadas (country hotels) in Spain and Portugal. An orientation map is provided for these country hotels. The entries include location, telephone, and a brief description of the area, including fishing sites. All choices for listing in the guide are based on the publisher's travel experience, and the information is updated from additional sources. SLB

SS 1004
South America on $10 a Day. 1966. bi-a. illus. Arthur Frommer, 380 Madison Ave, New York, NY 10017. Dist: Simon and Schuster, 1230 Ave of the Americas, New York, NY 10020. Examined: 1975/76. Arnold Greenberg and Harriet Greenberg. 311p. $4.50 pap.
Aud: Pl

The beginning chapter focuses on inexpensive ways to travel to South America and other related information. There are chapters on each country, with the emphasis on the major city within that country. Each chapter includes budget hotels and restaurants, day and night entertainment, shopping bargains, and useful information particular to that country. There is a brief discussion of the major sights in each country. The guide was published annually in 1968 and 1969. SLB

SS 1005
South American Handbook. ISSN 0081-2579. 1924. a. bibl. index. illus. Trade and Travel Publications, The Mendys Press, Parsonage Lane, Bath, BA1 1EN England. Dist: Rand McNally and Co., Box 7600, Chica-

go, IL 60680. Examined: 1977. John Brooks, ed. 1032p. $16.95. (1978. $17.95.)
Aud: Pl, Sa

The introduction makes it clear that the book can be used for more than a travel guide. The major portion of the book is arranged by country or island group, with a useful table of contents for each section. There is a physical description of the country, history of settlement and economic growth, people, and government. Under each region, cities and towns are described, including some demographic information not usual in a travel guide. Entries also cover transportation, in detail; hotels, with address, price and rating; restaurants; entertainment facilities; useful addresses; and sights. Before the country entries, there is a general section with information on health, general history, and people, and a demographic description of South America. There is a book and periodical index; British-Latin American Organizations; monetary equivalents and exchange; climatic tables; shipping services; index to advertisers; and index to places. There is a colored map insert, and black-and-white maps throughout. SLB

SS 1006

South Pacific Travel Digest. 1972. bi-a. index. illus. Paul Richmond and Co., 1100 Glendon Ave, Los Angeles, CA 90024. Examined: 1976. Charles Jacobs and Babette Jacobs, eds. 160p. $5.95 pap.
Aud: Pl

Presented in magazine format with many photographs and some maps. Includes entries for 13 countries and island groups. There is a strong emphasis on possible tours and sights, with descriptions and instructions on how to get there. For each country there are specific travel facts on entrance, climate, tipping, transportation, drinking and dining, and a hotel/motel directory arranged by city. Address, facilities, a brief comment on quality, and often a price rate are provided for each establishment listed. There is also a general section on traveling to and in the South Pacific and a calendar of colorful events. SLB

SS 1007

Spain and Morocco on $10 and $15 a Day. 1967. bi-a. illus. Arthur Frommer, 380 Madison Ave, New York, NY 10017. Dist: Simon and Schuster, 1230 Ave of the Americas, New York, NY 10020. Examined: 1977/78. Stanley Haggart and Darwin Porter. 384p. $3.95 pap.
Aud: Pl

The focus is on budget travel to Spain, Morocco, and the Canary Islands. After an introduction, there is a discussion of inexpensive ways to travel to and within Spain. There are chapters on Madrid, environs of Madrid, and the other regions of Spain. All chapters cover sights and entertainment and provide suggestions for budget hotels and restaurants. The sections on the Canary Islands and Morocco are also divided by area and include similar information. There are also menu translations, a capsule vocabulary, and currency conversions. A few area maps are included. SLB

SS 1008

Teton. ISSN 0049-3481. 1969. a. illus. Teton Magazine, Box 1903, Jackson, WY 83001. Examined: 1977. Ann Kesslen, ed. 64p. $1.50 pap.
Aud: Pl

A very high quality, magazine-format guide most notable for its magnificent color photographs. There are about seven feature articles on the history, life, and recreation of the area. A complete guide to the Jackson Hole area, which covers accommodations, dining, outdoor activities, services, and shopping, is provided. SLB

SS 1009

Traveler's Almanac. 1975. a. index. illus. Bill Muster, 6900 Santa Monica Blvd, Los Angeles, CA 90038. Examined: 1977. Nancy Meyer, ed. 320p. $6.95 pap.
Aud: Pl

Each chapter has a different author or authors. There are four chapters on transportation, including how to save money on air fare and seafare, overland trails, and automobile transportation. One chapter on touring America lists the top 500 sights to see. There are nine chapters on what to know before you go, including packaged tours, kindred spirit tours, vagabonding, freelancing, using a travel agent, photography for travelers, economy, shopping, 101 wonders of the modern world, and a worldwide touring guide. The touring guide is a country-by-country fact guide on transportation, tours, accommodations, sightseeing, and entertainment. The almanac is primarily a read-before-you-go guide. SLB

SS 1010

TWA Getaway Guide to Athens. 1971. bi-a. illus. Frommer/Pasmantier Publishing Corp., 380 Madison Ave, New York, NY 10017. Dist: Simon and Schuster, 1230 Ave of the Americas, New York, NY 10020. Examined: 1975/76. Ian Keown, ed. 207p. $1.50 pap.
Aud: Pl

The *TWA Getaway Guides* are intended to be brief,

easy-to-read travel guides for a particular country, area, or city. TWA notes that authors have complete editorial freedom and the only evidence of advertising are the discount coupons and an advertisement for TWA's credit card included in each book. This guide covers Greek history, a general description of Athens, hotels and restaurants arranged by price, nightlife, sightseeing, shopping, and other practical information. There are chapters on day trips from Athens, touring the country, and island highlights. A very brief vocabulary and area maps are also included. SLB

SS 1011
TWA Getaway Guide to Boston. 1971. bi-a. illus. Frommer/Pasmantier Publishing Corp., 380 Madison Ave, New York, NY 10017. Dist: Simon and Schuster, 1230 Ave of the Americas, New York, NY 10020. Examined: 1975/76. Faye Hammel. 206p. $1.50 pap.
Aud: Pl

Sections in this guide include an introduction to Boston, hotels, dining, sights, shopping, after dark, and beyond Boston. A section not included in other TWA guides is a student guide to Boston which notes inexpensive places to stay and free concerts and lectures. There are also several maps. SLB

SS 1012
TWA Getaway Guide to Denver and the Colorado Ski Country. 1971. bi-a. illus. Frommer/Pasmantier Publishing Corp., 380 Madison Ave, New York, NY 10017. Dist: Simon and Schuster, 1230 Ave of the Americas, New York, NY 10020. Examined: 1975/76. Rena Bulkin and John Foreman. 206p. $1.50 pap.
Aud: Pl

Provides detailed information on Denver and the Colorado Ski Country with emphasis on Aspen, Vail, Breckenridge, Steamboat Springs, and Denver area skiing. Several maps are included. SLB

SS 1013
TWA Getaway Guide to Honolulu. 1971. bi-a. illus. Frommer/Pasmantier Publishing Corp., 380 Madison Ave, New York, NY 10017. Dist: Simon and Schuster, 1230 Ave of the Americas, New York, NY 10020. Examined: 1975/76. Jill Michaels. 207p. $1.50 pap.
Aud: Pl

Sections in this guide include most for the money hotels, dining after dark, shopping, and three chapters on neighboring islands. There are some maps. SLB

SS 1014
TWA Getaway Guide to Ireland, Dublin/Shannon. 1974. bi-a. illus. Frommer/Pasmantier Publishing Corp., 380 Madison Ave, New York, NY 10017. Dist: Simon and Schuster, 1230 Ave of the Americas, New York, NY 10020. Examined: 1975/76. Beth Bryant and John Godwin. 207p. $1.50 pap.
Aud: Pl

Provides an introduction to the Irish people and several chapters on Dublin, listing hotels and restaurants arranged by price, Dublin pubs, sights, entertainment, and shopping. One-day excursions from Dublin, the Shannon area, and country hotels, restaurants, entertainment and pubs, and shops are also covered. The guide also features some unique Irish vacations, such as staying in a cottage and traveling in horse-drawn caravans. There is useful information and some maps. SLB

SS 1015
TWA Getaway Guide to Las Vegas. 1971. bi-a. illus. Frommer/Pasmantier Publishing Corp., 380 Madison Ave, New York, NY 10017. Dist: Simon and Schuster, 1230 Ave of the Americas, New York, NY 10020. Examined: 1975/76. Ralph H. Peck. 207p. $1.50 pap.
Aud: Pl

Chapters on where to stay, where to dine, evening spots, sports, and gambling and betting, and some information on areas outside Las Vegas are included. There are several maps. SLB

SS 1016
TWA Getaway Guide to Lisbon/Madrid; Costa Del Sol. 1971. bi-a. illus. Frommer/Pasmantier Publishing Corp., 380 Madison Ave, New York, NY 10017. Dist: Simon and Schuster, 1230 Ave of the Americas, New York, NY 10020. Examined: 1975/76. Stanley Haggart and Darwin Porter. 207p. $1.50 pap.
Aud: Pl

Sections in the guide include an introduction to Iberia, getting acquainted with each city, hotels, restaurants, sightseeing, shopping, and Spain and Portugal in a nutshell. There is one chapter on the beach strip, Costa Del Sol. The chapters on hotels and restaurants list selected hotels by quality and price. Entries provide the address, phone number, a brief description, and price. There are some maps. SLB

SS 1017
TWA Getaway Guide to London. 1971. bi-a. illus. Frommer/Pasmantier Publishing Corp., 380 Madison Ave, New York, NY 10017. Dist: Simon and Schuster, 1230 Ave of the Americas, New York, NY 10020. Ex-

amined: 1975/76. John Godwin. 206p. $1.50 pap.
Aud: Pl

The guide provides an orientation to the city and covers hotels, restaurants, and places to drink, arranged by price; sights; sporting events; theaters, after dark entertainment; shopping; children's London; and one-day excursions from the city. There is a chapter with very brief information on areas outside London in England and Wales. Also included are useful addresses, and area and city maps. SLB

SS 1018
TWA Getaway Guide to Los Angeles. 1971. bi-a. illus. Frommer/Pasmantier Publishing Corp., 380 Madison Ave, New York, NY 10017. Dist: Simon and Schuster, 1230 Ave of the Americas, New York, NY 10020. Examined: 1975/76. Stanley Haggart and Darwin Porter. 206p. $1.50 pap.
Aud: Pl

Includes chapters on settling in, finding a place in the sun, restaurants, sights, shopping, after dark, Anaheim, Disneyland and environs, and the California coast from Malibu to San Diego. SLB

SS 1019
TWA Getaway Guide to New York. 1971. bi-a. illus. Frommer/Pasmantier Publishing Corp., 380 Madison Ave, New York, NY 10017. Dist: Simon and Schuster, 1230 Ave of the Americas, New York, NY 10020. Examined: 1975/76. Faye Hammel. 207p. $1.50 pap.
Aud: Pl

Includes chapters on big city logistics, shopping, and excursions in the New York area. There is more emphasis on the best hotel and restaurant values than in other TWA guides. Maps are also included. SLB

SS 1020
TWA Getaway Guide to Paris. 1971. bi-a. illus. Frommer/Pasmantier Publishing Corp., 380 Madison Ave, New York, NY 10017. Dist: Simon and Schuster, 1230 Ave of the Americas, New York, NY 10020. Examined: 1975/76. Stanley Haggart and Darwin Porter. 206p. $1.50 pap.
Aud: Pl

The guide covers getting to know Paris, hotels and restaurants arranged by price, day and evening entertainment, museums and exhibitions, information on taking children to Paris, shopping, and one-day excursions from the city. There is a final chapter with very brief information on other areas in France. Maps of the various areas of the city are included. SLB

SS 1021
TWA Getaway Guide to Phoenix/Tucson. 1971. bi-a. illus. Frommer/Pasmantier Publishing Corp., 380 Madison Ave, New York, NY 10017. Dist: Simon and Schuster, 1230 Ave of the Americas, New York, NY 10020. Examined: 1975/76. John Godwin. 207p. $1.50 pap.
Aud: Pl

Unlike other *TWA Getaway Guides,* this book includes an introduction called "The Flying Start" which assumes that the reader will arrive on a TWA plane. There are chapters on dining, hotels, cultural events, sightseeing, sports, and auto excursions from the cities. There are several maps. SLB

SS 1022
TWA Getaway Guide to Rome. 1971. bi-a. illus. Frommer/Pasmantier Publishing Corp., 380 Madison Ave, New York, NY 10017. Dist: Simon and Schuster, 1230 Ave of the Americas, New York, NY 10020. Examined: 1975/76. Stanley Haggart and Darwin Porter. 207p. $1.50 pap.
Aud: Pl

The guide includes a basic orientation to Rome, hotels and restaurants arranged by prices, major sights with suggested walking tours, other attractions, shopping, and nighttime entertainment. There are also one-day trips from Rome and chapters on other areas and cities in Italy noting major sights and budget information. SLB

SS 1023
TWA Getaway Guide to San Francisco. 1971. bi-a. illus. Frommer/Pasmantier Publishing Corp., 380 Madison Ave, New York, NY 10017. Dist: Simon and Schuster, 1230 Ave of the Americas, New York, NY 10020. Examined: 1975/76. John Godwin and Beth Bryant. 206p. $1.50 pap.
Aud: Pl

Sections in this guide include where to stay, where to eat, strolling around, what to do by day, cultural events, for the kids, shopping, tours and excursions, and further afield. There are maps of the city and some outside areas. SLB

SS 1024
TWA Getaway Guide to Washington, D.C. 1971. bi-a. illus. Frommer/Pasmantier Publishing Corp., 380 Madison Ave, New York, NY 10017. Dist: Simon and Schuster, 1230 Ave of the Americas, New York, NY 10020. Examined: 1975/76. Ralph H. Peck. 207p. $1.50 pap.

Aud: Pl

Covers where to stay, where to eat, and evening entertainment in the nation's capital. This guide concentrates more strongly on historical aspects of the city than other *TWA Getaway Guides*. It includes a section for visiting foreigners, a section for children, and various maps. SLB

SS 1025
TWA Getaway Guide to Zurich/Geneva. 1971. bi-a. illus. Frommer/Pasmantier Publishing Corp., 380 Madison Ave, New York, NY 10017. Dist: Simon and Schuster, 1230 Ave of the Americas, New York, NY 10020. Examined: 1971. Ian M. Keown, ed. 191p. $1.50 pap.
Aud: Pl

Includes several chapters on Geneva, Zurich, and other areas of Switzerland. For each of these three areas, the guide covers hotels and restaurants arranged by price, shopping, sights, and entertainment, as well as useful names and addresses. There are maps scattered throughout. SLB

SS 1026
Thrum's All About Hawaii. (Continues: All About Hawaii; Almanac of the Pacific. ISSN 0065-6461.) 1875. a. bibl. illus. Star-Bulletin Co., Box 100, Honolulu, HI 96810. Examined: 1974. Arlene King Duncan, ed. 338p. $3.50 pap.
Aud: Pl

This is more than a travel guide. It includes much of the information that is usual in travel guides, such as sights, leisure time activities, and transportation available. However, there is also information commonly included in an almanac, such as demographic information. It begins with the state seal and flag and provides a description of each island, including industry, agriculture, and sights; detailed information on the people; a description of the military, government, and economy; a history of Hawaii; a 34-page section on the Hawaiian language; an extensive bibliography; recipes for Hawaiian cuisine; and sections on architecture, communications, and Hawaii's future. There are medium- to good-quality photographs throughout. SLB

SS 1027
Trailer Life's Recreational Vehicle Campground and Services Directory. ISSN 0093-4283. (Continues: Good Sam Club's Recreational Vehicle Owners Directory.) 1971. a. Trailer Life Publishing Co., 2345 Craftsman Rd, Calabasas, CA 91302. Examined: 1974. Art Rouse, ed. 944p. $5.95 pap. (1978. $6.95 pap.)
Aud: Pl

Subtitle: "Official directory for the Good Sam Club." Introductory articles cover recreational vehicle regulations for every state, trouble-shooting, and games for children to play while traveling. The major portion of the directory is arranged alphabetically by state, Canadian province, and Mexico. For each state there are firearms regulations, fishing/hunting information, and the address of the state's Good Sam Organization. Then follows, by city or town, a list of parks and campgrounds, with directions, facilities, season, regulations, and price. There are also listings of several types of services for vehicles, and an index to advertisers. SLB

SS 1028
Washington, D.C. on $10 and $15 a Day. (Continues: Washington, D.C. on $5 and $10 a Day; Washington, D.C. on $10 a Day.) 1965. bi-a. illus. Arthur Frommer, 380 Madison Ave, New York, NY 10017. Dist: Simon and Schuster, 1230 Ave of the Americas, New York, NY 10020. Examined: 1976. Beth Bryant, ed. 263p. $3.95 pap.
Aud: Pl

Includes sections on where to stay, where to eat, sights within the city, sights across the District lines, nighttown, shopping, outdoor activities, cultural activities, special activities and information for international visitors and for kids, and do-it-yourself tours. The 1976 edition has special materials for the Bicentennial and maps. Title changes over the years reflect inflation. SLB

SS 1029
Where to Stay USA from 50¢ to $10 a Night. 1974. a. bibl. illus. Council on International Educational Exchange, 777 United Nations Plaza, New York, NY 10017; Frommer/Pasmantier Publishing Corp., 380 Madison Ave, New York, NY 10017. Dist: Simon and Schuster, 1230 Ave of the Americas, New York, NY 10020. Examined: 1976. Marjorie Adoff Cohen. 335p. $2.95 pap.
Aud: Pl

The basic guide is a list of accommodations arranged by state and city which includes addresses, rates, and phone numbers. The "Getting Around" section covers all types of transportation, including hiking and hitchhiking, and suggests books to read. The "Staying

Awhile" section presents a variety of options from hotels to volunteerings. There is a special section for foreign visitors which lists hotlines and basic survival tips. SLB

SS 1030
Woodall's Campground Directory: Eastern Edition. (Continues: Woodall's Trailering Parks and Campgrounds: Eastern Edition.) 1974. a. illus. Woodall Publishing Co., 500 Hyacinth Place, Highland Park, IL 60035. Dist: Grosset and Dunlap, 51 Madison Ave, New York, NY 10010. Examined: 1975; 1976; 1977. 656p. $4.95 pap.
Aud: Pl

Woodall's apparently began as a single, national trailering parks and campgrounds directory in 1965. Then regional directories were published under separate cover, with the same material. The name changed to **Woodall's Campground Directory** in 1977. Two regional directories and a combined national directory are now available. The major portion of the book is arranged by state, then town. Each entry includes rating, address, size, facilities available, recreation offered, restrictions, and season open. There are also articles about such subjects as crossing international borders, fishing regulations, etc. The directory includes a listing of CB camps and road vehicle repair stations. Covers Eastern Canada, as well as the Eastern United States. SLB

SS 1031
Woodall's Campground Directory: North American Edition. ISSN 0084-1110. (Continues: Woodall's Trailering Parks and Campgrounds.) 1965. a. illus. Woodall Publishing Co., 500 Hyacinth Place, Highland Park, IL 60035. Dist: Grosset and Dunlap, 51 Madison Ave, New York, NY 10010. Examined: 1975; 1976; 1977. 1112p. $7.95 pap.
Aud: Pl

This directory combines the Eastern and Western editions of **Woodall's Campground Directory.** The pagination of the regional directories is retained, so that it is two books in one cover. See annotations for separate regional editions. SLB

SS 1032
Woodall's Campground Directory: Western Edition. (Continues: Woodall's Trailering Parks and Campgrounds: Western Edition.) 1974. a. illus. Woodall Publishing Co., 500 Hyacinth Place, Highland Park, IL 60035. Dist: Grosset and Dunlap, 51 Madison Ave, New York, NY 10010. Examined: 1976; 1977. 336p. $4.95 pap.
Aud: Pl

Beginning in 1974, the North American Edition of *Woodall's Trailering Parks and Campgrounds* was divided into two regional directories; the name of all directories was changed to **Woodall's Campground Directory** in 1977. The Western edition follows the same format and includes the same special articles as the Eastern edition; the territory covered is the Western United States and Canada. SLB

SCIENCE

GENERAL WORKS

SC 1

American Men and Women of Science. ISSN 0065-9347. (Continues: American Men and Women of Science: Physical and Biological Sciences.) 1906. irreg. index. R. R. Bowker, 1180 Ave of the Americas, New York, NY 10036. Dist: R. R. Bowker, Box 1807, Ann Arbor, MI 48106. Examined: 13th ed., 1976. Jaques Cattell Press, eds. 7v. 5776p. $300.
Aud: Cl, Pl, Sa

Lists approximately 110,000 men and women currently active in all areas of the sciences in the U.S. and Canada. Entries are arranged alphabetically by name in the first six volumes; the seventh volume contains geographic and discipline indexes. Entries provide full name, address, discipline, education, past and present positions, memberships, and research interest. Several discipline-oriented directories derived from this basic set are also available, including: **American Men and Women of Science; Biology; American Men and Women of Science: Chemistry; American Men and Women of Science: Consultants; American Men and Women of Science: Medical and Health Sciences; American Men and Women of Science: Physics, Astronomy, Mathematics, Statistics, and Computer Sciences;** and **American Men and Women of Science: Social and Behavioral Sciences.** JKM

SC 2

American Men and Women of Science: Consultants. ISSN 0146-0064. irreg. index. R. R. Bowker, 1180 Ave of the Americas, New York, NY 10036. Dist: R. R. Bowker, Box 1807, Ann Arbor, MI 48106. Examined: 1977. Jaques Cattell Press, eds. 1100p. $35.
Aud: Sa

Lists 15,447 U.S. and Canadian scientists with consulting experience. Entries are arranged alphabetically by name, and disciplinary and geographic indexes are provided. Each entry includes name, address, discipline, education, professional membership and honors, past and present positions, etc. Listings are derived from the seven-volume set **American Men and Women of Science.** This smaller, less expensive directory is designed for those who need easy access to consultants. Most libraries will find the basic set more valuable. JKM

SC 3

American Men and Women of Science: Physics, Astronomy, Mathematics, Statistics, and Computer Sciences. ISSN 0146-003X. irreg. index. R. R. Bowker, 1180 Ave of the Americas, New York, NY 10036. Dist: R. R. Bowker, Box 1807, Ann Arbor, MI 48106. Examined: 1977. Jaques Cattell Press, eds. 1294p. $45.
Aud: Cl, Sa

A disciplinary directory derived from the seven-volume set **American Men and Women of Science.** Covers U.S. and Canadian scientists currently active in the fields of "acoustics, astronomy, astrophysics, biophysics, crystallography, electricity and magnetism, mechanics, physics, atomic physics, experimental physics, nuclear and particle physics, optics, plasma physics, spectroscopy, and theoretical physics as well as in mathematics, statistics, and computer sciences." Entries provide the same biographical and career data as the full set. Although this title is less expensive and somewhat easier to use (since it is smaller), most libraries will probably find the full set a better value. Entries are arranged alphabetically by name and indexed by discipline and location. JKM

SC 4

Applied Science and Technology Index. ISSN 0003-6986. (Continues: Industrial Arts Index.) 1913. a. w/m. and q. suppls. H. W. Wilson, 950 University Ave, Bronx, NY 10452. Examined: 1977 suppls. service basis.
Aud: Jc, Cl, Sa

A cumulative subject index to nearly 300 English language periodicals in the fields of aeronautics and space science, chemistry, computer science, building and construction, energy, engineering, fire prevention, mathematics, mineralogy, metallurgy, oceanography, mining, transportation, and other related areas of the applied sciences and industrial arts. Includes a separate index of book reviews arranged by author. Like other Wilson indexes, a thorough and valuable guide to literature of the field. JKM

SC 5
Bibliographic Guide to Technology. ISSN 0360-2761. 1975. a. G. K. Hall, 70 Lincoln St, Boston, MA 02111. Examined: 1977. 2v. 925p. $110.
Aud: Cl

Presents complete cataloging information for materials in the fields of engineering, aeronautics/astronautics, building construction, food processing and manufacture, patents and trademarks, and production management. Represents Library of Congress MARC records entered during the year plus holdings of the Engineering Societies Library and the New York Public Library Research Libraries. Serials and monographs are listed in dictionary style, with entries for authors, subjects, titles, and series. EM

SC 6
General Science Index. 1978. a. w/m. and q. suppls. H. W. Wilson Co., 950 University Ave, Bronx, NY 10452. Examined: none. (begins July 1978. service basis.)
Aud: Hs, Jc, Cl, Pl

Although no issues of this new Wilson index were available for examination, it is listed here on the basis of the thorough, high-quality indexing provided in other Wilson publications. The publisher states that this work will be a subject index to 88 general science periodicals in the English language covering astronomy, atmospheric sciences, biological sciences, botany, chemistry, earth sciences, environment and conservation, food and nutrition, genetics, mathematics, medicine and health, microbiology, oceanography, psychology, physics, physiology, and zoology. Each issue will contain a separate index of book reviews. JKM

SC 7
Industrial Research Laboratories of the U.S. ISSN 0073-7623. (1975 is the 14th ed.) irreg. index. R. R. Bowker, 1180 Ave of the Americas, New York, NY 10036. Dist: R. R. Bowker, Box 1807, Ann Arbor, MI 48106. Examined: 15th ed., 1977. Jaques Cattell Press, ed. 828p. $65.
Aud: Cl, Sa

Consists chiefly of an alphabetical listing of industrial research laboratories arranged by name of company. Each entry covers areas of research, size and composition of staff, names of chief personnel, whether the laboratory will conduct research or provide consultation to outside organizations or individuals, etc. Includes a geographical index, a personnel index, and a subject index to research categories. EM

SC 8
McGraw-Hill Yearbook of Science and Technology. 1960. a. bibl. index. McGraw-Hill, 1221 Ave of the Americas, New York, NY 10020. Examined: 1976, 436p.; 1978. 430p. $31.50.
Aud: Jc, Cl, Pl

An annual supplement to the *McGraw-Hill Encyclopedia of Science and Technology*. The first part of the volume consists of signed essays on topics of current interest. In the 1976 edition topics covered included cryobiology, ozone in the atmosphere, behavior modification, etc. The second part of the volume consists of an alphabetically arranged update of the year's scientific developments. The articles in this section, which are substantial, have bibliographies appended to them and are signed. Includes a subject index. JKM

SC 9
Nature/Science Annual. ISSN 0085-3860. 1970. a. index. illus. Time-Life Books, Time and Life Bldg, Rockefeller Center, New York, NY 10020. Dist: Silver Burdett Co., 250 James St, Morristown, NJ 07960. Examined: 1977. Jane D. Alexander, ed. 192p. $7.95.
Aud: Jh, Hs, Jc, Cl, Pl

Consists of articles on a variety of science topics of current interest. Includes a 20-page brief summary of events and discoveries during the year covered, arranged by broad category. A list of the year's Nobel Prize winners, with photographs, includes a brief description of the work that led to the award. Well illustrated with color and black-and-white photographs, charts, and line drawings. Includes a subject index. JKM

SC 10
Science News Yearbook. ISSN 0080-7532. 1969. a. index. illus. Science Service, 597 Fifth Ave, New York, NY 10017. Examined: 1970. Warren Kornberg, ed. 373p. $9.95.
Aud: Hs, Jc, Cl, Pl

Based on material originally published in *Science News*. Contains unsigned essays by the *Science News* staff on the previous year's developments in the various fields of the natural sciences, medicine, and environmental sciences. Includes a report on the U.S. federal science policy and an illustrated listing of winners of science awards such as the Nobel Prize, National Medals of Science, and the Enrico Fermi Award. The entry for each award winner includes brief biographical data and a description of the work for which the award was given. There is a subject index. JKM

SC 11

Scientific and Technical Books and Serials in Print. ISSN 0000-054X. (Continues: Scientific and Technical Books in Print.) 1975. a. R. R. Bowker, 1180 Ave of the Americas, New York, NY 10036. Dist: R. R. Bowker, Box 1807, Ann Arbor, MI 48106. Examined: 4th ed., 1978. 2343p. (5th ed., 1979. 2400p. $52.50.)
Aud: Cl, Pl, Sa

Provides full bibliographic and ordering information for books and serials in the areas of the physical and biological sciences, engineering, technology, technical aspects of industry and architecture, biographical works, and philosophic works on historic technologies. Approximately 65,000 titles are indexed by author, title, and subject. Includes a directory of publishers represented with current addresses. Abstracting, indexing, and micropublishing information is included. JKM

SC 12

Scientific, Engineering, and Medical Societies Publications in Print. (Continues: Scientific, Technical and Engineering Societies Publications in Print.) 1974/75. irreg. index. R. R. Bowker, 1180 Ave of the Americas, New York, NY 10036. Dist: R. R. Bowker, Box 1807, Ann Arbor, MI 48106. Examined: 2nd ed., 1976/77. James M. Matarazzo and James M. Kyed, eds. 509p. $19.95.
Aud: Cl, Pl, Sa

Includes print and nonprint materials published by approximately 350 U.S. scientific, engineering, and medical societies and related organizations. Arranged alphabetically by name of the society with full address. Materials available are listed under each society with an indication of how payment should be made. Includes author and key word indexes. JKM

SC 13

Yearbook of Science and the Future. (Continues: Britannica Yearbook of Science and the Future. ISSN 0068-1199.) 1969. a. index. illus. Encyclopaedia Britannica, 425 N Michigan Ave, Chicago, IL 60611. Examined: 1972, 448p.; 13th ed., 1978. $14.95.
Aud: Jh, Hs, Jc, Pl

Approximately half of the volume consists of signed, in-depth essays on a variety of science topics of current interest. The other half of the volume is an alphabetically arranged update of the year's developments in pure and applied science: physics, biology, medicine, behavioral sciences, astronautics, etc. The length of these essays varies, but each is rather substantial and is signed. Obituaries are included in this second section. Well illustrated with color and black-and-white photographs, charts, drawings, and cartoons. JKM

AERONAUTICS

SC 14

Aerospace Facts and Figures. (1965 is 13th ed.). a. index. Aviation Week and Space Technology, 1221 Ave of the Americas, New York, NY 10020. Examined: 1975/76. 143p. $5.95. (1977/78.)
Aud: Cl

Contains a prose summary covering several aspects of the aerospace field, such as aircraft production, missile programs, space programs, and air transportation, followed by statistical data presented through tables and graphs. Statistics are given as far back as 25 years, but more frequently the tables cover the past 10-15 years. There is a subject index. EM

SC 15

Anglo-American Aeronautical Conference. Proceedings. (1969 is 11th ed.) irreg. Royal Aeronautical Society, 4 Hamilton Place, London W1V 0BQ, England. Dist: American Institute of Aeronautics and Astronautics, 1290 Ave of the Americas, New York, NY 10019. Examined: 15th ed., 1977. various paging. $11.
Aud: Cl

Includes the complete versions of papers presented at the annual Anglo-American Aeronautical Conference. There is no index of any sort. Papers cover such topics as aircraft noise, rotorcraft outlook, safety concepts, etc. EM

SC 16

National Aerospace Symposium. Proceedings. 1975. a. Institute of Navigation, 815 15th St, NW, Suite 832, Washington, DC 20005. Examined: 1976. 158p. $20.
Aud: Cl, Sa

Papers cover such topics as missile guidance systems, error reduction techniques, and inspection of navigation facilities. The table of contents provides the usual information on authors and titles. There is no index. EM

ASTRONOMY

SC 17

American Ephemeris and Nautical Almanac. ISSN 0065-8189. 1855; 1960. a. index. United States Nautical Almanac Office, 800 N Quincy St, Arlington, VA 22217. Dist: Superintendent of Documents, U.S. Government Printing Office, Washington, DC 20402. Examined: 1979. P. Kenneth Seidelmann, ed. 571p.
Aud: Pl

Beginning in 1960, the **American Ephemeris and Nautical Almanac** and the *Astronomical Ephemeris,* issued by Her Majesty's Nautical Almanac Office, are combined. Except for a few introductory pages, the two versions are identical. Contains tables showing the computed places of various celestial bodies for each day of the year or for other regular intervals based on standards set by the International Astronomical Union. An important resource for libraries serving anyone who is interested in the stars. The 1979 **Almanac** was published in 1977. NLE

SC 18

Annual Review of Astronomy and Astrophysics. ISSN 0066-4146. 1963. a. bibl. index. illus. Annual Reviews, 4139 El Camino Way, Palo Alto, CA 94306. Examined: v. 14, 1976. Geoffrey R. Burbidge, ed. 500p. $15.
Aud: Cl, Sa
Indexed in: *Chemical Abstracts; International Aerospace Abstracts; Multi-Media Reviews Index; Nuclear Science Abstracts; Science Abstracts.*

Each of the volumes in this series has the value of being a reporting medium for basic and generally new research and development in the field. The interstellar magnetic field, chemical evolution of the galaxies, stellar opacity, and physical processes in comets are among the topics. Some of the mathematics is quite demanding. Some of the articles are easily readable, even for someone with little background in the field. The bibliographies, which are in the form of citations in the text, are generally extensive. Many of the references are to titles easily found, but others are to titles many smaller libraries will not have. Important as a general resource for programs which have only a few courses in astronomy. NLE

SC 19

Ephemeris of the Sun, Polaris, and Other Selected Stars. ISSN 0071-0962. 1910. a. U.S. Department of the Interior, Bureau of Land Management, Washington, DC 20240. Dist: Superintendent of Documents, U.S. Government Printing Office, Washington, DC 20402. Examined: 69th ed., 1978. 30p. $.95.
Aud: Pl, Sa

An abbreviated version of the **American Ephemeris and Nautical Almanac**, designed for the purpose of land management and for farmers. Since this publication is limited and shortened, it will be appropriate for smaller collections. Contains tables of the apparent times of sunrise and sunset at the Greenwich meridian, tables of selected star positions by date at the Greenwich meridian, refractions in polar distances, and the companion trigonometric tables and formulas employed in these measurements. NLE

SC 20

Yearbook of Astronomy. ISSN 0084-3660. 1965. a. index. illus. W. W. Norton and Co., 500 Fifth Ave, New York, NY 10036. Examined: 1977; 1978. Patrick Moore, ed. 223p. $10.95.
Aud: Hs, Jc, Cl, Pl

Volumes include star charts showing relative locations in various areas of the sky; information on specific astronomical events during the year; charts showing phases of the moon and other sky phenomena; and separate sections on occultations, comets, meteors, and other classes of objects. The 1977 yearbook includes a section of notes and diagrams for sky observers in the Southern Hemisphere, which is expanded in the 1978 volume. The material is brief, compact, and readable. Recommended for anyone interested in the sky and what is found there, both natural and man-made. NLE

BIOLOGY

SC 21

Advances in Genetics. ISSN 0065-2660. 1947. irreg. bibl. index. illus. Academic Press, 111 Fifth Ave, New York, NY 10003. Examined: v. 17, 1977. E. W. Caspari, ed. 505p. $30.
Aud: Cl, Sa
Indexed in: *Index Medicus.*

Contains articles on current topics and issues in the field of genetics. The writing is serious, scientific, and scholarly. The bibliographies, or citation lists, lead the reader to challenging material in other sources. The 1977 volume contains articles on genes, behavior, evolutionary processes, and genetic control. Although the emphasis is on advanced research, these papers are important in any biological program. A compilation of papers such as this volume is a good way for a small collection to gather a large quantity of selected material on a specialized field. NLE

SC 22
Advances in Parasitology. ISSN 0065-308X. 1963. irreg. bibl. index. illus. Academic Press, 111 Fifth Ave, New York, NY 10003. Examined: v. 10, 1972. Ben Dawes, ed. 412p. $36.
Aud: Cl, Sa

Some consider parasitology one of "the" courses for the pre-med student. Passing this hurdle is a major step toward an M.D., and continuing knowledge is a must for many specialties. This topic can be quite tricky, and many of the articles are on very advanced topics. The series is probably needed by serious biology programs and students. The bibliographies are extensive, providing plenty of support and additional reading. NLE

SC 23
American Men and Women of Science: Biology. ISSN 0146-0048. irreg. index. R. R. Bowker, 1180 Ave of the Americas, New York, NY 10036. Dist: R. R. Bowker, Box 1807, Ann Arbor, MI 48106. Examined: 1977. Jaques Cattell Press, eds. 1134p. $49.95.
Aud: Cl, Sa

A disciplinary directory derived from the basic set **American Men and Women of Science**. The issue examined lists over 20,000 currently active biologists and biological scientists in the U.S. and Canada. Entries are arranged alphabetically and include: name, address, subject specialty, education, past and present positions, professional memberships and honors, and research interest. Includes disciplinary and geographic indexes. Most general libraries will be better off with the full seven-volume basic set, but special biology libraries may find this smaller, less expensive disciplinary directory sufficient for the needs of their clientele. JKM

SC 24
Annual Editions: Readings in Biology. ISSN 0090-4384. 1973. a. index. illus. Dushkin Publishing Group, Sluice Dock, Guilford, CT 06437. Examined: 1978/79. John Crane, ed. 256p. $5.95.
Aud: Hs, Jc, Cl, Pl

A collection of articles reproduced from newspapers, magazines, and science journals covering current issues and developments related to biology. Designed for use as a supplementary reader for biology courses at the high school and college level, volumes are also useful as a refresher or an introduction to the field for the general reader. Arranged under broad topics, with a subject index. JKM

SC 25
Annual Editions: Readings in Human Development. ISSN 0090-5348. 1972. a. index. illus. The Dushkin Publishing Group, Sluice Dock, Guilford, CT 06437. Examined: 1978/79. Bradley Glanville, ed. 320p. $6.55.
Aud: Hs, Jc, Cl, Pl

Reproduces articles from newspapers, magazines, and professional journals dealing with all aspects of human development. Articles are arranged under broad topics and indexed by subject. Like other works in the *Annual Editions* series, this collection is designed as a supplementary reader for human development courses at the high school and college levels, but it also provides a useful survey of the field for the general reader. JKM

SC 26
Annual Review of Biochemistry. ISSN 0066-4154. 1932. a. bibl. index. illus. Annual Reviews, 4139 El Camino Way, Palo Alto, CA 94306. Examined: v. 47, 1976. Esmond E. Snell, ed. 1011p. (v. 47, 1978. $18.)
Aud: Sa
Indexed in: *Chemical Abstracts; Multi-Media Reviews Index.*

A basic title for chemistry collections, each volume is a collection of scientific articles representing the latest research and thought in the field of biochemistry. The 1978 volume contains 48 articles. Most college libraries will find that this collection is heavily used. The series has improved with age, and it is recommended for any undergraduate collection in an institution which teaches chemistry. NLE

SC 27
Annual Review of Entomology. ISSN 0066-4170. 1956. a. bibl. index. illus. Annual Reviews, 4139 El Camino Way, Palo Alto, CA 94306. Examined: v. 24, 1978. Thomas E. Mittler, ed. 523p. $17.
Aud: Sa
Indexed in: *Apicultural Abstracts; Biological Abstracts; Chemical Abstracts; Multi-Media Reviews Index.*

A collection of articles covering current research and

developments in the field of entomology which are reprinted from a variety of scientific and technical journals. Volumes are designed for the expert or the student specializing in a study of the insect world, but they also include articles which relate to the fields of biology, environmental studies, agriculture, and genetics. The lists of citations and suggested readings included with the articles are extensive. The fact that this title is indexed in so many reference tools increases its value to libraries and their users. NLE

SC 28
Annual Review of Genetics. ISSN 0066-4197. 1967. a. bibl. index. illus. Annual Reviews, 4139 El Camino Way, Palo Alto, CA 94306. Examined: v. 11, 1977. Herschel L. Roman, ed. 505p. (v. 12, 1978. $17.)
Aud: Cl, Sa
Indexed in: *Animal Breeders Abstracts; Biological Abstracts; Chemical Abstracts; Multi-Media Reviews Index.*

An interest in genetic manipulation may generate associated interest in the wide-ranging articles in this series. This collection of scientific articles is generously indexed in several indexing tools and contains large and useful bibliographies which lead the reader to much additional material. Several aspects of the field of genetics are covered in each volume. The set is valuable as a support to research programs, since some of the experiments can be repeated easily, using the article as a guide. Should be of value, especially with a newly awakening interest in genetic engineering and its possible effect in such areas as population control. NLE

SC 29
Annual Review of Microbiology. ISSN 0066-4227. 1947. a. bibl. index. illus. Annual Reviews, 4139 El Camino Way, Palo Alto, CA 94306. Examined: v. 31, 1977. Mortimer P. Starr, ed. 695p. $17.
Aud: Cl, Pl
Indexed in: *Biological Abstracts; Chemical Abstracts; Multi-Media Reviews Index.*

Includes reprints of articles gathered from many sources. Some of the articles are extremely technical, but many provide useful information on current topics, e.g., "Oil Tankers and Pollution: A Microbiological Approach." Articles generally include extensive lists of citations. There is an excellent subject index. The 1977 volume includes 25 articles. NLE

SC 30
Annual Review of Physiology. ISSN 0066-4278. 1939. a. bibl. index. illus. Annual Reviews, 4139 El Camino Way, Palo Alto, CA 94306. Examined: v. 40, 1978. I. S. Edelman, ed. 604p. $17.
Aud: Cl
Indexed in: *Biological Abstracts; Chemical Abstracts; Child Development Abstracts; Multi-Media Reviews Index; Psychological Abstracts.*

A basic series in the field of physiology. Articles cover a wide range of topics, e.g., the 1978 volume covered such topics as muscle mechanics, sexual differentiation, respiratory mechanics, phasic activity in REM sleep, etc. The articles include long and complex bibliographies which are a help to both students and librarians. Since this series is indexed in so many outside sources, the volumes are valuable sources for smaller collections. Includes author and subject indexes. NLE

SC 31
Annual Review of Plant Physiology. ISSN 0066-4294. 1950. a. bibl. index. illus. Annual Reviews, 4139 El Camino Way, Palo Alto, CA 94306. Examined: v. 29, 1978. Winslow R. Briggs, ed. 620p. $17.
Aud: Cl
Indexed in: *Biological Abstracts; Chemical Abstracts; Multi-Media Reviews Index.*

A collection of essays and articles (27 in the volume examined) on recent research in plant physiology. The essays are gathered from many sources and deal with a wide range of topics, including molecules and metabolism, organelles and cells, tissues, organs, plants, population, and the environment. The volumes in this series contain excellent bibliographies, which lead the student to additional literature, and assist the smaller libraries in collection development. A topical collection. Some of the recent essays are relatively easy to read, and the whole series is recommended for undergraduate programs. NLE

SC 32
Annual Reviews of Biophysics and Bioengineering. ISSN 0084-6589. 1972. a. bibl. index. illus. Annual Reviews, 4139 El Camino Way, Palo Alto, CA 94306. Examined: v. 7, 1978. L. J. Mullins, ed. 601p. $17.
Aud: Cl, Sa
Indexed in: *Biological Abstracts; Chemical Abstracts; Multi-Media Reviews Index; Nuclear Science Abstracts; Science Abstracts.*

A multidisciplinary collection of articles covering such topics as microcomputers, signal processing in the retina, origin and maintenance of red blood shapes, phototaxis, etc. Articles include numerous citations and are written by experts in the field. There are numbering keys at the bottom of each article for ordering reprints, and an indication of the copyright fee if copies are made locally. One of the values of this series is that it is indexed in a number of outside sources. NLE

SC 33
Biological and Agricultural Index. ISSN 0006-3177. (Continues: The Agricultural Index.) 1964. a. index. H. W. Wilson Co., 950 University Ave, Bronx, NY 10542. Examined: v. 30, 1975/76; v. 31, 1976/77. Rita D. Goetz, ed. 1691p. service basis.
Aud: Cl, Pl, Sa

Originally published as the *Agricultural Index,* this serial changed its title when it broadened its scope in 1961. It is a "cumulative subject index to English language periodicals in the fields of agricultural chemicals, agricultural economics, agricultural engineering, agriculture and agricultural research, animal husbandry, bacteriology, biochemistry, biology, botany, conservation, dairying and dairy products, ecology, entomology, food science, forestry, genetics, horticulture, marine biology, microbiology, mycology, nutrition, pesticides, physiology, poultry, soil science, veterinary medicine, virology, and zoology." It includes a list of periodicals indexed with addresses and a separate index of book reviews. A basic, essential index which is recommended for biology programs at the college level and above. NLE

SC 34
Biosis List of Serials. ISSN 0067-8937. 1938. a. index. BioScience Information Service, 2100 Arch St, Philadelphia, PA 19103. Examined: 1977. 251p. $10 (included with subscription to *Biological Abstracts*).
Aud: Sa

Lists 8548 serial titles published in 117 countries which are covered in *Biological Abstracts.* Also included are 4000 "archival" titles no longer covered in the *Abstracts.* This is a comprehensive list for the biological sciences. The entries include an abbreviation, which is often the citation, and the title's CODEN which can lead to further bibliographical data through the CODEN lists or through various online data bases. Helpful as a selection or collection development tool. NLE

SC 35
Cold Spring Harbor Symposia on Quantitative Biology. ISSN 0091-7451. 1933. a. bibl. index. illus. Cold Spring Harbor Laboratory, Cold Spring Harbor, NY 11724. Examined: v. 41, 1976. 437p. $30.
Aud: Cl, Sa
Indexed in: *Biological Abstracts; Current Contents; Science Citation Index.*

A collection of papers presented at the Cold Spring Harbor Symposia. Each symposium focuses on a topic in the biological sciences. The quality of the articles is high. Appropriate for advanced programs in biology. NLE

SC 36
Developments in Industrial Microbiology. ISSN 0070-4563. 1960. a. bibl. index. illus. American Institute of Biological Sciences, 1401 Wilson Blvd, Arlington, VA 22209. Examined: v. 19, 1978. Leland A. Underkofler, ed. 624p. $32.95.
Aud: Cl, Sa

This series records the proceedings of the annual meetings of the Society for Industrial Microbiology. The papers contributed by specialists present a cross section of current work and concerns in the practical application of microbiology. Articles in volume 19 deal with esoteric topics such as plant cell culture and the microbial degradation of lignins; the patenting of microbiological inventions; and the relation of microbiology to ecology, industrial production, and foods. An abstract precedes each article. The volumes have author and subject indexes. ST/JKM

SC 37
Handbook of Biochemistry and Molecular Biology. (Continues: Handbook of Biochemistry. ISSN 0072-9736.) 1968. irreg. bibl. index. illus. CRC Press, 18901 Cranwood Pkwy, Cleveland, OH 44128. Examined: 1976. Gerald D. Fasman, ed. 2000p. $39.
Aud: Cl, Sa

This mammoth handbook is divided into four sections. The first section, Proteins, covers amino acids, peptides, polypeptides, and proteins. Section two covers nucleic acids, including purines, pyrimidines, nuclectides, oligonucleotides, tRNA, DNA, and RNA. Section three covers lipids, carbohydrates, and steroids. The fourth section includes physical and chemical data and miscellaneous information on such topics as ion exchange, chromatography, buffers, and vitamins. Each section is continuously updated. These volumes are basic to advanced collections. NLE

SC 38
Zoological Record. ISSN 0084-5604. 1864. a. bibl. index. The Zoological Society of London, Regent's

Park, London NWI 4RY, England. Examined: v. 109, 1972, 618p.; v. 111, 1974. $300.
Aud: Sa

Each volume is issued in fasicules throughout the year. The first of these is *Comprehensive Zoology,* followed by sections recording the year's literature relating to a phylum or to a class of the animal kingdom. The final section lists the new genera and subgenera covered in the volume. Volume 111 for 1974 will consist of 20 sections with two supplements, an indexing vocabulary and a list of serials indexed. Past volumes are available in reprint or in microform. The volumes currently cover about 6000 journals which are selectively indexed for appropriate items. The aim is to provide exhaustive coverage of serious material. The detail is enormous and almost overpowering. This is a basic, fundamental source. Necessary for any academic program in the biological sciences. NLE

BUILDING TECHNOLOGY

SC 39
American Institute of Steel Construction. Annual Report. 1922. a. American Institute of Steel Construction, 1221 Ave of the Americas, New York, NY 10020. Examined: 1976. Dan Farb, ed. 32p. free.
Aud: Cl

The Institute is composed of fabricators who erect structural steel for buildings and bridges. It encourages the development of new design and construction techniques and advises architects, consulting engineers, contractors, etc. as to the most suitable design and use of steel construction. The **Annual Report** includes a review of the year's activities, officers' reports, and reports on the annual convention, market research, awards, and financial studies. Also includes lists of officers and committee members. EM/JKM

SC 40
Associated General Contractors of America. Directory. 1921. a. Associated General Contractors of America, 1957 E St, NW, Washington, DC 20006. Examined: 1976/77. 336p. $25.
Aud: Sa

Lists member companies with their chief officials, addresses, and telephone numbers, by state and local chapter affiliation, followed by an alphabetical listing by name. EM

SC 41
Building Estimator's Reference Book. 1915. tri-a. index. Frank R. Walker Co., 5030 N Harlem Ave, Chicago, IL 60656. Examined: 1977. 1255p. $19.95.
Aud: Cl, Sa

Subtitle: "A practical and thoroughly reliable reference book for contractors and estimators engaged in estimating the cost of constructing all classes of modern buildings." Describes hundreds of building projects, such as erecting rafters for hip roofs or installing doors, with an estimate of the amount of time required by the average worker to complete the project and an estimate of the cost involved. Covers carpentry, concrete work, masonry, etc. There is a detailed subject index. EM

SC 42
Concrete Industries Yearbook. ISSN 0069-827X. (1969 is 31st ed.) a. Pit and Quarry Publications, 105 W Adams St, Chicago, IL 60603. Examined: 1977/78. 274p. $30.
Aud: Cl, Sa

Consists of short articles on different kinds of concrete projects or products, such as hot weather concreting, manufacturing of concrete blocks, etc. Includes descriptions of commercial equipment relative to the topics. EM

SC 43
Dodge Construction Systems Costs. 1974. a. index. McGraw-Hill Information Systems, 1221 Ave of the Americas, New York, NY 10020. Examined: 1977. John Farley, ed. 259p. $25. (5th ed., 1978. $38.60.)
Aud: Cl, Sa

Gives estimated costs of labor and materials for the performance of specific units of work, such as installing windows or doors, installing carpeting, preparing ceilings, etc. Allowances are made for different localities. There is a subject index. EM

SC 44
Engineering News Record. ENR Directory of Contractors. 1974/75. bi-a. index. Engineering News Record, 1221 Ave of the Americas, New York, NY 10020. Examined: 1976/77. James Sullivan, ed. 136p. $9.95.
Aud: Cl

Devotes two pages to describing the areas of activity of participating contracting companies, then lists the 400 largest U.S. contractors by size and by name. There is an alphabetical index. EM

SC 45
National Fire Protection Association. National Fire

Codes. ISSN 0077-4545. 1951. a. index. illus. National Fire Protection Agency, 470 Atlantic Ave, Boston, MA 02210. Examined: 1977. 16v. $75.
Aud: Cl

Describes in great detail the fire prevention standards, codes, and practices approved by the National Fire Protection Association. Well-illustrated and authoritative in nature. Volume one contains the indexes for the set. EM

CHEMISTRY

SC 46
Advances in Carbohydrate Chemistry and Biochemistry. ISSN 0065-2318. (Continues: Advances in Carbohydrate Chemistry.) 1945. irreg. bibl. index. illus. Academic Press, 111 Fifth Ave, New York, NY 10003. Examined: v. 34, 1977. R. Stuart Tipson and Derek Horton, eds. 439p. $48.40.
Aud: Cl, Sa

Beginning with volume 24, this series became interdisciplinary, expanding its coverage to include both biochemistry and carbohydrate chemistry. The emphasis is difficult to define, but chemistry is certainly one of the major interests. Many of the articles included are basic to courses at the upper college level; others are more technical, requiring advanced knowledge and experience and presupposing the availability of equipment. A challenge to the undergraduate, and an expansion of what is normally available in a college library. NLE

SC 47
Advances in Inorganic Chemistry and Radiochemistry. ISSN 0065-2792. 1959. irreg. bibl. index. illus. Academic Press, 111 Fifth Ave, New York, NY 10003. Examined: v. 20, 1977. H. J. Emeleus and A. G. Sharpe, eds. 374p. $35.
Aud: Cl, Sa

Although this series is highly technical, it can be an excellent background source for broad reading. A number of the items cited in the articles are relatively easy to locate in smaller collections. One article in volume 20, "Oxidation States of the Lanthanides," lists 593 citations, and a one-page appendix lists six more. A good choice for the advanced student who needs exposure to a broad range of information. NLE

SC 48
Advances in Organic Chemistry. ISSN 0065-3047. 1960. irreg. bibl. index. illus. Wiley Interscience, 605 Third Ave, New York, NY 10016. Examined: v. 9, 1976. E. C. Taylor, ed. 631p. $45.
Aud: Cl, Sa

Subtitle: "Methods and results." A monumental collection of scientific articles which is a basic source for any chemistry program. The aim of the publication is to cover new methods, reagents, ideas, and fields of application. Articles often serve as an overview of current knowledge or new concepts in a particular aspect of organic chemistry. Because the volumes are issued less frequently than most scientific journals, this collection has limited value as a source of current information. However, the cost of the annual volumes is much less than most journal subscriptions, a fact which smaller libraries with limited budgets will need to consider. NLE

SC 49
Advances in Physical Organic Chemistry. ISSN 0065-3160. 1963. a. bibl. index. illus. Academic Press, 111 Fifth Ave, New York, NY 10003. Examined: v. 13, 1976. V. Gold, ed. 450p. $19.
Aud: Cl, Sa

Articles in volume 13 include: "Calculation of Molecular Structure and Energy by Force-Field Methods"; "Protonation and Salvation in Strong Aqueous Acids"; and "Formation, Properties and Reactions of Cation Radicals in Solution." Such topics are typical throughout the series. The writing is clear and does not overpower the reader. Citations are excellent and serve as a good bibliography to the literature of the field. The advanced student will find much information that is basic to a continuing study in chemistry. NLE

SC 50
American Men and Women of Science: Chemistry. ISSN 0146-0056. irreg. index. R. R. Bowker, 1180 Ave of the Americas, New York, NY 10036. Dist: R. R. Bowker, Box 1807, Ann Arbor, MI 48106. Examined: 1977. Jaques Cattell Press, eds. 1672p. $45.
Aud: Cl, Sa

Lists approximately 29,700 U.S. and Canadian scientists currently active in the field of chemistry or related disciplines. Entries indicate name, address, discipline, education, past and present positions, professional memberships and honors, and research interest. Listings are derived from the seven-volume set **American Men and Women of Science**; special chemistry libraries may find this smaller, less expensive disciplinary directory sufficient for the needs of their clientele.

Includes disciplinary and geographic indexes. JKM

SC 51
Annual Review of Physical Chemistry. ISSN 0066-426X. 1950. a. bibl. index. illus. Annual Reviews, 4139 El Camino Way, Palo Alto, CA 94306. Examined: v. 28, 1977. B. S. Rabinovitch, ed. 570p. $17.
Aud: Cl, Sa
Indexed in: *Chemical Abstracts; Multi-Media Reviews Index; Nuclear Science Abstracts; Science Abstracts.*

Contains reprints of articles from a wide variety of journals in the fields of physical chemistry. An attempt is made to select the best articles, but the quality varies from volume to volume because of editorial opinion. The author and subject indexes make the volumes as good as textbooks, since such a wide variety of material is covered. The bibliographies are a major advantage — a relatively inexpensive way to collect information. A first-choice item for the smaller library which cannot afford subscriptions to a wide variety of journals. NLE

SC 52
CRC Handbook of Laboratory Safety. (Continues: Handbook of Laboratory Safety.) 1967. irreg. index. illus. The Chemical Rubber Company, 18901 Cranwood Parkway, Cleveland, OH 44128. Examined: 1967, Norman V. Steere, ed., 568p; 1971. 854p. $33.95.
Aud: Hs, Jc, Cl

The purpose of this handbook is "to provide useful and accurate information for preventing or controlling accidents, injuries, fires, and losses in laboratories, whether the laboratories are in educational institutions, in hospitals, in industry, or elsewhere." Many experts and sources were consulted for general information on protective equipment, ventilation, fire hazards, chemical reactions, toxic hazards, radiation hazards, electrical and mechanical hazards, water supplies, and other topics. Major feature is an extensive table of chemical hazards and information on over 1000 materials arranged by name. A condensed table is also provided. Contains useful information which should be available to anyone working with dangerous chemicals. Despite the age of the current edition, the volume should be a standard feature in school laboratories. NLE

SC 53
The Condensed Chemical Dictionary. 1919. irreg. index. Van Nostrand Reinhold Co., 7625 Empire Dr, Florence, KY 41042. Examined: 9th ed., 1977. Gessner G. Hawley, ed. 957p. $25.
Aud: Hs, Jc, Cl

A compendium of technical data and descriptive information covering thousands of chemicals and chemical phenomena. The level of this book lies between the *Glossary of Chemical Terms,* which is elementary, and *Encyclopedia of Chemistry,* a much more detailed and sophisticated volume, both of which are issued by the same publisher. The **Dictionary** presents technical descriptions of chemicals, raw materials, and processes; expanded definitions of chemical entities, phenomena, and terminology; and descriptions or identifications of a wide range of trademarked products used in the chemical industry. Covers names, synonyms, formulas, properties, sources, derivation, hazards, uses, and shipping regulations. An excellent source to accompany the handbooks containing the tables and formulas. NLE

SC 54
Handbook of Chemistry and Physics. 1918. a. index. Chemical Rubber Publishing Co., 18901 Cranwood Pkwy, Cleveland, OH 44128. Examined: 57th ed., 1976/77, 2393p.; 58th ed., 1977/78. Robert C. Weast, ed. 2345p. $38.50.
Aud: Cl, Sa

Subtitle: "A ready reference book of chemical and physical data." Each edition contains hundreds of tables of importance to chemists and physicists. There is a brief table of contents, and each edition has an index. The general organization covers mathematical tables, elements and inorganic compounds, organic compounds, general chemical, general physical constraints, etc. Recent editions also contain a list of National Standard Reference Data System publications which provide additional information in technical areas. End papers in the 58th edition contain the Periodic Table of the Elements, and tables showing melting and boiling points and atomic weights of the elements. A necessary resource to answer technical questions in the areas covered, but the user has to know the fields since access points to the information are not readily apparent to the novice. NLE

SC 55
Lange's Handbook of Chemistry. 1934. irreg. index. McGraw-Hill Book Co., 1221 Ave of the Americas, New York, NY 10020. Examined: 11th ed., 1973. John A. Dean, ed. 1581p. $19.50. (12th ed., 1978.)
Aud: Cl, Sa

A one-volume source of factual information for chemists, both students and professionals. Divided into ten sections: mathematics, general information and conversion tables, atomic and molecular structure, inorganic chemistry, analytical chemistry, electrochemistry, organic chemistry, spectroscopy, thermodynamic properties, and physical properties. Each section is subdivided into related groups of factual data. Each edition contains new and revised material and has broader coverage than the last. An extensive, cross-referenced subject index increases the work's value. Every chemistry collection should have this title, and all students should know about it. NLE

SS 56
Polymer Handbook. 1967. irreg. John Wiley and Sons, 605 Third Ave, New York, NY 10016. Examined: 2nd ed., 1975. J. Brandrup, ed. 1375p. $38.75.
Aud: Cl, Sa

Limited to synthetic polymers plus polysaccharides and derivatives. Does not include spectroscopic data since this information is available elsewhere. Many tables of a highly technical nature are included. Intended to assist in the search for data and constants needed in theoretical and experimental polymer work. Divided into broad sections: polymerization and depolymerization; solid state properties; solution properties; physical constants; and physical properties. A detailed and complex tool necessary only for those working in this specialized area of chemistry. Probably a necessary purchase for academic and technical institutions and for firms which have programs in this field. NLE

SC 57
Progress in Physical Organic Chemistry. ISSN 0079-6662. 1963. irreg. bibl. index. illus. Wiley Interscience, 605 Third Ave, New York, NY 10016. Examined: v. 12, 1976. Robert W. Taft, ed. 368p. $31.
Aud: Cl, Sa

This series is concerned with investigations of organic chemistry by quantitative and mathematical methods. The subjects covered include relationships with molecular structure, spectroscopy, molecular biology, and biophysics. This is an advanced source which may have limited utility for the undergraduate, but the articles serve as excellent springboards mto many related fields. Recommended because the articles cross many fields, and the citation lists are excellent, though they are not as extensive as those in other, similar series. NLE

SC 58-59
Reports on the Progress of Chemistry. (Continues: Chemical Society, London. Annual Reports on the Progress of Chemistry. ISSN 0069-3022.) 1904. a. bibl. index. illus. The Chemical Society, Burlington House, London W1V 0BN, England.
Aud: Cl, Sa

SC 58
Series A: Physical and Inorganic Chemistry ISSN 0308-6003. Examined: v. 73, 1976. 273p.

SC 59
Series B: Organic Chemistry. ISSN 0069-3030. Examined: v. 73, 1976. 456p.

The stated object in the 1904 edition was "to present an epitome of the principal definite steps in advance which have been accomplished in the preceding year, for the benefit of workers, students, or teachers of chemistry." In 1967 the reports split in two sections, separately issued and priced. **Series A, Physical and Inorganic Chemistry,** contains analytical and crystallographic material of significance to physical and inorganic chemists. **Series B** covers organic chemistry, biological chemistry, and other matters of interest to the organic chemist. The topics are selected each year to form a critical overview. The sections are crisp, cogent, and technical. The material is written by many authors, obviously specialists in each field. There are hundreds of citations. One of the top English-language publications in the field. Recommended as a knowledgeable series. NLE

COMPUTER SCIENCE

SC 60
Association for Computing Machinery. Annual Workshop on Microprogramming. Conference Record. 1968. a. bibl. Association for Computing Machinery, 1133 Ave of the Americas, New York, NY 10036. Examined: 10th ed., 1977. 133p. $12; $9 to members.
Aud: Sa

Contains papers presented at and a record of the workshop sessions. Topics covered include firmware engineering, future role of microprogramming, operational system support, etc. EM

SC 61
Association for Computing Machinery. Proceedings of the National Conference. ISSN 0066-9091. (1961 is 16th ed.) a. index. Association for Computing Machinery, 1133 Ave of the Americas, New York, NY 10036. Examined: 1976. 570p. $25.
Aud: Cl, Sa

Includes papers presented at the annual conference. Topics covered include computer applications, technology of information storage and retrieval, standardization of computer programs and data elements, computer design, etc. There is an index of participants. EM

SC 62

Computer Personnel Research Conference. Proceedings. ISSN 0069-8148. (1969 is 7th ed.) a. Association for Computing Machinery, 1133 Ave of the Americas, New York, NY 10036. Examined: 14th ed., 1976. 205p. $10.
Aud: Cl, Sa

Includes the entire texts of papers presented at the annual conference. Covers such topics as systems analysis, applications of computers to information systems, etc. EM

SC 63

Computer Yearbook. ISSN 0069-8180. (Continues: Data Processing Yearbook; Computer Yearbook and Directory.) 1952. irreg. International Electronics Information Services, Box 2658, Detroit, MI 48231. Examined: 1977. 500p. $40.
Aud: Sa

Brief "state-of-the-art" chapters provide overviews of the current status of computer technology. Seven major computer systems companies and several mini- and microcomputer firms are described. Some information on softwear, salaries, and career planning is provided. Major feature, and major portion of the issue examined, is an extensive glossary with helpful definitions but an unhelpful arrangement. There are cross references, and poking around among the terms is informative. Some phrases are invented, some are not. Does not contain the very latest information, but the inclusion of the smaller computer companies and computer systems makes this a good starting place for reference searches, even if it should not be considered as the final word. NLE

SC 64

Computers in Chemical and Biochemical Research. 1972. irreg. bibl. index. Academic Press, 111 Fifth Ave, New York, NY 10003. Examined: v. 2, 1974. C.E. Klopfenstein, ed. 276p. $26.
Aud: Cl, Sa

Reprints of published materials and original articles by practicing computer-chemists and biochemists provide retrospective and current reports of work in computer-assisted chemistry. Topics treated are delineations of design philosophies and laboratory computer systems; descriptions of hardware design to solve specific problems; algorithms; languages and programming techniques; applications of digital computer methods to specific problems; and training in computer use. Anticipated for future issues are articles dealing with computer networks, microprogrammed computers, advances in hardware technology, and new applications of information theory to chemistry and biochemistry research problems. The purpose of the series is to facilitate communication among workers and provide coverage of the state of the art. Each volume has a subject index. ST/JKM

SC 65

International Telemetering Conference. Proceedings. 1965. a. index. International Foundation for Telemetering, 19730 Ventura Blvd, Suite 6, Woodland Hills, CA 91364. Dist: Instrument Society of America, 400 Stanwix St, Pittsburgh, PA 15222. Examined: 1976. 737p. (v. 11, 1975. $30.)
Aud: Cl

Telemetering is the science of measuring the quantity or value of physical phenomena and transmitting the data to some remote point for recording. Papers presented at this annual conference, which is co-sponsored by the International Foundation for Telemetering and the Instrument Society of America, cover such topics as new devices for telemetering, computer communication systems, and worldwide communication systems. There is an author index. EM

SC 66

Winter Simulation Conference. Proceedings. 1969. a. index. Association for Computing Machinery, 1133 Ave of the Americas, New York, NY 10036. Examined: 1977. 2v. $40; $32 to members.
Aud: Cl

Subtitle: "Discrete-event simulation." Includes papers presented at the annual conference on applications of simulation. Topics covered range from statistical methods to military simulation to simulation of manufacturing systems. There are author and subject indexes. The proceedings are available on microfiche from the Society for Computer Simulation, Box 2228, La Jolla, CA 92038. EM

EARTH SCIENCES

SC 67

Advances in Ecological Research. ISSN 0065-2504. 1962. irreg. bibl. index. illus. Academic Press, 111 Fifth Ave, New York, NY 10003. Examined: v. 10, 1977. A. MacFadyen, ed. 177p.
Aud: Cl, Sa

While the volumes of this series are on the slender side, they do bring primary material together. Articles touch on a wide range of topics which stem from research in both the laboratory and the field. Many articles deal with the water systems and thus touch on current topics of interest to many students, e.g., steps that can be taken to protect the environment. Many of the experiments described can be repeated without too much difficulty and probably not too much money. Good bibliography and indexes. NLE

SC 68

Annual Review of Earth and Planetary Sciences. ISSN 0084-6597. 1973. a. bibl. index. illus. Annual Reviews, 4139 El Camino Way, Palo Alto, CA 94306. Examined: v. 5, 1977. Fred A. Donath, ed. 557p. $15. (v. 6, 1978. $17.)
Aud: Sa
Indexed in: *Chemistry Abstracts; International Aerospace Abstracts; Multi-Media Reviews Index*.

The volume examined includes 27 articles covering various topics in the fields of astronomy, biochemistry, ecology, geology, mineralogy, etc. Articles are reprinted from various scholarly journals, and some are duplicated in other Annual Reviews' titles, e.g., **Annual Review of Astronomy and Astrophysics**. While such volumes do not substitute for having the journals, having such a wide ranging source is an inspiration to the first- or second-year student. The articles provide hundreds of citations to the literature, some of which are easily available. The future of the planet and its resources is a topic of current interest, and this series provides an excellent start on a search of the scarce material. NLE

SC 69

Annual Review of Ecology and Systematics. ISSN 0066-4162. 1970. a. bibl. index. illus. Annual Reviews, 4139 El Camino Way, Palo Alto, CA 94306. Examined: v. 8, 1977. Richard J. Johnson, ed. 490p. $17. (v. 9, 1978.)
Aud: Cl, Sa
Indexed in: *Biology Abstracts; Chemistry Abstracts; Field Crop Abstracts; Herbage Abstracts; Multi-Media Reviews Index*.

Includes articles reprinted from various scholarly journals on topics in the fields of biology, botany, ecology, etc. The volume examined includes an article "Environmental Effects of Dams and Impoundments," which offers a fascinating account, easily readable by any college student, and one providing many arguments for ecological protection. As usual with the *Annual Reviews* series, the articles provide excellent bibliographies in the form of citations. While some other articles are difficult, many are appropriate for undergraduate programs. The volumes have good subject indexes. In addition, the contents are analyzed in a number of source indexes. Recommended for the current interest factor and for undergraduate programs. NLE

SC 70

Antarctic Bibliography. ISSN 0066-4626. 1965. 18 months. bibl. index. U.S. Library of Congress, Cold Regions Bibliography Project, Washington, DC 20540. Dist: Superintendent of Documents, U.S. Government Printing Office, Washington, DC 20402. Examined: v. 7, 1974. Geza T. Thuronyi, ed. $9.15.
Aud: Cl

A classified bibliography of current Antarctic literature. Entries are arranged into 13 categories: general, biological sciences, cartography, expeditions, geological sciences, ice and snow, logistics, equipment and supplies, medical sciences, meteorology, oceanography, atmospheric physics, terrestrial physics, and political geography. The 1975/76 volume contained 2452 abstracts. The scope is international. Annotations are descriptive rather than critical. There are author, subject, geographic, and grantee indexes. A companion volume, *Antarctic Bibliography 1951-1961* (349p., $4.75), provides retrospective coverage. A cumulative index is available for volumes one to seven. An excellent purchase for most colleges and advanced collections interested in the study of the South Pole. Updated on a monthly basis by *Current Antarctic Literature*, a new cumulation is issued every 18 months. NLE

SC 71

Bibliography and Index of Geology. ISSN 0098-2784. (Continues in part: Bibliography and Index of Geology Exclusive of North America. ISSN 0006-1522.) (v. 33 is 1969.) a. bibl. index. illus. The Geological Society of America, Publication Sales, 3300 Penrose Place, Boulder, CO 80301. Examined: v. 40, 1976. 4v. approx. 1000p. (v. 42, 1978. $750.)

Aud: Cl, Sa

The annual cumulations are in four volumes, two each for the bibliography and the index. Covers the earth sciences literature of the world. Books, serials, reports, maps, and North American theses are included. This publication combined the U.S. Geological Survey's *Bibliography and Index of North American Geology* which covered 1785 to 1970 and the Geological Society of America's *Bibliography and Index of Geology Exclusive of North America* which was issued from 1933 to 1968. The family of three titles is the basic set and should be in any collection covering the earth sciences, geography, or geology. The coverage is comprehensive. Should be used with **Geo Abstracts** for the most complete coverage. NLE

SC 72

United States Earthquakes. ISSN 0091-1429. 1928. a. illus. U.S. National Geophysical and Solar-Terrestrial Data Center, Boulder, CO 80303. Dist: Superintendent of Documents, U.S. Government Printing Office, Washington, DC 20402. Examined: 1975. Jerry L. Coffman and Carl W. Stover, eds. 136p. $2.30.
Aud: Cl

Co-sponsored by the National Oceanic and Atmospheric Administration and the U.S. Department of the Interior, Geological Survey. The basic purpose is to describe all earthquakes which occurred in the U.S. and nearby territories in the year of coverage. Intended to provide a continuous history of U.S. earthquakes for use in seismic risk studies, site evaluations for nuclear powerplants, design of earthquake-resistant structures, and for answering queries from the scientific community and the general public. Each description includes date, origin time, epicenter, epicenter source, maximum intensity, and macroseismic effects. Maps, tables, charts, and photographs enhance the data. Some text is descriptive; some is telegraphic, even cryptic. Interesting and full of information for geologists. Cumulative volumes were issued for 1928-35, 1936-40, and 1941-45. NLE

SC 73

U.S. Forest Service. Forest Resource Reports. ISSN 0071-755X. 1950. irreg. index. U.S. Forest Service, Department of Agriculture, Washington, DC 20250. Dist: Superintendent of Documents, U.S. Government Printing Office, Washington, DC 20402. Examined: 1975. 243p. (no. 21, 1977. $4.)
Aud: Sa

Each report focuses on a different topic, such as the renewable resources of forest, range, and inland waters. Provides an abundance of statistics and graphs, and there is a subject index. EM

SC 74

United States Geological Survey. Yearbook. 1880. a. index. illus. U.S. Department of the Interior, Washington, DC 20402. Dist: Superintendent of Documents, U.S. Government Printing Office, Washington, DC 20402. Examined: 1976, 212p., $3.60; 1977. 229p.
Aud: Cl, Sa

"Summarizes the progress made by the United States Geological Survey during fiscal year 1977 in its mandated role: to identify the nation's land, water, energy, and mineral resources; to classify Federally-owned mineral lands and water power sites; to regulate the exploration and development of energy and mineral resources on Federal and Indian lands; and to explore and appraise the petroleum potential of the National Petroleum Reserve in Alaska." In five parts: the year in review; perspectives; missions, organization, and budget; activities and accomplishments; and statistical tables. It is supplemented by the Survey's Professional Paper 1050: *Geological Survey Research in 1977.* Authoritative, basic, informative, readable, and easily available. Includes many tables and charts and a subject index. Recommended for libraries with collection interests in conservation, mineral resources, environmental studies, energy, water resources, etc. NLE

SC 75

U.S. National Park Service. Office of the Chief Scientist. Annual Report. ISSN 0095-5566. 1975. a. bibl. index. U.S. National Park Service, Office of the Chief Scientist, Washington, DC 20240. Examined: 1975. 556p.
Aud: Pl, Sa

Reports on research by service and non-service scientists from the U.S. and some foreign countries on animal species, geology, plants and vegetation, general ecology, fresh-water topics, human impact, marine studies, hydrology, sociology, fire ecology, meteorology, exotic species, and other miscellaneous topics. Divided into five sections: science projects underway, reports of progress in previous years, added reports in various areas, a bibliography, and author and subject indexes. Reports typically give investigator's name, the project title, a rationale, and a brief summary. Full of ideas for further research and details on current developments in many areas of earth sciences. Few libraries either want or need the full studies reported in such a compendium, but many will find such a collection of value and interest. Especially valuable for libraries with biological interests. NLE

SC 76
Weather Almanac. 1974. irreg. bibl. index. illus. Gale Research Co., Book Tower, Detroit, MI 48226. Examined: 2nd ed., 1977. James A. Ruffner and Frank E. Bair, eds. 728p. $25.
Aud: Pl

Subtitle: "A reference guide to weather, climate, and air quality of the United States and its key cities, comprising statistics, principles, and terminology." Provides detailed information on temperature, precipitation, snowfall, frost, and wind in the U.S. Includes sections on numerous severe weather conditions, from hurricanes to tsunami, and brief sections on air pollution and weather fundamentals. There are a wide range of clear, informative charts and tables. Certainly an excellent source for the weather novice, as well as a good reference compendium for the weather expert. Should be updated on a regular basis to remain of value for the smaller library. NLE

ELECTRICITY AND ELECTRONICS

SC 77
EEM (Electronic Engineers Master). ISSN 0423-9938. 1957. a. index. United Technical Publications, 645 Stewart Ave, Garden City, NY 11530. Examined: 20th ed., 1976/77. 2v. 3264p. $30.
Aud: Cl, Sa

A guide for buyers and specifiers of electronic components, systems, and equipment. Produced in two volumes. The directory volume includes a product index and an index to manufacturers and sales offices that includes addresses, names of local representatives, and other relevant information. The catalog volume presents manufacturers' listings or catalogs arranged in 43 product sections, e.g., resistors, microwave components, etc. EM/JKM

SC 78
Edison Electric Institute. Statistical Year Book of the Electrical Utility Industry. 1928. a. index. Edison Electric Institute, 90 Park Ave, New York, NY 10016. Examined: no. 44, 1977. 69p. $15; $10 to members.
Aud: Sa

Factual information, data, and statistics relating to the electric industry. Data are compiled from annual statistical reports and monthly reports from the Federal Power Commission, the Bureau of the Census, and other sources. Statistics are provided for the total U.S. electric utility industry, including all plants contributing to the public supply and industrial, railroad, and railway plants, except in the financial section where data for only investor-owned utilities are provided, due to the dissimilarity between investor-owned electric utilities and other component groups. Includes a subject index and a detailed table of contents. KR/JKM

SC 79
Electrical World Directory of Electric Utilities. (1976/77 is 85th ed.) a. index. Electrical World, 1221 Ave of the Americas, New York, NY 10020. Examined: 86th ed., 1977/78. 987p. $97.50.
Aud: Cl

Utility companies are listed first by state, then by type of utility. Each entry includes names of chief officers, sales data, number of customers, etc. There is an index of consulting engineers and an alphabetical index of company names. EM

SC 80
Electronic Components Conference. Proceedings. ISSN 0569-5503. 1950. a. index. Institute of Electrical and Electronics Engineers, 345 E 47th St, New York, NY 10017. Examined: 1977. 562p. $25.
Aud: Cl
Indexed in: *Engineering Index.*

Papers presented at the conference cover topics such as thin film technology, trends of component design, optical components, etc. There is an author index; the table of contents provides additional author/title data. EM

SC 81
Electronic Design's Gold Book. 1974. a. index. Hayden Publishing Co., 50 Essex St, Rochelle Park, NJ 07662. Examined: 1977/78. 3v. $30.
Aud: Cl

Published by *Electronic Design* magazine. Volume one contains listings of manufacturers by products and then alphabetically by name, with addresses. Also includes a trade name directory and a directory of distributors. Volume two contains pages from the catalogs of participating companies. Volume three examines the products of one sponsoring company. EM

SC 82
Electronic Industry Telephone Directory. ISSN 0422-

9053. 1963. a. index. Harris Publishing Co., 33140 Aurora Rd, Cleveland, OH 44139. Examined: 1976/77, $15; 1977/78. 408p. $16.75.
Aud: Cl, Sa

Divided into two main sections. The first lists electronic product manufacturers and related companies alphabetically by company name with addresses and telephone numbers. The second section lists manufacturers by products. EM

SC 83
Electronic Market Data Book. ISSN 0070-9867. (Continues: Electronic Industries Yearbook.) 1956. a. Electronic Industries Association, Marketing Services Department, 2001 Eye St, NW, Washington, DC 20006. Examined: 1975. 119p. $2.
Aud: Cl, Sa

A source book for the electronics industry. Presents detailed information in the form of text, tables, statistical charts, and pie graphs on production, sales, foreign trade, research and development, and government markets. Production and sales figures are obtained directly and voluntarily from over 500 companies. Chapters include: summary; consumer electronics; communications and industrial products; government products; electronic components; world trade; related information; and industry description. There is no index. KR/JKM

SC 84
Electronic News Financial Factbook and Directory. ISSN 0070-9875. 1962. a. index. Fairchild Publications, 7 E 12th St, New York, NY 10003. Examined: 1977. 652p. $75.
Aud: Cl

Offers an alphabetical listing of companies showing nature of their work, officers, affiliate companies, sales/earnings data, and other financial data. Has an alphabetical company name index. EM

SC 85
Electronics Buyers Guide. ISSN 0090-5291. 1945. a. index. Electronics, 1221 Ave of the Americas, New York, NY 10020. Examined: 1978. Regina Hera, ed. 1516p. $25.
Aud: Cl

Lists products under some 4000 terms, followed by an alphabetical index of manufacturers. Includes a directory of trade names and catalogs of participating companies. EM

SC 86
Frequency Control Symposium. Proceedings. (1970 is 24th ed.) a. Electronic Industries Association, 2001 Eye St, NW, Washington, DC 20006. Examined: 1977. 623p. $10.
Aud: Sa

Jointly sponsored by the Electronic Industries Association and the U.S. Army Electronics Command. Papers are arranged under subject categories such as quartz crystal devices, oscillator research, frequency standards, etc. Has a table of contents for author/title data. Separate indexes are available. EM

SC 87
International Electric Vehicle Symposium. Proceedings. 1969. Edison Electric Institute, Electric Vehicle Council, 90 Park Ave, New York, NY 10016. Examined: 1976. 777p. $75.
Aud: Cl

Papers presented at the international symposium are arranged under headings such as battery research, electric railways, and hybrid power system. An abstract precedes each article. EM

SC 88
Joint Power Generation Conference. Proceedings. a. Institute of Electrical and Electronic Engineers, 345 E 47th St, New York, NY 10017. Examined: 1977. various pagings. $16; $12 to members.
Aud: Cl

Contains the full texts of papers presented at the conference arranged by IEEE paper number. Topics covered include power station tests, hydroelectric planning, and noise control. EM

SC 89
National Electronics Conference Proceedings. ISSN 0077-4413. 1944. a. index. National Engineering Consortium, Oakbrook Executive Plaza, 1301 W 22nd St, Oak Brook, IL 60521. Examined: 1975. 353p. $10.
Aud: Cl
Indexed in: *Engineering Index.*

Includes all papers presented at the annual conference and summarizes seminar discussions. Papers cover such topics as telephone data communication, and display devices. There is an index to contributors. Cumulative indexes are issued every five years. EM

SC 90
National Research Council. Digest of Literature on

Dielectrics. ISSN 0070-4865. 1936. a. index. National Academy of Sciences, Division of Engineering, 2101 Constitution Ave, NW, Washington, DC 20008. Examined: 1973. 740p. $40.
Aud: Cl, Sa

Presents critical reviews of current dielectrics literature on topics such as electrical discharges, insulating films, conduction phenomena, etc. Covers many current scientific and engineering publications. EM

SC 91

Power Sources Symposium. Proceedings. ISSN 0079-4457. 1956. bi-a. PSC Publishing Committee, Box 891, Red Bank, NJ 07701. Examined: 1976. 218p. $15.
Aud: Cl

This symposium is sponsored by the U.S. Army Electronics Command. Papers presented at the symposium are arranged under categories such as electric vehicle batteries, primary and secondary batteries, fuel cells, etc. EM

SC 92

Who's Who in Electronics. ISSN 0083-9507. (Continues: Electronic Source Procurement.) 1949. a. index. Harris Publishing Co., 33140 Aurora Rd, Cleveland, OH 44139. Examined: 1977. various paging. $52.
Aud: Cl, Sa

Manufacturers of electronic equipment and components are listed alphabetically, then geographically. There is also a geographical list of distributors. EM

ENERGY AND ENVIRONMENTAL STUDIES

SC 93

American Nuclear Society. Directory: Who's Who in Nuclear Energy. ISSN 0092-8518. 1967. irreg. index. American Nuclear Society, 244 E Ogden Ave, Hinsdale, IL 60521. Examined: 1976. 142p.
Aud: Cl

Lists members of the American Nuclear Society alphabetically with home or professional addresses. Membership is comprised of physicists, chemists, mathematicians, engineers, metallurgists, and others with professional experience in nuclear science or nuclear engineering. In addition there are lists of officers, committee members, and divisions of the Society. EM/JKM

SC 94

American Petroleum Institute. Annual Statistical Review. 1946. a. bibl. index. American Petroleum Institute, 1801 K St, NW, Washington, DC 20006. Examined: 1964/1973; 1965/1974. 79p. $6.50.
Aud: Cl

Primarily consists of tabular data on all aspects of the petroleum industry, including number of wells producing, production (by state), exports and imports, energy consumption, transportation of oil, employment data, and world petroleum data. There is a bibliography of industry-related reference material. EM

SC 95

American Petroleum Institute. Petroleum Facts and Figures. 1928. irreg. American Petroleum Institute, 1801 K St, NW, Washington, DC 20006. Examined: 1971. 604p.
Aud: Cl

Provides prose and tabular accounts of petroleum production, refining, transport, marketing, prices, and general topics (e.g., labor, safety, etc.). EM

SC 96

Annual Review of Energy. 1976. a. bibl. Annual Reviews, 4139 El Camino Way, Palo Alto, CA 94306. Examined: none. (v. 3, 1978. J. M. Hollander, ed. $17.)
Aud: Jc, Cl, Pl, Sa

Although no copy was available for examination, this title is included on the basis of other works issued by Annual Reviews, e.g., **Annual Review of Astronomy and Astrophysics.** Volumes include scholarly articles on all aspects of energy written by experts in the field. Publisher's information indicates that volume three contains 24 articles including "Alternative Breeder Reactor Technologies"; "Energy, Employment, and Productivity"; "Passive Solar Energy Systems"; "Issues in Automobile Development: Efficiency Improvement and Environmental Control"; "Energy Use and the Quality of Life"; etc. Most of Annual Reviews, publications are aimed at an advanced audience, but it appears that this new title would be of interest to the general public or the beginning college student as well. JKM

SC 97

Annual Review of Nuclear Science. ISSN 0066-4243. 1952. a. bibl. index. illus. Annual Reviews, 4139 El Camino Way, Palo Alto, CA 94306. Examined: v. 27, 1977. Emilio Segre, ed. 568p. $17.50.

Aud: Cl, Sa

Indexed in: *Chemical Abstracts; Multi-Media Reviews Index; Nuclear Science Abstracts; Science Abstracts*.

A collection of articles by experts in the field of nuclear science. Like other works in the *Annual Reviews'* series, this collection has interdisciplinary value. Articles in the 1977 volume covered such topics as element production in the early universe, and the weak neutral current and its effects in stellar collapse. Articles in the 1978 volume covered high-intensity neutron sources, experimental nuclear astrophysics, nuonium chemistry, etc. Since the articles include numerous citations to additional sources, and the volume is indexed in so many of the science indexes, this series has great value for smaller collections. NLE

SC 98
Brown's Directory of North American Gas Companies. ISSN 0068-2888. 1887. a. index. Harcourt Brace Jovanovich, 757 Third Ave, New York, NY 10017. Examined: 1977. 664p. $96.50.
Aud: Cl

Following an alphabetical index of gas companies and municipal systems, there is a geographic listing of gas companies with operating statistics. Also includes lists of related public service commissions and gas associations. EM

SC 99
Conservation Directory. ISSN 0069-911X. 1953. a. bibl. index. National Wildlife Federation, 1412 16th St, NW, Washington, DC 20036. Examined: 20th ed., 1975. Gloria H. Decker, ed. 220p. (1977. $3.)
Aud: Jc, Cl, Pl, Sa

An extensive list of government agencies, organizations, and individuals whose activities are relevant to conservation. Includes U.S. congressional committees; members of Congress; U.S. executive departments and independent agencies; Canadian governmental agencies; international, national, and state commissions and organizations; U.S. and Canadian citizens groups; fish and game commissioners and directors; colleges and universities; and conservation/environment offices of foreign governments. Organizations are included on the basis of their stated objectives related to the conservation of natural resources; most listings note the relation of the person or organization to conservation. The bibliographic listings cover periodicals, directories, bibliographies, and sources of audiovisual materials. There are alphabetical indexes by types of organization and personal names. ST/JKM

SC 100
Directory of State Agencies Concerned with Land Pollution Control. 1971. bi-a. Freed Publishing Co., Box 1144 FDR Sta, New York, NY 10022. Examined: 1974.
Aud: Cl, Pl, Sa

A straightforward listing of state agencies which deal with land pollution control arranged alphabetically by state. Entries include name of agency, address, name of person in charge, telephone number, and a brief statement of the agency's function. There is no table of contents or index. PH/JKM

SC 101
Eastern Hemisphere Petroleum Directory. ISSN 0070-8224. 1970/71. a. index. Petroleum Publishing Co., Box 1260, Tulsa, OK 74101. Examined: 1974/75. Donald W. Wilson, ed. 459p. $45.
Aud: Cl

Provides geographical index of member companies by countries, followed by a government index. There are also indexes by company and personal executive name. EM

SC 102
Energy Index. ISSN 0094-6281. 1973. a. index. Environment Information Center, 292 Madison Ave, New York, NY 10017. Examined: 1977. 662p. $65. (6th ed., 1978.)
Aud: Cl, Sa

Contains abstracts of current literature arranged under broad subject categories, and a survey of energy-related research and news events during the preceding year. The abstracts are indexed by author, subject (keyword and subject headings), and Standard Industrial Classification (SIC) code. EM

SC 103
Environment Index. 1971. a. index. Environment Information Center, 292 Madison Ave, New York, NY 10017. Examined: 1976. 685p. $95.
Aud: Cl, Sa

Consists of abstracts of the current literature on environmental problems, arranged by broad subject categories. Includes author, subject, geographic, and Standard Industrial Classification (SIC) code indexes. Also includes summary articles on the year's activities related to the environment. EM

SC 104
Environmental Protection Directory. (Continues in

part: Directory of Consumer Protection and Environmental Agencies.) 1973. irreg. index. Marquis Academic Media, Marquis Who's Who, 200 E Ohio St, Chicago, IL 60611. Examined: 1975. Thaddeus C. Trzyna, ed. 526p. $44.50.
Aud: Jc, Cl, Pl, Sa

Subtitle: "A comprehensive guide to environmental organizations in the United States and Canada." Published under the auspices of the Center for California Public Affairs, an affiliate of the Claremont Colleges. Lists governmental and private agencies and organizations "concerned directly with the quality of the natural environment, protection and management of natural resources, and the effects of environmental factors on human health." Divided into five major sections. The first section identifies organizations by specific area of interest, e.g., air quality, economic aspects, environmental education, outdoor recreation resources, soil conservation, water resources, etc. The second section lists U.S. government organizations, ingate agencies, and national private organizations. It is followed by a state-by-state listing of environmental organizations. The fourth section lists government and private organizations in Canada, and the fifth section lists Canadian organizations by provinces. Entries include name of organization, address, telephone number, telex or TWX number, titles and names of key personnel, a description of functions and activities, a list of publications, and any regional offices, chapters, or subsidiary groups. There is also a listing of international organizations and indexes by subject, organization, personnel, and publications. PH/JKM

SC 105
Geothermal World Directory. ISSN 0094-9779. 1972. a. bibl. index. Geothermal World Publications, 18014 Sherman Way, Suite 169, Reseda, CA 91335. Examined: 1977/78. Alan Arthur Tratner, ed. 379p. $40.
Aud: Cl

Includes an alphabetical listing of private companies involved in geothermal energy, a state-by-state listing of pertinent government agencies, and a directory of individuals active in the field. There are also several articles on the technical aspects of geothermal energy development and use. EM

SC 106
Institute of Environmental Sciences. Annual Meeting. Proceedings. ISSN 0073-9227. 1960. a. index. Institute of Environmental Sciences, 940 E Northwest Hwy, Mt. Prospect, IL 60056. Examined: 1977. 437p. $20.
Aud: Cl, Sa

Each annual meeting focuses on a specific theme, e.g., "Environmental Progress in Science and Education" (1972), "Cost Effectiveness in the Environmental Sciences" (1974), and "Energy and the Environment." Papers presented at the 1977 conference covered such topics as solar energy, water quality assessment, reliability test equipment, etc. There is an author/title index in each volume; a cumulative index is available covering 1960-1971. EM/JKM

SC 107
International Atomic Energy Agency. Directory of Nuclear Reactors. (1967 is 6th ed.) a. index. International Atomic Energy Agency, Kaerntnerring 11, A-1010 Vienna, Austria. Dist: UNIPUB, Box 433, Murray Hill Sta, New York, NY 10016. Examined: 1977. 95p. $26.
Aud: Cl, Sa

Features reports on different types of reactors, such as power reactors or research reactors, with full details of their operational features. Includes a cumulative index to all previous volumes. EM

SC 108
International Petroleum Annual. ISSN 0074-7319. 1965. a. U.S. Bureau of Mines, Division of International Activities, Washington, DC 20240. Examined: 1975. 37p. free.
Aud: Cl

Presents petroleum statistics on a global basis, including figures on production, trade, demand, retail prices, crude oil reserve estimates, etc. EM

SC 109
International Solar Energy Society. American Section. Proceedings of the Annual Meeting. ISSN 0146-4566. 1977. a. index. International Solar Energy Society, U.S. Section, 300 State Rd 401, Cape Canaveral, FL 32930. Examined: 1977. Charles Beach, ed. 3v. $60.
Aud: Cl

Papers presented at the annual meetings are arranged under categories such as solar measurements, storage of energy, and combined energy systems. Includes an author index. EM

SC 110
Land Use Planning Abstracts. bi-a. 1971/73. index. EIC, Catalog Order Department, 292 Madison Ave, New York, NY 10017. Examined: 1976/77. 550p. $75.
Aud: Cl, Sa

Contains over 1800 abstracts drawn from newspapers,

periodicals, serials, and monographs on land use planning. Covers zoning regulations, control over population density, pollution problems, transportation, noise, energy needs, etc. Arranged by subject category with keyword, author, and SIC code indexes. Includes information on pending or recently enacted legislation, bibliographies of books and films on topics related to land use planning, and a lengthy statistical section. JKM

SC 111

Society of Petroleum Engineers of AIME. Membership Directory. ISSN 0560-6411. 1959. a. Society of Petroleum Engineers, 6200 N Central Expressway, Dallas, TX 75206. Examined: 1975, $3; 1977. 235p.
Aud: Cl

Members of this professional society of engineers in the field of petroleum engineering are listed alphabetically by name. There is a geographical index and an index by place of employment. EM

SC 112

Society of Petroleum Engineers of AIME. Transactions. ISSN 0081-1696. 1925. a. index. Society of Petroleum Engineers of AIME, 6200 N Central Expressway, Dallas, TX 75206. Examined: 1976. 360p. $15.
Aud: Cl

Indexed in: *Chemical Abstracts; Engineering Index; Gas Abstracts; Petroleum Abstracts.*

Includes lists of award winners, committee chairmen, and officers, and papers reprinted from *Journal of Petroleum Technology* and *Society of Petroleum Engineers Journal.* Papers cover petroleum technology, reservoir engineering, offshore drilling operations, etc. Has author and subject indexes. EM

SC 113

U.S. Council on Environmental Quality. Annual Report. 1970. a. index. U.S. Council on Environmental Quality, 722 Jackson Pl, NW, Washington, DC 20006. Dist: Superintendent of Documents, U.S. Government Printing Office, Washington, DC 20402. Examined: 1974, $.35; 1977. 445p.
Aud: Cl

Gives a detailed summary of the year's events in such areas as pollution, energy sources, natural resources, human settlements, global environment, major trends in environmental studies, etc. Includes copious tables and charts. There is a subject index. EM

SC 114

U.S. Department of the Interior. Water Resources Research Catalog. ISSN 0083-7695. 1965. a. index. U.S. Department of the Interior, Office of Water Research and Technology, Water Resources Scientific Information Center, Washington, DC 20402. Dist: Superintendent of Documents, U.S. Government Printing Office, Washington, DC 20402. Examined: v. 11, 1976. 1029p. $15.75.
Aud: Cl, Sa

Presents summary descriptions of current research on water resources problems. Volume 11 lists only new or continuing but modified projects. Continuing but unchanged projects are listed in volumes nine and ten, and these two volumes would be necessary for complete reference value. Earlier volumes are outdated. Provides a management tool for the administration of programs of research support. Also provides information on what is being done, by whom, and where. Over 2800 research projects are listed with principal investigator, sponsoring institution, title of project supported, and a succinct summary. The catalog includes an investigator index, a contractor index, a supporting agency index, and an index of definitions. There is also an extensive subject index which is based on a hierarchical structure developed for this topic. NLE

SC 115

U.S. Federal Power Commission. Annual Report. ISSN 0083-078X. 1920/21. a. illus. U.S. Federal Power Commission, 411 G St, NW, Washington, DC 20426. Dist: Superintendent of Documents, U.S. Government Printing Office, Washington, DC 20402. Examined: 1972. 101p. $1.25.
Aud: Cl

The annual report submitted by the Federal Power Commission to the U.S. Congress. It gives a rundown of the Commission's activities during the year. Beginning with a general summary of its major actions, changes in its rules and regulations, and its organization and personnel, it goes on to detail events in the fields of electric power, natural gas and the environment. Following these chapters, there are appendixes on litigation, legislation, changes in commission rules and regulations, the membership of its advisory committees, and tables of hydroelectric projects under major license. KSK

SC 116

U.S. Fish and Wild Life Service. Cooperative Research Units. Fishery and Wildlife Annual Report. a.

bibl. illus. U.S. Department of the Interior, Fish and Wildlife Service, Washington, DC 20240. Dist: Superintendent of Documents, U.S. Government Printing Office, Washington, DC 20402. Examined: 1974/75. James J. Kenelly and Richard L. Applegate, eds. 251p.
Aud: Sa

Since 1960, the Cooperative Unit program has included fishery as well as wildlife research units. In each section of the report, there is a subdivision for fisheries and for wildlife. A directory of unit and coordinating committee members, with area, names, addresses, and telephone numbers, is included. There are unit profiles which indicate honors, awards, and services, and statistics on teaching and workshops. The major portion of the report is a description of research, by broad subject area, including the objective and, sometimes, an abstract. There is a long list of publications and papers presented for the year. SLB

SC 117

U.S. Fish and Wildlife Service. Sport Fishery and Wildlife Research. ISSN 0362-0700. (Continues: U.S. Fish and Wildlife Service. Progress in Sport Fishery Research. ISSN 0079-6794.) 1958. a. bibl. illus. U.S. Department of the Interior, Fish and Wildlife Service, Washington, DC 20240. Dist: Superintendent of Documents, U.S. Government Printing Office, Washington, DC 20402. Examined: 1974/75. Van T. Harris and Paul H. Eschmeyer, eds. 138p.
Aud: Sa

A report of the activities in the Fish and Wildlife Service Division of Research for the fiscal year. Under ten broad categories such as animal damage control, endangered species, and reservoir fisheries, there is a description of projects conducted for the year arranged by the sponsoring research center or laboratory. Each entry includes the name of the project, a brief description, and the results. There is a long list of publications, primarily magazine articles, that have been produced as a result of these research projects. Also provides a directory of research facilities and personnel, including director and address. There are black-and-white photographs throughout. SLB

SC 118

World Directory of Environmental Research Centers. (Continues: Directory of Organizations Concerned with Environmental Research.) 1970. irreg. index. Oryx Press, 3930 E Camelback Rd, Phoenix, AZ 85018. Examined: 2nd ed., 1974. William K. Wilson, Morgan D. Dowd, and Phyllis Sholtys, eds. 330p. $19.50.
Aud: Cl, Sa

Sponsored by the Lake Erie Environmental Studies (LEES) Program, this directory lists approximately 4800 organizations or institutions throughout the world which conduct research on the environment. Includes educational institutions, field stations or labs, foundations, governmental organizations at all levels, industrial concerns, community and professional organizations, and research institutions. The main listing is arranged by subject or discipline, e.g., biology, chemistry, geology, physics, social sciences, interdisciplinary, etc. Each entry includes name and address of research center, name of director, size of staff engaged in research, area of the environment being studied (e.g., oceanographic, terrestrial, limnologic, or atmospheric environment), and nature of research. There is also a listing of research centers by country or by state in the U.S. PH/JKM

SC 119

World Energy Supplies. ISSN 0084-1749. 1952. tri-a. U.N. Department of Economic and Social Affairs, Statistical Office, New York, NY. Dist: United Nations Publications, LX 2300, New York, NY 10017. Examined: 1970/74. 825p. $38; $30 pap.
Aud: Cl

Presents data on energy production and consumption for over 200 countries. "The principal objective of the series is to provide a global framework of the comparable data on long-term trends and recent developments in the supply of all commercial forms of energy, as a basis for the examination of the characteristics of energy supply and demand." Tables include: production, trade and consumption of commercial energy by country or area; world movement of solid fuels; production of crude petroleum; petroleum products; kerosenes and jet fuels; world movement of natural gas; electrical energy; and nuclear fuels. Data for each type of fuel are shown for individual countries and territories and summarized into regional world totals. Data is compiled chiefly from annual questionnaires distributed by the U.N. Statistical Office, supplemented by official national statistical publications. KSK

SC 120

World Environmental Directory. ISSN 0094-4742. 1974. a. index. Business Publishers, 1101 Spring St, Silver Springs, MD 20910. Examined: v. 1, 1974. 508p. $50.
Aud: Cl, Pl, Sa

Lists approximately 6600 companies, agencies, organizations, and institutions concerned with various aspects of the environment. Entries include addresses, phone numbers, and names of top officials. Arranged in sections by type of activity, i.e., U.S. product manufacturers—air pollution control; U.S. product manufacturers—water pollution; U.S. waste services systems; U.S. government agencies; independent agencies and commissions; state and local governments; professional, scientific, trade, and public interest organizations; state water resources research institutes; universities and other educational institutions; corporate environmental officials; international organizations; etc. Includes an index to personnel. PH/JKM

SC 121

Worldwide Petrochemical Directory. ISSN 0084-2583. a. index. Petroleum Publishing Co., Box 1260, Tulsa, OK 74101. Examined: 1977. 256p. $40.
Aud: Cl, Sa

Provides a geographical directory of companies by country, followed by an alphabetical listing. Includes a company index and a personnel index. EM

ENGINEERING

SC 122

American Consulting Engineers Council. Directory. ISSN 0589-4882. (Continues: American Institute of Consulting Engineers.) 1973/74. a. index. American Consulting Engineers Council, 1155 15th St NW, Suite 713, Washington, DC 20005. Examined: 1978. 326p. $25; $12.50 to libraries.
Aud: Cl

Composed of consulting engineering firms engaged in private practice, the Council was formed in 1970 by a merger of the American Institute of Consulting Engineers and the Consulting Engineers. The **Directory** lists member firms by state, then alphabetically by firm name. Includes rosters of officers, staff members, and committee members; the council's code of ethics; and the bylaws. There are indexes by names of firms and by principals of each firm. EM

SC 123

American Council of Independent Laboratories. Directory. ISSN 0065-7964. 1952. bi-a. index. American Council of Independent Laboratories, 1725 K St, NW, Washington, DC 20006. Examined: 14th ed., 1976. 209p. free.
Aud: Cl

Consists of a directory of member laboratories, indexed alphabetically and geographically. Following that is an alphabetical list of laboratories, with descriptions of officers, services, members, branch officers, etc. An index of services (by subjects or materials) and the Council's code of ethics complete the volume. EM

SC 124

American Engineering Model Society. Membership Directory. 1972. a. American Engineering Model Society, Box 2066, Aiken, SC 29801. Examined: 1976. 25p.
Aud: Sa

A directory of the Society's members who include individuals, institutions, companies, and other groups engaged in the building and use of engineering models or interested in the application of those models. Includes a list of officers and committee members. EM/JKM

SC 125

American Society of Civil Engineers. Directory. (Continues: American Society of Civil Engineers. Yearbook.) 1872. bi-a. index. American Society of Civil Engineers, 345 E 47th St, New York, NY 10017. Examined: 1976. 792p. $8.
Aud: Sa

Lists both U.S. and foreign members of this professional society of civil engineers. Lists are arranged alphabetically by name, then geographically. Most entries provide both home and professional address. Honorary members are also listed. EM

SC 126

American Society of Civil Engineers. Transactions. ISSN 0066-0604. 1867. a. index. American Society of Civil Engineers, 345 E 47th St, New York, NY 10017. Examined: 1977. 808p. (143rd ed., 1978. $18; $14 to libraries.)
Aud: Cl

Contains abstracts of all papers issued as *Proceedings* contributions and of articles which appeared in the Society's journal, *Civil Engineering*, thus encompassing all the technical papers published by the Society. Also includes abstracts of manuals, reports, and miscellaneous publications, including memoirs of deceased members. Each volume contains author and subject indexes. Cumulative indexes are available for 1960-1969 and 1970-1974. EM

SC 127

**American Society of Heating, Refrigerating and Air

Conditioning Engineers. Transactions. (1976 is v. 82.) a. index. American Society of Heating, Refrigerating and Air Conditioning Engineers, 345 E 47th St, New York, NY 10017. Examined: v. 82, 1976. approx. 1850p. $80; $40 to members. (v. 83, 1977. 1417p. $100; $50 to members.)
Aud: Cl, Sa
Indexed in: *Engineering Index*.

Papers presented at the semi-annual and annual meetings are available in two semi-annual volumes (1977, $60 ea.) or as a single annual volume. The volumes include summaries of symposia, forums, and seminars; and lists of current and past officers, award winners, and committee members. Part one of the 1977 volume includes 74 papers on such topics as energy savings through shutdown of electric water heaters, efficiency of external combustion systems, alternate control strategies for home air conditioning, etc. Part two contains 34 papers on similar topics. There is an index to papers by titles and authors. EM/JKM

SC 128
American Society of Mechanical Engineers. Membership List. 1880. a. index. American Society of Mechanical Engineers, 345 E 47th St, New York, NY 10017. Examined: 1976. 719p. $25.
Aud: Sa

A professional society of mechanical engineers with members in the U.S., Canada, and Mexico. Members are listed first alphabetically by name, then by employers. Most entries include home and professional addresses, as well as the divisions of the Society to which the individual belongs. Also lists honorary members, Fellows of the Society, and current officers. EM

SC 129
American Society of Mechanical Engineers. Transactions. 1880. a. index. American Society of Mechanical Engineers, 345 E 47th St, New York, NY 10017. Examined: 1976. 4v. (1977. $250.)
Aud: Cl

Cumulates the contents of the Society's eight quarterly journals (i.e., Journals of: *Applied Mechanics; Dynamic Systems, Measurement, and Control; Engineering for Industry; Engineering for Power; Engineering Materials and Technology; Fluids Engineering; Heat Transfer; Lubrication Technology;* and *Pressure Technology*.) Includes abstracts of unpublished papers, and author and subject indexes. Cumulative indexes are available for volumes 1-45 (1880-1923) and for later volumes. The annual volumes are less expensive than separate subscriptions to all journals, but they are also less current—an important consideration to libraries supporting technical programs. EM

SC 130
American Society of Naval Engineers. Membership Lists. (Continues: Naval Engineering Journal.) 1958. a. American Society of Naval Engineers, 1012 14th St NW, Suite 807, Washington, DC 20005. Examined: 1977. 96p.
Aud: Sa

Includes lists of present and past officers of the Society, the bylaws, and an alphabetical listing of members which gives home and professional addresses in most cases. EM

SC 131
American Society of Sanitary Engineering. Year Book. ISSN 0066-068X. 1906. a. index. American Society of Sanitary Engineers, 960 Illumination Bldg, Cleveland, OH 44113. Examined: 1976. 356p. $5.
Aud: Sa

Presents the technical papers given at the Society's annual meeting, lists of officers and committee members, and a roster of members which is arranged geographically. The bylaws and a retrospective listing of award winners complete the volume. Cumulative indexes for 1906-1950, 1951-1963, and 1963-1970 are available. EM

SC 132
Association of Consulting Chemists and Chemical Engineers. Consulting Services. 1963. a. index. Association of Consulting Chemists and Chemical Engineers, 50 E 41st St, New York, NY 10017. Examined: 1977. $15.
Aud: Sa

Provides a listing of consulting organizations involved in chemical engineering, metallurgical engineering, analytical chemical engineering, and related fields. The one-page listings for each firm indicate experience, scope, staff size, etc. A subject index precedes the main listings. Also includes a geographical index and an index to personal members of the association who are employed in consulting organizations. EM

SC 133
Conference on Laser Engineering and Applications. Digest. ISSN 0069-858X. 1973. a. index. Institute of Electrical and Electronics Engineers, 345 E 47th St,

New York, NY 10017. Examined: 1977. 87p. $10; $5 to members.
Aud: Sa

Contains abstracts of technical papers presented at the conference arranged by broad topics such as remote sensing apparatus, medical applications, or optical communication. There is an author index. EM

SC 134
Engineering College Research and Graduate Study. (Continues: Directory of Engineering College Research and Graduate Study.) 1967. a. index. American Society for Engineering Education, One Dupont Circle, Washington, DC 20036. Examined: 1977. Cheryl J. Miller, ed. 243p. $7.
Aud: Cl, Pl
Indexed in: *Current Contents; Engineering Index*.

U.S. and Canadian institutions are listed alphabetically. Information provided for each is comprehensive and covers: admission requirements, officers' names, faculty, enrollment, fees, degrees offered, research funds, programs and fields of study, appointments available to graduate students. A sourcebook based on responses to questionnaires and not entirely complete owing to some lack of response. Indexes by field of study and areas of research are provided. Also available with a subscription to *Engineering Education*, which it supplements, and on microfilm and/or microfiche. BSM

SC 135
Engineering Index Annual. ISSN 0360-8557. 1884. a. index. Engineering Index, 345 E 47th St, New York, NY 10017. Examined: 1977. 5v. $390.
Aud: Cl

Cumulates the *Engineering Index Monthly,* an indexing and abstracting service with "transdisciplinary engineering coverage." More than 89,000 abstracts and citations culled from engineering periodicals and selected reports and monographs are included in the 1977 edition. Abstracts are arranged under 12,000 main engineering headings and subheadings. Includes a list of periodicals indexed, an author index, and an author affiliation index. EM

SC 136
Engineering News Record. ENR Directory of Design Firms. 1974/75. bi-a. index. Engineering News Record, 1221 Ave of the Americas, New York, NY 10020. Examined: 1976/77. James Sullivan, ed. 224p. $9.95.
Aud: Cl

Provides two-page descriptions of each company engaged in the design of buildings, structures, and industrial projects. Companies are listed alphabetically, then by location and by job type. Also includes a list of the 500 largest U.S. design firms, showing their areas of activity. EM

SC 137
Engineers' Council for Professional Development. Annual Report. 1932. a. Engineers' Council for Professional Development, 345 E 47th St, New York, NY 10017. Examined: 44th ed., 1976. 3v. $9. (45th ed., 1977. 3v. v. 1, 36p., $5; v. 2, 31p., $3; v. 3, 29p., $3.)
Aud: Cl

Volume one includes reports of officers and various committees, a financial statement, and a listing of officers and committee members. Volume two consists of a report on engineering education and accreditation. Volume three provides similar information for education related to engineering technology. EM

SC 138
Engineers Joint Council. Directory of Engineering Societies and Related Organizations. 1956. bi-a. index. Engineers Joint Council, 345 E 47th St, New York, NY 10017. Examined: 1976. 219p. $18.
Aud: Cl

Consists of an alphabetical listing of some 400 U.S. and Canadian engineering societies, showing names of staff members, founding date, size, dues, publications issued, etc. Has a geographical index and a keyword subject index derived from the titles of organizations. EM

SC 139
Engineers Joint Council. Directory of Engineering Society Management. 1975. a. Engineers Joint Council, 345 E 47th St, New York, NY 10017. Examined: 1976/77. 84p. $5.
Aud: Cl

Lists the chief elected officers of member societies of the Engineers Joint Council and other national engineering societies with a membership of 5000 or more. This is followed by a similar listing of the executive staff operating the headquarters of the societies listed. EM

SC 140
Engineers Joint Council. Engineering Manpower Commission. Professional Income of Engineers. ISSN 0071-0423. 1953. bi-a. Engineers Joint Council, Engi-

neering Manpower Commission, 345 E 47th St, New York, NY 10017. Examined: 1976. 92p. $8.
Aud: Cl

Uses graphs and tables to show salaries of engineers in different fields, and the effect of the amount of experience past the bachelor's degree on salary. EM

SC 141
Engineers Joint Council. Engineering Manpower Commission. Prospects of Engineering and Technology Graduates. ISSN 0071-0431. 1959. a. Engineers Joint Council, Engineering Manpower Commission, 345 E 47th St, New York, NY 10017. Examined: 1976. 31p. $10.
Aud: Cl

Shows overall employment and salary figures for new engineering and technology graduates by type of degree and by subject area. Includes two-year as well as graduate programs. EM

SC 142
Engineers Joint Council. Engineering Manpower Commission. Roster of Women and Minority Engineering and Technology Students. 1974. a. Engineers Joint Council, Engineering Manpower Commission, 345 E 47th St, New York, NY 10017. Examined: 1978. 152p. $60.
Aud: Hs, Jc, Cl, Sa

Lists the names of thousands of women and minority group members enrolled in engineering and technology programs in over 100 U.S. schools, arranged by state, school, name, year, and sex or minority group. Includes a list of contacts for each school for further information. EM

SC 143
Engineers Joint Council. Engineering Manpower Commission. Salaries of Engineering Technicians and Technologists. ISSN 0071-0474. 1966. bi-a. Engineers Joint Council, Engineering Manpower Commission, 345 E 47th St, New York, NY 10017. Examined: 1976. 112p. $45.
Aud: Cl

Subtitle: "Detailed industry report." Uses graphs and tables to show average salaries of technicians and technologists, as well as salary figures for specific industries. Includes a list of participating companies. EM

SC 144
Society of Logistics Engineers. Proceedings. ISSN 0081-1629. 1966. a. Society of Logistics Engineers, 3322 S Memorial Pkwy, Suite 65, Huntsville, AL 35801. Examined: 1976. 2v. $15.
Aud: Sa

Includes papers presented at the Society's annual International Symposium. Topics for sessions include logistics education, national transportation policy, and warranty programs. Author and title data are provided by the table of contents. EM

SC 145
Standards Engineers Society. Proceedings of Annual Meetings. ISSN 0081-430X. 1951. a. Standards Engineers Society, 6700 Pennsylvania Ave, Minneapolis, MN 55423. Examined: 1976. 180p. $20.
Aud: Cl

The Society is devoted to furthering knowledge and use of approved standards. The proceedings of the annual conferences include papers on such topics as computer-aided standardization, national standards programs, metric conversion, etc. EM

GEOGRAPHY

SC 146
American Society of Photogrammetry. Papers from the Annual Meeting. ISSN 0569-8413. (Continues: Technical Papers from the Annual Meeting. ISSN 0066-0663.) (1970 is 36th ed.) a. index. American Society of Photogrammetry, 105 N Virginia Ave, Falls Church, VA 22046. Examined: 1977. 709p. $5.
Aud: Sa

Contains papers presented at the annual meeting and the fall technical meeting. There is an author index to all papers included. Among the subjects covered are urban mapping, data bases for cartographers, etc. EM

SC 147
Bibliographie Cartographique Internationale. ISSN 0067-6934. 1946. a. illus. Librarie de la Faculte de Sciences, 12 Rue Pierre et Marie Curie, 75005 Paris, France. Dist: International Publications Service, 114 E 32nd St, New York, NY 10016. Examined: v. 27, 1974. P. Sommer, ed. 2v. 959p. $102.50.
Aud: Cl, Sa

UNESCO supports the gathering and editorial work of this important work which is issued through the efforts of the Laboratorie d'Information et de Documentation en Geographie and L'Union Geographique Internationale. Arranged by sections covering: Europe, Africa, North America, Canada, United States, Central America, South America, Asia, and Oceania. Each section has a separate list of regional maps and a list of maps of countries or states of the U.S. arranged by country and state name. For the U.S., maps produced by Geological Survey, the American Automobile Association, various state government departments, and commercial companies are listed. Though this list is probably not comprehensive, it still serves as a good checklist of cartographic publications. A necessary tool for the larger library collections. NLE

SC 148

Bibliographie Geographique Internationale. ISSN 0067-6993. (Continues: Annales de Geographie.) (1972 is v. 78.) a. index. Centre National de la Recherche Scientifique, 15 Quai Anatole, 75700 Paris, France. Examined: v. 82, 1975/76. 1029p.
Aud: Cl, Sa

L'Union Geographique International is assisted now by UNESCO in publishing this mammoth, basic bibliography of the field of geography. The listing is first divided by subject areas including methodology, historical geography, morphology, climatology, hydrology, biogeography, urban geography, and economic geography. Within these sections the listings are arranged geographically: first general, then France, then other countries. There is an author index, and the detailed table of contents serves as a subject index. A comprehensive scholarly work. NLE

SC 149

Geo Abstracts: Annual Index. (Continues: Geographical Abstracts: Annual Index.) 1972. a. bibl. index. Geo Abstracts, University of East Anglia, Norwich NR4 7TJ, England. Examined: 1976. K. M. Clayton, ed. 2v. 1149p. £40.
Aud: Cl, Sa

The annual index to the seven sections of *Geo Abstracts:* land forms and the quaternary, biogeography and climatology, sedimentology, remote sensing and cartography, economic geography, social geography and cartography, and regional and community planning. Based on KWIC indexing principles, each item is indexed an average of seven times. English and foreign titles as well as key words are grouped in various ways to enhance subject access. References are to the abstract number within each individual section. A superior reference work to be used with **Bibliography and Index of Geology** for the most complete coverage. Separate five-year cumulative indexes are available for each individual section. NLE

SC 150

Imago MVNDI; the Journal of the International Society for the History of Cartography. 1935. a. bibl. index. illus. Imago Mundi, c/o Lymprie Castle, Kent, England. Examined: v. 29, 1977. E. M. J. Campbell, ed. 128p. $16.50. (v. 30, 1978.)
Aud: Cl, Sa

"The complete file, from 1935, provides an unequaled body of reference material for the historian, the geographer, the collector, and makes an indispensable contribution to the systematic history of cartography." Several supplements devoted to individual topics have been issued. Each issue contains articles on maps, atlases, cartographic instruments, and individuals connected with cartography. Each issue also contains shorter notices and various news items. Several excellent book reviews and a bibliography of published literature are included. Includes advertisements for sellers of maps. Generally an excellent and worthwhile tool which can be used by anyone interested in cartography. NLE

SC 151

Progress in Geography. 1969. irreg. bibl. Edward Arnold Publishers, 41 Maddox St, London W1 8LL, England. Dist: St. Martin's Press, 175 Fifth Ave, New York, NY 10010. Examined: v. 1, 1969; v. 9, 1976. Christopher Board, et al, eds. 203p. $25.
Aud: Cl, Sa

Subtitle: "International reviews of current research." Attempts to "present regular, scholarly reviews of current developments within all branches of the field on a scale which will allow the specialist contributors an opportunity to develop broad geographical themes and to provide comprehensive bibliographic material." Covers regional and systematic geography and both traditional and contemporary modes of analysis. Both issues examined contained five reviews, each prefaced by a contents page in outline form. NLE/JKM

HORTICULTURE

SC 152

American Camellia Yearbook. ISSN 0065-762X. 1946. a. index. illus. American Camellia Society, Box 212, Fort Valley, GA 31030. Examined: v. 32, 1977. Milton H. Brown, ed. 221p. $5.
Aud: Sa

Contains articles on American and international camellia culture, research, and shows written for the general reader as well as the experienced gardener. A section called "Camellia Personalities" features biographical sketches of Society members and camellia authorities. Also includes news of the Society, a list of officers, and a list of award recipients. DA/JKM

SC 153
American Rose Annual. ISSN 0066-0000. 1916. a. index. illus. American Rose Society, Box 30000, Shreveport, LA 71130. Examined: no. 62, 1977. Harold S. Goldstein, ed. 228p. $9.50.
Aud: Cl

Contains over 20 articles dealing with roses throughout the world, including cultivation methods, diseases, rose varieties, shows, and organizations. Authors are amateur rose enthusiasts, active society members, researchers, and scientists. Several of the articles are reprinted from various horticultural periodicals. Also includes lists of the Society's officers and past presidents, medal and award winners, new roses of the world, and plant patents. A 50-page section entitled "Proof of the Pudding" includes evaluations of new rose varieties, with comments on cultivation, performance, growth characteristics, color, etc. Includes a subject index. JKM

SC 154
Better Homes and Gardens Garden Ideas and Outdoor Living. 1940. a. bibl. illus. Meredith Corp., Special Interest Publications, 1716 Locust St, Des Moines, IA 50036. Examined: 1974. Lorraine Burgess, ed. $1.50.
Aud: Pl

A collection of general articles for the beginning home gardener. Articles in the volume examined include: "Foolproof Annuals"; "Easy-Care Roses"; "Easy Maintenance Gardening"; "Living and Dining Outdoors"; "21 Favorite Outdoor Plans"; etc. There is a list of free and inexpensive brochures and pamphlets of garden ideas and product information. Includes several color illustrations. DA/JKM

SC 155
Herbarist. 1935. a. bibl. illus. Herb Society of America, 300 Massachusetts Ave, Boston, MA 02115. Examined: no. 4, 1978. 128p. $2.50.
Aud: Cl

Contains nine articles dealing with specific herbs, cultivation methods, uses of herbs, and environmental issues. Some articles include bibliographies and/or supplier information. There are brief biographical sketches of the authors who are herb enthusiasts and/or research scientists. There is a separate section of brief book reviews. A list of the Society's officers and publications, a list of herb nomenclature changes, and an index to advertisers complete the volume. JKM

SC 156
The Rose Annual. ISSN 0483-3686. 1910. a. illus. Royal National Rose Society, Cheswell Green Lane, St. Albans, Hertfordshire, AL2 3NR, England. Examined: 1977. Ken Lemmon, ed. 220p.
Aud: Sa

Consists of news of the Society and several articles on rose cultivation, shows, etc. Similar in format and content to the **American Rose Annual,** but the emphasis is more oriented to Commonwealth and European interests. There are separate sections of advertisements and book reviews. Includes many color plates and black-and-white illustrations. DA/JKM

SC 157
Time-Life Encyclopedia of Gardening. 1971. a. index. illus. Time-Life Books, Time and Life Bldg, New York, NY 10020. Examined: 1978. 160p. $8.95.
Aud: Cl, Pl

Provides a brief review of weather and gardening developments during the preceding year, including descriptions of new plants. There are many illustrations and a subject index. EM

INDUSTRIAL TECHNOLOGY

SC 158
Advances in Applied Mechanics. ISSN 0065-2156. 1948. a. bibl. index. illus. Academic Press, 111 Fifth Ave, New York, NY 10003. Examined: v. 17, 1977. Chia-Shun Yih, ed. 389p. $43.50.
Aud: Cl, Sa

Contains articles that treat a specific area of research in applied mechanics, review previous work in the area, and describe the research of the author. Apparently, the main purpose of the series is communication about areas of current research interest, and the results of current research, to workers and students in related fields. The volumes have author and subject indexes. ST/JKM

SC 159
Advances in Instrumentation. ISSN 0065-2814. (1970 is v. 25.) a. Instrument Society of America, 490 Stanwix St, Pittsburgh, PA 15222. Examined: v. 28, 1973, 4v., $64; v. 31, 1976. 4v. $75.

Aud: Cl, Sa
Indexed in: *Engineering Index; Index Medicus.*

Includes papers and proceedings of the international conference of the Instrument Society of America. Occasionally papers from other conferences are included, e.g., part three of the 1973 set included papers from the Joint Environmental Instrumentation and Control Symposium. Each four-volume set includes approximately 100 papers covering a wide range of topics related to instruments and their applications, e.g., environmental instrumentation, automatic control and data handling, process measurement, instrumentation in the mining and metallurgy industries, telemetry, etc. EM/JKM

SC 160

American Foundrymen's Society. Transactions. ISSN 0065-8375. 1896. a. index. American Foundrymen's Society, Golf and Wolf Rds, Des Plaines, IL 60016. Examined: v. 85, 1977. 634p. $70.
Aud: Cl, Sa

Includes the minutes of subcommittee reports and papers on the technical aspects of the process and science of metal castings. Each volume includes author and subject indexes, and there are ten-year cumulative indexes available for 1951-1960 and 1961-1970. EM

SC 161

American Gear Manufacturers Association. AGMA Directory. ISSN 0572-502X. 1969/70. a. American Gear Manufacturers Association, 1901 N Fort Meyer Dr, Suite 1100, Arlington, VA 22209. Examined: 1977/78. 44p.
Aud: Cl

Consists of an alphabetical and a geographical directory of members who include manufacturers of gears, geared speed changes, and related equipment and teachers of mechanical engineering. Also includes a roster of officers and committee members. EM/JKM

SC 162

American Society for Quality Control. Annual Technical Conference Transactions. ISSN 0066-0159. 1946. a. index. illus. American Society for Quality Control, 161 W Wisconsin Ave, Milwaukee, WI 53203. Examined: 31st ed., 1977. 618p. $13.
Aud: Cl
Indexed in: *Engineering Index.*

Presents technical papers on various aspects of quality control. Indexes to technical papers and authors are presented at the beginning of the volume followed by the papers themselves. Not all the papers presented at the conference are reprinted in full; some are presented only as one-page abstracts. The book is arranged in sessions, with each session devoted to one topic. There are two or three papers on various facets of that topic in each session. Session titles are: quality through process control, nuclear quality assurance, metals processing, medical research techniques, computer software quality assurance, drugs and GMP, experiences in worker participation, consumer safety, statistics—a working tool, home furnishings, international standards, and quality cost tutorial. The sessions are grouped under larger themes or subject headings (industrial quality, services/service industry, impact regulations, QA management, impact-consumer, general applications, and tutorial). Each conference is devoted to a theme; the 1977 theme is "Increased Productivity with Quality." Many of the articles contain bibliographies, and are illustrated with charts, graphs, drawings, figures, and statistics. KSK

SC 163

Annual Review of Fluid Mechanics. ISSN 0066-4189. 1969. a. bibl. index. illus. Annual Reviews, 4139 El Camino Way, Palo Alto, CA 94306. Examined: v. 10, 1978. Milton Van Dyke and J. V. Wehausen, eds. 475p. $17.
Aud: Cl, Sa
Indexed in: *Biological Abstracts; Chemical Abstracts; International Aerospace Abstracts; Multi-Media Reviews Index; Nuclear Science Abstracts; Oceanic Abstracts; Science Abstracts; Theoretical Chemical Engineering Abstracts.*

The 1978 volume includes 23 articles covering such topics as hydrodynamics of ships in restricted waters, dust explosions, objective methods for weather prediction, and river ice. The articles will be of interest to navigators, ecologists, and meterologists, among others. The articles in the 1978 volume include Copyright Clearing House information. One major reason for recommending this title is the heavy outside indexing which is done for the series. This serial will be of interest to most students involved in the sciences. NLE

SC 164

Davison's Textile Blue Book. ISSN 0070-2951. 1966. a. index. Davison Publishing Co., Box 477, Ridgewood, NJ 07451. Examined: 1978. 658p. $50.
Aud: Sa

Textile product manufacturers are listed under some 40 sections for different products, e.g., carpet backing, wool dealers, etc. There are indexes to mills by products manufactured and by process performed and an alphabetical index to all companies listed. EM

SC 165
Davison's Textile Catalog and Buyers Guide. ISSN 0070-296X. 1934. a. index. Davison Publishing Co., Box 477, Ridgewood, NJ 07451. Examined: 1977. 288p. $20.
Aud: Sa

Covers textile machinery and related supplies. Lists products alphabetically with sources. Another index lists suppliers alphabetically. EM

SC 166
Diesel and Gas Turbine World Wide Catalog. ISSN 0070-4822. 1935. a. Diesel and Gas Turbine Progress, Box 26308, Milwaukee, WI 53226. Examined: 1977. 1500p. $35.
Aud: Cl

Includes articles on topics such as machine tools, castings and forming, test equipment, etc. Appendixes provide information on horsepower ranges, the International Standards Symposium, conversion factors, etc. EM

SC 167
Human Factors Society. Directory and Yearbook. 1957. a. Human Factors Society, Box 1369, Santa Monica, CA 90406. Examined: 1977. 136p. $10. (21st ed., 1978.)
Aud: Cl, Sa

Presents an alphabetical and geographical listing of members of this professional society which is concerned with the study of human factors in the development of work systems and other aspects of human engineering. Members include psychologists, engineers, physiologists, and other related scientists. Includes the bylaws of the Society and list of officers. EM/JKM

SC 168
Human Factors Society. Proceedings of the Annual Meeting. (1972 is 16th ed.) a. Human Factors Society, Box 1369, Santa Monica, CA 90406. Examined: 20th ed., 1976. 563p. $20.
Aud: Cl

The proceedings of the annual meetings of this professional society concerned with human engineering. Past conference themes include: "Technology for Man" (1972); "The Consumer Factor" (1973); and "Human Factors in Our Expanding Technology."

Papers presented at the 1976 meeting cover subjects such as human factors in agriculture and industry, job enrichment, environmental effects in industry, hours of work, etc. EM/JKM

SC 169
Industrial Machinery and Equipment Printing Guide. ISSN 0091-8377. 1972. a. index. Van Nostrand Reinhold, 450 W 33rd St, New York, NY 10001. Examined: 1977/78. various paging. $29.95.
Aud: Sa

Lists new, used, and salvage prices for machinery in a dozen or so categories, such as machine tools, air conditioners, motors, etc. There is a subject index which includes names of specific products. EM

SC 170
Iron and Steel Society of AIME. Membership Directory. 1975. a. Iron and Steel Society of AIME, Box 411, Warrendale, PA 15086. Examined: 1976. 86p. $5; $2.50 to members.
Aud: Sa

The Iron and Steel Society is an affiliate of the American Institute of Mining, Metallurgical, and Petroleum Engineers and is comprised of men and women involved in the field of iron and steel processing and technology. The **Directory** lists members alphabetically, then geographically. EM/JKM

SC 171
Iron and Steel Society of AIME. Ironmaking Proceedings. 1941. a. Iron and Steel Society of AIME, Box 411, Warrendale, PA 15086. Examined: v. 36, 1977. 137p. $25; $11 to members.
Aud: Sa

The proceedings of the annual conference of the Ironmaking Division of the Iron and Steel Society. Papers are arranged under such categories as blast furnace dynamics, pollution control devices, and coke oven operations. Past conference proceedings are available on microfilm from University Microfilms, 300 N Zeeb Rd, Ann Arbor, MI 48106. EM/JKM

SC 172
Joint Automatic Control Conference. Record. ISSN 0075-3939. (1976 is 16th ed.) a. index. Institute of Electrical and Electronic Engineers, 345 E 47th St, New York, NY 10017. Examined: 1977. 2v. 1736p. $60; $45 to members.
Aud: Cl

Several societies sponsor this conference, which is concerned with such topics as power plant controls, applications of control systems, and microprocessors. Includes an author index. EM

SC 173
Machinery's Handbook. 1914. bi-a. index. Industrial Press, 200 Madison Ave, New York, NY 10016. Examined: v. 20, 1974/75. 2482p. (v. 22, 1978. $25.)
Aud: Cl

Subtitle: "A reference book for the mechanical engineer, draftsman, toolmaker, and machinist." Consists of dozens of sections on specific subjects such as gear materials, springs, iron castings, electric motors, etc. Includes many charts and tables, plus a detailed subject index. EM

SC 174
Material Handling Institute. Proceedings of the MHI Material Handling Seminar and MHI Inter-Society Material Handling Symposium. 1974. Material Handling Institute, 1326 Freeport Road, Pittsburgh, PA 15238. Examined: 1976. 202p. $35.
Aud: Cl

Sponsored by the Material Handling Institute, an association of manufacturers of industrial material handling equipment and systems. Papers cover many topics, including human engineering, how to establish materials handling departments, outlook for materials handling, etc. EM

SC 175
Microwaves Product Data Directory. 1973. a. illus. Hayden Publishing Co., 50 Essex St, Rochelle Park, NJ 07662. Examined: 1977/78. 928p. $15.
Aud: Sa

Part one is a product directory, arranged by types of products, showing manufacturers' locations and sales offices. Part two discusses and illustrates the products of a particular electronics product company. EM

SC 176
Modern Machine Shop NC/CAM Guidebook. (Continues: Machine Shop N/C Guidebook and Directory. ISSN 0076-9991.) 1970. a. Gardner Publications, 600 Main St, Cincinnati, OH 45202. Examined: 1977. 346p. $5.
Aud: Sa

A directory of manufacturers and shop operators involved in numerical control of equipment. Includes several short articles on numerical control and computer-aided design. EM

SC 177
Modern Plastics Encyclopedia. ISSN 0085-3518. (Continues: Modern Plastics Catalog; Plastics Catalog.) 1940. a. index. McGraw-Hill Publishing Co, 1221 Ave of the Americas, New York, NY 10020. Examined: 1977. Joan Agranoff, ed. various paging. $20. (1978/79.)
Aud: Cl

Originally published as the October issue of *Modern Plastics,* but available as a separate publication. Includes several short articles on plastics materials and applications, specifications for properties of plastics, a buyers' guide and directory of suppliers, and a subject index. EM

SC 178
National Association of Relay Manufacturers. Relay Conference Proceedings. 1952. a. National Association of Relay Manufacturers, Box 1649, Scottsdale, AZ 85252. Examined: 24th ed., 1976. various paging. $5.
Aud: Cl

Papers are arranged under such topics as materials for relays, design features, noise analysis, testing methods, etc. EM

SC 179
National Board of Boiler and Pressure Vessel Inspection. Proceedings of General Meeting. (1977 is v. 46) a. National Board of Boiler and Pressure Vessel Inspection, 1055 Crupper Ave, Columbus, OH 43229. Examined: v. 46, 1977. 196p.
Aud: Sa

The National Board is comprised of chief boiler inspectors of states and major cities in the U.S. and provinces of Canada. Its annual meetings are devoted to the design, inspection, and safety aspects of boilers and pressure vessels and the administration of relevant laws. The **Proceedings** include technical papers delivered at the meetings and the texts of speeches by invited guests. EM/JKM

SC 180
National Conference on Fluid Power. Proceedings. 1947. a. index. National Conference on Fluid Power, Illinois Institute of Technology, 10 W 32nd St, Chicago, IL 60616. Examined: v. 31, 1977. 736p. $25.
Aud: Sa
Indexed in: *Engineering Index.*

Title varies: National Conference on Industrial Hydraulics. Proceedings.

Papers are presented under various categories such as noise of fluid devices, design of pumps, and lubrications. Includes an author index. EM

SC 181
National Conference on Power Transmission. Proceedings. ISSN 0095-6481. 1974. a. index. National Conference on Power Transmission, Illinois Institute of Technology, 10 W 32nd St, Chicago, IL 60616. Examined: 1976. 417p. (v. 4, 1977. $25.)
Aud: Sa

Papers presented at the annual conference are arranged under such categories as bearings, lubrication systems, gearing, etc. There is an author index. EM

SC 182
Optical Industry and Systems Directory. ISSN 0078-5474. 1954. a. index. Optical Publishing Co., 59 Bartlett Ave, Pittsfield, MA 01201. Examined: 1977. 2v. $35.
Aud: Sa

Volume one includes an alphabetical index to products and services, a listing of products and services by product categories, a tabular listing of product specifications, and alphabetical and geographical listings of manufacturers. The second volume consists of an encyclopedia and technical directory. EM

SC 183
Package Engineering Annual Buyers Guide. (Continues: Package Machinery Catalog. ISSN 0552-7635.) 1963. a. index. Cahners Publishing Co., 5 S Wabash Ave, Chicago, IL 60603. Examined: 1977. 196p. $5.
Aud: Sa

A buyers' guide to machinery and supplies for the packaging industry. Includes an index to products and a supplier locator. There is also an index to trade names. EM

SC 184
Porcelain Enamel Institute. Forum Proceedings. ISSN 0079-3949. 1937. a. index. Porcelain Enamel Institute, 1911 N Fort Meyer Dr, Arlington, VA 22209. Examined: 1976. 158p.
Aud: Sa

Contains papers presented at the annual forum of the Porcelain Enamel Institute. Topics covered include reclaiming of enamels, powder coatings, low temperature enameling, etc. A cumulative index for the 1937-1970 volumes is available. EM

SC 185
Power Transmission and Bearing Handbook and Directory. ISSN 0554-890X. 1961/62. bi-a. index. Industrial Publishing Co., Power Transmission Design Magazine, 614 Superior Ave W, Cleveland, OH 44113. Examined: 1977/78. various paging. $20.
Aud: Sa

Title varies: Power Transmission and Bearing Handbook.

Includes a product index divided into four sections: bearings, controls, drives, and motors. Also contains a list of manufacturers with addresses, an index to trade names, a list of local sources, and several short articles on the technical aspects of power transmission and bearing products. EM

SC 186
Reliability and Maintainability Symposium. Proceedings. ISSN 0149-144X. (Continues: Institute of Electrical and Electronics Engineers. Symposium on Reliability.) 1964. a. index. Institute of Electrical and Electronics Engineers, 345 E 47th St, New York, NY 10017. Examined: 1978. 530p. $24; $16 to members.
Aud: Cl
Indexed in: *Science Citation Index*.

This symposium is sponsored jointly by the Institute of Electrical and Electronics Engineers' Reliability Group, the American Society for Quality Control, and other organizations. Sessions are devoted to topics such as consumer product reliability, theory of reliability, cost-effectiveness assurance programs, etc. Includes author and subject indexes. EM

SC 187
Society of Plastics Engineers. Annual Technical Conference. Technical Papers. 1954. a. Society of Plastics Engineers, 656 W Putnam Ave, Greenwich, CT 06830. Examined: v. 21, 1975, $25; v. 23, 1977. 553p. $25.
Aud: Sa

Typical session topics are thermosetting molding, plastics in building, physical properties of plastics, etc. Author/title data are provided by the contents page. EM

SC 188
Turbomachinery Symposium. Proceedings. 1972. a. Gas Turbine Laboratories, Department of Mechanical Engineering, Texas A and M University, College Station, TX 77843. Examined: 1975. 183p. (v. 5, 1976. $12.)

Aud: Sa

Papers cover gas turbine operation in extremes of weather, advanced power systems, blade failure analysis, etc. Includes short biographical sketches of conferences speakers and rosters of committee members. EM

SC 189
United States Foamed Plastic Markets and Directory. ISSN 0083-0968. 1963. a. Technomic Publishing Co., 265 W State St, Westport, CT 06880. Examined: 1975. 94p. $20. (v. 14, 1977.)
Aud: Sa

Title varies: International Foamed Plastic Markets and Directory.

Lists suppliers for various foamed plastics products, such as polyolefin foams, silicone foams, machinery, etc. Also contains a list of processors and a list of foamed plastic companies. EM

SC 190
Welding Data Book. ISSN 0511-4365. 1958. bi-a. illus. Industrial Publishing Corp., 614 Superior Ave W, Cleveland, OH 44113. Examined: 11th ed., 1978/79. various paging. $22.
Aud: Sa

Subtitle: "Product selector and source guide." The first section consists of manufacturers' catalogs, a trade name index, and a list of manufacturers with addresses. The second section lists local sources of welding supplies and related products, and the third section consists of short articles on welding techniques. EM

SC 191
Wire Journal Directory/Catalog. ISSN 0512-5405. 1969. a. index. Wire Journal, 1570 Boston Post Rd, Box 302, Guilford, CT 06437. Examined: 1976/77. 374p. $10.
Aud: Sa

Includes a product index, a manufacturers' catalog section, a directory of manufacturers, and a directory of wire associations. EM

MARINE SCIENCE

SC 192
Advances in Marine Biology. ISSN 0065-2881. 1963. irreg. bibl. index. illus. Academic Press, 111 Fifth Ave, New York, NY 10003. Examined: v. 14, 1976. Frederick C. Russell, ed. 497p. $38.
Aud: Cl, Sa
Indexed in: *Marine Science Abstracts.*

Each volume is divided into three or four large sections, each authored by one or several individuals. The scope is wide, dealing with many aspects of the subject. Taxonomic and subject indexes are usually detailed, although the indexing varies from volume to volume. Includes many illustrations and generous additional reading lists. The coverage includes fresh as well as salt water, and material on the inland water systems. The quality of the volumes varies, depending on the editor; still this series is recommended for advanced biology programs, even if they do not have specific courses in marine biology. NLE

SC 193
Directory of Marine Scientists in the United States. (Continues: Directory of Oceanographers in the United States. ISSN 0078-5969; International Directory of Oceanographers.) 1950. irreg. National Academy of Sciences, Ocean Affairs Board, 2101 Constitution Ave, NW, Washington, DC 20418. Examined: 1975. 325p. $6.50.
Aud: Pl

Provides the fullest information available on people working and conducting research in marine science. Data are gathered by questionnaires sent to more than 3000 individuals working in the areas covered. The first section lists names and zip codes; the second section is arranged by zip code and thus lists people and institutions geographically; the third section lists names under about 70 subject categories. If someone wants to identify people and institutions working in specialized subjects of marine science, this book will answer the question. An appendix lists the addresses of organization and laboratories which are covered by the directory. NLE

SC 194
Institute of Navigation. National Marine Navigation Meeting. Proceedings. 1971. a. bibl. Institute of Navigation, 815 15th St, NW, Suite 832, Washington, DC 20005. Examined: 1976. 87p. $20.
Aud: Cl

Title varies: ION National Marine Meeting. Proceedings.

Papers presented at the annual meeting deal with topics ranging from use of satellites to underwater navigation. EM

SC 195
Jane's Ocean Technology. ISSN 0360-4950. 1975. a. illus. Franklin Watts, 750 Fifth Ave, New York, NY 10019. Examined: 1978. Robert Trillo, ed. 800p. $72.50.
Aud: Cl, Sa

An annual survey of the latest developments in underwater technology, including submersible vehicles, underwater photography, offshore drilling, etc. Publisher states that this book is "the only single source of reference for the engineer or scientist working with underwater equipment or structures." Also of interest to the student or professional working in any aspect of marine science. As is true of most titles in the Jane's series, the volumes are well illustrated with color and black-and-white photographs. JKM

SC 196
Marine Technology Society. Annual Conference Proceedings. ISSN 0542-710X. 1965. a. bibl. Marine Technology Society, 1730 M St, NW, Washington, DC 20036. Examined: 1977. 2v. $30.
Aud: Cl

The papers of this conference, jointly sponsored by the Institute of Electrical and Electronic Engineers and the Marine Technology Society, are presented under broad categories such as undersea technology, undersea acoustics, and ocean mining. EM

SC 197
Ocean Yearbook. 1977. a. index. University of Chicago Press, 11030 Langley Ave, Chicago, IL 60628. Examined: 1977. Elisabeth Mann Borgese and Norton Ginsburg, ed. approx. 600p. $25.
Aud: Cl, Pl, Sa

Begins with a survey of the year's developments in the study and use of the ocean, scientific discoveries, related legislation, and other important ocean-related events. Articles written by leading experts in the various fields represented are then presented under the following categories: living resources, nonliving resources, transportation and communication, marine science and technology, environment, coastal management, military activities, and regional developments. The appendixes include: annual reports from international organizations concerned with ocean-related issues, e.g., Scientific Committee on Oceanic Research; documents and proceedings; directory of institutions; and tables on living resources, nonliving ocean resources, transportation and communication, and military activities. JKM

SC 198
Oceanography and Marine Biology. ISSN 0078-3218. 1963. a. bibl. index. George Allen and Unwin, 40 Museum St, London WC1, England. Dist: Hafner Press, 866 Third Ave, New York, NY 10022. Examined: v. 13, 1975. Harold Barnes, ed. 465p. (v. 15, 1977. $19.95.)
Aud: Cl, Sa

The objectives of this annual review are to "consider basic aspects of the field, returning to each at appropriate intervals, to deal with subjects of special or topical importance, and to add new ones as they arise." There were seven articles in the issue examined. The contributors also listed bibliographical sources and suggested works at the end of each article. Includes an author index, systematic index, and subject index. KR/JKM

SC 199
Offshore Technology Conference. Proceedings. 1969. a. Offshore Technology Conference, Executive Manager, 6200 N Central Expressway, Dallas, TX 75206. Examined: 1977. 4v. $35.
Aud: Cl

Co-sponsored by several major engineering societies, the proceedings cover topics ranging from ocean mining to drilling operations to offshore mobile platforms. EM

SC 200
Society of Naval Architects and Marine Engineers. Transactions. ISSN 0081-1661. 1893. a. index. Society of Naval Architects and Marine Engineers, One World Trade Center, Suite 1369, New York, NY 10048. Examined: 1976. 439p. $15; free to members.
Aud: Sa
Indexed in: *Engineering Index; Oceanic Abstracts; Pollution Abstracts.*

Papers discuss shipbuilding techniques, analysis of ship structures, bid preparation, and similar topics. Includes lists of present and past officers, committee members, and award winners, and annual meeting reports. EM

MATHEMATICS

SC 201
Chemical Rubber Company. CRC Standard Mathematical Tables. 1948. index. illus. CRC Press, 18901 Cranwood Pkwy, Cleveland, OH 44128. Examined: 24th ed., 1976. William H. Beyer. 565p. $9.95.

Aud: Cl, Sa

The updated 24th edition aims to provide an adequately broad range of traditional and modern mathematical data necessary for current scientific needs. A table of contents provides access to tables through groupings in categories, such as numerical tables; logarithm tables; special function tables; financial tables; formulas and tables in trigonometry; and calculus, including derivatives, integration and integrals. There is an alphabetical index. The publisher states that the information included was obtained from "authentic and highly regarded sources," but disclaims responsibility for the validity of all materials or the consequences of their use. The author is also the editor of *Mathematics and Statistics*. The volume includes a statement referring readers to other CRC handbooks, such as the *Handbook for Probability and Statistics,* for information not included in the volume. ST/JKM

SC 202

Handbook of Mathematical Tables and Formulas. 1933. irreg. bibl. index. McGraw-Hill Book Co., 1221 Ave of the Americas, New York, NY 10020. Examined: 5th ed., 1972. Richard Stevens Burington, ed. 500p. $10.50.
Aud: Hs, Jc, Cl

Compact summary of the more important formulas and theorems of algebra, geometry, trigonometry, calculus, vector analysis, and many areas of basic and applied mathematics. Generally displayed in a logical progression without much explanation. Designed for use by those having basic knowledge of mathematics or mathematics students. A good choice for schools and for libraries needing basic mathematics information, but it is not of much value for advanced students. Needs to be updated on a more regular basis. NLE

SC 203

Handbook of Tables for Mathematics. ISSN 0362-8191. 1962. irreg. Chemical Rubber Publishing Co., 18901 Cranwood Pkwy, Cleveland, OH 44128. Examined: 4th ed., 1975. Robert C. Weast, ed. 1152p. $45.
Aud: Hs, Jc, Cl

This edition has added new sections under astrodynamics, basic orbital equations, and astrodynamical terminology, notation, and usage. The integral tables have been reorganized and now include 150 additional formulas. The section on hyperbolic functions has been extended, and there is an upgraded section of financial tables that is better suited to the economic realities of modern interest rates and other matters. This may be the best single-volume collection of formulas and tables for mathematicians. The good student will find many answers here, and most libraries will find this to be an excellent source for formula and notation questions. NLE

SC 204

Mathematical Handbook for Scientists and Engineers. 1961. irreg. index. McGraw-Hill Book Co., 1221 Ave of the Americas, New York, NY 10020. Examined: 2nd ed., 1965. Granino A. Korn and Theresa M. Korn, eds. 1130p. $39.50.
Aud: Cl, Sa

Subtitle: "Definitions, theorems, and formulas for reference and review." Includes sections on Z-transforms, the matrix notation for systems of differential equations, representation of rotations, mathematical programming, optimal-control theory, random process, and decision theory. Designed as a comprehensive reference collection of mathematical definitions, theorems, and formulas for scientists, engineers, and students. The 21 chapters are divided into several sections of increasing complexity. There are six appendixes, the last including two dozen numerical tables. Although the volume is too advanced for many, it does contain the answers to many mathematical questions and should be in most larger libraries. A basic source for mathematical methods and techniques. NLE

MEDICAL AND HEALTH SCIENCES

SC 205

Abortion Bibliography. ISSN 0092-9522. 1970. a. bibl. index. Whitston Publishing Co., Box 322, Troy, NY 12181. Examined: 5th ed., 1975; 6th ed., 1976. Mary K. Floyd, ed. 360p. $15.
Aud: Cl, Pl

A list of books and periodical articles on abortion which were published during the preceding year. Twenty-nine indexing and abstracting services are used to locate pertinent items; entries from *Biological Abstracts, Psychological Abstracts,* or *Sociological Abstracts* include the original abstract number. Listings are divided into two sections, an alphabetical list of materials by title or main entry and a list of materials by subject. There are approximately 223 subject headings used. Includes an author index. MSB

SC 206

Accepted Dental Therapeutics. ISSN 0065-079X.

(Continues: Accepted Dental Remedies.) 1934. bi-a. bibl. index. illus. American Dental Association, 211 E Chicago Ave, Chicago, IL 60611. Examined: 37th ed. Gordon Schrofenboer, ed. 342p. $3.50.
Aud: Cl, Pl

The information is gathered by the Council on Dental Therapeutics to assist the dental profession in the selection and use of therapeutic agents and their adjuncts, and dental cosmetic agents. These materials may be prescription or over-the-counter preparations. Mouthwashes or dentifrices which do not claim therapeutic value; cleansers for artificial dentures; and sterilizers which employ steam or boiling water as the bactericidal agent are not included. There are four main sections: 1) general principles of medication which include adverse drug reactions and nutritional factors; 2) therapeutic agents; 3) preventive agents which include fluoride compounds and dentifrices; and 4) indexes which include distributors of dental materials, council reports, and a general index. MSB

SC 207

Admission Requirements of U.S. and Canadian Dental Schools. (Continues: Admission Requirements of American Dental Schools.) 1963. a. index. American Association of Dental Schools, 1625 Massachusetts Ave, Washington, DC 20036. Examined: 14th ed., 1976/77; 15th ed., 1978/79. 200p. $7.50.
Aud: Jc, Cl, Pl

Provides current, official information on predental preparation and admission requirements. Includes a chapter on financial aid and estimating costs of a dental education. Discusses curriculum, enrollment, licensing, and testing. Information on each school is extensive, covering admission requirements, selection factors, financial aid, application and acceptance timetable, estimated expenses, and housing. Includes a geographic guide to the schools. BSM

SC 208

Advances in X-Ray Analysis. ISSN 0069-8490. 1957. a. bibl. index. illus. Plenum Press, 227 W 17th St, New York, NY 10011. Examined: v. 21, 1977. 325p. $39.50.
Aud: Sa

Title varies: Conference on Application of X-Ray Analysis. Proceedings.

Papers by specialists review current work in the application of X-ray methods to the characterization of substances of scientific and industrial interest. Developments in techniques, instrumentation, and applications are discussed. Recent conferences have alternated emphasis between X-ray diffraction and X-ray spectrometry. Most of the papers recount the results of the research of the authors; there are some state-of-the-art reviews. Abstracts precede some papers. The volumes have author and subject indexes. ST/JKM

SC 209

Alcoholism Treatment Programs Directory. 1976. a. Information Planning Associates, Box 1523, Rockville, MD 20850. Dist: Alcoholism Treatment Programs Directory, Box 6318, 5632 Connecticut Ave, NW, Washington, DC 20015. Examined: 1st ed., 1976. 476p. $14.95.
Aud: Pl

A comprehensive listing of approximately 3400 programs throughout the U.S. and its territories which offer treatment for alcoholism and related problems. There are 51 individual sections, one for each state and an additional section for the territories. In addition to the name, address, phone number, and director's name, entries for each program list the type of program, fee, services offered, and admission requirements. Each section is organized alphabetically, first by city and then by the name of the program. MSB

SC 210

Allied Medical Education Directory. (Continues: Directory of Approved Allied Medical Educational Programs.) 1972. a. American Medical Association, 535 N Dearborn St, Chicago, IL 60610. Examined: 6th ed., 1976. Donna G. Smith, ed. 527p. $7.50.
Aud: Hs, Jc, Cl, Pl

A detailed listing of educational programs in 26 allied medical professions. The American Medical Association and 29 national organizations that accredit these educational programs worked to produce this list of the 2742 accredited programs available in the allied health fields. Discusses the requirements for accreditation and basic curriculum for each program, then provides a list by state of accredited institutions offering the program with address, prerequisites, class size, beginning of course, financial aid, length of course, and the graduating award which is usually a certificate or degree. There is also a section on financial aid which is useful for counselors and students. There is a reference section in the back of the volume listing the 29 national organizations with addresses and telephone numbers and a list of credentials and their abbreviations. There is no index. BSM/MSB

SC 211

American Dental Directory. ISSN 0065-8073. 1947. a. index. American Dental Association, 211 E Chicago Ave, Chicago, IL 60611. Examined: 1977. 1435p. $25.
Aud: Cl, Pl

Lists dentists, dental schools, and dental organizations and their officials. The major portion of the volume concerns itself with the listings of dentists. This first listing is arranged geographically and includes the character of the practice, year of birth, membership in the ADA, and coded information indicating dental school and year of graduation. The second list of dentists is alphabetical; each entry notes the city and state or branch of federal service. At the end of the volume is an alphabetical list of all the dentists with names, cities, and states. MSB

SC 212

American Hospital Association. Guide to the Health Care Field. ISSN 0094-8969. 1945. a. index. American Hospital Association, 840 N Lake Shore Dr, Chicago, IL 60611. Examined: 1977. Paul Pearson, ed. 630p. $20.
Aud: Cl, Pl

A central reference source for information on health care institutions, organizations, agencies, and educational programs in the health field. Provides information on the American Hospital Association, national hospital statistical data, and sources of products and services used in hospitals. The list of health care institutions covers long-term care facilities, osteopathic hospitals, and U.S. government hospitals outside the U.S. The book is separated by divider pages; each divider page indicates contents of the section and gives pertinent definition or information. The four main sections are health care institutions; AHA membership; organizations and educational programs; and a buyers guide. There is an index by subject in the back of the volume. MSB

SC 213

American Hospital Association. Hospital Statistics. ISSN 0090-6662. 1946. a. index. American Hospital Association, 840 N Lake Shore Dr, Chicago, IL 60611. Examined: 1974. 222p. $12.50.
Aud: Sa

Contains data from the American Hospital Association's annual survey for the previous year. The data is compiled from questionnaires submitted to all hospitals accepted for registration in the United States and associated areas. Excluded are U.S. government hospitals outside of the United States. A statistical summary profile of hospitals precedes detailed tables in 12 categories, covering hospital services, utilization, personnel, and financial statistics. The tables deal mainly with changes in data over the year, but also include longer trend analyses and a review of data in relationship to the economy and population. An alphabetical index to data on specific topics refers to table numbers. ST/JKM

SC 214

American Medical Directory. ISSN 0065-9339. 1906. irreg. index. American Medical Association, 535 Dearborn St, Chicago, IL 60610. Examined: 26th ed., 1973. 4v. 3827p. $125.
Aud: Pl, Sa

A directory of physicians in the U.S., Canal Zone, Puerto Rico, Virgin Islands, and certain Pacific islands; U.S. physicians temporarily located in foreign countries; doctors of osteopathy who are AA members or are in approved medical training programs; non-M.D. special affiliates; and medical students who are AMA members. A geographical register in three volumes provides the following information under each heading: address, year of birth, medical education, year of license, primary and secondary specialties, type of practice, and American Specialty Board certification. The information was compiled by the AMA from questionnaires submitted by physicians and data received from medical schools, state licensing boards, hospitals, American specialty boards, medical societies, and the Educational Council for Foreign Medical Graduates. ST/JKM

SC 215

American Men and Women of Science: Medical and Health Sciences. ISSN 0145-9996. (Continues: American Men and Women of Science: Medical Sciences. ISSN 0097-6148.) 1975. irreg. index. R. R. Bowker, 1180 Ave of the Americas, New York, NY 10036. Dist: R. R. Bowker, Box 1807, Ann Arbor, MI 48106. Examined: 1977. Jaques Cattell Press, eds. 1720p. $47.50.
Aud: Cl, Sa

Derived from the seven-volume set **American Men and Women of Science**, this directory lists 26,627 U.S. and Canadian scientists currently active in the fields of dentistry, health sciences, medicine, neurosciences, pharmacology, psychiatry, surgery, pharmaceutical medicine, veterinary medicine, and related areas. Entries cover name, discipline, address, education, professional experience, memberships, honors, etc. Entries are arranged alphabetically by name, and disciplinary and geographic indexes are provided. Smaller, discipline-oriented collections may find this smaller, less expensive directory a better purchase for their needs than the full seven-volume set it is drawn from. JKM

SC 216
American Speech and Hearing Association. ASHA Reports. 1965. irreg. bibl. American Speech and Hearing Association, 9030 Old Georgetown Rd, Washington, DC 20014. Examined: v. 3, 1968, 431p.; v. 9, 1973. Robert T. Wertz, ed. 68p. $5.
Aud: Cl

The reports cover various aspects of speech and communication problems including such diverse topics as noise pollution as a public health hazard to very technical and clinical studies on orofacial functions. There are different features in each volume; some have very extensive references and bibliographies, while others include only a few references at the end of each chapter. There are no indexes. MSB

SC 217
American Speech and Hearing Association. Directory. a. American Speech and Hearing Association, 9030 Old Georgetown Rd, Washington, DC 20014. Examined: 1976. Kenneth O. Johnson, ed. 760p. $25.
Aud: Cl, Pl

Contains an alphabetical list and a geographical list of the members of the American Speech and Hearing Association. Also included are lists of the recognized state associations, members of the legislative council, accredited training programs, and the ASHA requirements for selection of hearing aids. The alphabetical list of members includes such information as name, preferred address, educational history, employment history, clinical certification, fellowship, and recency of directory information. MSB

SC 218
Annual Editions: Readings in Health. ISSN 0360-9766. 1975. a. index. illus. The Dushkin Publishing Group, Sluice Dock, Guilford, CT 06437. Examined: 1978/79. Helene Sloan, ed. 256p. $5.95.
Aud: Hs, Jc, Cl, Pl

Contains reproductions of newspaper, magazine, and journal articles relating to all aspects of health care and the health sciences. Articles are arranged under broad topics and indexed by subject. Many articles contain statistical charts and tables and black-and-white illustrations. Some include lists of suggested readings. As with other titles in the *Annual Editions* series, this collection is designed as a supplementary reader for high school and college courses, but it is also recommended as an introduction to the field and an overview of current health issues for the general reader. JKM

SC 219
Association of American Medical Colleges. AAMC Directory of American Medical Education. (Continues: AAMC Directory.) 1971/72. a. index. Association of American Medical Colleges, One Dupont Circle, NW, Suite 200, Washington, DC 20036. Examined: 1977/78. Verna E. Groo, ed. 370p. $6.
Aud: Cl

Lists medical schools in the U.S. and Canada that are association members or affiliate members of the Association of American Medical Colleges. Entries include a very brief description of the school's history, address and telephone numbers, type of school (public or private), total enrollment, clinical facilities, the university officials, medical school administrative staff, and department chairmen. The index is an alphabetical list of individual members, officers, and the staffs of the medical schools. MSB

SC 220
Bibliography of Bioethics. 1975. a. bibl. index. Center for Bioethics, Kennedy Institute, Georgetown University, Washington, DC. Dist: Gale Research Co., Book Tower, Detroit, MI 48226. Examined: 3rd ed., 1977. LeRoy Walters, ed. 348p. $24.
Aud: Pl, Cl

This title concerns itself with a very broad and complex field, bioethics, which can be defined as the systematic study of value questions which arise in the biomedical and behavioral fields. Materials are listed under 15 major areas with subtopics for each area. There is a list of journals cited, a thesaurus, a subject entry section, a title index, and an author index. Each entry includes the following information: author, article title, name of journal, volume and issue number, pages and dates, number of references, number of footnotes, descriptors which summarize the content of each entry, and identifiers which refer to a particular person, organization, political entity, or time. MSB

SC 221
Bibliography of the History of Medicine. ISSN 0067-7280. 1965. a. w/quinquennial cum. U.S. National Li

brary of Medicine, Department of Health, Education and Welfare, 8600 Rockville Pike, Bethesda, MD 20014. Dist: Superintendent of Documents, U.S. Government Printing Office, Washington, DC 20402. Examined: 11th ed., 1975. 191p. (1977.)
Aud: Cl, Pl
Indexed in: *Index Medicus; Current Catalog.*

Focuses on the history of medicine and related sciences, professions, and institutions. All chronologic periods and geographic areas are covered. Journal articles, monographs, and analytic entries for symposia, congresses, and similar composite publications, as well as historical chapters in general monographs are included. The majority of the journal citations come from the National Library of Medicine's *Index Medicus,* while the majority of monographs are from the *Current Catalog* which lists all monographs and other works received and cataloged in the National Library of Medicine. The bibliography is divided into three main parts: biographies, subjects, and authors. Biographies include citations to works dealing with the medical history of famous non-medical persons; medical aspects of the works of literary figures, composers, artists, etc.; and biographies of physicians, scientists, and others in the health care field. MSB

SC 222

Bibliography on Smoking and Health. ISSN 0067-7361. 1967. a. index. U.S. National Clearinghouse for Smoking and Health Center for Disease Control, Bureau of Health Education, Technical Information Center, Bldg 14, Rm 5B-1, Atlanta, GA 30333. Examined: 1975. Donald R. Shopman, ed. 315p.
Aud: Cl, Pl

Covers 12 major subject areas in the area of smoking and health. Each section contains numbered citations which indicate author, article title, journal title, volume, issue, page, year, and language if other than English. Following the bibliographic information, there is a brief abstract of the article. Some of the topics covered include tobacco economics, bills and legislation, and smoking cessation methods. There is a cumulative author and organization index with references to citation numbers rather than pages. There is also a subject index listing major subjects and subheadings. MSB

SC 223

Black's Medical Dictionary. 1906. irreg. illus. Barnes and Noble Books, 10 E 53rd St, New York, NY 10022. Examined: 30th ed., 1974. William A. R. Thomson, 934p. $17.50.

Aud: Hs, Jc, Cl, Pl

Compiled by a physician, this medical dictionary is intended to be a tool for educating the layperson about the action of the body in health and disease so that the individual may preserve health, recognize and cope with the early signs of disease, and know when to consult a physician. Preceding the main alphabetical list are practical suggestions for use which note general categories, such as symptoms of diseases, action of drugs, management of children, and nursing, with references in these categories to specific headings in the main list. The main section includes important diseases under their own names, with diseases of less frequent occurrence under the name of the organ affected. Under organ headings, information on anatomy and physiology precedes diseases and injuries. Treatment covered is mainly that which the non-specialist can render. Drugs are discussed under general headings, with more important drugs listed under their generic name. The list includes cross-references. Frequently updated editions assure the currency of the information presented. ST/JKM

SC 224

Connecticut Health Services Research Series. 1971. irreg. bibl. illus. Connecticut Health Services Research Series, Box 504, North Haven, CT 06473. Examined: 1st ed., 1971, 113p.; 4th ed., 1973. Donald Riedel and James E. C. Walker, eds. 108p. price varies from $3 to $7.50. (6th ed. 86p.)
Aud: Cl

A series of monographs. Each volume deals with problems that face every state in this country; although some of the studies were conducted in Connecticut, the findings and materials can be applied to almost any state or region in this nation. Some of the studies deal with extended health care facilities and patient care assessment in such facilities in light of Medicare and Medicaid. Other articles discuss health care for the urban poor and problems of the inner city population. Some volumes have references; others have charts, tables, and graphs. MSB

SC 225

Cumulated Abridged Index Medicus. 1970. a. National Library of Medicine, 8600 Rockville Pike, Bethesda, MD 20014. Dist: Superintendent of Documents, U.S. Government Printing Office, Washington, DC 20402. Examined: v. 2, 1971. 1128p. $30. (1977.)
Aud: Cl

Cumulates the twelve monthly issues of *Abridged*

Index Medicus. It is designed to give rapid access to selected biomedical journal literature of immediate interest to those people in the biomedical field. It abstracts 100 English language journals and is based on the larger version, **Cumulated Index Medicus.** There is an author section which is arranged alphabetically and a subject index which is based on the Medical Subject Headings (MeSH). Each article is listed under several subject headings in order to give the most complete coverage of the central concepts of the article. MSB

SC 226

Cumulated Index Medicus. ISSN 0590-3408 or 0090-1423. (Continues: Current List of Medical Literature and Quarterly Cumulative Index Medicus.) 1960. a. National Library of Medicine, 8600 Rockville Pike, Bethesda, MD 20014. Dist: Superintendent of Documents, U.S. Government Printing Office, Washington, DC 20402. Examined: v. 17, 1976. 8v. $202.
Aud: Cl

Cumulates the National Library of Medicine's monthly bibliography of the literature of biomedicine. Contains citations to the serial journal literature and to selected monographs. Original journal articles, letters, biographies, editorials, and obituaries that have substantive contents are indexed. The monographs indexed include published proceedings of various congresses and symposia. A list of books indexed is provided in the first volume, along with medical subject headings, a list of journals indexed, and the bibliography of medical reviews. The first three volumes are author indexes, and the remaining five volumes are subject indexes. The subject indexes use the medical subject headings, with major headings and subdivisions under the main topic. MSB

SC 227

Current Medical Diagnosis and Treatment. ISSN 0070-1920. (Continues: Current Diagnosis and Treatment.) 1962. a. bibl. index. illus. Lange Medical Publications, Drawer L, Los Altos, CA 94022. Examined: 16th ed., 1977. 1066p. $16.
Aud: Cl

A compendium of articles on widely accepted techniques for medical diagnosis and treatment. Although this desk reference is intended to serve the practicing physician, it would be of interest to others outside the field. Each article or chapter is concerned with a specific disorder or disease. Some chapters have short bibliographies at the end. There is an appendix with tables of normal values, miscellaneous information, and abbreviations. There is also a subject index at the end of the book. MSB

SC 228

Current Therapy. ISSN 0070-2102. 1949. a. index. W. B. Saunders Co., W Washington Sq, Philadelphia, PA 19105. Examined: 1978. Howard F. Conn, ed. 947p. $18.
Aud: Cl

A sophisticated tool describing the latest approved methods of treatment for practicing physicians. Although some of the information is complicated, educated lay persons should be able to understand a fair portion of the material presented. An interesting aspect of this work is that each disease or illness is discussed by individual practitioners and each article is signed by that physician with city and state given under his or her name. There is a complete index by subject at the end of the volume. MSB

SC 229

Directory of Medical Specialists. ISSN 0070-5829. 1944. bi-a. index. Marquis Who's Who, 200 E Ohio St, Chicago, IL 60611. Examined: 1977/78. 2v. 3661p. $49.50.
Aud: Cl, Pl

This two-volume set is published for the American Board of Medical Specialties. It is the authorized publication of approved American Specialty Boards certifying physicians in 22 major medical specialties. Entries for each of the specialty boards include the officers or boards of directors, functions and objectives, eligibility for examination, and an alphabetical list of certified physicians in the specialty area by state and town. Biographical data is given in abbreviated form (abbreviations are given in the preface). Data includes education, internships and residencies, staff affiliations, and teaching positions. Addresses and telephone numbers are usually included. MSB

SC 230

Directory of On-Going Research in Smoking and Health. ISSN 0070-6000. 1967. bi-a. index. U.S. Public Health Service Center for Disease Control, U.S. National Clearinghouse for Smoking and Health, Atlanta, GA 30333. Dist: Superintendent of Documents, U.S. Government Printing Office, Washington, DC 20402. Examined: 6th ed., 1976. 397p. $2.
Aud: Cl, Pl

An international source document for research on smoking and health. Includes research resumes from 37 countries. The scope of the research reported covers activities in the agricultural, biochemical, medical, behavioral, and psychological sciences, as well as related fields. The resumes are arranged in alphabetical order by country, and by state and/or city within the country. There are indexes to principal investigators, organizations, sponsors, and subjects. MSB

SC 231
Directory of Osteopathic Specialists. 1974. irreg. index. Marquis Who's Who, 200 E Ohio St, Chicago, IL 60611. Examined: 1974. 247p. $20.
Aud: Pl

A biographical directory that lists certified osteopathic specialists and fellows and contains information about the certification requirements of the 13 osteopathic boards and the American Academy of Osteopathy's Board on Fellowship. It is prepared by the American Osteopathic Association and the American Academy of Osteopathy. There is a separate section on each board which includes descriptive material detailing certification requirements within that specialty, a listing of board officers, and biographical sketches of the specialists certified by that board. Biographies are arranged alphabetically by state and town. Each biography includes professional and personal information. The index lists the specialists and fellows alphabetically by surname. MSB

SC 232
Directory of Poison Control Centers. 1967. irreg. U.S. Department of Health, Education, and Welfare, Food and Drug Administration, Bureau of Product Safety, Division of Hazardous Substances and Poison Control, Washington, DC 20402. Dist: Superintendent of Documents, U.S. Government Printing Office, Washington, DC 20402. Examined: 1972. 50p. $.35.
Aud: Hs, Cl, Pl

A list of facilities which provide information on a 24-hour basis concerning the treatment and prevention of accidents involving ingestion of poisonous and potentially poisonous substances. It is arranged alphabetically by state. Each state section includes the name, address, and telephone number of the state coordinator and a list of poison control centers, arranged by cities or towns, with name, address, telephone numbers, and directors. There are no indexes or bibliographies. MSB

SC 233
Directory of Women Physicians in the U.S. ISSN 0094-5471. 1973. American Medical Association, 535 N Dearborn St, Chicago, IL 60610. Examined: 1973. 432p. $10.
Aud: Cl, Pl

Lists women physicians indicating membership in the AMA (if applicable); local address; year of birth; a code which identifies the state and school within the state and the year of graduation; year of license; primary specialty and secondary specialty; type of practice, such as intern or medical teaching; and American Board specialty. The book has two major sections. The first is an alphabetical index by name indicating city and state. The second part is a geographical index which lists physicians by state and city. This second list contains all pertinent information about the physician. There is a short list in the back of the volume listing U.S. physicians temporarily located abroad. MSB

SC 234
Drug Abuse Bibliography. ISSN 0093-2515. 1970. a. index. Whitson Publishing Co., Box 322, Troy, NY 12181. Examined: 6th ed., 1975. Jean C. Advena and C. W. Triche, eds. 566p. (1977.)
Aud: Hs, Cl, Pl

Supplements *Drugs of Addiction and Non-Addiction, Their Use and Abuse, A Comprehensive Bibliography, 1960-1969*. Each volume contains a near-complete bibliography of books and periodical literature surrounding drug abuse issued during the previous year. The volumes are divided into three sections: books and government publications; subject index to periodical literature; and an author index. Book and government publication entries are arranged in alphabetical order by author, when given. Entries in the periodical literature section are listed alphabetically by title under each subject heading. MSB

SC 235
Drugs in Current Use and New Drugs. ISSN 0070-7392. (Continues: Drugs in Current Use.) 1955. a. Springer Publishing Co., 200 Park Ave S, New York, NY 10003. Examined: 1977. Walter Modell, ed. 175p. $6.50 pap.
Aud: Cl, Pl

This two-part paperback consists of an alphabetic listing of drugs currently in use in clinical medicine including well established drugs, new drugs still on trial, old drugs which are of questionable value but may still be used, and some drugs that may have been withdrawn becasue their effects are toxic or cause poisoning but which should still be mentioned. The second part focuses on new drugs that have been introduced recently on the commercial drug market. The descriptions in part two are more detailed. All drugs are listed under non-proprietary names; cross references are provided from the proprietary name to the generic name. The drugs listed are only single chemical drugs. Oral contraceptives, vaccines, radioactive agents, antigens, and, other pharmaceutical materials used in making up medicaments have been omitted to conserve space. MSB

SC 236

Drugs of Choice. ISSN 0070-7406. 1958. bi-a. index. C. V. Mosby Co., 11830 Westline Industrial Dr, St Louis, MO 63141. Examined: 1978/79. Walter Modell, ed. 824p.
Aud: Cl

A guide to the selection of the best drug for a particular therapeutic problem. It is directed primarily at the practicing physician, but the major portion of the book is in text format with concise explanations of the disease or problem to be treated. The drugs in common use are listed after the illness or problem with dosage information, side effects, and other clinical information. All drugs are listed by generic name. There are several tables which give a brief summary of toxic effects or chemical structures of particular drugs. The index includes drug names; illnesses, diseases, etc.; and anatomic listings. MSB

SC 237

The Easter Seal Directory of Resident Camps for Persons with Special Health Needs. (Continues: Directory of Camps for the Handicapped.) 1971. bi-a. index. National Easter Seal Society for Crippled Children and Adults, 2023 W Ogden Ave, Chicago, IL 60612. Examined: 1971; 1975; 1977. 73p. $1.50 pap.
Aud: Pl, Sa

Lists resident camps by state. Each entry includes information on impairments accepted (e.g., diabetes, minimal brain dysfunction, etc.), name, address, age range, sessions, capacity, fees, if camperships are available, where to send inquiries, and other pertinent information (e.g., co-ed, etc.). There are indexes by disability group served and by name of camp. SLB

SC 238

Facts About Nursing. ISSN 0071-3651. 1935. a. index. illus. American Nurses Association, 2420 Pershing Ave, Kansas City, MO 64108. Examined: 1972/73. Aleda Roth, ed. 272p. $6.50.
Aud: Cl

The authoritative collection of fundamental data on the nursing profession and its practitioners. It provides information on trends in nurse distribution and characteristics which are useful in understanding the role of nursing in the nation's health care delivery system. There are six chapters. The first is concerned with the distribution of registered nurses, the second with nursing education, the third with the economic status of registered nurses, and the fourth with allied nursing personnel. The fifth chapter provides related information on facilities, utilization, expenditures for health care, etc. The sixth chapter is concerned with the functions and purpose of nursing organizations. There is a subject index. MSB

SC 239

Foreign Medical School Catalogue. ISSN 0085-0829. 1971. a. illus. Foreign Medical School Information Center, One E Main St, Bay Shore, NY 11706. Examined: 1977. Charles R. Modica, ed. 165p. $9.95.
Aud: Cl, Pl

Describes the system of medical education and lists medical schools in 66 countries. Provides brief information on each school covering administration (public or private), admission requirements, program, and application procedures. Photographs of the schools are included whenever possible, and there are maps showing the general location of each. Information on tuition is not included. The introductory material provides information on foreign language preparation programs, charter flights, the Educational Council for Foreign Medical Graduates examination which is required by most states for medical practice in the U.S., addresses of foreign consulates in the U.S., and the Coordinated Transfer Application System which assists in the evaluation of credentials of U.S. citizens who wish to transfer from foreign to U.S. medical schools. BSM

SC 240

Handbook of Nonprescription Drugs. 1967. bi-a. index. illus. American Pharmaceutical Association, 2215 Constitution Ave, NW, Washington, DC 20037. Examined: 5th ed., 1977. George B. Griffenhagen, ed. 3880.
Aud: Hs, Cl, Pl

Designed primarily as a tool for pharmacists and other health professionals to help them deal with the self-medicating person. With the great number of over-the-counter drugs available, it is estimated that up to 70 percent of the illnesses in the U.S. are treated with self-prescribed medications. Therefore when a person chooses an over-the-counter drug, there must be special care taken due to possible side effects. This handbook, while not specifically a self-help manual, can assist in the selection of nonprescription drugs while trying to avoid adverse reactions. It is divided into 32 sections covering such topics as cold and allergy products, infant formula products, and burn and sunburn products, to name a few. There is a product index at the back of the book. Though the book is supposed to be a biennial publication, there was a four-year span between the fourth edition (1973) and the fifth edition (1977). MSB

SC 241
The Health Care Directory. ISSN 0147-7846. 1977/78. freq. not determined. Medical Economics Co., Book Division, Box 49, Oradell, NJ 07649. Examined: 1977/78. Craig T. Norback and Peter G. Norback, eds. 1124p. $150.
Aud: Cl, Pl

An alphabetical list of health agencies starting with adoption information and ending with volunteer work organizations. It is a fairly complete list of agencies that are either directly involved in health care (such as specialized hospitals which are listed alphabetically by type and then by state) or peripherally involved with health care (such as equipment leasing and legal services). The volume is divided into 60 sections; each section is individually paged. There are no indexes. MSB

SC 242
Health Consequences of Smoking. 1967. a. bibl. index. U.S. Health Service Administration, Public Health Service Center for Disease Control, Atlanta, GA 30333. Dist: Superintendent of Documents, U.S. Government Printing Office, Washington, DC 20402. Examined: 1973, 261p.; 1975. 235p. $1.85.
Aud: Hs, Cl, Pl

Each year the Public Health Service publishes a review of the scientific data related to the health consequences of smoking. Major areas covered each year include cardiovascular disease, cancer, respiratory disease, pregnancy and smoking, and the effects of smoking on nonsmokers. There are bibliographies at the end of each chapter and indexes at the end of each volume. The 1975 volume has a cumulative index for the period 1964-1975. MSB

SC 243
The Health Sciences Video Directory. 1977. a. index. Shelter Books, 218 E 19th St, New York, NY 10003. Examined: 1st ed., 1977. Lawrence Eidelberg, ed. 270p. $27.50. (2nd ed., 1978.)
Aud: Jc, Cl, Sa

An annotated directory, limited to videocassette or videotape programs, of more than 4400 individual programs or series in health sciences education designed for use in undergraduate, continuing, in-service, and patient health programs. Materials for school and general college use are not included. Arranged alphabetically by title of the program, entries include order information, format, intended audience, authority, and an annotation. JKM

SC 244
International Review of Research in Mental Retardation. ISSN 0074-7750. 1966. irreg. bibl. index. Academic Press, 111 Fifth Ave, New York, NY 10003. Examined: v.9, 1978. Norman R. Ellis, ed. 301p. $19.50.
Aud: Cl, Sa

Contains reviews by specialists of current research, reflecting the aim of basing action programs for the mentally retarded on systematic scientific research. Articles in volume 19 include studies of basic mental processes, the ethic of work with the mentally retarded, and programs and projects such as public and community residential services and the mainstreaming of mentally retarded children in education. Volumes seven to nine include subject indexes; earlier volumes contain author and subject indexes. ST/JKM

SC 245
The Killers and Cripplers. 1953. irreg. bibl. illus. David McKay Co., 750 Third Ave, New York, NY 10017. Examined: 11th ed., 1976. National Health Education Committee, eds. 333p.
Aud: Hs, Cl, Pl

A source book of vital statistics on the principal causes of death and disability in the U.S. The book portrays the triumphs and deficits of efforts made against the major diseases. It provides background information for evaluating the progress of various health and medical research programs. It also points out where there are still great needs for further research. There are 18 areas discussed. Short bibliographies are provided at the end of each chapter. There are profuse illustrations and photographs throughout the book. MSB

SC 246
Medical and Health Annual. 1976. a. index. illus. Encyclopaedia Britannica, 425 N Michigan Ave, Chicago, IL 60611. Examined: 1977. 447p. $12.95.
Aud: Jc, Cl, Pl

A medical miscellany designed for the lay reader. Somewhat less than half of the volume is devoted to lengthy articles on various aspects of health, the history of medicine, and, in the 1977 volume, two specific health conditions—arthritis and menopause. The second section of the work is an alphabetically arranged list of articles on 56 health and medicine topics. Most of the articles in this section are one to three pages in length; a few are more substantial. The rest of the volume covers basic health education topics and includes a first-aid handbook. Includes statistics and some color illustrations. JKM

SC 247

Medical and Health Information Directory. 1977. bi-a. index. Gale Research Co., Book Tower, Detroit, MI 48226. Examined: 1977. Anthony T. Kruzas, ed. 664p. $48.
Aud: Hs, Cl, Pl

Covers the public and private agencies involved in medical education, research, planning, financing, and reporting. The purpose of the directory is to collect information from other sources concerning all aspects of health care except medical equipment suppliers, testing laboratories, and nursing homes. It provides names, addresses, and descriptions for more than 12,000 agencies, associations, institutions, publications, and services. Includes libraries, research centers, audiovisual services, newsletters, and database services. Coverage of the subject matter is broad and includes clinical medicine, the basic biomedical sciences, and the socioeconomic and technological aspects of health care. The emphasis is on institutions in the United States. There are a total of 32 sections with an index at the end of each section; there is no general or comprehensive index. MSB

SC 248

Medical Books and Serials in Print. ISSN 0000-0574. (Continues: Bowker's Medical Books in Print.) 1971. a. R. R. Bowker Co., 1180 Ave of the Americas, New York, NY 10036. Dist: R. R. Bowker, Box 1807, Ann Arbor, MI 48106. Examined: 7th ed., 1978. 1250p. $39.95.
Aud: Cl, Pl

Subtitle: "An index to literature in the health sciences." Lists medical books and serials in the medical, psychiatric, pharmaceutical, veterinary, dental, and nursing fields. Also covers the literature of the allied fields of health sciences. Special features include book indexes by subject, author, and title with full bibliographic information in each. The serials indexes (subject and title indexes) have full bibliographic entry under the main subject category of the publication. Cross reference entries appear under the secondary subjects in the title index. There are lists of micropublishers and abstracting and indexing services in the health sciences, and a directory of publishers represented in the volume. MSB

SC 249

Medical School Admission Requirements, U.S.A. and Canada. ISSN 0066-9423. 1950. a. Association of American Medical Colleges, One Dupont Circle, NW, Suite 200, Washington, DC 20035. Examined: 28th ed., 1977/78. 350p. $5.
Aud: Hs, Jc, Cl, Pl

Lists all medical schools in the U.S. and Canada, all of whom are members of the Association of American Medical Colleges. A two-page descriptive entry for each school outlines the instructional program, including required and elective course titles, duration of program, types of instruction, pre-medical preparation, and admission policies. Entries are arranged alphabetically by school. Descriptive statistics with frequency tables and categorical listings identify patterns of change and development in the medical school curriculum. General information on planning, expense, financial aid, loans, employment, minority group students, and foreign applicants is also provided. An authoritative resource. BSM/MSB

SC 250

The Merck Index: An Encyclopedia of Chemicals and Drugs. ISSN 0076-6518. 1889. irreg. bibl. index. illus. Merck and Co., Rahway, NJ 07065. Examined: 9th ed., 1976. Martha Windholz, ed. 1313p. $18.
Aud: Pl, Sa

This encyclopedia of the most important chemicals, drugs, pesticides and biological substances provides concise descriptions of the preparation and general properties of compounds; information on the use, principal pharmacological action, and toxicity of the substances; and correlation of trivial, generic and chemical names with structures, trademarks, and company affiliations. The numbered monographs are arranged alphabetically by name, and access is provided through a formula index and a cross-index of names whicher refer to the number of the monograph. A thumb index indicating number groups facilitates the location of information. The monographs include *Chemical Abstract* names, alternate names, empirical formula, molecular weight, percent composition, illustration of structure, physical data, derivatives, use, therapeutic category, and references to the literature from which the information was abstracted. Another feature is a section on organic name reactions. The ninth edition, compiled and written by an editorial staff, includes 1000 new entries, with over 50 percent of the old monographs revised and material of minor importance eliminated. ST/JKM

SC 251
Modern Drug Encyclopedia and Therapeutic Index. ISSN 0076-9959. 1934. bi-a. (tri-a. prior to 1973.) index. Yorke Medical Books, Dun-Donnelley Publishing Co., 666 Fifth Ave, New York, NY 10019. Examined: 1977. Arthur Lewis, ed. 1009p. $40.
Aud: Cl, Pl

Lists therapeutic preparations available from physicians by prescription. All preparations are listed alphabetically by generic name or primary ingredient of combination products. Trade names of generic drugs are given at the end of each description along with availability (dosages as packaged). There are three indexes: a therapeutic index which provides an alphabetical listing of products by therapeutic indication; a manufacturers' index which is an alphabetical listing of the manufacturers and their products; and a general index which contains alphabetized references to all preparations by generic and trade names. Each preparation described is broken down into the following parts: synonym, chemical name, description, indications (use), contraindications, warnings, precautions, adverse reactions, dosage and administration, and availability. New products are updated by supplements. MSB

SC 252
Monographs of the Rutgers Center of Alcohol Studies. ISSN 0080-4983. (Continues: Monographs of the Yale Center of Alcohol Studies.) 1958. bibl. index. Rutgers University, Center of Alcohol Studies, New Brunswick, NJ 08903. Examined: v. 8, 1974, 82p; v. 11, 1976. Mark Keller, ed. 158p.
Aud: Cl, Pl

A series of monographs that concern alcohol and different groups. The studies concern such topics as alcohol in ethnic cultural settings; problems of alcoholism in different groups, such as American men, American Indians, and teenagers; and alcoholism and the law. This collection of monographs is not a how-to collection; rather it presents hard data on a very important and emotional issue, alcoholism. It is a study of public atttitudes toward drinking, heavy drinking, and probtem drinkers. There are bibliographies in most of the volumes, and subject indexes in all of the volumes. MSB

SC 253
National Health Directory. 1977. a. illus. Science and Health Publications, 1129 20th St, NW, Suite 511, Washington, DC 20036. Examined: 1978. Kathy Murphy, ed. 500p. $22.50.
Aud: Hs, Cl, Pl

Includes the name, title, address, and telephone number of more than 7500 important information sources on health programs and legislation. It lists congressmen and their health legislative aides and appointment secretaries in Washington and district offices; major health committees in the 95th Congress; and agency decision-makers in 23 federal agencies. Provides complete state maps indicating the boundaries of every congressional district. Also lists state health officials and federal regional officials including officials in public service regional offices, health system agencies, state health planning and development agencies, Medicare/Medicaid fiscal intermediaries and agencies, governors, state health officers, and state health legislative committees. While there is no subject index at the end of the volume, there are name indexes and a summary of contents that assist in using this tool. MSB

SC 254
National Institute on Drug Abuse Research Monograph Series. (Title varies: NIDA Research Monograph Series.) 1975. irreg. bibl. illus. U.S. Department of Health, Education, and Welfare, National Institute on Drug Abuse, Division of Research, 5600 Fisher Lane, Rockville, MD 20857. Dist: Superintendent of Documents, U.S. Government Printing Office, Washington, DC 20402. Examined: 17th ed., 1977. Robert C. Petersen, ed. 381p.
Aud: Hs, Cl, Pl
Indexed in: *Index Medicus; Biosciences Information Service; Chemical Abstracts; Psychological Abstracts; Psychopharmacology Abstracts.*

The purpose of this series is to provide critical reviews of research problem areas and techniques, the content of state-of-the-art conferences, research reviews, and significant original research. Each volume has a different subject, but all are related to drug abuse. Some volumes are very clinical and research oriented. Some titles focus on the effect of drugs on different groups, such as "Drugs and Men Between the Ages of 20 and 30," or "Cocaine: Its Use and Misuse." Other volumes are bibliographies. Illustrations are usually in the form of graphs or tables. MSB

SC 255
National Institutes of Health. NIH Factbook. 1976.

freq. not determined. index. Marquis Who's Who, 200 E Ohio St, Chicago, IL 60611. Examined: 1st ed., 1976. 597p. $44.50.
Aud: Cl

Presents the history, current activities, and research grants of the institutes that comprise the National Institutes of Health. There are 12 biomedical research institutes and divisions that make up the NIH; these are discussed separately and as a whole. The work is divided into seven major sections: history, organization, statistics (which includes costs), advisory groups, research, public health service grants and awards, and subject and personnel indexes. Geographical references are included in the subject index. MSB

SC 256
Pharmacy School Admission Requirements. (1977/78 is 3rd ed.) bi-a. American Association of Colleges of Pharmacy, 4630 Montgomery Ave, Suite 201, Bethesda, MD 20014. Examined: 3rd ed., 1977/78. John F. Schlegel, ed. 138p. $5.
Aud: Hs, Cl

This book provides general information on each school, as well as specific information on admissions requirements, selection factors, and educational costs. Each school provides the information for the directory, and only accredited schools in the U.S. and Puerto Rico are included. The directory first lists all the accredited schools by state with just addresses, then those schools requiring the Pharmacy College Admission Test are listed, also by state. The major part of the directory follows with more detailed entries for each school. MSB

SC 257
Philosophy and Medicine. 1975. irreg. index. D. Reidel Publishing Co., Box 17, Dordrecht, The Netherlands. Dist: D. Reidel Publishing Co., 306 Dartmouth St, Boston, MA 02116. Examined: v. 1, 1975, 240p; v. 4, 1978. H. Tristram Engelhardt, Jr., and Stuart F. Spicker, eds. 302p.
Aud: Cl, Pl

Focuses on the two disciplines, philosophy and medicine, and how they interact in today's society. The series is meant to reflect and encourage a development of concern for the general philosophical issues in medicine and in medical ethics. With the advent of life-prolonging devices, the questions raised about the quality and the quantity of life must be looked at; it is these difficult questions that the series tackles. Each volume discusses a different aspect of medicine and the philosophical approaches to it. There is a combined author-subject index in each volume. MSB

SC 258
Programs and Services for the Deaf in the United States. (Continues: Directory of Services for the Deaf in the United States.) 1966. a. American Annals of the Deaf, 5034 Wisconsin Ave, NW, Washington, DC 20016. Examined: 1977. William Craig and Helen Craig, eds. 296p. $5.
Aud: Cl, Pl

This directory is actually a special issue of the journal, *American Annals of the Deaf*. It is published yearly as the April issue and can be purchased separately from the journal. The directory is divided into four major sections: 1) educational programs and services; 2) rehabilitation programs and services; 3) community programs and supportive services; and 4) research and information programs and services. The directory is intended not only for the professional in speech and hearing, but also for individuals who would find this information valuable for personal use. MSB

SC 259
Southern Conference on Gerontology. ISSN 0071-6111. 1951. a. bibl. Center for Gerontological Studies, University of Florida, Gainesville, FL 32601. Dist: University Presses of Florida, 15 NW 15th St, Gainesville, FL 32601. Examined: v. 21, 1972, 142p; v. 23, 1974, 172p.; v. 24, 1975. Carter C. Osterbind, ed. 168p.
Aud: Cl, Pl

The published proceedings of the annual Southern Conference on Gerontology. Each year a specific topic is examined and reported on at the conference. Each volume is made up of chapters written by different contributors whose credentials are listed in the table of contents. The contributors are leaders in such fields as psychology, sociology, social welfare, architecture, economics, nursing, medicine, and the allied health sciences; therefore each topic is covered from diverse viewpoints. Some of the topics which have been covered are: social goals, social programs, and the aging; aging and retirement; independent living for older people; and medical care and social security. There are some bibliographies (usually at the end of different chapters), and a list of registrants to the conference and cooperating agencies. There are no indexes. MSB

SC 260
Standard Medical Almanac. 1977. freq. not deter-

mined. index. Marquis Who's Who, 20 E Ohio St, Chicago, IL 60611. Examined: 1st ed., 1977. 606p. $34.50.
Aud: Cl, Pl

Designed to provide a profile of health care in the U.S. by presenting data from a variety of government and private sources. Provides data on health care professionals including statistics on supply and demand of trained personnel. Discusses medical costs, salaries, insurance costs and trends, education, accreditation procedures, schools, licensing procedures and agencies, and distribution and utilization of health care facilities. Includes statistics on disease, mortality and birth rates, and socioeconomic factors which affect health status. There is a list of federal health agencies, current and proposed legislation, and other aspects of federal involvement in health care. Arranged in six parts covering the topics outlined above. There are subject, organization, and geographic indexes. JKM

SC 261
State Approved Schools of Nursing-LPN/LVN. ISSN 0081-4423. 1958. a. index. National League for Nursing, 10 Columbus Circle, New York, NY 10019. Examined: 19th ed., 1977. 87p. $4.95. (1978.)
Aud: Hs, Jc, Pl

A list of U.S. schools that conducted programs preparing students for licensure as practical nurses (LPN) or vocational nurses (LVN). The programs have been classified as adult education programs, high school programs, and high school extended programs. Schools are listed by state, and there is an alphabetical list to schools by name. Entries indicate types of programs offered, accreditation, administrative control, financial support, length of program, educational requirements, admissions policies, enrollment, and graduates. There are lists of new schools and schools that have closed, and a directory of state boards of nursing. Covers 1257 schools conducting more than 1300 programs. BSM/MSB

SC 262
State-Approved Schools of Nursing—R.N. ISSN 0081-4431. 1943. a. index. National League for Nursing, 10 Columbus Circle, New York, NY 10019. Examined: 1976. Walter Johnson, ed. 87p. $4.25.
Aud: Hs, Pl

Listing of the 1360 schools that conduct 1375 programs for training registered nurses that are approved by the respective state boards. Program listings are complete for diploma, associate degree, and baccalaureate schools of nursing. Graduates of these programs may have differences in preparation, but all are eligible to take the licensing examination which leads to an R.N. The schools are listed by state, with the name of the school and director of the program, complete address, type of program, National League for Nursing accreditation, administrative control, financial support, education requirements, enrollments, admissions, graduates, and fall admissions. The index is an alphabetical list of schools by name. BSM/MSB

SC 263
State Legislation on Smoking and Health. 1975. a. U.S. Department of Health, Education, and Welfare, Center for Disease Control, Bureau of Health Education, National Clearinghouse for Smoking and Health, Atlanta, GA 30333. Dist: Superintendent of Documents, U.S. Government Printing Office, Washington, DC 20402. Examined: 1977. 79p. free.
Aud: Hs, Cl, Pl

A compilation of information on state laws concerning smoking and tobacco products. It lists smoking and health resolutions and bills introduced in the state legislatures. The information is given in table format by subject and state. It covers legislation based around seven major areas: limitations on smoking, commerce, smoking and schools, advertising of tobacco products, sales to minors, insurance, and "other areas." Each state is tabulated, and the list is alphabetical by state. There are no indexes. MSB

SC 264
Studies in Medical Geography. 1958. a. bibl. index. illus. Hafner Press, 866 Third Ave, New York, NY 10022. Examined: v. 9, 1970, 675p.; v. 12, 1973. Jacques M. May and Donna McClellan, eds. 490p.
Aud: Hs, Cl, Pl

This series is concerned with disease and environmental health. The major focus is on the ecology of malnutrition in different sections of the world. The studies include food resources, habits, deficiencies, and the diseases involved with such problems. There are bibliographies at the end of each chapter and a subject index at the end of each volume. There are maps in those volumes where specific areas are discussed. MSB

SC 265
Syncrisis: The Dynamics of Health. 1972. irreg. bibl. illus. Office of International Health, Division of Program Analysis, Washington, DC. Dist: Superintendent of Documents, U.S. Government Printing Office,

Washington, DC 20402. Examined: v. 13, 1975, 136p.; v. 19, 1976. 144p.
Aud: Cl, Pl

Consists of country profiles describing and analyzing health conditions in particular countries and the impact of those conditions on the country's socioeconomic development. It attempts to provide a concise and up-to-date introduction to the health situation in a country. It is also a source of parallel descriptions of health systems in countries with widely varying cultural, social, economic, and government systems. Items covered in each volume include a brief overview of the country, population, health status, nutrition, environmental health, health facilities, health manpower, and national health policies. Includes a list of international organizations and a bibliography at the end of the volume. There are appropriate tables and illustrations in each volume. MSB

SC 266
Transactions of the Association of Life Insurance Medical Directors of America. ISSN 0066-9598. 1889. a. index. Association of Life Insurance Medical Directors, 200 Berkley St, Boston, MA 02117. Examined: 60th ed., 1977. Paul S. Entmacher, ed. 270p. free.
Aud: Cl, Pl
Indexed in: *Index Medicus.*

Includes papers presented at the annual meetings of the Association of Life Insurance Medical Directors. The contributors, all from the field of life insurance, range from physicians to life insurance specialists. The subjects cover a wide variety of topics from medical advancements and education to the costs of national medical insurance. Each contributor is identified at the beginning of his or her chapter. There is an author index and a subject index. MSB

SC 267
USAN and the USP Dictionary of Drug Names. ISSN 0090-6816. 1961. a. index. United States Pharmacopeial Convention, 12601 Twinbrook Pkwy, Rockville, MD 10852. Examined: 1976. Mary C. Griffiths, ed. 362p. $18.50.
Aud: Cl

A dictionary of nonproprietary names, brand names, code designations, and chemical abstracts service registry numbers for drugs. The dictionary cumulates every year and supersedes each earlier edition. There are over 10,000 entries arranged alphabetically; 3000 are brand names, 2146 are code designations, and more than 2800 are chemical abstract service registry numbers. There is also a list of drugs by category of pharmacologic activity and a list of molecular formulas and corresponding U.S. Adopted Names (USAN). Also includes the names and addresses of firms that are involved with the drugs and compounds listed. MSB

SC 268
U.S. Facilities and Programs for Children with Severe Mental Illnesses; A Directory. (Continues: Directory of Facilities for Mentally Ill Children in the United States.) 1974. index. National Institute of Mental Health, 5600 Fishers Lane, Rockville, MD 20852. Dist: Superintendent of Documents, U.S. Government Printing Office, Washington, DC 20402. Examined: 1974. National Society for Autistic Children, comp. 448p.
Aud: Cl, Pl

A catalog of service programs for children with severe mental illnesses. Programs and facilities listed in the directory include those which serve children diagnosed as autistic, schizophrenic, or as having any of the other childhood psychoses or severe mental disorders. Facilities are listed by state with full name, address, telephone number, whether it is a day or residential facility, date of establishment, and executive director. This information is followed by a description of the facility covering capacity, fees, physical description, admission criteria (type of problem and geographic limitations), parent participation, staff, and program offered. The index of facilities lists the names of the facilities and their programs, such as preschool programs, adult programs, camps, etc. There is also a list of chapters of the National Society for Autistic Children and a list of other directories that are available. MSB

SC 269
University of Michigan. Institute of Gerontology. Occasional Papers on Gerontology. 1968. irreg. bibl. illus. University of Michigan, Institute of Gerontology, 543 Church St, Ann Arbor, MI 48104. Examined: v. 7, 1972, 80p.; v. 8, 1972, 54p.; v. 9, 1972, 62p.; v. 11, 1975. 121p. $2.95.
Aud: Cl, Pl

This series is concerned with the various aspects of gerontology. The topics range from social aspects of gerontology to the financial problems of the aged. There are references and illustrations in some of the volumes, but there are no indexes. Each volume has several authors, i.e., each chapter is written by a different person whose credentials are indicated. MSB

SC 270
Venereal Disease Bibliography. ISSN 0090-8479. 1972. a. index. Whitston Publishing Co., Box 322, Troy, NY 12181. Examined: 1973. Stephen H. Goode, ed. 276p. $10.
Aud: Cl, Pl

Supplements the *Venereal Disease Bibliography 1966-1970,* a bibliography covering the world literature on VD. There is a section for monographs and one for periodical literature, both arranged by title. The periodical section includes a subject index. There is a combined author index to both sections. MSB

SC 271
Who's Who in Health Care. 1977. freq. not determined. index. Hanover Publications, 200 Park Ave, Suite 303E, New York, NY 10017. Examined: 1st ed., 1977. Elliot Sainer, ed. 764p. $60.
Aud: Cl, Pl

A bibliographic compilation of leaders in the health care field. There are approximately 8000 biographical sketches in detailing professional background and achievements. Includes leaders in all aspects of the health care fields such as schools, pharmaceutical and insurance industries, voluntary associations, researchers, consultants, hospital executives, etc. There are two indexes. The first is a geographic index listing the state, then person; no page numbers are given because the main body of the material is arranged alphabetically by individual. The second is a classified index which lists individuals by their primary institutional or organizational affiliations. MSB

SC 272
World Directory of Schools for Medical Assistants; Repertoire Mondial des Ecoles d'Assistants Medicaux. 1973. irreg. World Health Organization, 1211 Geneva 27, Switzerland. Dist: WHO Publications Centre, 49 Sheridan Ave, Albany, NY 12210. Examined: 1973. 111p. $8. (1976.)
Aud: Hs, Cl, Pl

A compilation of schools for medical assistants. The text is in English and French. Medical assistants are defined as health workers with eight to nine years of basic general education, followed by two to three years of technical training that should enable him/her to recognize the most common diseases, to care for simple medical problems, and to promote health in his/her area. The directory lists countries or areas in alphabetical order. Entries for each country are divided into two parts: a table and general information. Training institutions are listed alphabetically by city, province, state, or republic, and then by institution. Information in the tables includes name and address, year started, primary and secondary education, entrance exam, other requirements, duration of course, name of diploma, language of course, total enrollment, first year admissions, and graduates. The general information covers instruction hours, curriculum, admissions, facilities, recognition, and functions. MSB

SC 273
World Directory of Schools of Pharmacy. ISSN 0512-2783. 1963. freq. not determined. World Health Organization, 1211 Geneva 27, Switzerland. Dist: WHO Publications Centre, 49 Sheridan Ave, Albany, NY 12210. Examined: 1963. 301p. $7.
Aud: Cl

Describes the important and prominent features of pharmaceutical education in 81 countries. There are descriptive accounts and numerical data that serve as a general guide for those seeking information on the facilities and resources for pharmaceutical training in a specific country. The material is arranged alphabetically by country. There is an appendix which breaks down the information into tables for each continent. MSB

SC 274
World Health Organization. Monograph Series. ISSN 0512-3038. 1951. irreg. bibl. index. illus. World Health Organization, 1211 Geneva 27, Switzerland. Dist: WHO Publications Centre, 49 Sheridan Ave, Albany, NY 12210. Examined: v. 16, 1953; v. 29, 1968. 335p. (1977.)
Aud: Cl
Indexed in: *Biological Abstracts; Index Medicus.*

The series includes technical guides and treatises on a single subject or a group of related subjects. Essentially the individual volumes are textbooks which deal with well-known facts and recent advances in the health field, as well as pointing the way to future developments. The topics are quite diverse, covering such areas as economics in health care, meat hygiene, child guidance centers, and surveillance of drinking water quality. Most volumes are indexed, some have illustrations, and many include bibliographies. MSB

SC 275
Yearbook and Directory of Osteopathic Physicians. (Continues: Directory of Osteopathic Physicians.) (1952 is 44th ed.) a. American Osteopathic Association, 212 E Ohio St, Chicago, IL 60611. Examined:

69th ed., 1977. George W. Northrup, ed. 498p. $35.
Aud: Cl, Pl

Lists osteopathic physicians who are members of the American Osteopathic Association. (Nonmembers are listed in a separate publication, the *Directory of Nonmember Osteopathic Physicians.*) There are over 15,000 osteopathic physicians (D.O.'s) listed who are qualified and licensed to practice. The directory includes information on the profession, its members, component societies, institutions, affiliates, and licensing boards. It lists osteopathic physicians in both alphabetical and geographical order; national officers and committees; divisional societies with their presidents and secretaries; boards of specialty certification; certified specialists; osteopathic colleges; accredited osteopathic hospitals; and the code of ethics. The general alphabetical listing of members gives each doctor's city and state, AOA membership number, osteopathic college, and year of graduation. The geographical listing gives, in addition, each doctor's address, type of practice, date of birth, divisional society affiliation, and national honors and awards. MSB

SC 276
Year Book of Cancer. ISSN 0084-3679. 1956. a. bibl. index. illus. Year Book Medical Publications, 35 E Wacker Dr, Chicago, IL 60601. Examined: 1977. Randolph Lee Clark and Russell W. Cumley, eds. 499p. $24.75.
Aud: Sa

Includes 283 abstracts of the "best current oncology literature" of the year as selected by the editors and the 160-member editorial board. Abstracts range in length from one paragraph to three pages and are supplemented by "additional readings" lists and brief editorial comments on the subject of the article. They are arranged under 32 topical chapter groupings, covering types of cancer (skin, breast, etc.), therapies (chemotherapy, radiation, etc.), and current research. Author and subject indexes are provided. KR/JKM

SC 277
Yearbook of Dentistry. ISSN 0084-3717. 1936. a. index. illus. Year Book Medical Publishers, 35 E Wacker Dr, Chicago, IL 60601. Examined: 1977. M. L. Hale, et al., eds. 432p.
Aud: Cl

A review of the year's literature on all aspects of dentistry. There are detailed abstracts of the articles (which are noted with full citation in footnote form at the bottom of the page) with author or authors and place of work in parentheses. The review material covers all aspects of dentistry including preventive dentistry, dental development, caries, and dental materials, to mention a few. There are two indexes, a subject index and an author index. MSB

SC 278
Year Book of Medicine. ISSN 0084-3873. 1933. a. index. illus. Year Book of Medical Publications, 35 E Wacker Dr, Chicago, IL 60601. Examined: 1978. David E. Rogers, ed. 639p. $23.50.
Aud: Sa

The format of this scholarly annual is similar to the **Year Book of Cancer.** It includes abstracts of current literature arranged under topical sections. Each section (infections; the chest; the blood and blood-forming organs; the heart and blood vessels; digestive system; metabolism; kidney, water, and electrolysis; etc.) has been edited by an authority in the field. Editorial comments follow each article; unlike the **Year Book of Cancer,** no "further reading" suggestions have been appended. One feature, the "Current Literature Quiz," tests doctor's familiarity with new diagnostic and therapeutic procedures, i.e. "What is currently thought to be the best antibiotic against the bacillus that causes legionnaires' disease?" Answers and references to abstracts are given in the back of the book. KR/JKM

METALLURGY

SC 279
Metal Finishing Guidebook and Directory. 1932. a. index. Metals and Plastics Publications, One University Plaza, Hackensack, NJ 07601. Examined: 46th ed., 1978. 922p. $4.95.
Aud: Cl

Comprised of short, signed articles discussing special techniques, such as analysis of plating solutions, electroforming, waste water treatment, etc. Includes a section of miscellaneous tables, a directory of trade schools and trade names, and a directory of manufacturers. EM

SC 280
Metal Statistics. ISSN 0076-6658. 1904. a. index. Fairchild Publications, 7 E 12th St, New York, NY 10003. Examined: 1977. 399p. $25.
Aud: Cl

Subtitle: "The purchasing guide of the metals industries." Contains chapters on approximately 25 metals, giving tabular data on their production, shipments, and prices. Both foreign and domestic data are included. Depending upon the table, figures for as many as ten years are given. Includes a directory of buyers of metals and an international directory of metal associations and metal exchanges. EM

SC 281

The Metallurgical Society of AIME. Membership Directory. 1957. a. Metallurgical Society of AIME, Box 430, Warrendale, PA 15086. Examined: 1977. John Ballande, ed. 126p. $50.
Aud: Cl

A professional society of metallurgists, metallurgical engineers, and materials scientists. Members are listed alphabetically by name, then geographically. Lists of officers and committee members are included. EM

SC 282

Metallurgical Society of AIME. Metallurgical Transactions. (Continues: Transactions of the Metallurgical Society of AIME and Transactions of American Society for Metals.) 1970. a. index. Metallurgical Society of AIME, 345 E 47th St, New York, NY 10017. Examined: 1977. 3v. $95.
Aud: Cl, Sa
Indexed in: *Social Sciences Index*.

Co-sponsored by the American Society for Metals. A cumulated, bound version of the quarterly journals *Process Metallurgy* and *Physical Metallurgy* and *Materials Science* with a combined subject index. EM

SC 283

Non-ferrous Metal Data. ISSN 0360-9553. (Continues: American Bureau of Metal Statistics. Yearbook. ISSN 0065-7611.) 1974. a. American Bureau of Metal Statistics, 420 Lexington Ave, New York, NY 10017. Examined: 1976. 149p. $15.50.
Aud: Sa

Gives tabular data on mining, smelter production, consumption, and trade of copper, lead, zinc, nickel, silver, gold, bauxite, aluminum, antimony, tin, cadmium, cobalt, molybdenum, magnesium, platinum, and various other metals through the world. Includes prices and lists of metallurgical plants and their capabilities. Most tables show data for the past five years. EM

MILITARY SCIENCE

SC 284

American Defense Preparedness Association. Annual Directory. ISSN 0092-1491. (Continues: American Ordnance Association. Annual Directory; Army Ordnance Association.) a. American Defense Preparedness Association, 819 Union Trust Bldg, Washington, DC 20005. Examined: 1976/77. 84p. $12.
Aud: Sa

Includes listings of association officers, local officials, and members of technical divisions and sections. EM

SC 285

Defense and Foreign Affairs Handbook. 1977. a. bibl. illus. Copley and Associates, Suite 602, 2030 M St, NW, Washington, DC 20036. Dist: Franklin Watts, 730 Fifth Ave, New York, NY 10019. Examined: 1978. Gregory R. Copley and David S. Harvey, eds. 757p. $50.
Aud: Cl, Pl

Covers 190 countries and political subdivisions. The chapter on each country presents the political leaders; history; general statistics (area, coastline, major cities, population, religion, language, literacy rate); political facts; economic facts; news media; defenses, including army and air force battle order and defense production (most often not available); and a list of major embassies abroad. The concluding chapters include a defense production section (suppliers of ground force, naval, air force, and electronic equipment), a who's who in defense and world politics, a description of NATO and the Warsaw Treaty Organization, missile tables, political and defense acronyms and nomenclature, and basic data on the world. SJV

SC 286

Jane's Fighting Ships. ISSN 0075-3025. 1898. a. index. illus. Jane's Yearbooks, Paulton House, 8 Shepherdess Walk, London, N1 7LW, England. Dist: Franklin Watts, 730 Fifth Ave, New York, NY 10019. Examined: 1977/78. John E. Moore, ed. 829p. $72.50.
Aud: Cl

Provides illustrations and descriptions of all types of ships, including submarines, aircraft carriers, minesweepers, etc., arranged by country, then by types. Has an index by names of ships and by names of classes of ships. Includes data on missiles, radar, torpedoes, etc. EM

SC 287

Jane's Weapon Systems. ISSN 0075-3068. 1969. a. illus. BPC Publishing, Paulton House, 8 Shepherdess Walk, London N1 7LW, England. Dist: Franklin Watts, 730 Fifth Ave, New York, NY 10019. Exam-

ined: 1977/78. Ronald Pretty, ed. 750p. $72.50.
Aud: Sa

An annual survey of modern weapon technology covering missiles, radar and guidance systems, strategic defense systems, and other types of military hardware. The information presented is authoritative and highly technical. Volumes are illustrated with color and black-and-white photographs. Designed primarily for anyone involved in the "manufacture, procurement, or operation of military systems and equipment." Any library serving readers who are interested in defense and the military will want this up-to-date reference source. The Jane's Series also includes a new title, *Jane's Infantry Weapons* (1978, 700p., $72.50), which is designed as a companion volume to **Jane's Weapon Systems**. No copy was available for examination, but based on the high quality of other works in the series, libraries with military collections should consider purchase of both titles. JKM

SC 288

Royal United Services Institute and Brassey's Defence Yearbook. (Continues: Brassey's Annual: The Armed Forces Yearbook. ISSN 0068-0702.) 1890. a. bibl. Brassey's Publishers, 12 Montagu St, Portman Square, London W1H 2TB, England. Dist: Westview Press, 1898 Flatiron Ct, Boulder, CO 80301. Examined: 88th ed., 1977/78. 430p. $28.95.
Aud: Sa

This British yearbook is divided in three parts. The first part, Strategic Reviews, contains reviews/essays by authorities in international government, diplomacy, economy, and military. The second part, Weapons Technology, presents a survey of recent developments in weapons technology which "is essential for the understanding of military questions." Some photographs are included. Part three contains a bibliography of the year's defense literature and a chronology of the year's events. KR/JKM

SC 289

Soviet Armed Forces Review Annual. ISSN 0148-0928. 1977. a. bibl. illus. Academic International, Box 555, Gulf Breeze, FL 32561. Examined: 1977. David R. Jones, ed. 277p. $29.50.
Aud: Sa

A new annual series on Soviet military capability prepared by scholars in the area of military studies. It will complement the *Military-Naval Encyclopedia of Russia* (forthcoming). The publication is divided into five parts: survey of military issues, current developments in the armed forces, essays on various topics, "Documentation," and bibliography. SJV

SC 290

The United Nations Disarmament Yearbook. 1976. a. United Nations, Sales Section, New York, NY 10017. Examined: v.1, 1976. 310p. $15.
Aud: Cl, Sa

Reviews the development and negotiations of the United Nations in the area of disarmament. Contains summaries of Assembly resolutions adopted, reports on the status of existing disarmament agreements, and information, as communicated by various governments, on topics such as military expenditures and production, arms trade, and foreign aid in the military field. Chapters are based mainly on General Assembly and Conference of the Committee on Disarmament documents. They include background information, description of the problem, and summaries of the United Nations' action. Chapters cover disarmament in general, nuclear disarmament, measures relating to non-nuclear weapons, and other approaches to disarmament and arms control. SJV

SC 291

U.S. Arms Control and Disarmament Agency. Annual Report to Congress. ISSN 0082-8969. (Continues: Arms Control and Disarmament Agency, Annual Report.) 1961. a. U.S. Arms Control and Disarmament Agency, Washington, DC 20451. Dist: Superintendent of Documents, U.S. Government Printing Office, Washington, DC 20402. Examined: 15th ed., 1976. 75p. $2.45.
Aud: Cl, Sa

A report on the present state of disarmament and arms control. The focus is on the U.S. and its efforts to achieve peace through disarmament. Completed agreements are summarized. Two chapters are devoted to nuclear proliferation and nuclear arms. Arms transfers and military expenditures are briefly reviewed. The status of multilateral arms control agreements is given as of the end of the preceding fiscal year. Basically a compilation of highlights from agency publications issued over the year. SJV

SC 292

U.S. Arms Control and Disarmament Agency. Arms Control and Disarmament Agreements. 1975. bi-a. illus. U.S. Arms Control and Disarmament Agency, Washington, DC 20451. Dist: Superintendent of Documents, U.S. Government Printing Office, Wash-

ington, DC 20402. Examined: 1975; 1976. 187p. $2.75.
Aud: Cl, Sa

Subtitle: "Texts and history of negotiations." Contains the texts of all major arms control and disarmament agreements since 1925 in which the U.S. has been a participant. The introduction provides an historical survey of the fate of these various agreements. For each agreement the history of the negotiations is given, followed by the text and the participants. The 1977 edition covers such agreements as the Geneva Protocol, The Antarctic Treaty, "Hot Line" Agreement, Limited Test Ban Treaty, Outer Space Treaty, Biological Weapons Convention, ABM Protocol, and Environmental Modification Ban. SJV

SC 293
U.S. Arms Control and Disarmament Agency. Documents on Disarmament. 1960. a. bibl. index. U.S. Arms Control and Disarmament Agency, Washington, DC 20451. Dist: Superintendent of Documents, U.S. Government Printing Office, Washington, DC 20402. Examined: 1975. 849p. $8.60.
Aud: Cl, Sa

An annual compilation of selected statements, proposals, letters, and documents of the U.S. and other countries dealing with disarmament. There is a topical list which serves as a table of contents; documents are presented in alphabetical order. There is a bibliography of additional material published by the United Nations, the U.S. Arms Control and Disarmament Agency, Congress, the Department of State, and other U.S. agencies. The 1975 volume was published in 1977. SJV

SC 294
World Armaments and Disarmament; SIPRI Yearbook. 1968/69. a. bibl. index. illus. Taylor and Francis, 10-14 Macklin St, London WC2B 5NF, England. Examined: 1977. Frank Barnaby, ed. 421p. £18.
Aud: Cl, Sa

An annual analysis of the world's arms races and any attempts at disarmament prepared by the Stockholm International Peace Research Institute (SIPRI). Part one reviews the previous year's activities. Topics covered include increases in international nuclear transactions, accidents of nuclear weapons systems, chemical warfare, military satellites, and a review of SIPRI publications for the last year. Part two covers developments in world armaments such as world expenditures and arms trading. Part three chronicles developments in arms control and disarmament such as treaties and agreements. Much of the material is presented in tabular or statistical format. Sources and references are copious. SJV

SC 295
World Military Expenditures and Arms Transfers. (Continues: World Military Expenditures and Arms Trade.) 1963/73. a. illus. U.S. Arms Control and Disarmament Agency, Washington, DC 20451. Dist: Superintendent of Documents, U.S. Government Printing Office, Washington, DC 20402. Examined: 1965/75. 850p. $1.50.
Aud: Cl, Pl

An expanded version of *World Military Expenditures*. Presents worldwide statistical information on national military spending, armed forces, and international transfer of arms. The introduction notes any discernable trends and explains the sources for the compilation of statistics. Table one provides military expenditures, Gross National Product, and population and armed forces by group and region. Table two provides the same information by country. Table three shows arms transfers by group and region, and table four by country. Each annual volume covers a ten-year period. SJV

MINING AND MINERALOGY

SC 296
Coal Facts. (Continues: Bituminous Coal Facts. ISSN 0067-8988.) 1948. bi-a. index. illus. National Coal Association, Coal Bldg, Washington, DC 20036. Examined: 1974/75. 95p. $5; free to libraries and educational institutions.
Aud: Cl, Pl, Sa

This "report by the coal industry" includes survey articles, tables, and graphs on coal and energy production, transportation, environment, research, NCA officers and staff, and local and operators associations. The "press, investment analysts, writers, and the academic community," as well as the coal and allied industries will find this handbook useful. Survey articles comprise the first half of the book, followed by a statistical index and a section of charts, graphs, tables, etc. KR/JKM

SC 297
Dana's Manual of Mineralogy. 1912. irreg. bibl. index. illus. John Wiley and Sons, 605 Third Ave, New York, NY 10016. Examined: 18th ed., 1971. Cornelius

S. Hurlbut, ed. 579p. $19.50.
Aud: Pl

Designed as a text for a beginning course in mineralogy. With this in mind, the arrangement is clear, concise, straightforward, developmental, and to the point. Diagrams are explained, terms are defined, and the approach taken is that of the classroom. Enough chemistry and physics are included to make the technical information complete but not overpowering in detail. The general organization of the book starts with crystallography and continues with physical, chemical, and descriptive mineralogy. The information is basic and usually takes only one approach, leaving added views for other courses and more advanced study. This is a good companion volume for more complex and detailed titles which may well be beyond the average student's need. NLE

SC 298
Engineering and Mining Journal. E/MJ International Directory of Mining and Mineral Processing Operations. 1968/69. a. index. Engineering and Mining Journal, 1221 Ave of the Americas, New York, NY 10020. Examined: 1976; 1978. Louis Bell, ed. $40.
Aud: Cl, Sa

Contains an alphabetical listing of mining companies, showing locations, officers, holdings, and financial data. Also lists mine or plant units of companies, and executives. Includes surveys, such as a survey of mine expansion plans. EM

SC 299
Gems: Their Sources, Descriptions and Identification. 1962. irreg. bibl. index. illus. Archon Books, 955 Sherman Ave, Hamden, CT 06514. Examined: 3rd ed., 1975. Robert Webster, ed. 931p. $50.
Aud: Pl

The history of this essential book can be traced back to 1937 when Webster's *Gemmologists Compendium* first appeared. The author, now deceased, subsequently produced several texts on gemstones of which this is the best. Any library which can afford at least one book on gems should have this title. The third edition includes information on man-made materials in chapters on synthetics and composites. Color plates of important examples, a number of line drawings and black-and-white photographs, identification tables, and many appendixes make up this standard work. Information on prices is not included since they are established by the open market and not necessarily by scientific means. Highly recommended in many reviewing sources. NLE

SC 300
International Coal. (Continues: World Coal Trade.) 1969. a. National Coal Association, Coal Bldg, 1130 17th St, NW, Washington, DC 20036. Examined: 1977. various paging. $25.
Aud: Cl, Sa

Provides statistics on coal production, and shipments, coal exports from the U.S., and statistics on the coal industry in selected foreign countries. EM

SC 301
Keystone Coal Industry Manual. (Continues: Coal Mine Directory.) 1918. a. index. McGraw-Hill Publishing Co., 1221 Ave of the Americas, New York, NY 10020. Examined: 1977. George Nielsen, ed. 1184p. $90. (1978. $99.50.)
Aud: Cl

Includes directories of coal wholesalers, mines, and docks, and short technical articles. A buyers' guide and special indexes of individuals and companies are also provided. EM

SC 302
Mining Annual Review. ISSN 0076-8995. 1936. a. index. The Mining Journal, 15 Wilson St, London EC2M 2TR, England. Examined: 1975. John Spooner, ed. 548p. $45 (includes subscription to *Mining Journal* and *Mining Magazine*).
Aud: Sa

Designed for the mining industry and for manufacturers requiring ore of any sort. The introduction surveys the year's developments in mining. An alphabetical format gives easy access to the company listings and industry information by metal or mineral, country, or type of technical progress report. The metal and mineral section (the largest section of the book) provides information on production, uses, prices, and outlook. Advertisements are interspersed throughout the glossy-paged review. Indexes to manufacturers, companies, and advertisers are also included. KR/JKM

SC 303
Pit and Quarry Handbook and Buyers Guide. ISSN 0146-1893. (Continues: Pit and Quarry Handbook and Purchasing Guide. ISSN 0079-2128.) 1907. a. index. Pit and Quarry, 105 W Adams St, Chicago, IL 60603. Examined: 1977/78. various paging. $60.
Aud: Sa

Subtitle: "Equipment and technical reference manual for nonmetallic industry." Includes short chapters on the following categories: mineral recovery, mineral preparation, handling and storage, power transmission, control devices, and maintenance. EM

SC 304
Rocky Mountain Coal Mining Institute. Proceedings. 1912. a. Rocky Mountain Coal Mining Institute, 356 Lafayette, Denver, CO 80218. Examined: 1976. 76p. free to libraries and universities.
Aud: Cl

Includes papers on the latest techniques of coal mining, a list of new members, and reports from the annual meeting. EM

SC 305
Society of Mining Engineers of AIME. Membership Directory. 1949. a. Society of Mining Engineers, 540 Arapeen Dr, Box 8800, Salt Lake City, UT 84108. Examined: 1977. 290p. $25.
Aud: Cl

Subtitle: "Who's who in mineral engineering." The membership lists are published each year in the July issue of *Mining Engineering* and are then made available as a separate publication. Members are listed alphabetically by name, then geographically. Includes lists of officers and committee members. EM

SC 306
Society of Mining Engineers of AIME. Mining Transactions. 1871. a. index. Society of Mining Engineers of AIME, 540 Arapeen Dr, Box 8800, Salt Lake City, UT 84108. Examined: 1976. 375p. $25. (1978.)
Aud: Cl

Cumulates the contents of the Society's quarterly *Transactions*. Includes articles and papers on such topics as coal mining, geothermal energy, open pit mining, rock mechanics, etc. There is an author/subject index. EM

SC 307
Symposium on Coal Mine Drainage Research. Papers. ISSN 0085-7068. 1965. bi-a. index. National Coal Association, The Coal Bldg, 1130 17th St, NW, Washington, DC 20036. Examined: 1976. 291p. $10.
Aud: Sa

Covers topics such as water quality near strip mines, water treatment techniques, and disposal of sludge. Has an author index which gives local addresses. Formerly sponsored by the Coal Industry Advisory Committee to the Ohio River Valley Water Sanitation Commission. EM

SC 308
U.S. Bureau of Mines. Mineral Facts and Problems. 1950. quinquennial. bibl. U.S. Department of the Interior, Bureau of Mines, 2401 E St, NW, Washington, DC 21241. Dist: Superintendent of Documents, U.S. Government Printing Office, Washington, DC 20402. Examined: 5th ed., 1975. 1259p. $17.
Aud: Hs, Jc, Cl, Pl

A standard reference on mineral commodities in the U.S. and Canada. Supplements the numerous periodical and annual Bureau of Mines publications. Includes appraisals of world reserves and resources; production capacities of smelters and plants producing many different minerals such as copper, lead, zinc, aluminum; graphic and tabular supply-demand profiles; recycling diagrams for major commodities; price histories; and much more. This bicentennial edition includes an excellent essay on the importance of minerals in the U.S. economy, 1776-1976. There are nearly 90 detailed essays, each written by one or more experts, dealing with a particular mineral. Each essay generally covers the industry, structure, uses, reserves, technology, supply and demand, operating factors, and the outlook. Most sections are subdivided, and most contain statistical information extracted from a number of government sources and data bases. NLE

SC 309
U.S. Bureau of Mines. Minerals Yearbook. ISSN 0076-8952. 1932. a. U.S. Department of the Interior, Bureau of Mines, 2401 E St, NW, Washington, DC 20241. Dist: Superintendent of Documents, U.S. Government Printing Office, Washington, DC 20402. Examined: 1975. 3v. v. 1, 1550p., $15; v. 2, 800p.; v. 3, 1193p., $11.
Aud: Cl, Pl, Sa

Competent, thorough, and imposing in detail. Volume one covers metals, minerals, and fuels, and contains chapters on virtually all metallic, nonmetallic, and mineral fuel commodities. Volume two is comprised of "area reports" on the 50 states and nearby countries. Volume three includes available mineral data on well over 100 countries. The statistical and narrative material is huge. If any library can have but one source on minerals, this title should at least be considered since it is both inexpensive and comprehensive. One drawback is the dated nature of the information, a failing in many government publications. The 1975 volumes were not published until 1977. NLE

SC 310
World Mines Register. ISSN 0095-4322. (Continues:

Mines Register.) 1976. irreg. index. Freeman Publications, 500 Howard St, San Francisco, CA. Examined: 1976/77. 398p. $35.
Aud: Cl, Sa

The first section lists mining companies by country with brief information on history, officers, property, etc. This is followed by an alphabetical list of companies. The volume includes a listing of companies by mineral products, a buyers' guide to products, and an alphabetical index of personnel. EM

SC 311
Zinc Institute. Review of the U.S. Zinc Industry, Including Statements from Other Countries. 1972. a. Zinc Institute, 292 Madison Ave, New York, NY 10017. Examined: 1976. 28p. free.
Aud: Cl

A compilation of important statistics on zinc production, shipments, consumption, and sales in the U.S. and selected foreign countries. EM

PHYSICS

SC 312
Acoustical Holography. ISSN 0065-0870. 1969. a. bibl. index. illus. Plenum Publishing Corp., 227 W 17th St, New York, NY 10011. Examined: v. 2, 1970. A. F. Metherell, ed. 376p.
Aud: Sa

Contains papers delivered at the International Symposium of Acoustical Holography. The papers were prepared by experts who were asked to participate in the meeting. Acoustical holography is a relatively new field which deals with various forms of three-dimensional observations which have wide applications in areas such as medical diagnosis, geology, and optical reconstruction techniques. The physics is rigorous, but the interdisciplinary implications make this title valuable for smaller collections. One of the features of the volume examined is a supplementary annotated bibliography of literature on the topic. NLE

SC 313
Advances in Nuclear Physics. ISSN 0065-2970. 1968. irreg. bibl. index. illus. Plenum Publishing Corp., 227 W 17th St, New York, NY 10011. Examined: v. 9, 1977. Michael Baranger, ed. 264p. $34.50.
Aud: Cl, Sa

The three articles in volume nine demonstrate the wide scope of the series. Heavy ion accelerators, the nuclear shell model, and the mathematical techniques for coping with the lowest eigenvalues of large matrices are typical of the information covered. Each of the "chapters" is a small monograph in its own right, written by an expert and fully documented. The articles are usually too long for the periodical literature and too short for separate publication, but each is of such quality that it should be published. An interdisciplinary series recommended for smaller collections. NLE

SC 314
American Institute of Physics Handbook. 1957. irreg. bibl. index. illus. American Institute of Physics, 335 E 45th St, New York, NY 10017. Dist: McGraw-Hill Book Company, 1221 Ave of the Americas, New York, NY 10020. Examined: 3rd ed., 1972. Dwight E. Gray, ed. 2352p. $59.50.
Aud: Cl, Sa

Divided into nine major sections: mathematics bibliography and SI units; mechanics; acoustics; heat; electricity and magnetism; optics; atomic and molecular physics; nuclear physics; and solid-state physics. Each section is further divided into sections dealing with a specific topic. These smaller sections are written by an expert in the field and are submitted to many levels of editing to maintain a consistently high level of quality. The sponsoring body, the American Institute of Physics, lends authority to the publication. This is a one-of-a-kind directory and guide. Any advanced program in any field of physics should have access to this title. NLE

SC 315
Progress in Optics. ISSN 0079-6638. 1961. irreg. bibl. index. illus. Elsivier, North Holland, 52 Vanderbilt Ave, New York, NY 10017. Examined: v. 15, 1977. E. Wolf, ed. 364p.
Aud: Cl, Sa

Each volume contains three to eight essays on various topics in the field of optics. The essays are highly technical and specialized. Each volume has a cumulative contents list. The theory and math are difficult, and the demands on equipment are often subtle. Some of the articles presume considerable previous experience and background. Nonetheless, the series supports many other subjects and the bibliographies and citations are valuable. This series is recommended for the advanced student, but it should also be in any collection which is trying to be complete for an undergraduate program. NLE

PSYCHOLOGY AND PSYCHIATRY

SC 316

Adolescent Psychiatry. ISSN 0065-2008. 1971. irreg. bibl. index. Jason Aronson, 59 Fourth Ave, New York, NY 10003. Examined: v. 5, 1977. Sherman C. Feinstein, ed. 515p. $20.50.
Aud: Sa

Subtitle: "Annals of the American Society for Adolescent Psychiatry: developmental and clinical studies." Includes studies of the adolescent process covering the emotional and psychosocial development of the adolescent, political and social issues which affect young people, and adolescent psychotherapy. The authors are specialists in psychiatry and related areas. The articles are grouped in broad categories: adolescence—general considerations, developmental issues and the adolescent process, psychopatholgy and adolescence, various perspectives on anorexia nervosa, and psychotherapy of adolescence. Volume five contains a list of the contents of the first four volumes. ST/JKM

SC 317

American Men and Women of Science: Social and Behavioral Sciences. ISSN 0065-9363. (1973 is 12th ed.) irreg. index. R. R. Bowker, 1180 Ave of the Americas, New York, NY 10036. Dist: R. R. Bowker, Box 1807, Ann Arbor, MI 48106. Examined: 13th ed., 1978. Jaques Cattell Press, eds. 1490p. $69.95.
Aud: Cl, Sa

Lists approximately 24,000 U.S. and Canadian scientists currently working in the fields of business administration, economics, political science, psychology, and sociology. Entries are derived from the seven-volume set **American Men and Women of Science** and provide the same biographical and career data as the original volumes; therefore libraries will not want to duplicate the two titles. This smaller, less expensive directory will probably be sufficient to meet the reference needs of smaller, discipline-oriented libraries. Entries are arranged alphabetically by name and indexed by discipline and location. JKM

SC 318

American Psychiatric Association. Biographical Directory. ISSN 0065-9827. 1958. irreg. R. R. Bowker Co./Jaques Cattell Press, 1180 Ave of the Americas, New York, NY 10036. Dist: R. R. Bowker, Box 1807, Ann Arbor, MI 48106. Examined: 6th ed., 1973. Dorothy Hancock, ed. 1088p. $38.50.
Aud: Cl, Pl

A compilation of psychiatrists who are members or fellows of the American Psychiatric Association. The first section of the book is an alphabetical list of the members and fellows giving name, gender, birthdate and place, school, internship, residency, certification, professional experience, military records, address, and telephone number. The second section is a geographic list by state and city (in alphabetic order) with the names of psychiatrists listed alphabetically under the cities. MSB

SC 319

American Psychoanalytic Association. Roster. 1957. bi-a. American Psychoanalytic Association, One E 57th St, New York, NY 10022. Examined: 1974. 193p. $6.
Aud: Cl, Pl

Primarily a listing of members of the American Psychoanalytic Association including active, associate, and affiliate members. Presents the usual listing of councils and executive boards, as well as a list of approved training institutions and affiliate societies. The major lists, active and associate members, are alphabetical with names, addresses, and telephone numbers. These lists are followed by a geographical listing of members and an alphabetical listing of members by local chapter. MSB

SC 320

American Psychological Association. Directory. ISSN 0090-9076. (Continues: Biographical Directory.) 1916. bi-a. index. American Psychological Association, 1200 17th St, NW, Washington, DC 20036. Examined: 1975. Thomas J. Willette, ed. 1531p. $40; $20 to members. (1978. $50.)
Aud: Cl, Pl

A biographical listing of approximately 28,500 members, giving name, address, telephone number, date of birth, education, present major field, psychological specialty areas, American Board of Professional Psychology Diplomates, American Board of Psychological Hypnosis Diplomates, state licensure or certification, school psychologist certification, principal and secondary position, past employment (up to ten positions), APA membership, and when the information was submitted. This listing is alphabetical; there is a geographical index listing the U.S. and its possessions. The states and towns within the states are given in alphabetical order. Canada's list follows the U.S. list, with other foreign countries listed next. The last section includes the divisional membership rosters which comprise 35 sections. The 1978 volume will list approximately 4000 psychologists. MSB

SC 321

Annual Editions: Readings in Personality and Adjustment. ISSN 0361-3836. 1975. a. index. illus. The Dushkin Publishing Group, Sluice Dock, Guilford, CT 06434. Examined: 1978/79. Gerri Schwartz, ed. 224p. $5.95.
Aud: Hs, Jc, Cl, Pl

A collection of articles reproduced from newspapers, magazines, and professional journals for use in high school or college level psychology and sociology courses which deal with personality and adjustment. Articles present a variety of disciplinary perspectives on all aspects of personality development and adjustment. Arranged by broad topics with a subject index. The treatment tends to be more popular than in similar collections; therefore this "classroom reader" could also serve as an introduction to the study of personality for the general reader. JKM

SC 322

Annual Editions: Readings in Psychology. 1971. a. index. illus. The Dushkin Publishing Group, Sluice Dock, Guilford, CT 06437. Examined: 1978/79. $6.55.
Aud: Hs, Jc, Cl, Pl

Reproduces newspaper, magazine, and journal articles for use as supplementary readings in high school and college psychology courses. Articles are arranged under broad topical categories and indexed by subject. Like other works in the *Annual Editions* series, this collection also has value as an introduction to the field for the general reader. JKM

SC 323

Annual Progress in Child Psychiatry and Child Development. ISSN 0066-4030. 1968. a. index. Brunner-Mazel, 19 Union Sq W, New York, NY 10003. Examined: 10th ed., 1977. Stella Chess and Alexander Thomas, eds. 782p. $15.
Aud: Cl, Pl

An annual compilation of journal articles in the field of child development and child psychiatry. The articles cover new works concerning the sociocultural, perceptual-cognitive, behavioral, clinical, and biochemical aspects of child development and psychiatry. There are anywhere from ten to twelve major topics covered with several articles for each topic. Each article includes the author and the journal it originated from listed on the first page of that chapter. Each article has a brief abstract at the beginning and references cited at the end. There is an author index and a subject index. The tenth edition includes a ten-year cumulative author index and a ten-year cumulative article index. MSB

SC 324

Annual Review of Behavior Therapy; Theory and Practice. ISSN 0091-6595. 1973. bibl. Brunner-Mazel, 19 Union Sq W, New York, NY 10003. Examined: v. 5, 1977. Cyril M. Franks, ed. 765p. $55.
Aud: Sa

Reviews developments in behavior therapy during the past year. Includes feature articles grouped under topical headings, with each group preceded by an extensive commentary by the editor that reviews the state of the art in the specific subfield. Many of the articles discuss original research and clinical work. The section containing references to the editors' commentaries constitutes an extensive bibliography. Some topics treated in volume five are: an overview of behavior therapy; relaxation training; systematic desensitization, flooding, modeling, cognitive restructuring, and assertion training; biofeedback; behavior therapy with children and adolescents; addictive behaviors; sexual disorders, marital disharmony, and depression; behavior modification in institutional settings; and behavior therapy in industry and community. ST/JKM

SC 325

Annual Review of Psychology. ISSN 0066-4308. 1950. a. index. Annual Reviews, 4139 El Camino Way, Palo Alto, CA 94306. Examined: 29th ed., 1978. Lyman Porter and Mark Rosenzweig, eds. 748p. $15.
Aud: Cl

Indexed in: *Biological Abstracts; Chemical Abstracts; Child Development Abstracts; DSH Abstracts; Social Science Citation Abstracts; Psychological Abstracts.*

Articles are concerned with the various aspects of psychology and examine new theories and positions brought forth each year. The chapters cover different areas and are written by various contributors who are identified at the beginning of each chapter. References are cited at the end of each chapter. There is an author index, a subject index, and in some cases, a five-year cumulative author and chapter title index. At the end of each volume is a list of the chapters planned for the subsequent volume. MSB

SC 326

Annual Review of the Schizophrenic Syndrome. ISSN 0090-287X. (Continues: Schizophrenic Syndrome.)

1971. a. index. Brunner-Mazel, 19 Union Sq W, New York, NY 10003. Examined: 4th ed., 1974/75. Robert Cancro, ed. 564p. $17.50.
Aud: Cl, Pl

A compilation of journal literature, individual chapters from different monographs, and original articles on the complex subject of the schizophrenic syndrome. Each volume is divided into eight to ten sections with a number of articles in each section. The topics are diverse, ranging from very clinical and research-oriented subjects to social and ethical concerns. Each article is contributed by a different author(s) and the original source is cited on the first page of that article. There is a combined author and subject index. MSB

SC 327
Association for Research in Nervous and Mental Disease. Research Publications. 1920. a. index. Raven Press, 1140 Ave of the Americas, New York, NY 10036. Examined: 54th ed., 1974. Daniel X. Freedman, ed. 372p.
Aud: Cl
Indexed in: *Current Contents; Index Medicus*.

Based on the annual meetings of the Association for Research in Nervous and Mental Disease. It attempts to assess the state of the art of psychiatry in a particular area of that field. Mental illness is divided into two sections: diagnosis and classification, and biological processes that affect the brain. These points of view are brought together in these volumes. Topics covered have included pain, social psychiatry, aggression, mental retardation, and addictive states, to mention a few. Each volume is made up of chapters by different contributors, and references are cited at the end of each chapter. There is a subject index at the end of each volume. Formerly published by Williams and Wilkins Co. (428 E Preston St, Baltimore, MD 21202). MSB

SC 328
Bibliographic Guide to Psychology. 1975. a. G. K. Hall, 70 Lincoln St, Boston, MA 02111. Examined: 1977. 228p. $50.
Aud: Sa

Lists all psychology materials cataloged during the preceding year by the Library of Congress and the Research Libraries of the New York Public Library. Provides complete Library of Congress cataloging. Entries are arranged in one alphabet under main entry, added entries, titles, series, and subject headings. All aspects of psychology are covered: sensation, cognition, perception, and intelligence, will, applied psychology, comparative psychology, child psychology, etc. JKM

SC 329
Chicorel Index to Mental Health Book Reviews. (Continues: Mental Health Book Review Index.) 1976. a. Chicorel Library Publishing Corp., 275 Central Park W, New York, NY 10024. Examined: 1976. Marietta Chicorel, ed. 256p. $25.
Aud: Cl, Pl

An annotated guide to books and book reviews in the behavioral sciences. It lists and annotates over 1200 books and cites over 4000 reviews in journals published in the previous year. In the main section, book titles are listed alphabetically by author. Each entry gives full ordering information, publisher, price, and pagination. Annotations and summaries of the book's content are provided for most titles. Approximately 90 journals were examined for reviews; each citation gives reviewer's name, journal title, volume and issue number, and pages where the review may be located. The journals cited are listed with their addresses, price, and frequency. There is a subject guide in the back of the book. MSB

SC 330
Current Psychiatric Therapies. ISSN 0070-2080. 1961. a. bibl. index. Grune and Stratton, 111 Fifth Ave, New York, NY 10003. Examined: v. 16, 1976. Jules H. Masserman, ed. 351p. $28.50.
Aud: Sa

Includes articles by specialists which review current developments in various subfields of psychiatric therapy. Volume 16 covers childhood and adolescence; adult psychotherapies; drug, hormonal, and somatic therapies; addictions; family, group, and institutional therapies; and psychiatric vectors in population control. The volumes have name and subject indexes. ST/JKM

SC 331
Graduate Study in Psychology. ISSN 0072-5277. 1968/69. bi-a. index. American Psychological Association, 1200 17th St, NW, Washington, DC 20036. Examined: 1977/78. Patricia Walsh, ed. 591p. $6.
Aud: Cl, Pl

Descriptions of graduate programs in psychology arranged by state. Provides full information on faculty, programs, tuition, financial aid, student statistics, admissions, and degree requirements. Comments on departmental orientation, objectives, and emphases are frequently included. Introduction discusses how to apply to graduate schools and government stipends, and provides information for foreign students. Appendix lists APA-approved doctoral programs in clinical, counseling, and school psychology and includes a table giving fields of study and degrees offered. There is an index of institutions. MSB

SC 332
Mental Health Directory. 1964. a. U.S. National Institute of Mental Health, 5600 Fishers Lane, Rockville, MD 20857. Dist: Superintendent of Documents, U.S. Government Printing Office, Washington, DC 20402. Examined: 1977. Betram Brown, ed. 620p. $3.75.
Aud: Cl, Pl

Lists a variety of information sources for both practitioners and planners in the field and individuals seeking help for themselves or for family members. State mental health facilities and services are listed by state and city, with complete addresses, telephone numbers, geographic areas served, auspices, and services offered for various age groups. The appendix includes voluntary mental health associations, self-help organizations for mental health, and national agencies listed by special problem categories. There are no indexes. MSB

SC 333
Minnesota Symposia on Child Psychology. ISSN 0076-9266. 1966. bibl. index. illus. Harper's College Press, 10 E 53rd St, New York, NY 10022. Examined: v. 10, 1975. Anne D. Pick, ed. 241p. (v. 11, 1976. $14.50.)
Aud: Cl, Sa

Contains reports of the symposia sponsored by the Institute of Child Development of the University of Minnesota. Each volume features six papers in which investigators present their programs of research. The presentations include discussions of other studies relevant to the theory or set of issues that guide the research program, integrating findings from published and unpublished work with the objectives, strategy, and outcomes of the program of the author(s). The aim of the series is to allow the general reader to learn about the different areas of development currently being explored and the strategies used to advance understanding of the developmental process. The material would be useful for teachers, students of education, and social workers, as well as people involved directly in the field of child psychology. ST/JKM

SC 334
National Association of Private Psychiatric Hospitals. Directory of Member Hospitals. 1963. a. National Association of Private Psychiatric Hospitals, One Farragut Sq S, Suite 201, Washington, DC 20006. Examined: 1968. 200p.
Aud: Cl, Pl

A listing of private psychiatric hospitals in the United States, Canada, and Puerto Rico. The list is arranged alphabetically by state. Information includes the name of the member institution, address, telephone number, chief administrative officers, treatment program, license, accreditation, training programs (interns and residents), year opened, number of beds, annual admissions, physical description, rates, admission policies, and visiting regulations. MSB

SC 335
Year Book of Psychiatry and Applied Mental Health. ISSN 0084-3970. (Continues: Year Book of Neurology, Psychiatry, and Neurosurgery.) 1970. a. index. Year Book Medical Publishers, 35 E Wacker Dr, Chicago, IL 60601. Examined:1977. F. J. Braceland, ed. 460p.
Aud: Cl

A review of the literature in all aspects of psychiatry and mental health published during the previous year. There are detailed abstracts of the articles which are noted with full citations in footnote form at the bottom of the page. The reviews cover all aspects of mental health and psychiatry, including such areas as child psychiatry, genetics, geriatrics, drug abuse and addiction, and suicide. There is a subject index and an author index. MSB

VETERINARY MEDICINE

SC 336
American Veterinary Medical Association. Directory. ISSN 0066-1147. (1970 is 24th ed.) bi-a. American Veterinary Medical Association, 600 S Michigan Ave, Chicago, IL 60605. Examined: 1970; 1978. various paging. $25.
Aud: Cl, Sa

An alphabetical listing of members of this professional society of veterinarians, followed by a geographical roster. A supplementary section includes such features as the bylaws of the association, government veterinarian agencies, state meat and animal inspectors, etc. EM

SC 337
The Merck Veterinary Manual. ISSN 0076-6542. 1955. irreg. index. Merck and Co., Rahway, NJ 07065. Ex-

amined: 4th ed., 1973. O. H. Siegmund, ed. 1618p. $13.
Aud: Sa

Subtitle: "A handbook of diagnosis and therapy for the veterinarian." Consists of eight parts: diseases of common domestic animals; toxicology; diseases of poultry; management and diseases of fur; laboratory and zoo animals; nutrition; an addendum covering various topics; prescriptions used in the manual; and an alphabetical index. Drugs usually are referred to by their generic names. A thumb index to the sections within the parts facilitates quick location of information. Includes a list of tables, a general table of contents, and a table of contents for each section. There is an alphabetical subject index with cross-references. ST/JKM

SC 338
The Veterinary Annual. ISSN 0083-5870. 1959. a. index. John Wright and Sons, 42-44 Triangle W, Bristol B54 5NV, England. Examined: 1974. C. S. G. Grunswell and F. W. G. Hill, eds. 331p.
Aud: Sa

This British publication collects current contributions (in the form of two- to five-page articles with references) to the field of veterinary science which "sum up the existing situation in respect of the more perennial topics and also those which report relatively new developments in various fields." The arrangement is by subject chapters; the first half covering various species, e.g., cattle, sheep, pigs, horses, small animals, and the second half being reviews. KR/JKM

SC 339
World Directory of Veterinary Schools. ISSN 0512-2783. 1959. irreg. World Health Organization, Distribution and Sales Section, 20 Ave Appia, CH 1211, Geneva 27, Switzerland. Examined: 1971. 260p. $14.40.
Aud: Cl

Lists veterinary schools by country, with a description of each school's curriculum, admission requirements, examination standards, etc. Volumes are too irregular to provide more than the most general information to students. EM

WHEN TO BUY WHAT

"When to Buy What" is a guide to the announced publication schedule of approximately 880 of the regularly-issued serial titles included in *Serials for Libraries.* It is arranged first by title or corporate author, then by the month or season when publications should be ordered. Most of the ordering information provided in this guide was supplied by the Baker and Taylor Company, although publishers' catalogs were also consulted for verification.

The purpose of this guide is twofold. First, it can be used as a "when to claim" guide for serial titles which are maintained on standing order. It was primarily designed, however, as a guide for purchasing those serial titles which are *not* maintained through standing orders. With the rapidly increasing cost of serial publications (indeed of all published materials!) and diminishing library acquisitions budgets, many libraries are finding that it is not feasible to purchase every annual or biennial revision of every serial title. But librarians may find it difficult to maintain proper control of serials orders without information on the approximate publication schedule of the various serial titles. For example, if an order for an annual publication is placed in August and a revised edition is not scheduled for publication until October, the publisher or distributor may send the library the soon-to-be-outdated edition rather than the desired revision. It is hoped that the information in this guide will enable librarians who wish to control their serials ordering independently to avoid some of these problems.

It should be noted that neither the compilers of this guide nor the publishers of various serial titles can guarantee that the month or season of publication will remain constant through the years, any more than the titles or frequencies of serial publications remain constant. This guide should not be considered, then, as a fail-safe cure for the problems associated with the acquisition of serials. Rather, it provides current information on the ordering schedule of a number of serial publications which, when used with the annotated entries in *Serials for Libraries,* should be of assistance in the acquisition and control of serials.

SERIALS BUYING SCHEDULE BY TITLE

AB Bookman's Yearbook. *SPRING*

Abortion Bibliography. *OCTOBER*

Accepted Dental Therapeutics. (bi-a.) *JUNE*

Access Index to Little Magazines. *FALL*

Access: The Supplementary Index to Periodicals. *FALL*

Accountants' Index. *MAY*

Accredited Institutions of Post-Secondary Education. *OCTOBER*

Acoustical Holography. *SUMMER*

Admission Requirements of U.S. and Canadian Dental Schools. *JUNE*

Advances in Librarianship. *WINTER*

Advances in Marine Biology. *WINTER*

Advances in Nuclear Physics. *WINTER*

Advances in Organic Chemistry. *WINTER*

Advances in Physical Organic Chemistry. *WINTER*

Aerospace Facts and Figures. *SUMMER*

Africa Contemporary Record: Annual Survey and Documents. *SUMMER*

Africa South of the Sahara. *OCTOBER*

Africa Year Book and Who's Who. *JANUARY*

African Literature Today. *WINTER*

Aircraft Owners and Pilots Association. AOPA's Airports U.S.A. *WINTER*

Airline Guide to Stewardess and Stewards Careers. *SUMMER*

Allied Medical Education Directory. *SPRING*

Almanac of American Politics. *NOVEMBER*

Amateur Athletic Union of the United States. Directory. *JANUARY*

Amateur Athletic Union of the United States. Official Handbook of the AAU Codes. *WINTER*

Amateur Athletic Union of the United States. Athletic Library. Official AAU Basketball Handbook. (bi-a.) *NOVEMBER*

Amateur Athletic Union of the United States. Athletic

Library. Official AAU Baton Twirling Handbook. (bi-a.) *FEBRUARY*

Amateur Athletic Union of the United States. Athletic Library. Official AAU Boxing Handbook. (quadrennial) *SEPTEMBER*

Amateur Athletic Union of the United States. Athletic Library. Official AAU Diving Rules. *WINTER*

Amateur Athletic Union of the United States. Athletic Library. Official AAU Judo Rules. (bi-a.) *MAY*

Amateur Athletic Union of the United States. Athletic Library. Official AAU Karate Rules. (bi-a.) *JULY*

Amateur Athletic Union of the United States. Athletic Library. Official AAU Physique Handbook. (bi-a.) *OCTOBER*

Amateur Athletic Union of the United States. Athletic Library. Official AAU Powerlifting Handbook. (bi-a.) *JUNE*

Amateur Athletic Union of the United States. Athletic Library. Official AAU Synchronized Swimming Handbook. *JANUARY*

Amateur Athletic Union of the United States. Athletic Library. Official AAU Track and Field Handbook. (bi-a.) *SPRING*

Amateur Athletic Union of the United States. Athletic Library. Official AAU Trampoline and Tumbling Handbook. (bi-a.) *SUMMER*

Amateur Athletic Union of the United States. Athletic Library. Official AAU Wrestling Handbook. *WINTER*

Amateur Athletic Union of the United States. Athletic Library. Official Rules for Competitive Swimming. *DECEMBER*

Amateur Athletic Union of the United States. Athletic Library. Official Rules for Water Polo. *JANUARY*

Amateur Softball Association of America. Official Guide and Rule Book. *MARCH*

America Votes. (bi-a.) *NOVEMBER*

American Alpine Journal. *JUNE*

American Anthropological Association. Annual Report and Directory. *NOVEMBER*

American Art Directory. (bi-a.) *SPRING*

American Association of Marriage and Family Counselors. Register. *NOVEMBER*

American Association of State Highway Officials. AASHO Reference Book of Member Department Personnel and Committees. *MAY*

American Baptist Churches in the U.S.A. Directory. *JUNE*

American Baptist Churches in the U.S.A. Yearbook. *AUGUST*

American Book Prices Current. *SPRING*

American Book Publishing Record. Annual Cumulation. *APRIL*

American Book Trade Directory. *OCTOBER*

American Catholic Philosophical Association. Proceedings. *SPRING*

American Consulting Engineers Council. Directory. *OCTOBER*

American Cooperation. *SUMMER*

American Correctional Association. Annual Congress of Corrections. Proceedings. *AUGUST*

American Dental Directory. *MARCH*

American Federation of Information Processing Societies. AFIPS Conference Proceedings. *JUNE*

American Foreign Relations: A Documentary Record. *SUMMER*

American Foundrymen's Society. Transactions. *JANUARY*

American Hospital Association. Guide to the Health Care Field. *AUGUST*

American Jewish Organizations. Directory. (bi-a.) *MARCH*

American Jewish Year Book. *WINTER*

American Journal of Jurisprudence. *OCTOBER*

American Library Association. ALA Membership Directory. *NOVEMBER*

American Library Association. ALA Yearbook. *SUMMER*

American Library Association. Handbook of Organization. *DECEMBER*

American Library Directory. (bi-a.) *OCTOBER*

American Literary Scholarship. *JUNE*

American Lutheran Church. Yearbook. *AUGUST*

American Marketing Association. Proceedings. *SPRING*

American Medical Directory. *APRIL*

American Philosophical Association. Proceedings and Addresses. *SEPTEMBER*

American Psychoanalytic Association. Roster. (bi-a.) *WINTER*

American Psychological Association. Directory. (bi-a.) *SEPTEMBER*

American Public Works Association. APWA Directory. (bi-a.) *MARCH*

American Reference Books Annual. *SPRING*

American Register of Exporters and Importers. *JUNE*

American Research Center in Egypt. Journal. *WINTER*

American Rose Annual. *OCTOBER*

American Society for Information Science. Proceedings. *NOVEMBER*

American Society for Quality Control. Annual Technical Conference. Transactions. *APRIL*

American Society of Civil Engineers. Transactions. *DECEMBER*

American Society of Heating, Refrigerating, and Air Conditioning Engineers. Transactions. *DECEMBER*

American Society of International Law. Proceedings. *OCTOBER*

American Society of Photogrammetry. Papers from the Annual Meeting. *MARCH*

American Society of Sanitary Engineers. Year Book. *SPRING*

American Society of University Composers. Proceedings of the Annual Conference. *MARCH*

American Speech and Hearing Association. Directory. *JANUARY*

American Statistical Association. Business and Economic Statistics Section. Proceedings. *WINTER*

American Statistics Index. Supplement. *MAY*

American Theatre Association. Directory of Members. *JANUARY*

American Veterinary Medical Association. Directory. *WINTER*

American Vocational Association. Yearbook. *DECEMBER*

Anglo American Trade Directory. (bi-a.) *OCTOBER*

Anglo-Saxon England. *NOVEMBER*

Annual Bibliography of British and Irish History. *SPRING*

Annual Editions: Readings in American Government. *SUMMER*

Annual Editions: Readings in Anthropology. *FALL*

Annual Editions: Readings in Biology. *JUNE*

Annual Editions: Readings in Business. *AUGUST*

Annual Editions: Readings in Criminal Justice. *OCTOBER*

Annual Editions: Readings in Early Childhood Education. *NOVEMBER*

Annual Editions: Readings in Economics. *NOVEMBER*

Annual Editions: Readings in Education. *WINTER*

Annual Editions: Readings in Health. *NOVEMBER*

Annual Editions: Readings in Human Development. *SUMMER*

Annual Editions: Readings in Marketing. *SPRING*

Annual Editions: Readings in Marriage and Family. *SPRING*

Annual Editions: Readings in Personality and Adjustment. *NOVEMBER*

Annual Editions: Readings in Psychology. *WINTER*

Annual Editions: Readings in Social Problems. *SUMMER*

Annual Editions: Readings in Social Psychology. *OCTOBER*

Annual Editions: Readings in Sociology. *SUMMER*

Annual Handbook for Group Facilitators. *JANUARY*

Annual Index to Popular Music Record Reviews. *OCTOBER*

Annual International Congress Calendar. *APRIL*

Annual of Advertising, Editorial, and Television Art and Design with Annual Copy Awards. *FALL*

Annual of Power and Conflict. *WINTER*

Annual Progress in Child Psychiatry and Child Development. *DECEMBER*

Annual Register of Grant Support. *FALL*

Annual Register. World Events. *AUGUST*

Annual Review of Anthropology. *OCTOBER*

Annual Review of Astronomy and Astrophysics. *SEPTEMBER*

Annual Review of Biochemistry. *JULY*

Annual Review of Earth and Planetary Sciences. *APRIL*

Annual Review of Ecology and Systematics. *NOVEMBER*

Annual Review of Entomology. *JANUARY*

Annual Review of Fluid Mechanics. *JANUARY*

Annual Review of Genetics. *DECEMBER*

Annual Review of Information Science and Technology. *FALL*

Annual Review of Microbiology. *OCTOBER*

Annual Review of Nuclear Science. *DECEMBER*

Annual Review of Physical Chemistry. *MARCH*

Annual Review of Physiology. *MARCH*

Annual Review of Plant Physiology. *JUNE*

Annual Review of Psychology. *FEBRUARY*

Annual Review of Sociology. *SEPTEMBER*

Annual Review of the Schizophrenic Syndrome. *DECEMBER*

Annual Reviews of Biophysics and Bioengineering. *JUNE*

Annual Survey of African Law. *NOVEMBER*

Annuale Mediavale. *NOVEMBER*

Antiques and Their Prices. (bi-a.) *SUMMER*

Archaeological Institute of America. Bulletin. *OCTOBER*

Architectural Schools in North America. *NOVEMBER*

Archives of Asian Art. *JUNE*

Art and Crafts Market. *OCTOBER*

Art at Auction: The Year at Sotheby's and Parke-Bernet. *OCTOBER*

Art Design Photo. *DECEMBER*

Art Prices Current. *JUNE*

Artists/USA. (bi-a.) *DECEMBER*

Assembling. *NOVEMBER*

Association for Computing Machinery. Annual Workshop on Microprogramming. Conference Record. *NOVEMBER*

Association for Computing Machinery. Proceedings of the National Conference. *JUNE*

Association of American Medical Colleges. AAMC Directory of American Medical Education. *SUMMER*

AudArena Stadium Guide and International Directory. *SEPTEMBER*

Audio-Visual Equipment Directory. *JUNE*

Audiovisual Market Place (AVMP). *JANUARY*

Augustinian Studies. *OCTOBER*

Automobile Association. AA Budget Guide to Europe. *SPRING*

Automobile Association. AA Guide to Camping and Caravaning. *WINTER*

Automobile Association. AA Guide to Camping and Caravaning on the Continent. *SPRING*

Automobile Association. AA Guide to Guesthouses, Farmhouses, and Inns. *SPRING*

Automobile Association. AA Guide to Stately Homes, Museums, Castles and Gardens. *WINTER*

Ayer Directory of Publications. *MARCH*

Bank Administration Institute. Biennial Survey of Personnal Policies and Practices. (bi-a.) *APRIL*

Baseball Blue Book. *APRIL*

Basebook. *NOVEMBER*

Baxter's Eurailpass Travel Guide. *WINTER*

Baxter's USA Rail Pass GXuide. *FEBRUARY*

Bazak Guide to Israel. *WINTER*

Bazak Guide to Italy. *SUMMER*

Berkeley Journal of Socioology: Critical Review. *AUGUST*

Best American Short Stories. *SEPTEMBER*

Best Books for Children. *SEPTEMBER*

Best Plays of (year). *NOVEMBER*

Best Sport Stories. *JULY*

Best's Safety Directory; Safety—Industrial Hygiene—Security. *OCTOBER*

Bibliographic Guide to Black Studies. *DECEMBER*

Bibliographic Guide to Government Publications—Foreign. *JANUARY*

Bibliographic Guide to Government Publications—U.S. *DECEMBER*

Bibliographic Guide to Psychology. *JANUARY*

Bibliographie Cartographique Internationale. *DECEMBER*

Bibliography of Asian bstudies. *SEPTEMBER*

Bibliography of Publications of University Bureaus of Business and Economic Research. *SEPTEMBER*

Bibliography of Society, Ethics, and Life Sciences. *OCTOBER*

Billboard International Buyer's Guide of the Music—Record Industry. *SEPTEMBER*

Billboard International Directory of Recording Equipment and Studio Directory. *MAY*

Blue Book of College Athletics. *SEPTEMBER*

Blue Book of Junior College Athletics. *JANUARY*

Boat Owner's Buyers guide. *JANUARY*

Book Auction Records. *MAY*

The Book of Baseball Records. *APRIL*

The Book of the States. (bi-a.) *JUNE*

Book Review Index. *SPRING*

Books for the Teen Age. *WINTER*

Books in Print. *FALL*

Books in Series in the United States. Supplement. *APRIL*

Boston College. Studies in Philosophy. *JULY*

Bowker Annual of Library and Book Trade Information. *MAY*

Braddock's Federal-State-Local Government Directory. *NOVEMBER*

Bradford's Directory of Marketing Research Agencies and Management Consultants in the United States and the World. *DECEMBER*

British Books in Print. *FALL*

British Humanities Index. *JULY*

Broadcasting Yearbook. *MARCH*

Brown's Directory of North American Gas Companies. *NOVEMBER*

Building Estimator's Reference Book. (tri-a.) *JANUARY*

Building Officials and Code Administrators International. BOCA Basic Housing-Property Maintenance Code. (tri-a.) *JULY*

Business Books and Serials in Print. *JULY*

Buying and Selling United States Coins. *APRIL*

CRC Handbook of Laboratory Safety. *JANUARY*

Camping and Caravaning France. *SPRING*

Canadian Almanac and Directory. *FEBRUARY*

Canadian Essay and Literature Index. *SPRING*

Canadian Periodical Index. *SUMMER*

Canadian Yearbook of International Law. *JUNE*

Cassell's Directory of Publishing in Great Britain, the Commonwealth, Ireland, South Africa, and Pakistan. (bi-a). *JANUARY*

Catholic Almanac. *NOVEMBER*

Catholic Press Directory. *WINTER*

Catholic Theological Society of America. Proceedings. *JANUARY*

Cavalcade and Directory of Acts and Attractions. *DECEMBER*

Charter Flight Directory. *WINTER*

Chases' Calendar of Annual Events. *FALL*

Chicorel Index to Mental Health Book Reviews. *NOVEMBER*

Child Welfare League of America. Directory of Member Agencies and Associates. *JANUARY*

Children's Books; Awards and Prizes. (bi-a.) *FALL*

Children's Books in Print. *WINTER*

Children's Literature: A Guide to Reference Sources. Supplement. (quinquennial.) *FALL*

Chilton's Auto Repair Manual. *NOVEMBER*

Coin World Almanac. *NOVEMBER*

College Blue Book. (bi-a.) SEPTEMBER

College Handbook. (tri-a.) SEPTEMBER

College Placement Annual. OCTOBER

The College Planning Search Book. NOVEMBER

College Theology Society. Proceedings. SPRING

Collegiate Summer Employment Guide. AUGUST

Comic Book Price Guide. APRIL

Commodity Year Book. JUNE

Commonwealth Universities Yearbook. AUGUST

Comparative Guide to Two-year Colleges and Career Programs. (bi-a.) SEPTEMBER

Composium Directory of New Music. MAY

Congress and the Nation. (quadrennial.) DECEMBER

Congressional Quarterly Almanac. JANUARY

Congressional Roll Call. APRIL

Congressional Staff Directory. SPRING

Connecticut Health Services Research Series. WINTER

Consumer Complaint Guide. WINTER

Consumer Reports Buying Guide. DECEMBER

Containerization: A Bibliography. DECEMBER

Contemporary Crafts Market Place. FALL

Corpus Almanac of Canada. FEBRUARY

Council of State Governments. Suggested State Legislation. OCTOBER

Country Vacations U.S.A. (bi-a.) WINTER

The County Year Book. SUMMER

Crafts Annual. AUGUST

Creative Camera International Year Book. FALL

Credit Manual of Commercial Laws. WINTER

Crime and Justice. MARCH

Current Biography Yearbook. WINTER

Current Medical Diagnosis and Treatment. JANUARY

Current Therapy. FEBRUARY

Cycle Buyers Guide. MARCH

Dance Magazine Annual. WINTER

Dance World. DECEMBER

Davison's Textile Blue Book. WINTER

Davison's Textile Catalog and Buyers Guide. APRIL

Decorative Art and Modern Interiors. SUMMER

Demographic Yearbook. JANUARY

Dickens Studies Annual. SEPTEMBER

Diesel and Gas Turbine World Wide Catalog. MAY

Direction of Trade. SEPTEMBER

Directory and Guide to the Mutual Savings Banks of the United States. SEPTEMBER

Directory: Juvenile and Adult Correctional Departments, Institutions, and Agencies and Paroling Authorities of the United States and Canada. SEPTEMBER

Directory of Agencies Serving the Visually Handicapped in the U.S. (bi-a.) MAY

Directory of American Philosophers. (bi-a.) FEBRUARY

Directory of American Savings and Loan Associations. JANUARY

Directory of Associations in Canada. WINTER

Directory of College Placement Offices. AUGUST

Directory of Counseling Services. JUNE

Directory of Executive Recruiters. WINTER

Directory of Historical Societies and Agencies in the United States and Canada. (bi-a.) SEPTEMBER

Directory of Hotel and Motel Systems. JULY

Directory of Law Libraries. (bi-a) JUNE

Directory of Medical Specialists. (bi-a.) WINTER

Directory of Music Faculties in Colleges and Universities, U.S. and Canada. DECEMBER

Directory of Overseas Summer Jobs. NOVEMBER

Directory of Research Grants. FALL

Directory of Shipowners, Shipbuilders, and Marine Engineers. OCTOBER

Directory of the College Student Press in America. (tri-a.) WINTER

Dodge Construction Systems Costs. WINTER

Dollar Wise Guide to California and Las Vegas. (bi-a.) SPRING

Dollar Wise Guide to England. (bi-a.) WINTER

Dollar Wise Guide to France. (bi-a.) WINTER

Dollar Wise Guide to Japan and Hong Kong. (bi-a.) SUMMER

Dollars and Cents of Shopping Centers. (tri-a.) APRIL

Downtown Mall Annual and Urban Design Report. MAY

Drug Abuse Bibliography. FEBRUARY

Drugs in Current Use and New Drugs. JANUARY

Drugs of Choice. (bi-a.) JANUARY

EEM (Electronic Engineering Master Catalog). AUGUST

Easter Seal Directory of Resident Camps for Persons with Special Health Needs. SPRING

Eastern Hemisphere Petroleum Directory. SEPTEMBER

Economic Survey of Europe. DECEMBER

Economic Survey of Latin America. MAY

Editor and Publisher International Yearbook. MAY

Editor and Publisher Market Guide. WINTER

Educational Media Yearbook. OCTOBER

Educators Guide to Free Audio and Video Materials. AUGUST

Educators Guide to Free Films. JULY

Educators Guide to Free Filmstrips. JULY

Educators Guide to Free Guidance Materials. AUGUST

Educators Guide to Free Health, Physical Education, and Recreation Materials. SEPTEMBER

Educators Guide to Free Science Materials. AUGUST

Educators Guide to Free Social Studies Materials. SEPTEMBER

Educators Guide to Free Tapes, Scripts, and Transcriptions. FALL

Educators Guide to Free Teaching Aids. AUGUST

Egon Ronay's Dunlop Guide: Hotels, Restaurants, and Inns in Great Britain and Ireland. WINTER

El-Hi Textbooks in Print. MARCH

Election Index. (bi-a.) SEPTEMBER

Electrical World Directory of Electric Utilities. OCTOBER

Electronic Components Conference. Proceedings. AUGUST

Electronic Industry Telephone Directory. JUNE

Electronic News Financial Factbook and Directory. SEPTEMBER

Electronics Buyers Guide. MARCH

Elementary Teachers Guide to Free Curriculum Materials. SUMMER

Empirical Research in Theatre. SUMMER

Encyclopedia Buying Guide. (bi-a.) JUNE

Encyclopedia of Football. OCTOBER

Energy Index. DECEMBER

Engineering Index Annual. MARCH

Engineers Council for Professional Development. Annual Report. APRIL

Engineers Joint Council. Directory of Engineering Societies Management. JUNE

Engineers Joint Council. Engineering Manpower Commission. Prospects of Engineering and Technology Graduates. FEBRUARY

Environment Index. DECEMBER

Episcopal Church Annual. JANUARY

E-R-C Directory; Employee Relocation Real Estate Services. MARCH

Essays and Studies. SUMMER

Essays by Divers Hands. (bi-a.) SPRING

Eurail Guide: How to Travel Europe by Train. WINTER

Europa Year Book. JUNE

Europe on $10 a Day. WINTER

Facts About Nursing. DECEMBER

Facts on File Yearbook. MAY

Fairchild's Financial Manual of Retail Stores. *NOVEMBER*

The Far East and Australasia. *NOVEMBER*

Federal Tax Handbook. *APRIL*

Fielding's Guide to the Caribbean Plus the Bahamas. *FALL*

Fielding's Low Cost Europe. *WINTER*

Fielding's Selected Favorites: Hotels and Inns, Europe. *WINTER*

Fielding's Selective Shopping Guide to Europe. *WINTER*

Fielding's Travel Guide to Europe. *WINTER*

Financial Aids for Higher Education. (bi-a.) *JANUARY*

Financial Assistance for Library Education. *AUGUST*

Fine Arts Marketplace. (bi-a.) *MAY*

Fitzgerald/Hemingway Annual. *DECEMBER*

Fodor's Austria. *WINTER*

Fodor's Belgium and Luxembourg. *WINTER*

Fodor's Caribbean, Bahamas, and Bermuda. *FALL*

Fodor's Cruises Everywhere. (bi-a.) *FALL*

Fodor's Czechoslovakia. (bi-a.) *WINTER*

Fodor's Europe. *FALL*

Fodor's France. *WINTER*

Fodor's Germany: East and West. *WINTER*

Fodor's Great Britain. *WINTER*

Fodor's Greece. *WINTER*

Fodor's Hawaii. *FALL*

Fodor's Holland. *WINTER*

Fodor's India. *WINTER*

Fodor's Ireland. *WINTER*

Fodor's Israel. *WINTER*

Fodor's Italy. *WINTER*

Fodor's Japan and Korea. *WINTER*

Fodor's London: A Companion Guide. *SPRING*

Fodor's Mexico. *FALL*

Fodor's Morocco. *WINTER*

Fodor's Portugal. *WINTER*

Fodor's Scandinavia. *WINTER*

Fodor's South America. *FALL*

Fodor's South-East Asia. (bi-a.) *FALL*

Fodor's Soviet Union. *WINTER*

Fodor's Spain. *WINTER*

Fodor's Switzerland. *WINTER*

Fodor's Tunisia. *FALL*

Fodor's Turkey. *WINTER*

Fodor's U.S.A. *SPRING*

Fodor's Yugoslavia. *WINTER*

Football Register. *AUGUST*

Foreign Medical School Catalogue. *MAY*

Franciscan Studies. *MARCH*

French XX Bibliography. *NOVEMBER*

Garuda. *WINTER*

Genealogical Periodical Annual Index. *APRIL*

Golf Magazine Yearbook. *MAY*

Government Reference Books. (bi-a.) *FALL*

Graduate Programs and Admissions Manual. *SEPTEMBER*

Grants Register. (bi-a.) *FALL*

Graphis Annual. *OCTOBER*

Graphis Posters. *APRIL*

Gratz College Annual of Jewish Studies. *JUNE*

Greece on $10 a Day. (bi-a.) *WINTER*

Greenwood's Guide to Great Lakes Shipping. *APRIL*

Guide Book of United States Coins. *JULY*

Guide to College Courses in Film and Television. (bi-a.) *FALL*

Guide to Consumer Markets. *OCTOBER*

Guide to Graduate Departments of Sociology. *JANUARY*

Guide to Independent Study through Correspondence Instruction. (bi-a.) *MAY*

Guide to Microforms in Print. *WINTER*

Guide to Reference Books for School Media Centers. (bi-a.) *JANUARY*

Guide to Reviews of Books from and about Hispanic America. *WINTER*

Guide to Summer Camps and Summer Schools. (bi-a.) *MAY*

Guinness Book of World Records. (cloth) *FALL*

Guinness Book of World Records. (pap.) *WINTER*

Guinness Sports Record Book. (bi-a.) *MARCH*

Gun Digest. *JULY*

Guns and Ammo Annual. *AUGUST*

Guns Illustrated. *SEPTEMBER*

Hammond Almanac of a Million Facts. *FALL*

Handbook of Chemistry and Physics. *JULY*

Handbook of Denominations in the United States. (quinquennial) *DECEMBER*

Handbook of Latin American Studies. *DECEMBER*

Handbook of Nonprescription Drugs. (bi-a.) *JANUARY*

Handbook of Private Schools. *SUMMER*

Harris Survey Yearbook of Public Opinion. *SPRING*

Harvard Studies in Classical Philology. *SUMMER*

Hawaii on $15 and $20 a Day. *WINTER*

Hebrew Union College Annual. *DECEMBER*

Help; The Useful Almanac. *JULY*

High Fidelity; Records in Review. *FALL*

High Fidelity's Test Reports. *JANUARY*

Historic Documents. *MARCH*

Hockey Register. *DECEMBER*

Hotel and Motel Red Book. *SPRING*

Human Factors Society. Directory and Yearbook. *MAY*

Illustrators. *MARCH*

Index of American Periodical Verse. *WINTER*

Index to Book Reviews in the Humanities. *AUGUST*

Index to Literature on the American Indian. *OCTOBER*

Index Translationum. *SUMMER*

The Indianapolis 500 Yearbook. *SEPTEMBER*

Industrial Machinery and Equipment Pricing Guide. *WINTER*

Information Please Almanac, Atlas, and Yearbook. *FALL*

Institute of Environmental Sciences. Annual Meeting. Proceedings. *WINTER*

International Art and Antiques Yearbook. *FEBRUARY*

International Association of Chiefs of Police. The Police Yearbook. *APRIL*

International Auction Records. *JULY*

International Bibliography of Historical Sciences. *DECEMBER*

International Bibliography of Political Sciences. *JUNE*

International Bibliography of Social and Cultural Anthropology. *SUMMER*

International Bibliography of Sociology. *JUNE*

International Book Trade Directory. *AUGUST*

International Directory of Little Magazines and Small Presses. *JUNE*

International Directory of Marketing Research Houses and Services. *FEBRUARY*

International Folk Music Council. Yearbook. *SEPTEMBER*

International Handbook of Universities and Other Institutions of Higher Education. (tri-a.) *SUMMER*

International Telemetering Conference. Proceedings. *WINTER*

International Literary Market Place. *OCTOBER*

International Mimes and Pantomimists. IMP Directory. *JANUARY*

International Music Guide. *WINTER*

International Publications. *SPRING*

International Symposium on Transport and Handling of Minerals. Minerals Transportation; Proceedings. (bi-a.) *WINTER*

International Television Almanac. *JANUARY*

International Who's Who. *FALL*

International Who's Who in Art and Antiques. (tri-a.) *DECEMBER*

International Who's Who in Music and Musicians Directory. (bi-a.) *FALL*

International Who's Who in Poetry. (bi-a.) *SEPTEMBER*

International Yearbook and Statesmen's Who's Who. *APRIL*

Inventory of Marriage and Family. *AUGUST*

Ireland on $10 a Day. (bi-a.) *SPRING*

Irregular Serials and Annuals. (bi-a.) *SUMMER*

Jane's All the World's Aircraft. *FALL*

Jane's Fighting Ships. *DECEMBER*

Jane's Freight Containers. *APRIL*

Jane's Major Companies of Europe. *JANUARY*

Jane's Surface Skimmers, Hovercraft and Hydrofoils. *NOVEMBER*

Jane's World Railways. *SEPTEMBER*

Jednota Annual: Furdek. *JUNE*

Jewish Book Annual. *SEPTEMBER*

Jewish Travel Guide. *SPRING*

J. K. Lasser's Your Income Tax. *OCTOBER*

Journal of Behavioral Economics. *WINTER*

Journal of Glass Studies. *JANUARY*

Keystone Coal Industry Manual. *JULY*

Kovels' Complete Antiques Price List. *SPRING*

Labor Relations Yearbook. *MAY*

Large Type Books in Print. *SUMMER*

Leahy's Hotel-Motel Guide and Travel Atlas. *WINTER*

Let's Go: The Student Guide to Europe. *WINTER*

Let's Go: The Student Guide to the United States and Canada. *WINTER*

Let's Halt Awhile in Great Britain and Ireland. *DECEMBER*

Library Journal Book Review. *WINTER*

Literary Market Place. *APRIL*

Lutheran Church in America. Yearbook. *NOVEMBER*

Lutheran Church—Missouri Synod. Lutheran Annual. *JANUARY*

The Lyle Official Antiques Review. *WINTER*

McGraw-Hill Yearbook of Science and Technology. *MARCH*

Machinery's Handbook. (bi-a.) *SUMMER*

Marine Technology Society. Annual Conference Proceedings. *SEPTEMBER*

Marketing Economics Key Plants. (bi-a.) *SUMMER*

Marquis Who's Who Publications: Index to All Books. *FALL*

Marsyas. (bi-a.) *FALL*

Medical and Health Annual. *MARCH*

Medical and Health Information Directory. (bi-a.) *AUGUST*

Medical Books and Serials in Print. *JUNE*

Medical School Admission Requirements, U.S.A. and Canada. *APRIL*

Mennonite Yearbook and Directory. *FEBRUARY*

Mexico and Guatemala on $10 a Day. (bi-a.) *SPRING*

Michelin Red Guide Series: Benelux. *SPRING*

Michelin Red Guide Series: France. *WINTER*

Michelin Red Guide Series: Germany. *WINTER*

Michelin Red Guide Series: Great Britain and Ireland. *WINTER*

Michelin Red Guide Series: Italy. *WINTER*

Michelin Red Guide Series: Paris and Environs. *WINTER*

Michelin Red Guide Series: Spain and Portugal. *SPRING*

Microform Market Place. (bi-a.) WINTER

Middle East and North Africa. OCTOBER

Midwest Media. MARCH

Milepost: All-the-North Travel Guide. WINTER

Milton Studies. DECEMBER

Minkus New American Stamp Catalog. FALL

Minkus New World Wide Stamp Catalog. (bi-a.) OCTOBER

Mission Handbook: North American Protestant Ministries Overseas. (tri-a.) FALL

Mobil Travel Guide: California and the West. SPRING

Mobil Travel Guide: Great Lakes Area. WINTER

Mobil Travel Guide: Middle Atlantic States. WINTER

Mobil Travel Guide: Northeastern States. WINTER

Mobil Travel Guide: Northwest and Great Plains States. WINTER

Mobil Travel Guide: Southeastern States. WINTER

Mobil Travel Guide: Southwest and South Central Area. WINTER

Mobil Vacation and Business Guide. SPRING

Modern Plastics Encyclopedia. OCTOBER

Motion Picture Market Place. MARCH

Motor Auto Repair Manual. NOVEMBER

Motor Truck Repair Manual. APRIL

The Municipal Year Book. MARCH

Music in Higher Education. OCTOBER

Musical America International Directory of the Performing Arts. OCTOBER

Myra Waldo's Travel and Motoring Guide to Europe. WINTER

Myra Waldo's Travel Guide to South America. (quadrennial) WINTER

National Basketball Association Official Guide. OCTOBER

National Collegiate Athletic Association. Annual Report. JANUARY

National Collegiate Athletic Association. Official Gymnastic Rules. NOVEMBER

National Collegiate Championships. SEPTEMBER

National Conference on Fluid Power. Proceedings. FALL

National Directory of College Athletics. (Women's Edition.) SEPTEMBER

National Directory of High School Coaches. OCTOBER

National Directory of Law Enforcement Administrators: Prosecution, Correctional, and Judicial Agencies. JUNE

National Directory of State Agencies. (bi-a.) OCTOBER

National Electronics Conference. Proceedings. OCTOBER

National Faculty Directory. DECEMBER

Fire Protection Association. National Fire Codes. APRIL

National Football Guide. AUGUST

National Football League. Official Record Manual. SEPTEMBER

National Health Directory. FEBRUARY

National Hockey League Guide. OCTOBER

National Institute of Municipal Law Officers. NIMLO Municipal Law Review. JANUARY

National Newspaper Association. NNA National Directory of Weekly Newspapers. MARCH

National Real Estate Directory. JULY

National Roster of Black Elected Officials. SUMMER

National Roster of Realtors. MAY

National Society for the Study of Education. Yearbook. SPRING

National Telecommunications Conference. Record. JANUARY

National Union of Christian Schools. Directory and Annual Report. AUGUST

Nature/Science Annual. JANUARY

New York Times Index. JULY

New Zealand on $10 a Day. (bi-a.) SPRING

News Dictionary. SPRING

NICEM Index to Educational Audio Tapes. (bi-a.) *OCTOBER*

NICEM Index to Educational Overhead Transparencies. (bi-a.) *APRIL*

NICEM Index to Educational Records. (bi-a.) *OCTOBER*

NICEM Index to Educational Slides. (bi-a.) *OCTOBER*

NICEM Index to Educational Videotapes. (bi-a.) *OCTOBER*

NICEM Index to 8mm Motion Cartridges. (bi-a.) *JANUARY*

NICEM Index to Environmental Studies—Multimedia. *FEBRUARY*

NICEM Index to Health and Safety Education—Multimedia. (bi-a.) *FEBRUARY*

NICEM Index to Producers and Distributors. (bi-a.) *OCTOBER*

NICEM Index to Psychology—Multimedia. (bi-a.) *JANUARY*

NICEM Index to 16mm Educational Films. (bi-a.) *OCTOBER*

NICEM Index to 35mm Educational Filmstrips. (bi-a.) *JANUARY*

NICEM Index to Vocational and Technical Education—Multimedia. (bi-a.) *FEBRUARY*

Non-ferrous Metal Data. *JULY*

Norwegian-American Studies. *AUGUST*

Occupational Outlook Handbook. *JUNE*

Official Baseball Guide. *APRIL*

Official Catholic Directory. *MAY*

Official Hotel-Motel Directory and Facilities Guide. *SUMMER*

Official National Collegiate Athletic Association Baseball Guide. *DECEMBER*

Official National Collegiate Athletic Association Basketball Guide. *OCTOBER*

Official National Collegiate Athletic Association Basketball Rules and Casebook. *JUNE*

Official National Collegiate Athletic Association Football Guide. *AUGUST*

Official National Collegiate Athletic Association Football Rules Interpretations. *APRIL*

Official National Collegiate Athletic Association Ice Hockey Guide. *AUGUST*

Official National Collegiate Athletic Association Skiing Rules. *NOVEMBER*

Official National Collegiate Athletic Association Soccer Guide. *JUNE*

Official National Collegiate Athletic Association Swimming Guide. *OCTOBER*

Official National Collegiate Athletic Association Water Polo Rules. *APRIL*

Official Read-Easy Football Rules. *APRIL*

Official Rules of Sport and Games. (bi-a.) *JANUARY*

Official World Series Records. *DECEMBER*

Offshore Technology Conference. Proceedings. *APRIL*

Optical Industry and Systems Directory. *OCTOBER*

Oxbridge Omnibus of Holiday Observances around the World. *FALL*

Oxford Slavonic Papers. *WINTER*

Packaging Engineering Annual Buyers Guide. *SEPTEMBER*

Parents' Guide to Accredited Camps. (all editions) *JANUARY*

Patent Law Review. *DECEMBER*

Patterson's American Education; School Systems and Schools Classified. *APRIL*

Pears Cyclopaedia. *FALL*

Penrose Graphic Arts International Annual. *APRIL*

Performing Arts Resources. *SPRING*

Peterson's Annual Guide to Undergraduate Study. *OCTOBER*

Peterson's Annual Guides to Graduate Study. *OCTOBER*

The Philosopher's Index. *APRIL*

Photographer's Market. *OCTOBER*

Photographis. *JUNE*

Photography Annual. *SEPTEMBER*

Photography Market Place. *APRIL*

Photography Year. *APRIL*

Photography Year Book. *OCTOBER*

Plant Location: The Industrial and Economic Workbook. *DECEMBER*

Police and Law Enforcement. *JUNE*

Police Yearbook. *APRIL*

Political Handbook of the World. *JUNE*

Popular Music Periodicals Index. *NOVEMBER*

Population and the Population Explosion: A Bibliography. *SPRING*

Ports of the World. *OCTOBER*

Power Sources Symposium. Proceedings. *JUNE*

Pre-Law Handbook. *SEPTEMBER*

Presidency (year). *APRIL*

Private Independent Schools. *MAY*

Private Press Books. *SUMMER*

Prize Stories. *APRIL*

Pro and Amateur Hockey Guide. *DECEMBER*

Pro Football Illustrated. *DECEMBER*

Progress in Geography. *SUMMER*

Progress in Optics. *FALL*

Progress in Physical Organic Chemistry. *OCTOBER*

Proof. *WINTER*

Public Welfare Directory. *SUMMER*

Publishers' International Directory. *WINTER*

Publishers' Trade List Annual. *FALL*

Radio Amateur's Handbook. *WINTER*

Railway Passenger Car Annual. *SUMMER*

Rand McNally Campground and Trailer Park Guide. *WINTER*

Rand McNally National Park Guide. *WINTER*

Rand McNally Road Atlas; U.S., Canada, Mexico. *FEBRUARY*

Reader's Digest Almanac and Yearbook. *WINTER*

Reference and Subscription Books Reviews. *WINTER*

Reference Sources. *JUNE*

Reliability and Maintainability Symposium. Proceedings. *APRIL*

Requirements for Certification of Teachers, Counselors, Librarians, and Administrators. *MAY*

Research in Economic History. *MAY*

Ring Boxing Encyclopedia and Record Book. *APRIL*

Royal Society of Canada. Transactions. *DECEMBER*

Runner's Almanac. *MARCH*

Sage Yearbooks in Politics and Public Policy. *NOVEMBER*

Sailboat and Sailboat Equipment Directory. *OCTOBER*

Scandinavian Political Studies. *DECEMBER*

Science Fiction Book Review Index. *NOVEMBER*

Scientific and Technical Books and Serials in Print. *NOVEMBER*

Scott's Specialized Catalogue of U.S. Stamps. *AUGUST*

Securities Law Review. *AUGUST*

Selective Guide to Materials for Mental Health and Family Life Education. (bi-a.) *JUNE*

Setting National Priorities; the (year) Budget. *JUNE*

Shakespeare Studies. *APRIL*

Shakespeare Survey. *DECEMBER*

Small Press Record of Books in Print. *WINTER*

Society of Mining Engineers of AIME. Mining Transactions. *MAY*

Society of Naval Architects and Marine Engineers. Transactions. *JUNE*

Society of Plastics Engineers. Annual Technical Conference. Technical Papers. *APRIL*

Sociological Methodology. *NOVEMBER*

Sociological Yearbook of Religion in Britain. *SEPTEMBER*

Sourcebook of Equal Educational Opportunity. *SEPTEMBER*

Sourcebook on Aging. *NOVEMBER*

Sources of Serials. *FALL*

South America on $10 a Day. (bi-a.) *WINTER*

South American Handbook. *WINTER*

South Pacific Travel Digest. (bi-a.) *SUMMER*

Southern Conference on Gerontology. *DECEMBER*

Spain and Morocco on $10 and $15 a Day. (bi-a.) *WINTER*

Standard Catalogue of Canadian Coins, Tokens, and Paper Money. *SEPTEMBER*

Standard Directory of Advertisers. (classified ed.) *APRIL*

Standard Directory of Advertisers. (geographical ed.) *AUGUST*

Standard Education Almanac. *SEPTEMBER*

Standard Medical Almanac. *SEPTEMBER*

Standard Periodical Directory. (bi-a.) *SPRING*

Stanford Journal of International Studies. *NOVEMBER*

State Approved Schools of Nursing—L.P.N./L.V.N. *WINTER*

State Approved Schools of Nursing—R.N. *WINTER*

Statesman's Year Book. *SEPTEMBER*

Steam Passenger Service Directory. *MAY*

Student Aid Annual. *OCTOBER*

Subject Guide to Books in Print. *NOVEMBER*

Subject Guide to Children's Books in Print. *WINTER*

Subject Guide to Microforms in Print. *WINTER*

Summer Employment Directory of the United States. *NOVEMBER*

Summer Study Abroad. *MARCH*

Supreme Court Review. *APRIL*

Technician Education Yearbook. (bi-a.) *OCTOBER*

Techniques of Marriage and Family Counseling. *AUGUST*

Television Factbook. *JANUARY*

Tennessee Studies in Literature. *OCTOBER*

Theatre Annual. *NOVEMBER*

Theatre World. *NOVEMBER*

Thomas Register of American Manufacturers and Thomas Register Catalog. *MARCH*

Time-Life Encyclopedia of Gardening. *MARCH*

Trademark Register of the United States. *JUNE*

Traditio. *OCTOBER*

Trailer Life's Recreational Vehicle Campground and Services Directory. *WINTER*

Transportation Research Forum. Proceedings. Annual Meeting. *NOVEMBER*

Travelers Almanac. *WINTER*

Tulane Studies in Philosophy. *DECEMBER*

TV Feature Film Source Book. *SEPTEMBER*

TV Season (year). *WINTER*

TWA Getaway Guide to Athens. (bi-a.) *WINTER*

TWA Getaway Guide to Boston. (bi-a.) *WINTER*

TWA Getaway Guide to Honolulu. (bi-a.) *WINTER*

TWA Getaway Guide to Ireland, Dublin/Shannon. (bi-a.) *WINTER*

TWA Getaway Guide to Las Vegas. (bi-a.) *WINTER*

TWA Getaway Guide to Lisbon/Madrid; Costa del Sol. (bi-a.) *WINTER*

TWA Getaway Guide to London. (bi-a.) *WINTER*

TWA Getaway Guide to Los Angeles. (bi-a.) *WINTER*

TWA Getaway Guide to New York. (bi-a.) *WINTER*

TWA Getaway Guide to Paris. (bi-a.) *WINTER*

TWA Getaway Guide to Rome. (bi-a.) *WINTER*

TWA Getaway Guide to San Francisco. (bi-a.) *WINTER*

TWA Getaway Guide to Washington, DC. (bi-a.) *WINTER*

USAN and the USP Dictionary of Drug Names. *NOVEMBER*

Ulrich's International Periodicals Directory. (bi-a.) *WINTER*

Unitarian Historical Society, London. Transactions. *FALL*

Unitarian Universalist Directory. *NOVEMBER*

United Nations. Department of Economic and Social Affairs. World Economic Survey. *SUMMER*

United Nations. Statistical Yearbook. *AUGUST*

United Nations. Yearbook. *OCTOBER*

United States Political Science Documents. *SEPTEMBER*

United States Tennis Association. The Official USTA Yearbook and Tennis Guide with the Official Rules. *APRIL*

Urban Affairs Annual Reviews. *MAY*

Used Book Price Guide. (quinquennial.) *NOVEMBER*

Venereal Disease Bibliography. *SUMMER*

Volleyball Guide. *SUMMER*

Volleyball Rules. *SUMMER*

Ward's Automotive Yearbook. *MAY*

Washington, D.C. on $10 and $15 a Day. (bi-a.) *WINTER*

Washington Information Directory. *MAY*

Waterway Guide: the Yachtsman's Bible: Mid-Atlantic. *JANUARY*

Waterway Guide; the Yachtsman's Bible: Northern. *MARCH*

Waterway Guide; the Yachtsman's Bible: Southern. *DECEMBER*

Weather Almanac. *OCTOBER*

Welding Data Book: Product Selector and Source Guide. (bi-a.) *JANUARY*

West Indies and Caribbean Yearbook. *SUMMER*

What They Said. *MAY*

Where to Retire on a Small Income. (bi-a.) *DECEMBER*

Where to Stay in the USA from 50¢ to $10 a Night. *WINTER*

Whitaker's Almanack. *WINTER*

Who Owns Whom: North American Edition. *APRIL*

Who Was Who in America. (tri-a.) *WINTER*

Whole World Handbook. *FEBRUARY*

Who's Who. SPRING

Who's Who Among Black Americans. (bi-a.) *WINTER*

Who's Who in America. (bi-a.) *SUMMER*

Who's Who in American Art. (bi-a.) *SUMMER*

Who's Who in American Law. *NOVEMBER*

Who's Who in American Politics. (bi-a.) *DECEMBER*

Who's Who in Art. (bi-a.) *NOVEMBER*

Who's Who in Canada. (bi-a.) *WINTER*

Who's Who in Electronics. *OCTOBER*

Who's Who in Government. (bi-a.) *NOVEMBER*

Who's Who in Religion. *OCTOBER*

Who's Who in the Arab World. (bi-a.) *WINTER*

Who's Who in the East. (bi-a.) *SUMMER*

Who's Who in the Midwest. (bi-a.) SPRING

Who's Who in the South and Southwest. (bi-a.) *WINTER*

Who's Who in the Theatre. (bi-a.) *WINTER*

Who's Who in the West. (bi-a.) *WINTER*

Who's Who in the World. (bi-a.) *FALL*

Who's Who of American Women. (bi-a.) *WINTER*

Willing's Press Guide. *MARCH*

Winterthur Portfolio. *APRIL*

Wire Journal Directory/Catalog. *SUMMER*

Woodall's Campground Directory: Eastern Edition. *WINTER*

Woodall's Campground Directory: North American Edition. *WINTER*

Woodall's Campground Directory: Western Edition. *WINTER*

Woodall's Directory of Mobile Home Communities. *DECEMBER*

Woodall's Retirement and Resort Communities. *FALL*

Working Press of the Nation. *JANUARY*

World Almanac and Book of Facts. *WINTER*

World Armaments and Disarmaments; SIPRI Yearbook. *JUNE*

World Book Yearbook. *MARCH*

World Collectors Annuary. *OCTOBER*

World Legal Directory. (bi-a.) *FEBRUARY*

World Mines Register. *OCTOBER*

World of Learning. *NOVEMBER*

World Radio TV Handbook. *MARCH*

World Trade Annual. *NOVEMBER*

World Wide Chamber of Commerce Directory. *JULY*

World Wide Summer Placement Directory. *FEBRUARY*

Worldwide Petrochemical Directory. *NOVEMBER*

Writers and Artists' Yearbook. *FEBRUARY*

Writer's Directory. (bi-a.) *MAY*

Writer's Handbook. *FEBRUARY*

Writer's Market. *OCTOBER*

Writer's Yearbook. *FEBRUARY*

The Year Book of World Affairs. *FEBRUARY*

Yearbook of Adult and Continuing Education. *OCTOBER*

Yearbook of American and Canadian Churches. *MAY*

Yearbook of Astronomy. *JANUARY*

Yearbook of Comparative and General Literature. *NOVEMBER*

Yearbook of Comparative Criticism. *JUNE*

Yearbook of Dentistry. *AUGUST*

Yearbook of Higher Education. *NOVEMBER*

Yearbook of International Organizations. (bi-a.) *WINTER*

Yearbook of International Trade Statistics. *WINTER*

Yearbook of Labour Statistics. *WINTER*

Yearbook of Psychiatry and Applied Mental Health. *MAY*

Yearbook of School Law. *OCTOBER*

Yearbook of Science and the Future. *MARCH*

Yearbook of Special Education. *SEPTEMBER*

Yearbook of the European Convention on Human Rights. *NOVEMBER*

Yearbook on Human Rights. (bi-a.) *MAY*

Yearbook on International Communist Affairs. *JUNE*

Year's Work in English Studies. *JUNE*

Year's Work in Modern Language Studies. *WINTER*

YIVO Annual of Jewish Social Sciences. (bi-a.) *NOVEMBER*

SERIALS BUYING SCHEDULE BY MONTH OR SEASON

WINTER

Advances in Librarianship.

Advances in Marine Biology.

Advances in Nuclear Physics.

Advances in Organic Chemistry.

Advances in Physical Organic Chemistry.

African Literature Today.

Aircraft Owners and Pilots Association. AOPA's Airports U.S.A.

Amateur Athletic Union of the United States. Official Handbook of the AAU Codes.

Amateur Athletic Union of the United States. Athletic Library. Official AAU Diving Rules.

Amateur Athletic Union of the United States. Athletic Library. Official AAU Wrestling Handbook.

American Jewish Year Book.

American Psychoanalytic Association. Roster. (bi-a.)

American Research Center in Egypt. Journal.

American Statistical Association. Business and Economic Statistics Section. Proceedings.

American Veterinary Medical Association. Directory.

Annual Editions: Readings in Education.

Annual Editions: Readings in Psychology.

Annual of Power and Conflict.

Automobile Association. AA Guide to Camping and Caravaning.

Automobile Association. AA Guide to Stately Homes, Museums, Castles, and Gardens.

Baxter's Eurailpass Travel Guide.

Bazak Guide to Israel.

Books for the Teen Age.

Catholic Press Directory.

Charter Flight Directory.

Children's Books in Print.

Connecticut Health Services Research Series.

Consumer Complaint Guide.

Country Vacations U.S.A. (bi-a.)

Credit Manual of Commercial Laws.

Current Biography Yearbook.

Dance Magazine Annual.

Davison's Textile Blue Book.

Directory of Associations in Canada.

Directory of Executive Recruiters.

Directory of Medical Specialists.

Directory of the College Student Press in America. (tri-a.)

Dodge Construction Systems Costs.

Dollar Wise Guide to England. (bi-a.)

Dollar Wise Guide to France. (bi-a.)

Editor and Publisher Market Guide.

Egon Ronay's Dunlop Guide: Hotels, Restaurants, and Inns in Great Britain and Ireland.

Eurail Guide: How to Travel Europe by Train.

Europe on $10 a Day.

Fielding's Low Cost Europe.

Fielding's Selected Favorites: Hotels and Inns, Europe.

Fielding's Selective Shopping Guide to Europe.

Fielding's Travel Guide to Europe.

Fodor's Austria.

Fodor's Belgium and Luxembourg.

Fodor's Czechoslovakia. (bi-a.)

Fodor's France.

Fodor's Germany: East and West.

Fodor's Great Britain.

Fodor's Greece.

Fodor's Holland.

Fodor's India.

Fodor's Ireland.

Fodor's Israel.

Fodor's Italy.

Fodor's Japan and Korea.

Fodor's Morocco.

Fodor's Portugal.

Fodor's Scandinavia.

Fodor's Soviet Union.

Fodor's Spain.

Fodor's Switzerland.

Fodor's Turkey.

Fodor's Yugoslavia.

Garuda.

Greece on $10 a Day. (bi-a.)

Guide to Microforms in Print.

Guide to Reviews of Books from and about Hispanic America.

Guinness Book of World Records. (pap.)

Hawaii on $15 and $20 a Day.

Index of American Periodical Verse.

Industrial Machinery and Equipment Pricing Guide.

Institute of Environmental Sciences. Annual Meeting. Proceedings.

International Music Guide.

International Telemetering Conference. Proceedings.

Journal of Behavioral Economics.

Leahy's Hotel-Motel Guide and Travel Atlas.

Let's Go: The Student Guide to Europe.

Let's Go: The Student Guide to the United States and Canada.

Library Journal Book Review.

The Lyle Official Antiques Review.

Michelin Red Guide Series: France.

Michelin Red Guide Series: Germany.

Michelin Red Guide Series: Great Britain and Ireland.

Michelin Red Guide Series: Paris and Environs.

Microform Market Place. (bi-a.)

Mobil Travel Guide: Great Lakes Area.

Mobil Travel Guide: Middle Atlantic States.

Mobil Travel Guide: Northeastern States.

Mobil Travel Guide: Southeastern States.

Mobil Travel Guide: Southwest and South Central Area.

Myra Waldo's Travel and Motoring Guide to Europe.

Myra Waldo's Travel Guide to South America. (quadrennial)

Oxford Slavonic Papers.

Proof.

Publishers' International Directory.

Radio Amateur's Handbook.

Rand McNally Campground and Trailer Park Guide.

Rand McNally National Park Guide.

Reader's Digest Almanac and Yearbook.

Reference Books Reviews.

Small Press Record of Books in Print.

South America on $10 a Day. (bi-a.)

South Pacific Travel Digest. (bi-a.)

Spain and Morocco on $10 and $15 a Day. (bi-a.)

State Approved Schools of Nursing—L.P.N./L.V.N.

State Approved Schools of Nursing—R.N.

Subject Guide to Children's Books in Print.

Subject Guide to Microforms in Print.

Trailer Life's Recreational Vehicle Campground and Services Directory.

Travelers Almanac.

TV Season (year).

TWA Getaway Guide to Athens. (bi-a.)

TWA Getaway Guide to Boston. (bi-a.)

TWA Getaway Guide to Honolulu. (bi-a.)

TWA Getaway Guide to Ireland, Dublin/Shannon. (bi-a.)

TWA Getaway Guide to Las Vegas. (bi-a.)

TWA Getaway Guide to Lisbon/Madrid; Costa del Sol. (bi-a.)

TWA Getaway Guide to London. (bi-a.)

TWA Getaway Guide to Los Angeles. (bi-a.)

TWA Getaway Guide to New York. (bi-a.)

TWA Getaway Guide to Paris. (bi-a.)

TWA Getaway Guide to Rome. (bi-a.)

TWA Getaway Guide to San Francisco. (bi-a.)

TWA Getaway Guide to Washington. (bi-a.)

Ulrich's International Periodicals Directory. (bi-a.)

Washington, D.C., on $10 and $15 a Day. (bi-a.)

Where to Stay in the USA from 50¢ to $10 a Night.

Whitaker's Almanack.

Who Was Who in America. (tri-a.)

Who's Who Among Black Americans. (bi-a.)

Who's Who in Canada. (bi-a.)

Who's Who in the Arab World. (bi-a.)

Who's Who in the South and Southwest. (bi-a.)

Who's Who in the Theatre. (bi-a.)

Who's Who in the West. (bi-a.)

Who's Who of American Women. (bi-a.)

Woodall's Campground Directory: Eastern Edition.

Woodall's Campground Directory: North American Edition.

Woodall's Campground Directory: Western Edition.

World Almanac and Book of Facts.

Yearbook of International Organizations. (bi-a.)

Yearbook of International Trade Statistics.

Yearbook of Labour Statistics.

Year's Work in Modern Language Studies.

JANUARY

Africa Year Book and Who's Who.

Amateur Athletic Union of the United States. Directory.

Amateur Athletic Union of the United States. Athletic Library. Official AAU Synchronized Swimming Handbook.

Amateur Athletic Union of the United States. Athletic Library. Official Rules for Water Polo.

American Foundrymen's Society. Transactions.

American Speech and Hearing Association. Directory.

American Theatre Association. Directory of Members.

Annual Handbook for Group Facilitators.

Annual Review of Entomology.

Annual Review of Fluid Mechanics.

Audiovisual Market Place. (AVMP).

Bibliographic Guide to Government Publications—Foreign.

Bibliographic Guide to Psychology.

Blue Book of Junior College Athletics.

Boat Owner's Buyers Guide.

Building Estimator's Reference Book. (tri-a.)

CRC Handbook of Laboratory Safety.

Cassell's Directory of Publishing in Great Britain, the Commonwealth, Ireland, South Africa, and Pakistan. (bi-a.)

Catholic Theological Society of America. Proceedings.

Child Welfare League of America. Directory of Member Agencies and Associates.

Congressional Quarterly Almanac.

Current Medical Diagnosis and Treatment.

Demographic Yearbook.

Directory of American Savings and Loan Associations.

Drugs in Current Use and New Drugs.

Drugs of Choice. (bi-a.)

Episcopal Church Annual.

Financial Aids for Higher Education. (bi-a.)

Guide to Graduate Departments of Sociology.

Guide to Reference Books for School Media Centers. (bi-a.)

Handbook of Nonprescription Drugs. (bi-a.)

High Fidelity's Test Reports.

International Mimes and Pantomimists. IMP Directory.

International Television Almanac.

Jane's Major Companies of Europe.

Journal of Glass Studies.

Lutheran Church—Missouri Synod. Lutheran Annual.

National Collegiate Athletic Association. Annual Report.

National Institute of Municipal Law Officers. NIMLO Municipal Law Review.

National Telecommunications Conference. Record.

Nature/Science Annual.

NICEM Index to 8mm Motion Cartridges. (bi-a.)

NICEM Index to Psychology—Multimedia. (bi-a.)

NICEM Index to 35mm Educational Filmstrips. (bi-a.)

Official Rules of Sport and Games. (bi-a.)

Parents' Guide to Accredited Camps.

Television Factbook.

Waterway Guide; the Yachtsman's Bible: Mid-Atlantic.

Welding Data Book. (bi-a.)

Working Press of the Nation.

Yearbook of Astronomy.

FEBRUARY

Amateur Athletic Union of the United States. Athletic Library. Official AAU Baton Twirling Handbook. (bi-a.)

Annual Review of Psychology.

Baxter's USA Rail Pass Guide.

Canadian Almanac and Directory.

Corpus Almanac of Canada.

Current Therapy.

Directory and Guide to the Mutual Savings Banks of the United States.

Directory of American Philosophers. (bi-a.)

Drug Abuse Bibliography.

Engineers Joint Council. Engineering Manpower Commission. Prospects of Engineering and Technology Graduates.

International Art and Antiques Yearbook.

International Directory of Marketing Research Houses and Services.

Mennonite Yearbook and Directory.

National Health Directory.

NICEM Index to Environmental Studies—Multimedia. (bi-a.)

NICEM Index to Health and Safety Education—Multimedia. (bi-a.)

NICEM Index to Vocational and Technical Education—Multimedia. (bi-a.)

Rand McNally Road Atlas; U.S., Canada, Mexico.

Whole World Handbook.

World Legal Directory. (bi-a.)

World Wide Summer Placement Directory.

Writers and Artists' Yearbook.

Writer's Handbook.

Writer's Yearbook.

Year Book of World Affairs.

MARCH

Amateur Softball Association of America. Official Guide and Rule Book.

American Dental Directory.

American Jewish Organizations. Directory. (bi-a.)

American Public Works Association. APWA Directory.

American Society of Photogrammetry. Papers from the Annual Meeting.

American Society of University Composers. Proceedings of the Annual Conference.

Annual Review of Physical Chemistry.

Annual Review of Physiology.

Ayer Directory of Publications.

Broadcasting Yearbook.

Crime and Justice.

Cycle Buyers Guide.

El-Hi Textbooks in Print.

Electronics Buyers Guide.

Engineering Index Annual.

E-R-C Directory; Employee Relocation Real Estate Services.

Franciscan Studies.

Guinness Sports Record Book. (bi-a.)

Historic Documents.

Illustrators.

McGraw-Hill Yearbook of Science and Technology.

Medical and Health Annual.

Midwest Media.

Motion Picture Market Place.

Municipal Year Book.

National Newspaper Association. NNA National Directory of Weekly Newspapers.

Runner's Almanac.

Summer Study Abroad.

Thomas Register of American Manufacturers and Thomas Register Catalog.

Time-Life Encyclopedia of Gardening.

Waterway Guide; the Yachtsman's Bible: Northern.

Willing's Press Guide.

World Book Yearbook.

World Radio TV Handbook.

Yearbook of Science and the Future.

SPRING

AB Bookman's Yearbook.

Allied Medical Education Directory.

Amateur Athletic Union of the United States. Athletic Library. Official AAU Track and Field Handbook. (bi-a.)

American Art Directory. (bi-a.)

American Book Prices Current.

American Catholic Philosophical Association. Proceedings.

American Marketing Association. Proceedings.

American Reference Books Annual.

American Society of Sanitary Engineers. Year Book.

Annual Bibliography of British and Irish History.

Annual Editions: Readings in Marketing.

Annual Editions: Readings in Marriage and Family.

Automobile Association. AA Budget Guide to Europe.

Automobile Association. AA Guide to Camping and Caravaning on the Continent.

Automobile Association. AA Guide to Guesthouses, Farmhouses, and Inns.

Book Review Index.

Camping and Caravaning in France.

Canadian Essay and Literature Index.

College Theology Society. Proceedings.

Congressional Staff Directory.

Dollar Wise Guide to California and Las Vegas. (bi-a.)

Easter Seal Directory of Resident Camps for Persons with Special Health Needs.

Essays by Divers Hands. (bi-a.)

Fodor's London: A Companion Guide.

Fodor's U.S.A.

Harris Survey Yearbook of Public Opinion.

Hotel and Motel Red Book.

International Publications.

Ireland on $10 a Day. (bi-a.)

Jewish Travel Guide.

Kovels' Complete Antiques Price List.

Literary Market Place.

Mexico and Guatemala on $10 a Day. (bi-a.)

Michelin Red Guide Series: Benelux.

Michelin Red Guide Series: Spain and Portugal.

Mobil Travel Guide: California and the West.

Mobil Vacation and Business Guide.

National Society for the Study of Education. Yearbook.

New Zealand on $10 a Day. (bi-a.)

News Dictionary.

Performing Arts Resources.

Population and the Population Explosion: A Bibliography.

Standard Periodical Directory.

Who's Who.

Who's Who in the Midwest. (bi-a.)

APRIL

American Book Publishing Record. Annual Cumulation.

American Medical Directory.

American Society for Quality Control. Annual Technical Conference. Transactions.

Annual International Congress Calendar.

Annual Review of Earth and Planetary Sciences.

Bank Administration Institute. Biennial Survey of Personnel Policies and Practices. (bi-a.)

Baseball Blue Book.

The Book of Baseball Records.

Books in Series in the United States. Supplement.

Buying and Selling United States Coins.

Comic Book Price Guide.

Congressional Roll Call.

Davison's Textile Catalog and Buyers Guide.

Dollars and Cents of Shopping Centers. (tri-a.)

Engineers Council for Professional Development. Annual Report.

Federal Tax Handbook.

Genealogical Periodical Annual Index.

Graphis Posters.

Greenwood's Guide to Great Lakes Shipping.

International Association of Chiefs of Police. The Police Yearbook.

International Yearbook and Statesmen's Who's Who.

Jane's Freight Containers.

Literary Market Place.

Medical School Admission Requirements, U.S.A. and Canada.

Motor Truck Repair Manual.

National Fire Protection Association. National Fire Codes.

NICEM Index to Educational Overhead Transparencies. (bi-a.)

Official Baseball Guide.

Official National Collegiate Athletic Association Football Rules Interpretations.

Official National Collegiate Athletic Association Water Polo Rules.

Official Read-Easy Football Rules.

Offshore Technology Conference. Proceedings.

Patterson's American Education; School Systems and Schools Classified.

Penrose Graphic Arts International Annual.

The Philosopher's Index.

Photography Market Place.

Photography Year.

Police Yearbook.

Presidency (year).

Prize Stories.

Reliability and Maintainability Symposium. Proceedings.

Ring Boxing Encyclopedia and Record Book.

Shakespeare Studies.

Society of Plastics Engineers. Annual Technical Conference. Technical Papers.

Standard Directory of Advertisers. (classified edition)

Supreme Court Review.

United States Tennis Association. The Official USTA Yearbook and Tennis Guide with the Official Rules.

Who Owns Whom: North American Edition.

Winterthur Portfolio.

MAY

Accountants' Index.

Amateur Athletic Union of the United States. Athletic Library. Official AAU Judo Rules. (bi-a.)

American Association of State Highway Officials. AASHO Reference Book of Member Departments.

American Statistics Index. Supplement.

Billboard International Directory of Recording Equipment and Studio Directory.

Book Auction Records.

Bowker Annual of Library and Book Trade Information.

Composium Directory of New Music.

Diesel and Gas Turbine World Wide Catalog.

Directory of Agencies Serving the Visually Handicapped in the U.S. (bi-a.)

Downtown Mall Annual and Urban Design Report.

Economic Survey of Latin America.

Editor and Publisher International Yearbook.

Facts on File Yearbook.

Fine Arts Marketplace. (bi-a.)

Foreign Medical School Catalogue.

Golf Magazine Yearbook.

Guide to Independent Study through Correspondence Instruction. (bi-a.)

Guide to Summer Camps and Summer Schools. (bi-a.)

Human Factors Society. Directory and Yearbook.

Labor Relations Yearbook.

National Roster of Realtors.

Official Catholic Directory.

Private Independent Schools.

Requirements for Certification of Teachers, Counselors, Librarians, and Administrators.

Research in Economic History.

Society of Mining Engineers of AIME. Mining Transactions.

Steam Passenger Service Directory.

Urban Affairs Annual Reviews.

Ward's Automotive Yearbook.

Washington Information Directory.

What They Said.

Writer's Directory. (bi-a.)

Yearbook of American and Canadian Churches.

Yearbook of Psychiatry and Applied Mental Health.

Yearbook on Human Rights. (bi-a.)

JUNE

Accepted Dental Therapeutics. (bi-a.)

Admission Requirements of U.S. and Canadian Dental Schools.

America Athletic Union of the United States. Athletic Library. Official AAU Powerlifting Handbook. (bi-a.)

American Alpine Journal.

American Baptist Churches in the U.S.A. Directory.

American Federation of Information Processing Societies. AFIPS Conference Proceedings.

American Literary Scholarship.

American Register of Exporters and Importers.

Annual Editions: Readings in Biology.

Annual Review of Plant Physiology.

Annual Reviews of Biophysics and Bioengineering.

Archives of Asian Art.

Art Prices Current.

Association for Computing Machinery. Proceedings of the National Conference.

Audio-Visual Equipment Directory.

The Book of the States. (bi-a.)

Canadian Yearbook of International Law.

Commodity Year Book.

Directory of Counseling Services.

Directory of Law Libraries. (bi-a.)

Electronic Industry Telephone Directory.

Encyclopedia Buying Guide. (bi-a.)

Engineers Joint Council. Directory of Engineering Societies Management.

Europa Year Book.

Gratz College Annual of Jewish Studies.

International Bibliography of Political Sciences.

International Bibliography of Sociology.

International Directory of Little Magazines and Small Presses.

International Symposium on Transport and Handling of Minerals. Minerals Transportation; Proceedings. (bi-a.)

Jednota Annual: Furdek.

Medical Books and Serials in Print.

National Directory of Law Enforcement Administrators: Prosecution, Correctional, and Judicial Agencies.

Occupational Outlook Handbook.

Official National Collegiate Athletic Association Basketball Rules and Casebook.

Official National Collegiate Athletic Association Soccer Guide.

Photographis.

Police and Law Enforcement.

Political Handbook of the World.

Power Sources Symposium. Proceedings.

Reference Sources.

Selective Guide to Materials for Mental Health and Family Life Education. (bi-a.)

Setting National Priorities; The (year) Budget.

Society of Naval Architects and Marine Engineers. Transactions.

World Armaments and Disarmaments; SIPRI Yearbook.

Yearbook of Comparative Criticism.

Yearbook on International Communist Affairs.

Year's Work in English Studies.

SUMMER

Acoustical Holography.

Aerospace Facts and Figures.

Africa Contemporary Record. Annual Survey and Documents.

Airline Guide to Stewardess and Stewards Careers.

Amateur Athletic Union of the United States. Athletic Library. Official AAU Trampoline and Tumbling Handbook. (bi-a.)

American Cooperation.

American Foreign Relations: A Documentary Record.

American Library Association. ALA Yearbook.

Annual Editions: Readings in American Government.

Annual Editions: Readings in Human Development.

Annual Editions: Readings in Social Problems.

Annual Editions: Readings in Sociology.

Antiques and Their Prices. (bi-a.)

Association of American Medical Colleges. AAMC Directory of American Medical Education.

Canadian Periodical Index.

The County Year Book.

Decorative Art and Modern Interiors.

Dollar Wise Guide to Japan and Hong Kong. (bi-a.)

Elementary Teachers Guide to Free Curriculum Materials.

Empirical Research in Theatre.

Essays and Studies.

Handbook of Private Schools.

Harvard Studies in Classical Philology.

Index Translationum.

International Bibliography of Social and Cultural Anthropology.

International Handbook of Universities and Other Institutions of Higher Education. (tri-a.)

Irregular Series and Annuals. (bi-a.)

Large Type Books in Print.

Machinery's Handbook. (bi-a.)

Marketing Economics Key Plants. (bi-a.)

National Roster of Black Elected Officials.

Official Hotel-Motel Directory and Facilities Guide.

Private Press Books.

Progress in Geography.

Public Welfare Directory.

Railway Passenger Car Annual.

South Pacific Travel Digest. (bi-a.)

United Nations. Department of Economic and Social Affairs. World Economic Survey.

Venereal Disease Bibliography.

Volleyball Guide.

Volleyball Rules.

West Indies and Caribbean Yearbook.

Who's Who in America. (bi-a.)

Who's Who in American Art. (bi-a.)

Who's Who in the East. (bi-a.)

Wire Journal Directory/Catalog.

JULY

Amateur Athletic Union of the United States. Athletic Library. Official AAU Karate Rules. (bi-a.)

Annual Review of Biochemistry.

Best Sport Stories.

Boston College. Studies in Philosophy.

British Humanities Index.

Building Officials and Code Administrators International. BOCA Basic Housing-Property Maintenance Code. (tri-a.)

Business Books and Serials in Print.

Directory of Hotel and Motel Systems.

Educators Guide to Free Films.

Educators Guide to Free Filmstrips.

Guide Book of United States Coins.

Gun Digest.

Handbook of Chemistry and Physics.

Help; The Useful Almanac.

International Auction Records.

Keystone Coal Industry Manual.

National Real Estate Directory.

New York Times Index.

Standard Directory of Advertisers. (geographical edition)

World Wide Chamber of Commerce Directory.

AUGUST

American Baptist Churches in the U.S.A. Yearbook.

American Correctional Association. Annual Congress of Corrections. Proceedings.

American Hospital Association. Guide to the Health Care Field.

American Lutheran Church. Yearbook.

Annual Editions: Readings in Business.

Annual Register. World Events.

Berkeley Journal of Sociology: Critical Review.

Collegiate Summer Employment Guide.

Commonwealth Universities Yearbook.

Crafts Annual.

Directory of College Placement Offices.

EEM (Electronic Engineering Master Catalog).

Educators Guide to Free Audio and Video Materials.

Educators Guide to Free Guidance Materials.

Educators Guide to Free Science Materials.

Educators Guide to Free Teaching Aids.

Electronic Components Conference. Proceedings.

Financial Assistance for Library Education.

Football Register.

Guns and Ammo Annual.

Index to Book Reviews in the Humanities.

International Book Trade Directory.

Medical and Health Information Directory. (bi-a.)

National Football Guide.

National Union of Christian Schools. Directory and Annual Report.

Norwegian-American Studies.

Official National Collegiate Athletic Association Football Guide.

Official National Collegiate Athletic Association Ice Hockey Guide.

Scott's Specialized Catalogue of U.S. Stamps.

Securities Law Review.

Standard Catalogue of Canadian Coins, Tokens, and Paper Money.

Techniques of Marriage and Family Counseling.

United Nations. Statistical Yearbook.

Yearbook of Dentistry.

SEPTEMBER

Amateur Athletic Union of the United States. Athletic Library. Official AAU Boxing Handbook. (quadrennial.)

American Psychological Association. Directory. (bi-a.)

Annual Review of Astronomy and Astrophysics.

Annual Review of Sociology.

AudArena Stadium Guide and International Directory.

Best American Short Stories.

Best Books for Children.

Bibliography of Asian Studies.

Bibliography of Publications of University Bureaus of Business and Economic Research.

Billboard International Buyer's Guide of the Music—Record Industry.

Blue Book of College Athletics.

College Blue Book. (bi-a.)

College Handbook. (tri-a.)

Comparative Guide to Two-year Colleges and Career Programs. (bi-a.)

Dickens Studies Annual.

Direction of Trade.

Directory: Juvenile and Adult Correctional Departments, Institutions, and Agencies, and Paroling Authorities, United States and Canada.

Directory of Historical Societies and Agencies in the United States and Canada. (bi-a.)

Eastern Hemisphere Petroleum Directory.

Educators Guide to Free Health, Physical Education, and Recreation Materials.

Educators Guide to Free Social Studies Materials.

Election Index. (bi-a.)

Electronic News Financial Factbook and Directory.

Graduate Programs and Admissions Manual.

Guns Illustrated.

The Indianapolis 500 Yearbook.

International Folk Music Council. Yearbook.

International Who's Who in Poetry. (bi-a.)

Inventory of Marriage and Family.

Jane's World Railways.

Jewish Book Annual.

Marine Technology Society. Annual Conference. Proceedings.

National Collegiate Championships.

National Directory of College Athletics. (Women's Edition.)

National Football League. Official Record Manual.

Official National Collegiate Athletic Association Swimming Guide.

Packaging Engineering Annual Buyers Guide.

Photography Annual.

Pre-Law Handbook.

A Sociological Yearbook of Religion in Britain.

Sourcebook of Equal Educational Opportunity.

Standard Education Almanac.

Standard Medical Almanac.

Statesman's Year Book.

TV Feature Film Source Book.

United States Political Science Documents.

Yearbook of Special Education.

FALL

Access Index to Little Magazines.

Access: The Supplementary Index to Periodicals.

Annual Editions: Readings in Anthropology.

Annual of Advertising, Editorial, and Television Art and Design with Annual Copy Awards.

Annual Register of Grant Support.

Annual Review of International Science and Technology.

Books in Print.

British Books in Print.

Chases' Calendar of Annual Events.

Children's Books; Awards and Prizes. (bi-a.)

Children's Literature: A Guide to Reference Sources. Supplement. (quinquennial.)

Contemporary Crafts Market Place.

Creative Camera International Year Book.

Directory of Research Grants.

Educators Guide to Free Tapes, Scripts, and Transcriptions.

Fielding's Guide to the Caribbean Plus the Bahamas.

Fodor's Caribbean, Bahamas, and Bermuda.

Fodor's Cruises Everywhere. (bi-a.)

Fodor's Europe.

Fodor's Hawaii.

Fodor's Mexico.

Fodor's South America.

Fodor's South-East Asia. (bi-a.)

Tunisia.

Government Reference Books. (bi-a.)

Grants Register. (bi-a.)

Guide to College Courses in Film and Television. (bi-a.)

Guiness Book of World Records. (cloth)

Hammond Almanac of a Million Facts.

High Fidelity; Records in Review.

Information Please Almanac, Atlas, and Yearbook.

International Who's Who.

International Who's Who in Music and Musicians Directory. (bi-a.)

Jane's All the World Aircraft.

Marquis Who's Who Publications: Index to All Books.

Marsyas. (bi-a.)

Minkus New American Stamp Catalog.

Mission Handbook: North American Protestant Ministries Overseas. (tri-a.)

National Conference on Fluid Power. Proceedings.

Oxbridge Omnibus of Holiday Observances around the World.

Pears Cyclopaedia.

Progress in Optics.

Publishers' Trade List Annual.

Sources of Serials.

Unitarian Historical Society, London. Transactions.

Who's Who in the World. (bi-a.)

Woodall's Retirement and Resort Communities.

OCTOBER

Abortion Bibliography.

Accredited Institutions of Post Secondary Education.

Africa South of the Sahara.

Amateur Athletic Union of the United States. Athletic Library. Official AAU Physique Handbook. (bi-a.)

American Book Trade Directory.

American Consulting Engineers Council. Directory.

American Journal of Jurisprudence.

American Library Directory. (bi-a.)

American Rose Annual.

American Society of International Law. Proceedings.

Anglo American Trade Directory. (bi-a.)

Annual Editions: Readings in Criminal Justice.

Annual Editions: Readings in Social Psychology.

Annual Index to Popular Music Record Reviews.

Annual Review of Anthropology.

Annual Review of Microbiology.

Archaeological Institute of America. Bulletin.

Art and Crafts Market.

Art at Auction: The Year at Sotheby's and Parke-Bernet.

Augustinian Studies.

Best's Safety Directory; Safety—Industrial Hygiene—Security.

Bibliography of Society, Ethics, and Life Sciences.

College Placement Annual.

Council of State Governments. Suggested State Legislation.

Directory of Shipowners, Shipbuilders, and Marine Engineers.

Educational Media Yearbook.

Electrical World Directory of Electric Utilities.

Encyclopedia of Football.

Graphis Annual.

Guide to Consumer Markets.

Index to Literature on the American Indian.

International Literary Market Place.

J. K. Lasser's Your Income Tax.

Middle East and North Africa.

Minkus New World Wide Stamp Catalog. (bi-a.)

Modern Plastics Encyclopedia.

Music in Higher Education.

Musical America International Directory of the Performing Arts.

National Basketball Association Official Guide.

National Directory of bhigh School Coaches.

National Directory of State Agencies. (bi-a.)

National Electronics Conference. Proceedings.

National Hockey League Guide.

NICEM Index to Educational Audio Tapes. (bi-a.)

NICEM Index to Educational Records. (bi-a.)

NICEM Index to Educational Slides. (bi-a.)

NICEM Index to Educational Videotapes. (bi-a.)

NICEM Index to 16mm Educational Films. (bi-a.)

Official National Collegiate Athletic Association Basketball Guide.

Optical Industry and Systems Directory.

Peterson's Annual Guide to Undergraduate Study.

Peterson's Annual Guides to Graduate Study.

Photographer's Market.

Photography Year Book.

Ports of the World.

Progress in Physical Organic Chemistry.

Sailboat and Sailboat Equipment Directory.

Student Aid Annual.

Technician Education Yearbook. (bi-a.)

Tennessee Studies in Literature.

Traditio.

United Nations. Yearbook.

Weather Almanac.

Who's Who in Electronics.

Who's Who in Religion.

World Collectors Annuary.

World Mines Register.

Writer's Market.

Yearbook of Adult and Continuing Education.

Yearbook of School Law.

NOVEMBER

Almanac of American Politics.

Amateur Athletic Union of the United States. Athletic Library. Official AAU Basketball Handbook. (bi-a.)

America Votes. (bi-a.)

American Anthropological Association. Annual Report and Directory.

American Association of Marriage and Family Counselors. Register.

American Library Association. ALA Membership Directory.

American Society for Information Science. Proceedings.

Anglo-Saxon England.

Annual Editions: Readings in Early Childhood Education.

Annual Editions: Readings in Economics.

Annual Editions: Readings in Health.

Annual Editions: Readings in Personality and Adjustment.

Annual Review of Ecology and Systematics.

Annual Survey of African Law.

Annuale Mediaevale.

Architectural Schools in North America.

Assembling.

Association for Computing Machinery. Annual Workshop on Microprogramming. Conference Record.

Basebook.

Best Plays of (year).

Braddock's Federal—State—Local Government Directory.

Brown's Directory of North American Gas Companies.

Catholic Almanac.

Chicorel Index to Mental Health Book Reviews.

Chilton's Auto Repair Manual.

Coin World Almanac.

The College of Planning Search Book.

Directory of Overseas Summer Jobs.

Fairchild's Financial Manual of Retail Stores.

The Far East and Australasia.

French XX Bibliography.

Jane's Surface Skimmers, Hovercraft, and Hydrofoils.

Lutheran Church in America. Yearbook.

Motor Auto Repair Manual.

National Collegiate Athletic Association. Annual Report.

Official National Collegiate Athletic Association Skiing Rules.

Popular Music Periodicals Index.

Sage Yearbooks in Politics and Public Policy.

Science Fiction Book Review Index.

Scientific and Technical Books and Serials in Print.

Sociological Methodology.

Sourcebook on Aging.

Stanford Journal of International Studies.

Subject Guide to Books in Print.

Summer Employment Directory of the United States.

Theatre Annual.

Theatre World.

Transportation Research Forum. Proceedings. Annual Meeting.

USAN and the USP Dictionary of Name Drugs.

Unitarian Universalist Directory.

Used Book Price Guide. (quinquennial)

Who's Who in American Law.

Who's Who in Art. (bi-a.)

Who's Who in Government. (bi-a.)

World of Learning.

World Trade Annual.

Worldwide Petrochemical Directory.

Yearbook of Comparative and General Literature.

Yearbook of Higher Education.

Yearbook of the European Convention on Human Rights.

YIVO Annual of Jewish Social Sciences. (bi-a.)

DECEMBER

Amateur Athletic Union of the United States. Athletic Library. Official Rules for Competitive Swimming.

American Library Association. Handbook of Organization.

American Society of Civil Engineers. Transactions.

American Society of Heating, Refrigerating, and Air Conditioning Engineers. Transactions.

American Vocational Association. Yearbook.

Annual Progress in Child Psychiatry and Child Development.

Annual Review of Genetics.

Annual Review of Nuclear Science.

Annual Review of the Schizophrenic Syndrome.

Art Design Photo.

Artists/USA. (bi-a.)

Bibliographic Guide to Black Studies.

Bibliographic Guide to Government Publications—U.S.

Bibliographie Cartographique Internationale.

Bradford's Directory of Marketing Research Agencies and Management Consultants in the United States and the World.

Cavalcade and Directory of Acts and Attractions.

Congress and the Nation. (quadrennial)

Consumer Reports Buying Guide.

Containerization: A Bibliography.

Dance World.

Directory of Music Faculties in Colleges and Universities, U.S. and Canada.

Economic Survey of Europe.

Energy Index.

Environment Index.

Facts About Nursing.

Fitzgerald/Hemingway Annual.

Handbook of Denominations in the United States. (quinquennial)

Handbook of Latin American Studies.

Hebrew Union College Annual.

Hockey Register.

International Bibliography of Historical Sciences.

International Who's Who in Art and Antiques. (tri-a.)

Jane's Fighting Ships.

Let's Halt Awhile in Great Britain and Ireland.

Milton Studies.

National Faculty Directory.

Official National Collegiate Athletic Association Baseball Guide.

Official World Series Records.

Patent Law Review.

Plant Location: The Industrial and Economic Workbook.

Pro and Amateur Hockey Guide.

Pro Football Illustrated.

Royal Society of Canada. Transactions.

Scandinavian Political Studies.

Shakespeare Survey.

Southern Conference on Gerontology.

Tulane Studies in Philosophy.

Waterway Guide; The Yachtman's Bible: Southern.

Where to Retire on a Small Income. (bi-a.)

Who's Who in American Politics. (bi-a.)

Woodall's Directory of Mobile Home Communities.

AUTHOR—TITLE INDEX

AAMC Directory of American Medical Education. *see* Association of American Medical Colleges. AAMC Directory of American Medical Education, SC 219

AB Bookman's Yearbook, SS 148

ACLU. Annual Report. *see* American Civil Liberties Union. Annual Report, SS 138

ACTION (Service Corps). Annual Report, SS 616

AIAW Handbook-Directory. *see* Association for Intercollegiate Athletics for Women. AIAW Directory, SS 691; Association for Intercollegiate Athletics for Women. AIAW Handbook of Policies and Operating Procedures, SS 692

AIP: An Index and Listing of Some Movement Publications Reflecting Today's Social Change Activites. *see* Alternatives in Print, GE 21

ALA Membership Directory. *see* American Library Association. ALA Membership Directory, HU 143

The ALA Yearbook. *see* American Library Association. The ALA Yearbook, HU 144

ARBA. *see* American Reference Books Annual, GE 83

ARL Statistics. *see* Association of Research Libraries. ARL Statistics, HU 152

ASHA Reports. *see* American Speech and Hearing Association. ASHA Reports, SC 216

Abortion Bibliography, SC 205

Abridged Readers' Guide to Periodical Literature, GE 113

Accepted Dental Remedies. *see* Accepted Dental Therapeutics, SC 206

Accepted Dental Therapeutics, SC 206

Access: The Supplementary Index to Periodicals, GE 114

Access Index to Little Magazines, GE 115

Accidents in North American Mountaineering, SS 657

Accountants' Index, SS 32

Accounting Trends and Techniques. *see* American Institute of Certified Public Accountants. Accounting Trends and Techniques, SS 33

Accredited Institutions of Higher Education. *see* Accredited Institutions of Postsecondary Education, ED 33

Accredited Institutions of Postsecondary Education, ED 33

Acoustical Holography, SC 312

Administrative Management Society. Salary and Benefit Information for Middle Management Personnel for U.S. and Canada. *see* Salary and Benefit Information for Middle Management Personnel for U.S. and Canada, SS 428

Admission Requirements of American Dental Schools. *see* Admission Requirements of U.S. and Canadian Dental Schools, SC 207

Admission Requirements of U.S. and Canadian Dental Schools, SC 207

Adolescent Psychiatry, SC 316

Advanced Placement Course Descriptions, ED 24

Advancement and Placement Institute. World-wide Summer Placement Directory. *see* World-wide Summer Placement Directory, SS 532

Advances in Applied Mechanics, SC 158

Advances in Carbohydrate Chemistry and Biochemistry, SC 46

Advances in Ecological Research, SC 67

Advances in Genetics, SC 21

Advances in Inorganic Chemistry and Radiochemistry, SC 47

Advances in Instrumentation, SC 159

Advances in Librarianship, HU 142

Advances in Marine Biology, SC 192

Advances in Nuclear Physics, SC 313

Advances in Organic Chemistry, SC 48

Advances in Parasitology, SC 22

Advances in Physical Organic Chemistry, SC 49

Advances in X-Ray Analysis, SC 208

Aerospace Facts and Figures, SC 14

Africa (year), SS 323

Africa Contemporary Record: Annual Survey and Documents, SS 324

Africa South of the Sahara, SS 325

Africa Year Book and Who's Who, SS 326

African Literature and the Arts. *see* New African Literature and the Arts, HU 117

African Literature Today, HU 85

African Music, HU 177

African Music Society. Newsletter. *see* African Music, HU 177

African Statistical Yearbook; Annuaire Statistique pour l'Afrique, GE 122

The Agricultural Index. *see* Biological and Agricultural Index, SC 33

Air Travel Bargains, SS 900

Aircraft Owners and Pilots Association. AOPA's Airports U.S.A., SS 846

Airline Guide to Stewardess and Stewards Careers, SS 522

Akademiska Dzive, SS 258

Alaska Fishing Guide, SS 658

Alaska Hunting Guide, SS 659

Alcoholism Treatment Programs Directory, SC 209

Alfred P. Sloan Foundation. Report, HU 1

All about Hawaii. *see* Thrum's All about Hawaii, SS 1026

Allied Medical Education Directory, SC 210

The Almanac of American Politics, SS 542

Almanac of the Pacific. see Thrum's All about Hawaii, SS 1026

Alternatives in Print, GE 21

Amateur Athletic Union of the United States. Directory, SS 660

Amateur Athletic Union of the United States. Official Handbook of the AAU Codes, SS 661

Amateur Athletic Union of the United States. Athletic Library. Official AAU Diving Rules, SS 662

Amateur Athletic Union of the United States. Athletic Library. Official AAU Judo Rules, SS 674

Amateur Athletic Union of the United States. Athletic Library. Official AAU Karate Rules, SS 675

Amateur Athletic Union of the United States. Athletic Library. Official AAU Tae Kwon Do Rules, SS 676

Amateur Athletic Union of the United States. Athletic Library. Official AAU Track and Field Handbook, SS 677

Amateur Athletic Union of the United States. Athletic Library. Official Rules for Competitive Swimming, SS 678

Amateur Athletic Union of the United States. Athletic Library. Official Rules for Water Polo, SS 679

Amateur Athletic Union of the United States. Athletic Library: Official AAU Handbook Series. Official AAU Basketball Handbook, SS 663

Amateur Athletic Union of the United States. Athletic Library: Official AAU Handbook Series. Official AAU Baton Twirling Handbook, SS 664

Amateur Athletic Union of the United States. Athletic Library: Official AAU Handbook Series. Official AAU Boxing Handbook, SS 665

Amateur Athletic Union of the United States. Athletic Library: Official AAU Handbook Series. Official AAU Gymnastics Handbook, SS 666

Amateur Athletic Union of the United States. Athletic Library: Official AAU Handbook Series. Official AAU Junior Olympics Handbook, SS 667

Amateur Athletic Union of the United States. Athletic Library: Official AAU Handbook Series. Official AAU Physique Handbook, SS 668

Amateur Athletic Union of the United States. Athletic Library: Official AAU Handbook Series. Official AAU Powerlifting Handbook, SS 669

Amateur Athletic Union of the United States. Athletic Library: Official AAU Handbook Series. Official AAU Synchronized Swimming Handbook, SS 670

Amateur Athletic Union of the United States. Athletic Library: Official AAU Handbook Series. Official AAU Trampoline and Tumbling Handbook, SS 671

Amateur Athletic Union of the United States. Athletic Library: Official AAU Handbook Series. Official AAU Weightlifting Handbook, SS 672

Amateur Athletic Union of the United States. Athletic Library: Official AAU Handbook Series. Official AAU Wrestling Handbook, SS 673

Amateur Hockey Association of the United States. Official Guide, SS 680

Amateur Hockey Association of the United States. Rule Book, SS 681

Amateur Skating Union of the United States. Official Handbook: Speed Skating, SS 682

Amateur Softball Association of America. Official Rule Book and Guide, SS 683

Amateur Trapshooting Association. Official Trapshooting Rules, SS 684

America: History and Life. Part C: American History Bibliography, SS 327

America Votes, SS 543

American Academy of Arts and Sciences. Proceedings. see American Academy of Arts and Sciences. Records of the Academy, HU 20

American Academy of Arts and Sciences. Records of the Academy, HU 20

American Alliance for Health, Physical Education, and Recreation. Dance Directory. see Dance Directory, HU 81

American Alliance for Health, Physical Education, and Recreation. Focus on Dance. see Focus on Dance, HU 84

The American Alpine Club. Accidents in North American Mountaineering. see Accidents in North American Mountaineering, SS 657

American Alpine Journal, SS 685

American Annals of the Deaf. Programs and Services for the Deaf in the United States. see Programs and Services for the Deaf in the United States, SC 258

American Anthropological Association. Annual Report and Directory, SS 7

American Architects Directory, HU 21

American Art Annual. see American Art Directory, HU 22; Who's Who in American Art, HU 62

American Art Directory, HU 22

American Association for State and Local History. Directory of Historical Societies and Agencies in the United States and Canada. see Directory of Historical Societies and Agencies in the United States and Canada, SS 338

American Association of Colleges of Pharmacy. Pharmacy School Admission Requirements. see Pharmacy School Admission Requirements, SC 256

American Association of Dental Schools. Admission Requirements of U.S. and Canadian Dental Schools. see Admission Requirements of U.S. and Canadian Dental Schools, SC 207

American Association of Law Libraries. Directory of

Law Libraries. *see* Directory of Law Libraries, SS 461

American Association of Marriage and Family Counselors. Register, SS 617

American Association of Law Schools. Directory of Law Teachers. *see* Directory of Law Teachers, SS 462

American Association of Law Schools. Directory of Teachers in Member Schools. *see* Directory of Law Teachers, SS 462

American Association of Museums. Official Museum Directory. *see* Official Museum Directory, HU 52

American Association of Physical Anthropologists. Yearbook of Physical Anthropology, SS 31

American Association of State Highway Officials. AASHO Reference Book of Member Department Personnel and Committees, SS 847

American Association of Theological Schools. Bulletin. *see* Association of Theological Schools in the United States and Canada. Bulletin, HU 252

American Baptist Churches in the U.S.A. Directory, HU 244

American Baptist Churches in the U.S.A. Yearbook, HU 245

American Baptist Convention. Yearbook. *see* American Baptist Churches in the U.S.A. Directory, HU 244; American Baptist Churches in the U.S.A. Yearbook, HU 245

American Bar Association. Directory of Lawyer Referral Services and Committees. *see* Directory of Lawyer Referral Services and Committees, SS 463

American Bar Association. Law Student Division. Federal Government Job Opportunities for Young Lawyers. *see* American Bar Association. Law Student Division. Federal Government Legal Career Opportunities, SS 444

American Bar Association. Law Student Division. Federal Government Legal Career Opportunities, SS 444

The American Bench, SS 445

American Bible Society. Annual Report, HU 246

American Board of Medical Specialists. Directory of Medical Specialists. *see* Directory of Medical Specialists, SC 229

American Book-Prices Current, SS 149

American Book Publishing Record. Annual Cumulation, GE 22

American Book Trade Directory, SS 150

American Book Trade Manual. *see* American Book Trade Directory, SS 150

American Bureau of Metal Statistics. Yearbook. *see* Non-Ferrous Metal Data, SC 283

American Camellia Yearbook, SC 152

American Catholic Philosophical Association. Proceedings, HU 214

American Chamber of Commerce (United Kingdom). Anglo American Trade Directory. *see* Anglo American Trade Directory, SS 56

American City Magazine. Municipal Index. *see* Municipal Index, SS 585

American Civil Liberties Union. Annual Report, SS 138

American Consulting Engineers Council. Directory, SC 122

American College Testing Program. The College Planning Search Book. *see* The College Planning Search Book, ED 39

American Collegiate Employment Institute. Collegiate Summer Employment Guide. *see* Collegiate Summer Employment Guide, SS 524

American Cooperation, SS 53

American Correctional Association. Annual Congress of Corrections. Proceedings, SS 228

American Correctional Association. Directory. *see* Directory: Juvenile and Adult Correctional Departments, Institutions and Agencies and Paroling Authorities of the United States and Canada, SS 233

American Council of Independent Laboratories. Directory, SC 123

American Council of Learned Societies. Annual Report, HU 2

American Council of Life Insurance. Life Insurance Fact Book. *see* Life Insurance Fact Book, SS 415

American Council of Life Insurance. Pension Facts. *see* Pension Facts, SS 417

American Council on Education. Accredited Institutions of Postsecondary Education. *see* Accredited Institutions of Postsecondary Education, ED 33

American Crafts Council. Contemporary Crafts Market Place. *see* Contemporary Crafts Market Place, SS 372

American Dance Therapy Association. Proceedings of the Annual Conference, HU 79

American Defense Preparedness Association. Annual Directory, SC 284

American Dental Association. Accepted Dental Therapeutics. *see* Accepted Dental Therapeutics, SC 206

American Dental Association. American Dental Directory. *see* American Dental Directory, SC 211

American Dental Directory, SC 211

American Drop-Shippers Directory, SS 496

American Education. *see* Patterson's American Education: School Systems and Schools Classified, ED 29

American Educational Theatre Association. Directory

of Members. *see* American Theatre Association. Directory of Members, HU 332
American Engineering Model Society. Membership Directory, SC 124
American Enterprise Institute for Public Policy Research Review: (year) Session of the Congress, SS 544
American Ephemeris and Nautical Almanac, SC 17
American Executive Travel Companion, SS 901
American Film Institute. Guide to College Courses in Film and Television. *see* Guide to College Courses in Film and Television, SS 182
American Foreign Relations: A Documentary Record, SS 545
American Foundation for the Blind. Directory of Agencies Serving the Visually Handicapped in the U.S. *see* Directory of Agencies Serving the Visually Handicapped in the U.S., SS 622
American Foundations and Their Fields. *see* Foundation Directory, GE 103
American Foundrymen's Society. Transactions, SC 160
American Gear Manufacturers Association. AGMA Directory, SC 161
American Hospital Association. Guide to the Health Care Field, SC 212
American Hospital Association. Hospital Statistics, SC 213
American Hotel and Motel Association. Directory of Hotel and Motel Systems. *see* Directory of Hotel and Motel Systems, SS 77
American Indian Calendar. *see* U.S. Bureau of Indian Affairs. American Indian Calendar, SS 276
American Industrial Real Estate Association Journal, SS 607
American Institute of Architects. American Architects Directory. *see* American Architects Directory, HU 21
American Institute of Biological Sciences. Developments in Industrial Microbiology. *see* Developments in Industrial Microbiology, SC 36
American Institute of Certified Public Accountants. Accounting Trends and Techniques, SS 33
American Institute of Certified Public Accountants. Accountants' Index. *see* Accountants Index, SS 32
American Institute of Consulting Engineers. Directory. *see* American Consulting Engineers Council. Directory, SC 122
American Institute of Cooperation. American Cooperation. *see* American Cooperation, SS 53
American Institute of Family Relations. Techniques of Marriage and Family Counseling. *see* Techniques of Marriage and Family Counseling, SS 635
American Institute of Musicology. Musica Disciplina. *see* Musica Disciplina, HU 201
American Institute of Physics. Handbook. SC 314
American Institute of Steel Construction. Annual Report, SC 39
American Instructors of the Deaf. Proceedings. *see* Convention of American Instructors of the Deaf. Proceedings, ED 93
American Irish Historical Society. The Recorder, SS 259
American Italian Historical Association. Proceedings of the Annual Conference, SS 260
American Jewish Committee. American Jewish Year Book. *see* American Jewish Year Book, HU 248
The American Jewish Committee. Institute of Human Relations. Jewish Organizations: A Worldwide Directory. *see* Jewish Organizations: A Worldwide Directory, GE 108
American Jewish Organizations. Directory, HU 247
American Jewish Year Book, HU 248
American Journal of Jurisprudence, SS 446
American Library Annual and Book Trade Almanac. *see* Bowker Annual of Library and Book Trade Information, SS 160
American Library Association. ALA Membership Directory, HU 143
American Library Association. The ALA Yearbook, HU 144
American Library Association. Audiocassette Programs from the Annual Conference, HU 145
American Library Association. Biographical Directory of Librarians in the United States and Canada. *see* Biographical Directory of Librarians in the United States and Canada, HU 153
American Library Association. Directory of Library Science Libraries, HU 146
American Library Association. Guides to Educational Media. *see* Guides to Educational Media, ED 75
American Library Association. Handbook of Organization, HU 147
American Library Association. Reference and Subscription Books Reviews. *see* Reference and Subscription Books Reviews, GE 91
American Library Association. Government Documents Round Table. Directory of Government Document Collections and Librarians. *see* Directory of Government Document Collections and Librarians, HU 156
American Library Association. Library Education Division. Fellowships, Scholarships, Grants-in-Aid, Loans, and Other Financial Assistance for Library Education. *see* Financial Assistance for Library Education, HU 158

American Library Association. Library Education Division. Financial Assistance for Library Education. *see* Financial Assistance for Library Education, HU 158

American Library Association. Social Responsibilites Round Table. Task Force on Alternatives in Print. Alternatives in Print. *see* Alternatives in Print, GE 21

American Library Directory, HU 148

American Literary Scholarship, HU 86

American Lutheran Church. A Biographical Directory of Clergymen of the American Lutheran Church. *see* A Biographical Directory of Clergymen of the American Lutheran Church, HU 256

American Lutheran Church. Yearbook, HU 249

American Marketing Association. Abstracts of Papers of the Conferences. *see* American Marketing Association. Proceedings, SS 497

American Marketing Association.Proceedings, SS 497

American Medical Association. Allied Medical Education Directory. *see* Allied Medical Education Directory, SC 210

American Medical Association. American Medical Directory. *see* American Medical Directory, SC 214

American Medical Association. Directory of Women Physicians in the U.S. *see* Directory of Women Physicians in the U.S., SC 233

American Medical Directory, SC 214

American Men and Women of Science, SC 1

American Men and Women of Science: Biology, SC 23

American Men and Women of Science: Chemistry, SC 50

American Men and Women of Science: Consultants, SC 2

American Men and Women of Science: Medical and Health Sciences, SC 215

American Men and Women of Science: Medical Sciences. *see* American Men and Women of Science: Medical and Health Sciences, SC 215

American Men and Women of Science: Physics, Astronomy, Mathematics, Statistics, and Computer Sciences, SC 3

American Men and Women of Science: Social and Behavioral Sciences, SC 317

American National Red Cross. Annual Report, SS 618

American Newspaper Markets Circulation, SS 151

American Nuclear Society. Directory: Who's Who in Nuclear Energy, SC 93

American Numismatic Society. Annual Report, SS 363

American Numismatic Society. Proceedings. *see* American Numismatic Society. Annual Report, SS 363

American Nurses Association. Facts about Nursing. *see* Facts about Nursing, SC 238

American Ordnance Association. Annual Directory. *see* American Defense Preparedness Association. Annual Directory, SC 284

American Osteopathic Association. Yearbook and Directory of Osteopathic Physicians. *see* Yearbook and Directory of Osteopathic Physicians, SC 275

American Petroleum Institute. Annual Statistical Review, SC 94

American Petroleum Institute. Petroleum Facts and Figures, SC 95

American Pharmaceutical Association. Handbook of Nonprescription Drugs. *see* Handbook of Nonprescription Drugs, SC 240

American Philological Association. Directory, HU 87

American Philosophical Association. Proceedings and Addresses, HU 215

American Political Science Association. Guide to Graduate Study in Political Science. *see* Guide to Graduate Study in Political Science, SS 556

American Prison Association. Proceedings. *see* American Correctional Association. Annual Congress of Corrections. Proceedings, SS 228

American Psychiatric Association. Biographical Directory, SC 318

American Psychoanalytic Association. Roster, SC 319

American Psychological Association. Biographical Directory. *see* American Psychological Association. Directory, SC 320

American Psychological Association. Directory, SC 320

American Psychological Association. Graduate Study in Psychology. *see* Graduate Study in Psychology, SC 331

American Public Transit Association. Transit Fact Book, SS 848

American Public Welfare Association. Public Welfare Directory. *see* Public Welfare Directory, SS 630

American Public Works Association. APWA Directory, SS 287

American Public Works Association. APWA Yearbook. *see* American Public Works Association. APWA Directory, SS 287

American Radio Relay League. Radio Amateur's Handbook. *see* Radio Amateur's Handbook, SS 202

American Reference Books Annual, GE 83

American Register of Exporters and Importers, SS 54

American Research Center in Egypt. Journal, HU 23

American Rose Annual, SC 153

American School of Classical Studies at Athens. Annual Report, HU 65

The American Sephardi, SS 261

American Society for Engineering Education. Engineering College Research and Graduate Study. *see* Engineering College Research and Graduate Study, SC 134

American Society for Information Science. Proceedings, HU 149

American Society for Information Science. Review of Information Science and Technology. *see* Annual Review of Information Science and Technology, HU 150

American Society for Political and Legal Philosophy. Nomos. *see* Nomos, HU 226

American Society for Quality Control. Annual Technical Conference Transactions, SC 162

American Society for Training and Development. Membership Directory. *see* Who's Who in Training and Development, SS 521

American Society of Appraisers. Bibliography of Appraisal Literature. *see* Bibliography of Appraisal Literature, SS 64

American Society of Civil Engineers. Directory, SC 125

American Society of Civil Engineers. Transactions, SC 126

American Society of Civil Engineers. Yearbook. *see* American Society of Civil Engineers. Directory, SC 125

American Society of Heating, Refrigerating and Air Conditioning Engineers. Transactions, SC 127

American Society of International Law. Proceedings, SS 447

American Society of Mechanical Engineers. Membership List, SC 128

American Society of Mechanical Engineers. Transactions, SC 129

American Society of Naval Engineers. Membership Lists, SC 130

American Society of Photogrammetry. Papers from the Annual Meeting, SC 146

American Society of Photogrammetry. Technical Papers from the Annual Meeting. *see* American Society of Photogrammetry. Papers from the Annual Meeting, SC 146

American Society of Planning Officials. Profiles of State Planning Associations in the United States. *see* Profiles of State Planning Associations in the United States, SS 308

American Society of Sanitary Engineers. Yearbook, SC 131

American Society of University Composers. Proceedings of the Annual Conference, HU 178

American Sociological Association. Guide to Graduate Departments of Sociology. *see* Guide to Graduate Departments of Sociology, SS 648

American Sociological Association. Proceedings of the Annual Meeting, SS 638

American Sociological Association. Sociological Methodology. *see* Sociological Methodology, SS 655

American Speech and Hearing Association. ASHA Reports, SC 216

American Speech and Hearing Association. Directory, SC 217

American Statistical Association. Business and Economics Statistics Section. Proceedings, SS 55

American Statistics Index. Supplement, GE 123

American Synagogue Directory. *see* American Jewish Organizations. Directory, HU 247

American Theatre Association. Directory of Members, HU 332

American Theological Library Association. Index to Religious Periodical Literature. *see* Index to Religious Periodical Literature, HU 289

American Transit Association. Transit Fact Book. *see* American Public Transit Association. Transit Fact Book, SS 848

American Trucking Associations. Report. *see* American Trucking Trends. Statistical Report, SS 849

American Trucking Trends. Statistical Report, SS 849

American Veterinary Medical Association. Directory, SC 336

American Vocational Association. Yearbook, ED 97

Americana Annual, GE 1

America's Educational Press, ED 1

Amnesty International. Annual Report. *see* Amnesty International Report, SS 546

Amnesty International Report, SS 546

Analysis of the World Tank Ship Fleet, SS 850

Analysis of Work Stoppages. *see* U.S. Bureau of Labor Statistics. Analysis of Work Stoppages, SS 429

Analysts Handbook, SS 34

Ancient Near Eastern Society of Columbia University. Journal. *see* The Journal of the Ancient Near Eastern Society of Columbia University, HU 74

Andrew W. Mellon Foundation. Annual Report, HU 3

Anglican Church of Canada. Anglican Yearbook. *see* Anglican Yearbook, HU 250

Anglican Yearbook, HU 250

Anglo-American Aeronautical Conference. Proceedings, SC 15

Anglo American Trade Directory, SS 56

Anglo-Saxon England, SS 328

Annales de Geographie. *see* Bibliographie Geographique Internationale, SC 148
Annual Abstract of Statistics, GE 124
Annual Basic Hobby Industry Trade Directory. *see* Craft, Model and Hobby Industry Annual Trade Directory, SS 373
Annual Bibliography of British and Irish History, SS 329
Annual Bibliography of English Language and Literature. *see* Modern Humanities Research Association. Annual Bibliography of English Language and Literature, HU 112
Annual Directory: Houses of Prayer, HU 251
Annual Editions: Readings in American Government, SS 288
Annual Editions: Readings in American History, Post-Civil War, SS 330
Annual Editions: Readings in American History, Pre-Civil War, SS 331
Annual Editions: Readings in Anthropology, SS 8
Annual Editions: Readings in Biology, SC 24
Annual Editions: Readings in Business, SS 57
Annual Editions: Readings in Criminal Justice, SS 229
Annual Editions: Readings in Early Childhood Education, ED 25
Annual Editions: Readings in Economics, SS 58
Annual Editions: Readings in Education, ED 2
Annual Editions: Readings in Health, SC 218
Annual Editions: Readings in Human Development, SC 25
Annual Editions: Readings in Marketing, SS 498
Annual Editions: Readings in Marriage and Family, SS 639
Annual Editions: Readings in Microeconomics, SS 59
Annual Editions: Readings in Personality and Adjustment, SC 321
Annual Editions: Readings in Psychology, SC 322
Annual Editions: Readings in Social Problems, SS 640
Annual Editions: Readings in Social Psychology, SS 641
Annual Editions: Readings in Sociology, SS 642
Annual Editions: Readings in Unexplored Deviance, SS 643
Annual Editions: Readings in Urban Society, SS 644
Annual Editions: Readings on Aging, SS 645
Annual Guide to Undergraduate Study. *see* Peterson's Annual Guide to Undergraduate Study, ED 51
Annual Guides to Graduate Study. *see* Peterson's Annual Guides to Graduate Study, ED 52
Annual Handbook for Group Facilitators, SS 619
Annual Index to Popular Music Record Reviews, HU 179
Annual Institute on Patent Law. Lectures, SS 533
Annual International Congress Calendar, GE 93
Annual Legal Bibliography, SS 448
Annual of Advertising and Editorial Art. *see* Annual of Advertising, Editorial, and Television Art and Design with the Annual Copy Awards, HU 24
Annual of Advertising, Editorial, and Television Art and Design. *see* Annual of Advertising, Editorial, and Television Art and Design with the Annual Copy Awards, HU 24
Annual of Advertising, Editorial, and Television Art and Design with the Annual Copy Awards, HU 24
The Annual of American Illustrations. *see* Illustrators, HU 42
Annual of Articles on Antiques. *see* The Antique Trader Weekly. Annual of Articles on Antiques, SS 364
Annual of Power and Conflict, SS 547
Annual Progress in Child Psychiatry and Child Development, SC 323
Annual Register of Grant Support, GE 94
The Annual Register. World Events in (year), GE 2
Annual Report of the Register of Copyrights. *see* U.S. Copyright Office. Annual Report of the Register of Copyrights, SS 538
Annual Review of Anthropology, SS 9
Annual Review of Astronomy and Astrophysics, SC 18
Annual Review of Behavior Therapy; Theory and Practice, SC 324
Annual Review of Biochemistry, SC 26
Annual Review of Earth and Planetary Sciences, SC 68
Annual Review of Ecology and Systematics, SC 69
Annual Review of Energy, SC 96
Annual Review of Entomology, SC 27
Annual Review of Fluid Mechanics, SC 163
Annual Review of Genetics, SC 28
Annual Review of Information Science and Technology, HU 150
Annual Review of Microbiology, SC 29
Annual Review of Nuclear Science, SC 97
Annual Review of Physical Chemistry, SC 51
Annual Review of Physiology, SC 30
Annual Review of Plant Physiology, SC 31
Annual Review of Population Law, SS 449
Annual Review of Psychology, SC 325
Annual Review of Sociology, SS 646
Annual Review of the Schizophrenic Syndrome, SC 326
Annual Review of United Nations Affairs, SS 548
Annual Reviews of Biophysics and Bioengineering, SC 32
Annual Survey of African Law, SS 450

Annual Survey of American Law, SS 451

Annuaire Canadien de Droit International. *see* Canadian Yearbook of International Law; Annuaire Canadien de Droit International, SS 454

Annuaire Demographique. *see* Demographic Yearbook; Annuaire Demographique, GE 125

Annuaire des Organizations Internationales. *see* Yearbook of International Organizations; Annuaire des Organizations Internationales, GE 112

Annuaire du Canada. *see* Canada Yearbook; Annuaire du Canada, SS 335

Annuaire Statistique pour l'Afrique. *see* African Statistical Yearbook; Annuaire Statistique pour l'Afrique, GE 122

Annuaire Statistique pour l'Asie et le Pacifique. *see* Statistical Yearbook for Asia and the Pacific; Annuaire Statistique pour l'Asie et le Pacifique, GE 133

Annuale Mediaevale, HU 4

Antarctic Bibliography, SC 70

Antiquarian Bookman. AB Bookman's Yearbook. *see* AB Bookman's Yearbook, SS 148

The Antique Trader Weekly. Annual of Articles on Antiques, SS 364

Antiques and Their Prices, SS 365

The Antiques Yearbook. *see* International Art and Antiques Yearbook, SS 379

Anuario Interamericano de Investigacion Musical. *see* Yearbook for Inter-American Musical Research; Anuario Interamericano de Investigacion Musical, HU 213

Applied Science and Technology Index, SC 4

Archaeological Institute of America. Annual Meeting Paper Abstracts, SS 10

Archaeological Institute of America. Bulletin, SS 11

Archaeological Institute of America. Fieldwork Opportunities Bulletin. *see* Fieldwork Opportunities Bulletin, SS 16

Archaeological Society of New Jersey. Bulletin, SS 12

Archaeological Society of North Carolina. Southern Indian Studies. *see* Southern Indian Studies, SS 27

Archaeological Survey Annual Report, SS 13

Archaeology of Eastern North America, SS 14

Archery-Fencing Guide. *see* Archery-Golf Guide, SS 686

Archery-Golf Guide, SS 686

Architectural History, HU 25

Architectural Schools in North America, HU 26

Archives of Asian Art, HU 27

Arena, Auditorium, Stadium Guide. *see* AudArena Stadium Guide and International Directory, SS 60

Argosy Boating Annual, SS 687

Argosy Fishing Annual, SS 688

Argosy Hockey Yearbook, SS 689

Argosy Hunting Annual, SS 690

Aristotelian Society for the Systematic Study of Philosophy. Proceedings, HU 216

Arizona State University. Music Department. International Percussion Reference Library. Catalogue. *see* International Percussion Reference Library. Catalogue, HU 196

Armenian Church of America. Directory of the Armenian Church in North America and Church Calendar. *see* Directory of the Armenian Church in North America and Church Calendar, HU 277

Arms Control and Disarmament Agency. Annual Report. *see* U.S. Arms Control and Disarmament Agency. Annual Report to Congress, SC 291

Ars Orientalis, HU 28

Art and Crafts Market, HU 29

Art at Auction: The Year at Sotheby's and Parke-Bernet, HU 30

Art Design Photo, HU 31

Art Directors Annual of Advertising Art. *see* Annual of Advertising, Editorial, and Television Art and Design with the Annual Copy Awards, HU 24

Art Galleries Year Book. *see* Libraries, Museums, and Art Galleries Year Book, HU 46

Art Index, HU 32

Art/Kunst, HU 33

Art Prices Current, HU 34

Artist's and Photographer's Market. *see* Art and Crafts Market, HU 29

Artist's Market. *see* Art and Crafts Market, HU 29

Artists/USA, HU 35

The Arts of Islam and the East. *see* Ars Orientalis, HU 28

Assembling, SS 152

Associated General Contractors of America. Directory, SC 40

Associated Press Almanac. *see* Hammond Almanac of a Million Facts, GE 10

Association for Asian Studies. Bibliography of Asian Studies. *see* Bibliography of Asian Studies, SS 333

Association for Childhood Education International. Bibliography: Books for Children. *see* Bibliography: Books for Children, Ge 29

Association for Computing Machinery. Annual Workshop on Microprogramming. Conference Record, SC 60

Association for Computing Machinery. Proceedings of the National Conference, SC 61

Association for Computing Machinery. Winter Simulation Conference. Proceedings. *see* Winter Simulation Conference. Proceedings, SC 66

Association for Intercollegiate Athletics for Women. AIAW Directory, SS 691

Association for Intercollegiate Athletics for Women. AIAW Handbook of Policies and Operating Procedures, SS 692

Association for Programmed Learning and Educational Technology. Yearbook. *see* International Yearbook of Educational and Instructional Technology, ED 76

Association for Research in Nervous and Mental Disease. Research Publications, SC 327

Association for Systems Management. Ideas for Management. Proceedings of the Annual Conference. *see* Ideas for Management. Proceedings of the Annual Conference, SS 495

Association for the Study of Religion. Measuring Mormonism. *see* Measuring Mormonism, HU 298

Association of American Law Schools. Pre-Law Handbook. *see* Pre-Law Handbook, SS 475

Association of American Library Schools. Directory, HU 151

Association of American Medical Colleges. AAMC Directory of American Medical Education, SC 219

Association of American Medical Colleges. Medical School Admission Requirements, U.S.A. and Canada. *see* Medical School Admission Requirements, U.S.A. and Canada, SC 249

Association of American Railroads. Yearbook of Railroad Facts. *see* Yearbook of Railroad Facts, SS 899

Association of Collegiate Schools of Architecture. Architectural Schools in North America. *see* Architectural Schools in North America, HU 26

Association of Commonwealth Universities. Commonwealth Universities Yearbook. *see* Commonwealth Universities Yearbook, ED 40

Association of Consulting Chemists and Chemical Engineers. Consulting Services, SC 132

Association of Research Libraries. ARL Statistics, HU 152

Association of Theological Schools. Directory. *see* Association of Theological Schools in the United States and Canada. Bulletin, HU 252

Association of Theological Schools. Fact Book on Theological Education. *see* Fact Book on Theological Education, HU 281

Association of Theological Schools in the United States and Canada. Bulletin, HU 252

AudArena Stadium Guide and International Directory, SS 60

Audio-Visual Equipment Directory, ED 60

Audiovisual Market Place (AVMP), SS 153

Augustana Annual Yearbook. *see* Lutheran Church in America. Yearbook, HU 296

Augustinian Studies, HU 66

Author Biographies Master Index, HU 88

Authors and Writers Who's Who. *see* International Authors and Writers Who's Who, HU 107

Automobile Association. AA Budget Guide to Europe, SS 902

Automobile Association. AA Guide to Camping and Caravanning, SS 903

Automobile Association. AA Guide to Camping and Caravanning on the Continent, SS 904

Automobile Association. AA Guide to Continental Motoring, SS 905

Automobile Association. AA Guide to Guesthouses, Farmhouses, and Inns, SS 906

Automobile Association. AA Guide to Holiday Houses, Cottages, and Chalets, SS 907

Automobile Association. AA Guide to Hotels and Restaurants in Great Britain and Ireland, SS 908

Automobile Association. AA Guide to Stately Homes, Museums, Castles and Gardens, SS 909

Automobile Facts and Figures. *see* MVMA Motor Vehicle Facts and Figures, SS 870

Avery Architectural Library. Avery Index to Architectural Periodicals. Supplement. *see* Avery Index to Architectural Periodicals. Supplement, HU 36

Avery Index to Architectural Periodicals. Supplement, HU 36

Awards, Honors, and Prizes, GE 95

Ayer Directory of Newspapers, Magazines, and Trade Publications. *see* Ayer Directory of Publications, SS 154

Ayer Directory of Publications, SS 154

BMAA Directory and Handbook. *see* Baptist Missionary Association of America. BMAA Directory and Handbook, HU 254

BOCA Basic Housing-Property Maintenance Code. *see* Building Officials and Code Administrators International. BOCA Basic Housing-Property Maintenance Code, SS 398

BOCA Basic Mechanical Code. *see* Building Officials and Code Administrators International. BOCA Basic Mechanical Code, SS 399

BOCA Basic Plumbing Code. *see* Building Officials and Code Administrators International. BOCA Basic Plumbing Code, SS 400

BPR Annual Cumulation. *see* American Book Publishing Record. Annual Cumulation, GE 22

Bank Administration Institute. Biennial Survey of Bank Office Salaries, SS 487

Bank Administration Institute. Biennial Survey of Bank Personnel Policies and Practices, SS 488

The Bankers Blue Book. see Rand McNally International Bankers Directory, SS 50
Baptist Federation of Canada. Proceedings; Minutes Report, HU 253
Baptist Handbook. see The Baptist Union Directory, HU 255
Baptist Missionary Association of America. BMAA Directory and Handbook, HU 254
Baptist News Service. Directory and Handbook. see Baptist Missionary Association of America. BMAA Directory and Handbook, HU 254
The Baptist Union Directory, HU 255
Barron's Guide to the Two-year Colleges, ED 98
Barron's Handbook of American College Financial Aid, ED 34
Barron's Handbook of College Transfer Information, ED 36
Barron's Profiles of American Colleges, ED 35
Baseball Blue Book, SS 693
Baseball Dope Book. see Official Baseball Dope Book, SS 783
Baseball Guidebook, SS 694
Baseball Illustrated, SS 695
Baseball Record Book, SS 696
Baseball Rule Book. see Baseball Rules, SS 697
Baseball Rules, SS 697
Basebook, SS 61
Basic Facts About the United Nations, SS 549
Basketball Case Book, SS 698
Basketball Guide, SS 699
Basketball Guide. see Basketball-Volleyball Tips and Techniques, SS 703
Basketball Handbook, SS 700
Basketball Rules, SS 701
Basketball Rules—Simplified and Illustrated, SS 702
Basketball-Volleyball Tips and Techniques, SS 703
Bass Master Fishing Annual, SS 704
Baxter's Eurailpass Travel Guide, SS 910
Baxter's USA Bus Travel Guide, SS 911
Baxter's USA Rail Pass Guide, SS 912
Baxter's USA Train Travel Guide. see Baxter's USA Rail Pass Guide, SS 912
Bazak Guide to Israel, SS 913
Bazak Guide to Italy, SS 914
Bazak Guide to Portugal, SS 915
Bazak Guide to Spain, SS 916
Benefit-Cost and Policy Analysis, SS 62
Berkeley Journal of Sociology: Critical Review, SS 647
Best American Short Stories, HU 89
Best Books for Children, GE 23
Best Editorial Cartoons of the Year, SS 155
Best in Covers, SS 156
Best Plays of (year), HU 333
Best Poems of (year), HU 90
Best Short Plays, HU 334
Best Short Stories. see Best American Short Stories, HU 89
Best Sports Stories, SS 705
Best's Environmental Control and Safety Directory. see Best's Safety Directory; Safety—Industrial Hygiene—Security, SS 489
Best's Safety Directory; Safety—Industrial Hygiene—Security, SS 489
Best's Safety Maintenance Directory. see Best's Safety Directory; Safety—Industrial Hygiene—Security, SS 489
Better Homes and Gardens Christmas Ideas, SS 389
Better Homes and Gardens Garden Ideas and Outdoor Living, SC 154
Better Homes and Gardens Travel Ideas, SS 917
Bibliographia Musicologica; Bibliography of Music Literature, HU 180
Bibliographic Annual In Speech Communication, HU 91
Bibliographic Guide to Art and Architecture, HU 37
Bibliographic Guide to Black Studies, GE 24
Bibliographic Guide to Business and Economics, SS 63
Bibliographic Guide to Conference Publications, GE 25
Bibliographic Guide to Dance, HU 80
Bibliographic Guide to Government Publications—Foreign, GE 26
Bibliographic Guide to Government Publications—U.S., GE 27
Bibliographic Guide to Law, SS 452
Bibliographic Guide to Music, HU 181
Bibliographic Guide to North American History, SS 332
Bibliographic Guide to Psychology, SC 328
Bibliographic Guide to Technology, SC 5
Bibliographic Guide to Theatre Arts, HU 335
Bibliographic Index, GE 28
Bibliographie Cartographique Internationale, SC 147
Bibliographie Geographique Internationale, SC 148
Bibliographie Linguistique; Linguistic Bibliography, HU 92
Bibliography: Books for Children, GE 29
Bibliography and Index of Geology, SC 71
Bibliography and Index of Geology Exclusive of North America. see Bibliography and Index of Geology, SC 71
Bibliography and Index of North American Geology. see Bibliography and Index of Geology, SC 71
Bibliography of Appraisal Literature, SS 64
Bibliography of Asian Studies, SS 333
Bibliography of Bioethics, SC 220

AUTHOR-TITLE INDEX/423

Bibliography of Boiotian Studies. see Teiresias, HU 75
Bibliography of Corporate Responsibility for Social Problems; Programs and Politics, SS 65
Bibliography of Economics of Containerization. see Containerization: A Bibliography, SS 854
Bibliography of Music Literature. see Bibliographia Musicologica; Bibliography of Music Literature, HU 180
Bibliography of Old Norse-Icelandic Studies, SS 334
Bibliography of Publications of University Bureaus of Business and Economic Research, SS 66
Bibliography of Society, Ethics, and the Life Sciences, HU 217
Bibliography of the History of Medicine, SC 221
Bibliography on Smoking and Health, SC 222
Biennial Review of Anthropology. see Annual Review of Anthropology, SS 9
Big Ten Records Book, SS 706
Billboard International Buyer's Guide of the Music-Record Industry, HU 182
Billboard International Directory of Recording Equipment and Studio Directory, HU 183
Billboard's Carnival and Circus Booking Guide. see Carnival and Circus Booking Guide, SS 70
Biographical Dictionaries Master List, GE 62
A Biographical Directory of Clergymen of the American Lutheran Church, HU 256
Biographical Directory of Librarians in the United States and Canada, HU 153
Biographical Directory of Negro Ministers, HU 257
Biography Index, GE 63
Biological and Agricultural Index, SC 33
Biosis List of Serials, SC 34
Bituminous Coal Facts. see Coal Facts, SC 296
Black Photographer's Annual, HU 233
Black Review, SS 262
Black's Medical Dictionary, SC 223
Blue Book: Leaders of the English-Speaking World, GE 64
Blue Book of College Athletics, SS 707
Blue Book of Junior College Athletics, SS 708
The Blue Book of Occupational Education. see College Blue Book, ED 37
Blue Book of U.S. Coins. see Handbook of United States Coins, with Premium List, SS 378
Blum, Daniel. Theatre World. see Theatre World, HU 351
Boat Owner's Buyers Guide, SS 851
Boating Industry Association. BIA Certification Handbook, SS 852
Bob Wallack's Hunter's Guns, SS 709
Bob Zwirz' Fishing Annual, SS 710
Bob Zwirz' Fishing Guide, SS 711

Book Auction Records, SS 157
Book Guide to Music. see Bibliographic Guide to Music, HU 181
The Book of Baseball Records, SS 712
The Book of the States, SS 289
Book Review Digest, GE 84
Book Review Index, GE 85
Bookman's Price Index, SS 158
Books for Children. see Bibliography: Books for Children, GE 29
Books for Secondary School Libraries, ED 61
Books for the Teen Age, GE 30
Books In Print, GE 31
Books in Series in the United States, GE 32
Borestone Mountain Poetry Awards. see Best Poems of (year), HU 90
Boston College. Studies in Philosophy, HU 218
Bow and Arrow Magazine's Bowhunter's Annual, SS 713
Bowker Annual of Library and Book Trade Information, SS 160
Bowling-Fencing Guide, SS 714
Boy's Gymnastics Rules, SS 715
Braddock's Federal-State-Local Government Directory, SS 290
Bradford's Directory of Marketing Research Agencies and Management Consultants in the United States and the World, SS 499
Bradford's Survey and Directory of Marketing Research Agencies in the U.S. and the World. see Bradford's Directory of Marketing Research Agencies and Management Consultants in the United States and the World, SS 499
Brassey's Annual: The Armed Forces Yearbook. see Royal United Services Institute and Brassey's Defence Yearbook, SC 288
Brassey's Defence Yearbook. see Royal United Services Institute and Brassey's Defence Yearbook, SC 288
Bricker's International Directory of University-Sponsored Executive Development Programs, SS 490
Britain: An Official Handbook. see Great Britain. Central Office of Information. Britain: An Official Handbook, SS 342
Britain's Heritage Guide to Stately Homes, Castles, and Gardens. see Automobile Association. AA Guide to Stately Homes, Museums, Castles, and Gardens, SS 909
Britannica Book of the Year, GE 3
Britannica Yearbook of Science and the Future. see Yearbook of Science and the Future, SC 13
British Academy, London. Proceedings, HU 5
The British Antiques Yearbook, SS 366

British Books in Print, GE 33
British Columbia Provincial Museum. Syesis. see Syesis, SS 28
British Humanities Index, HU 6
British Journal of Photographic Almanac. see British Journal of Photography Annual, HU 234
British Journal of Photography Annual, HU 234
British Librarianship and Information Science, HU 154
British Library Year Book. see Libraries, Museums, and Art Galleries Year Book, HU 46
British Music Yearbook, HU 184
British Numismatic Journal and Proceedings of the British Numismatic Society, SS 367
British Numismatic Society. British Numismatic Journal and Proceedings of the British Numismatic Society. see British Numismatic Journal and Proceedings of the British Numismatic Society, SS 367
The British School of Archaeology in Jerusalem. Levant. see Levant: Journal of the British School of Archaeology in Jerusalem, SS 21
British Yearbook of International Law, SS 453
Broadcast Information Bureau. Series, Serials, and Packages. see Series, Serials, and Packages, SS 203
Broadcast Information Bureau. TV Feature Film Source Book. see TV Feature Film Source Book, SS 204
Broadcast Yearbook—Marketbook Issue. see Broadcasting Yearbook, SS 162
Broadcasting Cable Sourcebook, SS 161
Broadcasting Yearbook, SS 162
Broadman Comments: On the International Bible Lessons for Christian Teaching, Convention Uniform Series, HU 258
Brookings Institution. Annual Report, SS 1
Brookings Institution. Setting National Priorities: The (year) Budget. see Setting National Priorities: The (year) Budget, SS 586
Brown's Directory of North American Gas Companies, SC 98
Budget Guide to Europe. see Automobile Association. AA Budget Guide to Europe, SS 902
Building Estimator's Reference Book, SC 41
Building Officials and Code Administrators International. BOCA Basic Housing-Property Maintenance Code, SS 398
Building Officials and Code Administrators International. BOCA Basic Mechanical Code, SS 399
Building Officials and Code Administrators International. BOCA Basic Plumbing Code, SS 400
Bulletin of Research in Music Education. see Pennsylvania Music Educators Association. Bulletin of Research in Music Education, HU 206
Bureau of the Census Catalog. see U.S. Bureau of the Census. Bureau of the Census Catalog, GE 60
Burns Mantle Best Plays. see Best Plays of (year), HU 333
Business Books and Serials in Print, SS 67
Business Books in Print. see Business Books and Serials in Print, SS 67
Business Periodicals Index, SS 68
Business Statistics, SS 69
Buyer's Guide to the World of Tape, HU 185
Buying and Selling United States Coins, SS 368
Byzantine and Modern Greek Studies, HU 67

CATV Buyer's Guide. see CATV Systems Directory, Map Service, and Handbook, SS 163
CATV Systems Directory, Map Service, and Handbook, SS 163
CBI. see Cumulative Book Index, GE 38
CBS News Almanac. see Hammond Almanac of a Million Facts, GE 10
CIS/Annual. see Congressional Information Service. CIS/Annual, SS 293
CRC Handbook of Biochemistry and Molecular Biology. see Handbook of Biochemistry and Molecular Biology, SC 37
CRC Handbook of Chemistry and Physics. see Handbook of Chemistry and Physics, SC 54
CRC Handbook of Laboratory Safety, SC 52
CRC Handbook of Tables for Mathematics. see Handbook of Tables for Mathematics, SC 203
CRC Standard Mathematical Tables. see Chemical Rubber Company. CRC Standard Mathematical Tables, SC 201
Calendar of Annual Events. see Chases' Calendar of Annual Events, GE 4
Calendar of Festivals, SS 279
Calendar of Folk Festivals and Related Events. see Calendar of Festivals, SS 279
California Studies in Classical Antiquity, HU 68
Camping and Caravanning France, SS 918
Camping and Caravanning Handbook. see Automobile Association. AA Guide to Camping and Caravanning, SS 903
Canada Yearbook: Annuaire du Canada, SS 335
Canadian Almanac and Directory, SS 336
Canadian Annual Review of Politics and Public Affairs, SS 550
Canadian Baptist Overseas Mission Board. Church Overseas. see Church Overseas, HU 267
Canadian Essay and Literature Index, GE 116
Canadian Football League. Official Record and Information Manual, SS 716

Canadian Index to Periodicals and Documentary Films. *see* Canadian Periodical Index, GE 117

Canadian Periodical Index; Index de Periodiques Canadiens, GE 117

Canadian Society for the Study of Religion. Proceedings; Société Canadienne pour l'Etude de la Religion. Actes, HU 259

Canadian Yearbook of International Law; Annuaire Canadien de Droit International, SS 454

Capital Punishment. *see* U.S. National Criminal Justice Information and Statistics Service. Capital Punishment, SS 253

Career and Vocational School Guide. *see* Lovejoy's Career and Vocational School Guide, ED 101

Carnegie Corporation of New York. Annual Report, HU 7

Carnival and Circus Booking Guide, SS 70

Cases Decided in the United States Court of Customs and Patent Appeals; Customs Cases Adjudged in the Court of Customs and Patent Appeals, SS 455

Cassell's Directory of Publishing in Great Britain, the Commonwealth, Ireland, South Africa, and Pakistan, SS 164

Catalog of Federal Assistance Programs, ED 3

Catalog of Federal Domestic Assistance. *see* Catalog of Federal Assistance Programs, ED 3

Catalog of Modern World Coins. *see* Current Coins of the World, SS 375

Catalogue: An Index to Indian Legal Materials and Resources in the National Indian Law Library, SS 456

Catholic Almanac, HU 260

Catholic Periodical and Literature Index, HU 261

Catholic Periodical Index. *see* Catholic Periodical and Literature Index, HU 261

Catholic Press Directory, SS 165

Catholic Telephone Guide, HU 262

Catholic Theological Society of America. Proceedings, HU 263

Cavalcade and Directory of Acts and Attractions, HU 336

Cavalcade and Directory of Fairs. *see* Directory of North American Fairs and Expositions, SS 79

Celebrate!, SS 390

Center for Bioethics. Bibliography of Bioethics. *see* Bibliography of Bioethics, SC 220

Center for California Public Affairs. Environmental Protection Directory. *see* Environmental Protection Directory, SC 104

Center for Gerontological Studies. Southern Conference on Gerontology. *see* Southern Conference on Gerontology, SC 259

Center for Intercultural Studies in Folklore and Oral History. Folklore Annual. *see* Folklore Annual, SS 280

Center for Medieval and Renaissance Studies. Comitatus. *see* Comitatus, HU 219

Center for Philosophic Exchange. Annual Proceedings. *see* Philosophic Exchange, HU 228

Central Conference of American Rabbis. Yearbook, HU 264

Chamber of Commerce of the United States of America. Employee Benefits, SS 419

Chamber of Commerce of the United States of America. Fringe Benefits. *see* Chamber of Commerce of the United States of America. Employee Benefits, SS 419

Charter Flight Directory, SS 919

Chases' Calendar of Annual Events, GE 4

Chemical Rubber Company. CRC Standard Mathematical Tables, SC 201

Chemical Society, London. Annual Reports on the Progress of Chemistry. *see* Reports on the Progress of Chemistry, SC 58-59

Chicorel Abstracts to Reading and Learning Disabilities Periodicals, ED 92

Chicorel Index to Mental Health Book Reviews, SC 329

Child Welfare League of America. Directory of Member Agencies and Associates, SS 620

Children's Book Review Index, GE 86

Children's Books; Awards and Prizes, GE 34

Children's Books for Schools and Libraries. *see* Children's Books in Print, GE 35

Children's Books in Print, GE 35

Children's Catalog, GE 36

Children's Literature: A Guide to Reference Sources. Supplement, GE 37

Children's Literature Review, HU 93

Children's Media Market Place, SS 166

Children's Record and Tape Guide. *see* Schwann Children's Record and Tape Guide, HU 210

Chilton's Auto Repair Manual, SS 853

Chinese Art Society of America. Archives. *see* Archives of Asian Art, HU 27

Christian Annual. *see* United Church of Christ. Yearbook, HU 322

Christian Church. Yearbook and Directory, HU 265

Christian Periodicals Index, HU 266

Church of Jesus Christ of Latter Day Saints. Deseret News Church Almanac. *see* Deseret News Church Almanac, HU 274

Church of Jesus Christ of Latter Day Saints. Index to Mormonism in Periodical Literature. *see* Index to Mormonism in Periodical Literature, HU 288

Church Overseas, HU 267

The Church Pulpit Year Book, HU 268
The Classical Association. Proceedings, HU 69
Clements' Encyclopedia of World Governments, SS 291
Clerical Directory of the Protestant Episcopal Church, HU 269
Clinic on Library Applications of Data Processing. Proceedings. *see* University of Illinois at Urbana-Champaign. Clinic on Library Applications of Data Processing. Proceedings, HU 170
Coal Facts, SC 296
Coal Mine Directory. *see* Keystone Coal Industry Manual, SC 301
Coin Collectors' Handbook, SS 369
Coin World Almanac, SS 370
Collected Studies in Criminological Research, SS 230
Cold Spring Harbor Symposia on Quantitative Biology, SC 35
College Blue Book, ED 37
College Blue Book: Occupational Education. *see* College Blue Book, ED 37
College Entrance Examination Board. Advanced Placement Course Descriptions. *see* Advanced Placement Course Descriptions, ED 24
College Entrance Examination Board. College Handbook. *see* College Handbook, ED 38
College Guide. *see* Lovejoy's College Guide, ED 49
College Handbook, ED 38
College Placement Annual, SS 523
College Placement Council. Directory of College Placement Offices. *see* Directory of College Placement Offices, SS 525
The College Planning Search Book, ED 39
College Theology Society. Proceedings, HU 270
Colleges and Universities. *see* Education Directory, ED 8
Collegiate Summer Employment Guide, SS 524
Collier's Yearbook, GE 5
Columbia University. Avery Architectural Library. Avery Index to Architectural Periodicals. Supplement. *see* Avery Index to Architectural Periodicals. Supplement, HU 36
Comic Book Price Guide, SS 371
Comitatus; A Journal of Medieval and Renaissance Studies, HU 219
Commodity Research Bureau. Commodity Year Book. *see* Commodity Year Book, SS 71
Commodity Year Book, SS 71
Commonwealth Universities Yearbook, ED 40
Communication Yearbook, SS 167
Comparative Guide to American Colleges for Students, Parents, and Counselors, ED 41

Comparative Guide to Two-year Colleges and Career Programs, ED 99
Comparative Judical Review. *see* Comparative Juridical Review, SS 457
Comparative Juridical Review, SS 457
Comparative Survey of Freedom. *see* Freedom in the World, SS 139
Complete Handbook of Pro Hockey, SS 717
Composium Directory of New Music, HU 186
Comprehensive Crime Control Plan. *see* New York State Division of Criminal Justice Services. Comprehensive Crime Control Plan, SS 242
Compton Yearbook, GE 6
Computer Personnel Research Conference. Proceedings, SC 62
Computer Yearbook, SC 63
Computer Yearbook and Directory. *see* Computer Yearbook, SC 63
Computers in Chemical and Biochemical Research, SC 64
Concrete Industries Yearbook, SC 42
The Condensed Chemical Dictionary, SC 53
The Conference Board. Cumulative Index, SS 72
Conference on Application of X-Ray Analysis. Proceedings. *see* Advances in X-Ray Analysis, SC 208
Conference on Laser Engineering and Applications. Digest, SC 133
Confessions in Dialogue, HU 271
Congress and the Nation: A Review of Government and Politics, SS 551
Congressional Directory, SS 292
Congressional Information Service. CIS/Annual, SS 293
Congressional Quarterly Almanac, SS 552
Congressional Roll Call, SS 553
Congressional Staff Directory, SS 294
Congregational Christian Churches. Yearbook. *see* United Church of Christ. Yearbook, HU 322
Congregational Yearbook. *see* United Church of Christ. Yearbook, HU 322
Connecticut Health Services Research Series, SC 224
Conservative Congregational Christian Conference. Annual Report, HU 272
Conservation Directory, SC 99
Consort; Journal of the Dolmetsch Foundation, HU 187
Consultation on Church Union. Digest, HU 273
Consumer Bulletin Annual. *see* Consumers' Research Magazine Handbook of Buying, SS 224
Consumer Complaint Guide, SS 219
Consumer Guide, SS 220
Consumer Protection Guide, SS 221
Consumer Reports Buying Guide, SS 222

Consumers Index to Product Evaluations and Information Sources, SS 223
Consumers' Research Magazine Handbook of Buying, SS 224
Consumers Union Reports. see Consumer Reports Buying Guide, SS 222
Containerization: A Bibliography, SS 854
Contemporary Authors, HU 94
Contemporary Crafts Market Place, SS 372
Contemporary Literary Criticism, HU 95
Continuing Education, ED 19
Continuing Education Resource Guide, ED 20
Contributions to Music Education, HU 188
Convention of American Instructors of the Deaf. Proceedings, ED 93
Copyright Laws and Treaties of the World. Supplements, SS 534
Cord Sportsfacts Fisherman Annual, SS 718
Cord Sportfacts Fishing Report, SS 719
Cord Sportfacts Guns Guide, SS 720
Cord Sportfacts Hockey Guide, SS 721
Cord Sportfacts Hunting, SS 722
Corning Museum of Glass. Journal of Glass Studies. see Journal of Glass Studies, HU 45
Corporate Counsel's Annual, SS 458
Corpus Almanac of Canada, SS 337
Corpus Canadian Almanac. see Corpus Almanac of Canada, SS 337
Council of Graduate Schools. Graduate Programs and Admissions Manual. see Graduate Programs and Admissions Manual, ED 45
Council of Jewish Federations and Welfare Funds. Jewish Social Service Year Book. see Jewish Social Service Year Book, SS 629
The Council of State Governments. The Book of the States. see The Book of the States, SS 289
The Council of State Governments. Suggested State Legislation, SS 295
Council of the Baptist Union of Great Britain and Ireland. Baptist Union Directory. see The Baptist Union Directory, HU 255
Countries of the World and Their Leaders, SS 296
Council on International Educational Exchange. Whole World Handbook. see Whole World Handbook, ED 57
Council on Library Resources. Report, HU 155
Council on Social Work Education. Schools of Social Work with Accredited Master's Programs. see Schools of Social Work with Accredited Master's Programs, SS 631
Country Vacations U.S.A., SS 920
County and City Data Book, SS 297
The County Year Book, SS 298

Craft, Model and Hobby Industry Annual Trade Directory, SS 373
Crafts Annual, SS 374
Creative Camera International Year Book, HU 235
Creative Christmas Ideas from Better Homes and Gardens. see Better Homes and Gardens Christmas Ideas, SS 389
The Credit Diary and Manual of Commercial Laws. see Credit Manual of Commercial Laws, SS 35
The Credit Man's Diary. see Credit Manual of Commercial Laws, SS 35
Credit Manual of Commercial Laws, SS 35
The Credit Manual of Commercial Laws with Diary. see Credit Manual of Commercial Laws, SS 35
Credit Union National Association. Credit Union Yearbook. see Credit Union Yearbook, SS 36
Credit Union Yearbook, SS 36
Crime and Justice, SS 231
Crime in the U.S. see U.S. Federal Bureau of Investigation. Uniform Crime Reports for the United States, SS 248
Criminal Justice Periodical Index, SS 232
Criminal Victimization in the United States. see U.S. National Criminal Justice Information and Statistics Service. Criminal Victimization in the United States: A Comparison of (year) and (year) Findings, SS 254
Croation Academy of America. Journal of Croation Studies. see Journal of Croation Studies, SS 271
Cumulated Abridged Index Medicus, SC 225
Cumulated Index Medicus, SC 226
Cumulative Book Index, GE 38
Current Biography Yearbook, GE 65
Current Book Review Citations, GE 87
Current British Directories, GE 96
Current Coins of the World, SS 375
Current Diagnosis and Treatment. see Current Medical Diagnosis and Treatment, SC 227
Current List of Medical Literature and Quarterly Cumulative Index Medicus. see Cumulated Index Medicus, SC 226
Current Medical Diagnosis and Treatment, SC 227
Current Psychiatric Therapies, SC 330
Current Research in British Studies by American and Canadian Scholars, HU 8
Current Research in British Studies by North American Scholars. see Current Research in British Studies by American and Canadian Scholars, HU 8
Current Therapy, SC 228
Current Trends in Linguistics, HU 96
Curriculum Information Center. School Universe Data Book. see School Universe Data Book, ED 31
Custom House Guide, SS 73

Customs Practices of Notaries Public and Digest of Notary Laws in the U.S., SS 459
Cycle Buyers Guide, SS 855
Cycle Tests, SS 856
Cycle World Road Test Annual and Buyer's Guide, SS 857

Daiwa Fishing Annual, SS 723
Dana's Manual of Mineralogy, SC 297
Dance Directory, HU 81
Dance Magazine Annual, HU 82
Dance World, HU 83
Danish Yearbook of Philosophy, HU 220
Data Processing Yearbook. see Computer Yearbook, SC 63
Daughters of the American Colonists Lineage Book, SS 283
Davison's Textile Blue Book, SC 164
Davison's Textile Catalog and Buyers Guide, SC 165
Decisions of the United States Courts Involving Copyrights, SS 535
Decorative Art and Modern Interiors, SS 391
Decorative Art in Modern Interiors. see Decorative Art and Modern Interiors, SS 391
Defense and Foreign Affairs Handbook, SC 285
Demographic Yearbook; Annuaire Demographique, GE 125
Deseret News Church Almanac, HU 274
Developments in Industrial Microbiology, SC 36
Dickens Studies Annual, HU 97
Dictionary of International Biography, GE 66
Dictionary of Labour Biography, SS 420
Diesel and Gas Turbine World Wide Catalog, SC 166
Digest of Educational Statistics, ED 4
Digest of Legal Activities of International Organizations and Other Institutions, SS 460
Direction of Trade, SS 74
Directors Guild of America. Directory of Members, HU 337
Directory and Guide to the Mutual Savings Banks of the United States, SS 37
Directory for Exceptional Children, ED 94
Directory for Reaching Minority Groups, SS 621
Directory: Juvenile and Adult Correctional Departments, Institutions and Agencies and Paroling Authorities of the United States and Canada, SS 233
Directory of Acts and Attractions. see Cavalcade and Directory of Acts and Attractions, HU 336
Directory of Agencies Serving the Visually Handicapped in the U.S., SS 622
Directory of American Fiction Writers, HU 98

Directory of American Firms Operating in Foreign Countries, SS 75
Directory of American Philosophers, HU 221
Directory of American Poets, HU 99
Directory of American Savings and Loan Associations, SS 38
Directory of American Scholars, ED 5
Directory of Approved Allied Medical Educational Programs. see Allied Medical Education Directory, SC 210
Directory of Approved Counseling Agencies. see Directory of Counseling Services, SS 623
Directory of Associations in Canada; Repertoir des Associations du Canada, GE 97
Directory of British Associations and Associations in Ireland, GE 98
Directory of Camps for the Handicapped. see The Easter Seal Directory of Resident Camps for Persons with Special Health Needs, SC 237
Directory of Campus Ministry, HU 275
Directory of College Placement Offices, SS 525
Directory of Consumer Protection and Environmental Agencies. see Environmental Protection Directory, SC 104
Directory of Corporate Affiliation of Major National Advertisers. see Directory of Corporate Affiliations, SS 500
Directory of Corporate Affiliations, SS 500
Directory of Correctional Institutions and Agencies of the United States of America. see Directory: Juvenile and Adult Correctional Departments, Institutions and Agencies and Paroling Authorities of the United States and Canada, SS 233
Directory of Counseling Services, SS 623
Directory of Engineering College Research and Graduate Study. see Engineering College Research and Graduate Study, SC 134
Directory of European Associations, GE 99
Directory of Executive Recruiters, SS 491
Directory of Facilities for Mentally Ill Children in the United States. see U.S. Facilities and Programs for Children with Severe Mental Illnesses; A Directory, SC 268
Directory of Federal Statistical Agencies. see Federal Statistical Directory, GE 126
Directory of Franchising Organizations, SS 76
Directory of Government Agencies Safeguarding Consumer and Environment, SS 225
Directory of Government Document Collections and Librarians, HU 156
Directory of Historical Societies and Agencies in the United States and Canada, SS 338
Directory of Hotel and Motel Systems, SS 77

Directory of Law Libraries, SS 461
Directory of Law Teachers, SS 462
Directory of Lawyer Referral Services and Committees, SS 463
Directory of Library Science Libraries. *see* American Library Association. Directory of Library Science Libraries, HU 146
Directory of Little Magazines and Small Presses. *see* The International Directory of Little Magazines and Small Presses, SS 185
Directory of Lutheran Churches in Canada, HU 276
Directory of Marine Scientists in the United States, SC 193
Directory of Marketing Research Houses and Services. *see* International Directory of Marketing Research Houses and Services, SS 507
Directory of Medical Specialists, SC 229
Directory of Municipal Management Assistants, SS 492
Directory of Music Faculties in American Colleges and Universities. *see* Directory of Music Faculties in Colleges and Universities U.S. and Canada, HU 189
Directory of Music Faculties in Colleges and Universities U.S. and Canada, HU 189
Directory of National and International Labor Unions in the United States. *see* Directory of National Unions and Employee Associations, SS 421
Directory of National Unions and Employee Associations, SS 421
Directory of New England Manufacturers, SS 78
Directory of New Music. *see* Composium Directory of New Music, HU 186
Directory of North American Fairs and Expositions, SS 79
Directory of North American Gas Companies. *see* Brown's Directory of North American Gas Companies, SC 98
Directory of Oceanographers in the United States. *see* Directory of Marine Scientists in the United States, SC 193
Directory of On-Going Research in Smoking and Health, SC 230
Directory of Organizations and Individuals Professionally Engaged in Governmental Research and Related Activities, GE 100
Directory of Organizations and Personnel in Educational Management, ED 6
Directory of Organizations and Personnel in Educational Administration. *see* Directory of Organizations and Personnel in Educational Management, ED 6
Directory of Organizations Concerned with Environmental Research. *see* World Directory of Environmental Research Centers, SC 118
Directory of Osteopathic Physicians. *see* Yearbook and Directory of Osteopathic Physicians, SC 275
Directory of Osteopathic Specialists, SC 231
The Directory of Overseas Summer Jobs, SS 526
Directory of Poison Control Centers, SC 232
Directory of Post Offices with ZIP Codes. *see* United States Postal Service. Directory of Post Offices with ZIP Codes, SS 208
Directory of Postsecondary Schools with Occupational Programs, ED 100
Directory of Predominately Black Colleges and Universities in the United States of America, ED 42
Directory of Professional Photography, HU 236
Directory of Research Grants, GE 101
Directory of Services for the Deaf in the United States. *see* Programs and Services for the Deaf in the United States, SC 258
Directory of Shipowners, Shipbuilders, and Marine Engineers, SS 858
Directory of Significant 20th Century Minority Women in the U.S.A., GE 67
Directory of Special Libraries and Information Centers, HU 157
Directory of State Agencies Concerned with Land Pollution Control, SC 100
Directory of Texas Manufacturers, SS 80
Directory of the Armenian Church in North America and Church Calendar, HU 277
Directory of the College Student Press in America, SS 168
Directory of U.S. Institutions of Higher Education. *see* Education Directory, ED 8
Directory of Women Physicians in the U.S., SC 233
Directory of Women Writing, HU 100
Disarmament Yearbook. *see* The United Nations Disarmament Yearbook, SC 290
Disciples of Christ. Yearbook and Directory. *see* Christian Church. Yearbook and Directory, HU 265
Dixie Gun Works Mussleloaders' Annual, SS 724
Documents on American Foreign Relations. *see* American Foreign Relations: A Documentary Record, SS 545
Dodge Construction Systems Costs, SC 43
Dod's Parliamentary Companion, SS 300
Dollar Wise Guide to California and Las Vegas, SS 921
Dollar Wise Guide to England, SS 922
Dollar Wise Guide to France, SS 923
Dollar Wise Guide to Japan and Hong Kong, SS 924
Dollars and Cents of Shopping Centers, SS 501

Dolmetsch Foundation. Journal. *see* Consort: Journal of the Dolmetsch Foundation, HU 187
The Dow Jones Investor's Handbook, SS 39
Dow Jones-Irwin Business Almanac, SS 81
Downtown Mall Annual and Urban Design Report, SS 401
Downtown Malls. *see* Downtown Mall Annual and Urban Design Report, SS 401
Drug Abuse Bibliography, SC 234
Drugs in Current Use and New Drugs, SC 235
Drugs of Choice, SC 236
Dun and Bradstreet. Exporters Encyclopedia World Market Guide. *see* Exporters Encyclopedia World Market Guide, SS 88
Dun and Bradstreet. Principal International Businesses. *see* Principal International Businesses, SS 515
Dun and Bradstreet International Market Guide; Continental Europe, SS 502
Dun and Bradstreet Middle Market Directory, SS 503
Dun and Bradstreet Million Dollar Directory, SS 504
Dun and Bradstreet Reference Book of Corporate Managements, SS 493

EEM (Electronic Engineers Master), SC 77
E/MJ International Directory of Mining and Mineral Processing Operations. *see* Engineering and Mining Journal. E/MJ International Directory of Mining and Mineral Processing Operations, SC 298
ENR Directory of Contractors. *see* Engineering News Record. ENR Directory of Contractors, SC 44
ENR Directory of Design Firms. *see* Engineering News Record. ENR Directory of Design Firms, SC 136
E-R-C Directory; Employee Relocation Real Estate Services, SS 608
ERIC Clearinghouse on Educational Management. Directory of Organizations and Personnel in Educational Management. *see* Directory of Organizations and Personnel in Educational Management, ED 6
ERIC Educational Documents Index, ED 7
The Easter Seal Directory of Resident Camps for Persons with Special Health Needs, SC 237
Eastern Hemisphere Petroleum Directory, SC 101
Eastern Manufacturers and Industrial Classified Directory and Buyers Guide, ED 82
Eastern States Archaeological Federation. Archaeology of Eastern North America. *see* Archaeology of Eastern North America, SS 14
Eastern States Archaeological Federation. Bulletin, SS 15

Economic and Social Progress in Latin America. Annual Report, SS 83
Economic Commission for Europe. Economic Survey of Europe. *see* Economic Survey of Europe, SS 84
Economic Commission for Latin America. Economic Survey of Latin America. *see* Economic Survey of Latin America, SS 85
Economic Survey of Europe, SS 84
Economic Survey of Latin America, SS 85
Economics: Encyclopedia, SS 86
Ecumenical Directory of Retreat and Conference Centers, HU 278
Edison Electric Institute. Statistical Year Book of the Electrical Utility Industry, SC 78
Edison Electric Institute. Electric Vehicle Council. International Electric Vehicle Symposium. Proceedings. *see* International Electric Vehicle Symposium Proceedings, SC 87
Editor and Publisher International Yearbook, SS 169
Editor and Publisher Market Guide, SS 170
Editor and Publisher Yearbook. *see* Editor and Publisher International Yearbook, SS 169
Educating the Disadvantaged, ED 95
Educational Associations. *see* Education Directory, ED 8
Education Directory, ED 8
Education Index, ED 9
Educational Media Yearbook, ED 62
Educational Press Association of America. America's Educational Press. *see* America's Educational Press, ED 1
Educational Testing Service. Graduate and Professional School Opportunities for Minority Students. *see* Graduate and Professional School Opportunities for Minority Students, ED 44
Educational Testing Service. Graduate Programs and Admissions Manual. *see* Graduate Programs and Admissions Manual, ED 45
Educators Guide to Free Audio and Video Materials, ED 63
Educators Guide to Free Films, ED 64
Educators Guide to Free Filmstrips, ED 65
Educators Guide to Free Guidance Materials, ED 66
Educators Guide to Free Health, Physical Education, and Recreation Materials, ED 67
Educators Guide to Free Science Materials, ED 68
Educators Guide to Free Social Studies Materials, ED 69
Educators Guide to Free Tapes, Scripts, and Transcriptions, ED 70
Educators Guide to Free Teaching Aids, ED 71
Educators Progress Service. Educators Guides. *see* Educators Guides, ED 63-71

Educators Progress Service. Elementary Teachers Guide to Free Curriculum Materials. *see* Elementary Teachers Guide to Free Curriculum Materials, ED 73

Egon Ronay's Dunlop Guide: Hotels, Restaurants and Inns in Great Britain and Ireland, SS 925

Election Index, SS 554

Electrical World Directory of Electric Utilities, SC 79

Electronic Components Conference. Proceedings, SC 80

Electronic Design's Gold Book, SC 81

Electronic Engineers Master. *see* EEM (Electronic Engineers Master), SC 77

Electronic Industries Association. Electronic Market Data Book. *see* Electronic Market Data Book, SC 83

Electronic Industries Association. Frequency Control Symposium. Proceedings. *see* Frequency Control Symposium. Proceedings, SC 86

Electronic Industries Yearbook. *see* Electronic Market Data Book, SC 83

Electronic Industry Telephone Directory, SC 82

Electronic Market Data Book, SC 83

Electronic News Financial Factbook and Directory, SC 84

Electronic Source Procurement. *see* Who's Who in Electronics, SC 92

Electronics Buyers' Guide, SC 85

Elementary and Secondary Schools. *see* Education Directory, ED 8

El-Hi Textbooks in Print, ED 72

Elementary Teachers Guide to Free Curriculum Materials, ED 73

Empirical Research in Theatre, HU 338

Employee Relocation Council. Employee Relocation Real Estate Services. *see* E-R-C Directory: Employee Relocation Real Estate Services, SS 608

Employment and Earnings Statistics for the United States. *see* Employment and Earnings: United States, SS 422

Employment and Earnings: United States, SS 422

Encore, HU 339

Encyclopaedia Britannica. *see* Britannica Book of the Year, GE 3

Encyclopaedia Britannica. Medical and Health Annual. *see* Medical and Health Annual SC 246

Encyclopedia Buying Guide, SS 226

Encyclopedia of Associations, GE 102

Encyclopedia of Business Information Sources, SS 87

An Encyclopedia of Chemicals and Drugs. *see* The Merck Index: An Encyclopedia of Chemicals and Drugs, SC 250

The Encyclopedia of Europe. *see* Europa Year Book, SS 555

The Encyclopedia of Football, SS 725

Encyclopedia of Government Officials: Federal and State. *see* Taylor's Encyclopedia of Government Officials: Federal and State, SS 312

Encyclopedia of Social Work, SS 624

Encyclopedia of World Governments. *see* Clements' Encyclopedia of World Governments, SS 291

Energy Index, SC 102

Engineering and Mining Journal. E/MJ International Directory of Mining and Mineral Processing Operations, SC 298

Engineering College Research and Graduate Study, SC 134

Engineering Index Annual, SC 135

Engineering Manpower Commission. Professional Income of Engineers. *see* Engineers Joint Council. Engineering Manpower Commission. Professional Income of Engineers, SC 140

Engineering Manpower Commission. Prospects of Engineering and Technology Graduates. *see* Engineers Joint Council. Engineering Manpower Commission. Prospects of Engineering and Technology Graduates, SC 141

Engineering Manpower Commission. Roster of Women and Minority Engineering and Technology Students. *see* Engineers Joint Council. Engineering Manpower Commission. Roster of Women and Minority Engineering and Technology Students, SC 142

Engineering Manpower Commission. Salaries of Engineering Technicians and Technologists. *see* Engineers Joint Council. Engineering Manpower Commission. Salaries of Engineering Technicians and Technologists, SC 143

Engineering News Record. ENR Directory of Contractors, SC 44

Engineering News Record. ENR Directory of Design Firms, SC 136

Engineers' Council for Professional Development. Annual Report, SC 137

Engineers Joint Council. Directory of Engineering Societies and Related Organizations, SC 138

Engineers Joint Council. Directory of Engineering Society Management, SC 139

Engineers Joint Council. Engineering Manpower Commission. Professional Income of Engineers, SC 140

Engineers Joint Council. Engineering Manpower Commission. Prospects of Engineering and Technology Graduates, SC 141

Engineers Joint Council. Engineering Manpower

Commission. Roster of Women and Minority Engineering and Technology Students, SC 142
Engineers Joint Council. Engineering Manpower Commission. Salaries of Engineering Technicians and Technologists, SC 143
English Studies. *see* Essays and Studies, HU 101
Environment Index, SC 103
Environment Information Center. Energy Index. *see* Energy Index, SC 102
Environment Information Center. Environment Index. *see* Environment Index, SC 103
Environment Law Review, SS 465
Environmental Protection Directory, SC 104
Ephemeris of the Sun, Polaris, and other Selected Stars, SC 19
Episcopal Church Annual, HU 279
Episcopal Church Calendar, HU 280
Episcopal Church Lesson Calendar. *see* Episcopal Church Calendar, HU 280
Equal Employment Opportunity Report. *see* U.S. Equal Employment Opportunity Commission. Equal Employment Opportunity Report, SS 437
Essay and General Literature Index, GE 118
Essays and Studies, HU 101
Essays by Divers Hands, HU 102
Ethnic Studies Bibliography, SS 263
Eurail Guide: How to Travel Europe by Train, SS 926
Eurailpass Travel Guide. *see* Baxter's Eurailpass Travel Guide, SS 910
Europa Year Book, SS 555
Europe on $10 a Day, SS 927
European Literary Market Place. *see* International Literary Market Place, SS 187
Executives' Guide to Information Sources. *see* Encyclopedia of Business Information Sources, SS 87
Exporters' Encyclopedia World Marketing Guide, SS 88

Face the Nation, SS 339
Fact Book on Theological Education, HU 281
Facts About Nursing, SC 238
Facts and Figures on Government Finance, SS 581
Facts on File Yearbook, GE 7
Fairchild's Financial Manual of Retail Stores, SS 494
Family Circle Great Ideas Christmas Helps, SS 392
Famous Literary Prizes and Their Winners. *see* Literary and Library Prizes, HU 110
The Far East and Australasia, SS 340
The Far East and Southwest Pacific, SS 341
Farm and Ranch Vacation Guide. *see* Country Vacations U.S.A., SS 920

Farm, Ranch and Countryside Guide. *see* Country Vacations U.S.A., SS 920
Fawcett's Hunting Journal, SS 726
Feature Films on 8mm and 16mm, SS 180
The Feature Writer and Syndicate Directory. *see* Working Press of the Nation, v. 4, SS 212
Federal Council Year Book. *see* Directory of American and Canadian Churches, HU 330
Federal Election Commission. Annual Report, SS 301
Federal Employees Almanac, SS 302
Federal Statistical Directory, GE 126
Federal Tax Handbook, SS 582
Federal Tax Regulations, SS 583
Female Artists Past and Present, HU 38
Fiction Catalog, HU 103
Field and Stream Bass Fishing Annual, SS 727
Field and Stream Fishing Annual, SS 728
Field and Stream Hunting Annual, SS 729
Field Hockey-LaCrosse Guide, SS 730
Field Hockey Rules: Boys and Girls, SS 731
Fielding's Guide to the Caribbean Plus the Bahamas, SS 928
Fielding's Low-Cost Europe, SS 929
Fielding's Selected Favorites: Hotels and Inns, Europe, SS 930
Fielding's Selective Shopping Guide to Europe, SS 931
Fielding's Super Economy Europe. *see* Fielding's Low-Cost Europe, SS 929
Fielding's Travel Guide to Europe, SS 932
Fieldwork Opportunities Bulletin, SS 16
Film Literature Index, HU 171
Film Review Digest Annual, HU 172
Films: The Visualization of Anthropology, SS 17
Finance Facts Yearbook, SS 40
Financial Aids for Higher Education, ED 43
Financial Assistance for Library Education, HU 158
Financial Characteristics by Indicators of Housing and Neighborhood Quality. *see* U.S. Bureau of the Census. Annual Housing Survey, SS 410
Financial Characteristics for the Housing Inventory. *see* U.S. Bureau of the Census. Annual Housing Survey, SS 407
Fine Arts Marketplace, HU 39
Finnish Americana, SS 264
Fishery and Wildlife Annual Report. *see* U.S. Fish and Wildlife Service. Cooperative Research Units. Fishery and Wildlife Annual Report, SC 116
Fishing Guidebook, SS 732
Fishing World Annual, SS 733
Fitzgerald/Hemingway Annual, HU 104
Five Years' Work in Librarianship. *see* British Librarianship and Information Science, HU 154
Focus on Dance, HU 84

Fodor's Austria, SS 933
Fodor's Belgium and Luxembourg, SS 934
Fodor's Caribbean, Bahamas, and Bermuda, SS 935
Fodor's Cruises Everywhere, SS 936
Fodor's Czechoslovakia, SS 937
Fodor's Europe, SS 938
Fodor's France, SS 939
Fodor's Germany; East and West, SS 940
Fodor's Great Britain, SS 941
Fodor's Greece, SS 942
Fodor's Guide to Japan and East Asia. see Fodor's Japan and Korea, SS 950; Fodor's South-East Asia, SS 957
Fodor's Hawaii, SS 943
Fodor's Holland, SS 944
Fodor's Hungary, SS 945
Fodor's India, SS 946
Fodor's Ireland, SS 947
Fodor's Israel, SS 948
Fodor's Italy, SS 949
Fodor's Japan and Korea, SS 950
Fodor's London: A Companion Guide, SS 951
Fodor's Mexico, SS 952
Fodor's Morocco, SS 953
Fodor's Portugal, SS 954
Fodor's Scandinavia, SS 955
Fodor's South America, SS 956
Fodor's South-East Asia, SS 957
Fodor's Soviet Union, SS 958
Fodor's Spain, SS 959
Fodor's Switzerland, SS 960
Fodor's Tunisia, SS 961
Fodor's Turkey, SS 962
Fodor's USA, SS 963
Fodor's Yugoslavia, SS 964
Folklore Annual, SS 280
Food and Agriculture Organization of the United Nations. Production Yearbook, SS 89
Food and Agriculture Organization of the United Nations. Trade Yearbook, SS 90
Food Co-Op Directory, SS 227
Football Action, SS 734
Football Case Book, SS 735
Football Handbook (Includes Flag Football), SS 736
Football Register, SS 737
Ford Foundation. Annual Report, HU 9
Foreign Commerce and Navigation in the United States. see U.S. Bureau of the Census. Foreign Commerce and Navigation in the United States, SS 125
Foreign Medical School Catalogue, SC 239
Foreign Trade Marketplace, SS 91
Forest Resource Reports. see U.S. Forest Service. Forest Resource Reports, SC 73
Fortune Double 500 Directory, SS 92
Foundation Directory, GE 103
Foundation Grants Index, GE 104
Franciscan Studies, HU 222
Franklin Mint. Limited Editions, SS 376
Franklin Mint. Numismatic Issues. see Franklin Mint. Limited Editions, SS 376
Freedom in the World: Political Rights and Civil Liberties, SS 139
Freer Gallery of Art. Ars Orientalis. see Ars Orientalis, HU 28
French VII Bibliography. see French XX Bibliography, HU 105
French XX Bibliography, HU 105
Frequency Control Symposium. Proceedings, SC 86
Friends Directory. see Friends World Conference Committee. American Section. Friends Directory, HU 282
Friends World Committee for Consultation. World Conference of Friends. see World Conference of Friends, HU 328
Friends World Conference Committee. American Section. Friends Directory, HU 282
Funspot Directory, SS 965

GRA Directory. see Directory of Organizations and Individuals Professionally Engaged in Governmental Research and Related Activities, GE 100
Galpin Society Journal, HU 190
Game Plan College Basketball, SS 738
Game Plan Pro Basketball, SS 739
Garden Ideas and Outdoor Living. see Better Homes and Gardens Garden Ideas and Outdoor Living, SC 154
Garuda, HU 283
Gebbie House Magazine Directory. see Working Press of the Nation, v. 5, SS 212
Gebbie Press All-in-One Directory, SS 181
Gemmologists Compendium. see Gems: Their Sources, Descriptions, and Identification, SC 299
Gems: Their Sources, Descriptions, and Identification, SC 299
Genealogical Periodical Annual Index, SS 284
General Association of Regular Baptist Churches. Yearbook, HU 284
The General Convention of the Protestant Episcopal Church. Journal. see Journal of the General Convention of the Protestant Episcopal Church, HU 294

General Housing Characteristics. *see* U.S. Bureau of the Census. Annual Housing Survey, SS 405
General Science Index, SC 6
Geo Abstracts. Annual Index, SC 149
Geographical Abstracts: Annual Index. *see* Geo Abstracts: Annual Index, SC 149
The Geological Society of America. Bibliography and Index of Geology. *see* Bibliography and Index of Geology, SC 71
Geothermal World Directory, SC 105
Giorgio Levi Della Vida Conference. Publications, HU 70
Girls Gymnastics Judging Manual, SS 740
Girls Gymnastics Manual. *see* Girls Gymnastics Judging Manual, SS 740
Girls Gymnastics Rules, SS 741
Glass Studies. *see* Journal of Glass Studies, HU 45
Global Automotive Market Survey and World Motor Census. *see* World Automotive Market, SS 895
Goal Post College Football, SS 742
Goal Post Pro Football, SS 743
Golf Digest Annual, SS 744
Golf Magazine Yearbook, SS 745
Golf Tips Annual, SS 746
Good Food Guide, SS 966
Good Old Days Christmas Annual, SS 281
Good Sam Club's Recreational Vehicle Owners Directory. *see* Trailer Life's Recreational Vehicle Campground and Services Directory, SS 1027
Government Reference Books, GE 39
Government Research Association. Directory of Organizations and Individuals Professionally Engaged in Governmental Research and Related Activities. *see* Directory of Organizations and Individuals Professionally Engaged in Governmental Research and Related Activities, GE 100
Graduate and Professional School Opportunities for Minority Students, ED 44
Graduate Professional Schools of Social Work in Canada and the U.S.A. *see* Schools of Social Work with Accredited Master's Programs, SS 631
Graduate Programs and Admissions Manual, ED 45
Graduate Record Examination Board. Graduate Programs and Admissions Manual. *see* Graduate Programs and Admissions Manual, ED 45
Graduate Study in Psychology, SC 331
Grant Data Quarterly. *see* Annual Register of Grant Support, GE 94
Grants Register, GE 105
Graphic Arts International Annual. *see* Penrose Graphic Arts International Annual, HU 55
Graphic Guide to Consumer Markets. *see* Guide to Consumer Markets, SS 505

Graphis Annual, HU 40
Graphis Posters, HU 41
Gratz College Annual of Jewish Studies, SS 265
Great Britain. Central Office of Information. Britain: An Official Handbook, SS 342
Great Britain. Central Statistics Office. Annual Abstract of Statistics. *see* Annual Abstract of Statistics, GE 124
Great Britain. Central Statistics Office. Guide to Official Statistics. *see* Guide to Official Statistics, GE 127
Great Ideas Today. *see* The Great Issues Today, GE 8
The Great Issues Today, GE 8
Greece and Yugoslavia on $5 and $10 a Day. *see* Greece on $10 a Day, SS 967
Greece on $10 a Day, SS 967
Greenwood's Guide to Great Lakes Shipping, SS 859
Greenwood's Library Year Book. *see* Libraries, Museums, and Art Galleries Year Book, HU 46
Gridiron News Pro Yearbook, SS 747
The Growth of World Industry. *see* Yearbook of Industrial Statistics, SS 136
Guggenheim Memorial Foundation. Reports of the President and the Treasurer. *see* John Simon Guggenheim Memorial Foundation. Reports of the President and the Treasurer, HU 12
Guía a las Reseñas de Libros de y sobre Hispanoamérica. *see* Guide to Reviews of Books from and about Hispanic America; Guía a las Reseñas de Libros de y sobre Hispanoamérica, GE 88
Guide Book of United States Coins, SS 377
A Guide for the College-Bound Student-Athlete, SS 748
Guide to American Directories, GE 106
Guide to American Educational Directories, ED 10
Guide to American Graduate Schools, ED 46
Guide to Camping and Caravanning. *see* Automobile Association. AA Guide to Camping and Caravanning, SS 903
Guide to Camping and Caravanning on the Continent. *see* Automobile Association. AA Guide to Camping and Caravanning on the Continent, SS 904
The Guide to Catholic Literature. *see* Catholic Periodical and Literature Index, HU 261
Guide to College Courses in Film and Television, SS 182
Guide to Consumer Markets, SS 505
Guide to Continental Motoring. *see* Automobile Association. AA Guide to Continental Motoring, SS 905
Guide to Correspondence Studies in Colleges and Universities. *see* Guide to Independent Study Through Correspondence Instruction, ED 21
Guide to Cross Country Skiing, SS 749

Guide to Free Audio and Video Materials. *see* Educators Guide to Free Audio and Video Materials, ED 63

Guide to Free Curriculum Materials. *see* Elementary Teachers Guide to Free Curriculum Materials, ED 73

Guide to Free Films. *see* Educators Guide to Free Films, ED 64

Guide to Free Filmstrips. *see* Educators Guide to Free Filmstrips, ED 65

Guide to Free Guidance Materials. *see* Educators Guide to Free Guidance Materials, ED 66

Guide to Free Health, Physical Education, and Recreation Materials. *see* Educators Guide to Free Health, Physical Education and Recreation Materials, ED 67

Guide to Free Science Materials. *see* Educators Guide to Free Science Materials, ED 68

Guide to Free Social Studies Materials. *see* Educators Guide to Free Social Studies Materials, ED 69

Guide to Free Tapes, Scripts, Transcriptions. *see* Educators Guide to Free Tapes, Scripts, Transcriptions, ED 70

Guide to Free Teaching Aids. *see* Educators Guide to Free Teaching Aids, ED 71

Guide to Graduate Departments of Sociology, SS 648

Guide to Graduate Study in Political Science, SS 556

Guide to Guesthouses, Farmhouses, and Inns. *see* Automobile Association. AA Guide to Guesthouses, Farmhouses, and Inns, SS 906

Guide to Holiday Houses, Cottages, and Chalets. *see* Automobile Association. AA Guide to Holiday Houses, Cottages, and Chalets, SS 907

Guide to Hotels and Restaurants in Great Britain and Ireland. *see* Automobile Association. AA Guide to Hotels and Restaurants in Great Britain and Ireland, SS 908

Guide to Independent Study through Correspondence Instruction, ED 21

Guide to Microforms in Print, GE 40

A Guide to Museum and Gallery Acquisitions in the U.S.A. and U.K. *see* On View, HU 54

Guide to Official Statistics, GE 127

Guide to Reference Books, GE 41

Guide to Reference Books for School Media Centers. Supplement, ED 74

Guide to Religious and Semi-religious Periodicals. *see* Guide to Social Science and Religion in Periodical Literature, HU 285

Guide to Reprints, GE 42

Guide to Reviews of Books from and about Hispanic America; Guía a las Reseñas de Libros de y sobre Hispanoamérica, GE 88

Guide to Self-Catering Holiday Accommodations. *see* Automobile Association. AA Guide to Holiday Houses, Cottages, and Chalets, SS 907

Guide to Social Science and Religion in Periodical Literature, HU 285

Guide to Stately Homes, Museums, Castles, and Gardens. *see* Automobile Association. AA Guide to Stately Homes, Museums, Castles, and Gardens, SS 909

A Guide to Study Abroad. *see* The New Guide to Study Abroad, ED 50

Guide to Summer Camps and Summer Schools, ED 26

Guide to the Health Care Field. *see* American Hospital Association. Guide to the Health Care Field, SC 212

Guide to the Two-Year Colleges. *see* Barron's Guide to the Two-Year Colleges, ED 98

Guide to Traveling on Business in 50 States. *see* American Executive Travel Companion, SS 901

Guides to Educational Media, ED 75

Guides to Newer Educational Media. *see* Guides to Educational Media, ED 75

Guinness Book of Olympic Records, SS 750

Guinness Book of Records. *see* Guinness Book of World Records, GE 9

Guinness Book of World Records, GE 9

Guinness Sports Record Book, SS 751

Gun Digest, SS 752

Gun Handbook Hunting Guide. *see* Hunting Guide, SS 760

Gun World Hunting Guide, SS 753

Guns and Ammo Annual, SS 754

Guns Annual Book of Handguns, SS 755

Guns Illustrated, SS 756

Gymnastics Guide, SS 757

Hammond Almanac of a Million Facts, GE 10

Handbook of American College Financial Aid. *see* Barron's Handbook of American College Financial Aid, ED 34

Handbook of Biochemistry and Molecular Biology, SC 37

Handbook of Chemistry and Physics, SC 54

Handbook of College Transfer Information. *see* Barron's Handbook of College Transfer Information, ED 36

Handbook of Denominations in the United States, HU 286

Handbook of Facts on Women Workers. *see* U.S. Women's Bureau. Handbook on Women Workers, SS 442

Handbook of Independent Advertising and Marketing Services, SS 506
Handbook of International Trade and Development Statistics, SS 93
Handbook of Labor Statistics. *see* U.S. Bureau of Labor Statistics. Handbook of Labor Statistics, SS 430
Handbook of Laboratory Safety. *see* CRC Handbook of Laboratory Safety, SC 52
Handbook of Latin American Studies, SS 343
Handbook of Mathematical Tables and Formulas, SC 202
Handbook of Nonprescription Drugs, SC 240
Handbook of Private Schools, ED 27
Handbook of Tables for Mathematics, SC 203
Handbook of the Churches. *see* Yearbook of American and Canadian Churches, HU 330
Handbook of United States Coins, with Premium Lists, SS 378
Handbook on International Study. *see* Handbook on International Study for U.S. Nationals, ED 47
Handbook on International Study for U.S. Nationals, ED 47
Handbook on Women Workers. *see* U.S. Women's Bureau. Handbook on Women Workers, SS 442
Hardy Year Book. *see* Thomas Hardy Year Book, HU 131
Harris Survey Yearbook of Public Opinion, SS 649
Harvard Studies in Classical Philology, HU 71
Harvard University. Department of Classics. Studies in Classical Philology. *see* Harvard Studies in Classical Philology, HU 71
Harvard University Seminar in Ukrainian Studies. Minutes, SS 266
Haviland, Virginia, ed. Children's Literature: A Guide to Reference Sources. Supplement. *see* Children's Literature: A Guide to Reference Sources, GE 37
Hawaii on $15 and $20 a Day, SS 968
The Health Care Directory, SC 241
Health Consequences of Smoking, SC 242
Health Insurance Institute. New Group Health Insurance. *see* New Group Health Insurance, SS 416
Health Insurance Institute. Source Book of Health Insurance Data. *see* Source Book of Health Insurance Data, SS 418
The Health Sciences Video Directory, SC 243
Hebrew Abstracts. *see* Hebrew Studies, HU 287
Hebrew Studies, HU 287
Hebrew Union College Annual, SS 267
Help; The Useful Almanac, SS 625
Herb Society of America. Herbarist. *see* Herbarist, SC 155
Herbarist, SC 155

Herdeg, Walter. Graphis Annual. *see* Graphis Annual, HU 40
Herdeg, Walter. Graphis Posters. *see* Graphis Posters, HU 41
Hereditary Register of the United States of America, SS 285
Herzl Year Book, SS 268
High Fidelity; Records in Review, HU 191
High Fidelity's Test Reports, HU 192
Historic Documents, SS 344
Historical Archaeology, SS 18
History as We Lived It. *see* The World in (year): History as We Lived It, GE 20
Hockey Register, SS 758
Horse and Rider All-Western Yearbook, SS 759
Hospital Statistics. *see* American Hospital Association. Hospital Statistics, SC 213
Hosteling Holidays, SS 969
Hotel and Motel Redbook, SS 94
Hotel-Motel Guide and Travel Atlas. *see* Leahy's Hotel-Motel Guide and Travel Atlas, SS 972
Hotel Redbook. *see* Hotel and Motel Redbook, SS 94
Hotel Sales Management Association. Official Hotel-Motel Directory and Facilities Guide. *see* Official Hotel-Motel Directory and Facilities Guide, SS 106
House and Garden Color Guide, SS 393
Houses of Prayer. *see* Annual Directory: Houses of Prayer, HU 251
Housing Characteristics of Recent Movers. *see* U.S. Bureau of the Census. Annual Housing Survey, SS 408
Hubbell's Legal Directory. *see* Martindale-Hubbell Law Directory, SS 474
Human Factors Society. Directory and Yearbook, SC 167
Human Factors Society. Proceedings of the Annual Meeting, SC 168
Human Rights Organizations and Periodicals Directory, SS 140
Humanidad, SS 626
Humanities Index, HU 10
Hunting Guide, SS 760

IMP Directory. *see* International Mimes and Pantomimists. IMP Directory, HU 340
ION National Marine Meeting. Proceedings. *see* Institute of Navigation. National Marine Navigation Meeting. Proceedings, SC 194
ISBN Publishers' Index. *see* Publishers' International Directory, SS 201

ISME Yearbook. *see* International Society for Music Education. ISME Yearbook, HU 197
Ice Rink Directory and Hockey Buyers Guide, SS 95
Ideas for Management. Proceedings of the Annual Conference, SS 495
Illustrators, HU 42
Imago MVNDI; The Journal of the International Society for the History of Cartography, SC 150
Index de Periodiques et Films Documentaire Canadiens. *see* Canadian Periodical Index, GE 117
Index Medicus, Cumulated. *see* Cumulated Index Medicus, SC 226
Index of American Periodical Verse, HU 106
Index to Book Reviews in Historical Periodicals, SS 345
Index to Book Reviews in the Humanities, HU 11
Index to Current Urban Documents, SS 303
Index to Educational Audio Tapes. *see* NICEM Index to Educational Audio Tapes, ED 77
Index to Educational Overhead Transparencies. *see* NICEM Index to Educational Overhead Transparencies, ED 78
Index to Educational Records. *see* NICEM Index to Educational Records, ED 79
Index to Educational Slides. *see* NICEM Index to Educational Slides, ED 80
Index to Educational Videotapes. *see* NICEM Index to Educational Videotapes, ED 81
Index to 8mm Motion Cartridges. *see* NICEM Index to 8mm Motion Cartridges, ED 82
Index to Environmental Studies—Multimedia. *see* NICEM Index to Environmental Studies—Multimedia, ED 83
Index to Health and Safety Education—Multimedia. *see* NICEM Index to Health and Safety Education—Multimedia, ED 84
Index to Legal Periodicals, SS 466
Index to Literature on the American Indian, SS 269
Index to Mormonism in Periodical Literature, HU 288
Index to Periodicals Related to Law, SS 467
Index to Periodiques Canadiens. *see* Canadian Periodical Index; Index de Periodiques Canadiens, GE 117
Index to Popular Music Record Reviews. *see* Annual Index to Popular Music Record Reviews, HU 179
Index to Producers and Distributors. *see* NICEM Index to Producers and Distributors, ED 85
Index to Psychology—Multimedia. *see* NICEM Index to Psychology—Multimedia, ED 86
Index to Record and Tape Reviews, HU 193
Index to Religious Periodical Literature, HU 289
Index to Short Stories. *see* Short Story Index, HU 126
Index to 16mm Educational Films. *see* NICEM Index to 16mm Educational Films, ED 87
Index to the Contemporary Scene, SS 183
Index to 35mm Educational Filmstrips. *see* NICEM Index to 35mm Educational Filmstrips, ED 88
Index to Vocational and Technical Education—Multimedia. *see* NICEM Index to Vocational and Technical Education—Multimedia, ED 89
Index Translationum, GE 43
Index to U.S. Government Periodicals, GE 119
Indian Historical Press. Index to Literature on the American Indian. *see* Index to Literature on the American Indian, SS 269
The Indianapolis 500 Yearbook, SS 761
Indicators of Housing and Neighborhood Quality. *see* U.S. Bureau of the Census. Annual Housing Survey, SS 406
Industrial Arts Index. *see* Applied Science and Technology Index, SC 4
Industrial Machinery and Equipment Pricing Guide, SC 169
Industrial Research Laboratories of the U.S., SC 7
Information Please Almanac, Atlas, and Yearbook, GE 11
Information Research Center for Mental Health and Family Hygiene. IRC Recommends. *see* A Selective Guide to Materials for Mental Health and Family Life Education, ED 91
Inland River Guide, SS 860
Institute for Life Insurance. Life Insurance Fact Book. *see* Life Insurance Fact Book, SS 415
Institute for Scientific Information. Social Sciences Citation Index. *see* Social Sciences Citation Index, SS 3
Institute for the Study of Conflict. Annual of Power and Conflict. *see* Annual of Power and Conflict, SS 547
Institute of Electrical and Electronics Engineers. Conference on Laser Engineering and Applications. Digest. *see* Conference on Laser Engineering and Applications. Digest, SC 133
Institute of Electrical and Electronics Engineers. Electronic Components Conference. Proceedings. *see* Electronic Components Conference. Proceedings, SC 80
Institute of Electrical and Electronics Engineers. Joint Automatic Control Conference. Record. *see* Joint Automatic Control Conference. Record, SC 172
Institute of Electrical and Electronics Engineers. Joint Power Generation Conference. Proceedings. *see* Joint Power Generation Conference. Proceedings, SC 88
Institute of Electrical and Electronics Engineers. Symposium on Reliability. *see* Reliability and Maintainability Symposium. Proceedings, SC 186

Institute of Environmental Sciences. Annual Meeting. Proceedings, SC 106
Institute of International Education. Handbook on International Study for U.S. Nationals. *see* Handbook on International Study for U.S. Nationals, ED 47
Institute of International Education. Summer Study Abroad. *see* Summer Study Abroad, ED 55
Institute of International Education. Teaching Abroad. *see* Teaching Abroad, SS 531
Institute of International Education. U.S. College Sponsored Programs Abroad: (academic year). *see* U.S. College Sponsored Programs Abroad: (academic year), ED 56
Institute of Jewish Studies. Bulletin, HU 290
Institute of Judicial Administration. Juvenile Justice Standards Project. Juvenile Law Litigation Directory. *see* Juvenile Law Litigation Directory, SS 469
Institute of Navigation. National Marine Navigation Meeting. Proceedings, SC 194
Institute of Society, Ethics, and the Life Sciences. Bibliography. *see* Bibliography of Society, Ethics, and the Life Sciences, HU 217
Institute of Surplus Dealers. Surplus Dealers Directory. *see* Surplus Dealers Directory, SS 517
Institute of Traffic Engineers. Membership Directory. *see* Institute of Transportation Engineers. Membership Directory, SS 861
Institute of Transportation Engineers. Membership Directory, SS 861
Instrument Society of America. Advances in Instrumentation. *see* Advances in Instrumentation, SC 159
Insurance Almanac, SS 414
Inter-American Development Bank. Economic and Social Progress in Latin America. Annual Report. *see* Economic and Social Progress in Latin America. Annual Report, SS 83
Interamerican Institute for Musical Research. Yearbook; Anuario. *see* Yearbook for Inter-American Musical Research; Anuario Interamericano de Investigacion Musical, HU 213
International Advisory Committee on Population and Law. Annual Review of Population Law. *see* Annual Review of Population Law, SS 449
International Annual of Advertising and Editorial Graphics. *see* Graphis Annual, HU 40
International Annual of Poster Art. *see* Graphis Posters, HU 41
The International Antiques Yearbook. *see* The British Antiques Yearbook, SS 366; International Art and Antiques Yearbook, SS 379
International Art and Antiques Yearbook, SS 379

International Association of Chiefs of Police. Law Enforcement and Criminal Justice Education Directory. *see* Law Enforcement and Criminal Justice Education Directory, SS 237
International Association of Chiefs of Polies. The Police Yearbook, SS 234
International Association of Chiefs of Police. Proceedings. *see* International Association of Chiefs of Police. The Police Yearbook, SS 234
International Association of Counseling Services. Directory of Counseling Services. *see* Directory of Counseling Services, SS 623
International Association of Universities. International Handbook of Universities and Other Institutions of Higher Education. *see* International Handbook of Universities and Other Institutions of Higher Education, ED 48
International Atomic Energy Agency. Directory of Nuclear Reactors, SC 107
International Auction Records, HU 43
International Authors and Writers Who's Who, HU 107
International Bankers Directory. *see* Rand McNally International Bankers Directory, SS 50
International Bibliography of Books and Articles on the Modern Languages and Literatures. *see* Modern Language Association of America. MLA International Bibliography of Books and Articles on the Modern Languages and Literatures, HU 114
International Bibliography of Directories; Internationals Bibliographie der Fachadressbuecher, GE 107
International Bibliography of Economics, SS 96
International Bibliography of Historical Sciences, SS 346
International Bibliography of Political Science, SS 557
International Bibliography of Research in Marriage and the Family. *see* Inventory of Marriage and Family Literature, SS 651
International Bibliography of Social and Cultural Anthropology, SS 19
International Bibliography of Sociology, SS 650
International Bibliography of the Social Sciences. *see* International Bibliography of Economics, SS 96; International Bibliography of Political Science, SS 557; International Bibliography of Social and Cultural Anthropology, SS 19; International Bibliography of Sociology, SS 650
International Book Trade Directory, SS 184
International Buyer's Guide of the Music-Record Industry. *see* Billboard International Buyer's Guide of the Music-Record Industry, HU 182
International Cable Address Directory. *see* Marconi's International Register, SS 191

International City Management Association. Directory of Municipal Management Assistants. see Directory of Municipal Management Assistants, SS 492

International City Management Association. The Municipal Year Book. see The Municipal Year Book, SS 305

International Coal, SC 300

International Committee on Linguistic Information. Current Trends in Linguistics. see Current Trends in Linguistics, HU 96

International Committee on Urgent Anthropological and Ethnological Research. Bulletin, SS 20

International Court of Justice. Yearbook, SS 468

International Credit Union. Yearbook. see Credit Union Yearbook, SS 36

The International Directory of Little Magazines and Small Presses, SS 185

International Directory of Marketing Research Houses and Services, SS 507

International Directory of Oceanographers. see Directory of Marine Scientists in the United States, SC 193

International Directory of Recording Equipment and Studio Directory. see Billboard International Directory of Recording Equipment and Studio Directory, HU 183

International Directory of the Performing Arts. see Musical America International Directory of the Performing Arts, HU 202

International Directory of University-Sponsored Executive Development Programs. see Bricker's International Directory of University-Sponsored Executive Development Programs, SS 490

International Electric Vehicle Symposium. Proceedings, SC 87

International Electronics Information Services. Computer Yearbook. see Computer Yearbook, SS 63

International Federation of Film Archives. International Index to Film Periodicals. see International Index to Film Periodicals, SS 186

International Film Guide, HU 173

International Foamed Plastic Markets and Directory. see United States Foamed Plastic Markets and Directory, SC 189

International Folk Music Council. Journal. see International Folk Music Council. Yearbook, HU 194

International Folk Music Council. Yearbook, HU 194

International Foundation for Telemetering. International Telemetering Conference. Proceedings. see International Telemetering Conference. Proceedings, SC 65

International Handbook of Universities and Other Institutions of Higher Education, ED 48

International Index to Film Periodicals, SS 186

International Index to Periodicals. see Humanities Index, HU 10; Social Sciences Index, SS 4

International Laborer Organization. Yearbook of Labour Statistics. see Yearbook of Labour Statistics, SS 443

International Literary Market Place, SS 187

International Market Guide; Continental Europe. see Dun and Bradstreet International Market Guide; Continental Europe, SS 502

International Mimes and Pantomimists. IMP Directory, HU 340

International Monetary Fund. Statistics Bureau. Direction of Trade. see Direction of Trade, SS 74

International Motion Picture Almanac, HU 174

International Music Educator. see International Society for Music Education. ISME Yearbook, HU 197

International Music Guide, HU 195

International Percussion Reference Library. Catalogue, HU 196

International Periodicals Directory. see Ulrich's International Periodicals Directory, GE 59

International Petroleum Annual, SC 108

International Publications, GE 44

International Rescue Committee. Annual Report, SS 627

International Review of Criminal Policy, SS 235

International Review of Research in Mental Retardation, SC 244

International Road Federation. World Survey of Current Research and Development on Roads and Road Transportation, SS 862

International Society for Music Education. ISME Yearbook, HU 197

International Society for the History of Cartography. Imago MVNDI; The Journal of the International Society for the History of Cartography. see Imago MVNDI; The Journal of the International Society for the History of Cartography, SC 150

International Solar Energy Society. American Section. Proceedings of the Annual Meeting, SC 109

The International Star Class Yacht Racing Association. Log of the Star Class: Official Rule Book. see Log of the Star Class: Official Rule Book, SS 869

International Studies in Philosophy, HU 223

International Symposium on Transport and Handling of Minerals. Minerals Transportation; Proceedings, SS 863

International Telemetering Conference. Proceedings, SC 65

International Television Almanac, SS 188

International Trade Statistics. *see* Yearbook of International Trade Statistics, SS 137
International Who's Who, GE 68
International Who's Who in Art and Antiques, HU 44
International Who's Who in Music and Musicians Directory, HU 198
International Who's Who in Poetry, HU 108
International Yearbook and Statesmen's Who's Who, SS 558
International Yearbook of Educational and Instructional Technology, ED 76
International Yearbook of Foreign Policy Analysis, SS 559
International Yearbook of Foreign Policy Studies, SS 560
International Yearbook of Sales. *see* International Auction Records, HU 43
International Yearbooks of Drug Addiction and Society, SS 236
Internationale Bibliographie der Fachadressbuecher. *see* International Bibliography of Directories; Internationale Bibliographie der Fachadressbuecher, GE 107
Inventory of Marriage and Family Literature, SS 651
Invest Your Summer. *see* Invest Yourself: Volunteer Service Opportunities, SS 628
Invest Yourself: Volunteer Service Opportunities, SS 628
Investment Companies, SS 41
Investment Companies and Their Securities. *see* Investment Companies, SS 41
Investment Company Institute. Mutual Fund Fact Book. *see* Mutual Fund Fact Book, SS 48
Involvement and Action: A Catalogue of Opportunities. *see* Invest Yourself: Volunteer Service Opportunities, SS 628
Ireland on $10 a Day, SS 970
Iron and Steel Society of AIME. Ironmaking Proceedings, SC 171
Iron and Steel Society of AIME. Membership Directory, SC 170
Irregular Serials and Annuals; An International Directory, GE 45
Ithacagun Hunting and Shooting Annual, SS 762
Ivory Hammer. *see* Art at Auction: The Year at Sotheby's and Parke-Bernet, HU 30

J.K. Lasser's Your Income Tax, SS 584
Jaeger and Waldmann World Telex Directory, SS 189
Jane's All the World's Aircraft, SS 864
Jane's Fighting Ships, SS 286
Jane's Freight Containers, SS 865

Jane's Major Companies of Europe, SS 97
Jane's Ocean Technology, SC 195
Jane's Surface Skimmers; Hovercraft and Hydrofoils, SS 866
Jane's Weapon Systems, SC 287
Jane's World Railways, SS 867
Japan Almanac, SS 347
Japan and Hong Kong on $10 a Day. *see* Dollar Wise Guide to Japan and Hong Kong, SS 924
Japan Economic Yearbook, SS 98
Japan on $10 a Day. *see* Dollar Wise Guide to Japan and Hong Kong, SS 924
Japan's 500 Leading Industrial Corporations. *see* President Directory, SS 110
Jednota Annual: Furdek, HU 291
Jednota: Katolicky Kalendar, HU 292
Jewish Book Annual, HU 109
Jewish Book Council. Jewish Book Annual. *see* Jewish Book Annual, HU 109
Jewish National Fund. Yearbook, SS 270
Jewish Organizations: A Worldwide Directory, GE 108
Jewish Social Service Year Book, SS 629
Jewish Travel Guide, SS 971
Joachimsthal Documentation. *see* Bibliographia Musicologica; Bibliography of Music Literature, HU 180
John Guggenheim Memorial Foundation. Reports of the President and the Treasurer, HU 12
Joint Automatic Control Conference. Record, SC 172
Joint Center for Political Studies. National Roster of Black Elected Officials. *see* National Roster of Black Elected Officials, SS 561
Joint Center for Political Studies. The State of Black Politics. *see* The State of Black Politics, SS 311
Joint Power Generation Conference. Proceedings, SC 88
A Journal for Players and Historians of Keyboard Instruments. *see* Organ Yearbook, HU 205
Journal of Behavioral Economics, SS 99
Journal of Croation Studies, SS 271
Journal of Glass Studies, HU 45
Journal of Hellenic Studies, HU 72
A Journal of Medieval and Renaissance Studies. *see* Comitatus, HU 219
Journal of Mexican American History, SS 272
Journal of Mormon History, HU 293
Journal of Renaissance and Baroque Music. *see* Musica Disciplina, HU 201
Journal of Roman Studies, HU 73
The Journal of the Ancient Near Eastern Society of Columbia University, HU 74
Journal of the British School of Archaeology in Jeru-

salem. *see* Levant: Journal of the British School of Archaeology in Jerusalem, SS 21
Journal of the Courtauld Institute. *see* Journal of the Warburg and Courtauld Institutes, HU 13
Journal of the Dolmetsch Foundation. *see* Consort: Journal of the Dolmetsch Foundation, HU 187
Journal of the General Convention of the Protestant Episcopal Church, HU 294
The Journal of the International Society for the History of Cartography. *see* Imago MVNDI: The Journal of the International Society for the History of Cartography, SC 150
Journal of the Philosophy of Sport, SS 763
Journal of the Warburg and Courtauld Institutes, HU 13
Journal of the Warburg Institute. *see* Journal of the Warburg and Courtauld Institutes, HU 13
Junior High School Library Catalog, GE 46
Juvenile and Adult Correctional Departments, Institutions and Agencies and Paroling Authorities of the United States and Canada. *see* Directory: Juvenile and Adult Correctional Departments, Institutions and Agencies and Paroling Authorities of the United States and Canada, SS 233
Juvenile Law Litigation Directory, SS 469

Katolicky Kalendar. *see* Jednota: Katolicky Kalendar, HU 292
Katz, William. Magazines for Libraries. *see* Magazines for Libraries, GE 49
Kelly's Manufacturers' and Merchants' Directory, SS 100
Keystone Coal Industry Manual, SC 301
The Killers and Cripplers, SC 245
Klein, Bernard. Guide to American Directories. *see* Guide to American Directories, GE 106
The Kovels' Complete Antiques Price List, SS 380

LIST: Library and Information Services Today, HU 159
LOMA; Literature on Modern Art. *see* Art Design Photo, HU 31
Labor Relations Yearbook, SS 423
Lake Erie Environmental Studies (LEES) Program. World Directory of Environmental Research Centers. *see* World Directory of Environmental Research Centers, SC 118
Land Use Planning Abstracts, SC 110
Lange's Handbook of Chemistry, SC 55
Large Type Books in Print, GE 47
Lasser's Your Income Tax. *see* J. K. Lasser's Your Income Tax, SS 584
Latin America (Stryker-Post), SS 348
Latin America (Facts on File), SS 349
Law Enforcement and Criminal Justice Education Directory, SS 237
Law Enforcement Desk Reference and Police Official Diary, SS 238
Law Enforcement Education Directory. *see* Law Enforcement and Criminal Justice Education Directory, SS 237
Law Libraries in the United States and Canada. *see* Directory of Law Libraries, SS 461
Lawyer's Desk Reference (LDR), SS 470
Lawyers Directory, SS 471
Leaders in Education, ED 11
Leaders of the English-Speaking World. *see* Blue Book: Leaders of the English-Speaking World, GE 64
Leahy's Hotel-Motel Guide and Travel Atlas, SS 972
Legal Aid Review, SS 472
Legal Medicine Almanac, SS 473
Let's Go: The Student Guide to Europe, SS 973
Let's Go: The Student Guide to the United States and Canada, SS 974
Let's Halt Awhile in Great Britain and Ireland, SS 975
Levant: Journal of the British School of Archaeology in Jerusalem, SS 21
Librarian's Guide. *see* Libraries, Museums, and Art Galleries Year Book, HU 46
Libraries, Museums, and Art Galleries Year Book, HU 46
Library and Information Services Today. *see* LIST: Library and Information Services Today, HU 159
Library Journal Book Review, GE 89
Library Lit: The Best of (year), HU 160
Library Networks, HU 161
Library of Congress Publications in Print, GE 48
Library Statistics of Colleges and Universities, HU 162
Life Insurance Fact Book, SS 415
Lilly Digest. *see* National Association of Chain Drug Stores. NACDS Lilly Digest, SS 512
Lilly Endowment, Inc. Report, HU 14
Linguistic Bibliography. *see* Bibliographie Linguistique; Linguistic Bibliography, HU 92
Literary and Library Prizes, HU 110
Literary Market Place, SS 190
Literary Prizes and Their Winners. *see* Literary and Library Prizes, HU 110
Little League Baseball Inc. Handbook With Rules and Regulations, SS 764
Little League Baseball Inc. Official Rules. *see* Little

League Baseball Inc. Handbook With Rules and Regulations, SS 764
Little Red Book of Baseball. *see* The Book of Baseball Records, SS 712
Lloyd's Register of American Yachts, SS 868
The Locke Newsletter, HU 224
Log of the Star Class; Official Rule Book, SS 869
Looking for Employment in Foreign Countries Reference Handbook, SS 527
Lovejoy's Career and Vocational School Guide, ED 101
Lovejoy's College Guide, ED 49
Lovejoy's Prep School Guide, ED 28
Lutheran Annual. *see* Lutheran Church—Missouri Synod. Lutheran Annual, HU 297
Lutheran Church in America. Minutes of Biennial Convention, HU 295
Lutheran Church in America. Yearbook, HU 296
Lutheran Church—Missouri Synod. Lutheran Annual, HU 297
Lutheran Council in Canada. Directory of Lutheran Churches in Canada. *see* Directory of Lutheran Churches in Canada, HU 276
The Lyle Official Antiques Review, SS 381

MHRA Annual Bibliography of English Language and Literature. *see* Modern Humanities Research Association. Annual Bibliography of English Language and Literature, HU 112
MHRA Annual Bulletin. *see* Modern Humanities Research Association. MHRA Annual Bulletin, HU 113
MLA International Bibliography of Books and Articles on the Modern Languages and Literatures. *see* Modern Language Association of America. MLA International Bibliography of Books and Articles on the Modern Languages and Literatures, HU 114
MVMA Motor Vehicle Facts and Figures, SS 870
McCall's Needlework and Crafts Christmas Make-It Ideas, SS 394
McGraw-Hill Yearbook of Science and Technology, SC 8
Machine Shop N/C Guidebook and Directory. *see* Modern Machine Shop. NC/CAM Guidebook, SC 176
Machinery's Handbook, SC 173
McKittrick Directory of Advertisers. *see* Standard Directory of Advertisers, SS 516
Madison Avenue Handbook, SS 508
The Magazine and Editorial Directory. *see* Working Press of the Nation, v. 2, SS 212

Magazines for Libraries, GE 49
Mail Order Business Directory, SS 101
Major League Year and Notebook, SS 765
Manchester Literary and Philosophical Society. Memoirs and Proceedings, HU 225
Manpower and Automation Research. *see* U.S. Department of Labor. Manpower and Automation Research, SS 435
Manual of Mineralogy. *see* Dana's Manual of Mineralogy, SC 297
Marathon Handbook, SS 766
Marconi's International Register, SS 191
Marine Technology Society. Annual Conference Proceedings, SC 196
Market Statistics Key Plants. *see* Marketing Economics Key Plants, SS 509
Marketing Economics Key Plants, SS 509
Marketing Guide, SS 510
Marquis Who's Who Publications: Index to All Books, GE 69
Marsyas, HU 47
Material Handling Institute. Proceedings of the MHI Material Handling Seminar and MHI Inter-Society Material Handling Symposium, SC 174
Martindale-Hubbell Law Directory, SS 474
Martindale's American Law Directory. *see* Martindale-Hubbell Law Directory, SS 474
Mathematical Handbook for Scientists and Engineers, SC 204
Measuring Mormonism, HU 298
Media Review Digest, GE 90
Media Report to Women. Index/Directory, SS 192
Medical and Health Annual, SC 246
Medical and Health Information Directory, SC 247
Medical Books and Serials in Print, SC 248
Medical School Admission Requirements, U.S.A. and Canada, SC 249
Medievalia et Humanistica: Studies in Medieval and Renaissance Culture, HU 15
Mellon Foundation. Annual Report. *see* Andrew W. Mellon Foundation. Annual Report, HU 3
Mennonite Yearbook and Directory, HU 299
Mental Health Book Review Index. *see* Chicorel Index to Mental Health Book Reviews, SC 329
Mental Health Directory, sec 332
Mental Health Materials Center. A Selective Guide to Materials for Mental Health and Family Life Education. *see* A Selective Guide to Materials for Mental Health and Family Life Education, ED 91
Merchandise and Operating Results of Department and Specialty Stores, SS 511
Merchant Vessels of the United States (Including Yachts), SS 871

The Merck Index: An Encyclopedia of Chemicals and Drugs, SC 250
The Merck Veterinary Manual, SC 337
Metal Finishing Guidebook and Directory, SC 279
Metal Statistics, SC 280
Metallurgical Society of AIME. Membership Directory, SS 281
Metropolitan Museum Journal, HU 48
Mexico and Guatemala on $10 a Day, SS 976
Michelin Camping and Caravaning France. see Camping and Caravaning France, SS 918
Michelin Red Guide Series: Benelux, SS 977
Michelin Red Guide Series: France, SS 978
Michelin Red Guide Series: Germany, SS 979
Michelin Red Guide Series: Great Britain and Ireland, SS 980
Michelin Red Guide Series: Italy, SS 981
Michelin Red Guide Series: Paris and Environs, SS 982
Michelin Red Guide Series: Spain and Portugal, SS 983
Microform Market Place, SS 193
Microforms: The Librarians' View, HU 163
The Micropublishers' Trade List Annual, SS 194
Microwaves Product Data Directory, SC 175
Middle East. see The Middle East and North Africa, SS 350
Middle East and North Africa, SS 350
The Middle East and South Asia, SS 351
Middle East Annual Review, SS 352
Middle East Contemporary Survey, SS 353
Middle East Yearbook, SS 354
Middle Market Directory. see Dun and Bradstreet Middle Market Directory, SS 503
Midwest Media, SS 195
Milepost: All-the-North Travel Guide, SS 984
Million Dollar Directory. see Dun and Bradstreet Million Dollar Directory, SS 504
Milton Studies, HU 111
Mineral Facts and Problems. see U.S. Bureau of Mines. Mineral Facts and Problems, SC 308
Minerals Yearbook. see U.S. Bureau of Mines. Minerals Yearbook, SC 309
Mines Register. see World Mines Register, SC 310
Mining Annual Review, SC 302
Minkus New American Stamp Catalog, SS 382
Minkus New World Wide Stamp Catalog, SS 383
Minnesota Symposia on Child Psychology, SC 333
Minor League Digest, SS 767
Minorities and Women in State and Local Government, SS 424
Minority Group Employment in the Federal Government, SS 425

Mission Handbook: North American Protestant Ministries Overseas, HU 300
Mission Yearbook of Prayer, HU 301
Mobil Travel Guide: California and the West, SS 985
Mobil Travel Guide: Great Lakes Area, SS 986
Mobil Travel Guide: Middle Atlantic States, SS 987
Mobil Travel Guide: Northeastern States, SS 988
Mobil Travel Guide: Northwest and Great Plains States, SS 989
Mobil Travel Guide: Southeastern States, SS 990
Mobil Travel Guide: Southwest and South Central Area, SS 991
Mobil Vacation and Business Guide, SS 992
Modern Drug Encyclopedia and Therapeutic Index, SC 251
Modern Humanities Research Association. Annual Bibliography of English Language and Literature, HU 112
Modern Humanities Research Association. MHRA Annual Bulletin, HU 113
Modern Humanities Research Association. Yearbook of English Studies. see Yearbook of English Studies, HU 138
Modern Humanities Research Association. Year's Work in Modern Language Studies. see Year's Work in Modern Language Studies, HU 140
Modern Language Association Conference on Research Opportunities in Renaissance Drama. see Research Opportunities in Renaissance Drama, HU 346
Modern Language Association of America. American Bibliography. see Modern Language Association of America. MLA International Bibliography of Books and Articles on the Modern Languages and Literatures, HU 114
Modern Language Association of America. Annual Bibliography. see Modern Language Association of America. MLA International Bibliography of Books and Articles on the Modern Languages and Literatures, HU 114
Modern Language Association of America. MLA International Bibliography of Books and Articles on the Modern Languages and Literature, HU 114
Modern Language Association of America. The Romantic Movement. see The Romantic Movement, HU 122
Modern Machine Shop. NC/CAM Guidebook, SC 176
Modern Plastics Catalog. see Modern Plastics Encyclopedia, SC 177
Modern Plastics Encyclopedia, SC 177
Monographs of the Rutgers Center of Alcohol Studies, SC 252

Monographs of the Yale Center of Alcohol Studies. *see* Monographs of the Rutgers Center of Alcohol Studies, SC 252
Moody's Bank and Finance Manual, SS 42
Moody's Dividend Record, SS 43
Moody's Handbook of Common Stocks, SS 44
Moody's Handbook of Corporate Managements. *see* Dun and Bradstreet Reference Book of Corporate Managements, SS 493
Moody's Handbook of Widely Held Common Stocks. *see* Moody's Handbook of Common Stocks, SS 44
Moody's Industrial Manual, SS 45
Moody's Manual of Investments: American and Foreign Government Securities. *see* Moody's Municipal and Government Manual, SS 304
Moody's Municipal and Government Manual, SS 304
Moody's Over-the-Counter (OTC) Industrial Manual, SS 46
Moody's Public Utilities Manual, SS 47
Moody's Transportation Manual, SS 872
Moravian Church in America Daily Texts and Directory and Statistics, HU 302
Mormon History Association. Journal of Mormon History. *see* Journal of Mormon History, HU 293
Motion Picture and Television Almanac. *see* International Motion Picture Almanac, HU 174
Motion Picture Market Place, SS 196
Motor Auto Repair Manual, SS 873
Motor Parts and Time Guide, SS 874
Motor Truck Facts. *see* MVMA Motor Vehicle Facts and Figures, SS 870
Motor Truck Repair Manual, SS 875
Motor Vehicle Facts and Figures. *see* MVMA Motor Vehicle Facts and Figures, SS 870
Motor Vehicle Manufacturers Association of the U.S. MVMA Motor Vehicle Facts and Figures. *see* MVMA Motor Vehicle Facts and Figures, SS 870
Motor's Flat Rate and Parts Manual. *see* Motor Parts and Time Guide, SS 874
Motor's Truck and Diesel Repair Manual. *see* Motor Truck Repair Manual, SS 875
Multi-Media Reviews Index. *see* Media Review Digest, GE 90
Municipal Index, SS 585
The Municipal Year Book, SS 305
Municipalities and the Law in Action. *see* National Institute of Municipal Law Officers. NIMLO Municipal Law Review, SS 241
Muse, SS 22
Museen der Welt. *see* Museums of the World; Museen der Welt, HU 50
Museum Notes, HU 49

Museums and Art Galleries Year Book. *see* Libraries, Museums, and Art Galleries Year Book, HU 46
Museums Directory of the United States and Canada. *see* Official Museum Directory, HU 52
Museums of the World; Museen der Welt, HU 50
Music and the Artists Directory, HU 199
Music Faculties in Colleges and Universities U.S. and Canada. *see* Directory of Music Faculties in Colleges and Universities U.S. and Canada, HU 189
Music in Higher Education, HU 200
Music Journal Artists' Directory. *see* Music and Artists Directory, HU 199
Music Yearbook. *see* British Music Yearbook, HU 184
Musica Disciplina, HU 201
Musical America and High Fidelity—Musical America Directory Issue. *see* Musical America International Directory of the Performing Arts, HU 202
Musical America International Directory of the Performing Arts, HU 202
Mutual Fund Fact Book, SS 48
Myra Waldo's Travel and Motoring Guide to Europe, SS 993
Myra Waldo's Travel Guide to South America, SS 994

N. W. Ayer and Son's Directory of Newspapers and Periodicals. *see* Ayer Directory of Publications, SS 154
NAACP Annual Report. *see* National Association for the Advancement of Colored People. NAACP Annual Report, SS 141
NACDS Lilly Digest. *see* National Association of Chain Drug Stores. NACDS Lilly Digest, SS 512
NAREIF Handbook of Member Trusts. *see* National Association of Real Estate Investment Trusts. REIT Handbook of Member Trusts, SS 609
NCLIS Annual Report to the President and Congress. *see* National Commission on Libraries and Information Science. Annual Report to the President and Congress, HU 164
NICEM Index to Educational Audio Tapes, ED 77
NICEM Index to Educational Overhead Transparencies, ED 78
NICEM Index to Educational Records, ED 79
NICEM Index to Educational Slides, ED 80
NICEM Index to Educational Videotapes, ED 81
NICEM Index to 8mm Motion Cartridges, ED 82
NICEM Index to Environmental Studies—Multimedia ED 83
NICEM Index to Health and Safety Education—Multimedia, ED 84
NICEM Index to Producers and Distributors, ED 85

NICEM Index to Psychology—Multimedia, ED 86
NICEM Index to 16mm Educational Films, ED 87
NICEM Index to 35mm Educational Filmstrips, ED 88
NICEM Index to Vocational and Technical Education—Multimedia, ED 89
NIDA Research Monograph Series. *see* National Institute on Drug Abuse Research. Monograph Series, SC 254
NIH Factbook. *see* National Institutes of Health. NIH Factbook, SC 255
NIMLO Municipal Law Review. *see* National Institute of Municipal Law Officers. NIMLO Municipal Law Review, SS 241
NNA National Directory of Weekly Newspapers. *see* National Newspaper Association. NNA National Directory of Weekly Newspapers, SS 197
The Nathaniel Hawthorne Journal, HU 115
National Academy of Sciences. National Research Council. Digest of Literature on Dielectrics. *see* National Research Council. Digest of Literature on Dielectrics, SC 90
National Aerospace Symposium. Proceedings, SC 16
National Alliance of Businessmen. Directory of Predominantly Black Colleges and Universities in the United States of America. *see* Directory of Predominantly Black Colleges and Universities in the United States of America, ED 42
National Association for Girls and Women in Sport. Basketball Guide. *see* Basketball Guide, SS 699
National Association for Girls and Women in Sport. Basketball-Volleyball Tips and Techniques. *see* Basketball-Volleyball Tips and Techniques, SS 703
National Association for Girls and Women in Sport. Bowling-Fencing Guide. *see* Bowling-Fencing Guide, SS 714
National Association for Girls and Women in Sport. Field Hockey-LaCrosse Guide. *see* Field Hockey-LaCrosse Guide, SS 730
National Association for Girls and Women in Sport. Gymnastics Guide. *see* Gymnastics Guide, SS 757
National Association for Girls and Women in Sport. Skiing Rules. *see* Skiing Rules, SS 815
National Association for Girls and Women in Sport. Softball Guide. *see* Softball Guide, SS 817
National Association for Girls and Women in Sport. Softball Rules. *see* Softball Rules, SS 818
National Association for Girls and Women in Sport. Tennis-Badminton-Squash Guide. *see* Tennis-Badminton-Squash Guide, SS 831
National Association for Girls and Women in Sport. Track and Field Guide. *see* Track and Field Guide, SS 832
National Association for Girls and Women in Sport. Volleyball Guide. *see* Volleyball Guide, SS 840
National Association for the Advancement of Colored People. NAACP Annual Report, SS 141
National Association of Catholic Chaplains. Annual Convention Proceedings, HU 303
National Association of Chain Drug Stores. NACDS Lilly Digest, SS 512
National Association of Counties. The County Year Book. *see* The County Year Book, SS 298
National Association of Credit Management. Credit Manual of Commercial Laws. *see* Credit Manual of Commercial Laws, SS 35
National Association of Dramatic and Speech Arts. Encore. *see* Encore, HU 339
National Association of Mutual Savings Banks. Directory and Guide to the Mutual Savings Banks of the United States. *see* Directory and Guide to the Mutual Savings Banks of the United States, SS 37
National Association of Mutual Savings Banks. National Fact Book of Mutual Savings Banks. *see* National Fact Book of Mutual Savings Banks, SS 49
National Association of Private Psychiatric Hospitals. Directory of Member Hospitals, SC 334
National Association of Real Estate Investment Trusts. REIT Handbook of Member Trusts, SS 609
National Association of Real Estate Investment Funds. NAREIF Handbook of Member Trusts. *see* National Association of Real Estate Investment Trusts. REIT Handbook of Member Trusts, SS 609
National Association of Regional Councils. Directory, SS 306
National Association of Relay Manufacturers. Relay Conference Proceedings, SC 178
National Association of Schools of Music. Directory, HU 203
National Association of Schools of Music. Music in Higher Education. *see* Music in Higher Education, HU 200
National Association of Schools of Music. Proceedings of the Annual Meeting, HU 204
National Association of Social Workers. Encyclopedia of Social Work. *see* Encyclopedia of Social Work, SS 624
National Audio-Visual Association. Audio-Visual Equipment Directory. *see* Audio-Visual Equipment Directory, ED 60
National Automotive Annual. *see* National Motorsports Annual, SS 781
National Baseball Congress. Official Baseball Annual, SS 768
National Basketball Association Official Guide, SS 769

National Basketball Committee. Official Basketball Guide. see Basketball Rules, SS 701

National Black Business Directory. see National Minority Business Directory, SS 103

National Board of Boiler and Pressure Vessel Inspection. Proceedings of General Meeting, SC 179

National Bureau of Economic Research. Annual Report, SS 102

National Buy-Black Campaign. National Minority Business Directory. see National Minority Business Directory, SS 103

National Catalog of Aids for Students Entering College. see Financial Aids for Higher Education, ED 43

National Catholic Almanac. see Catholic Almanac, HU 260

National Center for Educational Statistics. Digest of Educational Statistics. see Digest of Educational Statistics, ED 4

National Center for Educational Statistics. Directory of Postsecondary Schools with Occupational Programs. see Directory of Postsecondary Schools with Occupational Programs, ED 100

National Center for Educational Statistics. Education Directory. see Education Directory, ED 8

National Center for Educational Statistics. Projections of Educational Statistics to (year). see Projections of Educational Statistics to (year), ED 14

National Coal Association. Coal Facts. see Coal Facts, SC 296

National Coal Association. International Coal. see International Coal, SC 300

National Coal Association. Symposium on Coal Mine Drainage Research. Papers. see Symposium on Coal Mine Drainage Research. Papers, SC 307

National Collegiate Athletic Association. Annual Reports, SS 770

National Collegiate Athletic Association. Baseball Guide. see Official National Collegiate Athletic Association Baseball Guide, SS 787

National Collegiate Athletic Association. Basketball Guide. see Official National Collegiate Athletic Association Basketball Guide, SS 788

National Collegiate Athletic Association. Basketball Rules and Casebook. see Official National Collegiate Athletic Association Basketball Rules and Casebook, SS 789

National Collegiate Athletic Association. Football Guide. see Official National Collegiate Athletic Association Football Guide, SS 790

National Collegiate Athletic Association. Football Rules Interpretations. see Official National Collegiate Athletic Association Football Rules Interpretations, SS 791

National Collegiate Athletic Association. A Guide for the College-Bound Student-Athlete. see A Guide for the College-Bound Student-Athlete, SS 748

National Collegiate Athletic Association. Ice Hockey Guide. see Official National Collegiate Athletic Association Ice Hockey Guide, SS 792

National Collegiate Athletic Association. Official Gymnastics Rules, SS 771

National Collegiate Athletic Association. Official Read-Easy Football Rules. see Official Read-Easy Football Rules, SS 797

National Collegiate Athletic Association. Skiing Rules. see Official National Collegiate Athletic Association Skiing Rules, SS 793

National Collegiate Athletic Association. Soccer Guide. see Official National Collegiate Athletic Association Soccer Guide, SS 794

National Collegiate Athletic Association. Swimming Guide. see Official National Collegiate Athletic Association Swimming Guide, SS 795

National Collegiate Athletic Association. Water Polo Rules. see Official National Collegiate Athletic Association Water Polo Rules, SS 796

National Collegiate Athletic Association. Yearbook. see National Collegiate Athletic Association. Annual Reports, SS 770.

National Collegiate Championships, SS 772

National Commission on Libraries and Information Science. Annual Report to the President and Congress, HU 164

National Conference on Fluid Power. Proceedings, SC 180

National Conference on Industrial Hydraulics. Proceedings. see National Conference on Fluid Power. Proceedings, SC 180

National Conference on Power Transmission. Proceedings, SC 181

National Conference on Social Welfare. Social Work Practice. see Social Work Practice, SS 633

National Consumer Finance Association. Finance Facts Yearbook. see Finance Facts Yearbook, SS 40

National Council for the Social Studies. Yearbook, SS 2

The National Council for the Traditional Arts. Calendar of Festivals. see Calendar of Festivals, SS 279

National Council of Churches. Division of Overseas Ministries. Report, HU 304

National Council of Churches. Office of Research and Evaluation. Yearbook of American and Canadian Churches. see Yearbook of American and Canadian Churches, HU 330

National Council of College Publications Advisors. Directory of the College Student Press in America. *see* Directory of the College Student Press in America, SS 168

National Cutting Horse Association. Rule Book, SS 773

National Dance Association. Annual Conference. *see* Focus on Dance, HU 84

The National Dance Association. Focus on Dance. *see* Focus on Dance, HU 84

National Directory for the Performing Arts and Civic Centers, HU 341

National Directory of Accredited Camps for Boys and Girls. *see* Parents Guide to Accredited Camps: Midwestern Edition, SS 801; Parents Guide to Accredited Camps: Northeastern Edition, SS 802; Parents Guide to Accredited Camps: Southern Edition, SS 803; Parents Guide to Accredited Camps: Western Edition, SS 804

National Directory of College Athletics. Men's Edition, SS774

National Directory of College Athletics. Women's Edition, SS 775

National Directory of High School Coaches, SS 776

National Directory of Law Enforcement Administrators: Prosecution, Correctional and Judicial Agencies, SS 239

National Directory of State Agencies, SS 307

National Directory of Weekly Newspapers. *see* National Newspaper Association. NNA National Directory of Weekly Newspapers, SS 197

National Directory of Women's Athletics. *see* National Directory of College Athletics. Women's Edition, SS 775

National Easter Seal Society for Crippled Children and Adults. The Easter Seal Directory of Resident Camps for Persons with Special Health Needs. *see* The Easter Seal Directory of Resident Camps for Persons with Special Health Needs, SC 237

National Electronics Conference. Proceedings, SC 89

National Endowment for the Humanities. Annual Report, HU 16

National Engineering Consortium. National Electronics Conference. Proceedings. *see* National Electronics Conference. Proceedings, SC 89

National Fact Book of Mutual Savings Banks, SS 49

National Faculty Directory, ED 12

National Federation of State High School Associations. Baseball Rules. *see* Baseball Rules, SS 697

National Federation of State High School Associations. Basketball Case Book. *see* Basketball Case Book, SS 698

National Federation of State High School Associations. Basketball Handbook. *see* Basketball Handbook, SS 700

National Federation of State High School Associations. Basketball Rules. *see* Basketball Rules, SS 701

National Federation of State High School Associations. Basketball Rules—Simplified and Illustrated. *see* Basketball Rules—Simplified and Illustrated, SS 702

National Federation of State High School Associations. Boy's Gymnastics Rules. *see* Boy's Gymnastics Rules, SS 715

National Federation of State High School Associations. Field Hockey Rules: Boys and Girls. *see* Field Hockey Rules: Boys and Girls, SS 731

National Federation of State High School Associations. Football Case Book. *see* Football Case Book, SS 735

National Federation of State High School Associations. Football Handbook (Includes Flag Football). *see* Football Handbook (Includes Flag Football), SS 736

National Federation of State High School Associations. Girls Gymnastics Judging Manual. *see* Girls Gymnastics Judging Manual, SS 740

National Federation of State High School Associations. Girls Gymnastics Rules. *see* Girls Gymnastics Rules, SS 741

National Federation of State High School Associations. Official Football Rules. *see* Official Football Rules, SS 786

National Federation of State High School Associations. Official Handbook, SS 777

National Federation of State High School Associations. Soccer Rules. *see* Soccer Rules, SS 816

National Federation of State High School Associations. Swimming and Diving Case Book. *see* Swimming and Diving Case Book, SS 828

National Federation of State High School Associations. Swimming and Diving Rules and Records. *see* Swimming and Diving Rules and Records, SS 829

National Federation of State High School Associations. Track and Field Rules and Records; Boys and Girls. *see* Track and Field Rules and Records; Boys and Girls, SS 833

National Federation of State High School Associations. Volleyball Rules. *see* Volleyball Rules, SS 841

National Federation of State High School Associations. Wrestling Officials Manual. *see* Wrestling Officials Manual, SS 844

National Federation of State High School Associations. Wrestling Rules. *see* Wrestling Rules, SS 845

National Fire Codes. *see* National Fire Protection Association. National Fire Codes, SC 45

National Fire Protection Association. National Fire Codes, SC 45

National Football Guide, SS 778

National Football League. Official Record Manual, SS 779

National Football League. Record Manual. *see* National Football League. Official Record Manual, SS 779

National Gallery of Art. Annual Report. *see* U.S. National Gallery of Art. Annual Report, HU 58

National Gallery of Art. Studies in the History of Art. *see* U.S. National Gallery of Art. Studies in the History of Art, HU 59

National Health Directory, SC 253

National Health Education Committee. The Killers and Cripplers. *see* The Killers and Cripplers, SC 245

National Hockey League Guide, SS 780

National Information Bureau. Wise Giving Bulletin. *see* Wise Giving Bulletin, SS 637

National Information Center for Educational Media. NICEM Indexes. *see* NICEM Indexes, ED 77-89

National Institute for Architectural Education. Bulletin. *see* National Institute for Architectural Education. Yearbook, HU 51

National Institute for Architectural Education. Yearbook, HU 51

National Institute of Law Enforcement and Criminal Justice. Annual Report, SS 240

National Institute of Mental Health. U.S. Facilities and Programs for Children with Severe Mental Illnesses; A Directory. *see* U.S. Facilities and Programs for Children with Severe Mental Illnesses; A Directory, SC 268

National Institute of Municipal Law Officers. Municipalities and the Law in Action. *see* National Institute of Municipal Law Officers. NIMLO Municipal Law Review, SS 241

National Institute of Municipal Law Officers. NIMLO Municipal Law Review, SS 241

National Institute on Drug Abuse Research. Monograph Series, SC 254

National Institutes of Health. NIH Factbook, SC 255

National Law Forum. *see* American Journal of Jurisprudence, SS 446

National League of Nursing. State Approved Schools of Nursing—LPN/LVN. *see* State Approved Schools of Nursing—LPN/LVN, SC 261

National League of Nursing. State Approved Schools of Nursing—RN. *see* State Approved Schools of Nursing—RN, SC 262

National Minority Business Directory, SS 103

National Motorsports Annual, SS 781

National Newspaper Association. NNA National Directory of Weekly Newspapers, SS 197

National Notary Association. Customs and Practices of Notaries Public and Digest of Notary Laws in the U.S. *see* Customs and Practices of Notaries Public and Digest of Notary Laws in the U.S., SS 459

National Playwrights Directory, HU 342

National Police Chiefs and Sheriffs Information Bureau. National Directory. *see* National Directory of Law Enforcement Administrators: Prosecution, Correctional, and Judicial Agencies, SS 239

National Prisoner Statistics Bulletin. *see* U.S. Federal Bureau of Prisons. Statistical Report, SS 250

National Radio Publicity Directory, SS 198

National Real Estate Directory, SS 610

National Real Estate Investor Handbook and Directory. *see* National Real Estate Directory, SS 610

National Retail Merchants Association. Merchandise and Operating Results of Department and Specialty Stores. *see* Merchandise and Operating Results of Department and Specialty Stores, SS 511

National Research Council. Digest of Literature on Dielectrics, SC 90

National Roster of Black Elected Officials, SS 561

National Roster of Realtors, SS 611

National Society for the Study of Education. Yearbook, ED 90

National Society of Daughters of the American Colonists. Daughters of the American Colonists Lineage Book. *see* Daughters of the American Colonists Lineage Book, SS 283

National Telecommunications Conference. Record, SS 199

National Telemetering Conference. Proceedings. *see* National Telecommunications Conference. Record, SS 199

National Union of Christian Schools. Directory and Annual Reports, ED 13

National University Extension Association. Guide to Independent Study through Correspondence Instruction. *see* Guide to Independent Study through Correspondence Instruction. *see* Guide to Independent Study through correspondence Instruction, ED 21

National Urban League. The State of Black America. *see* The State of Black America, SS 274

National Wildlife Federation. Conservation Directory. *see* Conservation Directory, SC 99

Nationwide Directory of Apparel and Accessories Buyers Exclusive of New York Metropolitan Area, SS 513

Native American Rights Fund. Catalogue: An Index to

Indian Legal Materials and Resources in the National Indian Law Library. *see* Catalogue: An Index to Indian Legal Materials and Resources in the National Indian Law Library, SS 456
Nature/Science Annual, SC 9
Naval Engineering Journal. *see* American Society of Naval Engineers. Membership Lists, SC 130
Nebula Award Stories, HU 116
Needlework and Crafts Christmas Make-It Ideas. *see* McCall's Needlework and Crafts Christmas Make-It Ideas, SS 394
New African Literature and the Arts, HU 117
New African Yearbook, SS 355
New Dimensions. *see* New Dimensions Science Fiction, HU 118
New Dimensions Science Fiction, HU 118
New England Guide, SS 995
New Fishing, SS 782
New Group Health Insurance, SS 416
The New Guide to Study Abroad, ED 50
New Hampshire Archeologist, SS 23
New Jersey State Industrial Directory, SS 104
New Settler's Guide for Washington, D.C. and Communities in Nearby Maryland and Virginia, SS 996
New York on $15 a Day, SS 997
New York Public Library. Books for the Teen Age. *see* Books for the Teen Age, GE 30
New York Publicity Outlets, SS 514
New York State Division of Criminal Justice Services. Comprehensive Crime Control Plan, SS 242
New York State Industrial Directory, SS 105
New York Theatre Annual, HU 343
New York Times Encyclopedic Almanac. *see* Hammond Almanac of a Million Facts, GE 10
New York Times Film Reviews, HU 175
New York Times Index, GE 120
New Zealand on $10 a Day, SS 998
News Dictionary, GE 12
News Year. *see* News Dictionary, GE 12
Newspaper and Allied Services Directory. *see* Working Press of the Nation, v. 1, SS 212
Nomos, HU 226
Non-Ferrous Metal Data, SC 283
North American Film and Video Directory, SS 200
North American Protestant Ministries Overseas. *see* Mission Handbook, HU 300
Northeast Folklore, SS 282
Norwegian-American Studies, SS 273

OCLC Annual Report, HU 165

Occupational Outlook Handbook, SS 528
Occupations of Federal White-Collar Workers. *see* U.S. Civil Service Commission. Manpower Statistics Division. Occupations of Federal White-Collar Workers, SS 432
Ocean Yearbook, SC 197
Oceanography and Marine Biology, SC 198
Official Baseball Dope Book, SS 783
Official Baseball Guide, SS 784
Official Baseball Rules, SS 785
Official Catholic Directory, HU 305
The Official Encyclopedia of Football. *see* The Encyclopedia of Football, SS 725
Official Football Rules, SS 786
Official Hotel-Motel Directory and Facilities Guide, SS 106
The Official Hotel Redbook and Directory. *see* Hotel and Motel Redbook, SS 94
Official Museum Directory, HU 52
Official National Collegiate Athletic Association Baseball Guide, SS 787
Official National Collegiate Athletic Association Basketball Guide, SS 788
Official National Collegiate Athletic Association Basketball Rules and Casebook, SS 789
Official National Collegiate Athletic Association Boxing, Gymnastics, Skiing Rules. *see* Official National Collegiate Athletic Association Skiing Rules, SS 793
Official National Collegiate Athletic Association Football Guide, SS 790
Official National Collegiate Athletic Association Football Rules Interpretations, SS 791
Official National Collegiate Athletic Association Ice Hockey Guide, SS 792
Official National Collegiate Athletic Association Skiing Rules, SS 793
Official National Collegiate Athletic Association Soccer Guide, SS 794
Official National Collegiate Athletic Association Swimming Guide, SS 795
Official National Collegiate Athletic Association Water Polo Rules, SS 796
Official Read-Easy Football Rules, SS 797
Official Rules of Sports and Games, SS 798
Official United States Tennis Tournament Directory, SS 799
Official World Series Records, SS 800
Offshore Technology Conference. Proceedings, SC 199
Ohio College Library Center. Annual Report. *see* OCLC Annual Report, HU 165
Ohio Music Education Association. Contributions to

Music Education. *see* Contributions to Music Education, HU 188
Ohio State University, Columbus. OSU Theatre Collection. Bulletin. *see* Theatre Studies, HU 350
Omnibus of Holiday Observances around the World. *see* Oxbridge Omnibus of Holiday Observances around the World, GE 13
Oklahoma Anthropological Society. Bulletin, SS 24
On Site, HU 53
On View, HU 54
Ontario Archaeology, SS 25
Opportunities for Research in Renaissance Drama. *see* Research Opportunities in Renaissance Drama, HU 346
Optical Industry and Systems Directory, SC 182
Oral History Association Annual Colloquia. Proceedings. *see* Oral History Review, SS 356
Oral History Review, SS 356
Orbis Encyclopedia of Extra-European Countries. *see* Europa Year Book, SS 555
Organ Yearbook, HU 205
Organic Chemistry. *see* Reports on the Progress of Chemistry, SC 59
The Organization of the United Methodist Church, HU 306
Orthodox Church in America. Yearbook and Church Directory and Calendar, HU 307
Oxbridge Omnibus of Holiday Observances around the World, GE 13
Oxford Slavonic Papers, HU 119

PAIS. *see* Public Affairs Information Service. Bulletin, SS 564
PTLA. *see* Publishers' Trade List Annual, GE 52
Pacific Anthropologists, SS 26
Package Engineering Annual Buyers Guide, SC 183
Package Machinery Catalog. *see* Package Engineering Annual Buyers Guide, SC 183
Pan American Development Foundation. Annual Report, SS 107
Parents Guide to Accredited Camps; Midwestern Edition, SS 801
Parents Guide to Accredited Camps; Northeastern Edition, SS 802
Parents Guide to Accredited Camps; Southern Edition, SS 803
Parents Guide to Accredited Camps; Western Edition, SS 804
Passenger and Inflight Service Magazine. Airline Guide to Stewardess and Stewards Careers. *see* Airline Guide to Stewardess and Stewards Careers, SS 522
Patent Law Review, SS 536
Patterson's American Education, ED 29
Patterson's American Educational Directory. *see* Patterson's American Education, ED 29
Pay Structure of the Federal Civil Service. *see* U.S. Civil Service Commission. Manpower Statistics Division. Pay Structure of the Federal Civil Service, SS 433
Pears Cyclopaedia, GE 14
Pennsylvania Music Educators Association. Bulletin of Research in Music Education, HU 206
Penrose Annual. *see* Penrose Graphic Arts International Annual, HU 55
Penrose Graphic Arts International Annual, HU 55
Pension Facts, SS 417
Per Jacobsson Foundation. Proceedings of the Lecture Meeting, SS 108
Per Jacobsson Memorial Lecture. *see* Per Jacobsson Foundation. Proceedings of the Lecture Meeting, SS 108
The Performance Dynamics' Worldwide Directory of Job Changing Contacts, SS 529
Performing Arts Resoruces, HU 344
Periodicals Directory. *see* Ulrich's International Periodicals Directory, GE 59
Perspecta; The Yale Architectural Journal, HU 56
Perspectives in Jewish Learning. *see* Solomon Goldman Lectures; Perspectives in Jewish Learning, HU 313
Petersen's Pro Football Annual, SS 805
Peterson's Annual Guide to Undergraduate Study, ED 51
Peterson's Annual Guides to Graduate Study, ED 52
Pharmacy School Admission Requirements, SC 256
Philadelphia Yearly Meeting of the Religious Society of Friends. Proceedings and Yearbook, HU 308
The Philosopher's Index, HU 227
Philosophic Exchange, HU 228
Philosophic Society for the Study of Sport. Journal of the Philosophy of Sport. *see* Journal of the Philosophy of Sport, SS 763
Philosophy and Medicine, SC 257
Photographer's Market, HU 237
The Photographic Annual. *see* British Journal of Photography Annual, HU 234
Photographis, HU 238
Photography Annual, HU 239
Photography Market Place, HU 240
Photography Year, HU 241
Photography Year Book, HU 242
Photo-Lab Index, HU 243

Physical and Inorganic Chemistry. *see* Reports on the Progress of Chemistry, SC 58
Pick's Currency Yearbook, SS 384
Pit and Quarry Handbook and Buyers Guide, SC 303
Pit and Quarry Handbook and Purchasing Guide. *see* Pit and Quarry Handbook and Buyers Guide, SC 303
Plant Location, SS 109
Plastics Catalog. *see* Modern Plastics Encyclopedia, SC 177
Play Index, HU 345
Plays from Off-Off Broadway. *see* The Scene, HU 347
Pocket Data Book, U.S.A., GE 128
Police and Law Enforcement, SS 243
Police Yearbook, SS 244
The Police Yearbook. *see* International Association of Chiefs of Police. The Police Yearbook, SC 234
Political Handbook and Atlas of the World. *see* Political Handbook of the World, SS 562
Political Handbook of the World, SS 562
Polymer Handbook, SC 56
Poor's Register of Corporations, Directors, and Executives: U.S. and Canada. *see* Standard and Poor's Register of Corporations, Directors, and Executives, SS 117
Poor's Register of Directors of the U.S. and Canada. *see* Standard and Poor's Register of Corporations, Directors, and Executives, SS 117
Popular Cycling's Cycle Tests. *see* Cycle Tests, SS 856
Popular Music Periodicals Index, HU 207
Population and Family Planning Programs, SS 652
Population and the Population Explosion: A Bibliography, SS 653
The Population Council. Population and Family Planning Programs. *see* Population and Family Planning Programs, SS 652
Porcelain Enamel Institute. Forum Proceedings, SC 184
Ports of the World, SS 876
Power Boat Annual; Accessory Directory, SS 877
Power Sources Symposium. Proceedings, SC 91
Power Transmission and Bearing Handbook and Directory, SC 185
Predicasts Basebook. *see* Basebook, SS 61
Pre-Law Handbook, SS 475
Prep School Guide. *see* Lovejoy's Prep School Guide, ED 28
Presidency (year), SS 563
President Directory, SS 110
Principal International Businesses, SS 515
Prisoners in State and Federal Institutions. *see* U.S. National Criminal Justice Information and Statistics Service. Prisoners in State and Federal Institutions, SS 255

Private Independent Schools, ED 30
Private Press Books, GE 50
Prize Stories, HU 120
Pro and Amateur Hockey Guide, SS 806
Pro and Senior Hockey Guide. *see* Hockey Register, SS 758; Pro and Amateur Hockey Guide, SS 806
Pro Basketball Illustrated, SS 807
Pro Football Illustrated, SS 808
Pro Hockey, SS 809
Pro Quarterback, SS 810
Probation and Parole, SS 245
Probation and Parole Officers Association. Probation and Parole. *see* Probation and Parole, SS 245
Professional Income of Engineers. *see* Engineers Joint Council. Engineering Manpower Commission. Professional Income of Engineers, SC 140
Professional Photographer's Association of America. Directory of Professional Photography. *see* Directory of Professional Photography, HU 236
Profiles of American Colleges. *see* Barron's Profiles of American Colleges, ED 35
Profiles of State Planning Associations in the United States, SS 308
Programs and Services for the Deaf in the United States, SC 258
Progress in Geography, SC 151
Progress in Optics, SC 315
Progress in Physical Organic Chemistry, SC 57
Progress in Sport Fishery Research. *see* U.S. Fish and Wildlife Service. Sport Fishery and Wildlife Research, SC 117
Projections of Educational Statistics to (year), ED 14
Proof, HU 121
Prospects of Engineering and Technology Graduates. *see* Engineers Joint Council. Engineering Manpower Commission. Prospects of Engineering and Technology Graduates, SC 141
Public Affairs Information Service. Bulletin, SS 564
Public Employment, SS 426
Public Library Catalog, GE 51
Public Papers of the Presidents of the United States, SS 309
Public School Systems. *see* Education Directory, ED 8
Public Welfare Directory, SS 630
Publishers' International Directory, SS 201
Publishers' Trade List Annual, GE 52
Puerto Rico. Department of the Treasury. Office of Economic Research. Economy and Finances, SS 111

Question, HU 229

REIT Handbook of Member Trusts. *see* National Association of Real Estate Investment Trusts. REIT Handbook of Member Trusts, SS 609
Radio Amateur's Handbook, SS 202
The Radio and Television Directory. *see* Working Press of the Nation, v. 3, SS 212
Railroad Facts. *see* Yearbook of Railroad Facts, SS 899
Railroad Information. *see* Yearbook of Railroad Facts, SS 899
Railway Passenger Car Annual, SS 878
Rand McNally Campground and Trailer Park Guide, SS 999
Rand McNally Guidebook to Campgrounds. *see* Rand McNally Campground and Trailer Park Guide, SS 999
Rand McNally Historic America Guide, SS 1000
Rand McNally International Bankers Directory, SS 50
Rand McNally National Park Guide, SS 1001
Rand McNally Road Atlas of the United States, Canada, and Mexico, SS 1002
Rand McNally Travel Trailer Guide. *see* Rand McNally Campground and Trailer Park Guide, SS 999
Rand McNally Vacation Guide. *see* Rand McNally Historic America Guide, SS 1000
Rationalist Annual. *see* Question, HU 229
Reader's Digest Almanac and Yearbook, GE 12
Readers' Guide to Periodical Literature, GE 121
Readers' Guide to Periodical Literature, Abridged. *see* Abridged Readers' Guide to Periodical Literature, GE 113
Readings in American Government. *see* Annual Editions: Readings in American Government, SS 288
Readings in American History, Post-Civil War. *see* Annual Editions: Readings in American History, Post-Civil War, SS 330
Readings in American History, Pre-Civil War. *see* Annual Editions: Readings in American History, Pre-Civil War, SS 331
Readings in Anthropology. *see* Annual Editions: Readings in Anthropology, SS 8
Readings in Biology. *see* Annual Editions: Readings in Biology, SC 24
Readings in Business. *see* Annual Editions: Readings in Business, SS 57
Readings in Criminal Justice. *see* Annual Editions: Readings in Criminal Justice, SS 229
Readings in Early Childhood Education. *see* Annual Editions: Readings in Early Childhood Education, ED 25
Readings in Economics. *see* Annual Editions: Readings in Economics, SS 58
Readings in Education. *see* Annual Editions: Readings in Education, ED 2
Readings in Health. *see* Annual Editions: Readings in Health, SC 218
Readings in Human Development. *see* Annual Editions: Readings in Human Development, SC 25
Readings in Marriage and the Family. *see* Annual Editions: Readings in Marriage and the Family, SS 639
Readings in Marketing. *see* Annual Editions: Readings in Marketing, SS 498
Readings in Microeconomics. *see* Annual Editions: Readings in Microeconomics, SS 59
Readings in Personality and Adjustment. *see* Annual Editions: Readings in Personality and Adjustment, SC 321
Readings in Psychology. *see* Annual Editions: Readings in Psychology, SC 322
Readings in Social Problems. *see* Annual Editions: Readings in Social Problems, SS 640
Readings in Social Psychology. *see* Annual Editions: Readings in Social Psychology, SS 641
Readings in Sociology. *see* Annual Editions: Readings in Sociology, SS 642
Readings in Unexplored Deviance. *see* Annual Editions: Readings in Unexplored Deviance, SS 643
Readings in Urban Society. *see* Annual Editions: Readings in Urban Society, SS 644
Readings on Aging. *see* Annual Editions: Readings on Aging, SS 645
Recent Sociology, SS 654
Records in Review. *see* High Fidelity; Records in Review, HU 191
Reed's Nautical Almanac; American-East Coast Edition, SS 879
Reference and Subscription Books Reviews, GE 91
Reference Sources, GE 92
The Reference Catalogue of Current Literature. *see* British Books in Print, GE 33
Reliability and Maintainability Symposium. Proceedings, SC 186
Religious Books and Serials in Print, HU 309
The Religious Public Relations Council. Directory, HU 310
Religious Society of Friends. Handbook, HU 311
Religious Society of Friends. Proceedings and Yearbook of the Philadelphia Yearly Meeting. *see* Philadelphia Yearly Meeting of the Religious Society of Friends. Proceedings and Yearbook, HU 308
Renaissance and Modern Studies, HU 17
Renaissance Drama. *see* Research Opportunities in Renaissance Drama, HU 346
Repertoir des Associations du Canada. *see* Directory

of Associations in Canada; Repertoir des Associations du Canada, GE 97

Repertoire Mondial des Ecoles d'Assistants Medicaux. see World Directory of Schools for Medical Assistants; Repertoire Mondial des Ecoles d'Assistants Medicaux, SC 272

Report on National Survey of Compensation Paid Scientists and Engineers Engaged in Research and Development Activities to the U.S. Atomic Energy Commission, SS 427

Reports on the Progress of Chemistry, SC 58-59

Requirements for Certification for Elementary Schools, Secondary Schools, and Junior Colleges. see Requirements for Certification of Teachers, Counselors, Librarians, and Administrators, ED 15

Requirements for Certification of Teachers, Counselors, Librarians, and Administrators, ED 15

Research Centers Directory, GE 109

Research in Corporate Social Performance and Policy, SS 112

Research in Economic History, SS 113

Research in Experimental Economics, SS 114

Research in Finance, SS 115

Research in International Business and Finance, SS 116

Research Opportunities in Renaissance Drama, HU 346

Rhode Island School of Design. Museum of Art. Museum Notes. see Museum Notes, HU 49

Ring Boxing Encyclopedia and Record Book, SS 811

Rockefeller Foundation. Annual Report, HU 18

Rockefeller Foundation. The President's Review and Annual Report. see Rockefeller Foundation. Annual Report, HU 18

Rocky Mountain Coal Mining Institute. Proceedings, SC 304

Roll of Arms, SS 286

The Romantic Movement, HU 122

The Rose Annual, SC 156

Ross Carpenter's Hunter's Guns. see Bob Wallack's Hunter's Guns, SS 709

Roster of Women and Minority Engineering and Technology Students. see Engineers Joint Council. Engineering Manpower Commission. Roster of Women and Minority Engineering and Technology Students, SC 142

Royal Aeronautical Society. Anglo-American Aeronautical Conference. Proceedings. see Anglo-American Aeronautical Conference. Proceedings, SC 15

Royal Musical Association, London. Proceedings, HU 208

Royal National Rose Society. The Rose Annual. see The Rose Annual, SC 156

Royal Society. Transactions. see Essays by Divers Hands, HU 102

Royal Society of Canada. Transactions; Société Royale du Canada. Memoires, HU 230

Royal United Services Institute and Brassey's Defence Yearbook, SC 288

Runner's Almanac, SS 812

Rutgers Center of Alcohol Studies. Monographs. see Monographs of the Rutgers Center of Alcohol Studies, SC 252

SHARE: A Directory of Feminist Library Workers, HU 166

SIPRI Yearbook. see World Armaments and Disarmament; SIPRI Yearbook, SC 294

Sage Yearbooks in Politics and Public Policy, SS 565

Sailboat and Sailboat Equipment Directory, SS 880

Salaries of Engineering Technicians and Technologists. see Engineers Joint Council. Engineering Manpower Commission. Salaries of Engineering Technicians and Technologists, SC 143

Salary and Benefit Information for Middle Management Personnel for U.S. and Canada, SS 428

Sargent Guide to Summer Camps and Summer Schools. see Guide to Summer Camps and Summer Schools, ED 26

Savings and Loan Fact Book, SS 51

Sav*On*Hotels, SS 1003

Scandinavian Political Studies, SS 566

The Scene, HU 347

Schizophrenic Syndrome. see Annual Review of the Schizophrenic Syndrome, SC 326

Scholarships, Fellowships, Grants and Loans. see College Blue Book, ED 37

School Universe Data Book, ED 31

Schools Abroad of Interest to Americans, ED 32

Schools of Social Work with Accredited Master's Degree Programs, SS 631

Schwann Artist Issue Catalog. see Schwann Artists Catalog, HU 209

Schwann Artist Listing Long Playing Record Catalog. see Schwann Artists Catalog, HU 209

Schwann Artists Catalog, HU 209

Schwann Children's Record and Tape Guide, HU 210

Science Fiction Book Review Index, HU 123

Science Fiction Writers of America. Nebula Award Stories. see Nebula Award Stories, HU 116

Science News Yearbook, SC 10

Scientific and Technical Books and Serials in Print, SC 11

Scientific, Engineering, and Medical Societies Publications in Print, SC 12

Scientific, Technical and Engineering Societies Publications in Print. *see* Scientific, Engineering, and Medical Societies Publications in Print, SC 12
Scottish Studies, SS 357
Scott's Specialized Catalogue of U.S. Stamps, SS 385
Scott's Standard Postage Stamp Catalogue, SS 386
Screen World, HU 176
Securities Law Review, SS 52
Seeing Eye Annual Report, SS 632
A Selective Guide to Materials for Mental Health and Family Life Education, ED 91
Senior High School Library Catalog, GE 53
Series, Serials, and Packages, SS 203
Setting National Priorities: The (year) Budget, SS 586
The Sexual Barrier, SS 142
Shakespeare Studies, HU 124
Shakespeare Survey, HU 125
Sheehy, Eugene P. Guide to Reference Books. *see* Guide to Reference Books, GE 41
Short Story Index, HU 126
Sisters Have Resources Everywhere: A Directory of Feminist Library Workers. *see* SHARE: A Directory of Feminist Library Workers, HU 166
Site Selection Handbook, SS 612
Ski Info: The Equipment Book, SS 813
Ski Magazine's Guide to Cross Country Skiing, SS 814
Skiing Rules, SS 815
Sloan Foundation. Report. *see* Alfred P. Sloan Foundation. Report, HU 1
Small Press Record of Books in Print, GE 54
Smith, Dr. Jessie Carney. Directory of Significant 20th Century Minority Women in the U.S.A.. *see* Directory of Significant 20th Century Minority Women in the U.S.A., GE 67
Smithsonian Institution. Ars Orientalis. *see* Ars Orientalis, HU 28
Soccer Rules, SS 816
Social Science and Humanities Index. *see* Humanities Index, HU 10; Social Sciences Index, SS 4
Social Sciences Citation Index, SS 3
Social Sciences Index, SS 4
Social Work Practice, SS 633
Social Work Year Book. *see* Encyclopedia of Social Work, SS 624
Société Canadienne pour l'Etude de la Religion. Actes. *see* Canadian Society for the Study of Religion. Proceedings; Société Canadienne pour l'Etude de la Religion. Actes, HU 259
Société Royale du Canada. Memoires. *see* Royal Society of Canada. Transactions; Société Royale du Canada. Memoires, HU 230
The Society for Historical Archaeology. Historical Archaeology. *see* Historical Archaeology, SS 18

Society for the Advancement of Continuing Education for Ministry. Continuing Education Resource Guide. *see* Continuing Education Resource Guide, ED 20
Society for the Promotion of Hellenic Studies. Journal of Hellenic Studies. *see* Journal of Hellenic Studies, HU 72
Society for the Promotion of Roman Studies. Journal of Roman Studies. *see* Journal of Roman Studies, HU 73
Society of Architectural Historians of Great Britain. Architectural History. *see* Architectural History, HU 25
Society of Catholic College Teachers of Sacred Doctrine. Proceedings. *see* College Theology Society. Proceedings, HU 270
Society of Logistics Engineers. Proceedings, SC 144
Society of Mining Engineers of AIME. Membership Directory, SC 305
Society of Mining Engineers of AIME. Mining Transactions, SC 306
Society of Naval Architects and Marine Engineers. Transactions, SC 200
Society of Petroleum Engineers of AIME. Membership Directory, SC 111
Society of Petroleum Engineers of AIME. Transactions, SC 112
Society of Plastics Engineers. Annual Technical Conference. Technical Papers, SC 187
Socio-Economic Progress in Latin America. Annual Report. *see* Economic and Social Progress in Latin America. Annual Report, SS 83
Sociological Methodology, SS 655
A Sociological Yearbook of Religion in Britain, HU 312
Softball Guide, SS 817
Softball Rules, SS 818
Solomon Goldman Lectures; Perspectives in Jewish Learning, HU 313
Something About the Author, HU 127
Sotheby's Annual Review. *see* Art at Auction: The Year at Sotheby's and Parke-Bernet, HU 30
Soundings: A Music Journal, HU 211
Sourcebook of Criminal Justice Statistics. *see* U.S. National Criminal Justice Information and Statistics Service. Sourcebook of Criminal Justice Statistics, SS 256
Sourcebook of Equal Educational Opportunity, ED 16
Source Book of Health Insurance Data, SS 418
Sourcebook on Aging, SS 634
Sources of Information for the Trial Lawyer and the Legal Investigator. *see* Lawyer's Desk Reference (LDR), SS 470

Sources of Serials, GE 110
South America on $10 a Day, SS 1004
South American Handbook, SS 1005
South Pacific Travel Digest, SS 1006
Southern Baptist Convention. Southern Baptist Periodical Index. *see* Southern Baptist Periodical Index, HU 314
Southern Baptist Periodical Index, HU 314
Southern Conference on Gerontology, SC 259
Southern Indian Studies, SS 27
Soviet Armed Forces Review Annual, SC 289
The Soviet Union and Eastern Europe, SS 358
Spain and Morocco on $10 and $15 a Day, SS 1007
Spare-Time Furniture Projects, SS 395
Special Library Association. Annual Directory Issue, HU 167
Speech Association of America. Directory. *see* Speech Communication Association. Directory, HU 128
Speech Communication Association. Bibliographic Annual in Speech Communication. *see* Bibliographic Annual in Speech Communication, HU 91
Speech Communication Association. Directory, HU 128
Speech Index, HU 129
Spiritual Community Guide for North America, HU 315
Sport Fishery and Wildlife Research. *see* U.S. Fish and Wildlife Service. Sport Fishery and Wildlife Research, SC 117
Sports Afield Fishing Annual, SS 819
Sports Afield Gun Annual, SS 820
Sports Afield Hunting Annual, SS 821
Sports All Stars Baseball, SS 822
Standard Advertising Register. *see* Standard Directory of Advertisers, SS 516
Standard and Poor's. Analysts Handbook. *see* Analysts Handbook, SS 34
Standard and Poor's Register of Corporations, Directors, and Executives, SS 117
Standard Catalog of World Coins, SS 387
Standard Catalogue of Canadian Coins, Tokens, and Paper Money, SS 388
Standard Directory of Advertisers, SS 516
Standard Education Almanac, ED 17
Standards Engineers Society. Proceedings of Annual Meetings, SC 145
Standard Medical Almanac, SC 260
Standard Periodical Directory, GE 55
Stanford Journal of International Studies, SS 5
Stanford University. School of Law. International Society. Proceedings. *see* Stanford Journal of International Studies, SS 359
Stanford University School of Law. International Society. Proceedings. *see* Stanford Journal of International Studies, SS 5
State Approved Schools of Nursing—LPN/LVN, SC 261
State Approved Schools of Nursing—RN, SC 262
State Education Agency Officials. *see* Education Directory, ED 8
State Information and Federal Region Book, SS 310
State Legislation on Smoking and Health, SC 263
The State of Black America, SS 274
The State of Black Politics, SS 311
The State of Civil Rights: A Report of the United States Commission on Civil Rights. *see* U.S. Commission on Civil Rights. The State of Civil Rights: A Report of the United States Commission on Civil Rights, SS 143
State Tax Handbook, SS 587
Statesman's Year Book, GE 129
Statistical Abstract of Latin America, GE 130
Statistical Abstract of the United States, GE 131
Statistical Services of the United States Government, GE 132
Statistical Yearbook for Asia and the Pacific; Annuaire Statistique pour l'Asie et le Pacifique, GE 133
Statistical Year Book of the Electrical Utility Industry. *see* Edison Electric Institute. Statistical Year Book of the Electrical Utility Industry, SC 78
Statistical Yearbook of the League of Nations. *see* UNESCO. Statistical Yearbook; Annuaire Statistique, GE 136; United Nations. Statistical Yearbook; Annuaire Statistique, GE 137
Statistics Europe, GE 134
Statistics of Income: Business Income Tax Returns. *see* U.S. Internal Revenue Service. Statistics of Income: Business Income Tax Returns, SS 129
Statistics of Income: Corporation Income Tax Returns. *see* U.S. Internal Revenue Service. Statistics of Income: Corporation Income Tax Returns, SS 130
Statistics of Income: Individual Tax Returns. *see* U.S. Internal Revenue Service. Statistics of Income: Individual Tax Return, SS 598
Statistics Sources, GE 135
Steam Passenger Service Directory, SS 882
Steve Ferber's Hunter's Guns. *see* Bob Wallack's Hunter's Guns, SS 709
Stockholm International Peace Research Institute (SIPRI). World Armaments and Disarmament; SIPRI Yearbook. *see* World Armaments and Disarmament; SIPRI Yearbook, SC 294
The Story of the Olympic Games; 776 BC to (year), SS 823

Street and Smith's Baseball Yearbook, SS 824
Street and Smith's College and Pro Official Basketball Yearbook, SS 825
Street and Smith's Official Yearbook; College Football, SS 826
Street and Smith's Official Yearbook; Pro Football, SS 827
Structurist, HU 57
Student Aid Annual, ED 53
Studies in Criminological Research. see Collected Studies in Criminological Research, SS 230
Studies in Medical Geography, SC 264
Studies in Medieval and Renaissance Culture. see Medievalia et Humanistica: Studies in Medieval and Renaissance Culture, HU 15
Studies in Music, HU 212
Studies in the History of Art. see U.S. National Gallery of Art. Studies in the History of Art, HU 59
Study Abroad, ED 54
Study in Africa South of the Sahara. see Handbook on International Study for U.S. Nationals, ED 47
Study in East and South Asia and Oceania. see Handbook on International Study for U.S. Nationals, ED 47
Study in Europe. see Handbook on International Study for U.S. Nationals, ED 47
Study in the American Republics. see Handbook on International Study for U.S. Nationals, ED 47
Study in the Middle East and North Africa. see Handbook on International Study for U.S. Nationals, ED 47
Study of Employment of Women in the Federal Government. see U.S. Civil Service Commission. Manpower Statistics Division. Study of Employment of Women in the Federal Government, SS 434
Subject Bibliography Index. see U.S. Superintendent of Documents. Subject Bibliography Index, GE 61
Subject Directory of Special Libraries and Information Centers, HU 168
Subject Guide to Books in Print, GE 56
Subject Guide to Children's Books in Print, GE 57
Subject Guide to Microforms in Print, GE 58
Subject Index to Periodicals. see British Humanities Index, HU 6
Summer Camps and Summer Schools. see Guide to Summer Camps and Summer Schools, ED 26
Summer Employment Directory of the United States, SS 530
Summer Study Abroad, ED 55
Supreme Court Historical Society. Yearbook, SS 476
Supreme Court Review, SS 477
Surplus Dealers Directory, SS 517
Survey of Consumer Finances. see Surveys of Consumers, SS 118

Surveys of Consumers, SS 118
Swimming and Diving Case Book, SS 828
Swimming and Diving Rules and Records, SS 829
Swimming Pool Weekly and Swimming Pool Age Data and Reference Annual, SS 119
Swimming Rules. see Swimming and Diving Rules and Records, SS 829
Syesis, SS 28
Symposium on Coal Mine Drainage Research. Papers, SC 307
Syncrisis: The Dynamics of Health, SC 265

TV Directory: Television Rates and Fact Book. see Television Factbook, SS 207
TV Feature Film Source Book, SS 204
TV Free Film Source Book. see Series, Serials, and Packages, SS 203
TV Season (year), SS 205
TWA Getaway Guide to Athens, SS 1010
TWA Getaway Guide to Boston, SS 1011
TWA Getaway Guide to Denver and the Colorado Ski Country, SS 1012
TWA Getaway Guide to Honolulu, SS 1013
TWA Getaway Guide to Ireland, Dublin/Shannon, SS 1014
TWA Getaway Guide to Las Vegas, SS 1015
TWA Getaway Guide to Lisbon/Madrid; Costa del Sol, SS 1016
TWA Getaway Guide to London, SS 1017
TWA Getaway Guide to Los Angeles, SS 1018
TWA Getaway Guide to New York, SS 1019
TWA Getaway Guide to Paris, SS 1020
TWA Getaway Guide to Phoenix/Tucson, SS 1021
TWA Getaway Guide to Rome, SS 1022
TWA Getaway Guide to San Francisco, SS 1023
TWA Getaway Guide to Washington, D.C., SS 1024
TWA Getaway Guide to Zurich/Geneva, SS 1025
Tarbell's Teacher's Guide to the International Bible Lessons for Christian Teaching of the Uniform Course, HU 316
Task Force on Alternatives in Print. Alternatives in Print. see Alternatives in Print, GE 21
Tax Foundation. Facts and Figures on Government Finance. see Facts and Figures on Government Finance, SS 581
Taylor's Encyclopedia of Government Officials: Federal and State, SS 312
Teacher's Guide to the International Bible Lessons for Christian Teaching of the Uniform Course. see Tarbell's Teacher's Guide to the International Bible Lessons for Christian Teaching of the Uniform Course, HU 316

Teaching Abroad, SS 531
Technician Education Yearbook, ED 102
Techniques of Marriage and Family Counseling, SS 635
Teiresias, HU 75
Television Contacts, SS 206
Television Factbook, SS 207
Tennessee Studies in Literature, HU 130
Tennis Annual, SS 830
Tennis-Badminton-Squash Guide, SS 831
Teton, SS 1008
Texas Archaeological Society. Bulletin, SS 29
Textbooks in Print. see El-Hi Textbooks in Print, ED 172
Textile Blue Book. see Davison's Textile Blue Book, SC 164
Textile Catalog and Buyers Guide. see Davison's Textile Catalog and Buyers Guide, SC 165
Theatre Annual, HU 348
Theatre, Film, and Television Biographical Master Index, HU 349
Theatre Library Association. Performing Arts Resources. see Performing Arts Resources, HU 344
Theatre Studies, HU 350
Theatre World, HU 351
Theodor Herzl Institute. Herzl Year Book. see Herzl Year Book, SS 268
Thomas Grocery Register, SS 120
Thomas Hardy Year Book, HU 131
Thomas Register of American Manufacturers and Thomas Register Catalog File, SS 518
Three Thousand Books for Secondary School Libraries. see Books for Secondary School Libraries, ED 61
Thrum's All about Hawaii, SS 1026
Time-Life Encyclopedia of Gardening, SC 157
Track and Field Guide, SS 832
Track and Field Rules and Records; Boys and Girls, SS 833
Trademark Register of the United States, SS 537
The Trademark Renewal Register. see Trademark Register of the United States, SS 537
Traditio, HU 231
Trailer Life's Recreational Vehicle Campground and Services Directory, SS 1027
Training and Development Organizations Directory, ED 22
Transactions of the Association of Life Insurance Medical Directors of America, SC 266
Transit Fact Book. see American Public Transit Association. Transit Fact Book, SS 848
Transportation Research Forum. Proceedings: Annual Meeting, SS 883

Transportation Telephone Tickler, SS 884
Traveler's Almanac, SS 1009
Trinc's Blue Book of the Trucking Industry, SS 885
Trinity Journal, HU 317
Trinity Studies. see Trinity Journal, HU 317
Tri-State Regional Planning Commission. Annual Regional Report, SS 402
Tri-State Transportation Commission. Annual Report. see Tri-State Regional Planning Commission. Annual Regional Report, SS 402
Tulane Studies in English, HU 132
Tulane Studies in Philosophy, HU 232
Turbomachinery Symposium. Proceedings, SC 188
Twentieth Century Literary Criticism, HU 133

UNESCO. Annuaire Statistique. see UNESCO. Statistical Yearbook; Annuaire Statistique, GE 136
UNESCO. Copyright Laws and Treaties of the World. see Copyright Laws and Treaties of the World, SS 534
UNESCO. Index Translationum. see Index Translationum, GE 43
UNESCO. Statistical Yearbook; Annuaire Statistique, GE 136
UNESCO. Study Abroad. see Study Abroad, ED 54
USA Bus Travel Guide. see Baxter's USA Bus Travel Guide, SS 911
USA Rail Pass Guide. see Baxter's USA Rail Pass Guide, SS 912
USAN and the USP Dictionary of Drug Names, SC 267
Ukrainian Academy of Arts and Sciences in the United States. Annals, SS 275
Ulrich's International Periodicals Directory, GE 59
Union of International Associations. Annual International Congress Calendar. see Annual International Congress Calendar, GE 93
Union of International Associations. Yearbook of International Organizations; Annuaire des Organizations Internationales. see Yearbook of International Organizations; Annuaire des Organizations Internationales, GE 112
Union Wages and Hours Surveys; Local Transit Operating Employees. see U.S. Bureau of Labor Statistics. Union Wages and Hours Surveys; Local Transit Operating Employees, SS 431
Unitarian Historical Society, London. Transactions, HU 318
Unitarian Universalist Directory, HU 319
United Church Board for World Ministries. Annual Report and Calendar of Prayer, HU 320

United Church of Christ. General Synod. Minutes, HU 321

United Church of Christ. Yearbook, HU 322

United Lutheran Church in American. Yearbook. *see* Lutheran Church in America. Yearbook, HU 296

United Methodist Church. The Organization of the United Methodist Church. *see* The Organization of the United Methodist Church, HU 306

United Methodist Church (United States). General Minutes of the Annual Conference of the United Methodist Church, HU 323

United Nations. Annuaire Statistique. *see* United Nations. Statistical Yearbook; Annuaire Statistique, GE 137

United Nations. Delegations to the General Assembly, SS 567

United Nations. List of Delegations. *see* United Nations. Delegations to the General Assembly, SS 567

United Nations. Statistical Yearbook; Annuaire Statistique, GE 137

United Nations. Yearbook, SS 568

United Nations. Department of Economic Affairs. Yearbook of Industrial Statistics. *see* Yearbook of Industrial Statistics, SS 136

United Nations. Department of Economic and Social Affairs. World Economic Survey, SS 121

United Nations. Department of Economic and Social Affairs. World Energy Supplies. *see* World Energy Supplies, SC 119

The United Nations Disarmament Yearbook, SC 290

United Nations. Economic Commission for Europe. Economic Survey of Europe. *see* Economic Survey of Europe, SS 84

United Nations. Economic Commission for Latin America. Economic Survey of Latin America. *see* Economic Survey of Latin America, SS 85

United Nations Educational, Scientific, and Cultural Organization. Statistical Yearbook; Annuaire Statistique. *see* UNESCO. Statistical Yearbook; Annuaire Statistique, GE 136

United Nations Educational, Scientific, and Cultural Organization. Study Abroad. *see* Study Abroad, ED 54

United Nations. Food and Agriculture Organization. Production Yearbook. *see* Food and Agriculture Organization of the United Nations. Production Yearbook, SS 89

United Nations. Food and Agriculture Organization. Trade Yearbook. *see* Food and Agriculture Organization of the United Nations. Trade Yearbook, SS 90

United Nations. Office of Public Information. Basic Facts About the United Nations. *see* Basic Facts About the United Nations, SS 549

United Nations. Statistical Office. Demographic Yearbook; Annuaire Demographique. *see* Demographic Yearbook; Annuaire Demographique, GE 125

United Nations. Statistical Office. Yearbook of International Trade Statistics. *see* Yearbook of International Trade Statistics, SS 137

United Presbyterian Church. Mission Yearbook of Prayer. *see* Mission Yearbook of Prayer, HU 301

United Presbyterian Church in the U.S.A. Minutes of the General Assembly, HU 324

U.S. Academic Programs Abroad and Undergraduate Study Abroad. *see* U.S. College Sponsored Programs Abroad: (academic year), ED 56

U.S. Agency for International Development. Proposed Foreign Aid Program; Summary Presentation to Congress, SS 122

United States and Canadian Mailing Lists, SS 519

U.S. and the Developing World; Agenda for Action, SS 569

U.S. Arms Control and Disarmament Agency. Annual Report to Congress, SC 291

U.S. Arms Control and Disarmament Agency. Arms Control and Disarmament Agreements, SC 292

U.S. Arms Control and Disarmament Agency. Documents on Disarmament, SC 293

U.S. Arms Control and Disarmament Agency. World Military Expenditures and Arms Transfers. *see* World Military Expenditures and Arms Transfers, SC 295

U.S. Bureau of Economic Analysis. Business Statistics. *see* Business Statistics, SS 69

U.S. Bureau of Indian Affairs. American Indian Calendar, SS 276

U.S. Bureau of Labor Statistics. Analysis of Work Stoppages, SS 429

U.S. Bureau of Labor Statistics. Directory of National Unions and Employee Associations. *see* Directory of National Unions and Employee Associations, SS 421

U.S. Bureau of Labor Statistics. Employment and Earnings: United States. *see* Employment and Earnings: United States, SS 422

U.S. Bureau of Labor Statistics. Handbook of Labor Statisics, SS 430

U.S. Bureau of Labor Statistics. Union Wages and Hours Surveys; Local Transit Operating Employees, SS 431

U.S. Bureau of Land Management. Public Land Statistics, SS 613

U.S. Bureau of Mines. International Petroleum Annual. *see* International Petroleum Annual, SC 108

U.S. Bureau of Mines. Mineral Facts and Problems, SC 308

U.S. Bureau of Mines. Minerals Yearbook, SC 309

U.S. Bureau of National Affairs. Labor Relations Yearbook. *see* Labor Relations Yearbook, SS 423

U.S. Bureau of Prisons. National Prisoner Statistics: Executions. *see* U.S. National Criminal Justice Information Statistics Service. Capital Punishment, SS 253

U.S. Bureau of the Budget. Statistical Policy Division. Federal Statistical Directory. *see* Federal Statistical Directory, GE 126

U.S. Bureau of the Budget. Statistical Policy Division. Statistical Services of the United States Government. *see* Statistical Services of the United States Government, GE 132

U.S. Bureau of the Census. Annual Housing Survey, SS 405-410

U.S. Bureau of the Census. Bureau of the Census Catalog, GE 60

U.S. Bureau of the Census. Census of Governments, SS 313

U.S. Bureau of the Census. Census of Manufacturers, SS 123

U.S. Bureau of the Census. Census of Population, GE 138

U.S. Bureau of the Census. Chart Book of Governmental Data; Organization, Finances, and Employment, SS 314

U.S. Bureau of the Census. Chart Book on Government Finances and Employment. *see* U.S. Bureau of the Census. Chart Book of Governmental Data: Organization, Finances, and Employment, SS 314

U.S. Bureau of the Census. City Employment in (year), SS 315

U.S. Bureau of the Census. City Government Finances in (year), SS 588

U.S. Bureau of the Census. Congressional District Atlas, SS 570

U.S. Bureau of the Census. Congressional District Data Book, SS 571

U.S. Bureau of the Census. Consumer Income. *see* U.S. Bureau of the Census. Current Population Reports, GE 139

U.S. Bureau of the Census. County and City Data Book. *see* County and City Data Book, SS 297

U.S. Bureau of the Census. County Business Patterns, SS 124

U.S. Bureau of the Census. County Government Employment in (year), SS 316

U.S. Bureau of the Census. County Government Finances in (year), SS 589

U.S. Bureau of the Census. Current Population Reports, GE 139

U.S. Bureau of the Census. Farm Population. *see* U.S. Bureau of the Census. Current Population Reports, GE 139

U.S. Bureau of the Census. Federal-State Cooperative Program for Population Estimates. *see* U.S. Bureau of the Census. Current Population Reports, GE 139

U.S. Bureau of the Census. Finances of Employee-Retirement Systems of State and Local Governments in (year), SS 590

U.S. Bureau of the Census. Financial Characteristics by Indicators of Housing and Neighborhood Quality. *see* U.S. Bureau of the Census. Annual Housing Survey, SS 410

U.S. Bureau of U.S. Bureau of the Census. Financial Characteristics for the Housing Inventory. *see* U.S. Bureau of the Census. Annual Housing Survey, SS 407

U.S. Bureau of the Census. Foreign Commerce and Navigation of the United States, SS 125

U.S. Bureau of the Census. General Housing Characteristics. *see* U.S. Bureau of the Census. Annual Housing Survey, SS 405

U.S. Bureau of the Census. Governmental Finances in (year), SS 591

U.S. Bureau of the Census. Housing Characteristics of Recent Movers. *see* U.S. Bureau of the Census. Annual Housing Survey, SS 408

U.S. Bureau of the Census. Indicators of Housing and Neighborhood Quality. *see* U.S. Bureau of the Census. Annual Housing Survey, SS 406

U.S. Bureau of the Census. Local Government Employment in Selected Metropolitan Areas and Large Counties, SS 317

U.S. Bureau of the Census. Local Government Finances in Selected Metropolitan Areas and Large Counties: (Year), SS 592

U.S. Bureau of the Census. Pocket Data Book, U.S.A. *see* Pocket Data Book, U.S.A., GE 128

U.S. Bureau of the Census. Population Characteristics. *see* U.S. Bureau of the Census. Current Population Reports, GE 139

U.S. Bureau of the Census. Population Estimates and Projections. *see* U.S. Bureau of the Census. Current Population Reports, GE 139

U.S. Bureau of the Census. Prisoners in State and Federal Prisons and Reformatories. *see* U.S. Federal Bureau of Prisons. Statistical Report, SS 250

U.S. Bureau of the Census. Public Employment. *see* Public Employment, SS 426

U.S. Bureau of the Census. Public Employment in (year), SS 318

U.S. Bureau of the Census. Special Censuses. *see* U.S. Bureau of the Census. Current Population Reports, GE 139

U.S. Bureau of the Census. Special Studies. *see* U.S.

Bureau of the Census. Current Population Reports, GE 139

U.S. Bureau of the Census. State Government Finances in (year), SS 593

U.S. Bureau of the Census. State Tax Collections in (year), SS 594

U.S. Bureau of the Census. Statistical Abstract of the United States. *see* Statistical Abstract of the United States, GE 131

U.S. Bureau of the Census. Summary of City Finances in (year). *see* U.S. Bureau of the Census. City Government Finances in (year), SS 588

U.S. Bureau of the Census. Urban and Rural Housing Characteristics. *see* U.S. Bureau of the Census. Annual Housing Survey, SS 409

U.S. Catholic Conference. Directory of Campus Ministry. *see* Directory of Campus Ministry, HU 275

United States Catholic Mission Council. Mission Handbook, HU 325

United States Catholic Missionary Personnel Overseas. *see* United States Catholic Mission Council. Mission Handbook, HU 325

U.S. Citizens' Advisory Council on the Status of Women. Women in (year). *see* Women in (year), SS 144

U.S. Civil Aeronautics Board. Aircraft Operating Cost and Performance Report, SS 886

U.S. Civil Service Commission. Minority Group Employment in the Federal Government. *see* Minority Group Employment in the Federal Government, SS 425

U.S. Civil Service Commission. Manpower Statistics Division. Federal Civilian Employment of Women. *see* U.S. Civil Service Commission. Manpower Statistics Division. Study of Employment of Women in the Federal Government, SS 434

U.S. Civil Service Commission. Manpower Statistics Division. Occupations of Federal White-Collar Workers, SS 432

U.S. Civil Service Commission. Manpower Statistics Division. Pay Structure of the Federal Civil Service, SS 433

U.S. Civil Service Commission. Manpower Statistics Division. Study of Employment of Women in the Federal Government, SS 434

U.S. Coast Guard. Boating Statistics, SS 887

U.S. Coast Guard. Merchant Vessels of the United States (Including Yachts). *see* Merchant Vessels of the United States (Including Yachts), SS 871

U.S. Code Congressional and Administrative News, SS 478

U.S. College Sponsored Programs Abroad (academic year), ED 56

U.S. Commission on Civil Rights. The State of Civil Rights: A Report of the United States Commission on Civil Rights, SS 143

U.S. Congress. Congressional Directory. *see* Congressional Directory, SS 292

U.S. Copyright Office. Annual Report of the Register of Copyrights, SS 538

U.S. Copyright Office. Decisions of the United States Courts Involving Copyrights. *see* Decisions of the United States Courts Involving Copyrights, SS 535

U.S. Council on Environmental Quality. Annual Report, SC 113

U.S. Council on International Economic Policy. International Economic Report of the President Transmitted to the Congress, SS 126

U.S. Department of Commerce. U.S. Industrial Outlook; With Projections to (year). *see* U.S. Industrial Outlook; With Projections to (year), SS 128

U.S. Department of Health, Education, and Welfare. Directory of Poison Control Centers. *see* Directory of Poison Control Centers, SC 232

U.S. Department of Health, Education, and Welfare. Education Division. Library Statistics of Colleges and Universities. *see* Library Statistics of Colleges and Universities, HU 162

U.S. Department of Housing and Urban Development. Annual Report, SS 411

U.S. Department of Justice. Annual Report of the Attorney General of the United States, SS 246

U.S. Department of Justice. Office of the Attorney General. Report of the Attorney General to the Congress of the U.S. on the Foreign Agents Registration Act of 1938, as Amended, for the Calendar Year (date), SS 479

U.S. Department of Labor. Manpower and Automation Research, SS 435

U.S. Department of Labor. Occupational Outlook Handbook. *see* Occupational Outlook Handbook, SS 528

U.S. Department of Labor. Apprenticeship and Training Bureau. Directory for Reaching Minority Groups. *see* Directory for Reaching Minority Groups, SS 621

U.S. Department of Labor. Employment and Training Administration. Manpower Research and Development Projects. *see* U.S. Department of Labor. Employment and Training Administration. Research and Development Projects, SS 436

U.S. Department of Labor. Employment and Training Administration. Manpower Research Projects. *see* U.S. Department of Labor. Employment and Training Administration. Research and Development Projects, SS 436

U.S. Department of Labor. Employment and Training Administration. Research and Development Projects, SS 436

U.S. Department of State. Digest of International Law. *see* U.S. Department of State. Digest of United States Practice in International Law, SS 480

U.S. Department of State. Digest of United States Practice in International Law, SS 480

U.S. Department of State. Treaties in Force, SS 572

U.S. Department of State. United States Treaties and Other International Agreements, SS 573

U.S. Department of the Interior. United States Geological Survey. *see* United States Geological Survey, SC 74

U.S. Department of the Interior. Water Resources Research Catalog, SC 114

U.S. Department of the Interior. Fish and Wildlife Service. Fishery and Wildlife Annual Report. *see* U.S. Fish and Wildlife Service. Cooperative Research Units. Fishery and Wildlife Annual Report, SC 116

U.S. Department of the Interior. Fish and Wildlife Service. Sport Fishery and Wildlife Research. *see* U.S. Fish and Wildlife Service. Sport Fishery and Wildlife Research, SC 117

U.S. Department of Transportation. Annual Report, SS 888

United States Earthquakes, SC 72

U.S. Environmental Protection Agency. A Collection of Legal Opinions, SS 481

U.S. Equal Employment Opportunity Commission. Equal Employment Opportunity Report, SS 437

U.S. Equal Employment Opportunity Commission. Minorities and Women in State and Local Government. *see* Minorities and Women in State and Local Government, SS 424

U.S. Excise Tax Guide, SS 595

U.S. Facilities and Programs for Children with Severe Mental Illnesses; A Directory, SC 268

U.S. Federal Aviation Administration. Census of U.S. Civil Aircraft, SS 889

U.S. Federal Aviation Administration. Statistical Study of U.S. Civil Aircraft. *see* U.S. Federal Aviation Administration. Census of U.S. Civil Aircraft, SS 889

U.S. Federal Aviation Administration. U.S. Active Civil Aircraft by State and County. *see* U.S. Federal Aviation Administration. Census of U.S. Civil Aircraft, SS 889

U.S. Federal Bureau of Investigation. Annual Report, SS 247

U.S. Federal Bureau of Investigation. Uniform Crime Reports for the United States, SS 248

U.S. Federal Bureau of Prisons. Annual Report, SS 249

U.S. Federal Bureau of Prisons. Statistical Report, SS 250

U.S. Federal Mediation and Conciliation Service. Annual Report, SS 438

U.S. Federal Power Commission. Annual Report, SC 115

U.S. Federal Supply Bureau. Federal Standard Stock Catalogue, Section 4, Federal Specifications, Part I: Index to Federal Specifications, Standards, and Handbooks. *see* U.S. Federal Supply Service. Index of Federal Specifications and Standards, SS 127

U.S. Federal Supply Service. Index of Federal Specifications and Standards, SS 127

United States Figure Skating Association. Official USFSA Rulebook, SS 834

U.S. Fish and Wildlife Service. Progress in Sport Fishery Research. *see* U.S. Fish and Wildlife Service. Sport Fishery and Wildlife Research, SC 117

U.S. Fish and Wildlife Service. Sport Fishery and Wildlife Research, SC 117

U.S. Fish and Wildlife Service. Cooperative Research Units. Fishery and Wildlife Annual Report, SC 116

United States Foamed Plastic Markets and Directory, SC 189

U.S. Forest Service. Forest Resource Report, SC 73

U.S. Geological Survey. Yearbook, SC 74

United States Government Manual, SS 319

United States Government Organization Manual. *see* United States Government Manual, SS 319

U.S. Industrial Outlook; With Projections to (year), SS 128

U.S. Internal Revenue Service. Annual Report of the Commissioner, SS 596

U.S. Internal Revenue Service. Annual Report of the Secretary of the Treasury on the State of the Finances, SS 597

U.S. Internal Revenue Service. Statistics of Income: Business Income Tax Returns, SS 129

U.S. Internal Revenue Service. Statistics of Income: Corporation Income Tax Returns, SS 130

U.S. Internal Revenue Service. Statistics of Income: Individual Tax Returns, SS 598

U.S. Law Enforcement Assistance Administration. Annual Report, SS 251

U.S. Law Enforcement Assistance Administration. Expenditure and Employment Data for the Criminal Justice System, SS 252

United States Lawn Tennis Association. Yearbook. *see* United States Tennis Association. The Official USTA Yearbook and Tennis Guide with the Official Rules, SS 838

U.S. Library of Congress. Annual Report of the Librarian of Congress, HU 169

U.S. Library of Congress. Publications in Print. *see* Library of Congress Publications in Print, GE 48

U.S. Master Tax Guide, SS 599

U.S. National Archives and Records Service. Public Papers of the Presidents of the United States. *see* Public Papers of the Presidents of the United States, SS 309

U.S. National Burea of Standards. Annual Report, SS 131

U.S. National Bureau of Standards. Technical Highlights of the National Bureau of Standards. *see* U.S. National Bureau of Standards. Annual Report, SS 131

U.S. National Center for Educational Statistics. Digest of Educational Statistics. *see* Digest of Educational Statistics, ED 4

U.S. National Center for Educational Statistics. Directory of Postsecondary Schools with Occupational Programs. *see* Directory of Postsecondary Schools with Occupational Programs, ED 100

U.S. National Center for Educational Statistics. Education Directory. *see* Education Directory, ED 8

U.S. National Center for Educational Statistics. Projections of Educational Statistics to (year). *see* Projections of Educational Statistics to (year), ED 14

U.S. National Clearinghouse for Smoking and Health. Bibliography on Smoking and Health. *see* Bibliography on Smoking and Health, SC 222

U.S. National Clearinghouse for Smoking and Health. Directory of On-going Research in Smoking and Health. *see* Directory of On-Going Research in Smoking and Health, SC 230

U.S. National Clearinghouse for Smoking and Health. Health Consequences of Smoking. *see* Health Consequences of Smoking, SC 242

U.S. National Clearinghouse for Smoking and Health. State Legislation on Smoking and Health. *see* State Legislation on Smoking and Health, SC 263

U.S. National Criminal Justice Information and Statistics Service. Capital Punishment, SS 253

U.S. National Criminal Justice Information and Statistics Service. Criminal Victimization in the United States: A Comparison of (year) and (year) Findings, SS 254

U.S. National Criminal Justice Information and Statistics Service. Prisoners in State and Federal Institutions, SS 255

U.S. National Criminal Justice Information and Statistics Service. Sourcebook of Criminal Justice Statistics, SS 256

U.S. National Criminal Justice Information and Statistics Service. Trends in Expenditures and Employment Data for the Criminal Justice System, SS 257

U.S. National Gallery of Art. Annual Report, HU 58

U.S. National Gallery of Art. Report and Studies in the History of Art. *see* U.S. National Gallery of Art. Studies in the History of Art, HU 59

U.S. National Gallery of Art. Studies in the History of Art, HU 59

U.S. National Geophysical and Solar-Terrestrial Data Center. United States Earthquakes. *see* United States Earthquakes, SC 72

U.S. National Institute of Mental Health. Mental Health Directory. *see* Mental Health Directory, SC 332

U.S. National Labor Relations Board. Annual Report, SS 439

U.S. National Labor Relations Board. Digest and Index of Decisions of the National Relations Board. Annual Supplements, SS 440

U.S. National Library of Medicine. Bibliography of the History of Medicine. *see* Bibliography of the History of Medicine, SC 221

U.S. National Library of Medicine. Cumulated Abridged Index Medicus. *see* Cumulated Abridged Index Medicus, SC 225

U.S. National Library of Medicine. Cumulated Index Medicus. *see* Cumulated Index Medicus, SC 226

U.S. National Mediation Board. Annual Report, SS 441

U.S. National Park Service. Office of the Chief Scientist. Annual Report, SC 75

U.S. Office of Education. Office of Management. Catalog of Federal Assistance Programs. *see* Catalog of Federal Assistance Programs, ED 3

U.S. Office of International Health. Syncrisis: The Dynamics of Health. *see* Syncrisis: The Dynamics of Health, SC 265

U.S. Office of Management and Budget. The Budget of the United States Government, SS 600

U.S. Office of Management and Budget. The Budget of the United States Government. Appendix, SS 601

U.S. Office of Management and Budget. Catalog of Federal Domestic Assistance, SS 602

U.S. Office of Management and Budget. Issues 78, SS 603

U.S. Office of Management and Budget. Social Indicators, SS 656

U.S. Office of Management and Budget. Special Analysis Budget of the United States Government, SS 604

U.S. Office of Management and Budget. The United States Budget in Brief, SS 605

U.S. Official Hotel Directory. *see* Hotel and Motel Redbook, SS 94

U.S. Patent and Trademark Office. Commissioner of Patents and Trademarks. Annual Report, SS 539

U.S. Patent and Trademark Office. Index of Patents Issued from the U.S. Patent and Trademark Office, SS 540

U.S. Patent and Trademark Office. Index of Trademarks Issued from the U.S. Patent and Trademark Office, SS 541

United States Pharmacopeial Convention. USAN and the USP Dictionary of Drug Names. *see* USAN and the USP Dictionary of Drug Names, SC 267

United States Political Science Documents, SS 574

United States Polo Association. Yearbook, SS 835

United States Postal Service. Directory of Post Offices with ZIP Codes, SS 208

United States Postal Service. ZIP Code Directory, SS 209

United States Savings and Loan League. Savings and Loan Fact Book. *see* Savings and Loan Fact Book, SS 51

United States Ski Association. Directory, SS 836

United States Squash Racquets Association. Official Year Book, SS 837

United States Statutes at Large, SS 482

U.S. Superintendent of Documents. Subject Bibliography Index, GE 61

U.S. Tax Guide. *see* U.S. Master Tax Guide, SS 599

United States Tennis Association. The Official USTA Yearbook and Tennis Guide with the Official Rules, SS 838

United States Tennis Survey. Official United States Tennis Tournament Directory. *see* Official United States Tennis Tournament Directory, SS 799

U.S. Urban Mass Transit Administration. Urban Mass Transportation Abstracts, SS 890

United States Volleyball Association. Annual Official Volleyball Rules and Reference Guide, SS 839

U.S. Women's Bureau. Handbook of Facts on Women Workers. *see* U.S. Women's Bureau. Handbook on Women Workers, SS 442

U.S. Women's Bureau. Handbook on Women Workers, SS 442

U.S. Women's Bureau. Women of the (no.) Congress. *see* Women of the (no.) Congress, SS 322

The Universal Reference System: Political Science, Government and Public Policy Series. Annual Supplement, SS 575

University of California, Los Angeles. Department of Anthropology. Archaeological Survey Annual Report. *see* Archaeological Survey Annual Report, SS 13

University of Edinburgh. School of Scottish Studies. Scottish Studies. *see* Scottish Studies, SS 357

University of Illinois at Urbana-Champaign. Clinic on Library Applications of Data Processing. Proceedings, HU 170

University of Michigan, Ann Arbor. Institute for Social Research. Surveys of Consumers. *see* Surveys of Consumers, SS 118

University of Michigan. Institute of Gerontology. Occasional Papers in Gerontology, SC 269

University of Missouri-Columbia. Museum of Art and Archaeology. Muse. *see* Muse, SS 22

University of Texas at Austin. Bureau of Business Research. Directory of Texas Manufacturers. *see* Directory of Texas Manufacturers, SS 80

Urban Affairs Annual Reviews, SS 403

Urban and Rural Housing Characteristics. *see* U.S. Bureau of the Census. Annual Housing Survey, SS 409

Urban Institute. Annual Report, SS 404

Urban Land Institute. Dollars and Cents Shopping Centers. *see* Dollars and Cents Shopping Centers, SS 501

Urban Mass Transportation Abstracts. *see* U.S. Urban Mass Transit Administration. Urban Mass Transportation Abstracts, SS 890

Used Book Price Guide, SS 210

Venereal Disease Bibliography, SC 270

The Vergilian Society. Annual Report. *see* Vergilius, HU 76

Vergilius, HU 76

Vesak Annual. *see* World Buddhism; Vesak Annual, HU 327

Veterans Information Service. What Every Veteran Should Know. *see* What Every Veteran Should Know, SS 636

The Veterinary Annual, SC 338

Virgil Society. Proceedings, HU 77

The Visualization of Anthropology. *see* Films: The Visualization of Anthropology, SS 17

Volleyball Guide, SS 840

Volleyball Rules, SS 841

Walters Art Gallery. Journal, HU 60

The Warburg Institute. Journal of the Warburg and Courtauld Institutes. *see* Journal of the Warburg and Courtauld Institutes, HU 13

Ward's Automotive Yearbook, SS 891

Washington, D.C. on $10 and $15 a Day, SS 1028
Washington Information Directory, SS 320
Waterway Guide; The Yachtsman's Bible: Mid-Atlantic, SS 892
Waterway Guide; The Yachtsman's Bible: Northern, SS 893
Waterway Guide; The Yachtsman's Bible: Southern, SS 894
Weather Almanac, SC 76
Webster's Gemmologists Compendium. see Gems: Their Sources, Descriptions and Identification, SC 299
Welding Data Book, SC 190
Wenner-Gren Foundation for Anthropological Research. Report, SS 30
West Africa Annual, SS 360
The West Indies and Caribbean Yearbook, SS 361
Westchester Library System. Children's Books; Awards and Prizes. see Children's Books; Awards and Prizes, GE 34
What Every Veteran Should Know, SS 636
What They Said, GE 16
Where to Retire on a Small Income, SS 614
Where to Stay USA from 50¢ to $10 a Night, SS 1029
Whitaker's Almanack, GE 17
Whitney Museum of American Art. Whitney Review. see Whitney Review, HU 61
Whitney Review, HU 61
Who Owns Whom: International Subsidiaries of U.S. Companies. see Who Owns Whom: North American Edition, SS 520
Who Owns Whom: North American Edition, SS 520
Who Was Who in America, GE 70
Whole World Handbook, ED 57
Who's Who, GE 71
Who's Who Among Black Americans, GE 72
Who's Who in America, GE 73
Who's Who in American Art, HU 62
Who's Who in American Law, SS 483
Who's Who in American Politics, SS 576
Who's Who in Art, HU 63
Who's Who in Art and Antiques. see International Who's Who in Art and Antiques, HU 44
Who's Who in Baseball, SS 842
Who's Who in Canada, GE 74
Who's Who in Commerce and Industry. see Who's Who in Finance and Industry, SS 132
Who's Who in Electronics, SC 92
Who's Who in Finance and Industry, SS 132
Who's Who in Government, SS 321
Who's Who in Health Care, SC 271
Who's Who in Library Service. see Biographical Directory of Librarians in the United States and Canada, HU 153
Who's Who in Music and Musicians' International Directory. see International Who's Who in Music and Musicians Directory, HU 198
Who's Who in Nuclear Energy. see American Nuclear Society. Directory: Who's Who in Nuclear Energy, SC 93
Who's Who in Poetry. see International Who's Who in Poetry, HU 108
Who's Who in Religion, HU 326
Who's Who in the Arab World, GE 75
Who's Who in the East, GE 76
Who's Who in the Midwest, GE 77
Who's Who in the South and Southwest, GE 78
Who's Who in the Theatre, HU 352
Who's Who in the West, GE 79
Who's Who in the World, GE 80
Who's Who in Training and Development, SS 521
Who's Who of American Women, GE 81
Willing's Press Guide, SS 211
Willis, John. Screen World. see Screen World, HU 176
Winchell, Constance M. Guide to Reference Books. see Guide to Reference Books, GE 41
Winter Simulation Conference. Proceedings, SC 66
Winterthur Portfolio, HU 19
Wire Journal Directory/Catalog, SC 191
Wise Giving Bulletin, SS 637
Woman's Day Best Ideas for Christmas, SS 396
Woman's Day Granny Squares, SS 397
Women and Literature, HU 134
Women in (year), SS 144
Women of the (no.) Congress, SS 322
Women's History Research Center. Female Artists Past and Present. see Female Artists Past and Present, HU 38
Women's Organizations and Leaders Directory, GE 111
Women's Rights Almanac, SS 145
WomenSports Magazine; Scholarship Guide Issue, ED 58
Woodall's Campground Directory: Eastern Edition, SS 1030
Woodall's Campground Directory: North American Edition, SS 1031
Woodall's Campground Directory: Western Edition, SS 1032
Woodall's Directory of Mobile Home Communities, SS 412
Woodall's Mobile Home Park Directory. see Woodall's Directory of Mobile Home Communities, SS 412
Woodall's Mobile Home Parks and Retirement Com-

munities. *see* Woodall's Retirement and Resort Communities, SS 615
Woodall's Retirement and Resort Communities, SS 615
Woodall's Trailer Park Directory. *see* Woodall's Directory of Mobile Home Communities, SS 412
Woodall's Trailering Parks and Campgrounds. *see* Woodall's Campground Directory, SS 1030-1032
Working Press of the Nation, SS 212
World Almanac and Book of Facts, GE 18
World Armaments and Disarmament; SIPRI Yearbook, SC 294
World Automotive Market, SS 895
World Book Year Book, GE 19
World Buddhism; Vesak Annual, HU 327
World Cars, SS 896
World Coal Trade. *see* International Coal, SC 300
World Collectors Annuary, HU 64
World Conference of Friends. Report, HU 328
World Council of Churches. Confessions in Dialogue. *see* Confessions in Dialogue, HU 271
World Council of Churches. Minutes and Reports of the Central Committee Meetings, HU 329
World Directory of Environmental Research Centers, SC 118
World Directory of Schools for Medical Assistants; Repertoire Mondial des Ecoles d'Assistants Medicaux, SC 272
World Directory of Schools of Pharmacy, SC 273
World Directory of Veterinary Schools, SC 339
World Economic Survey. *see* United Nations. Department of Economic and Social Affairs. World Economic Survey, SS 121
World Energy Supplies, SC 119
World Environmental Directory, SC 120
World Events in (year). *see* The Annual Register. World Events in (year), GE 2
World Guide for Jewish Travellers. *see* Jewish Travel Guide, SS 971
World Health Organization. Monograph Series, SC 274
World Health Organization. World Directory of Schools for Medical Assistants; Repertoire Mondial des Ecoles d'Assistants Medicaux. *see* World Directory of Schools for Medical Assistants; Repertoire Mondial des Ecoles d'Assistants Medicaux, SC 272
World Health Organization. World Directory of Schools of Pharmacy. *see* World Directory of Schools of Pharmacy, SC 273
World Health Organization. World Directory of Veterinary Schools. *see* World Directory of Veterinary Schools, SC 339
World Ice Rink Directory. *see* Ice Rink Directory and Hockey Buyers Guide, SS 95

The World in (year): History as We Lived It, GE 20
World Intellectual Property Organization (WIPO). Copyright Laws and Treaties of the World. *see* Copyright Laws and Treaties of the World, SS 534
World Law Directory. *see* World Legal Directory, SS 484
World Legal Directory, SS 484
The World Marketing Directory. *see* Principal International Businesses, SS 515
World Military and Social Expenditures, SS 577
World Military Expenditures and Arms Trade. *see* World Military Expenditures and Arms Transfers, SC 295
World Military Expenditures and Arms Transfers, SC 295
World Mines Register, SC 310
World Motor Vehicle Data, SS 897
World of Learning, ED 18
World of Tennis, SS 843
World Peace Through Law Center. World Legal Directory. *see* World Legal Directory, SS 484
World Radio TV Handbook, SS 213
World Telex Directory. *see* Jaeger and Waldmann World Telex Directory, SS 189
World Trade Annual, SS 133
World Trade Annual. Supplement, SS 134
World Who's Who of Women, GE 82
World Wide Chamber of Commerce Directory, SS 135
Worldwide Petrochemical Directory, SC 121
World-wide Summer Placement Directory, SS 532
Worldwide Yacht Charter and Boat Rental Guide, SS 898
Wrestling Officials Manual, SS 844
Wrestling Rules, SS 845
Write on, Woman! HU 135
Writers and Artists Yearbook, SS 214
Writer's Directory, SS 215
Writer's Handbook, SS 216
Writer's Market, SS 217
Writer's Yearbook, SS 218
Writings on American History, SS 362
Writings on American History. *see* America: History and Life. Part C, American History Bibliography, SS 327

The Yachtsman's Bible. *see* Waterway Guides, SS 892-894
The Yale Architectural Journal. *see* Perspecta: The Yale Architectural Journal, HU 56
Yale Classical Studies, HU 78
The Year at Sotheby's and Parke-Bernet. *see* Art at

Auction: The Year at Sotheby's and Parke-Bernet, HU 30
Yearbook and Directory of Osteopathic Physicians, SC 275
Yearbook for Inter-American Musical Research; Anuario Interamericano de Investigacion Musical, HU 213
Yearbook of Adult and Continuing Education, ED 23
Yearbook of American and Canadian Churches, HU 330
The Yearbook of American Bibliographic and Textual Studies. see Proof, HU 121
Yearbook of American Churches. see Yearbook of American and Canadian Churches, HU 330
Yearbook of Astronomy, SC 20
Year Book of Cancer, SC 276
Yearbook of Comparative and General Literature, HU 136
Yearbook of Comparative Criticism, HU 137
Yearbook of Dentistry, SC 277
Yearbook of Educational and Instructional Technology. see International Yearbook of Educational and Instructional Technology, ED 76
Yearbook of English Studies, HU 138
Yearbook of Equal Educational Opportunity. see Sourcebook of Equal Educational Opportunity, ED 16
Yearbook of Food and Agricultural Statistics, Part One. see Food and Agriculture Organization of the United Nations. Production Yearbook, SS 89
Yearbook of Food and Agricultural Statistics, Part Two. see Food and Agriculture Organization of the United Nations. Trade Yearbook, SS 90
Yearbook of Higher Education, ED 59
Yearbook of Industrial Statistics, SS 136
Yearbook of International Organizations; Annuaire des Organizations Internationales, GE 112
Yearbook of International Trade Statistics, SS 137
Yearbook of Labour Statistics, SS 443
Year Book of Medicine, SC 278
Year Book of Neurology, Psychiatry and Neurosurgery. see Year Book of Psychiatry and Applied Mental Health, SC 335
The Year Book of Photography and Amateur's Guide. see British Journal of Photography Annual, HU 234
Yearbook of Physical Anthropology, SS 31
Year Book of Psychiatry and Applied Mental Health, SC 335
Yearbook of Railroad Facts, SS 899
Yearbook of Railroad Information. see Yearbook of Railroad Facts, SS 899
Yearbook of School Law, SS 485
Yearbook of Science and Technology. see McGraw-Hill Yearbook of Science and Technology, SC 8
Yearbook of Science and the Future, SC 13
Yearbook of Special Education, ED 96
Year Book of the Churches. see Yearbook of American and Canadian Churches, HU 330
Yearbook of the European Convention on Human Rights, SS 146
Yearbook of the History of Music, Medieval and Renaissance. see Musica Disciplina, HU 201
Yearbook of the International Law Commission, SS 486
Yearbook of the Lutheran Church in America. see Lutheran Church in America. Yearbook, HU 296
The Year Book of World Affairs, SS 579
Yearbook on Human Rights, SS 147
Yearbook on International Communist Affairs, SS 580
Year's Work in English Studies, HU 139
Year's Work in Librarianship. see British Librarianship and Information Science, HU 154
Year's Work in Modern Language Studies, HU 140
Yeshiva University. Sephardic Studies Program. The American Sephardi. see The American Sephardi, SS 261
Yesterday's Authors of Books for Children, HU 141
Yivo Annual of Jewish Social Sciences, SS 6
Yivo Bleter, SS 277
Your Federal Income Tax Annual, SS 606

ZIP Code Directory. see United States Postal Service. ZIP Code Directory, SS 209
Zapisy, SS 278
Zinc Institute. Review of the U.S. Zinc Industry, Including Statements from Other Countries, SC 311
Zionist Federation of Great Britain and Ireland. Zionist Year Book. see Zionist Year Book, HU 331
Zionist Year Book, HU 331
Zoological Record, SC 38
The Zoological Society of London. Zoological Record. see Zoological Record, SC 38

SUBJECT INDEX

Compiled by
Sanford Berman
Head Cataloger
Hennepin County Library
Edina, Minnesota

Abortion, SS 138, SS 145, SS 653
Abortion Bibliographies, SC 205
Academic Libraries, HU 146, HU 162
Academy Awards, HU 176
Accidents, SS 657, SS 887. *See also* Safety.
Accounting, SS 33
Accounting Bibliographies, SS 32
Acoustical Holography, SC 312
Accredited Schools, ED 33, ED 38, ED 59
Acting. *See* Theater Arts.
ACTION, SS 616
Addictions. *See* Alcoholism; Drug Abuse; Smoking and Health.
Adolescent Psychiatry, SC 316
Adoption Services, SS 620, SC 241
Adult Education, ED 19, ED 20, ED 23. *See also* Executive Training Programs; Job Training Programs.
Advanced Placement Programs, ED 24
Advertising Agencies, HU 29, HU 39, HU 238, SS 169, SS 197, SS 506
Advertising Photography, HU 238
Aeronautics, SC 15, SC 16. *See also* Aircraft; Airports.
Aerospace Industry, SS 866, SS 886, SS 889, SC 14
Affirmative Action Agencies and Groups, SS 621
Africa, SS 323, SS 324, SS 325, SS 326, SS 350, SS 355, SS 360. *See also* Apartheid and names of specific countries, e.g., Morocco, Tunisia.
African Art, HU 117
African Law, SS 450
African Literature, HU 85, HU 114, HU 117
African Music, HU 177
African Statistics, GE 122, SS 355
Afro-American Businesses, SS 103
Afro-American Colleges, ED 42, SS 621
Afro-American Government Workers, SS 425
Afro-American Ministers, HU 257
Afro-American Organizations, SS 621
Afro-American Photographers, HU 233
Afro-American Politicians, SS 311, SS 561
Afro-American Press, SS 181, SS 195, SS 212, SS 514
Afro-American Studies, GE 24
Afro-American Workers, SS 437
Afro-Americans, GE 24, GE 72, SS 262, SS 274, SS 638

Afro-Americans' Rights, SS 141
Ageism in Employment, SS 634
Aging, SS 634, SS 638, SS 645, SC 259, SC 269
Agricultural Co-ops. *See* Farm Co-ops.
Agricultural Education, ED 19
Agricultural Periodical Indexes, SC 33
Agricultural Statistics, SS 89, SS 90
Air Conditioning, SC 127
Air Cushion Vehicles, SS 866
Air Pollution, SS 225, SS 402, SC 76
Air Quality, SC 76, SC 104
Air Travel, SS 900, SS 910, SS 919, SS 971, SS 993, SS 1009
Aircraft, SS 864, SS 866, SS 889, SS 900
Aircraft Industry. *See* Aerospace Industry.
Airline Stewards and Stewardesses. *See* Flight Attendants.
Airports, SS 846, SS 992
Alaska, SS 658, SS 659, SS 984
Alcoholism, SC 252
Alcoholism Treatment Services, SC 209
Allied Medical Education, SC 210
Almanacs, GE 4, GE 10, GE 11, GE 15, GE 17, GE 18
Almanacs, Nautical. *See* Nautical Almanacs.
Alternative Press, GE 21, HU 135, SS 185
Amateur Radio, SS 202
America, SS 911, SS 912, SS 917, SS 920, SS 963, SS 969, SS 972, SS 974, SS 992, SS 999, SS 1000, SS 1002, SS 1009, SS 1029. *See also* National Parks and names of specific regions, states, and cities, e.g., Los Angeles, New England, Hawaii.
American Architecture, HU 53, HU 56
American Art, HU 22, HU 49, HU 62
American Biographies, GE 62, GE 63, GE 64, GE 65, GE 67, GE 69, GE 70, GE 72, GE 73, GE 76, GE 77, GE 78, GE 79, GE 81, ED 5, ED 11, HU 35, HU 62, HU 256, HU 257, HU 269, HU 326, HU 342, HU 349, SS 132, SS 292, SS 320, SS 322, SS 445, SS 483, SS 554, SS 576, SC 1, SC 3, SC 23, SC 50, SC 215, SC 271, SC 317, SC 318, SC 320
American Football League, SS 808, SS 827
American Foreign Relations, SS 545, SS 563, SS 569, SS 572, SS 573. *See also* Arms Control; Foreign Aid Programs; Treaties.
American History, GE 70, SS 327, SS 330, SS 331, SS

338, SS 362, SS 1000. *See also* Genealogy; Historical Societies; New Hampshire History; New Jersey History; Southern United States History; Texas History.

American History Bibliographies, SS 332

American Indian Studies. *See* Native American Studies.

American Institute of Certified Public Accountants, SS 32

American Law, SS 451, SS 471, SS 474, SS 478, SS 482. *See also* Legislation; Supreme Court.

American Literature, HU 86, HU 89, HU 98, HU 99, HU 104, HU 114, HU 115, HU 120, HU 121, HU 130, HU 132, SS 152

American Literature Periodical Indexes, HU 106

American Organizations, GE 100, GE 102, GE 105, ED 6, SS 621, SS 660, SC 104

American Periodicals, GE 113, GE 114, GE 115, GE 119, GE 120, GE 121, HU 135

American Politics and Government, GE 7, GE 10, GE 11, GE 15, GE 18, GE 19, SS 288, SS 290, SS 292, SS 301, SS 310, SS 312, SS 314, SS 319, SS 320, SS 321, SS 339, SS 542, SS 551, SS 570, SS 571, SS 576, SS 600, SS 601. *See also* Congress; Elections; Legislation; Local Government; Municipal Government; Presidents; State Government.

American Presidents. *See* Presidents.

American Publications, GE 21, GE 22, GE 31, GE 32, GE 35, GE 38, GE 39, GE 48, GE 52, GE 54, GE 56, GE 57, GE 60, HU 121, SS 67, SC 11, SC 12, SC 248

American Statistics, GE 123, GE 126, GE 128, GE 131, GE 132, GE 138, GE 139, SS 248, SS 297, SS 313, SS 314, SS 405, SS 406, SS 407, SS 408, SS 409, SS 410, SS 422, SS 430, SS 543, SS 571, SS 581, SS 591, SS 592, SS 598, SS 624, SS 656, SS 887, SC 68

American Studies, HU 19, SS 327. *See also* American Literature.

American Women, GE 67, GE 81, SS 142, SS 144, SS 145

Americana Encyclopedia, GE 1

Ameripass, SS 911

Amusement Industry. *See* Entertainment Industry.

Ancient Art, HU 60

Anglican Church, HU 250, HU 268. *See also* Episcopal Church.

Anglo-Saxon Studies, SS 328

Antarctica Bibliographies, SC 70

Anthropological Films, SS 17

Anthropological Research, SS 20, SS 26, SS 30

Anthropologists, SS 7, SS 26

Anthropology, SS 7, SS 9, SS 26, SS 31. *See also* Archaeology; Folk Dance; Folk Music; Folklore.

Anthropology Bibliographies, SS 9, SS 19

Anti-Poverty Programs, SS 602

Antiquarian Book Trade, SS 148, SS 149, SS 157, SS 158, SS 184, SS 210

Antique Trade, HU 44, SS 365, SS 366, SS 379

Antiques, SS 364, SS 365, SS 380, SS 381

Antitrust Law, SS 458

Apartheid, SS 548

Applied Mechanics, SC 158

Appraising, SS 64, SS 608, SS 610

Aquatic Sports. *See* Boating; Diving; Swimming; Water Polo.

Arab Biographies, GE 75

Arbitration and Mediation, SS 438, SS 439, SS 440, SS 441

Archaeology, HU 23, HU 72, SS 10, SS 11, SS 12, SS 13, SS 14, SS 15, SS 16, SS 18, SS 21, SS 23, SS 25, SS 28, SS 29. *See also* Museums; Native American History.

Archery, SS 686. *See also* Bowhunting.

Architects, HU 21

Architectural Barriers for Disabled Persons, ED 96

Architectural Education, HU 51

Architectural Schools, HU 26

Architecture, American. *See* American Architecture.

Architecture, British. *See* British Architecture.

Architecture Periodicals, HU 36

Archives, HU 157

Aristotelian Philosophy, HU 216

Arizona, SS 1021

Armed Forces, SC 285, SC 288, SC 289. *See also* Military Career Programs; Military Defense Organizations; Military Expenditures; Military Policy; Military Schools; Warships; Weapons Systems.

Armenian-Americans, HU 277

Armenian Church in America, HU 277

Arms Control, SS 545, SS 568, SS 579, SC 290, SC 291, SC 292, SC 293, SC 294

Art, HU 57

Art, American. *See* American Art.

Art, Asian. *See* Asian Art.

Art Auctions, HU 30, HU 34, HU 39, HU 43, HU 64

Art Bibliographies, HU 31, HU 33, HU 37

Art Collectors, HU 62, HU 63

Art Dealers, HU 29, HU 30, HU 39, HU 44, HU 62, SS 379

Art Galleries, HU 22, HU 29, HU 31, HU 44, HU 46, HU 48, HU 49, HU 50, HU 54, HU 58, HU 59, HU 60, HU 61, SS 909

Art History, HU 47, HU 48, HU 49, HU 59

Art Industries and Trade, HU 29, HU 30, HU 34, HU 39, HU 43, HU 44, SS 379

Art, Islamic. *See* Islamic Art.

Art Libraries, HU 22, HU 31, HU 46
Art, Modern. *See* Modern Art.
Art Periodical Indexes, HU 32
Art Schools, HU 22, HU 44
Artists, HU 31, HU 35, HU 38, HU 42, HU 44, HU 62, HU 63
Asia, SS 340, SS 341, SS 351. *See also* names of specific regions and countries, e.g., South Asia, Japan, Hong Kong.
Asian-American Government Workers, SS 425
Asian-American Workers, SS 437
Asian-Americans, SS 638
Asian Art, HU 27, HU 28
Asian Literature, HU 114
Asian Statistics, GE 133
Asian Studies Bibliographies, SS 333
Associations. *See* Organizations.
Astronomy, SC 18, SC 20, SC 68. *See also* Ephemerides.
Astrophysics, SC 18, SC 97
Atheism, HU 229
Athens, SS 1010. *See also* Greece.
Athletic Scholarships. *See* Sports Scholarships.
Athletics. *See* Sports.
Atlases, GE 14
Atomic Power *See* Nuclear Power.
Atomic Reactors. *See* Nuclear Reactors.
Auctions, Art. *See* Art Auctions.
Auctions, Book. *See* Book Auctions.
Audio Equipment. *See* Sound Equipment.
Audio Tapes. *See* Tapes.
Audio-Visual Education, ED 17, ED 62, ED 75. *See also* Educational Technology.
Audio-Visual Equipment, ED 60, HU 192, SS 153. *See also* Sound Equipment; Tape Players.
Audio-Visual Industry, ED 60, ED 62, ED 76, ED 85, HU 237, SS 153, SS 166. *See also* Film Industry; Microform Industry; Music Industry; Photography Dealers and Suppliers; Radio Industry; Record Industry; Tape Industry; Television Industry.
Audio-Visual Materials, ED 62, ED 63, ED 64, ED 65, ED 66, ED 67, ED 68, ED 69, ED 70, ED 71, ED 75, ED 77, ED 78, ED 79, ED 80, ED 81, ED 82, ED 83, ED 84, ED 85, ED 86, ED 87, ED 88, ED 89, SC 12. *See also* Films; Kits; Microforms; Records; Tapes.
Audio-Visual Reviews, GE 90, ED 75
Augustinian Studies, HU 66
Austria, SS 933
Authors, HU 88, HU 94, HU 98, HU 99, HU 100, HU 107, HU 108, HU 127, HU 141, HU 342, SS 212, SS 215
Authors' Handbooks, SS 187, SS 190, SS 214, SS 216, SS 217, SS 218

Autistic Children's Services, SC 268
Automatic Control Engineering, SC 172
Automation, SS 435. *See also* Computers.
Automobile Maintenance and Repair, SS 853, SS 873, SS 874
Automobile Racing, SS 761, SS 781
Automobile Safety, SS 225
Automobiles, SS 896
Automotive Industry, SS 870, SS 891, SS 895, SS 896, SS 897
Awards and Prizes, GE 1, GE 3, GE 11, GE 15, GE 18, GE 20, GE 34, GE 95, GE 105, HU 2, HU 16, HU 24, HU 51, HU 82, HU 108, HU 109, HU 110, HU 116, HU 120, HU 176, HU 198, HU 241, HU 333, HU 337, SS 153, SS 156, SS 160, SS 164, SS 169, SS 187, SS 188, SS 205, SS 217, SS 363, SS 390, SS 445, SS 584, SS 612, SS 705, SS 706, SS 777, SC 9, SC 10

Babe Ruth League, SS 693
Badminton, SS 831
Bahama Islands, SS 928
Banking Industry, SS 37, SS 38, SS 40, SS 42, SS 49, SS 50, SS 51, SS 92, SS 487, SS 488. *See also* Credit Unions.
Banking Law, SS 451
Baptist Church, HU 244, HU 245, HU 253, HU 254, HU 255, HU 267, HU 284, HU 314
Baseball, SS 693, SS 694, SS 695, SS 696, SS 697, SS 698, SS 712, SS 764, SS 765, SS 767, SS 768, SS 783, SS 784, SS 785, SS 787, SS 800, SS 822, SS 824, SS 842. *See also* Softball.
Basketball, SS 663, SS 699, SS 700, SS 701, SS 702, SS 703, SS 738, SS 739, SS 769, SS 788, SS 789, SS 807, SS 825
Bass Fishing, SS 688, SS 704, SS 723, SS 727
Baton Twirling, SS 663
Batteries, SC 87, SC 91
Bearings Industry, SC 185
Behavior Therapy, SC 324
Behavioral Scientists, SC 317, SC 319, SC 320
Belgium, SS 934, SS 977
Berlin, SS 940
Bermuda, SS 935
Best Books, GE 23, GE 29, GE 30, GE 36, GE 46, GE 51, GE 53, ED 61, ED 74, HU 103
Best Sellers, SS 160
Bible, HU 246, HU 258, HU 287, HU 290, HU 309, HU 316, HU 317
Bilingual Education, ED 17
Bilingual Materials, HU 40, HU 41, HU 213, HU 259, SS 261, SS 271, SS 457

Bibliographies, GE 28, GE 61, HU 121, SS 183. *See also* Abortion Bibliographies; Accounting Bibliographies; American History Bibliographies; Antarctica Bibliographies; Anthropology Bibliographies; Asian Studies Bibliographies; Art Bibliographies; Bioethics Bibliographies; British History Bibliographies; Business Bibliographies; Cartography Bibliographies; Dance Bibliographies; Drug Abuse Bibliographies; Economics Bibliographies; Ethnic Studies Bibliographies; Film Review Indexes; History Bibliographies; Latin American Studies Bibliographies; Law Bibliographies; Linguistics Bibliographies; Medical Bibliographies; Mental Health Bibliographies; Music Bibliographies; Native American Studies Bibliographies; Periodical Indexes; Play Bibliographies; Political Science Bibliographies; Record Reviews Indexes; Science Bibliographies; Speech Communication Bibliographies; Technology Bibliographies; Theater Arts Bibliographies.

Big Ten Sports, SS 706

Biochemistry, SC 26, SC 37, SC 46, SC 64, SC 68

Bioethics, HU 217

Bioethics Bibliographies, SC 220

Bioengineering, SC 32

Biofeedback Training, SC 324

Biographies, GE 62, GE 63, GE 64, GE 65, GE 66, GE 67, GE 68, GE 69, GE 70, GE 71, GE 72, GE 73, GE 74, GE 75, GE 76, GE 77, GE 78, GE 79, GE 80, GE 81, GE 82, ED 5, ED 11, HU 35, HU 44, HU 62, HU 63, HU 88, HU 94, HU 107, HU 108, HU 127, HU 141, HU 153, HU 198, HU 235, HU 256, HU 257, HU 260, HU 269, HU 326, HU 342, HU 349, HU 352, SS 132, SS 215, SS 292, SS 300, SS 321, SS 322, SS 325, SS 326, SS 340, SS 347, SS 350, SS 420, SS 445, SS 483, SS 558, SS 576, SC 1, SC 3, SC 23, SC 50, SC 215, SC 271, SC 317, SC 318, SC 320. *See also* Obituaries and Necrologies.

Biologists, SC 23

Biology, SC 24, SC 25, SC 35, SC 69. *See also* Biochemistry; Bioengineering; Biophysics; Entomology; Genetics; Microbiology; Parasitology; Physiology.

Biology, Marine. *See* Marine Biology.

Biology Periodical Indexes, SC 33

Biology Periodicals, SC 34

Biophysics, SC 32, SC 57

Birth Control, SS 653. *See also* Abortion; Family Planning; Population.

Birthdays, GE 4

Black Americans. *See* Afro-Americans.

Black Colleges. *See* Afro-American Colleges.

Black Studies, GE 24

Black Theater Movement, HU 339

Blind Persons, ED 96

Blind Persons' Projects and Services, SS 622, SS 632

Boarding Schools, ED 27, ED 30

Boating and Boats, SS 687, SS 851, SS 852, SS 877, SS 887, SS 898. *See also* Marine Engineering; Navigation; Navigation Guides; Ports; Sailboats; Shipping Industry; Tankers; Warships; Yachts.

Bodybuilding, SS 668. *See also* Weightlifting.

Boiler Inspection, SC 179

Bonds, SS 39, SS 42, SS 43, SS 46, SS 47, SS 304. *See also* Investments.

Book Auctions, SS 157

Book Distributors, GE 44

Book Jackets, SS 156

Book Review Indexes, HU 10, HU 11, HU 32, HU 123, SS 345, SS 329

Book Reviews, GE 83, GE 84, GE 85, GE 86, GE 87, GE 88, GE 89, GE 91, GE 92, GE 116

Book Trade, HU 39, SS 148, SS 149, SS 150, SS 157, SS 158, SS 160, SS 164, SS 166, SS 184, SS 187, SS 190, SS 201, SS 210. *See also* Publishers and Publishing.

Booking Agents, HU 82, HU 336, SS 60

Books for Visually Impaired Persons. *See* Large Print Books.

Books-in-Series. *See* Series' Books.

Boston, SS 1011

Botany, SC 69, SC 75

Bowhunting, SS 713

Bowling, SS 714

Boxing, SS 665, SS 811

Boys' Sports. *See* Men's Sports.

Britain, SS 342, SS 906, SS 907, SS 908, SS 909, SS 922, SS 925, SS 941, SS 966, SS 975, SS 980. *See also* London.

British Architecture, HU 25

British Art, HU 63

British Biographies, GE 64, GE 71, HU 63, SS 300, SS 420

British Columbia History, SS 28

British History, GE 14, HU 8, SS 328

British History Bibliographies, SS 329

British Organizations, GE 96, GE 98, GE 105, SS 1005

British Politics and Government, GE 2, GE 17, SS 300, SS 342

British Publications, GE 33, GE 38

British Statistics, GE 124, GE 127

British Studies, HU 8, HU 25. *See also* Anglo-Saxon Studies; English Literature; Scottish Studies.

Broadcasting Industry. *See* Cable Television; Radio Industry; Television Industry.

Broadway Theater, GE 333, , HU 343, HU 351, HU 352

Buddhism, HU 283, HU 327

Budget. *See* Public Finance.
Building Contractors, SC 40
Building Costs, SC 41, SC 43
Bus Travel, SS 911
Business, SS 57, SS 81. *See also* Accounting; Banking Industry; Bonds; Commercial law; Corporations; Economics; Exporters; Importers; Investments; Stocks; Trade.
Business Bibliographies, SS 63, SS 64, SS 65, SS 66, SS 67, SS 72, SS 87
Business Directories, SS 54, SS 60, SS 70, SS 75, SS 76, SS 77, SS 78, SS 79, SS 80, SS 82, SS 91, SS 94, SS 95, SS 97, SS 98, SS 100, SS 101, SS 103, SS 104, SS 105, SS 106, SS 117, SS 119, SS 120, SS 150, SS 153, SS 162, SS 163, SS 164, SS 166, SS 181, SS 184, SS 187, SS 189, SS 190, SS 191, SS 201, SS 212, SS 372, SS 373, SS 413, SS 414, SS 493, SS 494, SS 496, SS 502, SS 503, SS 504, SS 508, SS 509, SS 513, SS 515, SS 517, SS 518, SS 858, SS 859, SS 866, SS 872, SS 884, SS 891, SS 896, SC 77, SC 79, SC 81, SC 82, SC 84, SC 85, SC 92, SC 98, SC 101, SC 120, SC 121, SC 122, SC 136, SC 161, SC 164, SC 165, SC 175, SC 176, SC 177, SC 178, SC 182, SC 183, SC 185, SC 189, SC 191, SC 251, SC 279, SC 280, SC 301, SC 310. *See also* Periodical Directories.
Business Executives. *See* Executives.
Business Information Services, SS 87
Business Law. *See* Commercial Law.
Business Periodical Indexes, SS 68
Business Research, SS 66, SS 116, SS 118. *See also* Economics Research.
Business Schools, ED 98
Business Statistics, SS 55, SS 61, SS 69, SS 74, SS 81, SS 83, SS 84, SS 93, SS 121, SS 123, SS 124, SS 125, SS 126, SS 128, SS 129, SS 133, SS 134, SS 136, SS 137, SC 68
Byelorussian Studies, SS 278
Byzantine Studies, HU 67

Cable Television, SS 161, SS 163, SS 207, SS 404
Cake Decoration, SS 390
Caldecott Awards, GE 34
Calendars, GE 4, GE 11, GE 15, GE 93, SS 81, SS 160, SS 164, SS 276, SS 279
Calendars, Church. *See* Church Calendars.
California, SS 921, SS 985, SS 1018, SS 1023
California History, SS 13
Camellias, SC 152
Camps and Camping, ED 26, ED 27, HU 262, SS 628, SS 801, SS 802, SS 803, SS 804, SS 903, SS 904, SS 917, SS 918, SS 984, SS 999, SS 1030, SS 1031, SS 1032, SC 237. *See also* Mobile Home Parks.
Canada, SS 335, SS 336, SS 337, SS 912, SS 917, SS 974, SS 984, SS 999, SS 1002, SS 1032
Canadian Biographies, GE 74, ED 11, HU 326, SC 2, SC 3, SC 317
Canadian Folklore, SS 282
Canadian Football League, SS 716, SS 747, SS 827
Canadian Foreign Relations, SS 550
Canadian History, SS 338. *See also* British Columbia History; Ontario History.
Canadian Law, SS 471
Canadian Literature, GE 116
Canadian Organizations, GE 97, ED 6, SS 336, SS 337, SC 104
Canadian Periodicals, GE 116, GE 117
Canadian Politics and Government, SS 305, SS 335, SS 336, SS 337, SS 550
Canadian Studies, SS 327
Cancer, SC 276. *See also* Smoking and Health.
Capital Punishment, SS 138, SS 253, SS 256, SS 546
Carbohydrate Chemistry, SC 47
Career Centers, ED 20
Career Education. *See* Job Training Programs; Vocational Education.
Caribbean Area, SS 361, SS 928, SS 935. *See also* Bahama Islands; Bermuda; Puerto Rico.
Carnivals, SS 70
Cartography, SC 146, SC 150. *See also* Atlases; Road Maps.
Cartography Bibliographies, SC 147
Cartoons, Editorial. *See* Editorial Cartoons.
Cataloging, HU 142, HU 145, HU 165. *See also* Subject Headings.
Catholic Church, HU 251, HU 260, HU 262, HU 275, HU 291, HU 292, HU 305, HU 325. *See also* Ecumenism; Priests.
Catholic Periodical Indexes, HU 261
Catholic Philosophy, HU 214, HU 222, HU 231
Catholic Press, SS 165
Catholic Schools, HU 260, HU 305
Catholic Theology, HU 263
Celebrities, GE 11, GE 16, GE 63, GE 64, GE 65, GE 68, GE 71, GE 73, GE 74, GE 80
Celtic Literature, HU 114
Census Bureau, GE 60
Certification (Education), ED 15
Chambers of Commerce, SS 135
Charter Flights, SS 919
Chemical Engineers, SC 132
Chemical Dependency. *See* Alcoholism; Drug Abuse; Smoking and Health.
Chemicals, SC 53, SC 250. *See also* Drugs.
Chemists, SC 50, SC 132

Chemistry, SC 46, SC 52, SC 54, SC 55, SC 64. *See also* Biochemistry; Inorganic Chemistry; Organic Chemistry; Physical Chemistry; Polymers; Radiochemistry.
Chicago Media, SS 195
Chicanos, SS 272
Child Psychiatry, SC 323
Child Psychology, SC 333
Child Welfare Projects and Services, SS 620, SS 629, SC 268
Children's Literature, GE 23, GE 29, GE 34, GE 35, GE 36, GE 37, GE 46, GE 86, HU 93, HU 109, HU 127, HU 141
Children's Materials, SS 166
Children's Records, HU 210
Children's Tapes, HU 210
China, SS 5, SS 638
Christian Ministers. *See* Ministers.
Christian Missions. *See* Missionaries and Missions.
Christian Periodical Indexes, HU 261, HU 266, HU 288, HU 289, HU 314
Christian Schools, ED 13, ED 29, HU 284, HU 299
Christianity. *See* Anglican Church; Armenian Church in America; Baptist Church; Bible; Catholic Church; Catholic Philosophy; Christian Schools; Church Directories; Congregational Church; Disciples of Christ; Eastern Orthodox Church; Ecumenism; Episcopal Church; Friends Meetings; Lutheran Church; Mennonite Church; Methodist Church; Ministers; Moravian Church; Mormon Church; Parochial Schools; Presbyterian Church; Theological Education; Theology; Unitarian-Universalist Association; United Church of Christ.
Christmas, SS 281, SS 389, SS 392, SS 394, SS 396
Chronologies, GE 2, GE 3, GE 5, GE 10, GE 19, GE 20, GE 70
Church Calendars, HU 277, HU 280, HU 296, HU 302, HU 307, HU 320, HU 330
Church Directories, HU 244, HU 247, HU 249, HU 250, HU 251, HU 262, HU 265, HU 275, HU 276, HU 282, HU 284, HU 292, HU 296, HU 297, HU 299, HU 302, HU 305, HU 307, HU 319, HU 321, HU 322, HU 323, HU 324, HU 330
Church of the Latter-Day Saints. *See* Mormon Church.
Church Schools. *See* Parochial Schools.
Church Union. *See* Ecumenism.
Church Workers' Education, ED 20
Circuses, SS 70
City Planning. *See* Urban Planning.
Civil Engineering, SC 126
Civil Engineers, SC 125
Civil Liberties. *See* Human Rights.
Civil Rights. *See* Human Rights.
Civil Service, SS 302, SS 424, SS 425, SS 426, SS 432, SS 433, SS 434
Classical Music, HU 186, HU 187, HU 191, HU 193, HU 208, HU 209, HU 211, HU 212
Classical Studies, HU 65, HU 68, HU 69, HU 71, HU 74 HU 75, HU 78. *See also* Archaeology; Augustinian Studies; Byzantine Studies; Egyptian Studies; Greek Studies; Islamic Studies; Roman Studies.
Clergy. *See* Ministers; Missionaries and Missions; Priests; Rabbis.
Climate, SC 75, SC 76
Clothing Industry, SS 513
Coaches, Sports. *See* Sports Coaches.
Coal Industry, SC 296, SC 300, SC 301
Coal Mining, SC 304, SC 306, SC 307
Coats-of-Arms, SS 286
Coins and Coin Collecting, SS 363, SS 367, SS 368, SS 369, SS 370, SS 375, SS 376, SS 377, SS 378, SS 387, SS 388
College Directories, ED 8, ED 10, ED 18, ED 19, ED 20, ED 21, ED 24, ED 29, ED 33, ED 35, ED 37, ED 38, ED 39, ED 40, ED 41, ED 42, ED 44, ED 45, ED 46, ED 47, ED 48, ED 49, ED 51, ED 52, ED 59, ED 98, ED 100, ED 102. *See also* School Directories.
College Graduates, SS 523, SS 525, SC 141
College Libraries. *See* Academic Libraries, HU 146
College Preparatory Schools. *See* Prep Schools.
College Press. *See* Student Press.
Collegiate Sports. *See* School Sports.
Collier's Encyclopedia, GE 5
Colonies, SS 147, SS 568. *See also* International Relations; Puerto Rico; United Nations.
Colorado, SS 1012
Comic Book Collecting, SS 371
Commercial Art, HU 24, HU 40, SS 156
Commercial Law, SS 35, SS 52, SS 73, SS 450, SS 451, SS 455, SS 458
Commodity Exchanges, SS 71
Commonwealth Schools, ED 40
Communication, SS 167. *See also* Speech Communication.
Communism, SS 580
Community Colleges, ED 33, ED 37, ED 98
Community Development, SS 402, SS 411
Comparative Law, SS 457
Comparative Literature, HU 136, HU 137
Composers, HU 178
Compton's Encyclopedia, GE 6
Computer-Assisted Research, SC 64
Computer Industry, SC 63
Computer Simulation, SC 66

Computers, SC 60, SC 61, SC 62, SC 63, SC 65
Concrete Construction, SC 42
Conferences, GE 25, GE 55, GE 93, ED 19, ED 62, HU 278, SS 190, SS 217, SS 585
Congregational Church, HU 272
Congress, SS 292, SS 293, SS 294, SS 312, SS 320, SS 322, SS 482, SS 542, SS 544, SS 551, SS 552, SS 553, SS 570, SS 571. *See also* American Politics and Government; Elections; Legislation.
Congresses. *See* Conferences.
Conservation, SS 613. *See also* Environmental Protection; Natural Resources.
Conservation Agencies and Groups, SC 99
Conservation, Energy. *See* Energy Conservation.
Constitutional History, SS 476
Constitutional Law, SS 477. *See also* Supreme Court.
Construction Costs, SC 41, SC 43
Construction Industry, SC 39, SC 40, SC 42, SC 44
Consulates. *See* Diplomatic Service.
Consulting Engineers, SC 122, SC 132
Consumer Action, SS 219
Consumer Finance Companies, SS 40
Consumer Guides, SS 219, SS 220, SS 222, SS 223, SS 224, SS 226, SS 625
Consumer Agencies and Groups, SS 219, SS 221, SS 225, SS 226, SS 411, SC 104
Consumer Price Index, SS 430
Consumer Protection, SS 145, SS 221, SS 225, SS 451. *See also* Product Reliability.
Consumer Research, SS 118, SS 505
Containerization, SS 854, SS 865
Continuing Education. *See* Adult Education.
Cooking, Game and Fish. *See* Game and Fish Cooking.
Cooperatives, SS 53, SS 227
Copyright, HU 29, SS 160, SS 214, SS 217, SS 451, SS 471, SS 474, SS 533, SS 534, SS 535, SS 536, SS 538. *See also* Patents; Trademarks.
Corporate Accountability, SS 65, SS 112
Corporate Income, SS 34, SS 92, SS 130
Corporate Law, SS 458. *See also* Banking Law; Commercial Law; Labor Law; Trade Law.
Corporations, SS 45, SS 46, SS 92, SS 97, SS 98, SS 110, SS 117, SS 191, SS 493, SS 500, SS 503, SS 504, SS 516, SS 520. *See also* Antitrust Law; Business Directories; Commercial Law.
Corporations, Multinational. *See* Multinational Corporations.
Corrections, SS 228, SS 233, SS 235, SS 240, SS 257. *See also* Criminal Justice; Law Enforcement; Parole; Police; Prisoners; Prisons; Probation.
Correspondence Schools and Courses, ED 19, ED 21, ED 29

Cost-of-Living, SS 614. *See also* Consumer Price Index; Income; Income Tax; Pensions; Retirement Planning; Wages and Salaries.
Counselors and Counseling Services, SS 617, SS 623, SS 635. *See also* Mental Health Care Directories; Psychiatrists; Psychoanalysts.
Countries, GE 129, ED 18, SS 139, SS 291, SS 296, SS 323, SS 324, SS 326, SS 340, SS 341, SS 348, SS 349, SS 350, SS 351, SS 352, SS 354, SS 355, SS 358, SS 360, SS 361, SS 450, SS 546, SS 547, SS 555, SS 558, SS 562, SS 577, SS 580, SS 864, SS 897, SS 910, SS 1005, SS 1006, SC 265, SC 285. *See also* Travel and names of specific countries, e.g., Canada, Japan.
County Government. *See* Local Government.
Courts, SS 239, SS 240, SS 290, SS 336, SS 445. *See also* Corrections; Criminal Justice; Law Enforcement; Legal Services.
Crafts Fairs, SS 279
Crafts Trade, HU 29, SS 372, SS 373, SS 374
Credit, SS 35, SS 40, SS 634
Credit Unions, SS 36
Crime, SS 230, SS 231, SS 235, SS 243, SS 246, SS 247, SS 248. *See also* Corrections; Criminal Justice; Law Enforcement; Narcotics Traffic; Police; Rape; Terrorism; Victims of Crime.
Crime Statistics, SS 230, SS 242, SS 248, SS 250, SS 256
Crime Victims. *See* Victims of Crime.
Criminal Justice, SS 229, SS 235, SS 239, SS 246, SS 251, SS 252, SS 256, SS 257. *See also* Capital Punishment; Corrections; Courts; Crime; Forensic Medicine; Law Enforcement; Parole; Police; Prisoners; Prisons; Probation.
Criminal Justice Education, SS 237
Criminal Justice Periodical Indexes, SS 232
Criminal Justice Planning, SS 242
Criminal Justice Research, SS 240, SS 242
Criminal Law, SS 450, SS 451
Criticism, Literary. *See* Literary Criticism.
Croation-Americans, SS 271
Croatian-Language Materials, SS 271
Croation Studies, SS 271
Crocheting, SS 397
Cross-County Racing, SS 677
Cross Country Skiing, SS 749, SS 814
Crossword Puzzles, GE 11
Cruises, SS 936
Cuban Law, SS 457
Cultural Anthropology. *See* Anthropology.
Currency, SS 384, SS 388
Current History, GE 1, GE 2, GE 3, GE 5, GE 6, GE 7, GE 10, GE 11, GE 12, GE 15, GE 17, GE 18, GE 19, GE 20, GE 129, SS 183, SS 324, SS 326, SS 335,

SS 337, SS 339, SS 344, SS 347, SS 349, SS 353, SS 354
Current History Indexes, SS 564
Czechoslovakia, SS 937

Dance Bibliographies, HU 80
Dance Education, HU 81, HU 82
Dance History, HU 84
Dance Industry, HU 82, HU 83, HU 202
Dance Periodicals, HU 82
Dance Therapy, HU 79, HU 84
Dancers, HU 82
Data Processing, HU 170. *See also* Computers; Information Storage and Retrieval.
Day Care Centers, SS 620
Deaf Persons' Projects and Services, SC 258
Deaf Students, ED 93
Death Notices. *See* Obituaries and Necrologies.
Death Penalty. *See* Capital Punishment.
Debt, National. *See* Public Finance.
Decoration, SS 389, SS 390, SS 391, SS 392, SS 394, SS 396
Defense Policy. *See* Military Policy.
Demography. *See* Population.
Dental Schools, SC 207, SC 211
Dental Therapeutics, SC 206
Dentistry, SC 277
Dentists, SC 211
Denver, SS 1012
Design Industry, SC 136
"Developing" Countries. *See* Third World.
"Deviance," Social. *See* Social "Deviance."
Dickens Studies, HU 97
Dielectrics, SC 90
Diesel Engines, SC 166
Diplomatic Service, SS 292, SS 320, SS 471, SS 562, SS 567, SC 285
Direct-Mail Business, SS 519
Directory Guides, GE 96, GE 106, GE 107, ED 10
Disability Insurance, SS 630
Disabled Children, ED 94, ED 96
Disabled Persons, ED 96
Disabled Persons' Camps, SC 237
Disabled Persons' Projects and Services, SS 622, SS 630, SS 632, SC 258
Disabled Students, ED 21, ED 26, ED 49, ED 92, ED 94
Disarmament. *See* Arms Control.
Disciples of Christ, HU 265
Discographies, HU 184, HU 209, HU 210
Diseases, SC 245. *See also* Cancer; Medicine, Venereal Disease Bibliographies.

Displaced Workers, SS 435
Dividends. *See* Investments.
Diving, SS 662, SS 828, SS 829
Divorce, SS 145, SS 638
Doctors. *See* Dentists; Osteopaths; Physicians; Psychiatrists; Veterinarians.
Drama Schools. *See* Theater Arts Education.
Dramas. *See* Plays.
Dramatists. *See* Playwrights.
Drop-Shipping Industry, SS 496
Drug Abuse, SS 232, SS 236, SC 335. *See also* Narcotics Traffic.
Drug Abuse Bibliographies, SC 234
Drug Abuse Research, SC 254
Drug Abuse Services, SC 209
Drug Education, SS 236. *See also* Health Education; Narcotics Traffic.
Drug Industry, SC 251
Drug Stories, SS 512
Drugs, SC 235, SC 236, SC 240, SC 250, SC 251, SC 267
Dublin, SS 1014. *See also* Ireland.

Early Childhood Education. *See* Elementary Education; Preschool Education.
Earth Sciences. *See* Ecology; Environmental Studies; Geography; Geology; Natural Resources; Nature Study.
Earthquakes, SC 72
Eastern Europe, SS 358. *See also* Czechoslovakia; Hungary; Soviet Union; Yugoslavia.
Eastern Orthodox Church, HU 307
Eastern Religions, HU 315. *See also* Buddhism.
Ecology, ED 61, SC 67, SC 68, SC 69, SC 75. *See also* Environmental Studies.
Economic Forecasting, SS 128, SS 600
Economic History, SS 113
Economic Policy, SS 126, SS 586, SS 597. *See also* Public Finance; Trade Policy.
Economics, SS 58, SS 59, SS 108. *See also* Business; Corporations; Investments; Public Finance.
Economics Bibliographies, SS 63, SS 66, SS 67, SS 72, SS 96
Economics Dictionaries and Encyclopedias, SS 86
Economics Research, SS 99, SS 102, SS 113, SS 114, SS 115, SS 116
Ecumenism, HU 271, HU 273, HU 278, HU 330
Editorial Cartoons, SS 155
Education, ED 2, ED 4, ED 7, ED 16, ED 17, ED 90, SS 628, SS 656. *See also* Learning Disabilities; School Directories; School Law; Student Aid Pro-

grams; Student Exchange Programs; Student Press; Studying Abroad.
Education, Adult. *See* Adult Education.
Education, Architectural. *See* Architectural Education.
Education, Criminal Justice. *See* Criminal Justice Education.
Education, Dance. *See* Dance Education.
Education, Drug. *See* Drug Education.
Education, Elementary. *See* Elementary Education.
Education, Engineering. *See* Engineering Education.
Education, Environmental. *See* Environmental Education.
Education, Higher. *See* Higher Education.
Education, Library. *See* Library Education.
Education, Medical. *See* Allied Medical Education; Dental Schools; Medical Schools; Nursing Schools; Pharmacy Schools; Veterinary Schools.
Education, Minority. *See* Minority Education.
Education, Music. *See* Music Education.
Education Periodicals, ED 1, ED 9
Education, Philosophy. *See* Philosophy Education.
Education, Political Science. *See* Political Science Education.
Education, Preschool. *See* Preschool Education.
Education, Psychology. *See* Psychology Education.
Education, Secondary. *See* Secondary Education.
Education, Social Work. *See* Social Work Education.
Education, Sociology. *See* Sociology Education.
Education, Theater Arts. *See* Theater Arts Education.
Education, Vocational. *See* Vocational Education.
Educational Films, ED 64, ED 75, ED 82, ED 87
Educational Management, ED 6
Educational Media. *See* Audio-Visual Education; Audio-Visual Equipment; Audio-Visual Materials.
Educational Organizations, ED 10, ED 18, ED 23, ED 29, ED 30. *See also* Scholarly Organizations.
Educational Statistics, ED 4, ED 14, ED 23, ED 31, ED 59, HU 200
Educational Technology, ED 76. *See also* Audio-Visual Education; Audio-Visual Equipment; Audio-Visual Materials; Educational Television.
Educational Television, ED 19, SS 207, SS 212
Educators, ED 5, ED 11, ED 12, ED 29, ED 31, ED 40, HU 189, SS 462
Egyptican Studies, HU 23
Elections, SS 301, SS 305, SS 542, SS 543, SS 554. *See also* American Politics and Government; Congress; Presidents.
Electric Power, SC 88, SC 91, SC 115
Electric Power Plants, SC 78, SC 88
Electric Railroads, SC 87
Electric Utilities, SC 78, SC 79
Electric Vehicles, SC 87, SC 91
Electronics, SC 80, SC 86, SC 89
Electronics Industry, SC 77, SC 81, SC 82, SC 83, SC 84, SC 85, SC 92, SC 175
Elementary Education, ED 25
Elementary School Libraries, ED 74
Elementary Schools, ED 30, ED 32
Embassies. *See* Diplomatic Service.
Employee Benefits, SS 419, SS 428, SS 430. *See also* Pensions; Wages and Salaries.
Employee Training Programs. *See* Job Training Programs.
Employment Guides. *See* Job Hunting Guides.
Employment, Overseas. *See* Overseas Employment.
Employment Statistics, SS 124, SS 422, SS 426, SS 430, SS 432, SS 433, SS 434, SS 437, SS 443, SS 505, SS 656
Encyclopaedia Britannica, GE 3, GE 8
Encyclopedia Buying, SS 226
Encyclopedia Yearbooks, GE 1, GE 3, GE 5, GE 6, GE 19, SC 8
Energy, SC 96, SC 102, SC 296. *See also* Electric Power; Fuels; Hydroelectric Power; Nuclear Power; Solar Energy.
Energy Conservation, SS 888
Energy Industries. *See* Coal Industry; Electric Utilities; Gas Industry; Geothermal Energy Industry; Petroleum Industry.
Energy Policy, SS 597, SS 612
Energy Research, SC 102
Energy Resources, SC 74, SC 113. *See also* Mineral Resources; Petroleum Resources.
Energy Statistics, SC 68, SC 119
Engineering, Automatic Control. *See* Automatic Control Engineering.
Engineering Bibliographies, SC 12
Engineering, Civil. *See* Civil Engineering.
Engineering Education, SC 134, SC 137, SC 142, SC 144
Engineering, Human. *See* Human Engineering.
Engineering, Laser. *See* Laser Engineering.
Engineering, Marine. *See* Marine Engineering.
Engineering, Mechanical. *See* Mechanical Engineering.
Engineering, Metallurgical. *See* Metallurgical Engineering.
Engineering, Mineral. *See* Mining.
Engineering Models, SC 124
Engineering Periodical Indexes, SC 135
Engineering, Petroleum. *See* Petroleum Engineering.
Engineering, Quality Control. *See* Quality Control Engineering.
Engineering, Sanitary. *See* Sanitary Engineering.

Engineering Standards. *See* Standards.
Engineering Students, SC 142
Engineering Technicians, SC 143
Engineering, Transportation. *See* Transportation Engineering.
Engineers, SS 427, SS 861, SC 93, SC 111, SC 122, SC 125, SC 128, SC 130, SC 132, SC 138, SC 139, SC 140, SC 141, SC 167, SC 170, SC 281, SC 305
Engines. *See* Diesel Engines; Gas Turbines; Machinery; Mechanical Engineering.
English History. *See* British History.
English Language, HU 112, HU 138, HU 139
English Literature, HU 97, HU 101, HU 102, HU 111, HU 112, HU 114, HU 122, HU 124, HU 125, HU 131, HU 132, HU 138, HU 139
English Politics and Government. *See* British Politics and Government.
Enrico Fermi Awards, SC 10
Entertainers, HU 202, HU 336, HU 340, HU 349, HU 352
Entertainment Industry, HU 336, HU 341, SS 60, SS 70, SS 95, SS 196, SS 965. *See also* Dance Industry; Film Industry; Music Industry; Radio Industry; Record Industry; Tape Industry; Television Industry; Theatrical Directories.
Entomology, SC 27
Environmental Education, SC 104, SC 106
Environmental Law, SS 465, SS 481
Environmental Planning, SS 612
Environmental Protection, SS 481, SC 67. *See also* Conservation; Pollution Control.
Environmental Protection Agencies and Groups, SS 612, SC 104, SC 120
Environmental Research Centers, SC 118, SC 120
Environmental Studies, ED 83, HU 159, SC 10, SC 103, SC 106, SC 113. *See also* Ecology; Natural Resources.
Ephemerides, SC 17, SC 19
Episcopal Church, HU 269, HU 279, HU 294. *See also* Anglican Church.
Equal Educational Opportunity, ED 16, ED 17, ED 95
Equal Employment Opportunity, SS 424, SS 437, SS 621
Equal Rights Amendment, SS 144, SS 145
Essays, GE 118
Ethics, HU 217, HU 309
Ethnic Groups, HU 145, SS 139. *See also* Afro-American Studies; Afro-Americans; Anthropology; Armenian-Americans; Asian-Americans; Bilingual Education; Byelorussian Studies; Chicanos; Croatian Studies; Festivals; Finnish-Americans; Irish-Americans; Italian-Americans; Jewish-Americans; Jewish Studies; Jews; Latvians; Multicultural Education; Native American Studies; Native Americans; Norwegian-Americans; Scottish Studies; Slovak-Americans; Ukrainian Studies.
Ethnic Press, SS 195, SS 212
Ethnic Studies Bibliographies, SS 263
Ethnology. *See* Anthropology.
Eurailpass, SS 910, SS 919, SS 926
Europe, SS 902, SS 904, SS 905, SS 910, SS 926, SS 927, SS 929, SS 930, SS 931, SS 932, SS 938, SS 969, SS 973, SS 993, SS 1003. *See also* names of specific regions, countries, and cities, e.g., Britain, France, Portugal, London, Paris, Eastern Europe.
European Organizations, GE 99
European Statistics, GE 134, SS 84
Exceptional Children, ED 94, ED 96
Excise Tax, SS 595
Executive Recruitment, SS 491, SS 529
Executive Training Programs, SS 490
Executives, SS 132, SS 428, SS 487, SS 493
Experimental Theater, HU 333, HU 343, HU 347
Exporters, SS 54, SS 73, SS 88. *See also* Trade; Trade Fairs.

Factory Sites. *See* Plant Sites.
Fairs, SS 79, SS 81, SS 366. *See also* Crafts Fairs.
Family, SS 639, SS 651, SS 654
Family Associations, SS 284, SS 285
Family Counseling, SS 635
Family Counselors, SS 617
Family Life Education, ED 91, SS 629
Family Planning, SS 652. *See also* Abortion; Birth Control; Population.
Farm Co-ops, SS 53
Fashion, HU 31
Federal Aid to Education, ED 3, ED 59
Fellowships. *See* Scholarships and Fellowships.
Feminist Library Workers, HU 166
Feminist Organizations, GE 111, HU 166
Feminist Periodicals, HU 135
Fencing, SS 686, SS 714
Festivals, GE 4, SS 153, SS 279. *See also* Christmas; Film Festivals; Music Festivals.
Fiction, HU 89, HU 98, HU 103, HU 116, HU 118, HU 120, SS 152
Fiction Bibliographies, HU 126
Fiction Review Indexes, HU 123
Field Hockey, SS 730, SS 731
Figure Skating. *See* Ice Skating.
Film Catalogs, SS 17, SS 180, SS 203, SS 204
Film Cooperatives and Circuits, SS 200
Film Education, SS 182

Film Festivals, HU 173
Film Industry, HU 173, HU 174, SS 188, SS 196
Film Libraries, HU 344, SS 200
Film Periodical Indexes, HU 171, SS 186
Film Personalities, HU 349, SS 188
Film Reviews, HU 172, HU 175
Films, ED 64, ED 75, ED 82, ED 87, HU 176
Films, Anthropological. *See* Anthropological Films.
Filmstrips, ED 65, ED 75, ED 88
Finance, Public. *See* Public Finance.
Financial Aid for Students. *See* Student Aid Programs.
Finnish-Americans, SS 264
Fire Prevention, SC 45
Firearms. *See* Guns.
First Catholic Slovak Union, HU 291, HU 292
Fisheries Research, SC 116, SC 117
Fishing, SS 658, SS 659, SS 688, SS 704, SS 710, SS 711, SS 718, SS 719, SS 723, SS 727, SS 728, SS 732, SS 733, SS 782, SS 819, SS 984
Fitzgerald Studies, HU 104
Flag Football, SS 736
Flags, GE 18
Flight Attendants, SS 522
Flower Gardening, SC 152, SC 153, SC 154, SC 156
Fluid Mechanics, SC 163, SC 180
Foamed Plastic Industry, SC 189
Folk Dance, HU 84
Folk Festivals. *See* Festivals.
Folk Music, HU 184, HU 194, SS 282
Folk Societies. *See* Anthropology.
Folklore, HU 114, HU 117, SS 280, SS 282
Food Buying, SS 222, SS 223
Food Co-ops, SS 227
Food Industry, SS 120
Football, SS 716, SS 725, SS 734, SS 735, SS 736, SS 737, SS 742, SS 743, SS 747, SS 778, SS 779, SS 786, SS 790, SS 791, SS 797, SS 805, SS 808, SS 810, SS 826, SS 827
Foreign Agents, SS 479
Foreign Aid Programs, SS 122, SS 126, SS 569
Foreign Relations, American. *See* American Foreign Relations.
Foreign Relations, Canadian. *See* Canadian Foreign Relations.
Foreign Study. *See* Commonwealth Colleges; Studying Abroad.
Forensic Medicine, SS 473
Forests, SC 73
Foundations, GE 103, GE 104, GE 105, ED 37, ED 62, HU 1, HU 3, HU 7, HU 9, HU 12, HU 14, HU 16, HU 18, HU 155, SS 30, SS 107, SS 108
Founding, SC 160

France, SS 918, SS 923, SS 939, SS 978. *See also* Paris.
Franchises, SS 76, SS 610
Free Materials, GE 61, ED 63, ED 64, ED 65, ED 66, ED 67, ED 68, ED 69, ED 70, ED 71, ED 73, SS 203, SS 719, SS 720
Free Thought, HU 229
Freedom. *See* Human Rights.
French-Language Materials, HU 230, HU 259, SS 146, SS 282
French Literature, HU 105
Friends Meetings, HU 282, HU 308, HU 311, HU 328
Fuels, SC 119, SC 309. *See also* Energy Resources.
Fund Raising, SS 637. *See also* Foundations; Grants.
Furniture Making, SS 395

GI Benefits. *See* Veterans' Services.
Galleries. *See* Art Galleries.
Gambling, SS 1015. *See also* Las Vegas, Nevada; Sports Betting Guides.
Game and Fish Cooking, SS 690, SS 728, SS 729, SS 760, SS 782
Gardening, SC 154, SC 155, SC 157
Gardening, Flower. *See* Flower Gardening.
Gas Industry, SC 98
Gas Turbines, SC 166, SC 188
Gear Industry, SC 161
Gems, SC 299
Genealogical Societies, SS 338
Genealogy, SS 283, SS 285
Genealogy Periodical Indexes, SS 284
Genetics, SC 21, SC 28, SC 335
Geneva, SS 1025. *See also* Switzerland.
Geography, SC 149, SC 151. *See also* Climate; Ecology; Environmental Studies; Geology; Meteorology; Travel.
Geography Bibliographies, SC 148. *See also* Cartography Bibliographies.
Geography, Medical. *See* Medical Geography.
Geology, SC 68, SC 75. *See also* Earthquakes; Ecology; Environmental Studies.
Geology Bibliographies, SC 71
Geothermal Energy Industry, SC 105
Germany, SS 940, SS 979
Gerontology. *See* Aging.
Gifted Children, ED 96
Gifts, SS 389, SS 392, SS 394, SS 396
Girls' Sports. *See* Women's Sports.
Glassware, HU 45, SS 365
Golf, SS 686, SS 744, SS 745, SS 746
Government, American. *See* American Politics and Government.

Government Bonds, SS 304
Government, British. *See* British Politics and Government.
Government Finance. *See* Public Finance.
Government Grants and Loans, SS 602
Government Information Services, SS 320, SS 335
Government Lawyers, SS 444
Government, Local. *See* Local Government.
Government, Municipal. *See* Municipal Government.
Government Officials and Employees, SS 302, SS 312, SS 313, SS 314, SS 315, SS 316, SS 317, SS 318, SS 321, SS 424, SS 425, SS 426, SS 432, SS 433, SS 434. *See also* Congress; Parliament; Presidents.
Government Publications, GE 26, GE 27, GE 39, GE 44, GE 48, GE 55, GE 60, GE 61, GE 119, GE 123, SS 127
Government Publications Collections, HU 156
Government Publications Indexes, SS 303
Government Purchasing, SS 585
Government Research, GE 100, SS 435, SS 436
Government, State. *See* State Government.
Grade Schools. *See* Elementary Schools.
Graduate Study Programs, ED 38, ED 45, ED 46, ED 52, SS 556, SS 648, SC 134, SC 331
Grammar Schools. *See* Elementary Schools.
Grants, GE 94, GE 101, GE 103, GE 104, GE 105, ED 3, ED 34, ED 37, ED 54, ED 62, HU 2, HU 3, HU 7, HU 14, HU 16, HU 18, HU 44, HU 155, SS 602
Graphic Arts, HU 24, HU 31, HU 40, HU 41, HU 55
Great Books of the Western World, GE 8
Great Britain. *See* Britain.
Great Lakes Region, SS 986
Great Plains States, SS 989
Greece, SS 942, SS 967. *See also* Athens.
Greek Studies, HU 67, HU 72
Greyhound Bus Company, SS 911
Grocery Markets, SS 120
Group Dynamics, SS 619
Guatemala, SS 976
Guide Dogs, SS 632
Guided Missiles, SC 14, SC 16
Gun Control, SS 256
Guns, SS 690, SS 709, SS 720, SS 722, SS 724, SS 752, SS 754, SS 755, SS 756, SS 762, SS 820
Gymnastics, SS 666, SS 715, SS 740, SS 741, SS 757, SS 771. *See also* Trampoline; Tumbling.

Handicapped Students. *See* Disabled Students.
Handicraft Trade. *See* Crafts Trade.
Harbors. *See* Ports.
Hardy Studies, HU 131
Hawaii, SS 943, SS 968, SS 1013, SS 1026

Hawthorne Studies, HU 115
Health Care, SS 634, SS 654, SS 656, SC 218, SC 224, SC 260, SC 265, SC 274
Health Care Directories, SC 209, SC 212, SC 232, SC 241, SC 253, SC 268, SC 332, SC 334
Health Care Personnel, SC 271. *See also* Dentists; Medical Specialists; Osteopaths; Physicians; Psychiatrists.
Health Education, ED 66, ED 84, SC 218, SC 243, SC 246. *See also* Drug Education.
Health Information Services, SC 247, SC 253
Health Insurance, SS 415, SS 416, SS 418, SS 488, SS 630, SC 266. *See also* National Health Insurance.
Health Sciences Education. *See* Allied Medical Education; Dental Schools; Medical Schools; Nursing Schools; Pharmacy Schools; Veterinary Schools.
Hearing Aids, SC 217
Hearing Disorders, SC 216, SC 217. *See also* Deaf Persons' Projects and Services.
Heating, SC 127
Hebrew Language, HU 287
Hebrew-Language Materials, HU 109, HU 290, SS 267
Hellenic Studies. *See* Greek Studies.
Hemingway Studies, HU 104
Heraldry, SS 286
Herbs, SC 155
High School Education. *See* Secondary Education.
High School Libraries, GE 53, ED 61, ED 74
High School Sports. *See* School Sports.
High Schools, ED 29, ED 30, ED 32
Higher Education, ED 59. *See also* College Directories; Graduate Study Programs; Vocational-Technical Schools.
Highways. *See* Roads.
Historical Societies, SS 338
History, SS 344. *See also* Archaeology; Archives; Classical Studies; Genealogy.
History, Art. *See* Art History.
History Bibliographies, SS 346
History, British. *See* British History.
History, British Columbia. *See* British Columbia History.
History, California. *See* California History.
History, Canadian. *See* Canadian History.
History, Constitutional. *See* Constitutional History.
History, Current. *See* Current History.
History, Dance. *See* Dance History.
History, Economic. *See* Economic History.
History, English. *See* British History.
History, Jewish. *See* Jewish History.
History, Music. *See* Music History.
History, Native American. *See* Native American History.

History, North American. *See* North American History.
History, Oral. *See* Oral History.
History Periodical Indexes, SS 345
Hobby Industry, SS 373. *See also* Antique Trade; Crafts Trade; Photography Dealers and Suppliers.
Hockey, SS 95, SS 680, SS 681, SS 689, SS 717, SS 721, SS 758, SS 780, SS 792, SS 806, SS 809
Holiday Homes, SS 907
Holidays, GE 4, GE 13. *See also* Christmas.
Holland. *See* Netherlands.
Holography, Acoustical. *See* Acoustical Holography.
Home Decorating. *See* Interior Decoration.
Home Remodeling, SS 393
Home Study. *See* Correspondence Schools and Courses.
Hong Kong, SS 924
Honolulu, SS 1013. *See also* Hawaii.
Horse Showing, SS 773
Hospitals, SC 212, SC 213, SC 241, SC 334
Hostels, Youth. *See* Youth Hostels.
Hotels, SS 77, SS 94, SS 106, SS 614, SS 906, SS 908, SS 910, SS 911, SS 912, SS 925, SS 930, SS 972, SS 975, SS 977, SS 978, SS 979, SS 980, SS 981, SS 982, SS 983, SS 1003, SS 1029. *See also* Travel.
Hotlines, SS 1029
Hours of Work, SS 431, SS 443
Housing, SS 405, SS 406, SS 407, SS 408, SS 409, SS 410, SS 411, SS 629, SS 634, SS 638, SS 656
Housing Codes, SS 398, SS 399, SS 400
Human Engineering, SC 167, SC 168, SC 174
Human Rights, SS 138, SS 139, SS 143, SS 146, SS 147, SS 447, SS 451, SS 546, SS 548, SS 568. *See also* Equal Educational Opportunity; Equal Employment Opportunity; Equal Rights Amendment; Integrated Schools; Women's Rights.
Human Rights Organizations, SS 138, SS 140, SS 141, SS 143, SS 144, SS 546
Human Services, SS 616, SS 617, SS 618, SS 620, SS 622, SS 623, SS 624, SS 626, SS 627, SS 628, SS 629, SS 630, SS 632, SS 633, SS 634, SS 635. *See also* Alcoholism Treatment Services; Child Welfare Projects and Services; Counselors and Counseling Services; Disabled Persons' Projects and Services; Drug Abuse Services; Health Care Directories; Seniors' Projects and Services.
Humanities, HU 13, HU 17, HU 230. *See also* American Studies; Anglo-Saxon Studies; Black Studies; British Studies; Classical Studies; Egyptian Studies; Medieval Studies; Renaissance Studies; Slavonic Studies.
Humanities Bibliographies, SS 343
Humanities Periodical Indexes, HU 6, HU 10, HU 11
Humanities Programs and Research, HU 1, HU 2, HU 3, HU 7, HU 8, HU 9, HU 12, HU 14, HU 16, HU 18, HU 20, HU 48, HU 58, HU 65, HU 113
Hungary, SS 945
Hunting, SS 659, SS 690, SS 709, SS 713, SS 720, SS 722, SS 724, SS 726, SS 729, SS 753, SS 754, SS 760, SS 762, SS 821
Hydroelectric Power, SC 88, SC 115

Ice Hockey. *See* Hockey.
Ice Rink Equipment, SS 95
Ice Skating, SS 682, SS 834
Illustrators, HU 42, HU 127, HU 141
Importers, SS 54, SS 73
Imprints, American. *See* American Publications.
In-Print Books, GE 21, GE 22, GE 23, GE 31, GE 33, GE 35, GE 38, GE 39, GE 42, GE 43, GE 44, GE 47, GE 48, GE 50, GE 52, GE 54, GE 56, GE 57, GE 60, GE 61, ED 72, HU 309, SS 67, SC 11, SC 12, SC 248
In-Print Microforms, GE 40, GE 58, SS 194, SC 11
Income, SS 34, SS 92, SS 129, SS 130, SS 422, SS 423, SS 430, SS 598, SS 614, SS 656. *See also* Pensions; Personal Finance; Retirement Planning; Social Security; Wages and Salaries.
Income Tax, SS 584, SS 596, SS 598, SS 599, SS 606. *See also* Taxation.
Independent Schools. *See* Private Schools.
Independent Study Programs, ED 19, ED 21, ED 35, ED 50
India, SS 946
Indian Studies. *See* Native American Studies.
Industrial Directories. *See* Business Directories.
Industrial Hydraulics, SC 180
Industrial Microbiology, SC 36
Industrial Parks, SS 612
Industrial Relations. *See* Labor-Management Relations.
Industrial Research Laboratories, SC 7
Industrial Statistics. *See* Business Statistics; Employment Statistics.
Information Centers, HU 157, HU 168
Information Science, HU 149, HU 150, HU 154, HU 164
Information Services, Government. *See* Government Information Services.
Information Services, Health. *See* Health Information Services.
Information Storage and Retrieval, SC 61, SC 62
Inns. *See* Hotels; Restaurants.
Inorganic Chemistry, SC 47, SC 58

Instrumentation, SC 159. *See also* Computers.
Insurance Companies, SS 413, SS 414, SS 415
Insurance, Health. *See* Health Insurance.
Insurance Lawyers, SS 413
Insurance, Life. *See* Life Insurance.
Integrated Schools, ED 95, SS 138
Interethnic Relations, SS 139
Interior Decoration, SS 391, SS 393
Internal Security, SS 547
International Law, SS 447, SS 448, SS 452, SS 453, SS 454, SS 458, SS 468, SS 480, SS 486, SS 534, SS 548, SS 572, SS 573. *See also* Treaties.
International Organizations, GE 112, GE 129, SS 291, SS 292, SS 324, SS 325, SS 326, SS 460, SS 468, SS 555, SS 558, SS 562. *See also* United Nations.
International Relations, GE 2, SS 339, SS 353, SS 545, SS 559, SS 560, SS 579. *See also* American Foreign Relations; Arms Control; Canadian Foreign Relations; Diplomatic Service; United Nations.
International Statistics. *See* Statistics.
International Studies, SS 5
International Study. *See* Commonwealth Colleges; Studying Abroad.
International Trade. *See* Trade.
Interscholastic Sports. *See* School Sports.
Interviews, SS 339
Inventions. *See* Patents.
Investment Companies, SS 41, SS 42
Investment Law. *See* Commercial Law.
Investments, SS 39, SS 42, SS 43, SS 44, SS 45, SS 46, SS 47, SS 48, SS 71, SS 223, SS 304, SS 569, SS 609
Ireland, SS 259, SS 906, SS 908, SS 925, SS 947, SS 966, SS 970, SS 975, SS 980, SS 1014
Irish-Americans, SS 259
Irish History Bibliographies, SS 329
Irish Organizations, GE 98
Iron Metallurgy, SC 171
Islamic Art, HU 28
Islamic Studies, HU 70
Israel, HU 331, SS 270, SS 913, SS 948. *See also* Zionism.
Italian-Americans, SS 260
Italy, SS 914, SS 949, SS 981, SS 1022. *See also* Roman Studies.

Japan, SS 98, SS 347, SS 924, SS 950
Japanese Corporations, SS 98, SS 110, SS 347
Japanese Statistics, SS 347
Jewish-Americans, HU 248, SS 6, SS 261, SS 265, SS 270
Jewish Book Council, HU 109

Jewish History, SS 6, SS 265, SS 267, SS 277
Jewish Literature, HU 109
Jewish Organizations, GE 108, HU 247, HU 331, SS 971
Jewish Schools, HU 247
Jewish Social Services, SS 629
Jewish Studies, HU 287, HU 290, HU 313, SS 265, SS 267, SS 277
Jews, HU 248, SS 6, SS 261, SS 277. *See also* Israel; Judaism; Rabbis; Synagogues; Zionism.
Job Hunting Guides, SS 523, SS 524, SS 525, SS 526, SS 527, SS 529, SS 530, SS 531, SS 532. *See also* Vocational Guidance; Volunteer Programs.
Job Training Programs, ED 22, ED 99, ED 101, SS 488, SS 521, SS 621
Journalism Education, ED 19
Judaism, HU 264, HU 287, HU 290, SS 265. *See also* Rabbis; Synagogues.
Judiciary. *See* Courts; Criminal Justice.
Judo, SS 674
Junior College Libraries, ED 74
Junior Colleges, ED 33, ED 37, ED 98, SS 708
Junior High School Libraries, GE 46, ED 74
Junior High Schools, ED 29
Junior Olympics, SS 662, SS 665, SS 667
Juvenile Delinquents, SS 228. *See also* Corrections; Crime; Criminal Justice.
Juvenile Law, SS 469
Juvenile Literature. *See* Children's Literature.

Karate, SS 675
Kits, ED 75, ED 83, ED 84, ED 86, ED 89
Korea, SS 950
Kosher Restaurants, SS 913, SS 971

Labor Law, SS 423, SS 439, SS 440, SS 442, SS 451, SS 458
Labor Leaders, SS 420
Labor-Management Relations, SS 423, SS 429, SS 430, SS 438, SS 439, SS 440, SS 441
Labor Unions, SS 421, SS 430
Laboratory Directories, SC 7, SC 123
Laboratory Safety, SC 52
Lacrosse, SS 730
Land, SC 74
Land Management, SS 613, SC 19
Land Use Planning, SC 110
Large Print Books, GE 47, HU 103
Las Vegas, Nevada, SS 921, SS 1015

Laser Engineering, SC 133
Latin America, GE 88, SS 83, SS 85, SS 107, SS 348, SS 956, SS 994, SS 1004, SS 1005. *See also* names of specific regions and countries, e.g., Caribbean Area, Mexico.
Latin American Literature, HU 114
Latin American Music, HU 213
Latin American Statistics, GE 130, SS 83, SS 85
Latin American Studies Bibliographies, SS 343
Latin Literature, HU 76, HU 77
Latino Workers, SS 437
Latinos, SS 272, SS 425
Latter-Day Saints Church. *See* Mormon Church.
Latvian-Language Materials, SS 258
Latvians, SS 258
Law, African. *See* African Law.
Law, American. *See* American Law.
Law Bibliographies, SS 448, SS 452, SS 456
Law, Canadian. *See* Canadian Law.
Law, Commercial. *See* Commercial Law.
Law, Comparative. *See* Comparative Law.
Law, Constitutional. *See* Constitutional Law.
Law, Copyright. *See* Copyright.
Law, Cuban. *See* Cuban Law.
Law Enforcement, SS 232, SS 237, SS 239, SS 241, SS 243, SS 246, SS 247, SS 248. *See also* Corrections; Crime; Criminal Justice; Police.
Law Enforcement Handbooks, SS 238
Law, Environmental. *See* Environmental Law.
Law, International. *See* International Law.
Law, Juvenile. *See* Juvenile Law.
Law, Labor. *See* Labor Law.
Law Libraries, SS 461, SS 475
Law, Native American. *See* Native American Law.
Law, Natural. *See* Natural Law.
Law, Negligence. *See* Negligence Law.
Law, Patent. *See* Patents.
Law Periodical Indexes, SS 466, SS 467
Law, Population. *See* Population Law.
Law, School. *See* School Law.
Law Schools, SS 462, SS 475
Law, Trade. *See* Trade Law.
Lawyers, SS 471, SS 474, SS 483, SS 484
Lawyers, Government. *See* Government Lawyers.
Lawyers, Insurance. *See* Insurance Lawyers.
Lawyers, Women. *See* Women Lawyers.
Learned Societies. *See* Scholarly Organizations.
Learning Disabilities, ED 92
Legal Bibliographies. *See* Law Bibliographies.
Legal Directories, SS 445, SS 460, SS 462, SS 463, SS 464, SS 469, SS 471, SS 474, SS 483, SS 484
Legal Guides, SS 470, SS 471
Legal Medicine. *See* Forensic Medicine.
Legal Philosophy, HU 226, SS 446
Legal Services, SS 240, SS 252, SS 257, SS 463, SS 472, SS 474
Legislation, SS 293, SS 295, SS 301, SS 478, SS 482, SS 544, SS 551, SS 552. *See also* American Politics and Government; Congress; Smoking and Health Laws.
Leisure, SS 656. *See also* Retirement Planning; Recreation; Sports.
Lesbian Periodicals, HU 135
"Less-Developed" Countries. *See* Third World.
Librarians, HU 143, HU 153, HU 167
Librarianship, HU 142, HU 144, HU 145, HU 154, HU 160
Libraries, ED 18, HU 46, HU 144, HU 164, SS 160. *See also* Library of Congress; New York Public Library.
Libraries, Academic. *See* Academic Libraries.
Libraries, Art. *See* Art Libraries.
Libraries, Film. *See* Film Libraries.
Libraries, High School. *See* High School Libraries.
Libraries, Junior High School. *See* Junior High School Libraries.
Libraries, Law. *See* Law Libraries.
Libraries, Research. *See* Research Libraries.
Libraries, Special. *See* Special Libraries.
Library Associations, HU 143, HU 144, HU 145, HU 147, HU 167, SS 160, SS 187, SS 201
Library Automation, HU 170
Library Awards, HU 110, SS 160
Library Cataloging. *See* Cataloging.
Library Directories, HU 146, HU 148, HU 156, HU 157, HU 167, HU 168, HU 315, SS 187, SS 200, SS 337, SS 461
Library Education, ED 19, HU 142, HU 144, HU 146, HU 151, HU 158
Library Fees, HU 145
Library Networks, HU 161, HU 165
Library of Congress, GE 25, GE 26, GE 27, GE 48, HU 37, HU 80, HU 169, HU 181, HU 335, SS 63, SS 452, SC 5, SC 328
Library Research, HU 155, HU 159, HU 164
Library Statistics, HU 152, HU 162, HU 165, SS 160
Life Insurance, SS 415, SS 417, SS 584, SC 266
Lifelong Learning Programs. *See* Adult Education.
Linguistics, HU 96, HU 140
Linguistics Bibliographies, HU 92, HU 114
Lisbon, SS 1016. *See also* Portugal.
Literary Agents, SS 214
Literary Criticism, GE 118, HU 95, HU 117, HU 130, HU 133, HU 137
Literary Prizes, GE 34, HU 108, HU 109, HU 110, HU 116, HU 120, SS 160, SS 164, SS 187, SS 217
Literature, African. *See* African Literature.

Literature, American. *See* American Literature.
Literature, Celtic. *See* Celtic Literature.
Literature, Children's. *See* Children's Literature.
Literature, Comparative. *See* Comparative Literature.
Literature, English. *See* English Literature.
Literature, French. *See* French Literature.
Literature, Jewish. *See* Jewish Literature.
Literature, Latin American. *See* Latin American Literature.
Literature, Romantic. *See* Romantic Literature.
Literature, Teen-Agers'. *See* Teen-Agers' Literature.
Little League Baseball, SS 693, SS 764
Little Magazines, GE 115, SS 185
Little Presses. *See* Small Presses.
Little Theater Movement, HU 347
Loans, Government. *See* Government Grants and Loans.
Local Government, SS 241, SS 290, SS 297, SS 298, SS 303, SS 306, SS 313, SS 314, SS 316, SS 317, SS 318, SS 424, SS 581, SS 585, SS 589, SS 590, SS 591, SS 592
Locke Studies, HU 224
Logistics Engineering. *See* Transportation Engineering.
London, SS 951, SS 966, SS 1017. *See also* Britain.
Los Angeles, SS 1018. *See also* California.
Lutheran Church, HU 249, HU 256, HU 276, HU 295, HU 296, HU 297
Luxembourg, SS 934, SS 977

McGraw-Hill Encyclopedia of Science and Technology, SC 8
Machinery, SC 169, SC 173, SC 176. *See also* Diesel Engines; Gas Turbines; Gear Industry; Mechanical Engineering; Motor Vehicles.
Madrid, SS 1016. *See also* Spain.
Magazine Directories. *See* Periodical Directories.
Magazine Indexes. *See* Periodical Indexes.
Mail-Order Business, SS 101
Mailing Lists, SS 519
Malls, SS 401, SS 501
Malnutrition, SC 264
Management, SS 495
Management Education, ED 19, ED 22, SS 490
Management, Personnel. *See* Personnel Management.
Manufacturers' Directories. *See* Business Directories.
Maps and Mapping. *See* Cartography; Road Maps.
Marathon Running, SS 766
Marine Biology, SC 192, SC 198
Marine Engineering, SC 195, SC 196, SC 200
Marine Engineers, SC 130, SC 200

Marine Science, SC 197, SC 198
Marine Scientists, SC 193
Marine Technology. *See* Marine Engineering.
Marketing, SS 497, SS 498, SS 502, SS 505. *See also* Business Directories; Mail-Order Business; Retail Stores; Shopping Centers.
Marketing Research, SS 499, SS 507, SS 510. *See also* Consumer Research.
Marketing Services, SS 499, SS 506, SS 507
Marriage, SS 145, SS 639, SS 651, SS 654
Marriage Counseling, SS 635
Marriage Counselors, SS 617
Martial Arts, SS 674, SS 675, SS 676
Mass Transit. *See* Public Transportation.
Materials Handling, SS 863, SC 174
Maternity Homes, SS 620
Mathematical Tables, SC 201, SC 202, SC 203, SC 204
Mechanical Engineering, SC 129. *See also* Diesel Engines; Gas Turbines; Gear Industry; Machinery.
Mechanical Engineers, SC 128
Mechanics, Applied. *See* Applied Mechanics.
Mechanics, Fluid. *See* Fluid Mechanics.
Media Reviews. *See* Audio-Visual Reviews.
Mediation. *See* Arbitration and Mediation.
Medical Bibliographies, SC 12, SC 205, SC 220, SC 221, SC 222, SC 226, SC 234, SC 248, SC 270
Medical Costs, SC 260
Medical Dictionaries, SC 223
Medical Handbooks, SC 227, SC 236, SC 240, SC 250, SC 251, SC 267
Medical Geography, SC 264
Medical Information Services, SC 247, SC 253
Medical Periodical Indexes, SC 225, SC 226
Medical Periodicals, SC 248
Medical Philosophy, SC 257. *See also* Bioethics.
Medical Research, SC 255
Medical Schools, ED 37, SC 210, SC 219, SC 239, SC 249, SC 272. *See also* Dental Schools; Nursing Schools; Pharmacy Schools; Veterinary Schools.
Medical Specialists, SC 229
Medical Statistics, SC 245, SC 260, SC 265
Medicine, SC 10, SC 228, SC 246, SC 260, SC 266, SC 274, SC 278. *See also* Dentistry; Health Care; Mental Health; Nursing; Psychiatry.
Medicine, Forensic. *See* Forensic Medicine.
Medicine, Veterinary. *See* Veterinary Medicine.
Medieval Studies, HU 4, HU 15, HU 114, HU 201, HU 219, HU 231, HU 346
Mennonite Church, HU 299
Men's Sports, SS 665, SS 674, SS 675, SS 683, SS 693, SS 694, SS 695, SS 696, SS 701, SS 706, SS 712, SS 715, SS 716, SS 717, SS 721, SS 725, SS 731, SS 734, SS 735, SS 736, SS 737, SS 738, SS 739, SS 742, SS

743, SS 744, SS 747, SS 758, SS 765, SS 767, SS 768, SS 769, SS 774, SS 778, SS 779, SS 780, SS 783, SS 784, SS 785, SS 786, SS 787, SS 788, SS 789, SS 790, SS 791, SS 792, SS 794, SS 797, SS 800, SS 805, SS 806, SS 807, SS 808, SS 809, SS 810, SS 811, SS 816, SS 822, SS 824, SS 825, SS 826, SS 827, SS 833, SS 841

Mental Health, SC 335. *See also* Behavior Therapy; Counselors and Counseling Services; Psychology; Psychiatry.

Mental Health Bibliographies, SC 329

Mental Health Care Directories, SC 332

Mental Health Education, ED 91

Mental Illness, SC 327 *See also* Behavior Therapy; Counselors and Counseling Services; Psychiatry.

Mental "Retardation," SC 244

Mentally Disabled Persons, ED 96

Mentally Ill Children's Services, SC 268

Merchandising, SS 511, SS 513

Metal Casting, SC 160

Metallurgical Engineering, SC 282, SC 283

Metallurgical Engineers, SC 170, SC 281

Metallurgical Industry, SC 279, SC 280, SC 283

Meteorology, SC 75, SC 76

Methodist Church, HU 306, HU 323

Mexican-Americans, SS 272

Mexico, SS 952, SS 976, SS 1002

Microbiology, SC 29, SC 36

Microeconomics, SS 59

Microform Industry, SS 193, SS 194

Microforms, GE 40, GE 58, GE 115, HU 145, HU 163, SS 194

Microprogramming, SC 60

Microwave Product Industry, SC 175

Middle Ages. *See* Medieval Studies.

Middle Atlantic States, SS 987, SS 996

Middle East, SS 350, SS 351, SS 352, SS 353, SS 354. *See also* Arab Biographies; Israel; Turkey; Zionism.

Middle East History, HU 74

Military Career Programs, ED 101

Military Defense Organizations, SC 284

Military Expenditures, SS 577, SC 291, SC 295

Military Policy, SS 547, SS 550, SS 555, SC 289. *See also* Armed Forces; Arms Control; Warships; Weapons Systems.

Military Schools, ED 30

Milton Studies, HU 111

Mime, HU 340

Mineral Engineering. *See* Mining.

Mineral Resources, SC 74, SC 283, SC 308, SC 309

Mineralogy, SC 68, SC 297

Mining, SC 303, SC 304, SC 306

Mining Engineers, SC 305

Mining Industry, SC 298, SC 302, SC 308, SC 310, SC 311. *See also* Coal Industry.

Mining, Ocean. *See* Ocean Mining.

Ministers, HU 244, HU 249, HU 250, HU 255, HU 256, HU 257, HU 265, HU 269, HU 272, HU 276, HU 279, HU 284, HU 296, HU 297, HU 299, HU 302, HU 319, HU 322, HU 323, HU 324, HU 326. *See also* Priests; Rabbis.

Ministers' Education, ED 20

Minority Businesses, SS 103

Minority Education, ED 16, ED 17, ED 95

Minority Engineering Students, SC 142

Minority Government Workers, SS 424, SS 425

Minority Organizations, SS 621

Minority Students, ED 35, ED 38, ED 44

Minority Women, GE 67

Minority Workers, SS 437

Miscellaneous Facts, GE 1, GE 2, GE 3, GE 4, GE 5, GE 6, GE 9, GE 10, GE 11, GE 14, GE 15, GE 17, GE 18. *See also* Sports Records; World Records.

Missiles, Guided. *See* Guided Missiles.

Missionaries and Missions, HU 254, HU 267, HU 274, HU 284, HU 296, HU 300, HU 301, HU 304, HU 311, HU 320, HU 325

Mobile Home Parks, SS 412, SS 999, SS 1027

Mobile Homes, SS 615

Model Agencies, HU 240

Model Industry, SS 373

Models, Engineering. *See* Engineering Models.

Modern Art, HU 31, HU 57

Modern Music, HU 186, HU 212

Molecular Biology, SC 37, SC 57

Moravian Church, HU 302

Mormon Church, HU 274, HU 288, HU 293, HU 298

Morocco, SS 953, SS 1007

Mortgage Loans, SS 602

Motels, SS 77, SS 94, SS 106, SS 972, SS 1003

Motion Pictures. *See* Films.

Motor Vehicles, SS 870, SS 895, SS 897. *See also* Automobiles; Automotive Industry; Bus Travel; Mobile Homes; Motorcycles; Public Transportation; Recreational Vehicles; Truck Maintenance and Repair; Trucking Industry.

Motorcycles, SS 855, SS 856, SS 857

Motors. *See* Diesel Engines; Gas Turbines; Machinery; Mechanical Engineering.

Mountaineering, SS 657, SS 685

Movies. *See* Films.

Multicultural Education, ED 17

Multimedia Kits. *See* Kits.

Multinational Corporations, SS 5, SS 55, SS 75, SS 126, SS 520

Municipal Government, SS 241, SS 297, SS 305, SS 315, SS 336, SS 492, SS 585, SS 588, SS 592
Munitions Industry, SC 294, SC 295. *See also* Arms Control; Military Expenditures; Weapons Systems.
Museum Stores, HU 39
Museums, ED 18, HU 22, HU 46, HU 48, HU 49, HU 50, HU 52, HU 54, HU 58, HU 61, SS 22, SS 28, SS 337, SS 347, SS 882, SS 1000
Music, African. *See* African Music.
Music Bibliographies, HU 180, HU 181, HU 207
Music Catalogs, HU 186
Music, Classical. *See* Classical Music.
Music Education, HU 188, HU 189, HU 197, HU 200, HU 203, HU 204, HU 206
Music Festivals, HU 184, HU 199, HU 202, SS 279
Music History, HU 201, HU 211, HU 212
Music Industry, HU 182, HU 184, HU 195, HU 199, HU 336
Music, Latin American. *See* Latin American Music.
Music, Organ. *See* Organs and Organ Music.
Music Periodical Indexes, HU 207
Music, Percussion. *See* Percussion Music.
Music, Popular. *See* Popular Music.
Music Research, HU 201, HU 208, HU 211, HU 212, HU 213
Musical Instruments, HU 190, HU 205
Musicians, HU 178, HU 184, HU 198, HU 199, HU 202
Mutual Funds, SS 41, SS 48
Mutual Savings Banks, SS 37, SS 49
Muzzleloaders, SS 724

Narcotics Traffic, SS 230, SS 234, SS 236
National Basketball Association, SS 739, SS 769, SS 807
National Book Awards, GE 34
National Debt. *See* Public Finance.
National Football League, SS 725, SS 737, SS 779, SS 805, SS 808, SS 827
National Health Insurance, SS 404
National Hockey League, SS 780, SS 806, SS 809
National Jewish Book Awards, HU 109
National Parks, SS 1001
Nations. *See* Countries.
Native American Government Workers, SS 425
Native American History, SS 12, SS 24, SS 27
Native American Law, SS 456
Native American Periodicals, SS 269
Native American Studies, HU 159
Native American Studies Bibliographies, SS 269
Native American Workers, SS 437

Native Americans, SS 276, SS 279, SS 638
Natural Gas, SC 115, SC 119
Natural Law, SS 446
Natural Resources, SC 73, SC 74, SC 113. *See also* Conservation; Energy Resources; Environmental Protection; Forests; Land; Petroleum Resources; Water Resources.
Nature Study, SC 9
Nautical Almanacs, SS 879, SC 17, SC 19
Naval Engineering. *See* Marine Engineering.
Navigation, SC 194
Navigation Guides, SS 879, SS 892, SS 893, SS 894
Necrologies. *See* Obituaries and Necrologies.
Needlework, SS 394, SS 397
Negligence Law, SS 470
Netherlands, SS 944, SS 977
Networks, Library. *See* Library Networks.
"New Age" Bibliographies, SS 183
"New Age" Directories, HU 315
New England, SS 995
New England Folklore, SS 282
New Hampshire History, SS 23
New Jersey History, SS 12
New York City, SS 997, SS 1019
New York Public Library, GE 24, GE 25, GE 26, GE 27, HU 37, HU 80, HU 181, HU 335, SS 63, SS 452, SC 5, SC 328
New York Theater. *See* Broadway Theater; Off-Broadway Theater; Off-Off-Broadway Theater.
New Zealand, SS 998
Newbery Awards, GE 34
News Services, SS 212, SS 514
Newspaper Directories, SS 154, SS 165, SS 168, SS 169, SS 170, SS 181, SS 190, SS 197, SS 211, SS 212, SS 214, SS 514
Newspaper Indexes, GE 120
Newspaper Publishing, SS 151, SS 169, SS 170
Nobel Prizes, SC 9, SC 10
Noise Pollution, SC 216
Non-Print Reviews. *See* Audio-Visual Reviews.
Non-Self-Governing Territories. *See* Colonies.
Non-Traditional Education, ED 23, ED 35
North Africa, SS 350. *See also* Morocco; Tunisia.
North American History, SS 14, SS 15. *See also* American History; Canadian History.
Northeastern United States, SS 988
Northwestern United States, SS 989
Norwegian-Americans, SS 273
Notaries Public, SS 459
Nuclear Engineers, SC 93
Nuclear Physics, SC 313
Nuclear Power, SC 96
Nuclear Power Plants, SC 72

Nuclear Reactors, SC 107
Nuclear Science, SC 97
Nuclear Scientists, SC 93
Nuclear Weapons, SC 291, SC 294
Numerical Control, SC 176
Numismatics, SS 363, SS 367, SS 368, SS 369, SS 370, SS 375, SS 376, SS 377, SS 378, SS 387, SS 388
Nursing, SC 238
Nursing Schools, SC 261, SC 262

Obituaries and Necrologies, GE 2, GE 3, GE 10, GE 15, GE 20, GE 65, GE 68, GE 71, HU 21, HU 63, HU 176, HU 248, HU 264, HU 322, HU 352, SS 275, SC 13
Occultism, HU 309, SS 183
Occupational Education. See Vocational Education.
Occupational Guidance. See Vocational Guidance.
Occupational Schools. See Vocational-Technical Schools.
Ocean Mining, SC 196, SC 199
Ocean Travel, SS 936, SS 993, SS 1009
Oceanographers, SC 193
Oceanography, SC 197, SC 198. See also Marine Biology.
Off-Broadway Theater, HU 333, HU 343, HU 351, HU 352
Off-Off-Broadway Theater, HU 333, HU 343, HU 347
Offshore Oil Fields, SC 199
Ohio College Library Center, HU 165
Oil Industry. See Petroleum Industry.
Oil Resources. See Petroleum Resources.
Oklahoma History, SS 24
Old Norse-Icelandic Studies Bibliographies, SS 334
Olympic Games, SS 750, SS 823, SS 832. See also Junior Olympics.
One-Act Plays, HU 334
Ontario History, SS 25
Optical Industry, SC 182
Optics, SC 315
Oral History, SS 282, SS 356
Orchestras, HU 199, HU 202
Organic Chemistry, SC 48, SC 49, SC 57, SC 59. See also Biochemistry.
Organizations, GE 93, GE 94, GE 97, GE 98, GE 99, GE 100, GE 102, GE 103, GE 104, GE 105, GE 108, GE 109, GE 111, GE 112, ED 6. See also Afro-American Organizations; Chambers of Commerce; Conservation Agencies and Groups; Consumer Agencies and Groups; Educational Organizations; Foundations; Human Rights Organizations; International Organizations; Library Associations; Minority Organizations; Scholarly Organizations; Sports Organizations; Women's Organizations.
Organs and Organ Music, HU 205
Orthodox Church. See Eastern Orthodox Church.
Osteopaths, SC 231, SC 275
Overhead Transparencies. See Transparencies.
Overseas Employment, SS 526, SS 527, SS 529, SS 531, SS 532

Pacific Islands, SS 26, SS 340, SS 341, SS 1006
Pacific Northwest History, SS 28
Packaging Industry, SC 183
Pageants, GE 4
Palestinian History, SS 21
Pantomime, HU 340
Parasitology, SC 22
Paris, SS 939, SS 982, SS 1020. See also France.
Parliament, SS 300
Parochial Schools, ED 13, ED 29, ED 30, ED 31, HU 260, HU 299, HU 305, HU 330
Parole, SS 228, SS 233, SS 245. See also Criminal Justice.
Parties, SS 396
Pastors. See Ministers; Priests; Rabbis.
Pastors' Education. See Ministers' Education.
Patents, SS 471, SS 474, SS 533, SS 536, SS 539, SS 540. See also Copyright; Trademarks.
Patient Education, SC 243. See also Health Education.
Peace Corps, SS 616
Pensions, SS 417, SS 419, SS 428, SS 488, SS 584, SS 590. See also Social Security.
Percussion Music, HU 196
Performing Arts Directories. See Theatrical Directories.
Periodical Covers, SS 156
Periodical Directories, GE 49, GE 55, GE 59, ED 1, HU 36, HU 82, HU 135, HU 309, SS 140, SS 154, SS 165, SS 181, SS 185, SS 187, SS 190, SS 195, SS 211, SS 212, SS 214, SS 217, SS 269, SS 514, SC 11, SC 34, SC 248. See also Newspaper Directories.
Periodical Indexes, GE 63, GE 84, GE 85, GE 86, GE 87, GE 113, GE 114, GE 115, GE 116, GE 117, GE 119, GE 120, GE 121, ED 9, HU 6, HU 10, HU 11, HU 32, HU 106, HU 145, HU 171, HU 207, HU 227, HU 261, HU 266, HU 285, HU 288, HU 289, HU 314, SS 3, SS 4, SS 68, SS 186, SS 223, SS 232, SS 269, SS 284, SS 345, SS 466, SS 467, SS 564, SS 585, SC 4, SC 6, SC 33, SC 135, SC 225, SC 226, SC 234
Periodical Selection, GE 49

Personal Finance, SS 615, SS 625. *See also* Consumer Guides; Cost-of-Living; Income; Income Tax; Investments; Job Hunting Guides; Pensions; RetirementPlanning; Social Security; Veterans' Services; Wages and Salaries.
Personality, SC 321
Personnel Management, SS 488. *See also* Employee Benefits; Hours of Work; Job Training Programs; Labor-Management Relations; Labor Unions; Wages and Salaries.
Pesticides, SS 225
Petrochemical Industry, SC 121
Petroleum Engineering, SC 112, SC 199
Petroleum Engineers, SC 111
Petroleum Industry, SC 94, SC 95, SC 101, SC 108
Petroleum Resources, SC 74, SC 95, SC 108, SC 119
Pharmaceutical Handbooks, SC 235, SC 236, SC 240, SC 250, SC 251, SC 267
Pharmaceutical Industry, SC 251, SC 267
Pharmacies, SS 512
Pharmacy Schools, SC 256, SC 273
Philanthropy, SS 637. *See also* Foundations; Fund Raising; Grants.
Philately. *See* Stamps and Stamp Collecting.
Philologists, HU 87
Philosophers, HU 221
Philosophy, HU 214, HU 215, HU 216, HU 218, HU 220, HU 222, HU 223, HU 225, HU 226, HU 228, HU 231, HU 232, HU 309. *See also* Locke Studies; Rationalism.
Philosophy Education, HU 221
Philosophy, Medical. *See* Medical Philosophy.
Philosophy Periodical Indexes, HU 227
Philosophy, Sport. *See* Sport Philosophy.
Phoenix, Arizona, SS 1021
Photogrammetry, SC 146
Phonograph Records. *See* Records.
Photographers, HU 35, HU 82, HU 233, HU 235, HU 236, HU 241, SS 212
Photography, HU 24, HU 31, HU 233, HU 234, HU 235, HU 239, HU 240, HU 241, HU 242
Photography, Advertising. *See* Advertising Photography.
Photography Awards, HU 241, SS 705
Photography Dealers and Suppliers, HU 39, HU 236, HU 237, HU 240, SS 164
Photography Handbooks, HU 243
Physical Chemistry, SC 49, SC 51, SC 57, SC 58
Physical Education, ED 67, ED 96
Physical Organic Chemistry, SC 49, SC 57
Physically Disabled Persons. *See* Disabled Persons.
Physicians, SC 214, SC 229, SC 233
Physics, SC 54, SC 314. *See also* Acoustical Holography; Astrophysics; Biophysics; Nuclear Physics; Nuclear Science; Optics.
Physiology, SC 30
Physiology, Plant. *See* Plant Physiology.
Planning Associations, State. *See* State Planning Associations.
Planning, Criminal Justice. *See* Criminal Justice Planning.
Planning, Regional. *See* Regional Planning.
Planning, Retirement. *See* Retirement Planning.
Planning, Urban. *See* Urban Planning.
Plant Physiology, SC 31
Plant Sites, SS 109, SS 612
Plants. *See* Botany; Gardening.
Plastics, SC 177, SC 187
Plastics Industry, SC 177, SC 189
Play Bibliographies, HU 345
Plays, HU 333, HU 334, HU 339, HU 347, SS 273. *See also* Mime; Theater.
Playwrights, HU 342
Plumbing, SS 398, SS 400
Poetry, HU 17, HU 90, HU 117, SS 152, SS 262
Poetry Bibliographies, HU 106
Poets, HU 99, HU 108
Poison Control Centers, SC 232
Police, SS 234, SS 239, SS 243, SS 247. *See also* Corrections; Law Enforcement.
Police Examinations, SS 244
Police Handbooks, SS 238
Policy Analysis, SS 62, SS 559, SS 560, SS 565
Political Science, HU 226, SS 565, SS 566
Political Science Bibliographies, SS 557, SS 564, SS 574, SS 575
Political Science Education, SS 556
Pollution, SS 225, SS 402, SS 481, SC 113, SC 216
Pollution Control, SS 612
Pollution Control Agencies, SC 100, SC 120
Pollution Control Industry, SC 120
Polo, SS 835
Polymers, SS 56
Popular Culture, SS 183
Popular Music, HU 179, HU 195, HU 207
Population, GE 60, GE 125, GE 136, GE 137, GE 138, GE 139, SS 548, SS 656
Population Bibliographies, SS 653
Population Law, SS 449
Population Policy, SS 652
Porcelain Enameling, SC 184
Ports, SS 859, SS 860, SS 863, SS 865, SS 876, SS 883, SS 892, SS 936
Portugal, SS 915, SS 954, SS 983, SS 1016
Post Offices, SS 208

Postage Stamp Collecting. *See* Stamps and Stamp Collecting.
Posters, HU 41
Power Companies. *See* Electric Utilities.
Power, Fluid. *See* Fluid Mechanics.
Power Plants. *See* Electric Power Plants; Nuclear Power Plants.
Power Transmission, SC 181, SC 185, SC 303
Powerlifting. *See* Weightlifting.
Prehistory. *See* Archaeology.
Prep Schools, ED 28, ED 29, ED 30, ED 32
Presbyterian Church, HU 324
Preschool Education, ED 25
Presidents, SS 309, SS 312, SS 543, SS 563, SS 576, SS 600. *See also* American Politics and Government; Elections.
Pressure Vessel Inspection, SC 179
Priests, HU 262, HU 269, HU 275, HU 279, HU 292, HU 303, HU 305, HU 307, HU 325
Primary Schools. *See* Elementary Schools.
"Primitive" Societies. *See* Anthropology.
Printers, SS 212
Prisoners, SS 228, SS 233, SS 235, SS 249, SS 250, SS 253, SS 255, SS 256, SS 546. *See also* Corrections; Criminal Justice; Parole.
Prisons, SS 228, SS 233, SS 246, SS 249, SS 250. *See also* Corrections; Criminal Justice; Parole.
Privacy, SS 138, SS 320
Private Presses, GE 50
Private Schools, ED 27, ED 28, ED 29, ED 30, ED 31. *See also* Parochial Schools.
Prizefighting. *See* Boxing.
Probation, SS 245. *See also* Corrections; Criminal Justice.
Product Reliability, SC 186
Professional Baseball, SS 693, SS 694, SS 695, SS 696, SS 712, SS 765, SS 767, SS 783, SS 784, SS 785, SS 800, SS 822, SS 824, SS 842
Professional Basketball, SS 739, SS 769, SS 807, SS 825
Professional Education. *See* Vocational Education.
Professional Football, SS 716, SS 725, SS 734, SS 737, SS 743, SS 747, SS 778, SS 779, SS 805, SS 808, SS 810, SS 827
Professional Hockey, SS 717, SS 721, SS 758, SS 780, SS 806, SS 809
Professors. *See* Educators.
Profit Sharing Plans, SS 488
Programmed Instruction Materials, ED 75, ED 76
Propaganda, SS 479. *See also* Social Psychology.
Protestant Episcopal Church. *See* Episcopal Church.
Protestantism. *See* Anglican Church; Baptist Church; Christian Schools; Church Directories; Congregational Church; Disciples of Christ; Ecumenism; Episcopal Church; Friends Meetings; Lutheran Church; Mennonite Church; Methodist Church; Ministers; Moravian Church; Mormon Church; Parochial Schools; Presbyterian Church; Theological Education; Theology; Unitarian-Universalist Association; United Church of Christ.
Psychiatric Hospitals, SC 334
Psychiatrists, SC 318, SC 319
Psychiatry, SC 316, SC 323, SC 326, SC 330, SC 335
Psychoanalysts, SC 319
Psychologists, SC 320
Psychology, ED 86, HU 220, SC 321, SC 322, SC 325. *See also* Behavior Therapy; Psychiatry.
Psychology Bibliographies, SC 328
Psychology, Child. *See* Child Psychology.
Psychology Education, SC 331
Psychology, Social. *See* Social Psychology.
Public Administration, GE 100. *See also* Local Government; Municipal Government; Public Works; State Government.
Public Finance, SS 581, SS 585, SS 586, SS 588, SS 589, SS 590, SS 591, SS 592, SS 593, SS 597, SS 600, SS 601, SS 603, SS 604, SS 605. *See also* Government Grants and Loans; Military Expenditures; Taxation.
Public Interest Law Firms, SS 474
Public Lands, SS 613
Public Libraries, GE 51, HU 103, HU 142, HU 144
Public Opinion, SS 649. *See also* Elections; Propaganda; Social Psychology.
Public Relations Agencies, HU 237, HU 310
Public Service Commissions, SC 98
Public Television, SS 212
Public Transportation, SS 848, SS 883, SS 890
Public Utilities, SS 47, SC 78, SC 79, SC 98
Public Welfare Programs. *See* Welfare Programs.
Public Works, SS 287
Publications, American. *See* American Publications.
Publicity and Public Relations, SS 514. *See also* Advertising Agencies; Newspaper Directories; Periodical Directories; Radio Industry; Television Industry.
Publishers and Publishing, GE 21, GE 31, GE 33, GE 35, GE 36, GE 38, GE 42, GE 47, GE 50, GE 51, GE 52, GE 54, GE 56, GE 57, GE 58, GE 110, HU 39, HU 44, HU 82, HU 237, SS 67, SS 150, SS 151, SS 159, SS 160, SS 164, SS 165, SS 166, SS 168, SS 185, SS 187, SS 190, SS 193, SS 195, SS 201, SS 214, SS 215, SS 217, SS 337. *See also* Audio-Visual Industry; Book Trade; Periodical Directories.
Puerto Rico, SS 111, SS 348, SS 626, SS 972

Quaker Meetings. *See* Friends Meetings.
Quality Control Engineering, SC 162, SC 186
Quality of Life Indicators, SS 612
Quotations, GE 16

RSVP, SS 616
Rabbis, HU 264
Race Relations, ED 61, SS 139
Race Walking, SS 677, SS 766
Racing, Automobile. *See* Automobile Racing.
Racing, Marathon. *See* Marathon Running.
Racing, Yacht. *See* Yacht Racing.
Racism, SS 141. *See also* Apartheid.
Radical Publishers, GE 21
Radical Sociology, SS 647
Radicals, SS 420
Radio, Amateur. *See* Amateur Radio.
Radio History, HU 344
Radio Industry, SS 162, SS 181, SS 195, SS 212, SS 213, SS 514
Radiochemistry, SC 47
Railroads, SS 867, SS 8ii88888877 8, SS 882, SS 899, SS 910, SS 912, SS 926, SC 77
Rape, SS 145, SS 248, SS 254
Rationalism, HU 229
Reactors, Nuclear. *See* Nuclear Reactors.
Reading Disabilities, ED 92
Real Estate Business, SS 607, SS 608, SS 610, SS 611, SS 612
Real Estate Investment Trusts, SS 609
Record Catalogs, HU 209, HU 210
Record Covers, SS 156
Record Industry, HU 182, HU 183
Record Review Indexes, HU 179, HU 193
Record Reviews, HU 191
Recording Studios, HU 183
Records, GE 48, ED 75, ED 79
Records, Sports. *See* Sports Records.
Records, World. *See* World Records.
Recreation, ED 67, SS 656. *See also* Antiques; Camps and Camping; Coins and Coin Collecting; Needlework; Sports; Stamps and Stamp Collecting; Travel.
Recreational Vehicles, SS 1027
Red Cross, SS 618
Reference Books, GE 39, GE 41, GE 83, GE 91, GE 92, ED 74
Refrigeration, SC 127
Refugees, SS 627
Regional Planning, SS 402
Relay Industry, SC 178
Religion, HU 231, HU 259, HU 286, HU 317, HU 329, HU 330. *See also* Anglican Church; Armenian Church in America; Atheism; Baptist Church; Bible; Buddhism; Catholic Church; Catholic Philosophy; Christian Schools; Church Directories; Congregational Church; Disciples of Christ; Eastern Orthodox Church; Ecumenism; Episcopal Church; Free Thought; Friends Meetings; Jewish Schools; Jews; Judaism; Lutheran Church; Mennonite Church; Methodist Church; Moravian Church; Mormon Church; Parochial Schools; Presbyterian Church; Synagogues; Theological Education; Theology; Unitarian-Universalist Association; United Church of Christ.
Religion Bibliographies, HU 309, SS 183
Religions, Eastern. *See* Eastern Religions.
Religious Biographies, HU 326
Religious Periodical Indexes, HU 261, HU 266, HU 278, HU 288, HU 289, HU 314
Religious Retreats, HU 278
Religious Society of Friends, HU 308, HU 311
Religious Sociology, HU 312
Renaissance Studies, HU 15, HU 17, HU 201, HU 219, HU 346
Reprints, GE 42, GE 48
Research Centers, GE 109, ED 18, HU 23, HU 157, SS 340, SS 404. *See also* Environmental Research Centers; Industrial Research Laboratories.
Research Grants, GE 101, HU 2, HU 3, HU 7, HU 14, HU 16, HU 18, HU 155, SC 255
Research Libraries, HU 152, HU 169
Resorts, SS 615
Restaurants, SS 906, SS 908, SS 913, SS 914, SS 915, SS 916, SS 925, SS 966, SS 977, SS 978, SS 979, SS 980, SS 981, SS 982, SS 983. *See also* Travel.
Retail Stores, SS 494, SS 511, SS 513. *See also* Drug Stores; Grocery Markets; Shopping Centers.
"Retarded" Persons. *See* Mentally Disabled Persons.
"Retardation," Mental. *See* Mental Retardation.
Retirement Planning, SS 417, SS 614, SS 615. *See also* Consumer Guides; Cost-of-Living; Income; Income Tax; Pensions; Seniors' Projects and Services; Social Security; Veterans' Services.
Revolutionary Groups, SS 547
Road Maps, SS 1002
Roads, SS 847, SS 862
Roman Catholic Church. *See* Catholic Church.
Roman Studies, HU 73, HU 76, HU 77
Romantic Literature, HU 122
Rome, SS 1022. *See also* Italy.
Roses, SC 153, SC 154, SC 156
Royal Families, GE 68, GE 71, SS 300
Running, SS 812. *See also* Marathon Running; Track and Field.
Russia. *See* Soviet Union.

Safety, SS 489, SS 887. *See also* Accidents; Fire Prevention; Laboratory Safety.
Safety Education, ED 84
Sailboats, SS 880. *See also* Boats and Boating; Yachts.
Salaries. *See* Wages and Salaries.
San Francisco, SS 1023. *See also* California.
Sanitary Engineering, SC 131
Savings and Loan Associations, SS 38, SS 42, SS 51
Scandinavia, SS 566, SS 955
Schizophrenia, SC 326
Scholarly Organizations, HU 2, HU 5, HU 20, HU 69, HU 87, HU 128, HU 208, HU 214, HU 215, HU 216, HU 221, HU 225, HU 230, HU 293, SS 1, SS 7, SS 11, SS 12, SS 15, SS 23, SS 24, SS 102, SS 356
Scholars, ED 5, HU 5, HU 62, HU 87, SC 1, SC 3, SC 23, SC 50, SC 193, SC 215, SC 317
Scholarships and Fellowships, GE 105, ED 3, ED 28, ED 37, ED 43, ED 53, ED 54, ED 58, HU 44, HU 158, SS 11, SS 584, SS 602. *See also* Research Grants.
Schomburg Center for Research in Black Culture, GE 24
School Desegregation. *See* Integrated Schools.
School Directories, ED 8, ED 10, ED 13, ED 18, ED 19, ED 20, ED 21, ED 24, ED 26, ED 27, ED 28, ED 29, ED 31, ED 32, ED 33, ED 35, ED 37, ED 38, ED 39, ED 40, ED 41, ED 42, ED 44, ED 45, ED 46, ED 47, ED 48, ED 49, ED 51, ED 52, ED 59, ED 94, ED 98, ED 99, ED 100, ED 101, ED 102, HU 22, HU 26, HU 81, HU 151, HU 189, HU 203, HU 221, HU 247, HU 252, HU 277, HU 299, HU 305, HU 315, HU 332, SS 182, SS 237, SS 475, SS 556, SS 631, SS 648, SC 134, SC 207, SC 210, SC 219, SC 239, SC 249, SC 256, SC 261, SC 262, SC 272, SC 273, SC 279, SC 331, SC 339
School Law, SS 485
School Libraries, GE 46, GE 53, ED 61, ED 74
School Management. *See* Educational Management.
School Media Centers. *See* School Libraries.
School Media Programs. *See* Audio-Visual Education.
School Sports, SS 691, SS 692, SS 697, SS 698, SS 699, SS 700, SS 701, SS 702, SS 706, SS 707, SS 708, SS 715, SS 731, SS 735, SS 736, SS 738, SS 742, SS 748, SS 770, SS 771, SS 772, SS 774, SS 775, SS 776, SS 777, SS 786, SS 787, SS 788, SS 789, SS 790, SS 791, SS 792, SS 793, SS 794, SS 795, SS 796, SS 797, SS 816, SS 825, SS 826, SS 828, SS 829, SS 833, SS 841, SS 845
Science, HU 230
Science Bibliographies, SC 11, SC 12. *See also* Antarctica Bibliographies; Bioethics Bibliographies; Geography Bibliographies; Geology Bibliographies; Medical Bibliographies; Science Periodical Indexes; Social Science Bibliographies.
Science Consultants, SC 2
Science Education, ED 68
Science Experiments, SC 67
Science Fiction, HU 116, HU 118
Science Fiction Review Indexes, HU 123
Science Periodical Indexes, SC 4, SC 6, SC 33
Science Philosophy, HU 225
Science Policy, SC 10
Science Yearbooks, SC 8, SC 9, SC 10, SC 13
Scientists, SS 427, SC 1, SC 3, SC 23, SC 50, SC 93, SC 193, SC 215, SC 317
Scottish Studies, SS 357
Scripts, ED 70
Sea Travel. *See* Ocean Travel.
Secondary Education, ED 24, ED 40
"Seeing Eye" Dogs, SS 632
Senior High Schools. *See* High Schools.
Seniors' Education. *See* Adult Education.
Seniors' Housing, SS 629, SS 634. *See also* Retirement Planning.
Seniors' Projects and Services, SS 629, SS 634, SC 259. *See also* Social Security; Veterans' Services.
Sephardic Jews, SS 261
Serial Directories, GE 39, GE 45, GE 110. *See also* Periodical Directories.
Series' Books, GE 32, GE 91
Sermons, HU 268
Sexism, SS 142, SS 144
Shakespeare Festivals, HU 351
Shakespeare Studies, HU 124, HU 125, HU 139
Shipping Industry, SS 850, SS 858, SS 859, SS 860, SS 863, SS 865, SS 871
Shopping, SS 931, SS 932, SS 1009. *See also* Consumer Guides.
Shopping Centers, SS 401, SS 501
Short Stories, HU 89, HU 116, HU 118, HU 120, SS 262, SS 264
Short Story Bibliographies, HU 126
Shortwave Stations, SS 213
Sight-Saving Books. *See* Large Print Books.
Simulation, Computer. *See* Computer Simulation.
Site Selection. *See* Plant Sites.
Skiing, SS 793, SS 813, SS 814, SS 815, SS 836, SS 1012
Skiing, Cross Country. *See* Cross Country Skiing.
Slavonic Studies, HU 119, HU 140
Slides, ED 75, ED 80
Slovak-Americans, HU 291, HU 292
Slovak-Language Materials, HU 292
Small Presses, GE 21, GE 50, GE 54, SS 185
Smoking and Health, SC 242
Smoking and Health Bibliographies, SC 222
Smoking and Health Laws, SC 263
Smoking and Health Research, SC 230

Soccer, SS 794, SS 816
Social Anthropology. *See* Anthropology.
Social "Deviance," SS 643
Social Indicators, SS 656. *See also* Employment Statistics; Quality of Life Indicators.
Social Problems, SS 640. *See also* Ageism; Apartheid; Crime; Divorce; Racism; Rape; Unemployment.
Social Psychology, SS 641. *See also* Propaganda; Public Opinion.
Social Science Bibliographies, SS 183, SS 343, SS 650, SS 651, SS 653, SC 328
Social Science Periodical Indexes, HU 285, SS 3, SS 4
Social Science Research, SS 1, SS 99, SS 404, SS 655
Social Sciences, HU 230
Social Scientists, SC 317
Social Security, SS 634, SC 259
Social Services. *See* Human Services.
Social Studies, ED 69, SS 2
Social Work, SS 624, SS 626, SS 628, SS 633, SS 635. *See also* Human Services.
Social Work Education, SS 631
Sociology, SS 638, SS 642, SS 646, SS 647, SS 654, SS 655
Sociology Bibliographies, SS 650, SS 651
Sociology Education, SS 648
Sociology, Religious. *See* Religious Sociology.
Sociology, Urban. *See* Urban Studies.
Softball, SS 683, SS 817, SS 818
Soil Conservation, SC 104
Solar Energy, SC 96, SC 106, SC 109
Sound Equipment, HU 185, HU 192, HU 195
South America. *See* Latin America.
South Asia, SS 351, SS 957
South Central United States, SS 991
Southeastern United States, SS 990
Southern United States History, SS 27
Southwestern United States, SS 991
Soviet Union, SS 358, SS 958, SC 289
Space Sciences, SC 68. *See also* Astronomy.
Space Travel, ED 61
Spain, SS 916, SS 959, SS 983, SS 1007, SS 1016
Spanish-Language Materials, HU 213, SS 261, SS 457, SS 626
Special Education, ED 31, ED 92, ED 93, ED 94, ED 95, ED 96
Special Libraries, HU 156, HU 157, HU 167, HU 168
Speech Communication, HU 128
Speech Communication Bibliographies, HU 91, HU 129
Speech Disorders, SC 216, SC 217
Speeches, GE 16, SS 344. *See also* Interviews.
Speed Skating, SS 682
Sport Philosophy, SS 763

Sports, SS 705, SS 706, SS 707, SS 708. *See also* Archery; Automobile Racing; Badminton; Baseball; Basketball; Baton Twirling; Boating and Boats; Bodybuilding; Bowhunting; Bowling; Boxing; Cross Country Skiing; Diving; Fencing; Field Hockey; Fishing; Football; Golf; Gymnastics; Hockey; Hunting; Horse Showing; Ice Skating; Judo; Junior Olympics; Karate; Lacrosse; Marathon Running; Men's Sports; Mountaineering; Olympic Games; Polo; Skiing; Soccer; Softball; Squash Racquets; Swimming; Tae Kwon Do; Tennis; Track and Field; Trapshooting; Volleyball; Water Polo; Weightlifting; Western Riding; Women's Sports; Wrestling; Yacht Racing.
Sports Betting Guides, SS 734, SS 738, SS 739, SS 743, SS 805
Sports Coaches, SS 776, SS 844
Sports Equipment, SS 95, SS 119, SS 687, SS 688, SS 690, SS 704, SS 710, SS 711, SS 713, SS 718, SS 719, SS 726, SS 727, SS 729, SS 732, SS 733, SS 753, SS 760, SS 782, SS 813, SS 814, SS 819. *See also* Guns.
Sports Organizations, SS 660, SS 661, SS 681, SS 682, SS 684, SS 691, SS 692, SS 770, SS 777, SS 779, SS 780, SS 781, SS 798, SS 835, SS 836
Sports Records, GE 2, GE 3, GE 9, GE 15, GE 17, SS 665, SS 668, SS 678, SS 680, SS 682, SS 683, SS 689, SS 693, SS 694, SS 696, SS 706, SS 712, SS 716, SS 717, SS 721, SS 725, SS 744, SS 745, SS 747, SS 750, SS 751, SS 761, SS 765, SS 766, SS 767, SS 768, SS 769, SS 772, SS 776, SS 778, SS 779, SS 780, SS 783, SS 784, SS 788, SS 790, SS 792, SS 794, SS 795, SS 800, SS 806, SS 809, SS 811, SS 812, SS 822, SS 823, SS 825, SS 829, SS 830, SS 832, SS 833, SS 834, SS 838, SS 843, SS 869
Sports Rules, SS 661, SS 662, SS 663, SS 664, SS 665, SS 666, SS 667, SS 668, SS 669, SS 670, SS 671, SS 672, SS 673, SS 674, SS 675, SS 676, SS 677, SS 678, SS 679, SS 680, SS 681, SS 682, SS 683, SS 684, SS 686, SS 692, SS 697, SS 698, SS 699, SS 700, SS 701, SS 702, SS 714, SS 715, SS 730, SS 731, SS 735, SS 736, SS 741, SS 750, SS 764, SS 768, SS 771, SS 773, SS 785, SS 786, SS 789, SS 791, SS 793, SS 794, SS 795, SS 796, SS 797, SS 798, SS 815, SS 816, SS 817, SS 818, SS 828, SS 831, SS 833, SS 838, SS 839, SS 840, SS 841, SS 844, SS 845, SS 869
Sports Scholarships, ED 58, SS 692, SS 748
Squash Racquets, SS 831, SS 837
Stamps and Stamp Collecting, SS 382, SS 383, SS 385, SS 386
Standards, SS 127, SS 131, SS 489, SC 145. *See also* Housing Codes.
Star Charts, SC 20
State Government, SS 289, SS 290, SS 295, SS 303, SS

307, SS 310, SS 313, SS 314, SS 318, SS 424, SS 542, SS 581, SS 587, SS 590, SS 591, SS 593, SS 594, SS 847
State Planning Associations, SS 308
Statistical Services, GE 126, GE 127, GE 132, GE 134, GE 135, SS 55
Statistics, GE 125, GE 129, GE 136, GE 137, SS 443, SS 555, SS 569, SS 577, SS 652, SS 895. *See also* Sports Records; World Records.
Statistics, African. *See* African Statistics.
Statistics, Agricultural. *See* Agricultural Statistics.
Statistics, American. *See* American Statistics.
Statistics, Asian. *See* Asian Statistics.
Statistics, British. *See* British Statistics.
Statistics, Business. *See* Business Statistics.
Statistics, Crime. *See* Crime Statistics.
Statistics, Educational. *See* Educational Statistics.
Statistics, Energy. *See* Energy Statistics.
Statistics, European. *See* European Statistics.
Statistics, Japanese. *See* Japanese Statistics.
Statistics, Latin American. *See* Latin American Statistics.
Statistics, Library. *See* Library Statistics.
Statistics, Medical. *See* Medical Statistics.
Steel Construction, SC 39
Still Photography, HU 240
Stocks, SS 39, SS 43, SS 44, SS 45, SS 46, SS 47
Strikes, SS 429, SS 430
Student Aid Programs, ED 3, ED 34, ED 37, ED 38, ED 43, ED 44, ED 45, ED 46, ED 49, ED 53, ED 58, HU 158, SS 692, SS 748, SC 207, SC 210, SC 331
Student Exchange Programs, ED 47
Student Press, SS 168
Student Travel, SS 929, SS 973, SS 974. *See also* Student Exchange Programs; Studying Abroad; Youth Hostels.
Studying Abroad, ED 29, ED 30, ED 32, ED 47, ED 48, ED 50, ED 54, ED 55, ED 56, ED 57
Subject Headings, HU 145, SC 225, SC 226
Suicide, SC 335
Summer Camps. *See* Camps and Camping.
Summer Schools, ED 26, ED 27, ED 29, ED 50, ED 55, ED 57
Summer Work Programs, ED 50, ED 55, ED 57, SS 524, SS 526, SS 530, SS 532
Supervisory Education. *See* Management Education.
Supreme Court, SS 476, SS 477
Surplus Dealers, SS 517
Swimming, SS 668, SS 678, SS 776, SS 795, SS 828, SS 829. *See also* Diving.
Swimming Pools, SS 119
Switzerland, SS 960, SS 1025

Symposia. *See* Conferences.
Synagogues, HU 247, SS 971
Systems Analysis, SC 62

Talk Shows, SS 195, SS 198
Talmud, HU 290
Tankers, SS 850, SS 859
Tape Catalogs, HU 209, HU 210
Tape Industry, HU 182
Tape Players, HU 185
Tape Review Indexes, HU 193
Tape Reviews, HU 191
Tapes, ED 63, ED 70, ED 75, ED 77, HU 185
Tariff Law. *See* Trade Law.
Tax Law, SS 458, SS 471, SS 478, SS 582, SS 583, SS 599
Taxation, SS 542, SS 581, SS 582, SS 583, SS 584, SS 587, SS 594, SS 595, SS 596, HU 599, SS 606, SS 625. *See also* Public Finance.
Teachers. *See* Educators.
Teaching Materials, ED 62, ED 63, ED 64, ED 65, ED 66, ED 67, ED 68, ED 69, ED 70, ED 71, ED 72, ED 73, ED 75, ED 76, ED 77, ED 78, ED 79, ED 80, ED 81, ED 82, ED 83, ED 84, ED 85, ED 86, ED 87, ED 88, ED 89, ED 91
Technical Education. *See* Vocational Education.
Technical Schools. *See* Vocational-Technical Schools.
Technology Bibliographies, SC 5, SC 11, SC 12, SC 147
Technology Periodical Indexes, SC 4, SC 33, SC 135
Technology Yearbooks, SC 8
Teen-Agers, SC 316
Teen-Agers' Literature, GE 30, GE 46, GE 53, HU 93
Telecommunications, SS 199, SC 65
Telemetering, SC 65
Telephone Directories, HU 262
Television, Cable. *See* Cable Television.
Television Education, SS 182
Television, Educational. *See* Educational Television.
Television History, HU 344
Television Industry, HU 173, SS 162, SS 181, SS 188, SS 195, SS 196, SS 198, SS 205, SS 206, SS 207, SS 212, SS 213, SS 514
Television Personalities, HU 349, SS 188, SS 205
Telex/Teletype Directories, SS 189
Tennis, SS 799, SS 830, SS 831, SS 838, SS 843
Terrorism, SS 234, SS 247, SS 447, SS 568
Texas History, SS 29
Textbooks, ED 72
Textile Industry, SC 164, SC 165
Theater, HU 333, HU 339, HU 343, HU 348, HU 351.

See also Entertainers; Entertainment Industry; Mime; Musicians; Plays; Playwrights.
Theater Arts Bibliographies, HU 335, HU 340
Theater Arts Education, HU 332, SS 182
Theater Arts Research, HU 338, HU 344, HU 346, HU 348, HU 350
Theater Personalities, HU 337, HU 349, HU 351
Theatrical Awards, HU 333, HU 337
Theatrical Directories, HU 332, HU 336, HU 337, HU 340, HU 341, SS 217
Theatrical History, HU 344, HU 346, HU 348, HU 350
Theological Schools, HU 252, HU 281, HU 330
Theology, HU 263, HU 270, HU 309, HU 317
Therapists. *See* Counselors and Counseling Services; Psychiatrists; Psychoanalysts.
Therapy, Dance. *See* Dance Therapy.
Third World, SS 121, SS 122, SS 134, SS 454, SS 569, SS 577, SS 597, SS 652. *See also* Africa; Asia; Colonies; Latin America; Pacific Islands.
Torture, SS 546. *See also* Human Rights.
Touch Football, SS 736
Tourist Railways, SS 882
Track and Field, SS 677, SS 776, SS 832, SS 833. *See also* Marathon Running; Olympic Games; Running.
Trade, SS 74, SS 88, SS 90, SS 91, SS 93, SS 121, SS 125, SS 126, SS 133, SS 134, SS 137, SS 191, SS 568, SS 569. *See also* Commercial Law; Exporters; Importers.
Trade Policy, SS 597
Trade Fairs, SS 79, SS 81
Trade Law, SS 455, SS 458
Trade Unions. *See* Labor Unions.
Trademarks, SS 474, SS 536, SS 537, SS 539, SS 541. *See also* Copyright; Patents.
Trailer Parks. *See* Mobile Home Parks.
Trampoline, SS 671
Transfer Students, ED 35, ED 36
Transit Industry, SS 848
Transit Workers, SS 431
Translations, GE 43, HU 136
Transnational Corporations. *See* Multinational Corporations.
Transparencies, ED 75, ED 78
Transportation Engineering, SC 144
Transportation Engineers, SS 861
Transportation Industry, SS 872, SS 884. *See also* Aerospace Industry; Automotive Industry; Railroads; Shipping Industry; Trucking Industry.
Transportation Policy, SS 888, SC 144
Transportation Research, SS 883, SS 890
Trapshooting, SS 684

Travel, SS 901, SS 902, SS 905, SS 907, SS 909, SS 910, SS 913, SS 914, SS 915, SS 916, SS 917, SS 920, SS 921, SS 922, SS 923, SS 924, SS 927, SS 928, SS 929, SS 931, SS 932, SS 933, SS 934, SS 935, SS 936, SS 937, SS 938, SS 939, SS 949, SS 940, SS 941, SS 942, SS 943, SS 944, SS 945, SS 946, SS 947, SS 948, SS 949, SS 950, SS 951, SS 952, SS 953, SS 954, SS 955, SS 956, SS 957, SS 958, SS 959, SS 960, SS 961, SS 962, SS 963, SS 964, SS 967, SS 968, SS 970, SS 971, SS 972, SS 973, SS 974, SS 976, SS 984, SS 985, SS 986, SS 987, SS 988, SS 989, SS 990, SS 991, SS 992, SS 993, SS 994, SS 995, SS 997, SS 998, SS 1000, SS 1001, SS 1002, SS 1004, SS 1005, SS 1006, SS 1007, SS 1008, SS 1009, SS 1010, SS 1011, SS 1012, SS 1013, SS 1014, SS 1015, SS 1016, SS 1017, SS 1018, SS 1019, SS 1020, SS 1021, SS 1022, SS 1023, SS 1024, SS 1025, SS 1026, SS 1028. *See also* Air Travel; Bus Travel; Camps and Camping; Countries; Hotels; Motels; Railroads; Restaurants; Space Travel.
Treaties, SS 572, SS 573, SC 292, SC 294. *See also* Arms Control; International Law; International Relations.
Truck Maintenance and Repair, SS 875
Trucking Industry, SS 849, SS 885
Tucson, SS 1021
Tumbling, SS 671
Tunisia, SS 961
Turkey, SS 962
Turbines, Gas. *See* Gas Turbines.

Ukrainian Studies, SS 266, SS 275
"Underdeveloped" Countries. *See* Third World.
Underground Press. *See* Alternative Press.
Underwater Technology. *See* Marine Engineering.
Unemployment, SS 430, SS 443
Unions. *See* Credit Unions; Labor Unions.
Unitarian-Universalist Association, HU 318, HU 319
United Church of Christ, HU 321, HU 322
United Methodist Church. *See* Methodist Church.
United Nations, SS 548, SS 549, SS 558, SS 567, SS 568, SS 290. *See also* International Law; International Relations.
United States. *See* America.
United States Census Bureau. *See* Census Bureau.
United States Congress. *See* Congress.
United States History. *See* American History.
United States Library of Congress. *See* Library of Congress.
United States Politics and Government. *See* American Politics and Government.

United States Presidents. *See* Presidents.
United States Supreme Court. *See* Supreme Court.
University Directories. *See* College Directories.
Urban Planning, SS 401, SS 411
Urban Policy, SS 404, SS 411
Urban Studies, SS 303, SS 403, SS 404, SS 644, SS 646. *See also* Municipal Government.
Urban Transportation. *See* Public Transportation.
USARail Pass, SS 912
Utilities, Public. *See* Public Utilities.

Venereal Disease Bibliographies, SC 270
Veterans' Services, SS 630, SS 636
Veterinarians, SC 336
Veterinarians' Handbooks, SC 337
Veterinary Medicine, SC 338
Veterinary Schools, SC 339
Victims of Crime, SS 254. *See also* Crime.
Video Tapes, ED 63, ED 75, ED 81, SS 203, SS 204, SC 243
Virgil Studies, HU 76, HU 77
VISTA, SS 616
Visually Disabled Persons' Projects and Services, SS 622, SS 632
Vocational Education, ED 19, ED 20, ED 23, ED 89, ED 97, ED 99, ED 102
Vocational Guidance, ED 66, SS 523. *See also* Job Hunting Guides; Volunteer Programs.
Vocational Guidance for Minorities, SS 621
Vocational-Technical Schools, ED 37, ED 98, ED 99, ED 100, ED 101, ED 102, SC 279
Volleyball, SS 703, SS 839, SS 840, SS 841
Volunteer Programs, SS 616, SS 628, SS 629, SC 241

Wages and Salaries, SS 419, SS 422, SS 425, SS 427, SS 428, SS 430, SS 431, SS 432, SS 433, SS 434, SS 443, SS 487, SS 488, SC 140, SC 141, SC 143
Warships, SC 286
Washington, D.C., SS 303, SS 320, SS 996, SS 1001, SS 1024, SS 1028. *See also* American Politics and Government; Congress; Presidents.
Water Pollution, SS 225
Water Polo, SS 679, SS 796
Water Resources, SC 74, SC 104, SC 114
Water Sports. *See* Boating; Diving; Swimming; Water Polo; Yacht Racing.
Weapons Systems, SC 287, SC 288, SC 294, SC 295. *See also* Arms Control.
Weather, SC 75, SC 76
Weightlifting, SS 669, SS 672. *See also* Bodybuilding.

Welding, SC 190
Welfare Programs, SS 630. *See also* Human Services.
West Africa, SS 360
West Indies, SS 361, SS 928, SS 935
Western Riding, SS 759
Western United States, SS 985, SS 1032
Wildlife Research, SC 116, SC 117
Winter Sports. *See* Cross Country Skiing; Hockey; Ice Skating; Skiing.
Wire Industry, SC 191
Women, GE 82, GE 111, ED 61
Women, American. *See* American Women.
Women Artists, HU 38
Women Authors, HU 100, HU 134
Women Engineering Students, SC 142
Women Government Workers, SS 424, SS 434
Women Lawyers, SS 464
Women Legislators, SS 322
Women Librarians, HU 142, HU 166
Women, Minority. *See* Minority Women.
Women Physicians, SC 233
Women Police Officers, SS 234
Women Prisoners, SS 255
Women Workers, SS 142, SS 145, SS 422, SS 442
Women's Media, SS 192
Women's Organizations, GE 111, SS 145, SS 192
Women's Periodicals, HU 135
Women's Rights, SS 138, SS 142, SS 144, SS 145
Women's Scholarships and Fellowships, ED 58
Women's Sports, SS 664, SS 675, SS 686, SS 691, SS 692, SS 699, SS 703, SS 714, SS 730, SS 731, SS 740, SS 741, SS 744, SS 757, SS 775, SS 815, SS 817, SS 818, SS 829, SS 833, SS 837, SS 840, SS 841
Women's Studies, HU 159
Women's Studies Bibliographies, SS 651
Women's Writings, HU 134
Workers' Benefits. *See* Employee Benefits.
Workers' Compensation, SS 470
Workers, Government. *See* Government Officials and Employees.
Workers, Minority. *See* Minority Workers.
Workers, Women. *See* Women Workers.
Working Hours. *See* Hours of Work.
World Book Encyclopedia, GE 19
World History, GE 14
World Hockey League, SS 806, SS 809
World Leaders, SS 296, SS 339, SS 558
World Politics, GE 2, GE 7, SS 579, SS 285. *See also* Arms Control; Current History; International Relations; United Nations.
World Records, GE 9. *See also* Sports Records.
World Series, SS 712, SS 783, SS 800, SS 824. *See also* Professional Baseball.
World Trade. *See* Trade.

Wrestling, SS 673, SS 844, SS 845
Writers. *See* Authors.

X-Ray Analysis, SC 208

Yacht Racing, SS 869
Yachts, SS 868, SS 871, SS 898
Yiddish-Language Materials, HU 109, SS 277
Young Adult Literature. *See* Teen-Agers' Literature.

Youth Hostels, SS 969
Youth Challenge Program, SS 616
Yugoslavia, SS 964

Zinc Industry, SC 311
Zionism, HU 331, SS 268, SS 270
Zip Codes, GE 11, SS 208, SS 209
Zoology, SC 38, SC 75
Zoos, SS 909, SS 965
Zurich, SS 1025. *See also* Switzerland.

Ref
Z
1035.1
M27

AUG 16 1979

RAYMOND H. FOGLER LIBRARY
DATE DUE

BOOKS ARE SUBJECT TO
RECALL AFTER TWO WEEKS